Coll

JAPANESE
DICTIONARY
ESSENTIAL EDITION

日本語

Published by Collins
An imprint of HarperCollins Publishers
Westerhill Road
Bishopbriggs
Glasgow G64 2QT

2nd Edition 2018

10 9 8 7 6 5 4 3 2 1

© HarperCollins Publishers 2018

ISBN 978-0-00-827071-1

collinsdictionary.com

Typeset by Davidson Publishing
Solutions, Glasgow

Printed and bound by CPI Group (UK)
Ltd, Croydon, CR0 4YY

A catalogue record for this book is
available from the British Library.

If you would like to comment on any
aspect of this book, please contact us
at the given address or online.
E-mail: dictionaries@harpercollins.co.uk
 facebook.com/collinsdictionary
 @collinsdict

Acknowledgements
We would like to thank those authors
and publishers who kindly gave
permission for copyright material
to be used in the Collins Corpus.
We would also like to thank Times
Newspapers Ltd for providing
valuable data.

CONTENTS　　　　　内容

Introduction	iv	紹介
Abbreviations	v	略語
Japanese Romanization	vi	日本語のローマ字表記
Japanese Pronunciation	viii	日本語の発音
English Pronunciation	x	英語の発音
Numbers	xii	数字
Days of the Week	xiv	曜日
Months	xiv	月
JAPANESE – ENGLISH	1–223	日本語ー英語
Japanese Grammar	1–16	日本語文法
English Grammar	17–32	英文法
ENGLISH – JAPANESE	225–430	英語–日本語

NOTE ON TRADEMARKS
Words which we have reason to believe constitute trademarks have been designated as such. However, neither the presence nor absence of such designations should be regarded as affecting the legal status of any trademark.

商標に関する注意
商標とみなすべき根拠がある語には、登録商標マークが示されています。ただし、登録商標マーク記載の有無は、商標の法的地位に影響を与えるものではありません。

INTRODUCTION

We are delighted that you have decided to buy this dictionary and hope that you will enjoy and benefit from using it at home, on holiday or at work.

ごあいさつ

本書をお買い上げいただきまして、誠にありがとうございます。読者の皆様がご自宅にて、お仕事で、あるいはご旅行の際などに本書をご活用いただければ幸いです。

ABBREVIATIONS 略語

adjective	*adj*	形容詞
adverb	*adv*	副詞
conjunction	*conj*	接続詞
interjection	*intj*	感嘆詞
exclamation	*excl*	感嘆符
feminine	*f*	女性の言葉
masculine	*m*	男性の言葉
noun	*n*	名詞
plural	*pl*	複数形
preposition	*prep*	前置詞
pronoun	*pron*	代名詞
verb	*v*	動詞
intransitive verb	*vi*	自動詞
transitive verb	*vt*	他動詞

JAPANESE ROMANIZATION / 日本語のローマ字表記

There are several systems for writing Japanese in Roman characters, but the most understandable for English speakers is the Hepburn system. The following table illustrates this system, with its hiragana and katakana equivalents, as it has been adopted in this dictionary.

	a	i	u	e	o
	a	**i**	**u**	**e**	**o**
	あ	い	う	え	お
	ア	イ	ウ	エ	オ
k	**ka**	**ki**	**ku**	**ke**	**ko**
	か	き	く	け	こ
	カ	キ	ク	ケ	コ
s	**sa**	**shi**	**su**	**se**	**so**
	さ	し	す	せ	そ
	サ	シ	ス	セ	ソ
t	**ta**	**chi**	**tsu**	**te**	**to**
	た	ち	つ	て	と
	タ	チ	ツ	テ	ト
n	**na**	**ni**	**nu**	**ne**	**no**
	な	に	ぬ	ね	の
	ナ	ニ	ヌ	ネ	ノ
h	**ha**	**hi**	**fu**	**he**	**ho**
	は	ひ	ふ	へ	ほ
	ハ	ヒ	フ	ヘ	ホ
m	**ma**	**mi**	**mu**	**me**	**mo**
	ま	み	む	め	も
	マ	ミ	ム	メ	モ
	ya		**yu**		**yo**

	a	i	u	e	o
y	や ヤ		ゆ ユ		よ ヨ
r	**ra** ら ラ	**ri** り リ	**ru** る ル	**re** れ レ	**ro** ろ ロ
w	**wa** わ ワ				**o** を ヲ
					n ん ン
g	**ga** が ガ	**gi** ぎ ギ	**gu** ぐ グ	**ge** げ ゲ	**go** ご ゴ
z	**za** ざ ザ	**ji** じ ジ	**zu** ず ズ	**ze** ぜ ゼ	**zo** ぞ ゾ
d	**da** だ ダ	**ji** ぢ ヂ	**zu** づ ヅ	**de** で デ	**do** ど ド
b	**ba** ば バ	**bi** び ビ	**bu** ぶ ブ	**be** べ ベ	**bo** ぼ ボ
p	**pa** ぱ パ	**pi** ぴ ピ	**pu** ぷ プ	**pe** ぺ ペ	**po** ぽ ポ

JAPANESE PRONUNCIATION

VOWELS

	Japanese example	Explanation
[a]	秋 [aki]	Like *a* in father
[e]	枝 [eda]	Like *e* in set
[i]	犬 [inu]	Like *i* in machine
[o]	音 [oto]	Like *o* in open
[u]	歌 [uta]	Like *oo* in soon

However, generally the *u* at the end of syllables is barely pronounced. Common endings such as -*desu* and -*masu* are pronounced as "des" and "mas" respectively.

Doubled vowels such as *aa*, *ee*, *ii*, *oo*, and *uu* are pronounced as above but with twice the length. The diphthongs *ei* and *ou* are pronounced like the "ay" in say and the "ow" in crow respectively.

CONSONANTS

In Romanized Japanese, consonants are pronounced as in English but note the few differences.

	Japanese example	Explanation
[b]	晩 [ban]	Like *b* in bank
[d]	度 [do]	Like *d* in dog
[f]	藤 [fuji]	Like *f* in far or a cross between f and h
[g]	蛾 [ga]	Always like *g* in girl, never like in gin
[h]	葉 [ha]	Like *h* in happy
[j]	十 [juu]	Like *j* in jam
[k]	亀 [kame]	Like *k* in kettle
[m]	豆 [mame]	Like *m* in mother

[n]	名前 [namae]	Like *n* in not, but like *m* before b, m, p
[p]	パンク [panku]	Like *p* in pie
[r]	例 [rei]	Like *r* in three or a cross between l and r
[s]	先生 [sensei]	Like *s* in sister
[t]	手紙 [tegami]	Like *t* in tell
[w]	ワイン [wain]	Like *w* in wine
[y]	山 [yama]	Like *y* in yes
[z]	像 [zou]	Like *z* in zoo

[ch], [sh], [ts] - These are pronounced just as in English: ch as in chair, sh as in shout and ts as in hot soup.

Double consonants such as **kk**, **pp**, **ss**, **tt** are pronounced as double letters with a pause between each. Some sounds such as **ki**, **gi**, **ri**, etc. may combine with **ya**, **yu**, **yo** to form double consonant combinations such as *kya*, *kyu*, *gyo*, etc.

英語の発音 / ENGLISH PRONUNCIATION

母音

	単語例	発音のヒント
[ɑ:]	**fa**ther	口を大きく開けて、喉の奥から「アー」と言う。
[ʌ]	b**u**t, c**o**me	日本語の「ア」より少しだけ口を閉じて、短く「ア」と言う。
[æ]	m**a**n, c**a**t	「ア」と「エ」を同時に言う感じで「ア」と言う。
[ə]	fath**er**, **a**go	舌の前後の位置を口の真ん中に置き、「ア」と言う。
[ə:]	b**ir**d, h**ear**d	舌の前後の位置を口の真ん中に置き、「アー」と言う。
[ɛ]	g**e**t, b**e**d	日本語の「エ」より口を横に開いて発音する。
[ɪ]	**i**t, b**i**g	日本語の「イ」より口の両端を広げて発音する。
[ɔ]	h**o**t, w**a**sh	日本語の「オ」より口を開け、「ア」と「オ」の間発音。
[u]	p**u**t, b**oo**k	「ウ」と「オ」の中間の音。
[ʊ]	t**oo**, y**ou**	日本語の「ウ」より口をとがらせて発音する。

母音

	単語例	発音のヒント
[ai]	fl**y**, h**igh**	日本語の「ア」より大きく口を開け、「アィ」のように発音。
[au]	h**ow**, h**ou**se	日本語の「ア」より大きく口を開け、「アゥ」のように発音。
[ɛə]	th**ere**, b**ear**	日本語の「エ」よりやや口を広げ、「エァ」のように発音。
[ei]	d**ay**, ob**ey**	日本語の「エ」よりやや口を広げ、「エィ」のように発音。
[iə]	h**ere**, h**ear**	日本語の「イ」より口を広げ、「イァ」のように発音。
[əu]	g**o**, n**o**te	口をつぼめ気味にして、「オゥ」のように発音。
[əi]	b**oy**, **oi**l	日本語の「オ」より口を開け、「オィ」のように発音。
[uə]	p**oor**, s**ure**	あいまいな「ウ」から始め、「ウァ」のように発音。

母音

	単語例	発音のヒント
[b]	big, lobby	わせた上下の唇を、息と音を出しながらぱっと放す。
[d]	mended	舌先を上の歯茎の裏に付けて止めた息を、音と一緒に押し出す。
[g]	go, get, big	舌の根元でせき止めた息を、声と一緒に勢いよく出す。
[dʒ]	gin, judge	上の歯茎の裏に近づけた舌を、「ジャ」行の音を出しながら勢いよく放す。
[ŋ]	sing	鼻から空気を出すように、「ング」の「ン」で止める。
[h]	house, he	喉の奥から息を出して、「ハ」行の音を出す。
[j]	young, yes	いったん緊張させた舌をゆるめて、「ヤ」行の音を出す。
[k]	come, mock	舌の根元でせき止めた息を勢いよく出す。
[r]	red, tread	口を丸め、舌先をやや後ろに巻いて「ラ」行の音を出す。
[s]	sand, yes	日本語の「サ」行より強く空気を出す、「スィ」に近い音。
[z]	rose, zebra	日本語の「ザ」行より強く空気を出す。
[ʃ]	she, machine	唇を丸めて息を強く出しながら、「シャ」行の音を出す。
[tʃ]	chin, rich	舌先を上の歯茎の裏に近づけ、勢いよく舌を放す。
[v]	valley	下唇を軽くかみながら息と一緒に声を出す。
[w]	water, which	唇をしぼめて「ウ」の音を出す。
[ʒ]	vision	[ʃ] と同じ口の形で、声を加えて発音する。
[θ]	think, myth	舌先を上下の歯に挟んで、歯と舌の間から息だけ出す。
[ð]	this, the	舌先を上下の歯に挟んで、歯と舌の間から息と一緒に声を出す。

NUMBERS

数字

zero	0	ゼロ zero
uno	1	一 ichi
two	2	二 ni
three	3	三 san
four	4	四 shi, yon
five	5	五 go
six	6	六 roku
seven	7	七 shichi, nana
eight	8	八 hachi
nine	9	九 kyuu, kuu
ten	10	十 juu
eleven	11	十一 juuichi
twelve	12	十二 juuni
thirteen	13	十三 juusan
fourteen	14	十六 juuyon
fifteen	15	十五 juugo
sixteen	16	十六 juuroku
seventeen	17	十七 juunana
eighteen	18	十八 juuhachi
nineteen	19	十九 juukyuu
twenty	20	二十 nijuu
twenty-one	21	二十一 nijuuichi
twenty-two	22	二十二 nijuuni
twenty-three	23	二十三 nijuusan
thirty	30	三十 sanjuu
thirty-one	31	三十一 sanjuuichi
forty	40	四十 yonjuu
fifty	50	五十 gojuu
sixty	60	六十 rokujuu
seventy	70	七十 nanajuu, shichijuu
eighty	80	八十 hachijuu
ninety	90	九十 kyuujuu

one hundred	100	百 hyaku
one hundred and ten	110	百十 hyakujuu
two hundred	200	二百 nihyaku
two hundred and fifty	250	二百五十 nihyakugojuu
one thousand	1,000	千、一千 sen, issen
ten thousand	10,000	一万 ichiman
one million	1,000,000	十万 juuman

DAYS OF THE WEEK 曜日

Monday	月曜日 getsuyoobi
Tuesday	火曜日 kayoobi
Wednesday	水曜日 suiyoobi
Thursday	木曜日 mokuyoobi
Friday	金曜日 kinyoobi
Saturday	土曜日 doyoobi
Sunday	日曜日 nichiyoobi

MONTHS 月

January	一月 ichigatsu
February	二月 nigatsu
March	三月 sangatsu
April	四月 shigatsu
May	五月 gogatsu
June	六月 rokugatsu
July	七月 sichigatsu
August	八月 hachigatsu
September	九月 kugatsu
October	十月 juugatsu
November	十一月 juuichigatsu
December	十二月 nigatsu

Japanese – English

日本語－英語

a

your email address?; Eメールアドレスをお
持ちですか? [ii-meeru-adoresu o o-mochi
desu ka?] Do you have an email?; Eメール
アドレスを教えてもらえますか?
[ii-meeru-adoresu o oshiete moraemasu
ka?] Can I have your email?

アドリア海 [adoriakai] n Adriatic Sea; ア
ドリア海の [adoriakai no] adj Adriatic

亜鉛 [aen] n zinc

アフガニスタン [afuganisutan] n
Afghanistan; アフガニスタンの
[afuganisutan no] adj Afghan

アフガニスタン人 [afuganisutanjin] n
Afghan (person)

アフリカ [afurika] n Africa; 中央アフリカ
共和国 [chuuou afurika kyouwakoku] n
Central African Republic; アフリカの
[afurika no] adj African

アフリカーナー [afurikaanaa] n
Afrikaner

アフリカーンス語 [afurikaansugo] n
Afrikaans

アフリカ人 [afurikajin] n African (person)

上がる [agaru] v come up, go up

上げる [ageru] v raise; 速度を上げる
[sokudo-o ageru] v speed up; 金切り声を
上げる [kanagiri koe-o ageru] v scream

揚げる [age ru] 油で揚げた [abura de
ageta] adj fried; 油で揚げる [abura de
ageru] v deep-fry, fry

あご [ago] n chin, jaw

あごひげ [agohige] n beard; あごひげを
生やした [agohige-o hayashita] adj
bearded

アヒル [ahiru] n duck

愛 [ai] n love; 愛する [ai suru] v love

愛着 [aichaku] n attachment

間 [aida] n while; ・・・の間に [...no aida ni]
prep between

愛人 [aijin] n lover; 女性の愛人 [josei no
aijin] n mistress

愛情 [aijou] 愛情のこもった [aijou no
komotta] adj affectionate

愛国 [aikoku] 愛国的な [aikokuteki na] adj
patriotic

アーチ [aachi] n arch

アーモンド [aamondo] n almond

アーティチョーク [aatichouku] n
artichoke

アボカド [abokado] n avocado

アブダビ [abudabi] n Abu Dhabi

油 [abura] n oil; 油で揚げた [abura de
ageta] adj fried; 油で揚げる [abura de
ageru] v deep-fry, fry; 油を差す [abura-o
sasu] (注油) v oil

脂 [abura] 脂を含んだ [abura-o fukunda]
adj greasy

脂っこい [aburakkoi] 食べ物がとても脂っ
こいです [tabemono ga totemo aburakkoi
desu] The food is very greasy

あっち [atchi] あっちへ行ってください!
[atchi e itte kudasai!] Go away!

あちこち [achikochi] prep around

あだ名 [adana] ・・・とあだ名をつけられた
[...to adana-o tsukerareta] adj dubbed

アダプタ [adaputa] ソケットアダプタ
[soketto adaputa] n adaptor

アドレス [adoresu] n address; あなたのE
メールアドレスは何ですか? [anata no
ii-meeru-adoresu wa nan desu ka?] What is

愛国主義 [aikokushugi] 熱狂的愛国主義者 [nekkyoutekiaikokushugisha] n chauvinist

曖昧 [aimai] 曖昧な [aimai na] adj vague

アイライナー [airainaa] n eyeliner

アイロン [airon] アイロンをかける [airon-o kakeru] v iron; アイロンをかけるべきもの [airon-o kakerubeki mono] n ironing; アイロン台 [airondai] n ironing board; どこでこれにアイロンをかけてもらえますか? [doko de kore ni airon o kakete moraemasu ka?] Where can I get this ironed?; 私はアイロンが必要です [watashi wa airon ga hitsuyou desu] I need an iron

アイルランド [airurando] n Eire, Ireland

アイルランド人 [airurandojin] n Irish, Irishman, Irishwoman

アイルランドの [airurando no] adj Irish

挨拶 [aisatsu] n greeting; 挨拶する [aisatsu suru] v salute; ···に挨拶する [...ni aisatsu suru] v greet

アイシャドウ [aishadou] n eye shadow

アイシング [aishingu] n icing

アイス [aisu] アイスキャンディー [aisu kyandii] n ice lolly; アイスボックス [aisu bokkusu] n icebox

アイスホッケー [aisuhokkee] n ice hockey

アイスクリーム [aisukuriimu] n ice cream; 私はアイスクリームをいただきます [watashi wa aisukuriimu o itadakimasu] I'd like an ice cream

アイスキューブ [aisukyuubu] n ice cube

アイスランド [aisurando] n Iceland

アイスランド人 [aisurandojin] n Icelandic (person)

アイスランドの [aisurando no] adj Icelandic

愛する [ai suru] 私はあなたを愛しています [watashi wa anata o aishite imasu] I love you

アイススケート [aisusukeeto] n ice-skating; どこに行けばアイススケートができますか? [dokoni ikeba aisusukeeto ga dekimasu ka?] Where can we go ice-skating?

相手 [aite] n partner; 決まった相手がいる [kimatta aite ga iru] adj attached; 競争相手 [kyousouaite] n rival

合図 [aizu] n signal; 合図する [aizu suru] v signal

味 [aji] n flavour, taste; 味のない [aji no nai] adj tasteless; 味のよい [aji no yoi] adj tasty; 味をみる [aji-o miru] v taste; 味があまりよくありません [aji ga amari yoku arimasen] It doesn't taste very nice

アジア [ajia] n Asia; アジアの [ajia no] adj Asian, Asiatic

アジア人 [ajiajin] n Asian (person)

赤ちゃん [akachan] n baby; どこで赤ちゃんに授乳できますか? [doko de akachan ni junyuu dekimasu ka?] Where can I breast-feed the baby?; どこで赤ちゃんのおしめを替えられますか? [doko de akachan no oshime o kaeraremasu ka?] Where can I change the baby?; 赤ちゃんがいる両親のための設備はありますか? [akachan ga iru ryoushin no tame no setsubi wa arimasu ka?] Are there facilities for parents with babies?

赤ちゃん用ウェットティシュー [akachan-you uettotishuu] n baby wipe

赤毛 [akage] n redhead; 赤毛の [akage no] adj red-haired

赤い [akai] adj red; 赤十字社 [sekijuujisha] n Red Cross

赤身 [akami] 赤身肉 [akaminiku] n red meat

赤身肉 [akaminiku] 私は赤身肉を食べません [watashi wa akaminiku o tabemasen] I don't eat red meat

赤ん坊 [akanbou] n baby

明かり [akari] n light; 明かりがつきません [akari ga tsukimasen] The light doesn't work; 明かりをつけてもいいですか? [akari o tsukete mo ii desu ka?] Can I switch the light on?; 明かりを消してもいいですか? [akari o keshite mo ii desu ka?] Can I switch the light off?

明るい [akarui] adj bright, light (not dark); 明るいところに持っていってもいいですか? [akarui tokoro ni motte itte mo ii desu ka?]

May I take it over to the light?

赤ワイン [akawain] よい赤ワインを教えて もらえますか? [yoi aka-wain o oshiete moraemasu ka?] Can you recommend a good red wine?

あける [akeru] 穴をあけた [ana-o aketa] adj pierced; 穴をあける [ana-o akeru] v bore, drill; 錠をあける [jou-o akeru] v unlock

空ける [akeru] いつ部屋を空けなければな りませんか? [itsu heya o akenakereba narimasen ka?] When do I have to vacate the room?

開ける [akeru] v open; ファスナーを開ける [fasunaa-o hirakeru] v unzip; 窓を開けても いいですか? [mado o akete mo ii desu ka?] May I open the window?; 窓を開けられま せん [mado o akeraremasen] I can't open the window

秋 [aki] n autumn

空き瓶 [akibin] 空き瓶回収ボックス [akikan kaishuu bokkusu] n bottle bank

明らか [akiraka] 明らかな [akiraka na] adj apparent; 明らかに [akiraka ni] adv apparently, obviously; 明らかにする [akiraka ni suru] v clarify, disclose, reveal

明らかな [akiraka na] adj obvious

空き室 [akishitsu] n vacancy; 空き室はあ りますか? [akishitsu wa arimasu ka?] Do you have any vacancies?

悪化 [akka] 悪化する [akka suru] v deteriorate, worsen

あこがれる [akogareru] v adore

アコーディオン [akoodeion] n accordion

空く [aku] 空いている [aite iru] adj vacant; この席は空いていますか? [kono seki wa aite imasu ka?] Is this seat free?

あくび [akubi] あくびをする [akubi-o suru] v yawn

悪意 [akui] n venom; 悪意のある [akui no aru] adj malicious, malignant

悪魔 [akuma] n devil

悪夢 [akumu] n nightmare

アクセル [akuseru] n accelerator

アクセス [akusesu] アクセスする [akusesu suru] v access

悪臭 [akushuu] n stink; 悪臭を放つ [akushuu-o hanatsu] v stink

アクティビティ [akuteibitei] 子供向けの アクティビティはありますか? [kodomo muke no akutibiti wa arimasu ka?] Do you have activities for children?

アクティブ [akuteibu] アクティブホリデー [akutibu horidee] n activity holiday

悪徳 [akutoku] n vice

悪党 [akutou] n villain

アマチュア [amachua] n amateur

甘い [amai] adj sweet (taste); 甘いもの [amai mono] n sweet

甘味 [amami] 甘味料 [kanmiryou] n sweetener

余り [amari] n surplus

雨 [ame] n rain; 酸性雨 [sanseiu] n acid rain; 雨の [ame no] adj rainy; 雨が降る [ame ga furu] v rain; 雨が降っています [ame ga futte imasu] It's raining; 雨が降る と思いますか? [ame ga furu to omoimasu ka?] Do you think it's going to rain?

アメニティー [ameniteii] n amenities

アメリカ [amerika] n America; 中央アメリ カ [chuuou amerika] n Central America; アメリカの [amerika no] adj American

アメリカ人 [amerikajin] n American (person)

網 [ami] n net

編み [ami] 編み棒 [amibou] n knitting needle

編物 [amimono] n knitting

編む [amu] v knit

穴 [ana] n hole; 穴をあけた [ana-o aketa] adj pierced; 穴をあける [ana-o akeru] v bore, drill, pierce; 鼻の穴 [hana no ana] n nostril

アナグマ [anaguma] n badger

あなた [anata] n sir ▷ pron you (singular), you (singular polite); あなたの [anata no] adj your (singular polite); あなたの [anata no] adj your (singular), yours (singular), yours (singular polite); あなた方

[anatagata] *pron* you (plural); あなた方の [anatagata no] *adj* your (plural); あなた自身 [anata jishin] *pron* yourself (polite); あなた自身 [anata jishin] *pron* yourself, yourselves (polite); あなたは? [anata wa?] And you?

あなた方 [anatagata] あなた方の [anatagata no] *adj* yours (plural); あなた方自身 [anatagata jishin] *pron* yourselves (reflexive)

アンチウイルス [anchiuirusu] *n* antivirus

アンチョビー [anchobii] *n* anchovy

アンダーパス [andaapasu] *n* underpass

アンダースカート [andaasukaato] *n* underskirt

アンデス [andesu] アンデス山脈 [andesu sanmyaku] *n* Andes

アンドラ [andora] *n* Andorra

アンゴラ [angora] *n* Angola; アンゴラの [angora no] *adj* Angolan

アンゴラ人 [angorajin] *n* Angolan (person)

暗号 [angou] *n* code

アニシード [anishiido] *n* aniseed

アンケート [ankeeto] アンケート用紙 [ankeeto youshi] *n* questionnaire

案内 [annai] *n* information; 案内所 [annaijo] *n* information office, inquiries office; 案内書 [annaisho] *n* prospectus; 番号案内サービス [bangou annai saabisu] *n* directory enquiries; アパートメントを案内していただけますか? [apaatomento o annai shite itadakemasu ka?] Could you show us around the apartment?; 案内していただけますか? [annai shite itadakemasu ka?] Could you show us around?; 観光案内所はどこですか? [kankou annai-sho wa doko desu ka?] Where is the tourist office?

案内する [annai suru] *n* guide

あの [ano] *adj* that

アノラック [anorakku] *n* anorak

アンパイア [anpaia] *n* umpire

アンペア [anpea] *n* amp, ampere

アンプ [anpu] *n* amplifier

安楽 [anraku] *n* comfort; 安楽椅子 [anraku isu] *n* easy chair

安心 [anshin] *n* relief; 安心させる [anshin saseru] *v* reassure, relieve; 安心した [anshin shita] *adj* relieved

暗証 [anshou] 暗証番号 [anshobango] *n* PIN, personal identification number

安息 [ansoku] 安息日 [ansokubi] *n* Sabbath

安定 [antei] *n* stability; 安定した [antei shita] *adj* stable; 公共職業安定所 [koukyoushokugyou anteisho] *n* job centre

アンテナ [antena] *n* aerial

安全 [anzen] *n* safety; 安全ベルト [anzenberuto] *n* safety belt; 安全ピン [anzenpin] *n* safety pin

安全な [anzen na] *adj* safe, secure

青々 [aoao] 青々とした [aoao to shita] *adj* lush

青い [aoi] *adj* blue

青緑色 [aomidoriiro] 青緑色の [aomidori iro no] *adj* turquoise

アパート [apaato] *n* apartment; ワンルームのアパート [wanruumu no apaato] *n* bedsit

アパートメント [apaatomento] *n* apartment, flat; アパートメントを案内していただけますか? [apaatomento o annai shite itadakemasu ka?] Could you show us around the apartment?; 私たちはアパートメントを探しています [watashi-tachi wa apaatomento o sagashite imasu] We're looking for an apartment; ···の名前でアパートメントを予約してあります [...no namae de apaatomento o yoyaku shite arimasu] We've booked an apartment in the name of...

アペリチフ [aperichifu] *n* aperitif; アペリチフをいただきます [aperichifu o itadakimasu] We'd like an aperitif

アポストロフィ [aposutorofi] *n* apostrophe

アップグレード [appugureedo] *n* upgrade; 切符をアップグレードしたいのですが [kippu o appugureedo shitai no desu ga] I want to upgrade my ticket

アップル [appuru] アップルパイ [appurupai] n apple pie

アプリ [apuri] n app

アプリコット [apurikotto] n apricot

アプザイレン [apuzairen] 私はアプザイレンをしたいのですが [watashi wa apuzairen o shitai no desu ga] I'd like to go abseiling

アラビア [arabia] アラビアの [arabia no] adj Arab

アラビア語 [arabiago] n Arabic (language); アラビア語の [arabiago no] Arabic

アラビア人 [arabiajin] n Arab

アラブ首長国連邦 [arabu shuchoukokurenpou] n United Arab Emirates

洗える [araeru] 洗濯機で洗える [sentakuki de araeru] adj machine washable; それは洗えますか？ [sore wa araemasu ka?] Is it washable?

粗い [arai] adj rough; きめの粗い [kime no komakai] adj coarse

アライグマ [araiguma] n racoon

粗い砂 [araisuna] n grit

あらかじめ [arakajime] adv beforehand

嵐 [arashi] n storm; 嵐の [arashi no] adj stormy; 嵐になると思いますか？ [arashi ni naru to omoimasu ka?] Do you think there will be a storm?

洗う [arau] v wash; ごしごし洗う [goshigoshi arau] v scrub; 洗って片付ける [aratte katazukeru] v wash up; 食器洗い [shokkiarai] n washing-up; 食器洗い機 [shokkiaraiki] n dishwasher; 車を洗いたいのですが [kuruma o araitai no desu ga] I would like to wash the car; 食器洗い場はどこですか？ [shokki-araiba wa doko desu ka?] Where is the washing up area?

現れる [arawareru] v appear, show up

現す [arawasu] v signify; 姿を現す [sugata-o arawasu] v turn up

表す [arawasu] v stand for; 感謝を表さない [kansha-o arawasanai] adj ungrateful

あれ [are] pron that

アレチネズミ [arechinezumi] n gerbil

荒野 [areno] n moor

荒れる [areru] v deteriorate; 今日は海が荒れていますか？ [kyou wa umi ga arete imasu ka?] Is the sea rough today?

アレルギー [arerugii] n allergy; アレルギーの [arerugii no] adj allergic; 小麦アレルギー [komugi arerugii] n wheat intolerance

アリ [ari] n ant

アリバイ [aribai] n alibi

ありがとう [arigatou] Thank you; ありがとうございます [arigatou gozaimasu] Thank you very much

ありがとう! [arigatou] excl thanks!

ありそうもない [arisou mo nai] adj unlikely

ありそうな [arisou na] adj probable

アロマセラピー [aromaserapii] n aromatherapy

アッラー [arraa] n Allah

ある [aru] v have; …はありますか？ [...wa arimasu ka?] Have you got any...?; …へ行くバスはありますか？ [...e iku basu wa arimasu ka?] Is there a bus to...?

アルバム [arubamu] n (photo) album

アルバニア [arubania] n Albania; アルバニアの [arubania no] adj Albanian

アルバニア語 [arubaniago] n Albanian (language)

アルバニア人 [arubaniajin] n Albanian (person)

あるべき所にない [aru beki tokoro ni nai] v missing

アルファベット [arufabetto] n alphabet

アルジェリア [arujeria] n Algeria; アルジェリアの [arujeria no] adj Algerian

アルジェリア人 [arujeriajin] n Algerian (person)

歩き回る [arukimawaru] v wander

アルコール中毒 [arukooru chuudoku] アルコール中毒者 [arukooru chuudokusha] n alcoholic

アルコール [arukouru] n alcohol; 低アル

コールの [tei arukooru no] *adj*
low-alcohol; アルコール中毒者 [arukooru chuudokusha] *n* alcoholic; アルコールの [arukooru no] *adj* alcoholic; アルコールを含まない [arukooru o fukumanai] *adj* alcohol-free; それにはアルコールが入っていますか? [sore ni wa arukooru ga haitte imasu ka?] Does that contain alcohol?; 私はアルコールを飲みません [watashi wa arukooru o nomimasen] I don't drink alcohol

歩く [aruku] *v* walk; ぶらぶら歩き [burabura aruki] *n* stroll; 足をひきずって歩く [ashi-o hikizutte aruku] *v* shuffle; 夢遊病で歩く [muyuubyou de aruku] *v* sleepwalk; そこまで歩いて行けますか? [soko made aruite ikemasu ka?] Can I walk there?

アルメニア [arumenia] *n* Armenia; アルメニアの [arumenia no] *adj* Armenian

アルメニア語 [arumeniago] *n* Armenian (*language*)

アルメニア人 [arumeniajin] *n* Armenian (*person*)

アルミ [arumi] アルミ箔 [arumihaku] *n* tinfoil

アルミニウム [aruminiumu] *n* aluminium

アルプス [arupusu] アルプス山脈 [arupusu sanmyaku] *n* Alps

アルスター [arusutaa] *n* Ulster

アルゼンチン [aruzenchin] *n* Argentina; アルゼンチンの [aruzenchin no] *adj* Argentinian

アルゼンチン人 [aruzenchinjin] *n* Argentinian (*person*)

朝 [asa] *n* morning; 朝寝坊 [asanebou] *n* have a lie-in, lie in; 明日の朝 [asu no asa] tomorrow morning

麻 [asa] *n* linen

浅い [asai] *adj* shallow

あさって [asatte] the day after tomorrow

汗 [ase] *n* perspiration, sweat; 汗をかく [ase o kaku] *v* sweat

汗だらけ [asedarake] 汗だらけの [ase darake no] *adj* sweaty

褪せる [aseru] *v* fade

足 [ashi] *n* feet, foot; 足の指 [ashi no yubi] *n* toe; 足治療医 [ashichiryoui] *n* chiropodist; 動物の足 [doubutsu no ashi] *n* paw; 私は足が痛みます [watashi wa ashi ga itamimasu] My feet are sore; 私の足は六号です [watashi no ashi wa roku-gou desu] My feet are a size six

脚 [ashi] *n* leg; 私は脚がかゆみます [watashi wa ashi ga kayumimasu] My leg itches; 私は脚がつっています [watashi wa ashi ga tsutte imasu] I've got cramp in my leg; 私は脚を動かせません [watashi wa ashi o ugokasemasen] I can't move my leg; 彼は脚を動かせません [kare wa ashi o ugokasemasen] He can't move his leg; 彼女は脚を痛めました [kanojo wa ashi o itamemashita] She has hurt her leg

アシ [ashi] *n* (植物) reed

足跡 [ashiato] *n* footprint

足場 [ashiba] *n* scaffolding

足取り [ashidori] *n* footstep

遊び [asobi] *n* fun; 遊び時間 [asobi jikan] *n* playtime

遊び場 [asobiba] *n* playground

遊ぶ [asobu] *n* play; 楽しく遊ぶ [tanoshiku asobu] *v* have fun

あそこ [asoko] *adv* over there; あそこです [asoko desu] It's over there

明日 [asu] *adv* tomorrow; 明日何かなさりたいですか? [asu nani ka nasaritai desu ka?] Would you like to do something tomorrow?; 明日の朝 [asu no asa] tomorrow morning; 明日の午後 [asu no gogo] tomorrow afternoon; 明日電話してもいいですか? [asu denwa shite mo ii desu ka?] May I call you tomorrow?; 私は明日の朝10時に出発します [watashi wa asu no asa juu-ji ni shuppatsu shimasu] I will be leaving tomorrow morning at ten a.m.; 私は明日出発します [watashi wa asu shuppatsu shimasu] I'm leaving tomorrow

アスパラガス [asuparagasu] *n* asparagus

アスピリン [asupirin] *n* aspirin; アスピリ

ンが欲しいのですが [asupirin ga hoshii no desu ga] I'd like some aspirin; 私はアスピリンを飲めません [watashi wa asupirin o nomemasen] I can't take aspirin

与える [ataeru] v give; 不快感を与える [fukaikan-o ataeru] v offend; 権限を与える [kengen-o ataeru] v authorize; 衝撃を与える [shougeki-o ataeru] v shock; 食物を与える [tabemono o ataeru] v feed; 影響を与える [eikyou-o ataeru] v affect

値する [atai suru] v to be worth; ···に値する [...ni atai suru] v deserve

頭 [atama] n head (body part); 頭のはげた [atama no hageta] v bald; 頭のいい [atama no ii] adj brainy

新しい [atarashii] adj new; 全く新しいスタイルにしてください [mattaku atarashii sutairu ni shite kudasai] I want a completely new look

あたり [atari] あたりを見回す [atari-o miwatasu] v look round; 1時間あたりいくらですか? [ichi-jikan atari ikura desu ka?] How much is it per hour?

暖かい [atatakai] adj warm

暖まる [atatamaru] v warm up

温める [atatameru] これを温めてもらえますか? [kore o atatamete moraemasu ka?] Can you warm this up, please?

あて [ate] あてにならない [ate ni naranai] adj shifty; あてにする [ate ni suru] v depend, rely on

あてにならない [ate ni naranai] adj unreliable

跡 [ato] n trace; 汚れの跡 [yogore no ato] n stain; 汚れの跡をつける [yogore no ato-o tsukeru] v stain

あと [ato] あとで [ato de] adv later

あとで [ato de] あとでもう一度かけてもらえますか? [ato de mou ichido kakete moraemasu ka?] Can you try again later?; あとで出直しましょうか? [ato de denaoshimashou ka?] Shall I come back later?

熱い [atsui] adj hot; 食べ物が熱すぎます [tabemono ga atsu-sugimasu] The food is too hot

暑い [atsui] adj hot; うだるように暑い [udaru youni atsui] adj sweltering; とても暑いです [totemo atsui desu] It's very hot; 暑くて眠れません [atsukute nemuremasen] I can't sleep for the heat; 部屋が暑すぎます [heya ga atsu-sugimasu] The room is too hot; 少し暑すぎます [sukoshi atsu-sugimasu] It's a bit too hot

厚い [atsui] adj thick; 厚さ [atsusa] n thickness

扱う [atsukau] v deal with, treat; 巧みに扱う [takumi ni atsukau] v manipulate

厚く [atsuku] 厚く切ったもの [atsuku kitta mono] n chunk

集まる [atsumaru] v get together

集める [atsumeru] v collect, gather

圧力 [atsuryoku] n pressure; 圧力を加える [atsuryoku-o kuwaeru] v pressure

アットマー [attomaa] アットマークが見つかりません [atto-maaku ga mitsukarimasen] I can't find the at sign

会う [au] vi meet; 〜に会う [~ ni au] vt meet; どこでお会いしましょうか? [doko de o-ai shimashou ka?] Where shall we meet?; どこでお会いできますか? [doko de o-ai dekimasu ka?] Where can we meet?; あとでお会いしましょうか? [ato de o-ai shimashou ka?] Shall we meet afterwards?; お会いできてうれしいです [o-ai dekite ureshii desu] Pleased to meet you; お会いできて光栄でした [o-ai dekite kouei deshita] It was a pleasure to meet you; ロビーでお会いしましょう [robii de o-ai shimashou] I'll meet you in the lobby

合う [au] v fit; 分け合う [wakeau] v share out; 合った [atta] adj matching; それは私に合いません [sore wa watashi ni aimasen] It doesn't fit me

アウトドア [autodoa] adv outdoors; どんなアウトドア・アクティビティがありますか? [donna autodoa-akutibiti ga arimasu ka?] What outdoor activities are there?

泡 [awa] n bubble; 泡風呂 [awaburo] n bubble bath

泡立つ [awadatsu] シュシュと泡立つ [shushu to awadatsu] adj fizzy

哀れみ [awaremi] *n* pity

哀れむ [awaremu] *v* pity

哀れな [aware na] *adj* pitiful

合わせる [awaseru] *v* combine; 焦点を合わせる [shouten-o awaseru] *v* focus

泡立て器 [awatateki] *n* whisk

誤る [ayamaru] *v* err; 判断を誤る [handan-o ayamaru] *v* misjudge

謝る [ayamaru] *v* apologize

アヤメ [ayame] *n* iris

怪しげな [ayashige na] *adj* dubious

怪しむ [ayashimu] *v* wonder

歩み [ayumi] *n* step

あざける [azakeru] *v* mock, scoff

アザミ [azami] *n* thistle

アザラシ [azarashi] *n* seal *(animal)*

鮮やかな [azayaka na] *adj* vivid

アゼルバイジャン [azerubaijan] *n* Azerbaijan; アゼルバイジャンの [azerubaijan no] *adj* Azerbaijani

アゼルバイジャン人 [azerubaijanjin] *n* Azerbaijani *(person)*

預かり所 [azukarisho] 手荷物一時預かり所 [tenimotsu ichiji azukarisho] *n* left-luggage office

預ける [azukeru] 預けた手荷物 [azuketa tenimotsu] *n* left-luggage

b

場 [ba] *n* place; 火葬場 [kasouba] *n* crematorium

バー [baa] *n* (酒場) bar *(alcohol)*; どこかに感じの良いバーはありますか? [doko-ka ni kanji no yoi baa wa arimasu ka?] Where is there a nice bar?; バーはどこですか? [baa wa doko desu ka?] Where is the bar?

バーベキュー [baabekyuu] *n* barbecue; バーベキュー場はどこですか? [baabekyuu-jou wa doko desu ka?] Where is the barbecue area?

バーチャルリアリティー [baacharuriariteii] *n* virtual reality

バードウォッチング [baadowotchingu] *n* birdwatching

バーガー [baagaa] *n* burger; ビーフバーガー [biifu baagaa] *n* beefburger

場合 [baai] *n* case, occasion

バージ [baaji] *n* barge

バーナー [baanaa] CDバーナー [shiidii baanaa] *n* CD burner; DVDバーナー [diibuidii baanaa] *n* DVD burner

バーレーン [baareen] *n* Bahrain

バーテンダー [baatendaa] *n* barman, bartender; 女性バーテンダー [josei baatendaa] *n* barmaid

バチカン [bachikan] n Vatican

バドミントン [badominton] n badminton; バドミントンのシャトル [badominton no shatoru] n shuttlecock

バグパイプ [bagupaipu] n bagpipes

バハマ [bahama] n Bahamas

売買 [baibai] n buying and selling; 売買契約 [baibai keiyaku] n bargain

バイバイ [baibai] excl bye-bye!

売機 [bai ki] 券売機 [kenbaiki] n ticket machine

バイオリン [baiorin] n violin; バイオリン奏者 [baiorinsousha] n violinist

バイパス [baipasu] n bypass

バイリンガル [bairingaru] バイリンガルの [bairingaru no] adj bilingual

バイロウ® [bairou] n Biro®

陪審 [baishin] n jury

賠償 [baishou] n reparation; 賠償金 [baishoukin] n compensation

売春 [baishun] n prostitution; 売春婦 [baishunfu] n prostitute

買収 [baishuu] n buyout; 企業買収 [kigyou baishuu] n takeover

バジル [bajiru] n basil

バッジ [bajji] n badge

ばか [baka] n idiot, twit; ばかな [baka na] adj daft, idiotic

ばかげる [bakageru] ばかげた [bakageta] adj absurd, ridiculous

ばか者 [bakamono] n fool

バケツ [baketsu] n bucket, pail

罰金 [bakkin] n fine; どこで罰金を払うのですか? [doko de bakkin o harau no desu ka?] Where do I pay the fine?; 罰金はいくらですか? [bakkin wa ikura desu ka?] How much is the fine?

バックアップ [bakkuappu] n backup

バックミラー [bakkumiraa] n rear-view mirror

バックパッカー [bakkupakkaa] backpacker

バックパッキング [bakkupakkingu] backpacking

バックパック [bakkupakku] n backpack; バックパッカー [bakkupakkaa] n backpacker; バックパッキング [bakkupakkingu] n backpacking

バックル [bakkuru] n buckle

バックスラッシュ [bakkusurasshu] n backslash

爆弾 [bakudan] n bomb; 時限爆弾 [jigenbakudan] n time bomb; 原子爆弾 [genshibakudan] n atom bomb

爆撃 [bakugeki] n bombing; 爆撃する [bakugeki suru] v bomb

爆破 [bakuha] n blast, explosion; 爆破する [bakuha suru] v blow up

爆発 [bakuhatsu] n blast, explosion; 爆発する [bakuhatsu suru] v explode

爆発物 [bakuhatsubutsu] n explosive

バクテリア [bakuteria] n bacteria

場面 [bamen] n scene

番 [ban] 二十番目の [nijuu banme no] adj twentieth; 七番目 [shichi banme] n seventh; 七番目の [shichi banme no] adj seventh; 三番目 [san banme] n third; 三番目の [san banme no] adj third; 六番目の [roku banme no] adj sixth; 十二番目の [juuni banme no] adj twelfth; 十七番目の [juushichi banme no] adj seventeenth; 十三番目の [juusan banme no] adj thirteenth; 十番目 [juu banme] n tenth; 十番目の [juu banme no] adj tenth; 十六番目の [juuroku banme no] adj sixteenth; 千番目 [sen banme] n thousandth; 千番目の [sen banme no] adj thousandth; 誰の番ですか? [dare no ban desu ka?] Whose turn is it?

晩 [ban] n evening; 晩に [ban ni] in the evening; 晩にできることは何がありますか? [ban ni dekiru koto wa nani ga arimasu ka?] What is there to do in the evenings?

バン [ban] n (自動車) van, (食べ物) bun

バナナ [banana] n banana

バンド [bando] n (音楽グループ) band (musical group); ブラスバンド [burasubando] n brass band; 腕時計のバンド [udedokei no bando] n watch strap

バンドエイド [bandoeido] n Band-Aid®

ばね [bane] n spring (coil)

バンガロー [bangarou] n bungalow

番号 [bangou] 携帯電話番号 [keitai denwa bangou] n mobile number; 番号案内サービス [bangou annai saabisu] n directory enquiries; 電話番号 [denwabangou] n phone number; 口座番号 [kouzabangou] n account number; あなたの携帯電話番号は何番ですか? [anata no keitai-denwa-bangou wa nan-ban desu ka?] What is the number of your mobile?; 番号間違いです [bangou machigai desu] You have the wrong number; 私の携帯電話番号は···です [watashi no keitai-denwa-bangou wa ... desu] My mobile number is...; 電話番号は何番ですか? [denwa-bangou wa nan-ban desu ka?] What's the telephone number?

番組 [bangumi] n programme; リアリティーテレビ番組 [riariitii terebi bangumi] n reality TV

バングラデシュ [banguradeshu] n Bangladesh; バングラデシュの [banguradeshu no] adj Bangladeshi

バングラデシュ人 [banguradeshujin] n Bangladeshi (person)

バニオン [banion] n bunion

バニラ [banira] n vanilla

バンジージャンプ [banjiijanpu] n bungee jumping

バンジョー [banjoo] n banjo

番人 [bannin] n watchman; 番人のいない [bannin no inai] adj unattended

バンパー [banpaa] n bumper

ばんそうこう [bansoukou] n (sticking) plaster; ばんそうこうが欲しいのですが [bansoukou ga hoshii no desu ga] I'd like some plasters

万歳! [banzai] excl hooray!

バプテスト [baputesuto] n Baptist

バラ [bara] n (植物) rose

ばらばら [barabara] adj in pieces; ばらばらにする [barabara ni suru] v break up

バランス [baransu] n balance; バランスの

とれた [baransu no toreta] adj balanced

バレエ [baree] n ballet; バレエシューズ [baree shuuzu] n ballet shoes; バレエダンサー [bareedansaa] n ballet dancer; どこでそのバレエのチケットを買えますか? [doko de sono baree no chiketto o kaemasu ka?] Where can I buy tickets for the ballet?

バレーボール [bareebouru] n volleyball

バレリーナ [bareriina] n ballerina

バルバドス [barubadosu] n Barbados

バルカン [barukan] バルカン諸国の [barukan shokoku no] adj Balkan

バルコニー [barukonii] n balcony; バルコニー付きの部屋はありますか? [barukonii-tsuki no heya wa arimasu ka?] Do you have a room with a balcony?

場所 [basho] n location, place; 住む場所 [sumu basho] n accommodation; 屋外市を催す場所 [okugai ichi-o moyousu basho] n fairground; 待避場所 [taihi basho] n layby; 今いる場所は···です [ima iru basho wa...desu] My location is...

バス [basu] n (乗り物) bus, (声楽) bass; バスの切符 [basu no kippu] n bus ticket; バスターミナル [basutaaminaru] n bus station; バス停 [basutei] n bus stop; 空港バス [kuukou basu] n airport bus; 長距離バス [choukyori basu] n coach (vehicle); すみません、···へ行くバスはどれですか? [sumimasen, ... e iku basu wa dore desu ka?] Excuse me, which bus goes to...?; バスは二十分おきに出ています [basu wa nijup-pun oki ni dete imasu] The bus runs every twenty minutes; バスは何時に着きますか? [basu wa nan-ji ni tsukimasu ka?] What time does the bus arrive?; バスは何時に出ますか? [basu wa nan-ji ni demasu ka?] What time does the bus leave?; 最終のバスは何時ですか? [saishuu no basu wa nan-ji desu ka?] What time is the last bus?; ···へ行くバスはどのくらい出ていますか? [...e iku basu wa dono kurai dete imasu ka?] How often are the buses to...?; ···へ行く次のバスは何時ですか? [...e iku tsugi no basu wa nan-ji desu ka?] When is the next bus to...?; ···へ行く始発のバスは何時ですか? [...e iku shihatsu no basu wa nan-ji desu ka?] **When is the first bus to…?**

バスドラム [basudoramu] n **bass drum**

バスケットボール [basukettobouru] n **basketball**

バスク地方 [basuku chihou] バスク地方の [basuku chihou no] adj **Basque**

バスク語 [basukugo] n **Basque** (language)

バスク人 [basukujin] n **Basque** (person)

バスローブ [basuroubu] n **bathrobe**

バスルーム [basuruumu] n **bathroom**; その部屋に専用のバスルームはありますか? [sono heya ni senyou no basu-ruumu wa arimasu ka?] **Does the room have a private bathroom?**; バスルームに介助の手すりはありますか? [basu-ruumu ni kaijo no tesuri wa arimasu ka?] **Are there hand rails in the bathroom?**; バスルームが水浸しになっています [basu-ruumu ga mizu-bitashi ni natte imasu] **The bathroom is flooded**

バスターミナル [basu-taaminaru] n **bus station**; バスターミナルはどこですか? [basu-taaminaru wa doko desu ka?] **Where is the bus station?**; バスターミナルまでどのくらいありますか? [basu-taaminaru made dono kurai arimasu ka?] **How far are we from the bus station?**

バス停 [basutei] 一番近いバス停はどこですか? [ichiban chikai basu-tei wa doko desu ka?] **Where is the nearest bus stop?**; バス停までどのくらいの距離ですか? [basu-tei made dono kurai no kyori desu ka?] **How far is the bus stop?**

バスト [basuto] n **bust**

バター [bataa] n **butter**

罰 [batsu] n **punishment**; 罰する [bassuru] v **penalize, punish**

ばったり [battari] adv **accidentally**; ばったり出会う [battari deau] v **bump into**

バッテリー [batterii] n **battery**; バッテリーはありますか? [batterii wa arimasu ka?] **Do you have any batteries?**; バッテリーが上がってしまいました [batterii ga agatte shimaimashita] **The battery is flat**; 私は新しいバッテリーが必要です [watashi wa

atarashii batterii ga hitsuyou desu] **I need a new battery**

バット [batto] n **bat** (with ball)

ベビー [bebii] n **baby**; ベビーミルク [bebii miruku] n **baby milk**

ベビーカー [bebiikaa] n **pushchair**

ベビーシート [bebiishiito] n **baby seat**; ベビーシートはありますか? [bebii-shiito wa arimasu ka?] **Do you have a baby seat?**

ベビーシッター [bebiishittaa] n **babysitter**; ベビーシッターをする [bebiishittaa o suru] v **babysit**

ベッド [beddo] n **bed**; 二段ベッド [nidanbeddo] n **bunk beds**; キングサイズのベッド [kingu saizu no beddo] n **king-size bed**; キャンプベッド [kyanpubeddo] n **camp bed**; ベッドサイドランプ [beddosaido ranpu] n **bedside lamp**; ベッドカバー [beddokabaa] n **bedspread**; 持ち運び用ベッド [mochihakobi you beddo] n **carrycot**; 日光浴用ベッド [nikkouyoku you beddo] n **sunbed**; 小児用ベッド [shouni you beddo] n **cot**; ベッドの寝心地がよくありません [beddo no ne-gokochi ga yoku arimasen] **The bed is uncomfortable**

ベッド＆ブレックファースト [beddo burekkufaasuto] n **bed and breakfast, B&B**

ベッドリネン [beddorinen] n **bed linen**

ベッドサイド [beddosaido] n **bedside**; ベッドサイドテーブル [beddosaido teeburu] n **bedside table**

ベージュ [beeju] adj **beige**; ベージュの [beeju no] adj **beige**

ベーキング [beekingu] n **baking**; ベーキングパウダー [beekingupaudaa] n **baking powder**

ベーコン [beekon] n **bacon**

ベークドポテト [beekudopoteto] n **baked potato**

ベール [beeru] n **veil**

米国 [beikoku] n **United States, US, USA**

ベジタリアン [bejitarian] n **vegetarian**; ベジタリアンの [bejitarian no] adj **vegetarian**; ここにベジタリアン用のレストランはありますか? [koko ni bejitarian-you no resutoran wa arimasu ka?] **Are there any vegetarian restaurants here?**; これはベジタリアン向きですか? [kore wa bejitarian muki desu ka?] **Is this suitable for vegetarians?**; ベジタリアン料理はありますか? [bejitarian-ryouri wa arimasu ka?] **Do you have any vegetarian dishes?**; 私はベジタリアンです [watashi wa bejitarian desu] **I'm vegetarian**

別館 [bekkan] n **pavilion**

別個 [bekko] 別個に [bekko ni] adv **apart**

ベンチ [benchi] n **bench**

ベネチアンブラインド [benechianburaindo] n **Venetian blind**

ベネズエラ [benezuera] n **Venezuela**; ベネズエラ人 [benezuerajin] n **Venezuelan** (person); ベネズエラの [benezuera no] adj **Venezuelan**

弁護 [bengo] n **defence**; 弁護士 [bengoshi] n **attorney**

弁護士 [bengoshi] n **lawyer**; 事務弁護士 [jimubengoshi] n **solicitor**

ベニバナインゲン [benibanaingen] n **runner bean**

ベニヤ板 [beniyaita] n **plywood**

弁解 [benkai] n **excuse**; 弁解する [benkai suru] v **excuse**

便器 [benki] n **toilet**; 幼児用の便器 [youji-you no benki] n **potty**; 幼児用の便器はありますか? [youji-you no benki wa arimasu ka?] **Do you have a potty?**

勉強 [benkyou] 勉強する [benkyou suru] v **study**

便秘 [benpi] n **constipation**; 便秘した [benpi shita] adj **constipated**; 私は便秘しています [watashi wa benpi shite imasu] **I'm constipated**

便利 [benri] adj **convenient**; 便利な [benri na] adj **handy**

弁済 [bensai] 弁済する [bensai suru] v **reimburse**

弁当 [bentou] n **packed lunch**

ベラルーシ [beraruushi] n **Belarus**; ベラルーシの [beraruushi no] adj **Belarussian**

ベラルーシ語 [beraruushigo] n **Belarussian** (language)

ベラルーシ人 [beraruushijin] n **Belarussian** (person)

ベリー [berii] n **berry**

ベルギー [berugii] n **Belgium**; ベルギーの [berugii no] adj **Belgian**

ベルギー人 [berugiijin] n **Belgian**

ベルクロ® [berukuro] n **Velcro®**

ベルト [beruto] n **belt**; 救命ベルト [kyuumei beruto] n **lifebelt**; 安全ベルト [anzenberuto] n **safety belt**

別荘 [bessou] n **holiday home**

ベストセラー [besutoseraa] n **bestseller**

べたぼめ [betabome] n **rave**

べとべと [betobeto] べとべとした [betobeto shita] adj **sticky**

ベトナム [betonamu] n **Vietnam**; ベトナム人 [betonamujin] n **Vietnamese** (person); ベトナムの [betonamu no] adj **Vietnamese**; ベトナム語 [betonamugo] n **Vietnamese** (language)

別 [betsu] 男女の別 [danjo no betsu] n **sexuality**; ・・・は別として [...wa betsu to shite] prep **apart from**; 別々に [betsubetsu ni] adv **separately**; これの別の色はありますか? [kore no betsu no iro wa arimasu ka?] **Do you have this in another colour?**; 別のものが欲しいのですが [betsu no mono ga hoshii no desu ga] **I would like something different**

別名 [betsumei] n **alias**; ・・・の別名で知られる [...no betsumei de shirareru] prep **alias**

別な [betsu na] adj **another**; 別なふうに [betsu na fuuni] adv **otherwise**

美貌 [bibou] 美貌の [bibou no] adj **good-looking**

ビデオ [bideo] n **video**

ビデオゲーム [bideogeemu] n **video game**; ビデオゲームができますか? [bideo-geemu ga dekimasu ka?] **Can I play video games?**

ビデオカメラ [bideokamera] n **video camera**; このビデオカメラ用のテープをいただけますか? [kono bideo-kamera-you no teepu o itadakemasu ka?] **Can I have a tape for this video camera, please?**

美顔術 [biganjutsu] *n* **facial**

ビーバー [biibaa] *n* **beaver**

ビーチ [biichi] *n* **beach**; ビーチサンダル [biichi sandaru] *n* **flip-flops**; この近くにいいビーチはありますか? [kono chikaku ni ii biichi wa arimasu ka?] **Are there any good beaches near here?**; この近くに静かなビーチはありますか? [kono chikaku ni shizuka na biichi wa arimasu ka?] **Is there a quiet beach near here?**; ビーチまでどのくらいの距離ですか? [biichi made dono kurai no kyori desu ka?] **How far is the beach?**; ビーチまでどのくらいありますか? [biichi made dono kurai arimasu ka?] **How far are we from the beach?**; ビーチへ行くバスはありますか? [biichi e iku basu wa arimasu ka?] **Is there a bus to the beach?**; 私はビーチに行きます [watashi wa biichi ni ikimasu] **I'm going to the beach**

ビーフ [biifu] *n* **beef**; ビーフバーガー [biifu baagaa] *n* **beefburger**

ビーガン [biigan] *n* **vegan**; これはビーガン向きですか? [kore wa biigan muki desu ka?] **Is this suitable for vegans?**; ビーガン料理はありますか? [biigan-ryouri wa arimasu ka?] **Do you have any vegan dishes?**

ビール [biiru] *n* **beer**; ビールをもう一杯 [biiru o mou ippai] **another beer**

ビートルート [biitoruuto] *n* **beetroot**

ビーズ [biizu] *n* **bead**

ビジネス [bijinesu] *n* **business**; ビジネスクラス [bijinesu kurasu] *n* **business class**

ビジネスマン [bijinesuman] *n* **businessman**; 私はビジネスマンです [watashi wa bijinesu-man desu] **I'm a businessman**

ビジネスウーマン [bijinesuuuman] *n* **businesswoman**; 私はビジネスウーマンです [watashi wa bijinesu-uuman desu] **I'm a businesswoman**

ビジターセンター [bijitaasentaa] *n* **visitor centre**

美術 [bijutsu] *n* **art**; 美術館 [bijutsukan] *n* art gallery; 美術品 [bijutsuhin] *n* **work of art**; 美術学校 [bijutsugakkou] *n* **art school**

ビキニ [bikini] *n* **bikini**

びっこ [bikko] びっこの [bikko no] *adj* **lame**

びっこをひく [bikko o hiku] *v* **limp**

びっくり [bikkuri] びっくりさせる [bikkuri saseru] *v* **surprise**

微妙 [bimyou] 微妙な [bimyou na] *adj* **subtle**

便 [bin] *n* **flight**; チャーター便 [chaataa bin] *n* **charter flight**; 航空便 [koukuubin] *n* **airmail**; 定期便 [teikibin] *n* **scheduled flight**

瓶 [bin] *n* **jar**; ジャムの瓶 [jamu no bin] *n* **jam jar**; 哺乳瓶 [honyuubin] *n* **baby's bottle**

ビンディング [bindeingu] *npl* **bindings**; ビンディングを調節していただけますか? [bindingu o chousetsu shite itadakemasu ka?] **Can you adjust my bindings, please?**; ビンディングを締めていただけますか? [bindingu o shimete itadakemasu ka?] **Can you tighten my bindings, please?**

ビネグレットドレッシング [binegurettodoresshingu] *n* **vinaigrette**

ビンゴ [bingo] *n* **bingo**

ビニール [biniiru] *n* **vinyl**; ビニール袋 [biniiru bukuro] *n* **plastic bag**

便箋 [binsen] *n* **writing paper**

ビオラ [biora] *n* **viola**

ビリヤード [biriyaado] *n* **billiards**

ビロード [biroudo] *n* **velvet**

ビルマ [biruma] *n* **Burma**; ビルマの [biruma no] *adj* **Burmese**

ビルマ語 [birumago] *n* **Burmese** *(language)*

ビルマ人 [birumajin] *n* **Burmese** *(person)*

びしょぬれ [bishonure] びしょぬれにする [bishonure ni suru] *v* **drench**

微小 [bishou] 微小な [bishou na] *adj* **minute**

ビスケット [bisuketto] *n* **biscuit**

ビタミン [bitamin] *n* **vitamin**

美容 [biyou] 美容外科 [biyou geka] n cosmetic surgery

美容院 [biyouin] n beauty salon, hairdresser's

美容師 [biyoushi] n hairdresser

ビザ [biza] n visa; 私のビザです [watashi no biza desu] Here is my visa; 入国ビザを持っています [nyuukoku-biza o motte imasu] I have an entry visa

墓地 [bochi] n cemetery, graveyard

ボディービル [bodiibiru] n bodybuilding

ボディーガード [bodiigaado] n bodyguard

母音 [boin] n vowel

ボイラー [boiraa] n boiler

ボイスメール [boisumeeru] n voicemail

ボックス [bokkusu] n box; アイスボックス [aisu bokkusu] n icebox; グローブボックス [guroobubokkusu] n glove compartment; 空き瓶回収ボックス [akikan kaishuu bokkusu] n bottle bank; 電話ボックス [denwa bokkusu] n phonebox

母国 [bokoku] 母国語 [bokokugo] n mother tongue

母国語 [bokokugo] 母国語とする人 [bokokugo to suru hito] n native speaker

ボクサー [bokusaa] n boxer; ボクサーショーツ [bokusaa shootsu] n boxer shorts

牧師 [bokushi] 教区牧師 [kyouku bokushi] n vicar

ボクシング [bokushingu] n boxing

牧草地 [bokusouchi] n meadow

牧羊 [bokuyou] 牧羊犬 [bokuyouken] n sheepdog

盆 [bon] n (台所用品) tray

ボンネット [bonnetto] n bonnet (car)

ぼんやり [bon'yari] ぼんやりした [bonyari shita] adj absent-minded

勃発 [boppatsu] n outbreak

ボリビア [boribia] n Bolivia; ボリビアの [boribia no] adj Bolivian

ボリビア人 [boribiajin] n Bolivian (person)

ぼろきれ [borokire] n rag

ボルト [boruto] n (電圧) volt

ボリューム [boryuumu] n volume; ボリュームを上げてもいいですか? [boryuumu o agete mo ii desu ka?] May I turn the volume up?; ボリュームを下げてもらえますか? [boryuumu o sagete moraemasu ka?] Please could you lower the volume?

母性 [bosei] 母性の [bosei no] adj maternal

没収 [bosshuu] 没収する [bosshuu suru] v confiscate

ボス [bosu] n boss

ボスニア [bosunia] n Bosnia; ボスニアの [bosunia no] adj Bosnian

ボスニア・ヘルツェゴビナ [bosunia herutsuegobina] n Bosnia and Herzegovina

ボスニア人 [bosuniajin] n Bosnian (person)

ボタン [botan] n (服) button; どのボタンを押すのですか? [dono botan o osu no desu ka?] Which button do I press?

ボトル [botoru] n bottle; ボトルをもう1本持ってきてください [botoru o mou ippon motte kite kudasai] Please bring another bottle; ミネラルウォーターのボトル1本 [mineraruuootaa no botoru 1 hon] a bottle of mineral water; 赤ワインのボトルを1本 [aka-wain no botoru o ippon] a bottle of red wine

ボツワナ [botsuwana] n Botswana

棒 [bou] n bar (strip), pole, rod, staff (stick or rod); 棒切れ [bou kire] n stick; 編み棒 [amibou] n knitting needle

膨張 [bouchou] 膨張性の [bouchou sei no] adj inflatable

暴動 [boudou] n riot; 暴動を起こす [boudou-o okosu] v riot

望遠 [bouen] 望遠鏡 [bouenkyou] n telescope

防護 [bougo] n security

防御 [bougyo] n defence; 防御する [bougyo suru] v defend; 防御者 [bougyosha] n defender

ボーイフレンド [bouifurendo] n

boyfriend; 私にはボーイフレンドがいます [watashi ni wa booifurendo ga imasu] **I have a boyfriend**

防火壁 [boukaheki] n firewall

傍観 [boukan] 傍観者 [boukansha] n onlooker

冒険 [bouken] n adventure; 冒険好きな [bouken zuki na] adj adventurous

膀胱 [boukou] n bladder; 膀胱炎 [boukouen] n cystitis

亡命 [boumei] n asylum; 亡命者 [boumeisha] n asylum seeker

ボーナス [bounasu] n bonus

暴利 [bouri] n rip-off

ボウリング [bouringu] n bowling; ボウリング場 [bouringu jou] n bowling alley

ボウル [bouru] n bowl

ボール [bouru] n ball (toy)

ボール箱 [bourubako] n carton

ボール紙 [bourugami] n cardboard

ボールペン [bourupen] n ballpoint pen

暴力 [bouryoku] n violence; 暴力的な [bouryokuteki na] adj violent

帽子 [boushi] n hat; ベレー帽 [bereebou] n beret; 縁なし帽子 [fuchinashi boushi] n cap; 野球帽 [yakyuubou] n baseball cap

防水 [bousui] 防水の [bousui no] adj waterproof

防水布 [bousuifu] タール塗り防水布 [taaru nuri bousuifu] n tarpaulin

棒高跳び [bou taka tobi] n pole vault

ボート [bouto] n boat; ボートを漕ぐこと [booto-o kogu koto] n rowing; 救命ボート [kyuumeibooto] n lifeboat

部分 [bubun] n part, portion, section; 部分的な [bubunteki na] adj partial; 部分的に [bubunteki ni] adv partly

仏陀 [budda] n Buddha

ブドウ [budou] n grape; ブドウ園 [budouen] n vineyard

ブイ [bui] n buoy

侮辱 [bujoku] n insult; 侮辱する [bujoku suru] v insult

武器 [buki] n weapon

不器用 [bukiyou] 不器用な [bukiyou na] adj clumsy

仏教 [bukkyou] n Buddhism; 仏教の [bukkyou no] adj Buddhist; 仏教徒 [bukkyouto] n Buddhist

部門 [bumon] n category, department, sector

文 [bun] n (言葉) sentence (words); 引用文 [in-youbun] n quotation

ブナ [buna] n beech (tree)

無難な [bunan na] adj acceptable

分別 [bunbetsu] n discretion; 分別のない [funbetsu no nai] adj unwise; 分別のある [bunbetsu no aru] adj sensible

文房具 [bunbougu] n stationery; 文房具店 [bunbouguten] n stationer's

ブンブン [bunbun] n humming; ブンブンいう [bunbun iu] v hum

文学 [bungaku] n literature; 文学士 [bungakushi] n BA

文化 [bunka] n culture; 文化の [bunka no] adj cultural

分解 [bunkai] n dissolution; 生物分解性の [seibutsu bunkaisei no] adj biodegradable; 分解する [bunkai suru] v take apart

分割 [bunkatsu] n division; 分割払い [bunkatsu harai] n instalment

文明 [bunmei] n civilization

分派 [bunpa] n sect

文法 [bunpou] n grammar; 文法の [bunpou no] adj grammatical

分裂 [bunretsu] n division; 分裂する [bunretsu suru] v split up

分離 [bunri] n separation

分離帯付き [bunritaitsuki] 中央分離帯付き道路 [chuuou bunritai tsuki douro] n dual carriageway

分類 [bunrui] n class; 分類広告 [bunruikoukoku] n small ads

分量 [bunryou] どのくらいの分量を飲ませればよいのですか? [dono kurai no bunryou o nomasereba yoi no desu ka?] **How much should I give?**

分析 [bunseki] n analysis; 分析する [bunseki suru] v analyse

分子 [bunshi] n molecule

文書 [bunsho] n document

文書館 [bunshokan] n archive

文通 [buntsuu] n correspondence; 文通者 [buntsuusha] n correspondent

ぶらぶら [burabura] adv idly; ぶらぶら歩き [burabura aruki] n stroll

ブラインド [buraindo] n blind

ブラジャー [burajaa] n bra

ブラジル [burajiru] n Brazil; ブラジルの [burajiru no] adj Brazilian

ブラジル人 [burajirujin] n Brazilian (person)

ブラックベリー [burakkuberii] n blackberry

ブラックベリー® [burakkuberii] n BlackBerry®

ブラックチョコレート [burakku chokoreeto] n plain chocolate

ブランデー [burandee] n brandy; ブランデーをください [burandee o kudasai] I'll have a brandy

ブランド [burando] n brand; ブランド名 [burando mei] n brand name

ブラシ [burashi] n brush; ブラシをかける [burashi o kakeru] v brush; 歯ブラシ [haburashi] n toothbrush

ブラス [burasu] n brass; ブラスバンド [burasubando] n brass band

ブラウス [burausu] n blouse

ブラウザ [burauza] n browser

ブレーキ [bureeki] n brake; ブレーキをかける [bureeki-o kakeru] v brake; ブレーキランプ [bureeki ranpu] n brake light; ブレーキがききません [bureeki ga kikimasen] The brakes are not working, The brakes don't work

ブレンダー [burendaa] n blender

ブレサライザー® [buresaraizaa] n Breathalyser®

ブレスレット [buresuretto] n bracelet

ブレザー [burezaa] n blazer

ブリーフィング [buriifingu] n briefing

ブリーフ [buriifu] n briefs

ブリーフケース [buriifukeesu] n briefcase

ブリザード [burizaado] n blizzard

ブログ [burogu] n blog; ブログを書く [burogu-o kaku] v blog

ブロッコリー [burokkorii] n broccoli

ブロック [burokku] n block (buildings)

ブロンド [burondo] ブロンドの [burondo no] adj blonde; 私は生まれつきブロンドです [watashi wa umaretsuki burondo desu] My hair is naturally blonde

ブロンズ [buronzu] n bronze

ブロードライ [buroodorai] n blow-dry

ブローカー [burookaa] n broker

ブローチ [burouchi] n brooch

ブロードバンド [buroudobando] n broadband

ブルドーザー [burudouzaa] n bulldozer

ブルガリア [burugaria] n Bulgaria; ブルガリアの [burugaria no] adj Bulgarian

ブルガリア語 [burugariago] n Bulgarian (language)

ブルガリア人 [burugariajin] n Bulgarian (person)

ブルーベリー [buruuberii] n blueberry

ブルース [buruusu] n blues

武装 [busou] 武装した [busou shita] adj armed

物質 [busshitsu] n matter, substance; 抗生物質 [kousei busshitsu] n antibiotic

豚 [buta] n pig

豚肉 [butaniku] n pork; 私は豚肉を食べません [watashi wa butaniku o tabemasen] I don't eat pork

舞踏 [butou] 舞踏会 [butoukai] n ball (dance)

物理学 [butsurigaku] n physics

物理学者 [butsurigakusha] n physicist

物体 [buttai] 未確認飛行物体 [mikakunin hikoubuttai] n UFO

ブーケ [buuke] n bouquet

ブースターケーブル
[buusutaakeeburu] *npl* jump leads; ブースターケーブルはありますか?
[buusutaa-keeburu wa arimasu ka?] Do you have any jump leads?

ブースターコード [buusutaakoodo] *n* jump leads

ブーツ [buutsu] *n* boot

部族 [buzoku] *n* tribe

病 [byou] アルツハイマー病 [arutsuhaimaa byou] *n* Alzheimer's disease; 私は心臓病があります [watashi wa shinzou-byou ga arimasu] I have a heart condition

鋲 [byou] *n* stud

平等 [byoudou] *n* equality

病学 [byougaku] 老人病学の [roujinbyougaku no] *adj* geriatric

病院 [byouin] *n* hospital; 産科病院 [sanka byouin] *n* maternity hospital; 精神病院 [seishinbyouin] *n* psychiatric hospital; その病院へはどう行けばいいのですか? [sono byouin e wa dou ikeba ii no desu ka?] How do I get to the hospital?; 病院はどこですか? [byouin wa doko desu ka?] Where is the hospital?; 私は病院で働いています [watashi wa byouin de hataraite imasu] I work in a hospital; 私たちは彼を病院に連れて行かなければなりません [watashi-tachi wa kare o byouin ni tsurete ikanakereba narimasen] We must get him to hospital; 彼女は病院に行かなければなりませんか? [kanojo wa byouin ni ikanakereba narimasen ka?] Will she have to go to hospital?

病欠 [byouketsu] 病欠届け [byouketsu todoke] *n* sick note

病気 [byouki] *n* disease, illness, sickness; 病気休暇 [byoukikyuuka] *n* sick leave; 病気の [byouki no] *adj* ill

病人 [byounin] *n* invalid

病棟 [byoutou] *n* ward (*hospital room*); ···はどの病棟に入院していますか? […wa dono byoutou ni nyuuin shite imasu ka?] Which ward is … in?; 救急病棟 [kyuukyuubyoutou] *n* accident & emergency department

ビュッフェ [byuffe] *n* buffet; ビュッフェ車 [byuffesha] *n* buffet car; ビュッフェ車はどこですか? [byuffe-sha wa doko desu ka?] Where is the buffet car?; 電車にはビュッフェ車がありますか? [densha ni wa byuffe-sha ga arimasu ka?] Is there a buffet car on the train?

C

チャージ [chaaji] n charge; カバーチャージ [kabaa chaaji] n cover charge

チャーター [chaataa] n charter; チャーター便 [chaataa bin] n charter flight

チャド [chado] n Chad

チャイブ [chaibu] n chives

茶色 [chairo] adj brown; 茶色の [chairo no] adj brown

チャイルドマインダー [chairudomaindaa] n childminder

チャイルドシート [chairudoshiito] 2歳の子供用のチャイルドシートが欲しいのですが [ni-sai no kodomo-you no chairudo-shiito ga hoshii no desu ga] I'd like a child seat for a two-year-old child; チャイルドシートはありますか? [chairudo-shiito wa arimasu ka?] Do you have a child's seat?

着地 [chakuchi] n touchdown

着古す [chaku furusu] 着古した [kifurushita] adj worn

着陸 [chakuriku] 着陸する [chakuriku suru] v land; 緊急着陸 [kinkyuu chakuriku] n emergency landing

着席 [chakuseki] 着席する [chakuseki suru] v sit down

着信 [chakushin] 着信メロディ [chakushin merodi] n ringtone

着色 [chakushoku] n colouring

チャンネル [channeru] n channel

チャリティー [charitii] チャリティーショップ [charitii shoppu] n charity shop

チャット [chatto] チャットルーム [chatto ruumu] n chatroom

チャットする [chatto suru] v chat (in chatroom)

チェア [chea] n chair; デッキチェア [dekkichea] n deckchair

チェアリフト [chearifuto] n chairlift

チェチェン [chechien] チェチェン共和国 [chechen kyouwakoku] n Chechnya

チェッカー [chekkaa] n draughts

チェック [chekku] n tick; チェックの [chekku no] adj checked; チェックする [chekku suru] v tick off

チェックアウト [chekkuauto] n checkout; チェックアウトする [chekkuauto suru] v check out

チェックイン [chekkuin] n check-in; チェックインする [chekkuin suru] v check in

チェコ [cheko] チェコの [cheko no] adj Czech; チェコ共和国 [cheko kyouwakoku] n Czech Republic

チェコ語 [chekogo] n Czech (language)

チェコ人 [chekojin] n Czech (person)

チェロ [chero] n cello

チェス [chesu] n chess

血 [chi] n blood; 血を見るスポーツ [chi-o miru supootsu] n blood sports; 血圧 [ketsuatsu] n blood pressure

地 [chi] 沼地 [numachi] n swamp

治安 [chian] n public order; 治安判事 [chian hanji] n magistrate

チベット [chibetto] n Tibet; チベット人 [chibettojin] n Tibetan (person); チベットの [chibetto no] adj Tibetan; チベット語 [chibettogo] n Tibetan (language)

乳房 [chibusa] n breast

乳 [chichi] n milk; 乳を搾る [chichi-o shiboru] v milk

父 [chichi] n father; 継父 [mama chichi] n stepfather

地中海 [chichuukai] n Mediterranean; 地中海の [chichuukai no] adj Mediterranean

チフス [chifusu] 腸チフス [chouchifusu] n typhoid

違い [chigai] n difference

違う [chigau] adj different

地平 [chihei] 地平線 [chiheisen] n horizon

地方 [chihou] n region; 地方議会議員 [chihou gikai giin] n councillor; どこでその地方の地図を買えますか? [doko de sono chihou no chizu o kaemasu ka?] Where can I buy a map of the region?

地位 [chii] n job (rank)

地域 [chiiki] n area, region, territory; 地域の [chiiki no] adj regional; 地域社会 [chiiki shakai] n community; この地域ではどんなところを見物できますか? [kono chiiki de wa donna tokoro o kenbutsu dekimasu ka?] What can we visit in the area?

チーム [chiimu] n team

小い [chiisai] adj small; 小さくする [chiisaku suru] v turn down (volume)

小さな [chiisa na] adj tiny; 小さな袋 [chiisana fukuro] n sachet; 小さな包み [chiisana tsutsumi] n packet

小さい [chiisa na] adj little, small; 小さい方の [chiisai hou no] adj minor; それは小さすぎます [sore wa chiisa-sugimasu] It's too small

チーズ [chiizu] n cheese

縮む [chijimu] v shrink; 縮んだ [chijinda] adj shrunk

地下 [chika] 地下に [chika ni] adv underground; 地下運動 [chika undou] n underground (movement)

地下道 [chikadou] n subway

近づきやすい [chikadukiyasui] adj accessible

近づく [chikaduku] v approach

誓い [chikai] n oath

近い [chikai] adj close, near

地階 [chikai] n basement

近く [chikaku] すぐ近くの [sugu chikaku no] adj close by; 近くに [chikaku ni] adv close, near, nearby; 近くの [chikaku no] adj nearby; ···の近くに [...no chikaku ni] prep near; すぐ近くです [sugu chikaku desu] It's very near; 近くに銀行はありますか? [chikaku ni ginkou wa arimasu ka?] Is there a bank nearby?

近道 [chikamichi] n shortcut

力 [chikara] n strength; 意志の力 [ishi no chikara] n willpower; 説得力のある [settokuryoku no aru] adj convincing

地下牢 [chikarou] n dungeon

地下室 [chikashitsu] n cellar

地下鉄 [chikatetsu] n underground, metro; 地下鉄駅 [chikatetsu eki] n metro station, tube station; 一番近い地下鉄の駅はどこですか? [ichiban chikai chikatetsu no eki wa doko desu ka?] Where is the nearest tube station?; 一番近い地下鉄の駅へはどう行けばいいのですか? [ichiban chikai chikatetsu no eki e wa dou ikeba ii no desu ka?] How do I get to the nearest tube station?; 地下鉄のマップはありますか? [chikatetsu no mappu wa arimasu ka?] Do you have a map of the tube?; 地下鉄のマップをいただけますか? [chikatetsu no mappu o itadakemasu ka?] Could I have a map of the tube, please?

チケット [chiketto] n ticket; 今晩のチケットを2枚お願いします [konban no chiketto o nimai o-negai shimasu] Two tickets for tonight, please; どこでそのコンサートのチケットを買えますか? [doko de sono konsaato no chiketto o kaemasu ka?] Where can I buy tickets for the concert?; ここでそのチケットを買えますか? [koko de sono chiketto o kaemasu ka?] Can I buy the tickets here?; 私はチケットをなくしました [watashi wa chiketto o nakushimashita] I've lost my ticket; 私たちのためにそのチケットを予約してもらえますか? [watashi-tachi no tame ni sono chiketto o yoyaku shite moraemasu ka?] Can you book the tickets for us?; 駐車チケットを買わなければなりませんか? [chuusha-chiketto o kawanakereba narimasen ka?] Do I need to buy a car-parking ticket?; 子供のチケット [kodomo no chiketto] a child's ticket

地区 [chiku] n district; 指定地区 [shitei chiku] n precinct

畜牛 [chikugyuu] n cattle

地球 [chikyuu] n earth; 地球の [chikyuu no] adj global

地球儀 [chikyuugi] n globe

地球温暖化 [chikyuuondanka] n global warming

血まみれ [chimamire] 血まみれの [chi mamire no] adj bloody

致命 [chimei] 致命的な [chimeiteki na] adj fatal

賃借り [chingari] n hire; 賃借りする [chingari suru] v hire

賃金 [chingin] n wage

知能 [chinou] n intelligence; 知能指数 [chinoushisuu] n IQ

チンパンジー [chinpanjii] n chimpanzee

チンピラ [chinpira] n punk

鎮静 [chinsei] 鎮静剤 [chinseizai] n sedative

賃借 [chinshaku] 賃借人 [chinshakunin] n tenant

賃貸 [chintai] 賃貸する [chintai suru] v rent; 賃貸料 [chintairyou] n rent

賃貸借 [chintaishaku] 賃貸借する [chintaishaku suru] v lease; 賃貸借契約 [chintaishaku keiyaku] n lease

チップ [chippu] n (電子) chip (electronic), (心づけ) tip (reward); チップをやる [chippu-o yaru] (心づけ) v tip (reward); チップはいくら渡せばよいですか? [chippu wa ikura wataseba yoi desu ka?] How much should I give as a tip?; チップを渡すのは一般的なことですか? [chippu o watasu no wa ippan-teki na koto desu ka?] Is it usual to give a tip?

チップス [chippusu] n crisps; ポテトチップス [potetochippusu] n crisps

散らかす [chirakasu] v mess up; 散らかしたもの [chirakashita mono] n clutter

散らかった [chira katta] v messy

ちらし [chirashi] n (印刷物) leaflet

チリ [chiri] n Chile; チリの [chiri no] adj Chilean

地理学 [chirigaku] n geography

チリ人 [chirijin] n Chilean (person)

ちり取り [chiritori] n dustpan

治療 [chiryou] n cure, remedy, treatment

治療医 [chiryoui] 足治療医 [ashichiryoui] n chiropodist

治療室 [chiryoushitsu] 集中治療室 [shuuchuuchiryoushitsu, ICU aishiiyuu] n intensive care unit

知識 [chishiki] n information, knowledge; 一般知識 [ippan chishiki] n general knowledge; 知識を与える [chishiki-o ataeru] adj informative

知識人 [chishikijin] n intellectual

地質学 [chishitsugaku] n geology

窒素 [chisso] n nitrogen

窒息 [chissoku] 窒息する [chissoku suru] v suffocate

地帯 [chitai] n zone

知的 [chiteki] adj intellectual; 知的な [chiteki na] adj intellectual

地点 [chiten] n spot (place)

地図 [chizu] n map; 街路地図 [gairo chizu] n street map; 地図帳 [chizuchou] n atlas; どこでその街の地図を買えますか? [doko de sono machi no chizu o kaemasu ka?] Where can I buy a map of the city?; どこでその国の地図を買えますか? [doko de sono kuni no chizu o kaemasu ka?] Where can I buy a map of the country?; どこでその地方の地図を買えますか? [doko de sono chihou no chizu o kaemasu ka?] Where can I buy a map of the region?; 道順を示す地図を書いてもらえますか? [michijun o shimesu chizu o kaite moraemasu ka?] Can you draw me a map with directions?; 地図でそれがどこにあるか教えてもらえますか? [chizu de sore ga doko ni aru ka oshiete moraemasu ka?] Can you show me where it is on the map?; 地図で私たちがいる場所を教えてもらえます

か？ [chizu de watashi-tachi ga iru basho o oshiete moraemasu ka?] Can you show me where we are on the map?

宁金 [chokin] n savings; 貯金箱 [chokinbako] n piggybank

直角 [chokkaku] n right angle

直感 [chokkan] n intuition

直径 [chokkei] n diameter

直行 [chokkou] 直行で [chokkou de] adv non-stop

チョコレート [chokoreeto] n chocolate

直毛 [chokumou] 私は生まれつき直毛です [watashi wa umaretsuki chokumou desu] My hair is naturally straight

直接 [chokusetsu] 直接に [chokusetsu ni] adv directly; 直接自分で [chokusetsu jibun de] adv personally

直通 [chokutsuu] 直通のほうがいいのですが [chokutsuu no hou ga ii no desu ga] I'd prefer to go direct

著者 [chosha] n author

貯水 [chosui] 貯水池 [chosuichi] n reservoir

ちょっと [chotto] ちょっとの間 [chotto no aida] adv momentarily

腸 [chou] n bowels, gut; 腸チフス [chouchifusu] n typhoid

長 [chou] n (統率) head (principal), (統率) master

帳 [chou] n book; メモ帳 [memochou] n jotter; 電話帳 [denwachou] n telephone directory

チョウ [chou] n butterfly

・・・長 [...chou] n chief, head

諜報 [chouhou] 諜報機関 [chouhou kikan] n secret service

長方形 [chouhoukei] n rectangle; 長方形の [chouhoukei no] adj oblong, rectangular

頂上 [choujou] n summit

超過 [chouka] n excess; 超過手荷物 [choukatenimotsu] n excess baggage; 超過勤務 [chouka kinmu] n overtime

聴覚 [choukaku] v cancel; 聴覚の

[choukaku no] adj acoustic

帳消す [choukesu] v cancel; 帳消しにする [choukeshi ni suru] v cross out

彫刻 [choukoku] n sculpture; 彫刻家 [choukokuka] n sculptor

兆候 [choukou] n sign

チョーク [chouku] n (白墨) chalk

長距離 [choukyori] 長距離バス [choukyori basu] n coach (vehicle); 長距離バスは朝何時に出ますか？ [choukyori-basu wa asa nan-ji ni demasu ka?] When does the coach leave in the morning?

調味料 [choumiryou] n flavouring, seasoning

蝶ネクタイ [chounekutai] n bow tie

超音波 [chouonpa] n ultrasound

調理 [chouri] n cooking; 調理法 [chourihou] n recipe; 調理済みの [chouri zumi no] adj ready-cooked; これは十分調理されていません [kore wa juubun chouri sarete imasen] This isn't cooked properly

長老派 [chourouha] 長老派の [chourouha no] adj Presbyterian; 長老派の人 [chourouha no hito] n Presbyterian

聴力 [chouryoku] n hearing

調査 [chousa] n investigation, research, survey; 世論調査 [yoronchousa] n opinion poll, poll; 調査する [chousa suru] v explore; 綿密な調査 [menmitsu na chousa] n scan; 国勢調査 [kokuzeichousa] n census; 市場調査 [shijouchousa] n market research

調整 [chousei] n adjustment; 調整できる [chousei dekiru] adj adjustable

挑戦 [chousen] n challenge; 挑戦する [chousen suru] v challenge; 挑戦的な [chousenteki na] adj challenging

朝鮮 [chousen] n Korea; 朝鮮の [chousen no] adj Korean

朝鮮語 [chousengo] n Korean (language)

朝鮮人 [chousenjin] n Korean (person)

調子 [choushi] n pitch (sound)

超自然 [choushizen] 超自然の [choushizen no] adj supernatural

朝食 [choushoku] n breakfast; ヨーロッパ大陸式の簡単な朝食 [yooroppa tairikushiki no kantan na choushoku] n continental breakfast; 朝食付きで [choushoku-tsuki de] with breakfast; 朝食なしで [choushoku nashi de] without breakfast; 朝食には何を召し上がりますか? [choushoku ni wa nani o meshiagarimasu ka?] What would you like for breakfast?; 朝食は何時ですか? [choushoku wa nan-ji desu ka?] What time is breakfast?; 朝食はどこで取るのですか? [choushoku wa doko de toru no desu ka?] Where is breakfast served?; 朝食は含まれていますか? [choushoku wa fukumarete imasu ka?] Is breakfast included?; 自分の部屋で朝食を取ることができますか? [jibun no heya de choushoku o toru koto ga dekimasu ka?] Can I have breakfast in my room?

聴衆 [choushuu] n audience

調達 [choutatsu] n supply; 資金を調達する [shikin-o choutatsu suru] v finance

ちょうつがい [choutsugai] n hinge

調剤 [chouzai] 調剤師 [chouzaishi] n dispenser

チュニジア [chunijia] n Tunisia; チュニジア人 [chunijiajin] n Tunisian (person); チュニジアの [chunijia no] adj Tunisian

チューブ [chuubu] n tube

中風 [chuubuu] n stroke (apoplexy)

中断 [chuudan] n interruption; 中断する [chuudan suru] v interrupt

中毒 [chuudoku] n poisoning; 中毒者 [chuudokusha] n addict; アルコール中毒者 [arukooru chuudokusha] n alcoholic

中学 [chuugaku] 中学校 [chuugakkou] n secondary school

中国 [chuugoku] n China; 中国の [chuugoku no] adj Chinese

中国語 [chuugokugo] n Chinese (language)

中国人 [chuugokujin] n Chinese (person)

中尉 [chuui] n lieutenant

注意 [chuui] n attention, care, caution, notice (note); 注意をそらす [chuui-o

sorasu] v distract

注意深い [chuuibukai] adj careful

注意深く [chuuibukaku] adv carefully

チューインガム [chuuingamu] n chewing gum

注意せよ [chuui seyo] NB (nota bene)

忠実 [chuujitsu] 忠実な [chuujitsu na] adj faithful; 忠実に [chuujitsuni] adv faithfully

中間 [chuukan] 中間の [chuukan no] adj mid; 中間の [chuukan no] adj intermediate

中古 [chuuko] 中古の [chuuko no] adj secondhand, used

注文 [chuumon] n order; 注文する [chuumon suru] v order (request); 注文用紙 [chuumon youshi] n order form; これは私が注文したものと違います [kore wa watashi ga chuumon shita mono to chigaimasu] This isn't what I ordered; 注文していいですか? [chuumon shite ii desu ka?] Can I order now, please?

中年 [chuunen] 中年の [chuunen no] adj middle-aged

注入 [chuunyuu] ポンプで注入する [ponpu de chuunyuu suru] v pump

中央 [chuuou] n middle; 中央の [chuuou no] adj central; 中央アメリカ [chuuou amerika] n Central America; 中央アフリカ共和国 [chuuou afurika kyouwakoku] n Central African Republic; 中央分離帯付き道路 [chuuou bunritai tsuki douro] n dual carriageway

チューリップ [chuurippu] n tulip

中立 [chuuritsu] 中立の [chuuritsu no] adj neutral; 中立国 [chuuritsukoku] n neutral country

中流階級 [chuuryuu kaikyuu] 中流階級の [chuuryuu kaikyuu no] adj middle-class

仲裁 [chuusai] n arbitration

中世 [chuusei] n Middle Ages; 中世の [chuusei no] adj mediaeval

忠誠 [chuusei] n loyalty

注射 [chuusha] n injection; 注射する [chuusha suru] v inject; 注射器

[chuushaki] *n* syringe; 注射を打ってくださ
い [chuusha o utte kudasai] **Please give
me an injection**; 私は痛み止めの注射は欲
しくありません [watashi wa itami-dome no
chuusha wa hoshiku arimasen] **I don't
want an injection for the pain**

駐車 [chuusha] *n* parking; 駐車する
[chuusha suru] *v* park; 駐車違反切符
[chuushaihan kippu] *n* parking ticket

駐車場 [chuushajou] *n* car park; この近く
に駐車場はありますか? [kono chikaku ni
chuusha-jou wa arimasu ka?] **Is there a car
park near here?**

中止 [chuushi] *n* stop

中心 [chuushin] *n* centre; 街の中心部
[machi no chuushinbu] *n* city centre; 町の
中心部 [machi no chuushinbu] *n* town
centre; 街の中心部へ行く一番よい方法は
何ですか? [machi no chuushinbu e iku
ichiban yoi houhou wa nan desu ka?]
**What's the best way to get to the city
centre?**

中心部 [chuushinbu] *n* city centre, town
centre; 街の中心部までどのくらいあります
か? [machi no chuushinbu made dono
kurai arimasu ka?] **How far are we from
the town centre?**; 街の中心部までお願い
します [machi no chuushinbu made
o-negai shimasu] **Please take me to the
city centre**; ・・・の中心部へはどう行けば
いのですか? [...no chuushinbu e wa dou
ikeba ii no desu ka?] **How do I get to the
centre of...?**

昼食 [chuushoku] *n* lunch; 昼食にはどこで
停まりますか? [chuushoku ni wa doko de
tomarimasu ka?] **Where do we stop for
lunch?**; 昼食には時間があいています
[chuushoku ni wa jikan ga aite imasu] **I'm
free for lunch**; 昼食はいつ用意できます
か? [chuushoku wa itsu youi dekimasu
ka?] **When will lunch be ready?**; 昼食はす
ばらしかったです [chuushoku wa
subarashikatta desu] **The lunch was
excellent**; 昼食をご一緒できますか?
[chuushoku o go-issho dekimasu ka?] **Can
we meet for lunch?**

抽象 [chuushou] 抽象的な [chuushouteki
na] *adj* abstract

虫垂炎 [chuusuien] *n* appendicitis

中東 [chuutou] *n* Middle East

中絶 [chuuzetsu] 妊娠中絶
[ninshinchuuzetsu] *n* abortion

鋳造 [chuuzou] 貨幣鋳造所 [kahei
chuuzoujo] *n* mint *(coins)*

d

ダーツ [daatsu] n darts; ダーツ用の投げ矢 [daatsu you no nageya] n dart

打撲傷 [dabokushou] n bruise

だぶだぶ [dabudabu] だぶだぶの [dabudabu no] adj baggy

ダブル [daburu] ダブルの部屋がいいのですが [daburu no heya ga ii no desu ga] I'd like a room with a double bed

ダブルベッド [daburubeddo] n double bed

ダブルルーム [daburu-ruumu] n double room; ダブルルームを予約したいのですが [daburu-ruumu o yoyaku shitai no desu ga] I want to reserve a double room, I'd like to book a double room

ダチョウ [dachou] n ostrich

唾液 [daeki] n saliva

ダイビング [daibingu] n diving; ダイビングに最適の場所はどこですか? [daibingu ni saiteki no basho wa doko desu ka?] Where is the best place to dive?; ダイビングをしたいのですが [daibingu o shitai no desu ga] I'd like to go diving

大部分 [daibubun] n majority

台所 [daidokoro] n kitchen

ダイエット [daietto] n diet; ダイエットする [daietto suru] v diet; 私はダイエットしています [watashi wa daietto shite imasu] I'm on a diet

大学 [daigaku] n uni, university; 大学の [daigaku no] adj academic; 大学の卒業生 [daigaku no sotsugyousei] n graduate; 大学卒業 [daigaku sotsugyou] n graduation

大学院 [daigakuin] 大学院生 [daigakuinsei] n postgraduate

大虐殺 [daigyakusatsu] n massacre

代表 [daihyou] n delegate; 代表する [daihyou suru] adj represent, representative; 代表として派遣する [daihyou toshite haken suru] v delegate

第一 [daiichi] adj first; まず第一に [mazu daiichi ni] adv firstly; 第一の [daiichi no] adj primary

第一級 [daiikkyuu] 第一級の [daiikkyuu no] adj first-class

大臣 [daijin] n minister (government)

大丈夫 [daijoubu] adj alright; ぬれても大丈夫な [nurete mo daijoubu na] adj showerproof; 大丈夫ですか? [daijoubu desu ka?] Are you alright?

大工 [daiku] n carpenter; 大工仕事 [daikushigoto] n carpentry

題名 [daimei] n title

代名詞 [daimeishi] n pronoun

台無し [dainashi] 台無しにされた [dainashi ni sareta] adj ruined; 台無しにする [dainashi ni suru] v ruin

第二 [daini] 第二に [dai ni ni] adv secondly

ダイニング [dainingu] n dining; ダイニングルーム [dainingu ruumu] n dining room

代理 [dairi] n on behalf of; 代理母 [dairibo] n surrogate mother; 臨時代理の [rinji dairi no] adj acting

代理人 [dairinin] n agent

大理石 [dairiseki] n marble

代理店 [dairiten] n agency; 旅行代理店 [ryokoudairiten] n travel agency, travel agent's

大災害 [daisaigai] n catastrophe

第三 [daisan] 第三に [dai san ni] adv thirdly

第三者 [daisansha] n third party; 第三者賠償責任保険 [daisansha baishousekinin hoken] n third-party insurance

大聖堂 [daiseidou] n cathedral; その大聖堂はいつ開きますか? [sono daiseidou wa itsu hirakimasu ka?] When is the cathedral open?

大集会 [daishuukai] n rally

大好き [daisuki] 大好きな [daisuki na] adj favourite

大邸宅 [daiteitaku] n mansion

大統領 [daitouryou] n president

ダイヤモンド [daiyamondo] n diamond

ダイヤル [daiyaru] ダイヤルする [daiyaru suru] v dial

代用 [daiyou] n substitute; 代用する [daiyou suru] v substitute

大豆 [daizu] n soya bean

抱きしめる [dakishimeru] v cuddle, hug; 抱きしめること [dakishimeru koto] n hug

妥協 [dakyou] n compromise; 妥協する [dakyou suru] v compromise

黙る [damaru] v shut up

だます [damasu] v cheat, deceive, fool, trick

だめな [damena] adj rubbish

ダム [damu] n dam

暖房 [danbou] n heating; 暖房器具 [danbou kigu] n heater; その部屋に暖房はありますか? [sono heya ni danbou wa arimasu ka?] Does the room have heating?; 暖房はどうやって使うのですか? [danbou wa dou-yatte tsukau no desu ka?] How does the heating work?; 暖房がつきません [danbou ga tsukimasen] The heating doesn't work; 暖房を入れることができません [danbou o ireru koto ga dekimasen] I can't turn the heating on; 暖房を切ることができません [danbou o kiru koto ga dekimasen] I can't turn the heating off

団地 [danchi] 工業団地 [kougyoudanchi] n industrial estate

段地作り [dan chi tsukuri] 段地作りの [danchizukuri no] adj terraced

弾丸 [dangan] n bullet

ダンガリー [dangarii] ダンガリーのオーバーオール [dangarii no oobaaooru] n dungarees

断言 [dangen] n assertion; 断言する [dangen suru] v declare

男女 [danjo] 男女の別 [danjo no betsu] n sexuality

男女別 [danjobetsu] 男女別々の部屋はありますか? [danjo betsubetsu no heya wa arimasu ka?] Do you have any single sex dorms?

段階 [dankai] n stage

断固 [danko] 断固とした [dan ko to shita] adj determined; ···に断固たる措置を取る [...ni dankotaru sochi-o toru] v crack down on

ダンプリング [danpuringu] n dumpling

段落 [danraku] n paragraph

暖炉 [danro] n fireplace

ダンサー [dansaa] n dancer; バレエダンサー [bareedansaa] n ballet dancer

男性 [dansei] n male; 独身の男性 [dokushin no dansei] n bachelor; 男性の [dansei no] adj male; 男性用トイレ [dansei you toire] n gents'

弾性 [dansei] 弾性ゴム [dansei gomu] n rubber band, (for hair) elastic

男子 [danshi] 男子生徒 [danshiseito] n schoolboy

ダンス [dansu] n dance; 社交ダンス [shakou dansu] n ballroom dancing; どこに行けばダンスができますか? [doko ni ikeba dansu ga dekimasu ka?] Where can we go dancing?; ダンスはいかがですか? [dansu wa ikaga desu ka?] Would you like to dance?

団体 [dantai] n group; 慈善団体 [jizen dantai] n charity; 団体割引はありますか? [dantai-waribiki wa arimasu ka?] Are there any reductions for groups?

弾薬 [dan-yaku] n ammunition, cartridge, magazine (ammunition)

男優 [danyuu] n actor

だらけ [darake] prep full of; しみだらけの

[shimidarake no] *adj* spotty

堕落 [daraku] *n* depravity; 堕落した [daraku shita] *adj* vile

だらしのない [darashi no nai] *adj* untidy

誰 [dare] *pron* who; 誰の [dare no] *adj* whose; 誰のもの [dare no mono] *pron* whose; 誰を [dare-o] *pron* whom; 誰の番ですか? [dare no ban desu ka?] Whose round is it?

誰でも [dare demo] *pron* anybody, anyone

誰でも皆 [dare demo mina] *pron* everybody, everyone

誰か [dareka] *pron* somebody, someone

誰も・・・ない [daremo... nai] *pron* no one, nobody, none

脱脂 [dasshi] 脱脂乳 [dasshinyuu] *n* skimmed milk; 脱脂綿 [dasshimen] *n* cotton wool

ダッシュボード [dasshuboudo] *n* dashboard

脱水 [dassui] 脱水機 [dassuiki] *n* spin dryer

出す [dasu] 煙を出す [kemuri o dasu] *v* smoke; 金切り声を出す [kanakirigoe o dasu] *v* shriek; ごみはどこに出すのですか? [gomi wa doko ni dasu no desu ka?] Where do we leave the rubbish?

脱退 [dattai] ・・・から脱退する [...kara dattai suru] *v* opt out

ダウン [daun] ダウン症候群 [daun shoukougun] *n* Down's syndrome

ダウンロード [daunroudo] *n* download; ダウンロードする [daunroodo suru] *v* download; ここに写真をダウンロードできますか? [koko ni shashin o daunroodo dekimasu ka?] Can I download photos to here?

出会う [deau] *v* encounter; ばったり出会う [battari deau] *v* bump into

デビット [debitto] *n* debit

デビットカード [debitto kaado] *n* debit card; デビットカードは使えますか? [debitto-kaado wa tsukaemasu ka?] Do you take debit cards?

データ [deeta] *n* data

データベース [deetabeesu] *n* database

出口 [deguchi] *n* exit, way out; ・・・へ行く出口はどれですか? [...e iku deguchi wa dore desu ka?] Which exit for...?; 出口はどこですか? [deguchi wa doko desu ka?] Where is the exit?

で走る [de hashiru] ギャロップで走る [gyaroppu de hashiru] *v* gallop

ディーゼル [deiizeru] ディーゼルエンジン [diizeruenjin] *n* diesel

ディナー [deinaa] *n* dinner; ディナーの時刻 [dinaa no jikoku] *n* dinner time; ディナージャケット [dinaa jaketto] *n* dinner jacket; ディナーパーティー [dinaa paatii] *n* dinner party

ディンギー [deingii] *n* dinghy

ディスケット [deisuketto] *n* diskette

泥炭 [deitan] *n* peat

デジタル [dejitaru] デジタルの [dejitaru no] *adj* digital; デジタルカメラ [dejitaru kamera] *n* digital camera; デジタルラジオ [dejitaru rajio] *n* digital radio; デジタルテレビ [dejitaru terebi] *n* digital television; デジタル時計 [dejitaru tokei] *n* digital watch

デジタルカメラ [dejitaru kamera] このデジタルカメラ用のメモリカードをください [kono dejitaru-kamera-you no memori-kaado o kudasai] A memory card for this digital camera, please

出かける [dekakeru] *v* go out; 食事に出かけるのはいかがですか? [shokuji ni dekakeru no wa ikaga desu ka?] Would you like to go out for dinner?

出来事 [dekigoto] *n* event, incident, occurrence; 不幸な出来事 [fukou na dekigoto] *n* mishap; 悲惨な出来事 [hisan na dekigoto] *n* tragedy; 出来事の多い [dekigoto no ooi] *adj* eventful

・・・できない [...dekinai] *adj* unable to

できる [dekiru] *v* be able; 読み書きのできない [yomikaki no dekinai] *adj* illiterate; ・・・ができる [...ga dekiru] *adj* able, capable; ・・・できる [...dekiru] *v* can; 利用できる [riyou dekiru] *adj* available; ここで

できることは何がありますか? [koko de dekiru koto wa nani ga arimasu ka?] **What is there to do here?**; 晩にできることは何がありますか? [ban ni dekiru koto wa nani ga arimasu ka?] **What is there to do in the evenings?**

できるだけ [dekiru dake] *adv* **as ... as possible**; できるだけ早く [dekiru dake hayaku] *adv* **asap** (= as soon as possible)

溺死 [dekishi] 溺死する [dekishi suru] *v* **drown**

デッキ [dekki] *n* **deck**; デッキチェア [dekkichea] *n* **deckchair**; デッキに出られますか? [dekki ni deraremasu ka?] **Can we go out on deck?**

でこぼこ [dekoboko] でこぼこのある [dekoboko no aru] *adj* **bumpy**

でも [demo] *adv* **though**

デモ [demo] *n* **demo, demonstration**

デモンストレーター [demonsutoreetaa] *n* **demonstrator**

・・・でない [...denai] *adv* **not**

電圧 [den-atsu] *n* **voltage**; 電圧は何ボルトですか? [denatsu wa nan-boruto desu ka?] **What's the voltage?**

臀部 [denbu] *n* **backside, behind, buttocks**

電池 [denchi] *n* **battery**

伝言 [dengon] *n* **message**; 伝言をお願いできますか? [dengon o o-negai dekimasu ka?] **Can I leave a message?**; 私あての伝言がありますか? [watashi ate no dengon ga arimasu ka?] **Are there any messages for me?**; 彼の秘書に伝言を残すことはできますか? [kare no hisho ni dengon o nokosu koto wa dekimasu ka?] **Can I leave a message with his secretary?**

デニム [denimu] *n* **denim**

電荷 [denka] 電荷がもちません [denka ga mochimasen] **It's not holding its charge**

伝記 [denki] *n* **biography**

電気 [denki] *n* **electricity**; 電気に関する [denki ni kansuru] *adj* **electrical**; 電気の [denki no] *adj* **electric**; 電気コード [denki koodo] *n* **flex**; 電気毛布 [denkimoufu] *n* **electric blanket**; 電気技師 [denki gishi] *n* **electrician**; 電気掃除機 [denki soujiki] *n*

vacuum cleaner; 電気通信 [denkitsuushin] *n* **telecommunications**; 電気代は別に払わなければなりませんか? [denki-dai wa betsu ni harawanakereba narimasen ka?] **Do we have to pay extra for electricity?**; 電気代は含まれていますか? [denki-dai wa fukumarete imasu ka?] **Is the cost of electricity included?**; 電気のメーターはどこですか? [denki no meetaa wa doko desu ka?] **Where is the electricity meter?**; 電気がきていません [denki ga kite imasen] **There is no electricity**

電気系統 [denkikeitou] 電気系統に何か問題があります [denki-keitou ni nani ka mondai ga arimasu] **There is something wrong with the electrics**

電球 [denkyuu] *n* **bulb** (electricity), **light bulb**

デンマーク [denmaaku] *n* **Denmark**; デンマークの [denmaaku no] *adj* **Danish**

デンマーク語 [denmaakugo] *n* **Danish** (language)

デンマーク人 [denmaakujin] *n* **Dane**

電報 [denpou] *n* **telegram**; どこで電報を送ることができますか? [doko de denpou o okuru koto ga dekimasu ka?] **Where can I send a telegram from?**; ここから電報を送れますか? [koko kara denpou o okuremasu ka?] **Can I send a telegram from here?**; 私は電報を送りたいのですが [watashi wa denpou o okuritai no desu ga] **I want to send a telegram**

澱粉 [denpun] *n* **starch**

伝票 [denpyou] *n* **slip** (paper)

電流 [denryuu] *n* **current** (electricity)

伝染 [densen] 伝染性の [densensei no] *adj* **contagious**

伝染性 [densensei] 伝染性の [densensei no] *adj* **catching**

伝説 [densetsu] *n* **legend**

電車 [densha] *n* **train**; これは・・・行きの電車ですか? [kore wa ... iki no densha desu ka?] **Is this the train for...?**; 次に乗れる電車をお願いします [tsugi ni noreru densha o o-negai shimasu] **The next available train, please**; ・・・へ行く次の電車は何時で

すか? [...e iku tsugi no densha wa nan-ji desu ka?] **When is the next train to...?; ・・・へ行く電車にはどこで乗れますか?** [...e iku densha ni wa doko de noremasu ka?] **Where can I get a train to...?; ・・・へ行く電車は何時ですか?** [...e iku densha wa nan-ji desu ka?] **What time is the train to...?; 電車は何時に出ますか?** [densha wa nan-ji ni demasu ka?] **What time does the train leave?; 電車は・・・に停まりますか?** [densha wa ... ni tomarimasu ka?] **Does the train stop at...?; 電車は十分遅れています** [densha wa jup-puku okurete imasu] **The train is running ten minutes late**

電子 [denshi] *adj* **electronic; 電子の** [denshi no] *adj* **electronic; 電子書籍** [denshi shoseki] *n* **e-book; 電子工学** [denshikougaku] *n* **electronics**

電子メール [denshi meeru] *n* **email; 電子メールを送る** [denshi meeru-o okuru] *v* **email** (*a person*); **電子メールアドレス** [denshi meeru adoresu] *n* **email address**

電子レンジ [denshi renji] *n* **microwave oven**

伝承 [denshou] **伝承童謡** [denshou douyou] *n* **nursery rhyme; 民間伝承** [minkandenshou] *n* **folklore**

電卓 [dentaku] *n* **pocket calculator**

デンタル [dentaru] **デンタルフロス** [dentaru furosu] *n* **dental floss**

伝統 [dentou] *n* **tradition; 伝統的な** [dentouteki na] *adj* **classical, traditional**

電灯 [dentou] *n* **lamp; 懐中電灯** [kaichuudentou] *n* **torch**

電話 [denwa] *n* **phone, telephone; カメラ付き携帯電話** [kamera tsuki keitai denwa] *n* **camera phone; テレビ電話** [terebi denwa] *n* **videophone; 携帯電話** [keitai denwa] *n* **mobile phone; 留守番電話** [rusubandenwa] *n* **answerphone; 間違い電話** [machigai denwa] *n* **wrong number; 電話交換台** [denwa koukandai] *n* **switchboard; 電話しなおす** [denwa shinaosu] *v* **call back; 電話セールス** [denwa seerusu] *n* **telesales; 電話をかけなおす** [denwa-o kakenaosu] *v* **phone back, ring back; 電話をかける** [denwa-o

kakeru] *v* **phone, ring up; 電話を切る** [denwa o kiru] *v* **hang up; 電話番号** [denwabangou] *n* **phone number; 電話帳** [denwachou] *n* **phonebook, telephone directory; 公衆電話** [koushuudenwa] *n* **payphone; ここから電話をかけられますか?** [koko kara denwa o kakeraremasu ka?] **Can I phone from here?; ここから国際電話をかけられますか?** [koko kara kokusai-denwa o kakeraremasu ka?] **Can I phone internationally from here?; 私は電話をかけなければなりません** [watashi wa denwa o kakenakereba narimasen] **I must make a phone call; 電話をお借りできますか?** [denwa o o-kari dekimasu ka?] **Can I use your phone, please?, May I use your phone?; 電話をかけたいのですが** [denwa o kaketai no desu ga] **I want to make a phone call; 電話番号は何番ですか?** [denwa-bangou wa nan-ban desu ka?] **What's the telephone number?; 家に電話していいですか?** [ie ni denwa shite ii desu ka?] **May I phone home?; 国際電話用のテレホンカードを売っていますか?** [kokusai-denwa-you no terehon-kaado o utte imasu ka?] **Do you sell international phone cards?**

デオドラント [deodoranto] *n* **deodorant**

デパート [depaato] *n* **department store**

デリカテッセン [derikatessen] *n* **delicatessen**

出る [deru] *v* **leave, run; バスは二十分おきに出ています** [basu wa nijup-pun oki ni dete imasu] **The bus runs every twenty minutes; バスは何時に出ますか?** [basu wa nan-ji ni demasu ka?] **What time does the bus leave?; ・・・へ行くバスはどのくらい出ていますか?** [...e iku basu wa dono kurai dete imasu ka?] **How often are the buses to...?; 電車は何時に出ますか?** [densha wa nan-ji ni demasu ka?] **What time does the train leave?**

です [desu] *v* **is; ・・・です** [...desu] **This is ... (calling), I'm from...**

デスク [desuku] **照会デスク** [shoukai desuku] *n* **enquiry desk**

出て行く [deteiku] *adj* **outgoing**

ではまた [dewamata] *excl* **see you later, bye**

デザート [dezaato] n afters, dessert; デザートスプーン [dezaato supuun] n dessert spoon; デザートのメニューをください [dezaato no menyuu o kudasai] The dessert menu, please; 私たちはデザートをいただきます [watashi-tachi wa dezaato o itadakimasu] We'd like a dessert

デザイン [dezain] n design; デザインする [dezain suru] v design

デザイナー [dezainaa] n designer

痔 [ji] n haemorrhoids, piles

DVD [dii bui dii] n DVD [dii bui dii]; DVDバーナー [diibuidii baanaa] n DVD burner; DVDプレーヤー [diibuidii pureiyaa] n DVD player

DNA [dii enu ee] n DNA

ディーラー [diiraa] n dealer; 麻薬ディーラー [mayaku diiraa] n drug dealer

ディスコ [disuko] n disco

ディスク [disuku] n disc, disk; ディスクドライブ [disukudoraibu] n disk drive; フロッピーディスク [furoppi disuku] n floppy disk

ディスクジョッキー [disukujokkii] n disc jockey, DJ

度 [do] 度を超えた [do-o koeta] adj excessive

ドア [doa] n door; ドアハンドル [doahandoru] n door handle; ドアが閉まりません [doa ga shimarimasen] The door won't close; ドアが開きません [doa ga akimasen] The door won't open; ドアに鍵がかかりません [doa ni kagi ga kakarimasen] The door won't lock; ドアの取っ手が外れました [doa no totte ga hazuremashita] The door handle has come off

ドアマン [doaman] n doorman

ドブネズミ [dobunezumi] n rat

どちら [dochira] n どちらさまでしょうか? [dochira-sama deshou ka?] Who am I talking to?, Who's calling?

どちらも [dochiramo] pron either; どちらも・・・でない [dochiramo ... denai] pron neither

土台 [dodai] n base

どぎもを抜かれた [dogimo o nukareta] adj stunned

ドイツ [doitsu] n Germany

ドイツ語 [doitsugo] n German (language)

ドイツ人 [doitsujin] n German (person)

ドイツの [doitsu no] adj German

ドイツスズラン [doitsusuzuran] n lily of the valley

どけち [dokechi] n miser

ドック [dokku] n dock

どこ [doko] adv where; 三十号車はどこですか? [sanjuu-gou-sha wa doko desu ka?] Where is carriage number thirty?; どこに行けば・・・ができますか? [doko ni ikeba ... ga dekimasu ka?] Where can you go...?; どこが悪いのですか? [doko ga warui no desu ka?] What's wrong?; どこで払うのですか? [doko de harau no desu ka?] Where do I pay?; どこで電話をかけられますか? [doko de denwa o kakeraremasu ka?] Where can I make a phone call?; ここはどこですか? [koko wa doko desu ka?] Where are we?; エレベーターはどこですか? [erebeetaa wa doko desu ka?] Where is the lift?; ・・・はどこですか? [...wa doko desu ka?] Where is...?

どこでも [dokodemo] adv anywhere, everywhere

どこか [dokoka] どこかに [dokoka ni] adv someplace, somewhere

どこに [doko ni] adv where; どこにも・・・ない [dokonimo ... nai] conj nowhere

毒 [doku] n poison; 毒を盛る [doku-o moru] v poison; 毒キノコ [doku kinoko] n toadstool

独立 [dokuritsu] n independence; 独立した [dokuritsu shita] adj independent

独裁 [dokusai] 独裁者 [dokusaisha] n dictator

独占 [dokusen] n monopoly

読者 [dokusha] n reader

独身 [dokushin] 独身の男性 [dokushin no dansei] n bachelor; あなたは独身ですか? [anata wa dokushin desu ka?] Are you single?; ええ、私は独身です [ee, watashi wa dokushin desu]Yes, I'm single; 私は独身です [watashi wa dokushin desu] I'm single

独身女性 [dokushinjosei] n single woman, spinster; 独身女性の名字の前に付ける敬称 [dokushin josei no myouji no mae ni tsukeru keishou] n Miss

読唇術 [dokushinjutsu] 読唇術で解する [dokushinjutsu de kaisuru] v lip-read

読書 [dokusho] n reading

独創 [dokusou] 独創的な [dokusouteki na] adj ingenious

独特 [dokutoku] 独特の [dokutoku no] adj unique

ドキュメンタリー [dokyumentarii] n documentary

ドキュメンテーション [dokyumenteeshon] n documentation

ドキュメント [dokyumento] n documents

ドミニカ [dominika] ドミニカ共和国 [dominika kyouwakoku] n Dominican Republic

ドミノ [domino] n domino, dominoes

どもる [domoru] v stammer, stutter

ドナー [donaa] n donor

どなた [donata] pron who; どなたですか? [donata desu ka?] Who is it?

どんぐり [donguri] n acorn

鈍感 [donkan] 鈍感な [donkan na] adj insensitive

どの [dono] adj which

どのように [dono you ni] adv how

ドーナツ [doonatsu] n doughnut

ドライ [dorai] adj dry (wine); ドライシェリーをください [dorai-sherii o kudasai] A dry sherry, please

ドライバー [doraibaa] n (人) motorist, (道具) screwdriver

ドライブ [doraibu] n drive; ディスクドライブ [disukudoraibu] n disk drive

ドライクリーニング [doraikuriiningu] n dry-cleaning; ドライクリーニング屋 [doraikuriininguya] n dry-cleaner's

ドラマー [doramaa] n drummer

ドラム [doramu] n drum

どれ [dore] pron which

どれでも [dore de mo] pron any

奴隷 [dorei] n slave; 奴隷のように働く [dorei no youni hataraku] v slave

ドレッシングガウン [doresshingugaun] n dressing gown

ドリル [doriru] n drill; 空気ドリル [kuukidoriru] n pneumatic drill

泥 [doro] n mud

泥棒 [dorobou] n thief; 泥棒に入る [dorobou ni hairu] v burgle; 個人情報泥棒 [kojin jouhou dorobou] n identity theft

泥だらけ [dorodarake] 泥だらけの [doro darake no] adj muddy

泥よけ [doroyoke] n mudguard

ドル [doru] n dollar; ドルを使えますか? [doru o tsukaemasu ka?] Do you take dollars?

努力 [doryoku] n effort, try

土砂降り [doshaburi] n downpour

どっしり [dosshiri] どっしりした [dosshiri shita] adj massive

土手 [dote] n bank (ridge)

銅 [dou] n copper

堂 [dou] 軽食堂 [keishokudou] n snack bar

どう [dou] adv how, what; どうしたんですか? [dou shita n desu ka?] What happened?; どうすればいいのですか? [dou sureba ii no desu ka?] What do I do?; 気分はどうですか? [kibun wa dou desu ka?] How are you feeling now?

動物 [doubutsu] n animal; 齧歯動物 [gesshi doubutsu] n rodent; 動物の一腹子 [doubutsu no ippukushi] n litter (offspring); 動物の足 [doubutsu no ashi] n paw; 動物園 [doubutsuen] n zoo; 動物学 [doubutsugaku] n zoology; 哺乳動物 [honyuu doubutsu] n mammal

動物相 [doubutsusou] n fauna

道義心 [dougishin] n honour

道具 [dougu] n tool

胴衣 [doui] n waistcoat; 救命胴衣

[kyuumeidoui] n life jacket

同意 [doui] n agreement

どういたしまして [douitashimashite] You're welcome

同一 [douitsu] 同一の [douitsu no] adj identical

同時 [douji] 同時に [douji ni] adv simultaneously; 同時に起こる [douji ni okoru] v coincide; 同時の [douji no] adj simultaneous

同情 [doujou] n sympathy; 同情する [doujou suru] v sympathize; 同情的な [doujouteki na] adj sympathetic

動き [douki] n movement

動機 [douki] n motive; 動機づけ [douki zuke] n motivation; 動機づけられた [douki zukerareta] adj motivated

動悸 [douki] 動悸を打つ [douki-o utsu] v throb

瞳孔 [doukou] n pupil (eye)

同行 [doukou] 同行する [doukou suru] v accompany

同級生 [doukyuusei] n classmate

同盟 [doumei] 同盟国 [doumeikoku] n ally (country)

動脈 [doumyaku] n artery

道路 [douro] n road; 中央分離帯付き道路 [chuuou bunritai tsuki douro] n dual carriageway; 環状道路 [kanjoudouro] n ring road; 高速道路 [kousokudouro] n motorway; 道路標識 [dourohyoushiki] n road sign, signpost; 道路封鎖 [douro fuusa] n roadblock; 道路工事 [dourokouji] n roadworks; この地域の道路マップはありますか? [kono chiiki no douro-mappu wa arimasu ka?] Do you have a road map of this area?; 私は・・・の道路マップが必要です [watashi wa ... no douro-mappu ga hitsuyou desu] I need a road map of...; 道路は凍結していますか? [douro wa touketsu shite imasu ka?] Are the roads icy?

同僚 [douryou] n colleague

同棲 [dousei] 同棲する [dousei suru] v live together

動詞 [doushi] n verb

どうした [doushita] adv what; どうしたのですか? [dou shita no desu ka?] What's the matter?

同室者 [doushitsusha] n roommate; 私の同室者はとてもうるさいです [watashi no doushitsusha wa totemo urusai desu] My dorm-mates are very noisy

道徳 [doutoku] 不道徳な [fudoutoku na] adj immoral; 道徳の [doutoku no] adj moral

同等 [doutou] 同等のもの [doutou no mono] n equivalent

童謡 [douyou] n nursery rhyme; 伝承童謡 [denshou douyou] n nursery rhyme

土曜日 [doyoubi] n Saturday; 今週の土曜日に [konshuu no doyoubi ni] this Saturday; 毎週土曜日に [maishuu doyoubi ni] every Saturday; 毎土曜日に [mai-doyoubi ni] on Saturdays; 来週の土曜日に [raishuu no doyoubi ni] next Saturday; 先週の土曜日に [senshuu no doyoubi ni] last Saturday; 土曜日に [doyoubi ni] on Saturday

e

絵 [e] *n* picture; 絵のように美しい [e no youni utsukushii] *adj* picturesque; 絵を描く [e-o egaku] *v* paint; 開くと絵が飛び出す本 [hiraku to e ga tobidasu hon] *n* pop-up book

エアバッグ [eabaggu] *n* airbag

エアコン [eakon] *n* air conditioning; その部屋にエアコンはありますか? [sono heya ni eakon wa arimasu ka?] Does the room have air conditioning?; エアコンはついていますか? [eakon wa tsuite imasu ka?] Does it have air conditioning?; エアコンが動きません [eakon ga ugokimasen] The air conditioning doesn't work

エアロビクス [earobikusu] *n* aerobics

エアゾール [eazooru] *n* aerosol

エビ [ebi] 小エビ [koebi] *n* shrimp

エチオピア [echiopia] *n* Ethiopia; エチオピア人 [echiopiajin] *n* Ethiopian (person); エチオピアの [echiopia no] *adj* Ethiopian

枝 [eda] *n* branch

エーカー [eekaa] *n* acre

エープリルフール [eepurirufuuru] エープリルフールの日 [eepuriru fuuru no nichi] *n* April Fools' Day

エース [eesu] *n* ace

絵筆 [efude] *n* paintbrush

FAQ [efueekyuu] *abbr* FAQ [efueekyuu]

描く [egaku] *v* draw (sketch); スケッチを描く [suketchi-o egaku] *v* sketch; 絵を描く [e-o egaku] *v* paint

笑顔 [egao] *n* beam

エッグカップ [eggukappu] *n* eggcup

エグゼクティブ [eguzekuteibu] *n* executive

エホバ [ehoba] エホバの証人 [ehoba no shounin] *n* Jehovah's Witness

永遠 [eien] 永遠の [eien no] *adj* eternal; 永遠性 [eiensei] *n* eternity

映画 [eiga] *n* film, movie; ホラー映画 [horaa eiga] *n* horror film; 映画スター [eigasutaa] *n* film star; どこに行けば映画を見られますか? [doko ni ikeba eiga o miraremasu ka?] Where can we go to see a film?; 映画はいつ始まりますか? [eiga wa itsu hajimarimasu ka?] When does the film start?; 英語の映画はありますか? [eigo no eiga wa arimasu ka?] Are there any films in English?

映画館 [eigakan] *n* cinema; その映画館で今晩何が上映されますか? [sono eigakan de konban nani ga jouei saremasu ka?] What's on tonight at the cinema?; その映画館で何が上映されていますか? [sono eigakan de nani ga jouei sarete imasu ka?] What's on at the cinema?; その映画館でどの映画が上映されていますか? [sono eigakan de dono eiga ga jouei sarete imasu ka?] Which film is on at the cinema?

英語 [eigo] *n* English; あなたは英語を話しますか? [anata wa eigo o hanashimasu ka?] Do you speak English?; 誰か英語を話せる人はいますか? [dare ka eigo o hanaseru hito wa imasu ka?] Does anyone speak English?; 英語のガイドブックはありますか? [eigo no gaidobukku wa arimasu ka?] Do you have a guide book in English?; 英語を話せるお医者さんはいらっしゃいますか? [eigo o hanaseru o-isha-san wa irasshaimasu ka?] Is there a doctor who speaks English?; 私は英語をほとんど話せません [watashi wa eigo o hotondo hanasemasen] I speak very little English;

私は英語を話せません [watashi wa eigo o hanasemasen] I don't speak English

営業 [eigyou] 自営業の [jieigyou no] *adj* self-employed; 営業時間 [eigyoujikan] *n* office hours, opening hours; 営業していますか? [eigyou shite imasu ka?] Are you open?

英貨 [eika] *n* pound sterling

英国 [eikoku] *n* Britain, UK, United Kingdom; 英国の [eikoku no] *adj* British

英国人 [eikokujin] *n* British (person)

影響 [eikyou] *n* effect, impact, influence; 影響を与える [eikyou-o ataeru] *v* affect, influence

永久 [eikyuu] 永久に [eikyuu ni] *adv* forever, permanently; 永久の [eikyuu no] *adj* permanent

衛生 [eisei] *n* hygiene

衛星 [eisei] 人工衛星 [jinkou eisei] *n* satellite; 衛星ナビゲーション [eisei nabigeeshon] *n* sat nav; 衛星放送用パラボラアンテナ [eisei housou you parabora antena] *n* satellite dish

栄誉 [eiyo] *n* glory

栄養 [eiyou] *n* nutrition; 栄養不良 [eiyou furyou] *n* malnutrition; 栄養物摂取 [eiyoubutsu sesshu] *n* nutrition; 栄養分 [eiyoubun] *n* nutrient

エイズ [eizu] *n* AIDS

餌食 [ejiki] *n* prey

エジプト [ejiputo] *n* Egypt

エジプト人 [ejiputojin] *n* Egyptian (person)

エジプトの [ejiputo no] *adj* Egyptian

液 [eki] 不凍液 [futoueki] *n* antifreeze

駅 [eki] *n* station; 鉄道駅 [tetsudoueki] *n* railway station; 地下鉄駅 [chikatetsu eki] *n* metro station, tube station; 鉄道駅へ行く一番よい方法は何ですか? [tetsudou-eki e iku ichiban yoi houhou wa nan desu ka?] What's the best way to get to the railway station?

液体 [ekitai] *n* liquid

エキゾチック [ekizochikku] エキゾチックな [ekizochikku na] *adj* exotic

エキゾーストパイプ [ekizoosutopaipu] *n* exhaust pipe

エキゾースト [ekizousuto] エキゾーストが壊れています [ekizoosuto ga kowarete imasu] The exhaust is broken

X線 [ekkususen] *n* X-ray; X線写真を撮る [ekkusosen shashin-o toru] *v* X-ray

エコノミー [ekonomii] エコノミークラス [ekonomiikurasu] *n* economy class

エクアドル [ekuadoru] *n* Ecuador

エクスタシー [ekusutashii] *n* ecstasy

絵文字 [emoji] *n* emoji

MP4プレーヤー [emu pi foa pyreeyaa] *n* MP4 player

MP3プレーヤー [emu pi surii pureeyaa] *n* MP3 player

縁 [en] *n* rim

円 [en] *n* (丸) circle, round

エナメル [enameru] *n* enamel

延長 [enchou] *n* extension; サッカー・ラグビーなどで怪我の手当てなどに要した分の延長時間 [sakkaa / ragubii nado de kega no teate nado ni youshita bun no enchou jikan] *n* injury time; 延長コード [enchoukoodo] *n* extension cable

円柱 [enchuu] *n* column

演壇 [endan] *n* platform

エンドウ [endou] *n* peas

エネルギー [enerugii] *n* energy; 太陽エネルギー [taiyou enerugii] *n* solar power

沿岸 [engan] *n* coast; 沿岸警備隊 [engankeibitai] *n* coastguard

園芸 [engei] 園芸用品店 [engei youhinten] *n* garden centre

演劇 [engeki] 演劇の [engeki no] *adj* dramatic

演技 [engi] *n* acting

縁組 [engumi] 養子縁組 [youshiengumi] *n* adoption

縁組み [engumi] *n* match (partnership)

円グラフ [engurafu] *n* pie chart

エンジン [enjin] *n* engine; ディーゼルエンジン [diizeruenjin] *n* diesel; 検索エンジン [kensaku enjin] *n* search engine; エンジン

がオーバーヒートしています [enjin ga oobaahiito shite imasu] **The engine is overheating**

援助 [enjo] *n* aid, assistance, help

円形 [enkei] 円形の [enkei no] *adj* circular

延期 [enki] 延期する [enki suru] *v* postpone, put off

煙霧 [enmu] *n* fumes

縁日 [ennichi] *n* fair

鉛筆 [enpitsu] *n* pencil

鉛筆削り [enpitsukezuri] *n* pencil sharpener

遠慮 [enryo] 遠慮のない [enryo no nai] *adj* outspoken

遠視 [enshi] 私は遠視です [watashi wa enshi desu] I'm long-sighted

炎症 [enshou] *n* inflammation; 炎症を起こした [enshou-o okoshita] *adj* inflamed

塩素 [enso] *n* chlorine

遠足 [ensoku] *n* outing

演奏 [ensou] *n* performance *(artistic)*; 演奏する [ensou suru] *v* play *(music)*; 演奏者 [ensousha] *n* player *(instrumentalist)*

円錐形 [ensuikei] 円錐形のもの [ensuikei no mono] *n* cone

エンターテイナー [entaateinaa] *n* entertainer

煙突 [entotsu] *n* chimney

円筒 [entou] *n* cylinder

演説 [enzetsu] *n* address *(speech)*

エピソード [episoudo] *n* episode

エプロン [epuron] *n* apron, pinafore

選ぶ [erabu] *v* choose, pick, pick out, select; 選ばれた [erabareta] *adj* chosen

エラストプラスト® [erasutopurasuto] *n* Elastoplast®

エレベーター [erebeetaa] *n* lift *(up/down)*; エレベーターはどこですか? [erebeetaa wa doko desu ka?] Where is the lift?; エレベーターはありますか? [erebeetaa wa arimasu ka?] Is there a lift?; 車椅子用のエレベーターはありますか? [kuruma-isu-you no erebeetaa wa arimasu ka?] Do you have a lift for wheelchairs?;

建物内にエレベーターはありますか? [tatemono-nai ni erebeetaa wa arimasu ka?] Is there a lift in the building?

襟 [eri] *n* collar

エリア [eria] *n* area; 禁煙エリアはありますか? [kin'en-eria wa arimasu ka?] Is there a non-smoking area?; 喫煙エリアの席が欲しいのですが [kitsuen-eria no seki ga hoshii no desu ga] I'd like a seat in the smoking area

エリトリア [eritoria] *n* Eritrea

エロチックな [erochikku na] *adj* erotic

得る [eru] *v* gain, get; 利益を得る [rieki o eru] *v* benefit; 勝利を得た [shouri-o eta] *adj* winning

エッセイ [essei] *n* essay

エスカレーター [esukareetaa] *n* escalator

エステートカー [esuteetokaa] *n* estate car

エストニア [esutonia] *n* Estonia

エストニア語 [esutoniago] *n* Estonian *(language)*

エストニア人 [esutoniajin] *n* Estonian *(person)*

エストニアの [esutonia no] *adj* Estonian

閲覧履歴 [etsuran rireki] *n* (search) history

閲覧する [etsuran suru] *v* browse *(on internet)*

f

ミリールームを予約したいのですが [famirii-ruumu o yoyaku shitai no desu ga] I want to reserve a family room, I'd like to book a family room

ファンベルト [fanberuto] n fan belt

ファスナー [fasunaa] n zip; ファスナーを締める [fasunaa-o shimeru] v zip (up); ファスナーを開ける [fasunaa-o hirakeru] v unzip

ファウル [fauru] n foul

フェミニスト [feminisuto] n feminist

フェンネル [fenneru] n fennel

フェリー [ferii] n ferry; ・・・行きのフェリーはどこで乗るのですか? [...iki no ferii wa doko de noru no desu ka?] Where do we catch the ferry to...?; ・・・行きのフェリーはありますか? [...iki no ferii wa arimasu ka?] Is there a ferry to...?

フェロー [feroo] フェロー諸島 [feroo shotou] n Faroe Islands

フェルト [feruto] n felt

フェルトペン [ferutopen] n felt-tip pen

フェスティバル [fesutibaru] n festival

フィジー [fijii] n Fiji

フィクション [fikushon] n fiction

フィンランド [finrando] n Finland

フィンランド人 [finrandojin] n Finn

フィンランドの [finrando no] adj Finnish

フィリピン [firipin] フィリピン人 [firipinjin] n Filipino (person); フィリピンの [firipin no] adj Filipino

フィルム [firumu] n film; このフィルムを現像していただけますか? [kono firumu o genzou shite itadakemasu ka?] Can you develop this film, please?

フィットネス [fittonesu] n fitness; フィットネス運動 [fittonesu undou] n keep-fit

フォグランプ [foguranpu] n fog light

フォローする [foroo suru] v follow (on social media)

フォーク [fouku] n fork; フォークミュージック [fouku myuujikku] n folk music; 新しいフォークをいただけますか? [atarashii fouku o itadakemasu ka?] Could I have a clean fork please?

ファーストネーム [faasutoneemu] n first name

ファゴット [fagotto] n bassoon

ファイル [fairu] n file (folder); ファイルする [fairu suru] v file (folder)

ファックス [fakkusu] n fax; ファックスを送る [fakkusu-o okuru] v fax; あなたのファックスに問題があります [anata no fakkusu ni mondai ga arimasu] There is a problem with your fax; あなたのファックスを再送信してください [anata no fakkusu o sai-soushin shite kudasai] Please resend your fax; ここからファックスを送れますか? [koko kara fakkusu o okuremasu ka?] Can I send a fax from here?; ファックスがありますか? [fakkusu ga arimasu ka?] Do you have a fax?; ファックスを送るのはいくらですか? [fakkusu o okuru no wa ikura desu ka?] How much is it to send a fax?; ファックス番号は何番ですか? [fakkusu-bangou wa nan-ban desu ka?] What is the fax number?; 私はファックスを送りたいのですが [watashi wa fakkusu o okuritai no desu ga] I want to send a fax; 私が使えるファックス機はありますか? [watashi ga tsukaeru fakkusuki wa arimasu ka?] Is there a fax machine I can use?

ファミリールーム [famirii-ruumu] ファ

フォワードスラッシュ
[fowaadosurasshu] n forward slash

不 [fu] 不自然な [fushizen na] adj strained

符 [fu] 引用符 [in-youfu] n quotation marks

不安 [fuan] n uneasiness; 不安な [fuan na] adj uneasy

不安定 [fuantei] n instability; 不安定な [fuantei na] adj unstable, unsteady

不便 [fuben] n inconvenience; 不便な [fuben na] adj inconvenient

吹雪 [fubuki] n snowstorm

縁石 [fuchiishi] n kerb

不注意 [fuchuui] 不注意な [fuchuui na] adj careless; 不注意で [fuchuui de] adv inadvertently

不断 [fudan] adj casual; 優柔不断な [yuujuu fudan na] adj indecisive

筆箱 [fudebako] n pencil case

不動産 [fudousan] 不動産屋 [fudousanya] n estate agent

不道徳 [fudoutoku] 不道徳な [fudoutoku na] adj immoral

腐敗 [fuhai] n decay; 腐敗した [fuhai shita] adj corrupt

腐敗行為 [fuhaikoui] n corruption

不平 [fuhei] n complaint, grouse (complaint); 不平を言う [fuhei o iu] v complain

不必要 [fuhitsuyou] 不必要な [fuhitsuyou na] adj unnecessary

不法 [fuhou] 不法侵入者 [fuhou shinnyuusha] n burglar; 不法な [fuhou na] adj illegal

不意 [fui] 不意に [fui ni] adv unexpectedly; 不意の [fui no] adj unexpected

藤紫 [fujimurasaki] 藤紫色の [fuji murasaki iro no] adj mauve

婦人 [fujin] n lady; 婦人警官 [fujinkeikan] n policewoman

婦人科医 [fujinkai] n gynaecologist

不十分 [fujuubun] 不十分な [fujuubun na] adj inadequate, insufficient, skimpy

不従順 [fujuujun] 不従順な [fujuujun na] adj disobedient

深い [fukai] adj deep; 思慮深い [shiryobukai] adj thoughtful; 深さ [fukasa] n depth; 疑い深い [utagaibukai] adj sceptical; 嫉妬深い [shittobukai] adj jealous

不快感 [fukaikan] n insensitivity; 不快感を与える [fukaikan-o ataeru] v offend

不快な [fukai na] adj obnoxious

付加価値税 [fukakachizei] 付加価値税は含まれていますか? [fukakachi-zei wa fukumarete imasu ka?] Is VAT included?

不可欠 [fukaketsu] 不可欠な [fukaketsu na] adj indispensable

深く [fukaku] adv deeply

不確実 [fukakujitsu] n uncertainty; 不確実な [fukakujitsu na] adj uncertain

不可能 [fukanou] 不可能な [fukanou na] adj impossible

不完全 [fukanzen] 不完全な [fukanzen na] adj incomplete

深さ [fukasa] n depth; 海の深さはどのくらいありますか? [umi no fukasa wa dono kurai arimasu ka?] How deep is the water?

ふけ [fuke] n dandruff

不健康 [fukenkou] 不健康な [fukenkou na] adj unhealthy

不潔 [fuketsu] 不潔な [fuketsu na] adj filthy

吹き出物 [fukidemono] n pimple

不機嫌 [fukigen] 不機嫌な [fukigen na] adj cross

噴きこぼれる [fukikoboreru] v boil over

布巾 [fukin] n dish towel, dishcloth, tea towel

不吉 [fukitsu] 不吉な [fukitsu na] adj sinister

ふっかける [fukkakeru] v carry out; 法外な値をふっかける [hougai na ne-o fukkakeru] v rip off

復活 [fukkatsu] 復活する [fukkatsu suru] v revive

復活祭 [fukkatsusai] n Easter; 復活祭の

卵 [fukkatsusai no tamago] n Easter egg

腹腔 [fukkou] 腹腔の [fukkou no] adj coeliac

フック [fukku] n hook

不幸 [fukou] 不幸な [fukou na] adj unhappy; 不幸な出来事 [fukou na dekigoto] n mishap

不公平 [fukouhei] n injustice; 不公平な [fukouhei na] adj unfair

服 [fuku] n clothes; 服を脱ぐ [fuku o nugu] v undress; 服を着た [fuku o kita] adj dressed; 服を着る [fuku o kiru] v dress; 服のロッカーはどこですか? [fuku no rokkaa wa doko desu ka?] Where are the clothes lockers?; 服を干すところがありますか? [fuku o hosu tokoro ga arimasu ka?] Is there somewhere to dry clothes?; 私の服が湿っています [watashi no fuku ga shimette imasu] My clothes are damp

副 [fuku] 副作用 [fukusayou] n side effect

拭く [fuku] v wipe; 皿拭きをする [sarafuki-o suru] v wipe up

吹く [fuku] v blow; 口笛を吹く [kuchibue o fuku] v whistle

腹部 [fukubu] n belly

複合 [fukugou] 複合の [fukugou no] adj complex

複合体 [fukugoutai] n complex

福音 [fukuin] n gospel

含まる [fukumaru] v include; 含まれた [fukumareta] adj included; 料金には何が含まれていますか? [ryoukin ni wa nani ga fukumarete imasu ka?] What is included in the price?; 料金には総合自動車保険が含まれていますか? [ryoukin ni wa sougou-jidousha-hoken ga fukumarete imasu ka?] Is fully comprehensive insurance included in the price?; 総合自動車保険に加入する追加料金はいくらですか? [sougou-jidousha-hoken ni kanyuu suru tsuika-ryoukin wa ikura desu ka?] How much extra is comprehensive insurance cover?

含める [fukumeru] ···を含めて [...-o fukumete] prep including; 含めた [fukumeta] adj inclusive

含む [fukumu] v contain, include; アルコールを含まない [arukooru o fukumanai] adj alcohol-free; 脂を含んだ [abura-o fukunda] adj greasy; 付加価値税は含まれていますか? [fukakachi-zei wa fukumarete imasu ka?] Is VAT included?; 朝食は含まれていますか? [choushoku wa fukumarete imasu ka?] Is breakfast included?; 電気代は含まれていますか? [denki-dai wa fukumarete imasu ka?] Is the cost of electricity included?

膨らむ [fukuramu] v fill up; ポンプで膨らませる [ponpu de fukuramaseru] v pump up

袋 [fukuro] n bag; ビニール袋 [biniiru bukuro] n plastic bag; ポリエチレンの袋 [poriechiren no fukuro] n polythene bag; 買物袋 [kaimonobukuro] n carrier bag, shopping bag; 寝袋 [nebukuro] n sleeping bag; 小さな袋 [chiisana fukuro] n sachet; 余分に袋をいただけますか? [yobun ni fukuro o itadakemasu ka?] Can I have an extra bag, please?; 袋は要りません [fukuro wa irimasen] I don't need a bag, thanks; 袋をいただけますか? [fukuro o itadakemasu ka?] Can I have a bag, please?

フクロウ [fukurou] n owl

複製 [fukusei] n copy (reproduction); 複製する [fukusei suru] v copy

復讐 [fukushuu] n revenge

服装 [fukusou] n clothes; 服装倒錯 [fukusou tousaku] n transvestite; 服装の決まりがありますか? [fukusou no kimari ga arimasu ka?] Is there a dress-code?

複層 [fukusou] 複層ガラス [fukusou garasu] n double glazing

複数 [fukusuu] n plural

複数回 [fukusuukai] 複数回乗車できる切符はありますか? [fukusuukai jousha dekiru kippu wa arimasu ka?] Do you have multi-journey tickets?

服用 [fukuyou] 過量服用 [karyou fukuyou] n overdose

服用量 [fukuyouryou] n dose

複雑 [fukuzatsu] 複雑な [fukuzatsu na] adj complicated; 複雑な要因 [fukuzatsu na youin] *n* complication

不満 [fuman] *n* dissatisfaction; 不満な [fuman na] *adj* dissatisfied; 私はこれに不満です [watashi wa kore ni fuman desu] I'm not satisfied with this

不満足 [fumanzoku] 不満足な [fumanzoku na] *adj* unsatisfactory

不明 [fumei] *adj* missing; 私の息子が行方不明です [watashi no musuko ga yukue-fumei desu] My son is missing; 私の娘が行方不明です [watashi no musume ga yukue-fumei desu] My daughter is missing; 私の子供が行方不明です [watashi no kodomo ga yukue-fumei desu] My child is missing

不明瞭 [fumeiryou] 不明瞭な [fumeiryou na] *adj* unclear

不名誉 [fumeiyo] *n* disgrace; 不名誉な [fumeiyo na] *adj* disgraceful

踏切 [fumikiri] *n* level crossing

不眠症 [fuminshou] *n* insomnia

踏みつける [fumitsukeru] *v* stamp

踏む [fumu] *v* step on

不向き [fumuki] 不向きな [fumuki na] *adj* unfit

分 [fun] *n* minute

船乗り [funanori] *n* seaman

不慣れ [funare] 不慣れの [funare no] *adj* unfamiliar

船 [fune] *n* ship; 船に酔った [fune ni yotta] *adj* seasick; 宇宙船 [uchuusen] *n* spacecraft; 定期船 [teikisen] *n* liner

舟 [fune] *n* boat; 漕ぎ舟 [kogibune] *n* rowing boat

憤慨 [fungai] *n* indignation; 憤慨した [fungai shita] *adj* resentful; 憤慨する [fungai suru] *v* resent

噴火 [funka] 噴火口 [funkakou] *n* volcano

粉末 [funmatsu] *n* powder

粉末洗剤 [funmatsusenzai] *n* washing powder; 粉末洗剤はありますか? [funmatsu-senzai wa arimasu ka?] Do you have washing powder?

噴霧 [funmu] *n* spray; 噴霧する [funmu suru] *v* spray

紛失 [funshitsu] 私の手荷物が紛失しました [watashi no tenimotsu ga funshitsu shimashita] My luggage has been lost

噴水 [funsui] *n* fountain

フライ [furai] *adj* fried; フライパン [furaipan] *n* frying pan

フライドポテト [furaidopoteto] *n* chips

フライト [furaito] *n* flight; もっと早いフライトがいいのですが [motto hayai furaito ga ii no desu ga] I would prefer an earlier flight; フライトは遅れています [furaito wa okurete imasu] The flight has been delayed; フライトをキャンセルしたいのですが [furaito o kyanseru shitai no desu ga] I'd like to cancel my flight; フライトを変更したいのですが [furaito o henkou shitai no desu ga] I'd like to change my flight; 私はフライトに乗り遅れました [watashi wa furaito ni noriokuremashita] I've missed my flight; ···からのフライトの手荷物はどこですか? [...kara no furaito no tenimotsu wa doko desu ka?] Where is the luggage for the flight from...?; ···行きのフライトはどこでチェックインするのですか? [...iki no furaito wa doko de chekku-in suru no desu ka?] Where do I check in for the flight to...?; 安いフライトはありますか? [yasui furaito wa arimasu ka?] Are there any cheap flights?

フラン [furan] *n* (食べ物) flan

フランス [furansu] *n* France

フランス語 [furansugo] *n* French (language)

フランス人 [furansujin] *n* Frenchman, Frenchwoman

フランスの [furansu no] *adj* French

フラッシュ [furasshu] *n* flash; フラッシュが働きません [furasshu ga hatarakimasen] The flash is not working

フラット [furatto] *n* flat

フラットスクリーン [furattosukuriin] フラットスクリーンの [furatto sukuriin no] *adj* flat-screen

フレーバー [fureebaa] *n* flavour; どんなフレーバーがありますか? [donna fureebaa ga arimasu ka?] What flavours do you have?

フレックスタイム [furekkusutaimu] *n* flexitime

フレンチホルン [furenchihorun] *n* French horn

触れる [fureru] *v* touch

不利 [furi] *n* disadvantage

フリー [furii] *adj* free; フリーキック [furiikikku] *n* free kick

フリース [furiisu] *n* fleece

振替 [furikae] 自動振替 [jidoufurikae] *n* standing order

ふりをする [furi o suru] *v* pretend

風呂 [furo] 泡風呂 [awaburo] *n* bubble bath

フロントガラス [furonto-garasu] *n* windscreen; フロントガラスのワイパー [furonto-garasu no waipaa] *n* windscreen wiper; フロントガラスが割れています [furonto-garasu ga warete imasu] The windscreen is broken; フロントガラスを拭いてもらえますか? [furonto-garasu o fuite moraemasu ka?] Could you clean the windscreen?

フロントガラスのウォッシャー液 [furonto-garasu no uosshaa eki] フロントガラスのウォッシャー液を補充してもらえますか? [furonto-garasu no wosshaa-eki o hojuu shite moraemasu ka?] Can you top up the windscreen washers?

フロッピー [furoppii] フロッピーディスク [furoppii disuku] *n* floppy disk

浮浪者 [furousha] *n* tramp *(beggar)*

振る [furu] *vt* shake; 手を振る [te o furu] *v* wave

降る [furu] *v* fall *(rain, snow)*; みぞれが降る [mizore ga furu] *v* sleet; 雪が降る [yuki ga furu] *v* snow; 雪が降っています [yuki ga futte imasu] It's snowing; 雨が降っています [ame ga futte imasu] It's raining; 雨が降ると思いますか? [ame ga furu to omoimasu ka?] Do you think it's going to rain?

震える [furueru] *v* shiver, tremble

古い [furui] 古くなった [furuku natta] *adj* stale

古い [furui] *adj* old *(aged: things)*

振舞う [furumau] *v* behave

フルタイム [furutaimu] フルタイムの [furutaimu no] *adj* full-time; フルタイムで [furutaimu de] *adv* full-time

フルート [furuuto] *n* flute

フルーツ [furuutsu] *n* fruit; フルーツサラダ [furuutsusarada] *n* fruit salad; フルーツジュース [furuutsujuusu] *n* fruit juice

不良 [furyou] 消化不良 [shoukafuryou] *n* indigestion; 栄養不良 [eiyou furyou] *n* malnutrition

ふさ [fusa] 髪のふさ [kami no fusa] *n* lock *(hair)*

ふさぐ [fusagu] *v* block, (じゃま) obstruct

防ぐ [fusegu] *v* prevent

不正 [fusei] *adj* improper; 不正を働く [fusei-o hataraku] *v* misbehave

不正確 [fuseikaku] 不正確な [fuseikaku na] *adj* inaccurate, incorrect

不成功 [fuseikou] 不成功に終わった [fuseikou ni owatta] *adj* unsuccessful

不詳 [fushou] 身元不詳の [mimoto fushou no] *adj* unidentified

不正直 [fushoujiki] 不正直な [fushoujiki na] *adj* bent *(dishonest)*

不正直な [fushoujiki na] dishonest

不足 [fusoku] *n* shortage; 不足して [fusoku shite] *adj* scarce; 不足すること [fusoku suru koto] *n* shortfall

ふすま [fusuma] *n* (小麦外皮) bran

蓋 [futa] *n* lid

双子 [futago] *n* twin

双子座 [futagoza] *n* Gemini

再び [futatabi] *adv* again; 再び始められる [futatabi hajimerareru] *adj* renewable

不貞 [futei] 不貞な [futei na] *adj* unfaithful

不定詞 [futeishi] *n* infinitive

不適切 [futekisetsu] 不適切な [futekisetsu na] *adj* unsuitable

布団 [futon] *n* futon; キルトの掛け布団 [kiruto no kakebuton] *n* duvet

太りすぎ [futorisugi] 太りすぎの [futori sugi no] *adj* overweight

太る [futoru] 丸々太った [marumaru futotta] *adj* chubby, plump; 太った [futotta] *adj* fat

不凍 [futou] 不凍液 [futoueki] *n* antifreeze

不当 [futou] 不当な [futou na] *adj* unreasonable

埠頭 [futou] *n* pier, quay

二日酔い [futsukayoi] *n* hangover

普通 [futsuu] 普通に [futsu ni] *adv* normally; 普通は [futsuu wa] *adv* usually; 普通の [futsuu no] *adj* common, normal, ordinary, usual; 普通でない [futsuu de nai] *adj* unusual; 普通車 [futsuu-sha] a standard class cabin; 普通郵便でどのくらいの日数がかかりますか? [futsuu-yuubin de dono kurai no nissuu ga kakarimasu ka?] How long will it take by normal post?

普通駆け足 [futsuu kakeashi] 普通駆け足で行く [futsuu kakeashi de iku] *v* canter

フットボール [futtobouru] *n* football; アメリカンフットボール [amerikan futtobouru] *n* American football; フットボールの試合 [futtobouru no shiai] *n* football match; フットボール選手 [futtobouru senshu] *n* football player, footballer

フットプリント [futtopurinto] カーボンフットプリント [kaabon futtopurinto] *n* carbon footprint

沸騰 [futtou] 沸騰した [futtou shita] *adj* boiled; 沸騰する [futtou suru] *vi* boil

封 [fuu] 封をする [fuu-o suru] *v* seal

ふう [fuu] 別なふうに [betsu na fuuni] *adv* otherwise

フーバー® [fuubaa] *n* Hoover®

フード [fuudo] *n* hood

フードプロセッサー [fuudopurosessaa] *n* food processor

風変わり [fuugawari] 風変わりな [fuugawari na] *adj* eccentric

封印 [fuuin] *n* seal (mark)

風景 [fuukei] *n* landscape, scenery

不運 [fuun] *n* misfortune

封鎖 [fuusa] *n* blockage; 道路封鎖 [douro fuusa] *n* roadblock; 封鎖された [fuusa sareta] *adj* blocked

風船 [fuusen] *n* balloon

風車 [fuusha] 風車小屋 [fuushagoya] *n* windmill

風疹 [fuushin] *n* German measles

風習 [fuushuu] *n* custom

封筒 [fuutou] *n* envelope

不和 [fuwa] *n* disagreement; 不和になる [fuwa ni naru] *v* fall out

冬 [fuyu] *n* winter

富裕 [fuyuu] *n* wealth; 富裕な [fuyuu na] *adj* wealthy

不愉快 [fuyuukai] 不愉快な [fuyukai na] *adj* unpleasant

不在 [fuzai] *n* absence; 不在の [fuzai no] *adj* absent

付属 [fuzoku] 付属物 [fuzokubutsu] *n* accessory

ふぞろい [fuzoroi] ふぞろいの [fuzoroi no] *adj* irregular

g

蛾 [ga] *n* moth

ガーナ [gaana] *n* Ghana; ガーナの [gaana no] *adj* Ghanaian

ガーナ人 [gaanajin] *n* Ghanaian (*person*)

ガーリック [gaarikku] *n* garlic; それには ガーリックが入っていますか? [sore ni wa gaarikku ga haitte imasu ka?] Is there any garlic in it?

ガールフレンド [gaarufurendo] *n* girlfriend; 私にはガールフレンドがいます [watashi ni wa gaarufurendo ga imasu] I have a girlfriend

ガボン [gabon] *n* Gabon

画鋲 [gabyou] *n* drawing pin, thumb tack

ガチョウ [gachou] *n* goose

害 [gai] 害する [gai suru] *v* harm

ガイアナ [gaiana] *n* Guyana

外部 [gaibu] 外部の [gaibu no] *adj* external

害虫 [gaichuu] *n* pest

ガイド [gaido] *n* guide; ガイドツアーは何時 に始まりますか? [gaido-tsuaa wa nan-ji ni hajimarimasu ka?] What time does the guided tour begin?; 英語を話すガイドは いますか? [eigo o hanasu gaido wa imasu ka?] Is there a guide who speaks English?; 地元のウォーキングのガイドはいますか? [jimoto no wookingu no gaido wa imasu ka?] Do you have a guide to local walks?

ガイドブック [gaidobukku] *n* guidebook

ガイドツアー [gaidotsuaa] *n* guided tour

外貨 [gaika] *n* foreign currency; 外貨両替 所 [gaika ryougaesho] *n* bureau de change; ここに外貨両替所はありますか? [koko ni gaika ryougae-jo wa arimasu ka?] Is there a bureau de change here?; その外 貨両替所はいつ開きますか? [sono gaika ryougae-jo wa itsu hirakimasu ka?] When is the bureau de change open?

外国 [gaikoku] 外国人 [gaikokujin] *n* foreigner; 外国の [gaikoku no] *adj* foreign

外国語 [gaikokugo] *n* foreign language; 外国語慣用句集 [gaikokugo kan'youku shuu] *n* phrasebook

外国人 [gaikokujin] *n* foreigner

外交 [gaikou] 外交上の [gaikoujou no] *adj* diplomatic; 外交官 [gaikoukan] *n* diplomat

街路 [gairo] 街路計画 [gairo keikaku] *n* street plan; 街路地図 [gairo chizu] *n* street map

外線電話 [gaisendenwa] *n* external call; 外線電話をかけたいので、つないでもらえ ますか? [gaisen-denwa o kaketai no de, tsunaide moraemasu ka?] I want to make an outside call, can I have a line?

外傷 [gaishou] 外傷性の [gaishou sei no] *adj* traumatic

外出 [gaishutsu] 外出する [gaishutsu suru] *v* go out

外出する [gaishutsu suru] 彼は外出して います [kare wa gaishutsu shite imasu] He's out

街灯 [gaitou] *n* streetlamp; 街灯柱 [gaitouchuu] *n* lamppost

概要 [gaiyou] *n* outline

画家 [gaka] *n* painter

崖 [gake] *n* cliff

学会 [gakkai] *n* institute

がっかりする [gakkari suru] がっかりさ

せる [gakkari saseru] v let down; がっかり
させる [gakkari saseru] v disappointing

楽器 [gakki] n musical instrument

学期 [gakki] n term (division of year); 二学
期制度の一学期 [nigakki seido no
ichigakki] n semester; 学期中の中間休暇
[gakkichuu no chuukan kyuuka] n
half-term

学校 [gakkou] n school; 語学学校 [gogaku
gakkou] n language school; 美術学校
[bijutsugakkou] n art school; 寄宿学校
[kishuku gakkou] n boarding school; 夜間
学校 [yakangakkou] n night school; 学校
の制服 [gakkou no seifuku] n school
uniform; 小学校 [shougakkou] n
elementary school, primary school

学 [gaku] 社会学 [shakaigaku] n sociology;
心理学 [shinrigaku] n psychology; 動物学
[doubutsugaku] n zoology

学部 [gakubu] 学部学生 [gakubu gakusei]
n undergraduate

額縁 [gakubuchi] n picture frame

学童 [gakudou] n schoolchildren

楽譜 [gakufu nijuu] n score (of music)

岳救助隊 [gakukyuujotai] 一番近い山岳
救助隊はどこですか? [ichiban chikai
sangaku-kyuujo-tai wa doko desu ka?]
Where is the nearest mountain rescue
service post?

学問 [gakumon] n scholarship

学年 [gakunen] n academic year

学生 [gakusei] n student; 成人学生 [seijin
gakusei] n mature student; 学生割引
[gakusei waribiki] n student discount; 学
部学生 [gakubu gakusei] n
undergraduate; 私は学生です [watashi
wa gakusei desu] I'm a student; 学生割引
はありますか? [gakusei-waribiki wa
arimasu ka?] Are there any reductions for
students?

楽節 [gakusetsu] n passage (musical)

学者 [gakusha] n scholar; 言語学者
[gengogakusha] n linguist; 経済学者
[keizaigakusha] n economist; 心理学者
[shinrigakusha] n psychologist

学士院 [gakushiin] n academy

学習者 [gakushuusha] n learner

がみがみ [gamigami] がみがみ小言を言
う [gamigami kogoto-o iu] v nag

ガム [gamu] n gum; 風船ガム
[fuusengamu] n bubble gum

癌 [gan] n cancer (illness)

がんばる [ganbaru] v bear up

ガンビア [ganbia] n Gambia

頑固 [ganko] 頑固な [ganko na] adj
stubborn

頑固な [ganko na] adj obstinate,
stubborn

丸薬 [ganyaku] n pill

合併 [gappei] n merger; 合併する [gappei
suru] v merge

ガラガラヘビ [garagarahebi] n
rattlesnake

ガラガラいう音 [garagara iu oto] n
rattle

がらくた [garakuta] n junk

がらんとした [garan to shita] adj stark

ガラス [garasu] n glass, glass (vessel); ガラ
ス繊維 [garasu sen'i] n fibreglass; 複層ガ
ラス [fukusou garasu] n double glazing;
窓ガラス [madogarasu] n window pane

ガレージ [gareeji] n garage

ガリ勉 [gariben] ガリ勉する [gariben suru]
v swot

画廊 [garou] n gallery

餓死 [gashi] n starvation; 餓死する [gashi
suru] v starve

画素 [gaso] n pixel

ガソリン [gasorin] n petrol; 無鉛ガソリン
[muen gasorin] n unleaded petrol; ガソリ
ンが切れてしまいました [gasorin ga kirete
shimaimashita] I've run out of petrol, The
petrol has run out

ガソリンスタンド [gasorinsutando] n
petrol station, service station; この近くに
ガソリンスタンドはありますか? [kono
chikaku ni gasorin-sutando wa arimasu
ka?] Is there a petrol station near here?

ガソリンタンク [gasorintanku] n petrol
tank; ガソリンタンクが漏れています

[gasorin-tanku ga morete imasu] **The petrol tank is leaking**

ガス [gasu] *n* **gas**; キャンプ用ガス [kyanpu you gasu] *n* **camping gas**; 排気ガス [haikigasu] *n* **exhaust fumes**; 催涙ガス [sairuigasu] *n* **tear gas**; 天然ガス [tennengasu] *n* **natural gas**; ガスのにおいがします [gasu no nioi ga shimasu] **I can smell gas**

ガスケット [gasuketto] *n* **gasket**

ガスレンジ [gasurenji] *n* **gas cooker**

ガス点火器 [gasutenkaki] *n* **gas lighter**; ガス点火器用のカートリッジはありますか? [gasu-tenkaki-you no kaatorijji wa arimasu ka?] **Do you have a refill for my gas lighter?**

側 [gawa] *n* **side**

画像 [gazou] *n* **graphics**

ゲーム [geemu] *n* **game**; コンピューターゲーム [konpyuutaa geemu] *n* **computer game**; ゲームコンソール [geemu konsooru] *n* **games console**; ゲームセンター [geemu sentaa] *n* **amusement arcade**; ボードゲーム [boodo geemu] *n* **board game**

ゲート [geeto] *n* **gate**; …ゲートに行ってください […geeto ni itte kudasai] **Please go to gate…**

芸術 [geijutsu] *n* **art**; 芸術的な [geijutsuteki na] *adj* **artistic**; 芸術家 [geijutsuka] *n* **artist**

芸人 [geinin] *n* **performer**; 大道芸人 [daidougeinin] *n* **busker**

外科 [geka] 美容外科 [biyou geka] *n* **cosmetic surgery**; 外科医 [gekai] *n* **surgeon**; 形成外科 [keisei geka] *n* **plastic surgery**

劇 [geki] *n* **drama, play**

劇団 [gekidan] *n* **theatrical troupe**; レパートリー劇団 [repaatorii gekidan] *n* **rep**

激怒 [gekido] *n* **rage**; ドライバーが路上で激怒すること [doraibaa ga rojou de gekido suru koto] *n* **road rage**

激動 [gekidou] *n* **turbulence**

劇場 [gekijou] *n* **theatre**; その劇場で何が上演されていますか? [sono gekijou de nani ga jouen sarete imasu ka?] **What's on at the theatre?**

月経 [gekkei] *n* **menstruation**

現場 [genba] *n* **site**; 建設現場 [kensetsu genba] *n* **building site**

現代 [gendai] 現代の [gendai no] *adj* **contemporary, modern**; 現代語 [gendaigo] *n* **modern languages**; 現代化する [gendaika suru] *v* **modernize**

言語 [gengo] *n* **language**; 言語の [gengo no] *adj* **linguistic**; 言語学者 [gengogakusha] *n* **linguist**

原因 [gen'in] *n* **cause, reason**; この渋滞の原因は何ですか? [kono juutai no gen'in wa nan desu ka?] **What is causing this hold-up?**

現実 [genjitsu] *n* **reality**; 現実的な [genjitsuteki na] *adj* **realistic**

現実のものではない [genjitsu no mono dewa nai] *adj* **unreal**

現状 [genjou] *n* **status quo**

限界 [genkai] *n* **limit**

厳格 [genkaku] 厳格さ [genkakusa] *n* **austerity**

玄関 [genkan] *n* **hallway**; 玄関の呼び鈴 [genkan no yobisuzu] *n* **doorbell**

元気 [genki] *n* **energy**; 元気のよい [genki no yoi] *adj* **lively**

現金 [genkin] *n* **cash**; 現金自動支払い機 [genkin jidoushiharaiki] *n* **cash dispenser**; ここに現金自動支払い機がありますか? [koko ni genkin-jidou-shiharaiki ga arimasu ka?] **Is there a cash machine here?**; 現金で払うと割引がありますか? [genkin de harau to waribki ga arimasu ka?] **Do you offer a discount for cash?**; 私は現金がありません [watashi wa genkin ga arimasen] **I don't have any cash**; 私のカードを使って現金を引き出せますか? [watashi no kaado o tsukatte genkin o hikidasemasu ka?] **Can I use my card to get cash?**

現金化 [genkinka] ここで私のトラベラーズチェックを現金化できますか? [koko de watashi no toraberaazu-chekku o genkinka dekimasu ka?] **Can I change my traveller's cheques here?**; 小切手を現金化してくださ

い [kogitte o genkinka shite kudasai] **I want to cash a cheque, please**; 小切手を現金化できますか? [kogitte o genkinka dekimasu ka?] **Can I cash a cheque?**

げんこつ [genkotsu] n jab; げんこつをくらわす [genkotsu-o kurawasu] v punch

原稿 [genkou] n copy (written text), manuscript

玄米 [genmai] n brown rice

原子 [genshi] n atom; 原子炉 [genshiro] n reactor; 原子爆弾 [genshibakudan] n atom bomb; 原子力の [genshiryoku no] adj atomic

原子力 [genshiryoku] 原子力の [genshiryoku no] adj atomic, nuclear

減少 [genshou] n decrease, reduction; 減少する [genshou suru] v decrease

厳守 [genshu] 時間厳守の [jikangenshu no] adj punctual

現在 [genzai] n present (time being); 現在の [genzai no] adj current

現像 [genzou] このフィルムを現像していただけますか? [kono firumu o genzou shite itadakemasu ka?] **Can you develop this film, please?**

げっぷ [geppu] n (口) burp; げっぷをする [geppu o suru] v burp

ゲレンデ [gerende] n ski slope; 初心者用ゲレンデ [shoshinshayou gerende] n nursery slope; ゲレンデのマップはありますか? [gerende no mappu wa arimasu ka?] **Do you have a map of the ski runs?**

下痢 [geri] n diarrhoea; 私は下痢しています [watashi wa geri shite imasu] **I have diarrhoea**

下船 [gesen] n disembarkation; もう下船できますか? [mou gesen dekimasu ka?] **Can we go ashore now?**

下宿人 [geshukunin] n lodger

下水 [gesui] n sewer

ゲストハウス [gesutohausu] n guesthouse

月曜 [getsuyou] n Monday; 私は月曜から具合が悪いです [watashi wa getsuyou kara guai ga warui desu] **I've been sick since Monday**

月曜日 [getsuyoubi] n Monday; 月曜日に [getsuyoubi ni] on Monday; 六月十五日の月曜日です [roku-gatsu juugo-nichi no getsuyoubi desu] **It's Monday the fifteenth of June**

ギア [gia] n gear (mechanism); ギアがききません [gia ga kikimasen] **The gears don't work**; ギアが入りません [gia ga hairimasen] **The gears are not working**

ギアボックス [giabokkusu] n gear box

ギアレバー [giarebaa] n gear lever

ギアシフト [giashifuto] n gear stick, gearshift

義母 [gibo] n mother-in-law

議長 [gichou] n chairman

義父 [gifu] n father-in-law

ギフト [gifuto] n gift; ギフトショップ [gifuto shoppu] n gift shop; どこでギフトを買えますか? [doko de gifuto o kaemasu ka?] **Where can I buy gifts?**; それをギフト用にラッピングしていただけますか? [sore o gifuto-you ni rappingu shite itadakemasu ka?] **Please can you gift-wrap it?**

議員 [giin] n member; 地方議会議員 [chihou gikai giin] n councillor

議事 [giji] 議事日程 [giji nittei] n agenda

技術 [gijutsu] n technology; 情報技術 [jouhou gijutsu] n IT; 技術的な [gijutsuteki na] adj technological; 専門技術 [senmon gijutsu] n technique; 専門技術者 [senmon gijutsusha] n technician

議会 [gikai] n parliament; 地方議会議員 [chihou gikai giin] n councillor

義兄弟 [gikyoudai] n brother-in-law

疑問 [gimon] n query

疑問符 [gimonfu] n question mark

銀 [gin] n silver

ギニア [ginia] n Guinea; 赤道ギニア [sekidou ginia] n Equatorial Guinea

銀行 [ginkou] n bank (finance); 銀行の残高 [ginkou no zandaka] n bank balance; 銀行の手数料 [ginkou no tesuuryou] n bank charges; 銀行の明細書 [ginkou no meisaisho] n bank statement; 銀行家 [ginkouka] n banker; 銀行口座

[ginkoukouza] *n* bank account; ここに銀行はありますか? [koko ni ginkou wa arimasu ka?] Is there a bank here?; その銀行は今日開いていますか? [sono ginkou wa kyou hiraite imasu ka?] Is the bank open today?; その銀行はいつ閉まりますか? [sono ginkou wa itsu shimarimasu ka?] When does the bank close?; その銀行はいつ開きますか? [sono ginkou wa itsu hirakimasu ka?] When does the bank open?; 近くに銀行はありますか? [chikaku ni ginkou wa arimasu ka?] Is there a bank nearby?; ···にある取引銀行から送金したいのですが [...ni aru torihiki-ginkou kara soukin shitai no desu ga] I would like to transfer some money from my bank in...; 銀行までどのくらいの距離ですか? [ginkou made dono kurai no kyori desu ka?] How far is the bank?

儀礼 [girei] 儀礼的行為 [gireiteki koui] *n* formality

義理 [giri] 義理の姉妹 [giri no shimai] *n* sister-in-law

ギリシャ [girisha] *n* Greece

ギリシャ語 [girishago] *n* Greek (*language*)

ギリシャ人 [girishajin] *n* Greek (*person*)

ギリシャの [girisha no] *adj* Greek

犠牲 [gisei] *n* sacrifice, victim

議席 [giseki] *n* seat (*constituency*)

技師 [gishi] *n* engineer; 電気技師 [denki gishi] *n* electrician

儀式 [gishiki] *n* ceremony, ritual; 儀式の [gishiki no] *adj* ritual

偽証 [gishou] *n* perjury

ぎっしり [gisshiri] *adv* tightly; ぎっしり詰まった [gisshiri tsumatta] *adj* compact; ぎっしり詰め込んだ [gisshiri tsumekonda] *adj* jammed

ギター [gitaa] *n* guitar

偽造 [gizou] *n* forgery

五 [go] *number* five

五番目 [gobanme] 五番目の [go banme no] *adj* fifth

五分五分 [gobugobu] 五分五分の [gobugobu no] *adj* fifty-fifty; 五分五分で [gobugobu de] *adv* fifty-fifty

伍長 [gochou] *n* corporal

ゴッドファーザー [goddofaazaa] *n* godfather (*criminal leader*)

護衛 [goei] 護衛されている輸送車隊 [goei sareteiru yusoushatai] *n* convoy; 護衛する [goei suru] *v* escort

語学 [gogaku] *n* language study; 語学ラボ [gogaku rabo] *n* language laboratory; 語学学校 [gogaku gakkou] *n* language school

五月 [gogatsu] *n* May

午後 [gogo] *n* afternoon; 午後の [gogo no] *a* p.m.; 明日の午後 [asu no gogo] tomorrow afternoon; 午後に [gogo ni] in the afternoon

語彙 [goi] *n* vocabulary

ご一緒 [go issho] *adv* together; また近いうちにお仕事でご一緒できることを願っています [mata chikai uchi ni o-shigoto de go-issho dekiru koto o negatte imasu] I hope we can work together again soon

五時 [goji] 五時前に [go-ji mae ni] before five o'clock

五十 [gojuu] *number* fifty

誤解 [gokai] *n* misunderstanding; 誤解する [gokai suru] *v* misunderstand; 誤解を招きやすい [gokai-o manekiyasui] *adj* misleading; 誤解があります [gokai ga arimasu] There's been a misunderstanding

語形 [gokei] 語形変化 [gokei henka] *n* conjugation

ゴキブリ [gokiburi] *n* cockroach

ごめんなさい [gomen nasai] I'm sorry, Sorry; 本当にごめんなさい [hontou nigomennasai] I'm very sorry

ごめんなさい! [gomen nasai] *excl* sorry!

ごみ [gomi] *n* garbage, litter, refuse, rubbish; ごみ捨て場 [gomi suteba] *n* dump, rubbish dump; ごみ収集人 [gomishuushuunin] *n* dustman; ごみはどこに出すのですか? [gomi wa doko ni dasu no desu ka?] Where do we leave the rubbish?

ごみ箱 [gomibako] n bin, dustbin

ゴム [gomu] n rubber; ゴム手袋 [gomu tebukuro] n rubber gloves; 輪ゴム [wagomu] n rubber band; 弾性ゴム [dansei gomu] n rubber band, (for hair) elastic

娯楽 [goraku] n pastime

ゴリラ [gorira] n gorilla

ゴルフ [gorufu] n golf; ゴルフ用クラブ [gorufu you kurabu] n golf club (game); ゴルフ場 [gorufujou] n golf course; どこでゴルフができますか? [doko de gorufu ga dekimasu ka?] Where can I play golf?; この近くに公共のゴルフコースはありますか? [kono chikaku ni kookyou no gorufu-koosu wa arimasu ka?] Is there a public golf course near here?; ゴルフクラブを貸し出していますか? [gorufu-kurabu o kashidashite imasu ka?] Do they hire out golf clubs?

ゴルフクラブ [gorufukurabu] n golf club (society)

誤植 [goshoku] n misprint

ゴツン [gotsun] n whack; ゴツンと打つ [gotsun to utsu] v thump

強奪 [goudatsu] n mugging; 襲って強奪する [osotte goudatsu suru] v mug

合同 [goudou] 合同する [goudou suru] v club together

ゴーグル [gouguru] n goggles; ゴーグルを借りたいのですが [googuru o karitai no desu ga] I want to hire goggles

合法 [gouhou] 合法的な [gouhouteki na] adj legal

合意 [goui] n agreement; 合意された [goui sareta] adj agreed

合格 [goukaku] n pass (meets standard); 合格する [goukaku suru] v pass (an exam)

強姦 [goukan] 強姦者 [goukansha] n rapist

合計 [goukei] n sum, total; ···を合計する [...-o goukei suru] v add up

拷問 [goumon] n torture; 拷問にかける [goumon ni kakeru] v torture

合理 [gouri] 理にかなった [ri ni kanatta] adj rational

ゴール [gouru] n goal

ゴールキーパー [gourukiipaa] n goalkeeper

強盗 [goutou] n (人) mugger, (人) robber, (行為) robbery, (量・程度) hold-up

午前 [gozen] n morning; 午前の [gozen no] a a.m.; 午前中に [gozen-chuu ni] in the morning

具 [gu] 水彩絵の具 [suisai enogu] n watercolour

具合 [guai] n condition; 私は今朝から具合が悪いです [watashi wa kesa kara guai ga warui desu] I've been sick since this morning; 私は昨日から具合が悪いです [watashi wa kinou kara guai ga warui desu] I've been sick since yesterday; 彼は具合がよくありません [kare wa guai ga yoku arimasen] He's not well

グアテマラ [guatemara] n Guatemala

愚人 [gujin] n lunatic

グカード [gukaado] グリーティングカード [guriitingukaado] n greetings card

軍 [gun] 軍の [gun no] adj military; 空軍 [kuugun] n Air Force

軍人 [gunjin] n serviceman; 女性軍人 [josei gunjin] n servicewoman

群集 [gunshuu] n crowd

軍曹 [gunsou] n sergeant

軍隊 [guntai] n army, troops

グラフ [gurafu] n graph

グライダー [guraidaa] n glider; グライダー競技 [guraidaa kyougi] n gliding

グラム [guramu] n gramme

グラウンド [guraundo] n playing field

グレービーソース [gureebiisousu] n gravy

グレープフルーツ [gureepufuruutsu] n grapefruit

グレートブリテン [gureetoburiten] n Great Britain

グリッド [guriddo] n grid

グリーンランド [guriinrando] n Greenland

グリーティン [guriitin] n greeting; グリー

ティングカード [guriitingukaado] n
greetings card

グリル [guriru] n grill; グリルで焼く [guriru
de yaku] v grill; 網焼きにする [amiyaki ni
suru] adj grilled

グローバル [guroobaru] adj global; グロ
ーバル化 [guroobaruka] n globalization

グローバルポジショニングシステム
[guroobaru-pojishoningu-shisutemu]
n GPS; グローバルポジショニングシス
テムはついていますか? [guroobaru-
pojishoningu-shisutemu wa tsuite imasu
ka?] Does it have GPS?

グローブ [guroobu] グローブボックス
[guroobubokkusu] n glove compartment

グルジア [gurujia] n Georgia (country); グ
ルジアの [gurujia no] adj Georgian

グルジア人 [gurujiajin] n Georgian
(inhabitant of Georgia)

グルコース [gurukousu] n glucose

グルテン [guruten] n gluten; グルテンを
使っていない料理はありますか? [guruten
o tsukatte inai ryouri wa arimasu ka?] Do
you have gluten-free dishes?; グルテンを
使わずに食事を用意していただけますか?
[guruten o tsukawazu ni shokuji o youi
shite itadakemasu ka?] Could you prepare
a meal without gluten?

グループ [guruupu] n group

グーグル® [guuguru] グーグル®で調べ
る [guuguru de shiraberu] v Google®

偶然 [guuzen] n coincidence; 偶然に
[guuzen ni] adv accidentally, by chance,
by accident, casually; 偶然の [guuzen no]
adj accidental, casual

グーズベリー [guuzuberii] n gooseberry

逆 [gyaku] n reverse; 逆に [gyaku ni] adv
vice versa; 逆にする [gyaku ni suru] v
reverse

逆戻り [gyakumodori] n relapse

虐待 [gyakutai] n abuse; 虐待する
[gyakutai suru] v abuse; 児童虐待 [jidou
gyakutai] n child abuse

ギャンブラー [gyanburaa] n gambler

ギャンブル [gyanburu] n gambling

ギャング [gyangu] n gang; ギャングの一員
[gyangu no ichiin] n gangster

ギャロップ [gyaroppu] n gallop; ギャロッ
プで走る [gyaroppu de hashiru] v gallop

漁業 [gyogyou] n fishing

魚介類 [gyokairui] 魚介類を使わずに食
事を用意していただけますか? [gyokairui
o tsukawazu ni shokuji o youi shite
itadakemasu ka?] Could you prepare a
meal without seafood?

漁船 [gyosen] n fishing boat

ぎょっとさせる [gyotto saseru] v
frightening

業 [gyou] n industry; 旅行業 [ryokou gyou]
n tourism

行儀 [gyougi] n manners; 行儀のよい
[gyougi no yoi] adj well-behaved

業者 [gyousha] 旅行業者 [ryokou gyousha]
n tour operator, travel agent; 製造業者
[seizou gyousha] n manufacturer; 建築業
者 [kenchiku gyousha] n builder; 密輸業者
[mitsuyu gyousha] n smuggler; 出版業者
[shuppan gyousha] n publisher; 印刷業者
[insatsu gyousha] n printer (person); 卸売
業者 [oroshiuri gyousha] n distributor; 小
売業者 [kouri gyousha] n retailer

牛肉 [gyuuniku] n beef

牛乳 [gyuunyuu] n milk; 超高温殺菌牛乳
[choukouon sakkin gyuunyuu] n UHT milk;
あなたは牛乳を飲みますか? [anata wa
gyuunyuu o nomimasu ka?] Do you drink
milk?; それは低温殺菌していない牛乳を
使って作られていますか? [sore wa
teion-sakkin shite inai gyuunyuu o tsukatte
tsukurarete imasu ka?] Is it made with
unpasteurised milk?; 本物の牛乳はありま
すか? [honmono no gyuunyuu wa arimasu
ka?] Have you got real milk?

h

歯 [ha] *n* tooth; 歯の [ha no] *adj* dental; 歯が生える [ha ga haeru] *v* teethe; 歯ブラシ [haburashi] *n* toothbrush; 練り歯ミガキ [neri hamigaki] *n* toothpaste; 入れ歯 [ireba] *n* dentures; この歯が痛みます [kono ha ga itamimasu] This tooth hurts; 私は歯を折りました [watashi wa ha o orimashita] I've broken a tooth

派 [ha] *n* group; 過激派 [kagekiha] *n* extremist

葉 [ha] *n* leaf, leaves

刃 [ha] *n* blade; 安全かみそりの刃 [anzen kamisori no ha] *n* razor blade

ハーブ [haabu] *n* herbs

ハーブティー [haabuteii] *n* herbal tea

ハードボード [haadoboodo] *n* hardboard

ハードディスク [haadodisuku] *n* hard disk

ハードコピー [haadokopii] *n* hard copy, printout

ハードル [haadoru] *n* hurdle

ハードウェア [haadouea] *n* hardware

ハーフタイム [haafutaimu] *n* half-time

ハーモニカ [haamonika] *n* mouth organ

ハープ [haapu] *n* harp

幅 [haba] *n* width

幅木 [habaki] *n* skirting board

幅跳び [habatobi] *n* long jump

省く [habuku] *v* leave out

ハブキャップ [habukyappu] *n* hubcap

鉢 [hachi] *n* flower pot; 植木鉢 [uekibachi] *n* plant pot; 鉢植え植物 [hachiue shokubutsu] *n* pot plant

八 [hachi] *number* eight; 八時過ぎに [hachi-ji sugi ni] after eight o'clock

ハチ [hachi] *n* (昆虫) bee

八番目 [hachibanme] *n* eighth; 八番目の [hachi banme no] *adj* eighth

八月 [hachigatsu] *n* August

八十 [hachijuu] *number* eighty

蜂蜜 [hachimitsu] *n* honey

波長 [hachou] *n* wavelength

爬虫類 [hachuuurui] *n* reptile

肌 [hada] *n* skin; 鳥肌 [torihada] *n* goose pimples

肌着 [hadagi] *n* vest

裸 [hadaka] 裸の [hadaka no] *adj* naked, nude

裸足 [hadashi] 裸足の [hadashi no] *adj* barefoot; 裸足で [hadashi de] *adv* barefoot

派手な [hade na] *adj* gaudy

ハドック [hadokku] *n* haddock

ハエ [hae] *n* fly

生える [haeru] *v* grow; 歯が生える [ha ga haeru] *v* teethe

はがき [hagaki] *n* postcard; 郵便はがき [yuubin hagaki] *n* postcard; どこで郵便はがきを買えますか? [doko de yuubin-hagaki o o kaemasu ka?] Where can I buy some postcards?; 私は郵便はがきを探しています [watashi wa yuubin-hagaki o sagashite imasu] I'm looking for postcards; 郵便はがきはありますか? [yuubin-hagaki wa arimasu ka?] Do you have any postcards?

励み [hagemi] *n* encouragement; 励みになる [hagemi ni naru] *adj* encouraging

はげる [hageru] *v* go bald; 頭のはげた

[atama no hageta] *adj* bald

ハゲワシ [hagewashi] *n* vulture

はぐ [hagu] *v* strip

歯ぐき [haguki] *n* gums; 私は歯ぐきが痛みます [watashi wa haguki ga itamimasu] **My gums are sore**; 私は歯ぐきが出血しています [watashi wa haguki ga shukketsu shite imasu] **My gums are bleeding**

母 [haha] *n* mother; 代理母 [dairibo] *n* surrogate mother; 継母 [mama haha] *n* stepmother

破片 [hahen] *n* splinter

灰 [hai] *n* ash; 灰の水曜日 [hai no suiyoubi] *n* Ash Wednesday

肺 [hai] *n* lung

はい [hai] *excl* yes

配置 [haichi] *n* layout, placement

ハイチ [haichi] *n* Haiti

背泳 [haiei] *n* backstroke

肺炎 [haien] *n* pneumonia

ハイファイ [haifai] ハイファイ装置 [haifai souchi] *n* hifi

配布 [haifu] 配布する [haifu suru] *v* give out

ハイフン [haifun] *n* hyphen

配偶者 [haiguusha] *n* spouse

ハイヒール [haihiiru] *n* high heels; ハイヒールの [haihiiru no] *adj* high-heeled

灰色 [haiiro] 灰色の [hai iro no] *adj* grey

ハイジャック [haijakku] ハイジャックの犯人 [haijakku no hannin] *n* hijacker; ハイジャックする [haijakku suru] *v* hijack

排除 [haijo] 可能性を排除する [kanousei-o haijo suru] *v* rule out

ハイカー [haikaa] *n* rambler

配管 [haikan] *n* plumbing; 配管工 [haikankou] *n* plumber

背景 [haikei] *n* background

敗血症 [haiketsushou] *n* blood poisoning

排気 [haiki] 排気ガス [haikigasu] *n* exhaust fumes

廃棄 [haiki] 廃棄する [haiki suru] *v* scrap

ハイキング [haikingu] *n* hike, hiking

ハイライト [hairaito] *n* (やま場) highlight, (化粧品) highlighter; 私はハイライトを入れています [watashi wa hairaito o irete imasu] **My hair is highlighted**

入る [hairu] *v* come in, enter, go in; 中に入れない [naka ni irenai] *v* keep out; ひびの入った [hibi no haitta] *adj* cracked; お入りください! [o-hairi kudasai!] **Come in!**

敗者 [haisha] *n* loser

歯医者 [haisha] *n* dentist; 私は歯医者さんに診てもらわなければなりません [watashi wa haisha-san ni mite morawanakereba narimasen] **I need a dentist**

廃止 [haishi] *n* abolition; 廃止する [haishi suru] *v* abolish

排水 [haisui] 排水する [haisui suru] *v* drain; 排水口 [haisuikou] *n* plughole

排水管 [haisuikan] *n* drain, drainpipe; 排水管が詰まっています [haisuikan ga tsumatte imasu] **The drain is blocked**

配達 [haitatsu] *n* delivery; 新聞配達 [shinbun haitatsu] *n* paper round; 郵便配達人 [yuubin haitatsunin] *n* postman; 配達する [haitatsu suru] *v* deliver; 女性郵便配達人 [josei yuubin haitatsunin] *n* postwoman

俳優 [haiyuu] *n* actor; 喜劇俳優 [kigeki haiyuu] *n* comedian

灰皿 [haizara] *n* ashtray; 灰皿をいただけますか? [haizara o itadakemasu ka?] **May I have an ashtray?**

始まる [hajimaru] *vi* start

初め [hajime] *n* beginning; 初めは [hajime wa] *adv* originally; 六月の初めに [roku-gatsu no hajime ni] **at the beginning of June**

始め [hajime] *n* beginning

始める [hajimeru] *v* begin, start

恥じて [hajite] *adj* ashamed

波状 [hajou] 波状の [hajou no] *adj* wavy

墓 [haka] *n* grave, tomb

破壊 [hakai] *n* break, destruction; 故意に破壊する [koi ni hakai suru] *v* sabotage, vandalize; 故意の破壊 [koi no hakai] *n* sabotage; 破壊する [hakai suru] v destroy; 破壊行為 [hakai koui] n vandalism; 破壊者 [hakaisha] n vandal

墓石 [hakaishi] n gravestone

測る [hakaru] v gauge

博士号 [hakasegou] n PhD

派遣 [haken] 代表として派遣する [daihyou toshite haken suru] v delegate

破棄 [haki] 破棄する [haki suru] v rip up

吐き出す [hakidasu] 息を吐き出す [iki-o hakidasu] v breathe out

吐き気 [hakike] n nausea; つわりの時期の朝の吐き気 [tsuwari no jiki no asa no hakike] n morning sickness; 吐き気がする [hakike ga suru] v feel sick; 吐き気をもよおさせる [hakike-o moyousaseru] adj sickening

ハッカー [hakkaa] n hacker

発汗 [hakkan] 発汗抑制剤 [hakkan yokuseizai] n antiperspirant

発見 [hakken] 発見する [hakken suru] v discover, find out

白血病 [hakketsubyou] n leukaemia

はっきり [hakkiri] adv clearly

箱 [hako] n box; 貯金箱 [chokinbako] n piggybank

運び去る [hakobi saru] v take away

運ぶ [hakobu] v carry

箔 [haku] アルミ箔 [arumihaku] n tinfoil

掃く [haku] v sweep

吐く [haku] v throw up, vomit; つばを吐く [tsuba o haku] v spit

博物館 [hakubutsukan] n museum; その博物館はいつ開きますか? [sono hakubutsukan wa itsu hirakimasu ka?] When is the museum open?; その博物館は毎日開いていますか? [sono hakubutsukan wa mainichi hiraite imasu ka?] Is the museum open every day?; その博物館は日曜日は開いていますか? [sono hakubutsukan wa nichiyoubi wa hiraite imasu ka?] Is the museum open on Sundays?; その博物館は午後開いていますか? [sono hakubutsukan wa gogo hiraite imasu ka?] Is the museum open in the afternoon?; その博物館は午前中開いていますか? [sono hakubutsukan wa gozen-chuu hiraite imasu ka?] Is the museum open in the morning?

白鳥 [hakuchou] n swan

迫害 [hakugai] 迫害する [hakugai suru] v persecute

白状 [hakujou] n confession; すっかり白状する [sukkari hakujou suru] v own up

白内障 [hakunaishou] n cataract (eye)

白紙 [hakushi] 白紙の [hakushi no] adj blank

拍手 [hakushu] n applause; 拍手する [hakushu suru] v clap; 拍手を送る [hakushu-o okuru] v applaud

浜辺 [hamabe] n beach

葉巻き [hamaki] n cigar

ハム [hamu] n ham

ハムスター [hamusutaa] n hamster

版 [han] n edition, version

犯 [han] 凶悪犯 [kyouakuhan] n thug

班 [han] 交替班 [koutai han] n relay

半 [han] n half; 二時半です [ni-ji-han desu] It's half past two

花 [hana] n blossom, flower; 花が咲く [hana ga saku] v blossom, flower; 花屋 [hanaya] n florist

鼻 [hana] n nose; 鼻の穴 [hana no ana] n nostril; 鼻で吸う [hana de suu] v sniff

花火 [hanabi] n fireworks

鼻血 [hanaji] n nosebleed

花婿 [hanamuko] n bridegroom, groom

離れる [hanareru] v leave; 遠く離れて [touku hanarete] adv remotely; 遠く離れた [touku hanareta] adj remote; 離れて [hanarete] adv away; 離れて [hanarete] adv off; 離れた [hanareta] adj distant

離れわざ [hanarewaza] n stunt

話せる [hanaseru] どなたか・・・語を話せる方はいらっしゃいますか? [donata-ka ... go o hanaseru kata wa irasshaimasu ka?] Does anyone here speak...?

話 [hanashi] n tale, talk; 話に出す [hanashi ni dasu] v mention; 話がわかる

[hanashi ga wakaru] *adj* understanding; 話好きな [hanashi zuki na] *adj* talkative

話し [hanashi] 話し中の信号音 [hanashichuu no shingouon] *n* engaged tone; 話し手 [hanashite] *n* teller

話し合う [hanashiau] ・・・を話し合う [...-o hanashiau] *v* discuss

話し中 [hanashichuu] お話し中です [o-hanashi-chuu desu] It's engaged

話しかける [hanashikakeru] ・・・に話しかける [...ni hanashikakeru] *v* talk to

話します [hanashimasu] 何語が話せますか? [nani-go ga hanasemasu ka?] What languages do you speak?; あなたは英語を話しますか? [anata wa eigo o hanashimasu ka?] Do you speak English?; 誰か英語を話せる人はいますか? [dare ka eigo o hanaseru hito wa imasu ka?] Does anyone speak English?; 私は英語をほとんど話せません [watashi wa eigo o hotondo hanasemasen] I speak very little English; 私は英語を話せません [watashi wa eigo o hanasemasen] I don't speak English; 私は・・・を話します [watashi wa ... go o hanashimasu] I speak...

話す [hanasu] *v* speak, talk; 話す人 [hanasu hito] *n* speaker; 遠慮なく話す [enryo naku hanasu] *v* speak up; あなたと個人的にお話ができますか? [anata to kojin-teki ni o-hanashi ga dekimasu ka?] Can I speak to you in private?; お医者さんと話をしたいのですが [o-isha-san to hanashi o shitai no desu ga] I'd like to speak to a doctor; オーナーと話させていただけますか? [oonaa to hanasasete itadakemasu ka?] Could I speak to the owner, please?; もっとゆっくり話していただけますか? [motto yukkuri hanashite itadakemasu ka?] Could you speak more slowly, please?; もっと大きな声で話していただけますか? [motto ooki-na koe de hanashite itadakemasu ka?] Could you speak louder, please?; マネージャーと話させてください [maneejaa to hanasasete kudasai] I'd like to speak to the manager, please; 私は婦人警官と話したいのです [watashi wa fujin-keikan to hanashitai no desu] I want to speak to a policewoman

販売 [hanbai] *n* sale; 信用販売 [shinyou hanbai] *n* credit; 販売価格 [hanbai kakaku] *n* selling price; 販売スタッフ [hanbai sutaffu] *n* sales assistant; 販売期限 [hanbai kigen] *n* sell-by date; 販売員 [hanbaiin] *n* sales rep

販売機 [hanbaiki] 自動販売機 [jidouhanbaiki] *n* vending machine

販売店 [hanbaiten] *n* seller, vendor; 乳製品販売店 [nyuuseihin hanbaiten] *n* dairy; 新聞販売店 [shinbun hanbaiten] *n* newsagent

反駁 [hanbaku] *n* contradiction; 反駁する [hanbaku suru] *v* contradict

半分 [hanbun] *n* half; 半分の [hanbun no] *adj* half; 半分だけ [hanbun dake] *adv* half

判断 [handan] 判断する [handan suru] *v* reckon; 判断を誤る [handan-o ayamaru] *v* misjudge

半脱脂 [handasshi] 半脱脂乳 [han dasshi nyuu] *n* semi-skimmed milk

ハンディーキャップ [handiikyappu] あなたのハンディーキャップはどのくらいですか? [anata no handiikyappu wa dono kurai desu ka?] What's your handicap?; 私のハンディーキャップは・・・です [watashi no handiikyappu wa ... desu] My handicap is...

ハンドバッグ [handobaggu] *n* handbag

ハンドボール [handobooru] *n* handball

ハンドブック [handobukku] *n* handbook

ハンドブレーキ [handobureeki] *n* handbrake

判読しにくい [handokushinikui] *adj* illegible

ハンドメイド [handomeido] *adj* handmade; これはハンドメイドですか? [kore wa hando-meido desu ka?] Is this handmade?

ハンドル [handoru] *n* (自転車・バイク) handlebars, (取っ手) handle; ドアハンドル

[doahandoru] n door handle; 右ハンドル [migi handoru] n right-hand drive

反動 [handou] n repercussions

羽 [hane] n feather

繁栄 [han-ei] n prosperity

はねかける [hanekakeru] v splash

ハネムーン [hanemuun] n honeymoon; 私たちはハネムーン中です [watashi-tachi wa hanemuun-chuu desu] We are on our honeymoon

半円 [han'en] n semicircle

跳ねる [haneru] v leap; 飛び跳ねる [tobihaneru] v skip

ハンガー [hangaa] n coathanger, hanger

半額 [hangaku] 半額の [hangaku no] adj half-price; 半額で [hangaku de] adv half-price

ハンガリー [hangarii] n Hungary

ハンガリー人 [hangariijin] n Hungarian (person)

ハンガリーの [hangarii no] adj Hungarian

ハンググライディング [hanguguraideingu] n hang-gliding; 私はハンググライディングをしたいのですが [watashi wa hanguguraidingu o shitai no desu ga] I'd like to go hang-gliding

範囲 [han-i] n range (limits)

判事 [hanji] n judge; 治安判事 [chian hanji] n magistrate

繁華 [hanka] 繁華街へ [hankagai-e] adv downtown

ハンカチ [hankachi] n handkerchief, hankie

版権 [hanken] n copyright

判決 [hanketsu] 判決を下す [hanketsu-o kudasu] v sentence

反響 [hankyou] n echo

半狂乱 [hankyouran] 半狂乱の [hankyouran no] adj frantic

ハンマー [hanmaa] n hammer

ハンモック [hanmokku] n hammock

犯人 [hannin] n criminal; ハイジャックの犯人 [haijakku no hannin] n hijacker

反応 [hannou] n reaction; 反応する [hannou suru] v react

反復 [hanpuku] 反復性の [hanpuku sei no] adj repetitive

氾濫 [hanran] n flooding; 氾濫させる [hanran saseru] vt flood; 氾濫する [hanran suru] vi flood

伴る [hanru] 雷鳴を伴った [raimei-o tomonatta] adj thundery

ハンサム [hansamu] ハンサムな [hansamu na] adj handsome

反射 [hansha] n reflection; 反射作用 [hansha sayou] n reflex; 反射する [hansha suru] v reflect

繁殖 [hanshoku] n reproduction

繁殖力 [hanshokuryoku] n fertility; 繁殖力のない [hanshokuryoku no nai] adj infertile; 繁殖力のある [hanshokuryoku no aru] adj fertile

ハンター [hantaa] n hunter

反対 [hantai] n objection, opposition; 反対した [hantai shita] adj opposed; 反対する [hantai suru] adj oppose, opposing

半島 [hantou] n peninsula

犯罪 [hanzai] n crime; サイバー犯罪 [saibaa hanzai] n cybercrime; 犯罪の [hanzai no] adj criminal; 犯罪者 [hanzaisha] n criminal, culprit

ハンズフリー [hanzufurii] ハンズフリーの [hanzufurii no] adj hands-free; ハンズフリーキット [hanzu furii kitto] n hands-free kit

発砲 [happou] n shot

発表 [happyou] n announcement; 発表する [happyou suru] v announce

腹 [hara] n abdomen; 腹の減った [hara no hetta] adj hungry; 腹を立てた [hara-o tateta] adj mad (angry)

ハラール [haraaru] adj halal; ハラール料理はありますか? [haraaru-ryoui wa arimasu ka?] Do you have halal dishes?

腹立たしい [haradata shii] adj infuriating

払い戻し [haraimodoshi] n refund

払い戻す [haraimodosu] v pay back,

refund; 払い戻ししてもらえますか? [haraimodoshite moraemasu ka?] Can I have a refund?

払う [harau] v pay, sweep; ほこりを払う [hokori-o harau] v dust; 分割払い [bunkatsu harai] n instalment; 十分な額が払われていない [juubun na gaku ga harawarete inai] adj underpaid; どこで払うのですか? [doko de harau no desu ka?] Where do I pay?; どこで罰金を払うのですか? [doko de bakkin o harau no desu ka?] Where do I pay the fine?; あなたにいくら払えばいいですか? [anata ni ikura haraeba ii desu ka?] What do I owe you?; いつ払うのですか? [itsu harau no desu ka?] When do I pay?; それをすぐに払わなければなりませんか? [sore o sugu ni harawanakereba narimasen ka?] Do I have to pay it straightaway?; 払うのは今ですか、それとも後ですか? [harau no wa ima desu ka, sore tomo ato desu ka?] Do I pay now or later?; ···払ってください [... haratte kudasai] You owe me...; 電気代は別に払わなければなりませんか? [denki-dai wa betsu ni harawanakereba narimasen ka?] Do we have to pay extra for electricity?; 前もって払うのですか? [maemotte harau no desu ka?] Do I pay in advance?

晴れる [hareru] v be fine (weather); 晴れています [harete imasu] It's sunny; 晴れますか? [haremasu ka?] Is it going to be fine?

腫れる [hareru] v swell; 腫れた [hareta] adj swollen

破裂 [haretsu] 破裂する [haretsu suru] v burst; タイヤが破裂しました [taiya ga haretsu shimashita] The tyre has burst

針 [hari] n needle; 針と糸をお持ちですか? [hari to ito o o-mochi desu ka?] Do you have a needle and thread?

鍼 [hari] n acupuncture

針金 [harigane] n wire

ハリケーン [harikeen] n hurricane

ハリネズミ [harinezumi] n hedgehog

春 [haru] n spring (season)

張る [haru] v stretch; ぴんと張った [pin to hatta] adj tight; タイルを張った [tairu-o hatta] adj tiled; 虚勢を張る [kyosei-o haru] v bluff

はさみ [hasami] n clippers, scissors; 爪切りばさみ [tsume kiri basami] n nail scissors

破産 [hasan] 破産した [hasan shita] adj bankrupt, broke

端 [hashi] n edge

箸 [hashi] n chopsticks

橋 [hashi] n bridge

はしご [hashigo] n ladder

はしか [hashika] n measles; 私は最近はしかにかかりました [watashi wa saikin hashika ni kakarimashita] I had measles recently

柱 [hashira] n pillar, post (stake); 街灯柱 [gaitouchuu] n lamppost

走り書き [hashirigaki] 走り書きする [hashirigaki suru] v scribble

走り高跳ぶ [hashiritakatobu] 走り高跳び [hashiri takatobi] n high jump

走る [hashiru] vi run; を走る [-o hashiru] vt run; 走ること [hashiru koto] n run; 全力で走る [zenryoku de hashiru] v sprint

破傷風 [hashoufuu] n tetanus

破損 [hason] n damage; 着いた私のスーツケースが破損しています [tsuita watashi no suutsukeesu ga hason shite imasu] My suitcase has arrived damaged; 私の手荷物が破損しています [watashi no tenimotsu ga hason shite imasu] My luggage has been damaged

発生する [hassei suru] v occur; 繰り返し発生する [kurikaeshi hassei suru] adj recurring

発信 [hasshin] 発信音 [hasshin-on] n dialling tone

発疹 [hasshin] n rash; 私は発疹がでました [watashi wa hasshin ga demashita] I have a rash

発送 [hassou] 発送する [hassou suru] v send out

旗 [hata] n flag

働く [hataraku] v work; 奴隷のように働く [dorei no youni hataraku] v slave away; 共

同して働く [kyoudou shite hataraku] v collaborate; フラッシュが働きません [furasshu ga hatarakimasen] The flash is not working; 私はオフィスで働いています [watashi wa ofisu de hataraite imasu] I work in an office; 私は病院で働いています [watashi wa byouin de hataraite imasu] I work in a hospital; 私は働いています [watashi wa hataraite imasu] I work; 私は工場で働いています [watashi wa koujou de hataraite imasu] I work in a factory

働く人 [hatarakuhito] n worker

果たす [hatasu] v fulfil

ハッチバック [hatchibakku] n hatchback

鳩 [hato] n pigeon

ハト [hato] n dove

発電機 [hatsudenki] n generator

ハツカネズミ [hatsukanezumi] n mouse

発明 [hatsumei] n invention; 発明する [hatsumei suru] v invent; 発明者 [hatsumeisha] n inventor

発音 [hatsuon] n pronunciation; 発音する [hatsuon suru] v pronounce

発展 [hatten] n development, evolution; 発展させる [hatten saseru] vt develop; 発展する [hatten suru] vi develop; 発展途上国 [hattentojoukoku] n developing country

這う [hau] v crawl

ハウスワイン [hausuwain] n house wine; ハウスワインのボトルを1本 [hausu-wain no botoru o ippon] a bottle of the house wine

速足 [hayaashi] 速足で駆ける [hayaashi de kakeru] v trot

早い [hayai] adj early; より早く [yori hayaku] adv sooner; もっと早いフライトがいいのですが [motto hayai furaito ga ii no desu ga] I would prefer an earlier flight

速い [hayai] adj fast

早く [hayaku] adv early; できるだけ早く [dekiru dake hayaku] adv asap

速く [hayaku] adv fast

はやる [hayaru] はやらない [hayaranai] adj unfashionable

速さ [hayasa] n speed

早瀬 [hayase] n rapids

恥ずかしい [hazukashii] adj embarrassed; 恥ずかしい思い [hazukashii omoi] n shame

弾む [hazumu] v bounce

ヘア [hea] n hair; ヘアスタイル [heasutairu] n hairdo, hairstyle

ヘアバンド [heabando] n hairband

ヘアブラシ [heaburashi] n hairbrush

ヘアドライヤー [headoraiyaa] n hairdryer

ヘアジェル [heajieru] n hair gel

ヘアカット [heakatto] n haircut

ヘアピン [heapin] n hairgrip

ヘアスプレー [heasupuree] n hair spray

ヘビ [hebi] n snake

ヘッドホン [heddohon] n headphones; ヘッドホンはついていますか? [heddohon wa tsuite imasu ka?] Does it have headphones?

ヘッドライト [heddoraito] n headlight

ヘッドランプ [heddoranpu] n headlamp

ヘッドスカーフ [heddosukaafu] n headscarf

ヘーゼルナッツ [heezerunattsu] n hazelnut

兵 [hei] n soldier; 偵察兵 [teisatsuhei] n scout

平原 [heigen] n plain

平日 [heijitsu] n weekday

平価 [heika] 平価切下げ [heikakirisage] n devaluation

閉経 [heikei] 閉経期 [heikeiki] n menopause

平均 [heikin] n average; 平均の [heikin no] adj average

平行 [heikou] 平行の [heikou no] adj parallel

平面 [heimen] n plane (surface)

平穏 [heion] n peace

閉鎖 [heisa] n closure; 閉鎖する [heisa suru] v shut down

弊社 [heisha] n company; 弊社についての情報です [heisha ni tsuite no jouhou desu] Here's some information about my company

兵士 [heishi] n soldier

兵所 [heisho] n partition; 閉所恐怖症の [heisho kyoufushou no] adj claustrophobic

閉塞 [heisoku] 閉塞物 [heisokubutsu] n block (obstruction)

平坦な [heitan na] adj plain

閉店 [heiten] 閉店時刻 [heiten jikoku] n closing time

平和な [heiwa na] adj peaceful

へこみ [hekomi] n dent

へこむ [hekomu] v dent

変動 [hendou] 気候変動 [kikou hendo] n climate change

返事 [henji] n reply; 返事をする [henji-o suru] v reply

変化 [henka] n change, shift; 語形変化 [gokei henka] n conjugation; 変化する [henka suru] v range

偏見 [henken] n prejudice; 偏見をもった [henken-o motta] adj prejudiced

返金 [henkin] n refund; 返金してください [henkin shite kudasai] I want my money back; 返金してもらえますか? [henkin shite moraemasu ka?] Can I have my money back?

変更 [henkou] n modification; 変更する [henkou suru] v alter, modify

変な [hen na] adj odd, peculiar, weird

ヘンパーティー [henpaatii] n hen night

返品 [henpin] これを返品したいのですが [kore o henpin shitai no desu ga] I'd like to return this

返済 [hensai] n repayment; 返済する [hensai suru] v repay

編成 [hensei] 再編成する [saihensei suru] v reorganize, restructure

編集 [henshuu] 編集者 [henshuusha] n editor

変装 [hensou] 変装する [hensou suru] v disguise

扁桃 [hentou] n tonsils; 扁桃腺炎 [hentousen'en] n tonsillitis

返答 [hentou] n response; 返答する [hentou suru] v respond

変容 [henyou] 変容させる [hen'you saseru] v transform

片頭痛 [henzutsuu] n migraine

へら [hera] n spatula

減らす [herasu] v diminish, reduce

へり [heri] n margin

ヘリコプター [herikoputaa] n helicopter

ヘロイン [heroin] n heroin

減る [heru] v decrease; 腹の減った [hara no hetta] adj hungry

ヘルメット [herumetto] n helmet; ヘルメットをください [herumetto o kudasai] Can I have a helmet?

ヘルニア [herunia] n hernia

ヘルプライン [herupurain] n helpline

へそ [heso] n navel

部屋 [heya] n room; 子供部屋 [kodomobeya] n nursery; 今晩部屋はありますか? [konban heya wa arimasu ka?] Do you have a room for tonight?; これがあなたの部屋です [kore ga anata no heya desu] This is your room; その部屋にテレビはありますか? [sono heya ni terebi wa arimasu ka?] Does the room have a TV?; その部屋はいくらですか? [sono heya wa ikura desu ka?] How much is the room?; ダブルの部屋がいいのですが [daburu no heya ga ii no desu ga] I'd like a room with a double bed; ツインの部屋がいいのですが [tsuin no heya ga ii no desu ga] I'd like a room with twin beds; 自分の部屋で朝食を取ることができますか? [jibun no heya de choushoku o toru koto ga dekimasu ka?] Can I have breakfast in my room?; 禁煙の部屋がいいのですが [kin'en no heya ga ii no desu ga] I'd like a no smoking room; ···の名前で部屋を予約しました […no namae de heya o yoyaku shimashita] I booked a room in the name of...; 部屋に問題があります [heya ni mondai ga arimasu] There's a problem with the room; 部屋はありますか? [heya wa arimasu ka?] Do you have a room?; 部屋が狭すぎます [heya ga sema-sugimasu] **The room is too small**; 部屋を掃除してもらえますか? [heya o souji shite moraemasu ka?] **Can you clean the room, please?**; 部屋を替えることができますか? [heya o kaeru koto ga dekimasu ka?] **Can I switch rooms?**; 部屋を借りたいのですが [heya o karitai no desu ga] **I'd like to rent a room**; 山が見える部屋がいいのですが [yama ga mieru heya ga ii no desu ga] **I'd like a room with a view of the mountains**; 別の部屋がいいのですが [betsu no heya ga ii no desu ga] **I'd like another room**; 喫煙できる部屋がいいのですが [kitsuen dekiru heya ga ii no desu ga] **I'd like a smoking room**

ヘザー [hezaa] n **heather**

火 [hi] n **fire**; 火をもみ消す [hi-o momikesu] v **stub out**; 大かがり火 [oukagaribi] n **bonfire**

費 [hi] n **expense**; 生活費 [seikatsuhi] n **cost of living**

日当たり [hiatari] 日当たりのよい [hiatari no yoi] adj **sunny**

火花 [hibana] n **spark**

ひび [hibi] ひびの入った [hibi no haitta] adj **cracked**

ヒッチハイク [hitchihaiku] n **hitchhiking**; ヒッチハイクする [hitchihaiku suru] v **hitchhike**; ヒッチハイクをする人 [hitchihaiku o suru hito] n **hitchhiker**

左 [hidari] n **left**; 左に [hidari ni] adv **left**; 左の [hidari no] adj **left**; 左に曲がってください [hidari ni magatte kudasai] **Turn left**

左側 [hidarigawa] 左側の [hidarigawa no] adj **left-hand**; 左側通行 [hidarigawa tsuukou] n **left-hand drive**

左利き [hidarikiki] 左利きの [hidarikiki no] adj **left-handed**

左回り [hidarimawari] 左回りに [hidari mawari ni] adv **anticlockwise**

日照り [hideri] n **drought**

ひどい [hidoi] adj **awful, gross (fat), gross (income etc.), terrible, vicious**; ひどく [hidoku] adv **terribly**; 実にひどい [jitsu ni hidoi] adj **horrible**; なんてひどい天気でし

よう! [nante hidoi tenki deshou!] **What awful weather!**; サービスがひどかったです [saabisu ga hidokatta desu] **The service was terrible**

ひどく [hidoku] adv **awfully, grossly**

日付 [hiduke] n **date**

冷える [hieru] v **cool**

飛越 [hietsu] n **jumping**; 障害飛越 [shougaihietsu] n **show-jumping**

皮膚 [hifu] n **skin**

日帰り [higaeri] 日帰り往復割引切符 [higaeri oufuku waribiki kippu] n **day return**

東 [higashi] n **east**; 東の [higashi no] adj **east, eastern**; 東へ [higashi e] adv **east**

東行き [higashiiki] 東行きの [higashi yuki no] adj **eastbound**

ひげ [hige] n **whiskers**; ひげを剃っていない [hige-o sotte inai] adj **unshaven**; 口ひげ [kuchi hige] n **moustache**

非現実 [higenjitsu] 非現実的な [higenjitsuteki na] adj **unrealistic**

批判 [hihan] n **criticism**; 批判する [hihan suru] v **criticize**

批評 [hihyou] n **review**; 批評家 [hihyouka] n **critic**

ヒーロー [hiirou] n **hero**

ひじ [hiji] n **elbow**

肘掛け [hijikake] adj **reclining**; 肘掛け椅子 [hijikakeke isu] n **armchair**

非常 [hijou] 非常に [hijou ni] adv **very**; 非常階段 [hijoukaidan] n **fire escape**

非常口 [hijouguchi] n **emergency exit**

控えめ [hikae me] 控えめの [hikaeme no] adj **reserved**

比較 [hikaku] n **comparison**; 比較する [hikaku suru] v **compare**; 比較的 [hikakuteki] adv **comparatively, relatively**

悲観 [hikan] n **pessimism**; 悲観主義者 [hikanshugisha] n **pessimist**; 悲観的な [hikanteki na] adj **pessimistic**

ひからびる [hikarabiru] v **be parched**; ひからびた [hikarabita] adj **bone dry**

光 [hikari] n **light**

光り [hikari] n light; 光り輝く [hikari kagayaku] adj brilliant

光る [hikaru] v shine; 光った [hikatta] adj shiny

引き出し [hikidashi] n drawer; 引き出しが動きません [hikidashi ga ugokimasen] The drawer is jammed

ヒキガエル [hikigaeru] n toad

引換 [hikikae] 引換券 [hikikaeken] n voucher

引き返す [hikikaesu] v turn back

挽肉 [hikiniku] n mince

引き起こす [hikiokosu] v cause

引き落とす [hikiotosu] 口座引き落とし [kouza hikiotoshi] n direct debit

引き裂く [hikisaku] v rip; ずたずたに引き裂く [zutazuta ni hikisaku] v tear up

引き継ぐ [hikitsugu] v take over

ひきつける [hikitsukeru] v attract

引き分け [hikiwake] n (試合) draw (tie)

引き分ける [hikiwakeru] v draw (equal with)

ひきずる [hikizuru] v drag; 足をひきずって歩く [ashi-o hikizutte aruku] v shuffle

引っ掻く [hikkaku] v scratch

引っ込める [hikkomeru] 引っ込めること [hikkomeru koto] n withdrawal

引越し [hikkoshi] 引越しトラック [hikkoshi torakku] n removal van

ひっくり [hikkuri] ひっくり返す [hikkurigaesu] v overturn

被告 [hikoku] 被告人 [hikokunin] n accused

被告人 [hikokunin] n defendant

飛行 [hikou] n flight; 未確認飛行物体 [mikakunin hikoubuttai] n UFO

飛行機 [hikouki] n aeroplane, plane; 飛行機に酔った [hikouki ni yotta] adj airsick

非公認 [hikounin] 非公認の [hikounin no] adj unofficial

飛行士 [hikoushi] 宇宙飛行士 [uchuuhikoushi] n astronaut

挽く [hiku] v grind

轢く [hiku] v run over

引く [hiku] v pull, subtract; 下線を引く [kasen-o hiku] v underline; 綱引き [tsunahiki] n tug-of-war; ···を引いた [...-o hiita] prep minus

低い [hikui] adj low; より低い [yori hikui] adj lower

低く [hikuku] adv low

暇 [hima] n free time; 明日の午前中は暇です [asu no gozen-chuu wa hima desu] I'm free tomorrow morning

肥満 [himan] 肥満した [himan shita] adj obese

ヒマワリ [himawari] n sunflower

秘密 [himitsu] n confidence (secret), secret; 秘密に [himitsu ni] adv secretly; 秘密の [himitsu no] adj secret

ひも [himo] n string; 革ひも [kawa himo] n strap; 靴ひも [kutsuhimo] n shoelace; 帯状のひも [obijou no himo] n band (strip)

品 [hin] n product; 記念品 [kinenhin] n souvenir; 貴重品 [kichouhin] n valuables; 美術品 [bijutsuhin] n work of art; 免税品 [menzeihin] n duty-free; 在庫品 [zaikohin] n stock; 何かこの街の特産品はありますか? [nani ka kono machi no tokusanhin wa arimasu ka?] Have you anything typical of this town?; 何かこの地方の特産品はありますか? [nani ka kono chihou no tokusanhin wa arimasu ka?] Do you have anything typical of this region?

ヒナギク [hinagiku] n daisy

避難 [hinan] 避難させる [hinan saseru] v evacuate; 避難所 [hinanjo] n refuge, shelter; 避難者 [hinansha] n refugee

非難 [hinan] n accusation, blame; 非難する [hinan suru] v condemn

皮肉 [hiniku] n irony; 皮肉な [hiniku na] adj ironic

皮肉な [hiniku na] adj sarcastic

避妊 [hinin] n birth control, contraception; 私は避妊が必要です [watashi wa hinin ga hitsuyou desu] I need contraception

避妊具 [hiningu] n contraceptive

貧血 [hinketsu] 貧血の [hinketsu no] adj anaemic

貧困 [hinkon] n poverty

品行 [hinkou] n morals

頻発 [hinpatsu] n frequency

品種 [hinshu] n breed; 品種改良する [hinshu kairyou suru] v breed

ヒント [hinto] n hint

ヒンズー [hinzuu] ヒンズー教徒 [hinzuu kyouto] n Hindu

ヒンズー教 [hinzuukyou] n Hinduism; ヒンズー教の [hinzuu kyou no] adj Hindu

引っ張る [hipparu] v drag

ひっぱたく [hippataku] v spank

ヒッピー [hippii] n hippie

開く [hiraku] 開いた [aita] adj open; いつ開きますか? [itsu hirakimasu ka?] When does it open?; その銀行はいつ開きますか? [sono ginkou wa itsu hirakimasu ka?] When does the bank open?; それは今日開いていますか? [sore wa kyou hiraite imasu ka?] Is it open today?; それは明日開きますか? [sore wa asu hirakimasu ka?] Is it open tomorrow?; ドアが開きません [doa ga akimasen] The door won't open; 窓が開きません [mado ga akimasen] The window won't open; 郵便局はいつ開きますか? [yuubinkyoku wa itsu hirakimasu ka?] When does the post office open?; 鍵が開きません [kagi ga akimasen] The key doesn't work

ヒラマメ [hiramame] n lentils

平泳ぎ [hiraoyogi] n breaststroke

ひれ足 [hireashi] n flippers

比例 [hirei] 比例した [hirei shita] adj proportional

ヒレ肉 [hireniku] n fillet; ···からヒレ肉を取る [...kara hireniku-o toru] v fillet

卑劣 [hiretsu] 卑劣な [hiretsu na] adj lousy

比率 [hiritsu] n proportion, ratio

広がり [hirogari] n extent

広がる [hirogaru] 広がること [hirogaru koto] n spread

広げる [hirogeru] v spread, spread out, unroll

拾い [hiroi] adj random; 拾い読みする [hiroiyomi suru] v browse

広い [hiroi] adj broad, extensive, wide; 広く [hiroku] adv wide

ヒロイン [hiroin] n heroine

広く [hiroku] adv extensively

広まる [hiromaru] v pervade; 広まった [hiromatta] adj widespread

ヒル [hiru] ヒルウォーキングに行きたいのですが [hiru-wookingu ni ikitai no desu ga] I'd like to go hill walking

昼間 [hiruma] n daytime

ヒルウォーキング [hiruuookingu] n hill-walking

肥料 [hiryou] n fertilizer

悲惨 [hisan] 悲惨な [hisan na] adj tragic; 悲惨な出来事 [hisan na dekigoto] n tragedy

秘書 [hisho] n secretary; 個人秘書 [kojin hisho] n personal assistant, PA

被収 [hi shuu] n detainment; 被収容者 [hishuuyousha] n inmate

ひそめる [hisomeru] まゆをひそめる [mayu o hisomeru] v frown

必死 [hisshi] 必死の [hisshi no] adj desperate; 必死で [hisshi de] adv desperately

ヒスタミン [hisutamin] 抗ヒスタミン剤 [kouhisutaminzai] n antihistamine

額 [hitai] n (顔) forehead; 十分な額が払われていない [juubun na gaku ga harawarete inai] adj underpaid

悲嘆 [hitan] n mourning

浸す [hitasu] v soak; ちょっと浸す [chotto hitasu] v dip

否定 [hitei] 否定の [hitei no] adj negative; 否定の答え [hitei no kotae] n negative; 否定する [hitei suru] v deny; 否定できない [hitei dekinai] adj undeniable

人 [hito] n person; 人の住んでいない [hito no sunde inai] adj uninhabited; 人を車に乗せてあげること [hito-o kuruma ni nosete ageru koto] n lift (free ride); いとしい人 [itoshii hito] n darling; 有名人 [yuumeijin]

n celebrity; 食事する人 [shokuji suru hito] *n* diner

一晩 [hitoban] *adj* overnight; 私は一晩入院しなければなりませんか? [watashi wa hitoban nyuuin shinakereba narimasen ka?] Do I have to stay overnight?; ここに一晩駐車できますか? [koko ni hitoban chuusha dekimasu ka?] Can I park here overnight?

人々 [hitobito] *n* people

ひと針 [hitohari] *n* stitch

ひとひら [hitohira] ひとひらの雪 [hitohira no yuki] *n* snowflake

人質 [hitojichi] *n* hostage

ひと口 [hitokuchi] ひと口いただいてもいいですか? [hito-kuchi itadaite mo ii desu ka?] Can I taste it?

ひと組 [hitokumi] *n* pair

HIV [hitomen'ekifuzenuirusu] 私はHIVに感染しています [watashi wa eichi-ai-vui ni kansen shite imasu] I am HIV-positive

HIV陰性 [hitomenekizenuirusu negatibu] HIV陰性の [eichiaibui insei no] *adj* HIV-negative

HIV陽性 [hitomenekizenuirusu pojitibu] HIV陽性の [eichiaibui yousei no] *adj* HIV-positive

一人 [hitori] それは一人あたりいくらですか? [sore wa hitori atari ikura desu ka?] How much is it per person?

一人よがり [hitoriyogari] 一人よがりの [hitori yogari no] *adj* smug

ひとさじ [hitosaji] *n* spoonful

等しい [hitoshii] *adj* equal; 等しくする [hitoshiku suru] *v* equalize; 等しくすること [hitoshiku suru koto] *n* equation; ・・・に等しい [...ni hitoshii] *v* equal

一つ [hitotsu] *n* piece ▷ *pron* one; 一つの [hitotsu no] *art* a, an; もう一つの [mou hitotsu no] *adj* another

ひと続き [hitotsuduki] *n* series

ひつぎ [hitsugi] *n* coffin

羊 [hitsuji] *n* sheep; 羊の毛皮 [hitsuji no kegawa] *n* sheepskin; 羊飼い [hitsujikai] *n* shepherd

必要 [hitsuyou] *n* need; 必要とする [hitsuyou to suru] *v* need, require; 必要性 [hitsuyousei] *n* necessity; 何か必要ですか? [nani ka hitsuyou desu ka?] Do you need anything?; 私は介助が必要です [watashi wa kaijo ga hitsuyou desu] I need assistance; 私は避妊が必要です [watashi wa hinin ga hitsuyou desu] I need contraception; 食器がもっと必要です [shokki ga motto hitsuyou desu] We need more crockery

必要な [hitsuyou na] *adj* necessary

ひったくる [hittakuru] *v* snatch

匹敵 [hitteki] 匹敵する [hitteki suru] *adj* comparable

ひっつかむ [hittsukamu] *v* grab

日焼け [hiyake] *n* sunburn, tan; 日焼けした [hiyake shita] *adj* sunburnt; 日焼け色の [hiyake iro no] *adj* tanned; 小麦色の日焼け [komugi iro no hiyake] *n* suntan

日焼け止め [hiyakedome] *n* sunblock

ヒヤシンス [hiyashinsu] *n* hyacinth

冷やす [hiyasu] *v* chill

ひよこ [hiyoko] *n* chick

ヒヨコマメ [hiyokomame] *n* chickpea

費用 [hiyou] *n* cost; 参加費用はいくらですか? [sanka-hiyou wa ikura desu ka?] How much does it cost to get in?

ひざ [hiza] *n* knee, lap; ひざを曲げる [hiza-o mageru] *v* kneel

ひざがしら [hizagashira] *n* kneecap

ひざまずく [hizamazuku] *v* kneel down

帆 [ho] *n* sail

ホバークラフト [hobaakurafuto] *n* hovercraft

歩調 [hochou] *n* pace

補聴器 [hochouki] *n* hearing aid; 私は補聴器をつけています [watashi wa hochouki o tsukete imasu] I have a hearing aid

ほどく [hodoku] *v* undo, untie, unwind

歩道 [hodou] *n* pavement; 横断歩道 [oudanhodou] *n* pedestrian crossing

吠える [hoeru] *v* bark

保護 [hogo] *n* custody, protection; 保護す

る [hogo suru] v protect; 保護区 [hogoku] n reserve (land)

歩兵 [hohei] n infantry

ほほ笑み [hohoemi] n smile

ほほ笑む [hohoemu] v smile

ホイールがロック [hoiiru ga rokku] ホイールがロックします [hoiiru ga rokku shimasu] The wheels lock

保育園 [hoikuen] n nursery school

ホイップクリーム [hoippukuriimu] n whipped cream

ホイル [hoiru] n foil

補充 [hojuu] n supplement; 新人補充 [shinjin hojuu] n recruitment; 補充する [hojuu suru] v refill; タオルが補充されていません [taoru ga hojuu sarete imasen] The towels have run out

ほか [hoka] ほかの [hoka no] adj other; ほかに何かありますか? [hoka ni nani ka arimasu ka?] Have you anything else?; ほかの部屋はありますか? [hoka no heya wa arimasu ka?] Do you have any others?

保管 [hokan] n storage

補完 [hokan] 補完的な [hokanteki na] adj complementary

ほかに [hoka ni] そのほかに [sono hoka ni] adv other than that

保管所 [hokanjo] 死体保管所 [shitaihokanjo] n morgue

保険 [hoken] n insurance; 事故保険 [jiko hoken] n accident insurance; 保険に入った [hoken ni haitta] adj insured; 保険をかける [hoken-o kakeru] v insure; 旅行保険 [ryokou hoken] n travel insurance; 自動車保険 [jidousha hoken] n car insurance; 第三者賠償責任保険 [daisansha baishousekinin hoken] n third-party insurance; 生命保険 [seimeihoken] n life insurance; 保険でそれが補償されますか? [hoken de sore ga hoshou saremasu ka?] Will the insurance pay for it?; あなたは保険に入っていますか? [anata wa hoken ni haitte imasu ka?] Do you have insurance?; あなたの保険の詳細を教えてください [anata no hoken no shousai o oshiete kudasai] Give me your insurance details, please; あなたの保険証書を見せていただけますか? [anata no hoken-shousho o misete itadakemasu ka?] Can I see your insurance certificate please?; 私は保険に入っています [watashi wa hoken ni haitte imasu] I have insurance; 私は歯科保険に入っていません [watashi wa shika-hoken ni haitte imasen] I don't have dental insurance; 私の保険の詳細です [watashi no hoken no shousai desu] Here are my insurance details; 総合自動車保険に加入する追加料金はいくらですか? [sougou-jidousha-hoken ni kanyuu suru tsuika-ryoukin wa ikura desu ka?] How much extra is comprehensive insurance cover?; 個人傷害保険をかけたいのですが [kojin-shougai-hoken o kaketai no desu ga] I'd like to arrange personal accident insurance

北海 [hokkai] n North Sea

ホッケー [hokkee] n hockey

北極 [hokkyoku] n North Pole; 北極グマ [hokkyokuguma] n polar bear; 北極海 [hokkyokukai] n Arctic Ocean; 北極圏 [hokkyokuken] n Arctic Circle

誇り [hokori] n pride

ほこり [hokori] n (ごみ) dust; ほこりを払う [hokori-o harau] v dust

誇りに思う [hokori ni omou] adj proud

ほこりっぽい [hokorippoi] adj dusty

歩行 [hokou] n walking

歩行者 [hokousha] n pedestrian; 歩行者用の小道 [hokoushayou no komichi] n footpath; 歩行者用通路 [hokoushayou tsuuro] n walkway; 歩行者専用になった [hokousha sen'you ni natta] adj pedestrianized

歩行者天国 [hokoushatengoku] n pedestrian precinct

ほくろ [hokuro] n mole (skin)

北西 [hokusei] n northwest

北東 [hokutou] n northeast

補給 [hokyuu] n refill; 燃料を補給する [nenryou o hokyuu suru] v refuel

ほめことば [homekotoba] n compliment

ホメオパシー [homeopashii] n

homeopathy; ホメオパシーの [homeopashii no] adj homeopathic

ほめる [homeru] v compliment, praise

本 [hon] n (書物) book; 漫画本 [mangabon] n comic book; 料理の本 [ryouri no hon] n cookbook, cookery book; 開くと絵が飛び出す本 [hiraku to e ga tobidasu hon] n pop-up book

本箱 [honbako] n bookcase

本文 [honbun] n text

本棚 [hondana] n bookshelf

本土 [hondo] n mainland

骨 [hone] n bone; 頭蓋骨 [zugaikotsu] n skull

骨組み [honegumi] n frame

骨付き [honetsuki] 骨付き肉 [honetsuki niku] n joint (meat)

本位 [hon'i] 自己本位の [jiko hon'i no] adj self-centred

ホンジュラス [honjurasu] n Honduras

本管 [honkan] 本管で止めてください [honkan de tomete kudasai] Turn it off at the mains

本物 [honmono] 本物の [honmono no] adj authentic; 本物の [honmono no] adj genuine

ほんの [hon no] n mere

本能 [honnou] n instinct

ほのめかす [honomekasu] v hint

炎 [hono-o] n flame; 扁桃腺炎 [hentousen'en] n tonsillitis; 気管支炎 [kikanshien] n bronchitis; 膀胱炎 [boukouen] n cystitis; 喉頭炎 [koutouen] n laryngitis

本社 [honsha] n head office, headquarters, HQ

本当 [hontou] 本当の [hontou no] adj true

本当に [hontou ni] adv really

翻訳 [honyaku] n translation; 翻訳者 [hon'yakusha] n translator

哺乳 [honyuu] 哺乳瓶 [honyuubin] n baby's bottle; 哺乳動物 [honyuu doubutsu] n mammal

ほお [hoo] n cheek

ほお紅 [hoobeni] n blusher

ほお骨 [hoobone] n cheekbone

ホーム [hoomu] adj home; ホームの試合 [hoomu no shiai] n home match; …行きの電車のホームはここでいいのですか? [... iki no densha no hoomu wa koko de ii no desu ka?] Is this the right platform for the train to...?

ホームページ [hoomupeeji] n home page, website

ホームシック [hoomushikku] ホームシックの [hoomushikku no] adj homesick

洞 [hora] n sinus

ホラー [horaa] adj horror; ホラー映画 [horaa eiga] n horror film

ほら穴 [horaana] n cave

濠 [hori] n moat

ホリデー [horidee] アクティブホリデー [akutibu horidee] n activity holiday

ほろ酔い [horoyoi] ほろ酔いの [horo yoi no] adj tipsy

掘る [horu] v dig

彫る [horu] v carve, engrave

ホルダー [horudaa] n folder

ホルモン [horumon] n hormone

保釈 [hoshaku] 保釈金 [hoshakukin] n bail

星 [hoshi] n star (sky)

干しブドウ [hoshibudou] 小粒の種なし干しブドウ [kotsubu no tanenashi hoshibudou] n currant

欲しい [hoshii] v want

干し草 [hoshikusa] n hay; 干し草の山 [hoshikusa no yama] n haystack

星占い [hoshiuranai] n horoscope

保証 [hoshou] n guarantee, warranty; 信用を保証するもの [shin'you-o hoshou suru mono] n credentials; 保証する [hoshou suru] v ensure, guarantee; まだ保証期間内です [mada hoshou-kikan nai desu] It's still under guarantee; 車はまだ保証期間内です [kuruma wa mada hoshou-kikan nai desu] The car is still under warranty

保障 [hoshou] 社会保障 [shakaihoshou] n social security

補償 [hoshou] n compensation; 補償する [hoshou suru] v compensate; 保険でそれが補償されますか？ [hoken de sore ga hoshou saremasu ka?] Will the insurance pay for it?

保証金 [hoshoukin] n deposit; 保証金はいくらですか？ [hoshoukin wa ikura desu ka?] How much is the deposit?; 保証金を返していただけますか？ [hoshoukin o kaeshite itadakemasu ka?] Can I have my deposit back, please?

保守 [hoshu] 保守的な [hoshuteki na] adj conservative

補足 [hosoku] n supplement

発作 [hossa] n fit, seizure; 癲癇の発作 [tenkan no hossa] n epileptic fit; 心臓発作 [shinzouhossa] n heart attack

ほっそり [hossori] ほっそりした [hossori shita] adj slender, slim

干す [hosu] v dry; 服を干すところがありますか？ [fuku o hosu tokoro ga arimasu ka?] Is there somewhere to dry clothes?

ホステル [hosuteru] n hostel

ホスト [hosuto] n host (entertains)

ホタテガイ [hotategai] n scallop

ホテル [hoteru] n hotel; いいホテルを教えてもらえますか？ [ii hoteru o oshiete moraemasu ka?] Can you recommend a hotel?; おたくのホテルは車椅子で利用できますか？ [otaku no hoteru wa kuruma-isu de riyou dekimasu ka?] Is your hotel accessible to wheelchairs?; このホテルまでのタクシー料金はいくらですか？ [kono hoteru made no takushii-ryoukin wa ikura desu ka?] How much is the taxi fare to this hotel?; このホテルへ行く一番よい方法は何ですか？ [kono hoteru e iku ichiban yoi houhou wa nan desu ka?] What's the best way to get to this hotel?; 私はホテルに滞在しています [watashi wa hoteru ni taizai shite imasu] I'm staying at a hotel; 私のためにホテルの部屋を予約してもらえますか？ [watashi no tame ni hoteru no heya o yoyaku shite moraemasu ka?] Can you book me into a hotel?; 私たちはホテルを探しています [watashi-tachi wa hoteru o sagashite imasu] We're

looking for a hotel; 彼がホテルの経営者です [kare ga hoteru no keieisha desu] He runs the hotel

ほとんど [hotondo] adv almost, nearly; ほとんど・・・ない [hotondo ... nai] adv hardly, scarcely

ホットドッグ [hottodokku] n hot dog

法 [hou] n method; 調理法 [chourihou] n recipe

法案 [houan] n bill (legislation)

報知器 [houchiki] n alarm; 火災報知器 [kasai houchiki] n fire alarm

法外 [hougai] 法外な [hougai na] adj extortionate; 法外な値をふっかける [hougai na ne-o fukkakeru] v rip off

方言 [hougen] n dialect

方法 [houhou] n manner, method, way; 組織的な方法 [soshikiteki na houhou] n system

放火 [houka] n arson

放棄 [houki] 放棄する [houki suru] v waive

ほうき [houki] n broom

報告 [houkoku] n report; 報告する [houkoku suru] v report

方向 [houkou] n direction; 方向転換する [houkoutenkan suru] v turn round, turn around

芳香 [houkou] n aroma

訪問 [houmon] n visit; 訪問する [houmon suru] v visit; 訪問者 [houmonsha] n visitor

法王 [houou] ローマ法王 [rooma houou] n pope

ほうれん草 [hourensou] n spinach

法律 [houritsu] n law; 法律制定 [houritsu seitei] n legislation

砲声 [housei] n bang

宝石 [houseki] n gem, jewel; 宝石類 [housekirui] n jewellery; 宝石商 [housekishou] n jeweller, jeweller's

放射 [housha] n radiation; 放射性のある [houshasei no aru] adj radioactive

報酬 [houshuu] n reward

法則 [housoku] 法則化する [housokuka suru] v generalize

放送 [housou] n broadcast; 放送する [housou suru] v broadcast

包装 [housou] n wrapping; 包装を解く [housou-o toku] v unwrap; 包装紙 [housoushi] n wrapping paper; それを包装していただけますか? [sore o housou shite itadakemasu ka?] Could you wrap it up for me, please?

ホース [housu] n hose, hosepipe

包帯 [houtai] n bandage; 包帯をする [houtai-o suru] v bandage; 吊り包帯 [tsuri houtai] n sling; 新しい包帯をしてください [atarashii houtai o shite kudasai] I'd like a fresh bandage; 包帯をしてください [houtai o shite kudasai] I'd like a bandage

法廷 [houtei] n court

包擁 [houyou] n cuddle

ホワイティング [howaitingu] n (魚) whiting

ホワイトボード [howaitoboodo] n whiteboard

保全 [hozen] n conservation

保存 [hozon] 保存料 [hozonryou] n preservative

百科 [hyakka] 百科事典 [hyakka jiten] n encyclopaedia

百 [hyaku] number hundred

100万 [hyakuman] n million

百につき [hyaku ni tsuki] adv per cent

表 [hyou] n (作表) table (chart); 価格表 [kakakuhyou] n price list; 時刻表 [jikokuhyou] n timetable; 通知表 [tsuuchihyou] n report card

雹 [hyou] n hail

ヒョウ [hyou] n (動物) leopard, (動物) panther

評判 [hyouban] n reputation

氷河 [hyouga] n glacier

表現 [hyougen] n expression; 表現する [hyougen suru] v express

漂白 [hyouhaku] 漂白した [hyouhaku shita] adj bleached; 漂白剤 [hyouhakuzai] n bleach

標準 [hyoujun] n standard; 標準の [hyoujun no] adj standard; 標準時間帯 [hyoujun jikantai] n time zone

評価 [hyouka] 評価する [hyouka suru] v rate; 高く評価する [takaku hyouka suru] v appreciate; 過大評価する [kadai hyouka suru] v overestimate

評決 [hyouketsu] n verdict

表面 [hyoumen] n surface; 表面的な [hyoumenteki na] adj superficial

漂流 [hyouryuu] 漂流する [hyouryuu suru] v drift

標識 [hyoushiki] 道路標識 [dourohyoushiki] n road sign, signpost

標的 [hyouteki] n target

氷山 [hyouzan] n iceberg

ヒューズ [hyuuzu] n fuse; ヒューズがとびました [hyuuzu ga tobimashita] A fuse has blown; ヒューズを直してもらえますか? [hyuuzu o naoshite moraemasu ka?] Can you mend a fuse?

ヒューズボックス [hyuuzubokkusu] n fuse box

i

胃 [i] *n* stomach

医 [i] *n* doctor; 一般医 [ippan'i] *n* GP; 外科医 [gekai] *n* surgeon

威張る [ibaru] *v* look down on; 威張った [ibatta] *adj* bossy

イベント [ibento] *n* event; 私たちはどのスポーツイベントに行けますか? [watashi-tachi wa dono supootsu-ibento ni ikemasu ka?] Which sporting events can we go to?

いびき [ibiki] いびきをかく [ibiki o kaku] *v* snore

いぼ [ibo] *n* wart

イブニングドレス [ibuningu doresu] *n* evening dress

いぶす [ibusu] いぶした [ibushita] *adj* smoked

遺物 [ibutsu] *n* remains

一致 [itchi] 満場一致の [manjouitchi no] *adj* unanimous

一 [ichi] *number* one

位置 [ichi] *n* position; 位置している [ichi shite iru] *adj* situated

市場 [ichiba] *n* market, marketplace; 株式市場 [kabushikishijou] *n* stock market;

市場調査 [shijouchousa] *n* market research

一番 [ichiban] *adv* most; 一番上の [ichiban ue no] *adj* top; 一番若い [ichiban wakai] *adj* youngest

一度 [ichido] *adv* once; 年に一度 [nen ni ichido] *adv* yearly; 年に一度の [nen ni ichido no] *adj* yearly

一月 [ichigatsu] *n* January

一語 [ichigo] 一語です [ichi-go desu] all one word

イチゴ [ichigo] *n* strawberry

一腹子 [ichi hara ko] 動物の一腹子 [doubutsu no ippukushi] *n* litter (offspring)

イチイ [ichii] *n* yew

一時 [ichiji] 一時の [ichiji no] *adj* temporary; 一時解雇する [ichiji kaiko suru] *v* lay off; 一時停止 [ichiji teishi] *n* suspension; 一時です [ichi-ji desu] It's one o'clock

一時間 [ichijikan] *n* hour; 一時間ごとに [ichijikan goto ni] *adv* hourly; 一時間ごとの [ichijikan goto no] *adj* hourly; 1時間あたりいくらですか? [ichi-jikan atari ikura desu ka?] How much is it per hour?

一時期 [ichijiki] *n* spell (time)

イチジク [ichijiku] *n* fig

著しい [ichijirushii] *adj* remarkable; 著しく [ichijirushiku] *adv* remarkably

一覧表 [ichiranhyou] *n* list; 一覧表を作る [ichiranhyou-o tsukuru] *v* list

一流の芸術作品 [ichiryuu no geijutsusakuhin] *n* classic

遺伝 [iden] *n* heredity; 遺伝的な [identeki na] *adj* hereditary

遺伝学 [idengaku] *n* genetics

遺伝子 [idenshi] *n* gene; 遺伝子の [idenshi no] *adj* genetic; 遺伝子組み換えの [idenshi kumikae no] *adj* genetically-modified

イデオロギー [ideorogii] *n* ideology

井戸 [ido] *n* well

緯度 [ido] *n* latitude

移動 [idou] *n* move, removal; レッカー移

動する [rekkaa idou suru] v tow away; 移動する [idou suru] v travel; 移動性の [idousei no] adj migrant; 移動可能な [idoukanou na] n mobile

家 [ie] n house; 住む家のない [sumu ie no nai] adj homeless; 家にいる [ie ni iru] v stay in; 専門家 [senmonka] n specialist; 家はかなり大きいです [ie wa kanari ookii desu] The house is quite big

傷創膏 [iedomo chimakemu] n plaster (for wound)

イエメン [iemen] n Yemen

イエローページ® [ieroopeeji] n Yellow Pages®

イエス [iesu] n Jesus

衣服 [ifuku] n garment

意外な [igai na] adj surprising

医学 [igaku] n medicine; 医学の [igaku no] adj medical

威厳 [igen] n dignity, majesty

異議 [igi] n objection; 異議のない [igi no nai] adj undisputed

違反 [ihan] n offence; 駐車違反切符 [chuushaihan kippu] n parking ticket

いい [ii] adj appropriate; どのように飲めばいいのですか? [dono you ni nomeba ii no desu ka?] How should I take it?; いいですか? [ii desu ka?] Do you mind?; いいですとも [ii desu tomo] No problem; いいですよ [ii desu yo] I don't mind; 私は・・・のほうがいいです [watashi wa ... no hou ga ii desu] I prefer to...; ・・・行きの電車のホームはここでいいのですか? [...iki no densha no hoomu wa koko de ii no desu ka?] Is this the right platform for the train to...?

Eチケット [iichiketto] n e-ticket

いいえ [iie] adv no

いい加減 [iikagen] いい加減な [iikagen na] adj irresponsible

Eコマース [iikomaasu] n e-commerce

Eメール [iimeeru] n email; あなたのEメールアドレスは何ですか? [anata no ii-meeru-adoresu wa nan desu ka?] What is your email address?; 私のEメールが届きましたか? [watashi no ii-meeru ga

todokimashita ka?] Did you get my email?; 私のEメールアドレスは・・・です [watashi no ii-meeru-adoresu wa ... desu] My email address is...; Eメールを送っていいですか? [ii-meeru o okutte ii desu ka?] Can I send an email?; Eメールアドレスをお持ちですか? [ii-meeru-adoresu o o-mochi desu ka?] Do you have an email?; Eメールアドレスを教えてもらえますか? [ii-meeru-adoresu o oshiete moraemasu ka?] Can I have your email?

いいね [iine] excl like (on social media)

委員会 [iinkai] n committee; 裁定委員会 [saitei iinkai] n tribunal

EU [iiyuu] abbr EU

維持 [iji] n maintenance; 維持する [iji suru] v keep up, keep up with, maintain

意地 [iji] n stubbornness; 意地の悪い [iji no warui] adj spiteful

いじめる [ijimeru] v bully, pick on

意地悪 [ijiwaru] n spite; 意地悪をする [ijiwaru-o suru] v spite

以上 [ijou] adv not less than; それ以上の [sore ijou no] adj further; それ以上のこと [sore ijou nokoto] pron more

異常 [ijou] 異常な [ijou na] adj abnormal, extraordinary

移住 [ijuu] n immigration, migration; 移住する [ijuu suru] v emigrate; 移住者 [ijuusha] n immigrant, migrant

以下 [ika] 以下の [ika no] (次の) adj following

イカ [ika] n squid

いかだ [ikada] n raft

いかに [ika ni] いかに・・・であろうとも [ikani ... de aroutomo] adv however

錨 [ikari] n anchor

怒り [ikari] n anger

池 [ike] n pond; 貯水池 [chosuichi] n reservoir

意見 [iken] n feedback, opinion, remark; 意見の相違 [iken no soui] n disagreement; 意見が異なる [iken ga kotonaru] v disagree

息 [iki] n breath; 息が詰まる [iki ga

tsumaru] v choke; 息をする [iki-o suru] v breathe; 息を吐き出す [iki-o hakidasu] v breathe out; 息を吸い込む [iki-o suikomu] v breathe in

意気 [iki] n mood; 意気消沈した [ikishouchin shita] adj depressed

行き止まり [ikidomari] n dead end

行きづまる [ikidumaru] 行きづまった [ikizumatta] adj stuck

生き物 [ikimono] n creature

生き残る [ikinokoru] v survive

生きる [ikiru] v live; 生きている [ikite iru] adj live

行き渡る [ikiwataru] 皆に行き渡る [mina ni iki wataru] v go round

一か月 [ikkagetsu] 一か月後に [ikkagetsu go ni] in a month's time; 一か月前 [ikkagetsu mae] a month ago

一階 [ikkai] n ground floor

一回 [ikkai] adv once; 一回限りのこと [ikkai kagiri no koto] n one-off; 年一回の [nen'ikkai no] adj annual

一貫 [ikkan] 一貫した [ikkan shita] adj consistent

一貫性 [ikkansei] 一貫性のない [ikkansei no nai] adj inconsistent

一戸建て [ikkodate] 土地付き一戸建て家屋 [tochi tsuki ikkodate kaoku] n detached house

一行 [ikkou] n (集まり) party (group)

移行 [ikou] n transition

行く [iku] v go; まっすぐ行ってください [massugu itte kudasai] Go straight on; もう行く時間ですか? [mou iku jikan desu ka?] Is it time to go?; 私は・・・へ行きます [watashi wa ... e ikimasu] I'm going to...; 私たちは・・・に行きたいのですが [watashi-tachi wa ... ni ikitai no desu ga] We'd like to go to...; 私たちは・・・へ行きます [watashi-tachi wa ... e ikimasu] We're going to...; ・・・に行けますか? [...ni ikemasu ka?] Can we go to...?

育児 [ikuji] n 父親の育児休暇 [chichioya no ikuji kyuuka] n paternity leave

いくら [ikura] adv how much; 2食付きはい

くらですか? [ni-shoku tsuki wa ikura desu ka?] How much is half board?; 3食付きはいくらですか? [san-shoku tsuki wa ikura desu ka?] How much is full board?; 一泊いくらですか? [ippaku ikura desu ka?] How much is it per night?; あなたにいくら払えばいいですか? [anata ni ikura haraeba ii desu ka?] What do I owe you?; あれはいくらですか? [are wa ikura desu ka?] How much does that cost?; いくらでしょう? [ikura deshou?] How much will it be?; いくらですか? [ikura desu ka?] How much is it?; その部屋はいくらですか? [sono heya wa ikura desu ka?] How much is the room?; それは1週間あたりいくらですか? [sore wa isshuukan atari ikura desu ka?] How much is it per week?; それは一人あたりいくらですか? [sore wa hitori atari ikura desu ka?] How much is it per person?; それは一泊いくらですか? [sore wa ippaku ikura desu ka?] How much is it per night?; それはいくらですか? [sore wa ikura desu ka?] How much does it cost?; それはいくら分ですか? [sore wa ikura-bun desu ka?] How much is it worth?; ・・・に電話するのはいくらですか? [...ni denwa suru no wa ikura desu ka?] How much is it to telephone...?

いくらか [ikuraka] pron some; いくらかの [ikuraka no] adj some

いくつ [ikutsu] adv how old; おいくつですか? [o-ikutsu desu ka?] How old are you?

いくつか [ikutsuka] いくつかの [ikutsuka no] adj several

今 [ima] adv now; たった今 [tatta ima] adv just

居間 [ima] n living room, sitting room

今はやり [imahayari] 今はやりの [ima hayari no] adj trendy

いまいましい [imaimashii] adj damn

今まで [ima made] 今までに [ima made ni] adv ever

イメージ [imeeji] n image

意味 [imi] n meaning; 意味する [imi suru] v mean; 無意味な [muimi na] adj senseless

イモムシ [imomushi] n caterpillar

イモリ [imori] n newt

陰 [in] n shade

員 [in] 乗務員 [joumuin] n cabin crew; 警備員 [keibiin] n security guard; 店員 [ten-in] n shop assistant

イナゴ [inago] n grasshopper

以内 [inai] …以内で […inai de] prep within

田舎 [inaka] n countryside; 田舎の [inaka no] adj rural; 田舎屋 [inakaya] n cottage

いなくなる [inakunaru] v disappear; いなくなって [inaku natte] adj gone

インボイス [inboisu] n invoice; インボイスを送る [inboisu-o okuru] v invoice

陰謀 [inbou] n conspiracy

インチ [inchi] n inch

インド [indo] n India; インド洋 [indoyou] n Indian Ocean

インドア [indoa] adv indoors; どんなインドア・アクティビティがありますか? [donna indoa-akutibiti ga arimasu ka?] What indoor activities are there?

インド人 [indojin] n Indian (person)

インドネシア [indoneshia] n Indonesia

インドネシア人 [indoneshiajin] n Indonesian (person)

インドネシアの [indoneshia no] adj Indonesian

インドの [indo no] adj Indian

居眠り [inemuri] n snooze; 居眠りをする [inemuri-o suru] v snooze

インフラストラクチャー [infurasutorakuchaa] n infrastructure

インフレーション [infureeshon] n inflation

インフルエンザ [infuruenza] n flu, influenza; 鳥インフルエンザ [tori infuruenza] n bird flu; 私はインフルエンザにかかりました [watashi wa infuruenza ni kakarimashita] I've got flu; 私は最近インフルエンザにかかりました [watashi wa saikin infuruenza ni kakarimashita] I had flu recently

イングランド [ingurando] n England;

イングランドの [ingurando no] adj English

イングランド人 [ingurandojin] イングランド人男性 [ingurandojin dansei] n Englishman; イングランド人女性 [ingurandojin josei] n Englishwoman

イニシアチブ [inishiachibu] n initiative

陰気 [inki] 陰気な [inki na] adj dismal

インク [inku] n ink

インナーチューブ [innaachuubu] n inner tube

祈り [inori] n prayer

祈る [inoru] v pray

飲料 [inryou] 飲料水 [inryousui] n drinking water

印刷 [insatsu] 印刷する [insatsu suru] v print; 印刷業者 [insatsu gyousha] n printer (person); 印刷機 [insatsuki] n printer (machine); 印刷物 [insatsubutsu] n print; 印刷はいくらですか? [insatsu wa ikura desu ka?] How much is printing?

隕石 [inseki] n meteorite

姻戚 [inseki] n in-laws

印象 [inshou] n impression; 印象的な [inshouteki na] adj impressive

印象づける [inshoudukeru] 強く印象づける [tsuyoku inshou zukeru] v impress

飲酒 [inshu] n drinking; 飲酒運転 [inshu unten] n drink-driving

インシュリン [inshurin] n insulin

インターホン [intaahon] n entry phone

インターコム [intaakomu] n intercom

インターネット [intaanetto] n internet; インターネットサービスプロバイダ [intaanetto saabisu purobaida] n ISP; インターネット利用者 [intaanetto riyousha] n internet user; その部屋にインターネットの接続ポイントはありますか? [sono heya ni intaanetto no setsuzoku-pointo wa arimasu ka?] Is there an internet connection in the room?

インターネットカフェ [intaanetto kafe] n internet café; ここにインターネットカフェはありますか? [koko ni intaanetto kafe wa arimasu ka?] Are there any internet cafés here?

インテリアデザイナー [interiadezainaa] *n* interior designer

イントラネット [intoranetto] *n* intranet

犬 [inu] *n* dog; 牧羊犬 [bokuyouken] *n* sheepdog; 雑種の犬 [zasshu no inu] *n* mongrel

犬小屋 [inugoya] *n* kennel

引用 [inyou] 引用する [inyou suru] *v* quote; 引用文 [in-youbun] *n* quotation, quote

引用符 [in-youfu] *n* inverted commas, quotation marks

iPod® [ipod] *n* iPod®

一杯 [ippai] *n* (one) cup; コップ一杯の水 [koppu ippai no mizu] a glass of water; ビールをもう一杯 [biiru o mou ippai] another beer; 紅茶をもう一杯いただけますか？ [koucha o mou ippai itadakemasu ka?] Could we have another cup of tea, please?

いっぱい [ippai] *adj* full; いっぱいにする [ippai ni suru] *v* fill

一泊 [ippaku] *n* (one) night; 一泊いくらですか？ [ippaku ikura desu ka?] How much is it per night?; それは一泊いくらですか？ [sore wa ippaku ikura desu ka?] How much is it per night?; もう一泊したいのですが [mou ippaku shitai no desu ga] I want to stay an extra night

一般 [ippan] 一般に [ippan ni] *adv* generally; 一般の [ippan no] *adj* general; 一般知識 [ippan chishiki] *n* general knowledge; 一般医 [ippan'i] *n* GP

以来 [irai] その時以来 [sono toki irai] *adv* since; ・・・以来 [...irai] *prep* since; ・・・して以来 [...shite irai] *conj* since

依頼 [irai] 制作依頼 [seisaku irai] *n* commission

依頼人 [irainin] *n* client

いらいら [iraira] いらいらさせる [iraira saseru] *adj* irritating

いらいらした [irairashita] *adj* irritated, impatient

いらいらして [iraira shite] *adv* impatiently

いらいらしている [iraira shiteiru] *v* be impatient

イラク [iraku] *n* Iraq

イラク人 [irakujin] *n* Iraqi *(person)*

イラクの [iraku no] *adj* Iraqi

イラクサ [irakusa] *n* nettle

イラン [iran] *n* Iran

イラン人 [iranjin] *n* Iranian *(person)*

イランの [iran no] *n* Iranian

いらっしゃる [irassharu] *v* be; 今晩どこにいらっしゃりたいですか？ [konban doko ni irassharitai desu ka?] Where would you like to go tonight?; ・・・さんはいらっしゃいますか？ [...san wa irasshaimasu ka?] Is ... there?

入れ [ire] *n* pouch; 洗面用具入れ [senmen yougu ire] *n* sponge bag

入れ歯 [ireba] *n* dentures, false teeth; 私の入れ歯を修理してもらえますか？ [watashi no ireba o shuuri shite moraemasu ka?] Can you repair my dentures?

入れる [ireru] *v* let in; 香辛料を入れた [koushinryou-o ireta] *adj* spicy

入れ墨 [irezumi] *n* tattoo

入口 [iriguchi] *n* entrance, entry, way in; 入口の廊下 [iriguchi no rouka] *n* hall; 車椅子で利用できる入口はどこですか？ [kuruma-isu de riyou dekiru iriguchi wa doko desu ka?] Where is the wheelchair-accessible entrance?

炒り卵 [iritamago] *n* scrambled eggs

色 [iro] *n* colour; クリーム色の [kuriimuiro no] *adj* cream; ライラック色の [rairakku iro no] *adj* lilac; 日焼け色の [hiyake iro no] *adj* tanned; この色でお願いします [kono iro de o-negai shimasu] This colour, please; これの別の色はありますか？ [kore no betsu no iro wa arimasu ka?] Do you have this in another colour?; 色が好きではありません [iro ga suki de wa arimasen] I don't like the colour

色白 [irojiro] 色白の [irojiro no] *adj* fair *(light colour)*

いる [iru] *v* be; 家にいる [ie ni iru] *v* stay in

居る [iru] adj present

衣類 [irui] n clothing; 毛織物衣類 [keorimono irui] n woollens

イルカ [iruka] n dolphin

医療 [iryou] n medical treatment; 私は個人医療保険に入っています [watashi wa kojin-iryou-hoken ni haitte imasu] I have private health insurance; 私は医療保険に入っていません [watashi wa iryou-hoken ni haitte imasen] I don't have health insurance

異性愛 [iseiai] 異性愛の [iseiai no] adj heterosexual

医者 [isha] n doctor; お医者さんの予約を取れますか? [o-isha-san no yoyaku o toremasu ka?] Can I have an appointment with the doctor?; お医者さんと話をしたいのですが [o-isha-san to hanashi o shitai no desu ga] I'd like to speak to a doctor; 英語を話せるお医者さんはいらっしゃいますか? [eigo o hanaseru o-isha-san wa irasshaimasu ka?] Is there a doctor who speaks English?; 私はお医者さんに診てもらわなければなりません [watashi wa o-isha-san ni mite morawanakereba narimasen] I need a doctor; 医者を呼んで! [isha o yonde!] Call a doctor!

石 [ishi] n stone

意志 [ishi] n will (motivation); 意志の力 [ishi no chikara] n willpower

意識 [ishiki] n consciousness; 意識がある [ishiki ga aru] adj conscious; 意識を回復する [ishiki-o kaifuku suru] v come round; 意識を失った [ishiki o ushinatta] adj unconscious; 意識を失う [ishiki-o ushinau] v pass out; 自意識の強い [jiishiki no tsuyoi] adj self-conscious

遺失物 [ishitsubutsu] n lost-and-found; 遺失物取扱所 [ishitsubutsu toriatsukaijo] n lost-property office

移植 [ishoku] n transplant

移植ごて [ishokugote] n trowel

衣装 [ishou] 衣装一式 [ishou isshiki] n outfit

忙しい [isogashii] adj busy; ごめんなさい、忙しいのです [gomen nasai, isogashii

no desu] Sorry, I'm busy

急ぐ [isogu] v hurry, hurry up, rush; 大急ぎ [ooisogi] n hurry; 私は急いでいます [watashi wa isoide imasu] I'm in a hurry

急いで [isoide] adv hastily

一式 [isshiki] 用具一式 [yougu isshiki] n kit

一緒 [issho] adv together; ご一緒してもいいですか? [go-issho shite mo ii desu ka?] Can I join you?; 全部一緒にお勘定をお願いします [zenbu issho ni o-kanjou o o-negai shimasu] All together, please

一緒に [issho ni] adv together; ···と一緒に [...to issho ni] prep with

一周 [isshuu] n circuit

一週間 [isshuukan] n (one) week; 一週間後に [isshuukan go ni] in a week's time; 一週間前 [isshuukan mae] a week ago

一層 [issou] 一層悪い [issou warui] adj worse; 一層悪く [issou waruku] adv worse

椅子 [isu] n chair (furniture); 肘掛け椅子 [hijikakeke isu] n armchair; 安楽椅子 [anraku isu] n easy chair; 小児用の食事椅子 [shouni you no shokuji isu] n highchair; 子供用の椅子はありますか? [kodomo-you no isu wa arimasu ka?] Do you have a high chair?

イスラエル [isuraeru] n Israel

イスラエル人 [isuraerujin] n Israeli (person)

イスラエルの [isuraeru no] adj Israeli

イスラム教 [isuramukyou] n Islam; イスラム教の [isuramukyou no] adj Moslem, Muslim, Islamic; イスラム教徒 [isuramukyouto] n Moslem, Muslim

板 [ita] n board (wood); 掲示板 [keijiban] n bulletin board, notice board

イタチ [itachi] n weasel

痛い [itai] adj painful, sore; さわると痛いところ [sawaru to itai tokoro] n sore

痛める [itameru] v hurt; 私は肩を痛めました [watashi wa kata o itamemashita] I've hurt my shoulder; 私は背中を痛めました [watashi wa senaka o itamemashita] I've hurt my back

痛み [itami] n ache, pain; 耳の痛み [mimi no itami] n earache; 痛み止めに何かもらえますか? [itami-dome ni nani ka moraemasu ka?] Can you give me something for the pain?; 私は胸に痛みがあります [watashi wa mune ni itami ga arimasu] I have a pain in my chest

痛み止め [itamidome] n painkiller

痛む [itamu] v ache

イタリア [itaria] n Italy

イタリア語 [itariago] n Italian (language)

イタリア人 [itariajin] n Italian (person)

イタリアの [itaria no] adj Italian

いたずら [itazura] n mischief; いたずら好きな [itazura zuki na] adj mischievous

移転 [iten] n transfer; 移転する [iten suru] v transfer

射手座 [iteza] n Sagittarius

糸 [ito] n thread; 針と糸をお持ちですか? [hari to ito o o-mochi desu ka?] Do you have a needle and thread?

意図 [ito] n intention; 意図的な [itoteki na] adj intentional

いとこ [itoko] n cousin

営む [itonamu] v run (business); 私は自分で事業を営んでいます [watashi wa jibun de jigyou o itonande imasu] I run my own business

いとしい [itoshii] いとしい人 [itoshii hito] n darling

いとわない [itowanai] v willing

いつ [itsu] adv when; いつ仕上がりますか? [itsu shiagarimasu ka?] When will it be ready?

いつか [itsu ka] adv sometime

いつまでに [itsumadeni] それはいつまでに払わなければならないのですか? [sore wa itsu made ni harawanakereba naranai no desu ka?] When is it due to be paid?

胃痛 [itsuu] n stomachache

偽り [itsuwari] 偽りの [itsuwari no] adj false

偽る [itsuwaru] 偽りなく [itsuwari naku] adv truly

行って連れて来る [itte tsurete kuru] v fetch

言う [iu] v say; ブツブツ言う [butsubutsu iu] v mutter; 冗談を言う [joudan o iu] v joke; 大げさに言う [oogesa ni iu] v exaggerate

岩 [iwa] n rock; 石灰岩 [sekkaigan] n limestone

祝い [iwai] n celebration

いわせる [iwaseru] 世間をあっといわせるような [seken-o atto iwaseru you na] adj sensational

祝う [iwau] v celebrate, congratulate

いや [iya] いやな [iya na] adj foul, grim; いやだと思う [iyadato omou] v mind

いやがらせ [iyagarase] n harassment

イヤホン [iyahon] n earphones

いやいや [iyaiya] adv reluctantly; いやいやながらの [iyaiya nagara no] adj reluctant

嫌な [iya na] adj nasty, offensive, repellent; 実に嫌な [jitsu ni iya na] adj revolting

いやな [iya na] いやなにおいのする [iya na nioi no suru] adj smelly

イヤリング [iyaringu] n earring

以前 [izen] 以前に [izen ni] adv before; 以前は [izen wa] adv formerly; 以前の [izen no] adj former

以前に [izen ni] adv previously

以前の [izen no] adj previous

j

ジャージー [jaajii] n jersey

邪悪 [jaaku] 邪悪な [jaaku na] adj wicked

ジャーナリスト [jaanarisuto] n journalist

ジャーナリズム [jaanarizumu] n journalism

ジャガイモ [jagaimo] n potato

ジャグ [jagu] n jug

ジャケット [jaketto] n jacket; ディナージャケット [dinaa jaketto] n dinner jacket

ジャッキ [jakki] n jack

邪魔 [jama] n burden; 邪魔をする [jama-o suru] v disturb

ジャマイカ人 [jamaikajin] n Jamaican (person)

ジャマイカの [jamaika no] adj Jamaican

ジャム [jamu] n jam; ジャムの瓶 [jamu no bin] n jam jar

ジャンボジェット [janbojetto] n jumbo jet

ジャングル [janguru] n jungle

ジャンク [janku] ジャンクメール [janku meeru] n junk mail

ジャンクション [jankushon] n junction; 車は・・・番ジャンクションの近くです [kuruma wa ... ban jankushon no chikaku desu] The car is near junction number...; ・・・へ行くのはどのジャンクションですか? [...e iku no wa dono jankushon desu ka?] Which junction is it for...?

ジャンプ [janpu] n jump

砂利 [jari] n gravel

ジャズ [jazu] n jazz

ジェル [jeru] n gel

自爆 [jibaku] 自爆者 [jibakusha] n suicide bomber

自分 [jibun] ご自分で [go jibun de] pron yourself (intensifier), yourselves (intensifier); 直接自分で [chokusetsu jibun de] adv personally

自分自身 [jibunjishin] 自分自身の [jubunjishin no] adj own

自治 [jichi] 自治権のある [jichiken no aru] adj autonomous; 自治国家 [jichi kokka] n autonomy

時代 [jidai] n era; 青春時代 [seishun jidai] n youth; 子供時代 [kodomo jidai] n childhood

時代遅れ [jidaiokure] 時代遅れの [jidaiokure no] adj old-fashioned

自撮り [jidori] n selfie

自動 [jidou] adj automatic; 自動振替 [jidoufurikae] n standing order; 自動販売機 [jidouhanbaiki] n vending machine; 自動的な [jidouteki na] adj automatic; 自動的に [jidouteki ni] adv automatically

児童 [jidou] 児童虐待 [jidou gyakutai] n child abuse; 児童養護 [jidou yougo] n childcare

自動券売機 [jidoukenbaiki] n ticket machine; 自動券売機はどうやって使うのですか? [jidoukenbaiki wa dou-yatte tsukau no desu ka?] How does the ticket machine work?; 自動券売機はどこですか? [jidoukenbaiki wa doko desu ka?] Where is the ticket machine?; 自動券売機が故障しています [jidoukenbaiki ga koshou shite imasu] The ticket machine isn't working

自動車 [jidousha] n car; 自動車保険 [jidousha hoken] n car insurance; 自動車

整備士 [jidousha seibishi] *n* motor mechanic

自動車教習 [jidoushakyoushuu] *n* driving lesson; 自動車教習指導員 [jidousha kyoushuu shidouin] *n* driving instructor

自衛 [jiei] *n* self-defence

自営業 [jieigyou] 私は自営業です [watashi wa jieigyou desu] I'm self-employed

ジェット [jietto] ジェット機 [jettoki] *n* jet

時限 [jigen] 時限爆弾 [jigenbakudan] *n* time bomb

地獄 [jigoku] *n* hell

ジグソーパズル [jigusou pazuru] *n* jigsaw

事業 [jigyou] *n* enterprise; 政府の社会福祉事業 [seifu no shakai fukushi jigyou] *n* social services; 私は自分で事業を営んでいます [watashi wa jibun de jigyou o itonande imasu] I run my own business

自白 [jihaku] *n* confession; 自白する [jihaku suru] *v* confess

自発 [jihatsu] 自発的な [jihatsuteki na] *adj* spontaneous, voluntary; 自発的に [jihatsuteki ni] *adv* voluntarily; 自発的に申し出る [jihatsuteki ni moushideru] *v* volunteer

慈悲 [jihi] *n* mercy

寺院 [jiin] *n* temple; その寺院は一般公開されていますか? [sono jiin wa ippan-koukai sarete imasu ka?] Is the temple open to the public?; その寺院はいつ開きますか? [sono jiin wa itsu hirakimasu ka?] When is the temple open?

ジーンズ [jiinzu] *n* jeans

時事 [jiji] 時事的な [jijiteki na] *adj* topical; 時事問題 [jiji mondai] *n* current affairs

事実 [jijitsu] *n* fact, truth

自叙 [jijo] 自叙伝 [jijoden] *n* autobiography

事情 [jijou] *n* circumstances

時間 [jikan] *n* time; サッカー・ラグビーなどで怪我の手当てなどに要した分の延長時間 [sakkaa / ragubii nado de kega no teate nado ni youshita bun no enchou jikan] *n* injury time; コマーシャルの時間 [komaasharu no jikan] *n* commercial break; 欠勤時間 [kekkin jikan] *n* time off; 時間厳守の [jikangenshu no] *adj* punctual; 標準時間帯 [hyoujun jikantai] *n* time zone; 超過勤務 [chouka kinmu] *n* overtime; 食事時間 [shokuji jikan] *n* mealtime; 遊び時間 [asobi jikan] *n* playtime; 面会時間 [menkaijikan] *n* visiting hours; 営業時間 [eigyoujikan] *n* office hours, opening hours; もう行く時間ですか? [mou iku jikan desu ka?] Is it time to go?

時間がかかる [jikan gakakaru] *v* take (time)

自家製 [jikasei] 自家製の [jikasei no] *adj* home-made

磁器 [jiki] *n* china

時期 [jiki] 時期尚早の [jikishousou no] *adj* premature

実験 [jikken] *n* experiment

実験台 [jikkendai] *n* guinea pig (for experiment)

実験室 [jikkenshitsu] *n* laboratory

実行 [jikkou] 実行する [jikkou suru] *v* carry out; 実行可能な [jikkoukanou na] *adj* feasible

実況 [jikkyou] 実況解説 [jikkyou kaisetsu] *n* commentary

事故 [jiko] *n* accident; 事故保険 [jiko hoken] *n* accident insurance; 事故にあったらどうすればいいのですか? [jiko ni attara dou sureba ii no desu ka?] What do I do if I have an accident?; 事故がありました! [jiko ga arimashita!] There's been an accident!; 私は事故にあいました [watashi wa jiko ni aimashita] I've been in an accident, I've had an accident

自己 [jiko] 自己本位の [jiko hon'i no] *adj* self-centred; 自己訓練 [jiko kunren] *n* self-discipline

時刻 [jikoku] *n* time; ディナーの時刻 [dinaa no jikoku] *n* dinner time; 時刻表 [jikokuhyou] *n* timetable; 閉店時刻 [heiten jikoku] *n* closing time; 就寝時刻 [shuushin jikoku] *n* bedtime; 電車は時刻

どおりですか? [densha wa jikoku doori desu ka?] Is the train on time?

時刻表 [jikokuhyou] n timetable; 時刻表をいただけますか? [jikokuhyou o itadakemasu ka?] Can I have a timetable, please?

ジマー [jimaa] n Zimmer® frame

字幕 [jimaku] n subtitles; 字幕を入れた [jimaku-o ireta] adj subtitled

自慢 [jiman] 自慢する [jiman suru] v boast

地面 [jimen] n ground; 地面に置く [jimen ni oku] v ground

事務 [jimu] n office work; 事務弁護士 [jimubengoshi] n solicitor; 机上事務 [kijou jimu] n paperwork

ジム [jimu] n gym; ジムはどこですか? [jimu wa doko desu ka?] Where is the gym?

地虫 [jimushi] n grub

ジン [jin] n gin

ジンバブウェ [jinbabuwe] n Zimbabwe; ジンバブウェ人 [jinbabuwejin] n Zimbabwean; ジンバブウェの [jinbabuwe no] adj Zimbabwean

人道主義 [jindoushugi] 人道主義の [jindou shugi no] adj humanitarian

人員 [jin-in] n personnel

神社 [jinja] n shrine

人権 [jinken] n human rights

人口 [jinkou] n population

人工 [jinkou] 人工の [jinkou no] adj artificial; 人工衛星 [jinkou eisei] n satellite

人類 [jinrui] n mankind; 人類学 [jinruigaku] n anthropology

人種 [jinshu] n race (origin); 人種の [jinshu no] adj racial; 人種差別 [jinshusabetsu] n racism

人種差別 [jinshusabetsu] 人種差別主義者 [jinshusabetsushugisha] n racist; 人種差別主義者の [jinshusabetsushugisha no] adj racist

ジントニック [jintonikku] n gin and tonic; ジントニックをお願いします [jin-tonikku o o-negai shimasu] I'll have a

gin and tonic, please

地主 [jinushi] n landowner

人造 [jinzou] 人造の [jinzou no] adj man-made

腎臓 [jinzou] n kidney

ジプシー [jipushii] n gypsy

事例 [jirei] n instance

ジレンマ [jirenma] n dilemma

時差ぼけ [jisaboke] n jet lag; 私は時差ぼけに悩んでいます [watashi wa jisaboke ni nayande imasu] I'm suffering from jet lag

自殺 [jisatsu] n suicide

時制 [jisei] n tense

自制 [jisei] n self-control

磁石 [jishaku] n magnet; 磁石の [jishaku no] adj magnetic

自信 [jishin] n confidence (self-assurance); 自信のある [jishin no aru] adj self-assured

自身 [jishin] n oneself; あなた方自身 [anatagata jishin] pron yourselves (reflexive); あなた自身 [anata jishin] pron yourself (polite); あなた自身 [anata jishin] pron yourself, yourselves (polite); それ自身 [sore jishin] pron itself; 私たち自身 [watashi-tachi jishin] pron ourselves; 彼ら自身 [karera jishin] pron themselves; 彼自身 [kare jishin] pron himself; 彼女自身 [kanojo jishin] pron herself

地震 [jishin] n earthquake

辞書 [jisho] n dictionary

地所 [jisho] n estate

辞職 [jishoku] 辞職する [jishoku suru] v resign

実際 [jissai] 実際に [jissai ni] adv actually, practically; 実際の [jissai no] adj actual; 実際的な [jissaiteki na] adj practical; 実際的でない [jissaiteki denai] adj impractical

実施 [jisshi] レッスンを実施していますか? [ressun o jisshi shite imasu ka?] Do you give lessons?

実質 [jisshitsu] n substance; 実質上の [jisshitsujou no] adj virtual

地すべり [jisuberi] n landslide

自炊 [jisui] n self-catering

事態 [jitai] n situation; 緊急事態 [kinkyuujitai] n emergency; 緊急事態です! [kinkyuu-jitai desu!] It's an emergency!

自宅 [jitaku] n home; 自宅住所 [jitaku juusho] n home address

事典 [jiten] n dictionary; 百科事典 [hyakka jiten] n encyclopaedia

次点 [jiten] 次点者 [jitensha] n runner-up

自転車 [jitensha] n bicycle, bike, cycle (bike); タンデム自転車 [tandemu jitensha] n tandem; 自転車に乗る [jitensha ni noru] v cycle; 自転車ポンプ [jitensha ponpu] n bicycle pump; 一番近い自転車修理店はどこですか? [ichiban chikai jitensha shuuri-ten wa doko desu ka?] Where is the nearest bike repair shop?; どこで自転車をレンタルできますか? [doko de jitensha o rentaru dekimasu ka?] Where can I hire a bike?; ここに自転車を置いておけますか? [koko ni jitensha o oite okemasu ka?] Can I keep my bike here?; 自転車はいつ返すことになっていますか? [jitensha wa itsu kaesu koto ni natte imasu ka?] When is the bike due back?; 自転車はコースターブレーキ付きですか? [jitensha wa koosutaa-bureeki tsuki desu ka?] Does the bike have back-pedal brakes?; 自転車はギア付きですか? [jitensha wa gia tsuki desu ka?] Does the bike have gears?; 自転車はライト付きですか? [jitensha wa raito tsuki desu ka?] Does the bike have lights?; 自転車はブレーキ付きですか? [jitensha wa bureeki tsuki desu ka?] Does the bike have brakes?; 自転車を借りたいのですが [jitensha o karitai no desu ga] I want to hire a bike; ・・・へ行く自転車道はどこですか? [...e iku jitensha-dou wa doko desu ka?] Where is the cycle path to...?

実在 [jitsuzai] 実在の [jitsuzai no] adj real

じっと [jitto] adv still; じっと見つめる [jitto mitsumeru] v stare

滋養 [jiyou] 滋養のある [jiyou no aru] adj nutritious

自由 [jiyuu] n freedom; 自由な [jiyuu na] adj free (no restraint); 自由契約の [jiyuu keiyaku no] adj freelance; 自由契約で [jiyuu keiyaku de] adv freelance; ・・・を自由にする [...-o jiyuu ni suru] v free

自由選択 [jiyuusentaku] 自由選択の [jiyuusentakuno] adj optional

事前 [jizen] adv beforehand; 事前予約 [jizen yoyaku] n advance booking

慈善 [jizen] 慈善団体 [jizen dantai] n charity

持続 [jizoku] 持続性の [jizokusei no] adj persistent; 持続期間 [jizoku kikan] n duration

除外 [jogai] 除外する [jogai suru] v exclude

助言 [jogen] n advice, tip (suggestion); 助言する [jogen suru] v advise

ジョギング [jogingu] n jogging; ジョギングする [jogingu suru] v jog; どこに行けばジョギングができますか? [doko ni ikeba jogingu ga dekimasu ka?] Where can I go jogging?

除氷 [johyou] 除氷装置 [johyou souchi] n de-icer

女医 [joi] n female doctor; 女医さんと話をしたいのですが [joi-san to hanashi o shitai no desu ga] I'd like to speak to a female doctor

徐々 [jojo] 徐々に [jojo ni] adv gradually; 徐々の [jojo no] adj gradual

抒情 [jojou] 抒情詩 [jojoushi] n lyrics

除光液 [jokoueki] n nail-polish remover

除去 [jokyo] 除去する [jokyo suru] v eliminate

ジョージア [joojia] n Georgia (US state)

女王 [joou] n queen

助産婦 [josanpu] n midwife

女性 [josei] n female, woman; 独身女性 [dokushinjosei] n spinster; 女性の [josei no] adj female; 女性バーテンダー [josei baatendaa] n barmaid; 女性軍人 [josei gunjin] n servicewoman; 女性用トイレ [joseiyou toire] n ladies'; 女性店員 [josei ten'in] n saleswoman

助成金 [joseikin] n grant, subsidy; 助成金を支給する [joseikin-o shikyuu suru] v subsidize

除雪 [josetsu] 除雪車 [josetsusha] n snowplough

女子 [joshi] 女子修道院 [joshishuudouin] n convent; 女子生徒 [joshiseito] n schoolgirl

助手 [joshu] n assistant; 教室助手 [kyoushitsu joshu] n classroom assistant

除草 [josou] 除草剤 [josouzai] n weedkiller

錠 [jou] n lock (door); 錠をあける [jou-o akeru] v unlock; 錠剤 [jouzai] n tablet

乗馬 [jouba] n horse riding, riding; 乗馬に行きましょう [jouba ni ikimashou] Let's go horse riding; 乗馬に行けますか? [jouba ni ikemasu ka?] Can we go horse riding?

丈夫 [joubu] 丈夫な [joubu na] adj strong, durable

冗談 [joudan] n joke; 冗談を言う [joudan o iu] v joke

上演 [jouen] n performance; そのオペラ劇場で今晩何が上演されますか? [sono opera-gekijou de konban nani ga jouen saremasu ka?] What's on tonight at the opera?

定規 [jougi] n ruler (measure)

じょうご [jougo] n funnel

譲歩 [jouho] n concession

情報 [jouhou] n information; 情報技術 [jouho gijutsu] n IT; 個人情報泥棒 [kojin jouhou dorobou] n identity theft; ・・・に関する情報が欲しいのですが [...ni kansuru jouhou ga hoshii no desu ga] I'd like some information about...; 弊社についての情報です [heisha ni tsuite no jouhou desu] Here's some information about my company

浄化槽 [joukasou] n septic tank

条件付き [joukentsuki] 条件付きの [joukentsuki no] adj conditional

蒸気 [jouki] n steam

条項 [joukou] n clause

乗客 [joukyaku] n passenger

状況 [joukyou] n context, situation

上級官吏 [joukyuu kanri] n mandarin (official)

錠前屋 [joumaeya] n locksmith

乗務 [joumu] 乗務員 [joumuin] n cabin crew

乗務員 [joumuin] n crew member; 客室乗務員 [kyakushitsu joumuin] n flight attendant

静脈 [joumyaku] n vein

じょうろ [jouro] n watering can

蒸留 [jouryuu] 蒸留所 [jouryuujo] n distillery

乗車 [jousha] 複数回乗車できる切符はありますか? [fukusuukai jousha dekiru kippu wa arimasu ka?] Do you have multi-journey tickets?

常識 [joushiki] n common sense

上昇 [joushou] n rise

常習 [joushuu] 常習的な [joushuuteki na] adj addicted

状態 [joutai] n condition, state; 乱雑な状態 [ranzatsu na joutai] n shambles; 混乱状態 [konranjoutai] n muddle

条約 [jouyaku] n treaty

常用 [jouyou] 麻薬常用者 [mayaku jouyousha] n drug addict

醸造 [jouzou] 醸造所 [jouzoujo] n brewery

女優 [joyuu] n actress

授業 [jugyou] n lesson, tuition; 授業料 [jugyouryou] n tuition fees

受験 [juken] 再受験する [saijuken suru] v resit

熟 [juku] 熟した [juku shita] adj ripe

熟練 [jukuren] n skill; 熟練していない [jukuren shite inai] adj unskilled; 熟練した [jukuren shita] adj skilful, skilled; 熟練職業 [jukuren shokugyou] n craft

受給 [jukyuu] 老齢年金受給者 [rourei nenkin jukyuusha] n old-age pensioner

受給者 [jukyuusha] 年金受給者 [nenkin jukyuusha] n pensioner

呪文 [jumon] n spell (magic)

準・・・ [jun...] adj associate

順番 [junban] 順番待ち名簿 [junbanmachi meibo] n waiting list

準備 [junbi] n preparation; 準備する [junbi suru] v prepare, provide for

順序 [junjo] n sequence

準々決勝 [junjunkesshou] n quarter final

循環 [junkan] n circulation

準決勝 [junkesshou] n semifinal

巡航 [junkou] n cruise

殉教 [junkyou] 殉教者 [junkyousha] n martyr

順応 [junnou] 順応する [junnou suru] v adjust

巡礼 [junrei] n pilgrimage; 巡礼者 [junreisha] n pilgrim; 巡礼の旅 [junrei no tabi] n pilgrimage

純粋な [junsui na] adj pure

授乳 [junyuu] 授乳する [junyuu suru] v breast-feed; どこで赤ちゃんに授乳できますか? [doko de akachan ni junyuu dekimasu ka?] Where can I breast-feed the baby?; ここで授乳できますか? [koko de junyuu dekimasu ka?] Can I breast-feed here?

受領証 [juryoushou] n receipt

樹脂 [jushi] n resin

受信 [jushin] n reception; 受信機 [jushinki] n receiver (electronic)

授賞 [jushou] 授賞式 [jushoushiki] n prize-giving

受賞 [jushou] 受賞者 [jushousha] n prizewinner

十歳 [jussai] 彼は十歳です [kare wa jus-sai desu] He is ten years old

十進法 [jusshinhou] 十進法の [jusshinhou no] adj decimal

銃 [juu] n gun; ライフル銃 [raifuru juu] n rifle; 散弾銃 [sandanjuu] n shotgun

十 [juu] number ten; 十番目 [juu banme] n tenth; 十番目の [juu banme no] adj tenth

十分 [juubun] pron (量・程度) enough; 不十分な [fujuubun na] adj inadequate, insufficient; 十分な [juubun na] adj enough; 十分に [juubun ni] adv fully

十分な [juubun na] adj sufficient

重大 [juudai] adj serious; きわめて重大な [kiwamete juudai na] adj momentous, vital; 重大な [juudai na] adj critical, crucial; 重大局面 [juudai kyokumen] n crisis

十代 [juudai] n teens

充電 [juuden] n charge (electricity); 充電する [juuden suru] v charge (electricity); 再充電する [saijuuden suru] v recharge; どこで携帯電話を充電できますか? [doko de keitai-denwa o juuden dekimasu ka?] Where can I charge my mobile phone?; 充電されません [juuden saremasen] It's not charging

充電器 [juudenki] n charger

柔道 [juudou] n judo

十月 [juugatsu] n October; 十月三日の日曜日です [juu-gatsu mik-ka no nichiyoubi desu] It's Sunday third October

十五 [juugo] number fifteen

十五番目 [juugo banme] 十五番目の [juugobanme no] adj fifteenth

十五分 [juugofun] 二時十五分です [ni-ji juugo-fun desu] It's quarter past two

従業員 [juugyouin] n employee

十八 [juuhachi] number eighteen

十八番目 [juuhachibanme] 十八番目の [juuhachi banme no] adj eighteenth

獣医 [juui] n vet

十一 [juuichi] number eleven

十一番目 [juuichibanme] 十一番目の [juuichi banme no] adj eleventh

十一月 [juuichigatsu] n November

十字 [juuji] 赤十字社 [sekijuujisha] n Red Cross; 十字形 [juujigata] n cross

十字架 [juujika] n crucifix

従順 [juujun] adj obedient; 不従順な [fujuujun na] adj disobedient

従順な [juujun na] adj obedient

住居 [juukyo] n residence; 住居侵入罪 [juukyoshinnyuuzai] n burglary

十九 [juukyuu] number nineteen

十九番目 [juukyuubanme] 十九番目の [juukyuu banme no] adj nineteenth

十七 [juunana] number seventeen; 十七番目の [juushichi banme no] adj seventeenth

柔軟剤 [juunanzai] n fabric softener; 柔軟剤はありますか? [juunan-zai wa arimasu ka?] **Do you have softener?**

十年間 [juunenkan] *n* decade

十二 [juuni] *number* twelve; 十二番目の
[juuni banme no] *adj* twelfth

十二月 [juunigatsu] *n* December; 十二月
三十一日の金曜日に [juuni-gatsu
sanjuuichi-nichi no kinyoubi ni] **on Friday
the thirty first of December**

十二時 [juuniji] *n* twelve o'clock; 夜中の
十二時に [yonaka no juuni-ji ni] **at
midnight**

12個 [juuniko] *n* dozen

十二宮 [juunikyuu] *n* zodiac

住人 [juunin] *n* inhabitant

10億 [juuoku] *n* billion

十六 [juuroku] *number* sixteen; 十六番目
の [juuroku banme no] *adj* sixteenth

重量挙げ [juuryouage] *n* weightlifting;
重量挙げ選手 [juuryouage senshu] *n*
weightlifter

十三 [juusan] *number* thirteen; 十三番目
の [juusan banme no] *adj* thirteenth

獣脂 [juushi] *n* grease

住所 [juusho] *n* address *(location)*; 住所氏
名録 [juusho shimei roku] *n* directory; 住
所録 [juushoroku] *n* address book; 自宅住
所 [jitaku juusho] *n* home address; 私あて
の郵便物をこの住所に回送してください
[watashi ate no yuubinbutsu o kono juusho
ni kaisou shite kudasai] **Please send my
mail on to this address**

重症 [juushou] *n* serious condition; 重症
ですか? [juushou desu ka?] **Is it serious?**

ジュース [juusu] *n* juice; フルーツジュース
[furuutsujuusu] *n* fruit juice

渋滞 [juutai] 交通渋滞 [koutsuujuutai] *n*
traffic jam; この渋滞の原因は何ですか?
[kono juutai no gen'in wa nan desu ka?]
What is causing this hold-up?

住宅 [juutaku] *n* residence; 公営住宅
[koueijuutaku] *n* council house

住宅地 [juutakuchi] 住宅地の
[juutakuchi no] *adj* residential

重炭酸ソーダ [juutansansouda] *n*
bicarbonate of soda

十四 [juuyon] *number* fourteen

十四番目 [juuyonbanme] 十四番目の
[juuyon banme no] *adj* fourteenth

重要 [juuyou] *n* importance; 最も重要な
[mottomo juuyou na] *adj* essential; 重要
な [juuyou na] *adj* important, significant;
重要でない [juuyou de nai] *adj*
unimportant; 重要である [juuyou de aru]
v matter; 重要性 [juuyousei] *n*
importance, significance

k

cards?; クレジットカードで支払えますか？
[kurejitto-kaado de shiharaemasu ka?] **Can I pay by credit card?**; デビットカードは使えますか？ [debitto-kaado wa tsukaemasu ka?] **Do you take debit cards?**; バスのカードはどこで買えますか？ [basu no kaado wa doko de kaemasu ka?] **Where can I buy a bus card?**; 現金自動支払い機が私のカードを吸い込んでしまいました [genkin-jidou-shiharaiki ga watashi no kaado o suikonde shimaimashita] **The cash machine swallowed my card**; 私はカードをキャンセルしなければなりません [watashi wa kaado o kyanseru shinakereba narimasen] **I need to cancel my card**; 私のカードが盗まれました [watashi no kaado ga nusumaremashita] **My card has been stolen**; 私のカードです [watashi no kaado desu] **Here is my card**; 私のカードを使って現金を引き出せますか？ [watashi no kaado o tsukatte genkin o hikidasemasu ka?] **Can I use my card to get cash?**

科 [ka] 精神科の [seishinka no] *adj* **psychiatric**; 精神科医 [seishinka-i] *n* **psychiatrist**

課 [ka] 貴社には広報報道課がありますか？ [kisha ni wa kouhou-houdou-ka ga arimasu ka?] **Do you have a press office?**

蚊 [ka] *n* **mosquito**

カーボン [kaabon] カーボンフットプリント [kaabon futtopurinto] *n* **carbon footprint**

カーデッキ [kaadekki] カーデッキへはどう行けばいいのですか？ [kaa-dekki e wa dou ikeba ii no desu ka?] **How do I get to the car deck?**

カーディガン [kaadigan] *n* **cardigan**

カード [kaado] *n* **card**; カード式公衆電話 [kaado shiki koushuu denwa] *n* **cardphone**; クリスマスカード [kurisumasu kaado] *n* **Christmas card**; このカードをどこで投函できますか？ [kono kaado o doko de toukan dekimasu ka?] **Where can I post these cards?**; この現金自動支払い機で私のカードを使えますか？ [kono genkin-jidou-shiharaiki de watashi no kaado o tsukaemasu ka?] **Can I use my card with this cash machine?**; クレジットカードは使えますか？ [kurejitto-kaado wa tsukaemasu ka?] **Do you take credit**

カーフェリー [kaaferii] *n* **car-ferry**

カーネーション [kaaneeshon] *n* **carnation**

カーニバル [kaanibaru] *n* **carnival**

カーペット [kaapetto] *n* **carpet**

カーラー [kaaraa] *n* **curler**

カーソル [kaasoru] *n* **cursor**

カーステレオ [kaasutereo] *n* **car stereo**; カーステレオはついていますか？ [kaa-sutereo wa tsuite imasu ka?] **Does it have a stereo?**; 車にカーステレオはついていますか？ [kuruma ni kaa-sutereo wa tsuite imasu ka?] **Is there a stereo in the car?**

カーテン [kaaten] *n* **curtain**

カート [kaato] 手荷物カート [tenimotsu kaato] *n* **luggage trolley**

カートリッジ [kaatorijji] *n* **cartridge**; ガス点火器用のカートリッジはありますか？ [gasu-tenkaki-you no kaatorijji wa arimasu ka?] **Do you have a refill for my gas lighter?**

樺 [kaba] *n* **birch**

カバ [kaba] *n* (植物) **hippo**, (植物) **hippopotamus**

カバー [kabaa] カバーチャージ [kabaa chaaji] n cover charge; ベッドカバー [beddokabaa] n bedspread; 枕カバー [makurakabaa] n pillowcase

カバブ [kababu] n kebab

かばん [kaban] n bag; 一泊旅行用かばん [ippaku ryokou you kaban] n overnight bag; 肩掛けかばん [katakake kaban] n satchel; 通学かばん [tsuugaku kaban] n schoolbag; 大型の旅行かばん [ougata no ryokou kaban] n holdall; 誰かが私のかばんを盗みました [dare ka ga watashi no kaban o nusumimashita] Someone's stolen my bag; 私はタクシーにかばんを置き忘れました [watashi wa takushii ni kaban o okiwasuremashita] I left my bags in the taxi

壁 [kabe] n wall

壁紙 [kabegami] n wallpaper

カビ [kabi] n mould (fungus)

花瓶 [kabin] n vase

過敏な [kabin na] 神経過敏な [shinkeikabin na] adj neurotic

かびる [kabiru] かびた [kabita] adj mouldy

カボチャ [kabocha] n pumpkin

カブ [kabu] n (食べ物) turnip

株主 [kabunushi] n shareholder, stockholder

株式 [kabushiki] 株式仲買人 [kabushikinakagainin] n stockbroker; 株式市場 [kabushikishijou] n stock market

カブトムシ [kabutomushi] n beetle

価値 [kachi] n value; 価値のない [kachi no nai] adj worthless

カチカチ [kachikachi] カチッという音 [kachitto iu oto] n click; カチッと鳴る [kachitto naru] v click

家畜 [kachiku] 迷い出た家畜 [mayoideta kachiku] n stray

課長補佐 [kachouhosa] n deputy head

過大 [kadai] 過大評価する [kadai hyouka suru] v overestimate

過大な [kadai na] 過大請求する [kadai seikyuu suru] v overcharge

角 [kado] n corner; 2番目の角を左に曲がってください [ni-ban-me no kado o hidari ni magatte kudasai] Take the second turning on your left; その角です [sono kado desu] It's on the corner; その角を曲がったところです [sono kado o magatta tokoro desu] It's round the corner; 最初の角を右に曲がってください [saisho no kado o migi ni magatte kudasai] Take the first turning on your right

角 1 [kado] n (数学) angle

•••かどうか [...kadouka] conj whether

カエデ [kaede] n maple

火炎 [kaen] n blaze

変えられる [kaerareru] v convertible

帰る [kaeru] 帰ること [kaeru koto] n return (coming back); あなたが帰ってくるころには私たちは寝ています [anata ga kaette kuru koro ni wa watashi-tachi wa nete imasu] We'll be in bed when you get back; いつお国へお帰りになりますか? [itsu o-kuni e o-kaeri ni narimasu ka?] When do you go home?; 私は家に帰りたいです [watashi wa ie ni kaeritai desu] I'd like to go home

カエル [kaeru] n frog

変える [kaeru] v convert, switch, change; 向きを変える [muki o kaeru] v turn

返す [kaesu] v give back; ひっくり返す [hikkurigaesu] v knock over; もとへ返す [moto-e kaesu] v put back; 送り返す [okurikaesu] v send back

カフェ [kafe] n café; インターネットカフェ [intaanetto kafe] n internet café

カフェイン [kafein] n caffeine

カフェイン抜き [kafein nuki] カフェイン抜きの [kafein nuki no] adj decaffeinated; カフェイン抜きのコーヒー [kafein nuki no koohii] n decaffeinated coffee

カフェテリア [kafeteria] n cafeteria

カフカス [kafukasu] カフカス山脈 [kafukasu sanmyaku] n Caucasus

花粉 [kafun] n pollen

花粉症 [kafunshou] n hay fever

カフスリンク [kafusurinku] n cufflinks

科学 [kagaku] n science; コンピューター科

学 [konpyuutaa kagaku] n computer science; 科学の [kagaku no] adj scientific; 科学者 [kagakusha] n scientist

化学 [kagaku] n chemistry; 化学薬品 [kagakuyakuhin] n chemical

鏡 [kagami] n mirror; 望遠鏡 [bouenkyou] n telescope

かがむ [kagamu] v bend down, bend over

輝く [kagayaku] 光り輝く [hikari kagayaku] adj brilliant

影 [kage] n shadow

過激 [kageki] 過激主義 [kageki shugi] n extremism; 過激派 [kagekiha] n extremist

鍵 [kagi] n key (for lock); 車の鍵 [kuruma no kagi] n car keys; 鍵をかける [kagi-o kakeru] v lock; 202号室の鍵 [nihyaku-ni-gou-shitsu no kagi] the key for room number two hundred and two; このドアの鍵はどれですか? [kono doa no kagi wa dore desu ka?] Which is the key for this door?; この鍵は何のためですか? [kono kagi wa nan no tame desu ka?] What's this key for?; 正面玄関の鍵はどれですか? [shoumen-genkan no kagi wa dore desu ka?] Which is the key for the front door?; 裏口の鍵はどれですか? [uraguchi no kagi wa dore desu ka?] Which is the key for the back door?; 車庫の鍵はどれですか? [shako no kagi wa dore desu ka?] Which is the key for the garage?; 私は鍵を置き忘れました [watashi wa kagi o okiwasuremashita] I've forgotten the key; 私の鍵は開きません [watashi no kagi wa akimasen] My key doesn't work; ···の鍵はどこでもらえばいいのですか? [...no kagi wa doko de moraeba ii no desu ka?] Where do we get the key...?; 鍵に問題があります [kagi ni mondai ga arimasu] I'm having trouble with the key; 鍵がもう一つ必要です [kagi ga mou hitotsu hitsuyou desu] We need a second key; 鍵が開きません [kagi ga akimasen] The key doesn't work; 鍵をお願いします [kagi o o-negai shimasu] The key, please; 鍵をもらえますか? [kagi o moraemasu ka?] Can I have a key?

かぎ針編み [kagibariami] かぎ針編みをする [kagiamibari-o suru] v crochet

限り [kagiri] 一回限りのこと [ikkai kagiri no koto] n one-off

かぎづめ [kagizume] n claw

かご [kago] n basket, cage

家具 [kagu] n furniture; 家具付きの [kagu tsuki no] adj furnished

嗅ぐ [kagu] においを嗅ぐ [nioi-o kagu] vt smell

カグール [kaguuru] n cagoule

貨幣 [kahei] 貨幣鋳造所 [kahei chuuzoujo] n mint (coins)

貝 [kai] n shellfish

階 [kai] それは何階ですか? [sore wa nan-kai desu ka?] What floor is it on?

怪物 [kaibutsu] n monster

懐中 [kaichuu] 懐中電灯 [kaichuudentou] n torch

懐中電灯 [kaichuudentou] n flashlight

階段 [kaidan] n staircase, stairs; 非常階段 [hijoukaidan] n fire escape

回復 [kaifuku] n recovery; 意識を回復する [ishiki-o kaifuku suru] v come round; 回復する [kaifuku suru] v recover, regain

絵画 [kaiga] n painting

海外 [kaigai] 海外に [kaigai ni] adv abroad, overseas

海岸 [kaigan] n seashore, seaside; 海岸の遊歩道 [kaigan no yuuhodou] n promenade

会議 [kaigi] n conference, meeting

海軍 [kaigun] n navy; 海軍の [kaigun no] adj naval

解放 [kaihou] n liberation, release; 解放する [kaihou suru] v release

会員 [kaiin] n member; 会員でないといけないのですか? [kaiin de nai to ikenai no desu ka?] Do you have to be a member?; 会員でなければなりませんか? [kaiin de nakereba narimasen ka?] Do I have to be a member?

海事 [kaiji] 海事の [kaiji no] adj maritime

介助 [kaijo] 私は介助が必要です [watashi wa kaijo ga hitsuyou desu] I need assistance

会場 [kaijou] n venue

階下 [kaika] 階下の [kaika no] adj downstairs; 階下へ [kaika-e] adv downstairs

会計 [kaikei] n accountancy; 会計係 [kaikeigakari] n cashier, treasurer; 会計監査人 [kaikei kansanin] n auditor; 会計士 [kaikeishi] n accountant

会計年度 [kaikeinendo] n fiscal year

会見 [kaiken] 記者会見 [kishakaiken] n press conference

解決 [kaiketsu] n solution; 解決する [kaiketsu suru] v settle, solve, sort out

会期 [kaiki] n session

解雇 [kaiko] n sack (dismissal); 一時解雇する [ichiji kaiko suru] v lay off; 余剰人員の解雇 [yojoujin'in no kaiko] n redundancy; 余剰人員として解雇された [yojoujin'in to shite kaiko sareta] adj redundant; 解雇する [kaiko suru] v dismiss

開口部 [kaikoubu] n aperture

階級 [kaikyuu] n rank (status); 労働者階級の [roudoushakaikyuu no] adj working-class

買物 [kaimono] n shopping; 買物袋 [kaimonobukuro] n carrier bag, shopping bag

飼いならす [kainarasu] 飼いならされた [kainarasareta] adj tame

貝類 [kairui] 私は貝類のアレルギーがあります [watashi wa kairui no arerugii ga arimasu] I'm allergic to shellfish

改良 [kairyou] 品種改良する [hinshu kairyou suru] v breed

海流 [kairyuu] 海流がありますか? [kairyuu ga arimasu ka?] Are there currents?

改札 [kaisatsu] 改札係 [kaisatsugakari] n ticket collector; 改札口 [kaisatsuguchi] n ticket barrier; 回転式改札口 [kaitenshiki kaisatsuguchi] n turnstile

回線 [kaisen] n telephone line; 回線が悪いです [kaisen ga warui desu] It's a bad line

解説 [kaisetsu] 解説者 [kaisetsusha] n commentator; 実況解説 [jikkyou kaisetsu] n commentary

会社 [kaisha] n company, firm; 航空会社 [koukuu gaisha] n airline; 子会社 [kogaisha] n subsidiary; 会社についての情報を教えていただきたいのですが [kaisha ni tsuite no jouhou o oshiete itadakitai no desu ga] I would like some information about the company

解釈 [kaishaku] 解釈する [kaishaku suru] v interpret

開始 [kaishi] n start

快速 [kaisoku] 快速モーターボート [kaisoku mootaabooto] n speedboat

海藻 [kaisou] n seaweed

改装 [kaisou] 改装する [kaisou suru] v redecorate

回送 [kaisou] 私あての郵便物をこの住所に回送してください [watashi ate no yuubinbutsu o kono juusho ni kaisou shite kudasai] Please send my mail on to this address

海水 [kaisui] n sea water; 海水面 [kaisui men] n sea level

解する [kai suru] 読唇術で解する [dokushinjutsu de kaisuru] v lip-read

回数 [kaisuu] 回数券をください [kaisuuken o kudasai] A book of tickets, please

快適 [kaiteki] 快適な [kaiteki na] adj comfortable

回転 [kaiten] 回転木馬 [kaitenmokuba] n merry-go-round; 回転式乾燥機 [kaitenshiki kansouki] n tumble dryer; 回転式改札口 [kaitenshiki kaisatsuguchi] n turnstile

会話 [kaiwa] n conversation

海洋 [kaiyou] n ocean

潰瘍 [kaiyou] n ulcer

改善 [kaizen] n improvement; 改善する [kaizen suru] v improve

海賊 [kaizoku] n pirate

改造 [kaizou] n makeover

火事 [kaji] 火事だ! [kaji da!] Fire!

家事 [kaji] n housework

カジノ [kajino] n casino

果樹 [kaju] 果樹園 [kajuen] n orchard

価格 [kakaku] n price; 価格表 [kakakuhyou] n price list; 販売価格 [hanbai kakaku] n selling price; 小売価格 [kourikakaku] n retail price

係 [kakari] 会計係 [kaikeigakari] n cashier, treasurer; 改札係 [kaisatsugakari] n ticket collector; 検札係 [kensatsugakari] n ticket inspector

係官 [kakarikan] 税関係官 [zeikan kakarikan] n customs officer

かかる [kakaru] v (費用) cost

掛かる [kaka ru] vi hang

かかし [kakashi] n scarecrow

かかと [kakato] n heel

かかわらず [kakawarazu] ···にもかかわらず [...nimokakawarazu] conj though

かかわる [kakawaru] v be connected; 個人にかかわらない [kojin ni kakawaranai] adj impersonal

賭け [kake] bet; 賭け事 [kakegoto] n betting; 賭け屋 [kakeya] n betting shop

···掛け [...kake] n (帽子や洋服) rack

かけなおす [kakenaosu] 電話をかけなおす [denwa-o kakenaosu] v phone back, ring back; あとでかけなおします [ato de kakenaoshimasu] I'll call back later; かけなおしてください [kakenaoshite kudasai] Please call me back; 明日かけなおします [asu kakenaoshimasu] I'll call back tomorrow

かけら [kakera] n chip (small piece)

かけられる [kakerareru] ここから電話をかけられますか? [koko kara denwa o kakeraremasu ka?] Can I phone from here?

かける [kakeru] 保険をかける [hoken-o kakeru] v insure; やすりをかける [yasuri-o kakeru] v file (smoothing); アイロンをかける [airon-o kakeru] v iron; アイロンをかけるべきもの [airon-o kakerubeki mono] n ironing; 拷問にかける [goumon ni kakeru] v torture; 疑いをかける [utagai-o kakeru] v suspect; ご迷惑をかけてすみません [go-meiwaku o kakete sumimasen] I'm sorry to trouble you; 私は電話をかけなけ

ればなりません [watashi wa denwa o kakenakereba narimasen] I must make a phone call; 電話をかけたいのですが [denwa o kaketai no desu ga] I want to make a phone call

掛ける [kakeru] vt hang

賭ける [kakeru] v bet; 賭け事をする [kakegoto-o suru] v gamble

駆ける [kakeru] 速足で駆ける [hayaashi de kakeru] v trot

掛け算 [kakezan] n multiplication

牡蠣 [kaki] n oyster

夏季 [kaki] n summertime

かき集める [kakiatsumeru] v round up

かき傷 [kakikizu] n scratch

かき混ぜる [kakimazeru] v stir

垣根 [kakine] n hedge

書留 [kakitome] n registered mail; 簡易書留 [kan-i kakitome] n recorded delivery; 書留郵便でどのくらいの日数がかかりますか? [kakitome-yuubin de dono kurai no nissuu ga kakarimasu ka?] How long will it take by registered post?

書き留める [kakitomeru] v note down, write down; ちょっと書き留める [chotto kakitodomeru] v jot down

括弧 [kakko] n brackets

かっこいい [kakkoii] adj cool (stylish)

カッコウ [kakkou] n cuckoo

過去 [kako] n past

囲い [kakoi] n fold

囲む [kakomu] v surround

過越し [ka koshi] 過越しの祭 [sugikoshi no matsuri] n Passover

角2 [kaku] n (場所) corner

かく [kaku] 汗をかく [ase o kaku] v sweat

書く [kaku] v write; ブログを書く [burogu-o kaku] v blog; 書いたもの [kaita mono] n writing; その住所を紙に書いてもらえますか? [sono juusho o kami ni kaite moraemasu ka?] Will you write down the address, please?; それを書いていただけますか? [sore o kaite itadakemasu ka?] Could you write it down, please?; それを

紙に書いていただけませんか? [sore o kami ni kaite itadakemasen ka?] Could you write that down, please?; 値段を書いてください [nedan o kaite kudasai] Please write down the price

広大 [kakudai] n enlargement

広大鏡 [kakudaikyou] n magnifying glass

確実 [kakujitsu] 確実なこと [kakujitsu na koto] n certainty

革命 [kakumei] n revolution

革命的な [kakumeiteki na] adj revolutionary

確認 [kakunin] n confirmation; 確認する [kakunin suru] v confirm

かくれん坊 [kakurenbou] n hide-and-seek

隠れる [kakureru] vi hide

隠される [kakusareru] 隠された [kakusareta] adj hidden

確信 [kakushin] n confidence; 確信のない [kakushin no nai] adj unsure; 確信させる [kakushin saseru] v convince; 確信して [kakushin shite] adj confident; 確信している [kakushin shite iru] adj certain, positive; 確信している [kakushin shite iru] adj sure

革新 [kakushin] n innovation; 革新的な [kakushinteki na] adj innovative

各種 [kakushu] n assortment; 各種取り合わせ [kakushu toriawase] n assortment

隠す [kakusu] vt hide

カクテル [kakuteru] n cocktail; カクテルはありますか? [kakuteru wa arimasu ka?] Do you sell cocktails?

確約 [kakuyaku] 確約する [kakuyaku suru] v assure

下級 [kakyuu] 下級の [kakyuu no] adj junior

かまう [kamau] v care about; かまいませんよ [kamaimasen yo] It doesn't matter

カメ [kame] n (動物) tortoise, (動物) turtle

カメラ [kamera] n camera; カメラ付き携帯電話 [kamera tsuki keitai denwa] n camera phone; カメラマン [kameraman] n cameraman; デジタルカメラ [dejitaru

kamera] n digital camera; このカメラ用のバッテリーはありますか? [kono kamera-you no batterii wa arimasu ka?] Do you have batteries for this camera?; 私はこのカメラ用のカラーフィルムが必要です [watashi wa kono kamera-you no karaa-firumu ga hitsuyou desu] I need a colour film for this camera; 私のカメラが動きません [watashi no kamera ga ugokimasen] My camera is sticking

カメルーン [kameruun] n Cameroon

神 [kami] n god

紙 [kami] n paper; 包装紙 [housoushi] n wrapping paper

髪 [kami] n hair; 髪のふさ [kami no fusa] n lock of hair; 私のようなタイプの髪をカットしたことがありますか? [watashi no you na taipu no kami o katto shita koto ga arimasu ka?] Have you cut my type of hair before?; 私の髪には何がいいと思いますか? [watashi no kami ni wa nani ga ii to omoimasu ka?] What do you recommend for my hair?; 私の髪は乾性です [watashi no kami wa kansei desu] I have dry hair; 私の髪は脂性です [watashi no kami wa aburashou desu] I have greasy hair; 髪をまっすぐにしてもらえますか? [kami o massugu ni shite moraemasu ka?] Can you straighten my hair?; 髪を染めていただけますか? [kami o somete itadakemasu ka?] Can you dye my hair, please?

紙ばさみ [kamibasami] n portfolio

紙吹雪 [kamifubuki] n confetti

かみ傷 [kamikizu] このかみ傷は感染しています [kono kami-kizu wa kansen shite imasu] This bite is infected

紙巻きタバコ [kamimakitabako] n cigarette

雷 [kaminari] n lightning

かみそり [kamisori] n razor; 安全かみそりの刃 [anzen kamisori no ha] n razor blade

寡黙な [kamoku na] adj silent

カモメ [kamome] n seagull

貨物 [kamotsu] n cargo; 貨物輸送 [kamotsu yusou] n freight

かむ [kamu] v (歯) bite; かむこと [kamu koto] (歯) n bite; 私はかまれました [watashi wa kamaremashita] I have been bitten

噛む [kamu] v chew

カムコーダー [kamukoudaa] n camcorder

缶 [kan] 缶詰にした [kanzume ni shita] adj tinned; 缶切り [kankiri] n tin-opener

管 [kan] n tube; 排水管 [haisuikan] n drain, drainpipe; 試験管 [shikenkan] n test tube

艦 [kan] 潜水艦 [sensuikan] n submarine

官 [kan] 検査官 [kensakan] n inspector; 裁判官 [saibankan] n judge; 外交官 [gaikoukan] n diplomat

カナダ [kanada] n Canada; カナダの [kanada no] adj Canadian

カナダ人 [kanadajin] n Canadian (person)

金切り声 [kanakirigoe] n scream; 金切り声を上げる [kanagiri koe-o ageru] v scream; 金切り声を出す [kanakirigoe o dasu] v shriek

金物 [kanamono] 金物屋 [kanamonoya] n ironmonger's

必ず [kanarazu] adv necessarily

かなり [kanari] adv pretty, quite, rather; かなり遠いです [kanari tooi desu] It's quite far

カナリア [kanaria] n canary

カナリア諸島 [kanaria shotou] n Canaries

悲しい [kanashii] adj sad

悲しみ [kanashimi] 深い悲しみ [fukai kanashimi] n grief

悲しむ [kanashimu] 悲しんで [kanashinde] adv sadly

カンボジア [kanbojia] n Cambodia; カンボジアの [kanbojia no] adj Cambodian

カンボジア人 [kanbojiajin] n Cambodian (person)

寛大 [kandai] n generosity

感電 [kanden] n electric shock

感動 [kandou] 感動させる [kandou saseru] adj moving; 感動した [kandou shita] adj impressed, touched; 感動的な [kandouteki na] adj touching

鐘 [kane] n bell; 鐘の音 [kane no oto] n toll

金遣い [kanedukai] 金遣いが荒い [kanezukai ga arai] adj extravagant

金持ち [kanemochi] 金持ちの [kanemochi no] adj rich

肝炎 [kanen] n hepatitis

可燃 [kanen] 可燃性の [kanensei no] adj flammable

加熱 [kanetsu] 加熱する [kanetsu suru] v heat up

考え [kangae] n idea

考え出す [kangaedasu] v work out

考え直す [kangaenaosu] v reconsider

考える [kangaeru] v think

管楽器 [kangakki] 木管楽器 [mokkangakki] n woodwind

カンガルー [kangaruu] n kangaroo

歓迎 [kangei] n welcome; 歓迎する [kangei suru] v welcome

観劇 [kangeki] n play (theatre); どこに行けば観劇ができますか? [doko ni ikeba kangeki ga dekimasu ka?] Where can we go to see a play?

緩下剤 [kangezai] n laxative

看護 [kango] 看護師 [kangoshi] n nurse

看護師 [kangoshi] n nurse; 看護師さんと話をしたいのですが [kangoshi-san to hanashi o shitai no desu ga] I'd like to speak to a nurse

カニ [kani] n crab

蟹座 [kaniza] n Cancer (horoscope)

患者 [kanja] n patient; 老人病患者 [roujinbyou kanja] n geriatric; 糖尿病患者 [tounyoubyou kanja] n diabetic; 癲癇患者 [tenkan kanja] n epileptic

感じ [kanji] ぞくぞくする感じ [zokuzoku suru kanji] n thrill; 空虚な感じ [kuukyo na kanji] n void

感じる [kanjiru] v feel

環状 [kanjou] 環状交差路 [kanjou kousaro] n roundabout; 環状道路 [kanjoudouro] n ring road

感情 [kanjou] n emotion; 感情の [kanjou no] adj emotional

勘定 [kanjou] n bill; お勘定をお願いします [o-kanjou o o-negai shimasu] Please bring the bill; それを私の部屋の勘定につけておいてください [sore o watashi no heya no kanjou ni tsukete oite kudasai] Please charge it to my room; それを私の勘定につけておいてください [sore o watashi no kanjou ni tsukete oite kudasai] Put it on my bill; 別々にお勘定をお願いします [betsubetsu ni o-kanjou o o-negai shimasu] Separate bills, please

感覚 [kankaku] n sense; 感覚に訴える [kankaku ni uttaeru] adj sensuous; 感覚のない [kankaku no nai] adj numb

間隔 [kankaku] n interval

関係 [kankei] n connection, relation, relationship; 無関係な [mukankei na] adj irrelevant; 関係している [kankei shiteiru] adj concerned; 婚姻関係の有無 [kon'in kankei no umu] n marital status

簡潔 [kanketsu] 簡潔な [kanketsu na] adj concise

缶切り [kankiri] n can-opener

韓国 [kankoku] n South Korea

観光 [kankou] n sightseeing

観客 [kankyaku] n spectator

環境 [kankyou] n environment, surroundings; 環境にやさしい [kankyou ni yasashii] adj ecofriendly, environmentally friendly; 環境の [kankyou no] adj environmental

甘味料 [kanmiryou] 甘味料はありますか？ [kanmiryou wa arimasu ka?] Do you have any sweetener?

かんな [kanna] n (道具) plane (tool)

かんぬき [kannuki] n bolt

彼女 [kanojo] 彼女は [kanojo wa] pron she; 彼女の [kanojo no] adj her; 彼女のもの [kanojo no mono] pron hers; 彼女を [kanojo wo] pron her; 彼女自身 [kanojojishin] pron herself

可能 [kanou] 不可能な [fukanou na] adj impossible; 実行可能な [jikkoukanou na] adj feasible; 可能な [kanou na] adj possible; 可能性 [kanousei] n possibility, potential; 可能性のある [kanousei no aru] adj potential; 可能性を排除する [kanousei-o haijo suru] v rule out

乾杯 [kanpai] n toast (tribute)

乾杯！ [kanpai] excl cheers!

完璧 [kanpeki] n perfection; 完璧に [kanpeki ni] adv perfectly

完璧な [kanpeki na] adj perfect

歓楽街 [kanrakugai] 歓楽街での夜の楽しみ [kanrakugai deno yoru no tanoshimi] n nightlife

慣例 [kanrei] n custom; 慣例にのっとった [kanrei ni nottotta] adj conventional; 慣例に従わない [kanrei ni shitagawanai] adj unconventional

関連 [kanren] 関連する [kanren suru] adj relevant

管理 [kanri] n administration; 管理上の [kanrijou no] adj administrative; 管理者 [kanrisha] n director, warden

管理人 [kanrinin] n caretaker

官僚主義 [kanryoushugi] n bureaucracy

監査 [kansa] n audit; 会計監査人 [kaikei kansanin] n auditor; 監査する [kansa suru] v audit

観察 [kansatsu] 観察する [kansatsu suru] v observe; 観察者 [kansatsusha] n observer

観察力 [kansatsuryoku] 観察力の鋭い [kansatsuryoku no surudoi] adj observant

感染 [kansen] n infection; 感染性の [kansensei no] adj infectious

幹線道路 [kansendouro] n main road

間接 [kansetsu] 間接的な [kansetsuteki na] adj indirect

関節炎 [kansetsuen] n arthritis; 私は関節炎をわずらっています [watashi wa kansetsuen o wazuratte imasu] I suffer from arthritis

感謝 [kansha] n gratitude; 感謝している [kansha shite iru] adj grateful; 感謝する [kansha suru] v thank; 感謝を表さない [kansha-o arawasanai] adj ungrateful

かんしゃく [kanshaku] n tantrum, temper

監視 [kanshi] 交通監視員 [koutsuu kanshiin] n traffic warden

監視員 [kanshiin] 監視員はいますか? [kanshi-in wa imasu ka?] Is there a lifeguard?

感心 [kanshin] n admiration; 感心する [kanshin suru] v admire

関心 [kanshin] n concern

関して [kanshite] ···に関して [...ni kanshite] prep regarding

感傷 [kanshou] 感傷的な [kanshouteki na] adj sentimental

看守 [kanshu] n prison officer

観測所 [kansokujo] n observatory

乾燥 [kansou] 乾燥の [kansou no] adj dehydrated; 乾燥させた [kansou saseta] adj dried; 乾燥させる [kansou saseru] v dry; 乾燥した [kansou shita] adj dry; 乾燥機 [kansouki] n dryer

乾燥機 [kansouki] 回転式乾燥機 [kaitenshiki kansouki] n tumble dryer

関する [kan suru] ···に関して [...ni kanshite] prep concerning; 電気に関する [denki ni kansuru] adj electrical

歓待 [kantai] n hospitality, treat

艦隊 [kantai] n fleet

簡単 [kantan] 簡単な [kantan na] adj easy, simple; 簡単に [kantan ni] adv briefly, simply; 簡単にする [kantan ni suru] v simplify; 一番簡単なスロープはどれですか? [ichiban kantan na suroopu wa dore desu ka?] Which are the easiest runs?

感嘆符 [kantanfu] n exclamation mark

鑑定 [kantei] 鑑定士 [kanteishi] n surveyor

観点 [kanten] n perspective, viewpoint

監督 [kantoku] n oversight (supervision); 試験監督者 [shiken kantokusha] n invigilator; 監督する [kantoku suru] v direct, supervise; 監督者 [kantokusha] n supervisor; 監督生 [kantokusei] n prefect

カヌー [kanuu] n canoe; カヌー漕ぎ [kanuu kogi] n canoeing; どこに行けばカヌーをこげますか? [doko ni ikeba kanuu o kogemasu ka?] Where can we go canoeing?

慣用 [kanyou] 慣用句 [kan'youku] n phrase

寛容 [kanyou] 寛容な [kan'you na] adj tolerant

慣用句集 [kanyoukushuu] 外国語慣用句集 [gaikokugo kan'youku shuu] n phrasebook

加入 [kanyuu] 免責補償制度に加入したいのですが [menseki-hoshou-seido ni kanyuu shitai no desu ga] I'd like to arrange a collision damage waiver

関税 [kanzei] n customs, (customs) duty; 関税率 [kanzeiritsu] n tariff; これに関税を払わなければなりませんか? [kore ni kanzei o harawanakereba narimasen ka?] Do I have to pay duty on this?

完全 [kanzen] n perfect; 不完全な [fukanzen na] adj incomplete; 完全な [kanzen na] adj total; 完全に [kanzen ni] adv totally

肝臓 [kanzou] n liver

缶詰め [kanzume] 缶詰めにした [kanzume ni shita] adj canned

顔 [kao] n face; 顔の [kao no] adj facial

顔立ち [kaodachi] n feature

顔色 [kaoiro] n complexion

家屋 [kaoku] 土地付き一戸建て家屋 [tochi tsuki ikkodate kaoku] n detached house

顔文字 [kaomoji] n 'face' emoji

カップ [kappu] n cup

カップル [kappuru] n couple

カプセル [kapuseru] n capsule

殻 [kara] n shell

から [kara] ···から [...kara] prep from; ···だから [...dakara] conj because

カラー [karaa] カラーテレビ [karaaterebi] n colour television; このカラーコピーをお願いします [kono karaa-kopii o o-negai shimasu] I'd like a colour photocopy of this, please; カラーで [karaa de] in colour

カラーフィルム [karaafirumu] n colour film

カラープリンター [karaapurintaa] n colour printer; カラープリンターはありますか? [karaa-purintaa wa arimasu ka?] Is there a colour printer?

体 [karada] n body

カラフ [karafu] n carafe

からかう [karakau] v tease

カラオケ [karaoke] n karaoke

カラス [karasu] n crow, raven

空手 [karate] n karate

カラット [karatto] n carat

彼 [kare] 彼は [kare wa] pron he; 彼の [kare no] adj his; 彼のもの [kare no mono] pron his; 彼を [kare wo] pron him; 彼自身 [karejishin] pron himself

カレー [karee] カレー料理 [karee ryouri] n curry; カレー粉 [kareeko] n curry powder

華麗 [karei] 華麗な [karei na] adj gorgeous

カレッジ [karejji] n college

カレンダー [karendaa] n calendar

彼ら [karera] 彼らは [karera wa] pron they; 彼らの [karera no] adj their; 彼らのもの [karera no mono] pron theirs; 彼らを [karera wo] pron them; 彼ら自身 [karera jishin] pron themselves

仮 [kari] 仮の詰め物をしてもらえますか? [kari no tsumemono o shite moraemasu ka?] Can you do a temporary filling?

狩り [kari] n hunt, hunting; 狩りをする [kari-o suru] v hunt

借り [kari] 借りがある [kari ga aru] v owe

カリブ人 [karibujin] n Caribbean person

カリブ海 [karibukai] カリブ海の [karibukai no] adj Caribbean

カリフラワー [karifurawaa] n cauliflower

借方 [karikata] n debit; 借方に記入する [karikata ni kinyuu suru] v debit

刈り込み [karikomi] n clip

カリキュラム [karikyuramu] n curriculum

借りる [kariru] v borrow

カロリー [karorii] n calorie

かろうじて [karoujite] adv barely

刈る [karu] v mow

軽い [karui] adj light (not heavy)

軽く [karuku] 軽くたたくこと [karuku tataku koto] n tap

カルシウム [karushiumu] n calcium

軽業 [karuwaza] 軽業師 [karuwazashi] n acrobat

過量 [karyou] 過量服用 [karyou fukuyou] n overdose

傘 [kasa] n umbrella

火災 [kasai] 火災報知器 [kasai houchiki] n fire alarm

かさむ [kasamu] v mount up

カササギ [kasasagi] n magpie

稼ぐ [kasegu] v earn

下線 [kasen] 下線を引く [kasen-o hiku] v underline

カセット [kasetto] n cassette

貨車 [kasha] 無蓋貨車 [mugai kasha] n truck

呵責 [kashaku] 良心の呵責 [ryoushin no kashaku] n remorse

華氏 [kashi] 華氏温度 [kashi ondo] n degree Fahrenheit

菓子 [kashi] n gateau

賢い [kashikoi] adj clever, wise

カシミヤ [kashimiya] n cashmere

頭文字 [kashiramoji] n initials; 頭文字で署名する [atamamoji de shomei suru] v initial

貸し付ける [kashitsukeru] v loan; 貸し付け [kashizuke] n loan

過食症 [kashokushou] n bulimia

過小評価する [kashouhyouka suru] v underestimate

歌手 [kashu] n singer

カシューナッツ [kashuunattsu] n cashew

加速 [kasoku] n acceleration; 加速する [kasoku suru] v accelerate

火葬 [kasou] 火葬場 [kasouba] n crematorium

仮装服 [kasoufuku] n fancy dress

喝采 [kassai] n cheer

滑走 [kassou] 滑走路 [kassouro] n runway

貸す [kasu] v lend; お金をいくらか貸していただけますか? [o-kane o ikura ka kashite itadakemasu ka?] Could you lend me some money?; タオルを貸していただけますか? [taoru o kashite itadakemasu ka?] Could you lend me a towel?

かすか [kasuka] かすかな [kasuka na] adj faint

カスタード [kasutaado] n custard

カスタマイズ [kasutamaizu] カスタマイズされた [kasutamaizu sareta] adj customized

肩 [kata] n shoulder; 肩をすくめる [kata o sukumeru] v shrug; 肩掛けかばん [katakake kaban] n satchel; 肩甲骨 [kenkoukotsu] n shoulder blade; 私は肩を痛めました [watashi wa kata o itamemashita] I've hurt my shoulder

型 [kata] n mould (shape); 内蔵型の [naizougata no] adj self-contained

カタール [kataaru] n Qatar

片足 [kataashi] 片足スケート [kataashi sukeeto] n scooter

形 [katachi] n form, shape; 十字形 [juujigata] n cross

固い [katai] adj firm, hard (solid); 固く縛る [kataku shibaru] v tie up

堅い [katai] adj firm, hard (firm, rigid), stiff

塊 [katamari] n block (solid piece), lump; パンのひと塊 [pan no hitokatamari] n loaf

片道 [katamichi] 片道切符 [katamichi kippu] n one-way ticket, single ticket; 片道切符はいくらですか? [katamichi-kippu wa ikura desu ka?] How much is a single ticket?; ···行き片道 [...iki katamichi] a single to...

傾ける [katamukeru] v tip (incline)

片親 [kataoya] 片親で子育てをする人 [kataoya de kosodate-o suru hito] n single parent

カタログ [katarogu] n catalogue; カタログが欲しいのですが [katarogu ga hoshii no desu ga] I'd like a catalogue

カタル [kataru] n catarrh

カタツムリ [katatsumuri] n snail

偏らない [katayoranai] adj impartial

偏る [katayoru] 偏った [katayotta] adj biased

片付ける [katazukeru] v clear up, tidy; 洗って片付ける [aratte katazukeru] v wash up

仮定 [katei] n supposition; もし···と仮定するならば [moshi ... to katei surunaraba] conj supposing

課程 [katei] n course

過程 [katei] n course, process

カトリック [katorikku] カトリックの [katorikku no] adj Catholic; カトリック教徒 [katorikkukyouto] n Catholic

勝つ [katsu] v win; ···に勝つ [...ni katsu] v beat (outdo)

活動 [katsudou] n action, activity; 活動的な [katsudouteki na] adj active, dynamic

かつら [katsura] n toupee, wig

カッテージチーズ [katteeji chiizu] n cottage cheese

カット [katto] n haircut; カットとブローをお願いします [katto to buroo o o-negai shimasu] A cut and blow-dry, please

買う [kau] v buy; 買い手 [kaite] n buyer; どこでその地域の地図を買えますか? [doko de sono chiiki no chizu o kaemasu ka?] Where can I buy a map of the area?; どこでテレホンカードを買えますか? [doko de terehon-kaado o kaemasu ka?] Where can I buy a phonecard?

飼う [kau] 羊飼い [hitsujikai] n shepherd

カウボーイ [kauboui] n cowboy

カウチソファー [kauchisofaa] n couch

カウンター [kauntaa] n counter

皮 [kawa] n (果物・野菜) peel; 皮むき器 [kawamukiki] n potato peeler; 皮をむく [kawa-o muku] v peel

革 [kawa] n leather; 革ひも [kawa himo] n strap

川 [kawa] n river; その川の遊覧ツアーはあ

りますか? [sono kawa no yuuran-tsuaa wa arimasu ka?] **Are there any boat trips on the river?**; その川で泳げますか? [sono kawa de oyogemasu ka?] **Can one swim in the river?**

かわいい [kawaii] *adj* **cute**

渇く [kawaku] のどの渇き [nodo no kawaki] *n* **thirst**; のどが渇いた [nodo ga kawaita] *adj* **thirsty**

代わり [kawari] 代わりに [kawari ni] *adv* **alternatively**; 代わりの [kawari no] *adj* **alternative**; ・・・の代わりに [...no kawari ni] *prep* **instead of**

代わりに [kawari ni] その代わりに [sono kawari ni] *adv* **instead**

変わる [kawaru] *v* **vary, change**; 変わりやすい [kawariyasui] *adj* **changeable, variable**

為替 [kawase] *n* **exchange**; 為替レート [kawase reeto] *n* **exchange rate, rate of exchange**; 郵便為替 [yuubin kawase] *n* **postal order**; 為替レートはいくらですか? [kawase-reeto wa ikura desu ka?] **What's the exchange rate?**; ・・・を・・・に替える為替レートはいくらですか? [...o ... ni kaeru kawase-reeto wa ikura desu ka?] **What is the rate for ... to...?**

カワセミ [kawasemi] *n* **kingfisher**

変わっていない [kawatteinai] *adj* **unchanged**

カワウソ [kawauso] *n* **otter**

火曜日 [kayoubi] *n* **Tuesday**; 告解火曜日 [kokkai kayoubi] *n* **Shrove Tuesday**; 火曜日に [kayoubi ni] **on Tuesday**

かよわい [kayowai] *adj* **frail**

かゆい [kayui] *adj* **itchy** ▷ *v* **itch**

かゆむ [kayumu] 私は脚がかゆみます [watashi wa ashi ga kayumimasu] **My leg itches**

カザフスタン [kazafusutan] *n* **Kazakhstan**

風 [kaze] *n* **wind**; 風の強い [kaze no tsuyoi] *adj* **windy**

風邪 [kaze] *n* **cold**; おたふく風邪 [otafukukaze] *n* **mumps**; 私は風邪をひきました [watashi wa kaze o hikimashita]

I have a cold; 風邪に効くものが欲しいのですが [kaze ni kiku mono ga hoshii no desu ga] **I'd like something for a cold**

風通し [kazetooshi] *n* **ventilation**; 風通しの悪い [kazetoushi no warui] *adj* **stuffy**

数える [kazoeru] *v* **count**

家族 [kazoku] *n* **family, household**; 私は家族と来ています [watashi wa kazoku to kite imasu] **I'm here with my family**

数 [kazu] *n* **number**

毛深い [kebukai] *adj* **hairy**

ケチャップ [kechappu] *n* **ketchup**

けち [kechi] けちな [kechi na] *adj* **mean, stingy**

ケーブル [keeburu] *n* **cable**; ケーブルテレビ [keeburu terebii] *n* **cable television**

ケーブルカー [keeburukaa] *n* **cable car**

携帯電話 [keeitai denwa] 携帯電話番号 [keitai denwa bangou] *n* **mobile number**

ケーキ [keeki] *n* **cake**

ケース [keesu] *n* **case**; パンケース [pan keesu] *n* **bread bin**

ケータリング [keetaringu] *n* **catering**

怪我 [kega] *n* **injury**; サッカー・ラグビーなどで怪我の手当てなどに要した分の延長時間 [sakkaa / ragubii nado de kega no teate nado ni youshita bun no enchou jikan] *n* **injury time**

怪我人 [keganin] 怪我人がいます [keganin ga imasu] **There are some people injured**

毛皮 [kegawa] *n* **fur**; 羊の毛皮 [hitsuji no kegawa] *n* **sheepskin**

毛皮コート [kegawa kooto] 毛皮のコート [kegawa no kooto] *n* **fur coat**

系 [kei] 太陽系 [taiyoukei] *n* **solar system**

継 [kei] 継母 [mama haha] *n* **stepmother**; 継父 [mama chichi] *n* **stepfather**; 継兄弟 [mama kyoudai] *n* **stepbrother**; 継姉妹 [mama shimai] *n* **stepsister**; 継娘 [mama musume] *n* **stepdaughter**; 継子 [mamako] *n* **stepson**

計 [kei] 温度計 [ondokei] *n* **thermometer**; 速度計 [sokudokei] *n* **speedometer**

競馬 [keiba] n horse racing; 競馬騎手 [keiba kishu] n jockey; 競馬場 [keibajou] n racecourse

刑罰 [keibatsu] n penalty, sentence (punishment)

軽蔑 [keibetsu] n contempt; 軽蔑する [keibetsu suru] v despise

警備 [keibi] n guard; 沿岸警備隊 [engankeibitai] n coastguard; 警備員 [keibiin] n security guard

経度 [keido] n longitude

経営 [keiei] n running, management; 最高経営責任者 [saikou keiei sekininsha] n CEO; 経営陣 [keieijin] n management

経営者 [keieisha] n manager; 女性経営者 [josei keieisha] n manageress; 彼がホテルの経営者です [kare ga hoteru no keieisha desu] He runs the hotel

経費 [keihi] n expenses; 諸経費 [shokeihi] n overheads

警報 [keihou] n alarm; 警報を出す [keihou-o dasu] v alert; 盗難警報機 [tounankeihouki] n burglar alarm; 間違い警報 [machigai keihou] n false alarm

警報器 [keihouki] 煙警報器 [kemuri keihouki] n smoke alarm

敬意 [keii] n regard

掲示 [keiji] n notice; 掲示板 [keijiban] n bulletin board, notice board

刑事 [keiji] n detective

警戒 [keikai] 油断なく警戒して [yudan naku keikai shite] adj alert; 警戒心をいだかせる [keikaishin-o idakaseru] adj alarming

計画 [keikaku] n plan, planning, scheme; 街路計画 [gairo keikaku] n street plan; 計画する [keikaku suru] v plan; 都市計画 [toshikeikaku] n town planning

警官 [keikan] n cop, police officer; 婦人警官 [fujinkeikan] n female police officer

経験 [keiken] n experience; 経験のない [keiken no nai] adj inexperienced; 経験のある [keiken no aru] adj experienced; 経験する [keiken suru] v go through, undergo

景気 [keiki] n economic situation; 景気後退 [keikikoutai] n recession

計器 [keiki] n gauge

警告 [keikoku] n warning; 故障警告灯 [koshou keikokutou] n hazard warning lights; 警告する [keikoku suru] v warn

蛍光 [keikou] 蛍光性の [keikousei no] adj fluorescent

傾向 [keikou] n tendency, trend; 傾向がある [keikou ga aru] v tend

刑務所 [keimusho] n jail, prison

痙攣 [keirei] n spasm

計算 [keisan] n calculation, computing; 計算して出す [keisan dasu] v figure out; 計算する [keisan suru] v calculate; 計算機 [keisanki] n calculator

警察 [keisatsu] n police; 警察官 [keisatsukan] n police officer; 警察を! [keisatsu o!] Police!; 警察を呼んでください [keisatsu o yonde kudasai] Call the police; 私たちはそれを警察に届け出なければなりません [watashi-tachi wa sore o keisatsu ni todokedenakereba narimasen] We will have to report it to the police

警察署 [keisatsusho] n police station; 私は警察署をさがしています [watashi ha keisatsusho o sagashite imasu] I need to find a police station; 警察署はどこですか? [keisatsusho wa doko desu ka?] Where is the police station?

形成 [keisei] 形成外科 [keisei geka] n plastic surgery

傾斜面 [keishamen] n ramp

形式 [keishiki] 形式ばらない [keishikibaranai] adj informal; 形式を定める [keishiki-o sadameru] v format

軽食 [keishoku] n refreshments, snack; 軽食堂 [keishokudou] n snack bar

敬称 [keishou] n honorific; 既婚女性の名字の前に付ける敬称 [kikonjosei no myouji no mae ni tsukeru keishou] n Mrs; 未婚・既婚にかかわらず、女性に対する敬称 [mikon / kikon ni kakawarazu, josei ni taisuru keishou] n Ms; 独身女性の名字の前に付ける敬称 [dokushin josei no myouji no mae ni tsukeru keishou] n Miss; 男性の名字の前に付ける敬称 [dansei no myouji no mae ni tsukeru keishou] n Mr

景勝地 [keishouchi] n beauty spot

形態 [keitai] n shape; 図書形態 [tosho keitai] n format

携帯電話 [keitai denwa] n mobile phone; カメラ付き携帯電話 [kamera tsuki keitai denwa] n camera phone; あなたは携帯電話をお持ちですか？ [anata wa keitai-denwa o o-mochi desu ka?] Do you have a mobile?; あなたの携帯電話番号は何番ですか？ [anata no keitai-denwa-bangou wa nan-ban desu ka?] What is the number of your mobile?; 私の携帯電話番号は・・・です [watashi no keitai-denwa-bangou wa ... desu] My mobile number is...

契約 [keiyaku] n contract; 保険契約書 [hoken keiyakusho] n insurance certificate; 賃貸借契約 [chintaishaku keiyaku] n lease; 自由契約の [jiyuu keiyaku no] adj freelance; 自由契約で [jiyuu keiyaku de] adv freelance; 契約人 [keiyakunin] n contractor; 売買契約 [baibai keiyaku] n bargain

形容 [keiyou] 形容詞 [keiyoushi] n adjective

経由 [keiyu] ・・・経由で [...keiyu de] prep via

軽油 [keiyu] n diesel oil; ・・・分の軽油をお願いします [...bun no keiyu o o-negai shimasu] ... worth of diesel, please

経済 [keizai] n economy; 経済の [keizai no] adj economic; 経済的な [keizaiteki na] adj economical; 経済学者 [keizaigakusha] n economist

経済学 [keizaigaku] n economics

継続 [keizoku] 継続教育 [keizoku kyouiku] n further education; 継続的な [keizokuteki na] adj continual; 継続的に [keizokuteki ni] adv continually

結果 [kekka] n consequence, outcome, result; その結果 [sono kekka] adv consequently; 結果として生じる [kekka toshite shoujiru] v result in

結核 [kekkaku] n tuberculosis, TB

欠陥 [kekkan] n defect; 欠陥のある [kekkan no aru] adj faulty

欠勤 [kekkin] n absence; 欠勤時間 [kekkin jikan] n time off

結婚 [kekkon] n marriage; 結婚している [kekkon shite iru] adj married; 結婚する [kekkon suru] v marry; 結婚指輪 [kekkon yubiwa] n wedding ring; 結婚証明書 [kekkonshoumeisho] n marriage certificate; 結婚記念日 [kekkon kinenbi] n wedding anniversary; 結婚式 [kekkonshiki] n wedding; 女性の結婚前の旧姓 [josei no kekkonmae no kyuusei] n maiden name

結構 [kekkou] adj adequate; もう結構です [mou kekkou desu] That's enough, thank you

煙 [kemuri] n smoke; 煙を出す [kemuri o dasu] v smoke; 煙警報器 [kemuri keihouki] n smoke alarm

権 [ken] 拒否権 [kyohiken] n veto; 優先権 [yuusenken] n right of way

券 [ken] n ticket; 搭乗券 [toujouken] n boarding card, boarding pass; 引換券 [hikikaeken] n voucher; 定期券 [teikiken] n season ticket; 券売機 [kenbaiki] n ticket machine; 回数券をください [kaisuuken o kudasai] A book of tickets, please

ケナガイタチ [kenagaitachi] n ferret

けなす [kenasu] v slag off

顕微鏡 [kenbikyou] n microscope

見物 [kenbutsu] n sightseeing; この地域ではどんなところを見物できますか？ [kono chiiki de wa donna tokoro o kenbutsu dekimasu ka?] What can we visit in the area?

見地 [kenchi] n standpoint

建築 [kenchiku] n architechture; 高層建築 [kousou kenchiku] n high-rise; 建築業者 [kenchikugyousha] n builder; 建築様式 [kenchikuyoushiki] n architecture; 建築家 [kenchikuka] n architect

検疫 [ken'eki] 検疫期間 [ken'eki kikan] n quarantine

懸念 [kenen] n reservation

権限 [kengen] 権限を与える [kengen-o ataeru] v authorize

ケニア [kenia] n Kenya

ケニア人 [keniajin] n Kenyan

ケニアの [kenia no] n Kenyan

喧嘩 [kenka] n row (argument); 喧嘩する [kenka suru] v row (to argue)

けんか [kenka] n (争い) scrap (dispute)

見解 [kenkai] n view

健康 [kenkou] n health; 健康な [kenkou na] adj healthy; 健康診断 [kenkoushindan] n medical

謙虚 [kenkyo] 謙虚な [kenkyo na] adj humble, modest

研究者 [kenkyuusha] n researcher; 自然誌研究者 [shizenshi kenkyuusha] n naturalist

懸命 [kenmei] 懸命に [kenmei ni] adv hard

賢明 [kenmei] n wisdom; 賢明な [kenmei na] adj advisable

憲法 [kenpou] n constitution

権利 [kenri] n right

検査 [kensa] n check-up; 検査する [kensa suru] v inspect; 検査官 [kensakan] n inspector; 血液検査 [ketsueki kensa] n blood test; 身体検査 [shintai kensa] n physical; 塗沫検査 [tomatsu kensa] n smear test

検索 [kensaku] 検索エンジン [kensaku enjin] n search engine

検索する [kensaku suru] v search

検札 [kensatsu] 検札係 [kensatsugakari] n ticket inspector

建設 [kensetsu] n construction; 建設する [kensetsu suru] v construct; 建設現場 [kensetsu genba] n building site; 建設的な [kensetsuteki na] adj constructive

検死 [kenshi] 検死審問 [kenshi shinmon] n inquest

献身 [kenshin] n dedication; 献身的な [kenshinteki na] adj devoted

健全 [kenzen] 健全な [kenzen na] adj sound

毛織り [keori] 毛織りの [keori no] adj woollen

毛織物 [keorimono] 毛織物衣類 [keorimono irui] n woollens

潔白 [keppaku] 潔白な [keppaku na] adj innocent

蹴り [keri] n kick

蹴る [keru] v kick

今朝 [kesa] n this morning; 私は今朝から具合が悪いです [watashi wa kesa kara guai ga warui desu] I've been sick since this morning

ケシ [keshi] n poppy

消印 [keshiin] n postmark

化粧 [keshou] 洗面化粧用品 [senmen keshou youhin] n toiletries

化粧品 [keshouhin] n cosmetics

傑作 [kessaku] n masterpiece

決心 [kesshin] 決心がついていない [kesshin ga tsuite inai] adj undecided

決勝 [kesshou] n final

傑出 [kesshutsu] 傑出した [kesshutsu shita] adj outstanding

欠損 [kesson] n deficit

消す [kesu] v (消去) erase, (切る) turn out

ケトル [ketoru] n kettle

欠乏 [ketsubou] n lack

血液 [ketsueki] n blood; 血液検査 [ketsuekikensa] n blood test

血液型 [ketsuekigata] n blood group; 私の血液型はO型Rhプラスです [watashi no ketsueki-gata wa oo-gata aaru-eichi-purasu desu] My blood group is O positive

結合 [ketsugou] n conjunction, union; 結合する [ketsugou suru] v combine, unite

決意 [ketsui] n resolution

欠員 [ketsuin] n vacancy

結末 [ketsumatsu] n ending

結露 [ketsuro] n condensation

結論 [ketsuron] n conclusion; 結論を出す [ketsuron-o dasu] v conclude

決定 [kettei] n decision; 決定する [kettei suru] v decide; 決定的な [ketteiteki na] adj decisive; 決定的にする [ketteiteki ni suru]

v finalize; 有罪と決定する [yuuzai to kettei suru] *v* convict

欠点 [ketten] *n* drawback, shortcoming

血統の明らかな [kettou no akiraka na] *adj* pedigree

険しい [kewashii] *adj* steep; それはとても険しいですか? [sore wa totemo kewashii desu ka?] Is it very steep?

機 [ki] *n* device; 洗濯機 [sentakuki] *n* washing machine; 洗車機 [senshaki] *n* car wash; 脱水機 [dassuiki] *n* spin dryer; 盗難警報機 [tounankeihouki] *n* burglar alarm; 受信機 [jushinki] *n* receiver (electronic); 私が使えるファックス機はありますか? [watashi ga tsukaeru fakkusuki wa arimasu ka?] Is there a fax machine I can use?

木 [ki] *n* tree; 木管楽器 [mokkangakki] *n* woodwind; 添え木 [soegi] *n* splint

気 [ki] 気がついて [ki ga tsuite] *adj* aware; 気をもむ [ki-o momu] *v* fret

厳しい [kibishii] *adj* harsh, strict; 要求の厳しい [youkyuu no kibishii] *adj* demanding; 厳しく [kibishiku] *adv* strictly

希望 [kibou] *n* desire, hope; 希望が持てる [kibou ga moteru] *adj* hopeful; 希望する [kibou suru] *v* desire; 希望を持って [kibou-o motte] *adv* hopefully; 希望を失って [kibou-o ushinatte] *adj* hopeless

気分 [kibun] *n* mood; 気分のすぐれない [kibun no sugurenai] *adj* unwell; 私は気分が悪いのです [watashi wa kibun ga warui no desu] I feel ill

機知 [kichi] *n* wit; 機知に富んだ [kichi ni tonda] *adj* witty

気違い [kichigai] *n* nutter; 気違いのように [kichigai no youni] *adv* madly; 気違い男 [kichigai otoko] *n* madman

きちんと [kichin to] *adv* neatly; きちんとした [kichin to shita] *adj* decent, neat; きちんとした [kichin to shita] *adj* tidy

貴重品 [kichouhin] *npl* valuables; 貴重品はどこに置いておけますか? [kichouhin wa doko ni oite okemasu ka?] Where can I leave my valuables?; 私は貴重品を金庫に入れたいのですが [watashi wa kichouhin o kinko ni iretai no desu ga] I'd like to put my valuables in the safe

貴重な [kichou na] *adj* precious

気だてのよい [kidate no yoi] *adj* good-natured

消える [kieru] *v* vanish

寄付 [kifu] *n* contribution; 寄付する [kifu suru] *v* contribute, donate

着替える [kigaeru] *v* change, get changed; どこで着替えるのですか? [doko de kigaeru no desu ka?] Where do I change?

気がもめる [ki ga momeru] *v* worrying

喜劇 [kigeki] 喜劇俳優 [kigeki haiyuu] *n* comic

紀元 [kigen] 紀元前 [kigenzen] *prep* BC

機嫌 [kigen] 機嫌の悪い [kigen no warui] *adj* bad-tempered

期限 [kigen] 使用期限 [shiyou kigen] *n* expiry date; 期限が切れる [kigen ga kireru] *v* expire; 賞味期限 [shoumikigen] *n* best-before date; 販売期限 [hanbai kigen] *n* sell-by date; 締切り期限 [shimekiri kigen] *n* deadline

起源 [kigen] *n* origin

器具 [kigu] *n* apparatus, appliance, instrument; 暖房器具 [danbou kigu] *n* heater

木靴 [kigutsu] *n* clog

企業 [kigyou] 企業買収 [kigyou baishuu] *n* takeover; 多国籍企業 [takokuseki kigyou] *n* multinational

樹林 [ki hayashi] 土地の植物と樹木を見たいのですが [tochi no shokubutsu to jumoku o mitai no desu ga] We'd like to see local plants and trees

基本 [kihon] *n* basics; 基本的な [kihonteki na] *adj* basic; 基本的に [kihonteki ni] *adv* basically

キー [kii] *n* key (music/computer)

キーボード [kiiboudo] *n* keyboard

キーリング [kiiringu] *n* keyring

黄色 [kiiro] 黄色の [ki iro no] *adj* yellow

キーウィ [kiiui] *n* kiwi

キジ [kiji] n pheasant

生地 [kiji] n (料理) pastry

記事 [kiji] n article; トップ記事 [toppu kiji] n lead (position); 死亡記事 [shiboukiji] n obituary

机上 [kijou] 机上事務 [kijou jimu] n paperwork

基準 [kijun] n criterion

記述 [kijutsu] n description; 記述する [kijutsu suru] v describe

機会 [kikai] n opportunity

機械 [kikai] n machine; 乾燥機 [kansouki] n dryer; ジェット機 [jettoki] n jet; 機械の [kikai no] adj mechanical; 機械類 [kikairui] n machinery; 機械工 [kikaikou] n mechanic; 掘削機 [kussakuki] n digger; 食器洗い機 [shokkiaraiki] n dishwasher

企画 [kikaku] n project

機関 [kikan] n (組織) institution; 諜報機関 [chouhou kikan] n secret service; 公共交通機関 [koukyou koutsuu kikan] n public transport

期間 [kikan] n period; 持続期間 [jizoku kikan] n duration; 検疫期間 [ken'eki kikan] n quarantine; 試用期間 [shiyou kikan] n trial period

気管支 [kikan shi] 気管支炎 [kikanshien] n bronchitis

危険 [kiken] n danger, risk; 危険な [kiken na] adj dangerous, risky; 危険にさらす [kiken ni sarasu] v endanger, risk; なだれの危険はありますか? [nadare no kiken wa arimasu ka?] Is there a danger of avalanches?

飢饉 [kikin] n famine

聞き手 [kikite] n listener

聞き取る [kikitoru] v hear; ごめんなさい、聞き取れませんでした [gomen nasai, kikitoremasen deshita] Sorry, I didn't catch that

キック [kikku] フリーキック [furiikikku] n free kick

キックオフ [kikkuofu] n kick-off; キックオフする [kikkuofu suru] v kick off

聞こえる [kikoeru] v be audible; 私は耳が聞こえません [watashi wa mimi ga kikoemasen] I'm deaf

機構 [kikou] n (機械) mechanism

気候 [kikou] n climate; 気候変動 [kikou hendo] n climate change

帰航 [kikou] いつ帰航しますか? [itsu kikou shimasu ka?] When do we get back?

きく [kiku] 機転のきく [kiten no kiku] adj tactful

キク [kiku] n chrysanthemum

聞く [kiku] v hear, listen; 耳の聞こえない [mimi no kikoenai] adj deaf; ···を聞く [...-o kiku] v listen to

気前 [kimae] 気前のよい [kimae no yoi] adj generous

決りきる [kimarikiru] 決まりきった仕事 [kimarikitta shigoto] n routine

決まった [kimatta] 決まった相手がいる [kimatta aite ga iru] adj attached

きめ [kime] きめの粗い [kime no komakai] adj coarse

気味 [kimi] 気味の悪い [kimi no warui] adj spooky

黄身 [kimi] 卵の黄身 [tamago no kimi] n egg yolk

機密 [kimitsu] adj secret; 最高機密の [saikou kimitsu no] adj top-secret

気密 [kimitsu] 気密の [kimitsu no] adj airtight

気味悪い [kimiwarui] 薄気味悪い [usukimiwarui] adj creepy, spooky

気持ち [kimochi] n feeling

気むずかしい [kimuzukashii] adj grumpy

奇妙 [kimyou] 奇妙な [kimyou na] adj strange

金 [kin] n (金属) gold; 賠償金 [baishoukin] n compensation

緊張 [kinchou] n tension; 極度の緊張 [kyokudo no kinchou] n strain; 緊張させる [kinchou saseru] v strain; 緊張しきった [kinchou shikitta] adj uptight; 緊張した [kinchou shita] adj tense

禁煙 [kin'en] 禁煙の [kin'en no] adj

non-smoking; 禁煙の部屋がいいのですが [kin'en no heya ga ii no desu ga] I'd like a no smoking room; 禁煙エリアはありますか? [kin'en-eria wa arimasu ka?] Is there a non-smoking area?

記念 [kinen] n commemoration; 100周年記念祭 [hyakushuunen kinensai] n centenary; 記念碑 [kinenhi] n monument; 記念銘板 [kinen meiban] n plaque; 記念品 [kinenhin] n souvenir

記念日 [kinenbi] n anniversary; 結婚記念日 [kekkon kinenbi] n wedding anniversary

記念碑 [kinenhi] n memorial

禁煙席 [kin'enseki] 禁煙席が欲しいのですが [kin'en-seki ga hoshii no desu ga] I'd like a non-smoking seat; 禁煙席をお願いします [kin'en-seki o o-negai shimasu] Non-smoking, please

禁煙車 [kin'ensha] 禁煙車の席を予約したいのですが [kin'en-sha no seki o yoyaku shitai no desu ga] I want to book a seat in a non-smoking compartment

キングサイズ [kingusaizu] キングサイズのベッド [kingu saizu no beddo] n king-size bed

金魚 [kingyo] n goldfish

気に入る [ki ni iru] ···が気に入る [...ga ki ni iru] v fancy, like

近似 [kinji] 近似の [kinji no] adj approximate

禁じる [kinjiru] v forbid; 禁じられた [kinjirareta] adj forbidden

近所 [kinjo] n neighbourhood, vicinity; 近所の人 [kinjo no hito] n neighbour

金庫 [kinko] n safe; それを金庫に入れてください [sore o kinko ni irete kudasai] Put that in the safe, please; 私はジュエリーを金庫に入れたいのですが [watashi wa jueeri o kinko ni iretai no desu ga] I would like to put my jewellery in the safe; 私は貴重品を金庫に入れたいのですが [watashi wa kichouhin o kinko ni iretai no desu ga] I'd like to put my valuables in the safe; 金庫に入れたものがあります [kinko ni ireta mono ga arimasu] I have some things in the safe

筋骨 [kinkotsu] 筋骨たくましい [kinkotsu takumashii] adj muscular

緊急 [kinkyuu] n urgency; 緊急事態 [kinkyuujitai] n emergency; 緊急の [kinkyuu no] adj urgent; 緊急着陸 [kinkyu chakuriku] n emergency landing

金めっき [kinmekki] 金めっきの [kinmekki no] adj gold-plated

筋肉 [kinniku] n muscle

キノコ [kinoko] 毒キノコ [doku kinoko] n toadstool

昨日 [kinou, sakujitsu] adv yesterday

キンポウゲ [kinpouge] n buttercup

金製 [kinsei] 金製の [kinsei no] adj golden

金銭 [kinsen] n money

近接 [kinsetsu] n proximity; 近接した [kinsetsu shita] adj adjacent

禁止 [kinshi] n ban; 禁止された [kinshi sareta] adj banned, prohibited; 禁止する [kinshi suru] v ban, prohibit

近視 [kinshi] 近視の [kinshi no] adj near-sighted; 近視の [kinshi no] adj short-sighted; 私は近視です [watashi wa kinshi desu] I'm short-sighted

近親 [kinshin] 近親者 [kinshinsha] n next-of-kin

禁酒 [kinshu] 絶対禁酒の [zettai kinshu no] adj teetotal

絹 [kinu] n silk

金曜日 [kin-youbi] n Friday; 金曜日に [kinyoubi ni] on Friday; 十二月三十一日の金曜日に [juuni-gatsu sanjuuichi-nichi no kinyoubi ni] on Friday the thirty first of December

記入 [kinyuu] 記入する [kinyuu suru] v fill in, fill up; 借方に記入する [karikata ni kinyuu suru] v debit

金属 [kinzoku] n metal; 装飾用のぴかぴか光る金属片や糸 [soushoku you no pikapika hikaru kinzokuhen ya ito] n tinsel

記憶 [kioku] n memory; 記憶する [kioku suru] v memorize

気温 [kion] 気温は何度ですか? [kion wa nan-do desu ka?] What is the temperature?

キオスク [kiosuku] n kiosk

キッパー [kippaa] n kipper

切符 [kippu] n ticket; キャンセル待ちの切符 [kyanserumachi no kippu] n stand-by ticket; バスの切符 [basu no kippu] n bus ticket; 日帰り往復割引切符 [higaeri oufuku waribiki kippu] n day return; 片道切符 [katamichi kippu] n one-way ticket, single ticket; 往復切符 [oufuku kippu] n return ticket; 切符売場 [kippu uriba] n box office, ticket office; 今夜の切符を2枚ください [kon'ya no kippu o nimai kudasai] I'd like two tickets for tonight; 来週の金曜の切符を2枚ください [raishuu no kinyou no kippu o nimai kudasai] I'd like two tickets for next Friday; 片道切符はいくらですか？ [katamichi-kippu wa ikura desu ka?] How much is a single ticket?; ・・・行き往復切符2枚 [...iki oufuku-kippu nimai] two return tickets to...; 往復切符はいくらですか？ [oufuku-kippu wa ikura desu ka?] How much is a return ticket?; 切符はどこで買うのですか？ [kippu wa doko de kau no desu ka?] Where do I buy a ticket?; 切符はどこで買えますか？ [kippu wa doko de kaemasu ka?] Where can I get tickets?, Where can we get tickets?; 切符を2枚ください [kippu o nimai kudasai] I'd like two tickets, please; 切符をください [kippu o kudasai] A ticket, please; 切符をアップグレードしたいのですが [kippu o appugureedo shitai no desu ga] I want to upgrade my ticket; 切符を変更したいのですが [kippu o henkou shitai no desu ga] I want to change my ticket

キプロス [kipurosu] n Cyprus; キプロスの [kipurosu no] adj Cypriot

キプロス人 [kipurosujin] n Cypriot (person)

嫌い [kirai] adj distasteful; 私は・・・が大嫌いです [watashi wa ... ga daikirai desu] I hate...

嫌う [kirau] v dislike; ひどく嫌う [hidoku kirau] v loathe

きれい [kirei] adj clean; 部屋がきれいではありません [heya ga kirei de wa arimasen] The room isn't clean

きれいな [kirei na] adj pretty

きれいに [kirei ni] adv prettily

切れる [kireru] v cut; 棒切れ [bou kire] n stick; 期限が切れる [kigen ga kireru] v expire; ガソリンが切れてしまいました [gasorin ga kirete shimaimashita] I've run out of petrol, The petrol has run out; 電話が切れました [denwa ga kiremashita] I've been cut off

霧 [kiri] n fog; 霧の立ちこめた [kiri no tachikometa] adj foggy

切り離す [kirihanasu] v cut off

キリン [kirin] n giraffe

切り抜き [kirinuki] n cutting

切下げる [kirisageru] v devalue; 平価切下げ [heikakirisage] n devaluation

霧雨 [kirisame] n drizzle

キリスト [kirisuto] n Christ

キリスト教 [kirisutokyou] n Christianity; キリスト教の [kirisutokyou no] adj Christian; キリスト教徒 [kirisutokyouto] n Christian

伐り倒す [kiritaosu] v cut down

起立 [kiritsu] 起立する [kiritsu suru] v stand up

規律 [kiritsu] n discipline

切り分ける [kiriwakeru] v cut up

キロ [kiro] n kilo; 毎時・・・キロ [maiji ... kiro] adv km/h

記録 [kiroku] n record; テープに記録する [teepu ni kiroku suru] v tape; 記録係 [kirokugakari] n recorder (scribe); 記録する [kiroku suru] v record

キロメートル [kiromeetoru] n kilometre

着る [kiru] v put on (clothes); 服を着た [fuku-o kita] adj dressed; 服を着る [fuku o kiru] v dress; 何を着ればよいですか？ [nani o kireba yoi desu ka?] What should I wear?

切る [kiru] v cut, switch off; 薄く切る [usuku kiru] v slice; 厚く切ったもの [atsuku kitta mono] n chunk; あまりたくさん切らないでください [amari takusan kiranaide kudasai] Don't cut too much off

キルギスタン [kirugisutan] n Kyrgyzstan

キルト [kiruto] n (タータン) kilt, (ベッドの上掛け) quilt; キルトの掛け布団 [kiruto no kakebuton] n duvet

既製 [kisei] 既製の [kisei no] adj bought

規制 [kisei] n regulation

奇跡 [kiseki] n miracle

季節 [kisetsu] n season; 季節の [kisetsu no] adj seasonal

記者 [kisha] 記者会見 [kishakaiken] n press conference; 取材記者 [shuzai kisha] n reporter

希釈 [kishaku] 希釈した [kishaku shita] adj diluted; 希釈する [kishaku suru] v dilute

岸 [kishi] n shore

きしる [kishiru] v squeak

騎手 [kishu] 競馬騎手 [keiba kishu] n jockey

寄宿 [kishuku] 寄宿生 [kishukusei] n boarder; 寄宿学校 [kishuku gakkou] n boarding school

起訴 [kiso] 起訴する [kiso suru] v prosecute

基礎 [kiso] n basis, foundations

規則 [kisoku] n regulation, rule; 交通規則集 [koutsuu kisokushuu] n Highway Code

キス [kisu] n (口) kiss; キスする [kisu suru] v kiss

北 [kita] n north; 北に [kita ni] adv north; 北の [kita no] adj north, northern

北アフリカ [kita afurika] n North Africa; 北アフリカ人 [kita afurikajin] n North African; 北アフリカの [kita afurika no] adj North African

北アイルランド [kita airurando] n Northern Ireland

北アメリカ [kita amerika] n North America; 北アメリカ人 [kita amerikajin] n North American; 北アメリカの [kita amerika no] adj North American

北朝鮮 [kita chousen] n North Korea

期待 [kitai] 期待する [kitai suru] v expect

帰宅 [kitaku] 好きな時間に帰宅していいですよ [suki na jikan ni kitaku shite ii desu yo] Come home whenever you like; 午後11時までに帰宅してください [gogo juuichi-ji made ni kitaku shite kudasai] Please come home by 11p.m.

北大西洋条約機構 [kitataiseiyou jouyaku kikou] n NATO

北行き [kitayuki] 北行きの [kitayuki no] adj northbound

機転 [kiten] n tact; 機転のきかない [kiten no kikanai] adj tactless; 機転のきく [kiten no kiku] adj tactful

喫煙 [kitsuen] n smoking; 非喫煙者 [hikitsuensha] n non-smoker; 喫煙者 [kitsuensha] n smoker; 喫煙できる部屋がいいのですが [kitsuen dekiru heya ga ii no desu ga] I'd like a smoking room; 喫煙エリアの席が欲しいのですが [kitsuen-eria no seki ga hoshii no desu ga] I'd like a seat in the smoking area

喫煙席 [kitsuenseki] n smoking seat; 喫煙席をお願いします [kitsuen-seki o o-negai shimasu] Smoking, please

キツネ [kitsune] n fox

切手 [kitte] n stamp; どこで切手を買えますか? [doko de kitte o kaemasu ka?] Where can I buy stamps?; ・・・あての郵便はがき四枚分の切手をもらえますか? [...ate no yuubin-hagaki yonmai-bun no kitte o moraemasu ka?] Can I have stamps for four postcards to...; 切手を売っていますか? [kitte o utte imasu ka?] Do you sell stamps?; 切手を売っている一番近い店はどこですか? [kitte o utte iru ichiban chikai mise wa doko desu ka?] Where is the nearest shop which sells stamps?

キット [kitto] 修理キット [shuuri kitto] n repair kit; ハンズフリーキット [hanzu furii kitto] n hands-free kit; 救急処置キット [kyuukyuu shochi kitto] n first-aid kit

気をつける [ki o tsukeru] v be careful

器用 [kiyou] 不器用な [bukiyou na] adj awkward

気絶 [kizetsu] 気絶する [kizetsu suru] v faint; 彼女は気絶しました [kanojo wa kizetsu shimashita] She has fainted

傷 [kizu] n wound; 刺し傷 [sashi kizu] n sting

きず [kizu] *n* (損傷) flaw

傷痕 [kizuato] *n* scar

気づく [kizuku] *v* notice

傷つける [kizutsukeru] *v* hurt, injure, wound

傷つく [kizutsuku] 傷ついた [kizutsuita] *adj* hurt, injured; 傷つきやすい [kizutsukiyasui] *adj* sensitive, vulnerable

子 [ko] 継子 [mamako] *n* stepson; 馬の子 [uma no ko] *n* foal; 野獣の子 [yajuu no ko] *n* cub; 子会社 [kogaisha] *n* subsidiary; 子守り [komori] *n* babysitting

個別 [kobetsu] 個別指導 [kobetsu shidou] *n* tutorial; 個別指導教官 [kobetsu shidou kyoukan] *n* tutor

小人 [kobito] *n* person of small stature

こぼす [kobosu] *v* (漏らす) spill

こぶし [kobushi] 握りこぶし [nigiri kobushi] *n* fist

誇張 [kochou] *n* exaggeration

孤独 [kodoku] *n* loneliness; 孤独の [kodoku no] *adj* lonely, lonesome

子供 [kodomo] *n* child, kid; 子供時代 [kodomo jidai] *n* childhood; 子供用プール [kodomoyou puuru] *n* paddling pool; 子供部屋 [kodomobeya] *n* nursery; 一人前を子供用の量にできますか? [ichinin-mae o kodomo-you no ryou ni dekimasu ka?] Do you have children's portions?; それは子供にも安全ですか? [sore wa kodomo ni mo anzen desu ka?] Is it safe for children?; それは子供に安全ですか? [sore wa kodomo ni anzen desu ka?] Is it safe for children?; 私には子供が一人います [watashi ni wa kodomo ga hitori imasu] I have a child; 私には子供が三人います [watashi ni wa kodomo ga sannin imasu] I have three children; 私には子供がいません [watashi ni wa kodomo ga imasen] I don't have any children; 私の子供が病気です [watashi no kodomo ga byouki desu] My child is ill; 子供ができることは何がありますか? [kodomo ga dekiru koto wa nani ga arimasu ka?] What is there for children to do?; 子供たちが車の中にいます [kodomo-tachi ga kuruma no naka ni imasu] My children are in the car; 子供を連れて行っても大丈夫ですか? [kodomo o tsurete itte mo daijoubu desu ka?] Is it okay to take children?

子供じみた [kodomojimita] *v* childish

子供用 [kodomoyou] 子供用のプールはありますか? [kodomo-you no puuru wa arimasu ka?] Is there a children's pool?

声 [koe] *n* voice; 泣き叫ぶ声 [nakisakebu koe] *n* cry; 笑い声 [waraigoe] *n* laughter; 声を出して [koe o dashite] *adv* aloud

超える [koeru] *v* exceed; 度を超えた [do-o koeta] *adj* excessive

古風 [kofuu] 古風で趣のある [kofuu de omomuki no aru] *adj* quaint

小型 [kogata] 小型タクシー [kogata takushii] *n* minicab

こげる [kogeru] *v* row (boat); どこに行けばカヌーをこげますか? [doko ni ikeba kanuu o kogemasu ka?] Where can we go canoeing?; どこに行けばボートをこげますか? [doko ni ikeba booto o kogemasu ka] Where can we go rowing?

小切手 [kogitte] *n* cheque; 旅行者用小切手 [ryokousha you kogitte] *n* traveller's cheque; 白地小切手 [shiraji kogitte] *n* blank cheque; 小切手帳 [kogittechou] *n* chequebook; 小切手で支払えますか? [kogitte de shiharaemasu ka?] Can I pay by cheque?; 小切手を現金化してください [kogitte o genkinka shite kudasai] I want to cash a cheque, please; 小切手を現金化できますか? [kogitte o genkinka dekimasu ka?] Can I cash a cheque?

凍える [kogoeru] *v* be cold; 凍えるほどに寒いです [kogoeru hodo ni samui desu] It's freezing cold

小言 [kogoto] がみがみ小言を言う [gamigami kogoto-o iu] *v* nag

漕ぐ [kogu] *v* row (in boat); カヌー漕ぎ [kanuu kogi] *n* canoeing; パドルで漕ぐ [padoru de kogu] *v* paddle; ボートを漕ぐこと [booto-o kogu koto] *n* rowing; 漕ぎ舟 [kogibune] *n* rowing boat

琥珀 [kohaku] 琥珀色 [kohaku iro] *n* amber

子羊 [kohitsuji] *n* lamb

意 [koi] 故意に [koi ni] *adv* deliberately; 故意に破壊する [koi ni hakai suru] *v* sabotage, vandalize; 故意の [koi no] *adj* deliberate; 故意の破壊 [koi no hakai] *n* sabotage; 故意でない [koi de nai] *adj* unintentional

イン [koin] *n* coin; 電話に使うコインをいくらかお願いします [denwa ni tsukau koin o ikura ka o-negai shimasu] I'd like some coins for the phone, please

コインランドリー [koinrandorii] この近くにコインランドリーはありますか? [kono chikaku ni koin-randorii wa arimasu ka?] Is there a launderette near here?

コインロッカー [koinrokkaa] *n* left-luggage locker; コインロッカーはありますか? [koin-rokkaa wa arimasu ka?] Are there any luggage lockers?

子犬 [koinu] *n* puppy

小石 [koishi] *n* pebble

恋をもてあそぶ [koi o moteasobu] *v* flirt

孤児 [koji] *n* orphan

乞食 [kojiki] *n* beggar

個人 [kojin] *n* individual; 個人にかかわらない [kojin ni kakawaranai] *adj* impersonal; 個人の所有物 [kojin no shoyuubutsu] *n* private property; 個人情報泥棒 [kojin jouhou dorobou] *n* identity theft; 個人的な [kojinteki na] *adj* personal, private; 個人秘書 [kojin hisho] *n* personal assistant, PA; あなたと個人的にお話ができますか? [anata to kojin-teki ni o-hanashi ga dekimasu ka?] Can I speak to you in private?; それは私の個人用です [sore wa watashi no kojin-you desu] It is for my own personal use

コカイン [kokain] *n* cocaine

コカコーラ® [kokakoora] *n* Coke®

コケ [koke] *n* moss

こき使う [kokitsukau] *v* boss around

国歌 [kokka] *n* anthem, national anthem

国家 [kokka] *n* nation; 自治国家 [jichi kokka] *n* autonomy; 国家主義 [kokkashugi] *n* nationalism; 国家主義者 [kokkashugisha] *n* nationalist

告解 [kokkai] 告解火曜日 [kokkai kayoubi]

n Shrove Tuesday

骨格 [kokkaku] *n* skeleton

コックピット [kokkupitto] *n* cockpit

国境 [kokkyou] *n* frontier

ここ [koko] ここに [koko ni] *adv* here

個々 [koko] 個々の [koko no] *adj* individual

ココア [kokoa] *n* cocoa

心地 [kokochi] 居心地のよい [igokochi no yoi] *adj* cosy; 心地よくない [kokochi yokunai] *adj* uncomfortable

ココナツ [kokonatsu] *n* coconut

心 [kokoro] *n* mind, heart; 心の広い [kokoro no hiroi] *adj* broad-minded; 心から [kokoro kara] *adv* sincerely; 心からの [kokoro kara no] *adj* sincere

試み [kokoromi] *n* attempt, trial

試みる [kokoromiru] *v* attempt

心を強くとらえる [kokoro o tsuyoku toraeru] *adj* gripping

快い [kokoroyoi] *adj* sweet *(pleasing)*

黒板 [kokuban] *n* blackboard

国営 [kokuei] 国営にする [kokuei ni suru] *v* nationalize

克服 [kokufuku] 克服する [kokufuku suru] *v* overcome

国外 [kokugai] 国外退去させる [kokugai taikyo saseru] *v* deport

穀草 [koku kusa] *n* cereal crop

国民 [kokumin] *n* nation; 国民の [kokumin no] *adj* national

国内 [kokunai] 国内の [kokunai no] *adj* domestic

国立 [kokuritsu] 国立公園 [kokuritsu kouen] *n* national park

穀類 [kokurui] *n* cereal

国際 [kokusai] 国際的な [kokusaiteki na] *adj* international; どこで国際電話をかけられますか? [doko de kokusai-denwa o kakeraremasu ka?] Where can I make an international phone call?; ここから国際電話をかけられますか? [koko kara kokusai-denwa o kakeraremasu ka?] Can I phone internationally from here?; 国際電話用のテレホンカードをください

[kokusai-denwa-you no terehon-kaado o kudasai] An international phone card, please; 国際電話用のテレホンカードを売っていますか? [kokusai-denwa-kaado o utte imasu ka?] Do you sell international phone cards?

国際連合 [kokusairengou] n United Nations

国勢 [kokusei] 国勢調査 [kokuzeichousa] n census

国籍 [kokuseki] n nationality

告訴 [kokuso] n charge (accusation); 告訴する [kokuso suru] v charge (accuse)

穀粒 [kokutsubu] n grain

顧客 [kokyaku] n customer

呼吸 [kokyuu] n breathing

コマーシャル [komaasharu] n commercial; コマーシャルの時間 [komaasharu no jikan] n commercial break

コマドリ [komadori] n robin

細かい [komakai] 細かく調べる [komakaku shiraberu] v scan

細かいお金 [komakai okane] n small change; 細かいお金がありません [komakai o-kane ga arimasen] I don't have anything smaller

鼓膜 [komaku] n eardrum

困らせる [komaraseru] adj puzzling

困る [komaru] 困った [komatta] adj puzzled

米 [kome] n rice

コメディアン [komedian] n comedian

コメディー [komedii] n comedy

小道 [komichi] n path, track; 歩行者用の小道 [hokoushayou no komichi] n footpath

込み合う [komi gou ru] 込み合った [komiatta] adj crowded

小文字 [komoji] すべて小文字です [subete ko-moji desu] all lower case

顧問医 [komon-i] n consultant (adviser)

子守 [komori] n baby-sitter; 子守歌 [komoriuta] n lullaby

こもる [komoru] 愛情のこもった [aijou no

komotta] adj affectionate

小麦 [komugi] n wheat; 小麦アレルギー [komugi arerugii] n wheat intolerance

小麦粉 [komugiko] n flour

コミュニケーション [komyunikeeshon] n communication

根 [kon] n root

粉 [kona] n powder; カレー粉 [kareeko] n curry powder; パン粉 [panko] n breadcrumbs, crumb; 粉石鹸 [kona sekken] n soap powder; 粉砂糖 [konazatou] n icing sugar

コンバーター [konbaataa] 触媒コンバーター [shokubai konbaataa] n catalytic converter

コンバーティブル [konbaateiburu] n convertible

今晩 [konban] n tonight; 今晩どこにいらっしゃりたいですか? [konban doko ni irassharitai desu ka?] Where would you like to go tonight?; 今晩のご予定は? [konban no go-yotei wa?] What are you doing this evening?; 今晩のチケットを2枚お願いします [konban no chiketto o nimai o-negai shimasu] Two tickets for tonight, please; 今晩部屋はありますか? [konban heya wa arimasu ka?] Do you have a room for tonight?; 今晩八時に四人用のテーブルを予約したいのですが [konban hachi-ji ni yonin-you no teeburu o yoyaku shitai no desu ga] I'd like to book a table for four people for tonight at eight o'clock

こんばんは [konban wa] Good evening

コンベヤベルト [konbeyaberuto] n conveyor belt

棍棒 [konbou] n club (weapon)

コンチェルト [koncheruto] n concerto

昆虫 [konchuu] n insect

コンディショナー [kondeishonaa] n conditioner; コンディショナーを売っていますか? [kondishonaa o utte imasu ka?] Do you sell conditioner?

混同 [kondou] n confusion, mix-up; 混同する [kondou suru] v mix up

コンドーム [kondoumu] n condom

子猫 [koneko] n kitten

コンファレンスセンター
[konfarensusentaa] コンファレンスセン
ターまでお願いします [konfarensu-sentaa
made o-negai shimasu] Please take me to
the conference centre

懇願 [kangan] n appeal; 懇願する [kangan
suru] v appeal

コンゴ [kongo] n Congo

混合 [kongou] n mixture; 混合物
[kongoubutsu] n mix, mixture

混合する [kongou suru] 混合した
[kongou shita] adj mixed

婚姻 [kon'in] 婚姻関係の有無 [kon'in
kankei no umu] n marital status

婚活 [konkatsu] n search for a marriage
partner

コンクリート [konkuriito] n concrete

コンマ [konma] n comma

困難 [konnan] n difficulty, trouble; 困難な
[konnan na] adj difficult, hard (difficult)

こんにちは [konnichi wa] excl hello,
good afternoon

この [kono] adj this; このバスは・・・へ行き
ますか? [kono basu wa ... e ikimasu ka?]
Does this bus go to...?

このごろは [konogoro wa] adv nowadays

好ましい [konomashii] 好ましくない
[konomashikunai] adj unfavourable

好み [konomi] n preference

好む [konomu] v like; ・・・の方を好む [...no
hou o konomu] v prefer

好んで [kononde] adv preferably

コンパートメント [konpaatomento] n
compartment

コンパクトディスク [konpakuto
disuku] n compact disc

コンパス [konpasu] n compass

コンピュー ター [konpyuu taa] コンピュ
ーターゲーム [konpyuutaa geemu] n
computer game

コンピューター [konpyuutaa] n
computer; コンピューター科学
[konpyuutaa kagaku] n computer science;

あなたのコンピューターをお借りできます
か? [anata no konpyuutaa o o-kari
dekimasu ka?] May I use your computer?;
このコンピューターでCDを作成できます
か? [kono konpyuutaa de shii-dii o sakusei
dekimasu ka?] Can I make CDs at this
computer?; 私のコンピューターがフリーズ
しました [watashi no konpyuutaa ga furiizu
shimashita] My computer has frozen

コンピューター室 [konpyuutaa shitsu]
n computer room

混乱 [konran] 混乱させる [konran saseru]
v disrupt; 混乱状態 [konranjoutai] n
muddle; 大混乱 [daikonran] n chaos; 大
混乱した [daikonran shita] adj chaotic

コンサーバトリー [konsaabatorii] n
conservatory

コンサート [konsaato] n concert; 何かよ
いコンサートがありますか? [nani ka yoi
konsaato ga arimasu ka?] Are there any
good concerts on?; どこでそのコンサート
のチケットを買えますか? [doko de sono
konsaato no chiketto o kaemasu ka?]
Where can I buy tickets for the concert?

コンサートホール [konsaatohooru] n
concert hall; コンサートホールでは今晩何
をやっていますか? [konsaato-hooru de
wa konban nani o yatte imasu ka?] What's
on tonight at the concert hall?

コンセンサス [konsensasu] n consensus

コンセント [konsento] n socket; 電気カミ
ソリのコンセントはどこですか?
[denki-kamisori no konsento wa doko desu
ka?] Where is the socket for my electric
razor?

今週 [konshuu] 今週の土曜日に [konshuu
no doyoubi ni] this Saturday

コンソール [konsooru] ゲームコンソール
[geemu konsooru] n games console

昏睡 [konsui] n coma

コンタクトレンズ [kontakutorenzu] n
contact lenses; コンタクトレンズの洗浄液
[kontakuto-renzu no senjou-eki] cleansing
solution for contact lenses; 私はコンタク
トレンズをはめています [watashi wa
kontakuto-renzu o hamete imasu] I wear
contact lenses

コントラバス [kontorabasu] *n* double bass

困惑 [konwaku] *n* embarassment; 困惑させる [konwaku saseru] *adj* confuse, confusing; 困惑した [konwaku shita] *adj* baffled, bewildered

今夜 [konya] *adv* tonight; 今夜は寒くなりますか? [kon'ya wa samuku narimasu ka?] Will it be cold tonight?; 今夜の切符を2枚ください [kon'ya no kippu o nimai kudasai] I'd like two tickets for tonight

婚約 [konyaku] 婚約中の男性 [kon'yakuchuu no dansei] *n* fiancé; 婚約中の女性 [kon'yakuchuu no josei] *n* fiancée; 婚約している [konyaku shiteiru] *adj* engaged; 婚約指輪 [konyaku yubiwa] *n* engagement ring

コーデュロイ [koodeyuroi] *n* corduroy

コード [koodo] 電気コード [denki koodo] *n* flex; 延長コード [enchoukoodo] *n* extension cable

コードレス [koodoresu] コードレスの [koodoresu no] *adj* cordless

コーンフラワー [koonfurawaa] *n* cornflour

コオロギ [koorogi] *n* cricket (insect)

コール [kooru] コールセンター [kooru sentaa] *n* call centre

コーシャ [koosha] コーシャ料理はありますか? [koosha-ryouri wa arimasu ka?] Do you have kosher dishes?

コピー [kopii] *n* (複写) photocopy; コピーする [kopii suru] *v* photocopy; どこでコピーを取ってもらえますか? [doko de kopii o totte moraemasu ka?] Where can I get some photocopying done?; このコピーをお願いします [kono kopii o o-negai shimasu] I'd like a photocopy of this, please; このカラーコピーをお願いします [kono karaa-kopii o o-negai shimasu] I'd like a colour photocopy of this, please

コピー機 [kopiiki] *n* photocopier

コップ [koppu] *n* cup, glass; きれいなコップをもらえますか? [kirei na koppu o moraemasu ka?] Can I have a clean glass, please?; コップ一杯の水 [koppu ippai no mizu] a glass of water

これ [kore] *pron* this; これには何が入っていますか? [kore ni wa nani ga haitte imasu ka?] What is in this?; 私はこれをいただきます [watashi wa kore o itadakimasu] I'll have this

コレクション [korekushon] *n* collection

コレクトコール [korekutokooru] コレクトコールをかけたいのですが [korekuto-kooru o kaketai no desu ga] I'd like to make a reverse charge call

これら [korera] *pron* these; これらの [korera no] *adj* these

コレステロール [koresuterouru] *n* cholesterol

コリアンダー [koriandaa] *n* coriander

コリー [korii] *n* collie

孤立 [koritsu] 孤立した [koritsu shita] *adj* isolated

ころぶ [korobu] 彼女はころびました [kanojo wa korobimashita] She fell

転がる [korogaru] *v* roll; 転がり [korogari] *n* roll

ころも [koromo] (料理用の)ころも [(ryouriyou no) koromo] *n* batter

コロン [koron] *n* colon

コロンビア [koronbia] *n* Colombia

コロンビア人 [koronbiajin] *n* Colombian (person)

コロンビアの [koronbia no] *adj* Colombian

殺す [korosu] *v* kill

コルク [koruku] *n* cork; コルク栓抜き [koruku sennuki] *n* corkscrew

コルネット [korunetto] *n* cornet

個性 [kosei] *n* personality

腰 [koshi] *n* hip

腰掛け [koshikake] 窓下の腰掛け [mado shita no koshikake] *n* window seat

故障 [koshou] *n* breakdown; 故障した [koshou shita] *adj* broken down; 故障する [koshou suru] *v* break down; 故障警告灯 [koshou keikokutou] *n* hazard warning lights; 故障時緊急修理サービスを呼んで

ください [koshou-ji kinkyuu-shuuri-saabisu o yonde kudasai] Call the breakdown service, please

コショウ [koshou] n pepper

コショウひき [koshou hiki] n peppermill

コショウソウ [koshousou] n cress

コソボ [kosobo] n Kosovo

子育て [kosodate] 片親で子育てをする人 [kataoya de kosodate-o suru hito] n single parent; 私は子育てをしています [watashi wa kosodate o shite imasu] I'm a full-time parent

骨折 [kossetsu] n fracture

こする [kosuru] v rub

コスタリカ [kosutarika] n Costa Rica

コスト [kosuto] n cost

答え [kotae] n answer; 否定の答え [hitei no kotae] n negative

答える [kotaeru] v answer

固体 [kotai] 固体の [kotai no] adj solid

固定 [kotei] 固定した [kotei shita] adj fixed; 固定する [kotei suru] v fix

こと [koto] 電話をかけること [denwa-o kakeru koto] n phonecall

言葉 [kotoba] n word, speech

事柄 [kotogara] n affair

異なる [kotonaru] v differ; 意見が異なる [iken ga kotonaru] v disagree

ことによると [koto ni yoru to] adv perhaps, possibly

今年 [kotoshi] n this year

ことわざ [kotowaza] n proverb, saying

骨盤 [kotsuban] n pelvis

小粒の種なし [kotsubu no tane nashi] 小粒の種なし干しブドウ [kotsubu no tanenashi hoshibudou] n currant

骨髄 [kotsuzui] n marrow

骨董 [kottou] 骨董屋 [kottou ya] n antique shop; 骨董品 [kottouhin] n antique

抗 [kou] 抗ヒスタミン剤 [kouhisutaminzai] n antihistamine; 抗生物質 [kousei busshitsu] n antibiotic; 抗鬱剤 [kouutsuzai] n antidepressant

校 [kou] 中学校 [chuugakkou] n secondary school

腱 [kou] n tendon

考案 [kouan] 考案する [kouan suru] v devise

酵母菌 [koubokin] n yeast

鉱物 [koubutsu] n mineral; 鉱物の [koubutsu no] adj mineral

紅茶 [koucha] n (black) tea; 紅茶をくださ い [koucha o kudasai] A tea, please; 紅茶 をもう一杯いただけますか? [koucha o mou ippai itadakemasu ka?] Could we have another cup of tea, please?

コーチ [kouchi] n coach, trainer

校長 [kouchou] n headteacher, principal

甲冑 [kouchuu] n armour

高度 [koudo] n (海抜) altitude

購読 [koudoku] 定期購読 [teiki koudoku] n subscription

行動 [koudou] 行動する [koudou suru] v act

公営 [kouei] 公営住宅 [koueijuutaku] n council house

光栄 [kouei] n honour; お会いできて光栄 でした [o-ai dekite kouei deshita] It was a pleasure to meet you

後援 [kouen] n sponsorship; 後援者 [kouensha] n sponsor; 後援者となる [kouensha to naru] v sponsor

公演 [kouen] n performance; 公演は何時 に終わりますか? [kouen wa nan-ji ni owarimarimasu ka?] When does the performance end?; 公演は何時に始まりま すか? [kouen wa nan-ji ni hajimarimasu ka?] When does the performance begin?; 公演時間はどのくらいの長さですか? [kouen-jikan wa dono kurai no nagasa desu ka?] How long does the performance last?

公園 [kouen] n park; 国立公園 [kokuritsu kouen] n national park

公布 [koufu] 公布する [koufu suru] v issue

降伏 [koufuku] 降伏する [koufuku suru] v surrender

幸福 [koufuku] n happiness; 幸福な

[koufuku na] adj happy; 幸福に [koufuku ni] adv happily

興奮 [koufun] 興奮させる [koufun saseru] adj exciting; 興奮した [koufun shita] adj excited

郊外 [kougai] n outskirts, suburb; 郊外の [kougai no] adj suburban; 郊外の大型スーパー [kougai no ougata suupaa] n hypermarket

工学 [kougaku] n engineering; 電子工学 [denshikougaku] n electronics

攻撃 [kougeki] n attack; テロリストによる攻撃 [terorisuto niyoru kougeki] n terrorist attack; 攻撃する [kougeki suru] v attack; 攻撃的な [kougekiteki na] adj aggressive

抗議 [kougi] n protest; 抗議する [kougi suru] v protest

講義 [kougi] n lecture; 講義をする [kougi-o suru] v lecture

交互 [kougo] 交互の [kougo no] adj alternate

鉱業 [kougyou] n mining

工業 [kougyou] 工業団地 [kougyoudanchi] n industrial estate

荒廃 [kouhai] n ruin; 荒廃させる [kouhai saseru] v ruin

口辺ヘルペス [kouhenherupesu] n cold sore

コーヒー [kouhii] n coffee; コーヒーテーブル [koohii teeburu] n coffee table; コーヒーポット [koohiipotto] n coffeepot; コーヒー豆 [koohiimame] n coffee bean; カフェイン抜きのコーヒー [kafein nuki no koohii] n decaffeinated coffee; ブラックコーヒー [burakku koohii] n black coffee; コーヒーをください [koohii o kudasai] A coffee, please; コーヒーをもう一杯いただけますか? [koohii o mou ippai itadakemasu ka?] Could we have another cup of coffee, please?; ラウンジでコーヒーをいただけますか? [raunji de koohii o itadakemasu ka?] Could we have coffee in the lounge?; ミルク入りコーヒーをください [miruku-iri koohii o kudasai] A white coffee, please; 挽きたてのコーヒーはありますか? [hikitate no koohii wa arimasu ka?] Have you got fresh coffee?; 本物のコ

ーヒーはありますか? [honmono no koohii wa arimasu ka?] Have you got real coffee?

候補 [kouho] 選抜候補者リスト [senbatsu kouhosha risuto] n shortlist; 候補者 [kouhosha] n candidate

広報 [kouhou] n public relations

後方 [kouhou] 後方に [kouhou ni] adv backwards

行為 [koui] n act; スパイ行為 [supai koui] n espionage, spying; 破壊行為 [hakai koui] n vandalism; 儀礼的行為 [gireiteki koui] n formality

更衣室 [kouishitsu] n changing room

工事 [kouji] 道路工事 [dourokouji] n roadworks

口実 [koujitsu] n pretext

工場 [koujou] n factory; 製造工場 [seizou koujou] n plant (site/equipment); 私は工場で働いています [watashi wa koujou de hataraite imasu] I work in a factory

口述 [koujutsu] n dictation

硬貨 [kouka] n coin

高価 [kouka] 高価な [kouka na] adj expensive, valuable

効果 [kouka] 効果的な [koukateki na] adj effective; 効果的に [koukateki ni] adv effectively

狡猾 [koukai] 狡猾な [koukatsu na] adj cunning

紅海 [koukai] n Red Sea

航海 [koukai] n sailing; 航海する [koukai suru] v sail

後悔 [koukai] n regret; 後悔する [koukai suru] v regret

交換 [koukan] 交換する [koukan suru] v swap; これを交換したいのですが [kore o koukan shitai no desu ga] I'd like to exchange this; ···を交換できますか? [...o koukan dekimasu ka?] Can you replace...?

高価な [kouka na] adj dear (expensive)

交換台 [koukandai] 電話交換台 [denwa koukandai] n switchboard

後継 [koukei] 後継者 [koukeisha] n successor

考古学 [koukogaku] n archaeology; 考古学者 [koukogakusha] n archaeologist

広告 [koukoku] n ad, advert, advertisement; 広告する [koukoku suru] v advertise; 広告すること [koukoku suru koto] n advertising; 分類広告 [bunruikoukoku] n small ads

甲骨 [koukotsu] 肩甲骨 [kenkoukotsu] n shoulder blade

航空 [koukuu] 航空会社 [koukuu gaisha] n airline; 航空機 [koukuuki] n aircraft; 航空管制官 [koukuu kanseikan] n air-traffic controller

航空便 [koukuubin] n airmail; 航空便でどのくらいの日数がかかりますか? [koukuu-bin de dono kurai no nissuu ga kakarimasu ka?] How long will it take by air?

公共 [koukyou] 公共職業安定所 [koukyoushokugyou anteisho] n job centre

交響曲 [koukyoukyoku] n symphony

高慢ちき [koumanchiki] 高慢ちきな [koumanchiki na] adj stuck-up

公民権 [kouminken] n civil rights

項目 [koumoku] n item

コウモリ [koumori] n (動物) bat (mammal)

公務員 [koumuin] n civil servant

被る [koumuru] v suffer

コーンフレーク [kounfureeku] n cornflakes

購入 [kounyuu] 購入する [kounyuu suru] v purchase

行楽 [kouraku] 行楽地 [kourakuchi] n resort

コーラン [kouran] n Koran

高齢 [kourei] 高齢者 [koureisha] n senior citizen

氷 [koori] n ice; 路面の薄い透明な氷 [romen no usui toumei na kouri] n black ice; 氷を入れてください [koori o irete kudsai] With ice, please

小売 [kouri] 小売価格 [kourikakaku] n retail price; 小売業者 [kourigyousha] n retailer

小売り [kouri] n retail; 小売りする [kouri suru] v retail

効率 [kouritsu] 効率の悪い [kouritsu no warui] adj inefficient; 効率的な [kouritsuteki na] adj efficient

口論 [kouron] n argument, quarrel; つまらないことで口論する [tsumaranai koto de kouron suru] v squabble; 口論する [kouron suru] v quarrel

凍る [kouru] v freeze; 凍った [koutta] adj frozen; 凍るような [kouru you na] adj freezing

コールスロー [kourusurou] n coleslaw

考慮 [kouryo] •••を考慮すると [...-o kouryo suru to] prep considering

荒涼 [kouryou] 荒涼とした [kouryou to shita] adj bleak

拘留 [kouryuu] n detention

交差 [kousa] 環状交差路 [kanjou kousaro] n roundabout

交際 [kousai] ごめんなさい、交際している人がいます [gomen nasai, kousai shite iru hito ga imasu] Sorry, I'm in a relationship

交差路 [kousaro] n crossroads

交差点 [kousaten] n crossing, junction; 次の交差点で右に進んでください [tsugi no kousaten de migi ni susunde kudasai] Go right at the next junction; 次の交差点で左に進んでください [tsugi no kousaten de hidari ni susunde kudasai] Go left at the next junction

構成 [kousei] n composition; 構成している [kousei shite iru] adj component; 構成要素 [kousei youso] n component

公正 [kousei] n fairness; 公正な [kousei na] adj fair (reasonable); 公正に [kousei ni] adv fairly

校正刷り [kouseizuri] n proof (for checking)

鉱泉 [kousen] n spa

講師 [koushi] n lecturer

子牛 [koushi] n calf; 子牛の肉 [koushi no niku] n veal

公式 [koushiki] n formula

更新 [koushin] 更新する [koushin suru] v update

行進 [koushin] n march, procession; 行進する [koushin suru] v march

香辛料 [koushinryou] *n* spice; 香辛料を入れた [koushinryou-o ireta] *adj* spicy

交渉 [koushou] *n* negotiations; 交渉する [koushou suru] *v* negotiate; 交渉者 [koushousha] *n* negotiator

公衆 [koushuu] *n* public; 公衆の [koushuu no] *adj* public

公衆電話 [koushuudenwa] *n* payphone, public phone; カード式公衆電話 [kaado shiki koushuu denwa] *n* cardphone; 公衆電話ボックス [koushuu denwa bokkusu] *n* call box

拘束 [kousoku] *n* restriction

高速 [kousoku] 高速進行 [kousoku shinkou] *n* speeding; 高速道路 [kousokudouro] *n* motorway

高速道路 [kousokudouro] *n* motorway; 高速道路の進入退出路 [kousoku douro no shinnyuu taishutsuro] *n* slip road; この高速道路は有料ですか? [kono kousoku-douro wa yuuryou desu ka?] Is there a toll on this motorway?; 高速道路は交通量が多いですか? [kousoku-douro wa koutsuu-ryou ga ooi desu ka?] Is the traffic heavy on the motorway?; 高速道路へはどう行くのですか? [kousoku-douro e wa dou iku no desu ka?] How do I get to the motorway?

高層 [kousou] 高層建築 [kousou kenchiku] *n* high-rise

降霜 [kousou] *n* frosting

コース [kousu] *n* course; 再教育コース [saikyouiku koosu] *n* refresher course; この近くに公共のゴルフコースはありますか? [kono chikaku ni kookyou no gorufu-koosu wa arimasu ka?] Is there a public golf course near here?

香水 [kousui] *n* perfume

交替 [koutai] 交替班 [koutai han] *n* relay

抗体 [koutai] *n* antibody

後退 [koutai] 景気後退 [keikikoutai] *n* recession

後退する [koutai suru] 後退させる [koutai saseru] *v* back

皇帝 [koutei] *n* emperor

鋼鉄 [koutetsu] *n* steel

コート [kouto] *n (洋服)* coat

高等 [koutou] 高等教育 [koutoukyouiku] *n* higher education

口頭 [koutou] 口頭の [koutou no] *adj* oral; 口頭試験 [koutou shiken] *n* oral

喉頭 [koutou] 喉頭炎 [koutouen] *n* laryngitis

交通 [koutsuu] *n* traffic; 交通信号 [koutsuu shingou] *n* traffic lights; 交通渋滞 [koutsuujuutai] *n* traffic jam; 交通規則集 [koutsuu kisokushuu] *n* Highway Code; 交通監視員 [koutsuu kanshiin] *n* traffic warden; 公共交通機関 [koukyou koutsuu kikan] *n* public transport

幸運 [kouun] 幸運な [kouun na] *adj* fortunate; 幸運にも [kouun nimo] *adv* fortunately

口座 [kouza] *n* account; 銀行口座 [ginkoukouza] *n* bank account; 預金口座 [yokin kouza] *n* account *(in bank)*; 共同預金口座 [kyoudou yokin kouza] *n* joint account; 口座番号 [kouzabangou] *n* account number; 口座引き落とし [kouza hikiotoshi] *n* direct debit; 私の口座から送金したいのですが [watashi no kouza kara soukin shitai no desu ga] I would like to transfer some money from my account

鉱山 [kouzan] *n* mine

構造 [kouzou] *n* structure

洪水 [kouzui] *n* flood

怖がる [kowagaru] 怖がらせる [kowagaraseru] *v* frighten

怖い [kowai] *adj* scary; 怖がった [kowagatta] *adj* scared, terrified; 怖がらせる [kowagaraseru] *v* scare, terrify; ・・・が怖い [...ga kowai] *adj* afraid of...

壊れる [kowareru] これは壊れています [kore wa kowarete imasu] This is broken; ギアボックスが壊れています [gia-bokkusu ga kowarete imasu] The gearbox is broken; エキゾーストが壊れています [ekizoosuto ga kowarete imasu] The exhaust is broken; メーターが壊れています [meetaa ga kowarete imasu] The meter is broken; 鍵が壊れています [kagi ga kowarete imasu] The lock is broken

壊れやすい [kowareyasui] *adj* fragile

壊る [kowaru] 壊れた [kowareta] *adj* broken

壊す [kowasu] *v* break; 私は窓を壊してしまいました [watashi wa mado o kowashite shimaimashita] I've broken the window

壊すことのできない [kowasu koto no dekinai] *adj* unbreakable

小屋 [koya] *n* hut, shed; 馬小屋 [umagoya] *n* stable; 風車小屋 [fuushagoya] *n* windmill; 一番近い山小屋はどこですか? [ichiban chikai yama-goya wa doko desu ka?] Where is the nearest mountain hut?

雇用 [koyou] *n* employment; 雇用主 [koyounushi] *n* employer; 雇用する [koyou suru] *v* employ

小銭 [kozeni] *n* change; すみません、小銭がありません [sumimasen, kozeni ga arimasen] Sorry, I don't have any change; ···の小銭をいただけますか? [...no kozeni o itadakemasu ka?] Could you give me change of...?; 小銭がありますか? [kozeni ga arimasu ka?] Do you have any small change?; 小銭をいくらかいただけますか? [kozeni o ikura ka itadakemasu ka?] Can you give me some change, please?

小包 [kozutsumi] *n* package, parcel; この小包を送りたいのですが [kono kozutsumi o okuritai no desu ga] I'd like to send this parcel; この小包を送るのにいくらかかりますか? [kono kozutsumi o okuru no ni ikura kakarimasu ka?] How much is it to send this parcel?

区 [ku] *n* ward (area); 保護区 [hogoku] *n* reserve (land); 選挙区 [senkyoku] *n* constituency

句 [ku] 慣用句 [kan'youku] *n* phrase

配る [kubaru] *v* distribute

区別 [kubetsu] *n* distinction; 区別する [kubetsu suru] *v* distinguish

首 [kubi] *n* (体) neck; 首にする [kubi ni suru] *v* sack (employee)

口 [kuchi] *n* mouth; 改札口 [kaisatsuguchi] *n* ticket barrier; 口に出す [kuchi ni dasu] *v* refer; 口のきけない [kuchi no kikenai] *adj* speechless; 口ひげ [kuchi hige] *n* moustache

くちばし [kuchibashi] *n* beak

口紅 [kuchibeni] *n* lipstick

口火 [kuchibi] *n* pilot light

唇 [kuchibiru] *n* lip

口笛 [kuchibue] *n* whistle; 口笛を吹く [kuchibue o fuku] *v* whistle

口汚い [kuchi kitanai] *adj* abusive

果物 [kudamono] *n* fruit (botany), fruit (collectively)

くだらないこと [kudaranai koto] *n* trash

下さる [kudasaru] ···をください [...o kudasai] I'd like..., please

下す [kudasu] 判決を下す [hanketsu-o kudasu] *v* sentence

クエーカー [kueekaa] *n* Quaker

九月 [kugatsu] *n* September

釘 [kugi] *n* nail

クイズ [kuizu] *n* quiz

クジャク [kujaku] *n* peacock

くじ [kuji] *n* (抽選) draw (lottery)

くじく [kujiku] *v* sprain; ···の勇気をくじく [...no yuuki-o kujiku] *v* discourage

クジラ [kujira] *n* whale

苦情 [kujou] *n* complaint; 誰に苦情を言えばいいのですか? [dare ni kujou o ieba ii no desu ka?] Who can I complain to?; 苦情があるのですが [kujou ga aru no desu ga] I'd like to make a complaint; 私はサービスについて苦情があります [watashi wa saabisu ni tsuite kujou ga arimasu] I want to complain about the service

区画 [kukaku] 小区画 [shou kukaku] *n* plot (piece of land)

クマ [kuma] *n* (動物) bear; 北極グマ [hokkyokuguma] *n* polar bear

熊手 [kumade] *n* rake

組合 [kumiai] *n* 労働組合 [roudoukumiai] *n* trade union

組み合わせ [kumiawase] *n* combination

組み換える [kumikaeru] *v* modify; 遺伝子組み換えの [idenshi kumikae no] *adj* genetically-modified

組み込む [kumikomu] *v* fit in

クミン [kumin] n cumin

雲 [kumo] n cloud

クモ [kumo] n (動物) spider; クモの巣 [kumo no su] n spiderweb

苦悶 [kumon] n agony

くもの巣 [kumo no su] n cobweb

曇る [kumoru] 曇った [kumotta] adj cloudy, overcast; 曇っています [kumotte imasu] It's cloudy

国 [kuni] n country; 発展途上国 [hattentojoukoku] n developing country; どこでその国の地図を買えますか? [doko de sono kuni no chizu o kaemasu ka?] Where can I buy a map of the country?

国番号 [kunibangou] 英国の国番号は何番ですか? [eikoku no kuni-bangou wa nan-ban desu ka?] What is the dialling code for the UK?

訓練 [kunren] 自己訓練 [jiko kunren] n self-discipline; 訓練された [kunren sareta] adj trained; 訓練する [kunren suru] v train; 訓練を受けている人 [kunren-o ukete iru hito] n trainee

君主 [kunshu] n monarch; 君主制 [kunshusei] n monarchy

屈服 [kuppuku] 屈服する [kuppuku suru] v give in

クラブ [kurabu] n (集団) club (group); ゴルフ用クラブ [gorufu you kurabu] n golf club (game); どこかによいクラブはありますか? [doko-ka ni yoi kurabu wa arimasu ka?] Where is there a good club?; ゴルフクラブを貸し出していますか? [gorufu-kurabu o kashidashite imasu ka?] Do they hire out golf clubs?

クラゲ [kurage] n jellyfish; ここにクラゲはいますか? [koko ni kurage wa imasu ka?] Are there jellyfish here?

暗い [kurai] adj dark; 暗いです [kurai desu] It's dark

クライマー [kuraimaa] n climber

クライミング [kuraimingu] n climbing; 私はクライミングをしたいのですが [watashi wa kuraimingu o shitai no desu ga] I'd like to go climbing

クラッカー [kurakkaa] n cracker

クラック [kurakku] n crack (cocaine)

クランベリー [kuranberii] n cranberry

クラリネット [kurarinetto] n clarinet

暗さ [kurasa] n darkness

クラス [kurasu] n class; エコノミークラス [ekonomiikurasu] n economy class; ビジネスクラス [bijinesu kurasu] n business class; 夜間クラス [yakan kurasu] n evening class

暮らす [kurasu] ···にたよって暮らす [...ni tayotte kurasu] v live on

クラッチ [kuratchi] n clutch

くらわす [kurawasu] げんこつをくらわす [genkotsu-o kurawasu] v punch

クレームフォーム [kureemufoomu] n claim form

クレーン [kureen] n crane (for lifting)

クレジット [kurejitto] n credit

クレジットカード [kurejittokaado] n credit card; 私のクレジットカードでキャッシングが利用できますか? [watashi no kurejitto-kaado de kyasshingu ga riyou dekimasu ka?] Can I get a cash advance with my credit card?; クレジットカードは使えますか? [kurejitto-kaado wa tsukaemasu ka?] Do you take credit cards?

クレメンタイン [kurementain] n clementine

クレンジングローション [kurenjingurooshon] n cleansing lotion

クレンザー [kurenzaa] n cleanser

クレソン [kureson] n watercress

クレヨン [kureyon] n crayon

クリ [kuri] n chestnut

クリーム [kuriimu] n cream; クリーム色の [kuriimuiro no] adj cream

クリーニング [kuriiningu] n cleaning; どこでこれをクリーニングしてもらえますか? [doko de kore o kuriiningu shite moraemasu ka?] Where can I get this cleaned?; これをクリーニングして欲しいのですが [kore o kuriiningu shite hoshii no desu ga] I'd like to get these things cleaned

栗色 [kuriiro] 栗色の [kuri iro no] adj maroon

繰り返し [kurikaeshi] n repeat; 繰り返し発生する [kurikaeshi hassei suru] adj recurring

繰り返す [kurikaesu] v repeat; 繰り返して [kurikaeshite] adv repeatedly

クリケット [kuriketto] n cricket (game)

クリスマス [kurisumasu] n Christmas, Xmas; クリスマスカード [kurisumasu kaado] n Christmas card; メリークリスマス! [merii kurisumasu!] Merry Christmas!

クリスマスイブ [kurisumasu ibu] n Christmas Eve

クリスマスツリー [kurisumasu tsurii] n Christmas tree

クロアチア [kuroachia] n Croatia; クロアチアの [kuroachia no] adj Croatian

クロアチア語 [kuroachiago] n Croatian (language)

クロアチア人 [kuroachiajin] n Croatian (person)

黒い [kuroi] adj black

クロッカス [kurokkasu] n crocus

クロム [kuromu] n chrome

クロスグリ [kurosuguri] n blackcurrant

クロスカントリー [kurosukantorii] n cross-country

クロスカントリースキー [kurosukantoriisukii] n cross-country skiing; クロスカントリースキーに行くことは可能ですか? [kurosukantorii-sukii ni iku koto wa kanou desu ka?] Is it possible to go cross-country skiing?; クロスカントリースキーの板を借りたいのですが [kurosukantorii-sukii no ita o karitai no desu ga] I want to hire cross-country skis

クロスワードパズル [kurosuwaadopazuru] n crossword

クローブ [kuroubu] n clove

クローク [kurouku] n cloakroom

クローン [kuroun] n clone; クローンを作る [kuroon-o tsukuru] v clone

クロウタドリ [kuroutadori] n blackbird

繰る [kuru] 繰り上げる [kuriageru] v bring forward

来る [kuru] v come

くるぶし [kurubushi] n ankle

車 [kuruma] n car; 人を車に乗せてあげること [hito-o kuruma ni nosete ageru koto] n give a ride to; ビュッフェ車 [byuffesha] n buffet car; 車の鍵 [kuruma no kagi] n car keys; 社用車 [shayousha] n company car; 食堂車 [shokudousha] n dining car; 除雪車 [josetsusha] n snowplough; 寝台車 [shindaisha] n sleeping car; 寝台車コンパートメントの寝台 [shindaisha konpaatomento no shindai] n couchette; あなたの車を動かしていただけますか? [anata no kuruma o ugokashite itadakemasu ka?] Could you move your car, please?; レッカー車を手配してもらえますか? [rekkaa-sha o tehai shite moraemasu ka?] Can you send a breakdown van?; 普通車 [futsuu-sha] a standard class cabin; 車はいつ直りますか? [kuruma wa itsu naorimasu ka?] When will the car be ready?; 車を5日間借りたいのですが [kuruma o itsuka-kan karitai no desu ga] I want to hire a car for five days; 車を洗いたいのですが [kuruma o araitai no desu ga] I would like to wash the car; 車を週末借りたいのですが [kuruma o shuumatsu karitai no desu ga] I want to hire a car for the weekend; 車を借りたいのですが [kuruma o karitai no desu ga] I want to hire a car; 私は車に鍵を置き忘れました [watashi wa kuruma ni kagi o okiwasuremashita] I left the keys in the car; 私の車が故障しました [watashi no kuruma ga koshou shimashita] My car has broken down; 私の車が壊されて侵入されました [watashi no kuruma ga kowasarete shinnyuu saremashita] My car has been broken into; 私を車で連れて行ってもらえますか? [watashi o kuruma de tsurete itte moraemasu ka?] Can you take me by car?; 子供たちが車の中にいます [kodomo-tachi ga kuruma no naka ni imasu] My children are in the car

クルマエビ [kurumaebi] n prawn, scampi

車椅子 [kurumaisu] n wheelchair; おたくには車椅子がありますか? [otaku ni wa kuruma-isu ga arimasu ka?] **Do you have wheelchairs?**; おたくのホテルは車椅子で利用できますか? [otaku no hoteru wa kuruma-isu de riyou dekimasu ka?] **Is your hotel accessible to wheelchairs?**; 車椅子で···を訪れることができますか? [kuruma-isu de ... o otozureru koto ga dekimasu ka?] **Can you visit ... in a wheelchair?**; 車椅子で利用できる入口はどこですか? [kuruma-isu de riyou dekiru iriguchi wa doko desu ka?] **Where is the wheelchair-accessible entrance?**; 車椅子用のエレベーターはありますか? [kuruma-isu-you no erebeetaa wa arimasu ka?] **Do you have a lift for wheelchairs?**; 私は車椅子で入れる部屋が必要です [watashi wa kuruma-isu de haireru heya ga hitsuyou desu] **I need a room with wheelchair access**; 私は車椅子を使っています [watashi wa kuruma-isu o tsukatte imasu] **I use a wheelchair**; ···へ行くのに車椅子で利用しやすい交通手段はありますか? [...e iku no ni kuruma-isu de riyou shiyasui koutsuu-shudan wa arimasu ka?] **Is there wheelchair-friendly transport available to...?**; 電車は車椅子で乗れますか? [densha wa kuruma-isu de noremasu ka?] **Is the train wheelchair-accessible?**

クルミ [kurumi] n walnut

苦しい [kurushii] 苦しい体験 [kurushii taiken] n ordeal

狂う [kuruu] 怒り狂った [ikarikurutta] adj furious; 気の狂った [kino kurutta] adj mad (insane)

クルーカット [kuruukatto] n crew cut

草 [kusa] n grass (plant)

草刈り [kusakari] 草刈り機 [kusakariki] n mower

鎖 [kusari] n chain

腐る [kusaru] v rot; 腐った [kusatta] adj rotten

癖 [kuse] n habit

くせ毛 [kuseke] 私は生まれつきくせ毛です [watashi wa umaretsuki kusege desu] **My hair is naturally curly**

くしゃみ [kushami] くしゃみをする [kushami o suru] v sneeze

櫛 [kushi] n comb; 櫛でとかす [kushi de tokasu] v comb

掘削 [kussaku] 掘削機 [kussakuki] n digger; 掘削装置 [kussaku souchi] n rig

掘削装置 [kussaku souchi] 石油掘削装置 [sekiyu kussakusouchi] n oil rig

クッション [kusshon] n cushion

くすぐる [kusuguru] v tickle; くすぐったがる [kusuguttagaru] adj ticklish

薬 [kusuri] n drug, medicine; 目薬 [megusuri] n eye drops; 睡眠薬 [suimin-yaku] n sleeping pill; 局所麻酔薬 [kyokusho masuiyaku] n local anaesthetic; 咳止め薬 [sekidomegusuri] n cough mixture; 私はすでにこの薬を飲んでいます [watashi wa sudeni kono kusuri o nonde imasu] **I'm already taking this medicine**

苦闘 [kutou] n struggle; 苦闘する [kutou suru] v struggle

句読 [kutou] n punctuation

靴 [kutsu] n shoe; スケート靴 [sukeeto kutsu] n skates; ローラースケート靴 [rooraa sukeeto kutsu] n rollerskates; 靴ひも [kutsuhimo] n shoelace; 靴屋 [kutsuya] n shoe shop; 靴墨 [kutsuzumi] n shoe polish; この靴のヒールを付け直すことができますか? [kono kutsu no hiiru o tsukenaosu koto ga dekimasu ka?] **Can you re-heel these shoes?**; この靴を修理できますか? [kono kutsu o shuuri dekimasu ka?] **Can you repair these shoes?**; 靴に穴があきました [kutsu ni ana ga akimashita] **I have a hole in my shoe**; 靴は何階にありますか? [kutsu wa nan-kai ni arimasu ka?] **Which floor are shoes on?**

くつがえす [kutsugaesu] v overrule

くつろぐ [kutsurogu] v relax; くつろいだ [kutsuroida] adj laid-back, relaxed; くつろがせる [kutsurogaseru] adj relaxing; くつろぎ [kutsurogi] n relaxation

靴下 [kutsushita] 靴下留め [kutsushitadome] n suspenders

空調 [kuuchou] n air conditioning; 空調さ

れた [kuuchou sareta] adj air-conditioned

洞 [kuudou] 空洞の [kuudou no] adj hollow

ウェート [kuueeto] n Kuwait

ウェート人 [kuueetojin] n Kuwaiti (person)

ウェートの [kuueeto no] adj Kuwaiti

腹 [kuufuku] n hunger

間 [kuukan] n space

気 [kuuki] n air

気圧 [kuukiatsu] n air pressure; 空気圧を点検してもらえますか? [kuukiatsu o tenken shite moraemasu ka?] Can you check the air, please?

空港 [kuukou] n airport; 空港バス [kuukou basu] n airport bus; 空港までのタクシーはいくらですか? [kuukou made no takushii wa ikura desu ka?] How much is the taxi to the airport?; 空港へはどう行けばいいのですか? [kuukou e wa dou ikeba ii no desu ka?] How do I get to the airport?; 空港へ行くバスはありますか? [kuukou e iku basu wa arimasu ka?] Is there a bus to the airport?

空虚 [kuukyo] 空虚な感じ [kuukyo na kanji] n void

空欄 [kuuran] n blank

加える [kuwaeru] ・・・を加えて [...-o kuwaete] prep plus

加わる [kuwawaru] v join

くず紙 [kuzugami] n scrap paper

くずかご [kuzukago] n litter bin, wastepaper basket

崩れる [kuzureru] v collapse

キャベツ [kyabetsu] n cabbage; 芽キャベツ [mekyabetsu] n Brussels sprouts

キャビン [kyabin] n cabin; 5番のキャビンはどこですか? [go-ban no kyabin wa doko desu ka?] Where is cabin number five?

キャビネット [kyabinetto] n cabinet

キャブレター [kyaburetaa] n carburettor

客 [kyaku] n guest, customer

脚本 [kyakuhon] 脚本家 [kyakuhonka] n playwright

客車 [kyakusha] n carriage

客室 [kyakushitsu] n guest room; 客室乗務員 [kyakushitsu joumuin] n flight attendant; 客室係のメイド [kyakushitsugakari no meido] n chambermaid; 客室番号 [kyakushitsu bangou] n room number; 一階の客室がありますか? [ikkai no kyakushitsu ga arimasu ka?] Do you have any bedrooms on the ground floor?

キャンバス [kyanbasu] n canvas

キャンデー [kyandee] n sweets; 棒付きキャンデー [boutsuki kyandee] n lollipop, lolly

キャンディー [kyandii] アイスキャンディー [aisu kyandii] n ice lolly

キャニスター [kyanisutaa] n canister

キャンパス [kyanpasu] n campus

キャンピングカー [kyanpingukaa] n camper van; 4人用のキャンピングカーでいくらですか? [yonin-you no kyanpingukaa de ikura desu ka?] How much is it for a camper with four people?

キャンプ [kyanpu] n camp; キャンプする [kyanpu suru] v camp; キャンプする人 [kyanpu suru nin] n camper; キャンプベッド [kyanpubeddo] n camp bed; キャンプ生活 [kyanpu seikatsu] n camping; キャンプ用ガス [kyanpu you gasu] n camping gas; キャンプ場 [kyanpujou] n campsite; トレーラーハウスキャンプ場 [toreeraa hausu kyanpu jou] n caravan site; ここで一晩キャンプできますか? [koko de hitoban kyanpu dekimasu ka?] Can we camp here overnight?

キャンプ場 [kyanpujou] キャンプ場にレストランはありますか? [kyanpu-jou ni resutoran wa arimasu ka?] Is there a restaurant on the campsite?

キャンプする人 [kyanpu suru nin] n camper

キャンセル [kyanseru] n cancellation; キャンセル待ちの切符 [kyanserumachi no kippu] n stand-by ticket; キャンセルされたフライトはありますか? [kyanseru sareta furaito wa arimasu ka?] Are there any cancellations?

キャンティーン [kyantiin] n canteen

キャプション [kyapushon] n caption

キャラメル [kyarameru] n caramel

キャリア [kyaria] n career

キャロル [kyaroru] n carol

キャセロール [kyaserouru] n casserole

キャッシング [kyasshingu] n advance cash payment; 私のクレジットカードでキャッシングが利用できますか? [watashi no kurejitto-kaado de kyasshingu ga riyou dekimasu ka?] Can I get a cash advance with my credit card?

キャスト [kyasuto] n cast

脚立 [kyatatsu] n stepladder

巨大 [kyodai] 巨大な [kyodai na] adj enormous, giant, gigantic, huge, mammoth, tremendous

拒否 [kyohi] n refusal; 拒否する [kyohi suru] v refuse, reject, throw out; 拒否権 [kyohiken] n veto

巨人 [kyojin] n giant

居住 [kyojuu] 居住者 [kyojuusha] n resident

許可 [kyoka] n leave, permission; 許可証 [kyokashou] n pass, permit; 入場許可 [nyuujou kyoka] n admittance; 労働許可証 [roudou kyokashou] n work permit

極 [kyoku] 北極 [hokkyoku] n Arctic, the Arctic; 南極 [nankyoku] n the Antarctic, Antarctica

曲 [kyoku] n tune

局 [kyoku] ラジオ局 [rajio kyoku] n radio station; 郵便局 [yuubinkyoku] n post office

局番 [kyokuban] n dialling code

局部 [kyokubu] 局部の [kyokubu no] adj local

極地 [kyokuchi] 極地の [kyokuchi no] adj polar

極度 [kyokudo] 極度に [kyokudo ni] adv extremely; 極度の [kyokudo no] adj extreme; 極度の緊張 [kyokudo no kinchou] n strain

局面 [kyokumen] n aspect; 重大局面 [juudai kyokumen] n crisis

局所 [kyokusho] 局所麻酔薬 [kyokusho masuiyaku] n local anaesthetic

極東 [kyokutou] n Far East

去年 [kyonen] n last year

距離 [kyori] n distance; 短距離走者 [tankyori sousha] n sprinter; 短距離競走 [tankyorikyousou] n sprint

虚勢 [kyosei] n bluff; 虚勢を張る [kyosei-o haru] v bluff

拒食症 [kyoshokushou] 拒食症的な [kyoshokushouteki na] adj anorexic

興 [kyou] 人の興をそぐ人 [hito no kyou-o sogu hito] n spoilsport

今日 [kyou] adv today; 今日は何日ですか? [kyou wa nan-nichi desu ka?] What is today's date?; 今日は何曜日ですか? [kyou wa nan-youbi desu ka?] What day is it today?

凶悪 [kyouaku] 凶悪犯 [kyouakuhan] n thug

競売 [kyoubai] n auction

教母 [kyoubo] n godmother

凶暴 [kyoubou] 凶暴な [kyoubou na] adj fierce

強調 [kyouchou] 強調する [kyouchou suru] v emphasize, highlight, stress

強打 [kyouda] n bash, blow; 強打する [kyouda suru] v bash

鏡台 [kyoudai] n dressing table

兄弟 [kyoudai] n brother; 継兄弟 [mama kyoudai] n stepbrother

兄弟姉妹 [kyoudaishimai] n siblings

郷土料理 [kyoudoryouri] n local cuisine; 何か郷土料理を注文したいのですが [nani ka kyoudo-ryouri o chuumon shitai no desu ga] I'd like to order something local; おすすめの郷土料理はありますか? [osusume no kyoudo-ryouri wa arimasu ka?] Can you recommend a local dish?; 郷土料理は何ですか? [kyoudo-ryouri wa nan desu ka?] What's the local speciality?; 郷土料理はありますか? [kyoudo-ryouri wa arimasu ka?] Is there a local speciality?

共同 [kyoudou] 共同の [kyoudou no] adj

joint; 共同して働く [kyoudou shite hataraku] v collaborate; 共同資金 [kyoudou shikin] n pool (resources); 共同預金口座 [kyoudou yokin kouza] n joint account; 共同寝室 [kyoudoushinshitsu] n dormitory; 共同部屋がいいのですが [kyoudou-beya ga ii no desu ga] I'd like a dorm bed

共同所有権 [kyoudoushoyuuken] 休暇施設の共同所有権 [kyuuka shisetsu no kyoudou shoyuuken] n timeshare

恐怖 [kyoufu] n alarm, fright, horror, scare; 恐怖症 [kyoufushou] n phobia

教父 [kyoufu] n (名づけ親) godfather (baptism)

恐怖症 [kyoufushou] 閉所恐怖症の [heisho kyoufushou no] adj claustrophobic

強風 [kyoufuu] n gale

競技 [kyougi] 五種競技 [goshu kyougi] n pentathlon; グライダー競技 [guraidaa kyougi] n gliding; 競技を行う [kyougi-o okonau] v play (sport); 陸上競技 [rikujou kyougi] n athletics

共犯者 [kyouhansha] n accomplice

教育 [kyouiku] n education; 教育の [kyouiku no] adj educational; 教育のある [kyouiku no aru] adj educated; 継続教育 [keizoku kyouiku] n further education; 生涯教育 [shougai kyouiku] n adult education; 高等教育 [koutoukyouiku] n higher education; 再教育コース [saikyouiku koosu] n refresher course

教員 [kyouin] 臨時教員 [rinji kyouin] n supply teacher

狂人 [kyoujin] n maniac

教女 [kyoujo] n goddaughter

教授 [kyouju] n professor

教会 [kyoukai] n church; ローマカトリック教会の [rooma katorikku kyoukai no] adj Roman Catholic; 私たちがその教会を訪れることはできますか? [watashi-tachi ga sono kyoukai o otozureru koto wa dekimasu ka?] Can we visit the church?

協会 [kyoukai] n association

境界 [kyoukai] n border, boundary

教会区 [kyoukaiku] n parish

教科書 [kyoukasho] n schoolbook, textbook

恐喝 [kyoukatsu] n blackmail; 恐喝する [kyoukatsu suru] v blackmail

狂犬病 [kyoukenbyou] n rabies

狂気 [kyouki] n madness

教子 [kyouko] n (男女) godchild, (男子) godson

峡谷 [kyoukoku] n ravine

教区 [kyouku] 教区牧師 [kyouku bokushi] n vicar

教訓 [kyoukun] n moral

供給 [kyoukyuu] n supply; 供給する [kyoukyuu suru] v provide, supply; 供給者 [kyoukyuusha] n supplier

興味 [kyoumi] n interest (curiosity); 興味がある [kyoumi ga aru] adj interested; 興味を起こさせる [kyoumi-o okosaseru] v interest

興味深い [kyoumibukai] adj interesting

強烈 [kyouretsu] 強烈な [kyouretsu na] adj intense

協力 [kyouryoku] n cooperation

強力な [kyouryoku na] adj powerful

恐竜 [kyouryuu] n dinosaur

共産主義 [kyousanshugi] n communism; 共産主義の [kyousanshugi no] adj communist; 共産主義者 [kyousanshugisha] n communist

強制的な [kyouseiteki na] adj compulsory

教師 [kyoushi] n teacher; 学校教師 [gakkou kyoushi] n schoolteacher; 私は教師です [watashi wa kyoushi desu] I'm a teacher

教室 [kyoushitsu] n classroom; 教室助手 [kyoushitsu joshu] n classroom assistant

競争 [kyousou] n competition, contest, rivalry; 競争する [kyousou suru] adj compete, race, rival; 競争者 [kyousousha] n competitor, contestant; 競争的な [kyousouteki na] adj competitive; 競争相手 [kyousouaite] n rival

競走 [kyousou] 短距離競走

[tankyorikyousou] n sprint

強壮 [kyousou] 強壮剤 [kyousouzai] n tonic

競走馬 [kyousouba] n racehorse

教徒 [kyouto] n adherent; カトリック教徒 [katorrikkukyouto] n Catholic; シーク教徒 [shiiku kyouto] n Sikh; ヒンズー教徒 [hinzuu kyouto] n Hindu; ローマカトリック教徒 [rooma katorikku kyouto] n Roman Catholic

共和 [kyouwa] 共和政体 [kyouwa seitai] n republic

共和国 [kyouwakoku] 中央アフリカ共和国 [chuuou afurika kyouwakoku] n Central African Republic; チェコ共和国 [cheko kyouwakoku] n Czech Republic; チェチェン共和国 [chechen kyouwakoku] n Chechnya; ドミニカ共和国 [dominika kyouwakoku] n Dominican Republic

強要 [kyouyou] 強要する [kyouyou suru] v insist

共有 [kyouyuu] n communion

許容 [kyoyou] 無料手荷物許容量 [muryou tenimotsu kyoyouryou] n baggage allowance

九 [kyuu] number nine

急 [kyuu] 急にそれる [kyuu ni soreru] v swerve

キュー [kyuu] n cue (billiards)

キューバ [kyuuba] n Cuba

キューバ人 [kyuubajin] n Cuban (person)

九番目 [kyuubanme] n ninth; 九番目の [kyuu banme no] adj ninth

キューバの [kyuuba no] adj Cuban

宮殿 [kyuuden] n palace; その宮殿は一般公開されていますか? [sono kyuuden wa ippan-koukai sarete imasu ka?] Is the palace open to the public?; その宮殿はいつ開きますか? [sono kyuuden wa itsu hirakimasu ka?] When is the palace open?

臼砲 [kyuuhou] n mortar (military)

給仕 [kyuuji] 給仕する人 [kyuuji suru hito] n server (person)

休日 [kyuujitsu] 休日の仕事 [kyuujitsu no shigoto] n holiday job

救助 [kyuujo] n rescue

救助員 [kyuujoin] 水泳場の救助員 [suieijou no kyuujoin] n lifeguard; 救助員を呼んで! [kyuujoin o yonde!] Get the lifeguard!

救助艇 [kyuujotei] 救助艇を呼んで! [kyuujotei o yonde!] Call out the lifeboat!

九十 [kyuujuu] number ninety

休暇 [kyuuka] n holiday; 父親の育児休暇 [chichioya no ikuji kyuuka] n paternity leave; 病気休暇 [byoukikyuuka] n sick leave; 病気休暇中の手当て [byouki kyuukachuu no teate] n sick pay; 出産休暇 [shussan kyuuka] n maternity leave; 夏の休暇 [natsu no kyuuka] n summer holidays; 学期中の中間休暇 [gakkichuu no chuukan kyuuka] n half-term; 楽しい休暇を! [tanoshii kyuuka o!] Enjoy your holiday!; 私は休暇で来ています [watashi wa kyuuka de kite imasu] I'm here on holiday, I'm on holiday here

吸血鬼 [kyuuketsuki] n vampire

球根 [kyuukon] n bulb (plant)

救急 [kyuukyuu] 救急救命士 [kyuukyuu kyuumeishi] n paramedic; 救急車 [kyuukyuusha] n ambulance; 救急病棟 [kyuukyuubyoutou] n accident & emergency department; 救急処置 [kyuukyuu shochi] n first aid; 救急処置キット [kyuukyuu shochi kitto] n first-aid kit

救急病棟 [kyuukyuubyoutou] 救急病棟はどこですか? [kyuukyuu-byoutou wa doko desu ka?] Where is casualty?; 私は救急病棟に行かなければなりません [watashi wa kyuukyuu-byoutou ni ikanakereba narimasen] I need to go to casualty

救急医 [kyuukyuui] 救急医を呼んでください [kyuukyuu-i o yonde kudasai] Please call the emergency doctor

救急車 [kyuukyuusha] 救急車を呼んでください [kyuukyuu-sha o yonde kudasai] Call an ambulance

救命 [kyuumei] 救急救命士 [kyuukyuu kyuumeishi] n paramedic; 救命の [kyuumei no] adj life-saving; 救命ベルト [kyuumei beruto] n lifebelt; 救命ボート

[kyuumeibooto] *n* lifeboat; 救命胴衣 [kyuumeidoui] *n* life jacket

急な [kyuu na] *adj* (傾斜) steep

急難 [kyuunan] 救難信号 [kyuunan shingou] *n* SOS

吸入器 [kyuunyuuki] *n* inhaler

キュウリ [kyuuri] *n* cucumber

給料 [kyuuryou] *n* pay, salary; 給料のよい [kyuuryou no yoi] *adj* well-paid

旧姓 [kyuusei] 女性の結婚前の旧姓 [josei no kekkonmae no kyuusei] *n* maiden name

休戦 [kyuusen] *n* truce

急使 [kyuushi] *n* courier

マーチャントバンク [maachantobanku] *n* merchant bank

マーガリン [maagarin] *n* margarine

マーケティング [maaketeingu] *n* marketing

マーケット [maaketto] *n* market; マーケットが立つのはいつですか? [maaketto ga tatsu no wa itsu desu ka?] When is the market on?

まあまあ [maamaa] *adv* so-so

マーマレード [maamareedo] *n* marmalade

まばたき [mabataki] まばたきする [mabataki suru] *v* blink

まぶた [mabuta] *n* eyelid

マッチ [matchi] マッチさせる [matchi saseru] *v* match

町 [machi] *n* town; 町の中心部 [machi no chuushinbu] *n* town centre

街 [machi] *n* shopping district; スラム街 [suramugai] *n* slum; 街の中心部 [machi no chuushinbu] *n* city centre; 繁華街へ [hankagai-e] *adv* downtown; どこでその街の地図を買えますか? [doko de sono machi no chizu o kaemasu ka?] Where can I buy a map of the city?; その街のストリー

トマップが欲しいのですが [sono machi no sutoriito-mappu ga hoshii no desu ga] I want a street map of the city; 街の中心部までどのくらいありますか? [machi no chuushinbu made dono kurai arimasu ka] How far are we from the town centre?; 街の中心部までお願いします [machi no chuushinbu made o-negai shimasu] Please take me to the city centre; 街の中心部へ行く一番よい方法は何ですか? [machi no chuushinbu e iku ichiban yoi houhou wa nan desu ka?] What's the best way to get to the city centre?; 街へ行くバスはありますか? [machi e iku basu wa arimasu ka?] Is there a bus to the city?

待ち合わせ [machiawase] 待合室 [machiaishitsu] n waiting room

待ち合わせる [machiawaseru] v meet up

待ち伏せ [machifuse] n ambush

間違える [machigaeru] v mistake; 間違えた [machigaeta] adj mistaken

間違い [machigai] n error, mistake, slip, slip-up; 間違い警報 [machigai keihou] n false alarm; 間違い電話 [machigai denwa] n wrong number

間違う [machigau] v slip up; 間違って [machigatte] adv mistakenly, wrong; 間違った [machigatta] adj wrong

まだ [mada] adv still, yet (with negative)

マダガスカル [madagasukaru] n Madagascar

まで [made] ···まで [...made] prep until, till; ···の時まで [...no toki made] conj until

窓 [mado] n window; 窓下の腰掛け [mado shita no koshikake] n window seat; 窓の下枠 [mado no shitawaku] n windowsill; 窓ガラス [madogarasu] n window pane; 窓が開きません [mado ga akimasen] The window won't open; 窓を閉めてもいいですか? [mado o shimete mo ii desu ka?] May I close the window?; 窓を開けてもいいですか? [mado o akete mo ii desu ka?] May I open the window?; 窓を開けられません [mado o akeraremasen] I can't open the window; 私は窓を壊してしまいました [watashi wa mado o kowashite shimaimashita] I've broken the window

窓側 [madogawa] 窓側の席をお願いします [mado-gawa no seki o o-negai shimasu] I'd like a window seat

まどろむ [madoromu] v doze off

前 [mae] n front; ···の前に [...no mae ni] prep before; ···する前に [...suru mae ni] conj before; 前に [mae ni] adv ahead; 前に [mae ni] adv earlier; 前の [mae no] adj preceding; 前の [mae no] adj front

前髪 [maegami] 切下げ前髪 [kirisagemaegami] n fringe

前かがみ [maekagami] 前かがみになる [maekagami ni naru] v lean forward

マフラー [mafuraa] n muffler

まがい [magai] まがいの [magai no] adj mock

曲がる [magaru] v turn; 曲がった [magatta] adj bent (not straight); 曲がり [magari] n bend; 2番目の角を左に曲がってください [ni-ban-me no kado o hidari ni magatte kudasai] Take the second turning on your left; ここを曲がると···へ行きますか? [koko o magaru to ... e ikimasu ka?] Is this the turning for...?; その角を曲がったところです [sono kado o magatta tokoro desu] It's round the corner; 最初の角を右に曲がってください [saisho no kado o migi ni magatte kudasai] Take the first turning on your right; 右に曲がってください [migi ni magatte kudasai] Turn right; 左に曲がってください [hidari ni magatte kudasai] Turn left

曲げる [mageru] v bend; ひざを曲げる [hiza-o mageru] v kneel

曲げやすい [mageyasui] adj flexible

孫 [mago] n grandchild, grandchildren

孫息子 [magomusuko] n grandson

孫娘 [magomusume] n granddaughter

マグ [magu] n mug

マグロ [maguro] n tuna

麻痺 [mahi] 麻痺した [mahi shita] adj paralysed

真昼 [mahiru] n midday

ホガニー [mahoganii] n mahogany

法 [mahou] n magic; 魔法使い [mahoutsukai] n sorcerer; 魔法の [mahou no] adj magic

法瓶 [mahoubin] n flask

毎 [mai] 毎土曜日に [mai-doyoubi ni] on Saturdays

毎時 [maiji] 毎時···キロ [maiji ... kiro] adv km/h

イク [maiku] n mike

イクロバス [maikurobasu] n minibus

イクロチップ [maikurochippu] n microchip, silicon chip

イクロホン [maikurohon] n microphone; マイクロホンはついていますか? [maikurohon wa tsuite imasu ka?] Does it have a microphone?

毎日 [mainichi] adv daily; 毎日の [mainichi no] adj daily

イル [mairu] n mile; 毎時···マイル [maiji ... mairu] adv mph; 走行マイル計 [soukou mairu kei] n mileometer; 総マイル数 [sou mairu suu] n mileage

イルドな [mairudo na] adj mild

毎週 [maishuu] 毎週土曜日に [maishuu doyoubi ni] every Saturday

埋葬 [maisou] 埋葬する [maisou suru] v bury

毎月 [maitsuki] 毎月の [maitsuki no] adj monthly

マジパン [majipan] n marzipan

魔女 [majo] n witch

魔術 [majutsu] n magic; 魔術的な [majutsuteki na] adj magical; 魔術師 [majutsushi] n magician

マカロニ [makaroni] n macaroni

負かす [makasu] v defeat; 打ち負かす [uchimakasu] v knock out

負け [make] n defeat

負ける [makeru] vi lose

巻き毛 [makige] n curl; 巻き毛の [makige no] adj curly

巻尺 [makijaku] n tape measure

巻き戻す [makimodosu] v rewind

末期 [makki] 末期の [makki no] (終わりの時期) adj terminal; 末期的に [makkiteki ni] adv terminally

巻く [maku] v wind (coil around), wind (with a blow etc.)

枕 [makura] n pillow; 枕カバー [makurakabaa] n pillowcase; 追加の枕を持ってきてください [tsuika no makura o motte kite kudasai] Please bring me an extra pillow

まま [mama] ···のままである [...no mama de aru] v remain

ママ [mama] n mum, mummy (mother)

豆 [mame] n bean; コーヒー豆 [koohiimame] n coffee bean; 豆もやし [mame moyashi] n beansprouts

豆類 [mamerui] n pulses

まもなく [mamonaku] adv shortly, soon

守る [mamoru] 子守り [komori] n babysitting

学ぶ [manabu] v learn

間中 [manaka] ···の間中ずっと [...no aidajuu zutto] prep during

万引き [manbiki] n shoplifting

マンダリンオレンジ [mandarin orenji] n mandarin orange

マネーベルト [maneeberuto] n money belt

マネージャー [maneejaa] マネージャーと話させてください [maneejaa to hanasasete kudasai] I'd like to speak to the manager, please

マネキン [manekin] n dummy, mannequin

招く [maneku] 誤解を招きやすい [gokai-o manekiyasui] adj misleading

漫画 [manga] n cartoon; コマ割り漫画 [komawari manga] n comic strip; 漫画本 [mangabon] n comic book

満月 [mangetsu] n full moon

マンゴー [mangou] n mango

マニキュア [manikyua] n manicure; マニキュアを塗る [manikyua-o nuru] v manicure; マニキュア液 [manikyua eki] n nail polish, nail varnish

満場 [manjou] 満場一致の [manjouitchi no] *adj* unanimous

マンモス [manmosu] *n* mammoth

万年筆 [mannenhitsu] *n* fountain pen

満腹 [manpuku] *adj* satiated; 私は満腹です [watashi wa manpuku desu] I'm full

慢性 [mansei] 慢性の [mansei no] *adj* chronic

満タン [mantan] 満タンにしてください [mantan ni shite kudasai] Fill it up, please

マントルピース [mantorupiisu] *n* mantelpiece

マニュアル [manyuaru] *n* manual

マニュアル車 [manyuarusha] *n* manual car; マニュアル車をお願いします [manyuaru-sha o o-negai shimasu] A manual, please

満足 [manzoku] *n* satisfaction; 満足のいく [manzoku no iku] *adj* satisfactory; 満足した [manzoku shita] *adj* satisfied

マオリ [maori] マオリの [maori no] *adj* Maori; マオリ族 [maori zoku] *n* Maori (person); マオリ語 [maorigo] *n* Maori (language)

マップ [mappu] *n* map; この地域のサイクルマップはありますか? [kono chiiki no saikuru-mappu wa arimasu ka?] Is there a cycle map of this area?; この地域の道路マップはありますか? [kono chiiki no douro-mappu wa arimasu ka?] Do you have a road map of this area?; その街のストリートマップが欲しいのですが [sono machi no sutoriito-mappu ga hoshii no desu ga] I want a street map of the city; ゲレンデのマップはありますか? [gerende no mappu wa arimasu ka?] Do you have a map of the ski runs?; マップをください [mappu o kudasai] Can I have a map?; 私は・・・の道路マップが必要です [watashi wa ... no douro-mappu ga hitsuyou desu] I need a road map of...; 地下鉄のマップはありますか? [chikatetsu no mappu wa arimasu ka?] Do you have a map of the tube?; 地下鉄のマップをいただけますか? [chikatetsu no mappu o itadakemasu ka?] Could I have a map of the tube, please?

マラリア [mararia] *n* malaria

マラソン [marason] *n* marathon

マラウィ [maraui] *n* Malawi

マレーシア [mareeshia] *n* Malaysia; マレーシア人 [mareeshiajin] *n* Malaysian (person); マレーシアの [mareeshia no] *adj* Malaysian

マリファナ [marifana] *n* marijuana

マリーゴールド [mariigourudo] *n* marigold

マリーナ [mariina] *n* marina

マリネ [marine] *n* marinade; マリネにする [marine ni suru] *v* marinade

マルチメディアメッセージングサービス [maruchimedia messeejingu saabisu] *n* MMS

マルハナバチ [maruhanabachi] *n* bumblebee

丸い [marui] *adj* round

マルクス [marukusu] マルクス主義 [marukusushugi] *n* Marxism

丸太 [maruta] *n* log

マルタ [maruta] *n* Malta; マルタ人 [marutajin] *n* Maltese (person); マルタの [maruta no] *adj* Maltese; マルタ語 [marutago] *n* Maltese (language)

マシンガン [mashingan] *n* machine gun

マッサージ [massaaji] *n* massage

マッシュポテト [masshu poteto] *n* mashed potatoes

マッシュルーム [masshuruumu] *n* mushroom

まっすぐ [massugu] *adv* straight ahead; まっすぐ上に [massugu ueni] *adv* upright; まっすぐな [massugu na] *adj* straight; まっすぐに [massugu ni] *adv* straight on; まっすぐ行ってください [massugu itte kudasai] Go straight on; 髪をまっすぐにしてもらえますか? [kami o massugu ni shite moraemasu ka?] Can you straighten my hair?

マス [masu] *n* (魚) trout

増す [masu] *v* increase, multiply

麻酔 [masui] 麻酔薬 [masuiyaku] *n* anaesthetic; 局所麻酔薬 [kyokusho masuiyaku] *n* local anaesthetic; 全身麻酔 [zenshin masui] *n* general anaesthetic

スカラ [masukara] n mascara

スク [masuku] n mask; マスクをした [masuku-o shita] adj masked

すます [masumasu] adv increasingly

スメディア [masumedia] n media

スタード [masutaado] n mustard

スト [masuto] n mast

た [mata] adv (おなじく) too; また・・・でない [mata ... denai] conj neither; また近いうちに [mata chikai uchi ni] see you soon

たは [mata wa] conj or; ・・・かまたは・・・か [...ka matawa ... ka] conj either (.. or), either ... or

天楼 [matenrou] n skyscraper

トン [maton] n mutton

ツ [matsu] n pine

つ [matsu] v wait, wait for; そのまま待つ [sono mama matsu] v hang on; 寝ないで待つ [nenaide matsu] v wait up; ここで数分待ってもらえますか? [koko de suu-fun matte moraemasu ka?] Can you wait here for a few minutes?; 私が待っているあいだにできますか? [watashi ga matte iru aida ni dekimasu ka?] Can you do it while I wait?; 私たちはとても長いあいだ待っています [watashi-tachi wa totemo nagai aida matte imasu] We've been waiting for a very long time; 私たちは応対してもらうのをまだ待っています [watashi-tachi wa outai shite morau no o mada matte imasu] We are still waiting to be served; 私を待っていてください [watashi o matte ite kudasai] Please wait for me

松葉杖 [matsubadue] n crutch

まつげ [matsuge] n eyelash

祭 [matsuri] 過越しの祭 [sugikoshi no matsuri] n Passover

全く [mattaku] adv absolutely, altogether, completely, entirely, indeed; 全くの [mattaku no] adj complete; 全くの [mattaku no] adj sheer

マット [matto] n mat

マットレス [mattoresu] n mattress

マウンテンバイク [mauntenbaiku] n mountain bike

マウスパッド [mausupaddo] n mouse mat

マウスウォッシュ [mausu uosshu] n mouthwash

周り [mawari] 周りに [mawari ni] adv around

回り道 [mawarimichi] n detour

麻薬 [mayaku] n drugs, narcotics; 麻薬ディーラー [mayaku diiraa] n drug dealer; 麻薬常用者 [mayaku jouyousha] n drug addict

迷い出る [mayoideru] 迷い出た家畜 [mayoideta kachiku] n stray

真夜中 [mayonaka] n midnight

マヨネーズ [mayoneezu] n mayonnaise

マヨラナ [mayorana] n marjoram

迷う [mayou] v become confused; 私は道に迷いました [watashi wa michi ni mayoimashita] I'm lost; 私たちは道に迷いました [watashi-tachi wa michi ni mayoimashita] We're lost

眉 [mayu] n eyebrow

まゆ [mayu] まゆをひそめる [mayu o hisomeru] v frown

混ぜる [mazeru] v mix

まず [mazu] まず第一に [mazu daiichi ni] adv firstly

貧しい [mazushii] adj poor

目 [me] n eye; 目に見えない [me ni mienai] adj invisible; 目が覚める [me ga sameru] v awake, wake up; 目薬 [megusuri] n eye drops; 私は目に何か入っています [watashi wa me ni nani ka haitte imasu] I have something in my eye; 私は目が痛みます [watashi wa me ga itamimasu] My eyes are sore

芽 [me] 芽キャベツ [mekyabetsu] n Brussels sprouts

メダル [medaru] n medal; 大メダル [dai medaru] n medallion

目立つ [medatsu] adj noticeable ▷ v striking

メーキャップ [meekyappu] n make-up

メーリングリスト [meeringurisuto] n mailing list

メール [meeru] n mail; ジャンクメール [janku meeru] n junk mail; 電子メール [denshi meeru] n email; 電子メールを送る [denshi meeru-o okuru] v email (a person)

メールアドレス [meeruadoresu] 電子メールアドレス [denshi meeru adoresu] n email address

メーター [meetaa] n meter; パーキングメーター [paakingumeetaa] n parking meter; それではメーター料金より高いです [sore de wa meetaa-ryoukin yori takai desu] It's more than on the meter; メーターはありますか? [meetaa wa arimasu ka?] Do you have a meter? (taxi); メーターが壊れています [meetaa ga kowarete imasu] The meter is broken; メーターを使ってください [meetaa o tsukatte kudasai] Please use the meter; 電気のメーターはどこですか? [denki no meetaa wa doko desu ka?] Where is the electricity meter?

メートル [meetoru] n metre; メートル法の [meetoruhou no] adj metric

眼鏡 [megane] n glasses, specs, spectacles; 眼鏡士 [meganeshi] n optician

メガネ [megane] 遠近両用メガネ [enkin ryouyou megane] n bifocals; 私のメガネを修理できますか? [watashi no megane o shuuri dekimasu ka?] Can you repair my glasses?

雌羊 [mehitsuji] n ewe

銘 [mei] n inscription

姪 [mei] n niece

名簿 [meibo] 順番待ち名簿 [junbanmachi meibo] n waiting list

メイド [meido] 客室係のメイド [kyakushitsugakari no meido] n chambermaid

明白 [meihaku] 明白な [meihaku na] adj clear

明確 [meikaku] 明確な [meikaku na] adj definite; 明確に [meikaku ni] adv definitely

明記 [meiki] 明記する [meiki suru] v specify

メインコース [meinkoosu] n main course

命令 [meirei] n command, order; 命令する [meirei suru] n order (command)

迷路 [meiro] n maze

明細 [meisai] 請求書の明細をもらえますか? [seikyuusho no meisai o moraemasu ka?] Can I have an itemized bill?

明細書 [meisaisho] 銀行の明細書 [ginkou no meisaisho] n bank statement

名声 [meisei] n fame, prestige; 名声のある [meisei no aru] adj prestigious

名詞 [meishi] n noun

名刺 [meishi] n business card; お名刺をいただけますか? [o-meishi o itadakemasu ka?] Can I have your card?; お名刺をお持ちですか? [o-meishi o o-mochi desu ka?] Do you have a business card?; 私の名刺です [watashi no meishi desu] Here's my card

迷信 [meishin] 迷信的な [meishinteki na] adj superstitious

名所 [meisho] n tourist sight; ここにはどんな名所がありますか? [koko ni wa donna meisho ga arimasu ka?] What sights can you visit here?

瞑想 [meisou] n meditation

迷惑 [meiwaku] n trouble; ご迷惑をかけてすみません [go-meiwaku o kakete sumimasen] I'm sorry to trouble you

名誉 [meiyo] 不名誉な [fumeiyo na] adj disgraceful

メカジキ [mekajiki] n swordfish

目隠し [mekakushi] 目隠しする [mekakushi suru] v blindfold; 目隠し布 [mekakushi nuno] n blindfold

メキシコ [mekishiko] n Mexico; メキシコ人 [mekishikojin] n Mexican (person); メキシコの [mekishiko no] adj Mexican

メッカ [mekka] n Mecca

滅菌 [mekkin] 滅菌した [mekkin shita] adj sterile; 滅菌する [mekkin suru] v sterilize

めまい [memai] n vertigo; めまいがする [memai ga suru] adj dizzy; 私はめまいがします [watashi wa memai ga shimasu] I suffer from vertigo

メモ [memo] n memo, note (message); メモ

用紙 [memoyoushi] n notepaper; メモ帳 [memochou] n jotter

モパッド [memopaddo] n notepad

モリカード [memorikaado] n memory card; このデジタルカメラ用のメモリカードをください [kono dejitaru-kamera-you no memori-kaado o kudasai] A memory card for this digital camera, please

綿 [men] n cotton; 脱脂綿 [dasshimen] n cotton wool; 綿菓子 [watagashi] n candyfloss

面 [men] n surface; 海水面 [kaisui men] n sea level

メンバー [menbaa] n (会員) member, (会員資格) membership

メンバーカード [menbaakaado] n membership card

綿棒 [menbou] n cotton bud

麺棒 [menbou] n rolling pin

めんどり [mendori] n hen

面倒 [mendou] n annoyance; 私は今晩子供たちの面倒を見てくれる人が必要です [watashi wa konban kodomo-tachi no mendou o mite kureru hito ga hitsuyou desu] I need someone to look after the children tonight; 私は面倒なことになっています [watashi wa mendou na koto ni natte imasu] I am in trouble

免疫系 [men'ekikei] n immune system

免状 [menjou] n diploma

面会 [menkai] n interview; 面会時間 [menkaijikan] n visiting hours; 面会時間はいつですか? [menkai-jikan wa itsu desu ka?] When are visiting hours?

免許 [menkyo] n licence; 酒類販売免許 [sakerui hanbai menkyo] n off-licence

免許証 [menkyoshou] n licence; 運転免許証 [untenmenkyoshou] n driving licence; 私の運転免許証です [watashi no unten-menkyoshou desu] Here is my driving licence; 私の運転免許証番号は···です [watashi no unten-menkyoshou bangou wa ... desu] My driving licence number is...

綿密 [menmitsu] 綿密な調査 [menmitsu na chousa] n scan

目の見えない [me no mienai] adj blind

免責補償制度 [mensekihoshouseido] 免責補償制度に加入したいのですが [menseki-hoshou-seido ni kanyuu shitai no desu ga] I'd like to arrange a collision damage waiver

面接 [mensetsu] n interview; 面接する [mensetsu suru] v interview; 面接者 [mensetsusha] n interviewer

メニュー [menyuu] n menu; セットメニューをください [setto-menyuu o kudasai] We'll take the set menu; メニューをください [menyuu o kudasai] The menu, please; デザートのメニューをください [dezaato no menyuu o kudasai] The dessert menu, please; 子供用のメニューはありますか? [kodomo-you no menyuu wa arimasu ka?] Do you have a children's menu?

免税 [menzei] 免税の [menzei no] adj duty-free; 免税品 [menzeihin] n duty-free

免税店 [menzeiten] 免税店はどこですか? [menzei-ten wa doko desu ka?] Where is the duty-free shopping?

メレンゲ [merenge] n meringue

メロディ [merodi] 着信メロディ [chakushin merodi] n ringtone

メロディー [merodii] n melody

メロン [meron] n melon

召し上がる [meshiagaru] v eat, drink; 何か召し上がりますか? [nani ka meshiagarimasu ka?] Would you like something to eat?; 何を召し上がりますか? [nani o meshiagarimasu ka?] What would you like to eat?

目下 [meshita] adv (今) currently; 目下の者 [meshita no mono] n inferior

メソジスト派 [mesojisutoha] メソジスト派の [mesojisuto ha no] adj Methodist

メッセンジャー [messenjaa] メッセンジャープログラムを使えますか? [messenjaa-puroguramu o tsukaemasu ka?] Can I use messenger programmes?

雌 [mesu] 雌ライオン [mesuraion] n lioness

雌犬 [mesuinu] n bitch (dog)

目つき [metsuki] n look

めったに [mettani] めったに・・・しない [mettani ... shinai] adv rarely, seldom

雌馬 [meuma] n mare

雌牛 [meushi] n cow

目覚まし [mezamashi] 目覚まし時計 [mezamashi tokei] n alarm clock

珍しい [mezurashii] adj rare (uncommon)

身 [mi] n one's body; ・・・から身を乗り出す [...kara mi-o noridasu] v lean out

見当たる [miataru] 息子の姿が見当たりません [musuko no sugata ga miatarimasen] My son is lost; 娘の姿が見当たりません [musume no sugata ga miatarimasen] My daughter is lost

未払 [mibarai] 未払金 [miharaikin] n arrears

未亡人 [miboujin] n widow

身分 [mibun] n status; 身分証明 [mibun shoumei] n identification; 身分証明書 [mibunshomeisho] n ID card

身振り [miburi] n gesture

身震い [miburui] 身震いする [miburui suru] v shudder

路 [michi] ドライバーが路上で激怒すること [doraibaa ga rojou de gekido suru koto] n road rage; 滑走路 [kassouro] n runway

道 [michi] n road; 小道 [komichi] n lane; この道はどこにつながっていますか？ [kono michi wa doko ni tsunagatte imasu ka?] Where does this path lead?; 混雑を避けられる道はありますか？ [konzatsu o sakerareru michi wa arimasu ka?] Is there a route that avoids the traffic?; ・・・へ行くにはどの道を走ればいいのですか？ [...e iku ni wa dono michi o hashireba ii no desu ka?] Which road do I take for...?; ・・・へ行く自転車道はどこですか？ [...e iku jitensha-dou wa doko desu ka?] Where is the cycle path to...?; 道に沿って進んでください [michi ni sotte susunde kudasai] Keep to the path; 彼女は道を譲りませんでした [kanojo wa michi o yuzurimasen deshita] She didn't give way

未知 [michi] 未知の [michi no] adj unknown

導く [michibiku] v lead

満ちる [michiru] 満ちた [michita] adj full

満ち潮 [michishio] n high tide; 満ち潮はいつですか？ [michi-shio wa itsu desu ka?] When is high tide?

見出し [midashi] n headline

三重 [mie] 三重の [mie no] adj triple

見えなくなる [mienaku naru] 見えなくなること [mienaku naru koto] n disappearance

見える [mieru] v be visible; 見えなくなる [mienaku naru] v disappear; 目に見えない [me ni mienai] adj invisible; 目に見える [me ni mieru] adj visible; 透けて見える [sukete mieru] adj see-through; 私は目が見えません [watashi wa me ga miemasen] I'm blind

ミガキ [migaki] 練り歯ミガキ [neri hamigaki] n toothpaste

右 [migi] 右の [migi no] adj right (not left); 右ハンドル [migi handoru] n right-hand drive; 右に曲がってください [migi ni magatte kudasai] Turn right

右側 [migigawa] 右側の [migigawa no] adj right-hand

右利き [migikiki] 右利きの [migikiki no] adj right-handed

右回り [migimawari] 右回りに [migimawari ni] adv clockwise

見事 [migoto] 見事な [migoto na] adj fine; 見事に [migoto ni] adv fine

見張り [mihari] n guard

見張る [miharu] v guard, spy

見本 [mihon] n sample

ミイラ [miira] n mummy (body)

ミーティング [miitingu] n meeting; ・・・さんとのミーティングを設定したいのですが [...san to no miitingu o settei shitai no desu ga] I'd like to arrange a meeting with...

ミートボール [miitobouru] n meatball

短い [mijikai] adj brief, short

惨めな [mijime na] adj miserable

惨めさ [mijimesa] n misery

未熟 [mijuku] adj unripe; 未熟な [mijuku na]

(経験不足) adj green (inexperienced)

みかげ石 [mikageishi] n granite

未開 [mikai] 未開の [mikai no] adj uncivilized

幹 [miki] n trunk

ミキサー [mikisaa] n liquidizer, mixer

密告 [mikkoku] 密告者 [mikkokusha] n grass (informer)

ミックスサラダ [mikkususarada] n mixed salad

見込み [mikomi] n chance, probability

未婚 [mikon] 未婚の [mikon no] adj unmarried

見回す [mimawasu] あたりを見回す [atari-o miwatasu] v look round

耳 [mimi] n ear; 耳の聞こえない [mimi no kikoenai] adj deaf; 耳の痛み [mimi no itami] n earache; 耳を聾するような [mimi-o rousuru you na] adj deafening

耳栓 [mimisen] n earplugs

身元 [mimoto] n identity; 身元不詳の [mimoto fushou no] adj unidentified

南 [minami] n south; 南に [minami ni] adv south; 南の [minami no] adj south, southern

南アフリカ [minami afurika] n South Africa; 南アフリカ人 [minami afurikajin] n South African; 南アフリカの [minami afurika no] adj South African

南アメリカ [minami amerika] n South America; 南アメリカ人 [minami amerikajin] n South American (person); 南アメリカの [minami amerika no] adj South American

南行き [minami yuki] 南行きの [minami yuki no] adj southbound

見習う [minarau] 見習い [minarai] n apprentice

身なり [minari] n costume

みなす [minasu] v consider, regard

港 [minato] n harbour, port (ships)

民営 [min'ei] 民営化する [min'eika suru] v privatize

ミネラルウォーター [mineraru

uootaa] n mineral water; ミネラルウォーターのボトル1本 [mineraruuootaa no botoru 1 hon] a bottle of mineral water; 炭酸なしミネラルウォーターのボトル1本 [tansan-nashi mineraru-wootaa no botoru ippon] a bottle of still mineral water; 炭酸入りミネラルウォーターのボトル1本 [tansan-iri mineraru-wootaa no botoru ippon] a bottle of sparkling mineral water

ミニバー [minibaa] n minibar

ミニチュア [minichua] n miniature; ミニチュアの [minichua no] adj miniature

醜い [minikui] adj ugly

ミニスカート [minisukaato] n miniskirt

身に着ける [mi ni tsukeru] 身に着けている [mi ni tsukete iru] v wear

民間 [minkan] 民間伝承 [minkandenshou] n folklore; 民間の [minkan no] adj civilian

民間人 [minkanjin] n civilian

ミンク [minku] n mink

見逃す [minogasu] v miss

身代金 [minoshirokin] n ransom

民主 [minshu] 民主主義 [minshu shugi] n democracy; 民主主義の [minshu shugi no] adj democratic

ミント [minto] n mint (herb/sweet)

民族 [minzoku] 民族の [minzoku no] adj ethnic

見落とし [miotoshi] n oversight (mistake)

見落とす [miotosu] v overlook

未来 [mirai] n future; 未来の [mirai no] adj future

ミリメートル [mirimeetoru] n millimetre

みる [miru] 試してみる [tameshite miru] v try out

見る [miru] v look, see; ちらっと見る [chiratto miru] v glance; ちらっと見ること [chiratto miru koto] n glance; じっと見る [jitto miru] v stare; 見る人 [miru hito] n viewer; ···をよく見る [...-o yoku miru] v look at; 夢を見る [yume o miru] v dream; ちょっと見ているだけです [chotto mite iru dake desu] I'm just looking

ミルク [miruku] n milk; ベビーミルク [bebii miruku] n baby milk; ミルクは別にく

ください [miruku wa betsu ni kudasai] with the milk separate

ミルクチョコレート [mirukuchokoreeto] n milk chocolate

ミルク入り [miruku iri] ミルク入りコーヒーをください [miruku-iri koohii o kudasai] A white coffee, please

ミルクシェイク [mirukusheiku] n milkshake

魅力 [miryoku] n attraction, charm; 魅力的な [miryokuteki na] adj attractive, glamorous

魅力的な [miryokuteki na] adj charming

ミサ [misa] n mass (church); ミサはいつですか? [misa wa itsu desu ka?] When is mass?

ミサイル [misairu] n missile

店 [mise] n shop, store; 文房具店 [bunbouguten] n stationer's; 店主 [tenshu] n shopkeeper; 店員 [ten-in] n shop assistant; お店は何時に閉まりますか? [o-mise wa nan-ji ni shimarimasu ka?] What time do the shops close?; 新聞を売っている一番近い店はどこですか? [shinbun o utte iru ichiban chikai mise wa doko desu ka?] Where is the nearest shop which sells newspapers?; 写真用品を売っている一番近い店はどこですか? [shashin-youhin o utte iru ichiban chikai mise wa doko desu ka?] Where is the nearest shop which sells photographic equipment?; 切手を売っている一番近い店はどこですか? [kitte o utte iru ichiban chikai mise wa doko desu ka?] Where is the nearest shop which sells stamps?

見せびらかす [misebirakasu] v show off; 見せびらかし [misebirakashi] n show-off

未成年 [miseinen] 未成年の [miseinen no] adj underage; 未成年者 [miseinensha] n minor

見せる [miseru] v show; 見せていただけますか? [misete itadakemasu ka?] Could you show me please?

ミシン [mishin] n sewing machine

ミソサザイ [misosazai] n wren

密集 [misshuu] n congestion, density; 密集した [misshuu shita] adj dense

みすぼらしい [misuborashii] adj shabby

見捨てる [misuteru] v abandon

認める [mitomeru] v admit (confess)

ミトン [miton] n mitten

見通し [mitoushi] n outlook, prospect

三つ子 [mitsugo] n triplets

見つかる [mitsukaru] アットマークが見つかりません [atto-maaku ga mitsukarimasen] I can't find the at sign

見つけ出す [mitsukedasu] 跡をたどって見つけ出す [ato-o tadotte mitsukedasu] v track down

見つける [mitsukeru] v find, spot

見つめる [mitsumeru] v gaze; じっと見つめる [jitto mitsumeru] v stare

見積もり [mitsumori] n estimate

見積もる [mitsumoru] v estimate

密漁 [mitsuryou] 密漁した [mitsuryou shita] adj poached (caught illegally)

密輸 [mitsuyu] n smuggling; 密輸する [mitsuyu suru] v smuggle; 密輸業者 [mitsuyu gyousha] n smuggler

魅惑 [miwaku] 魅惑的な [miwakuteki na] adj fascinating

溝 [mizo] n ditch; 深くて細長い溝 [fukakute hosonagai mizo] n trench

みぞれ [mizore] n sleet; みぞれが降る [mizore ga furu] v sleet

水 [mizu] n water; 水上スキー [suijousukii] n water-skiing; 水をやる [mizu-o yaru] v water; 飲料水 [inryousui] n drinking water; 水をもっと持ってきてください [mizu o motto motte kite kudasai] Please bring more water; 水差し一杯の水 [mizusashi ippai no mizu] a jug of water

水疱瘡 [mizubousou] n chickenpox

水ぶくれ [mizubukure] n blister

水瓶座 [mizugameza] n Aquarius

水着 [mizugi] n bathing suit, swimming costume, swimsuit

水切り [mizukiri] n colander

水切り板 [mizukiriban] n draining board

水たまり [mizutamari] n puddle

湖 [mizu-umi] n lake

···も [...mo] adv also

モビールハウス [mobiiruhausu] n mobile home

持ち上げる [mochiageru] v lift, pick up

持ち運び [mochihakobi] 持ち運びできる [mochihakobi dekiru] adj portable

持ち運ぶ [mochihakobu] 持ち運び用ベッド [mochihakobi you beddo] n carrycot

持ちこたえる [mochikotaeru] v hold up

持ち続ける [mochitsudukeru] v keep

モデム [modemu] n modem

戻る [modoru] v get back, go back, return; 戻ってくる [modotte kuru] v come back

戻す [modosu] v bring back, return

モグラ [mogura] n mole (mammal)

模範 [mohan] n example; 模範的な [mohanteki na] adj model

模倣 [mohou] 模倣する [mohou suru] v imitate

モイスチャライザー [moisucharaizaa] n moisturizer

文字 [moji] n letter (a, b, c); 文字どおりに [mojidouri ni] adv literally

モジュール [mojuuru] n module

模型 [mokei] n model; 模型を作る [mokei-o tsukuru] v model

木工 [mokkou] 木工部 [mokkoubu] n woodwork

木馬 [mokuba] 揺り木馬 [yurimokuba] n rocking horse

目撃者 [mokugekisha] n witness; 私の目撃者になってもらえますか? [watashi no mokugeki-sha ni natte moraemasu ka?] Can you be a witness for me?

目次 [mokuji] n contents (list)

目録 [mokuroku] n inventory; 目録に載っていない [mokuroku ni notte inai] adj unlisted

木製 [mokusei] 木製の [mokusei no] adj wooden

木炭 [mokutan] n charcoal

目的 [mokuteki] n aim, objective, purpose

目的地 [mokutekichi] n destination

木曜日 [mokuyoubi] n Thursday; 木曜日に [mokuyoubi ni] on Thursday

もまた [momata] ···もまた [...momata] (否定) adv either (with negative); ···もまた···でない [...momata...denai] conj neither; ···もまた···ない [...momata...nai] conj nor

もめごと [momegoto] もめごとを起こす人 [momegoto-o okosu hito] n troublemaker

モミ [momi] n fir (tree)

もみ消す [momikesu] 火をもみ消す [hi-o momikesu] v stub out

腿 [momo] n thigh

モモ [momo] n peach

門 [mon] n gate

モナコ [monako] n Monaco

問題 [mondai] n problem; 時事問題 [jiji mondai] n current affairs; あなたのファックスに問題があります [anata no fakkusu ni mondai ga arimasu] There is a problem with your fax; 問題があったときに誰に連絡すればいいのですか? [mondai ga atta toki ni dare ni renraku sureba ii no desu ka?] Who do we contact if there are problems?

門限 [mongen] n curfew; 門限はありますか? [mongen wa arimasu ka?] Is there a curfew?

モンゴル [mongoru] n Mongolia; モンゴル人 [mongorujin] n Mongolian (person); モンゴルの [mongoru no] adj Mongolian; モンゴル語 [mongorugo] n Mongolian (language)

モニター [monitaa] n monitor

物 [mono] n object, thing; 洗濯物 [sentakumono] n laundry, washing

者 [mono] 目下の者 [meshita no mono] n inferior

もの [mono] n (材料) stuff; ···のものである [...no mono de aru] v belong to

物語 [monogatari] n story, tale

物乞い [monogoi] 物乞いをする [monogoi-o suru] v beg

物干し [monohoshi] 物干し綱 [monohoshi tsuna] *n* washing line

物まね [monomane] 物まねをする [monomane-o suru] *v* mimic

ものすごい [monosugoi] *adj* terrific

モンスーン [monsuun] *n* monsoon

モーニング [mooningu] モーニングコール [mooningukooru] *n* alarm call

モーリシャス [moorishasu] *n* Mauritius

モーリタニア [mooritania] *n* Mauritania

モールス [moorusu] モールス信号 [moorusu shingou] *n* Morse

モーターバイク [mootaabaiku] *n* motorbike

モーターレース [mootaareesu] *n* motor racing

モペッド [mopeddo] *n* moped

モペット [mopetto] モペットを借りたいのですが [mopetto o karitai no desu ga] I want to hire a moped

もっぱら [moppara] *adv* exclusively

モップ [moppu] *n* mop; モップでぬぐい取る [moppu de nuguitoru] *v* mop up

漏れ口 [moreguchi] *n* leak

漏れる [moreru] *v* leak; ガソリンタンクが漏れています [gasorin-tanku ga morete imasu] The petrol tank is leaking; ラジエーターに漏れがあります [rajieetaa ni more ga arimasu] There is a leak in the radiator

森 [mori] *n* forest, wood

モロッコ [morokko] *n* Morocco; モロッコ人 [morokkojin] *n* Moroccan; モロッコの [morokko no] *adj* Moroccan

漏る [moru] *v* leak; 天井が漏っています [tenjou ga motte imasu] The roof leaks

モルドバ [morudoba] *n* Moldova; モルドバ人 [morudobajin] *n* Moldovan; モルドバの [morudoba no] *adj* Moldovan

モルヒネ [moruhine] *n* morphine

モルモット [morumotto] *n* (動物) guinea pig (rodent)

モルタル [morutaru] *n* mortar (plaster)

モルトウイスキー [moruto uisukii] *n* malt whisky

もし [moshi] *conj* if; もし・・・とすれば [moshi ... tosureba] *conj* provided, providing; もし・・・でなければ [moshi ... denakereba] *conj* unless

もしかしたら [moshikashitara] *adv* maybe

もしも [moshimo] もしも・・・ならば [moshimo ... naraba] *conj* if

モスク [mosuku] *n* mosque; どこかにモスクはありますか? [doko-ka ni mosuku wa arimasu ka?] Where is there a mosque?

もたれる [motareru] *v* (寄りかかる) lean; ・・・にもたれて [...ni motarete] *prep* against

素 [moto] 固形スープの素 [kokei suupu no moto] *n* stock cube

求める [motomeru] ・・・を求める [...-o motomeru] *v* ask for

基づく [motozuku] ・・・に基づく [...ni motozuku] *adj* based

持つ [motsu] 手に持つ [te ni motsu] *v* hold; 持っている [motte iru] *v* have; 持ってくる [motte kuru] *v* bring; 希望が持てる [kibou ga moteru] *adj* hopeful; 希望を持って [kibou-o motte] *adv* hopefully; これを持っていていただけますか? [kore o motte ite itadakemasu ka?] Could you hold this for me?; それはどのくらい日持ちしますか? [sore wa dono kurai himochi shimasu ka?] How long will it keep?

最も [mottomo] 最もよい [mottomo yoi] *adj* best; 最もよく [mottomo yoku] *adv* best; 最も重要な [mottomo juuyou na] *adj* essential; 最も少ない [mottomo sukunai] *adj* least

最も多い [mottomo ooi] *adj* most; 最も多く [mottomo ouku] *adv* most (superlative)

もっとのんびりする [motto nonbiri suru] *v* slow down

もう [mou] *adv* yet; もう一つの [mou hitotsu no] *adj* another

盲導犬 [moudouken] *n* guide dog; 私は盲導犬を連れています [watashi wa moudouken o tsurete imasu] I have a guide dog

毛布 [moufu] *n* blanket; 電気毛布

[denkimoufu] n **electric blanket**; 毛布がもっと必要です [moufu ga motto hitsuyou desu] **We need more blankets**; 追加の毛布を持ってきてください [tsuika no moufu o motte kite kudasai] **Please bring me an extra blanket**

もう一度 [mou ichido] あとでもう一度かけてもらえますか? [ato de mou ichido kakete moraemasu ka?] **Can you try again later?**; もう一度言っていただけますか? [mou ichido itte itadakemasu ka?] **Could you repeat that, please?**; もう一度言ってください [mou ichido itsutte kudasai] **Pardon?**

儲かる [moukaru] v **lucrative**

猛禽 [moukin] n **bird of prey**

モーニングコール [mouningukouru] n **wake-up call, alarm call**; 明日の朝7時にモーニングコールをお願いします [asu no asa shichi-ji ni mooningu-kooru o o-negai shimasu] **I'd like an alarm call for tomorrow morning at seven o'clock**

申し分 [moushibun] 申し分ない [moushibun nai] adj **well**; 申し分なく [moushibun naku] adv **all right, well**

申し出る [moushideru] 自発的に申し出る [jihatsuteki ni moushideru] v **volunteer**

申込 [moushikomi] 申込書 [moushikomisho] n **application form**

申し込む [moushikomu] v **apply**; 申し込み [moushikomi] n **application**

申し立て [moushitate] n **allegation**

申し立てられた [moushitaterareta] v **alleged**

申し訳ない [moushiwakenai] 大変申し訳ありません、規則を知りませんでした [taihen moushiwake arimasen, kisoku o shirimasen deshita] **I'm very sorry, I didn't know the regulations**

モーター [moutaa] n **motor**

モーターボート [moutaabouto] n **motorboat**; 快速モーターボート [kaisoku mootaabooto] n **speedboat**

モーテル [mouteru] n **motel**

もや [moya] n **mist**; もやの立ち込めた [moya no tachikometa] adj **misty**

もやし [moyashi] 豆もやし [mame moyashi] n **beansprouts**

燃やす [moyasu] v **burn**

催す [moyoosu] 屋外市を催す場所 [okugai ichi-o moyousu basho] n **fairground**

模様 [moyou] n **pattern**

モザイク [mozaiku] n **mosaic**

モザンビーク [mozanbiiku] n **Mozambique**

模造 [mozou] 模造の [mozou no] adj **fake**

模造品 [mozouhin] n **fake, imitation**

無 [mu] 無意味な [muimi na] adj **senseless**

無茶な [mucha na] adj **crazy**

鞭 [muchi] n **whip**

無知 [muchi] n **ignorance**; 無知の [muchi no] adj **ignorant**

無鉛 [muen] 無鉛の [muen no] adj **lead-free**; 無鉛ガソリン [muen gasorin] n **unleaded petrol**; ···分の無鉛プレミアムガソリンをお願いします [...bun no muen-puremiamu-gasorin o o-negai shimasu] **... worth of premium unleaded, please**

無蓋 [mugai] 無蓋貨車 [mugai kasha] n **truck**

無害 [mugai] 無害な [mugai na] adj **harmless**

麦 [mugi] 大麦 [oumugi] n **barley**

麦わら [mugiwara] n **straw**

謀反 [muhon] 謀反の [muhon no] adj **rebellious**

無為 [mui] 無為に過ごす [mui ni sugosu] v **mess about**

無意味な [muimi na] adj **pointless**

無慈悲な [mujihi na] adj **ruthless**

無人 [mujin] 無人島 [mujintou] n **desert island**

無条件 [mujouken] 無条件の [mujouken no] adj **unconditional**

向かい側 [mukaigawa] 向かい側に [mukaigawa ni] adv **opposite**; 向かい側の [mukaigawa no] adj **opposite**

無関係 [mukankei] 無関係な [mukankei

na] *adj* irrelevant

むかつく [mukatsuku] *n* (腹が立つ) disgusted; むかつくような [mukatsuku you na] (腹が立つ) *adj* repulsive; むかむかする [mukamuka suru] (腹が立つ) *adj* disgusting

向かう [mukau] ···に向かう [...ni mukau] (方角) *v* face

向き [muki] 向きを変える [muki o kaeru] *v* turn

むき出す [mukidasu] むき出しにする [mukidashi ni suru] *v* bare; むき出しの [mukidashi no] *adj* bare

無効 [mukou] 無効の [mukou no] *adj* void

向こう [mukou] ···の向こうに [...no mukou ni] *prep* beyond

むこうずね [mukouzune] *n* shin

向く [muku] *v* face; 反対に向きを変えなければなりません [hantai ni muki o kaenakereba narimasen] You have to turn round

報い [mukui] 報いのある [mukui no aru] *adj* rewarding

無給 [mukyuu] 無給の [mukyuu no] *adj* unpaid

胸 [mune] *n* chest (body part); 私は胸に痛みがあります [watashi wa mune ni itami ga arimasu] I have a pain in my chest

胸焼け [muneyake] *n* heartburn

無能 [munou] 無能な [munou na] *adj* incompetent

村 [mura] *n* village

紫色 [murasakiiro] 紫色の [murasakiiro no] *adj* purple

群れ [mure] *n* a lot, flock, herd

無料 [muryou] 無料の [muryou no] *adj* free (no cost)

無線 [musen] *adj* wireless; 無線制御の [musen seigyo no] *adj* radio-controlled; その部屋で無線インターネット接続を利用できますか? [sono heya de musen-intaanetto-setsuzoku o riyou dekimasu ka?] Does the room have wireless internet access?

虫 [mushi] *n* bug, worm; 私の部屋に虫がいます [watashi no heya ni mushi ga imasu] There are bugs in my room

無視 [mushi] 無視する [mushi suru] *v* ignore

蒸し暑い [mushiatsui] 蒸し暑いです [mushiatsui desu] It's muggy

無神論 [mushinron] 無神論者 [mushinronsha] *n* atheist

無思慮 [mu shiryo] 無思慮な [mushiryo na] *adj* thoughtless

虫よけ [mushiyoke] *n* insect repellent; 虫よけはありますか? [mushi-yoke wa arimasu ka?] Do you have insect repellent?

結び目 [musubime] *n* knot

息子 [musuko] *n* son; 息子の妻 [musuko no tsuma] *n* daughter-in-law; 息子の姿が見当たりません [musuko no sugata ga miatarimasen] My son is lost; 私の息子が行方不明です [watashi no musuko ga yukue-fumei desu] My son is missing

娘 [musume] *n* daughter; おてんば娘 [otemba musume] *n* tomboy; 継娘 [mama musume] *n* stepdaughter; 娘の夫 [musume no otto] *n* son-in-law; 私の娘が行方不明です [watashi no musume ga yukue-fumei desu] My daughter is missing; 娘の姿が見当たりません [musume no sugata ga miatarimasen] My daughter is lost

むっとする [muttosuru] *v* (息詰まる) stifling

むっつり [muttsuri] むっつりした [muttsuri shita] *adj* moody

ムール貝 [muurugai] *n* mussel

ムース [muusu] *n* mousse

夢遊病 [muyuubyou] 夢遊病で歩く [muyuubyou de aruku] *v* sleepwalk

難しい [muzukashii] *adj* difficult

脈拍 [myakuhaku] *n* pulse

ミャンマー [myanmaa] *n* Myanmar

ミュージカル [myuujikaru] *n* musical

ミュージック [myuujikku] フォークミュージック [fooku myuujikku] *n* folk music

ミューズリー [myuuzurii] *n* muesli

n

ナビゲーション [nabigeeshon] 衛星ナビゲーション [eisei nabigeeshon] n sat nav

なだれ [nadare] n avalanche; なだれの危険はありますか？ [nadare no kiken wa arimasu ka?] Is there a danger of avalanches?

なでる [naderu] v stroke; なでること [naderu koto] n stroke (hit)

など [nado] ・・・など [...nado] adv etc

長い [nagai] adj long; ひょろ長い [hyoro nagai] adj lanky; 長さ [nagasa] n length; 私たちはとても長いあいだ待っています [watashi-tachi wa totemo nagai aida matte imasu] We've been waiting for a very long time

長椅子 [nagaisu] 背付きの長椅子 [setsuki no nagaisu] n settee

長く [nagaku] adv long; より長く [yori nagaku] adv longer

眺め [nagame] n view; 壮観な眺めを見たいのですが [soukan na nagame o mitai no desu ga] We'd like to see spectacular views

流れ [nagare] n current (flow)

流れる [nagareru] v flow

長さ [nagasa] この長さでお願いします [kono nagasa de o-negai shimasu] This length, please

流す [nagasu] v pour

投げる [nageru] v pitch, throw; 投げ飛ばす [nagetobasu] v fling; 軽く投げる [karuku nageru] v toss

投げ捨てる [nagesuteru] v dump

投げ矢 [nageya] ダーツ用の投げ矢 [daatsu you no nageya] n dart

投げ槍 [nageyari] n javelin

ない [nai] adj no

内部 [naibu] 内部の [naibu no] adj internal

ナイフ [naifu] n knife

ナイジェリア [naijeria] n Nigeria; ナイジェリア人 [naijeriajin] n Nigerian (person); ナイジェリアの [naijeria no] adj Nigerian

内密 [naimitsu] 内密の [naimitsu no] adj confidential

ナイロン [nairon] n nylon

内線 [naisen] 内線番号 [naisen-bangou] extension

内戦 [naisen] n civil war

ナイトクラブ [naitokurabu] n nightclub

内蔵 [naizou] 内蔵型の [naizougata no] adj self-contained

中 [naka] 中に入れない [naka ni irenai] v keep out; 中くらいの [naka kurai no] adj medium (between extremes); ・・・の中に [...no naka ni] prep in; ・・・の中で [...no naka de] prep among; ・・・の中へ [...no naka-e] prep into; 午前中に [gozen-chuu ni] in the morning

仲買人 [nakagainin] 株式仲買人 [kabushikinakagainin] n stockbroker

中程 [nakahodo] 中程で [nakahodo de] adv halfway

仲間 [nakama] n companion, mate

中身 [nakami] n content

中庭 [nakaniwa] n courtyard

泣きじゃくる [nakijakuru] v sob

泣き叫ぶ [nakisakebu] 泣き叫ぶ声 [nakisakebu koe] n cry

泣く [naku] v cry, weep

なくす [nakusu] *vt* lose

生ビール [namabiiru] 生ビールをください [nama-biiru o kudasai] **A draught beer, please**

名前 [namae] *n* name; 洗礼名 [senreimei] *n* Christian name; あなたのお名前は? [anata no o-namae wa?] **What's your name?**; 私の名前は・・・です [watashi no namae wa ... desu] **My name is...**

生意気 [namaiki] 生意気な [namaiki na] *adj* cheeky

生の [nama no] *n* raw

なまぬるい [namanurui] *adj* lukewarm

鉛 [namari] *n* lead (*metal*)

生卵 [namatamago] *n* raw egg; 私は生卵を食べられません [watashi wa nama-tamago o taberaremasen] **I can't eat raw eggs**

生焼け [namayake] 生焼けの [namayake no] *adj* rare (*undercooked*)

ナメクジ [namekuji] *n* slug

滑らかな [nameraka na] *adj* smooth

なめる [nameru] *v* (舌) lick

波 [nami] *n* wave; 打ち寄せる波 [uchiyoseru nami] *n* surf

涙 [namida] *n* tear (*from eye*)

何 [nan] *pron* what; 何の [nan no] *adj* what; これには何が入っていますか? [kore ni wa nani ga haitte imasu ka?] **What is in this?**; それは何ですか? [sore wa nan desu ka?] **What is it?**; ・・・は何といいますか? [...wa nan to iimasu ka?] **What is the word for...?**

ナナフシ [nanafushi] *n* stick insect

ナンバープレート [nanbaapureeto] *n* number plate

何でも [nandemo] *pron* anything

何語 [nanigo] 何語が話せますか? [nani-go ga hanasemasu ka?] **What languages do you speak?**

何か [nanika] *pron* something

何も [nanimo] 何もしない [nanimo shinai] *adj* idle; 何も・・・ない [nanimo ... nai] *n* nothing

何曜日 [nan-youbi] 今日は何曜日ですか? [kyou wa nan-youbi desu ka?] **What day is it today?**

何時 [nanji] 今何時か教えていただけますか? [ima nan-ji ka oshiete itadakemasu ka?] **What time is it, please?**; 何時に終わりますか? [nan-ji ni owarimasu ka?] **When will you have finished?**; ・・・へ行く電車は何時にありますか? [...e iku densha wa nan-ji ni arimasu ka?] **What times are the trains to...?**; ・・・へ行く電車は何時ですか? [...e iku densha wa nan-ji desu ka?] **What time is the train to...?**; 電車は・・・に何時に着きますか? [densha wa ... ni nan-ji ni tsukimasu ka?] **What time does the train arrive in...?**

南京錠 [nankinjou] *n* padlock

軟膏 [nankou] *n* ointment

南極 [nankyoku] *n* South Pole; 南極大陸 [nankyoku tairiku] *n* Antarctic

難問 [nanmon] *n* puzzle

何日 [nannichi] 今日は何日ですか? [kyou wa nan-nichi desu ka?] **What is today's date?**; 何日ですか? [nan-nichi desu ka?] **What is the date?**

難破 [nanpa] *n* shipwreck; 難破した [nanpa shita] *adj* shipwrecked

南西 [nansei] *n* southwest

ナンセンス [nansensu] *n* nonsense

なんてことを! [nantekoto wo] *excl* no!

何とか [nantoka] *adv* somehow

何とおっしゃいましたか? [nan to osshaimashita ka] *excl* pardon?

南東 [nantou] *n* southeast

治る [naoru] *v* heal

直す [naosu] *v* mend; ヒューズを直してもらえますか? [hyuuzu o naoshite moraemasu ka?] **Can you mend a fuse?**

治す [naosu] *v* cure

直す [naosu] 天気がもち直すといいですね [tenki ga mochinaosu to ii desu ne] **I hope the weather improves**

ナプキン [napukin] *n* napkin, serviette; 生理用ナプキン [seiriyou napukin] *n* sanitary towel

並べる [naraberu] v set out

鳴らす [narasu] v ring; ゴロゴロとのどを鳴らす [gorogoro to nodo-o narasu] v purr; 鳴らすこと [narasu koto] n ring

なる [naru] ···になる [...ni naru] v become; それはいくらになりますか? [sore wa ikura ni narimasu ka?] How much does that come to?

成る [naru] ···から成る [...kara naru] v consist of

鳴る [naru] カチッと鳴る [kachitto naru] v click

なさる [nasaru] 今日は何をなさりたいですか? [kyou wa nani o nasaritai desu ka?] What would you like to do today?

なし [nashi] 袖なしの [sode nashi no] adj sleeveless; ···なしで [...nashide] prep without; 砂糖なしで [satou nashi de] no sugar; ···なしでお願いします [...nashi de o-negai shimasu] I'd like it without..., please

ナス [nasu] n aubergine

夏 [natsu] n summer; 夏の休暇 [natsu no kyuuka] n summer holidays; 夏に [natsu ni] in summer; 夏の間 [natsu no aida] during the summer; 夏の後に [natsu no ato ni] after summer; 夏の前に [natsu no mae ni] before summer

ナツメグ [natsumegu] n nutmeg

ナット [natto] n nut (device)

ナッツ [nattsu] n nut (food); ナッツを使わずに食事を用意していただけますか? [nattsu o tsukawazu ni shokuji o youi shite itadakemasu ka?] Could you prepare a meal without nuts?

ナッツアレルギー [nattsuarerugii] n nut allergy

納屋 [naya] n barn

悩ます [nayamasu] v bother; 神経を悩ます [shinkei-o nayamasu] adj nerve-racking

悩む [nayamu] 悩ませる [nayamaseru] v pester; 私は時差ぼけに悩んでいます [watashi wa jisaboke ni nayande imasu] I'm suffering from jet lag

なぜ [naze] adv why

謎 [nazo] n mystery

謎めく [nazomeku] 謎めいた [nazomeita] adj mysterious

寝坊 [nebou] 朝寝坊 [asanebou] n have a lie-in, lie in

値段 [nedan] 値段を書いてください [nedan o kaite kudasai] Please write down the price

願い [negai] n wish

願う [negau] v wish

ネギ [negi] n leek, spring onion

値切る [negiru] うるさく値切る [urusaku negiru] v haggle

ネグリジェ [negurije] n nightie

ねじ [neji] n screw; ねじを緩める [neji-o yurumeru] v unscrew; ねじがゆるくなっています [neji ga yuruku natte imasu] The screw has come loose

ねじる [nejiru] v twist, wrench; ねじり [nejiri] n wrench

ネックレス [nekkuresu] n necklace

熱狂 [nekkyou] 熱狂者 [nekkyousha] n fanatic; 熱狂的愛国主義者 [nekkyoutekiaikokushugisha] n chauvinist

猫 [neko] n cat

ネクタイ [nekutai] n tie

ネクタリン [nekutarin] n nectarine

ねまき [nemaki] n nightdress

眠い [nemui] adj drowsy, sleepy

眠らずに [nemurazu ni] v awake

眠り [nemuri] n sleep

眠る [nemuru] v sleep; 眠って [nemutte] adj asleep; うるさくて眠れません [urusakute nemuremasen] I can't sleep for the noise; よく眠れましたか? [yoku nemuremashita ka?] Did you sleep well?; 暑くて眠れません [atsukute nemuremasen] I can't sleep for the heat

年 [nen, toshi] n year; うるう年 [uruudoshi] n leap year; 年一回の [nen'ikkai no] adj annual; 年に一度 [nen ni ichido] adv yearly

粘土 [nendo] n clay

年一回 [nen'ikkai] adv annually

念入 [nen'iri] 念入りな [nen'iri na] *adj* conscientious

年次 [nenji] *adj* annual; 年次総会 [nenjisoukai] *n* AGM

年金 [nenkin] *n* pension; 年金受給者 [nenkin jukyuusha] *n* pensioner

年配 [nenpai] 年配の [nenpai no] *adj* elderly

年齢 [nenrei] *n* age; 年齢制限 [nenreiseigen] *n* age limit

燃料 [nenryou] *n* fuel; 燃料を補給する [nenryou o hokyuu suru] *v* refuel

粘性ゴム [nenseigomu] *n* gum

捻挫 [nenza] *n* sprain

ネオン [neon] *n* neon

ネパール [nepaaru] *n* Nepal

ねらう [nerau] *v* aim

寝る [neru] *v* sleep; いっしょに寝る [issho ni neru] *v* sleep together; 誰とでも寝る [dare todemo neru] *v* sleep around; あなたが帰ってくるころには私たちは寝ています [anata ga kaette kuru koro ni wa watashi-tachi wa nete imasu] We'll be in bed when you get back

熱心 [nesshin] 熱心な [nesshin na] *adj* enthusiastic, keen

寝過ごす [nesugosu] *v* oversleep, sleep in

ねたみ [netami] *n* envy

熱 [netsu] *n* fever, heat; 熱する [nessuru] *v* heat; ···熱 [...netsu] (熱狂) *n* mania; 彼は熱があります [kare wa netsu ga arimasu] He has a fever

熱意 [netsui] *n* enthusiasm

熱情 [netsujou] *n* passion

熱帯 [nettai] 熱帯の [nettai no] *adj* tropical

熱帯雨林 [nettai urin] *n* rainforest

ネット [netto] *n* internet

ネットボール [nettobouru] *n* netball

ネットワーク [nettowaaku] *n* network; ネットワークにつながりません [nettowaaku ni tsunagarimasen] I can't get a network

二 [ni] *num* two

荷 [ni] *n* load; 荷を解く [ni-o toku] *v* unpack; 荷を積む [ni-o tsumu] *v* load; 荷を降ろす [ni-o orosu] *v* unload

···に [...ni] *prep* at, to

似合う [niau] *v* suit

2倍 [nibai] 2倍にする [nibai ni suru] *v* double; 2倍の [nibai no] *adj* double

二番目 [nibanme] *n* second; 二番目の [ni banme no] *adj* second

荷馬車 [nibasha] *n* cart

鈍い [nibui] *adj* blunt

日 [nichi] *n* day; 日の出 [hi no de] *n* sunrise; なんてすばらしい日でしょう! [nante subarashii hi deshou!] What a lovely day!

日没 [nichibotsu] *n* sunset

日曜日 [nichiyoubi] *n* Sunday; 日曜日に [nichiyoubi ni] on Sunday; 十月三日の日曜日です [juu-gatsu mik-ka no nichiyoubi desu] It's Sunday third October

日曜大工 [nichiyoudaiku] *n* DIY

二段 [nidan] 二段ベッド [nidanbeddo] *n* bunk beds

煮出し汁 [nidashijiru] *n* broth

二度 [nido] *adv* twice

にがい [nigai] *adj* bitter

二月 [nigatsu] *n* February

逃げ出す [nigedasu] *v* run away

逃げる [nigeru] *v* escape, flee, get away

二泊 [nihaku] 二泊したいのですが [nihaku shitai no desu ga] I'd like to stay for two nights

日本 [nihon] *n* Japan

日本人 [nihonjin] *n* Japanese (*person*)

日本の [nihon no] *adj* Japanese

日本語 [nihongo] *n* Japanese (*language*)

虹 [niji] *n* rainbow

二時 [niji] 二時です [ni-ji desu] It's two o'clock; 二時十五分です [ni-ji juugo-fun desu] It's quarter past two; 二時半です [ni-ji-han desu] It's half past two; もうすぐ二時半です [mousugu ni-ji han desu] It's almost half past two

ニジェール [nijieeru] *n* Niger

二十 [nijuu] *number* twenty; 二十番目の [nijuu banme no] *adj* twentieth

ニカラグア [nikaragua] *n* Nicaragua; ニカラグア人 [nikaraguajin] *n* Nicaraguan (person); ニカラグアの [nikaragua no] *adj* Nicaraguan

にきび [nikibi] *n* acne, zit

日記 [nikki] *n* diary

日光 [nikkou] *n* sunlight, sunshine

日光浴 [nikkouyoku] 日光浴をする [nikkouyoku o suru] *v* sunbathe; 日光浴用ベッド [nikkouyoku you beddo] *n* sunbed

ニックネーム [nikkuneemu] *n* nickname

ニコチン [nikochin] *n* nicotine

二戸建て住宅 [nikodate juutaku] *n* semi-detached house

肉 [niku] *n* meat; 赤身肉 [akaminiku] *n* red meat; 肉屋 [nikuya] *n* butcher; 骨付き肉 [honetsuki niku] *n* joint (meat); 子牛の肉 [koushi no niku] *n* veal; この肉はいたんでいます [kono niku wa itande imasu] This meat is off; これは肉のストックで料理してありますか? [kore wa niku no sutokku de ryouri shite arimasu ka?] Is this cooked in meat stock?; 肉が冷たいです [niku ga tsumetai desu] The meat is cold; 私は肉が好きではありません [watashi wa niku ga suki de wa arimasen] I don't like meat; 私は肉を食べません [watashi wa niku o tabemasen] I don't eat meat

憎む [nikumu] *v* hate

憎しみ [nikushimi] *n* hatred

肉体労働者 [nikutairoudousha] workman

・・・にもかかわらず [... nimokakawarazu] *prep* despite

荷物 [nimotsu] *n* burden, pack, baggage; 超過手荷物 [choukatenimotsu] *n* excess baggage; これから荷物を詰めなければなりません [kore kara nimotsu o tsumenakereba narimasen] I need to pack now

人間 [ningen] *n* human being; 人間の [ningen no] *adj* human

人魚 [ningyo] *n* mermaid

人形 [ningyou] *n* doll; あやつり人形 [ayatsuri ningyou] *n* puppet

ニンジン [ninjin] *n* carrot

人気 [ninki] *n* (評判) popularity; 人気のない [ninki no nai] *adj* unpopular; 人気のある [ninki no aru] *adj* popular

任命する [ninmei suru] *v* appoint

任者 [nin mono] 前任者 [zenninsha] *n* predecessor

任務 [ninmu] *n* duty, task

ニンニク [ninniku] *n* garlic

認識 [ninshiki] 認識できる [ninshiki dekiru] *adj* recognizable

妊娠 [ninshin] *n* pregnancy; 妊娠中絶 [ninshinchuuzetsu] *n* abortion; 妊娠した [ninshin shita] *adj* pregnant

忍耐 [nintai] *n* patience

忍耐強い [nintaizuyoi] *adj* patient

におい [nioi] *n* odour, scent, smell; においがする [nioi ga suru] *vi* smell; においを嗅ぐ [nioi-o kagu] *vt* smell; ガスのにおいがします [gasu no nioi ga shimasu] I can smell gas

にらみつける [niramitsukeru] *v* glare

ニレ [nire] *n* elm

似る [niru] 似ている [niteiru] *v* resemble; ・・・に似る [...ni niru] *v* take after, look like

煮る [niru] *v* cook; 弱火でとろとろ煮る [yowabi de torotoro niru] *v* simmer

二流 [niryuu] 二流の [niryuu no] *adj* second-rate

西 [nishi] *n* west; 西に [nishi ni] *adv* west; 西の [nishi no] *adj* west, western

西インド諸島 [nishi indo shotou] *n* West Indies; 西インド諸島の [nishi indo shotou no] *adj* West Indian; 西インド諸島の人 [nishi indo shotou no hito] *n* West Indian (person)

ニシン [nishin] *n* herring

西行き [nishiyuki] 西行きの [nishi yuki no] *adj* westbound

二食付き [nishokutsuki] *n* half board

二週間 [nishuukan] *n* fortnight

尼僧 [nisou] *n* nun

日射病 [nisshabyou] *n* sunstroke

ニス [nisu] *n* varnish; ニスを塗る [nisu-o nuru] *v* varnish

日常の食べ物 [nichijou no tabemono] *n* diet

二等 [nitou] *n* second class; 二等の [nitou no] *adj* second-class

・・・について [...nitsuite] *prep* about

について行く [ni tsuiteiku] ・・・について行く [...ni tsuite iku] *v* follow

・・・につき [...nitsuki] *prep* per

日程 [nittei] 議事日程 [giji nittei] *n* agenda

庭 [niwa] *n* garden, yard (enclosure); 庭仕事 [niwa shigoto] *n* gardening

庭師 [niwashi] *n* gardener

鶏 [niwatori] *n* chicken

による [ni yoru] ・・・によって [...ni yotte] *prep* by

荷造りをする [nizukuri o suru] *v* pack; 荷造りが済んで [nizukuri ga sunde] *adj* packed

・・・の [...no] *prep* of

述べる [noberu] *v* state

伸びる [nobiru] *v* stretch, stretchy

登る [noboru] *v* climb

昇る [noboru] 最後に昇るのはいつですか? [saigo ni noboru no wa itsu desu ka?] When is the last ascent?

のぼる [noboru] *v* mount, climb

ノブ [nobu] *n* knob

後 [nochi] ・・・の後に [...no nochi ni] *prep* after; ・・・した後に [...shita nochi ni] *conj* after; 後で [ato de] *adv* afterwards

のど [nodo] *n* throat; のどの渇き [nodo no kawaki] *n* thirst; のどが渇いた [nodo ga kawaita] *adj* thirsty; ゴロゴロとのどを鳴らす [gorogoro to nodo-o narasu] *v* purr

野原 [nohara] *n* field

・・・の方へ [...no hou e] *prep* towards

のこぎり [nokogiri] *n* saw

残り [nokori] 残りの [nokori no] *adj* remaining

蚤 [nomi] *n* flea

飲み込む [nomikomu] *vi* swallow; を飲み込む [-o nomikomu] *vt* swallow

飲み物 [nomimono] *n* drink; お飲み物はいかがですか? [o-nomimono wa ikaga desu ka?] Would you like a drink?; お飲み物を持ってきましょうか? [o-nomimono o motte kimashou ka?] Can I get you a drink?; 飲み物は私のおごりです [nomimono wa watashi no ogori desu] The drinks are on me

ノミの市 [nomi no ichi] *n* flea market

飲む [nomu] *v* drink; 飲み騒ぐこと [nomisawagu koto] *n* binge drinking; 何をお飲みになりますか? [nani o o-nomi ni narimasu ka?] What would you like to drink?

・・・の向かい側に [...no mukaigawa ni] *prep* opposite

ののしり [nonoshiri] *n* curse, swearword

ののしる [nonoshiru] *v* swear

・・・のおかげで [no okagede] *prep* owing to

乗り場 [noriba] タクシー乗り場 [takushii noriba] *n* taxi rank; タクシー乗り場はどこですか? [takushii-noriba wa doko desu ka?] Where is the taxi stand?

乗り出す [noridasu] ・・・から身を乗り出す [...kara mi-o noridasu] *v* lean out

乗り換え [norikae] *n* transfer; あなたは・・・で乗り換えなければなりません [anata wa ... de norikaenakereba narimasen] You have to transfer at...

乗り換える [norikaeru] *v* change, transfer; 乗り換えなければなりませんか? [norikaenakereba narimasen ka?] Do I have to change?; どこで乗り換えるのですか? [doko de norikaeru no desu ka?] Where do I change?; ・・・へ行くにはどこで乗り換えるのですか? [...e iku ni wa doko de norikaeru no desu ka?] Where do I change for...?

乗組員 [norikumiin] *n* crew

乗り物 [norimono] *n* vehicle

乗り遅れる [noriokureru] *v* be late for; 私はフライトに乗り遅れました [watashi wa furaito ni noriokuremashita] **I've missed my flight**

乗り手 [norite] *n* **rider**

乗り継ぎ [noritsugi] 私は乗り継ぎを逃しました [watashi wa noritsugi o nogashimashita] **I've missed my connection**

乗る [noru] *n* **board, get in, get on, ride**

載る [noru] 目録に載っていない [mokuroku ni notte inai] *adj* **unlisted**

ノルウェー [norwuee] *n* **Norway**; ノルウェー人 [norwueejin] *n* **Norwegian (person)**; ノルウェーの [norwuee no] *adj* **Norwegian**; ノルウェー語 [norwueego] *n* **Norwegian (language)**

乗せる [noseru] 人を車に乗せてあげること [hito-o kuruma ni nosete ageru koto] *v* **give a ride to**; 自動車修理工場まで私を乗せていってもらえますか? [jidousha-shuuri-koujou made watashi o nosete itte moraemasu ka?] **Can you give me a lift to the garage?**

・・・の下に [...no shita ni] *prep* **under, underneath**

・・・の外側に [...no sotogawa ni] *prep* **outside**

のっとる [nottoru] 慣例にのっとった [kanrei ni nottotta] *adj* **conventional**

脳 [nou] *n* **brain**; 脳震盪 [noushintou] *n* **concussion**

農業 [nougyou] *n* **agriculture, farming**; 農業の [nougyou no] *adj* **agricultural**

ノウハウ [nouhau] *n* **know-how**

囊胞 [nouhou] *n* **cyst**

農場 [noujou] *n* **farm**

農場主 [noujoushu] *n* **farmer**

農家 [nouka] *n* **farmhouse**

濃紺 [noukon] 濃紺の [noukon no] *adj* **navy-blue**

能力 [nouryoku] *n* **ability, power**

農作物 [nousakubutsu] *n* **crop**

ノート [nouto] *n* **notebook**

農薬 [nouyaku] *n* **pesticide**

膿瘍 [nouyou] *n* **abscess**; 私は膿瘍があり

ます [watashi wa nouyou ga arimasu] **I have an abscess**

納税 [nouzei] 納税者 [nouzeisha] *n* **tax payer**

除く [nozoku] ・・・を除いて [...-o nozoite] *prep* **excluding**; ・・・を除いては [...-o nozoite wa] *prep* **except**

望む [nozomu] *v* **hope**

脱ぐ [nugu] *v* **take off**; 服を脱ぐ [fuku o nugu] *v* **undress**

ぬぐい取る [nuguitoru] モップでぬぐい取る [moppu de nuguitoru] *v* **mop up**

縫い合わせる [nuiawaseru] *v* **sew up**

縫い針 [nuihari] *n* **needle**

縫い目 [nuime] *n* **seam**

ぬかるみ [nukarumi] *n* **slush**

抜き取る [nukitoru] *v* **withdraw**

抜く [nuku] *v* **pull out**; プラグを抜いて電源を断つ [puragu-o nuite dengen-o tatsu] *v* **unplug**

沼 [numa] *n* **bog, marsh**; 沼地 [numachi] *n* **swamp**

布 [nuno] 目隠し布 [mekakushi nuno] *n* **blindfold**

布地 [nunoji] *n* **cloth**

ぬれる [nureru] ぬれても大丈夫な [nurete mo daijoubu na] *adj* **showerproof**

濡れる [nureru] *v* **get wet**; 濡れた [nureta] *adj* **wet**

塗る [nuru] *v* **paint**; ニスを塗る [nisu-o nuru] *v* **varnish**; マニキュアを塗る [manikyua-o nuru] *v* **manicure**; 漆喰を塗る [shikkui-o nuru] *v* **whitewash**

盗み [nusumi] *n* **theft**

盗む [nusumu] *v* **steal**; 誰かが私のトラベラーズチェックを盗みました [dare ka ga watashi no toraberaazu-chekku o nusumimashita] **Someone's stolen my traveller's cheques**; 私のカードが盗まれました [watashi no kaado ga nusumaremashita] **My card has been stolen**

縫う [nuu] *v* **sew, stitch**

ヌードル [nuudoru] *n* **noodles**

尿 [nyou] n urine

入院 [nyuuin] n hospitalization; 私は一晩入院しなければなりませんか? [watashi wa hitoban nyuuin shinakereba narimasen ka?] Do I have to stay overnight?

ニュージーランド [nyuujiirando] n New Zealand; ニュージーランド人 [nyuujiirandojin] n New Zealander

入場 [nyuujou] n admission; 入場を許す [nyuujou-o yurusu] v admit (allow in); 入場料 [nyuujouryou] n admission charge; 入場許可 [nyuujou kyoka] n admittance

入場料 [nyuujouryou] n entrance fee

入札 [nyuusatsu] n bid; 入札する [nyuusatsu suru] v bid (at auction)

乳製品 [nyuuseihin] n dairy produce, dairy products; 乳製品販売店 [nyuuseihin hanbaiten] n dairy

ニュース [nyuusu] n news; ニュースはいつですか? [nyuusu wa itsu desu ka?] When is the news?

ニュースキャスター [nyuusukyasutaa] n newsreader

O

尾 [o] n tail

オアシス [oashisu] n oasis

おば [oba] n (伯母・叔母) aunt; おばちゃん [obachan] n auntie

おばあちゃん [obaachan] n grandma, granny

おべっか [obekka] n lip salve

帯 [obi] 帯状のひも [obijou no himo] n band (strip)

おびえる [obieru] おびえた [obieta] adj frightened

おぼれる [oboreru] v drown; 誰かおぼれています! [dare ka oborete imasu!] Someone is drowning!

汚物 [obutsu] n dirt

お茶 [o-cha] n tea

落ちる [ochiru] v drop, fall

落ち着く [ochitsuku] v (住居) settle down, (気分) calm down; 落ち着いた [ochitsuita] adj calm; 落ち着かない [ochitsukanai] adj restless

おだてる [odateru] v flatter; おだてられた [odaterareta] adj flattered

踊り場 [odoriba] n landing

驚き [odoroki] n surprise

驚く [odoroku] 驚いた [odoroita] adj surprised; 驚かす [odorokasu] v astonish; 驚くべき [odorokubeki] adj amazing

踊る [odoru] v dance; ワルツを踊る [warutsu o odoru] v waltz; 踊ること [odoru koto] n dancing; 私は本当に踊りません [watashi wa hontou ni odorimasen] I don't really dance; 私は踊りたい気分です [watashi wa odoritai kibun desu] I feel like dancing

脅す [odosu] v threaten; 脅し [odoshi] n threat; 脅すような [odosu you na] adj threatening

終える [oeru] v finish; 終えた [oeta] adj finished

オフィス [ofisu] n office; 予約オフィス [yoyaku ofisu] n booking office; 貴社のオフィスへ伺うにはどう行けばいいでしょうか? [kisha no ofisu e ukagau ni wa dou ikeba ii deshou ka?] How do I get to your office?; 私はオフィスで働いています [watashi wa ofisu de hataraite imasu] I work in an office

オフ [ofu] シーズンオフ [shiizun'ofu] n low season

オフラインの [ofurain no] adj offline; オフラインで [ofurain de] adv offline

オフサイド [ofusaido] オフサイドの [ofusaido no] adj offside

おがくず [ogakuzu] n sawdust

小川 [ogawa] n stream

おごり [ogori] n treat; 飲み物は私のおごりです [nomimono wa watashi no ogori desu] The drinks are on me

おはよう [ohayou] おはようございます [ohayou gozaimasu] Good morning

おへそ [oheso] n belly button

雄羊 [ohitsuji] 去勢していない雄羊 [kyosei shite inai ohitsuji] n ram

牡羊座 [ohitsujiza] n Aries

甥 [oi] n nephew

追い出す [oidasu] v expel

追い払う [oiharau] v send off

追い越す [oikosu] v overtake

オイル警告灯 [oiru keikokutou] オイル

警告灯が消えません [oiru keikoku-tou ga kiemasen] The oil warning light won't go off

おいしい [oishii] adj delicious; おいしかったです [oishikatta desu] That was delicious; とてもおいしいです [totemo oishii desu] It's very tasty; 食事はおいしかったです [shokuji wa oishikatta desu] The meal was delicious

美味しい [oishii] adj delicious

追いつく [oitsuku] v catch up

おじ [oji] n (伯父・叔父) uncle

お辞儀 [ojigi] n bow; お辞儀をする [ojigi-o suru] v bow

おじいちゃん [ojiichan] n granddad, grandpa

おじけづかせる [ojikedukaseru] v intimidate

丘 [oka] n hill

おかげ [okage] prep thanks to; ええ、おかげさまで [ee, okagesama de] Fine, thanks

お菓子 [okashi] 綿菓子 [watagashi] n candyfloss

犯す [okasu] v commit (crime)

桶 [oke] かいば桶 [kaibaoke] n trough

置場 [okiba] 食料置場 [shokuryou okiba] n larder

置き換え [okikae] n replacement

お金 [okin] どこでお金を両替できますか? [doko de o-kane o ryougae dekimasu ka?] Where can I change some money?; お金をいくらか至急送ってもらうように手配してもらえますか? [o-kane o ikura ka shikyuu okutte morau you ni tehai shite moraemasu ka?] Can you arrange to have some money sent over urgently?; 私はお金がありません [watashi wa o-kane ga arimasen] I have no money; 私はお金を使い果たしてしまいました [watashi wa o-kane o tsukaihatashite shimaimashita] I have run out of money

お気に入り [o-kiniiri] n favourite

起きる [okiru] v get up; 起きている [okite iru] v getting up; あなたは何時に起きますか? [anata wa nan-ji ni okimasu ka?]

What time do you get up?

置き去り [okizari] 私は置き去りにされました [watashi wa okizari ni saremashita] I've been left behind

オッケー！ [okkee] OK!

行う [okonau] v conduct, perform

怒りっぽい [okorippoi] adj irritable

怒る [okoru] 怒ってうなる [ikatte unaru] v growl; 怒った [okotta] adj angry; 怒りっぽい [okorippoi] adj touchy; 怒り狂った [ikarikurutta] adj furious

起こる [okoru] v happen, occur; いつ起こったのですか？ [itsu okotta no desu ka?] When did it happen?

起こす [okosu] 興味を起こさせる [kyoumi-o okosaseru] v interest; 炎症を起こした [enshou-o okoshita] adj inflamed; 起こしてあげましょうか？ [okoshite agemashou ka?] Shall I wake you up?

置く [oku] v lay, place, put; 置き忘れる [okiwasureru] v mislay; 在庫を置く [zaiko-o oku] v stock; 地面に置く [jimen ni oku] v ground; そこへ置いてください [soko e oite kudasai] Put it down over there, please

臆病 [okubyou] 臆病な [okubyou na] adj cowardly; 臆病者 [okubyoumono] n coward

屋外 [okugai] 屋外の [okugai no] adj outdoor; 屋外で [okugai de] adv out-of-doors, outdoors

屋外市 [okugaiichi] 屋外市を催す場所 [okugai ichi-o moyousu basho] n fairground

屋内 [okunai] 屋内の [okunai no] adj indoor; 屋内で [okunai de] adv indoors

遅れ [okure] n delay

遅れる [okureru] v delay, lag behind; 遅れた [okureta] adj late (delayed); フライトは遅れています [furaito wa okurete imasu] The flight has been delayed

遅れずに [okurezu ni] adv on time

贈り物 [okurimono] n gift

送る [okuru] v send; インボイスを送る [inboisu-o okuru] v invoice; テキストメッセージを送る [tekisuto messeeji-o okuru] v text; ファックスを送る [fakkusu-o okuru] v fax; 送り主 [okurinushi] n sender; 送り返す [okurikaesu] v send back; 電子メールを送る [denshi meeru-o okuru] v email (a person); ここからファックスを送れますか？ [koko kara fakkusu o okuremasu ka?] Can I send a fax from here?; 私は荷物を前もって送りました [watashi ha nimotsu o mae motte okuri mashita] I sent my luggage on in advance

奥様 [okusama] n madam

オマーン [omaan] n Oman

おめでとう [omedetou] n congratulations

お目にかかる [ome ni kakaru] ついにお目にかかれて光栄です [tsuini o-me ni kakarete kouei desu] I'm delighted to meet you at last

おみごと！ [omigoto] excl well done!

おみやげ [omiyage] n souvenirs; おみやげはありますか？ [o-miyage wa arimasu ka?] Do you have souvenirs?

おもちゃ [omocha] n toy

思い [omoi] 恥ずかしい思い [hazukashii omoi] n shame

重い [omoi] adj heavy; 重さ [omosa] n weight; 重さが・・・ある [omosa ga ... aru] weigh; これは重すぎます [kore wa omo-sugimasu] This is too heavy

思い出す [omoidasu] v remember; 思い出させる [omoidasaseru] v remind; 思い出させるもの [omoidasaseru mono] n reminder

思い出 [omoide] n recollection; 思い出の品 [omoide no shina] n memento

思い描く [omoiegaku] v visualize

思いがけなく [omoigakenaku] adv unexpectedly

思い切る [omoikiru] 思い切ったスタイルにしたくありません [omoikitta sutairu ni shitaku arimasen] I don't want anything drastic

思い切った [omoikitta] 思い切って・・・る [omoikitte ... suru] v dare

思い切って [omoikitte] 思い切った

[omoikitta] *adj* daring

思いやり [omoiyari] 思いやりのある [omoiyari no aru] *adj* considerate

思いやりのある [omoiyari no aru] *v* caring

重く [omoku] *adv* heavily

趣 [omomuki] 古風で趣のある [kofuu de omomuki no aru] *adj* quaint

主な [omo na] *adj* principal

面白い [omoshiroi] *adj* funny, interesting; 面白くない [omoshirokunai] *adj* dull, boring

おもしろい [omoshiroi] どこかおもしろい場所を教えてもらえますか? [doko-ka omoshiroi basho o oshiete moraemasu ka?] Can you suggest somewhere interesting to go?

思うに [omou ni] *adv* presumably

オムレツ [omuretsu] *n* omelette

おむつ [omutsu] *n* nappy

同じ [onaji] *adj* same; ···と同じくらい [...to onaji kurai] *adv* as; 私にも同じものをください [watashi ni mo onaji mono o kudasai] I'll have the same

おなか [onaka] *n* tummy, stomach

温度 [ondo] *n* temperature; 摂氏温度 [sesshi ondo] *n* degree centigrade; 温度計 [ondokei] *n* thermometer; 華氏温度 [kashi ondo] *n* degree Fahrenheit

おんどり [ondori] *n* cock; 若いおんどり [wakai ondori] *n* cockerel

お願い [onegai] お願いします [o-negai shimasu] Please; 喫煙席をお願いします [kitsuen-seki o o-negai shimasu] Smoking, please

お願い! [onegai] *excl* please

音楽 [ongaku] *n* music; 音楽の [ongaku no] *adj* musical; 音楽家 [ongakuka] *n* musician

女らしい [onnarashii] *adj* feminine

女相 [onna sou] 女相続人 [onna souzokunin] *n* heiress

斧 [ono] *n* axe

音符 [onpu] *n* note (music)

オンライン [onrain] オンラインの [onrain no] *adj* online; オンラインで [onrain de] *adv* online

音節 [onsetsu] *n* syllable

温室 [onshitsu] *n* greenhouse

オンス [onsu] *n* ounce

温水 [onsui] プールは温水ですか? [puuru wa onsui desu ka?] Is the pool heated?

温水器 [onsuiki] 温水器はどうやって使うのですか? [onsuiki wa dou-yatte tsukau no desu ka?] How does the water heater work?

オーバーヘッドプロジェクター [oobaaheddopurojekutaa] *n* overhead projector

オーバーヒート [oobaahiito] エンジンがオーバーヒートしています [enjin ga oobaahiito shite imasu] The engine is overheating

大袋 [oobukuro] *n* sack (container)

オーブンミット [oobunmitto] *n* oven glove

大金持ち [ooganemochi] *n* millionaire

大型 [oogata] 大型の旅行かばん [ougata no ryokou kaban] *n* holdall; 大型輸送車 [ougata yusousha] *n* HGV

オーガズム [oogazumu] *n* orgasm

大げさ [oogesa] 大げさに言う [oogesa ni iu] *v* exaggerate

大声 [oogoe] 大声の [oogoe no] *adj* loud; 大声で [oogoe de] *adv* loudly

多い [ooi] さらに多い [sarani ooi] *adj* more; 出来事の多い [dekigoto no ooi] *adj* eventful; 多くの [ouku no] *adj* many, much; それには···が多すぎます [sore ni wa ... ga oo-sugimasu] There's too much ... in it

大い [ooi] 大いに [ooi ni] *adv* much

大かがり [ookagari] 大かがり火 [ookagaribi] *n* bonfire

オーケー! [ookee] *excl* okay!, OK!

大きい [ookii] *adj* big, large; より大きい [yori ookii] *adj* bigger; 大きな [ooki na] *adj* great; 大きい方の [ookii hou no] *adj* major; これより大きな部屋はありますか?

[kore yori ooki-na heya wa arimasu ka?] Do you have a bigger one?; それは大きすぎます [sore wa ooki-sugimasu] It's too big

大昔 [oomukashi] 大昔の [oumukashi no] adj ancient

オーナー [oonaa] n owner; オーナーと話させていただけますか? [oonaa to hanasasete itadakemasu ka?] Could I speak to the owner, please?

オーペア [oopea] n au pair

オーストラレーシア [oosutorareeshia] n Australasia

オートバイ乗り [ootobainori] n motorcyclist

オートマ車 [ootomasha] それはオートマ車ですか? [sore wa ootoma-sha desu ka?] Is it an automatic car?; オートマ車をお願いします [ootoma-sha o o-negai shimasu] An automatic, please

オート麦 [ooto mugi] n oats

覆う [oou] v cover

公になる [ooyake ni naru] v come out

大雪 [ooyuki] 大雪です [ooyuki desu] The snow is very heavy

オペラ [opera] n opera

オペレーター [opereetaa] n operator

オランダ [oranda] n Holland, Netherlands

オランダ語 [orandago] n Dutch (language)

オランダ人 [orandajin] n Dutch; オランダ男性 [orandajin dansei] n Dutchman; オランダ人女性 [orandajin josei] n Dutchwoman

オランダの [oranda no] n Dutch

オレガノ [oregano] n oregano

オレンジ [orenji] n orange

オレンジ色 [orenjiiro] オレンジ色の [orenjiiro no] adj orange

オレンジジュース [orenjijuusu] n orange juice

オリーブ [oriibu] n olive, olive tree; オリーブ油 [oriibuyu] n olive oil

折り目 [orime] n crease; 折り目をつけた [orime-o tsuketa] adj creased

織物 [orimono] n fabric, textile

降りる [oriru] v descend, get off; 降りてくる [orite kuru] v come down; いつ降りればいいのか教えてください [itsu orireba ii no ka oshiete kudasai] Please tell me when to get off

折りたたみ [oritatami] 折りたたみの [oritatami no] adj folding

折りたたむ [oritatamu] v fold

愚かな [oroka na] adj silly, stupid

卸売 [oroshiuri] 卸売業者 [oroshiuri gyousha] n distributor

卸売り [oroshiuri] n wholesale; 卸売りの [oroshiuri no] adj wholesale

おろそか [orosoka] おろそかにされた [orosoka ni sareta] adj neglected; おろそかにする [orosoka ni suru] v neglect

降ろす [orosu] 荷を降ろす [ni-o orosu] v unload; 降ろしてください [oroshite kudasai] Please let me off

折る [oru] ポキッと折る [pokittto oru] v snap

オルガン [orugan] n organ (music)

おさげ [osage] n pigtail, plait

収める [osameru] 勝利を収める [shouri-o osameru] v triumph

オセアニア [oseania] n Oceania

汚染 [osen] n pollution; 汚染された [osen sareta] adj polluted; 汚染する [osen suru] v pollute

おしゃべり [o-shaberi] n chat

押しボタン信号式横断歩道 [oshibotan shingoushiki oudanhodou] n pelican crossing

教える [oshieru] v teach; 教えること [oshieru koto] n teaching

押し入る [oshiiru] v break in, break in (on); 押し入ること [oshiiru koto] n break-in

おしめ [oshime] どこで赤ちゃんのおしめを替えられますか? [doko de akachan no oshime o kaeraremasu ka?] Where can I change the baby?

押し流される [oshinagasareru] 押し流れるもの [oshinagasareru mono] n drift

お尻 [oshiri] n bum

押しつぶす [oshitsubusu] v crush, squash

御しやすい [o shiyasui] adj manageable

遅い [osoi] adj slow; 接続がとても遅いようです [setsuzoku ga totemo osoi you desu] The connection seems very slow

遅く [osoku] adv slowly

おそらく [osoraku] adv supposedly

恐れる [osoreru] v fear

恐ろしい [osoroshii] adj dreadful, horrendous

遅すぎる [ososugiru] 遅すぎます [oso-sugimasu] It's too late

襲う [osou] vi strike; 襲って強奪する [osotte goudatsu suru] v mug

押す [osu] v press, push; 強く押す [tsuyoku osu] v squeeze; 押してもらえますか? [oshite moraemasu ka?] Can you give me a push?

おすすめ [osusume] 何がおすすめですか? [nani ga osusume desu ka?] What do you recommend?; おすすめの郷土料理はありますか? [osusume no kyoudo-ryouri wa arimasu ka?] Can you recommend a local dish?

おたふく [otafuku] おたふく風邪 [otafukukaze] n mumps

お玉 [otama] n ladle

オタマジャクシ [otamajakushi] n tadpole

おてんば [otenba] おてんば娘 [otemba musume] n tomboy

お手伝い [otetsudai] n (使用人) maid

音 [oto] n sound; カチッという音 [kachitto iu oto] n click; やかましい音 [yakamashii oto] n din; 発信音 [hasshin-on] n dialling tone; 鐘の音 [kane no oto] n toll

おとぎ話 [otogibanashi] n fairytale

男 [otoko] n bloke, chap, guy, man; 男らしい [otokorashii] adj masculine

男やもめ [otokoyamome] n widower

乙女座 [otomeza] n Virgo

大人 [otona] n adult; 大人になる [otona ni naru] v grow up

衰える [otoroeru] v decay

劣る [otoru] 劣った [ototta] adj inferior

落とす [otosu] v drop; このしみを落とすことができますか? [kono shimi o otosu koto ga dekimasu ka?] Can you remove this stain?; スピードを落としてください! [supiido o otoshite kudasai!] Slow down!

おととい [ototoi] the day before yesterday

訪れる [otozureru] 車椅子で…を訪れることができますか? [kuruma-isu de … o otozureru koto ga dekimasu ka?] Can you visit … in a wheelchair?; 私たちがその街を訪れる時間はありますか? [watashi-tachi ga sono machi o otozureru jikan wa arimasu ka?] Do we have time to visit the town?

お釣り [otsuri] n change (money); お釣りはとっておいてください [o-tsuri wa totte oite kudasai] Keep the change; お釣りが間違っていると思います [o-tsuri ga machigatte iru to omoimasu] I think you've given me the wrong change; この紙幣でお釣りがありますか? [kono shihei de o-tsuri ga arimasu ka?] Do you have change for this note?

夫 [otto] n husband; 娘の夫 [musume no otto] n son-in-law; 私は夫へのプレゼントを探しています [watashi wa otto e no purezento o sagashite imasu] I'm looking for a present for my husband; 私の夫です [watashi no otto desu] This is my husband

王 [ou] n king

追う [ou] …を追う […-o ou] v pursue…, follow…

オーバー [oubaa] n overcoat

オーバーオール [oubaaouru] n overalls; ダンガリーのオーバーオール [dangarii no oobaaooru] n dungarees

応募 [oubo] 応募者 [oubosha] n applicant

オーボエ [ouboe] n oboe

オーブン [oubun] n oven; オーブン耐熱性の [oobun tainetsusei no] adj ovenproof

横断 [oudan] 横断歩道 [oudanhodou] n pedestrian crossing

黄疸 [oudan] n jaundice

横断歩道 [oudanhodou] 太い白線の縞模様で示した横断歩道 [futoi hakusen no shimamoyou de shimeshita oudanhodou] n zebra crossing

オーディション [oudishon] n audition

往復 [oufuku] n round trip; 日帰り往復割引切符 [higaeri oufuku waribiki kippu] n day return; 往復切符 [oufuku kippu] n return ticket; 定期往復便 [teiki oufuku bin] n shuttle

横柄な [ouhei na] adj arrogant

覆い [oui] n cover

王子 [ouji] n prince

応じる [oujiru] v comply with; それに応じて [sore ni oujite] adv accordingly

王女 [oujo] n princess

オオカミ [oukami] n wolf

王冠 [oukan] n crown

オーケー [oukee] adj okay

オーケストラ [oukesutora] n orchestra

王国 [oukoku] n kingdom

オーク [ouku] n oak

オウム [oumu] n parrot

オール [ouru] n oar

牡牛 [oushi] 牡牛座 [oushiza] n Taurus

雄牛 [oushi] n bull

王室 [oushitsu] 王室の [oushitsu no] adj royal

欧州 [oushuu] 欧州連合 [oushuu rengou] n European Union

オーストラリア [ousutoraria] n Australia; オーストラリアの [oosutoraria no] adj Australian

オーストラリア人 [ousutorariajin] n Australian (person)

オーストリア [ousutoria] n Austria; オーストリアの [oosutoria no] adj Austrian

オーストリア人 [ousutoriajin] n Austrian (person)

応対 [outai] 私たちは応対してもらうのをまだ待っています [watashi-tachi wa outai shite morau no o mada matte imasu] We are still waiting to be served

オートバイ [outobai] n motorcycle

オートミール [outomiiru] n oatmeal

王座 [ouza] n throne

終わり [owari] n end, finish; 六月の終わりに [roku-gatsu no owari ni] at the end of June

終わりから2番目の [owari kara ni banme no] n penultimate

終わりのない [owari no nai] adj endless

終わる [owaru] v end; 終わって [owatte] adj over

親 [oya] n parent

親知らず [oyashirazu] n wisdom tooth

親指 [oyayubi] n thumb

泳ぐ [oyogu] v bathe, swim; どこに行けば泳げますか? [doko ni ikeba oyogemasu ka?] Where can I go swimming?; ここで泳いで安全ですか? [koko de oyoide anzen desu ka?] Is it safe to swim here?; ここで泳げますか? [koko de oyogemasu ka?] Can you swim here?; その川で泳げますか? [sono kawa de oyogemasu ka?] Can one swim in the river?; 泳ぎに行きましょう [oyogi ni ikimashou] Let's go swimming

泳ぐ人 [oyogu hito] n swimmer

およそ [oyoso] adv about, approximately, roughly

お湯 [oyu] n hot water; お湯は料金に含まれていますか? [o-yu wa ryoukin ni fukumarete imasu ka?] Is hot water included in the price?; お湯がありません [o-yu ga arimasen] There is no hot water

オゾン [ozon] n ozone; オゾン層 [ozonsou] n ozone layer

p

パーキングメーター [paakingumeetaa] *n* parking meter; パーキングメーターが壊れています [paakingumeetaa ga kowarete imasu] The parking meter is broken; パーキングメーター用の小銭をお持ちですか? [paakingu-meetaa-you no kozeni o o-mochi desu ka?] Do you have change for the parking meter?

パーマ [paama] *n* perm; 私はパーマをかけています [watashi wa paama o kakete imasu] My hair is permed

パーセンテージ [paasenteeji] *n* percentage

パーソナルステレオ [paasonarusutereo] *n* personal stereo

パースニップ [paasunippu] *n* parsnip

パーティー [paateii] *n* party (social gathering); ディナーパーティー [dinaa paatii] *n* dinner party

パートナー [paatonaa] *n* partner; 私にはパートナーがいます [watashi ni wa paatonaa ga imasu] I have a partner; 私のパートナーです [watashi no paatonaa desu] This is my partner

パートタイム [paatotaimu] パートタイムの [paatotaimu no] *adj* part-time; パートタイムで [paatotaimu de] *adv* part-time

パーツ [paatsu] *n* parts; トヨタ車のパーツはありますか? [toyota-sha no paatsu wa arimasu ka?] Do you have parts for a Toyota?

パブ [pabu] *n* pub; パブの主人 [pabu no shujin] *n* publican

パブリックスクール [paburikkusukuuru] *n* public school

パッド [paddo] *n* pad

パドル [padoru] *n* paddle; パドルで漕ぐ [padoru de kogu] *v* paddle

パフペースト [pafupeesuto] *n* puff pastry

パイ [pai] *n* pie; アップルパイ [appurupai] *n* apple pie

パイナップル [painappuru] *n* pineapple

パイント [painto] *n* pint

パイプ [paipu] *n* pipe

パイプライン [paipurain] *n* pipeline

パイロット [pairotto] *n* pilot

パジャマ [pajama] *n* pyjamas

パキスタン [pakisutan] *n* Pakistan; パキスタン人 [pakisutanjin] *n* Pakistani (person); パキスタンの [pakisutan no] *adj* Pakistani

パッケージ [pakkeeji] *n* packaging

パック [pakku] パック旅行 [pakku ryokou] *n* package holiday, package tour

パン [pan] *n* bread; パンのひと塊 [pan no hitokatamari] *n* loaf; パンケース [pan keesu] *n* bread bin; パン粉 [panko] *n* breadcrumbs, crumb; パン屋 [pan-ya] *n* bakery; パン屋の主人 [pan ya no shujin] *n* baker; フライパン [furaipan] *n* frying pan; 黒パン [kuropan] *n* brown bread; パンはいかがですか? [pan wa ikaga desu ka?] Would you like some bread?; パンをもっと持ってきてください [pan o motto motte kite kudasai] Please bring more bread

パナマ [panama] *n* Panama

パンチ [panchi] *n* (殴打) punch (blow), (飲み物) punch (hot drink)

パンダ [panda] *n* panda

パンフレット [panfuretto] n brochure, pamphlet

パニック [panikku] n panic

パンケーキ [pankeeki] n pancake

パン生地 [pankiji] n dough

パンク [panku] n flat tyre; タイヤがパンクしました [taiya ga panku shimashita] I have a flat tyre

パンティー [pantii] n panties

パントマイム [pantomaimu] n pantomime

パンツ [pantsu] n (下着) underpants, (洋服) pants

パパ [papa] n dad, daddy

パプリカ [papurika] n paprika

パラボラアンテナ [paraboraantena] 衛星放送用パラボラアンテナ [eisei housou you parabora antena] n satellite dish

パラフィン [parafin] n paraffin

パラグアイ [paraguai] n Paraguay; パラグアイ人 [paraguaijin] n Paraguayan (person); パラグアイの [paraguai no] adj Paraguayan

パラグライディング [paraguraidingu] n paragliding; どこに行けばパラグライディングができますか? [doko ni ikeba paraguraidingu ga dekimasu ka?] Where can you go paragliding?

パラセーリング [paraseeringu] n para-sailing; どこでパラセーリングができますか? [doko de paraseeringu ga dekimasu ka?] Where can you go para-sailing?

パラセンディング [parasendeingu] n parascending; 私はパラセンディングをしたいのですが [watashi wa parasendingu o shitai no desu ga] I'd like to go parascending

パラセタモール [parasetamooru] パラセタモールが欲しいのですが [parasetamooru ga hoshii no desu ga] I'd like some paracetamol

パラシュート [parashuuto] n parachute

パレード [pareedo] n parade

パレスチナ [paresuchina] n Palestine; パレスチナ人 [paresuchinajin] n Palestinian (person); パレスチナの [paresuchina no] adj Palestinian

パリパリ [paripari] パリパリした [paripari shita] adj crisp; パリパリする [paripari suru] adj crispy

パセリ [paseri] n parsley

パッションフルーツ [passhonfuruutsu] n passion fruit

パス [pasu] n path, pass; サイクルパス [saikuru pasu] n cycle path; スキー場のパス [sukii jou no pasu] n ski pass; 1日スキーパスが欲しいのですが [ichinichi sukii-pasu ga hoshii no desu ga] I'd like a ski pass for a day; 1日パスはいくらですか? [ichinichi pasu wa ikura desu ka?] How much is a pass for a day?; 1週間スキーパスが欲しいのですが [isshuukan sukii-pasu ga hoshii no desu ga] I'd like a ski pass for a week; 1週間パスはいくらですか? [isshuukan pasu wa ikura desu ka?] How much is a pass per week?; どこでスキーパスを買えますか? [doko de sukii-pasu o kaemasu ka?] Where can I buy a ski pass?; スキーパスはいくらですか? [sukii-pasu wa ikura desu ka?] How much is a ski pass?

パスポート [pasupouto] n passport; パスポート審査窓口 [pasupooto shinsa madoguchi] n passport control; 私はパスポートをなくしました [watashi wa pasupooto o nakushimashita] I've lost my passport; 私はパスポートを置き忘れました [watashi wa pasupooto o okiwasuremashita] I've forgotten my passport; 私のパスポートが盗まれました [watashi no pasupooto ga nusumaremashita] My passport has been stolen; 私のパスポートです [watashi no pasupooto desu] Here is my passport; 私のパスポートを返してください [watashi no pasupooto o kaeshite kudasai] Please give me my passport back; 子供はこのパスポートに載っています [kodomo wa kono pasupooto ni notte imasu] The child is on this passport

パスタ [pasuta] n pasta; スターターにパスタをいただきます [sutaataa ni pasuta o itadakimasu] I'd like pasta as a starter

パスワード [pasuwaado] n password

パタパタ動かす [patapata ugokasu] v flap

パティオ [pateio] n patio

パトロールカー [patoroorukaa] n patrol car

パトロール [patorouru] n patrol

パッと発火する [patsu to hakka suru] v flash

パウダー [paudaa] n powder; ベーキングパウダー [beekingupaudaa] n baking powder

ペダル [pedaru] n pedal

ページ [peeji] n page; 次ページへ続く [jipeji he tsuduku] PTO

ペーパー [peepaa] トイレットペーパーがありません [toiretto-peepaa ga arimasen] There is no toilet paper

ペーパーバック [peepaabakku] n paperback

ペーパークリップ [peepaakurippu] n paperclip

ペーパーウェイト [peepaaueito] n paperweight

ペースメーカー [peesumeekaa] n pacemaker

ペースト [peesuto] n paste

ペグ [pegu] n peg

北京 [pekin] n Beijing

ペキニーズ [pekiniizu] n Pekinese

ペン [pen] n pen; ペンをお借りできますか? [pen o o-kari dekimasu ka?] Do you have a pen I could borrow?

ペンダント [pendanto] n pendant

ペンギン [pengin] n penguin

ペニー [penii] n penny

ペニシリン [penishirin] n penicillin

ペンキ [penki] n paint

ペンナイフ [pennaifu] n penknife

ペンネーム [penneemu] n pseudonym

ペンパル [penparu] n penfriend

ペパーミント [pepaaminto] n peppermint

ペリカン [perikan] n pelican

ペルシャ [perusha] ペルシャの [perusha no] adj Persian

ペルー [peruu] n Peru; ペルー人 [peruujin] n Peruvian (person); ペルーの [peruu no] adj Peruvian

ペテン師 [petenshi] n crook (swindler)

ペット [petto] n pet

ピアニスト [pianisuto] n pianist

ピアノ [piano] n piano

ピアス [piasu] n piercing

ピエロ [piero] n clown

PDF [piidiiefu] n PDF

ピーク時 [piikuji] n peak hours; ピーク時でなく [piikuji denaku] adv off-peak

ピーナッツ [piinattsu] n peanut; それにはピーナッツが入っていますか? [sore ni wa piinattsu ga haitte imasu ka?] Does that contain peanuts?; 私はピーナッツのアレルギーがあります [watashi wa piinattsu no arerugii ga arimasu] I'm allergic to peanuts

ピーナッツアレルギー [piinattsu arerugii] n peanut allergy

ピーナッツバター [piinattsubataa] n peanut butter

PC [piishii] n PC

ピクニック [pikunikku] n picnic

ピン [pin] n pin; 安全ピン [anzenpin] n safety pin; 私は安全ピンが必要です [watashi wa anzen-pin ga hitsuyou desu] I need a safety pin

ピンク色 [pinkuiro] ピンク色の [pinkuiro no] adj pink

ピンセット [pinsetto] n tweezers

ピラミッド [piramiddo] n pyramid

ピル [piru] n pill; 私はピルを飲んでいます [watashi wa piru o nonde imasu] I'm on the pill; 私はピルを飲んでいません [watashi wa piru o nonde imasen] I'm not on the pill

ピストン [pisuton] n piston

ピストル [pisutoru] n pistol

ピッチ [pitchi] n (競技場) pitch (sport)

ぴったり [pittari] adv tightly; ぴったり体に合う [pittari karada ni au] adj skin-tight; ぴったりと [pittarito] adv closely; ぴったり合うように敷かれたカーペット [pittari au youni shikareta kaapetto] n fitted carpet; マットレスにぴったり合うシーツ [mattoresu ni pittari au shiitsu] n fitted sheet

ピザ [piza] n pizza

ポッドキャスト [poddokyasuto] n podcast

ポケット [poketto] n pocket

ポケットベル [poketto beru] n bleeper, pager; ポケットベルで呼び出す [poketto beru de yobidasu] v page

ポケットマネー [pokettomanee] n pocket money

ポンド [pondo] n pound; 英貨ポンド [eika pondo] n pound sterling

ポニー [ponii] n pony; 私はポニートレッキングに行きたいのですが [watashi wa ponii-torekkingu ni ikitai no desu ga] I'd like to go pony trekking

ポニーテール [poniiteeru] n ponytail

ポニートレッキング [poniitorekkingu] n pony trekking

ポンプ [ponpu] n pump; ポンプで注入する [ponpu de chuunyuu suru] v pump; ポンプで膨らませる [ponpu de fukuramaseru] v pump up; 自転車ポンプ [jitensha ponpu] n bicycle pump; 3番のポンプをお願いします [san-ban no ponpu o o-negai shimasu] Pump number three, please

ポーチ [poochi] n porch

ポーチする [poochi suru] ポーチした [poochi shita] adj poached (simmered gently)

ポーカー [pookaa] n poker

ポーク [pooku] n pork

ポークチョップ [pookuchoppu] n pork chop

ポップコーン [poppukoun] n popcorn

ポプラ [popura] n poplar

ポリエチレン [poriechiren] ポリエチレンの袋 [poriechiren no fukuro] n polythene bag

ポリッジ [porijji] n porridge

ポリネシア [porineshia] n Polynesia; ポリネシア人 [porineshiajin] n Polynesian (person); ポリネシアの [porineshia no] adj Polynesian; ポリネシア語 [porineshiago] n Polynesian (language)

ポリオ [porio] n polio

ポロシャツ [poroshatsu] n polo shirt

ポルノ [poruno] n porn, pornography; ポルノの [poruno no] adj pornographic

ポルトガル [porutogaru] n Portugal; ポルトガル人 [porutogarujin] n Portuguese (person); ポルトガルの [porutogaru no] adj Portuguese; ポルトガル語 [porutogarugo] n Portuguese (language)

ポスター [posutaa] n poster

ポテト [poteto] n potato; ジャケットポテト [jaketto poteto] n jacket potato; ポテトチップス [potetochippusu] n crisps

ポット [potto] n pot; コーヒーポット [koohiipotto] n coffeepot

ポットホール [pottohooru] n pothole

ポーランド語 [pourandogo] n Polish (language)

ポーランド [pourando] n Poland; ポーランド人 [pourandojin] n Pole, Polish person; ポーランドの [pourando no] adj Polish

ポーター [poutaa] n porter

ポートワイン [poutowain] n port (wine)

プディング [pudingu] n pudding

プエルトリコ [puerutoriko] n Puerto Rico

プラチナ [purachina] n platinum

プラグ [puragu] n plug; プラグで接続する [puragu de setsuzoku suru] v plug in; プラグを抜いて電源を断つ [puragu-o nuite dengen-o tatsu] v unplug

プライバシー [puraibashii] n privacy

プライヤー [puraiyaa] n pliers

プラム [puramu] n plum

プラスチック [purasuchikku] n plastic; プラスチックの [purasuchikku no] adj plastic

プラズマスクリーン
[purazumasukuriin] n plasma screen

プラズマテレビ [purazumaterebi] n
plasma TV

プレーパーク [pureepaaku] n play park;
この近くにプレーパークはありますか?
[kono chikaku ni puree-paaku wa arimasu
ka?] Is there a play park near here?

プレーヤー [pureeyaa] CDプレーヤー
[shiidii pureiyaa] n CD player; DVDプレー
ヤー [diibuidii pureiyaa] n DVD player

プレイグループ [pureiguruupu] n
playgroup

プレイステーション®
[pureisuteeshon] n PlayStation®

プレス機 [puresuki] n press

プレゼンター [purezentaa] n presenter

プレゼント [purezento] n present (gift);
私は子供へのプレゼントを探しています
[watashi wa kodomo e no purezento o
sagashite imasu] I'm looking for a present
for a child

プリペイド [puripeido] プリペイドの
[puripeido no] adj prepaid

プロバイダ [purobaida] インターネットサ
ービスプロバイダ [intaanetto saabisu
purobaida] n ISP

プロデューサー [purodyuusaa] n
producer

プログラマー [puroguramaa] n
programmer

プログラム [puroguramu] n program,
programme; プログラム作成
[puroguramu sakusei] n programming; プ
ログラムを作成する [puroguramu-o
sakusei suru] v program; メッセンジャープ
ログラムを使えますか? [messenjaa-
proguramu o tsukaemasu ka?] Can I use
messenger programmes?

プロジェクター [purojekutaa] n
projector

プロパガンダ [puropaganda] n
propaganda

プロテスタント [purotesutanto] n
Protestant; プロテスタントの
[purotesutanto no] adj Protestant

プルオーバー [puruoobaa] n pullover

プルーン [puruun] n prune

プードル [puudoru] n poodle

プール [puuru] n (水泳) pool (water); 子供
用プール [kodomoyou puuru] n paddling
pool; それは屋外プールですか? [sore wa
okugai-puuru desu ka?] Is it an outdoor
pool?; スイミングプールはありますか?
[suimingu-puuru wa arimasu ka?] Is there
a swimming pool?; プールは温水ですか?
[puuru wa onsui desu ka?] Is the pool
heated?; 子供用のプールはありますか?
[kodomo-you no puuru wa arimasu ka?] Is
there a children's pool?

r

ラバ [raba] n mule

ラベンダー [rabendaa] n lavender

ラベル [raberu] n label

ラビ [rabi] n rabbi

ラボ [rabo] n lab; 語学ラボ [gogaku rabo] n language laboratory

ラディッシュ [radisshu] n radish

ラガー [ragaa] n lager

ラグ [ragu] n rug

ラグビー [ragubii] n rugby

ライブミュージック [raibumyuujikku] n live music; どこでライブミュージックを聴けますか? [doko de raibu-myuujikku o kikemasu ka?] Where can we hear live music?

ライチョウ [raichou] n grouse (game bird)

ライフル [raifuru] ライフル銃 [raifuru juu] n rifle

ライフスタイル [raifusutairu] n lifestyle

雷鳴 [raimei] n thunder; 雷鳴を伴った [raimei-o tomonatta] adj thundery

ライム [raimu] n lime (fruit)

ライ麦 [raimugi] n rye

来年 [rainen] n next year

ライオン [raion] n lion; 雌ライオン [mesuraion] n lioness

ライラック [rairakku] n lilac; ライラック色の [rairakku iro no] adj lilac

ライロー® [rairoo] n Lilo®

来週 [raishuu] n next week; 再来週 [saraishuu] the week after next

ライター [raitaa] n lighter; シガレットライター [shigaretto raitaa] n cigarette lighter

雷雨 [raiu] n thunderstorm

ラジエーター [rajieetaa] n radiator; ラジエーターに漏れがあります [rajieetaa ni more ga arimasu] There is a leak in the radiator

ラジオ [rajio] n radio; ラジオ局 [rajio kyoku] n radio station; デジタルラジオ [dejitaru rajio] n digital radio; ラジオをつけてもいいですか? [rajio o tsukete mo ii desu ka?] Can I switch the radio on?; ラジオを消してもいいですか? [rajio o keshite mo ii desu ka?] Can I switch the radio off?

ラケット [raketto] n racquet

落下 [rakka] n fall

ラッカー [rakkaa] n lacquer

楽観主義 [rakkanshugi] n optimism

ラクダ [rakuda] n camel

楽園 [rakuen] n paradise

落書き [rakugaki] n graffiti

楽観 [rakukan] 楽観主義者 [rakkan shugisha] n optimist; 楽観的な [rakkanteki na] adj optimistic

ラマダーン [ramadaan] n Ramadan

ラム [ramu] n (酒) rum

ラン [ran] n orchid

ランチタイム [ranchitaimu] n lunchtime

ランドマーク [randomaaku] n landmark

ランドリーサービス [randoriisaabisu] ランドリーサービスはありますか? [randorii-saabisu wa arimasu ka?] Is there a laundry service?

ランジェリー [ranjerii] n lingerie; ランジェリー売り場はどこですか? [ranjerii-uriba wa doko desu ka?] Where is the lingerie department?

卵形 [rankei] 卵形の [tamagogata no] *adj* oval

ランク付け [rankuzuke] ランク付けする [ranku zuke suru] *v* rank

ランナー [rannaa] *n* runner

ランニング [ranningu] *n* running

ランプ [ranpu] *n* lamp; ブレーキランプ [bureeki ranpu] *n* brake light; ランプがつきません [ranpu ga tsukimasen] The lamp is not working

ランプシェード [ranpusheedo] *n* lampshade

ランプステーキ [ranpusuteeki] *n* rump steak

卵巣 [ransou] *n* ovary

濫用 [ranyou] 濫用する [ran'you suru] *v* abuse

乱雑 [ranzatsu] 乱雑な状態 [ranzatsu na joutai] *n* shambles

ラオス [raosu] *n* Laos

ラッパズイセン [rappazuisen] *n* daffodil

ラッピング [rappingu] *n* wrapping; それをギフト用にラッピングしていただけますか? [sore o gifuto-you ni rappingu shite itadakemasu ka?] Please can you gift-wrap it?

ラップトップ [rapputoppu] *n* laptop; ここで自分のラップトップを使えますか? [koko de jibun no rappu-toppu o tsukaemasu ka?] Can I use my own laptop here?

ラッシュアワー [rasshuawaa] *n* rush hour

ラスク [rasuku] *n* rusk

裸体 [ratai] *n* nude; 裸体主義者 [rataishugisha] *n* nudist

ラテンアメリカ [raten amerika] *n* Latin America

ラテンアメリカの [raten amerika no] *adj* Latin American

ラテン語 [ratengo] *n* Latin

ラトビア [ratobia] *n* Latvia

ラトビア語 [ratobiago] *n* Latvian (language)

ラトビア人 [ratobiajin] *n* Latvian (person)

ラトビアの [ratobia no] *adj* Latvian

ラウンジ [raunji] *n* lounge; 通過ラウンジ [tsuuka raunji] *n* transit lounge; 出発ラウンジ [shuppatsu raunji] *n* departure lounge; ラウンジでコーヒーをいただけますか? [raunji de koohii o itadakemasu ka?] Could we have coffee in the lounge?

ラズベリー [razuberii] *n* raspberry

レバー [rebaa] *n* (操作ハンドル) lever

レバノン [rebanon] *n* Lebanon

レバノン人 [rebanonjin] *n* Lebanese (person)

レバノンの [rebanon no] *adj* Lebanese

レーダー [reedaa] *n* radar

レーサー [reesaa] *n* racer

レーシングドライバー [reeshingudoraibaa] *n* racing driver

レーシングカー [reeshingukaa] *n* racing car

レース [reesu] *n* (競争) race (contest), (布) lace

レーストラック [reesutorakku] *n* racetrack

レート [reeto] *n* rate; 為替レート [kawase reeto] *n* exchange rate, rate of exchange; 為替レートはいくらですか? [kawase-reeto wa ikura desu ka?] What's the exchange rate?; ···を···に替える為替レートはいくらですか? [...o ... ni kaeru kawase-reeto wa ikura desu ka?] What is the rate for ... to...?

レーザー [reezaa] *n* laser

レーズン [reezun] *n* raisin

レフェリー [referii] *n* referee

レギングス [regingusu] *n* leggings

例 [rei] *n* example

零 [rei] *n* nil, nought, zero

例外 [reigai] *n* exception; 例外的な [reigaiteki na] *adj* exceptional

礼拝 [reihai] 礼拝する [reihai suru] *v* worship

礼拝堂 [reihaidou] *n* chapel

冷却水 [reikyakusui] *n* coolant; 冷却水を点検してもらえますか? [reikyakusui o tenken shite moraemasu ka?] **Can you check the water, please?**

レインコート [reinkooto] *n* **mac, raincoat**

レイプ [reipu] *n* **rape** *(sexual attack)*; レイプする [reipu suru] *v* **rape**; 私はレイプされました [watashi wa reipu saremashita] **I've been raped**

冷凍庫 [reitouko] *n* **freezer**

レイヨウ [reiyou] *n* **antelope**

冷蔵庫 [reizouko] *n* **fridge, refrigerator**

レジャー [rejaa] レジャーセンター [rejaasentaa] *n* **leisure centre**

レジ [reji] *n* **cash register, till**

レジスターオフィス [rejisutaaofisu] *n* **registry office**

歴史 [rekishi] *n* **history**; 歴史上の [rekishijou no] *adj* **historical**; 歴史家 [rekishika] *n* **historian**

レッカー [rekkaa] レッカー移動する [rekkaa idou suru] *v* **tow away**; レッカー車を手配してもらえますか？ [rekkaa-sha o tehai shite moraemasu ka?] **Can you send a breakdown van?**

レッカー車 [rekkaasha] *n* **breakdown truck, breakdown van**

レモン [remon] *n* **lemon**; レモン入りで [remon-iri de] **with lemon**

レモネード [remoneedo] *n* **lemonade**; コップ一杯のレモネードをください [koppu ippai no remoneedo o kudasai] **A glass of lemonade, please**

レモンゼスト [remonzesuto] *n* **lemon zest**

恋愛 [ren-ai] *n* **love**

煉瓦 [renga] *n* **brick**; 煉瓦職人 [renga shokunin] *n* **bricklayer**

連合 [rengou] *n* **union**; 欧州連合 [oushuu rengou] *n* **European Union**; 国際連合 [kokusairengou] *n* **UN**

レンジ [renji] 料理用レンジ [ryouri you renji] *n* **cooker, stove**

連盟 [renmei] *n* **league**

連絡 [renraku] *n* **contact**; 連絡を取る [renraku-o toru] *v* **contact**; どこであなたに連絡を取れますか？ [doko de anata ni renraku o toremasu ka?] **Where can I contact you?**; 問題があったときに誰に連絡すればいいのですか？ [mondai ga atta toki ni dare ni renraku sureba ii no desu ka?] **Who do we contact if there are problems?**

練習 [renshuu] *n* **practice**; 練習する [renshuu suru] *v* **practise**

連隊 [rentai] *n* **regiment**

レンタカー [rentakaa] *n* **car hire, car rental, hire car, hired car, rental car**

レンタル [rentaru] *n* **rental**

レンタルDVD [rentaru dvd] レンタルDVDはありますか？ [rentaru dii-vui-dii wa arimasu ka?] **Do you rent DVDs?**

連続 [renzoku] *n* **round** *(series)*; 連続する [renzoku suru] *adj* **successive**; 連続もの [renzokumono] *n* **serial**; 連続的な [renzokuteki na] *adj* **consecutive, continuous**

レンズ [renzu] *n* **lens**; コンタクトレンズ [kontakutorenzu] *n* **contact lenses**; ズームレンズ [zuumurenzu] *n* **zoom lens**

レオタード [reotaado] *n* **leotard**

レパートリー [repaatorii] レパートリー劇団 [repaatorii gekidan] *n* **rep**

レプリカ [repurika] *n* **replica**

レシート [reshiito] *n* **receipt**; レシートをください [reshiito o kudasai] **I need a receipt, please**; 私は保険請求のためにレシートが必要です [watashi wa hoken-seikyuu no tame ni reshiito ga hitsuyou desu] **I need a receipt for the insurance**

列車 [ressha] *n* **train**

レッスン [ressun] *n* **lesson**; スキーのレッスンを企画していますか？ [sukii no ressun o kikaku shite imasu ka?] **Do you organise skiing lessons?**; スノーボードのレッスンを企画していますか？ [sunooboodo no ressun o kikaku shite imasu ka?] **Do you organise snowboarding lessons?**; レッスンを実施していますか？ [ressun o jisshi shite imasu ka?] **Do you give lessons?**; レッスンを受けられますか？ [ressun o ukeraremasu ka?] **Can we take lessons?**

レスラー [resuraa] *n* **wrestler**

レスリング [resuringu] n wrestling

レストラン [resutoran] n restaurant; ここにベジタリアン用のレストランはありますか? [koko ni bejitarian-you no resutoran wa arimasu ka?] Are there any vegetarian restaurants here?; よいレストランを教えてもらえますか? [yoi resutoran o oshiete moraemasu ka?] Can you recommend a good restaurant?; キャンプ場にレストランはありますか? [kyanpu-jou ni resutoran wa arimasu ka?] Is there a restaurant on the campsite?

レタス [retasu] n lettuce

列 [retsu] n queue, rank (line), row (line); 列を作る [retsu o tsukuru] v queue; ここが列の最後ですか? [koko ga retsu no saigo desu ka?] Is this the end of the queue?

リベート [ribeeto] n rebate

リベラル [riberaru] リベラルな [riberaru na] adj liberal

リベリア [riberia] n Liberia

リベリア人 [riberiajin] n Liberian (person)

リベリアの [riberia no] adj Liberian

リビア [ribia] n Libya

リビア人 [ribiajin] n Libyan (person)

リビアの [ribia no] adj Libyan

リボン [ribon] n ribbon

リボルバー [riborubaa] n revolver

利益 [rieki] n (もうけ) benefit; 利益を得る [rieki o eru] v benefit

リフト [rifuto] スキー場のリフト [sukii jou no rifuto] n ski lift

理学 [rigaku] 理学療法 [rigaku ryouhou] n physiotherapy; 理学療法士 [rigaku ryouhoushi] n physiotherapist

リハーサル [rihaasaru] n rehearsal; リハーサルをする [rihaasaru-o suru] v rehearse

リヒテンシュタイン [rihitenshutain] n Liechtenstein

リーダー [riidaa] n leader

リードシンガー [riidoshingaa] n lead singer

リーフレット [riifuretto] n leaflet; リーフ

レットはありますか? [riifuretto wa arimasu ka?] Do you have any leaflets?; 英語のリーフレットはありますか? [eigo no riifuretto wa arimasu ka?] Do you have a leaflet in English?; ···に関するリーフレットはありますか? [...ni kansuru riifuretto wa arimasu ka?] Do you have any leaflets about...?

リール [riiru] n reel

理解 [rikai] n comprehension; 理解する [rikai suru] v understand; 理解できる [rikai dekiru] adj understandable; 十分に理解する [juubun ni rikai suru] v realize

利己 [riko] 利己的な [rikoteki na] adj selfish

離婚 [rikon] n divorce; 私は離婚しています [watashi wa rikon shite imasu] I'm divorced

離婚する [rikon suru] v divorce; 離婚した [rikonshita] adj divorced

利口 [rikou] 利口な [rikou na] adj intelligent

リコーダー [rikoudaa] n recorder (music)

陸 [riku] n land

陸上 [rikujou] 陸上競技 [rikujou kyougi] n athletics

リクライニング式 [rikurainingu shiki] リクライニング式の [rikurainingu shiki no] adj reclining

リキュール [rikyuuru] n liqueur; どんなリキュールがありますか? [donna rikyuuru ga arimasu ka?] What liqueurs do you have?

リメイク [rimeiku] n remake

リモコン [rimokon] n remote control

リムジン [rimujin] n limousine

りんご [ringo] りんご酒 [ringoshu] n cider

リンゴ [ringo] n apple

リングバインダー [ringubaindaa] n ring binder

理にかなう [ri ni kanau] 理にかなって [ri ni kanatte] adv reasonably; 理にかなった [ri ni kanatta] adj reasonable

臨時 [rinji] 臨時代理の [rinji dairi no] adj acting; 臨時教員 [rinji kyouin] n supply teacher; 臨時職員 [rinjishokuin] n temp

リンク [rinku] スケートリンク [sukeetorinku] n ice rink

リノリウム [rinoriumu] n lino

倫理 [rinri] 倫理的な [rinriteki na] adj ethical

立方 [rippou] 立方の [rippou no] adj cubic

立方体 [rippoutai] n cube

履歴書 [rirekisho] n curriculum vitae, CV

離陸 [ririku] n takeoff

利率 [riritsu] n interest rate

理論 [riron] n theory

リサイクル [risaikuru] n recycling

利息 [risoku] n interest (income)

理想 [risou] 理想的な [risouteki na] adj ideal; 理想的に [risouteki ni] adv ideally

立証 [risshou] 立証する [risshou suru] v argue, demonstrate, prove

リス [risu] n squirrel

リトアニア [ritoania] n Lithuania

リトアニア語 [ritoaniago] n Lithuanian (language)

リトアニア人 [ritoaniajin] n Lithuanian (person)

リトアニアの [ritoania no] adj Lithuanian

利得 [ritoku] n gain

率 [ritsu] 関税率 [kanzeiritsu] n tariff

率的 [ritsu teki] 効率的に [kouritsuteki ni] adv efficiently

立体 [rittai] 立体的な [rittaiteki na] adj three-dimensional

リットル [rittoru] n litre

リウマチ [riumachi] n rheumatism

利用 [riyou] n use; 自動車の道路利用税 [jidousha no douro riyou zei] n road tax; 再生利用する [saisei riyou suru] v recycle; 利用する [riyou suru] v exploit; 利用できる [riyou dekiru] adj available; 最低利用時間はどれだけですか? [saitei-riyou-jikan wa dore dake desu ka?] What's the minimum amount of time?

利用者 [riyousha] インターネット利用者 [intaanetto riyousha] n internet user

理由 [riyuu] n cause (reason), reason

リズム [rizumu] n rhythm

炉 [ro] 原子炉 [genshiro] n reactor

ロバ [roba] n donkey

ロビー [robii] ロビーでお会いしましょう [robii de o-ai shimashou] I'll meet you in the lobby

ロボット [robotto] n robot

ロブスター [robusutaa] n lobster

ロゴ [rogo] n logo

ログアウト [roguauto] ログアウトする [roguauto suru] v log out

ログイン [roguin] ログインする [roguin suru] v log in

ログオフ [roguofu] ログオフする [roguofu suru] v log off

ログオン [roguon] ログオンする [roguon suru] v log on; 1時間ログオンするのにいくらですか? [ichi-jikan roguon suru no ni ikura desu ka?] How much is it to log on for an hour?; ログオンできません [roguon dekimasen] I can't log on

路地 [roji] n alley

濾過 [roka] 濾過する [roka suru] v filter

濾過器 [rokaki] n filter

路肩 [rokata] n hard shoulder

ロケット [roketto] n locket, rocket

ロッカー [rokkaa] n locker; コインロッカー [koinrokkaa] n left-luggage locker; どれが私のロッカーですか? [dore ga watashi no rokkaa desu ka?] Which locker is mine?; 服のロッカーはどこですか? [fuku no rokkaa wa doko desu ka?] Where are the clothes lockers?

ロッキングチェア [rokkinguchea] n rocking chair

肋骨 [rokkotsu] n rib

ロック [rokku] n lock; ドアをロックしておいてください [doa o rokku shite oite kudasai] Keep the door locked; ロックをください [rokku o kudasai] Can I have a lock?

ロッククライミング [rokkukuraimingu] n rock climbing

露骨 [rokotsu] 露骨な [rokotsu na] adj blatant

六 [roku] *number* six; 六番目の [roku banme no] *adj* sixth

六月 [rokugatsu] *n* June; 六月の終わりに [roku-gatsu no owari ni] at the end of June; 六月の初めに [roku-gatsu no hajime ni] at the beginning of June; 六月いっぱい [roku-gatsu ippai] for the whole of June; 六月十五日の月曜日です [roku-gatsu juugo-nichi no getsuyoubi desu] It's Monday fifteenth June

六時 [rokuji] 六時です [roku-ji desu] It's six o'clock

六十 [rokujuu] *number* sixty

録音 [rokuon] *n* recording

ロマンチックな [romanchikku na] *adj* romantic

ロマネスク [romanesuku] ロマネスク様式の [romanesuku youshiki no] *adj* Romanesque

路面 [romen] 路面電車 [romendensha] *n* tram

ロンドン [rondon] *n* London

論評 [ronpyou] *n* comment; 論評する [ronpyou suru] *v* comment

論理 [ronri] 論理的な [ronriteki na] *adj* logical

論争 [ronsou] 論争の [ronsou no] *adj* controversial

論点 [ronten] *n* issue

ロードマップ [roodomappu] *n* road map

ローマ [rooma] ローマの [rooma no] *adj* Roman

ローマカトリック [roomakatorikku] ローマカトリック教会の [rooma katorikku kyoukai no] *adj* Roman Catholic; ローマカトリック教徒 [rooma katorikku kyouto] *n* Roman Catholic

ローンドレット® [roondoretto] *n* Launderette®

ローラーコースター [rooraakoosutaa] *n* rollercoaster

ロースクール [roosukuuru] *n* law school

路線 [rosen] *n* route; ···へ行くにはどの路線を使えばいいのですか? [...e iku ni wa dono rosen o tsukaeba ii no desu ka?]

Which line should I take for...?

ロシア [roshia] *n* Russia; ロシア人 [roshiajin] *n* Russian (person); ロシアの [roshia no] *adj* Russian; ロシア語 [roshiago] *n* Russian (language)

聾 [rou] 耳を聾するような [mimi-o rousuru you na] *adj* deafening

蝋 [rou] *n* wax

狼狽 [roubai] 狼狽した [roubai shita] *adj* upset

労働 [roudou] *n* labour, work; 労働体験 [roudou taiken] *n* work experience; 労働許可証 [roudou kyokashou] *n* work permit; 労働組合 [roudoukumiai] *n* trade union; 労働組合主義者 [roudoukumiai shugisha] *n* trade unionist; 労働力 [roudouryoku] *n* manpower

労働者 [roudousha] *n* labourer; 肉体労働者 [nikutairoudousha] *n* workman; 炭坑労働者 [tankou roudousha] *n* miner; 労働者階級の [roudoushakaikyuu no] *adj* working-class

浪費 [rouhi] *n* waste; 浪費する [rouhi suru] *v* squander, waste

老人 [roujin] 老人ホーム [roujin hoomu] *n* nursing home; 老人病患者 [roujinbyou kanja] *n* geriatric; 老人病学の [roujinbyougaku no] *adj* geriatric

廊下 [rouka] *n* corridor; 入口の廊下 [iriguchi no rouka] *n* hall

ロープ [roupu] *n* rope; 洗濯ロープ [sentaku roopu] *n* clothes line

ローラー [rouraa] *n* roller

ローラースケート [rouraasukeeto] *n* rollerskating; ローラースケート靴 [rooraa sukeeto kutsu] *n* rollerskates

老齢年金 [roureinenkin] 老齢年金受給者 [rourei nenkin jukyuusha] *n* old-age pensioner

老練 [rouren] 老練な [rouren na] *adj* veteran; 老練な人 [rouren na hito] *n* veteran

ローリエ [rourie] *n* bay leaf

ロールパン [rourupan] *n* bread roll

ローション [roushon] *n* lotion; アフターサ

ンローション [afutaasan rooshon] n after sun lotion; アフターシェーブローション [afutaasheeburooshon] n aftershave

ろうそく [rousoku] n candle

ろうそく立て [rousokutate] n candlestick

ローズマリー [rouzumarii] n rosemary

ロゼワイン [rozewain] n rosé; よいロゼワインを教えてもらえますか? [yoi roze-wain o oshiete moraemasu ka?] Can you recommend a good rosé wine?

ルバーブ [rubaabu] n rhubarb

類 [rui] 機械類 [kikairui] n machinery; 宝石類 [housekirui] n jewellery

類似 [ruiji] n resemblance, similarity; 類似した [ruiji shita] adj similar

ルクセンブルク [rukusenburuku] n Luxembourg

留守番 [rusuban] 留守番電話 [rusubandenwa] n answering machine, answerphone

ルーフラック [ruufurakku] n roof rack

ルーマニア [ruumania] n Romania; ルーマニア人 [ruumaniajin] n Romanian (person); ルーマニアの [ruumania no] adj Romanian; ルーマニア語 [ruumaniago] n Romanian (language)

ルーム [ruumu] ダイニングルーム [dainingu ruumu] n dining room; ダブルルーム [daburu ruumu] n double room; チャットルーム [chatto ruumu] n chatroom

ルームメート [ruumumeeto] n roommate

ルームサービス [ruumusaabisu] n room service; ルームサービスはありますか? [ruumusaabisu wa arimasu ka?] Is there room service?

ルーレット [ruuretto] n roulette

ルート [ruuto] n route

略語 [ryakugo] n abbreviation

旅行 [ryokou] n journey, tour, travel, travelling, trip; パック旅行 [pakku ryokou] n package holiday, package tour; 旅行代理店 [ryokoudairiten] n travel agency, travel agent's; 旅行保険 [ryokou hoken] n travel insurance; 旅行する [ryokou suru] v

tour; 旅行業 [ryokou gyou] n tourism; 旅行業者 [ryokougyousha] n tour operator, travel agent; 旅行者 [ryokousha] n tourist, traveller; 旅行者用小切手 [ryokousha you kogitte] n traveller's cheque; 徒歩旅行 [tohoryokou] n tramp (long walk); 大型の旅行かばん [ougata no ryokou kaban] n holdall; よいご旅行を! [yoi go-ryokou o!] Have a good trip!; 私は一人で旅行しています [watashi wa hitori de ryokou shite imasu] I'm travelling alone; 私は旅行保険に入っていません [watashi wa ryokou-hoken ni haitte imasen] I don't have travel insurance; ···への旅行はこれが初めてです [...e no ryokou wa kore ga hajimete desu] This is my first trip to...

緑色 [ryokushoku] n green; 緑色の [midori iro no] adj green (colour)

旅程 [ryotei] n itinerary

料 [ryou] n fee; サービス料 [saabisuryou] n service charge; 授業料 [jugyouryou] n tuition fees; 賃貸料 [chintairyou] n rent; 調味料 [choumiryou] n seasoning; 甘味料 [kanmiryou] n sweetener; 送金料がかかりますか? [soukin-ryou ga kakarimasu ka?] Is there a transfer charge?

量 [ryou] n amount, quantity; 量を決める [ryou-o kimeru] v quantify

両替 [ryougae] 外貨両替所 [gaika ryougaesho] n bureau de change; どこでお金を両替できますか? [doko de o-kane o ryougae dekimasu ka?] Where can I change some money?; ここに外貨両替所はありますか? [koko ni gaika ryougae-jo wa arimasu ka?] Is there a bureau de change here?; 百···を···に両替したいのですが [hyaku ... o ... ni ryougae shitai no desu ga] I'd like to change one hundred ... into...; 私は外貨両替所をさがしています [watashi ha gaikaryougae tokoro o sagashite imasu] I need to find a bureau de change; ···を···に両替したいのですが [...o ... ni ryougae shitai no desu ga] I want to change some ... into...

両方 [ryouhou] pron both; 両方の [ryouhou no] adj both

療法 [ryouhou] n therapy; 理学療法

[rigaku ryouhou] *n* physiotherapy; 理学療法士 [rigaku ryouhoushi] *n* physiotherapist; 心理療法 [shinri ryouhou] *n* psychotherapy

領事 [ryouji] *n* consul

領事館 [ryoujikan] *n* consulate

了見 [ryouken] 了見の狭い [ryouken no semai] *adj* narrow-minded

料金 [ryoukin] *n* charge *(price)*, fee; 追加料金 [tsuikaryoukin] *n* surcharge; 郵便料金 [yuubin ryoukin] *n* postage; 予約料金がかかりますか? [yoyaku-ryoukin ga kakarimasu ka?] Is there a booking fee to pay?; サービスに料金がかかりますか? [saabisu ni ryoukin ga kakarimasu ka?] Is there a charge for the service?; 走行距離に対して料金がかかりますか? [soukou-kyori ni taishite ryoukin ga kakarimasu ka?] Is there a mileage charge?

領空 [ryoukuu] *n* airspace

料理 [ryouri] *n* cooking, dish *(food)*; カレー料理 [karee ryouri] *n* curry; 料理の本 [ryouri no hon] *n* cookbook, cookery book; 料理する [ryouri suru] *v* cook; 料理用レンジ [ryouri you renji] *n* cooker, stove; 今日のおすすめ料理は何ですか? [kyou no osusume ryouri wa nan desu ka?] What is the dish of the day?; おすすめの郷土料理はありますか? [osusume no kyoudo-ryouri wa arimasu ka?] Can you recommend a local dish?; この料理には何が入っていますか? [kono ryouri ni wa nani ga haitte imasu ka?] What is in this dish?; この料理はどのように作るのですか? [kono ryouri wa dono you ni tsukuru no desu ka?] How do you cook this dish?; この料理はどのように出てくるのですか? [kono ryouri wa dono you ni dete kuru no desu ka?] How is this dish served?; コーシャ料理はありますか? [koosha-ryouri wa arimasu ka?] Do you have kosher dishes?; グルテンを使っていない料理はありますか? [guruten o tsukatte inai ryouri wa arimasu ka?] Do you have gluten-free dishes?; ハラール料理はありますか? [haraaru-ryouri wa arimasu ka?] Do you have halal dishes?; ビーガン料理はありますか? [biigan-ryouri wa arimasu ka?] Do you have any vegan dishes?; ベジタリアン料理はありますか? [bejitarian-ryouri wa arimasu ka?] Do you have any vegetarian dishes?; 肉/魚の入っていない料理はどれですか? [niku / sakana no haitte inai ryouri wa dore desu ka?] Which dishes have no meat / fish?

料理法 [ryourihou] *n* cookery

料理人 [ryourinin] *n* cook

両立 [ryouritsu] 両立できる [ryouritsu dekiru] *adj* compatible

漁師 [ryoushi] *n* fisherman

両親 [ryoushin] *n* parents

良心 [ryoushin] *n* conscience; 良心の呵責 [ryoushin no kashaku] *n* remorse

リュックサック [ryukkusakku] *n* rucksack

竜 [ryuu] *n* dragon

流暢 [ryuuchou] 流暢な [ryuuchou na] *adj* fluent

流行 [ryuukou] *n* fashion; 流行の [ryuukou no] *adj* fashionable

流行病 [ryuukoubyou] *n* epidemic

流産 [ryuuzan] *n* miscarriage

S

サーバー [saabaa] n server (computer)

サービス [saabisu] n service; サービスを
提供する [saabisu-o teikyou suru] v
service; サービス料 [saabisuryou] n
service charge; インターネットサービスプ
ロバイダ [intaanetto saabisu purobaida] n
ISP; 番号案内サービス [bangou annai
saabisu] n directory enquiries; サービスに
料金がかかりますか? [saabisu ni ryoukin
ga kakarimasu ka?] Is there a charge for
the service?; サービスがひどかったです
[saabisu ga hidokatta desu] The service
was terrible; 故障時緊急修理サービスを
呼んでください [koshou-ji
kinkyuu-shuuri-saabisu o yonde kudasai]
Call the breakdown service, please; 託児
サービスはありますか? [takuji saabisu wa
arimasu ka?] Is there a child-minding
service?; 私はサービスについて苦情があ
ります [watashi wa saabisu ni tsuite kujou
ga arimasu] I want to complain about the
service

サービスエリア [saabisu eria] n service
area

サーブ [saabu] n serve

サーディン [saadein] n sardine

サーファー [saafaa] n surfer

サーフィン [saafin] n surfing; サーフィン
をする [saafin-o suru] v surf; どこでサーフ
ィンができますか? [doko de saafin ga
dekimasu ka?] Where can you go surfing?

サーフボード [saafuboudo] n surfboard

サーカス [saakasu] n circus

サーモス® [saamosu] n Thermos®

サーモスタット [saamosutatto] n
thermostat

サバ [saba] n mackerel

砂漠 [sabaku] n desert; サハラ砂漠
[sahara sabaku] n Sahara

差別 [sabetsu] n discrimination; 人種差別
[jinshusabetsu] n racism; 性差別主義
[seisabetsu shugi] n sexism; 性差別主義の
[seisabetsu shugi no] adj sexist

さび [sabi] n (腐食) rust

さびる [sabiru] さびた [sabita] adj rusty

サボる [saboru] v play truant; 仕事をサボ
る [shigoto-o saboru] v skive

サボテン [saboten] n cactus

定める [sadameru] v set; 形式を定める
[keishiki-o sadameru] v format

サドル [sadoru] n saddle

サドルバッグ [sadorubaggu] n
saddlebag

さえ [sae] ・・・でさえ [...de sae] adv even

さえない [saenai] v drab

サファイア [safaia] n sapphire

サファリ [safari] n safari

サフラン [safuran] n saffron

砂岩 [sagan] n sandstone

下がる [sagaru] v go down; 後ろに下がる
[ushiro ni sagaru] v move back

捜す [sagasu] v seek

探す [sagasu] 私は警察署をさがしています
[watashi wa keisatsusho o sagashite
imasu] I need to find a police station; 私
は外貨両替所をさがしています [watashi
wa gaikaryougae tokoro o sagashite imasu]
I need to find a bureau de change; 私たち
はアパートメントを探しています
[watashi-tachi wa apaatomento o
sagashite imasu] We're looking for an

apartment; 私たちは・・・を探しています [watashi-tachi wa ... o sagashite imasu] We're looking for...

さがす [sagasu] ・・・をさがす [...-o sagasu] v look for

下げる [sageru] v lower

サギ [sagi] n (鳥) heron

詐欺 [sagi] n fraud, scam

詐欺師 [sagishi] n cheat

作業 [sagyou] n operation (undertaking); 作業スペース [sagyou supeesu] n workspace; 作業要員 [sagyou youin] n workforce

左派 [saha] 左派の [saha no] adj left-wing

再 [sai] prefix re-; 再使用する [saishiyou suru] v reuse; 再編成する [saihensei suru] v reorganize, restructure; 再受験する [saijuken suru] v resit

最悪 [saiaku] 最悪の [saiaku no] adj worst

サイバー [saibaa] サイバー犯罪 [saibaa hanzai] n cybercrime

サイバーいじめ [saibaa ijime] n cyberbullying

サイバーカフェ [saibaakafe] n cybercafé

裁判 [saiban] n trial; 裁判官 [saibankan] n judge

細胞 [saibou] n cell

細部 [saibu] n detail

最大 [saidai] 最大の [saidai no] adj maximum

最大限 [saidaigen] n maximum

祭壇 [saidan] n altar

サイドミラー [saidomiraa] n wing mirror

サイドランプ [saidoranpu] ベッドサイドランプ [beddosaido ranpu] n bedside lamp

サイエンスフィクション [saiensu fikushon] n science fiction, scifi

財布 [saifu] n purse, wallet; 私は財布をなくしました [watashi wa saifu o nakushimashita] I've lost my wallet; 私の財布が盗まれました [watashi no saifu ga nusumaremashita] My wallet has been stolen

災害 [saigai] n disaster; 大災害の

[daisaigai no] adj disastrous

最後 [saigo] 最後に [saigo ni] adv last, lastly; 最後の [saigo no] adj last; 最後通牒 [saigo tsuuchou] n ultimatum

裁縫 [saihou] n sewing

祭日 [saijitsu] 聖バレンタインの祭日 [sei barentain no saijitsu] n Valentine's Day; 祝祭日 [shukusaijitsu] n bank holiday

最盛 [saijou] 最盛期 [saiseiki] n high season

再会 [saikai] n reunion

再開 [saikai] 再開する [saikai suru] v renew, resume

再建 [saiken] 再建する [saiken suru] v rebuild

細菌 [saikin] n germ

最近 [saikin] adv lately, recently; 最近の [saikin no] adj recent

再婚 [saikon] 再婚する [saikon suru] v remarry

さいころ [saikoro] n dice

最高 [saikou] 最高機密の [saikou kimitsu no] adj top-secret; 最高経営責任者 [saikou keiei sekininsha] n CEO

サイクリング [saikuringu] n cycling; サイクリングに行きましょう [saikuringu ni ikimashou] Let's go cycling; 私たちはサイクリングに行きたいのですが [watashi-tachi wa saikuringu ni ikitai no desu ga] We would like to go cycling

サイクリスト [saikurisuto] n cyclist

サイクロン [saikuron] n cyclone

サイクル [saikuru] サイクルパス [saikuru pasu] n cycle path; この地域のサイクルマップはありますか? [kono chiiki no saikuru-mappu wa arimasu ka?] Is there a cycle map of this area?

サイクルレーン [saikurureen] n cycle lane

サイン [sain] n autograph

最年長 [sainenchou] 最年長の [sainenchou no] adj eldest

才能 [sainou] n talent; 才能のある [sainou no aru] adj talented; 生まれつき才能のある [umaretsuki sainou no aru] adj gifted

サイレン [sairen] n siren

催涙 [sairui] 催涙ガス [sairuigasu] n tear gas

再生 [saisei] n replay; 再生する [saisei suru] v replay; 再生利用する [saisei riyou suru] v recycle

採石 [saiseki] 採石場 [saisekijou] n quarry

最新 [saishin] 最新の [saishin no] adj up-to-date; 最新設備 [saishin setsubi] n mod cons

最初 [saisho] n outset; 最初に [saisho ni] adv first, initially; 最初の [saisho no] adj first, original; 最初の [saisho no] adj initial; 最初のもの [saisho no mono] n first

最小 [saishou] 最小の [saishou no] adj minimum

最小限 [saishougen] n minimum; 最小限の [saishougen no] adj minimal; 最小限度にする [saishougendo ni suru] v minimize

最終 [saishuu] 最終の [saishuu no] adj final; 最終的な [saishuuteki na] adj ultimate; 最終的に [saishuuteki ni] adv ultimately; 最終のバスは何時ですか? [saishuu no basu wa nan-ji desu ka?] What time is the last bus?; 最終の船は何時ですか? [saishuu no fune wa nan-ji desu ka?] When is the last boat?; ・・・へ行く最終のバスは何時ですか? [...e iku saishuu no basu wa nan-ji desu ka?] When is the last bus to...?; ・・・へ行く最終の電車は何時ですか? [...e iku saishuu no densha wa nan-ji desu ka?] When is the last train to...?

最多数 [saitasuu] pron most (majority)

裁定 [saitei] 裁定委員会 [saitei iinkai] n tribunal

採点 [saiten] 採点する [saiten suru] v mark (grade)

サイト [saito] テント用のサイトが欲しいのですが [tento-you no saito ga hoshii no desu ga] We'd like a site for a tent

サイズ [saizu] n measurements, size; 中サイズの [naka saizu no] adj medium-sized; これの大きなサイズはありますか? [kore no ooki-na saizu wa arimasu ka?] Do you have this in a bigger size?; これの小さなサイズはありますか? [kore no chiisa-na saizu wa arimasu ka?] Do you have this in a smaller size?; 私のサイズは十六号です [watashi no saizu wa juuroku-gou desu] I'm a size 16

坂 [saka] n slope

魚 [sakana] n fish; 魚を捕る [sakana-o toru] v fish; 魚釣り [sakana tsuri] n angling; 魚屋 [sakanaya] n fishmonger; これは魚のストックで料理してありますか? [kore wa sakana no sutokku de ryouri shite arimasu ka?] Is this cooked in fish stock?; 私はこの魚をいただきます [watashi wa kono sakana o itadakimasu] I'll have the fish; 私は魚を食べません [watashi wa sakana o tabemasen] I don't eat fish; 魚は生鮮品ですか、それとも冷凍品ですか? [sakana wa seisen-hin desu ka, sore tomo reitou-hin desu ka?] Is the fish fresh or frozen?; 魚を使わずに食事を用意していただけますか? [sakana o tsukawazu ni shokuji o youi shite itadakemasu ka?] Could you prepare a meal without fish?

魚を釣る人 [sakana o tsuru hito] n angler

坂の上 [saka no ue] 坂の上へ [saka no ue-e] adv uphill

逆さま [sakasama] 逆さまに [sakasama ni] adv upside down

酒 [sake] n sake, rice wine, alcohol; りんご酒 [ringoshu] n cider

サケ [sake] n (魚) salmon

叫び [sakebi] n shout

叫ぶ [sakebu] v shout, yell

避ける [sakeru] v avoid; さっと身をかわして避ける [satto mi-o kawashite sakeru] v dodge; 避けられない [sakerarenai] adj inevitable, unavoidable

作家 [sakka] n writer

サッカー [sakkaa] n football; サッカーをしましょう [sakkaa o shimashou] Let's play football; 私はサッカーの試合が観たいのですが [watashi wa sakkaa no shiai ga mitai no desu ga] I'd like to see a football match

錯覚 [sakkaku] n illusion

殺菌 [sakkin] n sterilization; 低温殺菌した [teion sakkin shita] adj pasteurized; 殺菌剤 [sakkinzai] n antiseptic; 超高温殺菌牛乳 [choukouon sakkin gyuunyuu] n UHT milk

作曲 [sakkyoku] 作曲家 [sakkyokuka] n composer

鎖骨 [sakotsu] n collarbone

柵 [saku] n barrier, fence

鑿 [saku] n chisel

咲く [saku] 花が咲く [hana ga saku] v blossom, flower

索引 [sakuin] n index (list)

削除 [sakujo] 削除する [sakujo suru] v delete

サクランボ [sakuranbo] n cherry

サクラソウ [sakurasou] n primrose

策略 [sakuryaku] n trick

作成 [sakusei] プログラム作成 [puroguramu sakusei] n programming; プログラムを作成する [puroguramu-o sakusei suru] v program; このコンピュータでCDを作成できますか? [kono konpyuutaa de shii-dii o sakusei dekimasu ka?] Can I make CDs at this computer?

搾取 [sakushu] n exploitation

サクソフォーン [sakusofoon] n saxophone

昨夜 [sakuya] n last night

砂丘 [sakyuu] n sand dune

さま [sama] どちらさまでしょうか? [dochira-sama deshou ka?] Who am I talking to?, Who's calling?

妨げる [samatageru] 妨げ [samatage] n setback

さまざま [samazama] さまざまな [samazama na] adj varied, various

サメ [same] n shark

覚める [sameru] 目が覚める [me ga sameru] v awake, wake up

さもないと [sa mo nai to] conj otherwise

寒い [samui] adj chilly, cold; 今夜は寒くなりますか? [kon'ya wa samuku narimasu ka?] Will it be cold tonight?; 部屋が寒すぎます [heya ga samu-sugimasu] The room is too cold; 寒いです [samui desu] I'm cold; 凍えるほどに寒いです [kogoeru hodo ni samui desu] It's freezing cold

寒気 [samuke] 私は寒気がします [watashi wa samuke ga shimasu] I feel cold

寒さ [samusa] n cold

三 [san] number three; 三番目 [san banme] n third; 三番目の [san banme no] adj third; 第三世界 [dai san sekai] n Third World

酸 [san] n acid; 酸性雨 [sanseiu] n acid rain

三倍 [sanbai] 三倍にする [sanbai ni suru] v treble

賛美 [sanbi] 賛美歌 [sanbika] n hymn

産物 [sanbutsu] 主要産物 [shuyou sanbutsu] n staple (commodity)

散弾 [sandan] 散弾銃 [sandanjuu] n shotgun

サンダル [sandaru] n sandal; ビーチサンダル [biichi sandaru] n flip-flops

サンドイッチ [sandoitchi] n sandwich; どんなサンドイッチがありますか? [donna sandoitchi ga arimasu ka?] What kind of sandwiches do you have?

サンドペーパー [sandopeepaa] n sandpaper

三月 [sangatsu] n March

珊瑚 [sango] n coral

サングラス [sangurasu] n sunglasses

産業 [sangyou] n industry; 産業の [sangyou no] adj industrial

三時 [sanji] 三時に [san-ji ni] at three o'clock; 三時です [san-ji desu] It's three o'clock

三十分 [sanjuppun] n half-hour

三十 [sanjuu] number thirty

産科 [sanka] 産科病院 [sanka byouin] n maternity hospital

参加 [sanka] n participation; ストライキ参加者 [sutoraiki sankasha] n striker; 参加する [sanka suru] v participate; 参加費用はいくらですか? [sanka-hiyou wa ikura desu ka?] How much does it cost to get in?

三角形 [sankakkei] n triangle

参考 [sankou] n reference

サンクリーム [sankuriimu] n suncream

サンマリノ [sanmarino] n San Marino

山脈 [sanmyaku] n range (mountains); カ
フカス山脈 [kafukasu sanmyaku] n
Caucasus; アンデス山脈 [andesu
sanmyaku] n Andes; アルプス山脈
[arupusu sanmyaku] n Alps

散歩 [sanpo] n walk

散乱 [sanran] n mess

三輪車 [sanrinsha] n tricycle

サンルーフ [sanruufu] n sunroof

賛成 [sansei] n favour; 賛成する [sansei
suru] v agree

酸性 [sansei] 酸性雨 [sanseiu] n acid rain

参照 [sanshou] 参照番号 [sanshou
bangou] n reference number

酸素 [sanso] n oxygen

サンスクリーン [sansukuriin] n
sunscreen

サンタンオイル [santan oiru] n suntan
oil

サンタンローション [santanrooshon] n
suntan lotion

さんざん [sanzan] さんざんな [sanzan na]
adj devastating

サンザシ [sanzashi] n hawthorn

皿 [sara] n dish (plate); 皿拭きをする
[sarafuki-o suru] v wipe up

さらば! [saraba] excl farewell!

サラダ [sarada] n salad; グリーンサラダ
[guriin sarada] n green salad; フルーツサ
ラダ [furuutsusarada] n fruit salad

サラダドレッシング
[saradadoresshingu] n salad dressing

サラミ [sarami] n salami

さらに [sara ni] adv further

さらに多く [sara ni ooku] adv more

さらす [sarasu] 危険にさらす [kiken ni
sarasu] v risk

サル [saru] n monkey

去る [saru] 飛び去る [tobisaru] v fly away

支え [sasae] n support

支える [sasaeru] v (支持) bear, (支持)
support

些細 [sasai] 些細な [sasai na] adj trivial

ささやく [sasayaku] v whisper

左遷 [sasen] 左遷する [sasen suru] v
relegate

刺し穴 [sashiana] n puncture

挿絵 [sashie] n illustration

差し引く [sashihiku] v deduct

指し示す [sashishimesu] v point

誘い込む [sasoikomu] 人を誘い込む
[hito-o sasoi komu] v rope in

サソリ [sasori] n scorpion

蠍座 [sasoriza] n Scorpio

誘う [sasou] v invite

早速 [sassoku] adv immediately; 早速の
[sassoku no] adj immediate

刺す [sasu] v sting; チクリと刺す [chikuri to
sasu] v prick; 刺し傷 [sashi kizu] n sting;
私は虫に刺されました [watashi wa mushi
ni sasaremashita] I've been stung

差す [sasu] 人差し指 [hitosashi yubi] n
index finger; 油を差す [abura-o sasu] (注
油) v oil

里子 [satogo] n foster child

砂糖 [satou] n sugar; 砂糖を含まない
[satou-o fukumanai] adj sugar-free; 粉砂
糖 [konazatou] n icing sugar; 砂糖なしで
[satou nashi de] no sugar

撮影 [satsuei] 撮影する [satsuei suru] v
photograph; 写真撮影 [shashinsatsuei] n
photography

殺害 [satsugai] 殺害する [satsugai suru] v
murder

殺人 [satsujin] n murder; 殺人者
[satsujinsha] n murderer

殺人者 [satsujinsha] n killer

サウジアラビア [saujiarabia] n Saudi
Arabia; サウジアラビア人 [saujiarabiajin]
n Saudi, Saudi Arabian (person); サウジア
ラビアの [saujiarabia no] adj Saudi, Saudi
Arabian

サウナ [sauna] n sauna

サウンドトラック [saundotorakku] n soundtrack

騒ぎ [sawagi] n racket (racquet)

騒ぐ [sawagu] 大騒ぎ [ousawagi] n fuss

さわる [sawaru] さわると痛いところ [sawaru to itai tokoro] n sore

さわやかな [sawayaka na] adj refreshing

サヤエンドウ [sayaendou] n mangetout

サヤインゲン [saya ingen] n French beans

さよなら [sayonara] excl bye!

作用 [sayou] 副作用 [fukusayou] n side effect; 反射作用 [hansha sayou] n reflex

さようなら [sayounara] excl goodbye!

背骨 [sebone] n backbone

世代 [sedai] n generation

セダン [sedan] n saloon, saloon car

セールス [seerusu] 電話セールス [denwa seerusu] n telesales

セールスマン [seerusuman] n salesman

セーター [seetaa] n jumper, sweater; とっくり襟のセーター [tokkuri eri no seetaa] n polo-necked sweater

性 [sei] n gender; 性差別主義 [seisabetsu shugi] n sexism; 性差別主義の [seisabetsu shugi no] adj sexist

姓 [sei] n surname

・・・製 [...sei] n make

聖バレンタイン [seibarentain] 聖バレンタインの祭日 [sei barentain no saijitsu] n Valentine's Day

性別 [seibetsu] n sex

整備士 [seibishi] 自動車整備士 [jidousha seibishi] n motor mechanic

生物 [seibutsu] 生物分解性の [seibutsu bunkaisei no] adj biodegradable; 野生生物 [yaseiseibutsu] n wildlife

生物学 [seibutsugaku] n biology; 生物学の [seibutsugaku no] adj biological

生物測定 [seibutsusokutei] 生物測定の [seibutsu sokutei no] adj biometric

成長 [seichou] n growth

成長する [seichou suru] vi grow

声援 [seien] 声援する [seien suru] v cheer

政府 [seifu] n government

征服 [seifuku] 征服する [seifuku suru] v conquer

制服 [seifuku] n uniform; 学校の制服 [gakkou no seifuku] n school uniform

製粉所 [seifunjou] n mill

制限 [seigen] n limit; 年齢制限 [nenreiseigen] n age limit; 制限する [seigen suru] v restrict

制限速度 [seigensokudo] n speed limit; この道の制限速度はどうなっていますか? [kono michi no seigen-sokudo wa dou natte imasu ka?] What is the speed limit on this road?

正義 [seigi] n justice

制御 [seigyo] 無線制御の [musen seigyo no] adj radio-controlled

制御できない [seigyodekinai] adj uncontrollable

制御装置 [seigyosouchi] npl controls; 制御装置の使い方を教えてもらえますか? [seigyo-souchi no tsukaikata o oshiete moraemasu ka?] Can you show me how the controls work?; 制御装置が動かなくなりました [seigyo-souchi ga ugokanaku narimashita] The controls have jammed

正反対 [seihantai] n contrary

製品 [seihin] n product

正方形 [seihoukei] n square; 正方形の [seihoukei no] adj square

誠意 [seii] 誠意のない [seii no nai] adj insincere

政治 [seiji] n politics; 政治の [seiji no] adj political; 政治家 [seijika] n politician

成人 [seijin] n grown-up; 成人学生 [seijin gakusei] n mature student

聖人 [seijin] n saint

清浄 [seijou] ユダヤ教の掟に従って料理された清浄な [yudaya kyou no okite ni shitagatte ryouri sareta seijou na] adj kosher

成熟 [seijuku] 成熟した [seijuku shita] adj mature; 未成熟の [miseijuku no] adj immature

生化学 [seikagaku] n biochemistry

正確 [seikaku] adj accurate; 不正確な [fuseikaku na] adj inaccurate, incorrect; 正確に [seikaku ni] adv accurately, exactly, precisely; 正確さ [seikakusa] n accuracy

正確な [seikaku na] adj accurate, exact, precise

聖歌隊 [seikatai] n choir

生活 [seikatsu] n living; キャンプ生活 [kyanpu seikatsu] n camping; 生活水準 [seikatsusuijun] n standard of living; 生活費 [seikatsuhi] n cost of living

清潔 [seiketsu] 清潔な [seiketsu na] adj clean

世紀 [seiki] n century

聖金曜日 [seikinyoubi] n Good Friday

性交 [seikou] n sexual intercourse

成功 [seikou] n success; 成功した [seikou shita] adj successful; 成功する [seikou suru] v succeed

請求 [seikyuu] 請求する [seikyuu suru] v charge (price); 過大請求する [kadai seikyuu suru] v overcharge; なぜそんなにたくさん請求するのですか? [naze sonna ni takusan seikyuu suru no desu ka?] Why are you charging me so much?; 私は余分に請求されています [watashi wa yobun ni seikyuu sarete imasu] I've been overcharged

請求書 [seikyuusho] n bill (account); 電話の請求書 [denwa no seikyuusho] n phone bill; 請求書の明細をもらえますか? [seikyuusho no meisai o moraemasu ka?] Can I have an itemized bill?; 請求書が間違っています [seikyuusho ga machigatte imasu] The bill is wrong; 請求書を用意してください [seikyuusho o youi shite kudasai] Please prepare the bill

生命 [seimei] n life; 生命保険 [seimeihoken] n life insurance

声明 [seimei] n statement

西暦 [seireki] n AD

生理 [seiri] 生理用ナプキン [seiriyou napukin] n sanitary towel

整理 [seiri] 整理だんす [seiridansu] n chest of drawers

精力 [seiryoku] 精力的な [seiryokuteki na] adj energetic

制作 [seisaku] 制作依頼 [seisaku irai] n commission

生産 [seisan] n production; 生産する [seisan suru] v produce; 生産性 [seisansei] n productivity

精製 [seisei] 石油精製所 [sekiyu seiseijo] n oil refinery; 精製所 [seiseijo] n refinery

精子 [seishi] n sperm

正式 [seishiki] 正式の [seishiki no] adj formal

精神 [seishin] n spirit; 精神の [seishin no] adj mental; 精神構造 [seishin kouzou] n mentality; 精神病院 [seishinbyouin] n psychiatric hospital; 精神的な [seishinteki na] adj spiritual; 精神科の [seishinka no] adj psychiatric; 精神科医 [seishinka-i] n psychiatrist; 精神安定剤 [seishin anteizai] n tranquilizer

聖書 [seisho] n Bible

聖職 [seishoku] n ministry (religion); 聖職者 [seishokusha] n minister (clergy)

青春 [seishun] 青春時代 [seishun jidai] n youth

盛装 [seisou] 盛装する [seisou suru] v dress up

精巣 [seisou] n testicle

清掃人 [seisounin] n cleaner; 清掃人はいつ来ますか? [seisou-nin wa itsu kimasu ka?] When does the cleaner come?

政体 [seitai] 共和政体 [kyouwa seitai] n republic

生態学 [seitaigaku] n ecology; 生態学の [seitaigaku no] adj ecological

制定 [seitei] 法律制定 [houritsu seitei] n legislation

性的 [seiteki] 性的な [seiteki na] adj sexual

生徒 [seito] n cadet, pupil (learner); 男子生徒 [danshiseito] n schoolboy; 女子生徒 [joshiseito] n schoolgirl

整頓 [seiton] 整頓する [seiton suru] v tidy up

正当 [seitou] 正当な [seitou na] adj valid;

正当化する [seitouka suru] v justify

精通 [seitsuu] ···に精通している [...ni seitsuu shiteiru] adj knowledgeable

セイウチ [seiuchi] n walrus

性欲 [seiyoku] n lust

セイヨウアブラナ [seiyouaburana] n rape (plant)

セイヨウヒイラギ [seiyouhiiragi] n holly

西洋ナシ [seiyounashi] n pear

セイヨウワサビ [seiyouwasabi] n horseradish

生存 [seizon] n survival; 生存者 [seizonsha] n survivor

製造 [seizou] n production; 製造する [seizou suru] v manufacture; 製造業者 [seizougyousha] n manufacturer; 製造工場 [seizou koujou] n plant (site/equipment)

聖像 [seizou] n icon

世界 [sekai] n world; 第三世界 [dai san sekai] n Third World

咳 [seki] n cough; 咳をする [seki-o suru] v cough; 咳止め薬 [sekidomegusuri] n cough mixture; 私は咳がでます [watashi wa seki ga demasu] I have a cough

席 [seki] 通路側の席 [tsuurogawa no seki] n aisle seat; この席には誰か座っていますか? [kono seki ni wa dare ka suwatte imasu ka?] Is this seat taken?; この席は空いていますか? [kono seki wa aite imasu ka?] Is this seat free?; すみません、それは私の席です [sumimasen, sore wa watashi no seki desu] Excuse me, that's my seat; 進行方向に向いた席をお願いします [shinkou-houkou ni muita seki o o-negai shimasu] Facing the front, please

赤道 [sekidou] n equator; 赤道ギニア [sekidou ginia] n Equatorial Guinea

潟湖 [sekiko] n lagoon

赤面 [sekimen] n flush; 赤面する [sekimen suru] v blush, flush

責任 [sekinin] n fault (defect), fault (mistake), responsibility; 最高経営責任者 [saikou keiei sekininsha] n CEO; 説明する責任がある [setsumei suru sekinin ga aru] adj accountable; それは私の責任ではありません [sore wa watashi no sekinin de wa arimasen] It wasn't my fault

責任がある [sekinin ga aru] adj responsible

セキセイインコ [sekiseiinko] n budgerigar, budgie

積雪 [sekisetsu] ···へ行く道は積雪していますか? [...e iku michi wa sekisetsu shite imasu ka?] Is the road to ... snowed up?

石炭 [sekitan] n coal

脊椎 [sekitsui] n spine

石油 [sekiyu] 石油掘削装置 [sekiyu kussakusouchi] n oil rig; 石油精製所 [sekiyu seiseijo] n oil refinery

脊髄 [sekizui] n spinal cord

石灰 [sekkai] n lime (compound); 石灰岩 [sekkaigan] n limestone

せっかく [sekkaku] adv kindly; せっかくですが、私は飲みません [sekkaku desu ga, watashi wa nomimasen] I'm not drinking, thank you

赤褐色 [sekkasshoku] 赤褐色の [akakasshoku no] adj auburn

石鹸 [sekken] n soap; 石鹸入れ [sekken ire] n soap dish; 粉石鹸 [kona sekken] n soap powder; 石鹸がありません [sekken ga arimasen] There is no soap

接近 [sekkin] n access

説教 [sekkyou] n sermon

セクシー [sekushii] セクシーな [sekushii na] adj sexy

狭い [semai] adj narrow; 了見の狭い [ryouken no semai] adj narrow-minded

セメント [semento] n cement

責める [semeru] v blame

セミコロン [semikoron] n semicolon

線 [sen] n line; 地平線 [chiheisen] n horizon

栓 [sen] n plug

腺 [sen] n gland

千 [sen] number thousand; 千番目 [sen banme] n thousandth; 千番目の [sen banme no] adj thousandth

背中 [senaka] n back; 私は背中が痛みます

[watashi wa senaka ga itamimasu] I've got a bad back, My back is sore; 私は背中を痛めました [watashi wa senaka o itamemashita] I've hurt my back

選抜 [senbatsu] 選抜候補者リスト [senbatsu kouhosha risuto] n shortlist

センチメートル [senchimeetoru] n centimetre

センチメンタル [senchimentaru] いやにセンチメンタルな [iya ni senchimentaru na] adj soppy

船長 [senchou] n captain

宣伝 [senden] n publicity

セネガル [senegaru] n Senegal; セネガル人 [senegarujin] n Senegalese (person); セネガルの [senegaru no] adj Senegalese

繊維 [sen-i] n fibre; ガラス繊維 [garasu sen'i] n fibreglass

船員 [sen'in] n sailor

戦術 [senjutsu] n tactics

戦艦 [senkan] n battleship

閃光 [senkou] n flash

選挙 [senkyo] n election; 総選挙 [sousenkyo] n general election; 選挙する [senkyo suru] v elect; 選挙区 [senkyoku] n constituency

選挙人 [senkyonin] n electorate

宣教 [senkyou] 宣教師 [senkyoushi] n missionary

洗面 [senmen] 洗面用タオル [senmen you taoru] n face cloth; 洗面用具バッグ [senmen yougu baggu] n toilet bag; 洗面用具入れ [senmen yougu ire] n sponge bag; 洗面化粧用品 [senmen keshou youhin] n toiletries; 洗面台 [senmendai] n washbasin

洗面台 [senmendai] 洗面台が汚れています [senmendai ga yogorete imasu] The washbasin is dirty

洗面器 [senmenki] n basin

洗面する [senmen suru] v freshen up

専門 [senmon] n speciality; 専門にする [senmon ni suru] v specialize; 専門技術 [senmon gijutsu] n technique; 専門技術者 [senmon gijutsusha] n technician; 専門的な [senmonteki na] adj technical; 専門家 [senmonka] n expert, professional, specialist

船内 [sennai] 船内にトイレはありますか? [sennai ni toire wa arimasu ka?] Is there a toilet on board?; 船内で何か食べられるところはありますか? [sennai de nani ka taberareru tokoro wa arimasu ka?] Is there somewhere to eat on the boat?

千年間 [sennenkan] n millennium

栓抜き [sennuki] n bottle-opener; コルク栓抜き [koruku sennuki] n corkscrew

先輩 [senpai] 先輩の [senpai no] adj senior

先夫 [senpu] n ex-husband

扇風機 [senpuuki] n fan; その部屋に扇風機はありますか? [sono heya ni senpuuki wa arimasu ka?] Does the room have a fan?

洗礼 [senrei] n christening; 洗礼名 [senreimei] n Christian name

先例 [senrei] 先例のない [senrei no nai] adj unprecedented

洗練 [senren] 洗練された [senren sareta] adj sophisticated

戦略 [senryaku] n strategy; 戦略的な [senryakuteki na] adj strategic

染料 [senryou] n dye

占領 [senryou] n occupation (invasion)

先妻 [sensai] n ex-wife

詮索 [sensaku] 詮索する [sensaku suru] v pry; 詮索好きな [sensaku zuki na] adj inquisitive, nosy

占星術 [senseijutsu] n astrology

戦車 [sensha] n tank (combat vehicle)

洗車 [sensha] 洗車機 [senshaki] n car wash

洗車機 [senshaki] n car wash; 洗車機はどう使うのですか? [senshaki wa dou tsukau no desu ka?] How do I use the car wash?

選手 [senshu] n player (of sport); テニス選手 [tenisusenshu] n tennis player; フットボール選手 [futtobooru senshu] n football player, footballer; 運動選手 [undousenshu] n athlete; 重量挙げ選手 [juuryouage senshu] n weightlifter

選手権 [senshuken] n championship

先週 [senshuu] n last week; 先々週 [sensenshuu] the week before last

戦争 [sensou] n war

センス [sensu] ユーモアのセンス [yuumoa no sensu] n sense of humour

潜水 [sensui] 潜水艦 [sensuikan] n submarine

潜水夫 [sensuifu] n diver

センター [sentaa] n centre; コールセンター [kooru sentaa] n call centre; レジャーセンター [rejaasentaa] n leisure centre

船体 [sentai] n hull

洗濯 [sentaku] n washing, laundry; 洗濯ロープ [sentaku roopu] n clothes line; 洗濯機 [sentakuki] n washing machine; 洗濯物 [sentakumono] n laundry, washing; どこで洗濯ができますか? [doko de sentaku ga dekimasu ka?] Where can I do some washing?; この近くにコインランドリーはありますか? [kono chikaku ni koin-randorii wa arimasu ka?] Is there a Launderette® near here?; これを洗濯して欲しいのですが [kore o sentaku shite hoshii no desu ga] I'd like to get these things washed; ランドリーサービスはありますか? [randorii-saabisu wa arimasu ka?] Is there a laundry service?

選択 [sentaku] n choice, option, pick, selection; 選択肢 [sentakushi] n alternative

洗濯ばさみ [sentakubasami] n clothes peg

洗濯機 [sentakuki] 洗濯機で洗える [sentakuki de araeru] adj machine washable; 洗濯機はどうやって使うのですか? [sentakuki wa dou-yatte tsukau no desu ka?] How does the washing machine work?; 洗濯機はどこですか? [sentakuki wa doko desu ka?] Where are the washing machines?

先端 [sentan] n tip (end of object)

尖端 [sentan] n peak

セント [sento] n cent

セントラルヒーティング [sentoraruhiitingu] n central heating

戦闘 [sentou] n battle

先頭 [sentou] ・・・の先頭に立つ [...no sentou ni tatsu] v head

尖塔 [sentou] n spire, steeple

専用 [senyou] 歩行者専用になった [hokousha sen'you ni natta] adj pedestrianized; 専用の [sen'you no] adj dedicated

洗剤 [senzai] n detergent; 粉末洗剤 [funmatsusenzai] n washing powder; 食器洗い用液体洗剤 [shokkiarai you ekitai senzai] n washing-up liquid

先祖 [senzo] n ancestor

セラミック [seramikku] セラミックの [seramikku no] adj ceramic

セロリ [serori] n celery

セロテープ® [seroteepu] n Sellotape®

セルビア [serubia] n Serbia; セルビア人 [serubiajin] n Serbian (person); セルビアの [serubia no] adj Serbian; セルビア語 [serubiago] n Serbian (language)

セルフサービス [serufusaabisu] セルフサービスの [serufusaabisu no] adj self-service

摂氏 [sesshi] 摂氏温度 [sesshi ondo] n degree centigrade

接種 [sesshu] 予防接種 [yobou sesshu] n vaccination; 予防接種をする [yobou sesshu-o suru] v vaccinate; 私は予防接種が必要です [watashi wa yobou-sesshu ga hitsuyou desu] I need a vaccination

摂取 [sesshu] 栄養物摂取 [eiyoubutsu sesshu] n nutrition

接着剤 [setchakuzai] n glue; 接着剤でつける [setchakuzai de tsukeru] v glue

設備 [setsubi] n facilities; 最新設備 [saishin setsubi] n mod cons

切望 [setsubou] 切望する [setsubou suru] v long

切断 [setsudan] n cut

説明 [setsumei] n account (report), explanation; 説明する [setsumei suru] v explain; ・・・の説明がつく [...no setsumei ga tsuku] v account for

節約 [setsuyaku] 節約する [setsuyaku suru] v economize

接続 [setsuzoku] 接続を断つ [setsuzoku-o tatsu] v disconnect; その部屋にインターネットの接続ポイントはありますか? [sono heya ni iintaanetto no setsuzoku-pointo wa arimasu ka?] Is there an internet connection in the room?; 接続がとても遅いようです [setsuzoku ga totemo osoi you desu] The connection seems very slow

接続する [setsuzoku suru] v connect; プラグで接続する [puragu de setsuzoku suru] v plug in

設定 [settei] ···さんとのミーティングを設定したいのですが [...san to no miitingu o settei shitai no desu ga] I'd like to arrange a meeting with...

説得 [settoku] 説得する [settoku suru] v persuade; 説得力のある [settokuryoku no aru] adj convincing, persuasive

セットメニュー [settomenyuu] n set menu; セットメニューはありますか? [setto-menyuu wa arimasu ka?] Do you have a set-price menu?; セットメニューはいくらですか? [setto-menyuu wa ikura desu ka?] How much is the set menu?

世話 [sewa] ···の世話をする [...no sewa-o suru] v look after

しゃべり [shaberi] おしゃべりする [o-shaberi suru] v chat

シャベル [shaberu] n shovel

社長 [shachou] n managing director; 社長さまのお名前を教えていただけますか? [shachou-sama no o-namae o oshiete itadakemasu ka?] What is the name of the managing director?

車道 [shadou] n driveway

射撃 [shageki] n shooting

車軸 [shajiku] n axle

社会 [shakai] n society; 社会保障 [shakaihoshou] n social security; 社会主義 [shakaishugi] n socialism; 社会の [shakai no] adj social; 社会学 [shakaigaku] n sociology; 地域社会 [chiiki shakai] n community

社会福祉 [shakaifukushi] 政府の社会福祉事業 [seifu no shakai fukushi jigyou] n social services

社会主義 [shakaishugi] 社会主義の [shakaishugi no] adj socialist; 社会主義者 [shakaishugisha] n socialist

車検 [shaken] n MOT

借金 [shakkin] n debt

しゃっくり [shakkuri] n hiccups

社交 [shakou] 社交ダンス [shakou dansu] n ballroom dancing; 社交的な [shakouteki na] adj sociable

尺度 [shakudo] n scale (measure)

釈放 [shakuhou] 仮釈放 [kari shakuhou] n parole

シャンパン [shanpan] n champagne

シャンプー [shanpuu] n shampoo; シャンプーを売っていますか? [shanpuu o utte imasu ka?] Do you sell shampoo?

車輪 [sharin] n wheel

車両 [sharyou] n vehicle; 1等車に乗りたいのですが [ittou-sha ni noritai no desu ga] I would like to travel first-class; 2人用の車両はいくらですか? [futari-you no sharyou wa ikura desu ka?] How much is it for a car with two people?; 私の車両書類です [watashi no sharyou-shorui desu] Here are my vehicle documents

車線 [shasen] n lane (driving); 車線から出る [shasen kara deru] v pull out; あなたは間違った車線にいます [anata wa machigatta shasen ni imasu] You are in the wrong lane

斜視 [shashi] 斜視である [shashi de aru] v squint

写真 [shashin] n photo, photograph; スナップ写真 [sunappu shashin] n snapshot; 写真撮影 [shashinsatsuei] n photography; 写真家 [shashinka] n photographer; X線写真を撮る [x-sen shashin-o toru] v X-ray; この写真をCDに焼き付けていただけますか? [kono shashin o shii-dii ni yakitsukete itadakemasu ka?] Can you put these photos on CD, please?; ここに写真をダウンロードできますか? [koko ni shashin o daunroodo dekimasu ka?] Can I download photos to here?; 写真代はいくらですか?

[shashin-dai wa ikura desu ka?] **How much do the photos cost?**; 写真はいつできますか? [shashin wa itsu dekimasu ka?] **When will the photos be ready?**; 写真はマット仕上げにしてください [shashin wa matto-shiage ni shite kudasai] **I'd like the photos matt**; 写真は光沢仕上げにしてください [shashin wa koutaku-shiage ni shite kudasai] **I'd like the photos glossy**

写真用品 [shashinyouhin] 写真用品を売っている一番近い店はどこですか? [shashin-youhin o utte iru ichiban chikai mise wa doko desu ka?] **Where is the nearest shop which sells photographic equipment?**

車掌 [shashou] バスの車掌 [basu no shashou] n **bus conductor**; 車掌を見ましたか? [shashou o mimashita ka?] **Have you seen the guard?**

シャトル [shatoru] バドミントンのシャトル [badominton no shatoru] n **shuttlecock**

シャッター [shattaa] n **shutters**

シャワー [shawaa] n **shower**; シャワーはどこですか? [shawaa wa doko desu ka?] **Where are the showers?**; シャワーはありますか? [shawaa wa arimasu ka?] **Are there showers?**; シャワーが汚れています [shawaa ga yogorete imasu] **The shower is dirty**; シャワーが冷たいです [shawaa ga tsumetai desu] **The showers are cold**; シャワーが出ません [shawaa ga demasen] **The shower doesn't work**

シャワージェル [shawaajieru] n **shower gel**

シャワーキャップ [shawaakyappu] n **shower cap**

社用 [shayou] 社用車 [shayousha] n **company car**

シェーバー [sheebaa] n **shaver**

シェービングフォーム [sheebingufoomu] n **shaving foam**

シェービングクリーム [sheebingukuriimu] n **shaving cream**

シェフ [shefu] n **chef**; シェフの得意料理は何ですか? [shefu no tokui-ryouri wa nan desu ka?] **What's the chef's speciality?**

シェリー [sherii] n **sherry**; ドライシェリーをください [dorai-sherii o kudasai] **A dry sherry, please**

シェルスーツ [sherusuutsu] n **shell suit**

死 [shi] n **death**

詩 [shi] n **poem**; 抒情詩 [jojoushi] n **lyrics**

詞 [shi] 副詞 [fukushi] n **adverb**; 形容詞 [keiyoushi] n **adjective**

四 [shi] number **four**

仕上がる [shiagaru] v **finish**; いつ仕上がりますか? [itsu shiagarimasu ka?] **When will it be ready?**

試合 [shiai] n **match** (sport); アウェーの試合 [auee no shiai] n **away match**; フットボールの試合 [futtobooru no shiai] n **football match**; ホームの試合 [hoomu no shiai] n **home match**; 私はサッカーの試合が観たいのですが [watashi wa sakkaa no shiai ga mitai no desu ga] **I'd like to see a football match**

芝生 [shibafu] n **lawn**

芝刈り機 [shibakariki] n **lawnmower**

縛る [shibaru] v **tie**; 縛るもの [shibaru mono] n **bond**; 固く縛る [kataku shibaru] v **tie up**

しばしば [shibashiba] adv **often**

シベリア [shiberia] n **Siberia**

死別 [shibetsu] 私は配偶者と死別しました [watashi wa haiguusha to shibetsu shimashita] **I'm widowed**

搾る [shiboru] 乳を搾る [chichi-o shiboru] v **milk**

死亡 [shibou] 死亡記事 [shiboukiji] n **obituary**

脂肪 [shibou] n **fat**; 低脂肪の [teishibou no] adj **low-fat**

試着 [shichaku] 試着する [shichaku suru] v **try on**; 試着室 [shichakushitsu] n **fitting room**; このズボンを試着していいですか? [kono zubon o shichaku shite ii desu ka?] **Can I try on these trousers?**; このワンピースを試着していいですか? [kono wanpiisu o shichaku shite ii desu ka?] **Can I try on this dress?**; それを試着していいですか? [sore o shichaku shite ii desu ka?] **Can I try it on?**

試着室 [shichakushitsu] 試着室はどこで
すか? [shichaku-shitsu wa doko desu ka?]
Where are the changing rooms?

七 [shichi] *number* **seven**; 七番目 [shichi
banme] *n* **seventh**; 七番目の [shichi
banme no] *adj* **seventh**

七月 [shichigatsu] *n* **July**

七十 [shichijuu] *number* **seventy**

七面鳥 [shichimenchou] *n* **turkey**

質屋 [shichiya] *n* **pawnbroker**

市長 [shichou] *n* **mayor**

シチュエーションコメディー
[shichueeshonkomedii] *n* **sitcom**

シチュー [shichuu] *n* **stew**

シダ [shida] *n* **fern**

指導 [shidou] 指導者 [shidousha] *n*
instructor; 個別指導 [kobetsu shidou] *n*
tutorial; 個別指導教官 [kobetsu shidou
kyoukan] *n* **tutor**

始動 [shidou] 車が始動しません [kuruma
ga shidou shimasen] **The car won't start**

指導員 [shidouin] 自動車教習指導員
[jidousha kyoushuu shidouin] *n* **driving
instructor**

支援 [shien] *n* **backing**; 支援する [shien
suru] *v* **back up**

至福 [shifuku] *n* **bliss**

志願者 [shigansha] *n* **volunteer**

シガレット [shigaretto] シガレットライタ
ー [shigaretto raitaa] *n* **cigarette lighter**

四月 [shigatsu] *n* **April**

茂み [shigemi] *n* **bush** (thicket)

資源 [shigen] *n* **resource**; 天然資源
[tennenshigen] *n* **natural resources**

仕事 [shigoto] *n* **work**; 仕事をサボる
[shigoto-o saboru] *v* **skive**; 仕事場
[shigotoba] *n* **workshop**; 休日の仕事
[kyuujitsu no shigoto] *n* **holiday job**; つ
らない仕事 [tsumaranai shigoto] *n*
drudgery; 決まりきった仕事 [kimarikitta
shigoto] *n* **routine**; 仕事で来ました
[shigoto de kimashita] **I'm here on
business**; また近いうちにお仕事でご一緒

できることを願っています [mata chikai
uchi ni o-shigoto de go-issho dekiru koto o
negatte imasu] **I hope we can work
together again soon**; お仕事は何をなさって
いますか? [o-shigoto wa nani o nasatte
imasu ka?] **What do you do?**; 私は仕事で
来ています [watashi wa shigoto de kite
imasu] **I'm here for work**

支配 [shihai] *n* **control**; 支配する [shihai
suru] *v* **control, master**; 支配者
[shihaisha] *n* **ruler** (commander)

支払い [shiharai] *n* **payment**; 支払い済み
の [shiharaizumi no] *adj* **paid**

支払い機 [shiharai ki] *n* **cash machine**;
一番近い現金自動支払い機はどこですか?
[ichiban chikai genkin-jidou-shiharaiki wa
doko desu ka?] **Where is the nearest cash
machine?**; この現金自動支払い機で私の
カードを使えますか? [kono
genkin-jidou-shiharaiki de watashi no
kaado o tsukaemasu ka?] **Can I use my
card with this cash machine?**; ここに現金
自動支払い機がありますか? [koko ni
genkin-jidou-shiharaiki ga arimasu ka?] **Is
there a cash machine here?**; 現金自動支
払い機が私のカードを吸い込んでしまいま
した [genkin-jidou-shiharaiki ga watashi
no kaado o suikonde shimaimashita] **The
cash machine swallowed my card**

支払う [shiharau] *v* **pay**; 現金自動支払い
機 [genkin jidoushiharaiki] *n* **cash
dispenser**; 私は支払わなければなりませ
んか? [watashi wa shiharawanakereba
narimasu ka?] **Will I have to pay?**

支払うべき [shiharaubeki] *adj* **payable**

始発 [shihatsu] ・・・へ行く始発のバスは何
時ですか? [...e iku shihatsu no basu wa
nan-ji desu ka?] **When is the first bus to...?**;
・・・へ行く始発の電車は何時ですか? [...e
iku shihatsu no densha wa nan-ji desu ka?]
When is the first train to...?; 始発の船は
何時ですか? [shihatsu no fune wa nan-ji
desu ka?] **When is the first boat?**

紙幣 [shihei] *n* **banknote, note** (banknote);
この紙幣でお釣りがありますか? [kono
shihei de o-tsuri ga arimasu ka?] **Do you
have change for this note?**

資本主義 [shihonshugi] *n* **capitalism**

指標 [shihyou] n indicator

シーア派 [shiiaha] シーア派の信徒の [shiia ha no shinto no] adj Shiite

シーフード [shiifuudo] n seafood; シーフードはお好きですか? [shii-fuudo wa o-suki desu ka?] Do you like seafood?

詩歌 [shiika] n poetry

飼育係 [shiikugakari] 馬の飼育係 [uma no shiikugakari] n groom

シーク教 [shiikukyou] シーク教の [shiiku kyou no] adj Sikh; シーク教徒 [shiiku kyouto] n Sikh

子音 [shiin] n consonant

仕入れる [shiireru] v stock up on

強いる [shiiru] v force

シーソー [shiisou] n seesaw

シート [shiito] n seat; シートが低すぎます [shiito ga hiku-sugimasu] The seat is too low; シートが高すぎます [shiito ga taka-sugimasu] The seat is too high

シートベルト [shiitoberuto] n seatbelt

シーツ [shiitsu] n sheet; シーツがもっと必要です [shiitsu ga motto hitsuyou desu] We need more sheets; シーツが汚れています [shiitsu ga yogorete imasu] The sheets are dirty; 私のシーツは汚れています [watashi no shiitsu wa yogorete imasu] My sheets are dirty

シーズン [shiizun] シーズンオフ [shiizun'ofu] n low season

シーズンオフ [shiizun'ofu] シーズンオフに [shiizun'ofu ni] adv off-season; シーズンオフの [shiizun'ofu no] adj off-season

指示 [shiji] n directions, instructions; 指示する [shiji suru] v instruct

支持 [shiji] 支持者 [shijisha] n supporter

詩人 [shijin] n poet

四旬節 [shijunsetsu] n Lent

四十 [shijuu] number forty

四重奏 [shijuusou] n quartet

シカ [shika] n deer

歯科 [shika] n dentistry; 私は歯科保険に入っていません [watashi wa shika-hoken ni haitte imasen] I don't have dental insurance; 私は歯科保険に入っているのかどうかわかりません [watashi wa shika-hoken ni haitte iru no ka dou ka wakarimasen] I don't know if I have dental insurance

視界 [shikai] n visibility

司会 [shikai] 司会者 [shikaisha] n compere

歯科医 [shikai] n dentist

資格 [shikaku] n qualification; 資格を取る [shikaku o toru] v qualify; ···の資格を取り上げる [...no shikaku-o toriageru] v disqualify

視覚 [shikaku] 視覚の [shikaku no] adj visual; 私は視覚障害があります [watashi wa shikaku-shougai ga arimasu] I'm visually impaired

資格のある [shikaku no aru] adj qualified

士官 [shikan] n officer

鹿肉 [shika niku] n venison

しかる [shikaru] v scold, tell off

しかし [shikashi] conj but

死刑 [shikei] n capital punishment

試験 [shiken] n exam, examination (medical), examination (school), test; 試験する [shiken suru] v examine, test; 試験管 [shikenkan] n test tube; 試験監督者 [shiken kantokusha] n invigilator; 運転免許試験 [untenmenkyoshiken] n driving test; 口頭試験 [koutou shiken] n oral

試験官 [shikenkan] n examiner

式 [shiki] 授賞式 [jushoushiki] n prize-giving; 結婚式 [kekkonshiki] n wedding

士気 [shiki] n morale

識別 [shikibetsu] 識別する [shikibetsu suru] v identify

敷地 [shikichi] n site

色盲 [shikimou] 色盲の [shikimou no] adj colour-blind

資金 [shikin] n funds; 資金を調達する [shikin-o choutatsu suru] v finance; 共同資金 [kyoudou shikin] n pool (resources)

仕切り [shikiri] 仕切りをする [shikiri-o suru] v screen (off)

色彩 [shikisai] 色彩に富んだ [shikisai ni tonda] *adj* colourful

指揮者 [shikisha] *n* conductor

しっかり [shikkari] しっかりした [shikkari shita] *adj* steady

湿気 [shikke] *n* humidity, moisture; 湿気のある [shikke no aru] *adj* damp; 湿気の多い [shikke no oui] *adj* humid

漆喰 [shikkui] *n* plaster *(for wall)*; 漆喰を塗る [shikkui-o nuru] *v* whitewash

思考 [shikou] *n* thought

支給 [shikyuu] 助成金を支給する [joseikin-o shikyuu suru] *v* subsidize

至急 [shikyuu] *adv* immediately; お金をいくらか至急送ってもらうように手配してもらえますか? [o-kane o ikura ka shikyuu okutte morau you ni tehai shite moraemasu ka?] Can you arrange to have some money sent over urgently?

縞 [shima] *n* stripe; 縞のある [shima no aru] *adj* striped; 縞の入った [shima no haitta] *adj* stripy

島 [shima] *n* island; 無人島 [mujintou] *n* desert island

姉妹 [shimai] *n* sister; 継姉妹 [mama shimai] *n* stepsister; 義理の姉妹 [giri no shimai] *n* sister-in-law

閉まる [shimaru] 閉まっている [shimatte iru] *adj* closed; 何時に閉まりますか? [nan-ji ni shimarimasu ka?] What time do you close?; いつ閉まりますか? [itsu shimarimasu ka?] When does it close?; お店は何時に閉まりますか? [o-mise wa nan-ji ni shimarimasu ka?] What time do the shops close?; その銀行はいつ閉まりますか? [sono ginkou wa itsu shimarimasu ka?] When does the bank close?; ドアが閉まりません [doa ga shimarimasen] The door won't close

シマウマ [shimauma] *n* zebra

締め出す [shimedasu] *v* lock out

指名 [shimei] *n* nomination; 指名する [shimei suru] *v* nominate

締切り [shimekiri] 締切り期限 [shimekiri kigen] *n* deadline

絞め殺す [shimekorosu] *v* strangle

湿る [shimeru] 湿った [shimetta] *adj* moist

締める [shimeru] *v* tighten; ファスナーを締める [fasunaa-o shimeru] *v* zip (up)

閉める [shimeru] *v* close, shut; バタンと閉める [batan to shimeru] *v* slam; 窓を閉めてもいいですか? [mado o shimete mo ii desu ka?] May I close the window?

占める [shimeru] *v* occupy

示す [shimesu] *v* indicate

しみ [shimi] *n* spot *(blemish)*, stain; しみのない [shimi no nai] *adj* spotless; しみがつく [shimi ga tsuku] *v* stain; しみだらけの [shimidarake no] *adj* stained; このしみはコーヒーです [kono shimi wa koohii desu] This stain is coffee; このしみはワインです [kono shimi wa wain desu] This stain is wine; このしみは油です [kono shimi wa abura desu] This stain is oil; このしみは血です [kono shimi wa chi desu] This stain is blood; このしみを落とすことができますか? [kono shimi o otosu koto ga dekimasu ka?] Can you remove this stain?

市民 [shimin] *n* citizen

市民権 [shiminken] *n* citizenship

しみ抜き [shiminuki] しみ抜き剤 [shiminuki zai] *n* stain remover

霜 [shimo] *n* frost

指紋 [shimon] *n* fingerprint

霜の降りる [shimo no oriru] *adj* frosty

芯 [shin] *n* core

シナゴーグ [shinagoogu] *n* synagogue; どこかにシナゴーグはありますか? [doko-ka ni shinagoogu wa arimasu ka?] Where is there a synagogue?

親愛 [shin'ai] 親愛な [shin'ai na] *adj* dear *(loved)*

しなければならない [shinakereba naranai] ・・・しなければならない [... shinakereba naranai] *v* have to, must

シナモン [shinamon] *n* cinnamon

シンバル [shinbaru] *n* cymbals

辛抱 [shinbou] 辛抱する [shinbou suru] *v* persevere

新聞 [shinbun] *n* newspaper; 新聞販売店 [shinbunhanbaiten] *n* newsagent; 新聞配

達 [shinbun haitatsu] n paper round; どこで新聞を買えますか? [doko de shinbun o kaemasu ka?] **Where can I buy a newspaper?**; 新聞はありますか? [shinbun wa arimasu ka?] **Do you have newspapers?**; 新聞をください [shinbun o kudasai] **I would like a newspaper**; 新聞を売っている一番近い店はどこですか? [shinbun o utte iru ichiban chikai mise wa doko desu ka?] **Where is the nearest shop which sells newspapers?**

慎重 [shinchou] 慎重な [shinchou na] adj cautious; 慎重に [shinchou ni] adv cautiously

身長 [shinchou] あなたの身長はどのくらいありますか? [anata no shinchou wa dono kurai arimasu ka?] **How tall are you?**

真鍮 [shinchuu] n brass

寝台 [shindai] n berth; 作り付け寝台 [tsukuri zuke shindai] n bunk; 寝台車 [shindaisha] n sleeping car; 寝台車コンパートメントの寝台 [shindaisha konpaatomento no shindai] n couchette

寝台車 [shindaisha] ···行きの寝台車を予約したいのですが [...iki no shindai-sha o yoyaku shitai no desu ga] **I want to book a sleeper to...**; 寝台車を予約できますか? [shindai-sha o yoyaku dekimasu ka?] **Can I reserve a sleeper?**

診断 [shindan] n diagnosis; 健康診断 [kenkoushindan] n medical

診断書 [shindansho] n medical certificate

神学 [shingaku] n theology

審議会 [shingikai] n council

信号 [shingou] 交通信号 [koutsuu shingou] n traffic lights; 救難信号 [kyuunan shingou] n SOS; 話し中を示す信号 [hanashichuu-o shimesu shingou] n busy signal

信号音 [shingouon] 話し中の信号音 [hanashichuu no shingouon] n engaged tone

寝具 [shingu] n bedclothes, bedding; 予備の寝具はありますか? [yobi no shingu wa arimasu ka?] **Is there any spare bedding?**

シングル [shinguru] n single

シングルベッド [shingurubeddo] n single bed

シングルルーム [shinguru ruumu] n single room; シングルルームを予約したいのですが [shinguru ruumu o yoyaku shitai no desu ga] **I want to reserve a single room, I'd like to book a single room**

シングルス [shingurusu] n singles

新人 [shinjin] 新人補充 [shinjin hojuu] n recruitment; 最近来た人 [saikin kita hito] n newcomer

信じられない [shinjirarenai] adj incredible, unbelievable

信じる [shinjiru] vt believe; 信じている [shinjite iru] adj trusting

真珠 [shinju] n pearl

神経 [shinkei] n nerve (to/from brain); 神経を悩ます [shinkei-o nayamasu] adj nerve-racking; 神経衰弱 [shinkeisuijaku] n nervous breakdown; 神経過敏な [shinkeikabin na] adj neurotic

神経質な [shinkeishitsu na] adj nervous

申告 [shinkoku] 所得申告 [shotoku shinkoku] n tax return; 申告するスピリッツが1本あります [shinkoku suru supirittsu ga ippon arimasu] **I have a bottle of spirits to declare**; 申告するものは何もありません [shinkoku suru mono wa nani mo arimasen] **I have nothing to declare**; 申告する免税範囲のタバコがあります [shinkoku suru menzei-han'i no tabako ga arimasu] **I have the allowed amount of tobacco to declare**

深刻 [shinkoku] 深刻な [shinkoku na] adj serious; 深刻に [shinkoku ni] adv seriously

信仰 [shinkou] 信仰する [shinkou suru] vi believe

進行 [shinkou] n proceedings; 高速進行 [kousoku shinkou] n speeding

進行方向 [shinkouhoukou] 進行方向に向いた席をお願いします [shinkou-houkou ni muita seki o o-negai shimasu] **Facing the front, please**

シンク [shinku] n sink

深紅色 [shinku shoku] 深紅色の [shinkoushoku no] adj scarlet

新芽 [shinme] n sprouts

審問 [shinmon] 検死審問 [kenshi shinmon] n inquest

深鍋 [shin nabe] n pot

信念 [shinnen] n faith

新年 [shinnen] n New Year

侵入 [shinnyuu] n invasion; 侵入者 [shinnyuusha] n intruder; 不法侵入者 [fuhou shinnyuusha] n burglar; 住居侵入罪 [juukyoshinnyuuzai] n burglary; 私の車が壊されて侵入されました [watashi no kuruma ga kowasarete shinnyuu saremashita] My car has been broken into

心配 [shinpai] n anxiety, concern; 心配して [shinpai shite] adj apprehensive; 心配している [shinpai shite iru] adj worried; 心配する [shinpai suru] v care, worry

新品 [shinpin] 新品の [shinpin no] adj brand-new

進歩 [shinpo] n progress; 進歩した [shinpo shita] adj advanced

新婦 [shinpu] 新婦の付添い役 [shinpu no tsukisoiyaku] n bridesmaid

信頼 [shinrai] n belief, confidence (trust), trust; 信頼する [shinrai suru] v trust; 信頼できる [shinrai dekiru] adj reliable, reputable

心理 [shinri] 心理療法 [shinri ryouhou] n psychotherapy; 心理的な [shinriteki na] adj psychological; 心理学 [shinrigaku] n psychology; 心理学者 [shinrigakusha] n psychologist

新郎 [shinrou] 新郎の付添い役 [shinrou no tsukisoiyaku] n best man

親類 [shinrui] 親類の [shinrui no] adj related

侵略 [shinryaku] 侵略する [shinryaku suru] v invade

診療 [shinryou] 診療所 [shinryoujo] n clinic, infirmary, surgery (doctor's)

審査 [shinsa] パスポート審査窓口 [pasupooto shinsa madoguchi] n passport control; 審査する [shinsa suru] v judge

神聖 [shinsei] 神聖な [shinsei na] adj holy

神聖な [shinsei na] adj sacred

親戚 [shinseki] n relative

新鮮 [shinsen] 新鮮な [shinsen na] adj fresh

親切 [shinsetsu] n kindness; 不親切な [fushinsetsu na] adj unfriendly; 親切な [shinsetsu na] adj kind; 親切に [shinsetsu ni] adv kindly

紳士 [shinshi] n gentleman

紳士気取りの俗物 [shinshi kidori no zokubutsu] n snob

寝室 [shinshitsu] n bedroom; 予備の寝室 [yobi no shinshitsu] n spare room; 共同寝室 [kyoudoushinshitsu] n dormitory

進水 [shinsui] 進水させる [shinsui saseru] v launch

身体 [shintai] 体の不自由な [karada no fujiyuu na] adj disabled; 身体の [shintai no] adj physical; 身体検査 [shintai kensa] n physical; 身体障害 [shintaishougai] n disability; 身体障害者 [shintaishougaisha] n disabled person

身体障害者 [shintaishougaisha] n disabled person; 身体障害者のためのスロープなどがありますか? [shintai-shougaisha no tame no suroopu nado ga arimasu ka?] Do you provide access for people with disabilities?; 身体障害者用のどんな設備をそなえていますか? [shintai-shougaisha-you no donna setsubi o sonaete imasu ka?] What facilities do you have for people with disabilities?; 身体障害者用のトイレはありますか? [shintai-shougaisha-you no toire wa arimasu ka?] Are there any accessible toilets?; 身体障害者用の割引がありますか? [shintai-shougaisha-you no waribiki ga arimasu ka?] Is there a reduction for people with disabilities?

信徒 [shinto] シーア派の信徒の [shiia ha no shinto no] adj Shiite

神道 [shintou] n Shinto

死ぬ [shinu] v die; 死んだ [shinda] adj dead

神話 [shinwa] n myth; 神話体系 [shinwa taikei] n mythology

信用 [shinyou] 信用できる [shinyou dekiru] adj credible; 信用を保証するもの [shin'you-o hoshou suru mono] n credentials; 信用販売 [shinyou hanbai] n credit

信用販売 [shinyou hanbai] n credit

針葉樹 [shin-youju] n conifer

心臓 [shinzou] n heart; 心臓発作 [shinzouhossa] n heart attack; 私は心臓病があります [watashi wa shinzou-byou ga arimasu] I have a heart condition

潮 [shio] n tide

塩 [shio] n salt; 塩を取っていただけますか? [shio o totte itadakemasu ka?] Pass the salt, please

塩味 [shioaji] 塩味の [shioaji no] adj savoury; 食べ物に塩味がききすぎています [tabemono ni shioaji ga kiki-sugite imasu] The food is too salty

塩気 [shioke] 塩気のある [shioke no aru] adj salty

塩水 [shiomizu] 塩水の [shiomizu no] adj saltwater

しおれる [shioreru] v wilt

しおり [shiori] n bookmark

失敗 [shippai] n failure, flop; 失敗する [shippai suru] v fail; 大失敗 [daishippai] n blunder

調べる [shiraberu] v check, look up; グーグル®で調べる [guuguru de shiraberu] v Google®; 細かく調べる [komakaku shiraberu] v scan

しらふ [shirafu] しらふの [shirafu no] adj sober

白髪 [shiraga] 白髪のある [shiraga no aru] adj grey-haired

シラミ [shirami] n lice

知らない人 [shiranai hito] n stranger

知らせる [shiraseru] v inform

シリア [shiria] n Syria; シリア人 [shiriajin] n Syrian (person); シリアの [shiria no] adj Syrian

知りたがる [shiritagaru] v curious

城 [shiro] n castle; 砂のお城 [suna no oshiro] n sandcastle; その城は一般公開さ れていますか? [sono shiro wa ippan-koukai sarete imasu ka?] Is the castle open to the public?; 私たちがその城を訪れることはできますか? [watashi-tachi ga sono shiro o otozureru koto wa dekimasu ka?] Can we visit the castle?

シロホン [shirohon] n xylophone

白い [shiroi] adj white

白黒 [shirokuro] 白黒で [shiro-kuro de] in black and white

白目 [shirome] n pewter

白身 [shiromi] 卵の白身 [tamago no shiromi] n egg white

シロップ [shiroppu] n syrup

白ワイン [shirowain] n white wine; よい白ワインを教えてもらえますか? [yoi shiro-wain o oshiete moraemasu ka?] Can you recommend a good white wine?

知る [shiru] v know; よく知られている [yoku shirarete iru] adj well-known, familiar; 知っている [shitte iru] v know; 知られている [shirarete iru] adj known; これのやり方をご存知ですか? [kore no yarikata o go-zonji desu ka?] Do you know how to do this?; 彼を知っていますか? [kare o shitte imasu ka?] Do you know him?

しるし [shirushi] n (現れ) token

思慮 [shiryo] 思慮深い [shiryobukai] adj thoughtful

視力 [shiryoku] n eyesight, sight

司祭 [shisai] n priest

資産 [shisan] n worth

施設 [shisetsu] n facility; どんなスポーツ施設がありますか? [donna supootsu-shisetsu ga arimasu ka?] What sports facilities are there?

使者 [shisha] n messenger

獅子座 [shishiza] n Leo

支障 [shishou] 道はいつ支障がなくなるのですか? [michi wa itsu shishou ga nakunaru no desu ka?] When will the road be clear?

死傷 [shishou] 死傷者 [shishousha] n casualty

思春期 [shishunki] n adolescence

支出 [shishutsu] n expenditure

刺繍 [shishuu] n embroidery; 刺繍する [shishuu suru] v embroider

湿疹 [shisshin] n eczema

システムアナリスト [shisutemu anarisuto] n systems analyst

システムコンポ [shisutemukonpo] n music centre

指数 [shisuu] n index (numerical scale); 知能指数 [chinoushisuu, IQ aikyuu] n IQ

下 [shita] 下に [shita ni] adv below, underneath; 下へ [shita e] adv down; ···の下に [...no shita ni] prep beneath; ···より下に [...yori shitani] prep below

舌 [shita] n tongue

下書き [shitagaki] n draft

従って [shitagatte] adv therefore; ···に従って [...ni shitagatte] prep according to

従う [shitagau] v obey; ···に従って [...ni shitagatte] prep according to; ···に従わない [...ni shitagawanai] v disobey

下着 [shitagi] n underwear

死体 [shitai] n corpse; 死体保管所 [shitaihokanjo] n morgue

···したことがない [...shita koto ga nai] adv never

親しい [shitashii] adj friendly, intimate

したたり [shitatari] n drip

したたる [shitataru] v drip

指定 [shitei] 指定地区 [shitei chiku] n precinct; 8時指定で2人分 [hachi-ji shitei de futari-bun] two for the eight o'clock showing

···して以来 [... shite irai] conj since

指摘 [shiteki] 指摘する [shiteki suru] v point out

質 [shitsu] n quality

室 [shitsu] 手術室 [shujutsushitsu] n operating theatre; 試着室 [shichakushitsu] n fitting room; 職員室 [shokuinshitsu] n staffroom; 待合室 [machiaishitsu] n waiting room

失望 [shitsubou] n disappointment; 失望させる [shitsubou saseru] v disappoint; 失望した [shitsubou shita] adj disappointed

失読症 [shitsudokushou] n dyslexia; 失読症の [shitsudokushou no] adj dyslexic; 失読症の人 [shitsudokushou no hito] n dyslexic

室外 [shitsugai] それは屋外プールですか? [sore wa okugai-puuru desu ka?] Is it an outdoor pool?

失業 [shitsugyou] n unemployment; 失業中の [shitsugyouchuu no] adj jobless; 失業している [shitsugyou shite iru] adj unemployed; 失業手当 [shitsugyouteate] n dole; 失業登録をする [shitsugyou touroku-o suru] v sign on

しつけ [shitsuke] n upbringing

質問 [shitsumon] n question; 質問する [shitsumon suru] v interrogate, question

室内 [shitsunai] 室内装飾家 [shitsunai soushokuka] n decorator

失礼 [shitsurei] 失礼な [shitsurei na] adj rude

失恋 [shitsuren] 失恋した [shitsuren shita] adj heartbroken

歯痛 [shitsuu] n toothache

知ったかぶりをする人 [shitta kaburi o suru hito] n know-all

嫉妬 [shitto] 嫉妬深い [shittobukai] adj jealous

しわ [shiwa] n wrinkle; しわの寄った [shiwa no yotta] adj wrinkled

使用 [shiyou] n use; 使用人 [shiyounin] n servant; 使用する [shiyou suru] v use; 使用期限 [shiyou kigen] n expiry date; 使用者 [shiyousha] n user; 再使用する [saishiyou suru] v reuse

試用 [shiyou] 試用期間 [shiyou kikan] n trial period

自然 [shizen] n nature; 不自然な [fushizen na] adj unnatural; 自然食品 [shizen shokuhin] n wholefoods

自然誌 [shizen shi] 自然誌研究者 [shizenshi kenkyuusha] n naturalist

静か [shizuka] 静かな [shizuka na] adj still; 一日中自分たちだけになれる静かな

ところがいいのですが [ichinichi-juu jibun-tachi dake ni nareru shizuka na tokoro ga ii no desu ga] We'd like to see nobody but us all day!; 静かな部屋がいいのですが [shizuka na heya ga ii no desu ga] I'd like a quiet room

静かな [shizuka na] adj quiet

静かに [shizuka ni] adv quietly

静けさ [shizukesa] n silence

しずく [shizuku] n drop

沈む [shizumu] v sink

暑 [sho] 暑すぎます [atsu-sugimasu] I'm too hot

諸 [sho] 諸経費 [shokeihi] n overheads

処罰 [shobatsu] n punishment

処置 [shochi] 救急処置 [kyuukyuu shochi] n first aid; 救急処置キット [kyuukyuu shochi kitto] n first-aid kit

初演 [shoen] n premiere

処方 [shohou] 処方する [shohou suru] v prescribe; 処方箋 [shohousen] n prescription

処方箋 [shohousen] n prescription; どこでこの処方箋の薬を出してもらえますか? [doko de kono shohousen no kusuri o dashite moraemasu ka?] Where can I get this prescription made up?

所持 [shoji] 所持品 [shojihin] n belongings

処女 [shojo] n virgin

処刑 [shokei] n execution; 処刑する [shokei suru] v execute

初期 [shoki] 初期の [shoki no] adj primitive

食器 [shokki] n tableware; 食器棚 [shokkidana] n dresser, sideboard; 食器洗い [shokkiarai] n washing-up; 食器洗い機 [shokkiaraiki] n dishwasher; 食器洗い用液体洗剤 [shokkiarai you ekitai senzai] n washing-up liquid; 食器がもっと必要です [shokki ga motto hitsuyou desu] We need more crockery; 食器洗い場はどこですか? [shokki-araiba wa doko desu ka?] Where is the washing up area?

ショッキング [shokkingu] ショッキングな [shokkingu na] adj shocking

職 [shoku] n job; 職場 [shokuba] n workplace

触媒 [shokubai] 触媒コンバーター [shokubai konbaataa] n catalytic converter

植物 [shokubutsu] n plant; つる植物 [tsuru shokubutsu] n vine; 鉢植え植物 [hachiue shokubutsu] n pot plant; 土地の植物と樹木を見たいのですが [tochi no shokubutsu to jumoku o mitai no desu ga] We'd like to see local plants and trees

植物相 [shokubutsusou] n flora

食中毒 [shokuchuudoku] n food poisoning

食堂 [shokudou] 食堂車 [shokudousha] n dining car

職業 [shokugyou] n occupation (work), profession; 職業上の [shokugyou jou no] adj vocational; 職業的な [shokugyouteki na] adj professional; 職業的に [shokugyouteki ni] adv professionally; 熟練職業 [jukuren shokugyou] n craft; 公共職業安定所 [koukyoushokugyou anteisho] n job centre

食品 [shokuhin] 自然食品 [shizen shokuhin] n wholefoods

職員 [shokuin] n staff (workers); 職員室 [shokuinshitsu] n staffroom; 臨時職員 [rinjishokuin] n temp

食事 [shokuji] n meal; 食事する人 [shokuji suru hito] n diner; 食事時間 [shokuji jikan] n mealtime; 小児用の食事椅子 [shouni you no shokuji isu] n highchair; お食事をお楽しみください! [o-shokuji o o-tanoshimi kudasai!] Enjoy your meal!; グルテンを使わずに食事を用意していただけますか? [guruten o tsukawazu ni shokuji o youi shite itadakemasu ka?] Could you prepare a meal without gluten?; ナッツを使わずに食事を用意していただけますか? [nattsu o tsukawazu ni shokuji o youi shite itadakemasu ka?] Could you prepare a meal without nuts?; 食事はおいしかったです [shokuji wa oishikatta desu] The meal was delicious; 魚介類を使わずに食事を用意していただけますか? [gyokairui o tsukawazu ni shokuji o youi shite itadakemasu ka?] **Could you prepare a meal without seafood?**; 魚を使わずに食事を用意していただけますか? [sakana o tsukawazu ni shokuji o youi shite itadakemasu ka?] **Could you prepare a meal without fish?**; 卵を使わずに食事を用意していただけますか? [tamago o tsukawazu ni shokuji o youi shite itadakemasu ka?] **Could you prepare a meal without eggs?**

職務 [shokumu] 職務上の [shokumujou no] *adj* **official**

職人 [shokunin] *n* **craftsman**; 煉瓦職人 [renga shokunin] *n* **bricklayer**

食糧 [shokuryou] *n* **supplies**

食料 [shokuryou] 食料置場 [shokuryou okiba] *n* **larder**; 食料雑貨類 [shokuryou zakkarui] *n* **groceries**; 食料雑貨店 [shokuryou zakkaten] *n* **grocer's**; 食料雑貨商 [shokuryou zakkashou] *n* **grocer**

食卓用ナイフ・フォーク・スプーン類 [shokutaku you naifu, fouku, supuun rui] *n* **cutlery**

食欲 [shokuyoku] *n* **appetite**

署名 [shomei] *n* **signature**; 署名する [shomei suru] *v* **sign**; 頭文字で署名する [atamamoji de shomei suru] *v* **initial**

ショービジネス [shoobijinesu] *n* **show business**

ショートクラスト [shootokurasuto] *n* **shortcrust pastry**

ショートメッセージサービス [shootomesseejisaabisu] *n* **SMS**

ショーウィンドウ [shoouindou] *n* **shop window**

ショッピングカート [shoppingukaato] *n* **shopping trolley**

ショッピングセンター [shoppingu sentaa] *n* **shopping centre**

ショップ [shoppu] ギフトショップ [gifuto shoppu] *n* **gift shop**; チャリティーショップ [charitii shoppu] *n* **charity shop**

書類 [shorui] *n* **document**; この書類のコピーを取りたいのですが [kono shorui no kopii o toritai no desu ga] **I want to copy this document**; 私の車両書類です [watashi no sharyou-shorui desu] **Here are my vehicle documents**

書類受け [shoruiuke] *n* **inbox**

書籍 [shoseki] 電子書籍 [denshi shoseki] *n* **e-book**

初心者 [shoshinsha] *n* **beginner**; 初心者用ゲレンデ [shoshinshayou gerende] *n* **nursery slope**

書店 [shoten] *n* **bookshop**

所得 [shotoku] *n* **earnings, income**; 所得申告 [shotoku shinkoku] *n* **tax return**; 所得税 [shotokuzei] *n* **income tax**

諸島 [shotou] フェロー諸島 [feroo shotou] *n* **Faroe Islands**

章 [shou] *n* **chapter**

症 [shou] 拒食症 [kyoshokushou] *n* **anorexia**; 狭心症 [kyoushinshou] *n* **angina**

省 [shou] *n* **ministry** (*government*)

賞 [shou] *n* **award, prize**

商 [shou] 宝石商 [housekishou] *n* **jeweller, jeweller's**

ショー [shou] *n* **show**; どこに行けばショーを見られますか? [doko ni ikeba shoo o miraremasu ka?] **Where can we go to see a show?**

商売 [shoubai] *n* **trade**

消防士 [shouboushi] *n* **firefighter**

消防隊 [shouboutai] *n* **fire brigade**; 消防隊を呼んでください [shoubou-tai o yonde kudasai] **Please call the fire brigade**

消沈 [shouchin] 意気消沈した [ikishouchin shita] *adj* **depressed**

象徴 [shouchou] *n* **symbol**

消毒剤 [shoudokuzai] *n* **disinfectant**

収益 [shoueki] *n* **proceeds, profit, return** (*yield*); 収益の多い [shuueki no oui] *adj* **profitable**

ショウガ [shouga] *n* **ginger**; ショウガ色の [shouga iro no] *adj* **ginger**

生涯 [shougai] 生涯教育 [shougai kyouiku] *n* **adult education**

障害 [shougai] *n* **hitch**; 体の不自由な

[karada no fujiyuu na] *adj* disabled; 身体障害 [shintaishougai] *n* disability; 身体障害者 [shintaishougaisha] *n* disabled person; 障害のある [shougai no aru] *adj* disabled; 障害飛越 [shougaihietsu] *n* show-jumping

傷害 [shougai] 個人傷害保険をかけたいのですが [kojin-shougai-hoken o kaketai no desu ga] I'd like to arrange personal accident insurance

障害物 [shougaibutsu] *n* obstacle

衝撃 [shougeki] *n* shock; 衝撃を与える [shougeki-o ataeru] *v* shock

正午 [shougo] *n* noon

照合 [shougou] *n* check

照合の印 [shougou no in] *n* tick; 照合の印をつける [shougou no in-o tsukeru] *v* tick

将軍 [shougun] *n* general

小片 [shouhen] *n* bit, scrap (*small piece*)

消費 [shouhi] 消費者 [shouhisha] *n* consumer

商品 [shouhin] *n* goods

商品券 [shouhinken] *n* gift voucher

商標 [shouhyou] *n* trademark

正直 [shoujiki] *n* honesty; 不正直な [fushoujiki na] *adj* dishonest; 正直な [shoujiki na] *adj* honest, truthful; 正直に [shoujiki ni] *adv* honestly

生じる [shoujiru] 結果として生じる [kekka toshite shoujiru] *v* result in

少女 [shoujo] *n* girl, lass

症状 [shoujou] *n* symptom

消化 [shouka] *n* digestion; 消化不良 [shoukafuryou] *n* indigestion; 消化する [shouka suru] *v* digest

照会 [shoukai] 照会デスク [shoukai desuku] *n* enquiry desk

紹介 [shoukai] *n* introduction, presentation; 紹介する [shoukai suru] *v* introduce, present

消火器 [shoukaki] *n* extinguisher, fire extinguisher

証券 [shouken] 証券取引所 [shouken torihikijo] *n* stock exchange

正気 [shouki] 正気でない [shouki de nai] *adj* insane

賞金 [shoukin] 多額の賞金 [tagaku no shoukin] *n* jackpot

証拠 [shouko] *n* evidence, proof

症候群 [shoukougun] ダウン症候群 [daun shoukougun] *n* Down's syndrome

小球 [shoukyuu] *n* pellet

小休止 [shoukyuushi] *n* pause

照明 [shoumei] *n* lighting; 投光照明 [toukou shoumei] *n* floodlight

証明 [shoumei] 身分証明 [mibun shoumei] *n* identification

証明書 [shoumeisho] *n* certificate; 身分証明書 [mibunshomeisho] *n* ID card; 結婚証明書 [kekkonshoumeisho] *n* marriage certificate; 出生証明書 [shusshou shoumeisho] *n* birth certificate; 私は「飛行機搭乗の適性」証明書が必要です [watashi wa "hikouki-toujou no tekisei" shoumei-sho ga hitsuyou desu] I need a 'fit to fly' certificate

正味 [shoumi] *n* Net

賞味 [shoumi] 賞味期限 [shoumikigen] *n* best-before date

小虫 [shou mushi] *n* midge

少年 [shounen] *n* boy, lad

小児 [shouni] *n* child, infant; 小児用の食事椅子 [shouni you no shokuji isu] *n* highchair; 小児用ベッド [shouni you beddo] *n* cot; 小児用のベッドはありますか? [shouni-you no beddo wa arimasu ka?] Do you have a cot?

小児科医 [shounikai] *n* paediatrician; いい小児科医を教えてもらえますか? [ii shounika-i o oshiete moraemasu ka?] Can you recommend a paediatrician?

承認 [shounin] *n* acknowledgement, approval; 承認する [shounin suru] *v* approve

証人 [shounin] エホバの証人 [ehoba no shounin] *n* Jehovah's Witness

小児性愛者 [shouniseiaimono] *n* paedophile

消音 [shouon] 消音装置 [shouon souchi] n silencer

将来 [shourai] 将来有望な [shourai yuubou na] adj promising

奨励 [shourei] n encouragement, incentive

勝利 [shouri] n triumph, victory; 勝利を得た [shouri-o eta] adj winning; 勝利を収める [shouri-o osameru] v triumph

ショール [shouru] n shawl

少量 [shouryou] より少量 [yori shouryou] pron less

詳細 [shousai] 詳細な [shousai na] adj detailed; 私の保険の詳細です [watashi no hoken no shousai desu] Here are my insurance details

称賛 [shousan] n admiration; 称賛の [shousan no] adj complimentary

小冊子 [shousasshi] n booklet

小説 [shousetsu] n novel; 短篇小説 [tanpen shousetsu] n short story; 小説家 [shousetsuka] n novelist

勝者 [shousha] n winner

証書 [shousho] n certificate; 保険証書 [hokenshousho] n insurance policy; あなたの保険証書を見せていただけますか? [anata no hoken-shousho o misete itadakemasu ka?] Can I see your insurance certificate please?

少々 [shoushou] 少々お待ちください [shoushou o-machi kudasai] Just a moment, please

尚早 [shousou] 時期尚早の [jikishousou no] adj premature

少数 [shousuu] pron few; 少数派 [shousuuha] n minority

招待 [shoutai] n invitation

焦点 [shouten] n focus; 焦点を合わせる [shouten-o awaseru] v focus

衝突 [shoutotsu] n bump, collision, conflict, crash, hit, percussion; 衝突させる [shoutotsu saseru] vt crash; 衝突する [shoutotsu suru] vi collide, crash; 衝突がありました [shoutotsu ga arimashita] There's been a crash; 私は自分の車を衝突させました [watashi wa jibun no kuruma o shoutotsu sasemashita] I've crashed my car

衝突する [shoutotsu suru] v clash

ショーツ [shoutsu] n knickers; ボクサーショーツ [bokusaa shootsu] n boxer shorts

醤油 [shouyu] n soy sauce

肖像画 [shouzouga] n portrait

所要 [shoyou] 所要時間は二時間です [shoyou-jikan wa ni-jikan desu] The journey takes two hours; 所要時間はどのくらいですか? [shoyou-jikan wa dono kurai desu ka?] How long is the journey?, How long will it take?

所有 [shoyuu] n possession; 所有する [shoyuu suru] v own, possess; 所有者 [shoyuusha] n owner; 所有物 [shoyuubutsu] n property; 個人の所有物 [kojin no shoyuubutsu] n private property

所属 [shozoku] 所属する [shozoku suru] v belong

種 [shu] n (果実) pip

種1 [shu] n (生物) species

主張 [shuchou] n claim; 主張する [shuchou suru] v claim

主題 [shudai] n subject

手段 [shudan] n means

主演 [shuen] 主演する [shuen suru] v star

主婦 [shufu] n housewife

主義 [shugi] n principle; 性差別主義 [seisabetsu shugi] n sexism; 性差別主義の [seisabetsu shugi no] adj sexist; 民主主義 [minshushugi] n democracy; 民主主義の [minshu shugi no] adj democratic; 社会主義 [shakaishugi] n socialism; 過激主義 [kageki shugi] n extremism; 国家主義 [kokkashugi] n nationalism

主義者 [shugisha] 人種差別主義者 [jinshusabetsushugisha] n racist; 人種差別主義者の [jinshu sabetsu shugisha no] adj racist; 楽観主義者 [rakkan shugisha] n optimist; 悲観主義者 [hikanshugisha] n pessimist; 裸体主義者 [rataishugisha] n nudist; 労働組合主義者 [roudoukumiai shugisha] n trade unionist; 国家主義者 [kokkashugisha] n nationalist

主人 [shujin] パン屋の主人 [pan ya no shujin] n baker; パブの主人 [pabu no shujin] n publican

手術 [shujutsu] n operation (surgery), surgery (operation); 手術する [shujutsu suru] v operate (to perform surgery); 手術室 [shujutsushitsu] n operating theatre

出血 [shukketsu] 出血する [shukketsu suru] v bleed

出航 [shukkou] いつ出航しますか? [itsu shukkou shimasu ka?] When do we sail?; ・・・行きの次の出航は何時ですか? [...iki no tsugi no shukkou wa nan-ji desu ka?] When is the next sailing to...?; ・・・行きの最終の出航は何時ですか? [...iki no saishuu no shukkou wa nan-ji desu ka?] When is the last sailing to...?

宿題 [shukudai] n homework

祝福 [shukufuku] 祝福する [shukufuku suru] v bless

宿泊 [shukuhaku] 月曜から水曜まで宿泊したいのですが [getsuyou kara suiyou made shukuhaku shitai no desu ga] I want to stay from Monday till Wednesday

祝日 [shukujitsu] 祝祭日 [shukusaijitsu] n bank holiday

祝祭 [shukusai] 祝祭日 [shukusaijitsu] n public holiday

縮小 [shukushou] n cutback

主教 [shukyou] n bishop; 大主教 [dai shukyou] n archbishop

趣味 [shumi] n hobby; 趣味のよい [shumi no yoi] adj tasteful; 趣味が悪い [shumi ga warui] adj naff

瞬間 [shunkan] n moment; 瞬間の [shunkan no] adj momentary

春季 [shunki] n springtime; 春季の大掃除 [shunki no ousouji] n spring-cleaning

シュノーケリング [shunookeringu] シュノーケリングをしたいのですが [shunookeringu o shitai no desu ga] I'd like to go snorkelling

シュノーケル [shunookeru] n snorkel

主 [shu/nushi] 主な [omo na] adj main; 主に [omo ni] adv mainly; 主として [shutoshite] adv largely; 送り主

[okurinushi] n sender; 雇用主 [koyounushi] n employer; 店主 [tenshu] n shopkeeper

出版 [shuppan] n publication; 出版する [shuppan suru] v publish; 出版業者 [shuppan gyousha] n publisher

出発 [shuppatsu] n departure; 出発する [shuppatsu suru] v depart, leave, set off; 出発ラウンジ [shuppatsu raunji] n departure lounge

種類 [shurui] n kind, sort, type

酒類販売 [shuruihanbai] 酒類販売免許 [sakerui hanbai menkyo] n off-licence

首相 [shushou] n prime minister

出産 [shussan] 出産休暇 [shussan kyuuka] n maternity leave; 出産前の [shussanmae no] adj antenatal; 私は五か月後に出産予定です [watashi wa gokagetsu-go ni shussan yotei desu] I'm due in five months

出生地 [shusseichi] 出生地の [shusseichi no] adj native

出席 [shusseki] n attendance; 出席する [shusseki suru] v attend

出身 [shusshin] ・・・の出身である [...no shusshin de aru] v come from; ご出身はどちらですか? [go-shusshin wa dochira desu ka?] Where are you from?; ご出身は・・・のどちらですか? [go-shusshin wa ... no dochira desu ka?] What part of ... are you from?

出生 [shusshou] 出生証明書 [shusshou (shussei) shoumeisho] n birth certificate; 出生地 [shusseichi] n place of birth

出張 [shutchou] n business trip

首都 [shuto] n capital

主として [shutoshite] adv primarily

出没 [shutsubotsu] 幽霊が出没する [yuurei ga shutsubotsu suru] adj haunted

出現 [shutsugen] n advent, appearance

週 [shuu] n week; 1週間パスはいくらですか? [isshuukan pasu wa ikura desu ka?] How much is a pass per week?; 再来週 [saraishuu] the week after next

執着 [shuuchaku] n obsession; 執着した [shuuchaku shita] adj obsessed

集中 [shuuchuu] n concentration; 集中する [shuuchuu suru] v concentrate; 集中治療室 [shuuchuuchiryoushitsu, ICU aishiiyuu] n intensive care unit; 集中的な [shuuchuuteki na] adj intensive

集団 [shuudan] n collective; 集団の [shuudan no] adj collective

修道 [shuudou] 修道院 [shuudouin] n monastery; 修道士 [shuudoushi] n monk

修道院 [shuudouin] 女子修道院 [joshishuudouin] n convent; その修道院は一般公開されていますか？ [sono shuudouin wa ippan-koukai sarete imasu ka?] Is the monastery open to the public?

修復 [shuufuku] 修復する [shuufuku suru] v restore

襲撃 [shuugeki] n raid; 襲撃する [shuugeki suru] v raid

囚人 [shuujin] n prisoner

集会 [shuukai] n assembly

収穫 [shuukaku] n crop, harvest; 収穫する [shuukaku suru] v harvest

週間 [shuukan] 1週間でいくらですか？ [isshuukan de ikura desu ka?] How much is it for a week?; それは1週間あたりいくらですか？ [sore wa isshuukan atari ikura desu ka?] How much is it per week?

就活 [shuukatsu] n job-hunting

周期 [shuuki] n cycle (recurring period)

宗教 [shuukyou] n religion; 宗教の [shuukyou no] adj religious

週末 [shuumatsu] n weekend

周年 [shuunen] 100周年記念祭 [hyakushuunen kinensai] n centenary

収納箱 [shuunoubako] n chest (storage)

収入 [shuunyuu] n revenue, takings

修理 [shuuri] n repair; 修理する [shuuri suru] v repair; 修理キット [shuuri kitto] n repair kit; 修理にどのくらいの時間がかかりますか？ [shuuri ni dono kurai no jikan ga kakarimasu ka?] How long will it take to repair?; 修理してもらえますか？ [shuuri shite moraemasu ka?] Can you repair it?; 修理する価値がありますか？ [shuuri suru kachi ga arimasu ka?] Is it worth

repairing?; どこでこれを修理してもらえますか？ [doko de kore o shuuri shite moraemasu ka?] Where can I get this repaired?; この靴を修理できますか？ [kono kutsu o shuuri dekimasu ka?] Can you repair these shoes?; これを修理できますか？ [kore o shuuri dekimasu ka?] Can you repair this?; それを修理できますか？ [sore o shuuri dekimasu ka?] Can you repair it?; 私のメガネを修理できますか？ [watashi no megane o shuuri dekimasu ka?] Can you repair my glasses?; 私の時計を修理できますか？ [watashi no tokei o shuuri dekimasu ka?] Can you repair my watch?; 私の入れ歯を修理してもらえますか？ [watashi no ireba o shuuri shite moraemasu ka?] Can you repair my dentures?

修理代 [shuuridai] 修理代はいくらかかりますか？ [shuuri-dai wa ikura kakarimasu ka?] How much will the repairs cost?

修理キット [shuuri kitto] 修理キットはありますか？ [shuuri-kitto wa arimasu ka?] Do you have a repair kit?; 修理キットをください [shuuri-kitto o kudasai] Can I have a repair kit?

修理工 [shuurikou] n mechanic; 修理工を手配してもらえますか？ [shuuri-kou o tehai shite moraemasu ka?] Can you send a mechanic?

修理店 [shuuriten] n repair shop; 一番近い自転車修理店はどこですか？ [ichiban chikai jitensha shuuri-ten wa doko desu ka?] Where is the nearest bike repair shop?; 一番近くの車椅子修理店はどこですか？ [ichiban chikaku no kuruma-isu shuuri-ten wa doko desu ka?] Where is the nearest repair shop for wheelchairs?

終了 [shuuryou] 終了した [shuuryou shita] adj done

修正 [shuusei] n revision; 修正する [shuusei suru] v rectify, revise

終止符 [shuushifu] n full stop

就寝 [shuushin] 就寝時刻 [shuushin jikoku] n bedtime

収集 [shuushuu] ごみ収集人 [gomishuushuunin] n dustman; 収集家

[shuushuuka] n collector

収容 [shuuyou] 収容力 [shuuyouryoku] n capacity

修繕 [shuuzen] 修繕する [shuuzen suru] v renovate

シューズ [shuuzu] バレエシューズ [baree shuuzu] n ballet shoes

手話 [shuwa] n sign language

主役 [shuyaku] n lead (in play/film)

主要 [shuyou] 主要産物 [shuyou sanbutsu] n staple (commodity)

腫瘍 [shuyou] n tumour

主要な [shuyou na] adj chief

取材 [shuzai] 取材記者 [shuzai kisha] n reporter

CD [siidii] n CD [siidii]; CDバーナー [shiidii baanaa] n CD burner; CDプレーヤー [shiidii pureiyaa] n CD player; CDはいつできますか? [shii-dii wa itsu dekimasu ka?] When will the CD be ready?

CD-ROM [siidii romu] n CD-ROM [siidii romu]

そば [soba] ···のそばに [...no soba ni] prep beside

そばかす [sobakasu] n freckles

祖母 [sobo] n grandmother

率直 [sotchoku] 率直な [sotchoku na] adj direct, straightforward; 率直に [sotchoku ni] adv frankly

育てる [sodateru] v bring up, grow

袖 [sode] n sleeve; 袖なしの [sode nashi no] adj sleeveless; 半袖の [hansode no] adj short-sleeved

祖伝来 [sodenrai] 先祖伝来のもの [senzo denrai no mono] n heritage

添える [soeru] 添え木 [soegi] n splint

ソファー [sofaa] n sofa

ソファーベッド [sofaabeddo] n sofa bed

祖父 [sofu] n grandfather

祖父母 [sofubo] n grandparents

ソフトドリンク [sofutodorinku] n soft drink

ソフトウェア [sofutouea] n software

そぐ [sogu] 人の興をそぐ人 [hito no kyou-o sogu hito] n spoilsport

ソケット [soketto] ソケットアダプタ [soketto adaputa] n adaptor

速記 [sokki] n shorthand

ソックス [sokkusu] n sock

底 [soko] n bottom; 底の [soko no] adj bottom

そこ [soko] そこに [soko ni] adv there

祖国 [sokoku] n homeland

損なわれていない [sokonawareteinai] adj intact

速度 [sokudo] 速度を上げる [sokudo-o ageru] v speed up; 速度計 [sokudokei] n speedometer; 制限速度 [seigensokudo] n speed limit

促進 [sokushin] n promotion; 促進する [sokushin suru] v promote

測定 [sokutei] 測定する [sokutei suru] v measure

側灯 [sokutou] n sidelight

即座 [sokuza] 即座に [sokuza ni] adv instantly; 即座の [sokuza no] adj instant

即座に [sokuza ni] adv promptly

即座の [sokuza no] n prompt

ソマリア [somaria] n Somalia; ソマリア人 [somariajin] n Somali (person); ソマリアの [somaria no] adj Somali; ソマリア語 [somariago] n Somali (language)

染める [someru] v dye; 根元を染めていただけますか? [nemoto o somete itadakemasu ka?] Can you dye my roots, please?; 髪を染めていただけますか? [kami o somete itadakemasu ka?] Can you dye my hair, please?

備える [sonaeru] 備えた [sonaeta] adj equipped

尊重 [sonchou] n respect; 尊重する [sonchou suru] v respect

尊敬 [sonkei] 尊敬すべき [sonkeisubeki] adj respectable

そんな [sonna] そんなに [sonna ni] adv such

そんなに [sonna ni] adv so

園 [sono] 果樹園 [kajuen] n orchard; 動物園 [doubutsuen] n zoo

その [sono] art the

その間 [sono aida] その間に [sono aida ni] adv meantime, meanwhile

そのほか [sonohoka] そのほかに [sono hoka ni] adv other than that

その時 [sono toki] adv then

その上 [sono ue] adv besides

そのような [sono youna] adj such

損傷 [sonshou] n damage; 損傷する [sonshou suru] v damage

存在 [sonzai] n presence; 存在する [sonzai suru] v exist

ソーダ割り [soodawari] ウイスキーのソーダ割り [uisukii no sooda wari] a whisky and soda

ソープオペラ [soopuopera] n soap opera

ソプラノ [sopurano] n soprano

空 [sora] n (天) sky; 空にする [kara ni suru] v empty; 空の [kara no] adj empty

ソラマメ [soramame] n broad bean

そらす [sorasu] 注意をそらす [chuui-o sorasu] v distract

それ [sore] それは [sore wa] pron it; それの [sore no] adj its; それ自身 [sore jishin] pron itself; それは何ですか? [sore wa nan desu ka?] What is it?

それでも [soredemo] adv nevertheless

それなら [sorenara] conj then

それにもかかわらず [sorenimokakawarazu] conj yet (nevertheless)

それら [sorera] pron those; それらの [sorera no] adj those

それる [soreru] 急にそれる [kyuu ni soreru] v swerve

逸れる [soreru] 逸れること [soreru koto] n turn

それぞれ [sorezore] adv respectively ▷ pron each; それぞれの [sorezore no] adj each

そり [sori] n sledge; どこに行けばそりに乗れますか? [doko ni ikeba sori ni noremasu ka?] Where can we go sledging?

ソリスト [sorisuto] n soloist

ソロ [soro] n solo

そろい [soroi] ひとそろい [hitosoroi] n set

剃る [soru] v shave

ソルベ [sorube] n sorbet

組織 [soshiki] n (生物) tissue (anatomy), (生物) tissue (paper), (団体) organization; 組織する [soshiki suru] v organize; 組織的な方法 [soshikiteki na houhou] n system

外 [soto] 外に [hoka ni] adv out; 外の [hoka no] adj out

外側 [sotogawa] n outside; 外側に [sotogawa ni] adv outside; 外側の [sotogawa no] adj outside; 外側の [sotogawa no] adj exterior

卒業 [sotsugyou] 大学卒業 [daigaku sotsugyou] n graduation

卒業生 [sotsugyousei] 大学の卒業生 [daigaku no sotsugyousei] n graduate

層 [sou] n layer; オゾン層 [ozonsou] n ozone layer

沿う [sou] ···に沿って [...ni sotte] prep along; 道に沿って進んでください [michi ni sotte susunde kudasai] Keep to the path

装置 [souchi] n device, equipment; ハイファイ装置 [haifai souchi] n hifi; 消音装置 [shouon souchi] n silencer; 掘削装置 [kussaku souchi] n rig; 点火装置 [tenkasouchi] n ignition; 除氷装置 [johyou souchi] n de-icer

壮大 [soudai] 壮大な [sodai na] adj grand, magnificent

相談 [soudan] 相談する [soudan suru] v consult

双眼鏡 [sougankyou] n binoculars

葬儀 [sougi] 葬儀屋 [sougiya] n undertaker

葬儀場 [sougiba] n funeral parlour

相互 [sougo] 相互の [sougo no] adj mutual

総合 [sougou] 総合的な [sougouteki na] adj comprehensive

相違 [soui] n contrast; 意見の相違 [iken no soui] n disagreement

僧院 [souin] n abbey

掃除 [souji] n cleaning; 掃除する [souji suru] v clean; 掃除機で掃除する [soujiki de souji suru] v hoover; 春季の大掃除 [shunki no ousouji] n spring-cleaning; 電気掃除機で掃除する [denki soujiki de souji suru] v vacuum

掃除婦 [soujifu] n cleaning lady

掃除機 [soujiki] 掃除機で掃除する [soujiki de souji suru] v hoover; 電気掃除機 [denki soujiki] n vacuum cleaner; 電気掃除機で掃除する [denki soujiki de souji suru] v vacuum

操縦桿 [soujuukan] n joystick

壮観 [soukan] 壮観な [soukan na] adj spectacular

送金 [soukin] n remittance; 私の口座から送金したいのですが [watashi no kouza kara soukin shitai no desu ga] I would like to transfer some money from my account; 送金にかかる期間はどのくらいですか [soukin ni kakaru kikan wa dono kurai desu ka?] How long will it take to transfer?; 送金料がかかりますか? [soukin-ryou ga kakarimasu ka?] Is there a transfer charge?

倉庫 [souko] n warehouse

走行 [soukou] 走行マイル計 [soukou mairu kei] n mileometer

草木 [soumoku] n vegetation

騒音 [souon] n noise

騒る [sou ru] 騒ぎたてる [sawagitateru] adj fussy

操作 [sousa] 操作する [sousa suru] v operate (to function)

捜索 [sousaku] n search; 捜索する [sousaku suru] v search; 捜索隊 [sousakutai] n search party

ソーセージ [souseeji] n sausage

走者 [sousha] 短距離走者 [tankyori sousha] n sprinter

奏者 [sousha] バイオリン奏者 [baiorinsousha] n violinist

ソーシャルワーカー [sousharuwaakaa] n social worker

葬式 [soushiki] n funeral

喪失 [soushitsu] n loss

装飾 [soushoku] 装飾する [soushoku suru] v decorate; 装飾用のぴかぴか光る金属片や糸 [soushoku you no pikapika hikaru kinzokuhen ya ito] n tinsel; 室内装飾家 [shitsunai soushokuka] n decorator

装飾品 [soushokuhin] n ornament

曾祖母 [sousobo] n great-grandmother

曾祖父 [sousofu] n great-grandfather

ソース [sousu] n sauce; ディップソース [dippu sousu] n dip

ソースパン [sousupan] n saucepan

想定 [soutei] 想定する [soutei suru] v assume, suppose

総売上高 [souuriagedaka] n turnover

相続 [souzoku] n inheritance; 相続する [souzoku suru] v inherit

相続人 [souzokunin] n heir

想像 [souzou] n imagination; 想像の [souzou no] adj imaginary; 想像する [souzou suru] v imagine

創造 [souzou] n creation; 創造する [souzou suru] v create; 創造的な [souzouteki na] adj creative

そよ風 [soyokaze] n breeze

粗雑 [sozatsu] 粗雑な [sozatsu na] adj crude

酢 [su] n vinegar

巣 [su] n nest; クモの巣 [kumo no su] n web

すばらしい [subarashii] adj excellent, fabulous, fantastic, glorious, marvellous, smashing, splendid, stunning, super, superb, wonderful; 昼食はすばらしかったです [chuushoku wa subarashikatta desu] The lunch was excellent

素早い [subayai] adj quick; 素早く [subayaku] adv quickly

滑る [suberu] v slide, slip; 滑りやすい [suberiyasui] adj slippery; 滑ること [suberu koto] n slide

すべて [subete] pron everything; すべての [subete no] adj every

スチュワーデス [suchuwaadesu] *n* air hostess

スチュワード [suchuwaado] *n* steward

すでに [sude ni] *adv* already

スエード [sueedo] *n* suede

スエットシャツ [suettoshatsu] *n* sweatshirt

姿 [sugata] 姿を現す [sugata-o arawasu] *v* turn up

過ぎ [sugi] 八時過ぎに [hachi-ji sugi ni] after eight o'clock

過ぎる [sugiru] *vi* pass; ···を過ぎる [...-o sugiru] *v* go past

過ぎ去る [sugisaru] 過ぎ去った [sugisatta] *adj* past

過ごす [sugosu] 無為に過ごす [mui ni sugosu] *v* mess about; 私たちは楽しい時を過ごしています [watashi-tachi wa tanoshii toki o sugoshite imasu] We are having a nice time

すぐ [sugu] *adv* immediately; すぐにしてもらえますか? [sugu ni shite moraemasu ka?] Can you do it straightaway?

すぐに [sugu ni] *adv* readily

優れる [sugureru] 優れた [sugureta] *adj* superior

スグリ [suguri] 赤スグリ [aka suguri] *n* redcurrant

垂直 [suichoku] 垂直の [suichoku no] *adj* vertical

水中 [suichuu] 水中に [suichuu ni] *adv* underwater

水泳 [suiei] *n* swimming

水泳場 [suieijou] 水泳場の救助員 [suieijou no kyuujoin] *n* lifeguard

水銀 [suigin] *n* mercury

水牛 [suigyuu] *n* buffalo

水平 [suihei] *n* level; 水平な [suihei na] *adj* horizontal; 水平の [suihei no] *adj* level

スイート [suiito] *n* suite

衰弱 [suijaku] 神経衰弱 [shinkeisuijaku] *n* nervous breakdown

水上スキー [suijousukii] どこで水上スキーができますか? [doko de suijou-sukii ga dekimasu ka?] Where can you go waterskiing?; ここで水上スキーはできますか? [koko de suijou-sukii wa dekimasu ka?] Is it possible to go water-skiing here?

水準 [suijun] 生活水準 [seikatsusuijun] *n* standard of living

スイカ [suika] *n* watermelon

スイカズラ [suikazura] *n* honeysuckle

吸い込む [suikomu] 息を吸い込む [iki-o suikomu] *v* breathe in; 現金自動支払い機が私のカードを吸い込んでしまいました [genkin-jidou-shiharaiki ga watashi no kaado o suikonde shimaimashita] The cash machine swallowed my card

遂行 [suikou] *n* performance (functioning)

睡眠 [suimin] 睡眠薬 [suimin-yaku] *n* sleeping pill

スイミングプール [suimingupuuru] *n* swimming pool; スイミングプールはありますか? [suimingu-puuru wa arimasu ka?] Is there a swimming pool?; 公共のスイミングプールはどこですか? [koukyou no suimingu-puuru wa doko desu ka?] Where is the public swimming pool?

スイミングトランクス [suimingutorankusu] *n* swimming trunks

水彩絵 [suisaie] 水彩絵の具 [suisai enogu] *n* watercolour

彗星 [suisei] *n* comet

水晶 [suishou] *n* crystal

水素 [suiso] *n* hydrogen

推測 [suisoku] *n* guess; 推測する [suisoku suru] *v* guess, speculate

水槽 [suisou] *n* aquarium

スイス [suisu] *n* Switzerland; スイス人 [suisujin] *n* Swiss (person); スイスの [suisu no] *adj* Swiss

スイッチ [suitchi] *n* switch

推定 [suitei] 推定する [suitei suru] *v* presume

水曜日 [suiyoubi] *n* Wednesday; 灰の水曜日 [hai no suiyoubi] *n* Ash Wednesday; 水曜日に [suiyoubi ni] on Wednesday

スカーフ [sukaafu] *n* scarf

スカート [sukaato] n skirt

スカンジナビア [sukanjinabia] n Scandinavia; スカンジナビアの [sukanjinabia no] adj Scandinavian

スカッシュ [sukasshu] n squash

スケート [sukeeto] n skating; スケートをする [sukeeto o suru] v skate; スケートリンク [sukeetorinku] n ice rink; スケート靴 [sukeeto kutsu] n skates; 片足スケート [kataashi sukeeto] n scooter

スケートボーディング [sukeetoboodeingu] n skateboarding

スケートボード [sukeetoboodo] n skateboard; 私はスケートボードをしたいのですが [watashi wa sukeetoboodo o shitai no desu ga] I'd like to go skateboarding

スケートリンク [sukeetorinku] n rink, skating rink

透ける [sukeru] 透けて見える [sukete mieru] adj see-through

スケッチ [suketchi] n sketch; スケッチを描く [suketchi-o egaku] v sketch

鋤 [suki] n plough, spade

好き [suki] n fondness; スポーツ好きの [supootsuzuki no] adj sporty; 話好きな [hanashi zuki na] adj talkative; 詮索好きな [sensaku zuki na] adj inquisitive; ···が好きになる [...ga suki ni naru] v fall for; それも好きではありません [sore mo suki de wa arimasen] I don't like it either; 私はあなたがとても好きです [watashi wa anata ga totemo suki desu] I like you very much; 私は···が好きではありません [watashi wa ... ga suki de wa arimasen] I don't like...; 私は···が好きです [watashi wa ... ga suki desu] I like...; 私は···が大好きです [watashi wa ... ga daisuki desu] I love...

スキー [sukii] n ski, skiing; スキーをする [sukii o suru] v ski; 水上スキー [suijousukii] n water-skiing; 1日スキーパスが欲しいのですが [ichinichi sukii-pasu ga hoshii no desu ga] I'd like a ski pass for a day; 1週間スキーパスが欲しいのですが [isshuukan sukii-pasu ga hoshii no desu ga] I'd like a ski pass for a week; どこでスキーパスを買えますか? [doko de sukii-pasu o kaemasu ka?] Where can I buy a ski pass?; どこでスキー用具を借りられますか? [doko de sukii-yougu o kariraremasu ka?] Where can I hire skiing equipment?; スキーに行きたいのですが [sukii ni ikitai no desu ga] I'd like to go skiing; スキーのレッスンを企画していますか? [sukii no ressun o kikaku shite imasu ka?] Do you organise skiing lessons?; スキースクールはありますか? [sukii-sukuuru wa arimasu ka?] Is there a ski school?; スキーパスはいくらですか? [sukii-pasu wa ikura desu ka?] How much is a ski pass?; ダウンヒルスキーの板を借りたいのですが [daunhiru-sukii no ita o karitai no desu ga] I want to hire downhill skis

スキー板 [sukiiita] ここでスキー板を借りられますか? [koko de sukii-ita o kariraremasu ka?] Can we hire skis here?; スキー板を借りたいのですが [sukii-ita o karitai no desu ga] I want to hire skis

スキー場 [sukiijou] n ski area; スキー場のリフト [sukii jou no rifuto] n ski lift; スキー場のパス [sukii jou no pasu] n ski pass

スキーヤー [sukiiyaa] n skier

隙間 [sukima] n gap

隙間風 [sukimakaze] n draught

好きな [suki na] 詮索好きな [sensaku zuki na] adj nosy

スキンヘッド [sukinheddo] n skinhead

すっかり [sukkari] すっかり白状する [sukkari hakujou suru] v own up

少し [sukoshi] 少しの [sukoshi no] adj few

スコットランド [sukottorando] n Scotland; スコットランド人 [sukottorandojin] n Scot; スコットランド人男性 [sukottorandojin dansei] n Scotsman; スコットランド人女性 [sukottorandojin josei] n Scotswoman; スコットランドの [sukottorando no] adj Scots, Scottish

すく [suku] 私はおなかがすいています [watashi wa onaka ga suite imasu] I'm hungry; 私はおなかがすいていません [watashi wa onaka ga suite imasen] I'm not hungry

すくめる [sukumeru] 肩をすくめる [kata o sukumeru] v shrug

すくむ [sukumu] v be petrified

少ない [sukunai] 最も少ない [mottomo sukunai] adj least

少なく [sukunaku] adv less

少なくとも [sukunakutomo] adv at least

スクラップブック [sukurappubukku] n scrapbook

スクリーン [sukuriin] n screen

スクリーンセーバー [sukuriinseebaa] n screensaver

スクロールする [sukurooru suru] v scroll

救う [sukuu] v rescue, save

スクール [sukuuru] スキースクールはありますか? [sukii-sukuuru wa arimasu ka?] Is there a ski school?

スキャナー [sukyanaa] n scanner

スキャンダル [sukyandaru] n scandal

スキューバダイビング [sukyuubadaibingu] n scuba diving

スマート [sumaato] スマートな [sumaato na] adj smart

スマートフォン [sumaatofon] or スマホ [sumaho] n smart phone

スマイリー [sumairii] n smiley

済ます [sumasu] ･･･なしで済ます [... nashide sumasu] v do without

済み [sumi] 支払い済みの [shiharaizumi no] adj paid; 調理済みの [chouri zumi no] adj ready-cooked

隅から隅まで [sumi kara sumi made] ･･･の隅から隅まで [...no sumi kara sumi made] prep throughout

すみません [sumimasen] excuse me

住む [sumu] v live; 人の住んでいない [hito no sunde inai] adj uninhabited; 住む家のない [sumu ie no nai] adj homeless; 住む場所 [sumu basho] n accommodation; どちらにお住まいですか? [dochira ni o-sumai desu ka?] Where do you live?; 私は･･･に住んでいます [watashi wa ... ni sunde imasu] I live in...; 私たちは･･･に住んでいます [watashi-tachi wa ... ni sunde imasu] We live in...

砂 [suna] n sand; 砂のお城 [suna no oshiro] n sandcastle

砂場 [sunaba] n sandpit

スナップ [sunappu] スナップ写真 [sunappu shashin] n snapshot

すなわち [sunawachi] conj i.e.

すねる [suneru] v sulk; すねた [suneta] adj sulky

スニーカー [suniikaa] n sneakers

スノーボード [sunooboodo] スノーボードのレッスンを企画していますか? [sunooboodo no ressun o kikaku shite imasu ka?] Do you organise snowboarding lessons?; スノーボードを借りたいのですが [sunooboodo o karitai no desu ga] I want to hire a snowboard

スノーチェーン [sunoocheen] スノーチェーンは必要ですか? [sunoo-cheen wa hitsuyou desu ka?] Do I need snow chains?

寸法 [sunpou] n dimension

スヌーカー [sunuukaa] n snooker

スパークプラグ [supaakupuragu] n spark plug

スパゲッティ [supagetti] n spaghetti

スパイ [supai] n mole, spy; スパイ行為 [supai koui] n espionage, spying

スパムメール [supamumeeru] n spam

スパナ [supana] n spanner

スパニエル [supanieru] n spaniel

スペアホイール [supeahoiiru] n spare wheel

スペアパーツ [supeapaatsu] n spare part

スペアタイヤ [supeataiya] n spare tyre

スペース [supeesu] n space; 作業スペース [sagyou supeesu] n workspace; 頭上スペース [zujou supeesu] n headroom

スペイン [supein] n Spain; スペイン語 [supeingo] n Spanish (language); スペイン人 [supeinjin] n Spaniard, Spanish person; スペインの [supein no] adj Spanish

スペルチェッカー [superuchekkaa] n spellchecker

スピード [supiido] n speed; あなたはスピードを出しすぎていました [anata wa supiido o dashi-sugite imashita] You were driving too fast; スピードを落としてください! [supiido o otoshite kudasai!] Slow down!; 彼はスピードを出しすぎていました [kare wa supiido o dashi-sugite imashita] He was driving too fast

スピーカー [supiikaa] n loudspeaker

スピリッツ [supirittsu] n spirits

スポンジ [suponji] n sponge (for washing)

スポンジケーキ [suponji keeki] n sponge cake

スポークスパーソン [supookusupaason] n spokesperson

スポークスウーマン [supookusuuuman] n spokeswoman

スポットライト [supottoraito] n spotlight

スポーク [supouku] n spoke

スポークスマン [supoukusuman] n spokesman

スポーツ [supoutsu] n sport; スポーツ好きの [supootsuzuki no] adj sporty; 血を見るスポーツ [chi-o miru supootsu] n blood sports; どんなスポーツ施設がありますか? [donna supootsu-shisetsu ga arimasu ka?] What sports facilities are there?; 私たちはどのスポーツイベントに行けますか? [watashi-tachi wa dono supootsu-ibento ni ikemasu ka?] Which sporting events can we go to?

スポーツマン [supoutsuman] n sportsman

スポーツウェア [supoutsuuea] n sportswear

スポーツウーマン [supoutsuuuman] n sportswoman

酸っぱい [suppai] adj sour

スプレッドシート [supureddoshiito] n spreadsheet

スプリンクラー [supurinkuraa] n sprinkler

スプーン [supuun] n spoon; デザートスプーン [dezaato supuun] n dessert spoon;

新しいスプーンをいただけますか? [atarashii supuun o itadakemasu ka?] Could I have a clean spoon, please?

スラム [suramu] スラム街 [suramugai] n slum

スレート [sureeto] n slate

スレッジング [surejjingu] n sledging

スリ [suri] n pickpocket

すりおろす [suriorosu] v grate

スリッパ [surippa] n slipper

スリップ [surippu] n (下着) slip (underwear)

スリラー [suriraa] n thriller

スリランカ [suriranka] n Sri Lanka

スロバキア [surobakia] n Slovakia; スロバキア人 [surobakiajin] n Slovak (person); スロバキアの [surobakia no] adj Slovak; スロバキア語 [surobakiago] n Slovak (language)

スロベニア [surobenia] n Slovenia; スロベニア人 [surobeniajin] n Slovenian (person); スロベニアの [surobenia no] adj Slovenian; スロベニア語 [surobeniago] n Slovenian (language)

スロープ [suroopu] n slope; 一番簡単なスロープはどれですか? [ichiban kantan na suroopu wa dore desu ka?] Which are the easiest runs?; このスロープはどのくらい難しいですか? [kono suroopu wa dono kurai muzukashii desu ka?] How difficult is this slope?; 身体障害者のためのスロープなどがありますか? [shintai-shougaisha no tame no suroopu nado ga arimasu ka?] Do you provide access for people with disabilities?; 初心者用のスロープはどこですか? [shoshinsha-you no suroopu wa doko desu ka?] Where are the beginners' slopes?

スロット [surotto] n slot

スロットマシン [surottomashin] n fruit machine, slot machine

する [suru] v do; ···させる [...saseru] v let; ···しそうな [...shisou na] adj likely; ···をする [...-o suru] v do; ···する間 [...suru aida] conj while; ···する時まで [...suru toki made] conj till; ···する時は [...suru toki ni] conj when; ···する所に

[...suru tokoro ni] *conj* where; ···するつもりだ [...suru tsumori da] *v* intend to; 今日は何をなさりたいですか? [kyou wa nani o nasaritai desu ka?] **What would you like to do today?**; すぐにしてもらえますか? [sugu ni shite moraemasu ka?] **Can you do it straightaway?**

鋭い [surudoi] *adj* sharp; 観察力の鋭い [kansatsuryoku no surudoi] *adj* observant

スルタナ [surutana] *n* sultana

すす [susu] *n* soot

すすぐ [susugu] *v* rinse; すすぎ [susugi] *n* rinse

勧め [susume] *n* recommendation

勧める [susumeru] *v* recommend

進む [susumu] *v* advance; 先へ進む [saki-e susumu] *v* go ahead; 前へ進む [mae-e susumu] *v* move forward; 次の交差点で右に進んでください [tsugi no kousaten de migi ni susunde kudasai] **Go right at the next junction**; 次の交差点で左に進んでください [tsugi no kousaten de hidari ni susunde kudasai] **Go left at the next junction**; 私の時計は進んでいると思います [watashi no tokei wa susunde iru to omoimasu] **I think my watch is fast**

進んで [susunde] *adv* willingly

スター [sutaa] *n* star (*person*); 映画スター [eigasutaa] *n* film star

スターター [sutaataa] *n* starter; スターターにパスタをいただきます [sutaataa ni pasuta o itadakimasu] **I'd like pasta as a starter**

スタッフ [sutaffu] 販売スタッフ [hanbai sutaffu] *n* sales assistant

スタッグパーティー [sutaggupaateii] *n* stag night

スタイリング [sutairingu] スタイリング用品を売っていますか? [sutairingu youhin o utte imasu ka?] **Do you sell styling products?**

スタイリスト [sutairisuto] *n* stylist

スタイル [sutairu] *n* style; ヘアスタイル [heasutairu] *n* hairdo, hairstyle; このスタイルでお願いします [kono sutairu de o-negai shimasu] **This style, please**; 全く新

しいスタイルにしてください [mattaku atarashii sutairu ni shite kudasai] **I want a completely new look**

スタジアム [sutajiamu] *n* stadium; そのスタジアムにはどうやって行くのですか? [sono sutajiamu ni wa dou-yatte iku no desu ka?] **How do we get to the stadium?**

スタジオ [sutajio] *n* studio

スタジオフラット [sutajiofuratto] *n* studio flat

スタミナ [sutamina] *n* stamina

スタンド [sutando] *n* stands

スタントマン [sutantoman] *n* stuntman

すたれる [sutareru] すたれた [sutareta] *adj* obsolete

ステアリング [sutearingu] *n* steering

ステアリングホイール [sutearinguhoiiru] *n* steering wheel

ステーキ [suteeki] *n* steak

ステープラー [suteepuraa] *n* stapler

ステープル [suteepuru] *n* staple (*wire*); ステープルで留める [suteepuru de todomeru] *v* staple

ステイルメイト [suteirumeito] *n* stalemate

すてきな [sutekina] *adj* nice

ステッカー [sutekkaa] *n* sticker

ステッキ [sutekki] *n* walking stick

ステンドグラス [sutendogurasu] *n* stained glass

ステンレススチール [sutenresusuchiiru] *n* stainless steel

ステレオ [sutereo] *n* stereo

ステレオタイプ [sutereotaipu] *n* stereotype

ステロイド [suteroido] *n* steroid

捨てる [suteru] *v* ditch, throw away; 使い捨ての [tsukaisute no] *adj* disposable; ごみ捨て場 [gomi suteba] *n* dump, rubbish dump

スティック [sutikku] ディップスティック [dippu sutikku] *n* dipstick

ストッキング [sutokkingu] *n* stocking

ストック [sutokku] n ski poles; ストックを借りたいのですが [sutokku o karitai no desu ga] I want to hire ski poles; 料金にはストック代が含まれていますか? [ryoukin ni wa sutokku-dai ga fukumarete imasu ka?] Does the price include poles?

ストップウオッチ [sutoppuuotchi] n stopwatch

ストライキ [sutoraiki] n strike; ストライキ参加者 [sutoraiki sankasha] n striker; ストライキがあったからです [sutoraiki ga atta kara desu] because of a strike

ストライキをする [sutoraiki o suru] strike (suspend work)

ストレイトナー [sutoreitonaa] n straighteners

ストレス [sutoresu] n stress; ストレスの多い [sutoresu no oui] adj stressful; ストレスがたまった [sutoresu ga tamatta] adj stressed

ストリーミング [sutoriimingu] n streaming

ストリート [sutoriito] n street; その街のストリートマップが欲しいのですが [sono machi no sutoriito-mappu ga hoshii no desu ga] I want a street map of the city

ストリッパー [sutorippaa] n stripper

ストリップ [sutorippu] n strip

スツール [sutsuuru] n stool

吸う [suu] v suck; 鼻で吸う [hana de suu] v sniff

スーダン [suudan] n Sudan; スーダン人 [suudanjin] n Sudanese person; スーダンの [suudan no] adj Sudanese

スウェーデン [suueeden] n Sweden; スウェーデン人 [suueedenjin] n Swede, Swedish person; スウェーデンの [suueeden no] adj Swedish

スウェーデンカブ [suueedenkabu] n swede

数分 [suufun] ここで数分待ってもらえますか? [koko de suu-fun matte moraemasu ka?] Can you wait here for a few minutes?

数学 [suugaku] n mathematics, maths; 数学の [suugaku no] adj mathematical

数字 [suuji] n figure

数個 [suuko] pron several

スーパー [suupaa] adj super; スーパー [suupaa] n supermarket; 郊外の大型スーパー [kougai no ougata suupaa] n hypermarket

スーパーマーケット [suupaamaaketto] n supermarket; 私はスーパーマーケットをさがしています [watashi wa suupaamaaketto o sagashite imasu] I need to find a supermarket

スープ [suupu] n soup; 固形スープの素 [kokei suupu no moto] n stock cube; 今日のおすすめスープは何ですか? [kyou no osusume suupu wa nan desu ka?] What is the soup of the day?

スーツ [suutsu] n suit

スーツケース [suutsukeesu] n suitcase

スワジランド [suwajirando] n Swaziland

すわり心地 [suwarigokochi] すわり心地がよくありません [suwari-gokochi ga yoku arimasen] The seat is uncomfy

座る [suwaru] v sit; どこに座ればいいですか? [doko ni suwareba ii desu ka?] Where can I sit down?; どこか座れる場所がありますか? [doko-ka suwareru basho ga arimasu ka?] Is there somewhere I can sit down?; ここに座ってもいいですか? [koko ni suwatte mo ii desu ka?] Can I sit here?

錫 [suzu] n tin

スズメ [suzume] n sparrow

スズメバチ [suzumebachi] n wasp

涼しい [suzushii] adj cool, cold

た

[taberareru] *adj* edible; 何を召し上がりますか? [nani o meshiagarimasu ka?] **What would you like to eat?**; テラスで食べられますか? [terasu de taberaremasu ka?] **Can I eat on the terrace?**; 私は肉を食べません [watashi wa niku o tabemasen] **I don't eat meat**

食付き [tabetsuki] 2食付きはいくらですか? [ni-shoku tsuki wa ikura desu ka?] **How much is half board?**; 3食付きはいくらですか? [san-shoku tsuki wa ikura desu ka?] **How much is full board?**

旅 [tabi] 苦難に満ちた旅 [kunan ni michita tabi] *n* trek; 苦難に耐えつつ旅をする [kunan ni taetsutsu tabi-o suru] *v* trek

旅立つ [tabidatsu] *v* start off

たびたび [tabitabi] たびたびの [tabitabi no] *adj* frequent

多分 [tabun] *adv* probably

タブレット [taburetto] *n* tablet (*computer*)

タブー [tabuu] *n* taboo; タブーとなっている [tabuu to natte iru] *adj* taboo

タッチパッド [tatchipaddo] *n* touch pad

タッチライン [tatchirain] *n* touchline

立ち上がる [tachiagaru] *v* rise

立ち直る [tachinaoru] *v* get over

立ち往生 [tachioujou] 立ち往生した [tachioujou shita] *adj* stranded

立ち去る [tachisaru] *v* clear off, go away

立ち退く [tachishirizoku] *v* vacate

太刀打ち [tachiuchi] 太刀打ちできない [tachiuchi dekinai] *adj* unbeatable

立ち寄る [tachiyoru] 立ち寄ること [tachiyoru koto] *n* stopover

ただ [tada] ただ一人の [tada hitori no] *adj* alone

正しい [tadashii] *adj* correct, right; 正しく [tadashiku] *adv* right

正しく [tadashiku] *adv* correctly, rightly

たどりなおす [tadorinaosu] *v* retrace

たどる [tadoru] 跡をたどって見つけ出す [ato-o tadotte mitsukedasu] *v* track down

耐える [taeru] 耐えられない [taerarenai] *adj* intolerant, unbearable

ターミナル [taaminaru] *n* terminal; バスターミナル [basutaaminaru] *n* bus station

タールマカダム [taarumakadamu] *n* tarmac

タータン [taatan] タータンの [taatan no] *adj* tartan

束 [taba] *n* (ひとまとめ) bunch

タバコ [tabako] *n* tobacco; タバコ屋 [tabakoya] *n* tobacconist's

食物 [tabemono] 食物を与える [tabemono o ataeru] *v* feed

食べ物 [tabemono] *n* food; 食べ物に香辛料がききすぎています [tabemono ni koushinryou ga kiki-sugite imasu] **The food is too spicy**; 食べ物に塩味がききすぎています [tabemono ni shioaji ga kiki-sugite imasu] **The food is too salty**; 食べ物はありますか? [tabemono wa arimasu ka?] **Do you have food?**; 食べ物がとても脂っこいです [tabemono ga totemo aburakkoi desu] **The food is very greasy**; 食べ物が熱すぎます [tabemono ga atsu-sugimasu] **The food is too hot**; 食べ物が冷たすぎます [tabemono ga tsumeta-sugimasu] **The food is too cold**

食べ残し [tabenokoshi] *n* leftovers

食べる [taberu] *v* eat; 食べられる

絶えず [taezu] v constantly; 絶えず続く [taezu tsuzuku] adj constant

多額 [tagaku] 多額の賞金 [tagaku no shoukin] n jackpot

耕す [tagayasu] v plough

多発性硬化症 [tahatsusei koukashou] n multiple sclerosis, MS

タヒチ [tahichi] n Tahiti

多方面 [tahoumen] 多方面の [tahoumen no] adj versatile

隊 [tai] n group; 捜索隊 [sousakutai] n search party; 沿岸警備隊 [engankeibitai] n coastguard

タイ [tai] n (国) Thailand; タイ人 [taijin] n Thai (person); タイの [tai no] adj Thai; タイ語 [taigo] n Thai (language)

体調 [taichou] 体調が悪い [taichou ga warui] adj poorly

怠惰 [taida] 怠惰な [taida na] adj lazy

態度 [taido] n attitude, behaviour

大義 [taigi] n cause (ideals)

大破 [taiha] n wreck; 大破する [taiha suru] v wreck

太平洋 [taiheiyou] n Pacific

大変 [taihen] adv extremely; 大変申し訳ありません、規則を知りませんでした [taihen moushiwake arimasen, kisoku o shirimasen deshita] I'm very sorry, I didn't know the regulations

待避 [taihi] 待避場所 [taihi basho] n layby

堆肥 [taihi] n manure

逮捕 [taiho] n arrest; 逮捕する [taiho suru] v arrest

退院 [taiin] 私はいつ退院できますか？ [watashi wa itsu taiin dekimasu ka?] When will I be discharged?; 彼はいつ退院できますか？ [kare wa itsu taiin dekimasu ka?] When will he be discharged?

胎児 [taiji] n foetus

体重 [taijuu] n body weight; あなたの体重はどのくらいありますか？ [anata no taijuu wa dono kurai arimasu ka?] How much do you weigh?

対角 [taikaku] 対角の [taikaku no] adj diagonal

体系 [taikei] 体系的な [taikeiteki na] adj systematic; 神話体系 [shinwa taikei] n mythology

体刑 [taikei] n corporal punishment

体験 [taiken] 苦しい体験 [kurushii taiken] n ordeal; 労働体験 [roudou taiken] n work experience

大気 [taiki] n atmosphere

大金 [taikin] n fortune

退屈 [taikutsu] n boredom; 退屈な [taikutsu na] adj boring; 退屈した [taikutsu shita] adj bored

退去 [taikyo] 国外退去させる [kokugai taikyo saseru] v deport

大麻 [taima] n cannabis

タイマー [taimaa] n timer

怠慢 [taiman] n neglect

タイム [taimu] n thyme

耐熱 [tainetsu] オーブン耐熱性の [oobun tainetsusei no] adj ovenproof

タイピスト [taipisuto] n typist

タイプ [taipu] タイプする [taipu suru] v type

タイプライター [taipuraitaa] n typewriter

平 [taira] 平らな [taira na] adj flat

平らな [taira na] adj even

平なべ [taira nabe] n pan

平皿 [taira sara] n plate

大陸 [tairiku] n continent; 南極大陸 [nankyoku tairiku] n Antarctic

タイル [tairu] n tile; タイルを張った [tairu-o hatta] adj tiled

大量 [tairyou] n mass (amount)

大佐 [taisa] n colonel

大西洋 [taiseiyou] n Atlantic

代謝 [taisha] n metabolism

貸借 [taishaku] 貸借対照表 [taishakutaishouhyou] n balance sheet

大使 [taishi] n ambassador

大使館 [taishikan] n embassy; 私は大使

館に電話したいのですが [watashi wa taishikan ni denwa shitai no desu ga] I'd like to phone my embassy; 私は大使館に電話をしなければなりません [watashi wa taishikan ni denwa o shinakereba narimasen] I need to call my embassy

対処 [taisho] うまく対処する [umaku taisho suru] v cope (with)

退職 [taishoku] n retirement; 退職した [taishoku shita] adj retired; 退職する [taishoku suru] v retire

対称 [taishou] 左右対称の [sayuu taishou no] adj symmetrical

体操 [taisou] n gymnastics; 体操家 [taisouka] n gymnast

たいてい [taitei] adv mostly

タイツ [taitsu] n tights

対話 [taiwa] n dialogue

台湾 [taiwan] n Taiwan; 台湾人 [taiwanjin] n Taiwanese (person); 台湾の [taiwan no] adj Taiwanese

タイヤ [taiya] n tyre; タイヤがパンクしています [taiya ga panku shite imasu] I've a flat tyre; タイヤがパンクしました [taiya ga panku shimashita] I have a flat tyre; タイヤが破裂しました [taiya ga haretsu shimashita] The tyre has burst; タイヤを点検してもらえますか? [taiya o tenken shite moraemasu ka?] Can you check the tyres, please?

タイヤ圧 [taiyaatsu] n tyre pressure; 適正なタイヤ圧はどのくらいですか? [tekisei na taiyaatsu wa dono kurai desu ka?] What should the tyre pressure be?

太陽 [taiyou] n sun; 太陽の [taiyou no] adj solar; 太陽エネルギー [taiyou enerugii] n solar power; 太陽系 [taiyoukei] n solar system

滞在 [taizai] n stay; 私はホテルに滞在しています [watashi wa hoteru ni taizai shite imasu] I'm staying at a hotel

タジキスタン [tajikisutan] n Tajikistan

高い [takai] adj (高低) high, (高低) tall

高く [takaku] adv high

高まる [takamaru] 高まり [takamari] n surge

高める [takameru] v boost

宝くじ [takarakuji] n lottery

高さ [takasa] n height

竹 [take] n bamboo

滝 [taki] n waterfall; 大きな滝 [ouki na taki] n cataract (waterfall)

タキシード [takishiido] n tuxedo

タックル [takkuru] n tackle

卓球 [takkyuu] n table tennis

凧 [tako] n kite

タコ [tako] n (動物) octopus

多国籍 [takokuseki] 多国籍企業 [takokuseki kigyou] n multinational; 多国籍の [takokuseki no] adj multinational

宅配 [takuhai] これを宅配便で送りたいのですが [kore o takuhai-bin de okuritai no desu ga] I want to send this by courier

託児 [takuji] 託児所 [takujisho] n crèche; 託児サービスはありますか? [takuji saabisu wa arimasu ka?] Is there a child-minding service?

たくましい [takumashii] 筋骨たくましい [kinkotsu takumashii] adj muscular

巧む [takumu] 巧みに扱う [takumi ni atsukau] v manipulate

たくらむ [takura-mu] v plot, conspire

たくさん [takusan] pron much

タクシー [takushii] n cab, taxi; タクシー乗り場 [takushii noriba] n taxi rank; タクシー運転手 [takushii untenshu] n taxi driver; 小型タクシー [kogata takushii] n minicab; どこでタクシーに乗れますか? [doko de takushii ni noremasu ka?] Where can I get a taxi?; タクシー乗り場はどこですか? [takushii-noriba wa doko desu ka?] Where is the taxi stand?; タクシーを呼んでください [takushii o yonde kudasai] Please order me a taxi; 街までのタクシー料金はいくらですか? [machi made no takushii-ryoukin wa ikura desu ka?] How much is the taxi fare into town?; 荷物をタクシーに運んでください [nimotsu o takushii ni hakonde kudasai] Please take my luggage to a taxi; 私はタクシーにかばんを置き忘れました [watashi wa takushii ni kaban o okiwasuremashita] **I left my bags in the taxi**; 私はタクシーが必要です [watashi wa takushii ga hitsuyou desu] **I need a taxi**; 私たちはタクシーを相乗りすることもできます [watashi-tachi wa takushii o ainori suru koto mo dekimasu] **We could share a taxi**; 八時にタクシーを呼んでください [hachi-ji ni takushii o yonde kudasai] **Please order me a taxi for 8 o'clock**

蓄え [takuwae] n reserve (retention)

蓄える [takuwaeru] v save up, store

卵 [tamago] n egg; ゆで卵 [yudetamago] n boiled egg; 復活祭の卵 [fukkatsusai no tamago] n Easter egg; 卵の白身 [tamago no shiromi] n egg white; 卵の黄身 [tamago no kimi] n egg yolk, yolk; 卵を使わずに食事を用意していただけますか? [tamago o tsukawazu ni shokuji o youi shite itadakemasu ka?] **Could you prepare a meal without eggs?**

タマネギ [tamanegi] n onion

たまる [tamaru] ストレスがたまった [sutoresu ga tamatta] adj stressed

魂 [tamashii] n soul

ため [tame] ・・・のために [...no tame ni] prep (関係) for, (原因) due to; ・・・するために [...suru tame ni] conj so (that)

ため息 [tameiki] n sigh; ため息をつく [tameiki o tsuku] v sigh

ためらう [tamerau] v hesitate

試しす [tameshi su] 試してみる [tameshite miru] v try out

試す [tamesu] v test; 試してみてもいいですか? [tameshite mite mo ii desu ka?] **Can I test it, please?**

単 [tan] 単に [tan ni] adv only

棚 [tana] n shelf; 手荷物置き棚 [tenimotsu okidana] n luggage rack; 食器棚 [shokkidana] n dresser, sideboard

単調 [tanchou] 単調な [tanchou na] adj monotonous

タンデム [tandemu] タンデム自転車 [tandemu jitensha] n tandem

単独 [tandoku] 単独の [tandoku no] adj separate

種 [tane] n (植物) seed

嘆願 [tangan] 嘆願書 [tangansho] n petition

単語 [tango] n word

谷間 [taniai] n valley

単一体 [tan'itsutai] n unit

タンジェリン [tanjierin] n tangerine

誕生 [tanjou] n birth

誕生日 [tanjoubi] n birthday; お誕生日おめでとう! [o-tanjoubi omedetou!] **Happy birthday!**

担架 [tanka] n stretcher

タンカー [tankaa] n tanker

探検 [tanken] n expedition; 探検家 [tankenka] n explorer

短気 [tanki] n impatience

炭鉱 [tankou] n colliery

炭坑 [tankou] 炭坑労働者 [tankou roudousha] n miner

タンク [tanku] n tank (large container)

胆嚢 [tannou] n gall bladder

頼み [tanomi] n request

頼む [tanomu] v request

楽しい [tanoshii] adj delightful, enjoyable, fun, pleasant; 楽しく遊ぶ [tanoshiku asobu] v have fun

楽しみ [tanoshimi] n fun, pleasure; 歓楽街での夜の楽しみ [kanrakugai deno yoru no tanoshimi] n nightlife

楽む [tanoshimu] 楽しませる [tanoshimaseru] v amuse

楽しむ [tanoshimu] v enjoy; 楽しませる [tanoshimaseru] v entertain; お食事をお楽しみください! [o-shokuji o o-tanoshimi kudasai!] **Enjoy your meal!**

蛋白質 [tanpakushitsu] n protein

短篇 [tanpen] 短篇小説 [tanpen shousetsu] n short story

タンポン [tanpon] n tampon

タンポポ [tanpopo] n dandelion

炭酸 [tansan] 炭酸なしミネラルウォーターのボトル1本 [tansan-nashi mineraru-wootaa no botoru ippon] **a** bottle of still mineral water

炭酸 [tansan] 炭酸水 [tansansui] n sparkling water

胆石 [tanseki] n gallstone

炭素 [tanso] n carbon

たんす [tansu] 整理だんす [seiridansu] n chest of drawers

淡水魚 [tansuigyo] n freshwater fish

炭水化物 [tansuikabutsu] n carbohydrate

単数 [tansuu] n singular

タンザニア [tanzania] n Tanzania; タンザニア人 [tanzaniajin] n Tanzanian (person); タンザニアの [tanzania no] adj Tanzanian

鍛造 [tanzou] 鍛造する [tanzou suru] v forge

倒れる [taoreru] v fall down

タオル [taoru] n towel; バスタオル [basutaoru] n bath towel; 浴用タオル [yokuyou taoru] n flannel; 洗面用タオル [senmen you taoru] n face cloth; タオルが補充されていません [taoru ga hojuu sarete imasen] The towels have run out; タオルをもっと持ってきてください [taoru o motto motte kite kudasai] Please bring me more towels; タオルを貸していただけますか? [taoru o kashite itadakemasu ka?] Could you lend me a towel?

倒す [taosu] 打ち倒す [uchitaosu] v knock down

タップダンス [tappudansu] n tap-dancing

たっぷり [tappuri] n plenty

タラ [tara] n cod

タラゴン [taragon] n tarragon

樽 [taru] n barrel

タルカムパウダー [tarukamupaudaa] n talcum powder

たるむ [tarumu] たるんだ [tarunda] adj flabby

タルト [taruto] n tart

確かに [tashika ni] adv certainly, surely

達成 [tassei] n achievement; 達成する [tassei suru] v achieve

足す [tasu] v add

助ける [tasukeru] v help; すぐに助けを呼んで! [sugu ni tasuke o yonde!] Fetch help quickly!; 助けていただけますか? [tasukete itadakemasu ka?] Can you help me, please?; 助けてもらえますか? [tasukete moraemasu ka?] Can you help me?; 助けて! [tasukete] Help!

助けて! [tasukete] excl help!

タスマニア [tasumania] n Tasmania

多数 [tasuu] n host (multitude) ▷ pron many; 多数の [tasuu no] adj numerous

戦い [tatakai] n fight, fighting

戦う [tatakau] v fight

たたき切る [tatakikiru] v chop, hack; たたき切ること [tatakikiru koto] n chop

たたく [tataku] v knock, knock (on the door etc.); たたくこと [tataku koto] n knock; 軽くたたくこと [karuku tataku koto] n tap

盾 [tate] n shield

建具 [tategu] 建具屋 [tateguya] n joiner

建物 [tatemono] n building; 土地建物 [tochi tatemono] n premises

立てる [tateru] 腹を立てた [hara-o tateta] adj mad (angry)

建てる [tateru] v build, put up

たとえば [tatoeba] adv for example

立つ [tatsu] v stand; ・・・の先頭に立つ [... no sentou ni tatsu] v head

断つ [tatsu] 接続を断つ [setsuzoku-o tatsu] v disconnect

竜巻 [tatsumaki] n tornado

たった一つ [tatta hitotsu] たった一つの [tatta hitotsu no] adj single

タウンホール [taunhooru] n town hall

たわごと [tawagoto] たわごとを並べる [tawagoto-o naraberu] v waffle

戯れ [tawamure] n prank

頼る [tayoru] v resort to; ・・・に頼る [...ni tayoru] v count on

たよる [tayoru] ・・・にたよって暮らす [...ni tayotte kurasu] v live on

多様 [tayou] 多様性 [tayousei] n variety

手綱 [tazuna] n reins

訪ねる [tazuneru] v visit; 私たちは・・・を訪れたいのですが [watashi-tachi wa ... o otozuretai no desu ga] We'd like to visit...; 友人を訪ねるために来ました [yuujin o tazuneru tame ni kimashita] I'm here visiting friends

尋ねる [tazuneru] v ask, inquire, query

手 [te] n hand; 手に持つ [te ni motsu] v hold; 手に入れる [te ni ireru] v obtain; 手を振る [te o furu] v wave; 話し手 [hanashite] n teller; どこで手を洗えばいいのですか? [doko de te o araeba ii no desu ka?] Where can I wash my hands?

手当たり次第 [teatarishidai] 手当たり次第の [teatari shidai no] adj random

手当 [teate] 失業手当 [shitsugyouteate] n dole

手当て [teate] 病気休暇中の手当て [byouki kyuukachuu no teate] n sick pay

手放す [tebanasu] ・・・を手放す [...-o tebanasu] v part with

手袋 [tebukuro] n glove; ゴム手袋 [gomu tebukuro] n rubber gloves

手帳 [techou] システム手帳 [shisutemu techou] n personal organizer

テディーベア [tedeiibea] n teddy bear

テーブル [teeburu] n table (furniture); コーヒーテーブル [koohii teeburu] n coffee table; ベッドサイドテーブル [beddosaido teeburu] n bedside table; 今晩九時にテーブルを予約しました [konban ku-ji ni teeburu o yoyaku shimashita] The table is booked for nine o'clock this evening; 今晩三人用のテーブルを予約したいのですが [konban sannin-you no teeburu o yoyaku shitai no desu ga] I'd like to book a table for three people for tonight; 明日の晩二人用のテーブルを予約したいのですが [asu no ban futari-you no teeburu o yoyaku shitai no desu ga] I'd like to book a table for two people for tomorrow night; 四人用のテーブルをお願いします [yonin-you no teeburu o o-negai shimasu] A table for four people, please

テーブルチャージ [teeburuchaaji] テーブルチャージがかかりますか? [teeburu-chaaji ga kakarimasu ka?] Is there a cover charge?

テーブルクロス [teeburukurosu] n tablecloth

テーブルスプーン [teeburusupuun] n tablespoon

テーブルワイン [teeburuwain] n table wine

テークアウト [teekuauto] n takeaway

テーマ [teema] n theme

テーマパーク [teemapaaku] n theme park

テープ [teepu] n tape; テープに記録する [teepu ni kiroku suru] v tape; このビデオカメラ用のテープをいただけますか? [kono bideo-kamera-you no teepu o itadakemasu ka?] Can I have a tape for this video camera, please?

テープレコーダー [teepurekoudaa] n tape recorder

テーラー [teeraa] n tailor

手がかり [tegakari] n clue

手書き [tegaki] n handwriting

手紙 [tegami] n letter (message); この手紙を送りたいのですが [kono tegami o okuritai no desu ga] I'd like to send this letter

手ごろな [tegoro na] adj affordable

手配 [tehai] n arrangement; 手配する [tehai suru] v arrange

低 [tei] 低アルコールの [tei arukooru no] adj low-alcohol; 低脂肪の [teishibou no] adj low-fat

提案 [teian] n proposal, suggestion; 提案する [teian suru] v propose, suggest

低木 [teiboku] n bush, shrub

堤防 [teibou] n embankment

停電 [teiden] n power cut

程度 [teido] n degree

庭園 [teien] n garden; 私たちがその庭園を訪れることはできますか? [watashi-tachi ga sono teien o otozureru koto wa dekimasu ka?] Can we visit the gardens?

定義 [teigi] n definition; 定義する [teigi suru] v define

停泊 [teihaku] n 停泊させる [teihaku saseru] v moor

提携 [teikei] n alliance; 提携者 [teikeisha] n associate

定期 [teiki] n routine; 定期便 [teikibin] n scheduled flight; 定期購読 [teiki koudoku] n subscription; 定期船 [teikisen] n liner; 定期的な [teikiteki na] adj regular; 定期的に [teikiteki ni] adv regularly; 定期往復便 [teiki oufuku bin] n shuttle; 定期券 [teikiken] n season ticket

帝国 [teikoku] n empire

抵抗 [teikou] n resistance; 抵抗する [teikou suru] v resist

提供 [teikyou] n offer; サービスを提供する [saabisu-o teikyou suru] v service; 提供する [teikyou suru] v offer

丁寧 [teinei] n politeness

丁寧な [teinei na] adj polite

丁寧に [teinei ni] adv politely

定年 [teinen] 私は定年退職しています [watashi wa teinen-taishoku shite imasu] I'm retired

低温 [teion] 低温殺菌した [teion sakkin shita] adj pasteurized

停留所 [teiryuusho] バス停 [basutei] n bus stop

偵察 [teisatsu] 偵察兵 [teisatsuhei] n scout

訂正 [teisei] n correction; 訂正する [teisei suru] v correct

停戦 [teisen] n ceasefire

停車 [teisha] ···に停車しますか? [...ni teisha shimasu ka?] Do we stop at...?

停止 [teishi] n halt; 一時停止 [ichiji teishi] n suspension

定食 [teishoku] n set menu

提唱 [teishou] 提唱する [teishou suru] v put forward

邸宅 [teitaku] 大邸宅 [daiteitaku] n stately home, villa

蹄鉄 [teitetsu] n horseshoe

抵当 [teitou] n mortgage; 抵当に入れる [teitou ni ireru] v mortgage

低俗 [teizoku] 低俗な [teizoku na] adj vulgar

手品 [tejina] n sleight of hand

手品師 [tejinashi] n conjurer, juggler

手錠 [tejou] n handcuffs

敵 [teki] n enemy; 敵にまわす [teki ni mawasu] v antagonize

適度 [tekido] n moderation; 適度の [tekido no] adj moderate

適合 [tekigou] 適合させる [tekigou saseru] v adapt

敵意 [tekii] 敵意のある [teki-i no aru] adj hostile

的な [teki na] 活動的な [katsudouteki na] adj dynamic

適切 [tekisetsu] 適切な [tekisetsu na] adj appropriate, suitable; 適切に [tekisetsu ni] adv properly

適切な [tekisetsu na] adj proper

適する [teki suru] v fit; 適した [tekishita] adj fit

テキストメッセージ [tekisutomesseeji] n text message; テキストメッセージを送る [tekisuto messeeji-o okuru] v text

敵対 [tekitai] 敵対者 [tekitaisha] n adversary, opponent

摘要 [tekiyou] n syllabus

手首 [tekubi] n wrist

テクノポップ [tekunopoppu] n techno music

点 [ten] n (符号) dot; 点を取る [ten-o toru] v score

天秤 [tenbin] n scales

天秤座 [tenbinza] n Libra

天国 [tengoku] n heaven

手荷物 [tenimotsu] n baggage, hand luggage, luggage; 手荷物一時預かり所 [tenimotsu ichiji azukarisho] n left-luggage office; 手荷物カート [tenimotsu kaato] n luggage trolley; 手荷物置き棚 [tenimotsu okidana] n luggage rack; 手荷物受取所 [tenimotsu uketorisho] n baggage reclaim; 無料手荷物許容量 [muryou tenimotsu kyoyouryou] n baggage allowance; 預けた手荷物 [azuketa tenimotsu] n left-luggage; 手荷物に保険をかけられますか? [tenimotsu ni hoken o kakeraremasu ka?] Can I insure my luggage?; 手荷物のチェックインはどこでするのですか? [tenimotsu no chekku-in wa doko de suru no desu ka?] Where do I check in my luggage?; 無料手荷物許容量はどう規定されていますか? [muryou-tenimotsu-kyoyouryou wa dou kitei sarete imasu ka?] What is the baggage allowance?; 私の手荷物が着いていません [watashi no tenimotsu ga tsuite imasen] My luggage hasn't arrived; 私の手荷物が破損しています [watashi no tenimotsu ga hason shite imasu] My luggage has been damaged; 私の手荷物が紛失しました [watashi no tenimotsu ga funshitsu shimashita] My luggage has been lost; 私たちの手荷物が着いていません [watashi-tachi no tenimotsu ga tsuite imasen] Our luggage has not arrived; ・・・からのフライトの手荷物はどこですか? [... kara no furaito no tenimotsu wa doko desu ka?] Where is the luggage for the flight from...?

店員 [ten-in] n salesperson; 女性店員 [josei ten'in] n saleswoman

テニス [tenisu] n tennis; テニス選手 [tenisusenshu] n tennis player; どこでテニスができますか? [doko de tenisu ga dekimasu ka?] Where can I play tennis?; 私たちはテニスがしたいのですが [watashi-tachi wa tenisu ga shitai no desu ga] We'd like to play tennis

テニスコート [tenisukouto] n tennis court; テニスコートを借りるのはいくらですか? [tenisu-kooto o kariru no wa ikura desu ka?] How much is it to hire a tennis court?

テニスラケット [tenisuraketto] n tennis racket

手に取る [te ni toru] v take

展示 [tenji] n display, exhibition, showing; 展示する [tenji suru] v display

天井 [tenjou] n ceiling

点火 [tenka] 点火装置 [tenkasouchi] n ignition

添加 [tenka] 添加剤 [tenkazai] n additive

癲癇 [tenkan] 癲癇の発作 [tenkan no hossa] n epileptic fit; 癲癇患者 [tenkan kanja] n epileptic

転換 [tenkan] 方向転換する [houkoutenkan suru] v turn round, turn around

典型 [tenkei] 典型的な [tenkeiteki na] adj classic, typical

点検 [tenken] n inspection; タイヤを点検してもらえますか? [taiya o tenken shite moraemasu ka?] Can you check the tyres, please?; 空気圧を点検してもらえますか? [kuukiatsu o tenken shite moraemasu ka?] Can you check the air, please?; 冷却水を点検してもらえますか? [reikyakusui o tenken shite moraemasu ka?] Can you check the water, please?

天気 [tenki] n weather; 天気予報 [tenkiyohou] n forecast, weather forecast; なんてひどい天気でしょう! [nante hidoi tenki deshou!] What awful weather!; 明日はどんな天気でしょう? [asu wa donna tenki deshou?] What will the weather be like tomorrow?; 天気予報はどうですか? [tenki-yohou wa dou desu ka?] What's the weather forecast?; 天気は変わりますか? [tenki wa kawarimasu ka?] Is the weather going to change?; 天気がこのまま続いてくれるといいですね [tenki ga kono-mama tsuzuite kureru to ii desu ne] I hope the weather stays like this; 天気がもち直すといいですね [tenki ga mochinaosu to ii desu ne] I hope the weather improves

点呼 [tenko] n roll call

転居 [tenkyo] ・・・に転居する [...ni tenkyo suru] v move in

天文学 [tenmongaku] n astronomy

天然 [tennen] 天然ガス [tennengasu] n natural gas; 天然資源 [tennenshigen] n natural resources

手のひら [tenohira] n palm (part of hand)

テノール [tenouru] n tenor

テンピンボウリング [tenpinbouringu] n tenpin bowling

転覆 [tenpuku] 転覆する [tenpuku suru] v capsize

天才 [tensai] n genius

天使 [tenshi] n angel

転送 [tensou] 転送する [tensou suru] v forward

テント [tento] n tent; ここにテントを張ってもいいですか? [koko ni tento o hatte mo ii desu ka?] Can we pitch our tent here?; テント一つにつき1週間でいくらですか? [tento hitotsu ni tsuki isshuukan de ikura desu ka?] How much is it per week for a tent?; テント一つにつき一晩でいくらですか? [tento hitotsu ni tsuki hitoban de ikura desu ka?] How much is it per night for a tent?; テント用のサイトが欲しいのですが [tento-you no saito ga hoshii no desu ga] We'd like a site for a tent

テントペグ [tentopegu] n tent peg

テントポール [tentopooru] n tent pole

テントウムシ [tentoumushi] n ladybird

手押し車 [teoshiguruma] n wheelbarrow

テラス [terasu] n terrace; テラスで食べられますか? [terasu de taberaremasu ka?] Can I eat on the terrace?

テラスハウス [terasuhausu] n terrace

テレビ [terebi] n television, telly, TV; ケーブルテレビ [keeburu terebi] n cable television; カラーテレビ [karaaterebi] n colour television; リアリティーテレビ番組 [riaritii terebi bangumi] n reality TV; テレビ電話 [terebi denwa] n videophone; デジタルテレビ [dejitaru terebi] n digital television; 閉回路テレビ [heikairo terebi] n CCTV; その部屋にテレビはありますか? [sono heya ni terebi wa arimasu ka?] Does the room have a TV?; テレビはどこですか? [terebi wa doko desu ka?] Where is the television?

テレビラウンジ [terebiraunji] n television lounge; テレビラウンジはありますか? [terebi-raunji wa arimasu ka?] Is there a television lounge?

テレホンカード [terehon kaado] n phonecard; どこでテレホンカードを買えますか? [doko de terehon-kaado o kaemasu ka?] Where can I buy a phonecard?; テレホンカードをください [terehon-kaado o kudasai] A phonecard, please

テリア [teria] n terrier

テロリスト [terorisuto] n terrorist; テロリストによる攻撃 [terorisuto niyoru kougeki] n terrorist attack

テロリズム [terorizumu] n terrorism

手探り [tesaguri] 手探りする [tesaguri suru] v grope

手製 [tesei] 手製の [tesei no] adj handmade

鉄線 [tessen] 有刺鉄線 [yuushitessen] n barbed wire

手すり [tesuri] n banister, rail, railings

手数料 [tesuuryou] n handling fee; 銀行の手数料 [ginkou no tesuuryou] n bank charges; 手数料はいくらですか? [tesuuryou wa ikura desu ka?] What's the commission?; 手数料がかかりますか? [tesuuryou ga kakarimasu ka?] Do you charge commission?

鉄 [tetsu] n iron

手伝う [tetsudau] v help; 私が乗るのを手伝っていただけますか? [watashi ga noru no o tetsudatte itadakemasu ka?] Can you help me get on, please?

鉄道 [tetsudou] n rail, railway; 鉄道駅 [tetsudoueki] n railway station; 鉄道割引証 [tetsudou waribikishou] n railcard; 鉄道駅へ行く一番よい方法は何ですか? [tetsudou-eki e iku ichiban yoi houhou wa nan desu ka?] What's the best way to get to the railway station?

哲学 [tetsugaku] n philosophy

徹底 [tettei] 徹底的な [tetteiteki na] adj thorough; 徹底的に [tetteiteki ni] adv thoroughly

鉄塔 [tettou] n pylon

手渡す [tewatasu] v hand

ティー [tii] n (ゴルフ) tee

ティーバッグ [tiibaggu] n tea bag

ティーカップ [tiikappu] n teacup

ティーンエージャー [tiineejaa] n teenager

ティーポット [tiipotto] n teapot

Tシャツ [tiishatsu] n tee-shirt, T-shirt

ティースプーン [tiisupuun] n teaspoon

ティータイム [tiitaimu] n teatime

・・・と・・・ [...to...] conj and

飛ばす [tobasu] 投げ飛ばす [nagetobasu] v fling

跳びはねる [tobihaneru] v jump

飛込台 [tobikomidai] n diving board

飛び込む [tobikomu] v dive; 飛び込み [tobikomi] n dive, diving

トボガン [tobogan] n toboggan, tobogganing

飛ぶ [tobu] v fly; 飛び跳ねる [tobihaneru] v skip; 飛び去る [tobisaru] v fly away

土地 [tochi] n land; 土地建物 [tochi tatemono] n premises; 何かこの土地のものを試したいのですが [nani ka kono tochi no mono o tameshitai no desu ga] I'd like to try something local, please

・・・と違って [...tochigatte] prep unlike

土地付き [tochitsuki] 土地付き一戸建て家屋 [tochi tsuki ikkodate kaoku] n detached house

途中 [tochuu] adv on the way; 私たちは・・・へ向かう途中です [watashi-tachi wa ... e mukau tochuu desu] We are on our way to...

戸棚 [todana] n cupboard

届け [todoke] 病欠届け [byouketsu todoke] n sick note

届け出る [todokede ru] 私は盗難の届出をしたいのです [watashi wa tounan no todokede o shitai no desu] I want to report a theft; 私たちはそれを警察に届け出なければなりません [watashi-tachi wa sore o keisatsu ni todokedenakereba narimasen] We will have to report it to the police

届く [todoku] v be received; 私のEメールが届きましたか? [watashi no ii-meeru ga todokimashita ka?] Did you get my email?

とどまる [todomaru] v stay

留める [todomeru] ステープルで留める [suteepuru de todomeru] v staple

トフィー [tofii] n toffee

とげ [toge] n thorn

戸口の上がり段 [toguchi no agaridan] n doorstep

徒歩 [toho] 徒歩旅行 [tohoryokou] n hike

問い合わせ [toiawase] n enquiry, inquiry

問い合わせる [toiawaseru] v enquire

トイレ [toire] n lavatory, loo, toilet; 男性用トイレ [dansei-you toire] n gents'; 女性用トイレ [josei-you toire] n ladies'; トイレはどこですか? [toire wa doko desu ka?] Where are the toilets?; トイレが流れません [toire ga nagaremasen] The toilet won't flush; トイレをお借りできますか? [toire o o-kari dekimasu ka?] Can I use the toilet?; 身体障害者用のトイレはありますか? [shintai-shougaisha-you no toire wa arimasu ka?] Are there any accessible toilets?; 車内にトイレはありますか? [shanai ni toire wa arimasu ka?] Is there a toilet on board?

トイレット [toiretto] トイレットペーパーがありません [toiretto-peepaa ga arimasen] There is no toilet paper

トイレットペーパー [toirettopeepaa] n toilet paper

トイレットペーパーロール [toirettopeepaarooru] n toilet roll

ということ [to iu koto] ・・・ということ [...to iu koto] conj that

トカゲ [tokage] n lizard

とかす [tokasu] 櫛でとかす [kushi de tokasu] v comb

溶かす [tokasu] v dissolve, melt

時計 [tokei] n clock; デジタル時計 [dejitaru tokei] n digital watch; 腕時計 [udedokei] n watch; 目覚まし時計 [mezamashi tokei] n alarm clock

溶ける [tokeru] vi melt

解ける [tokeru] 雪解けしています

[yukidoke shite imasu] **It's thawing**

時 [toki] *n* **time**; ···している時 [...shite iru toki] *conj* **as**; 何時に閉まりますか? [nan-ji ni shimarimasu ka?] **What time do you close?**; 何時までにですか? [nan-ji made ni desu ka?] **By what time?**

とき [toki] すばらしいときを過ごせました [subarashii toki o sugosemashita] **I've had a great time**

時々 [tokidoki] *adv* **sometimes**

時折 [tokiori] *n* **occasionally**; 時折の [tokiori no] *adj* **occasional**

特権 [tokken] *n* **privilege**

所 [tokoro] 案内所 [annaijo] *n* **information office, inquiries office**; 蒸留所 [jouryuujo] *n* **distillery**; 診療所 [shinryoujo] *n* **clinic, infirmary, surgery** (*doctor's*); 託児所 [takujisho] *n* **crèche**; 造船所 [zousenjo] *n* **shipyard**; 避難所 [hinanjo] *n* **refuge, shelter**; ここでの見どころは何があります か? [koko de no midokoro wa nani ga arimasu ka?] **What is there to see here?**

ところ [tokoro] *n* **place**; よいところをご存知 ですか? [yoi tokoro o go-zonji desu ka?] **Do you know a good place to go?**

床屋 [tokoya] *n* **barber**

解く [toku] 荷を解く [ni-o toku] *v* **unpack**; 包装を解く [housou-o toku] *v* **unwrap**; 荷 物を解かなければなりません [nimotsu o tokanakereba narimasen] **I have to unpack**

特別 [tokubetsu] 特別に [tokubetsu ni] *adv* **specially**; 特別の [tokubetsu no] *adj* **particular**; 特別の [tokubetsu no] *adj* **special**; 特別売り出し [tokubetsu uridashi] *n* **special offer**

特徴 [tokuchou] *n* **characteristic**; 特徴的 な [tokuchouteki na] *adj* **distinctive**

特大 [tokudai] 特大の [tokudai no] *adj* **outsize**

得意料理 [tokuiryouri] レストランの得意 料理は何ですか? [resutoran no tokui-ryouri wa nan desu ka?] **What is the house speciality?**

匿名 [tokumei] 匿名の [tokumei no] *adj* **anonymous**

特に [toku ni] *adv* **especially, particularly, specifically**

特質 [tokushitsu] *n* **character**

特定 [tokutei] 特定の [tokutei no] *adj* **specific**

得点 [tokuten] *n* **score** (*in game*)

泊まる [tomaru] *v* **stay**; どちらにお泊まりで すか? [dochira ni o-tomari desu ka?] **Where are you staying?**

止まる [tomaru] *v* **go off, stop**; 私の時計が 止まってしまいました [watashi no tokei ga tomatte shimaimashita] **My watch has stopped**

停まる [tomaru] *v* **stop**; 次はいつ停まりま すか? [tsugi wa itsu tomarimasu ka?] **When do we stop next?**; 電車は···に停ま りますか? [densha wa ... ni tomarimasu ka?] **Does the train stop at...?**

トマト [tomato] *n* **tomato**

トマトソース [tomatosoosu] *n* **tomato sauce**

塗沫 [tomatsu] 塗沫検査 [tomatsu kensa] *n* **smear test**

留め [tome] 靴下留め [kutsushitadome] *n* **suspenders**

留め金 [tomegane] *n* **clasp**

止める [tomeru] *v* **pull up, stop**

停める [tomeru] *v* **stop**; ここで停めてくださ い [koko de tomete kudasai] **Stop here, please**; バスを停めてください [basu o tomete kudasai] **Please stop the bus**

富くじ [tomikuji] *n* **raffle**

友だち [tomodachi] *n* **friend, pal**; 私は友 だちと来ています [watashi wa tomodachi to kite imasu] **I'm here with my friends**

伴う [tomonau] *v* **involve**

灯 [tomoshibi] 故障警告灯 [koshou keikokutou] *n* **hazard warning lights**

ともす [tomosu] *v* **light**

富む [tomu] 機知に富んだ [kichi ni tonda] *adj* **witty**; 色彩に富んだ [shikisai ni tonda] *adj* **colourful**

トン [ton] *n* **ton**

トナカイ [tonakai] *n* **reindeer**

隣 [tonari] ···の隣に [...no tonari ni] prep next to

トンボ [tonbo] n dragonfly

とんでもない [tonde mo nai] adj outrageous

トンガ [tonga] n Tonga

とにかく [tonikaku] adv anyhow, anyway

トンネル [tonneru] n tunnel

遠吠えする [tooboe suru] v howl

トーゴ [toogo] n Togo

遠く [tooku] 遠くに [touku ni] adv far; かなり遠いです [kanari tooi desu] It's quite far; 遠くありません [tooku arimasen] It's not far

トークショー [tookushoo] n chat show

とおりに [toorini] 文字どおりに [mojidouri ni] adv literally

通す [toosu] 通してください [tooshite kudasai] Please let me through

トップ [toppu] トップ記事 [toppu kiji] n lead (position)

トップアップカード [toppuappukaado] どこでトップアップカードを買えますか? [doko de toppu-appu-kaado o kaemasu ka?] Where can I buy a top-up card?

突風 [toppuu] n gust

トラ [tora] n tiger

トラベラーズチェック [toraberaazu chekku] n traveller's cheque; このトラベラーズチェックを現金化したいのですが [kono toraberaazu-chekku o genkinka shitai no desu ga] I want to change these traveller's cheques; ここで私のトラベラーズチェックを現金化できますか? [koko de watashi no toraberaazu-chekku o genkinka dekimasu ka?] Can I change my traveller's cheques here?; トラベラーズチェックは使えますか? [toraberaazu-chekku wa tsukaemasu ka?] Do you accept traveller's cheques?; 誰かが私のトラベラーズチェックを盗みました [dare ka ga watashi no toraberaazu-chekku o nusumimashita] Someone's stolen my traveller's cheques

捕える [toraeru] v capture

トラック [torakku] n lorry; トラック運転手 [torakku untenshu] n lorry driver, truck driver; 引越しトラック [hikkoshi torakku] n removal van

トラックスーツ [torakkusuutsu] n tracksuit

トラクター [torakutaa] n tractor

トランジスター [toranjisutaa] n transistor

トランクス [torankusu] n trunks

トランペット [toranpetto] n trumpet

トランポリン [toranporin] n trampoline

トランプ [toranpu] n playing card

トランシーバー [toranshiibaa] n walkie-talkie

トレーニング [toreeningu] n training

トレーニングコース [toreeningukoosu] n training course

トレーニングシューズ [toreeningushuuzu] n trainers

トレーラー [toreeraa] n trailer

トレーラーハウス [toreeraahausu] n caravan; トレーラーハウスキャンプ場 [toreeraa hausu kyanpu jou] n caravan site; ここにトレーラーハウスを駐車してもいいですか? [koko ni toreeraa-hausu o chuusha shite mo ii desu ka?] Can we park our caravan here?; トレーラーハウスのサイトが欲しいのですが [toreeraa-hausu no saito ga hoshii no desu ga] We'd like a site for a caravan

トレース紙 [toreesushi] n tracing paper

トレッキング [torekkingu] n trekking; 私はポニートレッキングに行きたいのですが [watashi wa ponii-torekkingu ni ikitai no desu ga] I'd like to go pony trekking

鳥 [tori] n bird; 鳥インフルエンザ [tori infuruenza] n bird flu; 鳥肌 [torihada] n goose pimples

取り上げる [toriageru] v take up; ···の資格を取り上げる [...no shikaku-o toriageru] v disqualify

取扱所 [toriatsukaijo] 遺失物取扱所 [ishitsubutsu toriatsukaijo] n lost-property office

取り扱う [toriatsukau] *v* handle

取り合わせ [toriawase] 各種取り合わせ [kakushu toriawase] *n* assortment

砦 [toride] *n* fort

取り外す [torihazusu] 取り外せる [torihazuseru] *adj* removable

取引 [torihiki] *n* deal, transaction

取引所 [torihikijo] 証券取引所 [shouken torihikijo] *n* stock exchange

取り交わす [torikawasu] *v* exchange

取り消す [torikesu] *v* cancel, take back; 約束を取り消す [yakusoku-o torikesu] *v* back out

取り壊す [torikowasu] *v* demolish, pull down

取り組む [torikumu] *v* tackle

トリニダード・トバゴ [torinidaado tobago] *n* Trinidad and Tobago

取り付ける [toritsukeru] *v* attach

取りやめる [toriyameru] *v* call off

トロフィー [torofii] *n* trophy

トロンボーン [toronboun] *n* trombone

捕る [toru] 魚を捕る [sakana-o toru] *v* fish

取る [toru] …からヒレ肉を取る [...kara hireniku-o toru] *v* fillet; 連絡を取る [renraku-o toru] *v* contact

トルコ [toruko] *n* Turkey; トルコ人 [torukojin] *n* Turk; トルコの [toruko no] *adj* Turkish; トルコ語 [torukogo] *n* Turkish (language)

歳 [toshi] 私は五十歳です [watashi wa gojus-sai desu] I'm fifty years old; 彼女は十二歳です [kanojo wa juuni-sai desu] She is twelve years old

都市 [toshi] *n* city; 都市計画 [toshikeikaku] *n* town planning

年老いる [toshioiru] 年老いた [toshi oita] *adj* aged

年下 [toshishita] 年下の方の [toshishita no hou no] *adj* younger

…として [...toshite] *prep* as

年取った [toshitotta] *v* old

年上 [toshiue] 年上の [toshiue no] *adj* elder

図書 [tosho] 図書形態 [tosho keitai] *n* format

図書館 [toshokan] *n* library

図書館員 [toshokan-in] *n* librarian

突進 [tosshin] *n* rush; 突進する [tosshin suru] *v* dash

突出 [tosshutsu] 突出する [tosshutsu suru] *v* stand out

とても [totemo] *adv* too

とても大きい [totemo ookii] *adj* mega

十時 [totoki] 十時です [juu-ji desu] It's ten o'clock

整える [totonoeru] *v* trim; 髪を整えてもらえますか? [kami o totonoete moraemasu ka?] Can I have a trim?

取っ手 [totte] ドアの取っ手が外れました [doa no totte ga hazuremashita] The door handle has come off; 取っ手が外れました [totte ga hazuremashita] The handle has come off

突然 [totsuzen] 突然に [totsuzen ni] *adv* suddenly; 突然の [totsuzen no] *adj* sudden

突堤 [tottei] *n* jetty

取って代わる [tottekawaru] *v* replace

取っておく [totteoku] *v* put aside, put away, reserve

塔 [tou] *n* tower

逃亡 [toubou] *n* escape

到着 [touchaku] *n* arrival; …に到着する [...ni touchaku suru] *v* get into

灯台 [toudai] *n* lighthouse

トウガラシ [tougarashi] *n* red pepper

峠 [touge] *n* pass (in mountains)

討議 [tougi] *n* discussion

投獄 [tougoku] 投獄する [tougoku suru] *v* jail

統合失調症 [tougoushitchoushou] 統合失調症の [tougou shitchoushou no] *adj* schizophrenic

投光 [touhikari] 投光照明 [toukou shoumei] *n* floodlight

投票 [touhyou] *n* vote; 投票する [touhyou suru] *v* vote; 投票を頼んで回る

[touhyou-o tanonde mawaru] n canvass

遠い [toui] adj far; 遠く離れて [touku hanarete] adv remotely; 遠く離れた [touku hanareta] adj remote; 遠いですか? [tooi desu ka?] Is it far?

頭字語 [toujigo] n acronym

搭乗 [toujou] n boarding; 搭乗はいつ始まりますか? [toujou wa itsu hajimarimasu ka?] When does boarding begin?; ···行きフライトの搭乗ゲートはどれですか? [...iki furaito no toujou-geeto wa dore desu ka?] Which gate for the flight to...?

搭乗券 [toujouken] n boarding card, boarding pass; 私の搭乗券です [watashi no toujou-ken desu] Here is my boarding card

灯火管制 [toukakansei] n blackout

投函 [toukan] このカードをどこで投函できますか? [kono kaado o doko de toukan dekimasu ka?] Where can I post these cards?

統計 [toukei] n statistics

凍結 [touketsu] 道路は凍結していますか? [douro wa touketsu shite imasu ka?] Are the roads icy?

凍結した [touketsu shita] v icy

陶器 [touki] n pottery

投稿する [toukou suru] v post (on computer)

等級 [toukyuu] n grade

透明 [toumei] 透明な [toumei na] adj transparent

糖蜜 [toumitsu] n treacle

トウモロコシ [toumorokoshi] n maize, sweetcorn

トーナメント [tounamento] n tournament

盗難 [tounan] 盗難警報機 [tounankeihouki] n burglar alarm; 私は盗難の届出をしたいのです [watashi wa tounan no todokede o shitai no desu] I want to report a theft

糖尿病 [tounyoubyou] n diabetes; 糖尿病の [tounyoubyou no] adj diabetic; 糖尿病患者 [tounyoubyoukanja] n diabetic

投入 [tounyuu] 投入する [tounyuu suru] v put in

通り [touri] n street; 大通り [oudouri] n avenue

登録 [touroku] n registration; 登録した [touroku shita] adj registered; 登録する [touroku suru] v register; 登録簿 [tourokubo] n register; 失業登録をする [shitsugyou touroku-o suru] v sign on

討論 [touron] n debate; 討論する [touron suru] v debate

等車 [tousha] 1等車 [ittou-sha] a first-class cabin; ···行き1等車往復 [...iki ittou-sha oufuku] a first-class return to...

投資 [toushi] n investment; 投資する [toushi suru] v invest; 投資者 [toushisha] n investor

トースター [tousutaa] n toaster

トースト [tousuto] n toast (grilled bread)

当惑 [touwaku] 当惑させるような [touwaku saseru you na] adj embarrassing; 当惑した [touwaku shita] adj confused; 当惑した [touwaku shita] adj embarrassed

東洋 [touyou] n Far East; 東洋の [touyou no] adj far-eastern

灯油 [touyu] n kerosene

当座 [touza] 当座預金 [touzayokin] n current account

当座借越し [touzakarikoshi] n overdraft; 当座借越しをした [touza karikoshi-o shita] adj overdrawn

当然 [touzen] adv naturally; 当然の [touzen no] adj natural

···とはいえ [...towaie] conj although

トヨタ車 [toyotasha] トヨタ車のパーツはありますか? [toyota-sha no paatsu wa arimasu ka?] Do you have parts for a Toyota?

登山 [tozan] n mountaineering; 登山者 [tozansha] n mountaineer

ツアー [tsuaa] n tour; その街のバスツアーはいつですか? [sono machi no basu-tsuaa wa itsu desu ka?] When is the bus tour of the town?; その街の観光ツアーはあります

か? [sono machi no kankou-tsuaa wa arimasu ka?] **Are there any sightseeing tours of the town?**; その川の遊覧ツアーはありますか? [sono kawa no yuuran-tsuaa wa arimasu ka?] **Are there any boat trips on the river?**; ガイドツアーは何時に始まりますか? [gaido-tsuaa wa nan-ji ni hajimarimasu ka?] **What time does the guided tour begin?**; ツアーは楽しかったです [tsuaa wa tanoshikatta desu] **I enjoyed the tour**; ツアーは…時頃に始まります [tsuaa wa ... ji goro ni hajimarimasu] **The tour starts at about...**; ツアーの所要時間はどのくらいですか? [tsuaa no shoyou-jikan wa dono kurai desu ka?] **How long does the tour take?**; …に行く日帰りツアーを実施していますか? [...ni iku higaeri-tsuaa o jisshi shite imasu ka?] **Do you run day trips to...?**

ツアーガイド [tsuaagaido] *n* **tour guide**

つば [tsuba] *n* (唾液) **spit**; つばを吐く [tsuba o haku] *v* **spit**

翼 [tsubasa] *n* **wing**

土 [tsuchi] *n* **soil**

つづる [tsuduru] *v* **spell**; それはどうつづりますか? [sore wa dou tsuzurimasu ka?] **How do you spell it?**

告げる [tsugeru] *v* **tell**

つぎ [tsugi] *n* (布きれ) **patch**; つぎを当てた [tsugi-o ateta] *adj* **patched**

継ぎ目 [tsugime] *n* **joint** (junction)

次に [tsugi ni] *adv* **next**

次の [tsugi no] *adj* **next**; 次の駅はどこですか? [tsugi no eki wa doko desu ka?] **What is the next stop?**; …へ行く次のバスは何時ですか? [...e iku tsugi no basu wa nan-ji desu ka?] **When is the next bus to...?**

都合 [tsugou] 都合のよい [tsugou no yoi] *adj* **convenient**

ツグミ [tsugumi] *n* **thrush**

対 [tsui] …対 [...tai] *prep* **versus**

つい [tsui] ついに [tsuini] *adv* **eventually**

追放 [tsuihou] *n* **exile**

追加 [tsuika] *n* **addition**; 追加の [tsuika no] *adj* **additional**; 追加料金 [tsuikaryoukin] *n* **surcharge**; 追加の支払いがありますか? [tsuika no shiharai ga arimasu ka?] **Is there a supplement to pay?**; 追加料金がかかりますか? [tsuika-ryoukin ga kakarimasu ka?] **Is there a supplement to pay?**

追加カード [tsuikakaado] 度数追加カード [dosuu tsuika kaado] *n* **top-up card**

椎間板ヘルニア [tsuikanban herunia] *n* **slipped disc**

ツイン [tsuin] ツインの部屋がいいのですが [tsuin no heya ga ii no desu ga] **I'd like a room with twin beds**

ツインベッド [tsuinbeddo] *n* **twin beds**

ツインベッドルーム [tsuinbeddoruumu] *n* **twin-bedded room**

ついに [tsuini] *adv* **finally**

対になる [tsui ni naru] 対になった [tsui ni natta] *adj* **twinned**

ツインルーム [tsuinruumu] *n* **twin room**

一日 [tsuitachi] *n* **the first** (day of the month)

費やす [tsuiyasu] *v* **spend**

仕える [tsukaeru] *v* **serve**

使い果たす [tsukaihatasu] *v* **use up**; …を使い果たす [...-o tsukaihatasu] *v* **run out of**

使い残り [tsukainokori] *n* **stub, remains**

つかまえる [tsukamaeru] *v* **catch**

つかまる [tsukamaru] しっかりつかまる [shikkari tsukamaru] *v* **hold on**

つかむ [tsukamu] ぐいとつかむ [guito tsukamu] *v* **seize**; しっかりつかむ [shikkari tsukamu] *v* **grasp, grip**

疲れる [tsukareru] *v* **tiring**; 疲れきった [tsukarekitta] *adj* **exhausted**; 疲れた [tsukareta] *adj* **tired**

使う [tsukau] *v* **use**; 使いやすい [tsukaiyasui] *adj* **user-friendly**; 使い捨ての [tsukaisute no] *adj* **disposable**; 賄賂を使う [wairo-o tsukau] *v* **bribe**; これはどうやって使うのですか? [kore wa dou-yatte tsukau no desu ka?] **How does this work?**

つける [tsukeru] v (スイッチ) **switch on**, (スイッチ) **turn on**; 折り目をつけた [orime-o tsuketa] adj **creased**; 接着剤でつける [setchakuzai de tsukeru] v **glue**; 照合の印をつける [shougou no in-o tsukeru] v **tick**; どうやってつけるのですか？ [dou-yatte tsukeru no desu ka?] **How do you switch it on?**; ラジオをつけてもいいですか？ [rajio o tsukete mo ii desu ka?] **Can I switch the radio on?**; 明かりをつけてもいいですか？ [akari o tsukete mo ii desu ka?] **Can I switch the light on?**

付け札 [tsuke satsu] n **tag**

月 [tsuki] n (暦) **month**, (天体) **moon**

突き [tsuki] n **jab**

突き出す [tsukidasu] v **stick out**

突き刺す [tsukisasu] v **stab**; 突き刺さる [tsukisasaru] v **prick**

付添 [tsukisoi] 新郎の付添い役 [shinrou no tsukisoiyaku] n **best man**

付添う [tsukisoiu] 新婦の付添い役 [shinpu no tsukisoiyaku] n **bridesmaid**

突っ込む [tsukkomu] v **plunge**

つく [tsuku] しみがつく [shimi ga tsuku] v **stain**; つきません [tsukimasen] **It won't turn on**

着く [tsuku] v **arrive**, **get** (to a place), **reach**; そこに着くのに時間はどのくらいかかりますか？ [soko ni tsuku no ni jikan wa dono kurai kakarimasu ka?] **How long will it take to get there?**; バスは何時に着きますか？ [basu wa nan-ji ni tsukimasu ka?] **What time does the bus arrive?**; 着いた私のスーツケースが破損しています [tsuita watashi no suutsukeesu ga hason shite imasu] **My suitcase has arrived damaged**; 私は着いたばかりです [watashi wa tsuita bakari desu] **I've just arrived**; 私たちは早く／遅く着きました [watashi-tachi wa hayaku / osoku tsukimashita] **We arrived early/late**; 私たちの手荷物が着いていません [watashi-tachi no tenimotsu ga tsuite imasen] **Our luggage has not arrived**; ···に何時に着きますか？ [...ni nan-ji ni tsukimasu ka?] **What time do we get to...?**; ···に着いたら教えてください [...ni tsuitara

oshiete kudasai] **Please let me know when we get to...**; ···に着くのに時間はどのくらいかかりますか？ [...ni tsuku no ni jikan wa dono kurai kakarimasu ka?] **How long will it take to get to...?**

机 [tsukue] n **desk**; あなたの机をお借りできますか？ [anata no tsukue o o-kari dekimasu ka?] **May I use your desk?**

造り主 [tsukurinushi] n **maker** (God)

造り付けのキッチン [tsukuritsuke no kitchin] n **fitted kitchen**

作り付け [tsukurizuke] 作り付け寝台 [tsukuri zuke shindai] n **bunk**

作る [tsukuru] v **make**; 一覧表を作る [ichiranhyou-o tsukuru] v **list**

尽くす [tsukusu] 売り尽くす [uritsukusu] v **sell out**

妻 [tsuma] n **wife**; 息子の妻 [musuko no tsuma] n **daughter-in-law**; 私は妻へのプレゼントを探しています [watashi wa tsuma e no purezento o sagashite imasu] **I'm looking for a present for my wife**; 私の妻です [watashi no tsuma desu] **This is my wife**

つまらない [tsumaranai] つまらない仕事 [tsumaranai shigoto] n **fag**; つまらないもの [tsumaranai mono] n **trifle**

詰まる [tsumaru] v **be full**; ぎっしり詰まった [gisshiri tsumatta] adj **compact**; 息が詰まる [iki ga tsumaru] v **choke**

つまさき [tsumasaki] n **tiptoe**

つま楊枝 [tsuma youji] n **toothpick**

つまずく [tsumazuku] v **stumble**, **trip** (up)

爪 [tsume] 指の爪 [yubi no tsume] n **fingernail**; 爪切りばさみ [tsume kiri basami] n **nail scissors**

詰 [tsume] 缶詰にした [kanzume ni shita] adj **tinned**

爪ブラシ [tsumeburashi] n **nailbrush**

詰め込む [tsumekomu] v **cram**; ぎっしり詰め込んだ [gisshiri tsumekonda] adj **jammed**; 詰め込んだ [tsumekonda] adj **crammed**

詰め物 [tsumemono] 仮の詰め物をしてもらえますか？ [kari no tsumemono o shite moraemasu ka?] Can you do a temporary filling?; 詰め物がとれてしまいました [tsumemono ga torete shimaimashita] A filling has fallen out

詰める [tsumeru] v stuff; これから荷物を詰めなければなりません [kore kara nimotsu o tsumenakereba narimasen] I need to pack now

冷たい [tsumetai] adj cold; シャワーが冷たいです [shawaa ga tsumetai desu] The showers are cold; 食べ物が冷たすぎます [tabemono ga tsumeta-sugimasu] The food is too cold

爪やすり [tsumeyasuri] n nailfile

罪 [tsumi] n (宗教・道徳) sin

積み重なる [tsumikasanaru] v amass; 積み重なったもの [tsumikasanatta mono] n heap

積み重ね [tsumikasane] n pile, stack

積み荷 [tsumini] n shipment

積む [tsumu] 荷を積む [ni-o tsumu] v load

綱 [tsuna] 綱引き [tsunahiki] n tug-of-war; 物干し綱 [monohoshi tsuna] n washing line

つなぐ [tsunagu] v link (up)

津波 [tsunami] n tsunami

常 [tsune] 常に [tsune ni] adv always

つねる [tsuneru] v pinch

角3 [tsuno] n (動物) horn

突っ張り [tsuppari] n brace (fastening)

連れる [tsureru] v take sb along; 私を車で連れて行ってもらえますか? [watashi o kuruma de tsurete itte moraemasu ka?] Can you take me by car?; 私を連れて行っていただけますか? [watashi o tsurete itte itadakemasu ka?] Can you guide me, please?

釣り [tsuri] n fishing; どこに行けば釣りができますか? [doko ni ikeba tsuri ga dekimasu ka?] Where can I go fishing?; ここで釣りができますか? [koko de tsuri ga dekimasu ka?] Can we fish here?; ここで釣りをしていいのですか? [koko de tsuri o shite ii no desu ka?] Am I allowed to fish here?; 釣りの許可が要りますか? [tsuri no kyoka ga irimasu ka?] Do you need a fishing permit?

吊り [tsuri] 吊り包帯 [tsuri houtai] n sling

吊橋 [tsuribashi] n suspension bridge

釣具 [tsurigu] n fishing tackle

釣竿 [tsurizao] n fishing rod

ツル [tsuru] n (鳥) crane (bird)

釣る [tsuru] 魚釣り [sakana tsuri] n angling

剣 [tsurugi] n sword

つるす [tsurusu] v suspend

ツタ [tsuta] n ivy

伝える [tsutaeru] v communicate

努める [tsutomeru] v try

勤める [tsutomeru] v work; どちらにお勤めですか? [dochira ni o-tsutome desu ka?] Where do you work?; 私は・・・に勤めています [watashi wa ... ni tsutomete imasu] I work for...

つつく [tsutsuku] v poke

包み [tsutsumi] 小さな包み [chiisana tsutsumi] n packet

包む [tsutsumi] v do up, wrap, wrap up

通知 [tsuuchi] n notification; 通知する [tsuuchi suru] v notify; 通知表 [tsuuchihyou] n report card

通牒 [tsuuchou] 最後通牒 [saigo tsuuchou] n ultimatum

通学 [tsuugaku] 通学かばん [tsuugaku kaban] n schoolbag

通貨 [tsuuka] n currency; 通貨の [tsuuka no] adj monetary

通過 [tsuuka] 通過する [tsuuka suru] vt go by, pass; 通過ラウンジ [tsuuka raunji] n transit lounge

通勤 [tsuukin] 通勤する [tsuukin suru] v commute; 通勤者 [tsuukinsha] n commuter

通告 [tsuukoku] n (解雇) notice (termination)

通行 [tsuukou] 左側通行 [hidarigawa tsuukou] n left-hand drive

ツーリストオフィス [tsuurisutoofisu] n tourist office

通路 [tsuuro] n aisle, passage (route); 歩行者用通路 [hokoushayou tsuuro] n walkway

通路側 [tsuurogawa] 通路側の席をお願いします [tsuuro-gawa no seki o o-negai shimasu] **I'd like an aisle seat**

通信 [tsuushin] 電気通信 [denkitsuushin] *n* **telecommunications**

通訳 [tsuuyaku] *n* **interpretation;** 通訳者 [tsuuyakusha] *n* **interpreter;** 私は通訳が必要です [watashi wa tsuuyaku ga hitsuyou desu] **I need an interpreter;** 私たちの通訳をしていただけませんか? [watashi-tachi no tsuuyaku o shite itadakemasen ka?] **Could you act as an interpreter for us, please?**

つわり [tsuwari] つわりの時期の朝の吐き気 [tsuwari no jiki no asa no hakike] *n* **morning sickness**

つや [tsuya] つやを出す [tsuya-o dasu] *v* **polish**

つや出し [tsuyadashi] つや出し剤 [tsuyadashi zai] *n* **polish**

強い [tsuyoi] *adj* **strong;** うぬぼれの強い [unubore no tsuyoi] *adj* **vain;** 自意識の強い [jiishiki no tsuyoi] *adj* **self-conscious;** 風の強い [kaze no tsuyoi] *adj* **windy;** 強み [tsuyomi] *n* **asset, assets;** 強く [tsuyoku] *adv* **strongly;** 強くする [tsuyoku suru] *v* **strengthen;** 強さ [tsuyosa] *n* **strength;** 私はもっと強い薬が必要です [watashi wa motto tsuyoi kusuri ga hitsuyou desu] **I need something stronger**

強く [tsuyoku] 強く印象づける [tsuyoku inshou zukeru] *v* **impress**

続ける [tsuzukeru] *v* **carry on, go on, continue**

続く [tsuzuku] *v* **last, continue;** 絶えず続く [taezu tsuzuku] *adj* **constant**

つづり [tsuzuri] *n* **spelling**

乳母 [uba] *n* **nanny**

乳母車 [ubaguruma] *n* **buggy, pram**

奪う [ubau] *v* **rob**

うぶな [ubuna] *adj* **naive**

打ち上げる [uchiage ru] *v* **launch**

内側 [uchigawa] *n* **inside, interior;** ･･･の内側に [...no uchigawa ni] *prep* **inside;** 内側に [uchigawa ni] *adv* **inside;** 内側の [uchigawa no] *adj* **inner;** 内側です [uchigawa desu] **It's inside**

打ち固める [uchikatameru] *v* **ram**

内気な [uchiki na] *adj* **shy**

打ち砕く [uchikudaku] *v* **smash**

打ちのめされる [uchinomesareru] 打ちのめされた [uchinomesareta] *adj* **devastated**

打ち寄せる [uchiyoseru] 打ち寄せる波 [uchiyoseru nami] *n* **surf**

宇宙 [uchuu] *n* **universe;** 宇宙船 [uchuusen] *n* **spacecraft;** 宇宙飛行士 [uchuuhikoushi] *n* **astronaut**

腕 [ude] *n* **arm;** 腕時計 [udedokei] *n* **watch;** 私は腕を動かせません [watashi wa ude o ugokasemasen] **I can't move my arm;** 彼は腕を痛めました [kare wa ude o itamemashita] **He has hurt his arm**

腕時計 [udedokei] 腕時計のバンド [udedokei no bando] *n* **watch strap**

腕立て伏せ [udetatefuse] *n* **press-up, push-up**

上 [ue] *n* **top**; 一番上の [ichiban ue no] *adj* **top**; 上の [ue no] *adj* **upper**; 上へ [ue-e] *adv* **up**; まっすぐ上に [massugu ueni] *adv* **upright**; 物の上に載って [mono no ueni notte] *adv* **on**; ···の上に [...no ue ni] *prep* **above, on, over**

ウエハース [uehaasu] *n* **wafer**

上へ向かって [ue he mukatte] *adv* **upwards**

植木 [ueki] 植木鉢 [uekibachi] *n* **plant pot**

上の階 [ue no kai] 上の階に [ueno kai ni] *adv* **upstairs**

植える [ueru] *v* **plant**

飢える [ueru] 飢えた [ueta] *adj* **ravenous**

ウエスト [uesuto] *n* **waist**

ウエストバッグ [uesutobaggu] *n* **bum bag**

ウエストコート [uesutokooto] *n* **waistcoat**

ウガンダ [uganda] *n* **Uganda**; ウガンダ人 [ugandajin] *n* **Ugandan** *(person)*; ウガンダの [uganda no] *adj* **Ugandan**

動かない [ugokanai] 動かなくなりました [ugokanaku narimashita] **It's stuck**

動かなくなる [ugokanakunaru] 動かなくなりました [ugokanaku narimashita] **It's stuck**

動かす [ugokasu] *vt* **move**; 彼は脚を動かせません [kare wa ashi o ugokasemasen] **He can't move his leg**; 彼を動かさないでください [kare o ugokasanaide kudasai] **Don't move him**

動く [ugoku] *vi* **move**; 動かない [ugokanai] *adj* **motionless**; あなたの車を動かしていただけますか? [anata no kuruma o ugokashite itadakemasu ka?] **Could you move your car, please?**; 彼女は動けません [kanojo wa ugokemasen] **She can't move**

右派 [uha] 右派の [uha no] *adj* **right-wing**

ウインドサーフィン [uindosaafin] *n* **windsurfing**

ウインク [uinku] ウインクする [uinku suru] *v* **wink**

ウイルス [uirusu] *n* **virus**

ウイスキー [uisukii] *n* **whisky**; ウイスキーのソーダ割り [uisukii no sooda wari] **a whisky and soda**; ウイスキーをください [uisukii o kudasai] **I'll have a whisky**

うじ [uji] *n* (虫) **maggot**

迂回路 [ukairo] *n* **diversion**; 迂回路はありますか? [ukairo wa arimasu ka?] **Is there a diversion?**

受け入れる [ukeireru] *v* **accept**

受身 [ukemi] 受身の [ukemi no] *adj* **passive**

受ける [ukeru] レッスンを受けられますか? [ressun o ukeraremasu ka?] **Can we take lessons?**

受取人 [uketorinin] *n* **receiver** *(person)*, **recipient**

受け取る [uketoru] *v* **receive**; 手荷物受取所 [tenimotsu uketorisho] *n* **baggage reclaim**

受付 [uketsuke] *n* **reception**; 受付係 [uketsukegakari] *n* **receptionist**

受け皿 [ukezara] *n* **saucer**

浮き [uki] *n* **float**

浮く [uku] *v* **float**

ウクライナ [ukuraina] *n* **Ukraine**; ウクライナ人 [ukurainajin] *n* **Ukrainian** *(person)*; ウクライナの [ukuraina no] *adj* **Ukrainian**; ウクライナ語 [ukurainago] *n* **Ukrainian** *(language)*

馬 [uma] *n* **horse**; 馬の飼育係 [uma no shiikugakari] *n* **groom**; 馬の子 [uma no ko] *n* **foal**; 馬小屋 [umagoya] *n* **stable**

うまく [umaku] *adv* **successfully**; うまく···する [umaku ... suru] *v* **manage**; うまく対処する [umaku taisho suru] *v* **cope (with)**

生まれながら [umarenagara] 生まれながらの [umare nagara no] *adj* **born**

生まれたばかり [umaretabakari] 生まれたばかりの [umareta bakari no] *adj* **newborn**

生る [umaru] *v* **be born**; 生きている [ikite iru] *adj* **alive**

埋め合わせる [umeawaseru] *v* make up

うめく [umeku] *v* moan

海 [umi] *n* sea; 北極海 [hokkyokukai] *n* Arctic Ocean; 今日は海が荒れていますか? [kyou wa umi ga arete imasu ka?] Is the sea rough today?; 海が見える部屋がいいのですが [umi ga mieru heya ga ii no desu ga] I'd like a room with a view of the sea

膿 [umi] *n* pus

生む [umu] *v* (利益) yield

運 [un] *n* luck; 運のよい [un no yoi] *adj* lucky; 運の悪い [un no warui] *adj* unlucky; 運悪く [unwaruku] *adv* unfortunately

ウナギ [unagi] *n* eel

うなる [unaru] *v* groan; 怒ってうなる [ikatte unaru] *v* growl; 歯をむきだしてうなる [ha-o mukidashite unaru] *v* snarl

うなずく [unazuku] *v* nod

運賃 [unchin] *n* fare

運動 [undou] *n* (行動) campaign, (身体) exercise; フィットネス運動 [fittonesu undou] *n* keep-fit; 運動選手 [undousenshu] *n* athlete; 地下運動 [chika undou] *n* underground

運動選手 [undousenshu] 運動選手らしい [undou senshu rashii] *adj* athletic

運河 [unga] *n* canal

運命 [unmei] *n* destiny, fate

運転 [unten] *n* driving; 仮免許運転者 [karimenkyo untensha] *n* learner driver; 飲酒運転 [inshu unten] *n* drink-driving; 運転する [unten suru] *v* drive; 運転試験 [untenmenkyoshiken] *n* driving test

運転免許証 [untenmenkyoshou] *n* driving licence; 私は運転免許証を携帯していません [watashi wa unten-menkyoshou o keitai shite imasen] I don't have my driving licence on me; 私の運転免許証です [watashi no unten-menkyoshou desu] Here is my driving licence; 私の運転免許証番号は・・・です [watashi no unten-menkyoshou bangou wa ... desu] My driving licence number is...

運転手 [untenshu] *n* driver; おかかえ運

転手 [okakae untenshu] *n* chauffeur; タクシー運転手 [takushii untenshu] *n* taxi driver; トラック運転手 [torakku untenshu] *n* lorry driver, truck driver

うぬぼれ [unbore] うぬぼれの強い [unbore no tsuyoi] *adj* vain

うぬぼれた [unboreta] *adj* bigheaded

運よく [un yoku] *adv* luckily

うんざりする [unzari suru] うんざりして [unzari shite] *adj* fed up

ウォッカ [uokka] *n* vodka

ウォーキング [uookingu] *n* walking; そのウォーキングは何キロですか? [sono wookingu wa nan-kiro desu ka?] How many kilometres is the walk?; ガイド付きウォーキングはありますか? [gaido-tsuki wookingu wa arimasu ka?] Are there any guided walks?; ヒルウォーキングに行きたいのですが [hiru-wookingu ni ikitai no desu ga] I'd like to go hill walking; 地元のウォーキングのガイドはいますか? [jimoto no wookingu no gaido wa imasu ka?] Do you have a guide to local walks?

魚座 [uoza] *n* Pisces

裏 [ura] 屋根裏 [yaneura] *n* loft

裏切る [uragiru] *v* betray

裏地 [uraji] *n* lining

裏目 [urame] 裏目に出る [urame ni deru] *v* backfire

恨み [urami] *n* grudge

ウラニウム [uraniumu] *n* uranium

うらやましそうな [urayamashisouna] *adj* envious

うらやむ [urayamu] *v* envy

嬉しい [ureshii] *adj* glad, pleased

うれしい [ureshii] *adj* happy; お会いできてうれしいです [o-ai dekite ureshii desu] Pleased to meet you

売場 [uriba] 切符売場 [kippu uriba] *n* box office, ticket office

売り出し [uridashi] 特別売り出し [tokubetsu uridashi] *n* special offer

売切れ [urikire] 売切れの [urikire no] *adj* sold out

うろこ [uroko] n scale (tiny piece)

うろたえる [urotaeru] v panic

売る [uru] v sell; 売り払う [uriharau] v sell off; 売り尽くす [uritsukusu] v sell out; 売る人 [uru hito] n vendor; テレホンカードを売っていますか? [terehon-kaado o utte imasu ka?] Do you sell phone cards?

ウルグアイ [uruguai] n Uruguay; ウルグアイ人 [uruguaijin] n Uruguayan (person); ウルグアイの [uruguai no] adj Uruguayan

うるさがらせる [urusagaraseru] v annoy

うるさい [urusai] adj annoying

うるう [uruu] うるう年 [uruudoshi] n leap year

ウサギ [usagi] n rabbit; 野ウサギ [nousagi] n hare

失う [ushinau] 意識を失った [ishiki o ushinatta] adj unconscious; 意識を失う [ishiki-o ushinau] v pass out; 失った [utta] adj lost; 希望を失って [kibou-o ushinatte] adj hopeless

後ろ [ushiro] n rear; ···の後ろに [...no ushiro ni] prep behind; 後ろに [ushiro ni] adv back, behind; 後ろに下がる [ushiro ni sagaru] v move back; 後ろの [ushiro no] adj back, rear

嘘 [uso] n lie; 嘘をつく [uso-o tsuku] v lie

嘘つき [usotsuki] n liar

薄切り [usugiri] n slice

薄暗い [usugurai] adj dim

薄い [usui] adj (住居) pale, (厚み) thin; 薄く色を着けた [usuku iro-o tsuketa] adj tinted; 薄く切る [usuku kiru] v slice

薄い肉片 [usui nikuhen] n cutlet

歌 [uta] n song; 賛美歌 [sanbika] n hymn; 子守歌 [komoriuta] n lullaby

疑い [utagai] n doubt; 疑いなく [utagainaku] adv undoubtedly; 疑いをかける [utagai-o kakeru] v suspect

疑う [utagau] v doubt; 疑い深い [utagaibukai] adj sceptical

疑わしい [utagawashii] adj doubtful, suspicious

うたたね [utatane] n nap

うたた寝 [utatane] うたた寝する [utatane suru] v doze

歌う [utau] v sing; 歌うこと [utau koto] n singing

鬱 [utsu] 抗鬱剤 [kouutsuzai] n antidepressant

ウッ [utsu] excl ugh

打つ [utsu] v hit, strike; ゴツンと打つ [gotsun to utsu] v thump; バンと打つ [ban to utsu] v bang; ピシャリと打つ [pishari to utsu] v slap, smack, swat; 打ち負かす [uchimakasu] v knock out; 打ち倒す [uchitaosu] v knock down; 打つこと [utsu koto] n beat; 続けざまに打つ [tsuzukezama ni utsu] v beat (strike); 動悸を打つ [douki-o utsu] v throb

撃つ [utsu] v shoot

美しい [utsukushii] adj beautiful, lovely; 絵のように美しい [e no youni utsukushii] adj picturesque; 美しさ [utsukushisa] n beauty

美しく [utsukushiku] adv beautifully

写し [utsushi] n transcript

移す [utsusu] v remove, shift

器 [utsuwa] 注射器 [chuushaki] n syringe; 皮むき器 [kawamukiki] n potato peeler

訴える [uttaeru] v accuse, sue; 感覚に訴える [kankaku ni uttaeru] adj sensuous

浮気 [uwaki] 浮気者 [uwakimono] n flirt

うわさ [uwasa] n rumour

うわさ話 [uwasabanashi] n gossip; うわさ話をする [uwasabanashi-o suru] v gossip

上役 [uwayaku] n superior

ウズベキスタン [uzubekisutan] n Uzbekistan

うずくまる [uzukumaru] v crouch down

ウズラ [uzura] n quail

V W

ヴィラ [vira] n villa; ヴィラを借りたいのですが [vira o karitai no desu ga] I'd like to rent a villa

輪 [wa] n ring; 輪ゴム [wagomu] n rubber band

ワークステーション [waakusuteeshon] n work station, workstation

ワールドカップ [waarudokappu] n World Cup

詫び [wabi] n apology

話題 [wadai] n topic

ワッフル [waffuru] n waffle

我が [waga] 我が家へ [wagaya-e] adv home

輪ゴム [wagomu] n elastic band

ワゴン [wagon] n trolley

ワイファイ [waifai] n WiFi

ワイン [wain] n wine; 赤ワイン [aka-wain] n red wine; このワインは冷えていません [kono wain wa hiete imasen] This wine is not chilled; よいワインを教えてもらえますか? [yoi wain o oshiete moraemasu ka?] Can you recommend a good wine?; ワインは冷えていますか? [wain wa hiete imasu ka?] Is the wine chilled?; ハウスワインをカラフで1本 [hausu-wain o karafu de ippon] a carafe of the house wine; 赤ワインのボトルを1本 [aka-wain no botoru o ippon] a bottle of red wine; 赤ワインをカ

ラフで1本 [aka-wain o karafu de ippon] a carafe of red wine; 白ワインのボトルを1本 [shiro-wain no botoru o ippon] a bottle of white wine; 白ワインをカラフで1本 [shiro-wain o karafu de ippon] a carafe of white wine; 私はワインは全く飲みません [watashi wa wain wa mattaku nomimasen] I never drink wine

ワイングラス [waingurasu] n wineglass

ワインリスト [wainrisuto] n wine list; ワインリストをください [wain-risuto o kudasai] The wine list, please

ワイパー [waipaa] フロントガラスのワイパー [furonto garasu no waipaa] n windscreen wiper

賄賂 [wairo] 賄賂を使う [wairo-o tsukau] v bribe

猥褻な [waisetu] adj obscene

ワイシャツ [waishatsu] n shirt

若い [wakai] adj young; 一番若い [ichiban wakai] adj youngest; 若いおんどり [wakai ondori] n cockerel

若者 [wakamono] n adolescent

別れ [wakare] n parting

分かれ道 [wakaremichi] n turning

わかります [wakarimasu] I understand; わかりません [wakarimasen] I don't understand

わかる [wakaru] 話がわかる [hanashi ga wakaru] adj understanding

分かる [wakaru] v recognize

沸かす [wakasu] vt boil

分け前 [wakemae] n share

分ける [wakeru] v divide, separate, share; 分け合う [wakeau] v share out

腋 [waki] 腋の下 [waki no shita] n armpit

わき道 [wakimichi] わき道へ入る [wakimichi-e hairu] v turn off

枠 [waku] 窓の下枠 [mado no shitawaku] n windowsill

沸く [waku] 沸き立つ [wakitatsu] adj boiling

惑星 [wakusei] n planet

わめく [wameku] v rave

湾 [wan] n bay

わな [wana] n trap

ワニ [wani] n alligator, crocodile

湾曲 [wankyoku] n crook

腕白 [wanpaku] 腕白な [wanpaku na] adj naughty

ワンピース [wanpiisu] n dress; このワンピースを試着していいですか? [kono wanpiisu o shichaku shite ii desu ka?] Can I try on this dress?

ワンルーム [wanruumu] n studio flat; ワンルームのアパート [wanruumu no apaato] n bedsit

笑う [warau] v laugh; にこにこ笑い [nikoniko warai] n grin; にやにや笑う [niyaniya warau] v snigger; くすくす笑う [kusukusu warau] v giggle; 歯を見せてにっこり笑う [ha-o misete nikkori warau] v grin; 笑い [warai] n laugh; 笑い声 [waraigoe] n laughter

割れ目 [wareme] n crack (fracture)

割れる [wareru] v crack

割合 [wariai] n rate

割当て [wariate] n quota

割り当て [wariate] n assignment

割引 [waribiki] n discount; 日帰り往復割引切符 [higaeri oufuku waribiki kippu] n day return; 鉄道割引証 [tetsudou waribikishou] n railcard; 学生割引 [gakusei waribiki] n student discount; 現金で払うと割引がありますか? [genkin de harau to waribiki ga arimasu ka?] Do you offer a discount for cash?

割り込む [warikomu] v squeeze in

割る [waru] v break, split

悪がき [warugaki] n brat

悪い [warui] adj bad, evil; 一層悪い [issou warui] adj worse; 一層悪く [issou waruku] adv worse; 機嫌の悪い [kigen no warui] adj bad-tempered; 意地の悪い [iji no warui] adj spiteful; 気味の悪い [kimi no warui] adj spooky; 運悪く [unwaruku] adv unfortunately; 風通しの悪い [kazetoushi no warui] adj stuffy; 効率の悪い [kouritsu no warui] adj inefficient

悪く [waruku] adv badly

ワルツ [warutsu] n waltz; ワルツを踊る [warutsu o odoru] v waltz

ワシ [washi] n eagle

忘れる [wasureru] v forget; 置き忘れる [okiwasureru] v mislay; 忘れられない [wasurerarenai] adj unforgettable; 忘れられた [wasurerareta] adj forgotten

私 [watashi] pron I; 私の [watashi no] adj my

私自身 [watashijishin] pron myself

私のもの [watashi no mono] pron mine

私を [watashi o] pron me

私たち [watashi-tachi] 私たちは [watashi-tachi wa] pron we; 私たちの [watashi-tachi no] adj our; 私たちのもの [watashi-tachi no mono] pron ours; 私たちを [watashi-tachi-o] pron us; 私たち自身 [watashi-tachi jishin] pron ourselves

渡す [watasu] v hand in; 出るときに鍵はどこに渡せばいいのですか? [deru toki ni kagi wa doko ni wataseba ii no desu ka?] Where do we hand in the key when we're leaving?

わずか [wazuka] わずかな [wazuka na] adj slight; わずかに [wazuka ni] adv slightly

•••を離れて [...o hanarete] prep off

•••を囲んで [...o kakonde] prep round

•••を過ぎて [...o sugite] prep past

•••を通って [...o tootte] prep through

ウェブアドレス [webuadoresu] n web address

ウェブブラウザ [webuburauza] n web browser

ウェブジン [webujin] n webzine

ウェブカム [webukamu] n webcam

ウェブマスター [webumasutaa] n webmaster

ウェブサイト [webusaito] n website

ウェブサイトアドレス [webusaitoadoresu] ウェブサイトアドレスは•••です [webusaito adoresu wa ... desu] The website address is...

ウェブ2.0 [webutsuu] n Web 2.0

ウェディングドレス [wedingudoresu] n wedding dress

ウェールズ [weeruzu] n Wales; ウェールズの [weeruzu no] adj Welsh; ウェールズ語 [weeruzugo] n Welsh (language)

ウェイター [weitaa] n waiter

ウェイトレス [weitoresu] n waitress

ウェリントンブーツ [werintonbuutsu] n wellies, wellingtons

ウェスタン [wesutan] n western

ウェットスーツ [wettosuutsu] n wetsuit

ウィンタースポーツ [wintaasupootsu] n winter sports

Y

night school

夜間外出禁止令 [yakan gaishutsu kinshirei] *n* curfew

火傷 [yakedo] *n* burn

焼け落ちる [yakeochiru] *v* burn down

焼き串 [yakigushi] *n* skewer

夜勤 [yakin] *n* night shift

厄介 [yakkai] 厄介なもの [yakkai na mono] *n* nuisance

薬局 [yakkyoku] *n* chemist('s), pharmacy; 一番近い薬局はどこですか? [ichiban chikai yakkyoku wa doko desu ka?] **Where is the nearest chemist?**; どの薬局が夜間休日サービスを実施していますか? [dono yakkyoku ga yakan-kyuujitsu-saabisu o jisshi shite imasu ka?] **Which pharmacy provides emergency service?**

焼く [yaku] *v* bake; グリルで焼く [guriru de yaku] *v* grill; 網焼きにする [amiyaki ni suru] *adj* grilled; 焼いた [yaita] *adj* baked, roast

薬品 [yakuhin] 化学薬品 [kagakuyakuhin] *n* chemical

役員 [yakuin] 役員会 [yakuinkai] *n* board (*meeting*)

役に立たない [yaku ni tatanai] *adj* unhelpful, useless

役に立つ [yaku ni tatsu] *adj* helpful, useful

約束 [yakusoku] *n* engagement, promise; 会う約束 [au yakusoku] *n* rendezvous; 約束する [yakusoku suru] *v* promise; 約束を取り消す [yakusoku-o torikesu] *v* back out

訳す [yakusu] *v* translate; これを訳してもらえますか? [kore o yakushite moraemasu ka?] **Can you translate this for me?**

役割 [yakuwari] *n* role

薬剤 [yakuzai] *n* medicine

薬剤師 [yakuzaishi] *n* chemist, pharmacist

野球 [yakyuu] *n* baseball; 野球帽 [yakyuubou] *n* baseball cap

矢 [ya] *n* arrow

屋 [ya] タバコ屋 [tabakoya] *n* tobacconist's; 葬儀屋 [sougiya] *n* undertaker

やあ [yaa] *excl* hi!

ヤード [yaado] *n* yard (*measurement*)

野蛮 [yaban] 野蛮な [yaban na] *adj* barbaric

破れる [yabureru] 破れ目 [yabureme] *n* tear (*split*)

破る [yaburu] *v* tear

宿 [yado] 宿を提供する [yado-o teikyou suru] *v* accommodate; 宿屋 [yadoya] *n* inn

ヤドリギ [yadorigi] *n* mistletoe

やがて [yagate] *adv* presently

ヤギ [yagi] *n* goat

ヤギが子を産む [yagi ga ko o umu] *v* kid

山羊座 [yagiza] *n* Capricorn

野獣 [yajuu] 野獣の子 [yajuu no ko] *n* cub

やかましい [yakamashii] *adj* noisy; やかましい音 [yakamashii oto] *n* din

夜間 [yakan] 夜間クラス [yakan kurasu] *n* evening class; 夜間学校 [yakangakkou] *n*

山 [yama] *n* mountain; 山の多い [yama no oui] *adj* mountainous; 干し草の山 [hoshikusa no yama] *n* haystack; 一番近

い山小屋はどこですか? [ichiban chikai yama-goya wa doko desu ka?] **Where is the nearest mountain hut?**

山積み [yamazumi] n pile-up

やめる [yameru] v (よす) give up, (よす) quit

闇 [yami] n dark

ヤナギ [yanagi] n willow

屋根 [yane] n roof; 萱葺き屋根の [kayabuki yane no] adj thatched; 屋根裏 [yaneura] n attic, loft

家主 [yanushi] n landlord; 女家主 [onna yanushi] n landlady

八百屋 [yaoya] n greengrocer's

やり方 [yarikata] これのやり方をご存知ですか? [kore no yarikata o go-zonji desu ka?] **Do you know how to do this?**

やり直す [yarinaosu] v redo

やりすぎ [yarisugi] やりすぎの [yarisugi no] adj overdone

野菜 [yasai] n vegetable; 野菜は生鮮品ですか、それとも冷凍品ですか? [yasai wa seisen-hin desu ka, sore tomo reitou-hin desu ka?] **Are the vegetables fresh or frozen?**; 野菜も付いてきますか? [yasai mo tsuite kimasu ka?] **Are the vegetables included?**

優しい [yasashii] adj gentle

優しく [yasashiku] adv gently

野生 [yasei] 野生の [yasei no] adj wild; 野生生物 [yaseiseibutsu] n wildlife

野生生物 [yaseiseibutsu] n wildlife; 野生生物を見たいのですが [yasei-seibutsu o mitai no desu ga] **We'd like to see wildlife**

やせこけた [yasekoketa] v skinny

ヤシ [yashi] n palm (tree)

野心 [yashin] n ambition; 野心的な [yashinteki na] adj ambitious

安い [yasui] adj cheap, inexpensive; 一番安い方法がいいのですが [ichiban yasui houhou ga ii no desu ga] **I'd like the cheapest option**; もっと安いものが欲しいのです [motto yasui mono ga hoshii no desu] **I want something cheaper**; 安いフライトはありますか? [yasui furaito wa

arimasu ka?] **Are there any cheap flights?**; 安い電車料金はありますか? [yasui densha-ryoukin wa arimasu ka?] **Are there any cheap train fares?**; 安めのものはありますか? [yasume no mono wa arimasu ka?] **Do you have anything cheaper?**

休み [yasumi] n rest, the rest; 昼休み [hiruyasumi] n lunch break

休む [yasumu] v rest

やすり [yasuri] n file (tool); やすりをかける [yasuri-o kakeru] v file (smoothing)

屋台 [yatai] n stall

柔らかい [yawarakai] adj soft, tender

夜明け [yoake] n dawn

予備 [yobi] 予備の寝室 [yobi no shinshitsu] n spare room; 予備の寝具はありますか? [yobi no shingu wa arimasu ka?] **Is there any spare bedding?**

呼び出す [yobidasu] ポケットベルで呼び出す [poketto beru de yobidasu] v page; ···さんをポケットベルで呼び出してもらえますか? [...san o pokettoberu de yobidashite moraemasu ka?] **Can you page...?**

呼び声 [yobigoe] n call

呼び鈴 [yobisuzu] 玄関の呼び鈴 [genkan no yobisuzu] n doorbell

呼び止める [yobitomeru] v hail

予防 [yobou] n prevention; 予防接種 [yobou sesshu] n vaccination; 予防接種をする [yobou sesshu-o suru] v vaccinate

呼ぶ [yobu] v call; 消防隊を呼んでください [shoubou-tai o yonde kudasai] **Please call the fire brigade**; 救急車を呼んでください [kyuukyuu-sha o yonde kudasai] **Call an ambulance**; 救急医を呼んでください [kyuukyuu-i o yonde kudasai] **Please call the emergency doctor**; 救助艇を呼んで! [kyuujotei o yonde!] **Call out the lifeboat!**; 警察を呼んでください [keisatsu o yonde kudasai] **Call the police**; 医者を呼んで! [isha o yonde!] **Call a doctor!**

余分 [yobun] 余分な [yobun na] adj surplus; 余分に [yobun ni] adv extra; 余分の [yobun no] adj extra, spare; 余分に袋をいただけますか? [yobun ni fukuro o itadakemasu ka?] Can I have an extra bag, please?; 私は余分に請求されています [watashi wa yobun ni seikyuu sarete imasu] I've been overcharged; ・・・を余分につけてお願いします [...o yobun ni tsukete o-negai shimasu] I'd like it with extra...., please

よだれ掛け [yodarekake] n bib

ヨガ [yoga] n yoga

汚れ [yogore] n smudge; 汚れの跡 [yogore no ato] n mark; 汚れの跡をつける [yogore no ato-o tsukeru] v stain

汚れる [yogoreru] v be dirty; 汚れています [yogorete imasu] It's dirty; 洗面台が汚れています [senmendai ga yogorete imasu] The washbasin is dirty; 私のシーツは汚れています [watashi no shiitsu wa yogorete imasu] My sheets are dirty; 私のナイフやフォークが汚れています [watashi no naifu ya fooku ga yogorete imasu] My cutlery is dirty; 部屋が汚れています [heya ga yogorete imasu] The room is dirty

汚る [yogoru] 汚れた [yogoreta] adj dirty

予報 [yohou] 天気予報 [tenkiyohou] n forecast, weather forecast; 天気予報はどうですか? [tenki-yohou wa dou desu ka?] What's the weather forecast?

よい [yoi] 居心地のよい [igokochi no yoi] adj cosy; よいところをご存知ですか? [yoi tokoro o go-zonji desu ka?] Do you know a good place to go?

良い [yoi] adj good

余剰 [yojou] 余剰人員の解雇 [yojoujin'in no kaiko] n redundancy; 余剰人員として解雇された [yojoujin'in to shite kaiko sareta] adj redundant

余暇 [yoka] n leisure, spare time

予感 [yokan] n premonition

予見 [yoken] 予見する [yoken suru] v foresee

予期 [yoki] 予期しない [yoki shinai] adj unexpected

預金 [yokin] n deposit; 預金口座 [yokin kouza] n account (in bank); 共同預金口座 [kyoudou yokin kouza] n joint account; 当座預金 [touzayokin] n current account

横丁 [yokochou] n side street

横切る [yokogiru] v cross; ・・・を横切って [...-o yokogitte] prep across

横向き [yokomuki] 横向きに [yokomuki ni] adv sideways

横すべり [yoko suberi] 横すべりする [yokosuberi suru] v skid; 車が横すべりしました [kuruma ga yokosuberi shimashita] The car skidded

よく [yoku] 最もよく [mottomo yoku] adv best; よく眠れましたか? [yoku nemuremashita ka?] Did you sleep well?

抑圧 [yokuatsu] n inhibition

欲ばり [yokubari] 欲ばりの [yokubari no] adj greedy

浴場 [yokujou] 公衆浴場 [koushuu yokujou] n baths

抑制 [yokusei] 発汗抑制剤 [hakkan yokuseizai] n antiperspirant

浴槽 [yokusou] n bath, bathtub

読み上げる [yomiageru] v read out

読み書き [yomikaki] 読み書きのできない [yomikaki no dekinai] adj illiterate

読みやすい [yomiyasui] adj legible

読む [yomu] v read; 拾い読みする [hiroiyomi suru] v browse; それは読めません [sore wa yomemasen] I can't read it

夜中 [yonaka] 夜中の十二時に [yonaka no juuni-ji ni] at midnight

世慣れる [yonareru] 世慣れた [yonareta] adj streetwise

四番目 [yonbanme] 四番目の [yon banme no] adj fourth

4分の1 [yonbun no ichi] n quarter

余念 [yonen] ・・・に余念がない [...ni yonen ga nai] adj preoccupied

四輪駆動 [yonrinkudou] n four-wheel drive

ヨーロッパ [yooroppa] n Europe; ヨーロッパ人 [yooroppajin] n European (person); ヨーロッパの [yooroppa no] adj European; ヨーロッパ大陸式の簡単な朝食 [yooroppa tairikushiki no kantan na choushoku] n continental breakfast

ヨーロッパヤマウズラ
[yooroppayamauzura] n partridge

酔っぱらい [yopparai] n drunk

酔っぱらう [yopparau] 酔っぱらって
[yopparatte] adj hammered; 酔っぱらった
[yopparatta] adj drunk

より [yori] より早く [yori hayaku] adv sooner

よりも [yorimo] ···よりも [...yorimo] conj
than

より少ない [yori sukunai] adj fewer

よりよい [yoriyoi] adj better

よりよく [yoriyoku] adv better

喜び [yorokobi] n joy; 大喜び [ooyorokobi]
n delight; 大喜びの [ooyorokobi no] adj
delighted

喜ぶ [yorokobu] v be happy; ええ、喜んで
[ee, yorokonde] Yes, I'd love to; 喜んで!
[yorokonde!] With pleasure!

よろめく [yoromeku] v stagger

世論 [yoron] n public opinion; 世論調査
[yoronchousa] n opinion poll, poll

よろよろ [yoroyoro] よろよろする
[yoroyoro suru] adj shaky

夜 [yoru] n night; 明日の夜 [asu no yoru]
tomorrow night; 夜に [yoru ni] at night

ヨルダン [yorudan] n Jordan

ヨルダン人 [yorudanjin] n Jordanian
(person)

ヨルダンの [yorudan no] adj Jordanian

予算 [yosan] n budget

よそ [yoso] どこかよそで [dokoka yoso de]
adv elsewhere

予測 [yosoku] 予測できない [yosoku
dekinai] adj unpredictable

予想 [yosou] 予想する [yosou suru] v
predict; 予想できる [yosou dekiru] adj
predictable

予定 [yotei] n schedule; ···する予定で [...
suru yotei de] adj due; 私たちは予定どおり
です [watashi-tachi wa yotei doori desu]
We are on schedule; 私たちは予定より少
し遅れています [watashi-tachi wa yotei
yori sukoshi okurete imasu] We are slightly
behind schedule

ヨット [yotto] n sailing boat, yacht

洋 [you] インド洋 [indoyou] n Indian Ocean

よう [you] ように思われる [youni
omowareru] v seem; ···のような [...no
you na] prep like

酔う [you] 船に酔った [fune ni yotta] adj
seasick; 飛行機に酔った [hikouki ni yotta]
adj airsick; 酔った [yotta] adj drunk

幼稚園 [youchien] n infant school

洋服だんす [youfukudansu] n wardrobe

溶岩 [yougan] n lava

容疑 [yougi] 容疑者 [yougisha] n suspect

用語 [yougo] n term (description)

養護 [yougo] 児童養護 [jidou yougo] n
childcare

用具 [yougu] n gear (equipment); 洗面用具
バッグ [senmen yougu baggu] n toilet bag;
用具一式 [yougu isshiki] n kit

ヨーグルト [youguruto] n yoghurt

用品 [youhin] n product; 園芸用品店
[engei youhinten] n garden centre; スタイ
リング用品を売っていますか? [sutairingu
youhin o utte imasu ka?] Do you sell
styling products?

用意 [youi] adj ready; 用意のできた [youi
no dekita] adj ready; 用意ができた [youi
ga dekita] adj prepared; 用意はできました
か? [youi wa dekimashita ka?] Are you
ready?; 用意できていません [youi dekite
imasen] I'm not ready; 用意できました
[youi dekimashita] I'm ready; ···を使わず
にこれを用意していただけますか? [...o
tsukawazu ni kore o youi shite itadakemasu
ka?] Could you prepare this one
without...?

容易 [youi] 容易に [youi ni] adv easily

養育 [youiku] 養育する [youiku suru] v
foster

要員 [youin] 作業要員 [sagyou youin] n
workforce

要因 [youin] 複雑な要因 [fukuzatsu na
youin] n complication

幼児 [youji] よちよち歩きの幼児
[yochiyochi aruki no youji] n toddler; 幼児
用の便器 [youjiyou no benki] n potty; 幼児

用の便器はありますか? [youji-you no benki wa arimasu ka?] Do you have a potty?

用心 [youjin] n precaution

容器 [youki] n container

陽気な [youki na] adj cheerful, merry

ようこそ! [youkoso] excl welcome!

要求 [youkyuu] n demand, requirement; 要求の厳しい [youkyuu no kibishii] adj demanding; 要求する [youkyuu suru] v call for

要求する [youkyuu suru] v demand

容者 [you mono] 被収容者 [hishuuyousha] n inmate

羊毛 [youmou] n wool

用務員 [youmuin] n janitor

容認 [younin] 容認できない [younin dekinai] adj unacceptable

妖精 [yousei] n fairy

容積 [youseki] n volume

容赦 [yousha] 容赦する [yousha suru] v spare

用紙 [youshi] n form; アンケート用紙 [ankeeto youshi] n questionnaire; メモ用紙 [memo youshi] n notepaper; 注文用紙 [chuumon youshi] n order form

養子 [youshi] 養子になった [youshi ni natta] adj adopted; 養子にする [youshi ni suru] v adopt; 養子縁組 [youshiengumi] n adoption

様式 [youshiki] n style; ロマネスク様式の [romanesuku youshiki no] adj Romanesque; 建築様式 [kenchiku youshiki] n architecture

要素 [youso] n element; 構成要素 [kousei youso] n component

要点 [youten] n point

腰痛 [youtsuu] n back pain, backache

要約 [youyaku] n summary; 要約する [youyaku suru] v sum up, summarize

溶剤 [youzai] n solvent

弱火 [yowabi] 弱火でとろとろ煮る [yowabi de torotoro niru] v simmer

弱い [yowai] adj weak; 弱いこと [yowai koto] n weakness

弱い者いじめをする者 [yowai mono ijime o suru mono] n bully

予約 [yoyaku] n appointment, booking; 予約する [yoyaku suru] v book; 予約オフィス [yoyaku ofisu] n booking office; 事前予約 [jizen yoyaku] n advance booking; 予約をキャンセルしたいのですが [yoyaku o kyanseru shitai no desu ga] I want to cancel my booking; 予約を取りたいのですが [yoyaku o toritai no desu ga] I'd like to make an appointment; 予約料がかかりますか? [yoyaku-ryou ga kakarimasu ka?] Is there a booking fee?; 予約料金がかかりますか? [yoyaku-ryoukin ga kakarimasu ka?] Is there a booking fee to pay?; お医者さんの予約を取れますか? [o-isha-san no yoyaku o toremasu ka?] Can I have an appointment with the doctor?; 私は手紙で予約を確認しました [watashi wa tegami de yoyaku o kakunin shimashita] I confirmed my booking by letter

予約する [yoyaku suru] どこでコートを予約できますか? [doko de kooto o yoyaku dekimasu ka?] Where can I book a court?

余裕 [yoyuu] ···する余裕がある [...suru yoyuu ga aru] v afford

指 [yubi] 人差し指 [hitosashi yubi] n index finger; 手の指 [te no yubi] n finger; 足の指 [ashi no yubi] n toe

指輪 [yubiwa] n ring; 結婚指輪 [kekkon yubiwa] n wedding ring; 婚約指輪 [kon'yaku yubiwa] n engagement ring

油断 [yudan] 油断のならない [yudan no naranai] adj tricky

ユダヤ人 [yudayajin] n Jew

ユダヤ人の [yudayajin no] adj Jewish

ユダヤ教 [yudayakyou] ユダヤ教の掟に従って料理された清浄な [yudaya kyou no okite ni shitagatte ryouri sareta seijou na] adj kosher

ゆでる [yuderu] ゆで卵 [yudetamago] n boiled egg

故··· [yue...] adj late (dead)

遺言 [yuigon] n will (document)

唯一 [yuiitsu] 唯一の [yuiitsu no] adj only

床 [yuka] n floor

愉快 [yukai] 愉快な [yukai na] *adj* entertaining

輸血 [yuketsu] *n* blood transfusion, transfusion

雪 [yuki] *n* snow; ひとひらの雪 [hitohira no yuki] *n* snowflake; 雪が降る [yuki ga furu] *v* snow; 雪の状態はどうですか? [yuki no joutai wa dou desu ka?] **What are the snow conditions?**; 雪が降っています [yuki ga futte imasu] **It's snowing**; 雪が降ると思いますか? [yuki ga furu to omoimasu ka?] **Do you think it will snow?**

雪だるま [yukidaruma] *n* snowman

雪つぶて [yukitsubute] *n* snowball

ゆっくり [yukkuri] もっとゆっくり話していただけますか? [motto yukkuri hanashite itadakemasu ka?] **Could you speak more slowly, please?**

行方 [yukue] 私の息子が行方不明です [watashi no musuko ga yukue-fumei desu] **My son is missing**; 私の娘が行方不明です [watashi no musume ga yukue-fumei desu] **My daughter is missing**

油膜 [yumaku] *n* oil slick

夢 [yume] *n* dream; 夢を見る [yume o miru] *v* dream

弓 [yumi] *n* bow *(weapon)*

優美 [yumi] 優美な [yuubi na] *adj* delicate, graceful

輸入 [yunyuu] *n* import; 輸入する [yunyuu suru] *v* import

揺れ [yure] *n* swing

揺れる [yureru] *v* rock, swing, shake

ユリ [yuri] *n* lily

揺りかご [yurikago] *n* cradle

揺る [yuru] 揺り木馬 [yurimokuba] *n* rocking horse

緩い [yurui] *adj* loose, slack

緩める [yurumeru] ねじを緩める [neji-o yurumeru] *v* unscrew

許し [yurushi] *n* pardon

許す [yurusu] *v* allow, forgive; 入場を許す [nyuujou-o yurusu] *v* admit *(allow in)*

揺さぶる [yusa buru] 揺さぶられた [yusaburareta] *adj* shaken

油井 [yusei] *n* oil well

輸出 [yushutsu] *n* export; 輸出する [yushutsu suru] *v* export

輸送 [yusou] *n* transit, transport; 輸送する [yusou suru] *v* transport; 貨物輸送 [kamotsu yusou] *n* freight

輸送車 [yusousha] 護衛されている輸送車隊 [goei sareteiru yusoushatai] *n* convoy; 大型輸送車 [ougata yusousha] *n* HGV

ゆすぶる [yusuburu] *v* sway

湯たんぽ [yutanpo] *n* hot-water bottle

ゆったり [yuttari] ゆったりとした [yuttarito shita] *adj* easy-going

URL [yuuaarueru] *n* URL

郵便 [yuubin] *n* mail, post *(mail)*; 郵便料金 [yuubin ryoukin] *n* postage; 郵便為替 [yuubin kawase] *n* postal order; 郵便番号 [yuubin bangou] *n* postcode; 郵便配達人 [yuubin haitatsunin] *n* postman; 女性郵便配達人 [josei yuubin haitatsunin] *n* postwoman; 普通郵便でどのくらいの日数がかかりますか? [futsuu-yuubin de dono kurai no nissuu ga kakarimasu ka?] **How long will it take by normal post?**; 書留郵便でどのくらいの日数がかかりますか? [kakitome-yuubin de dono kurai no nissuu ga kakarimasu ka?] **How long will it take by registered post?**; 私あての郵便物がありますか? [watashi ate no yuubinbutsu ga arimasu ka?] **Is there any mail for me?**; 優先郵便でどのくらいの日数がかかりますか? [yuusen-yuubin de dono kurai no nissuu ga kakarimasu ka?] **How long will it take by priority post?**

郵便物 [yuubinbutsu] *n* mail, post; 私あての郵便物をこの住所に回送してください [watashi ate no yuubinbutsu o kono juusho ni kaisou shite kudasai] **Please send my mail on to this address**

郵便受 [yuubinju] *n* letterbox, mailbox

郵便局 [yuubinkyoku] *n* post office; 郵便局はいつ開きますか? [yuubinkyoku wa itsu hirakimasu ka?] **When does the post office open?**

有望な [yuubou na] 将来有望な [shourai yuubou na] *adj* promising

有毒 [yuudoku] 有毒な [yuudoku na] *adj* toxic

有毒な [yuudoku na] *adj* poisonous

誘導 [yuudou] 誘導ループはありますか? [yuudou-ruupu wa arimasu ka?] Is there an induction loop?

遊園地 [yuuenchi] *n* funfair

USBメモリー [yuu esu bii memorii] *n* USB stick

裕福 [yuufuku] 裕福な [yuufuku na] *adj* well-off

優雅 [yuuga] 優雅な [yuuga na] *adj* elegant

有害 [yuugai] 有害な [yuugai na] *adj* harmful

夕暮れ [yuugure] *n* dusk

遊歩道 [yuuhodou] 海岸の遊歩道 [kaigan no yuuhodou] *n* promenade; 近くにおもしろい遊歩道はありますか? [chikaku ni omoshiroi yuuhodou wa arimasu ka?] Are there any interesting walks nearby?

友情 [yuujou] *n* friendship

優柔 [yuujuu] 優柔不断な [yuujuu fudan na] *adj* indecisive

誘拐 [yuukai] 誘拐する [yuukai suru] *v* abduct, kidnap

勇敢 [yuukan] *n* bravery; 勇敢な [yuukan na] *adj* brave

勇気 [yuuki] *n* courage; ・・・の勇気をくじく [...no yuuki-o kujiku] *v* discourage; 勇気のある [yuuki no aru] *adj* courageous

有機体 [yuukitai] *n* organism; 有機体の [yuukitai no] *adj* organic

勇気づける [yuukizukeru] *v* encourage

有名 [yuumei] *n* fame; 有名人 [yuumeijin] *n* celebrity

有名な [yuumei na] *adj* famous, renowned, well-known

ユーモア [yuumoa] *n* humour; ユーモアのある [yuumoa no aru] *adj* humorous; ユーモアのセンス [yuumoa no sensu] *n* sense of humour

有能 [yuunou] 有能な [yuunou na] *adj* competent

遊覧 [yuuran] その川の遊覧ツアーはありますか? [sono kawa no yuuran-tsuaa wa arimasu ka?] Are there any boat trips on the river?

幽霊 [yuurei] *n* ghost; 幽霊が出没する [yuurei ga shutsubotsu suru] *adj* haunted

有利 [yuuri] *n* advantage

ユーロ [yuuro] *n* euro

有料 [yuuryou] *n* toll; この高速道路は有料ですか? [kono kousoku-douro wa yuuryou desu ka?] Is there a toll on this motorway?

優先 [yuusen] *n* priority; 優先権 [yuusenken] *n* right of way; 優先郵便でどのくらいの日数がかかりますか? [yuusen-yuubin de dono kurai no nissuu ga kakarimasu ka?] How long will it take by priority post?

優先権 [yuusenken] あなたには優先権がありませんでした [anata ni wa yuusen-ken ga arimasen deshita] It wasn't your right of way

有史前 [yuushimae] 有史前の [yuushi mae no] *adj* prehistoric

夕食 [yuushoku] *n* supper

優勝 [yuushou] 優勝者 [yuushousha] *n* champion

郵送 [yuusou] 郵送する [yuusou suru] *v* mail, post

ユースホステル [yuusuhosuteru] *n* youth hostel; 近くにユースホステルはありますか? [chikaku ni yuusuhosuteru wa arimasu ka?] Is there a youth hostel nearby?

ユースクラブ [yuusukurabu] *n* youth club

Uターン [yuutaan] *n* U-turn

ユーティリティールーム [yuutiritii ruumu] *n* utility room

憂鬱 [yuuutsu] *n* depression; 憂鬱な [yuuutsu na] *adj* depressing, gloomy

誘惑 [yuuwaku] *n* temptation; 誘惑する [yuuwaku suru] *adj* tempt; 誘惑する [yuuwaku suru] *adj* tempting

有用 [yuuyou] 有用性 [yuuyousei] n availability

有罪 [yuuzai] n guilt; 有罪の [yuuzai no] adj guilty; 有罪と決定する [yuuzai to kettei suru] v convict

譲る [yuzuru] v give way; 彼女は道を譲りませんでした [kanojo wa michi o yuzurimasen deshita] She didn't give way

Z

座 [za] 牡牛座 [oushiza] n Taurus

剤 [zai] しみ抜き剤 [shiminuki zai] n stain remover; 殺菌剤 [sakkinzai] n antiseptic; 抗ヒスタミン剤 [kouhisutaminzai] n antihistamine; 抗鬱剤 [kouutsuzai] n antidepressant; 解毒剤 [gedokuzai] n antidote; 発汗抑制剤 [hakkan yokuseizai] n antiperspirant; 精神安定剤 [seishin anteizai] n tranquillizer; 錠剤 [jouzai] n tablet; 鎮静剤 [chinseizai] n sedative; 除草剤 [josouzai] n weedkiller; 強壮剤 [kyousouzai] n tonic

財宝 [zaihou] n treasure

在庫 [zaiko] 在庫を置く [zaiko-o oku] v stock; 在庫品 [zaikohin] n stock

材木 [zaimoku] n timber, wood (material)

財務 [zaimu] n finance; 財務の [zaimu no] adj financial

材料 [zairyou] n ingredient, material; 材料は何ですか? [zairyou wa nan desu ka?] What is the material?

財政 [zaisei] 財政の [zaisei no] adj fiscal

雑貨 [zakka] 食料雑貨類 [shokuryou zakkarui] n groceries; 食料雑貨店 [shokuryou zakkaten] n grocer's; 食料雑貨商 [shokuryou zakkashou] n grocer

ザクロ [zakuro] n pomegranate

ザンビア [zanbia] n Zambia; ザンビア人 [zanbiajin] n Zambian (person); ザンビアの [zanbia no] adj Zambian

残高 [zandaka] 銀行の残高 [ginkou no zandaka] n bank balance

残骸 [zangai] n wreckage

残酷 [zankoku] n cruelty; 残酷な [zankoku na] adj cruel

残忍 [zannin] 残忍な [zannin na] adj brutal

暫定 [zantei] 暫定的な [zanteiteki na] adj provisional

ザリガニ [zarigani] n crayfish

座席 [zaseki] n seat (furniture); 今夜の座席を2つ予約したいのですが [kon'ya no zaseki o futatsu yoyaku shitai no desu ga] We'd like to reserve two seats for tonight; 一緒の座席を取れますか? [issho no zaseki o toremasu ka?] Can we have seats together?; 私は座席予約をしてあります [watashi wa zaseki-yoyaku o shite arimasu] I have a seat reservation

挫折 [zasetsu] 挫折した [zasetsu shita] adj frustrated

雑誌 [zasshi] n magazine (periodical); どこで雑誌を買えますか? [doko de zasshi o kaemasu ka?] Where can I buy a magazine?

雑種 [zasshu] 雑種の犬 [zasshu no inu] n mongrel

雑草 [zassou] n weed

雑多 [zatta] 雑多な [zatta na] adj miscellaneous

税 [zei] n tax; 付加価値税 [fukakachizei] n VAT; 所得税 [shotokuzei] n income tax; 自動車の道路利用税 [jidousha no douro riyou zei] n road tax

税関 [zeikan] 税関係官 [zeikan kakarikan] n customs officer

税金 [zeikin] n tax

贅沢 [zeitaku] n luxury; 贅沢な [zeitaku na] adj luxurious

全部 [zenbu] pron all

前景 [zenkei] n foreground

前方 [zenpou] 前方へ [zenpou-e] adv forward

全力 [zenryoku] 全力で走る [zenryoku de hashiru] v sprint

全粒小麦 [zenryuukomugi] 全粒小麦の [zenryuu komugi no] adj wholemeal

全身 [zenshin] 全身麻酔 [zenshin masui] n general anaesthetic

前進 [zenshin] n advance; 前進する [zenshin suru] v advance

喘息 [zensoku] n asthma; 私は喘息 があります [watashi ha zensoku gaarimasu] I suffer from asthma

全体 [zentai] n whole; 全体の [zentai no] adj entire; 全体の [zentai no] adj whole; 全体的に [zentaiteki ni] adv overall

前夜 [zenya] n eve

ゼラニウム [zeraniumu] n geranium

ゼリー [zerii] n jelly

絶望 [zetsubou] n despair

絶縁材 [zetsuenzai] n insulation

絶滅 [zetsumetsu] 絶滅した [zetsumetsu shita] adj extinct

絶対 [zettai] 絶対禁酒の [zettai kinshu no] adj teetotal

俗語 [zokugo] n slang

続篇 [zokuhen] n sequel

続人 [zoku nin] 女相続人 [onna souzokunin] n heiress

ぞくぞく [zokuzoku] ぞくぞくさせる [zokuzoku saseru] adj thrilling; ぞくぞくした [zokuzoku shita] adj thrilled; ぞくぞくする感じ [zokuzoku suru kanji] n thrill

ぞっと [zotto] ぞっとさせる [zotto saseru] adj horrifying; ぞっとするような [zotto suru you na] adj appalling

ぞっとする [zotto suru] v gruesome, hideous

像 [zou] n statue

ゾウ [zou] n elephant

増築 [zouchiku] n extension

象牙 [zouge] n ivory

増加 [zouka] n increase

臓器 [zouki] *n* organ *(body part)*

造船 [zousen] *n* shipbuilding; 造船所 [zousenjo] *n* shipyard

贈収賄 [zoushuuwai] *n* bribery

図 [zu] *n* diagram, drawing

ズボン [zubon] *n* trousers; 半ズボン [hanzubon] *n* shorts; このズボンを試着していいですか? [kono zubon o shichaku shite ii desu ka?] Can I try on these trousers?

ズボン吊り [zubontsuri] *n* braces

ずぶぬれ [zubunure] ずぶぬれの [zubunure no] *adj* soaked, soggy

ずぶとい [zubutoi] ずぶとさ [zubutosa] *n* nerve *(boldness)*

頭蓋 [zugai] 頭蓋骨 [zugaikotsu] *n* skull

図表 [zuhyou] *n* chart

髄膜 [zuimaku] 髄膜炎 [zuimakuen] *n* meningitis

ズッキーニ [zukkiini] *n* courgette, zucchini

ずるい [zurui] *adj* sly

ずさんな [zusanna] *adj* sloppy

ずたずた [zutazuta] ずたずたに引き裂く [zutazuta ni hikisaku] *v* tear up

頭痛 [zutsuu] *n* headache; 頭痛に効くものが欲しいのですが [zutsuu ni kiku mono ga hoshii no desu ga] I'd like something for a headache

ズーム [zuumu] ズームレンズ [zuumurenzu] *n* zoom lens

Japanese Grammar

Introduction	2
Sentence structure	3
Particles	3
Word order	6
Verbs	7
Questions	11
Expressing desire	11
Inviting, offering and suggesting	11
Making a request	12
Asking permission	13
Possibility/Ability	14
Adjectives	14
Question words	16

Introduction

This is a guide to some of the basic concepts and rules of Japanese grammar. It is designed to enable you to form simple sentences. There are different levels of politeness in Japanese, but polite forms, suitable for learners to use without being rude, have been used in the example sentences in the dictionary and in this grammar section. In the dictionary headwords, the verbs are in the plain form. This is the form used among family members and close friends, and to form more complex structures, so you may hear people using it. However, it is safest if you stick to using the polite form to avoid appearing over-familiar or rude.

Although the Japanese writing system is rather complicated because of the different scripts and the large number of Chinese characters, Japanese grammar is simple in many ways compared to most European languages. For example: there is no gender and there are no definite or indefinite articles; there is no difference between singular and plural; and verbs only have past and non-past (present or future) forms and do not change for grammatical person, i.e. according to who is performing an action.

Sentence structure

The basic Japanese sentence has a topic and a comment section. The topic (which is indicated by the topic marker **wa**) usually comes at the beginning of the sentence, but if the topic is understood among the speakers or from the context, it is often omitted.

> **(Watashi wa) Yamashita desu.**
> *(I) am Yamashita.*

Because the subject is often omitted and the verb form does not change according to grammatical person, the sentence **Kyouto ni ikimasu** can mean *I/you/he/she/we/they (will) go to Kyoto*, but the subject should be clear from the context.

In the example **Watashi wa Yamashita desu**, the topic is also the subject of the sentence, but in other cases the topic may be the object.

> **Sakana wa tabemasu.**
> *(I) eat <u>fish</u> (but there are other things I don't eat).*

Particles

Japanese has small words called particles that show how different parts of the sentence relate to each other. Some work in a similar way to English prepositions, but in Japanese they come after the nouns they refer to. These particles have the following functions.

wa	topic marker
ga	subject marker
o	direct object marker
ni	indirect object marker, goal and location marker
to	connects nouns, means 'and' or 'with'
de	indicates means by which an action is carried out, or place where an action takes place
no	Indicates that second noun is described in some way by first noun, e.g. possession
mo	means 'too/also/as well'
kara	means 'from/since'
made	means 'until/as far as'

Dare ga keeki o tabemashita ka?
Who ate the cake?

Densha de Kyouto ni ikimasu.
I/you/he/she/we/they will go to Kyoto by train.

Nihon no tabemono wa oishii desu.
Japanese food is delicious.

Furansu no tabemono mo oishii desu.
French food is also delicious.

Tanaka-san wa Yamada-san to sushiya ni ikimashita.
Mr/Ms Tanaka went with Mr/Ms Yamada to a sushi restaurant.

Toukyou kara Kyouto made dono kurai kakarimasu ka?
How long does it take from Tokyo to Kyoto?

Other particles are found at the end of sentences to change the meaning from a straightforward statement. Here are the most common ones.

ka	question marker
ne	asks for agreement or confirmation
yo	adds emphasis

Watashi no nimotsu wa doko ni arimasu <u>ka</u>?
Where is my luggage?

Atsui desu <u>ne</u>.
It's hot, isn't it.

Ii desu <u>yo</u>.
It's all right/I don't mind.

A: Kaimasen <u>ne</u>.
B: Iie, kaimasu <u>yo</u>.

A: You're not going to buy it, are you?
B: Yes, I am going to buy it.

Note in the last example above that **hai** (*yes*) and **iie** (*no*) are used rather differently from their English equivalents. In Japanese, you agree or disagree with the assumption underlying the question.

Finally, some particles are used to link clauses to make more complex sentences. Two of the most useful are **kara** (*because/so*) and **ga** (*but*). Note that **kara** always comes <u>after</u> the reason or cause, and usually follows the plain form (see below) of verbs and adjectives.

Kinou wa byouki datta <u>kara</u>, gakkou ni ikimasen deshita.
I was ill yesterday, so I didn't go to school/I didn't go to school yesterday, because I was ill.

In speech, the polite form is usually used before **ga**.

Nihongo wa muzukashii desu <u>ga</u>, omoshiroi desu.
Japanese is difficult, but interesting.

Word order

Japanese word order is: subject – object – verb. The verb comes at the end of the sentence. Therefore, *I eat sushi* becomes *I sushi eat*; **Watashi wa sushi o tabemasu**. When the comment part is long, for example, *I will eat sushi with my friend in London tomorrow*, as long as you put *I* (the topic) and *will eat* (the verb) in their respective places and you move the other words together with the necessary particles, the other parts of the sentence can be in any order. However, the most neutral order is: time – manner – place: **Watashi wa ashita tomodachi to Rondon de sushi o tabemasu** literally means *I tomorrow with (my) friend in London sushi will eat.*

In the polite form, Japanese verbs end with **masu**.

Ashita Nara ni iki<u>masu</u>.
I'm going to Tokyo tomorrow.

Sentences in the polite form ending in nouns or adjectives end with a special verb called the copula: **desu**.

Suzuki-san wa gakusei <u>desu</u>.
Mr/Ms Suzuki is a student.

Shinkansen wa totemo hayai <u>desu</u>.
The bullet train is very fast.

Negative sentences can be made by changing the verb or adjective at the end of the sentence to a negative form – see tables and examples below.

Verbs

To be

The English verb *to be* covers a range of meanings, but Japanese distinguishes between describing something and saying that something exists. The copula **desu** is used when you want to describe something or someone in some way.

Are wa ginkou <u>desu</u>.
That is a bank.

Ueno-san wa kenchikuka <u>desu</u>.
Mr/Ms Ueno is an architect.

NON-PAST POSITIVE	NON-PAST NEGATIVE	PAST POSITIVE	PAST NEGATIVE
desu	dewa arimasen or **ja arimasen**	deshita	dewa arimasen deshita or **ja arimasen deshita**

In the negative form of **desu**, **ja** is a contracted form of **dewa**.

Hon <u>desu</u>.
It is a book.

7

Hon <u>dewa/ja arimasen</u>.
It is not a book.

Hon <u>deshita</u>.
It was a book.

Hon <u>dewa/ja arimasen deshita</u>.
It was not a book.

When talking about whether something or someone exists – for example, to say that something or someone is in a particular place – you need to use different verbs for animate and inanimate objects. To refer to people and animals, use **imasu**, and to refer to things, use **arimasu**.

Kawaguchi-san wa doko ni <u>imasu</u> ka?
Where is Mr/Ms Kawaguchi?

Koko ni ginkou ga <u>arimasu</u> ka?
Is there a bank here?

Verb forms
Apart from the special case of the copula (**desu**), all Japanese verbs end in **masu** in the non-past positive polite form.

Mado o akemasu.
I (will) open the window.

The **masu** ending changes for negative and past forms.

NON-PAST POSITIVE	NON-PAST NEGATIVE	PAST POSITIVE	PAST NEGATIVE
-masu	-masen	-mashita	-masen deshita

sushi o tabe-<u>masu</u>.
I eat sushi.

sushi o tabe-<u>masen</u>.
I don't eat sushi.

Sushi o tabe-<u>mashita</u>.
I ate sushi.

Sushi o tabe-<u>masen deshita</u>.
I didn't eat sushi.

The verbs are divided into three groups, depending on their endings in the plain form. Most fall into two groups, but there are also two irregular verbs. The following chart shows how to make the polite **masu** form from the plain forms, which you will find as headwords in the dictionary. Note that there are sound changes for verbs ending in **su** and **tsu**.

	PLAIN FORM		POLITE FORM
group 1 verbs ending in **u**, **ku**, **gu**, **nu**, **bu**, **mu**, **ru**	**ka-u** *to buy*	change final **u** to **i** and add **masu**	**ka-<u>i-masu</u>**
	kak-u *to write*		**kak-<u>i-masu</u>**
	nom-u *to drink*		**nom-<u>i-masu</u>**
	kaer-u* *to return*		**kaer-<u>i-masu</u>**
group 1 verbs ending in **su**, **tsu**	**hana-su** *to talk*	change final **su** to **shi** and add **masu**	**hana<u>shi-masu</u>**
	mats-u *to wait*	change final **tsu** to **chi** and add **masu**	**ma<u>chi-masu</u>**

group 2 verbs most verbs ending in **eru** or **iru**	**mi-ru** *to see/watch/look* **tabe-ru** *to eat*	replace final **ru** with **masu**	mi-<u>**masu**</u> tabe-<u>**masu**</u>
irregular verbs	**suru** *to do* **kuru** *to come*	change **su** to **shi** and add **masu** change final **ru** to **masu**	shi-<u>**masu**</u> ki-<u>**masu**</u>

* There are some exceptions: for example, the verbs **kaeru** (*to return*), **hashiru** (*to run*), and **iru** (*to need*) look like group 2 verbs, but are in fact group 1 verbs.

Some Japanese verbs are a combination of a noun and the verb **shimasu** (*to do*), for example, **benkyou shimasu** (*to study*).

Transitive and intransitive verbs

In English, many verbs can be either transitive (these need to be followed by an object) or intransitive (these are not followed by an object). For example, in English, we can say both *I opened the door* (here *the door* is the object) and *The door opened* (no object) using the same verb. In Japanese, however, transitive and intransitive verbs are always slightly different, so the equivalent sentences would be **Watashi wa doa o ake̱mashita** and **Doa ga aki̱mashita** respectively.

Questions

You can create a question by simply adding the question marker **ka** at the end of the sentence.

> **Tokyo desu.**
> *This is Tokyo.*

> **Tokyo desu <u>ka</u>?**
> *Is it Tokyo?*

> **Sumida-san wa eigo o hanashimasu.**
> *Mr/Ms Sumida speaks English.*

> **Sumida-san wa eigo o hanashimasu <u>ka</u>?**
> *Does Mr/Ms Sumida speak English?*

Expressing desire

Change the **masu** polite verb ending to **tai desu**, for example, **tabe-masu** to **tabe-tai desu** (*I would like to eat*), and **nomi-masu** to **nomi-tai desu** (*I would like to drink*).

Inviting, offering and suggesting

It is generally considered impolite to use **tai desu** to ask someone else if they would like to do something. Instead, use the negative form with the question marker **ka**.

> **Ocha o nomi<u>masen</u> ka?**
> *Would you like to drink some tea?*

> **Issho ni eiga o mi<u>masen</u> ka?**
> *Would you like to see a film with me?*

11

To suggest doing something by saying *let's*, change the **masu** verb ending to **mashou**.

> **Oyogi ni iki<u>mashou</u>.**
> *Let's go swimming.*

Turn it into a question by adding **ka**.

> **Oyogi ni ikimashou <u>ka</u>?**
> *Shall we go swimming?*

Making a request

In order to make a request or ask permission, you need to know how to make the so-called **te** form of the verbs, which is based on the plain form, apart from the two irregular verbs.

		PLAIN FORM	te FORM
group 1 verbs verbs ending in **u**, **tsu**, **ru**	change **u/tsu/ru** ending to **tte**	ka-u *to buy* mats-u *to wait*	ka-<u>tte</u> ma-<u>tte</u>
verbs ending in **ku***	change **ku** ending to **ite**	ki-ku *to listen/hear*	ki-<u>ite</u>
verbs ending in **gu**	change **gu** ending to **ide**	iso-gu *to hurry*	iso-<u>ide</u>
verbs ending in **su**	change **su** ending to **shite**	hana-su *to speak*	hana-<u>shite</u>
verbs ending in **nu**, **bu**, **mu**	change **nu/bu/mu** ending to **nde**	no-mu *to drink*	no-<u>nde</u>

group 2 verbs	change final **ru** to **te**	**mi-ru** *to see/watch/ look*	**mi-te**
		tabe-ru *to eat*	**tabe-te**
irregular verbs	change **masu** to **te**	**shi-masu** *to do*	**shi-te**
		ki-masu *to come*	**ki-te**

*The verb **iku** is irregular in the **te** form: **itte**.

If you would like someone to provide you with something, you can use the words **kudasai** (*please give me*) or **onegai shimasu** (*please*). For example, **Reshiito o kudasai** (*Can I have a receipt please*) or **Reshiito, onegai shimasu** (*Receipt please*). The particle **o** marks the direct object.

If you want to ask someone to do something for you, use the **te** form of the verb, then add **kudasai** at the end: for example, **hanashite kudasai** (*please speak*); **katte kudasai** (*please buy*); **tabete kudasai** (*please eat*).

Asking permission

Use the **te** form of the verb and add **mo ii desu ka**.

> **Tabete <u>mo ii desu ka</u>?**
> *Is it all right to eat?*

> **Shashin o totte <u>mo ii desu ka</u>?**
> *Is it all right to take a photo?*

Possibility/Ability

For verbs that are a combination of a noun plus **shimasu**, simply change **shimasu** to **dekimasu**, for example, **benkyou dekimasu**.

> **Toshokan de yoku benkyou <u>dekimasu</u>.**
> *I am able to study well in the library.*

To ask whether it is possible to do something or if someone is able to do something, simply add the question marker **ka** at the end of the sentence.

> **Koko ni chuusha dekimasu <u>ka</u>?**
> *Can we park here?*

There are two ways of expressing possibility or ability for other verbs. The simplest way is to add **koto ga dekiru** to the plain form of the verb; remember that **dekiru** changes to **dekimasu** in the polite form.

> **Watashi wa uma ni noru <u>koto ga dekimasu</u>.**
> *I can ride a horse.*

Adjectives

There are two kinds of adjectives in Japanese.

One kind changes its endings like a verb; because these end in **i** in the non-past form, they are often called **i** adjectives. They can be used directly before a noun, for example, **oishii sakana** (*delicious fish*), or followed by **desu** to make a sentence in the polite form.

NON-PAST POSITIVE	NON-PAST NEGATIVE	PAST POSITIVE	PAST NEGATIVE
oishi-i (is delicious, tasty)	oishi-kunai (is not delicious)	oishi-katta (was delicious)	oishi-kunakatta (was not delicious)

Oishii desu.
(It) is delicious.

Sakana wa oishii desu.
The fish is delicious.

Sakana wa oishikatta desu.
The fish was delicious.

Oishii sakana desu ne.
It's delicious fish, isn't it.

The other kind of adjective works more like a noun, and is followed by some form of **desu**, including the special form **na**, which is used before a noun; these are therefore often called **na** adjectives.

Shizuka desu.
It is quiet.

Shizuka dewa/ja arimasen.
It is not quiet.

Shizuka deshita.
It was quiet.

Shizuka dewa/ja arimasen deshita.
It was not quiet.

Shizuka na apaato desu.
It's a quiet apartment.

Shizuka <u>na</u> apaato dewa/ja arimasen deshita.
It was not a quiet apartment.

Some English verbs are adjectives in Japanese. For example, *to want* is an **i** adjective in Japanese, **hoshii** and **suki** (*to like*) and **kirai** (*to dislike*) are both **na** adjectives.

Kuruma ga <u>hoshikatta</u> desu.
I wanted a car.

Nihon ga <u>suki</u> desu.
I like Japan.

<u>Kirai na</u> tabemono wa nan desu ka?
What food do you dislike?

Question words

dare	who
doko	where
dore	which one (of three or more)
dochira	which one (of two)/which direction
dono	which (before noun)
donna	what kind of
dou	how
itsu	when
nan/nani	what

英文法

はじめに	18
動詞	18
助動詞	19
句動詞（群動詞）	20
代名詞	21
形容詞	23
副詞	25
限定詞	26
前置詞	27
接続詞	27
時制	28
主部（主語）・目的語	30
呼応	31

はじめに

本章では日本人英語学習者を対象に英文法の基礎を説明します。

動詞

動作や状態を表す語を**動詞**と呼びます。**動詞**には**他動詞**と**自動詞**があります。

　　　他動詞として用いる場合は動詞の後に**目的語**が必要です。次の例文では **likes** が**他動詞**で、beer が**目的語**です。

Peter **likes** beer.
ピーターはビールが好きです。

単に"He likes."では不完全な文となります。**目的語**、つまり**何が**好きなのかを動詞の後に言わなければなりません。

　　　自動詞は**目的語なし**で用いられます。次の例文では **sneezed** の後に目的語はなく**自動詞**として使われています。

I **sneezed**.
私はくしゃみをした。

sneeze（くしゃみをする）の後にはloudly（大きな声で）のように動詞を修飾する副詞を続けることはできますが、「何を」にあたる目的語を置くことはできません。

　　　日本語では「増やす」（他動詞）、「増える」（自動詞）のように他動詞と自動詞ではふつう形が異なります。ところが英語ではそのどちらの意味にもincreaseが使われます。つまり同じ綴りでも他動詞としても自動詞としても使われる動詞が多くあります。

We have **increased** our spending on training.
当社は、研修費を増やした。（他動詞）

Sales levels have **increased**.
売上が増えた。（自動詞）

ただし、lay（〜を置く、横たえる）・lie（横になる、存在する）、raise（〜を上げる）・rise（上がる、増加する）のように他動詞と自動詞の形が異なるものもあります。例えば、「その店は価格を上げた」は "The store has **raised** prices."、「私の収入が増えた」は"My income has **risen**."となります。

助動詞

助動詞としてのbe, have, do

be, have, doなどの動詞は助動詞としての用法もあり、動詞と共に用いられて、さまざまな時制を表したり、疑問文や否定文を作ったりします。beやhaveと共に用いられ、進行形（〜しているところ）や完了形（〜したことがある）などの時制を表すことができます。

　　＜be＋現在分詞（動詞の-ing形）＞は、過去や現在において動作が進行中であることを表します。

I **am working** now.
私は今仕事中です。

＜be＋動詞の過去分詞形（ふつう動詞の-ed形）＞で、受身（〜される）を表します。

Mark **was arrested** yesterday.
マークは昨日逮捕されました。

＜have＋動詞の過去分詞形（ふつう動詞の-ed形）＞で、「過去と今をつなぐ」現在完了形や＜had＋動詞の過去分詞形＞「過去とそれ以前の過去をつなぐ」過去完了形を作ることができます。

Paul **has** just **finished** fixing the car.
ポールは、ちょうど車の修理を終えたところです。

doは動詞の原形と共に用いられ、否定文や疑問文、強調構文を作ります。

I **do** not **like** sausages.
私はソーセージが好きではありません。

Do you **like** prawns?
あなたはエビが好きですか。

話し言葉やくだけた書き言葉では、I'm, she's, they'veのように短縮形が
使われることがよくあります。

その他の助動詞

その他の助動詞は、動詞の原形と共に用いられて、能力・可能・必要性など
の意味を表すことができます。主な助動詞は次の通りです。
can, could, may, might, must, ought, shall, will, would
　　このような助動詞は、be, have, doなどの助動詞と異なり、主語によっ
て形が変わることはありません。

I **can** ride a horse.
私は、馬に乗ることができます。

She **can** ride a horse.
彼女は、馬に乗ることができます。

くだけた話し言葉では、助動詞willはI'll, they'llのように'llと短縮されるこ
とがよくあります。またwouldは、I'd, they'dのように'dと短縮されます。

句動詞（群動詞）

動詞に副詞や前置詞がつき、語のまとまりとして1つの動詞と同じ働きを
するものを**句動詞（群動詞）**と呼びます。
　　動詞＋副詞 には、take off（離陸する）、blow up（爆破する）などがあり
ます。
　　動詞＋前置詞には、pick on〜（〜をからかう）、look after（〜の世話を
する）などがあります。
　　動詞＋副詞＋前置詞には、put up with 〜（〜をがまんする）、get out
of 〜（〜を逃れる）などがあります。
　　句動詞は、動詞や副詞・前置詞が持つもともとの意味とはまったく異な
った意味を持つことがよくあるので、1つのまとまりとして覚えるとよいで
しょう。

名詞

事や物、考えなどを表す語を**名詞**と呼びます。

固有名詞
固有名詞とは、人や土地、物の名前を表し、大文字で始めます。
例：John Lennon（ジョン・レノン）、China（中国）、Mount Fuji（富士山）、
Thursday（木曜日）

可算名詞
可算名詞とは、one cat（ネコ1匹）、two cats（ネコ2匹）、several cats
（ネコ数匹）のように数えられるものを指す名詞で、単数形と複数形があ
ります。単数形は、不定冠詞のaあるいは定冠詞theと共に用いられます。
複数形は、ふつう名詞に-sをつけます。

We've bought six new **chairs**.
私たちは、新しい椅子を6脚買いました。

不可算名詞
不可算名詞とは、液体や気体のように「ひとつ、ふたつ...」と数えられない
ものを指す名詞です。数えられない名詞には複数形はありません。現在時
制の場合は、動詞に-s/esをつけます（三人称単数現在）。ただし、不定冠詞
のaは用いられません。an adviceやa moneyなどという表現は誤りです。

I asked Emiko for some **advice**.
私は、エミコにアドバイスを求めました。

代名詞

代名詞とは、「名詞の代わりをする言葉」です。1つの文や段落内での名詞
の繰り返しを避けるために代名詞が使われます。日本語には必ずしも訳す
必要がないこともよくあります。

Ken was hungry so **he** stopped at a burger bar.
ケンはお腹がすいていたので、ハンバーガー店に立ち寄りました。

代名詞は、使い方や意味によって、いくつかの種類に分類されます。
　　人称代名詞は、主語あるいは目的語として使われます。

He gave **her** a ring.
彼は彼女に指輪を贈りました。

再帰代名詞は人称代名詞の所有格あるいは目的格に-selfまたは-selves
のついた形をとり、動詞や前置詞の目的語として用いられます。動詞によ
っては決まった表現の一部として用いられることもあります。

I've just cut **myself** on a piece of glass.
（私は）ガラスの破片で切ってしまった。

再帰代名詞は強調の意味を表すために用いられることもあります。

The professor **himself** did not know the answer.
教授でさえその答えを知らなかった。

所有代名詞は、所有（誰のものか）を表す代名詞で単独で用いられます。
後に名詞を伴わず、「私の本」と言うときmine bookと言うのは誤りです。
正しくはmy bookあるいは「本」の話であることが明らかであればmineと
言います。

Give it back, it's **mine**.
返して。ボクのだよ。

指示代名詞は、特定の人やものを表します。指しているものが近くにある
か、遠くにあるか、複数か、単数かによってthis, these, that, thoseを使い
分けます。

This is Margaret's and **that** is Norman's.
これがマーガレットので、あれがノーマンのだよ。

関係代名詞は、「名詞を説明する節」と「説明される名詞（あるいは名詞句）」
を結びつけるために使われます。

I have friends **who** live in Canada.
私には、カナダに住んでいる友人がいます。

疑問代名詞は、尋ねたい事柄が名詞の場合に使われます。

What would you like for lunch?
昼食には、何がいいですか。

人称代名詞には、主格（I, you, he, she, it, we, they）と目的格（me, you, him, her, us, them）があります。主語が固有名詞と代名詞の両方を含む場合など、使い分けが難しいこともあります。
　　代名詞が他の名詞と共に主語として用いられる場合は、主格を用います。

Riku and **I** play rugby every Sunday.
リクと私は、毎週日曜日にラグビーをします。

Riku and **me** are ...と言うのはよくある間違いです。
　　代名詞が他の名詞と共に目的語として用いられる場合は、目的格を使います。

Ken helped Mike and **me**.
ケンは、マイクと私を手伝ってくれた。

形容詞

名詞を説明するときに**形容詞**が使われます。形容詞を使うことにより、具体的に何を表しているのかが明確になります。
　　a man（男性）→ a tall man（背の高い男性）
　　their TV（彼らのテレビ）→ their new, wide-screen TV（新しいワイドテレビ）
　　the cat（そのネコ）→ the fat, black-and-white cat（太った、白黒のネコ）

複数の形容詞を用いる場合は、ふつう形容詞と形容詞の間にコンマを入

れます。ただし、コンマなしで形容詞が続くことも珍しくありません。いくつかの形容詞を続けても構いませんが、5つ以上連続して使うことはまれです。

a happy young blonde German girl
うれしそうな、若い金髪のドイツ人の女の子

比較級

二つのもの（二人）を比べて「〜がより・・・だ」と述べる場合、**比較級**が用いられます。

Anna is **taller** than Mary, but Mary is **older**.
アナはメアリーよりも背が高いのですが、メアリーの方が年上です。

最上級

三つ以上のもの（三人以上）を比べて、「〜が一番・・・だ」と述べる場合、**最上級**が用いられます。

That is **the smallest** camera I have ever seen.
それは、私が今までに見た中で一番小さいカメラです。

形容詞の比較級・最上級の作り方は二通りあります。

　1音節（発音する母音の数が1つ）の形容詞には、語尾に-er（比較級）、-est（最上級）をつけます。例えば、long（長い）はlonger、the longestと変化します。

　語尾が –eで終わる語は、-e をとってから-er、-estをつけます。-yで終わる語は、ふつう-yを-iに変えてから –er、-estをつけます。「1短母音＋１子音」の形容詞の場合、子音字を重ねてから –er、-estをつけます。例: wise-wiser-the wisest, pretty-prettier-the prettiest, big-bigger-the biggest

　3音節以上ある形容詞には、形容詞の前に more、mostを置きます。例えば、fortunate（幸運な）は、more fortunate、the most fortunateとなります。また動詞の分詞形（現在分詞、過去分詞）が形容詞として用いられている場合もこの形をとります。例: boring → more boring, the most boring

　2音節の形容詞（すでに語尾が-erの語も含む）は、上記のどちら型を使

うこともできます。迷った場合は、more/most型を使うとよいでしょう。例えば、polite（丁寧な）は、politer/politestと言うこともmore polite/the most politeと言うこともできます。

　good/better/the best、bad/worse/the worstのように上記の規則に当てはまらない形容詞もまれにあります。

　1つの文でmore/mostと-er/-estの両方を用いるのは、よくある間違いですが、正しい英語ではないので、使わないようにしましょう。例えば、「一番賢い人」と言うときに、the most cleverest personとするのは誤りです。

副詞

副詞には、様々な用法があるために見分けることが難しい場合があります。基本的には、動作がどのように行われているか、いつ・どこで行われているか、を説明するのが副詞です。

　副詞には、形容詞に –lyをつけたものが多くあります。例:
slow（遅い）→ slowly（ゆっくりと）、clever（賢い）→ cleverly（賢く）

　-bleで終わる形容詞は –eをとってから–lyをつけます。true（本当の）も同様に活用します。sensible（分別のある）→ sensibly（賢明に）、suitable（適切な）→ suitably（適切に）、true（本当の）→ truly（本当に）

　ただし、一般的に–eで終わる形容詞には、単に –lyをつけます。
例: extreme（極端な）/extremely（極端に）, free（自由な）/freely（自由に）

　-yで終わる形容詞は、-yを –iに変えてから–lyをつけます。
例: happy（幸せな）→ happily（幸せに）、greedy（貪欲な）→ greedily（貪欲に）。ただし、sly（ずる賢い）のように1音節の形容詞はslylyのように単に-lyをつけます。

　late（遅れた、遅く）、early（早朝の、早く）のように形容詞と副詞が同じ綴りの場合もあります。そのような語では、動詞や形容詞を説明している場合は副詞であり、名詞を説明している場合は形容詞であると判断します。

an **early** meeting
早朝の会議

He arrived ten minutes **early**.
彼は、10分早く到着した。

文修飾をする副詞は、文や節の冒頭に置かれます。これには –lyで終わる副詞のほか、nevertheless（それにもかかわらず）, however（しかしながら）のような他の副詞も含まれます。

Foolishly, I gave him my address.
愚かにも、彼に住所を教えてしまった。

形容詞と同様に、副詞にも比較級と最上級があります。ほとんどの場合は more /mostを副詞の前に置くことにより、比較級・最上級を作ることができます。

Could you speak **more slowly**, please?
もっとゆっくり話していただけませんか。

well/better/ best、badly/worse/worstのように不規則変化をする副詞もあります。

限定詞

限定詞には、「人、もの、考えなど後に続く名詞に具体的な情報を与える」という役割があります。this carと言えば、話題となっている車がすぐ近くにあることがわかります。一方、my carと言えば、車の所有者が自分であることを明らかにしています。

限定詞は、以下が含まれます。
- a/anやtheなどの冠詞
- this, that, these, thoseなど距離感覚を示す指示限定詞
- my, your, his, its, our, theirなど誰のものであるかを示す所有限定詞
- some, any, few, enough, muchなど数や量を表す数量詞
- one, two, threeなどの基数やfirst, second, thirdなどの序数

前置詞

前置詞は、基本的に名詞の前に置かれ、文中の他の語との関係を示します。ほとんどの前置詞は、いくつかの意味を持ち合わせています。

　　ふつうin, on, underのように1語からなる語を前置詞と呼びますが、due to, together with, on top of, in spite of, out ofのように2語以上のまとまりが、前置詞と同じ働きをすることもあります。

　　下記の語はすべてよく使われる前置詞です。ただし、above, acrossのように文脈によっては副詞として使われる語も含まれています。前置詞には、他動詞と同様に後に目的語が続きます。

> aboard, about, above, across, after, against, along,
> alongside, amid, among, around, as, at, bar, before, behind,
> below, beneath, beside, between, beyond, by, despite, down,
> during, for, from, in, inside, into, like, near, of, off, on, onto,
> opposite, outside, over, past, pending, per, prior, pro, re,
> regarding, round, since, than, through, throughout, till, to,
> towards, under, underneath, until, unto, up, upon, via,
> with, within, without

接続詞

接続詞は、2つ以上の名詞あるいは節をつなぐ言葉です。

Lauren bought some bread, **but** she forgot to get the milk.
ローレンはパンを買ったが、ミルクを買い忘れた。

正式な文章（書き言葉）では、接続詞で文を始めるのはよくないとみなされます。ただし、クリエイティブな文章では、それが効果的になることもあります。

時制

動詞が表現する行為や状態がいつのことなのか、つまり現在・過去・未来など時間の前後関係を表すのが**時制**です。

　英語の時制では、動詞の活用形のみ（つまり1語）で表す単純時制と、beやhaveなどの助動詞の現在形あるいは過去形に-ing/-ed形を加えて表現する複合時制の二つがあります。

現在形
現在の行為・状態について述べる場合は、現在形を用います。I, youあるいは複数が主語の場合は動詞の原形と同じ形です。主語がI, you 以外（三人称）で単数の場合はふつう動詞の原形に-sをつけます（-s, -x, -ch, -sh, <子音字+o>で終わる動詞には-esをつける）。

I **go** to London Metropolitan University, but William **goes** to University of Bath.
私はロンドン・メトロポリタン大学に行っていますが、ウィリアムはバース大学です。

過去形
過去の行為・状態について述べる場合は、過去形を用います。形は、play → playedのように主語にかかわらず、ふつう動詞の原形に-edをつけます（-eで終わる動詞は語尾に-dだけをつける）。ただし、cost → cost, tell → toldのように不規則に活用する動詞もあります。

Harry **saw** a squirrel.
ハリーはリスを見かけた。

未来形
未来の行為・状態について述べる場合、未来形を用います。主語にかかわらず、動詞の原型の前に助動詞willを置きます。

We **will give** you the book.
私たちはあなたにその本をあげましょう。

現在完了形

過去を今の状況とつなげて表現する場合、現在完了形を用います。<have + 動詞の過去分詞>の形をとります（he/she/itなど三人称単数が主語の場合はhas + 動詞の過去分詞）。過去分詞は過去形と同様、ふつう動詞の原形に-edをつけますが、不規則に活用する動詞もあります。

This illness **has ruined** my life.
その病気で私の人生が台無しになった。

現在進行形

「今～している」と動作が進行中であることを表す場合は、現在進行形を用います。<be動詞の現在形 + 現在分詞>の形をとります。現在分詞は、ふつう動詞の原形に-ingをつけます。be動詞は、主語に合わせてam, is, areから適切なものを使います。

James **is finishing** his meal.
ジェームズは、食事を食べ終えるところです。

過去進行形

過去のある時点に動作が進行中であったことを表す場合は、過去進行形を用います。<be動詞の過去形 + 現在分詞>の形をとります。be動詞は、主語に合わせてwas, wereのどちらかを使います。

Sam **was listening** to his iPod then.
サムは、そのときiPodを聞いていました。

未来進行形

未来のあるときに進行中であろう動作を表す場合は、未来進行形を用います。主語にかかわらず、<will be + 現在分詞>の形をとります。

Japan **will be playing** England in the Wold Cup semi-final.
日本は、ワールドカップの準決勝戦でイングランドと対決します。

主部（主語）・目的語

文の中で「〜は／〜が」にあたる部分を**主語**と呼びます。主語になれるのは、名詞と代名詞です。名詞の働きをする句や節を主語と同じように用いることができます。その場合は、主部と呼びます。

Kentaro plays the clarinet.
健太朗はクラリネットを演奏します。

The man in the red coat asked me some questions.
赤いコートを着た男性が、私に質問をしました。

英語の文には必ず主語（主部）が必要です。
文の**目的語**はふつう動詞の後に置かれます。目的語になれるのは、名詞、名詞句、代名詞です。

Serge spilled **the milk**.
サージはミルクをこぼしました。

We were able to fix **the broken shelf**.
私たちは、壊れた棚を直すことができました。

動詞が自動詞として用いられていれば、目的語が置かれません。

Erica was writing.
エリカが執筆していました。（目的語なし）

Erica was writing **a letter**.
エリカが手紙を書いていました。（目的語あり）

動詞によっては「〜に」「〜を」と目的語が二つ続くことがあります。目的語を二つ取る動詞にはgive, find, oweなどがあります。

Nancy gave **me a box of chocolates**.
ナンシーは私にチョコレートをくれました。

呼応

主語や動詞、代名詞などをそれぞれ関連した語に合わせて適切に活用させて用いることを**呼応**と呼びます。

主語・動詞の呼応

動詞の形は、主語に呼応させなければなりません。例えば"The house is very large.（その家はとても大きい）"という文では、主語が三人称単数なので動詞はisを用います。"The stars are very bright.（星が光り輝いている）"では、主語が複数形なので動詞も複数形areで受けます。長い文、特に主語と動詞が離れている場合は、誤りを犯しやすいので気をつけましょう。

andで二つ以上の名詞がつながれている場合、複数形の動詞で受けます。

Simon and Natalie are going to Paris.
サイモンとナタリーはパリに行きます。

ただしandでつながれたものが1つのものとみなされている場合は、動詞は単数形を用います。

Fish and chips is my favourite meal.
フィッシュ・アンド・チップスは、お気に入りの料理です。注：「フィッシュ・アンド・チップス」は料理の名前

主語が each, every, noなどの語を伴う場合は、単数形の動詞を用います。

Every seat **was** taken already.
すべての席がすでに取られていました。

or, nor, neither/nor, either/or, not only/but alsoなどの語でつながれた名詞が主部（主語）になっている場合は、単数形の動詞を用います。

Either Mrs Green **or** Mr Brown **takes** the children to football.
グリーンさんかブラウンさんが子供たちをサッカーに連れて行きます。

本、映画、歌などのタイトルは、たとえタイトルに複数形が使われていても動詞は単数形を用います。

'The Birds' is a really scary film.
『鳥』は本当に怖い映画だ。

代名詞の呼応

代名詞が何を指しているかによって適切な代名詞が決まります。代名詞が指しているものは、別の文にあることもよくあります。

The car started fine, but **it** broke down half way to Manchester.
クルマは快調に走り出したが、マンチェスターに行く途中で故障してしまった。

集合名詞の呼応

committeeやparliamentのように集団を総括的に表す名詞を集合名詞と呼びます。イギリス英語では集合名詞が主語の場合、動詞は単数形でも複数形でも構いません。ただし、どちらかに統一する必要があります。アメリカ英語では、集合名詞は単数形の動詞で受けます。

The army **was** marching towards us./The army **were** marching towards us.
軍隊がこちらに向かって行進していた。

時制の呼応

文あるいは段落内で関連している時制が互いに呼応しなければなりません。「待っている間に映画を見た」と言う場合、"While I was waiting, I **seen** a film." は過去分詞を使っているため誤った表現で、正しくは"While I was waiting, I **saw** a film."と過去形を用います。

　　また「お昼までに50通以上の返事を書いた」と言う場合は、過去のある時点で動作が完了しているため、"By midday, I **answered** over 50 letters."は誤った表現で、正しくは"By midday, I **had answered** over 50 letters."と過去完了形を用います。

English – Japanese

英語-日本語

a

a [ə, eɪ] *art* 一つの [hitotsu no]

abandon [ə'bændən] *v* 見捨てる [misuteru]

abbey ['æbɪ] *n* 僧院 [souin]

abbreviation [ə,briːvɪ'eɪʃən] *n* 略語 [ryakugo]

abdomen ['æbdəmən; æb'dəʊ-] *n* 腹 [hara]

abduct [æb'dʌkt] *v* 誘拐する [yuukai suru]

ability [ə'bɪlɪtɪ] *n* 能力 [nouryoku]

able ['eɪbəl] *adj* ・・・ができる [...ga dekiru]

abnormal [æb'nɔːməl] *adj* 異常な [ijou na]

abolish [ə'bɒlɪʃ] *v* 廃止する [haishi suru]

abolition [,æbə'lɪʃən] *n* 廃止 [haishi]

abortion [ə'bɔːʃən] *n* 妊娠中絶 [ninshinchuuzetsu]

about [ə'baʊt] *adv* およそ [oyoso] ▷ *prep* ・・・について [...nitsuite]

above [ə'bʌv] *prep* ・・・の上に [...no ue ni]

abroad [ə'brɔːd] *adv* 海外に [kaigai ni]

abrupt [ə'brʌpt] *adj* 不意の [fui no]

abruptly [ə'brʌptlɪ] *adv* 不意に [fui ni]

abscess ['æbsɛs; -sɪs] *n* 膿瘍 [nouyou]; **I have an abscess** 私は膿瘍があります

[watashi wa nouyou ga arimasu]

absence ['æbsəns] *n* 不在 [fuzai]

absent ['æbsənt] *adj* 不在の [fuzai no]

absent-minded [,æbsən't'maɪndɪd] *adj* ぼんやりした [bon'yari shita]

absolutely [,æbsə'luːtlɪ] *adv* 全く [mattaku]

abstract ['æbstrækt] *adj* 抽象的な [chuushouteki na]

absurd [əb'sɜːd] *adj* ばかげた [bakageta]

Abu Dhabi ['æbuː 'dɑːbɪ] *n* アブダビ [abudabi]

abuse *n* [ə'bjuːs] 虐待 [gyakutai] ▷ *v* [ə'bjuːz] 濫用する [ran'you suru]; **child abuse** *n* 児童虐待 [jidou gyakutai]

abusive [ə'bjuːsɪv] *adj* 口汚い [kuchi kitanai]

academic [,ækə'dɛmɪk] *adj* 大学の [daigaku no]; **academic year** *n* 学年 [gakunen]

academy [ə'kædəmɪ] *n* 学士院 [gakushiin]

accelerate [æk'sɛlə,reɪt] *v* 加速する [kasoku suru]

acceleration [æk,sɛlə'reɪʃən] *n* 加速 [kasoku]

accelerator [æk'sɛlə,reɪtə] *n* アクセル [akuseru]

accept [ək'sɛpt] *v* 受け入れる [ukeireru]

acceptable [ək'sɛptəbəl] *adj* 無難な [bunan na]

access ['æksɛs] *n* 接近 [sekkin] ▷ *v* アクセスする [akusesu suru]

accessible [ək'sɛsəbəl] *adj* 近づきやすい [chikadukiyasui]

accessory [ək'sɛsərɪ] *n* 付属物 [fuzokubutsu]

accident ['æksɪdənt] *n* 事故 [jiko]; **accident & emergency department** *n* 救急病棟 [kyuukyuubyoutou]; **accident insurance** *n* 事故保険 [jiko hoken]; **by accident** *adv* 偶然に [guuzen ni]; **I've had an accident** 私は事故にあいました [watashi wa jiko ni aimashita]; **There's been an accident!** 事故がありました! [jiko ga arimashita!]; **What do I do if I**

have an accident? 事故にあったらどうすればいいのですか？ [jiko ni attara dou sureba ii no desu ka?]

accidental [ˌæksɪˈdɛntəl] *adj* 偶然の [guuzen no]

accidentally [ˌæksɪˈdɛntəlɪ] *adv* 偶然に [guuzen ni]

accommodate [əˈkɒmədeɪt] *v* 宿を提供する [yado-o teikyou suru]

accommodation [əˌkɒməˈdeɪʃən] *n* 住む場所 [sumu basho]

accompany [əˈkʌmpənɪ; əˈkʌmpnɪ] *v* 同行する [doukou suru]

accomplice [əˈkɒmplɪs; əˈkʌm-] *n* 共犯者 [kyouhansha]

according [əˈkɔːdɪŋ] *prep* **according to** *prep* ･･･に従って [...ni shitagatte]

accordingly [əˈkɔːdɪŋlɪ] *adv* それに応じて [sore ni oujite]

accordion [əˈkɔːdɪən] *n* アコーディオン [akoodeion]

account [əˈkaʊnt] *n* (in bank) 預金口座 [yokin kouza], (report) 説明 [setsumei]; **account number** *n* 口座番号 [kouzabangou]; **bank account** *n* 銀行口座 [ginkoukouza]; **current account** *n* 当座預金 [touzayokin]; **joint account** *n* 共同預金口座 [kyoudou yokin kouza]

accountable [əˈkaʊntəbəl] *adj* 説明する責任がある [setsumei suru sekinin ga aru]

accountancy [əˈkaʊntənsɪ] *n* 会計 [kaikei]

accountant [əˈkaʊntənt] *n* 会計士 [kaikeishi]

account for [əˈkaʊnt fɔː] *v* ･･･の説明がつく [...no setsumei ga tsuku]

accuracy [ˈækjʊrəsɪ] *n* 正確さ [seikakusa]

accurate [ˈækjərɪt] *adj* 正確な [seikaku na]

accurately [ˈækjərɪtlɪ] *adv* 正確に [seikaku ni]

accusation [ˌækjʊˈzeɪʃən] *n* 非難 [hinan]

accuse [əˈkjuːz] *v* 訴える [uttaeru]

accused [əˈkjuːzd] *n* 被告人 [hikokunin]

ace [eɪs] *n* エース [eesu]

ache [eɪk] *n* 痛み [itami] ▷ *v* 痛む [itamu]

achieve [əˈtʃiːv] *v* 達成する [tassei suru]

achievement [əˈtʃiːvmənt] *n* 達成 [tassei]

acid [ˈæsɪd] *n* 酸 [san]; **acid rain** *n* 酸性雨 [sanseiu]

acknowledgement [əkˈnɒlɪdʒmənt] *n* 承認 [shounin]

acne [ˈæknɪ] *n* にきび [nikibi]

acorn [ˈeɪkɔːn] *n* どんぐり [donguri]

acoustic [əˈkuːstɪk] *adj* 聴覚の [choukaku no]

acre [ˈeɪkə] *n* エーカー [eekaa]

acrobat [ˈækrəˌbæt] *n* 軽業師 [karuwazashi]

acronym [ˈækrənɪm] *n* 頭字語 [toujigo]

across [əˈkrɒs] *prep* ･･･を横切って [...-o yokogitte]

act [ækt] *n* 行為 [koui] ▷ *v* 行動する [koudou suru]

acting [ˈæktɪŋ] *adj* 臨時代理の [rinji dairi no] ▷ *n* 演技 [engi]

action [ˈækʃən] *n* 活動 [katsudou]

active [ˈæktɪv] *adj* 活動的な [katsudouteki na]

activity [ækˈtɪvɪtɪ] *n* 活動 [katsudou]; **activity holiday** *n* アクティブホリデー [akutibu horidee]

actor [ˈæktə] *n* 男優 [danyuu]

actress [ˈæktrɪs] *n* 女優 [joyuu]

actual [ˈæktjʊəl] *adj* 実際の [jissai no]

actually [ˈæktʃʊəlɪ] *adv* 実際に [jissai ni]

acupuncture [ˈækjʊˌpʌŋktʃə] *n* 鍼 [hari]

ad [æd] *abbr* 広告 [koukoku]; **small ads** *npl* 分類広告 [bunruikoukoku]

AD [eɪ diː] *abbr* 西暦 [seireki]

adapt [əˈdæpt] *v* 適合させる [tekigou saseru]

adaptor [əˈdæptə] *n* ソケットアダプタ [soketto adaputa]

add [æd] *v* 足す [tasu]

addict [ˈædɪkt] *n* 中毒者 [chuudokusha]; **drug addict** *n* 麻薬常用者 [mayaku jouyousha]

addicted [ə'dɪktɪd] *adj* 常習的な
[joushuuteki na]

additional [ə'dɪʃənᵊl] *adj* 追加の
[tsuika no]

additive ['ædɪtɪv] *n* 添加剤 [tenkazai]

address [ə'drɛs] *n* (*location*) 住所
[juusho], (*speech*) 演説 [enzetsu];
address book *n* 住所録 [juushoroku];
home address *n* 自宅住所 [jitaku
juusho]; **web address** *n* ウェブアドレス
[webuadoresu]; **Please send my mail
on to this address** 私あての郵便物をこ
の住所に回送してください [watashi ate
no yuubinbutsu o kono juusho ni kaisou
shite kudasai]; **Will you write down the
address, please?** その住所を紙に書い
てもらえますか? [sono juusho o kami ni
kaite moraemasu ka?]

add up [æd ʌp] *v* …を合計する [...-o
goukei suru]

adjacent [ə'dʒeɪsᵊnt] *adj* 近接した
[kinsetsu shita]

adjective ['ædʒɪktɪv] *n* 形容詞
[keiyoushi]

adjust [ə'dʒʌst] *v* 順応する [junnou
suru]

adjustable [ə'dʒʌstəbᵊl] *adj* 調整できる
[chousei dekiru]

adjustment [ə'dʒʌstmənt] *n* 調整
[chousei]

administration [əd,mɪnɪ'streɪʃən] *n*
管理 [kanri]

administrative [əd'mɪnɪ,strətɪv] *adj*
管理上の [kanrijou no]

admiration [,ædmə'reɪʃən] *n* 称賛
[shousan]

admire [əd'maɪə] *v* 感心する [kanshin
suru]

admission [əd'mɪʃən] *n* 入場 [nyuujou];
admission charge *n* 入場料
[nyuujouryou]

admit [əd'mɪt] *v* (*allow in*) 入場を許す
[nyuujou-o yurusu], (*confess*) 認める
[mitomeru]

admittance [əd'mɪtᵊns] *n* 入場許可
[nyuujou kyoka]

adolescence [,ædə'lɛsᵊns] *n* 思春期
[shishunki]

adolescent [,ædə'lɛsᵊnt] *n* 若者
[wakamono]

adopt [ə'dɒpt] *v* 養子にする [youshi ni
suru]

adopted [ə'dɒptɪd] *adj* 養子になった
[youshi ni natta]

adoption [ə'dɒpʃən] *n* 養子縁組
[youshiengumi]

adore [ə'dɔ:] *v* あこがれる [akogareru]

Adriatic [,eɪdrɪ'ætɪk] *adj* アドリア海の
[adoriakai no]

Adriatic Sea [,eɪdrɪ'ætɪk si:] *n* アドリア
海 [adoriakai]

adult ['ædʌlt; ə'dʌlt] *n* 大人 [otona];
adult education *n* 生涯教育 [shougai
kyouiku]

advance [əd'vɑ:ns] *n* 前進 [zenshin] ▷ *v*
前進する [zenshin suru]; **advance
booking** *n* 事前予約 [jizen yoyaku]

advanced [əd'vɑ:nst] *adj* 進歩した
[shinpo shita]

advantage [əd'vɑ:ntɪdʒ] *n* 有利 [yuuri]

advent ['ædvɛnt; -vənt] *n* 出現
[shutsugen]

adventure [əd'vɛntʃə] *n* 冒険 [bouken]

adventurous [əd'vɛntʃərəs] *adj* 冒険
好きな [bouken zuki na]

adverb ['ædvɜ:b] *n* 副詞 [fukushi]

adversary ['ædvəsərɪ] *n* 敵対者
[tekitaisha]

advert ['ædvɜ:t] *n* 広告 [koukoku]

advertise ['ædvə,taɪz] *v* 広告する
[koukoku suru]

advertisement [əd'vɜ:tɪsmənt; -tɪz-]
n 広告 [koukoku]

advertising ['ædvə,taɪzɪŋ] *n* 広告する
こと [koukoku suru koto]

advice [əd'vaɪs] *n* 助言 [jogen]

advisable [əd'vaɪzəbᵊl] *adj* 賢明な
[kenmei na]

advise [əd'vaɪz] *v* 助言する [jogen suru]

aerial ['ɛərɪəl] *n* アンテナ [antena]

aerobics [ɛə'rəʊbɪks] *npl* エアロビクス
[earobikusu]

aerosol ['ɛərəˌsɒl] n エアゾール [eazooru]

affair [ə'fɛə] n 事柄 [kotogara]

affect [ə'fɛkt] v 影響を与える [eikyou-o ataeru]

affectionate [ə'fɛkʃənɪt] adj 愛情のこもった [aijou no komotta]

afford [ə'fɔːd] v ・・・する余裕がある [...suru yoyuu ga aru]

affordable [ə'fɔːdəbəl] adj 手ごろな [tegoro na]

Afghan ['æfgæn; -gən] adj アフガニスタンの [afuganisutan no] ▷ n アフガニスタン人 [afuganisutanjin]

Afghanistan [æf'gænɪˌstɑːn; -ˌstæn] n アフガニスタン [afuganisutan]

afraid [ə'freɪd] adj ・・・が怖い [...ga kowai]

Africa ['æfrɪkə] n アフリカ [afurika]; **North Africa** n 北アフリカ [kita afurika]; **South Africa** n 南アフリカ [minami afurika]

African ['æfrɪkən] adj アフリカの [afurika no] ▷ n アフリカ人 [afurikajin]; **Central African Republic** n 中央アフリカ共和国 [chuuou afurika kyouwakoku]; **North African** n 北アフリカ人 [kita afurikajin], 北アフリカの [kita afurika no]; **South African** n 南アフリカ人 [minami afurikajin], 南アフリカの [minami afurika no]

Afrikaans [ˌæfrɪ'kɑːns; -'kɑːnz] n アフリカーンス語 [afurikaansugo]

Afrikaner [afri'kɑːnə; ˌæfrɪ'kɑːnə] n アフリカーナー [afurikaanaa]

after ['ɑːftə] conj ・・・した後に [...shita nochi ni] ▷ prep ・・・の後に [...no nochi ni]

afternoon [ˌɑːftə'nuːn] n 午後 [gogo]; **in the afternoon** 午後に [gogo ni]; **tomorrow afternoon** 明日の午後 [asu no gogo]

afters ['ɑːftəz] npl デザート [dezaato]

aftershave ['ɑːftəˌʃeɪv] n アフターシェーブローション [afutaasheeburooshon]

afterwards ['ɑːftəwədz] adv 後で [ato de]

again [ə'gɛn; ə'geɪn] adv 再び [futatabi]

against [ə'gɛnst; ə'geɪnst] prep ・・・にもたれて [...ni motarete]

age [eɪdʒ] n 年齢 [nenrei]; **age limit** n 年齢制限 [nenreiseigen]; **Middle Ages** npl 中世 [chuusei]

aged ['eɪdʒɪd] adj 年老いた [toshi oita]

agency ['eɪdʒənsɪ] n 代理店 [dairiten]; **travel agency** n 旅行代理店 [ryokoudairiten]

agenda [ə'dʒɛndə] n 議事日程 [giji nittei]

agent ['eɪdʒənt] n 代理人 [dairinin]; **estate agent** n 不動産屋 [fudousanya]; **travel agent** n 旅行業者 [ryokougyousha]

aggressive [ə'grɛsɪv] adj 攻撃的な [kougekiteki na]

AGM [eɪ dʒiː ɛm] abbr 年次総会 [nenjisoukai]

ago [ə'gəʊ] adv **a month ago** 一か月前 [ikkagetsu mae]; **a week ago** 一週間前 [isshuukan mae]

agony ['ægənɪ] n 苦悶 [kumon]

agree [ə'griː] v 賛成する [sansei suru]

agreed [ə'griːd] adj 合意された [goui sareta]

agreement [ə'griːmənt] n 同意 [doui]

agricultural ['ægrɪˌkʌltʃərəl] adj 農業の [nougyou no]

agriculture ['ægrɪˌkʌltʃə] n 農業 [nougyou]

ahead [ə'hɛd] adv 前に [mae ni]

aid [eɪd] n 援助 [enjo]; **first aid** n 救急処置 [kyuukyuu shochi]; **first-aid kit** n 救急処置キット [kyuukyuu shochi kitto]; **hearing aid** n 補聴器 [hochouki]

AIDS [eɪdz] n エイズ [eizu]

aim [eɪm] n 目的 [mokuteki] ▷ v ねらう [nerau]

air [ɛə] n 空気 [kuuki]; **air hostess** n スチュワーデス [suchuwaadesu]; **air-traffic controller** n 航空管制官 [koukuu kanseikan]; **Air Force** n 空軍 [kuugun]; **Can you check the air, please?** 空気圧を点検してもらえますか? [kuukiatsu o tenken shite moraemasu ka?]

airbag [ɛəbæg] n エアバッグ [eabaggu]

air-conditioned [ɛəkənˈdɪʃənd] adj 空調された [kuuchou sareta]

air conditioning [ɛə kənˈdɪʃənɪŋ] n 空調 [kuuchou]

aircraft [ˈɛəˌkrɑːft] n 航空機 [koukuuki]

airline [ˈɛəˌlaɪn] n 航空会社 [koukuu gaisha]

airmail [ˈɛəˌmeɪl] n 航空便 [koukuubin]

airport [ˈɛəˌpɔːt] n 空港 [kuukou]; **airport bus** n 空港バス [kuukou basu]; **How do I get to the airport?** 空港へはどう行けばいいのですか？ [kuukou e wa dou ikeba ii no desu ka?]; **How much is the taxi to the airport?** 空港までのタクシーはいくらですか？ [kuukou made no takushii wa ikura desu ka?]; **Is there a bus to the airport?** 空港へ行くバスはありますか？ [kuukou e iku basu wa arimasu ka?]

airsick [ˈɛəˌsɪk] adj 飛行機に酔った [hikouki ni yotta]

airspace [ˈɛəˌspeɪs] n 領空 [ryoukuu]

airtight [ˈɛəˌtaɪt] adj 気密の [kimitsu no]

aisle [aɪl] n 通路 [tsuuro]; **I'd like an aisle seat** 通路側の席をお願いします [tsuuro-gawa no seki o o-negai shimasu]

alarm [əˈlɑːm] n 恐怖 [kyoufu]; **alarm call** n モーニングコール [mooningukooru]; **alarm clock** n 目覚まし時計 [mezamashi tokei]; **false alarm** n 間違い警報 [machigai keihou]; **fire alarm** n 火災報知機 [kasai houchiki]; **smoke alarm** n 煙警報器 [kemuri keihouki]

alarming [əˈlɑːmɪŋ] adj 警戒心をいだかせる [keikaishin-o idakaseru]

Albania [ælˈbeɪnɪə] n アルバニア [arubania]

Albanian [ælˈbeɪnɪən] adj アルバニアの [arubania no] ▷ n (language) アルバニア語 [arubaniago], (person) アルバニア人 [arubaniajin]

album [ˈælbəm] n アルバム [arubamu]; **photo album** n アルバム [arubamu]

alcohol [ˈælkəˌhɒl] n アルコール [arukooru]; **Does that contain alcohol?** それにはアルコールが入っていますか？ [sore ni wa arukooru ga haitte imasu ka?]; **I don't drink alcohol** 私はアルコールを飲みません [watashi wa arukooru o nomimasen]

alcohol-free [ˈælkəˌhɒlfriː] adj アルコールを含まない [arukooru o fukumanai]

alcoholic [ˌælkəˈhɒlɪk] adj アルコールの [arukooru no] ▷ n アルコール中毒者 [arukooru chuudokusha]

alert [əˈlɜːt] adj 油断なく警戒して [yudan naku keikai shite] ▷ v 警報を出す [keihou-o dasu]

Algeria [ælˈdʒɪərɪə] n アルジェリア [arujeria]

Algerian [ælˈdʒɪərɪən] adj アルジェリアの [arujeria no] ▷ n アルジェリア人 [arujeriajin]

alias [ˈeɪlɪəs] adv 別名 [betsumei] ▷ prep ・・・の別名で知られる [...no betsumei de shirareru]

alibi [ˈælɪˌbaɪ] n アリバイ [aribai]

alien [ˈeɪljən; ˈeɪlɪən] n 外国人 [gaikokujin]

alive [əˈlaɪv] adj 生きている [ikite iru]

all [ɔːl] adj できるかぎりの [dekiru kagiri no] ▷ pron 全部 [zenbu]

Allah [ˈælə] n アッラー [arraa]

allegation [ˌælɪˈgeɪʃən] n 申し立て [moushitate]

alleged [əˈlɛdʒd] adj 申し立てられた [moushitaterareta]

allergic [əˈlɜːdʒɪk] adj アレルギーの [arerugii no]

allergy [ˈælədʒɪ] n アレルギー [arerugii]; **peanut allergy** n ピーナッツアレルギー [piinattsu arerugii]

alley [ˈælɪ] n 路地 [roji]

alliance [əˈlaɪəns] n 提携 [teikei]

alligator [ˈælɪˌgeɪtə] n ワニ [wani]

allow [əˈlaʊ] v 許す [yurusu]

all right [ɔːl raɪt] adv 申し分なく [moushibun naku]

ally [ˈælaɪ; əˈlaɪ] n 同盟国 [doumeikoku]

almond [ˈɑːmənd] n アーモンド [aamondo]

almost ['ɔːlməʊst] *adv* ほとんど [hotondo]

alone [ə'ləʊn] *adj* ただ一人の [tada hitori no]

along [ə'lɒŋ] *prep* ···に沿って [...ni sotte]

aloud [ə'laʊd] *adv* 声を出して [koe o dashite]

alphabet ['ælfə,bɛt] *n* アルファベット [arufabetto]

Alps [ælps] *npl* アルプス山脈 [arupusu sanmyaku]

already [ɔːl'rɛdɪ] *adv* すでに [sude ni]

alright [ɔːl'raɪt] *adv* **Are you alright?** 大丈夫ですか? [daijoubu desu ka?]

also ['ɔːlsəʊ] *adv* ···も [...mo]

altar ['ɔːltə] *n* 祭壇 [saidan]

alter ['ɔːltə] *v* 変更する [henkou suru]

alternate [ɔːl'tɜːnɪt] *adj* 交互の [kougo no]

alternative [ɔːl'tɜːnətɪv] *adj* 代わりの [kawari no] ▷ *n* 選択肢 [sentakushi]

alternatively [ɔːl'tɜːnətɪvlɪ] *adv* 代わりに [kawari ni]

although [ɔːl'ðəʊ] *conj* ···とはいえ [...towaie]

altitude ['æltɪˌtjuːd] *n* 高度 [koudo] (海抜)

altogether [ˌɔːltə'gɛðə; 'ɔːltəˌgɛðə] *adv* 全く [mattaku]

aluminium [ˌæljʊ'mɪnɪəm] *n* アルミニウム [aruminiumu]

always ['ɔːlweɪz; -wɪz] *adv* 常に [tsune ni]

a.m. [eɪɛm] *abbr* 午前の [gozen no]

amateur ['æmətə; -tʃə; -ˌtjʊə; ˌæmə'tɜː] *n* アマチュア [amachua]

amaze [ə'meɪz] *v* 驚かせる [odoroka seru]

amazed [ə'meɪzd] *adj* 驚いて [odoroi te]

amazing [ə'meɪzɪŋ] *adj* 驚くべき [odorokubeki]

ambassador [æm'bæsədə] *n* 大使 [taishi]

amber ['æmbə] *n* 琥珀色 [kohaku iro]

ambition [æm'bɪʃən] *n* 野心 [yashin]

ambitious [æm'bɪʃəs] *adj* 野心的な [yashinteki na]

ambulance ['æmbjʊləns] *n* 救急車 [kyuukyuusha]; **Call an ambulance** 救急車を呼んでください [kyuukyuu-sha o yonde kudasai]

ambush ['æmbʊʃ] *n* 待ち伏せ [machifuse]

amenities [ə'miːnɪtɪz] *npl* アメニティー [ameniteii]

America [ə'mɛrɪkə] *n* アメリカ [amerika]; **Central America** *n* 中央アメリカ [chuuou amerika]; **North America** *n* 北アメリカ [kita amerika]; **South America** *n* 南アメリカ [minami amerika]

American [ə'mɛrɪkən] *adj* アメリカの [amerika no] ▷ *n* アメリカ人 [amerikajin]; **American football** *n* アメリカンフットボール [amerikan futtobooru]; **North American** *n* 北アメリカ人 [kita amerikajin], 北アメリカの [kita amerika no]; **South American** *n* 南アメリカ人 [minami amerikajin], 南アメリカの [minami amerika no]

ammunition [ˌæmjʊ'nɪʃən] *n* 弾薬 [dan-yaku]

among [ə'mʌŋ] *prep* ···の中で [...no naka de]

amount [ə'maʊnt] *n* 量 [ryou]

amp [æmp] *n* アンペア [anpea]

amplifier ['æmplɪˌfaɪə] *n* アンプ [anpu]

amuse [ə'mjuːz] *v* 楽しませる [tanoshimaseru]; **amusement arcade** *n* ゲームセンター [geemu sentaa]

an [ɑːn] *art* 一つの [hitotsu no]

anaemic [ə'niːmɪk] *adj* 貧血の [hinketsu no]

anaesthetic [ˌænɪs'θɛtɪk] *n* 麻酔薬 [masuiyaku]; **general anaesthetic** *n* 全身麻酔 [zenshin masui]; **local anaesthetic** *n* 局所麻酔薬 [kyokusho masuiyaku]

analyse ['ænəˌlaɪz] *v* 分析する [bunseki suru]

analysis [ə'nælɪsɪs] *n* 分析 [bunseki]

ancestor ['ænsɛstə] *n* 先祖 [senzo]

anchor ['æŋkə] n 錨 [ikari]

anchovy ['ænt∫əvi] n アンチョビー [anchobii]

ancient ['eɪn∫ənt] adj 大昔の [oumukashi no]

and [ænd; ənd; ən] conj …と… […to…]

Andes ['ændiːz] npl アンデス山脈 [andesu sanmyaku]

Andorra [æn'dɔːrə] n アンドラ [andora]

angel ['eɪndʒəl] n 天使 [tenshi]

anger ['æŋgə] n 怒り [ikari]

angina [æn'dʒaɪnə] n 狭心症 [kyoushinshou]

angle ['æŋgəl] n 角 [kado] (数学); **right angle** n 直角 [chokkaku]

angler ['æŋglə] n 魚を釣る人 [sakana o tsuru hito]

angling ['æŋglɪŋ] n 魚釣り [sakana tsuri]

Angola [æŋ'gəʊlə] n アンゴラ [angora]

Angolan [æŋ'gəʊlən] adj アンゴラの [angora no] ▷ n アンゴラ人 [angorajin]

angry ['æŋgrɪ] adj 怒った [okotta]

animal ['ænɪməl] n 動物 [doubutsu]

aniseed ['ænɪˌsiːd] n アニシード [anishiido]

ankle ['æŋkəl] n くるぶし [kurubushi]

anniversary [ˌænɪ'vɜːsərɪ] n 記念日 [kinenbi]; **wedding anniversary** n 結婚記念日 [kekkon kinenbi]

announce [ə'naʊns] v 発表する [happyou suru]

announcement [ə'naʊnsmənt] n 発表 [happyou]

annoy [ə'nɔɪ] v うるさがらせる [urusagaraseru]

annoying [ə'nɔɪɪŋ; an'noying] adj うるさい [urusai]

annual ['ænjʊəl] adj 年一回の [nen'ikkai no]

annually ['ænjʊəlɪ] adv 年一回 [nen'ikkai]

anonymous [ə'nɒnɪməs] adj 匿名の [tokumei no]

anorak ['ænəˌræk] n アノラック [anorakku]

anorexia [ˌænɒ'rɛksɪə] n 拒食症 [kyoshokushou]

anorexic [ˌænɒ'rɛksɪk] adj 拒食症的な [kyoshokushouteki na]

another [ə'nʌðə] adj もう一つの [mou hitotsu no]

answer ['ɑːnsə] n 答え [kotae] ▷ v 答える [kotaeru]

answerphone ['ɑːnsəfəʊn] n 留守番電話 [rusubandenwa]

ant [ænt] n アリ [ari]

antagonize [æn'tægəˌnaɪz] v 敵にまわす [teki ni mawasu]

Antarctic [ænt'ɑːktɪk] adj 南極大陸 [nankyoku tairiku]; **the Antarctic** n 南極 [nankyoku]

Antarctica [ænt'ɑːktɪkə] n 南極 [nankyoku]

antelope ['æntɪˌləʊp] n レイヨウ [reiyou]

antenatal [ˌæntɪ'neɪtəl] adj 出産前の [shussanmae no]

anthem ['ænθəm] n 国歌 [kokka]

anthropology [ˌænθrə'pɒlədʒɪ] n 人類学 [jinruigaku]

antibiotic [ˌæntɪbaɪ'ɒtɪk] n 抗生物質 [kousei busshitsu]

antibody ['æntɪˌbɒdɪ] n 抗体 [koutai]

anticlockwise [ˌæntɪ'klɒkˌwaɪz] adv 左回りに [hidari mawari ni]

antidepressant [ˌæntɪdɪ'prɛsənt] n 抗鬱剤 [kouutsuzai]

antidote ['æntɪˌdəʊt] n 解毒剤 [gedokuzai]

antifreeze ['æntɪˌfriːz] n 不凍液 [futoueki]

antihistamine [ˌæntɪ'hɪstəˌmiːn; -mɪn] n 抗ヒスタミン剤 [kouhisutaminzai]

antiperspirant [ˌæntɪ'pɜːspərənt] n 発汗抑制剤 [hakkan yokuseizai]

antique [æn'tiːk] n 骨董品 [kottouhin]; **antique shop** n 骨董屋 [kottou ya]

antiseptic [ˌæntɪ'sɛptɪk] n 殺菌剤 [sakkinzai]

antivirus ['æntɪˌvaɪrəs] n アンチウイルス [anchiuirusu]

anxiety [æŋ'zaɪɪtɪ] n 心配 [shinpai]

any ['ɛnɪ] pron どれでも [dore de mo]

anybody ['ɛnɪˌbɒdɪ; -bədɪ] pron 誰でも [dare demo]

anyhow ['ɛnɪˌhaʊ] adv とにかく [tonikaku]

anyone ['ɛnɪˌwʌn; -wən] pron 誰でも [dare demo]

anything ['ɛnɪˌθɪŋ] pron 何でも [nandemo]

anyway ['ɛnɪˌweɪ] adv とにかく [tonikaku]

anywhere ['ɛnɪˌwɛə] adv どこでも [dokodemo]

apart [ə'pɑːt] adv 別個に [bekko ni]

apart from [ə'pɑːf frɒm] prep ・・・は別として [...wa betsu to shite]

apartment [ə'pɑːtmənt] n アパート [apaato]; **We're looking for an apartment** 私たちはアパートメントを探しています [watashi-tachi wa apaatomento o sagashite imasu]; **We've booked an apartment in the name of...** ・・・の名前でアパートメントを予約してあります [...no namae de apaatomento o yoyaku shite arimasu]

aperitif [ɑːˌpɛrɪ'tiːf] n アペリチフ [aperichifu]; **We'd like an aperitif** アペリチフをいただきます [aperichifu o itadakimasu]

apologize [ə'pɒləˌdʒaɪz] v 謝る [ayamaru]

apology [ə'pɒlədʒɪ] n 詫び [wabi]

apostrophe [ə'pɒstrəfɪ] n アポストロフィ [aposutorofi]

app [æp] n アプリ [apuri]

appalling [ə'pɔːlɪŋ] adj ぞっとするような [zotto suru you na]

apparatus [ˌæpə'reɪtəs; -'rɑːtəs; 'æpəˌreɪtəs] n 器具 [kigu]

apparent [ə'pærənt; ə'pɛər-] adj 明らかな [akiraka na]

apparently [ə'pærəntlɪ; ə'pɛər-] adv 明らかに [akiraka ni]

appeal [ə'piːl] n 懇願 [kongan] ▷ v 懇願する [kongan suru]

appear [ə'pɪə] v 現れる [arawareru]

appearance [ə'pɪərəns] n 出現 [shutsugen]

appendicitis [əˌpɛndɪ'saɪtɪs] n 虫垂炎 [chuusuien]

appetite ['æpɪˌtaɪt] n 食欲 [shokuyoku]

applaud [ə'plɔːd] v 拍手を送る [hakushu-o okuru]

applause [ə'plɔːz] n 拍手 [hakushu]

apple ['æpəl] n リンゴ [ringo]; **apple pie** n アップルパイ [appurupai]

appliance [ə'plaɪəns] n 器具 [kigu]

applicant ['æplɪkənt] n 応募者 [oubosha]

application [ˌæplɪ'keɪʃən] n 申し込み [moushikomi]; **application form** n 申込書 [moushikomisho]

apply [ə'plaɪ] v 申し込む [moushikomu]

appoint [ə'pɔɪnt] v 任命する [ninmei suru]

appointment [ə'pɔɪntmənt] n 予約 [yoyaku]; **Can I have an appointment with the doctor?** お医者さんの予約を取れますか? [o-isha-san no yoyaku o toremasu ka?]; **I'd like to make an appointment** 予約を取りたいのですが [yoyaku o toritai no desu ga]

appreciate [ə'priːʃɪˌeɪt; -sɪ-] v 高く評価する [takaku hyouka suru]

apprehensive [ˌæprɪ'hɛnsɪv] adj 心配して [shinpai shite]

apprentice [ə'prɛntɪs] n 見習い [minarai]

approach [ə'prəʊtʃ] v 近づく [chikaduku]

appropriate [ə'prəʊprɪɪt] adj 適切な [tekisetsu na]

approval [ə'pruːvəl] n 承認 [shounin]

approve [ə'pruːv] v 承認する [shounin suru]

approximate [ə'prɒksɪmɪt] adj 近似の [kinji no]

approximately [ə'prɒksɪmɪtlɪ] adv およそ [oyoso]

apricot ['eɪprɪˌkɒt] n アプリコット [apurikotto]

April ['eɪprəl] n 四月 [shigatsu]; **April**

Fools' Day n エープリルフールの日 [eepuriru fuuru no nichi]

apron ['eɪprən] n エプロン [epuron]

aquarium [ə'kwɛərɪəm] n 水槽 [suisou]

Aquarius [ə'kwɛərɪəs] n 水瓶座 [mizugameza]

Arab ['ærəb] adj アラビアの [arabia no] ▷ n アラビア人 [arabiajin]; **United Arab Emirates** npl アラブ首長国連邦 [arabu shuchoukokurenpou]

Arabic ['ærəbɪk] adj アラビア語の [arabiago no] ▷ n (language) アラビア語 [arabiago]

arbitration [ˌɑːbɪ'treɪʃən] n 仲裁 [chuusai]

arch [ɑːtʃ] n アーチ [aachi]

archaeologist [ˌɑːkɪ'ɒlədʒɪst] n 考古学者 [koukogakusha]

archaeology [ˌɑːkɪ'ɒlədʒɪ] n 考古学 [koukogaku]

archbishop ['ɑːtʃ'bɪʃəp] n 大主教 [dai shukyou]

architect ['ɑːkɪˌtɛkt] n 建築家 [kenchikuka]

architecture ['ɑːkɪˌtɛktʃə] n 建築様式 [kenchikuyoushiki]

archive ['ɑːkaɪv] n 文書館 [bunshokan]

Arctic ['ɑːktɪk] adj 北極 [hokkyoku]; **Arctic Circle** n 北極圏 [hokkyokuken]; **Arctic Ocean** n 北極海 [hokkyokukai]; **the Arctic** n 北極 [hokkyoku]

area ['ɛərɪə] n 地域 [chiiki]; **service area** n サービスエリア [saabisu eria]

Argentina [ˌɑːdʒən'tiːnə] n アルゼンチン [aruzenchin]

Argentinian [ˌɑːdʒən'tɪnɪən] adj アルゼンチンの [aruzenchin no] ▷ n (person) アルゼンチン人 [aruzenchinjin]

argue ['ɑːgjuː] v 立証する [risshou suru]

argument ['ɑːgjʊmənt] n 口論 [kouron]

Aries ['ɛəriːz] n 牡羊座 [ohitsujiza]

arm [ɑːm] n 腕 [ude]; **I can't move my arm** 私は腕を動かせません [watashi wa ude o ugokasemasen]

armchair ['ɑːmˌtʃɛə] n 肘掛け椅子 [hijikakeke isu]

armed [ɑːmd] adj 武装した [busou shita]

Armenia [ɑː'miːnɪə] n アルメニア [arumenia]

Armenian [ɑː'miːnɪən] adj アルメニアの [arumenia no] ▷ n (language) アルメニア語 [arumeniago], (person) アルメニア人 [arumeniajin]

armour ['ɑːmə] n 甲冑 [kouchuu]

armpit ['ɑːmˌpɪt] n 腋の下 [waki no shita]

army ['ɑːmɪ] n 軍隊 [guntai]

aroma [ə'rəʊmə] n 芳香 [houkou]

aromatherapy [əˌrəʊmə'θɛrəpɪ] n アロマセラピー [aromaserapii]

around [ə'raʊnd] adv 周りに [mawari ni] ▷ prep あちこち [achikochi]

arrange [ə'reɪndʒ] v 手配する [tehai suru]

arrangement [ə'reɪndʒmənt] n 手配 [tehai]

arrears [ə'rɪəz] npl 未払金 [miharaikin]

arrest [ə'rɛst] n 逮捕 [taiho] ▷ v 逮捕する [taiho suru]

arrival [ə'raɪvəl] n 到着 [touchaku]

arrive [ə'raɪv] v 着く [tsuku]

arrogant ['ærəgənt] adj 横柄な [ouhei na]

arrow ['ærəʊ] n 矢 [ya]

arson ['ɑːsən] n 放火 [houka]

art [ɑːt] n 美術 [bijutsu]; **art gallery** n 美術館 [bijutsukan]; **art school** n 美術学校 [bijutsugakkou]; **work of art** n 美術品 [bijutsuhin]

artery ['ɑːtərɪ] n 動脈 [doumyaku]

arthritis [ɑː'θraɪtɪs] n 関節炎 [kansetsuen]; **I suffer from arthritis** 私は関節炎をわずらっています [watashi wa kansetsuen o wazuratte imasu]

artichoke ['ɑːtɪˌtʃəʊk] n アーティチョーク [aatichooku]

article ['ɑːtɪkəl] n 記事 [kiji]

artificial [ˌɑːtɪ'fɪʃəl] adj 人工の [jinkou no]

artist ['ɑːtɪst] n 芸術家 [geijutsuka]

artistic [ɑː'tɪstɪk; ar'tistic] adj 芸術的な [geijutsuteki na]

as [əz] *adv* ・・・と同じくらい [...to onaji kurai] ▷ *conj* ・・・している時 [...shite iru toki] ▷ *prep* ・・・として [...toshite]

asap [eɪsæp] *abbr* (= *as soon as possible*) できるだけ早く [dekiru dake hayaku]

ascent [ə'sɛnt] *n* **When is the last ascent?** 最後に昇るのはいつですか? [saigo ni noboru no wa itsu desu ka?]

ashamed [ə'ʃeɪmd] *adj* 恥じて [hajite]

ashore [ə'ʃɔː] *adv* **Can we go ashore now?** もう下船できますか? [mou gesen dekimasu ka?]

ashtray ['æʃtreɪ] *n* 灰皿 [haizara]; **May I have an ashtray?** 灰皿をいただけますか? [haizara o itadakemasu ka?]

Asia ['eɪʃə; 'eɪʒə] *n* アジア [ajia]

Asian ['eɪʃən; 'eɪʒən] *adj* アジアの [ajia no] ▷ *n* アジア人 [ajiajin]

Asiatic [ˌeɪʃɪ'ætɪk; -zɪ-] *adj* アジアの [ajia no]

ask [ɑːsk] *v* 尋ねる [tazuneru]

ask for [ɑːsk fɔː] *v* ・・・を求める [...-o motomeru]

asleep [ə'sliːp] *adj* 眠って [nemutte]

asparagus [ə'spærəgəs] *n* アスパラガス [asuparagasu]

aspect ['æspɛkt] *n* 局面 [kyokumen]

aspirin ['æsprɪn] *n* アスピリン [asupirin]; **I can't take aspirin** 私はアスピリンを飲めません [watashi wa asupirin o nomemasen]; **I'd like some aspirin** アスピリンが欲しいのですが [asupirin ga hoshii no desu ga]

assembly [ə'sɛmblɪ] *n* 集会 [shuukai]

asset ['æsɛt] *n* 強み [tsuyomi]; **assets** *npl* 強み [tsuyomi]

assignment [ə'saɪnmənt] *n* 割り当て [wariate]

assistance [ə'sɪstəns] *n* 援助 [enjo]

assistant [ə'sɪstənt] *n* 助手 [joshu]; **personal assistant** *n* 個人秘書 [kojin hisho]; **sales assistant** *n* 販売スタッフ [hanbai sutaffu]; **shop assistant** *n* 店員 [ten-in]

associate *adj* [ə'səʊʃɪɪt] 準・・・ [jun...] ▷ *n* [ə'səʊʃɪɪt] 提携者 [teikeisha]

association [əˌsəʊsɪ'eɪʃən; -ʃɪ-] *n* 協会 [kyoukai]

assortment [ə'sɔːtmənt] *n* 各種取り合わせ [kakushu toriawase]

assume [ə'sjuːm] *v* 想定する [soutei suru]

assure [ə'ʃʊə] *v* 確約する [kakuyaku suru]

asthma ['æsmə] *n* 喘息 [zensoku]

astonish [ə'stɒnɪʃ] *v* 驚かす [odorokasu]

astonished [ə'stɒnɪʃt] *adj* 驚いた [odoroita]

astonishing [ə'stɒnɪʃɪŋ] *adj* 驚くばかりの [odoroku bakarino]

astrology [ə'strɒlədʒɪ] *n* 占星術 [senseijutsu]

astronaut ['æstrəˌnɔːt] *n* 宇宙飛行士 [uchuuhikoushi]

astronomy [ə'strɒnəmɪ] *n* 天文学 [tenmongaku]

asylum [ə'saɪləm] *n* 亡命 [boumei]; **asylum seeker** *n* 亡命者 [boumeisha]

at [æt] *prep* ・・・に [...ni]; **at least** *adv* 少なくとも [sukunakutomo]; **Do we stop at...?** ・・・に停車しますか? [...ni teisha shimasu ka?]

atheist ['eɪθɪˌɪst] *n* 無神論者 [mushinronsha]

athlete ['æθliːt] *n* 運動選手 [undousenshu]

athletic [æθ'lɛtɪk] *adj* 運動選手らしい [undou senshu rashii]

athletics [æθ'lɛtɪks] *npl* 陸上競技 [rikujou kyougi]

Atlantic [ət'læntɪk] *n* 大西洋 [taiseiyo]

atlas ['ætləs] *n* 地図帳 [chizuchou]

atmosphere ['ætməsˌfɪə] *n* 大気 [taiki]

atom ['ætəm] *n* 原子 [genshi]; **atom bomb** *n* 原子爆弾 [genshibakudan]

atomic [ə'tɒmɪk] *adj* 原子力の [genshiryoku no]

attach [ə'tætʃ] *v* 取り付ける [toritsuker]

attached [ə'tætʃt] *adj* 決まった相手がいる [kimatta aite ga iru]

attachment [ə'tætʃmənt] *n* 愛着 [aichaku]

attack [ə'tæk] n 攻撃 [kougeki] ▷ v 攻撃する [kougeki suru]; **heart attack** n 心臓発作 [shinzouhossa]; **terrorist attack** n テロリストによる攻撃 [terorisuto niyoru kougeki]

attempt [ə'tɛmpt] n 試み [kokoromi] ▷ v 試みる [kokoromiru]

attend [ə'tɛnd] v 出席する [shusseki suru]

attendance [ə'tɛndəns] n 出席 [shusseki]

attendant [ə'tɛndənt] n **flight attendant** n 客室乗務員 [kyakushitsu joumuin]

attention [ə'tɛnʃən] n 注意 [chuui]

attic ['ætɪk] n 屋根裏 [yaneura]

attitude ['ætɪ,tjuːd] n 態度 [taido]

attorney [ə'tɜːnɪ] n 弁護士 [bengoshi]

attract [ə'trækt] v ひきつける [hikitsukeru]

attraction [ə'trækʃən] n 魅力 [miryoku]

attractive [ə'træktɪv] adj 魅力的な [miryokuteki na]

aubergine ['əʊbəʒiːn] n ナス [nasu]

auburn ['ɔːbən] adj 赤褐色の [akakasshoku no]

auction ['ɔːkʃən] n 競売 [kyoubai]

audience ['ɔːdɪəns] n 聴衆 [choushuu]

audit ['ɔːdɪt] n 監査 [kansa] ▷ v 監査する [kansa suru]

audition [ɔːˈdɪʃən] n オーディション [oodishon]

auditor ['ɔːdɪtə] n 会計監査人 [kaikei kansanin]

August ['ɔːgəst] n 八月 [hachigatsu]

aunt [ɑːnt] n おば [oba] (伯母・叔母)

auntie ['ɑːntɪ] n おばちゃん [obachan]

au pair [əʊ 'pɛə; o pɛr] n オーペア [oopea]

austerity [ɒ'stɛrɪtɪ] n 厳格さ [genkakusa]

Australasia [,ɒstrə'leɪzɪə] n オーストラレーシア [oosutorareeshia]

Australia [ɒ'streɪlɪə] n オーストラリア [oosutoraria]

Australian [ɒ'streɪlɪən] adj オーストラリアの [oosutoraria no] ▷ n オーストラリア人 [oosutorariajin]

Austria ['ɒstrɪə] n オーストリア [oosutoria]

Austrian ['ɒstrɪən] adj オーストリアの [oosutoria no] ▷ n オーストリア人 [oosutoriajin]

authentic [ɔː'θɛntɪk] adj 本物の [honmono no]

author, authoress ['ɔːθə, 'ɔːθə,rɛs] n 著者 [chosha]

authorize ['ɔːθə,raɪz] v 権限を与える [kengen-o ataeru]

autobiography [,ɔːtəʊbaɪ'ɒgrəfɪ; ,ɔː'təbaɪ-] n 自叙伝 [jijoden]

autograph ['ɔːtə,grɑːf; -,græf] n サイン [sain]

automatic [,ɔːtə'mætɪk] adj 自動的な [jidouteki na]

automatically [,ɔːtə'mætɪklɪ] adv 自動的に [jidouteki ni]

autonomous [ɔː'tɒnəməs] adj 自治権のある [jichiken no aru]

autonomy [ɔː'tɒnəmɪ] n 自治国家 [jichi kokka]

autumn ['ɔːtəm] n 秋 [aki]

availability [ə'veɪləbɪlɪtɪ] n 有用性 [yuuyousei]

available [ə'veɪləbəl] adj 利用できる [riyou dekiru]

avalanche ['ævə,lɑːntʃ] n なだれ [nadare]; **Is there a danger of avalanches?** なだれの危険はありますか? [nadare no kiken wa arimasu ka?]

avenue ['ævɪ,njuː] n 大通り [oudouri]

average ['ævərɪdʒ; 'ævrɪdʒ] adj 平均の [heikin no] ▷ n 平均 [heikin]

avocado, avocados [,ævə'kɑːdəʊ, ,ævə'kɑːdəʊs] n アボカド [abokado]

avoid [ə'vɔɪd] v 避ける [sakeru]

awake [ə'weɪk] adj 眠らずに [nemurazu ni] ▷ v 目が覚める [me ga sameru]

award [ə'wɔːd] n 賞 [shou]

aware [ə'wɛə] adj 気がついて [ki ga tsuite]

away [ə'weɪ] *adv* 離れて [hanarete]; **away match** *n* アウェーの試合 [auee no shiai]

awful ['ɔːfʊl] *adj* ひどい [hidoi]; **What awful weather!** なんてひどい天気でしょう! [nante hidoi tenki deshou!]

awfully ['ɔːfəlɪ; 'ɔːflɪ] *adv* ひどく [hidoku]

awkward ['ɔːkwəd] *adj* 不器用な [bukiyou na]

axe [æks] *n* 斧 [ono]

axle ['æksəl] *n* 車軸 [shajiku]

Azerbaijan [ˌæzəbaɪ'dʒɑːn] *n* アゼルバイジャン [azerubaijan]

Azerbaijani [ˌæzəbaɪ'dʒɑːnɪ] *adj* アゼルバイジャンの [azerubaijan no] ▷ *n* (*person*) アゼルバイジャン人 [azerubaijanjin]

B&B [bi: ænd bi:] *n* ベッド&ブレックファースト [beddo burekkufaasuto]

BA [bɑː] *abbr* 文学士 [bungakushi]

baby ['beɪbɪ] *n* 赤ん坊 [akanbou]; **baby milk** *n* ベビーミルク [bebii miruku]; **baby wipe** *n* 赤ちゃん用ウェットティシュー [akachanyouuettotishuu]; **baby's bottle** *n* 哺乳瓶 [honyuubin]

babysit ['beɪbɪsɪt] *v* ベビーシッターをする [bebiishittaa o suru]

babysitter ['beɪbɪsɪtə] *n* ベビーシッター [bebiishittaa]

babysitting ['beɪbɪsɪtɪŋ] *n* 子守り [komori]

bachelor ['bætʃələ; 'bætʃlə] *n* 独身の男性 [dokushin no dansei]

back [bæk] *adj* 後ろの [ushiro no] ▷ *adv* 後ろに [ushiro ni] ▷ *n* 背中 [senaka] ▷ *v* 後退させる [koutai saseru]; **back pain** *n* 腰痛 [youtsuu]; **I've got a bad back** 私は背中が痛みます [watashi wa senaka ga itamimasu]; **I've hurt my back** 私は背中を痛めました [watashi wa senaka o itamemashita]

backache ['bæk,eɪk] *n* 腰痛 [youtsuu]

backbone ['bæk,bəʊn] *n* 背骨 [sebone]

backfire [ˌbækˈfaɪə] v 裏目に出る [urame ni deru]

background [ˈbækˌɡraʊnd] n 背景 [haikei]

backing [ˈbækɪŋ] n 支援 [shien]

back out [bæk aʊt] v 約束を取り消す [yakusoku-o torikesu]

backpack [ˈbækˌpæk] n バックパック [bakkupakku]

backpacker [ˈbækˌpækə] n バックパッカー [bakkupakkaa]

backpacking [ˈbækˌpækɪŋ] n バックパッキング [bakkupakkingu]

backside [ˌbækˈsaɪd] n 臀部 [denbu]

backslash [ˈbækˌslæʃ] n バックスラッシュ [bakkusurasshu]

backstroke [ˈbækˌstrəʊk] n 背泳 [haiei]

back up [bæk ʌp] v 支援する [shien suru]

backup [bækʌp] n バックアップ [bakkuappu]

backwards [ˈbækwədz] adv 後方に [kouhou ni]

bacon [ˈbeɪkən] n ベーコン [beekon]

bacteria [bækˈtɪərɪə] npl バクテリア [bakuteria]

bad [bæd] adj 悪い [warui]; **It's a bad line** 回線が悪いです [kaisen ga warui desu]

badge [bædʒ] n バッジ [bajji]

badger [ˈbædʒə] n アナグマ [anaguma]

badly [ˈbædlɪ] adv 悪く [waruku]

badminton [ˈbædmɪntən] n バドミントン [badominton]

bad-tempered [bædˈtɛmpəd] adj 機嫌の悪い [kigen no warui]

baffled [ˈbæfᵊld] adj 困惑した [konwaku shita]

bag [bæg] n かばん [kaban]; **bum bag** n ウエストバッグ [uesutobaggu]; **carrier bag** n 買物袋 [kaimonobukuro]; **overnight bag** n 一泊旅行用かばん [ippaku ryokou you kaban]; **plastic bag** n ビニール袋 [biniiru bukuro]; **polythene bag** n ポリエチレンの袋 [poriechiren no fukuro]; **shopping bag** n 買物袋 [kaimonobukuro]; **sleeping bag** n 寝袋 [nebukuro]; **tea bag** n ティーバッグ [tiibaggu]; **toilet bag** n 洗面用具バッグ [senmen yougu baggu]; **Could you watch my bag for a minute, please?** ちょっと私のかばんを見張っていただけますか? [chotto watashi no kaban o mihatte itadakemasu ka?]; **Someone's stolen my bag** 誰かが私のかばんを盗みました [dare ka ga watashi no kaban o nusumimashita]

baggage [ˈbægɪdʒ] n 手荷物 [tenimotsu]; **baggage allowance** n 無料手荷物許容量 [muryou tenimotsu kyouryou]; **baggage reclaim** n 手荷物受取所 [tenimotsu uketorisho]; **excess baggage** n 超過手荷物 [choukatenimotsu]; **What is the baggage allowance?** 無料手荷物許容量はどう規定されていますか? [muryou-tenimotsu-kyouryou wa dou kitei sarete imasu ka?]

baggy [ˈbægɪ] adj だぶだぶの [dabudabu no]

bagpipes [ˈbægˌpaɪps] npl バグパイプ [bagupaipu]

Bahamas [bəˈhɑːməz] npl バハマ [bahama]

Bahrain [bɑːˈreɪn] n バーレーン [baareen]

bail [beɪl] n 保釈金 [hoshakukin]

bake [beɪk] v 焼く [yaku]

baked [beɪkt] adj 焼いた [yaita]; **baked potato** n ベークドポテト [beekudopoteto]

baker [ˈbeɪkə] n パン屋の主人 [pan ya no shujin]

bakery [ˈbeɪkərɪ] n パン屋 [pan-ya]

baking [ˈbeɪkɪŋ] n ベーキング [beekingu]; **baking powder** n ベーキングパウダー [beekingupaudaa]

balance [ˈbæləns] n バランス [baransu]; **balance sheet** n 貸借対照表 [taishakutaishouhyou]; **bank balance** n 銀行の残高 [ginkou no zandaka]

balanced [ˈbælənst] adj バランスのとれた [baransu no toreta]

balcony ['bælkənɪ] n バルコニー [barukonii]; **Do you have a room with a balcony?** バルコニー付きの部屋はありますか？ [barukonii-tsuki no heya wa arimasu ka?]

bald [bɔːld] adj 頭のはげた [atama no hageta]

Balkan ['bɔːlkən] adj バルカン諸国の [barukan shokoku no]

ball [bɔːl] n (dance) 舞踏会 [butoukai], (toy) ボール [booru]

ballerina [ˌbælə'riːnə] n バレリーナ [bareriina]

ballet ['bæleɪ; bæ'leɪ] n バレエ [baree]; **ballet dancer** n バレエダンサー [bareedansaa]; **ballet shoes** npl バレエシューズ [baree shuuzu]; **Where can I buy tickets for the ballet?** どこでそのバレエのチケットを買えますか？ [doko de sono baree no chiketto o kaemasu ka?]

balloon [bə'luːn] n 風船 [fuusen]

bamboo [bæm'buː] n 竹 [take]

ban [bæn] n 禁止 [kinshi] ▷ v 禁止する [kinshi suru]

banana [bə'nɑːnə] n バナナ [banana]

band [bænd] n (musical group) バンド [bando] (音楽グループ), (strip) 帯状のひも [obijou no himo]; **brass band** n ブラスバンド [burasubando]; **elastic band** n 輪ゴム [wagomu]; **rubber band** n 輪ゴム [wagomu]

bandage ['bændɪdʒ] n 包帯 [houtai] ▷ v 包帯をする [houtai-o suru]; **I'd like a bandage** 包帯をしてください [houtai o shite kudasai]; **I'd like a fresh bandage** 新しい包帯をしてください [atarashii houtai o shite kudasai]

Band-Aid [bændeɪd] n バンドエイド [bandoeido]

bang [bæŋ] n 砲声 [housei] ▷ v バンと打つ [ban to utsu]

Bangladesh [ˌbɑːŋglə'dɛʃ; ˌbæŋ-] n バングラデシュ [banguradeshu]

Bangladeshi [ˌbɑːŋglə'dɛʃɪ; bæŋ-] adj バングラデシュの [banguradeshu no] ▷ n バングラデシュ人 [banguradeshujin]

banister ['bænɪstə] n 手すり [tesuri]

banjo ['bændʒəʊ] n バンジョー [banjoo]

bank [bæŋk] n (finance) 銀行 [ginkou], (ridge) 土手 [dote]; **bank account** n 銀行口座 [ginkoukouza]; **bank balance** n 銀行の残高 [ginkou no zandaka]; **bank charges** npl 銀行の手数料 [ginkou no tesuuryou]; **bank holiday** n 祝祭日 [shukusaijitsu]; **bank statement** n 銀行の明細書 [ginkou no meisaisho]; **bottle bank** n 空き瓶回収ボックス [akikan kaishuu bokkusu]; **merchant bank** n マーチャントバンク [maachantobanku]; **How far is the bank?** 銀行までのどのくらいの距離ですか？ [ginkou made dono kurai no kyori desu ka?]; **I would like to transfer some money from my bank in...** ···にある取引銀行から送金したいのですが [...ni aru torihiki-ginkou kara soukin shitai no desu ga]; **Is the bank open today?** その銀行は今日開いていますか？ [sono ginkou wa kyou hiraite imasu ka?]; **Is there a bank here?** ここに銀行はありますか？ [koko ni ginkou wa arimasu ka?]; **When does the bank close?** その銀行はいつ閉まりますか？ [sono ginkou wa itsu shimarimasu ka?]

banker ['bæŋkə] n 銀行家 [ginkouka]

banknote ['bæŋkˌnəʊt] n 紙幣 [shihei]

bankrupt ['bæŋkrʌpt; -rəpt] adj 破産した [hasan shita]

banned [bænd] adj 禁止された [kinshi sareta]

Baptist ['bæptɪst] n バプテスト [baputesuto]

bar [bɑː] n (alcohol) バー [baa] (酒場), (metal) 棒 [bou]; **snack bar** n 軽食堂 [keishokudou]; **Where is the bar?** バーはどこですか？ [baa wa doko desu ka?]; **Where is there a nice bar?** どこかに感じの良いバーはありますか？ [doko-ka ni kanji no yoi baa wa arimasu ka?]

Barbados [bɑː'beɪdəʊs; -dəʊz; -dɒs] n バルバドス [barubadosu]

barbaric [bɑː'bærɪk] adj 野蛮な [yaban na]

barbecue ['bɑːbɪˌkjuː] n バーベキュー

[baabekyuu]; **Where is the barbecue area?** バーベキュー場はどこですか? [baabekyuu-jou wa doko desu ka?]

barber ['bɑːbə] n 床屋 [tokoya]

bare [bɛə] adj むき出しの [mukidashi no] ▷ v むき出しにする [mukidashi ni suru]

barefoot ['bɛəˌfʊt] adj 裸足の [hadashi no] ▷ adv 裸足で [hadashi de]

barely ['bɛəlɪ] adv かろうじて [karoujite]

bargain ['bɑːgɪn] n 売買契約 [baibai keiyaku]

barge [bɑːdʒ] n バージ [baaji]

bark [bɑːk] v 吠える [hoeru]

barley ['bɑːlɪ] n 大麦 [oumugi]

barmaid ['bɑːˌmeɪd] n 女性バーテンダー [josei baatendaa]

barman, barmen ['bɑːmən, 'bɑːmɛn] n バーテンダー [baatendaa]

barn [bɑːn] n 納屋 [naya]

barrel ['bærəl] n 樽 [taru]

barrier ['bærɪə] n 柵 [saku]; **ticket barrier** n 改札口 [kaisatsuguchi]

bartender ['bɑːˌtɛndə] n バーテンダー [baatendaa]

base [beɪs] n 土台 [dodai]

baseball ['beɪsˌbɔːl] n 野球 [yakyuu]; **baseball cap** n 野球帽 [yakyuubou]

based [beɪst] adj ···に基づく [...ni motozuku]

basement ['beɪsmənt] n 地階 [chikai]

bash [bæʃ] n 強打 [kyouda] ▷ v 強打する [kyouda suru]

basic ['beɪsɪk] adj 基本的な [kihonteki na]

basically ['beɪsɪklɪ] adv 基本的に [kihonteki ni]

basics ['beɪsɪks] npl 基本 [kihon]

basil ['bæzəl] n バジル [bajiru]

basin ['beɪsən] n 洗面器 [senmenki]

basis ['beɪsɪs] n 基礎 [kiso]

basket ['bɑːskɪt] n かご [kago]; **wastepaper basket** n くずかご [kuzukago]

basketball ['bɑːskɪtˌbɔːl] n バスケットボール [basukettobooru]

Basque [bæsk; bɑːsk] adj バスク地方の [basuku chihou no] ▷ n (language) バスク語 [basukugo], (person) バスク人 [basukujin]

bass [beɪs] n バス [basu] (声楽); **bass drum** n バスドラム [basudoramu]; **double bass** n コントラバス [kontorabasu]

bassoon [bə'suːn] n ファゴット [fagotto]

bat [bæt] n (mammal) コウモリ [koumori] (動物), (with ball) バット [batto]

bath [bɑːθ] n **bubble bath** n 泡風呂 [awaburo]

bathe [beɪð] v 泳ぐ [oyogu]

bathrobe ['bɑːθˌrəʊb] n バスローブ [basuroobu]

bathroom ['bɑːθˌruːm; -ˌrʊm] n バスルーム [basuruumu]; **Are there hand rails in the bathroom?** バスルームに介助の手すりはありますか? [basu-ruumu ni kaijo no tesuri wa arimasu ka?]; **Does the room have a private bathroom?** その部屋に専用のバスルームはありますか? [sono heya ni senyou no basu-ruumu wa arimasu ka?]; **The bathroom is flooded** バスルームが水浸しになっています [basu-ruumu ga mizu-bitashi ni natte imasu]

baths [bɑːθz] npl 公衆浴場 [koushuu yokujou]

bathtub ['bɑːθˌtʌb] n 浴槽 [yokusou]

batter ['bætə] n (料理用の)ころも [(ryouriyou no) koromo]

battery ['bætərɪ] n 電池 [denchi]

battle ['bætəl] n 戦闘 [sentou]

battleship ['bætəlˌʃɪp] n 戦艦 [senkan]

bay [beɪ] n 湾 [wan]; **bay leaf** n ローリエ [roorie]

BC [biː siː] abbr 紀元前 [kigenzen]

be [biː; bɪ] v いる [iru]

beach [biːtʃ] n 浜辺 [hamabe]

bead [biːd] n ビーズ [biizu]

beak [biːk] n くちばし [kuchibashi]

beam [biːm] n 笑顔 [egao]

bean [biːn] n 豆 [mame]; **broad bean** n ソラマメ [soramame]; **coffee bean** n コーヒー豆 [koohiimame]; **French beans** npl サヤインゲン [saya ingen]; **runner**

bean n ベニバナインゲン [benibanaingen]

beansprout ['bi:nsprɑʊt] n
beansprouts npl 豆もやし [mame moyashi]

bear [bɛə] n クマ [kuma] (動物) ▷v 支える [sasaeru] (支持); **polar bear** n 北極グマ [hokkyokuguma]; **teddy bear** n テディーベア [tedeiibea]

beard [bɪəd] n あごひげ [agohige]

bearded [bɪədɪd] adj あごひげを生やした [agohige-o hayashita]

bear up [bɛə ʌp] v がんばる [ganbaru]

beat [bi:t] n 打つこと [utsu koto] ▷v (outdo) ···に勝つ [...ni katsu], (strike) 続けざまに打つ [tsuzukezama ni utsu]

beautiful ['bju:tɪfʊl] adj 美しい [utsukushii]

beautifully ['bju:tɪflɪ] adv 美しく [utsukushiku]

beauty ['bju:tɪ] n 美しさ [utsukushisa]; **beauty salon** n 美容院 [biyouin]; **beauty spot** n 景勝地 [keishouchi]

beaver ['bi:və] n ビーバー [biibaa]

because [bɪˈkɒz; -ˈkəz] conj ···だから [...dakara]

become [bɪˈkʌm] v ···になる [...ni naru]

bed [bɛd] n ベッド [beddo]; **bed and breakfast** n ベッド&ブレックファースト [beddo burekkufaasuto]; **bunk beds** npl 二段ベッド [nidanbeddo]; **camp bed** n キャンプベッド [kyanpubeddo]; **double bed** n ダブルベッド [daburubeddo]; **king-size bed** n キングサイズのベッド [kingu saizu no beddo]; **single bed** n シングルベッド [shingurubeddo]; **sofa bed** n ソファーベッド [sofaabeddo]; **twin beds** npl ツインベッド [tsuinbeddo]; **The bed is uncomfortable** ベッドの寝心地がよくありません [beddo no ne-gokochi ga yoku arimasen]

bedclothes ['bɛd,kləʊðz] npl 寝具 [shingu]

bedding ['bɛdɪŋ] n 寝具 [shingu]; **Is there any spare bedding?** 予備の寝具はありますか? [yobi no shingu wa arimasu ka?]

bedroom ['bɛd,ru:m; -,rʊm] n 寝室 [shinshitsu]

bedsit ['bɛd,sɪt] n ワンルームのアパート [wanruumu no apaato]

bedspread ['bɛd,sprɛd] n ベッドカバー [beddokabaa]

bedtime ['bɛd,taɪm] n 就寝時刻 [shuushin jikoku]

bee [bi:] n ハチ [hachi] (昆虫)

beech [bi:tʃ] n **beech (tree)** n ブナ [buna]

beef [bi:f] n 牛肉 [gyuuniku]

beefburger ['bi:f,bɜ:gə] n ビーフバーガー [biifu baagaa]

beer [bɪə] n ビール [biiru]; **another beer** ビールをもう一杯 [biiru o mou ippai]; **A draught beer, please** 生ビールをください [nama-biiru o kudasai]

beetle ['bi:tºl] n カブトムシ [kabutomushi]

beetroot ['bi:t,ru:t] n ビートルート [biitoruuto]

before [bɪˈfɔ:] adv 以前に [izen ni] ▷conj ···する前に [...suru mae ni] ▷prep ···の前に [...no mae ni]

beforehand [bɪˈfɔ:,hænd] adv あらかじめ [arakajime]

beg [bɛg] v 物乞いをする [monogoi-o suru]

beggar ['bɛgə] n 乞食 [kojiki]

begin [bɪˈgɪn] v 始める [hajimeru]

beginner [bɪˈgɪnə] n 初心者 [shoshinsha]

beginning [bɪˈgɪnɪŋ] n 始め [hajime]

behave [bɪˈheɪv] v 振舞う [furumau]

behaviour [bɪˈheɪvjə] n 態度 [taido]

behind [bɪˈhaɪnd] adv 後ろに [ushiro ni] ▷n 臀部 [denbu] ▷prep ···の後ろに [...no ushiro ni]; **lag behind** v 遅れる [okureru]

beige [beɪʒ] adj ベージュの [beeju no]

Beijing ['beɪˈdʒɪŋ] n 北京 [pekin]

Belarus ['bɛlə,rʌs; -,rʊs] n ベラルーシ [beraruushi]

Belarussian [,bɛləʊˈrʌʃən; ,bjɛl-] adj ベラルーシの [beraruushi no] ▷n (language) ベラルーシ語 [beraruushigo], (person) ベラルーシ人 [beraruushijin]

Belgian ['bɛldʒən] *adj* ベルギーの [berugii no] ▷ *n* ベルギー人 [berugiijin]

Belgium ['bɛldʒəm] *n* ベルギー [berugii]

belief [bɪ'liːf] *n* 信頼 [shinrai]

believe [bɪ'liːv] *vi* 信仰する [shinkou suru] ▷ *vt* 信じる [shinjiru]

bell [bɛl] *n* 鐘 [kane]

belly ['bɛlɪ] *n* 腹部 [fukubu]; **belly button** *n* おへそ [oheso]

belong [bɪ'lɒŋ] *v* 所属する [shozoku suru]; **belong to** *v* ・・・のものである [...no mono de aru]

belongings [bɪ'lɒŋɪŋz] *npl* 所持品 [shojihin]

below [bɪ'ləʊ] *adv* 下に [shita ni] ▷ *prep* ・・・より下に [...yori shitani]

belt [bɛlt] *n* ベルト [beruto]; **conveyor belt** *n* コンベヤベルト [konbeyaberuto]; **money belt** *n* マネーベルト [maneeberuto]; **safety belt** *n* 安全ベルト [anzenberuto]

bench [bɛntʃ] *n* ベンチ [benchi]

bend [bɛnd] *n* 曲がり [magari] ▷ *v* 曲げる [mageru]; **bend down** *v* かがむ [kagamu]; **bend over** *v* かがむ [kagamu]

beneath [bɪ'niːθ] *prep* ・・・の下に [...no shita ni]

benefit ['bɛnɪfɪt] *n* 利益 [rieki] (もうけ) ▷ *v* 利益を得る [rieki o eru]

bent [bɛnt] *adj* (not straight) 曲がった [magatta], (dishonest) 不正直な [fushoujiki na]

beret ['bɛreɪ] *n* ベレー帽 [bereebou]

berry ['bɛrɪ] *n* ベリー [berii]

berth [bɜːθ] *n* 寝台 [shindai]

beside [bɪ'saɪd] *prep* ・・・のそばに [...no soba ni]

besides [bɪ'saɪdz] *adv* その上 [sono ue]

best [bɛst] *adj* 最もよい [mottomo yoi] ▷ *adv* 最もよく [mottomo yoku]; **best man** *n* 新郎の付添い役 [shinrou no tsukisoiyaku]

bestseller [ˌbɛst'sɛlə] *n* ベストセラー [besutoseraa]

bet [bɛt] *n* 賭け [kake] ▷ *v* 賭ける [kakeru]

betray [bɪ'treɪ] *v* 裏切る [uragiru]

better ['bɛtə] *adj* よりよい [yoriyoi] ▷ *adv* よりよく [yoriyoku]

betting ['bɛtɪŋ] *n* 賭け事 [kakegoto]; **betting shop** *n* 賭け屋 [kakeya]

between [bɪ'twiːn] *prep* ・・・の間に [...no aida ni]

bewildered [bɪ'wɪldəd] *adj* 困惑した [konwaku shita]

beyond [bɪ'jɒnd] *prep* ・・・の向こうに [...no mukou ni]

biased ['baɪəst] *adj* 偏った [katayotta]

bib [bɪb] *n* よだれ掛け [yodarekake]

Bible ['baɪbəl] *n* 聖書 [seisho]

bicarbonate [baɪ'kɑːbənɪt; -ˌneɪt] *n* **bicarbonate of soda** *n* 重炭酸ソーダ [juutansansooda]

bicycle ['baɪsɪkəl] *n* 自転車 [jitensha]; **bicycle pump** *n* 自転車ポンプ [jitensha ponpu]

bid [bɪd] *n* 入札 [nyuusatsu] ▷ *v* (at auction) 入札する [nyuusatsu suru]

bifocals [baɪ'fəʊkəlz] *npl* 遠近両用メガネ [enkin ryouyou megane]

big [bɪg] *adj* 大きい [ookii]; **The house is quite big** 家はかなり大きいです [ie wa kanari ookii desu]

bigger ['bɪgə] *adj* より大きい [yori oukii]

bigheaded ['bɪgˌhɛdɪd] *adj* うぬぼれた [unuboreta]

bike [baɪk] *n* 自転車 [jitensha]; **mountain bike** *n* マウンテンバイク [mauntenbaiku]; **Can I keep my bike here?** ここに自転車を置いておけますか? [koko ni jitensha o oite okemasu ka?]; **Does the bike have brakes?** 自転車はブレーキ付きですか? [jitensha wa bureeki tsuki desu ka?]; **Does the bike have gears?** 自転車はギア付きですか? [jitensha wa gia tsuki desu ka?]; **I want to hire a bike** 自転車を借りたいのですが [jitensha o karitai no desu ga]; **Where is the nearest bike repair shop?** 一番近い自転車修理店はどこですか? [ichiban chikai jitensha shuuri-ten wa doko desu ka?]

bikini [bɪ'kiːnɪ] *n* ビキニ [bikini]

bilingual [baɪˈlɪŋgwəl] *adj* バイリンガルの [bairingaru no]

bill [bɪl] *n* (account) 請求書 [seikyuusho], (legislation) 法案 [houan]; **phone bill** *n* 電話の請求書 [denwa no seikyuusho]; **Can I have an itemized bill?** 請求書の明細をもらえますか？ [seikyuusho no meisai o moraemasu ka?]; **Please prepare the bill** 請求書を用意してください [seikyuusho o youi shite kudasai]; **The bill is wrong** 請求書が間違っています [seikyuusho ga machigatte imasu]

billiards [ˈbɪljədz] *npl* ビリヤード [biriyaado]

billion [ˈbɪljən] *n* 10億 [juuoku]

bin [bɪn] *n* ごみ箱 [gomibako]; **litter bin** *n* くずかご [kuzukago]

binding [ˈbaɪndɪŋ] *n* **Can you adjust my bindings, please?** ビンディングを調節していただけますか？ [bindingu o chousetsu shite itadakemasu ka?]; **Can you tighten my bindings, please?** ビンディングを締めていただけますか？ [bindingu o shimete itadakemasu ka?]

bingo [ˈbɪŋgəʊ] *n* ビンゴ [bingo]

binoculars [bɪˈnɒkjʊləz; baɪ-] *npl* 双眼鏡 [sougankyou]

biochemistry [ˌbaɪəʊˈkɛmɪstrɪ] *n* 生化学 [seikagaku]

biodegradable [ˌbaɪəʊdɪˈgreɪdəbəl] *adj* 生物分解性の [seibutsu bunkaisei no]

biography [baɪˈɒgrəfɪ] *n* 伝記 [denki]

biological [ˌbaɪəˈlɒdʒɪkəl] *adj* 生物学の [seibutsugaku no]

biology [baɪˈɒlədʒɪ] *n* 生物学 [seibutsugaku]

biometric [ˌbaɪəʊˈmɛtrɪk] *adj* 生物測定の [seibutsu sokutei no]

birch [bɜːtʃ] *n* 樺 [kaba]

bird [bɜːd] *n* 鳥 [tori]; **bird flu** *n* 鳥インフルエンザ [tori infuruenza]; **bird of prey** *n* 猛禽 [moukin]

birdwatching [bɜːdwɒtʃɪŋ] *n* バードウォッチング [baadowotchingu]

Biro® [ˈbaɪrəʊ] *n* バイロウ® [bairou]

birth [bɜːθ] *n* 誕生 [tanjou]; **birth certificate** *n* 出生証明書 [shusshou shoumeisho]; **birth control** *n* 避妊 [hinin]; **place of birth** *n* 出生地 [shusseichi]

birthday [ˈbɜːθˌdeɪ] *n* 誕生日 [tanjoubi]; **Happy birthday!** お誕生日おめでとう！ [o-tanjoubi omedetou!]

birthplace [ˈbɜːθˌpleɪs] *n* 出生地 [shusseichi]

biscuit [ˈbɪskɪt] *n* ビスケット [bisuketto]

bishop [ˈbɪʃəp] *n* 主教 [shukyou]

bit [bɪt] *n* 小片 [shouhen]

bitch [bɪtʃ] *n* (dog) 雌犬 [mesuinu]

bite [baɪt] *n* かむこと [kamu koto] (歯) ▷ *v* かむ [kamu] (歯)

bitter [ˈbɪtə] *adj* にがい [nigai]

black [blæk] *adj* 黒い [kuroi]; **black ice** *n* 路面の薄い透明な氷 [romen no usui toumei na kouri]

blackberry [ˈblækbərɪ] *n* ブラックベリー [burakkuberii]

blackbird [ˈblækˌbɜːd] *n* クロウタドリ [kuroutadori]

blackboard [ˈblækˌbɔːd] *n* 黒板 [kokuban]

blackcurrant [ˌblækˈkʌrənt] *n* クロスグリ [kurosuguri]

blackmail [ˈblækˌmeɪl] *n* 恐喝 [kyoukatsu] ▷ *v* 恐喝する [kyoukatsu suru]

blackout [ˈblækaʊt] *n* 灯火管制 [toukakansei]

bladder [ˈblædə] *n* 膀胱 [boukou]; **gall bladder** *n* 胆嚢 [tannou]

blade [bleɪd] *n* 刃 [ha]; **razor blade** *n* 安全かみそりの刃 [anzen kamisori no ha]; **shoulder blade** *n* 肩甲骨 [kenkoukotsu]

blame [bleɪm] *n* 非難 [hinan] ▷ *v* 責める [semeru]

blank [blæŋk] *adj* 白紙の [hakushi no] ▷ *n* 空欄 [kuuran]; **blank cheque** *n* 白地小切手 [shiraji kogitte]

blanket [ˈblæŋkɪt] *n* 毛布 [moufu]; **electric blanket** *n* 電気毛布 [denkimoufu]; **Please bring me an extra blanket** 追加の毛布を持ってきてください [tsuika no moufu o motte kite kudasai]; **We need more blankets** 毛布がもっと必要です [moufu ga motto hitsuyou desu]

blast [blɑːst] *n* 爆発 [bakuhatsu]

blatant ['bleɪtənt] *adj* 露骨な [rokotsu na]

blaze [bleɪz] *n* 火炎 [kaen]

blazer ['bleɪzə] *n* ブレザー [burezaa]

bleach [bliːtʃ] *n* 漂白剤 [hyouhakuzai]

bleached [bliːtʃt] *adj* 漂白した [hyouhaku shita]

bleak [bliːk] *adj* 荒涼とした [kouryou to shita]

bleed [bliːd] *v* 出血する [shukketsu suru]

bleeper ['bliːpə] *n* ポケットベル [poketto beru]

blender ['blɛndə] *n* ブレンダー [burendaa]

bless [blɛs] *v* 祝福する [shukufuku suru]

blind [blaɪnd] *adj* 目の見えない [me no mienai] ▷ *n* ブラインド [buraindo]; **Venetian blind** *n* ベネチアンブラインド [benechianburaindo]

blindfold ['blaɪnd,fəʊld] *n* 目隠し布 [mekakushi nuno] ▷ *v* 目隠しする [mekakushi suru]

blink [blɪŋk] *v* まばたきする [mabataki suru]

bliss [blɪs] *n* 至福 [shifuku]

blister ['blɪstə] *n* 水ぶくれ [mizubukure]

blizzard ['blɪzəd] *n* ブリザード [burizaado]

block [blɒk] *n* (buildings) ブロック [burokku], (obstruction) 閉塞物 [heisokubutsu], (solid piece) 塊 [katamari] ▷ *v* ふさぐ [fusagu]

blockage ['blɒkɪdʒ] *n* 封鎖 [fuusa]

blocked [blɒkt] *adj* 封鎖された [fuusa sareta]

blog [blɒg] *n* ブログ [burogu] ▷ *v* ブログを書く [burogu-o kaku]; **blogger** ['blɒgə] *n* ブロガー [burogaa]; **blogpost** ['blɒgpəʊst] *n* ブログ投稿 [burogu toukou];

bloke [bləʊk] *n* 男 [otoko]

blonde [blɒnd] *adj* ブロンドの [burondo no]

blood [blʌd] *n* 血 [chi]; **blood group** *n* 血液型 [ketsuekigata]; **blood poisoning** *n* 敗血症 [haiketsushou]; **blood pressure** *n* 血圧 [ketsuatsu]; **blood sports** *n* 血を見るスポーツ [chi-o miru supootsu]; **blood test** *n* 血液検査 [ketsuekikensa]; **blood transfusion** *n* 輸血 [yuketsu]; **My blood group is O positive** 私の血液型はO型Rhプラスです [watashi no ketsueki-gata wa oo-gata aaru-eichi-purasu desu]

bloody ['blʌdɪ] *adj* 血まみれの [chi mamire no]

blossom ['blɒsəm] *n* 花 [hana] ▷ *v* 花が咲く [hana ga saku]

blouse [blaʊz] *n* ブラウス [burausu]

blow [bləʊ] *n* 強打 [kyouda] ▷ *v* 吹く [fuku]

blow-dry [bləʊdraɪ] *n* ブロードライ [buroodorai]

blow up [bləʊ ʌp] *v* 爆破する [bakuha suru]

blue [bluː] *adj* 青い [aoi]

blueberry ['bluːbərɪ; -brɪ] *n* ブルーベリー [buruuberii]

blues [bluːz] *npl* ブルース [buruusu]

bluff [blʌf] *n* 虚勢 [kyosei] ▷ *v* 虚勢を張る [kyosei-o haru]

blunder ['blʌndə] *n* 大失敗 [daishippai]

blunt [blʌnt] *adj* 鈍い [nibui]

blush [blʌʃ] *v* 赤面する [sekimen suru]

blusher ['blʌʃə] *n* ほお紅 [hoobeni]

board [bɔːd] *n* (meeting) 役員会 [yakuinkai], (wood) 板 [ita] ▷ *v* (go aboard) 乗る [noru]; **board game** *n* ボードゲーム [boodo geemu]; **boarding card, boarding pass** *n* 搭乗券 [toujouken]; **boarding school** *n* 寄宿学校 [kishuku gakkou]; **bulletin board** *n* 掲示板 [keijiban]; **diving board** *n* 飛込台 [tobikomidai]; **draining board** *n* 水切り板 [mizukiriban]; **half board** *n* 二食付き [nishokutsuki]; **ironing board** *n* アイロン台 [airondai]; **notice board** *n* 掲示板 [keijiban]; **skirting board** *n* 幅木 [habaki]

boarder ['bɔːdə] n 寄宿生 [kishukusei]

boast [bəʊst] v 自慢する [jiman suru]

boat [bəʊt] n ボート [booto]; **fishing boat** n 漁船 [gyosen]; **rowing boat** n 漕ぎ舟 [kogibune]; **sailing boat** n ヨット [yotto]

body ['bɒdɪ] n 体 [karada]

bodybuilding ['bɒdɪˌbɪldɪŋ] n ボディービル [bodiibiru]

bodyguard ['bɒdɪˌgɑːd] n ボディーガード [bodiigaado]

bog [bɒg] n 沼 [numa]

boil [bɔɪl] vi 沸騰する [futtou suru] ▷ vt 沸かす [wakasu]

boiled [bɔɪld] adj 沸騰した [futtou shita]; **boiled egg** n ゆで卵 [yudetamago]

boiler ['bɔɪlə] n ボイラー [boiraa]

boiling ['bɔɪlɪŋ] adj 沸き立つ [wakitatsu]

boil over [bɔɪl 'əʊvə] v 噴きこぼれる [fukikoboreru]

Bolivia [bə'lɪvɪə] n ボリビア [boribia]

Bolivian [bə'lɪvɪən] adj ボリビアの [boribia no] ▷ n ボリビア人 [boribiajin]

bolt [bəʊlt] n かんぬき [kannuki]

bomb [bɒm] n 爆弾 [bakudan] ▷ v 爆撃する [bakugeki suru]; **atom bomb** n 原子爆弾 [genshibakudan]

bombing [bɒmɪŋ] n 爆撃 [bakugeki]

bond [bɒnd] n 縛るもの [shibaru mono]

bone [bəʊn] n 骨 [hone]; **bone dry** adj ひからびた [hikarabita]

bonfire ['bɒnˌfaɪə] n 大かがり火 [oukagaribi]

bonnet ['bɒnɪt] n (car) ボンネット [bonnetto]

bonus ['bəʊnəs] n ボーナス [boonasu]

book [bʊk] n 本 [hon] (書物) ▷ v 予約する [yoyaku suru]; **address book** n 住所録 [juushoroku]

bookcase ['bʊkˌkeɪs] n 本箱 [honbako]

booking ['bʊkɪŋ] n 予約 [yoyaku]; **advance booking** n 事前予約 [jizen yoyaku]; **booking office** n 予約オフィス [yoyaku ofisu]; **Can I change my booking?** 私の予約を変更できますか? [watashi no yoyaku o henkou dekimasu ka?];

I want to cancel my booking 予約をキャンセルしたいのですが [yoyaku o kyanseru shitai no desu ga]; **Is there a booking fee?** 予約料がかかりますか? [yoyaku-ryou ga kakarimasu ka?]

booklet ['bʊklɪt] n 小冊子 [shousasshi]

bookmark ['bʊkˌmɑːk] n しおり [shiori]

bookshelf ['bʊkˌʃelf] n 本棚 [hondana]

bookshop ['bʊkˌʃɒp] n 書店 [shoten]

boost [buːst] v 高める [takameru]

boot [buːt] n ブーツ [buutsu]

booze [buːz] n 酒 [sake]

border ['bɔːdə] n 境界 [kyoukai]

bore [bɔː] v (be dull) 穴をあける [ana-o akeru], (drill) 穴をあける [ana-o akeru]

bored [bɔːd] adj 退屈した [taikutsu shita]

boredom ['bɔːdəm] n 退屈 [taikutsu]

boring ['bɔːrɪŋ] adj 退屈な [taikutsu na]

born [bɔːn] adj 生まれながらの [umare nagara no]

borrow ['bɒrəʊ] v 借りる [kariru]

Bosnia ['bɒznɪə] n ボスニア [bosunia]; **Bosnia and Herzegovina** n ボスニア・ヘルツェゴビナ [bosunia herutsuegobina]

Bosnian ['bɒznɪən] adj ボスニアの [bosunia no] ▷ n (person) ボスニア人 [bosuniajin]

boss [bɒs] n ボス [bosu]

boss around [bɒs ə'raʊnd] v こき使う [kokitsukau]

bossy ['bɒsɪ] adj 威張った [ibatta]

both [bəʊθ] adj 両方の [ryouhou no] ▷ pron 両方 [ryouhou]

bother ['bɒðə] v 悩ます [nayamasu]

Botswana [bʊ'tʃwɑːnə; bʊt'swɑːnə; bɒt-] n ボツワナ [botsuwana]

bottle ['bɒtəl] n ボトル [botoru]; **baby's bottle** n 哺乳瓶 [honyuubin]; **bottle bank** n 空き瓶回収ボックス [akikan kaishuu bokkusu]; **hot-water bottle** n 湯たんぽ [yutanpo]; **a bottle of mineral water** ミネラルウォーターのボトル1本 [mineraruuootaa no botoru 1 hon]; **a bottle of red wine** 赤ワインのボトルを1本 [aka-wain no botoru o ippon]; **Please bring another bottle** ボトルをもう1本

持ってきてください [botoru o mou ippon motte kite kudasai]

ottle-opener ['bɒt³l'əʊpənə] *n* 栓抜き [sennuki]

ottom ['bɒtəm] *adj* 底の [soko no] ▷ *n* 底 [soko]

ought [bɔːt] *adj* 既製の [kisei no]

ounce [baʊns] *v* 弾む [hazumu]

ouncer ['baʊnsə] *n* 用心棒 [youjinbou] (バーでなどの)

oundary ['baʊndərɪ; -drɪ] *n* 境界 [kyoukai]

ouquet ['buːkeɪ] *n* ブーケ [buuke]

ow *n* [bəʊ] *(weapon)* 弓 [yumi] ▷ *v* [baʊ] お辞儀をする [ojigi-o suru]

owels ['baʊəlz] *npl* 腸 [chou]

owl [bəʊl] *n* ボウル [bouru]

owling ['bəʊlɪŋ] *n* ボウリング [bouringu]; **bowling alley** *n* ボウリング場 [bouringu jou]; **tenpin bowling** *n* テンピンボウリング [tenpinbouringu]

ow tie [bəʊ] *n* **bow tie** *n* 蝶ネクタイ [chounekutai]

ox [bɒks] *n* 箱 [hako]; **box office** *n* 切符売場 [kippu uriba]; **call box** *n* 公衆電話ボックス [koushuu denwa bokkusu]; **fuse box** *n* ヒューズボックス [hyuuzubokkusu]; **gear box** *n* ギアボックス [giabokkusu]

oxer ['bɒksə] *n* ボクサー [bokusaa]; **boxer shorts** *npl* ボクサーショーツ [bokusaa shootsu]

oxing ['bɒksɪŋ] *n* ボクシング [bokushingu]

oy [bɔɪ] *n* 少年 [shounen]

oyfriend ['bɔɪˌfrɛnd] *n* ボーイフレンド [booifurendo]; **I have a boyfriend** 私にはボーイフレンドがいます [watashi ni wa booifurendo ga imasu]

ra [brɑː] *n* ブラジャー [burajaa]

race [breɪs] *n (fastening)* 突っ張り [tsuppari]

racelet ['breɪslɪt] *n* ブレスレット [buresuretto]

races ['breɪsɪz] *npl* ズボン吊り [zubontsuri]

rackets ['brækɪts] *npl* 括弧 [kakko]

brain [breɪn] *n* 脳 [nou]

brainy ['breɪnɪ] *adj* 頭のいい [atama no ii]

brake [breɪk] *n* ブレーキ [bureeki] ▷ *v* ブレーキをかける [bureeki-o kakeru]; **brake light** *n* ブレーキランプ [bureeki ranpu]; **Does the bike have back-pedal brakes?** 自転車はコースターブレーキ付きですか? [jitensha wa koosutaa-bureeki tsuki desu ka?]; **The brakes don't work** ブレーキがききません [bureeki ga kikimasen]

bran [bræn] *n* ふすま [fusuma] (小麦外皮)

branch [brɑːntʃ] *n* 枝 [eda]

brand [brænd] *n* ブランド [burando]; **brand name** *n* ブランド名 [burando mei]

brand-new [brænd'njuː] *adj* 新品の [shinpin no]

brandy ['brændɪ] *n* ブランデー [burandee]; **I'll have a brandy** ブランデーをください [burandee o kudasai]

brass [brɑːs] *n* 真鍮 [shinchuu]; **brass band** *n* ブラスバンド [burasubando]

brat [bræt] *n* 悪がき [warugaki]

brave [breɪv] *adj* 勇敢な [yuukan na]

bravery ['breɪvərɪ] *n* 勇敢 [yuukan]

Brazil [brə'zɪl] *n* ブラジル [burajiru]

Brazilian [brə'zɪljən] *adj* ブラジルの [burajiru no] ▷ *n* ブラジル人 [burajirujin]

bread [brɛd] *n* パン [pan]; **bread roll** *n* ロールパン [roorupan]; **brown bread** *n* 黒パン [kuropan]; **Please bring more bread** パンをもっと持ってきてください [pan o motto motte kite kudasai]; **Would you like some bread?** パンはいかがですか? [pan wa ikaga desu ka?]

bread bin [brɛdbɪn] *n* パンケース [pan keesu]

breadcrumbs ['brɛdˌkrʌmz] *npl* パン粉 [panko]

break [breɪk] *n* 破壊 [hakai] ▷ *v* 割る [waru]; **lunch break** *n* 昼休み [hiruyasumi]

break down [breɪk daʊn] *v* 故障する [koshou suru]

breakdown ['breɪkdaʊn] *n* 故障 [koshou]; **breakdown truck** *n* レッカー車 [rekkaasha]; **breakdown van** *n* レッカー車 [rekkaasha]; **nervous breakdown** *n* 神経衰弱 [shinkeisuijaku]; **Call the breakdown service, please** 故障時緊急修理サービスを呼んでください [koshou-ji kinkyuu-shuuri-saabisu o yonde kudasai]

breakfast ['brɛkfəst] *n* 朝食 [choushoku]; **bed and breakfast** *n* ベッド&ブレックファースト [beddo burekkufaasuto]; **continental breakfast** *n* ヨーロッパ大陸式の簡単な朝食 [yooroppa tairikushiki no kantan na choushoku]; **Can I have breakfast in my room?** 自分の部屋で朝食を取ることができますか？ [jibun no heya de choushoku o toru koto ga dekimasu ka?]; **Is breakfast included?** 朝食は含まれていますか？ [choushoku wa fukumarete imasu ka?]; **with breakfast** 朝食付きで [choushoku-tsuki de]; **without breakfast** 朝食なしで [choushoku nashi de]; **What time is breakfast?** 朝食は何時ですか？ [choushoku wa nan-ji desu ka?]; **What would you like for breakfast?** 朝食には何を召し上がりますか？ [choushoku ni wa nani o meshiagarimasu ka?]

break in [breɪk ɪn] *v* 押し入る [oshiiru]; **break in (on)** *v* 押し入る [oshiiru]

break-in [breɪkɪn] *n* 押し入ること [oshiiru koto]

break up [breɪk ʌp] *v* ばらばらにする [barabara ni suru]

breast [brɛst] *n* 乳房 [chibusa]

breast-feed ['brɛst͵fiːd] *v* 授乳する [junyuu suru]

breaststroke ['brɛst͵strəʊk] *n* 平泳ぎ [hiraoyogi]

breath [brɛθ] *n* 息 [iki]

Breathalyser® ['brɛθə͵laɪzə] *n* ブレサライザー® [buresaraizaa]

breathe [briːð] *v* 息をする [iki-o suru]

breathe in [briːð ɪn] *v* 息を吸い込む [iki-o suikomu]

breathe out [briːð aʊt] *v* 息を吐き出す [iki-o hakidasu]

breathing ['briːðɪŋ] *n* 呼吸 [kokyuu]

breed [briːd] *n* 品種 [hinshu] ▷ *v* 品種改良する [hinshu kairyou suru]

breeze [briːz] *n* そよ風 [soyokaze]

brewery ['brʊərɪ] *n* 醸造所 [jouzoujo]

bribe [braɪb] *v* 賄賂を使う [wairo-o tsukau]

bribery ['braɪbərɪ; 'bribery] *n* 贈収賄 [zoushuuwai]

brick [brɪk] *n* 煉瓦 [renga]

bricklayer ['brɪk͵leɪə] *n* 煉瓦職人 [renga shokunin]

bride [braɪd] *n* 花嫁 [hanayome]

bridegroom ['braɪd͵gruːm; -͵grʊm] *n* 花婿 [hanamuko]

bridesmaid ['braɪdz͵meɪd] *n* 新婦の付添い役 [shinpu no tsukisoiyaku]

bridge [brɪdʒ] *n* 橋 [hashi]; **suspension bridge** *n* 吊橋 [tsuribashi]

brief [briːf] *adj* 短い [mijikai]

briefcase ['briːf͵keɪs] *n* ブリーフケース [buriifukeesu]

briefing ['briːfɪŋ] *n* ブリーフィング [buriifingu]

briefly ['briːflɪ] *adv* 簡単に [kantan ni]

briefs [briːfs] *npl* ブリーフ [buriifu]

bright [braɪt] *adj* 明るい [akarui]

brilliant ['brɪljənt] *adj* 光り輝く [hikari kagayaku]

bring [brɪŋ] *v* 持ってくる [motte kuru]

bring back [brɪŋ bæk] *v* 戻す [modosu]

bring forward [brɪŋ 'fɔːwəd] *v* 繰り上げる [kuriageru]

bring up [brɪŋ ʌp] *v* 育てる [sodateru]

Britain ['brɪtᵊn] *n* 英国 [eikoku]

British ['brɪtɪʃ] *adj* 英国の [eikoku no] ▷ *n* 英国人 [eikokujin]

broad [brɔːd] *adj* 広い [hiroi]

broadband ['brɔːd͵bænd] *n* ブロードバンド [buroodobando]

broadcast ['brɔːd͵kɑːst] *n* 放送 [housou] ▷ *v* 放送する [housou suru]

broad-minded [brɔːd'maɪndɪd] *adj* 心の広い [kokoro no hiroi]

roccoli ['brɒkəlɪ] n ブロッコリー [burokkorii]

rochure ['brəʊʃjʊə; -ʃə] n パンフレット [panfuretto]

roke [brəʊk] adj 破産した [hasan shita]

roken ['brəʊkən] adj 壊れた [kowareta]; **broken down** adj 故障した [koshou shita]

roker ['brəʊkə] n ブローカー [burookaa]

ronchitis [brɒŋ'kaɪtɪs] n 気管支炎 [kikanshien]

ronze [brɒnz] n ブロンズ [buronzu]

rooch [brəʊtʃ] n ブローチ [buroochi]

room [bru:m; brʊm] n ほうき [houki]

roth [brɒθ] n 煮出し汁 [nidashijiru]

rother ['brʌðə] n 兄弟 [kyoudai]

rother-in-law ['brʌðə ɪn lɔ:] n 義兄弟 [gikyoudai]

rown [braʊn] adj 茶色の [chairo no]; **brown bread** n 黒パン [kuropan]; **brown rice** n 玄米 [genmai]

rowse [braʊz] v 拾い読みする [hiroiyomi suru]; (on internet) 閲覧する [etsuran suru]

rowser ['braʊzə] n ブラウザ [burauza]

ruise [bru:z] n 打撲傷 [dabokushou]

rush [brʌʃ] n ブラシ [burashi] ▷ v ブラシをかける [burashi o kakeru]

rutal ['bru:tᵊl] adj 残忍な [zannin na]

ubble ['bʌbᵊl] n 泡 [awa]; **bubble bath** n 泡風呂 [awaburo]; **bubble gum** n 風船ガム [fuusengamu]

ucket ['bʌkɪt] n バケツ [baketsu]

uckle ['bʌkᵊl] n バックル [bakkuru]

uddha ['bʊdə] n 仏陀 [budda]

uddhism ['bʊdɪzəm] n 仏教 [bukkyou]

uddhist ['bʊdɪst] adj 仏教の [bukkyou no] ▷ n 仏教徒 [bukkyouto]

udgerigar ['bʌdʒərɪ,gɑ:] n セキセイインコ [sekiseiinko]

udget ['bʌdʒɪt] n 予算 [yosan]

udgie ['bʌdʒɪ] n セキセイインコ [sekiseiinko]

uffet ['bʊfeɪ] n ビュッフェ [byuffe]; **buffet car** n ビュッフェ車 [byuffesha]; **Is there a buffet car on the train?** 電車にはビュッフェ車がありますか? [densha ni wa byuffe-sha ga arimasu ka?]; **Where is the buffet car?** ビュッフェ車はどこですか? [byuffe-sha wa doko desu ka?]

bug [bʌg] n 虫 [mushi]; **There are bugs in my room** 私の部屋に虫がいます [watashi no heya ni mushi ga imasu]

bugged ['bʌgd] adj いらいらした [irairashita]

buggy ['bʌgɪ] n 乳母車 [ubaguruma]

build [bɪld] v 建てる [tateru]

builder ['bɪldə] n 建築業者 [kenchikugyousha]

building ['bɪldɪŋ] n 建物 [tatemono]; **building site** n 建設現場 [kensetsu genba]

bulb [bʌlb] n (electricity) 電球 [denkyuu], (plant) 球根 [kyuukon]

Bulgaria [bʌl'gɛərɪə; bʊl-] n ブルガリア [burugaria]

Bulgarian [bʌl'gɛərɪən; bʊl-] adj ブルガリアの [burugaria no] ▷ n (language) ブルガリア語 [burugariago], (person) ブルガリア人 [burugariajin]

bulimia [bju:'lɪmɪə] n 過食症 [kashokushou]

bull [bʊl] n 雄牛 [oushi]

bulldozer ['bʊl,dəʊzə] n ブルドーザー [burudoozaa]

bullet ['bʊlɪt] n 弾丸 [dangan]

bully ['bʊlɪ] n 弱い者いじめをする者 [yowai mono ijime o suru mono] ▷ v いじめる [ijimeru]

bum [bʌm] n お尻 [oshiri]; **bum bag** n ウエストバッグ [uesutobaggu]

bumblebee ['bʌmbᵊl,bi:] n マルハナバチ [maruhanabachi]

bump [bʌmp] n 衝突 [shoutotsu]; **bump into** v ばったり出会う [battari deau]

bumper ['bʌmpə] n バンパー [banpaa]

bumpy ['bʌmpɪ] adj でこぼこのある [dekoboko no aru]

bun [bʌn] n バン [ban] (食べ物)

bunch [bʌntʃ] n 束 [taba] (ひとまとめ)

bungalow ['bʌŋgə,ləʊ] n バンガロー [bangaroo]

bungee jumping ['bʌndʒɪ] n バンジージャンプ [banjiijanpu]; **Where can I go bungee jumping?** どこに行けばバンジージャンプができますか? [doko ni ikeba banjii-janpu ga dekimasu ka?]

bunion ['bʌnjən] n バニオン [banion]

bunk [bʌŋk] n 作り付け寝台 [tsukuri zuke shindai]; **bunk beds** npl 二段ベッド [nidanbeddo]

buoy [bɔɪ; 'buːɪ] n ブイ [bui]

burden ['bɜːdᵊn] n 荷物 [nimotsu]

bureaucracy [bjʊəˈrɒkrəsɪ] n 官僚主義 [kanryoushugi]

bureau de change ['bjʊərəʊ də ˈʃɒnʒ] n bureau de change n 外貨両替所 [gaika ryougaesho]; **I need to find a bureau de change** 私は外貨両替所をさがしています [watashi wa gaikaryougae tokoro o sagashite imasu]; **Is there a bureau de change here?** ここに外貨両替所はありますか? [koko ni gaika ryougae-jo wa arimasu ka?]; **When is the bureau de change open?** その外貨両替所はいつ開きますか? [sono gaika ryougae-jo wa itsu hirakimasu ka?]

burger ['bɜːgə] n バーガー [baagaa]

burglar ['bɜːglə] n 不法侵入者 [fuhou shinnyuusha]; **burglar alarm** n 盗難警報機 [tounankeihouki]

burglary ['bɜːglərɪ] n 住居侵入罪 [juukyoshinnyuuzai]

burgle ['bɜːgᵊl] v 泥棒に入る [dorobou ni hairu]

Burma ['bɜːmə] n ビルマ [biruma]

Burmese [bɜːˈmiːz] adj ビルマの [biruma no] ▷ n (language) ビルマ語 [birumago], (person) ビルマ人 [birumajin]

burn [bɜːn] n 火傷 [yakedo] ▷ v 燃やす [moyasu]

burn down [bɜːn daʊn] v 焼け落ちる [yakeochiru]

burp [bɜːp] n げっぷ [geppu] (口) ▷ v げっぷをする [geppu o suru]

burst [bɜːst] v 破裂する [haretsu suru]

bury ['bɛrɪ] v 埋葬する [maisou suru]

bus [bʌs] n バス [basu] (乗り物); **airport bus** n 空港バス [kuukou basu]; **bus station** n バスターミナル [basutaaminaru]; **bus stop** n バス停 [basutei]; **bus ticket** n バスの切符 [bas no kippu]; **Does this bus go to...?** このバスは・・・へ行きますか? [kono basu v ... e ikimasu ka?]; **Excuse me, which b goes to...?** すみません、・・・へ行くバス どれですか? [sumimasen, ... e iku basu dore desu ka?]; **How often are the buses to...?** ・・・へ行くバスはどのくらい 出ていますか? [...e iku basu wa dono kurai dete imasu ka?]; **Is there a bus to the airport?** 空港へ行くバスはありま か? [kuukou e iku basu wa arimasu ka?]; **What time does the bus leave?** バス は何時に出ますか? [basu wa nan-ji ni demasu ka?]; **What time is the last bus?** 最終のバスは何時ですか? [saish no basu wa nan-ji desu ka?]; **When is th next bus to...?** ・・・へ行く次のバスは 時ですか? [...e iku tsugi no basu wa nar desu ka?]; **Where can I buy a bus car** バスのカードはどこで買えますか? [ba no kaado wa doko de kaemasu ka?]; **Where can I get a bus to...?** ・・・へ行 バスにはどこで乗れますか? [...e iku ba ni wa doko de noremasu ka?]; **Where is the bus station?** バスターミナルはど ですか? [basu-taaminaru wa doko desu ka?]

bush [bʊʃ] n (shrub) 低木 [teiboku], (thicket) 茂み [shigemi]

business ['bɪznɪs] n ビジネス [bijinesu business class n ビジネスクラス [bijinesu kurasu]; **business trip** n 出張 [shutchou]; **show business** n ショービ ネス [shoobijinesu]

businessman, businessmen ['bɪznɪsˌmæn, 'bɪznɪsˌmɛn] n ビジ スマン [bijinesuman]; **I'm a businessman** 私はビジネスマンです [watashi wa bijinesu-man desu]

businesswoman, businesswomen ['bɪznɪsˌwʊmən, 'bɪznɪsˌwɪmɪn] n ジネスウーマン [bijinesuuuman]; **I'm a**

businesswoman 私はビジネスウーマンです [watashi wa bijinesu-uuman desu]

busker ['bʌskə] *n* 大道芸人 [daidougeinin]

bust [bʌst] *n* バスト [basuto]

busy ['bɪzɪ] *adj* 忙しい [isogashii]; **busy signal** *n* 話し中を示す信号 [hanashichuu-o shimesu shingou]; **Sorry, I'm busy** ごめんなさい、忙しいのです [gomen nasai, isogashii no desu]

but [bʌt] *conj* しかし [shikashi]

butcher ['bʊtʃə] *n* 肉屋 [nikuya]

butcher's ['bʊtʃəz] *n* 肉屋 [nikuya]

butter ['bʌtə] *n* バター [bataa]; **peanut butter** *n* ピーナッツバター [piinattsubataa]

buttercup ['bʌtə,kʌp] *n* キンポウゲ [kinpouge]

butterfly ['bʌtə,flaɪ] *n* チョウ [chou]

buttocks ['bʌtəkz] *npl* 臀部 [denbu]

button ['bʌtⁿn] *n* ボタン [botan] (服); **belly button** *n* おへそ [oheso]; **Which button do I press?** どのボタンを押すのですか? [dono botan o osu no desu ka?]

buy [baɪ] *v* 買う [kau]; **Where do I buy a ticket?** 切符はどこで買うのですか? [kippu wa doko de kau no desu ka?]

buyer ['baɪə] *n* 買い手 [kaite]

buyout ['baɪ,aʊt] *n* 買収 [baishuu]

by [baɪ] *prep* ・・・によって [...ni yotte]

bye [baɪ] *excl* さよなら! [sayonara]

bye-bye [baɪbaɪ] *excl* バイバイ! [baibai]

bypass ['baɪ,pɑːs] *n* バイパス [baipasu]

C

cab [kæb] *n* タクシー [takushii]

cabbage ['kæbɪdʒ] *n* キャベツ [kyabetsu]

cabin ['kæbɪn] *n* キャビン [kyabin]; **cabin crew** *n* 乗務員 [joumuin]; **Where is cabin number five?** 5番のキャビンはどこですか? [go-ban no kyabin wa doko desu ka?]

cabinet ['kæbɪnɪt] *n* キャビネット [kyabinetto]

cable ['keɪbⁿl] *n* ケーブル [keeburu]; **cable car** *n* ケーブルカー [keeburukaa]; **cable television** *n* ケーブルテレビ [keeburu terebi]

cactus ['kæktəs] *n* サボテン [saboten]

cadet [kə'dɛt] *n* 生徒 [seito]

café ['kæfeɪ; 'kæfɪ] *n* カフェ [kafe]; **internet café** *n* インターネットカフェ [intaanetto kafe]; **Are there any internet cafés here?** ここにインターネットカフェはありますか? [koko ni intaanetto-kafe wa arimasu ka?]

cafeteria [,kæfɪ'tɪərɪə] *n* カフェテリア [kafeteria]

caffeine ['kæfiːn] *n* カフェイン [kafein]

cage [keɪdʒ] *n* かご [kago]

cagoule [kə'guːl] *n* カグール [kaguuru]

cake [keɪk] n ケーキ [keeki]

calcium ['kælsɪəm] n カルシウム [karushiumu]

calculate ['kælkjʊˌleɪt] v 計算する [keisan suru]

calculation [ˌkælkjʊ'leɪʃən] n 計算 [keisan]

calculator ['kælkjʊˌleɪtə] n 計算機 [keisanki]; **pocket calculator** n 電卓 [dentaku]

calendar ['kælɪndə] n カレンダー [karendaa]

calf, calves [kɑːf, kɑːvz] n 子牛 [koushi]

call [kɔːl] n 呼び声 [yobigoe] ▷ v 呼ぶ [yobu]; **alarm call** n モーニングコール [mooningukooru]; **call box** n 公衆電話ボックス [koushuu denwa bokkusu]; **call centre** n コールセンター [kooru sentaa]; **roll call** n 点呼 [tenko]

call back [kɔːl bæk] v 電話しなおす [denwa shinaosu]

call for [kɔːl fɔː] v 要求する [youkyuu suru]

call off [kɔːl ɒf] v 取りやめる [toriyameru]

calm [kɑːm] adj 落ち着いた [ochitsuita]

calm down [kɑːm daʊn] v 落ち着く [ochitsuku] (気分)

calorie ['kælərɪ] n カロリー [karorii]

Cambodia [kæm'bəʊdɪə] n カンボジア [kanbojia]

Cambodian [kæm'bəʊdɪən] adj カンボジアの [kanbojia no] ▷ n (person) カンボジア人 [kanbojiajin]

camcorder ['kæmˌkɔːdə] n カムコーダー [kamukoodaa]

camel ['kæməl] n ラクダ [rakuda]

camera ['kæmərə; 'kæmrə] n カメラ [kamera]; **camera phone** n カメラ付き携帯電話 [kamera tsuki keitai denwa]; **digital camera** n デジタルカメラ [dejitaru kamera]; **video camera** n ビデオカメラ [bideokamera]

cameraman, cameramen ['kæmrəˌmæn, 'kæmrəˌmɛn] n カメラマン [kameraman]

Cameroon [ˌkæmə'ruːn; 'kæməˌruːn] n カメルーン [kameruun]

camp [kæmp] n キャンプ [kyanpu] ▷ v キャンプする [kyanpu suru]; **camp bed** n キャンプベッド [kyanpubeddo]; **Can we camp here overnight?** ここで一晩キャンプできますか? [koko de hitoban kyanpu dekimasu ka?]

campaign [kæm'peɪn] n 運動 [undou] (行動)

camper ['kæmpə] n キャンプする人 [kyanpu suru nin]

camping ['kæmpɪŋ] n キャンプ生活 [kyanpu seikatsu]; **camping gas** n キャンプ用ガス [kyanpu you gasu]

campsite ['kæmpˌsaɪt] n キャンプ場 [kyanpujou]; **Is there a campsite here?** ここにキャンプ場はありますか? [koko ni kyanpu-jou wa arimasu ka?]; **Is there a restaurant on the campsite?** キャンプ場にレストランはありますか? [kyanpu-jou ni resutoran wa arimasu ka?]

campus ['kæmpəs] n キャンパス [kyanpasu]

can [kæn] v …できる […dekiru]; **watering can** n じょうろ [jouro]

Canada ['kænədə] n カナダ [kanada]

Canadian [kə'neɪdɪən] adj カナダの [kanada no] ▷ n カナダ人 [kanadajin]

canal [kə'næl] n 運河 [unga]

Canaries [kə'nɛərɪːz] npl カナリア諸島 [kanaria shotou]

canary [kə'nɛərɪ] n カナリア [kanaria]

cancel ['kænsəl] v 取り消す [torikesu]

cancellation [ˌkænsɪ'leɪʃən] n キャンセル [kyanseru]; **Are there any cancellations?** キャンセルされたフライトはありますか? [kyanseru sareta furaito wa arimasu ka?]

cancer ['kænsə] n (illness) 癌 [gan]

Cancer ['kænsə] n (horoscope) 蟹座 [kaniza]

candidate ['kændɪˌdeɪt; -dɪt] n 候補者 [kouhosha]

candle ['kændəl] n ろうそく [rousoku]

candlestick ['kændəlˌstɪk] n ろうそく立て [rousokutate]

candyfloss ['kændɪˌflɒs] n 綿菓子 [watagashi]

canister ['kænɪstə] n キャニスター [kyanisutaa]

cannabis ['kænəbɪs] n 大麻 [taima]

canned [kænd] adj 缶詰めにした [kanzume ni shita]

canoe [kə'nuː] n カヌー [kanuu]

canoeing [kə'nuːɪŋ] n カヌー漕ぎ [kanuu kogi]

can-opener ['kæn'əʊpənə] n 缶切り [kankiri]

canteen [kæn'tiːn] n キャンティーン [kyantiin]

canter ['kæntə] v 普通駆け足で行く [futsuu kakeashi de iku]

canvas ['kænvəs] n キャンバス [kyanbasu]

canvass ['kænvəs] v 投票を頼んで回る [touhyou-o tanonde mawaru]

cap [kæp] n 縁なし帽子 [fuchinashi boushi]; **baseball cap** n 野球帽 [yakyuubou]

capable ['keɪpəbəl] adj ···ができる [...ga dekiru]

capacity [kə'pæsɪtɪ] n 収容力 [shuuyouryoku]

capital ['kæpɪtəl] n 首都 [shuto]

capitalism ['kæpɪtəˌlɪzəm] n 資本主義 [shihonshugi]

Capricorn ['kæprɪˌkɔːn] n 山羊座 [yagiza]

capsize [kæp'saɪz] v 転覆する [tenpuku suru]

capsule ['kæpsjuːl] n カプセル [kapuseru]

captain ['kæptɪn] n 船長 [senchou]

caption ['kæpʃən] n キャプション [kyapushon]

capture ['kæptʃə] v 捕える [toraeru]

car [kɑː] n 自動車 [jidousha]; **buffet car** n ビュッフェ車 [byuffesha]; **cable car** n ケーブルカー [keeburukaa]; **car hire** n レンタカー [rentakaa]; **car park** n 駐車場 [chuushajou]; **car rental** n レンタカー [rentakaa]; **car wash** n 洗車機 [senshaki];

company car n 社用車 [shayousha]; **dining car** n 食堂車 [shokudousha]; **estate car** n エステートカー [esuteetokaa]; **hired car** n レンタカー [rentakaa]; **patrol car** n パトロールカー [patoroorukaa]; **racing car** n レーシングカー [reeshingukaa]; **rental car** n レンタカー [rentakaa]; **saloon car** n セダン [sedan]; **sleeping car** n 寝台車 [shindaisha]

carafe [kə'ræf; -'rɑːf] n カラフ [karafu]; **a carafe of the house wine** ハウスワインをカラフで1本 [hausu-wain o karafu de ippon]

caramel ['kærəməl; -ˌmɛl] n キャラメル [kyarameru]

carat ['kærət] n カラット [karatto]

caravan ['kærəˌvæn] n トレーラーハウス [toreeraahausu]; **caravan site** n トレーラーハウスキャンプ場 [toreeraa hausu kyanpu jou]; **Can we park our caravan here?** ここにトレーラーハウスを駐車してもいいですか? [koko ni toreeraa-hausu o chuusha shite mo ii desu ka?]; **We'd like a site for a caravan** トレーラーハウスのサイトが欲しいのですが [toreeraa-hausu no saito ga hoshii no desu ga]

carbohydrate [ˌkɑːbəʊ'haɪdreɪt] n 炭水化物 [tansuikabutsu]

carbon ['kɑːbən] n 炭素 [tanso]; **carbon footprint** n カーボンフットプリント [kaabon futtopurinto]

carburettor [ˌkɑːbjʊ'rɛtə; -bə-] n キャブレター [kyaburetaa]

card [kɑːd] n カード [kaado]; **boarding card** n 搭乗券 [toujouken]; **credit card** n クレジットカード [kurejittokaado]; **debit card** n デビットカード [debitto kaado]; **greetings card** n グリーティングカード [guriitingukaado]; **ID card** abbr 身分証明書 [mibunshoumeisho]; **membership card** n メンバーカード [menbaakaado]; **playing card** n トランプ [toranpu]; **report card** n 通知表 [tsuuchihyou]; **top-up card** n 度数追加カード [dosuu tsuika kaado]; **A memory card for this digital camera, please** このデジタルカメラ用のメモリカードをください [kono dejitaru-kamera-you no memori-kaado o kudasai]; **Can I use my card to get cash?** 私のカードを使って現金を引き出せますか? [watashi no kaado o tsukatte genkin o hikidasemasu ka?]; **Do you sell phone cards?** テレホンカードを売っていますか? [terehon-kaado o utte imasu ka?]; **Do you take credit cards?** クレジットカードは使えますか? [kurejitto-kaado wa tsukaemasu ka?]; **Do you take debit cards?** デビットカードは使えますか? [debitto-kaado wa tsukaemasu ka?]; **I need to cancel my card** 私はカードをキャンセルしなければなりません [watashi wa kaado o kyanseru shinakereba narimasen]; **My card has been stolen** 私のカードが盗まれました [watashi no kaado ga nusuma remashita]; **Where can I post these cards?** このカードをどこで投函できますか? [kono kaado o doko de toukan dekimasu ka?]

cardboard [ˈkɑːdˌbɔːd] n ボール紙 [boorugami]

cardigan [ˈkɑːdɪɡən] n カーディガン [kaadigan]

cardphone [ˈkɑːdfəʊn] n カード式公衆電話 [kaado shiki koushuu denwa]

care [kɛə] n 注意 [chuui] ▷ v 心配する [shinpai suru]; **intensive care unit** n 集中治療室 [shuuchuuchiryoushitsu, ICU aishiiyuu]

career [kəˈrɪə] n キャリア [kyaria]

careful [ˈkɛəfʊl] adj 注意深い [chuuibukai]

carefully [ˈkɛəfʊlɪ] adv 注意深く [chuuibukaku]

careless [ˈkɛəlɪs] adj 不注意な [fuchuui na]

caretaker [ˈkɛəˌteɪkə] n 管理人 [kanrinin]

car ferry [ˈkɑːfɛrɪ] n カーフェリー [kaaferii]

cargo [ˈkɑːɡəʊ] n 貨物 [kamotsu]

Caribbean [ˌkærɪˈbiːən; kəˈrɪbɪən] adj カリブ海の [karibukai no] ▷ n カリブ人 [karibujin]

caring [ˈkɛərɪŋ] adj 思いやりのある [omoiyari no aru]

carnation [kɑːˈneɪʃən] n カーネーション [kaaneeshon]

carnival [ˈkɑːnɪvəl] n カーニバル [kaanibaru]

carol [ˈkærəl] n キャロル [kyaroru]

carpenter [ˈkɑːpɪntə] n 大工 [daiku]

carpentry [ˈkɑːpɪntrɪ] n 大工仕事 [daikushigoto]

carpet [ˈkɑːpɪt] n カーペット [kaapetto]; **fitted carpet** n ぴったり合うように敷かれたカーペット [pittari au youni shikareta kaapetto]

carriage [ˈkærɪdʒ] n 客車 [kyakusha]

carriageway [ˈkærɪdʒˌweɪ] n dual carriageway n 中央分離帯付き道路 [chuuou bunritai tsuki douro]

carrot [ˈkærət] n ニンジン [ninjin]

carry [ˈkærɪ] v 運ぶ [hakobu]

carrycot [ˈkærɪˌkɒt] n 持ち運び用ベッド [mochihakobi you beddo]

carry on [ˈkærɪ ɒn] v 続ける [tsuzukeru]

carry out [ˈkærɪ aʊt] v 実行する [jikkou suru]

cart [kɑːt] n 荷馬車 [nibasha]

carton [ˈkɑːtən] n ボール箱 [boorubako]

cartoon [kɑːˈtuːn] n 漫画 [manga]

cartridge [ˈkɑːtrɪdʒ] n 弾薬 [dan-yaku]

carve [kɑːv] v 彫る [horu]

case [keɪs] n 場合 [baai]; **pencil case** n 筆箱 [fudebako]

cash [kæʃ] n 現金 [genkin]; **cash dispenser** n 現金自動支払い機 [genkin jidoushiharaiki]; **cash register** n レジ [reji]; **Do you offer a discount for cash?** 現金で払うと割引がありますか? [genkin de harau to waribiki ga arimasu ka?]; **I don't have any cash** 私は現金がありません [watashi wa genkin ga arimasen]; **I want to cash a cheque, please** 小切手を現金化してください [kogitte o genkinka shite kudasai];

Is there a cash machine here? ここに現金自動支払い機がありますか？ [koko ni genkin-jidou-shiharaiki ga arimasu ka?]; **Where is the nearest cash machine?** 一番近い現金自動支払い機はどこですか？ [ichiban chikai genkin-jidou-shiharaiki wa doko desu ka?]

cashew ['kæʃuː; kæ'ʃuː] n カシューナッツ [kashuunattsu]

cashier [kæ'ʃɪə] n 会計係 [kaikeigakari]

cashmere ['kæʃmɪə] n カシミヤ [kashimiya]

casino [kə'siːnəʊ] n カジノ [kajino]

casserole ['kæsə,rəʊl] n キャセロール [kyaserooru]

cassette [kæ'sɛt] n カセット [kasetto]

cast [kɑːst] n キャスト [kyasuto]

castle ['kɑːsəl] n 城 [shiro]

casual ['kæʒjʊəl] adj 偶然の [guuzen no]

casually ['kæʒjʊəlɪ] adv 偶然に [guuzen ni]

casualty ['kæʒjʊəltɪ] n 死傷者 [shishousha]

cat [kæt] n 猫 [neko]

catalogue ['kætə,lɒg] n カタログ [katarogu]; **I'd like a catalogue** カタログが欲しいのですが [katarogu ga hoshii no desu ga]

cataract ['kætə,rækt] n (eye) 白内障 [hakunaishou], (waterfall) 大きな滝 [ouki na taki]

catarrh [kə'tɑː] n カタル [kataru]

catastrophe [kə'tæstrəfɪ] n 大災害 [daisaigai]

catch [kætʃ] v つかまえる [tsukamaeru]

catching ['kætʃɪŋ] adj 伝染性の [densensei no]

catch up [kætʃ ʌp] v 追いつく [oitsuku]

category ['kætɪgərɪ] n 部門 [bumon]

catering ['keɪtərɪŋ] n ケータリング [keetaringu]

caterpillar ['kætə,pɪlə] n イモムシ [imomushi]

cathedral [kə'θiːdrəl] n 大聖堂 [daiseidou]; **When is the cathedral open?** その大聖堂はいつ開きますか？ [sono daiseidou wa itsu hirakimasu ka?]

Catholic ['kæθəlɪk; 'kæθlɪk] adj カトリックの [katorikku no] ▷ n カトリック教徒 [katorikkukyouto]; **Roman Catholic** n ローマカトリック教会の [rooma katorikku kyoukai no], ローマカトリック教徒 [rooma katorikku kyouto]

cattle ['kætəl] npl 畜牛 [chikugyuu]

Caucasus ['kɔːkəsəs] n カフカス山脈 [kafukasu sanmyaku]

cauliflower ['kɒlɪ,flaʊə] n カリフラワー [karifurawaa]

cause [kɔːz] n (ideals) 大義 [taigi], (reason) 理由 [riyuu] ▷ v 引き起こす [hikiokosu]

caution ['kɔːʃən] n 注意 [chuui]

cautious ['kɔːʃəs] adj 慎重な [shinchou na]

cautiously ['kɔːʃəslɪ] adv 慎重に [shinchou ni]

cave [keɪv] n ほら穴 [horaana]

CCTV [siː siː tiː viː] abbr 閉回路テレビ [heikairo terebi]

CD [siː diː] n CD [siidii]; **CD burner** n CDバーナー [shiidii baanaa]; **CD player** n CDプレーヤー [shiidii pureiyaa]; **Can I make CDs at this computer?** このコンピューターでCDを作成できますか？ [kono konpyuutaa de shii-dii o sakusei dekimasu ka?]

CD-ROM [-'rɒm] n CD-ROM [siidii romu]

ceasefire ['siːs'faɪə] n 停戦 [teisen]

ceiling ['siːlɪŋ] n 天井 [tenjou]

celebrate ['sɛlɪ,breɪt] v 祝う [iwau]

celebration ['sɛlɪ,breɪʃən] n 祝い [iwai]

celebrity [sɪ'lɛbrɪtɪ] n 有名人 [yuumeijin]

celery ['sɛlərɪ] n セロリ [serori]

cell [sɛl] n 細胞 [saibou]

cellar ['sɛlə] n 地下室 [chikashitsu]

cello ['tʃɛləʊ] n チェロ [chero]

cement [sɪ'mɛnt] n セメント [semento]

cemetery ['sɛmɪtrɪ] n 墓地 [bochi]

census ['sɛnsəs] n 国勢調査 [kokuzeichousa]

cent [sɛnt] n セント [sento]

centenary [sɛn'tiːnərɪ] n 100周年記念祭 [hyakushuunen kinensai]

centimetre ['sɛntɪ,miːtə] n センチメートル [senchimeetoru]

central ['sɛntrəl] adj 中央の [chuuou no]; **central heating** n セントラルヒーティング [sentoraruhiitingu]; **Central America** n 中央アメリカ [chuuou amerika]

centre ['sɛntə] n 中心 [chuushin]; **call centre** n コールセンター [kooru sentaa]; **city centre** n 街の中心部 [machi no chuushinbu]; **job centre** n 公共職業安定所 [koukyoushokugyou anteisho]; **leisure centre** n レジャーセンター [rejaasentaa]; **shopping centre** n ショッピングセンター [shoppingu sentaa]; **town centre** n 町の中心部 [machi no chuushinbu]; **visitor centre** n ビジターセンター [bijitaasentaa]; **How do I get to the centre of...?** ・・・の中心部へはどう行けばいいのですか? [...no chuushinbu e wa dou ikeba ii no desu ka?]

century ['sɛntʃərɪ] n 世紀 [seiki]

CEO [siː iː əʊ] abbr 最高経営責任者 [saikou keiei sekininsha]

ceramic [sɪˈræmɪk] adj セラミックの [seramikku no]

cereal ['sɪərɪəl] n 穀類 [kokurui]

ceremony ['sɛrɪmənɪ] n 儀式 [gishiki]

certain ['sɜːtən] adj 確信している [kakushin shite iru]

certainly ['sɜːtənlɪ] adv 確かに [tashika ni]

certainty ['sɜːtəntɪ] n 確実なこと [kakujitsu na koto]

certificate [səˈtɪfɪkɪt] n 証明書 [shoumeisho]; **birth certificate** n 出生証明書 [shusshou (shussei) shoumeisho]; **marriage certificate** n 結婚証明書 [kekkonshoumeisho]; **medical certificate** n 診断書 [shindansho]; **I need a 'fit to fly' certificate** 私は「飛行機搭乗の適性」証明書が必要です [watashi wa "hikouki-toujou no tekisei" shoumei-sho ga hitsuyou desu]

Chad [tʃæd] n チャド [chado]

chain [tʃeɪn] n 鎖 [kusari]

chair [tʃɛə] n (furniture) 椅子 [isu]; **easy chair** n 安楽椅子 [anraku isu]; **rocking chair** n ロッキングチェア [rokkinguchea]; **Do you have a high chair?** 子供用の椅子はありますか? [kodomo-you no isu wa arimasu ka?]

chairlift ['tʃɛə,lɪft] n チェアリフト [chearifuto]; **When does the first chair-lift go?** 最初のチェアリフトはいつ出ますか? [saisho no chea-rifuto wa itsu demasu ka?]

chairman, chairmen ['tʃɛəmən, 'tʃɛəmɛn] n 議長 [gichou]

chalk [tʃɔːk] n チョーク [chooku] (白墨)

challenge ['tʃælɪndʒ] n 挑戦 [chousen] ▷ v 挑戦する [chousen suru]

challenging ['tʃælɪndʒɪŋ] adj 挑戦的な [chousenteki na]

chambermaid ['tʃeɪmbə,meɪd] n 客室係のメイド [kyakushitsugakari no meido]

champagne [ʃæmˈpeɪn] n シャンパン [shanpan]

champion ['tʃæmpɪən] n 優勝者 [yuushousha]

championship ['tʃæmpɪən,ʃɪp] n 選手権 [senshuken]

chance [tʃɑːns] n 見込み [mikomi]; **by chance** adv 偶然に [guuzen ni]

change [tʃeɪndʒ] n 変化 [henka] ▷ vi 変わる [kawaru] ▷ vt 変える [kaeru]; **changing room** n 更衣室 [kouishitsu]

changeable ['tʃeɪndʒəbəl] adj 変わりやすい [kawariyasui]

channel ['tʃænəl] n チャンネル [channeru]

chaos ['keɪɒs] n 大混乱 [daikonran]

chaotic ['keɪˈɒtɪk] adj 大混乱した [daikonran shita]

chap [tʃæp] n 男 [otoko]

chapel ['tʃæpəl] n 礼拝堂 [reihaidou]

chapter ['tʃæptə] n 章 [shou]

character ['kærɪktə] n 特質 [tokushitsu]

characteristic [,kærɪktəˈrɪstɪk] n 特徴 [tokuchou]

charcoal ['tʃɑː,kəʊl] n 木炭 [mokutan]

charge [tʃɑːdʒ] n (accusation) 告訴

[kokuso], *(electricity)* 充電 [juuden], *(price)* 料金 [ryoukin] ▷ v *(accuse)* 告訴する [kokuso suru], *(electricity)* 充電する [juuden suru], *(price)* 請求する [seikyuu suru]; **admission charge** n 入場料 [nyuujouryou]; **cover charge** n カバーチャージ [kabaa chaaji]; **service charge** n サービス料 [saabisuryou]; **Is there a charge for the service?** サービスに料金がかかりますか? [saabisu ni ryoukin ga kakarimasu ka?]; **Is there a mileage charge?** 走行距離に対して料金がかかりますか? [soukou-kyori ni taishite ryoukin ga kakarimasu ka?]; **It's not charging** 充電されません [juuden saremasen]; **Where can I charge my mobile phone?** どこで携帯電話を充電できますか? [doko de keitai-denwa o juuden dekimasu ka?]; **Why are you charging me so much?** なぜそんなにたくさん請求するのですか? [naze sonna ni takusan seikyuu suru no desu ka?]

charger ['tʃɑːdʒə] n 充電器 [juudenki]

charity ['tʃærɪtɪ] n 慈善団体 [jizen dantai]; **charity shop** n チャリティーショップ [charitii shoppu]

charm [tʃɑːm] n 魅力 [miryoku]

charming ['tʃɑːmɪŋ] adj 魅力的な [miryokuteki na]

chart [tʃɑːt] n 図表 [zuhyou]

chase [tʃeɪs] n 追跡 [tsuiseki] ▷ v 追跡する [tsuiseki suru]

chat [tʃæt] n おしゃべり [o-shaberi] ▷ v おしゃべりする [o-shaberi suru], *(on computer)* チャットする [chatto suru]; **chatroom** ['tʃæt,ruːm; -,rʊm] n チャットルーム [chatto ruumu]; **chat show** n トークショー [tookushoo]

chauffeur ['ʃəʊfə; ʃəʊ'fɜː] n おかかえ運転手 [okakae untenshu]

chauvinist ['ʃəʊvɪ,nɪst] n 熱狂的な愛国主義者 [nekkyouteki aikokushugisha]

cheap [tʃiːp] adj 安い [yasui]; **I'd like the cheapest option** 一番安い方法がいいのですが [ichiban yasui houhou ga ii no desu ga]

cheat [tʃiːt] n 詐欺師 [sagishi] ▷ v だます [damasu]

Chechnya ['tʃetʃnjə] n チェチェン共和国 [chechen kyouwakoku]

check [tʃɛk] n 照合 [shougou] ▷ v 調べる [shiraberu]

checked [tʃɛkt] adj チェックの [chekku no]

check in [tʃɛk ɪn] v チェックインする [chekkuin suru]; **Where do I check in for the flight to...?** ・・・行きのフライトはどこでチェックインするのですか? [...iki no furaito wa doko de chekku-in suru no desu ka?]

check-in [tʃɛkɪn] n チェックイン [chekkuin]

check out [tʃɛk aʊt] v チェックアウトする [chekkuauto suru]

checkout ['tʃɛkaʊt] n チェックアウト [chekkuauto]

check-up [tʃɛkʌp] n 検査 [kensa]

cheek [tʃiːk] n ほお [hoo]

cheekbone ['tʃiːk,bəʊn] n ほお骨 [hoobone]

cheeky ['tʃiːkɪ] adj 生意気な [namaiki na]

cheer [tʃɪə] n 喝采 [kassai] ▷ v 声援する [seien suru]

cheerful ['tʃɪəfʊl] adj 陽気な [youki na]

cheerio [,tʃɪərɪ'əʊ] excl ではまた! [dewamata]

cheers [tʃɪəz] excl 乾杯! [kanpai]

cheese [tʃiːz] n チーズ [chiizu]; **cottage cheese** n カッテージチーズ [katteeji chiizu]; **What sort of cheese?** どんなチーズですか? [donna cheezu desu ka?]

chef [ʃɛf] n シェフ [shiefu]; **What is the chef's speciality?** シェフの得意料理は何ですか? [shefu no tokui-ryouri wa nan desu ka?]

chemical ['kɛmɪkəl] n 化学薬品 [kagakuyakuhin]

chemist ['kɛmɪst] n 薬剤師 [yakuzaishi]; **chemist('s)** n 薬局 [yakkyoku]

chemistry ['kɛmɪstrɪ] n 化学 [kagaku]

cheque [tʃɛk] n 小切手 [kogitte]; **blank cheque** n 白地小切手 [shiraji kogitte];

traveller's cheque n 旅行者用小切手 [ryokousha you kogitte]; **Can I cash a cheque?** 小切手を現金化できますか? [kogitte o genkinka dekimasu ka?]; **Can I pay by cheque?** 小切手で支払えますか? [kogitte de shiharaemasu ka?]

chequebook ['tʃɛkˌbʊk] n 小切手帳 [kogittechou]

cherry ['tʃɛrɪ] n サクランボ [sakuranbo]

chess [tʃɛs] n チェス [chesu]

chest [tʃɛst] n (body part) 胸 [mune], (storage) 収納箱 [shuunoubako]; **chest of drawers** n 整理だんす [seiridansu]; **I have a pain in my chest** 私は胸に痛みがあります [watashi wa mune ni itami ga arimasu]

chestnut ['tʃɛsˌnʌt] n クリ [kuri]

chew [tʃuː] v 噛む [kamu]; **chewing gum** n チューインガム [chuuingamu]

chick [tʃɪk] n ひよこ [hiyoko]

chicken ['tʃɪkɪn] n 鶏 [niwatori]

chickenpox ['tʃɪkɪnˌpɒks] n 水疱瘡 [mizubousou]

chickpea ['tʃɪkˌpiː] n ヒヨコマメ [hiyokomame]

chief [tʃiːf] adj 主要な [shuyou na] ▷ n ・・・長 [...chou] (統率)

child, children [tʃaɪld, 'tʃɪldrən] n 子供 [kodomo]; **child abuse** n 児童虐待 [jidou gyakutai]; **Do you have a children's menu?** 子供用のメニューはありますか? [kodomo-you no menyuu wa arimasu ka?]; **I don't have any children** 私には子供がいません [watashi ni wa kodomo ga imasen]; **I have three children** 私には子供が三人います [watashi ni wa kodomo ga sannin imasu]; **I need someone to look after the children tonight** 私は今晩子供たちの面倒を見てくれる人が必要です [watashi wa konban kodomo-tachi no mendou o mite kureru hito ga hitsuyou desu]; **I'd like a child seat for a two-year-old child** 2歳の子供用のチャイルドシートが欲しいのですが [ni-sai no kodomo-you no chairudo-shiito ga hoshii no desu ga]; **I'm looking for a present for a child** 私は子供へのプレゼントを探しています [watashi wa kodomo e no purezento o sagashite imasu]; **Is it safe for children?** それは子供にも安全ですか? [sore wa kodomo ni mo anzen desu ka?]; **My child is ill** 私の子供が病気です [watashi no kodomo ga byouki desu]; **My child is missing** 私の子供が行方不明です [watashi no kodomo ga yukue-fumei desu]; **My children are in the car** 子供たちが車の中にいます [kodomo-tachi ga kuruma no naka ni imasu]; **The child is on this passport** 子供はこのパスポートに載っています [kodomo wa kono pasupooto ni notte imasu]; **What is there for children to do?** 子供ができることは何がありますか? [kodomo ga dekiru koto wa nani ga arimasu ka?]

childcare ['tʃaɪldˌkɛə] n 児童養護 [jidou yougo]

childhood ['tʃaɪldhʊd] n 子供時代 [kodomo jidai]

childish ['tʃaɪldɪʃ] adj 子供じみた [kodomojimita]

childminder ['tʃaɪldˌmaɪndə] n チャイルドマインダー [chairudomaindaa]

Chile ['tʃɪlɪ] n チリ [chiri]

Chilean ['tʃɪlɪən] adj チリの [chiri no] ▷ n チリ人 [chirijin]

chill [tʃɪl] v 冷やす [hiyasu]

chilli ['tʃɪlɪ] n トウガラシ [tougarashi]

chilly ['tʃɪlɪ] adj 寒い [samui]

chimney ['tʃɪmnɪ] n 煙突 [entotsu]

chimpanzee [ˌtʃɪmpæn'ziː] n チンパンジー [chinpanjii]

chin [tʃɪn] n あご [ago]

china ['tʃaɪnə] n 磁器 [jiki]

China ['tʃaɪnə] n 中国 [chuugoku]

Chinese [tʃaɪ'niːz] adj 中国の [chuugoku no] ▷ n (language) 中国語 [chuugokugo], (person) 中国人 [chuugokujin]

chip [tʃɪp] n (electronic) チップ [chippu] (電子), (small piece) かけら [kakera]; **silicon chip** n マイクロチップ [maikurochippu]

chips [tʃɪps] *npl* フライドポテト [furaidopoteto]

chiropodist [kɪˈrɒpədɪst] *n* 足治療医 [ashichiryoui]

chisel [ˈtʃɪzəl] *n* 鑿 [saku]

chives [tʃaɪvz] *npl* チャイブ [chaibu]

chlorine [ˈklɔːriːn] *n* 塩素 [enso]

chocolate [ˈtʃɒkəlɪt; ˈtʃɒklɪt; -lət] *n* チョコレート [chokoreeto]; **milk chocolate** *n* ミルクチョコレート [mirukuchokoreeto]; **plain chocolate** *n* ブラックチョコレート [burakku chokoreeto]

choice [tʃɔɪs] *n* 選択 [sentaku]

choir [kwaɪə] *n* 聖歌隊 [seikatai]

choke [tʃəʊk] *v* 息が詰まる [iki ga tsumaru]

cholesterol [kəˈlɛstəˌrɒl] *n* コレステロール [koresuterooru]

choose [tʃuːz] *v* 選ぶ [erabu]

chop [tʃɒp] *n* たたき切ること [tatakikiru koto] ▷ *v* たたき切る [tatakikiru]; **pork chop** *n* ポークチョップ [pookuchoppu]

chopsticks [ˈtʃɒpstɪks] *npl* 箸 [hashi]

chosen [ˈtʃəʊzən] *adj* 選ばれた [erabareta]

Christ [kraɪst] *n* キリスト [kirisuto]

christening [ˈkrɪsənɪŋ] *n* 洗礼 [senrei]

Christian [ˈkrɪstʃən] *adj* キリスト教の [kirisutokyou no] ▷ *n* キリスト教徒 [kirisutokyouto]; **Christian name** *n* 洗礼名 [senreimei]

Christianity [ˌkrɪstɪˈænɪtɪ] *n* キリスト教 [kirisutokyou]

Christmas [ˈkrɪsməs] *n* クリスマス [kurisumasu]; **Christmas card** *n* クリスマスカード [kurisumasu kaado]; **Christmas Eve** *n* クリスマスイブ [kurisumasu ibu]; **Christmas tree** *n* クリスマスツリー [kurisumasu tsurii]; **Merry Christmas!** メリークリスマス! [merii kurisumasu!]

chrome [krəʊm] *n* クロム [kuromu]

chronic [ˈkrɒnɪk] *adj* 慢性の [mansei no]

chrysanthemum [krɪˈsænθəməm] *n* キク [kiku]

chubby [ˈtʃʌbɪ] *adj* 丸々太った [marumaru futotta]

chunk [tʃʌŋk] *n* 厚く切ったもの [atsuku kitta mono]

church [tʃɜːtʃ] *n* 教会 [kyoukai]; **Can we visit the church?** 私たちがその教会を訪れることはできますか? [watashi-tachi ga sono kyoukai o otozureru koto wa dekimasu ka?]

cider [ˈsaɪdə] *n* りんご酒 [ringoshu]

cigar [sɪˈgɑː] *n* 葉巻き [hamaki]

cigarette [ˌsɪgəˈrɛt] *n* 紙巻きタバコ [kamimakitabako]; **cigarette lighter** *n* シガレットライター [shigaretto raitaa]

cinema [ˈsɪnɪmə] *n* 映画館 [eigakan]; **What's on at the cinema?** その映画館で何が上映されていますか? [sono eigakan de nani ga jouei sarete imasu ka?]

cinnamon [ˈsɪnəmən] *n* シナモン [shinamon]

circle [ˈsɜːkəl] *n* 円 [en] (丸); **Arctic Circle** *n* 北極圏 [hokkyokuken]

circuit [ˈsɜːkɪt] *n* 一周 [isshuu]

circular [ˈsɜːkjʊlə] *adj* 円形の [enkei no]

circulation [ˌsɜːkjʊˈleɪʃən] *n* 循環 [junkan]

circumstances [ˈsɜːkəmstənsɪz] *npl* 事情 [jijou]

circus [ˈsɜːkəs] *n* サーカス [saakasu]

citizen [ˈsɪtɪzən] *n* 市民 [shimin]; **senior citizen** *n* 高齢者 [koureisha]

citizenship [ˈsɪtɪzənˌʃɪp] *n* 市民権 [shiminken]

city [ˈsɪtɪ] *n* 都市 [toshi]; **city centre** *n* 街の中心部 [machi no chuushinbu]

civilian [sɪˈvɪljən] *adj* 民間の [minkan no] ▷ *n* 民間人 [minkanjin]

civilization [ˌsɪvɪlaɪˈzeɪʃən] *n* 文明 [bunmei]

claim [kleɪm] *n* 主張 [shuchou] ▷ *v* 主張する [shuchou suru]; **claim form** *n* クレームフォーム [kureemufoomu]

clap [klæp] *v* 拍手する [hakushu suru]

clarify [ˈklærɪˌfaɪ] *v* 明らかにする [akiraka ni suru]

clarinet [ˌklærɪˈnɛt] *n* クラリネット [kurarinetto]

clash [klæʃ] v 衝突する [shoutotsu suru]

clasp [klɑːsp] n 留め金 [tomegane]

class [klɑːs] n 分類 [bunrui]; **business class** n ビジネスクラス [bijinesu kurasu]; **economy class** n エコノミークラス [ekonomiikurasu]; **second class** n 二等 [nitou]

classic ['klæsɪk] adj 典型的な [tenkeiteki na] ▷ n 一流の芸術作品 [ichiryuu no geijutsusakuhin]

classical ['klæsɪkəl] adj 伝統的な [dentouteki na]

classmate ['klɑːsˌmeɪt] n 同級生 [doukyuusei]

classroom ['klɑːsˌruːm; -ˌrʊm] n 教室 [kyoushitsu]; **classroom assistant** n 教室助手 [kyoushitsu joshu]

clause [klɔːz] n 条項 [joukou]

claustrophobic [ˌklɔːstrəˈfəʊbɪk; ˌklɒs-] adj 閉所恐怖症の [heisho kyoufushou no]

claw [klɔː] n かぎづめ [kagizume]

clay [kleɪ] n 粘土 [nendo]

clean [kliːn] adj 清潔な [seiketsu na] ▷ v 掃除する [souji suru]

cleaner ['kliːnə] n 清掃人 [seisounin]; **When does the cleaner come?** 清掃人はいつ来ますか? [seisou-nin wa itsu kimasu ka?]

cleaning ['kliːnɪŋ] n 掃除 [souji]; **cleaning lady** n 掃除婦 [soujifu]

cleanser ['klɛnzə] n クレンザー [kurenzaa]

clear [klɪə] adj 明白な [meihaku na]

clearly ['klɪəlɪ] adv はっきり [hakkiri]

clear off [klɪə ɒf] v 立ち去る [tachisaru]

clear up [klɪə ʌp] v 片付ける [katazukeru]

clementine ['klɛmənˌtiːn; -ˌtaɪn] n クレメンタイン [kurementain]

clever ['klɛvə] adj 賢い [kashikoi]

click [klɪk] n カチッという音 [kachitto iu oto] ▷ v カチッと鳴る [kachitto naru]

client ['klaɪənt] n 依頼人 [irainin]

cliff [klɪf] n 崖 [gake]

climate ['klaɪmɪt] n 気候 [kikou];

climate change n 気候変動 [kikou hendo]

climb [klaɪm] v 登る [noboru]

climber ['klaɪmə] n クライマー [kuraimaa]

climbing ['klaɪmɪŋ] n クライミング [kuraimingu]

clinic ['klɪnɪk] n 診療所 [shinryoujo]

clip [klɪp] n 刈り込み [karikomi]

clippers ['klɪpəz] npl はさみ [hasami]

cloakroom ['kləʊkˌruːm; -ˌrʊm] n クローク [kurooku]

clock [klɒk] n 時計 [tokei]; **alarm clock** n 目覚まし時計 [mezamashi tokei]

clockwise ['klɒkˌwaɪz] adv 右回りに [migimawari ni]

clog [klɒg] n 木靴 [kigutsu]

clone [kləʊn] n クローン [kuroon] ▷ v クローンを作る [kuroon-o tsukuru]

close adj [kləʊs] 近い [chikai] ▷ adv [kləʊs] 近くに [chikaku ni] ▷ v [kləʊz] 閉める [shimeru]; **close by** adj すぐ近くの [sugu chikaku no]; **closing time** n 閉店時刻 [heiten jikoku]

closed [kləʊzd] adj 閉まっている [shimatte iru]

closely [kləʊslɪ] adv ぴったりと [pittarito]

closure ['kləʊʒə] n 閉鎖 [heisa]

cloth [klɒθ] n 布地 [nunoji]

clothes [kləʊðz] npl 服 [fuku]; **clothes line** n 洗濯ロープ [sentaku roopu]; **clothes peg** n 洗濯ばさみ [sentakubasami]; **Is there somewhere to dry clothes?** 服を干すところがありますか? [fuku o hosu tokoro ga arimasu ka?]; **My clothes are damp** 私の服が湿っています [watashi no fuku ga shimette imasu]

clothing ['kləʊðɪŋ] n 衣類 [irui]

cloud [klaʊd] n 雲 [kumo]

cloudy ['klaʊdɪ] adj 曇った [kumotta]

clove [kləʊv] n クローブ [kuroobu]

clown [klaʊn] n ピエロ [piero]

club [klʌb] n (group) クラブ [kurabu] (集団), (weapon) 棍棒 [konbou]; **golf club** n (game) ゴルフ用クラブ [gorufu you kurabu], (society) ゴルフクラブ [gorufukurabu]; **Do they hire out golf clubs?** ゴルフクラブを貸し出しています か? [gorufu-kurabu o kashidashite imasu ka?]; **Where is there a good club?** どこ かによいクラブはありますか? [doko-ka ni yoi kurabu wa arimasu ka?]

club together [klʌb təˈgɛðə] v 合同す る [goudou suru]

clue [kluː] n 手がかり [tegakari]

clumsy [ˈklʌmzɪ] adj 不器用な [bukiyou na]

clutch [klʌtʃ] n クラッチ [kuratchi]

clutter [ˈklʌtə] n 散らかしたもの [chirakashita mono]

coach [kəʊtʃ] n (trainer) コーチ [koochi], (vehicle) 長距離バス [choukyori basu]; **The coach has left without me** 長距 離バスが私を乗せずに出発してしまいま した [choukyori-basu ga watashi o nosezu ni shuppatsu shite shimaimashita]; **When does the coach leave in the morning?** 長距離バスは朝何時に出ま すか? [choukyori-basu wa asa nan-ji ni demasu ka?]

coal [kəʊl] n 石炭 [sekitan]

coarse [kɔːs] adj きめの粗い [kime no komakai]

coast [kəʊst] n 沿岸 [engan]

coastguard [ˈkəʊstˌɡɑːd] n 沿岸警備隊 [engankeibitai]

coat [kəʊt] n コート [kooto] (洋服); **fur coat** n 毛皮のコート [kegawa no kooto]

coathanger [ˈkəʊtˌhæŋə] n ハンガー [hangaa]

cobweb [ˈkɒbˌwɛb] n くもの巣 [kumo no su]

cocaine [kəˈkeɪn] n コカイン [kokain]

cock [kɒk] n おんどり [ondori]

cockerel [ˈkɒkərəl; ˈkɒkrəl] n 若いおん どり [wakai ondori]

cockpit [ˈkɒkˌpɪt] n コックピット [kokkupitto]

cockroach [ˈkɒkˌrəʊtʃ] n ゴキブリ [gokiburi]

cocktail [ˈkɒkˌteɪl] n カクテル [kakuteru];

Do you sell cocktails? カクテルはあり ますか? [kakuteru wa arimasu ka?]

cocoa [ˈkəʊkəʊ] n ココア [kokoa]

coconut [ˈkəʊkəˌnʌt] n ココナツ [kokonatsu]

cod [kɒd] n タラ [tara]

code [kəʊd] n 暗号 [angou]; **dialling code** n 局番 [kyokuban]; **Highway Code** n 交通規則集 [koutsuu kisokushuu]

coeliac [ˈsiːlɪæk] adj 腹腔の [fukkou no]

coffee [ˈkɒfɪ] n コーヒー [koohii]; **black coffee** n ブラックコーヒー [burakku koohii]; **coffee bean** n コーヒー豆 [koohiimame]; **decaffeinated coffee** n カフェイン抜きのコーヒー [kafein nuki no koohii]; **A white coffee, please** ミルク入 りコーヒーをください [miruku-iri koohii o kudasai]; **Could we have another cup of coffee, please?** コーヒーをもう一杯 いただけますか? [koohii o mou ippai itadakemasu ka?]; **Have you got fresh coffee?** 挽きたてのコーヒーはあります か? [hikitate no koohii wa arimasu ka?]

coffeepot [ˈkɒfɪˌpɒt] n コーヒーポット [koohiipotto]

coffin [ˈkɒfɪn] n ひつぎ [hitsugi]

coin [kɔɪn] n 硬貨 [kouka]

coincide [ˌkəʊɪnˈsaɪd] v 同時に起こる [douji ni okoru]

coincidence [kəʊˈɪnsɪdəns] n 偶然 [guuzen]

Coke® [kəʊk] n コカコーラ® [kokakoora]

colander [ˈkɒləndə; ˈkʌl-] n 水切り [mizukiri]

cold [kəʊld] adj 寒い [samui] ▷ n 寒さ [samusa]; **cold sore** n 口辺ヘルペス [kouhenherupesu]; **I'm cold** 寒いです [samui desu]; **It's freezing cold** 凍えるほ どに寒いです [kogoeru hodo ni samui desu]

coleslaw [ˈkəʊlˌslɔː] n コールスロー [koorusuroo]

collaborate [kəˈlæbəˌreɪt] v 共同して働 く [kyoudou shite hataraku]

collapse [kəˈlæps] v 崩れる [kuzureru]

collar [ˈkɒlə] n 襟 [eri]

collarbone [ˈkɒləˌbəʊn] n 鎖骨 [sakotsu]

colleague [ˈkɒliːɡ] n 同僚 [douryou]

collect [kəˈlɛkt] v 集める [atsumeru]

collection [kəˈlɛkʃən] n コレクション [korekushon]

collective [kəˈlɛktɪv] adj 集団の [shuudan no] ▷ n 集団 [shuudan]

collector [kəˈlɛktə] n 収集家 [shuushuuka]; **ticket collector** n 改札係 [kaisatsugakari]

college [ˈkɒlɪdʒ] n カレッジ [karejji]

collide [kəˈlaɪd] v 衝突する [shoutotsu suru]

collie [ˈkɒlɪ] n コリー [korii]

colliery [ˈkɒljərɪ] n 炭鉱 [tankou]

collision [kəˈlɪʒən] n 衝突 [shoutotsu]

Colombia [kəˈlɒmbɪə] n コロンビア [koronbia]

Colombian [kəˈlɒmbɪən] adj コロンビアの [koronbia no] ▷ n コロンビア人 [koronbiajin]

colon [ˈkəʊlən] n コロン [koron]

colonel [ˈkɜːnəl] n 大佐 [taisa]

colour [ˈkʌlə] n 色 [iro]; **Do you have this in another colour?** これの別の色はありますか? [kore no betsu no iro wa arimasu ka?]; **I don't like the colour** 色が好きではありません [iro ga suki de wa arimasen]

colour-blind [ˈkʌləˈblaɪnd] adj 色盲の [shikimou no]

colourful [ˈkʌləfʊl] adj 色彩に富んだ [shikisai ni tonda]

colouring [ˈkʌlərɪŋ] n 着色 [chakushoku]

column [ˈkɒləm] n 円柱 [enchuu]

coma [ˈkəʊmə] n 昏睡 [konsui]

comb [kəʊm] n 櫛 [kushi] ▷ v 櫛でとかす [kushi de tokasu]

combination [ˌkɒmbɪˈneɪʃən] n 組み合わせ [kumiawase]

combine [kəmˈbaɪn] v 結合する [ketsugou suru]

come [kʌm] v 来る [kuru]

come back [kʌm bæk] v 戻ってくる [modotte kuru]

comedian [kəˈmiːdɪən] n コメディアン [komedian]

come down [kʌm daʊn] v 降りてくる [orite kuru]

comedy [ˈkɒmɪdɪ] n コメディー [komedii]

come from [kʌm frəm] v ・・・の出身である [...no shusshin de aru]

come in [kʌm ɪn] v 入る [hairu]

come off [kʌm ɒf] v **The handle has come off** 取っ手が外れました [totte ga hazuremashita]

come out [kʌm aʊt] v 公になる [ooyake ni naru]

come round [kʌm raʊnd] v 意識を回復する [ishiki-o kaifuku suru]

comet [ˈkɒmɪt] n 彗星 [suisei]

come up [kʌm ʌp] v 上がる [agaru]

comfortable [ˈkʌmftəbˀl; ˈkʌmfətəbˀl] adj 快適な [kaiteki na]

comic [ˈkɒmɪk] n 喜劇俳優 [kigeki haiyuu]; **comic book** n 漫画本 [mangabon]; **comic strip** n コマ割り漫画 [komawari manga]

coming [ˈkʌmɪŋ] adj 次の [tsugi no]

comma [ˈkɒmə] n コンマ [konma]; **inverted commas** npl 引用符 [in-youfu]

command [kəˈmɑːnd] n 命令 [meirei]

comment [ˈkɒmɛnt] n 論評 [ronpyou] ▷ v 論評する [ronpyou suru]

commentary [ˈkɒməntərɪ; -trɪ] n 実況解説 [jikkyou kaisetsu]

commentator [ˈkɒmənˌteɪtə] n 解説者 [kaisetsusha]

commercial [kəˈmɜːʃəl] n コマーシャル [komaasharu]; **commercial break** n コマーシャルの時間 [komaasharu no jikan]

commission [kəˈmɪʃən] n 制作依頼 [seisaku irai]

commit [kəˈmɪt] v (crime) 犯す [okasu]

committee [kəˈmɪtɪ] n 委員会 [iinkai]

common [ˈkɒmən] adj 普通の [futsuu no]; **common sense** n 常識 [joushiki]

communicate [kəˈmjuːnɪˌkeɪt] v 伝える [tsutaeru]

communication [kə,mjuːnɪ'keɪʃən] n コミュニケーション [komyunikeeshon]

communion [kə'mjuːnjən] n 共有 [kyouyuu]

communism ['kɒmjʊˌnɪzəm] n 共産主義 [kyousanshugi]

communist ['kɒmjʊnɪst] adj 共産主義の [kyousanshugi no] ▷ n 共産主義者 [kyousanshugisha]

community [kə'mjuːnɪtɪ] n 地域社会 [chiiki shakai]

commute [kə'mjuːt] v 通勤する [tsuukin suru]

commuter [kə'mjuːtə] n 通勤者 [tsuukinsha]

compact ['kəm'pækt] adj ぎっしり詰まった [gisshiri tsumatta]; **compact disc** n コンパクトディスク [konpakuto disuku]

companion [kəm'pænjən] n 仲間 [nakama]

company ['kʌmpənɪ] n 会社 [kaisha]; **company car** n 社用車 [shayousha]; **I would like some information about the company** 会社についての情報を教えていただきたいのですが [kaisha ni tsuite no jouhou o oshiete itadakitai no desu ga]

comparable ['kɒmpərəbəl] adj 匹敵する [hitteki suru]

comparatively [kəm'pærətɪvlɪ] adv 比較的 [hikakuteki]

compare [kəm'pɛə] v 比較する [hikaku suru]

comparison [kəm'pærɪsən] n 比較 [hikaku]

compartment [kəm'pɑːtmənt] n コンパートメント [konpaatomento]

compass ['kʌmpəs] n コンパス [konpasu]

compatible [kəm'pætəbəl] adj 両立できる [ryouritsu dekiru]

compensate ['kɒmpɛnˌseɪt] v 補償する [hoshou suru]

compensation [,kɒmpɛn'seɪʃən] n 賠償金 [baishoukin]

compere ['kɒmpɛə] n 司会者 [shikaisha]

compete [kəm'piːt] v 競争する [kyousou suru]

competent ['kɒmpɪtənt] adj 有能な [yuunou na]

competition [,kɒmpɪ'tɪʃən] n 競争 [kyousou]

competitive [kəm'pɛtɪtɪv] adj 競争的な [kyousouteki na]

competitor [kəm'pɛtɪtə] n 競争者 [kyousousha]

complain [kəm'pleɪn] v 不平を言う [fuhei o iu]

complaint [kəm'pleɪnt] n 不平 [fuhei]

complementary [,kɒmplɪ'mɛntərɪ; -trɪ] adj 補完的な [hokanteki na]

complete [kəm'pliːt] adj 全くの [mattaku no]

completely [kəm'pliːtlɪ] adv 全く [mattaku]; **I want a completely new look** 全く新しいスタイルにしてください [mattaku atarashii sutairu ni shite kudasai]

complex ['kɒmplɛks] adj 複合の [fukugou no] ▷ n 複合体 [fukugoutai]

complexion [kəm'plɛkʃən] n 顔色 [kaoiro]

complicated ['kɒmplɪˌkeɪtɪd] adj 複雑な [fukuzatsu na]

complication [,kɒmplɪ'keɪʃən] n 複雑な要因 [fukuzatsu na youin]

compliment n ['kɒmplɪmənt] ほめことば [homekotoba] ▷ v ['kɒmplɪˌmɛnt] ほめる [homeru]

complimentary [,kɒmplɪ'mɛntərɪ; -trɪ] adj 称賛の [shousan no]

component [kəm'pəʊnənt] adj 構成している [kousei shite iru] ▷ n 構成要素 [kousei youso]

composer [kəm'pəʊzə] n 作曲家 [sakkyokuka]

composition [,kɒmpə'zɪʃən] n 構成 [kousei]

comprehension [,kɒmprɪ'hɛnʃən] n 理解 [rikai]

comprehensive [,kɒmprɪ'hɛnsɪv] adj 総合的な [sougouteki na]

compromise ['kɒmprə,maɪz] *n* 妥協 [dakyou] ▷ *v* 妥協する [dakyou suru]

compulsory [kəm'pʌlsərɪ] *adj* 強制的な [kyouseiteki na]

computer [kəm'pju:tə] *n* コンピューター [konpyuutaa]; **computer game** *n* コンピューターゲーム [konpyuutaa geemu]; **computer science** *n* コンピューター科学 [konpyuutaa kagaku]; **May I use your computer?** あなたのコンピューターをお借りできますか? [anata no konpyuutaa o o-kari dekimasu ka?]; **My computer has frozen** 私のコンピューターがフリーズしました [watashi no konpyuutaa ga furiizu shimashita]; **Where is the computer room?** コンピューター室はどこですか? [konpyuutaa-shitsu wa doko desu ka?]

computing [kəm'pju:tɪŋ] *n* 計算 [keisan]

concentrate ['kɒnsən,treɪt] *v* 集中する [shuuchuu suru]

concentration [,kɒnsən'treɪʃən] *n* 集中 [shuuchuu]

concern [kən'sɜːn] *n* 心配 [shinpai]

concerned [kən'sɜːnd] *adj* 関係している [kankei shiteiru]

concerning [kən'sɜːnɪŋ] *prep* ···に関して [...ni kanshite]

concert ['kɒnsɜːt; -sət] *n* コンサート [konsaato]; **Are there any good concerts on?** 何かよいコンサートがありますか? [nani ka yoi konsaato ga arimasu ka?]; **What's on tonight at the concert hall?** コンサートホールでは今晩何をやっていますか? [konsaato-hooru de wa konban nani o yatte imasu ka?]; **Where can I buy tickets for the concert?** どこでそのコンサートのチケットを買えますか? [doko de sono konsaato no chiketto o kaemasu ka?]

concerto, concerti [kən'tʃɛətəʊ, kən'tʃɛətɪ] *n* コンチェルト [koncheruto]

concession [kən'sɛʃən] *n* 譲歩 [jouho]

concise [kən'saɪs] *adj* 簡潔な [kanketsu na]

conclude [kən'klu:d] *v* 結論を出す [ketsuron-o dasu]

conclusion [kən'klu:ʒən] *n* 結論 [ketsuron]

concrete ['kɒnkri:t] *n* コンクリート [konkuriito]

concussion [kən'kʌʃən] *n* 脳震盪 [noushintou]

condemn [kən'dɛm] *v* 非難する [hinan suru]

condensation [,kɒndɛn'seɪʃən] *n* 結露 [ketsuro]

condition [kən'dɪʃən] *n* 状態 [joutai]; **What are the snow conditions?** 雪の状態はどんなですか? [yuki no joutai wa donna desu ka?]

conditional [kən'dɪʃənᵊl] *adj* 条件付きの [joukentsuki no]

conditioner [kən'dɪʃənə] *n* コンディショナー [kondeishonaa]; **Do you sell conditioner?** コンディショナーを売っていますか? [kondishonaa o utte imasu ka?]

condom ['kɒndɒm; 'kɒndəm] *n* コンドーム [kondoomu]

conduct [kən'dʌkt] *v* 行う [okonau]

conductor [kən'dʌktə] *n* 指揮者 [shikisha]; **bus conductor** *n* バスの車掌 [basu no shashou]

cone [kəʊn] *n* 円錐形のもの [ensuikei no mono]

conference ['kɒnfərəns; -frəns] *n* 会議 [kaigi]; **press conference** *n* 記者会見 [kishakaiken]

confess [kən'fɛs] *v* 自白する [jihaku suru]

confession [kən'fɛʃən] *n* 自白 [jihaku]

confetti [kən'fɛtɪ] *npl* 紙吹雪 [kamifubuki]

confidence ['kɒnfɪdəns] *n* (secret) 秘密 [himitsu], (self-assurance) 自信 [jishin], (trust) 信頼 [shinrai]

confident ['kɒnfɪdənt] *adj* 確信して [kakushin shite]

confidential [,kɒnfɪ'dɛnʃəl] *adj* 内密の [naimitsu no]

confirm [kən'fɜːm] *v* 確認する [kakunin suru]

confirmation [ˌkɒnfə'meɪʃən] n 確認 [kakunin]

confiscate ['kɒnfɪˌskeɪt] v 没収する [bosshuu suru]

conflict ['kɒnflɪkt] n 衝突 [shoutotsu]

confuse [kən'fjuːz] v 困惑させる [konwaku saseru]

confused [kən'fjuːzd] adj 当惑した [touwaku shita]

confusing [kən'fjuːzɪŋ] adj 困惑させる [konwaku saseru]

confusion [kən'fjuːʒən] n 混同 [kondou]

congestion [kən'dʒɛstʃən] n 密集 [misshuu]

Congo ['kɒŋgəʊ] n コンゴ [kongo]

congratulate [kən'grætjʊˌleɪt] v 祝う [iwau]

congratulations [kənˌgrætjʊ'leɪʃənz] npl おめでとう [omedetou]

conifer ['kəʊnɪfə; 'kɒn-] n 針葉樹 [shin-youju]

conjugation [ˌkɒndʒʊ'geɪʃən] n 語形変化 [gokei henka]

conjunction [kən'dʒʌŋkʃən] n 結合 [ketsugou]

conjurer ['kʌndʒərə] n 手品師 [tejinashi]

connect [kə'nɛkt] v 接続する [setsuzoku suru]

connection [kə'nɛkʃən] n 関係 [kankei]

conquer ['kɒŋkə] v 征服する [seifuku suru]

conscience ['kɒnʃəns] n 良心 [ryoushin]

conscientious [ˌkɒnʃɪ'ɛnʃəs] adj 念入りな [nen'iri na]

conscious ['kɒnʃəs] adj 意識がある [ishiki ga aru]

consciousness ['kɒnʃəsnɪs] n 意識 [ishiki]

consecutive [kən'sɛkjʊtɪv] adj 連続的な [renzokuteki na]

consensus [kən'sɛnsəs] n コンセンサス [konsensasu]

consequence ['kɒnsɪkwəns] n 結果 [kekka]

consequently ['kɒnsɪkwəntlɪ] adv その結果 [sono kekka]

conservation [ˌkɒnsə'veɪʃən] n 保全 [hozen]

conservative [kən'sɜːvətɪv] adj 保守的な [hoshuteki na]

conservatory [kən'sɜːvətrɪ] n コンサーバトリー [konsaabatorii]

consider [kən'sɪdə] v みなす [minasu]

considerate [kən'sɪdərɪt] adj 思いやりのある [omoiyari no aru]

considering [kən'sɪdərɪŋ] prep ···を考慮すると [...-o kouryo suru to]

consist [kən'sɪst] v **consist of** v ···から成る [...kara naru]

consistent [kən'sɪstənt] adj 一貫した [ikkan shita]

consonant ['kɒnsənənt] n 子音 [shiin]

conspiracy [kən'spɪrəsɪ] n 陰謀 [inbou]

constant ['kɒnstənt] adj 絶えず続く [taezu tsuzuku]

constantly ['kɒnstəntlɪ] adv 絶えず [taezu]

constipated ['kɒnstɪˌpeɪtɪd] adj 便秘した [benpi shita]

constituency [kən'stɪtjʊənsɪ] n 選挙区 [senkyoku]

constitution [ˌkɒnstɪ'tjuːʃən] n 憲法 [kenpou]

construct [kən'strʌkt] v 建設する [kensetsu suru]

construction [kən'strʌkʃən] n 建設 [kensetsu]

constructive [kən'strʌktɪv] adj 建設的な [kensetsuteki na]

consul ['kɒnsəl] n 領事 [ryouji]

consulate ['kɒnsjʊlɪt] n 領事館 [ryoujikan]

consult [kən'sʌlt] v 相談する [soudan suru]

consultant [kən'sʌltənt] n (adviser) 顧問医 [komon-i]

consumer [kən'sjuːmə] n 消費者 [shouhisha]

contact n ['kɒntækt] 連絡 [renraku] ▷ v [kən'tækt] 連絡を取る [renraku-o toru]; **contact lenses** npl コンタクトレンズ [kontakutorenzu]; **Where can I contact**

you? どこであなたに連絡を取れますか? [doko de anata ni renraku o toremasu ka?];
Who do we contact if there are problems? 問題があったときに誰に連絡すればいいのですか? [mondai ga atta toki ni dare ni renraku sureba ii no desu ka?];
contactless ['kɒntæktlɪs] *adj* コンタクトレスの [kontakutoresu no]

contagious [kən'teɪdʒəs] *adj* 伝染性の [densensei no]

contain [kən'teɪn] *v* 含む [fukumu]

container [kən'teɪnə] *n* 容器 [youki]

contemporary [kən'tɛmprərɪ] *adj* 現代の [gendai no]

contempt [kən'tɛmpt] *n* 軽蔑 [keibetsu]

content ['kɒntɛnt] *n* 中身 [nakami];
contents *(list)* *npl* 目次 [mokuji]

contest ['kɒntɛst] *n* 競争 [kyousou]

contestant [kən'tɛstənt] *n* 競争者 [kyousousha]

context ['kɒntɛkst] *n* 状況 [joukyou]

continent ['kɒntɪnənt] *n* 大陸 [tairiku]

continual [kən'tɪnjʊəl] *adj* 継続的な [keizokuteki na]

continually [kən'tɪnjʊəlɪ] *adv* 継続的に [keizokuteki ni]

continue [kən'tɪnjuː] *vi* 続く [tsuzuku] ▷ *vt* 続ける [tsuzukeru]

continuous [kən'tɪnjʊəs] *adj* 連続的な [renzokuteki na]

contraception [ˌkɒntrə'sɛpʃən] *n* 避妊 [hinin]; **I need contraception** 私は避妊が必要です [watashi wa hinin ga hitsuyou desu]

contraceptive [ˌkɒntrə'sɛptɪv] *n* 避妊具 [hiningu]

contract ['kɒntrækt] *n* 契約 [keiyaku]

contractor ['kɒntræktə; kən'træk-] *n* 契約人 [keiyakunin]

contradict [ˌkɒntrə'dɪkt] *v* 反駁する [hanbaku suru]

contradiction [ˌkɒntrə'dɪkʃən] *n* 反駁 [hanbaku]

contrary ['kɒntrərɪ] *n* 正反対 [seihantai]

contrast ['kɒntrɑːst] *n* 相違 [soui]

contribute [kən'trɪbjuːt] *v* 寄付する [kifu suru]

contribution [ˌkɒntrɪ'bjuːʃən] *n* 寄付 [kifu]

control [kən'trəʊl] *n* 支配 [shihai] ▷ *v* 支配する [shihai suru]; **birth control** *n* 避妊 [hinin]; **passport control** *n* パスポート審査窓口 [pasupooto shinsa madoguchi]; **remote control** *n* リモコン [rimokon]

controller [kən'trəʊlə] *n* **air-traffic controller** *n* 航空管制官 [koukuu kanseikan]

controversial ['kɒntrə'vɜːʃəl] *adj* 論争の [ronsou no]

convenient [kən'viːnɪənt] *adj* 都合のよい [tsugou no yoi]

convent ['kɒnvənt] *n* 女子修道院 [joshishuudouin]

conventional [kən'vɛnʃənªl] *adj* 慣例にのっとった [kanrei ni nottotta]

conversation [ˌkɒnvə'seɪʃən] *n* 会話 [kaiwa]

convert [kən'vɜːt] *v* 変える [kaeru]; **catalytic converter** *n* 触媒コンバーター [shokubai konbaataa]

convertible [kən'vɜːtəbªl] *adj* 変えられる [kaerareru] ▷ *n* コンバーティブル [konbaateiburu]

convict [kən'vɪkt] *v* 有罪と決定する [yuuzai to kettei suru]

convince [kən'vɪns] *v* 確信させる [kakushin saseru]

convincing [kən'vɪnsɪŋ; con'vincing] *adj* 説得力のある [settokuryoku no aru]

convoy ['kɒnvɔɪ] *n* 護衛されている輸送車隊 [goei sareteiru yusoushatai]

cook [kʊk] *n* 料理人 [ryourinin] ▷ *v* 料理する [ryouri suru]

cookbook ['kʊkˌbʊk] *n* 料理の本 [ryouri no hon]

cooker ['kʊkə] *n* 料理用レンジ [ryouri you renji]; **gas cooker** *n* ガスレンジ [gasurenji]

cookery ['kʊkərɪ] *n* 料理法 [ryourihou]; **cookery book** *n* 料理の本 [ryouri no hon]

cooking ['kʊkɪŋ] n 料理 [ryouri]

cool [kuːl] adj (cold) 涼しい [suzushii], (stylish) かっこいい [kakkoii]

cooperation [kəʊˌɒpəˈreɪʃən] n 協力 [kyouryoku]

cop [kɒp] n 警官 [keikan]

cope [kəʊp] v cope (with) v うまく対処する [umaku taisho suru]

copper ['kɒpə] n 銅 [dou]

copy ['kɒpɪ] n (reproduction) 複製 [fukusei], (written text) 原稿 [genkou] ▷ v 複製する [fukusei suru]

copyright ['kɒpɪˌraɪt] n 版権 [hanken]

coral ['kɒrəl] n 珊瑚 [sango]

cord [kɔːd] n spinal cord n 脊髄 [sekizui]

cordless ['kɔːdlɪs] adj コードレスの [koodoresu no]

corduroy ['kɔːdəˌrɔɪ; ˌkɔːdəˈrɔɪ] n コーデュロイ [koodeyuroi]

core [kɔː] n 芯 [shin]

coriander [ˌkɒrɪˈændə] n コリアンダー [koriandaa]

cork [kɔːk] n コルク [koruku]

corkscrew ['kɔːkˌskruː] n コルク栓抜き [koruku sennuki]

corn [kɔːn] n 穀草 [koku kusa]

corner ['kɔːnə] n 角 [kado] (場所); It's on the corner その角です [sono kado desu]; It's round the corner その角を曲がったところです [sono kado o magatta tokoro desu]

cornet ['kɔːnɪt] n コルネット [korunetto]

cornflakes ['kɔːnˌfleɪks] npl コーンフレーク [koonfureeku]

cornflour ['kɔːnˌflaʊə] n コーンフラワー [koonfurawaa]

corporal ['kɔːpərəl; -prəl] n 伍長 [gochou]

corpse [kɔːps] n 死体 [shitai]

correct [kəˈrɛkt] adj 正しい [tadashii] ▷ v 訂正する [teisei suru]

correction [kəˈrɛkʃən] n 訂正 [teisei]

correctly [kəˈrɛktlɪ] adv 正しく [tadashiku]

correspondence [ˌkɒrɪˈspɒndəns] n 文通 [buntsuu]

correspondent [ˌkɒrɪˈspɒndənt] n 文通者 [buntsuusha]

corridor ['kɒrɪˌdɔː] n 廊下 [rouka]

corrupt [kəˈrʌpt] adj 腐敗した [fuhai shita]

corruption [kəˈrʌpʃən] n 腐敗行為 [fuhaikoui]

cosmetics [kɒzˈmɛtɪks] npl 化粧品 [keshouhin]

cost [kɒst] n コスト [kosuto] ▷ v かかる [kakaru] (費用); **cost of living** n 生活費 [seikatsuhi]

Costa Rica ['kɒstə 'riːkə] n コスタリカ [kosutarika]

costume ['kɒstjuːm] n 身なり [minari]; **swimming costume** n 水着 [mizugi]

cosy ['kəʊzɪ] adj 居心地のよい [igokochi no yoi]

cot [kɒt] n 小児用ベッド [shouni you beddo]

cottage ['kɒtɪdʒ] n 田舎屋 [inakaya]; **cottage cheese** n カッテージチーズ [katteeji chiizu]

cotton ['kɒtⁿn] n 綿 [men]; **cotton bud** n 綿棒 [menbou]; **cotton wool** n 脱脂綿 [dasshimen]

couch [kaʊtʃ] n カウチソファー [kauchisofaa]

couchette [kuːˈʃɛt] n 寝台車コンパートメントの寝台 [shindaisha konpaatomento no shindai]

cough [kɒf] n 咳 [seki] ▷ v 咳をする [seki-o suru]; **cough mixture** n 咳止め薬 [sekidomegusuri]; **I have a cough** 私は咳がでます [watashi wa seki ga demasu]

council ['kaʊnsəl] n 審議会 [shingikai]; **council house** n 公営住宅 [koueijuutaku]

councillor ['kaʊnsələ] n 地方議会議員 [chihou gikai giin]

count [kaʊnt] v 数える [kazoeru]

counter ['kaʊntə] n カウンター [kauntaa]

count on [kaʊnt ɒn] v ・・・に頼る [...ni tayoru]

country [ˈkʌntrɪ] n 国 [kuni]; **developing country** n 発展途上国 [hattentojoukoku]; **Where can I buy a map of the country?** どこでその国の地図を買えますか? [doko de sono kuni no chizu o kaemasu ka?]

countryside [ˈkʌntrɪˌsaɪd] n 田舎 [inaka]

couple [ˈkʌpəl] n カップル [kappuru]

courage [ˈkʌrɪdʒ] n 勇気 [yuuki]

courageous [kəˈreɪdʒəs] adj 勇気のある [yuuki no aru]

courgette [kʊəˈʒɛt] n ズッキーニ [zukkiini]

courier [ˈkʊərɪə] n 急使 [kyuushi]

course [kɔːs] n 過程 [katei]; **golf course** n ゴルフ場 [gorufujou]; **main course** n メインコース [meinkoosu]; **refresher course** n 再教育コース [saikyouiku koosu]; **training course** n トレーニングコース [toreeningukoosu]

court [kɔːt] n 法廷 [houtei]; **tennis court** n テニスコート [tenisukooto]

courtyard [ˈkɔːtˌjɑːd] n 中庭 [nakaniwa]

cousin [ˈkʌzən] n いとこ [itoko]

cover [ˈkʌvə] n 覆い [oui] ▷ v 覆う [oou]; **cover charge** n カバーチャージ [kabaa chaaji]

cow [kaʊ] n 雌牛 [meushi]

coward [ˈkaʊəd] n 臆病者 [okubyoumono]

cowardly [ˈkaʊədlɪ] adj 臆病な [okubyou na]

cowboy [ˈkaʊˌbɔɪ] n カウボーイ [kaubooi]

crab [kræb] n カニ [kani]

crack [kræk] n (cocaine) クラック [kurakku], (fracture) 割れ目 [wareme] ▷ v 割れる [wareru]; **crack down on** v …に断固たる措置を取る […ni dankotaru sochi-o toru]

cracked [krækt] adj ひびの入った [hibi no haitta]

cracker [ˈkrækə] n クラッカー [kurakkaa]

cradle [ˈkreɪdəl] n 揺りかご [yurikago]

craft [krɑːft] n 熟練職業 [jukuren shokugyou]

craftsman [ˈkrɑːftsmən] n 職人 [shokunin]

cram [kræm] v 詰め込む [tsumekomu]

crammed [kræmd] adj 詰め込んだ [tsumekonda]

cranberry [ˈkrænbərɪ; -brɪ] n クランベリー [kuranberii]

crane [kreɪn] n (bird) ツル [tsuru] (鳥), (for lifting) クレーン [kureen]

crash [kræʃ] n 衝突 [shoutotsu] ▷ vi 衝突する [shoutotsu suru] ▷ vt 衝突させる [shoutotsu saseru]; **I've crashed my car** 私は自分の車を衝突させました [watashi wa jibun no kuruma o shoutotsu sasemashita]; **There's been a crash** 衝突がありました [shoutotsu ga arimashita]

crawl [krɔːl] v 這う [hau]

crayfish [ˈkreɪˌfɪʃ] n ザリガニ [zarigani]

crayon [ˈkreɪən; -ɒn] n クレヨン [kureyon]

crazy [ˈkreɪzɪ] adj 無茶な [mucha na]

cream [kriːm] adj クリーム色の [kuriimuiro no] ▷ n クリーム [kuriimu]; **ice cream** n アイスクリーム [aisukuriimu]; **shaving cream** n シェービングクリーム [sheebingukuriimu]; **whipped cream** n ホイップクリーム [hoippukuriimu]

crease [kriːs] n 折り目 [orime]

creased [kriːst] adj 折り目をつけた [orime-o tsuketa]

create [kriːˈeɪt] v 創造する [souzou suru]

creation [kriːˈeɪʃən] n 創造 [souzou]

creative [kriːˈeɪtɪv] adj 創造的な [souzouteki na]

creature [ˈkriːtʃə] n 生き物 [ikimono]

crèche [krɛʃ] n 託児所 [takujisho]

credentials [krɪˈdɛnʃəlz] npl 信用を保証するもの [shin'you-o hoshou suru mono]

credible [ˈkrɛdɪbəl] adj 信用できる [shinyou dekiru]

credit [ˈkrɛdɪt] n 信用販売 [shinyou hanbai]; **credit card** n クレジットカード [kurejittokaado]

crematorium, crematoria [ˌkrɛməˈtɔːrɪəm, ˌkrɛməˈtɔːrɪə] n 火葬場 [kasouba]

cress [krɛs] n コショウソウ [koshousou]

crew [kruː] n 乗組員 [norikumiin]; **crew cut** n クルーカット [kuruukatto]

cricket ['krɪkɪt] n (game) クリケット [kuriketto], (insect) コオロギ [koorogi]

crime [kraɪm] n 犯罪 [hanzai]

criminal ['krɪmɪnᵊl] adj 犯罪の [hanzai no] ▷ n 犯罪者 [hanzaisha]

crisis ['kraɪsɪs] n 重大局面 [juudai kyokumen]

crisp [krɪsp] adj パリパリした [paripari shita]

crisps [krɪsps] npl ポテトチップス [potetochippusu]

crispy ['krɪspɪ] adj パリパリする [paripari suru]

criterion, criteria [kraɪˈtɪərɪən, kraɪˈtɪərɪə] n 基準 [kijun]

critic ['krɪtɪk] n 批評家 [hihyouka]

critical ['krɪtɪkᵊl] adj 重大な [juudai na]

criticism ['krɪtɪˌsɪzəm] n 批判 [hihan]

criticize ['krɪtɪˌsaɪz] v 批判する [hihan suru]

Croatia [krəʊˈeɪʃə] n クロアチア [kuroachia]

Croatian [krəʊˈeɪʃən] adj クロアチアの [kuroachia no] ▷ n (language) クロアチア語 [kuroachiago], (person) クロアチア人 [kuroachiajin]

crochet ['krəʊʃeɪ; -ʃɪ] v かぎ針編みをする [kagiamibari-o suru]

crockery ['krɒkərɪ] n We need more crockery 食器がもっと必要です [shokki ga motto hitsuyou desu]

crocodile ['krɒkəˌdaɪl] n ワニ [wani]

crocus ['krəʊkəs] n クロッカス [kurokkasu]

crook [krʊk] n 湾曲 [wankyoku], (swindler) ペテン師 [petenshi]

crop [krɒp] n 農作物 [nousakubutsu], 収穫 [shuukaku]

cross [krɒs] adj 不機嫌な [fukigen na] ▷ n 十字形 [juujigata] ▷ v 横切る [yokogiru]; **Red Cross** n 赤十字社 [sekijuujisha]

cross-country ['krɒsˈkʌntrɪ] n クロスカントリー [kurosukantorii]; **I want to hire cross-country skis** クロスカントリースキーの板を借りたいのですが [kurosukantorii-sukii no ita o karitai no desu ga]; **Is it possible to go cross-country skiing?** クロスカントリースキーに行くことは可能ですか？ [kurosukantorii-sukii ni iku koto wa kanou desu ka?]

crossing ['krɒsɪŋ] n 交差点 [kousaten]; **level crossing** n 踏切 [fumikiri]; **pedestrian crossing** n 横断歩道 [oudanhodou]; **pelican crossing** n 押しボタン信号式横断歩道 [oshibotan shingoushiki oudanhodou]; **zebra crossing** n 太い白線の縞模様で示した横断歩道 [futoi hakusen no shimamoyou de shimeshita oudanhodou]

cross out [krɒs aʊt] v 帳消しにする [choukeshi ni suru]

crossroads ['krɒsˌrəʊdz] n 交差路 [kousaro]

crossword ['krɒsˌwɜːd] n クロスワードパズル [kurosuwaadopazuru]

crow [krəʊ] n カラス [karasu]

crowd [kraʊd] n 群集 [gunshuu]

crowded [kraʊdɪd] adj 込み合った [komiatta]

crowdfunding ['kraʊdfʌndɪŋ] n クラウドファンディング [kuraudofandingu]

crown [kraʊn] n 王冠 [oukan]

crucial ['kruːʃəl] adj 重大な [juudai na]

crucifix ['kruːsɪfɪks] n 十字架 [juujika]

crude [kruːd] adj 粗雑な [sozatsu na]

cruel ['kruːəl] adj 残酷な [zankoku na]

cruelty ['kruːəltɪ] n 残酷 [zankoku]

cruise [kruːz] n 巡航 [junkou]

crumb [krʌm] n パン粉 [panko]

crush [krʌʃ] v 押しつぶす [oshitsubusu]

crutch [krʌtʃ] n 松葉杖 [matsubadue]

cry [kraɪ] n 泣き叫ぶ声 [nakisakebu koe] ▷ v 泣く [naku]

crystal ['krɪstᵊl] n 水晶 [suishou]

cub [kʌb] n 野獣の子 [yajuu no ko]

Cuba ['kjuːbə] n キューバ [kyuuba]

Cuban ['kjuːbən] adj キューバの [kyuuba no] ▷ n キューバ人 [kyuubajin]

cube [kjuːb] *n* 立方体 [rippoutai]; **ice cube** *n* アイスキューブ [aisukyuubu]; **stock cube** *n* 固形スープの素 [kokei suupu no moto]

cubic ['kjuːbɪk] *adj* 立方の [rippou no]

cuckoo ['kʊkuː] *n* カッコウ [kakkou]

cucumber ['kjuːˌkʌmbə] *n* キュウリ [kyuuri]

cuddle ['kʌdəl] *n* 抱擁 [houyou] ▷ *v* 抱きしめる [dakishimeru]

cue [kjuː] *n* (billiards) キュー [kyuu]

cufflinks ['kʌflɪŋks] *npl* カフスリンク [kafusurinku]

culprit ['kʌlprɪt] *n* 犯罪者 [hanzaisha]

cultural ['kʌltʃərəl] *adj* 文化の [bunka no]

culture ['kʌltʃə] *n* 文化 [bunka]

cumin ['kʌmɪn] *n* クミン [kumin]

cunning ['kʌnɪŋ] *adj* 狡猾な [koukatsu na]

cup [kʌp] *n* カップ [kappu]; **World Cup** *n* ワールドカップ [waarudokappu]

cupboard ['kʌbəd] *n* 戸棚 [todana]

curb [kɜːb] *n* 拘束 [kousoku]

cure [kjʊə] *n* 治療 [chiryou] ▷ *v* 治す [naosu]

curfew ['kɜːfjuː] *n* 夜間外出禁止令 [yakan gaishutsu kinshirei]

curious ['kjʊərɪəs] *adj* 知りたがる [shiritagaru]

curl [kɜːl] *n* 巻き毛 [makige]

curler ['kɜːlə] *n* カーラー [kaaraa]

curly ['kɜːlɪ] *adj* 巻き毛の [makige no]

currant ['kʌrənt] *n* 小粒の種なし干しブドウ [kotsubu no tanenashi hoshibudou]

currency ['kʌrənsɪ] *n* 通貨 [tsuuka]

current ['kʌrənt] *adj* 現在の [genzai no] ▷ *n* (electricity) 電流 [denryuu], (flow) 流れ [nagare]; **current account** *n* 当座預金 [touzayokin]; **current affairs** *npl* 時事問題 [jiji mondai]

currently ['kʌrəntlɪ] *adv* 目下 [meshita] (今)

curriculum [kə'rɪkjʊləm] *n* カリキュラム [karikyuramu]; **curriculum vitae** *n* 履歴書 [rirekisho]

curry ['kʌrɪ] *n* カレー料理 [karee ryouri]; **curry powder** *n* カレー粉 [kareeko]

curse [kɜːs] *n* ののしり [nonoshiri]

cursor ['kɜːsə] *n* カーソル [kaasoru]

curtain ['kɜːtən] *n* カーテン [kaaten]

cushion ['kʊʃən] *n* クッション [kusshon]

custard ['kʌstəd] *n* カスタード [kasutaado]

custody ['kʌstədɪ] *n* 保護 [hogo]

custom ['kʌstəm] *n* 風習 [fuushuu]

customer ['kʌstəmə] *n* 顧客 [kokyaku]

customized ['kʌstəˌmaɪzd] *adj* カスタマイズされた [kasutamaizu sareta]

customs ['kʌstəmz] *npl* 関税 [kanzei]; **customs officer** *n* 税関係官 [zeikan kakarikan]

cut [kʌt] *n* 切断 [setsudan] ▷ *v* 切る [kiru]; **crew cut** *n* クルーカット [kuruukatto]; **power cut** *n* 停電 [teiden]

cutback ['kʌtˌbæk] *n* 縮小 [shukushou]

cut down [kʌt daʊn] *v* 伐り倒す [kiritaosu]

cute [kjuːt] *adj* かわいい [kawaii]

cutlery ['kʌtlərɪ] *n* 食卓用ナイフ・フォーク・スプーン類 [shokutaku yoo naifu. fouku. supuun rui]

cutlet ['kʌtlɪt] *n* 薄い肉片 [usui nikuhen]

cut off [kʌt ɒf] *v* 切り離す [kirihanasu]

cutting ['kʌtɪŋ] *n* 切り抜き [kirinuki]

cut up [kʌt ʌp] *v* 切り分ける [kiriwakeru]

CV [siː viː] *abbr* 履歴書 [rirekisho]

cyberbullying ['saɪbəbʊlɪɪŋ] *n* サイバーいじめ [saibaa ijime]

cybercafé ['saɪbəˌkæfeɪ; -ˌkæfɪ] *n* サイバーカフェ [saibaakafe]

cybercrime ['saɪbəˌkraɪm] *n* サイバー犯罪 [saibaa hanzai]

cycle ['saɪkəl] *n* (bike) 自転車 [jitensha], (recurring period) 周期 [shuuki] ▷ *v* 自転車に乗る [jitensha ni noru]; **cycle lane** *n* サイクルレーン [saikurureen]; **cycle path** *n* サイクルパス [saikuru pasu]; **Where is the cycle path to...?** ···へ行く自転車道はどこですか? [...e iku jitensha-dou wa doko desu ka?]

cycling ['saɪklɪŋ] *n* サイクリング

[saikuringu]; **Let's go cycling** サイクリングに行きましょう [saikuringu ni ikimashou]; **We would like to go cycling** 私たちはサイクリングに行きたいのですが [watashi-tachi wa saikuringu ni ikitai no desu ga]

cyclist ['saɪklɪst] *n* サイクリスト [saikurisuto]

cyclone ['saɪkləʊn] *n* サイクロン [saikuron]

cylinder ['sɪlɪndə] *n* 円筒 [entou]

cymbals ['sɪmbəlz] *npl* シンバル [shinbaru]

Cypriot ['sɪprɪət] *adj* キプロスの [kipurosu no] ▷ *n (person)* キプロス人 [kipurosujin]

Cyprus ['saɪprəs] *n* キプロス [kipurosu]

cyst [sɪst] *n* 嚢胞 [nouhou]

cystitis [sɪ'staɪtɪs] *n* 膀胱炎 [boukouen]

Czech [tʃɛk] *adj* チェコの [cheko no] ▷ *n (language)* チェコ語 [chekogo], *(person)* チェコ人 [chekojin]; **Czech Republic** *n* チェコ共和国 [cheko kyouwakoku]

d

dad [dæd] *n* パパ [papa]

daddy ['dædɪ] *n* パパ [papa]

daffodil ['dæfədɪl] *n* ラッパズイセン [rappazuisen]

daft [dɑːft] *adj* ばかな [baka na]

daily ['deɪlɪ] *adj* 毎日の [mainichi no] ▷ *adv* 毎日 [mainichi]

dairy ['dɛərɪ] *n* 乳製品販売店 [nyuuseihin hanbaiten]; **dairy produce** *n* 乳製品 [nyuuseihin]; **dairy products** *npl* 乳製品 [nyuuseihin]

daisy ['deɪzɪ] *n* ヒナギク [hinagiku]

dam [dæm] *n* ダム [damu]

damage ['dæmɪdʒ] *n* 損傷 [sonshou] ▷ *v* 損傷する [sonshou suru]

damaged ['dæmɪdʒd] *adj* **My luggage has been damaged** 私の手荷物が破損しています [watashi no tenimotsu ga hason shite imasu]; **My suitcase has arrived damaged** 着いた私のスーツケースが破損しています [tsuita watashi no suutsukeesu ga hason shite imasu]

damn [dæm] *adj* いまいましい [imaimashii]

damp [dæmp] *adj* 湿気のある [shikke no aru]

dance [dɑːns] n ダンス [dansu] ▷ v 踊る [odoru]; **Would you like to dance?** ダンスはいかがですか? [dansu wa ikaga desu ka?]

dancer ['dɑːnsə] n ダンサー [dansaa]

dancing ['dɑːnsɪŋ] n 踊ること [odoru koto]; **ballroom dancing** n 社交ダンス [shakou dansu]

dandelion ['dændɪ,laɪən] n タンポポ [tanpopo]

dandruff ['dændrəf] n ふけ [fuke]

Dane [deɪn] n デンマーク人 [denmaakujin]

danger ['deɪndʒə] n 危険 [kiken]; **Is there a danger of avalanches?** なだれの危険はありますか? [nadare no kiken wa arimasu ka?]

dangerous ['deɪndʒərəs] adj 危険な [kiken na]

Danish ['deɪnɪʃ] adj デンマークの [denmaaku no] ▷ n (language) デンマーク語 [denmaakugo]

dare [dɛə] v 思い切って···する [omoikitte...suru]

daring ['dɛərɪŋ] adj 思い切った [omoikitta]

dark [dɑːk] adj 暗い [kurai] ▷ n 闇 [yami]; **It's dark** 暗いです [kurai desu]

darkness ['dɑːknɪs] n 暗さ [kurasa]

darling ['dɑːlɪŋ] n いとしい人 [itoshii hito]

darts [dɑːts] npl ダーツ [daatsu]

dash [dæʃ] v 突進する [tosshin suru]

dashboard ['dæʃ,bɔːd] n ダッシュボード [dasshuboodo]

dashcam ['dæʃkæm] n 車載カメラ [shasai kamera]

data ['deɪtə; 'dɑːtə] npl データ [deeta]

database ['deɪtə,beɪs] n データベース [deetabeesu]

date [deɪt] n 日付 [hiduke]; **best-before date** n 賞味期限 [shoumikigen]; **expiry date** n 使用期限 [shiyou kigen]; **sell-by date** n 販売期限 [hanbai kigen]

daughter ['dɔːtə] n 娘 [musume]; **My daughter is lost** 娘の姿が見当たりません [musume no sugata ga miatarimasen]; **My daughter is missing** 私の娘が行方不明です [watashi no musume ga yukue-fumei desu]

daughter-in-law ['dɔːtə ɪn lɔː] (daughters-in-law) n 息子の妻 [musuko no tsuma]

dawn [dɔːn] n 夜明け [yoake]

day [deɪ] n 一日 [tsuitachi]; **day return** n 日帰り往復割引切符 [higaeri oufuku waribiki kippu]; **Valentine's Day** n 聖バレンタインの祭日 [sei barentain no saijitsu]

daytime ['deɪ,taɪm] n 昼間 [hiruma]

dead [dɛd] adj 死んだ [shinda]; **dead end** n 行き止まり [ikidomari]

deadline ['dɛd,laɪn] n 締切り期限 [shimekiri kigen]

deaf [dɛf] adj 耳の聞こえない [mimi no kikoenai]

deafening ['dɛfᵊnɪŋ] adj 耳を聾するような [mimi-o rousuru you na]

deal [diːl] n 取引 [torihiki]

dealer ['diːlə] n ディーラー [diiraa]; **drug dealer** n 麻薬ディーラー [mayaku diiraa]

deal with [diːl wɪð] v 扱う [atsukau]

dear [dɪə] adj (expensive) 高価な [kouka na], (loved) 親愛な [shin'ai na]

death [dɛθ] n 死 [shi]

debate [dɪˈbeɪt] n 討論 [touron] ▷ v 討論する [touron suru]

debit ['dɛbɪt] n 借方 [karikata] ▷ v 借方に記入する [karikata ni kinyuu suru]; **debit card** n デビットカード [debitto kaado]; **direct debit** n 口座引き落とし [kouza hikiotoshi]

debt [dɛt] n 借金 [shakkin]

decade ['dɛkeɪd; dɪˈkeɪd] n 十年間 [juunenkan]

decaffeinated [dɪˈkæfɪ,neɪtɪd] adj カフェイン抜きの [kafein nuki no]; **decaffeinated coffee** n カフェイン抜きのコーヒー [kafein nuki no koohii]

decay [dɪˈkeɪ] v 衰える [otoroeru]

deceive [dɪˈsiːv] v だます [damasu]

December [dɪˈsɛmbə] n 十二月

[juunigatsu]; **on Friday the thirty first of December** 十二月三十一日の金曜日に [juuni-gatsu sanjuuichi-nichi no kinyoubi ni]

decent ['di:sᵊnt] *adj* きちんとした [kichin to shita]

decide [dɪˈsaɪd] *v* 決定する [kettei suru]

decimal ['dɛsɪməl] *adj* 十進法の [jusshinhou no]

decision [dɪˈsɪʒən] *n* 決定 [kettei]

decisive [dɪˈsaɪsɪv] *adj* 決定的な [ketteiteki na]

deck [dɛk] *n* デッキ [dekki]; **Can we go out on deck?** デッキに出られますか? [dekki ni deraremasu ka?]; **How do I get to the car deck?** カーデッキへはどう行けばいいのですか? [kaa-dekki e wa dou ikeba ii no desu ka?]

deckchair ['dɛk.tʃɛə] *n* デッキチェア [dekkichea]

declare [dɪˈklɛə] *v* 断言する [dangen suru]

decorate ['dɛkəˌreɪt] *v* 装飾する [soushoku suru]

decorator ['dɛkəˌreɪtə] *n* 室内装飾家 [shitsunai soushokuka]

decrease *n* ['di:kri:s] 減少 [genshou] ▷ *v* [dɪˈkri:s] 減少する [genshou suru]

dedicated ['dɛdɪˌkeɪtɪd] *adj* 専用の [sen'you no]

dedication [ˌdɛdɪˈkeɪʃən] *n* 献身 [kenshin]

deduct [dɪˈdʌkt] *v* 差し引く [sashihiku]

deep [di:p] *adj* 深い [fukai]

deep-fry [di:pˈfraɪ] *v* 油で揚げる [abura de ageru]

deeply ['di:plɪ] *adv* 深く [fukaku]

deer [dɪə] *n* シカ [shika]

defeat [dɪˈfi:t] *n* 負け [make] ▷ *v* 負かす [makasu]

defect [dɪˈfɛkt] *n* 欠陥 [kekkan]

defence [dɪˈfɛns] *n* 防御 [bougyo]

defend [dɪˈfɛnd] *v* 防御する [bougyo suru]

defendant [dɪˈfɛndənt] *n* 被告人 [hikokunin]

defender [dɪˈfɛndə] *n* 防御者 [bougyosha]

deficit ['dɛfɪsɪt; dɪˈfɪsɪt] *n* 欠損 [kesson]

define [dɪˈfaɪn] *v* 定義する [teigi suru]

definite ['dɛfɪnɪt] *adj* 明確な [meikaku na]

definitely ['dɛfɪnɪtlɪ] *adv* 明確に [meikaku ni]

definition [ˌdɛfɪˈnɪʃən] *n* 定義 [teigi]

degree [dɪˈgri:] *n* 程度 [teido]; **degree centigrade** *n* 摂氏温度 [sesshi ondo]; **degree Celsius** *n* 摂氏温度 [sesshi ondo]; **degree Fahrenheit** *n* 華氏温度 [kashi ondo]

dehydrated [di:ˈhaɪdreɪtɪd] *adj* 乾燥の [kansou no]

de-icer [di:ˈaɪsə] *n* 除氷装置 [johyou souchi]

delay [dɪˈleɪ] *n* 遅れ [okure] ▷ *v* 遅れる [okureru]

delayed [dɪˈleɪd] *adj* 遅れた [okureta]

delegate *n* ['dɛlɪˌgeɪt] 代表 [daihyou] ▷ *v* ['dɛlɪˌgeɪt] 代表として派遣する [daihyou toshite haken suru]

delete [dɪˈli:t] *v* 削除する [sakujo suru]

deliberate [dɪˈlɪbərɪt] *adj* 故意の [koi no]

deliberately [dɪˈlɪbərətlɪ] *adv* 故意に [koi ni]

delicate ['dɛlɪkɪt] *adj* 優美な [yuubi na]

delicatessen [ˌdɛlɪkəˈtɛsᵊn] *n* デリカテッセン [derikatessen]

delicious [dɪˈlɪʃəs] *adj* 美味しい [oishii]

delight [dɪˈlaɪt] *n* 大喜び [ooyorokobi]

delighted [dɪˈlaɪtɪd] *adj* 大喜びの [ooyorokobi no]

delightful [dɪˈlaɪtfʊl] *adj* 楽しい [tanoshii]

deliver [dɪˈlɪvə] *v* 配達する [haitatsu suru]

delivery [dɪˈlɪvərɪ] *n* 配達 [haitatsu]; **recorded delivery** *n* 簡易書留 [kan-i kakitome]

demand [dɪˈmɑ:nd] *n* 要求 [youkyuu] ▷ *v* 要求する [youkyuu suru]

demanding [dɪˈmɑ:ndɪŋ] *adj* 要求の厳しい [youkyuu no kibishii]

demo, demos ['dɛməʊ, 'di:mɒs] n
デモ [demo]

democracy [dɪ'mɒkrəsɪ] n 民主主義
[minshushugi]

democratic [,dɛmə'krætɪk] adj 民主主
義の [minshu shugi no]

demolish [dɪ'mɒlɪʃ] v 取り壊す
[torikowasu]

demonstrate ['dɛmən,streɪt] v 立証す
る [risshou suru]

demonstration [,dɛmən'streɪʃən] n
デモ [demo]

demonstrator ['dɛmən,streɪtə] n デモ
ンストレーター [demonsutoreetaa]

denim ['dɛnɪm] n デニム [denimu]

Denmark ['dɛnmɑːk] n デンマーク
[denmaaku]

dense [dɛns] adj 密集した [misshuu shita]

density ['dɛnsɪtɪ] n 密集 [misshuu]

dent [dɛnt] n へこみ [hekomi] ▷ v へこむ
[hekomu]

dental ['dɛntəl] adj 歯の [ha no]; **dental
floss** n デンタルフロス [dentaru furosu]

dentist ['dɛntɪst] n 歯科医 [shikai]

dentures ['dɛntʃəz] npl 入れ歯 [ireba];
Can you repair my dentures?
私の入れ歯を修理してもらえますか?
[watashi no ireba o shuuri shite
moraemasu ka?]

deny [dɪ'naɪ] v 否定する [hitei suru]

deodorant [diː'əʊdərənt] n デオドラン
ト [deodoranto]

depart [dɪ'pɑːt] v 出発する [shuppatsu
suru]

department [dɪ'pɑːtmənt] n 部門
[bumon]; **accident & emergency
department** n 救急病棟
[kyuukyuubyoutou]; **department store**
n デパート [depaato]

departure [dɪ'pɑːtʃə] n 出発
[shuppatsu]; **departure lounge** n 出発ラ
ウンジ [shuppatsu raunji]

depend [dɪ'pɛnd] v あてにする [ate ni
suru]

deport [dɪ'pɔːt] v 国外退去させる
[kokugai taikyo saseru]

deposit [dɪ'pɒzɪt] n 預金 [yokin]

depressed [dɪ'prɛst] adj 意気消沈した
[ikishouchin shita]

depressing [dɪ'prɛsɪŋ] adj 憂鬱な
[yuuutsu na]

depression [dɪ'prɛʃən] n 憂鬱 [yuuutsu]

depth [dɛpθ] n 深さ [fukasa]

descend [dɪ'sɛnd] v 降りる [oriru]

describe [dɪ'skraɪb] v 記述する [kijutsu
suru]

description [dɪ'skrɪpʃən] n 記述 [kijutsu]

desert ['dɛzət] n 砂漠 [sabaku]; **desert
island** n 無人島 [mujintou]

deserve [dɪ'zɜːv] v ・・・に値する [...ni atai
suru]

design [dɪ'zaɪn] n デザイン [dezain] ▷ v
デザインする [dezain suru]

designer [dɪ'zaɪnə] n デザイナー
[dezainaa]; **interior designer** n インテリ
アデザイナー [interiadezainaa]

desire [dɪ'zaɪə] n 希望 [kibou] ▷ v 希望す
る [kibou suru]

desk [dɛsk] n 机 [tsukue]; **enquiry desk**
n 照会デスク [shoukai desuku]; **May I use
your desk?** あなたの机をお借りできま
すか? [anata no tsukue o o-kari dekimasu
ka?]

despair [dɪ'spɛə] n 絶望 [zetsubou]

desperate ['dɛspərɪt; -prɪt] adj 必死の
[hisshi no]

desperately ['dɛspərɪtlɪ] adv 必死で
[hisshi de]

despise [dɪ'spaɪz] v 軽蔑する [keibetsu
suru]

despite [dɪ'spaɪt] prep ・・・にもかかわら
ず [...nimokakawarazu]

dessert [dɪ'zɜːt] n デザート [dezaato];
dessert spoon n デザートスプーン
[dezaato supuun]; **The dessert menu,
please** デザートのメニューをください
[dezaato no menyuu o kudasai]; **We'd like
a dessert** 私たちはデザートをいただき
ます [watashi-tachi wa dezaato o
itadakimasu]

destination [,dɛstɪ'neɪʃən] n 目的地
[mokutekichi]

destiny ['dɛstɪnɪ] n 運命 [unmei]

destroy [dɪ'strɔɪ] v 破壊する [hakai suru]

destruction [dɪ'strʌkʃən] n 破壊 [hakai]

detail ['di:teɪl] n 細部 [saibu]

detailed ['di:teɪld] adj 詳細な [shousai na]

detective [dɪ'tɛktɪv] n 刑事 [keiji]

detention [dɪ'tɛnʃən] n 拘留 [kouryuu]

detergent [dɪ'tɜ:dʒənt] n 洗剤 [senzai]

deteriorate [dɪ'tɪərɪəˌreɪt] v 悪化する [akka suru]

determined [dɪ'tɜ:mɪnd] adj 断固とした [dan ko to shita]

detour ['di:tʊə] n 回り道 [mawarimichi]

devaluation [di:ˌvælju:'eɪʃən] n 平価切下げ [heikakirisage]

devastated ['dɛvəˌsteɪtɪd] adj 打ちのめされた [uchinomesareta]

devastating ['dɛvəˌsteɪtɪŋ] adj さんざんな [sanzan na]

develop [dɪ'vɛləp] vi 発展する [hatten suru] ▷ vt 発展させる [hatten saseru]; **developing country** n 発展途上国 [hattentojoukoku]

development [dɪ'vɛləpmənt] n 発展 [hatten]

device [dɪ'vaɪs] n 装置 [souchi]

devil ['dɛvəl] n 悪魔 [akuma]

devise [dɪ'vaɪz] v 考案する [kouan suru]

devoted [dɪ'vəʊtɪd] adj 献身的な [kenshinteki na]

diabetes [ˌdaɪə'bi:tɪs; -ti:z] n 糖尿病 [tounyoubyou]

diabetic [ˌdaɪə'bɛtɪk] adj 糖尿病の [tounyoubyou no] ▷ n 糖尿病患者 [tounyoubyoukanja]

diagnosis [ˌdaɪəg'nəʊsɪs] n 診断 [shindan]

diagonal [daɪ'ægənəl] adj 対角の [taikaku no]

diagram ['daɪəˌgræm] n 図 [zu]

dial ['daɪəl; daɪl] v ダイヤルする [daiyaru suru]; **dialling code** n 局番 [kyokuban]; **dialling tone** n 発信音 [hasshin-on]

dialect ['daɪəˌlɛkt] n 方言 [hougen]

dialogue ['daɪəˌlɒg] n 対話 [taiwa]

diameter [daɪ'æmɪtə] n 直径 [chokkei]

diamond ['daɪəmənd] n ダイヤモンド [daiyamondo]

diarrhoea [ˌdaɪə'rɪə] n 下痢 [geri]; I **have diarrhoea** 私は下痢しています [watashi wa geri shite imasu]

diary ['daɪərɪ] n 日記 [nikki]

dice, die [daɪs, daɪ] npl さいころ [saikoro]

dictation [dɪk'teɪʃən] n 口述 [koujutsu]

dictator [dɪk'teɪtə] n 独裁者 [dokusaisha]

dictionary ['dɪkʃənərɪ; -ʃənrɪ] n 辞書 [jisho]

die [daɪ] v 死ぬ [shinu]

diesel ['di:zəl] n ディーゼルエンジン [diizeruenjin]

diet ['daɪət] n 日常の食べ物 [nitchijou no tabemono] ▷ v ダイエットする [daietto suru]

difference ['dɪfərəns; 'dɪfrəns] n 違い [chigai]

different ['dɪfərənt; 'dɪfrənt] adj 違う [chigau]

difficult ['dɪfɪkəlt] adj 難しい [muzukashii]

difficulty ['dɪfɪkəltɪ] n 困難 [konnan]

dig [dɪg] v 掘る [horu]

digest [dɪ'dʒɛst; daɪ-] v 消化する [shouka suru]

digestion [dɪ'dʒɛstʃən; daɪ-] n 消化 [shouka]

digger ['dɪgə] n 掘削機 [kussakuki]

digital ['dɪdʒɪtəl] adj デジタルの [dejitaru no]; **digital camera** n デジタルカメラ [dejitaru kamera]; **digital radio** n デジタルラジオ [dejitaru rajio]; **digital television** n デジタルテレビ [dejitaru terebi]; **digital watch** n デジタル時計 [dejitaru tokei]

dignity ['dɪgnɪtɪ] n 威厳 [igen]

dilemma [dɪ'lɛmə; daɪ-] n ジレンマ [jirenma]

dilute [daɪ'lu:t] v 希釈する [kishaku suru]

diluted [daɪ'lu:tɪd] adj 希釈した [kishaku shita]

dim [dɪm] *adj* 薄暗い [usugurai]

dimension [dɪˈmɛnʃən] *n* 寸法 [sunpou]

diminish [dɪˈmɪnɪʃ] *v* 減らす [herasu]

din [dɪn] *n* やかましい音 [yakamashii oto]

diner [ˈdaɪnə] *n* 食事する人 [shokuji suru hito]

dinghy [ˈdɪŋɪ] *n* ディンギー [deingii]

dinner [ˈdɪnə] *n* ディナー [deinaa]; **dinner jacket** *n* ディナージャケット [dinaa jaketto]; **dinner party** *n* ディナーパーティー [dinaa paatii]; **dinner time** *n* ディナーの時刻 [dinaa no jikoku]

dinosaur [ˈdaɪnəˌsɔː] *n* 恐竜 [kyouryuu]

dip [dɪp] *n* (food/sauce) ディップソース [dippu sousu] ▷ *v* ちょっと浸す [chotto hitasu]

diploma [dɪˈpləʊmə] *n* 免状 [menjou]

diplomat [ˈdɪpləˌmæt] *n* 外交官 [gaikoukan]

diplomatic [ˌdɪpləˈmætɪk] *adj* 外交上の [gaikoujou no]

dipstick [ˈdɪpˌstɪk] *n* ディップスティック [dippu sutikku]

direct [dɪˈrɛkt; daɪ-] *adj* 率直な [sotchoku na] ▷ *v* 監督する [kantoku suru]; **direct debit** *n* 口座引き落とし [kouza hikiotoshi]

direction [dɪˈrɛkʃən; daɪ-] *n* 方向 [houkou]

directions [dɪˈrɛkʃənz; daɪ-] *npl* 指示 [shiji]

directly [dɪˈrɛktlɪ; daɪ-] *adv* 直接に [chokusetsu ni]

director [dɪˈrɛktə; daɪ-] *n* 管理者 [kanrisha]; **managing director** *n* 社長 [shachou]

directory [dɪˈrɛktərɪ; -trɪ; daɪ-] *n* 住所氏名録 [juusho shimei roku]; **directory enquiries** *npl* 番号案内サービス [bangou annai saabisu]; **telephone directory** *n* 電話帳 [denwachou]

dirt [dɜːt] *n* 汚物 [obutsu]

dirty [ˈdɜːtɪ] *adj* 汚れた [yogoreta]

disability [ˌdɪsəˈbɪlɪtɪ] *n* 身体障害 [shintaishougai]

disabled [dɪˈseɪbəld] *adj* 体の不自由な [karada no fujiyuu na]; **disabled people** 身体障害者 [shintaishougaisha]; **Are there any toilets for disabled people?** 身体障害者用のトイレはありますか? [shintai-shougaisha-you no toire wa arimasu ka?]; **Do you provide access for disabled people?** 身体障害者のためのスロープなどがありますか? [shintai-shougaisha no tame no suroopu nado ga arimasu ka?]; **Is there a reduction for disabled people?** 身体障害者用の割引がありますか? [shintai-shougaisha-you no waribiki ga arimasu ka?]; **What facilities do you have for disabled people?** 身体障害者用のどんな設備をそなえていますか? [shintai-shougaisha-you no donna setsubi o sonaete imasu ka?]

disadvantage [ˌdɪsədˈvɑːntɪdʒ] *n* 不利 [furi]

disagree [ˌdɪsəˈɡriː] *v* 意見が異なる [iken ga kotonaru]

disagreement [ˌdɪsəˈɡriːmənt] *n* 意見の相違 [iken no soui]

disappear [ˌdɪsəˈpɪə] *v* 見えなくなる [mienaku naru]

disappearance [ˌdɪsəˈpɪərəns] *n* 見えなくなること [mienaku naru koto]

disappoint [ˌdɪsəˈpɔɪnt] *v* 失望させる [shitsubou saseru]

disappointed [ˌdɪsəˈpɔɪntɪd] *adj* 失望した [shitsubou shita]

disappointing [ˌdɪsəˈpɔɪntɪŋ] *adj* がっかりさせる [gakkari saseru]

disappointment [ˌdɪsəˈpɔɪntmənt] *n* 失望 [shitsubou]

disaster [dɪˈzɑːstə] *n* 災害 [saigai]

disastrous [dɪˈzɑːstrəs] *adj* 大災害の [daisaigai no]

disc [dɪsk] *n* ディスク [disuku]; **compact disc** *n* コンパクトディスク [konpakuto disuku]; **disc jockey** *n* ディスクジョッキー [disukujokkii]; **slipped disc** *n* 椎間板ヘルニア [tsuikanban herunia]

discharge [dɪsˈtʃɑːdʒ] *v* **When will I be discharged?** 私はいつ退院できますか?

[watashi wa itsu taiin dekimasu ka?]

discipline ['dɪsɪplɪn] n 規律 [kiritsu]

disclose [dɪs'kləʊz] v 明らかにする [akiraka ni suru]

disco ['dɪskəʊ] n ディスコ [disuko]

disconnect [ˌdɪskə'nɛkt] v 接続を断つ [setsuzoku-o tatsu]

discount ['dɪskaʊnt] n 割引 [waribiki]; **student discount** n 学生割引 [gakusei waribiki]; **Do you offer a discount for cash?** 現金で払うと割引がありますか? [genkin de harau to waribki ga arimasu ka?]

discourage [dɪs'kʌrɪdʒ] v ・・・の勇気を くじく [...no yuuki-o kujiku]

discover [dɪs'kʌvə] v 発見する [hakken suru]

discretion [dɪ'skrɛʃən] n 分別 [bunbetsu]

discrimination [dɪˌskrɪmɪ'neɪʃən] n 差別 [sabetsu]

discuss [dɪ'skʌs] v ・・・を話し合う [...-o hanashiau]

discussion [dɪ'skʌʃən] n 討議 [tougi]

disease [dɪ'ziːz] n 病気 [byouki]; **Alzheimer's disease** n アルツハイマー 病 [arutsuhaimaa byou]

disgraceful [dɪs'greɪsfʊl] adj 不名誉な [fumeiyo na]

disguise [dɪs'gaɪz] v 変装する [hensou suru]

disgusted [dɪs'gʌstɪd] adj むかつく [mukatsuku] (腹が立つ)

disgusting [dɪs'gʌstɪŋ] adj むかむかす る [mukamuka suru] (腹が立つ)

dish [dɪʃ] n (food) 料理 [ryouri], (plate) 皿 [sara]; **dish towel** n 布巾 [fukin]; **satellite dish** n 衛星放送用パラボラア ンテナ [eisei housou you parabora antena]; **soap dish** n 石鹸入れ [sekken ire]; **Can you recommend a local dish?** おすす めの郷土料理はありますか? [osusume no kyoudo-ryouri wa arimasu ka?]; **Do you have any vegetarian dishes?** ベジタリ アン料理はありますか? [bejitarian-ryouri wa arimasu ka?]; **Do you have halal dishes?** ハラール料理はありますか?

[haraaru-ryouri wa arimasu ka?]; **Do you have kosher dishes?** コーシャ料理はあ りますか? [koosha-ryouri wa arimasu ka?]; **How do you cook this dish?** この料理 はどのように作るのですか? [kono ryouri wa dono you ni tsukuru no desu ka?]; **How is this dish served?** この料理はどのよう に出てくるのですか? [kono ryouri wa dono you ni dete kuru no desu ka?]; **What fish dishes do you have?** どんな魚料 理がありますか? [donna sakana-ryouri ga arimasu ka?]; **What is in this dish?** この 料理には何が入っていますか? [kono ryouri ni wa nani ga haitte imasu ka?]; **What is the dish of the day?** 今日のお すすめ料理は何ですか? [kyou no osusume ryouri wa nan desu ka?]; **Which dishes have no meat / fish?** 肉／魚の 入っていない料理はどれですか? [niku / sakana no haitte inai ryouri wa dore desu ka?]

dishcloth ['dɪʃˌklɒθ] n 布巾 [fukin]

dishonest [dɪs'ɒnɪst] adj 不正直な [fushoujiki na]

dishwasher ['dɪʃˌwɒʃə] n 食器洗い機 [shokkiaraiki]

disinfectant [ˌdɪsɪn'fɛktənt] n 消毒剤 [shoudokuzai]

disk [dɪsk] n ディスク [disuku]; **disk drive** n ディスクドライブ [disukudoraibu]

diskette [dɪs'kɛt] n ディスケット [deisuketto]

dislike [dɪs'laɪk] v 嫌う [kirau]

dismal ['dɪzməl] adj 陰気な [inki na]

dismiss [dɪs'mɪs] v 解雇する [kaiko suru]

disobedient [ˌdɪsə'biːdɪənt] adj 不従順 な [fujuujun na]

disobey [ˌdɪsə'beɪ] v ・・・に従わない [...ni shitagawanai]

dispenser [dɪ'spɛnsə] n 調剤師 [chouzaishi]; **cash dispenser** n 現金自動 支払い機 [genkin jidoushiharaiki]

display [dɪ'spleɪ] n 展示 [tenji] ▷ v 展示 する [tenji suru]

disposable [dɪ'spəʊzəbəl] adj 使い捨て の [tsukaisute no]

disqualify [dɪs'kwɒlɪ,faɪ] v ···の資格を取り上げる [...no shikaku-o toriageru]

disrupt [dɪs'rʌpt] v 混乱させる [konran saseru]

dissatisfied [dɪs'sætɪs,faɪd] adj 不満な [fuman na]

dissolve [dɪ'zɒlv] v 溶かす [tokasu]

distance ['dɪstəns] n 距離 [kyori]

distant ['dɪstənt] adj 離れた [hanareta]

distillery [dɪ'stɪləri] n 蒸留所 [jouryuujo]

distinction [dɪ'stɪŋkʃən] n 区別 [kubetsu]

distinctive [dɪ'stɪŋktɪv] adj 特徴的な [tokuchouteki na]

distinguish [dɪ'stɪŋgwɪʃ] v 区別する [kubetsu suru]

distract [dɪ'strækt] v 注意をそらす [chuui-o sorasu]

distribute [dɪ'strɪbju:t] v 配る [kubaru]

distributor [dɪ'strɪbjutə] n 卸売業者 [oroshiuri gyousha]

district ['dɪstrɪkt] n 地区 [chiku]

disturb [dɪ'stɜ:b] v 邪魔をする [jama-o suru]

ditch [dɪtʃ] n 溝 [mizo] ▷ v 捨てる [suteru]

dive [daɪv] n 飛び込み [tobikomi] ▷ v 飛び込む [tobikomu]

diver ['daɪvə] n 潜水夫 [sensuifu]

diversion [daɪ'vɜ:ʃən] n 迂回路 [ukairo]; **Is there a diversion?** 迂回路はありますか? [ukairo wa arimasu ka?]

divide [dɪ'vaɪd] v 分ける [wakeru]

diving ['daɪvɪŋ] n 飛び込み [tobikomi]; **diving board** n 飛込台 [tobikomidai]; **scuba diving** n スキューバダイビング [sukyuubadaibingu]

division [dɪ'vɪʒən] n 分割 [bunkatsu]

divorce [dɪ'vɔ:s] n 離婚 [rikon] ▷ v 離婚する [rikon suru]

divorced [dɪ'vɔ:st] adj 離婚した [rikonshita]

DIY [di: aɪ waɪ] abbr 日曜大工 [nichiyoudaiku]

dizzy ['dɪzɪ] adj めまいがする [memai ga suru]

DJ [di: dʒeɪ] abbr ディスクジョッキー [disukujokkii]

DNA [di: ɛn eɪ] n DNA [dii enu ee]

do [du] v ···をする [...-o suru]

dock [dɒk] n ドック [dokku]

doctor ['dɒktə] n 医者 [isha]; **Call a doctor!** 医者を呼んで! [isha o yonde!]; **I need a doctor** 私はお医者さんに診てもらわなければなりません [watashi wa o-isha-san ni mite morawanakereba narimasen]; **Is there a doctor who speaks English?** 英語を話せるお医者さんはいらっしゃいますか? [eigo o hanaseru o-isha-san wa irasshaimasu ka?]

document ['dɒkjumənt] n 文書 [bunsho]

documentary [,dɒkju'mɛntəri; -trɪ] n ドキュメンタリー [dokyumentarii]

documentation [,dɒkjumen'teɪʃən] n ドキュメンテーション [dokyumenteeshon]

documents [,dɒkjuments] npl ドキュメント [dokyumento]

dodge [dɒdʒ] v さっと身をかわして避ける [satto mi-o kawashite sakeru]

dog [dɒg] n 犬 [inu]; **guide dog** n 盲導犬 [moudouken]; **hot dog** n ホットドック [hottodokku]

dole [dəʊl] n 失業手当 [shitsugyouteate]

doll [dɒl] n 人形 [ningyou]

dollar ['dɒlə] n ドル [doru]; **Do you take dollars?** ドルを使えますか? [doru o tsukaemasu ka?]

dolphin ['dɒlfɪn] n イルカ [iruka]

domestic [də'mɛstɪk] adj 国内の [kokunai no]

Dominican Republic [də'mɪnɪkən rɪ'pʌblɪk] n ドミニカ共和国 [dominika kyouwakoku]

domino ['dɒmɪ,nəʊ] n ドミノ [domino]

dominoes ['dɒmɪ,nəʊz] npl ドミノ [domino]

donate [dəʊ'neɪt] v 寄付する [kifu suru]

done [dʌn] adj 終了した [shuuryou shita]

donkey ['dɒŋkɪ] n ロバ [roba]

donor ['dəʊnə] n ドナー [donaa]

door [dɔ:] n ドア [doa]; **door handle** n ド

アハンドル [doahandoru]; **Keep the door locked** ドアをロックしておいてください [doa o rokku shite oite kudasai]; **The door handle has come off** ドアの取っ手が外れました [doa no totte ga hazuremashita]; **The door won't close** ドアが閉まりません [doa ga shimarimasen]; **The door won't lock** ドアに鍵がかかりません [doa ni kagi ga kakarimasen]; **The door won't open** ドアが開きません [doa ga akimasen]

doorbell ['dɔːˌbɛl] n 玄関の呼び鈴 [genkan no yobisuzu]

doorman, doormen ['dɔːˌmæn; -mən, 'dɔːˌmɛn] n ドアマン [doaman]

doorstep ['dɔːˌstɛp] n 戸口の上がり段 [toguchi no agaridan]

dorm [dɔːm] n **Do you have any single sex dorms?** 男女別々の部屋はありますか? [danjo betsubetsu no heya wa arimasu ka?]

dormitory ['dɔːmɪtərɪ; -trɪ] n 共同寝室 [kyoudoushinshitsu]

dose [dəʊs] n 服用量 [fukuyouryou]

dot [dɒt] n 点 [ten] (符号)

double ['dʌbəl] adj 2倍の [nibai no] ▷ v 2倍にする [nibai ni suru]; **double bass** n コントラバス [kontorabasu]; **double bed** n ダブルベッド [daburubeddo]; **double glazing** n 複層ガラス [fukusou garasu]; **double room** n ダブルルーム [dabururuumu]

doubt [daʊt] n 疑い [utagai] ▷ v 疑う [utagau]

doubtful ['daʊtfʊl] adj 疑わしい [utagawashii]

dough [dəʊ] n パン生地 [pankiji]

doughnut ['dəʊnʌt] n ドーナツ [doonatsu]

do up [dʊ ʌp] v 包む [tsutsumu]

dove [dʌv] n ハト [hato]

do without [dʊ wɪ'ðaʊt] v ···なしで済ます [...nashide sumasu]

down [daʊn] adv 下へ [shita e]

download ['daʊnˌləʊd] n ダウンロード [daunroodo] ▷ v ダウンロードする

[daunroodo suru]; **Can I download photos to here?** ここに写真をダウンロードできますか? [koko ni shashin o daunroodo dekimasu ka?]

downpour ['daʊnˌpɔː] n 土砂降り [doshaburi]

downstairs ['daʊn'stɛəz] adj 階下の [kaika no] ▷ adv 階下へ [kaika-e]

downtown ['daʊn'taʊn] adv 繁華街へ [hankagai-e]

doze [dəʊz] v うたた寝する [utatane suru]

dozen ['dʌzən] n 12個 [juuniko]

doze off [dəʊz ɒf] v まどろむ [madoromu]

drab [dræb] adj さえない [saenai]

draft [drɑːft] n 下書き [shitagaki]

drag [dræg] v 引っ張る [hipparu]

dragon ['drægən] n 竜 [ryuu]

dragonfly ['drægənˌflaɪ] n トンボ [tonbo]

drain [dreɪn] n 排水管 [haisuikan] ▷ v 排水する [haisui suru]; **draining board** n 水切り板 [mizukiriban]; **The drain is blocked** 排水管が詰まっています [haisuikan ga tsumatte imasu]

drainpipe ['dreɪnˌpaɪp] n 排水管 [haisuikan]

drama ['drɑːmə] n 劇 [geki]

dramatic [drə'mætɪk] adj 演劇の [engeki no]

drastic ['dræstɪk] adj 思い切った [omoikitta]; **I don't want anything drastic** 思い切ったスタイルにしたくありません [omoikitta sutairu ni shitaku arimasen]

draught [drɑːft] n 隙間風 [sukimakaze]

draughts [drɑːfts] npl チェッカー [chekkaa]

draw [drɔː] n (lottery) くじ [kuji] (抽選), (tie) 引き分け [hikiwake] (試合) ▷ v (equal with) 引き分ける [hikiwakeru], (sketch) 描く [egaku]

drawback ['drɔːˌbæk] n 欠点 [ketten]

drawer ['drɔːə] n 引き出し [hikidashi]; **The drawer is jammed** 引き出しが動きません [hikidashi ga ugokimasen]

drawers [drɔːz] n **chest of drawers** n 整理だんす [seiridansu]

drawing ['drɔːɪŋ] n 図 [zu]

drawing pin ['drɔːɪŋ pɪn] n **drawing pin** n 画鋲 [gabyou]

dreadful ['drɛdfʊl] adj 恐しい [osoroshii]

dream [driːm] n 夢 [yume] ▷ v 夢を見る [yume o miru]

drench [drɛntʃ] v びしょぬれにする [bishonure ni suru]

dress [drɛs] n ワンピース [wanpiisu] ▷ v 服を着る [fuku o kiru]; **evening dress** n イブニングドレス [ibuningu doresu]; **wedding dress** n ウェディングドレス [uedeingudoresu]; **Can I try on this dress?** このワンピースを試着していいですか? [kono wanpiisu o shichaku shite ii desu ka?]

dressed [drɛst] adj 服を着た [fuku-o kita]

dresser ['drɛsə] n 食器棚 [shokkidana]

dressing ['drɛsɪŋ] n **salad dressing** n サラダドレッシング [saradadoresshingu]

dressing gown ['drɛsɪŋ gaʊn] n **dressing gown** n ドレッシングガウン [doresshingugaun]

dressing table ['drɛsɪŋ 'teɪbəl] n **dressing table** n 鏡台 [kyoudai]

dress up [drɛs ʌp] v 盛装する [seisou suru]

dried [draɪd] adj 乾燥させた [kansou saseta]

drift [drɪft] n 押し流されるもの [oshinagasareru mono] ▷ v 漂流する [hyouryuu suru]

drill [drɪl] n ドリル [doriru] ▷ v 穴をあける [ana-o akeru]; **pneumatic drill** n 空気ドリル [kuukidoriru]

drink [drɪŋk] n 飲み物 [nomimono] ▷ v 飲む [nomu]; **binge drinking** n 飲み騒ぐこと [nomisawagu koto]; **drinking water** n 飲料水 [inryousui]; **soft drink** n ソフトドリンク [sofutodorinku]; **Can I get you a drink?** お飲み物を持ってきましょうか? [o-nomimono o motte kimashou ka?];

The drinks are on me 飲み物は私のおごりです [nomimono wa watashi no ogori desu]; **What is your favourite drink?** お好きな飲み物は何ですか? [o-suki na nomimono wa nan desu ka?]; **Would you like a drink?** お飲み物はいかがですか? [o-nomimono wa ikaga desu ka?]

drink-driving ['drɪŋk'draɪvɪŋ] n 飲酒運転 [inshu unten]

drip [drɪp] n したたり [shitatari] ▷ v したたる [shitataru]

drive [draɪv] n ドライブ [doraibu] ▷ v 運転する [unten suru]; **driving instructor** n 自動車教習指導員 [jidousha kyoushuu shidouin]; **four-wheel drive** n 四輪駆動 [yonrinkudou]; **left-hand drive** n 左側通行 [hidarigawa tsuukou]; **right-hand drive** n 右ハンドル [migi handoru]

driver ['draɪvə] n 運転手 [untenshu]; **learner driver** n 仮免許運転者 [karimenkyo untensha]; **lorry driver** n トラック運転手 [torakku untenshu]; **racing driver** n レーシングドライバー [reeshingudoraibaa]; **truck driver** n トラック運転手 [torakku untenshu]

driveway ['draɪvweɪ] n 車道 [shadou]

driving lesson ['draɪvɪŋ 'lɛsən] n 自動車教習 [jidoushakyoushuu]

driving licence ['draɪvɪŋ 'laɪsəns] n 運転免許証 [untenmenkyoshou]; **Here is my driving licence** 私の運転免許証です [watashi no unten-menkyoshou desu]; **I don't have my driving licence on me** 私は運転免許証を携帯していません [watashi wa unten-menkyoshou o keitai shite imasen]; **My driving licence number is...** 私の運転免許証番号は・・・です [watashi no unten-menkyoshou bangou wa ... desu]

driving test ['draɪvɪŋ 'tɛst] n **driving test** n 運転免許試験 [untenmenkyoshiken]

drizzle ['drɪzəl] n 霧雨 [kirisame]

drop [drɒp] n しずく [shizuku] ▷ v 落ちる [ochiru]; **eye drops** npl 目薬 [megusuri]

drought [draʊt] *n* 日照り [hideri]

drown [draʊn] *v* 溺死する [dekishi suru]

drowsy ['draʊzɪ] *adj* 眠い [nemui]

drug [drʌg] *n* 薬 [kusuri]; **drug addict** *n* 麻薬常用者 [mayaku jouyousha]; **drug dealer** *n* 麻薬ディーラー [mayaku diiraa]

drum [drʌm] *n* ドラム [doramu]

drummer ['drʌmə] *n* ドラマー [doramaa]

drunk [drʌŋk] *adj* 酔った [yotta] ▷ *n* 酔っぱらい [yopparai]

dry [draɪ] *adj* 乾燥した [kansou shita] ▷ *v* 乾燥させる [kansou saseru]; **bone dry** *adj* ひからびた [hikarabita]

dry-cleaner's ['draɪ'kliːnəz] *n* ドライクリーニング屋 [doraikuriininguya]

dry-cleaning ['draɪ'kliːnɪŋ] *n* ドライクリーニング [doraikuriiningu]

dryer ['draɪə] *n* 乾燥機 [kansouki]; **spin dryer** *n* 脱水機 [dassuiki]; **tumble dryer** *n* 回転式乾燥機 [kaitenshiki kansouki]

dual ['djuːəl] *adj* **dual carriageway** *n* 中央分離帯付き道路 [chuuou bunritai tsuki douro]

dubbed [dʌbt] *adj* ・・・とあだ名をつけられた [...to adana-o tsukerareta]

dubious ['djuːbɪəs] *adj* 怪しげな [ayashige na]

duck [dʌk] *n* アヒル [ahiru]

due [djuː] *adj* ・・・する予定で [...suru yotei de]

due to [djuː tʊ] *prep* ・・・のために [...no tame ni] (原因)

dull [dʌl] *adj* 面白くない [omoshirokunai]

dummy ['dʌmɪ] *n* マネキン [manekin]

dump [dʌmp] *n* ごみ捨て場 [gomi suteba] ▷ *v* 投げ捨てる [nagesuteru]; **rubbish dump** *n* ごみ捨て場 [gomi suteba]

dumpling ['dʌmplɪŋ] *n* ダンプリング [danpuringu]

dune [djuːn] *n* **sand dune** *n* 砂丘 [sakyuu]

dungarees [ˌdʌŋɡə'riːz] *npl* ダンガリーのオーバーオール [dangarii no oobaaooru]

dungeon ['dʌndʒən] *n* 地下牢 [chikarou]

duration [djʊ'reɪʃən] *n* 持続期間 [jizoku kikan]

during ['djʊərɪŋ] *prep* ・・・の間中ずっと [...no aidajuu zutto]

dusk [dʌsk] *n* 夕暮れ [yuugure]

dust [dʌst] *n* ほこり [hokori] (ごみ) ▷ *v* ほこりを払う [hokori-o harau]

dustbin ['dʌstˌbɪn] *n* ごみ箱 [gomibako]

dustman, dustmen ['dʌstmən, 'dʌstmen] *n* ごみ収集人 [gomishuushuunin]

dustpan ['dʌstˌpæn] *n* ちり取り [chiritori]

dusty ['dʌstɪ] *adj* ほこりっぽい [hokorippoi]

Dutch [dʌtʃ] *adj* オランダの [oranda no] ▷ *n* オランダ人 [orandajin]; *(language)* オランダ語 [orandago]

Dutchman, Dutchmen ['dʌtʃmən, 'dʌtʃmen] *n* オランダ人男性 [orandajin dansei]

Dutchwoman, Dutchwomen [ˌdʌtʃwʊmən, 'dʌtʃwɪmɪn] *n* オランダ人女性 [orandajin josei]

duty ['djuːtɪ] *n* 任務 [ninmu]; **(customs) duty** *n* 関税 [kanzei]

duty-free ['djuːtɪ'friː] *adj* 免税の [menzei no] ▷ *n* 免税品 [menzeihin]

duvet ['duːveɪ] *n* キルトの掛け布団 [kiruto no kakebuton]

DVD [diː viː diː] *n* DVD [dii bui dii]; **DVD burner** *n* DVDバーナー [diibuidii baanaa]; **DVD player** *n* DVDプレーヤー [diibuidii pureiyaa]

dye [daɪ] *n* 染料 [senryou] ▷ *v* 染める [someru]

dynamic [daɪ'næmɪk] *adj* 活動的な [katsudouteki na]

dyslexia [dɪs'lɛksɪə] *n* 失読症 [shitsudokushou]

dyslexic [dɪs'lɛksɪk] *adj* 失読症の [shitsudokushou no] ▷ *n* 失読症の人 [shitsudokushou no hito]

e

each [iːtʃ] *adj* それぞれの [sorezore no] ▷ *pron* それぞれ [sorezore]

eagle [ˈiːgəl] *n* ワシ [washi]

ear [ɪə] *n* 耳 [mimi]

earache [ˈɪərˌeɪk] *n* 耳の痛み [mimi no itami]

eardrum [ˈɪəˌdrʌm] *n* 鼓膜 [komaku]

earlier [ˈɜːlɪə] *adv* 前に [mae ni]

early [ˈɜːlɪ] *adj* 早い [hayai] ▷ *adv* 早く [hayaku]; **We arrived early/late** 私たちは早く／遅く着きました [watashi-tachi wa hayaku / osoku tsukimashita]

earn [ɜːn] *v* 稼ぐ [kasegu]

earnings [ˈɜːnɪŋz] *npl* 所得 [shotoku]

earphones [ˈɪəˌfəʊnz] *npl* イヤホン [iyahon]

earplugs [ˈɪəˌplʌgz] *npl* 耳栓 [mimisen]

earring [ˈɪəˌrɪŋ] *n* イヤリング [iyaringu]

earth [ɜːθ] *n* 地球 [chikyuu]

earthquake [ˈɜːθˌkweɪk] *n* 地震 [jishin]

easily [ˈiːzɪlɪ] *adv* 容易に [youi ni]

east [iːst] *adj* 東の [higashi no] ▷ *adv* 東へ [higashi e] ▷ *n* 東 [higashi]; **Far East** *n* 極東 [kyokutou]; **Middle East** *n* 中東 [chuutou]

eastbound [ˈiːstˌbaʊnd] *adj* 東行きの [higashi yuki no]

Easter [ˈiːstə] *n* 復活祭 [fukkatsusai]; **Easter egg** *n* 復活祭の卵 [fukkatsusai no tamago]

eastern [ˈiːstən] *adj* 東の [higashi no]

easy [ˈiːzɪ] *adj* 簡単な [kantan na]; **easy chair** *n* 安楽椅子 [anraku isu]

easy-going [ˈiːzɪˌgəʊɪŋ] *adj* ゆったりとした [yuttarito shita]

eat [iːt] *v* 食べる [taberu]

e-book [ˈiːˈbʊk] *n* 電子書籍 [denshi shoseki]

eccentric [ɪkˈsɛntrɪk] *adj* 風変わりな [fuugawari na]

echo [ˈɛkəʊ] *n* 反響 [hankyou]

ecofriendly [ˈiːkəʊˌfrɛndlɪ] *adj* 環境にやさしい [kankyou ni yasashii]

ecological [ˌiːkəˈlɒdʒɪkəl] *adj* 生態学の [seitaigaku no]

ecology [ɪˈkɒlədʒɪ] *n* 生態学 [seitaigaku]

e-commerce [ˈiːkɒmɜːs] *n* Eコマース [iikomaasu]

economic [ˌiːkəˈnɒmɪk; ˌɛkə-] *adj* 経済の [keizai no]

economical [ˌiːkəˈnɒmɪkəl; ˌɛkə-] *adj* 経済的な [keizaiteki na]

economics [ˌiːkəˈnɒmɪks; ˌɛkə-] *npl* 経済学 [keizaigaku]

economist [ɪˈkɒnəmɪst] *n* 経済学者 [keizaigakusha]

economize [ɪˈkɒnəˌmaɪz] *v* 節約する [setsuyaku suru]

economy [ɪˈkɒnəmɪ] *n* 経済 [keizai]; **economy class** *n* エコノミークラス [ekonomiikurasu]

ecstasy [ˈɛkstəsɪ] *n* エクスタシー [ekusutashii]

Ecuador [ˈɛkwəˌdɔː] *n* エクアドル [ekuadoru]

eczema [ˈɛksɪmə; ɪgˈziːmə] *n* 湿疹 [shisshin]

edge [ɛdʒ] *n* 端 [hashi]

edgy [ˈɛdʒɪ] *adj* いらいらした [irairashita]

edible [ˈɛdɪbəl] *adj* 食べられる [taberareru]

edition [ɪˈdɪʃən] *n* 版 [han]

editor ['ɛdɪtə] n 編集者 [henshuusha]

educated ['ɛdjʊˌkeɪtɪd] adj 教育のある [kyoiku no aru]

education [ˌɛdjʊ'keɪʃən] n 教育 [kyoiku]; **adult education** n 生涯教育 [shougai kyoiku]; **higher education** n 高等教育 [koutoukyouiku]

educational [ˌɛdjʊ'keɪʃənəl] adj 教育の [kyouiku no]

eel [i:l] n ウナギ [unagi]

effect [ɪ'fɛkt] n 影響 [eikyou]; **side effect** n 副作用 [fukusayou]

effective [ɪ'fɛktɪv] adj 効果的な [koukateki na]

effectively [ɪ'fɛktɪvlɪ] adv 効果的に [koukateki ni]

efficient [ɪ'fɪʃənt] adj 効率的な [kouritsuteki na]

efficiently [ɪ'fɪʃəntlɪ] adv 効率的に [kouritsuteki ni]

effort ['ɛfət] n 努力 [doryoku]

e.g. [i: dʒi:] abbr たとえば [tatoeba]

egg [ɛg] n 卵 [tamago]; **boiled egg** n ゆで卵 [yudetamago]; **egg white** n 卵の白身 [tamago no shiromi]; **egg yolk** n 卵の黄身 [tamago no kimi]; **Easter egg** n 復活祭の卵 [fukkatsusai no tamago]; **scrambled eggs** npl 炒り卵 [iritamago]; **Could you prepare a meal without eggs?** 卵を使わずに食事を用意していただけますか? [tamago o tsukawazu ni shokuji o youi shite itadakemasu ka?]; **I can't eat raw eggs** 私は生卵を食べられません [watashi wa nama-tamago o taberaremasen]

eggcup ['ɛgˌkʌp] n エッグカップ [eggukappu]

Egypt ['i:dʒɪpt] n エジプト [ejiputo]

Egyptian [ɪ'dʒɪpʃən] adj エジプトの [ejiputo no] ▷ n エジプト人 [ejiputojin]

eight [eɪt] number 八 [hachi]

eighteen ['eɪ'ti:n] number 十八 [juuhachi]

eighteenth ['eɪ'ti:nθ] adj 十八番目の [juuhachi banme no]

eighth [eɪtθ] adj 八番目の [hachi banme

no] ▷ n 八番目 [hachibanme]

eighty ['eɪtɪ] number 八十 [hachijuu]

Eire ['ɛərə] n アイルランド [airurando]

either ['aɪðə; 'i:ðə] adv (with negative) ・・・もまた [...momata] (否定) ▷ conj (... or) ・・・かまたは・・・か [...ka matawa ... ka] ▷ pron どちらも [dochiramo]; **either ... or** conj ・・・かまたは・・・か [...ka matawa ... ka]

elastic [ɪ'læstɪk] n 弾性ゴム [dansei gomu]; **elastic band** n 輪ゴム [wagomu]

Elastoplast® [ɪ'læstəˌplɑ:st] n エラストプラスト® [erasutopurasuto]

elbow ['ɛlbəʊ] n ひじ [hiji]

elder ['ɛldə] adj 年上の [toshiue no]

elderly ['ɛldəlɪ] adj 年配の [nenpai no]

eldest ['ɛldɪst] adj 最年長の [sainenchou no]

elect [ɪ'lɛkt] v 選挙する [senkyo suru]

election [ɪ'lɛkʃən] n 選挙 [senkyo]; **general election** n 総選挙 [sousenkyo]

electorate [ɪ'lɛktərɪt] n 選挙人 [senkyonin]

electric [ɪ'lɛktrɪk] adj 電気の [denki no]; **electric blanket** n 電気毛布 [denkimoufu]; **electric shock** n 感電 [kanden]

electrical [ɪ'lɛktrɪkəl] adj 電気に関する [denki ni kansuru]

electrician [ɪlɛk'trɪʃən; ˌi:lɛk-] n 電気技師 [denki gishi]

electricity [ɪlɛk'trɪsɪtɪ; ˌi:lɛk-] n 電気 [denki]; **Do we have to pay extra for electricity?** 電気代は別に払わなければなりませんか? [denki-dai wa betsu ni harawanakereba narimasen ka?]; **Is the cost of electricity included?** 電気代は含まれていますか? [denki-dai wa fukumarete imasu ka?]; **There is no electricity** 電気がきていません [denki ga kite imasen]; **Where is the electricity meter?** 電気のメーターはどこですか? [denki no meetaa wa doko desu ka?]

electronic [ɪlɛk'trɒnɪk; ˌi:lɛk-] adj 電子の [denshi no]

electronics [ɪlɛk'trɒnɪks; ˌiːlɛk-] *npl* 電子工学 [denshikougaku]

elegant ['ɛlɪɡənt] *adj* 優雅な [yuuga na]

element ['ɛlɪmənt] *n* 要素 [youso]

elephant ['ɛlɪfənt] *n* ゾウ [zou]

eleven [ɪ'lɛvᵊn] *number* 十一 [juuichi]

eleventh [ɪ'lɛvᵊnθ] *adj* 十一番目の [juuichi banme no]

eliminate [ɪ'lɪmɪˌneɪt] *v* 除去する [jokyo suru]

elm [ɛlm] *n* ニレ [nire]

else [ɛls] *adj* そのほかに [sono hoka ni]

elsewhere [ˌɛls'wɛə] *adv* どこかよそで [dokoka yoso de]

email ['iːmeɪl] *n* 電子メール [denshi meeru] ▷ *vt (a person)* 電子メールを送る [denshi meeru-o okuru]; **email address** *n* 電子メールアドレス [denshi meeru adoresu]

embankment [ɪm'bæŋkmənt] *n* 堤防 [teibou]

embarrassed [ˌɪm'bærəst] *adj* 当惑した [touwaku shita]

embarrassing [ɪm'bærəsɪŋ;] *adj* 当惑させるような [touwaku saseru you na]

embassy ['ɛmbəsɪ] *n* 大使館 [taishikan]; **I need to call my embassy** 私は大使館に電話をしなければなりません [watashi wa taishikan ni denwa o shinakereba narimasen]

embroider [ɪm'brɔɪdə] *v* 刺繍する [shishuu suru]

embroidery [ɪm'brɔɪdərɪ] *n* 刺繍 [shishuu]

emergency [ɪ'mɜːdʒənsɪ] *n* 緊急事態 [kinkyuujitai]; **accident & emergency department** *n* 救急病棟 [kyuukyuubyoutou]; **emergency exit** *n* 非常口 [hijouguchi]; **emergency landing** *n* 緊急着陸 [kinkyuu chakuriku]; **It's an emergency!** 緊急事態です! [kinkyuu-jitai desu!]

emigrate ['ɛmɪˌɡreɪt] *v* 移住する [ijuu suru]

emoji [ɪ'məʊdʒɪ] *n* 絵文字 [emoji]

emotion [ɪ'məʊʃən] *n* 感情 [kanjou]

emotional [ɪ'məʊʃənᵊl] *adj* 感情の [kanjou no]

emperor, empress ['ɛmpərə, 'ɛmprɪs] *n* 皇帝 [koutei]

emphasize ['ɛmfəˌsaɪz] *v* 強調する [kyouchou suru]

empire ['ɛmpaɪə] *n* 帝国 [teikoku]

employ [ɪm'plɔɪ] *v* 雇用する [koyou suru]

employee [ɛm'plɔɪiː; ˌɛmplɔɪ'iː] *n* 従業員 [juugyouin]

employer [ɪm'plɔɪə] *n* 雇用主 [koyounushi]

employment [ɪm'plɔɪmənt] *n* 雇用 [koyou]

empty ['ɛmptɪ] *adj* 空の [kara no] ▷ *v* 空にする [kara ni suru]

enamel [ɪ'næməl] *n* エナメル [enameru]

encourage [ɪn'kʌrɪdʒ] *v* 勇気づける [yuukizukeru]

encouragement [ɪn'kʌrɪdʒmənt] *n* 奨励 [shourei]

encouraging [ɪn'kʌrɪdʒɪŋ] *adj* 励みになる [hagemi ni naru]

encyclopaedia [ɛnˌsaɪkləʊ'piːdɪə] *n* 百科事典 [hyakka jiten]

end [ɛnd] *n* 終わり [owari] ▷ *v* 終わる [owaru]; **dead end** *n* 行き止まり [ikidomari]; **at the end of June** 六月の終わりに [roku-gatsu no owari ni]

endanger [ɪn'deɪndʒə] *v* 危険にさらす [kiken ni sarasu]

ending ['ɛndɪŋ] *n* 結末 [ketsumatsu]

endless ['ɛndlɪs] *adj* 終わりのない [owari no nai]

enemy ['ɛnəmɪ] *n* 敵 [teki]

energetic [ˌɛnə'dʒɛtɪk] *adj* 精力的な [seiryokuteki na]

energy ['ɛnədʒɪ] *n* 元気 [genki]

engaged [ɪn'ɡeɪdʒd] *adj* 婚約している [konyaku shiteiru]; **engaged tone** *n* 話し中の信号音 [hanashichuu no shingouon]

engagement [ɪn'ɡeɪdʒmənt] *n* 約束 [yakusoku]; **engagement ring** *n* 婚約指輪 [kon'yaku yubiwa]

engine ['ɛndʒɪn] *n* エンジン [enjin]; **search engine** *n* 検索エンジン [kensaku enjin]; **The engine is overheating** エンジンがオーバーヒートしています [enjin ga oobaahiito shite imasu]

engineer [ˌɛndʒɪ'nɪə] n 技師 [gishi]

engineering [ˌɛndʒɪ'nɪərɪŋ] n 工学 [kougaku]

England ['ɪŋɡlənd] n イングランド [ingurando]

English ['ɪŋɡlɪʃ] adj イングランドの [inngurando no] ▷ n 英語 [eigo]; **Do you speak English?** あなたは英語を話しますか? [anata wa eigo o hanashimasu ka?]; **Does anyone speak English?** 誰か英語を話せる人はいますか? [dare ka eigo o hanaseru hito wa imasu ka?]; **I don't speak English** 私は英語を話せません [watashi wa eigo o hanasemasen]; **I speak very little English** 私は英語をほとんど話せません [watashi wa eigo o hotondo hanasemasen]

Englishman, Englishmen ['ɪŋɡlɪʃmən, 'ɪŋɡlɪʃmɛn] n イングランド人男性 [ingurandojin dansei]

Englishwoman, Englishwomen ['ɪŋɡlɪʃwumən, 'ɪŋɡlɪʃwimin] n イングランド人女性 [ingurandojin josei]

engrave [ɪn'ɡreɪv] v 彫る [horu]

enjoy [ɪn'dʒɔɪ] v 楽しむ [tanoshimu]

enjoyable [ɪn'dʒɔɪəbəl] adj 楽しい [tanoshii]

enlargement [ɪn'lɑːdʒmənt] n 拡大 [kakudai]

enormous [ɪ'nɔːməs] adj 巨大な [kyodai na]

enough [ɪ'nʌf] adj 十分な [juubun na] ▷ pron 十分 [juubun] (量・程度)

enquire [ɪn'kwaɪə] v 問い合わせる [toiawaseru]

enquiry [ɪn'kwaɪərɪ] n 問い合わせ [toiawase]; **enquiry desk** n 照会デスク [shoukai desuku]

ensure [ɛn'ʃuə; -'ʃɔː] v 保証する [hoshou suru]

enter ['ɛntə] v 入る [hairu]

entertain [ˌɛntə'teɪn] v 楽しませる [tanoshimaseru]

entertainer [ˌɛntə'teɪnə] n エンターテイナー [entaateinaa]

entertaining [ˌɛntə'teɪnɪŋ] adj 愉快な [yukai na]

entertainment [ˌɛntə'teɪnmənt] n **What entertainment is there?** どんな娯楽がありますか? [donna goraku ga arimasu ka?]

enthusiasm [ɪn'θjuːzɪˌæzəm] n 熱意 [netsui]

enthusiastic [ɪnˌθjuːzɪ'æstɪk] adj 熱心な [nesshin na]

entire [ɪn'taɪə] adj 全体の [zentai no]

entirely [ɪn'taɪəlɪ] adv 全く [mattaku]

entrance ['ɛntrəns] n 入口 [iriguchi]; **entrance fee** n 入場料 [nyuujouryou]; **Where is the wheelchair-accessible entrance?** 車椅子で利用できる入口はどこですか? [kuruma-isu de riyou dekiru iriguchi wa doko desu ka?]

entry ['ɛntrɪ] n 入口 [iriguchi]; **entry phone** n インターホン [intaahon]

envelope ['ɛnvəˌləʊp; 'ɒn-] n 封筒 [fuutou]

envious ['ɛnvɪəs] adj うらやましそうな [urayamashisouna]

environment [ɪn'vaɪrənmənt] n 環境 [kankyou]

environmental [ɪnˌvaɪrən'mɛntəl] adj 環境の [kankyou no]; **environmentally friendly** adj 環境にやさしい [kankyou ni yasashii]

envy ['ɛnvɪ] n ねたみ [netami] ▷ v うらやむ [urayamu]

epidemic [ˌɛpɪ'dɛmɪk] n 流行病 [ryuukoubyou]

epileptic [ˌɛpɪ'lɛptɪk] n 癲癇患者 [tenkan kanja]; **epileptic fit** n 癲癇の発作 [tenkan no hossa]

episode ['ɛpɪˌsəʊd] n エピソード [episoodo]

equal ['iːkwəl] adj 等しい [hitoshii] ▷ v ･･･に等しい [...ni hitoshii]

equality [ɪ'kwɒlɪtɪ] n 平等 [byoudou]

equalize ['iːkwəˌlaɪz] v 等しくする [hitoshiku suru]

equation | 284

equation [ɪˈkweɪʒən; -ʃən] n 等しくすること [hitoshiku suru koto]

equator [ɪˈkweɪtə] n 赤道 [sekidou]

Equatorial Guinea [ˌɛkwəˈtɔːrɪəl ˈɡɪnɪ] n 赤道ギニア [sekidou ginia]

equipment [ɪˈkwɪpmənt] n 装置 [souchi]

equipped [ɪˈkwɪpt] adj 備えた [sonaeta]

equivalent [ɪˈkwɪvələnt] n 同等のもの [doutou no mono]

erase [ɪˈreɪz] v 消す [kesu] (消去)

Eritrea [ˌɛrɪˈtreɪə] n エリトリア [eritoria]

erotic [ɪˈrɒtɪk] adj エロチックな [erochikku na]

error [ˈɛrə] n 間違い [machigai]

escalator [ˈɛskəˌleɪtə] n エスカレーター [esukareetaa]

escape [ɪˈskeɪp] n 逃亡 [toubou] ▷ v 逃げる [nigeru]; **fire escape** n 非常階段 [hijoukaidan]

escort [ɪsˈkɔːt] v 護衛する [goei suru]

especially [ɪˈspɛʃəlɪ] adv 特に [toku ni]

espionage [ˈɛspɪəˌnɑːʒ, ˌɛspɪəˈnɑːʒ, ˈɛspɪənɪdʒ] n スパイ行為 [supai koui]

essay [ˈɛseɪ] n エッセイ [essei]

essential [ɪˈsɛnʃəl] adj 最も重要な [mottomo juuyou na]

estate [ɪˈsteɪt] n 地所 [jisho]; **estate agent** n 不動産屋 [fudousanya]; **estate car** n エステートカー [esuteetokaa]

estimate n [ˈɛstɪmɪt] 見積もり [mitsumori] ▷ v [ˈɛstɪˌmeɪt] 見積もる [mitsumoru]

Estonia [ɛˈstəʊnɪə] n エストニア [esutonia]

Estonian [ɛˈstəʊnɪən] adj エストニアの [esutonia no] ▷ n (language) エストニア語 [esutoniago], (person) エストニア人 [esutoniajin]

etc [ɪt ˈsɛtrə] abbr ・・・など [...nado]

eternal [ɪˈtɜːnəl] adj 永遠の [eien no]

eternity [ɪˈtɜːnɪtɪ] n 永遠性 [eiensei]

ethical [ˈɛθɪkəl] adj 倫理的な [rinriteki na]

Ethiopia [ˌiːθɪˈəʊpɪə] n エチオピア [echiopia]

Ethiopian [ˌiːθɪˈəʊpɪən] adj エチオピアの [echiopia no] ▷ n エチオピア人 [echiopiajin]

ethnic [ˈɛθnɪk] adj 民族の [minzoku no]

e-ticket [ˈiːˈtɪkɪt] n Eチケット [iichiketto]

EU [iː juː] abbr (= European Union) EU [iiyuu]

euro [ˈjʊərəʊ] n ユーロ [yuuro]

Europe [ˈjʊərəp] n ヨーロッパ [yooroppa]

European [ˌjʊərəˈpɪən] adj ヨーロッパの [yooroppa no] ▷ n ヨーロッパ人 [yooroppajin]; **European Union** n 欧州連合 [oushuu rengou]

evacuate [ɪˈvækjʊˌeɪt] v 避難させる [hinan saseru]

eve [iːv] n 前夜 [zenya]

even [ˈiːvən] adj 平らな [taira na] ▷ adv ・・・でさえ [...de sae]

evening [ˈiːvnɪŋ] n 晩 [ban]; **evening class** n 夜間クラス [yakan kurasu]; **evening dress** n イブニングドレス [ibuningu doresu]; **in the evening** 晩に [ban ni]; **The table is booked for nine o'clock this evening** 今晩九時にテーブルを予約しました [konban ku-ji ni teeburu o yoyaku shimashita]; **What are you doing this evening?** 今晩のご予定は? [konban no go-yotei wa?]; **What is there to do in the evenings?** 晩にできることは何がありますか? [ban ni dekiru koto wa nani ga arimasu ka?]

event [ɪˈvɛnt] n 出来事 [dekigoto]

eventful [ɪˈvɛntfʊl] adj 出来事の多い [dekigoto no ooi]

eventually [ɪˈvɛntʃʊəlɪ] adv ついに [tsuini]

ever [ˈɛvə] adv 今までに [ima made ni]

every [ˈɛvrɪ] adj すべての [subete no]

everybody [ˈɛvrɪˌbɒdɪ] pron 誰でも皆 [dare demo mina]

everyone [ˈɛvrɪˌwʌn; -wən] pron 誰でも皆 [dare demo mina]

everything [ˈɛvrɪθɪŋ] pron すべて [subete]

everywhere [ˈɛvrɪˌwɛə] adv どこでも [dokodemo]

evidence [ˈɛvɪdəns] n 証拠 [shouko]

evil ['iːvªl] *adj* 悪い [warui]

evolution [ˌiːvəˈluːʃən] *n* 発展 [hatten]

ewe [juː] *n* 雌羊 [mehitsuji]

exact [ɪgˈzækt] *adj* 正確な [seikaku na]

exactly [ɪgˈzæktlɪ] *adv* 正確に [seikaku ni]

exaggerate [ɪgˈzædʒəˌreɪt] *v* 大げさに言う [oogesa ni iu]

exaggeration [ɪgˈzædʒəˌreɪʃən] *n* 誇張 [kochou]

exam [ɪgˈzæm] *n* 試験 [shiken]

examination [ɪgˌzæmɪˈneɪʃən] *n* (*medical*) 試験 [shiken], (*school*) 試験 [shiken]

examine [ɪgˈzæmɪn] *v* 試験する [shiken suru]

examiner [ɪgˈzæmɪnə] *n* 試験官 [shikenkan]

example [ɪgˈzɑːmpªl] *n* 例 [rei]

excellent ['ɛksələnt] *adj* すばらしい [subarashii]

except [ɪkˈsɛpt] *prep* ···を除いては [...-o nozoite wa]

exception [ɪkˈsɛpʃən] *n* 例外 [reigai]

exceptional [ɪkˈsɛpʃənªl] *adj* 例外的な [reigaiteki na]

excessive [ɪkˈsɛsɪv] *adj* 度を超えた [do-o koeta]

exchange [ɪksˈtʃeɪndʒ] *v* 取り交わす [torikawasu]; **exchange rate** *n* 為替レート [kawase reeto]; **rate of exchange** *n* 為替レート [kawase reeto]; **stock exchange** *n* 証券取引所 [shouken torihikijo]

excited [ɪkˈsaɪtɪd] *adj* 興奮した [koufun shita]

exciting [ɪkˈsaɪtɪŋ] *adj* 興奮させる [koufun saseru]

exclude [ɪkˈskluːd] *v* 除外する [jogai suru]

excluding [ɪkˈskluːdɪŋ] *prep* ···を除いて [...-o nozoite]

exclusively [ɪkˈskluːsɪvlɪ] *adv* もっぱら [moppara]

excuse *n* [ɪkˈskjuːs] 弁解 [benkai] ▷ *v* [ɪkˈskjuːz] 弁解する [benkai suru]

execute ['ɛksɪˌkjuːt] *v* 処刑する [shokei suru]

execution [ˌɛksɪˈkjuːʃən] *n* 処刑 [shokei]

executive [ɪgˈzɛkjʊtɪv] *n* エグゼクティブ [eguzekuteibu]

exercise ['ɛksəˌsaɪz] *n* 運動 [undou] (身体)

exhaust [ɪgˈzɔːst] *n* **The exhaust is broken** エキゾーストが壊れています [ekizoosuto ga kowarete imasu]

exhausted [ɪgˈzɔːstɪd] *adj* 疲れきった [tsukarekitta]

exhibition [ˌɛksɪˈbɪʃən] *n* 展示 [tenji]

ex-husband [ɛksˈhʌzbənd] *n* 先夫 [senpu]

exile ['ɛgzaɪl; 'ɛksaɪl] *n* 追放 [tsuihou]

exist [ɪgˈzɪst] *v* 存在する [sonzai suru]

exit ['ɛgzɪt; 'ɛksɪt] *n* 出口 [deguchi]; **emergency exit** *n* 非常口 [hijouguchi]; **Where is the exit?** 出口はどこですか? [deguchi wa doko desu ka?]; **Which exit for...?** ···へ行く出口はどれですか? [...e iku deguchi wa dore desu ka?]

exotic [ɪgˈzɒtɪk] *adj* エキゾチックな [ekizochikku na]

expect [ɪkˈspɛkt] *v* 期待する [kitai suru]

expedition [ˌɛkspɪˈdɪʃən] *n* 探検 [tanken]

expel [ɪkˈspɛl] *v* 追い出す [oidasu]

expenditure [ɪkˈspɛndɪtʃə] *n* 支出 [shishutsu]

expenses [ɪkˈspɛnsɪz] *npl* 経費 [keihi]

expensive [ɪkˈspɛnsɪv] *adj* 高価な [kouka na]

experience [ɪkˈspɪərɪəns] *n* 経験 [keiken]; **work experience** *n* 労働体験 [roudou taiken]

experienced [ɪkˈspɪərɪənst] *adj* 経験のある [keiken no aru]

experiment [ɪkˈspɛrɪmənt] *n* 実験 [jikken]

expert ['ɛkspɜːt] *n* 専門家 [senmonka]

expire [ɪkˈspaɪə] *v* 期限が切れる [kigen ga kireru]

explain [ɪk'spleɪn] v 説明する [setsumei suru]

explanation [,ɛksplə'neɪʃən] n 説明 [setsumei]

explode [ɪk'spləʊd] v 爆発する [bakuhatsu suru]

exploit [ɪk'splɔɪt] v 利用する [riyou suru]

exploitation [,ɛksplɔɪ'teɪʃən] n 搾取 [sakushu]

explore [ɪk'splɔː] v 調査する [chousa suru]

explorer [ɪk'splɔrə] n 探検家 [tankenka]

explosion [ɪk'spləʊʒən] n 爆発 [bakuhatsu]

explosive [ɪk'spləʊsɪv] n 爆発物 [bakuhatsubutsu]

export n ['ɛkspɔːt] 輸出 [yushutsu] ▷ v [ɪk'spɔːt] 輸出する [yushutsu suru]

express [ɪk'sprɛs] v 表現する [hyougen suru]

expression [ɪk'sprɛʃən] n 表現 [hyougen]

extension [ɪk'stɛnʃən] n 増築 [zouchiku]; **extension cable** n 延長コード [enchoukoodo]

extensive [ɪk'stɛnsɪv] adj 広い [hiroi]

extensively [ɪk'stɛnsɪvlɪ] adv 広く [hiroku]

extent [ɪk'stɛnt] n 広がり [hirogari]

exterior [ɪk'stɪərɪə] adj 外側の [sotogawa no]

external [ɪk'stɜːnᵊl] adj 外部の [gaibu no]

extinct [ɪk'stɪŋkt] adj 絶滅した [zetsumetsu shita]

extinguisher [ɪk'stɪŋgwɪʃə] n 消火器 [shoukaki]

extortionate [ɪk'stɔːʃənɪt] adj 法外な [hougai na]

extra ['ɛkstrə] adj 余分の [yobun no] ▷ adv 余分に [yobun ni]; **Can I have an extra bag, please?** 余分に袋をいただけますか? [yobun ni fukuro o itadakemasu ka?]; **I'd like it with extra..., please** ···を余分につけてお願いします [...o yobun ni tsukete o-negai shimasu]

extraordinary [ɪk'strɔːdᵊnrɪ; -dᵊnərɪ] adj 異常な [ijou na]

extravagant [ɪk'strævɪgənt] adj 金遣いが荒い [kanezukai ga arai]

extreme [ɪk'striːm] adj 極度の [kyokudo no]

extremely [ɪk'striːmlɪ] adv 極度に [kyokudo ni]

extremism [ɪk'striːmɪzəm] n 過激主義 [kageki shugi]

extremist [ɪk'striːmɪst] n 過激派 [kagekiha]

ex-wife [ɛks'waɪf] n 先妻 [sensai]

eye [aɪ] n 目 [me]; **eye drops** npl 目薬 [megusuri]; **eye shadow** n アイシャドウ [aishadou]; **I have something in my eye** 私は目に何か入っています [watashi wa me ni nani ka haitte imasu]; **My eyes are sore** 私は目が痛みます [watashi wa me ga itamimasu]

eyebrow ['aɪ,braʊ] n 眉 [mayu]

eyelash ['aɪ,læʃ] n まつげ [matsuge]

eyelid ['aɪ,lɪd] n まぶた [mabuta]

eyeliner ['aɪ,laɪnə] n アイライナー [airainaa]

eyesight ['aɪ,saɪt] n 視力 [shiryoku]

f

fabric ['fæbrɪk] *n* 織物 [orimono]

fabulous ['fæbjʊləs] *adj* すばらしい [subarashii]

face [feɪs] *n* 顔 [kao] ▷ *v* ···に向かう [...ni mukau] (方角); **face cloth** *n* 洗面用タオル [senmen you taoru]

facial ['feɪʃəl] *adj* 顔の [kao no] ▷ *n* 美顔術 [biganjutsu]

facilities [fə'sɪlɪtɪz] *npl* 設備 [setsubi]; **Do you have facilities for children?** 子供用の設備はありますか? [kodomo-you no setsubi wa arimasu ka?]; **What facilities do you have for people with disabilities?** 身体障害者用のどんな設備をそなえていますか? [shintai-shougaisha-you no donna setsubi o sonaete imasu ka?]; **What facilities do you have here?** ここにはどんな設備がありますか? [koko ni wa donna setsubi ga arimasu ka?]

fact [fækt] *n* 事実 [jijitsu]

factory ['fæktərɪ] *n* 工場 [koujou]; **I work in a factory** 私は工場で働いています [watashi wa koujou de hataraite imasu]

fade [feɪd] *v* 褪せる [aseru]

fag [fæg] *n* つまらない仕事 [tsumaranai shigoto]

fail [feɪl] *v* 失敗する [shippai suru]

failure ['feɪljə] *n* 失敗 [shippai]

faint [feɪnt] *adj* かすかな [kasuka na] ▷ *v* 気絶する [kizetsu suru]

fair [fɛə] *adj (light colour)* 色白の [irojiro no], *(reasonable)* 公正な [kousei na] ▷ *n* 縁日 [ennichi]

fairground ['fɛə,graʊnd] *n* 屋外市を催す場所 [okugai ichi-o moyousu basho]

fairly ['fɛəlɪ] *adv* 公正に [kousei ni]

fairness ['fɛənɪs] *n* 公正 [kousei]

fairy ['fɛərɪ] *n* 妖精 [yousei]

fairytale ['fɛərɪ,teɪl] *n* おとぎ話 [otogibanashi]

faith [feɪθ] *n* 信念 [shinnen]

faithful ['feɪθfʊl] *adj* 忠実な [chuujitsu na]

faithfully ['feɪθfʊlɪ] *adv* 忠実に [chuujitsuni]

fake [feɪk] *adj* 模造の [mozou no] ▷ *n* 模造品 [mozouhin]

fall [fɔːl] *n* 落下 [rakka] ▷ *v* 落ちる [ochiru]

fall down [fɔːl daʊn] *v* 倒れる [taoreru]

fall for [fɔːl fɔː] *v* ···が好きになる [...ga suki ni naru]

fall out [fɔːl aʊt] *v* 不和になる [fuwa ni naru]

false [fɔːls] *adj* 偽りの [itsuwari no]; **false alarm** *n* 間違い警報 [machigai keihou]

fame [feɪm] *n* 名声 [meisei]

familiar [fə'mɪlɪə] *adj* よく知られている [yoku shirarete iru]

family ['fæmɪlɪ; 'fæmlɪ] *n* 家族 [kazoku]; **I'm here with my family** 私は家族と来ています [watashi wa kazoku to kite imasu]

famine ['fæmɪn] *n* 飢饉 [kikin]

famous ['feɪməs] *adj* 有名な [yuumei na]

fan [fæn] *n* 扇風機 [senpuuki]; **fan belt** *n* ファンベルト [fanberuto]; **Does the room have a fan?** その部屋に扇風機はありますか? [sono heya ni senpuuki wa arimasu ka?]

fanatic [fə'nætɪk] *n* 熱狂者 [nekkyousha]

fancy ['fænsɪ] v ···が気に入る [...ga ki ni iru]; **fancy dress** n 仮装服 [kasoufuku]

fantastic [fæn'tæstɪk] adj すばらしい [subarashii]

FAQ [ɛf eɪ kjuː] abbr FAQ [efueekyuu]

far [fɑː] adj 遠い [toui] ▷ adv 遠くに [touku ni]; **Far East** n 極東 [kyokutou]; **Is it far?** 遠いですか? [tooi desu ka?]; **It's quite far** かなり遠いです [kanari tooi desu]

fare [fɛə] n 運賃 [unchin]

farewell [ˌfɛə'wɛl] excl さらば! [saraba]

farm [fɑːm] n 農場 [noujou]

farmer ['fɑːmə] n 農場主 [noujoushu]

farmhouse ['fɑːmˌhaʊs] n 農家 [nouka]

farming ['fɑːmɪŋ] n 農業 [nougyou]

Faroe Islands ['fɛərəʊ 'aɪləndz] npl フェロー諸島 [feroo shotou]

fascinating ['fæsɪˌneɪtɪŋ] adj 魅惑的な [miwakuteki na]

fashion ['fæʃən] n 流行 [ryuukou]

fashionable ['fæʃənəbəl] adj 流行の [ryuukou no]

fast [fɑːst] adj 速い [hayai] ▷ adv 速く [hayaku]

fat [fæt] adj 太った [futotta] ▷ n 脂肪 [shibou]

fatal ['feɪtəl] adj 致命的な [chimeiteki na]

fate [feɪt] n 運命 [unmei]

father ['fɑːðə] n 父 [chichi]

father-in-law ['fɑːðə ɪn lɔː] (fathers-in-law) n 義父 [gifu]

fault [fɔːlt] n (defect) 責任 [sekinin], (mistake) 責任 [sekinin]; **It wasn't my fault** それは私の責任ではありません [sore wa watashi no sekinin de wa arimasen]

faulty ['fɔːltɪ] adj 欠陥のある [kekkan no aru]

fauna ['fɔːnə] npl 動物相 [doubutsusou]

favour ['feɪvə] n 賛成 [sansei]

favourite ['feɪvərɪt; 'feɪvrɪt] adj 大好きな [daisuki na] ▷ n お気に入り [o-kiniiri]

fax [fæks] n ファックス [fakkusu] ▷ v ファックスを送る [fakkusu-o okuru]; **Do you have a fax?** ファックスがありますか? [fakkusu ga arimasu ka?]; **How much is it to send a fax?** ファックスを送るのはいくらですか? [fakkusu o okuru no wa ikura desu ka?]; **I want to send a fax** 私はファックスを送りたいのですが [watashi wa fakkusu o okuritai no desu ga]; **Is there a fax machine I can use?** 私が使えるファックス機はありますか? [watashi ga tsukaeru fakkusuki wa arimasu ka?]; **Please resend your fax** あなたのファックスを再送信してください [anata no fakkusu o sai-soushin shite kudasai]; **There is a problem with your fax** あなたのファックスに問題があります [anata no fakkusu ni mondai ga arimasu]; **What is the fax number?** ファックス番号は何番ですか? [fakkusu-bangou wa nan-ban desu ka?]

fear [fɪə] n 不安 [fuan] ▷ v 恐れる [osoreru]

feasible ['fiːzəbəl] adj 実行可能な [jikkoukanou na]

feather ['fɛðə] n 羽 [hane]

feature ['fiːtʃə] n 顔立ち [kaodachi]

February ['fɛbrʊərɪ] n 二月 [nigatsu]

fed up [fɛd ʌp] adj うんざりして [unzari shite]

fee [fiː] n 料金 [ryoukin]; **entrance fee** n 入場料 [nyuujouryou]; **tuition fees** npl 授業料 [jugyouryou]; **Is there a booking fee to pay?** 予約料金がかかりますか? [yoyaku-ryoukin ga kakarimasu ka?]

feed [fiːd] v 食物を与える [tabemono o ataeru] ▷ n フィード [fiido]

feedback ['fiːdˌbæk] n 意見 [iken]

feel [fiːl] v 感じる [kanjiru]

feeling ['fiːlɪŋ] n 気持ち [kimochi]

feet [fiːt] npl 足 [ashi]; **My feet are a size six** 私の足は六号です [watashi no ashi wa roku-gou desu]; **My feet are sore** 私は足が痛みます [watashi wa ashi ga itamimasu]

felt [fɛlt] n フェルト [feruto]

female ['fiːmeɪl] adj 女性の [josei no] ▷ n 女性 [josei]

feminine ['fɛmɪnɪn] adj 女らしい [onnarashii]

feminist ['fɛmɪnɪst] n フェミニスト [feminisuto]

fence [fɛns] n 柵 [saku]

fennel ['fɛnᵊl] n フェンネル [fenneru]

fern [fɜːn] n シダ [shida]

ferret ['fɛrɪt] n ケナガイタチ [kenagaitachi]

ferry ['fɛrɪ] n フェリー [ferii]; **Is there a ferry to...?** ···行きのフェリーはありますか? [...iki no ferii no arimasu ka?]; **Where do we catch the ferry to...?** ···行きのフェリーはどこで乗るのですか? [...iki no ferii wa doko de noru no desu ka?]

fertile ['fɜːtaɪl] adj 繁殖力のある [hanshokuryoku no aru]

fertilizer ['fɜːtɪˌlaɪzə] n 肥料 [hiryou]

festival ['fɛstɪvᵊl] n フェスティバル [fesutibaru]

fetch [fɛtʃ] v 行って連れて来る [itte tsurete kuru]

fever ['fiːvə] n 熱 [netsu]; **hay fever** n 花粉症 [kafunshou]; **He has a fever** 彼は熱があります [kare wa netsu ga arimasu]

few [fjuː] adj 少しの [sukoshi no] ▷ pron 少数 [shousuu]

fewer ['fjuːə] adj より少ない [yori sukunai]

fiancé [fɪˈɒnseɪ] n 婚約中の男性 [kon'yakuchuu no dansei]

fiancée [fɪˈɒnseɪ] n 婚約中の女性 [kon'yakuchuu no josei]

fibre ['faɪbə] n 繊維 [sen-i]

fibreglass ['faɪbəˌɡlɑːs] n ガラス繊維 [garasu sen'i]

fiction ['fɪkʃən] n フィクション [fikushon]; **science fiction** n サイエンスフィクション [saiensu fikushon]

field [fiːld] n 野原 [nohara]; **playing field** n グラウンド [guraundo]

fierce [fɪəs] adj 凶暴な [kyoubou na]

fifteen ['fɪf'tiːn] number 十五 [juugo]

fifteenth ['fɪf'tiːnθ] adj 十五番目の [juugo banme no]

fifth [fɪfθ] adj 五番目の [go banme no]

fifty ['fɪftɪ] number 五十 [gojuu]

fifty-fifty ['fɪftɪ'fɪftɪ] adj 五分五分の [gobugobu no] ▷ adv 五分五分で [gobugobu de]

fig [fɪg] n イチジク [ichijiku]

fight [faɪt] n 戦い [tatakai] ▷ v 戦う [tatakau]

fighting [faɪtɪŋ] n 戦い [tatakai]

figure ['fɪgə; 'fɪgjər] n 数字 [suuji]

figure out ['fɪgə aʊt] v 計算して出す [keisan shite dasu]

Fiji ['fiːdʒiː; fiːˈdʒiː] n フィジー [fijii]

file [faɪl] n (folder) ファイル [fairu], (tool) やすり [yasuri] ▷ v (folder) ファイルする [fairu suru], (smoothing) やすりをかける [yasuri-o kakeru]

Filipino, Filipina [ˌfɪlɪˈpiːnəʊ, ˌfɪlɪˈpiːna] adj フィリピンの [firipin no] ▷ n フィリピン人 [firipinjin]

fill [fɪl] v いっぱいにする [ippai ni suru]

fillet ['fɪlɪt] n ヒレ肉 [hireniku] ▷ v ···からヒレ肉を取る [...kara hireniku-o toru]

fill in [fɪl ɪn] v 記入する [kinyuu suru]

filling ['fɪlɪŋ] n **A filling has fallen out** 詰め物がとれてしまいました [tsumemono ga torete shimaimashita]; **Can you do a temporary filling?** 仮の詰め物をしてもらえますか? [kari no tsumemono o shite moraemasu ka?]

fill up [fɪl ʌp] v 記入する [kinyuu suru]

film [fɪlm] n 映画 [eiga]; **film star** n 映画スター [eigasutaa]; **horror film** n ホラー映画 [horaa eiga]; **Are there any films in English?** 英語の映画はありますか? [eigo no eiga wa arimasu ka?]; **When does the film start?** 映画はいつ始まりますか? [eiga wa itsu hajimarimasu ka?]; **Where can we go to see a film?** どこに行けば映画を見られますか? [doko ni ikeba eiga o miraremasu ka?]; **Which film is on at the cinema?** その映画館でどの映画が上映されていますか? [sono eigakan de dono eiga ga jouei sarete imasu ka?]

filter ['fɪltə] n 濾過器 [rokaki] ▷ v 濾過する [roka suru]

filthy ['fɪlθɪ] adj 不潔な [fuketsu na]

final ['faɪnᵊl] *adj* 最終の [saishuu no] ▷ *n* 決勝 [kesshou]

finalize ['faɪnə,laɪz] *v* 決定的にする [ketteiteki ni suru]

finally ['faɪnəlɪ] *adv* ついに [tsuini]

finance [fɪ'næns; 'faɪnæns] *n* 財務 [zaimu] ▷ *v* 資金を調達する [shikin-o choutatsu suru]

financial [fɪ'nænʃəl; faɪ-] *adj* 財務の [zaimu no]; **financial year** *n* 会計年度 [kaikeinendo]

find [faɪnd] *v* 見つける [mitsukeru]

find out [faɪnd aʊt] *v* 発見する [hakken suru]

fine [faɪn] *adj* 見事な [migoto na] ▷ *adv* 見事に [migoto ni] ▷ *n* 罰金 [bakkin]; **How much is the fine?** 罰金はいくらですか？ [bakkin wa ikura desu ka?]; **Where do I pay the fine?** どこで罰金を払うのですか？ [doko de bakkin o harau no desu ka?]

finger ['fɪŋɡə] *n* 手の指 [te no yubi]; **index finger** *n* 人差し指 [hitosashi yubi]

fingernail ['fɪŋɡə,neɪl] *n* 指の爪 [yubi no tsume]

fingerprint ['fɪŋɡə,prɪnt] *n* 指紋 [shimon]

finish ['fɪnɪʃ] *n* 終わり [owari] ▷ *v* 終える [oeru]; **When does it finish?** いつ終わりますか？ [itsu owarimasu ka?]; **When will you have finished?** 何時に終わりますか？ [nan-ji ni owarimasu ka?]

finished ['fɪnɪʃt] *adj* 終えた [oeta]

Finland ['fɪnlənd] *n* フィンランド [finrando]

Finn ['fɪn] *n* フィンランド人 [finrandojin]

Finnish ['fɪnɪʃ] *adj* フィンランドの [finrando no] ▷ *n* フィンランド人 [finrandojin]; *(language)* フィンランド語 [finrandogo]

fir [fɜː] *n* **fir (tree)** *n* モミ [momi]

fire [faɪə] *n* 火 [hi]; **fire alarm** *n* 火災報知器 [kasai houchiki]; **fire brigade** *n* 消防隊 [shouboutai]; **fire escape** *n* 非常階段 [hijoukaidan]; **fire extinguisher** *n* 消火器 [shoukaki]; **Fire!** 火事だ！ [kaji da!]

firefighter ['faɪəfaɪtə] *n* 消防士 [shouboushi]

fireplace ['faɪə,pleɪs] *n* 暖炉 [danro]

firewall ['faɪə,wɔːl] *n* 防火壁 [boukaheki]

fireworks ['faɪə,wɜːks] *npl* 花火 [hanabi]

firm [fɜːm] *adj* 堅い [katai] ▷ *n* 会社 [kaisha]

first [fɜːst] *adj* 最初の [saisho no] ▷ *adv* 最初に [saisho ni] ▷ *n* 最初のもの [saisho no mono]; **first aid** *n* 救急処置 [kyuukyuu shochi]; **first name** *n* ファーストネーム [faasutoneemu]; **When does the first chair-lift go?** 最初のチェアリフトはいつ出ますか？ [saisho no chea-rifuto wa itsu demasu ka?]

first-class ['fɜːst'klɑːs] *adj* 第一級の [daiikkyuu no]

firstly ['fɜːstlɪ] *adv* まず第一に [mazu daiichi ni]

fiscal ['fɪskᵊl] *adj* 財政の [zaisei no]; **fiscal year** *n* 会計年度 [kaikeinendo]

fish [fɪʃ] *n* 魚 [sakana] ▷ *v* 魚を捕る [sakana-o toru]; **freshwater fish** *n* 淡水魚 [tansuigyo]; **Could you prepare a meal without fish?** 魚を使わずに食事を用意していただけますか？ [sakana o tsukawazu ni shokuji o youi shite itadakemasu ka?]; **I don't eat fish** 私は魚を食べません [watashi wa sakana o tabemasen]; **I'll have the fish** 私はこの魚をいただきます [watashi wa kono sakana o itadakimasu]; **Is the fish fresh or frozen?** 魚は生鮮品ですか、それとも冷凍品ですか？ [sakana wa seisen-hin desu ka, sore tomo reitou-hin desu ka?]; **Is this cooked in fish stock?** これは魚のストックで料理してありますか？ [kore wa sakana no sutokku de ryouri shite arimasu ka?]; **What fish dishes do you have?** どんな魚料理がありますか？ [donna sakana-ryouri ga arimasu ka?]

fisherman, fishermen ['fɪʃəmən, 'fɪʃəmɛn] *n* 漁師 [ryoushi]

fishing ['fɪʃɪŋ] *n* 漁業 [gyogyou]; **fishing boat** *n* 漁船 [gyosen]; **fishing rod** *n* 釣竿 [tsurizao]; **fishing tackle** *n* 釣具 [tsurigu]

fishmonger ['fɪʃˌmʌŋgə] *n* 魚屋 [sakanaya]

fist [fɪst] *n* 握りこぶし [nigiri kobushi]

fit [fɪt] *adj* 適した [tekishita] ▷ *n* 発作 [hossa] ▷ *v* 適する [teki suru]; **epileptic fit** *n* 癲癇の発作 [tenkan no hossa]; **fitted kitchen** *n* 造り付けのキッチン [tsukuritsuke no kitchin]; **fitted sheet** *n* マットレスにぴったり合うシーツ [mattoresu ni pittari au shiitsu]; **fitting room** *n* 試着室 [shichakushitsu]

fit in [fɪt ɪn] *v* 組み込む [kumikomu]

five [faɪv] *number* 五 [go]

fix [fɪks] *v* 固定する [kotei suru]

fixed [fɪkst] *adj* 固定した [kotei shita]

fizzy ['fɪzɪ] *adj* シュシュと泡立つ [shushu to awadatsu]

flabby ['flæbɪ] *adj* たるんだ [tarunda]

flag [flæg] *n* 旗 [hata]

flame [fleɪm] *n* 炎 [hono-o]

flamingo [flə'mɪŋgəʊ] *n* フラミンゴ [furamingo]

flammable ['flæməbəl] *adj* 可燃性の [kanensei no]

flan [flæn] *n* フラン [furan] (食べ物)

flannel ['flænəl] *n* 浴用タオル [yokuyou taoru]

flap [flæp] *v* パタパタ動かす [patapata ugokasu]

flash [flæʃ] *n* 閃光 [senkou] ▷ *v* パッと発火する [patsu to hakka suru]

flashlight ['flæʃˌlaɪt] *n* 懐中電灯 [kaichuudentou]

flask [flɑːsk] *n* 魔法瓶 [mahoubin]

flat [flæt] *adj* 平らな [taira na] ▷ *n* フラット [furatto]; **studio flat** *n* スタジオフラット [sutajiofuratto]

flat-screen ['flætˌskriːn] *adj* フラットスクリーンの [furatto sukuriin no]

flatter ['flætə] *v* おだてる [odateru]

flattered ['flætəd] *adj* おだてられた [odaterareta]

flavour ['fleɪvə] *n* 味 [aji]

flavouring ['fleɪvərɪŋ] *n* 調味料 [choumiryou]

flaw [flɔː] *n* きず [kizu] (損傷)

flea [fliː] *n* 蚤 [nomi]; **flea market** *n* ノミの市 [nomi no ichi]

flee [fliː] *v* 逃げる [nigeru]

fleece [fliːs] *n* フリース [furiisu]

fleet [fliːt] *n* 艦隊 [kantai]

flex [flɛks] *n* 電気コード [denki koodo]

flexible ['flɛksɪbəl] *adj* 曲げやすい [mageyasui]

flexitime ['flɛksɪˌtaɪm] *n* フレックスタイム [furekkusutaimu]

flight [flaɪt] *n* フライト [furaito]; **charter flight** *n* チャーター便 [chaataa bin]; **flight attendant** *n* 客室乗務員 [kyakushitsu joumuin]; **scheduled flight** *n* 定期便 [teikibin]; **Are there any cheap flights?** 安いフライトはありますか？ [yasui furaito wa arimasu ka?]; **I would prefer an earlier flight** もっと早いフライトがいいのですが [motto hayai furaito ga ii no desu ga]; **I'd like to cancel my flight** フライトをキャンセルしたいのですが [furaito o kyanseru shitai no desu ga]; **I'd like to change my flight** フライトを変更したいのですが [furaito o henkou shitai no desu ga]; **I've missed my flight** 私はフライトに乗り遅れました [watashi wa furaito ni noriokuremashita]; **The flight has been delayed** フライトは遅れています [furaito wa okurete imasu]; **Where do I check in for the flight to...?** ・・・行きのフライトはどこでチェックインするのですか？ [...iki no furaito wa doko de chekku-in suru no desu ka?]; **Where is the luggage for the flight from...?** ・・・からのフライトの手荷物はどこですか？ [...kara no furaito no tenimotsu wa doko desu ka?]; **Which gate for the flight to...?** ・・・行きフライトの搭乗ゲートはどれですか？ [...iki furaito no toujou-geeto wa dore desu ka?]

fling [flɪŋ] *v* 投げ飛ばす [nagetobasu]

flip-flops ['flɪp'flɒpz] *npl* ビーチサンダル [biichi sandaru]

flippers ['flɪpəz] *npl* ひれ足 [hireashi]

flirt [flɜːt] *n* 浮気者 [uwakimono] ▷ *v* 恋を

もてあそぶ [koi o moteasobu]

float [fləʊt] n 浮き [uki] ▷ v 浮く [uku]

flock [flɒk] n 群れ [mure]

flood [flʌd] n 洪水 [kouzui] ▷ vi 氾濫する [hanran suru] ▷ vt 氾濫させる [hanran saseru]

flooding ['flʌdɪŋ] n 氾濫 [hanran]

floodlight ['flʌd,laɪt] n 投光照明 [toukou shoumei]

floor [flɔː] n 床 [yuka]; **ground floor** n 一階 [ikkai]

flop [flɒp] n 失敗 [shippai]

flora ['flɔːrə] npl 植物相 [shokubutsusou]

florist ['flɒrɪst] n 花屋 [hanaya]

flour ['flaʊə] n 小麦粉 [komugiko]

flow [fləʊ] v 流れる [nagareru]

flower ['flaʊə] n 花 [hana] ▷ v 花が咲く [hana ga saku]

flu [fluː] n インフルエンザ [infuruenza]; **bird flu** n 鳥インフルエンザ [tori infuruenza]; **I had flu recently** 私は最近インフルエンザにかかりました [watashi wa saikin infuruenza ni kakarimashita]; **I've got flu** 私はインフルエンザにかかりました [watashi wa infuruenza ni kakarimashita]

fluent ['fluːənt] adj 流暢な [ryuuchou na]

fluorescent [,flʊə'rɛsᵊnt] adj 蛍光性の [keikousei no]

flush [flʌʃ] n 赤面 [sekimen] ▷ v 赤面する [sekimen suru]

flute [fluːt] n フルート [furuuto]

fly [flaɪ] n ハエ [hae] ▷ v 飛ぶ [tobu]

fly away [flaɪ ə'weɪ] v 飛び去る [tobisaru]

foal [fəʊl] n 馬の子 [uma no ko]

foam [fəʊm] n **shaving foam** n シェービングフォーム [shieebingufoomu]

focus ['fəʊkəs] n 焦点 [shouten] ▷ v 焦点を合わせる [shouten-o awaseru]

foetus ['fiːtəs] n 胎児 [taiji]

fog [fɒg] n 霧 [kiri]; **fog light** n フォグランプ [foguranpu]

foggy ['fɒgɪ] adj 霧の立ちこめた [kiri no tachikometa]

foil [fɔɪl] n ホイル [hoiru]

fold [fəʊld] n 囲い [kakoi] ▷ v 折りたたむ [oritatamu]

folder ['fəʊldə] n ホルダー [horudaa]

folding [fəʊldɪŋ] adj 折りたたみの [oritatami no]

folklore ['fəʊk,lɔː] n 民間伝承 [minkandenshou]

follow ['fɒləʊ] v ···について行く [...ni tsuite iku], (on Twitter) をフォローする [o foroo suru]

following ['fɒləʊɪŋ] adj 以下の [ika no] (次の)

food [fuːd] n 食べ物 [tabemono]; **food poisoning** n 食中毒 [shokuchuudoku]; **food processor** n フードプロセッサー [fuudopurosessaa]; **Do you have food?** 食べ物はありますか? [tabemono wa arimasu ka?]; **The food is too hot** 食べ物が熱すぎます [tabemono ga atsu-sugimasu]; **The food is very greasy** 食べ物がとても脂っこいです [tabemono ga totemo aburakkoi desu]

fool [fuːl] n ばか者 [bakamono] ▷ v だます [damasu]

foot, feet [fʊt, fiːt] n 足 [ashi]; **My feet are a size six** 私の足は六号です [watashi no ashi wa roku-gou desu]

football ['fʊt,bɔːl] n フットボール [futtobooru]; **American football** n アメリカンフットボール [amerikan futtobooru]; **football match** n フットボールの試合 [futtobooru no shiai]; **football player** n フットボール選手 [futtobooru senshu]

footballer ['fʊt,bɔːlə] n フットボール選手 [futtobooru senshu]

footpath ['fʊt,pɑːθ] n 歩行者用の小道 [hokoushayou no komichi]

footprint ['fʊt,prɪnt] n 足跡 [ashiato]

footstep ['fʊt,stɛp] n 足取り [ashidori]

for [fɔː, fə] prep ···のために [...no tame ni] (関係)

forbid [fə'bɪd] v 禁じる [kinjiru]

forbidden [fə'bɪdᵊn] adj 禁じられた [kinjirareta]

force [fɔːs] n 力 [chikara] ▷ v 強いる

[shiiru]; **Air Force** n 空軍 [kuugun]

orecast ['fɔː,kɑːst] n 天気予報 [tenkiyohou]; **What's the weather forecast?** 天気予報はどうですか? [tenki-yohou wa dou desu ka?]

oreground ['fɔː,graʊnd] n 前景 [zenkei]

orehead ['fɒrɪd; 'fɔː,hɛd] n 額 [hitai] (顔)

oreign ['fɒrɪn] adj 外国の [gaikoku no]

oreigner ['fɒrɪnə] n 外国人 [gaikokujin]

oresee [fɔː'siː] v 予見する [yoken suru]

orest ['fɒrɪst] n 森 [mori]

orever [fɔː'rɛvə; fə-] adv 永久に [eikyuu ni]

orge [fɔːdʒ] v 鍛造する [tanzou suru]

orgery ['fɔːdʒərɪ] n 偽造 [gizou]

orget [fə'gɛt] v 忘れる [wasureru]

orgive [fə'gɪv] v 許す [yurusu]

orgotten [fə'gɒtʰn] adj 忘れられた [wasurerareta]

ork [fɔːk] n フォーク [fooku]; **Could I have a clean fork please?** 新しいフォークをいただけますか? [atarashii fooku o itadakemasu ka?]

orm [fɔːm] n 形 [katachi]; **application form** n 申込書 [moushikomisho]; **order form** n 注文用紙 [chuumon youshi]

ormal ['fɔːməl] adj 正式の [seishiki no]

ormality [fɔː'mælɪtɪ] n 儀礼的行為 [gireiteki koui]

ormat ['fɔːmæt] n 図書形態 [tosho keitai] ▷ v 形式を定める [keishiki-o sadameru]

ormer ['fɔːmə] adj 以前の [izen no]

ormerly ['fɔːməlɪ] adv 以前は [izen wa]

ormula ['fɔːmjʊlə] n 公式 [koushiki]

ort [fɔːt] n 砦 [toride]

ortnight ['fɔːt,naɪt] n 二週間 [nishuukan]

ortunate ['fɔːtʃənɪt] adj 幸運な [kouun na]

ortunately ['fɔːtʃənɪtlɪ] adv 幸運にも [kouun nimo]

ortune ['fɔːtʃən] n 大金 [taikin]

orty ['fɔːtɪ] number 四十 [shijuu]

forum ['fɔːrəm] n フォーラム [fooramu]

forward ['fɔːwəd] adv 前方へ [zenpou-e] ▷ v 転送する [tensou suru]; **forward slash** n フォワードスラッシュ [fowaadosurasshu]; **lean forward** v 前かがみになる [maekagami ni naru]

foster ['fɒstə] v 養育する [youiku suru]; **foster child** n 里子 [satogo]

foul [faʊl] adj いやな [iya na] ▷ n ファウル [fauru]

foundations [faʊn'deɪʃənz] npl 基礎 [kiso]

fountain ['faʊntɪn] n 噴水 [funsui]; **fountain pen** n 万年筆 [mannenhitsu]

four [fɔː] number 四 [shi]

fourteen ['fɔː'tiːn] number 十四 [juuyon]

fourteenth ['fɔː'tiːnθ] adj 十四番目の [juuyon banme no]

fourth [fɔːθ] adj 四番目の [yon banme no]

fox [fɒks] n キツネ [kitsune]

fracture ['fræktʃə] n 骨折 [kossetsu]

fragile ['frædʒaɪl] adj 壊れやすい [kowareyasui]

frail [freɪl] adj かよわい [kayowai]

frame [freɪm] n 骨組み [honegumi]; **picture frame** n 額縁 [gakubuchi]; **Zimmer® frame** n ジマー [jimaa]

France [frɑːns] n フランス [furansu]

frankly ['fræŋklɪ] adv 率直に [sotchoku ni]

frantic ['fræntɪk] adj 半狂乱の [hankyouran no]

fraud [frɔːd] n 詐欺 [sagi]

freckles ['frɛkªlz] npl そばかす [sobakasu]

free [friː] adj (no cost) 無料の [muryou no], (no restraint) 自由な [jiyuu na] ▷ v ···を自由にする [...-o jiyuu ni suru]; **free kick** n フリーキック [furiikikku]

freedom ['friːdəm] n 自由 [jiyuu]

freelance ['friː,lɑːns] adj 自由契約の [jiyuu keiyaku no] ▷ adv 自由契約で [jiyuu keiyaku de]

freeze [friːz] v 凍る [kouru]

freezer ['friːzə] n 冷凍庫 [reitouko]

freezing ['fri:zɪŋ] *adj* 凍るような [kouru you na]

freight [freɪt] *n* 貨物輸送 [kamotsu yusou]

French [frɛntʃ] *adj* フランスの [furansu no] ▷ *n* フランス人 [furansujin]; *(language)* フランス語 [furansugo]; **French beans** *npl* サヤインゲン [saya ingen]; **French horn** *n* フレンチホルン [furenchihorun]

Frenchman, Frenchmen ['frɛntʃmən, 'frɛntʃmɛn] *n* フランス人 [furansujin]

Frenchwoman, Frenchwomen ['frɛntʃwʊmən, 'frɛntʃwɪmɪn] *n* フランス人 [furansujin]

frequency ['fri:kwənsɪ] *n* 頻発 [hinpatsu]

frequent ['fri:kwənt] *adj* たびたびの [tabitabi no]

fresh [frɛʃ] *adj* 新鮮な [shinsen na]

freshen up ['frɛʃən ʌp] *v* 洗面する [senmen suru]

fret [frɛt] *v* 気をもむ [ki-o momu]

Friday ['fraɪdɪ] *n* 金曜日 [kin-youbi]; **Good Friday** *n* 聖金曜日 [seikinyoubi]; **on Friday the thirty first of December** 十二月三十一日の金曜日に [juuni-gatsu sanjuuichi-nichi no kinyoubi ni]; **on Friday** 金曜日に [kinyoubi ni]

fridge [frɪdʒ] *n* 冷蔵庫 [reizouko]

fried [fraɪd] *adj* 油で揚げた [abura de ageta]

friend [frɛnd] *n* 友だち [tomodachi] ▷ *v* と友達になる [to tomodachi ni naru]; **I'm here with my friends** 私は友だちと来ています [watashi wa tomodachi to kite imasu]

friendly ['frɛndlɪ] *adj* 親しい [shitashii]

friendship ['frɛndʃɪp] *n* 友情 [yuujou]

fright [fraɪt] *n* 恐怖 [kyoufu]

frighten ['fraɪtᵊn] *v* 怖がらせる [kowagaraseru]

frightened ['fraɪtənd] *adj* おびえた [obieta]

frightening ['fraɪtᵊnɪŋ] *adj* ぎょっとさせる [gyotto saseru]

fringe [frɪndʒ] *n* 切下げ前髪 [kirisagemaegami]

frog [frɒg] *n* カエル [kaeru]

from [frɒm; frəm] *prep* ・・・から [...kara]

front [frʌnt] *adj* 前の [mae no] ▷ *n* 前 [mae]

frontier ['frʌntɪə; frʌn'tɪə] *n* 国境 [kokkyou]

frost [frɒst] *n* 霜 [shimo]

frosting ['frɒstɪŋ] *n* 降霜 [kousou]

frosty ['frɒstɪ] *adj* 霜の降りる [shimo no oriru]

frown [fraʊn] *v* まゆをひそめる [mayu o hisomeru]

frozen ['frəʊzᵊn] *adj* 凍った [koutta]

fruit [fru:t] *n (botany)* 果物 [kudamono], *(collectively)* 果物 [kudamono]; **fruit juice** *n* フルーツジュース [furuutsujuusu]; **fruit machine** *n* スロットマシン [surottomashin]; **fruit salad** *n* フルーツサラダ [furuutsusarada]; **passion fruit** *n* パッションフルーツ [passhonfuruutsu]

frustrated [frʌ'streɪtɪd] *adj* 挫折した [zasetsu shita]

fry [fraɪ] *v* 油で揚げる [abura de ageru]; **frying pan** *n* フライパン [furaipan]

fuel [fjʊəl] *n* 燃料 [nenryou]

fulfil [fʊl'fɪl] *v* 果たす [hatasu]

full [fʊl] *adj* 満ちた [michita]; **full moon** *n* 満月 [mangetsu]; **full stop** *n* 終止符 [shuushifu]

full-time ['fʊlˌtaɪm] *adj* フルタイムの [furutaimu no] ▷ *adv* フルタイムで [furutaimu de]

fully ['fʊlɪ] *adv* 十分に [juubun ni]

fumes [fju:mz] *npl* 煙霧 [enmu]; **exhaust fumes** *npl* 排気ガス [haikigasu]

fun [fʌn] *adj* 楽しい [tanoshii] ▷ *n* 楽しみ [tanoshimi]

funds [fʌndz] *npl* 資金 [shikin]

funeral ['fju:nərəl] *n* 葬式 [soushiki]; **funeral parlour** *n* 葬儀場 [sougiba]

funfair ['fʌnˌfɛə] *n* 遊園地 [yuuenchi]

funnel ['fʌnəl] *n* じょうご [jougo]

funny ['fʌnɪ] *adj* 面白い [omoshiroi]

fur [fɜː] *n* 毛皮 [kegawa]; **fur coat** *n* 毛皮のコート [kegawa no kooto]

furious ['fjʊərɪəs] *adj* 怒り狂った [ikarikurutta]

furnished ['fɜːnɪʃt] *adj* 家具付きの [kagu tsuki no]

furniture ['fɜːnɪtʃə] *n* 家具 [kagu]

further ['fɜːðə] *adj* それ以上の [sore ijou no] ▷ *adv* さらに [sara ni]; **further education** *n* 継続教育 [keizoku kyouiku]

fuse [fjuːz] *n* ヒューズ [hyuuzu]; **fuse box** *n* ヒューズボックス [hyuuzubokkusu]; **A fuse has blown** ヒューズがとびました [hyuuzu ga tobimashita]; **Can you mend a fuse?** ヒューズを直してもらえますか? [hyuuzu o naoshite moraemasu ka?]

fusebox ['fjuːzˌbɒks] *n* **Where is the fusebox?** ヒューズボックスはどこですか? [hyuuzu-bokkusu wa doko desu ka?]

fuss [fʌs] *n* 大騒ぎ [ousawagi]

fussy ['fʌsɪ] *adj* 騒ぎたてる [sawagitateru]

future ['fjuːtʃə] *adj* 未来の [mirai no] ▷ *n* 未来 [mirai]

g

Gabon [gəˈbɒn] *n* ガボン [gabon]

gain [geɪn] *n* 利得 [ritoku] ▷ *v* 得る [eru]

gale [geɪl] *n* 強風 [kyoufuu]

gallery ['gælərɪ] *n* 画廊 [garou]; **art gallery** *n* 美術館 [bijutsukan]

gallop ['gæləp] *n* ギャロップ [gyaroppu] ▷ *v* ギャロップで走る [gyaroppu de hashiru]

gallstone ['gɔːlˌstəʊn] *n* 胆石 [tanseki]

Gambia ['gæmbɪə] *n* ガンビア [ganbia]

gamble ['gæmbəl] *v* 賭け事をする [kakegoto-o suru]

gambler ['gæmblə] *n* ギャンブラー [gyanburaa]

gambling ['gæmblɪŋ] *n* ギャンブル [gyanburu]

game [geɪm] *n* ゲーム [geemu]; **board game** *n* ボードゲーム [boodo geemu]; **games console** *n* ゲームコンソール [geemu konsooru]; **Can I play video games?** ビデオゲームができますか? [bideo-geemu ga dekimasu ka?]

gang [gæŋ] *n* ギャング [gyangu]

gangster ['gæŋstə] *n* ギャングの一員 [gyangu no ichiin]

gap [gæp] *n* 隙間 [sukima]

garage ['gærɑːʒ; -rɪdʒ] *n* ガレージ [gareeji]

garbage ['gɑːbɪdʒ] *n* ごみ [gomi]

garden ['gɑːdⁿn] *n* 庭 [niwa]; **garden centre** *n* 園芸用品店 [engei youhinten]; **Can we visit the gardens?** 私たちがその庭園を訪れることはできますか? [watashi-tachi ga sono teien o otozureru koto wa dekimasu ka?]

gardener ['gɑːdnə] *n* 庭師 [niwashi]

gardening ['gɑːdⁿnɪŋ] *n* 庭仕事 [niwa shigoto]

garlic ['gɑːlɪk] *n* ニンニク [ninniku]

garment ['gɑːmənt] *n* 衣服 [ifuku]

gas [gæs] *n* ガス [gasu]; **gas cooker** *n* ガスレンジ [gasurenji]; **natural gas** *n* 天然ガス [tennengasu]; **I can smell gas** ガスのにおいがします [gasu no nioi ga shimasu]; **Where is the gas meter?** ガスのメーターはどこですか? [gasu no meetaa wa doko desu ka?]

gasket ['gæskɪt] *n* ガスケット [gasuketto]

gate [geɪt] *n* 門 [mon]

gateau, gateaux ['gætəʊ, 'gætəʊz] *n* 菓子 [kashi]

gather ['gæðə] *v* 集める [atsumeru]

gauge [geɪdʒ] *n* 計器 [keiki] ▷ *v* 測る [hakaru]

gaze [geɪz] *v* 見つめる [mitsumeru]

gear [gɪə] *n* (equipment) 用具 [yougu], (mechanism) ギア [gia]; **gear box** *n* ギアボックス [giabokkusu]; **gear lever** *n* ギアレバー [giarebaa]; **gear stick** *n* ギアシフト [giashifuto]; **Does the bike have gears?** 自転車はギア付きですか? [jitensha wa gia tsuki desu ka?]; **The gears don't work** ギアがききません [gia ga kikimasen]

gearbox ['gɪəˌbɒks] *n* **The gearbox is broken** ギアボックスが壊れています [gia-bokkusu ga kowarete imasu]

gearshift ['gɪəˌʃɪft] *n* ギアシフト [giashifuto]

gel [dʒɛl] *n* ジェル [jeru]; **hair gel** *n* ヘアジェル [heajieru]

gem [dʒɛm] *n* 宝石 [houseki]

Gemini ['dʒɛmɪˌnaɪ; -ˌniː] *n* 双子座 [futagoza]

gender ['dʒɛndə] *n* 性 [sei]

gene [dʒiːn] *n* 遺伝子 [idenshi]

general ['dʒɛnərəl; 'dʒɛnrəl] *adj* 一般の [ippan no] ▷ *n* 将軍 [shougun]; **general anaesthetic** *n* 全身麻酔 [zenshin masui]; **general election** *n* 総選挙 [sousenkyo]; **general knowledge** *n* 一般知識 [ippan chishiki]

generalize ['dʒɛnrəˌlaɪz] *v* 法則化する [housokuka suru]

generally ['dʒɛnrəlɪ] *adv* 一般に [ippan ni]

generation [ˌdʒɛnə'reɪʃən] *n* 世代 [sedai]

generator ['dʒɛnəˌreɪtə] *n* 発電機 [hatsudenki]

generosity [ˌdʒɛnə'rɒsɪtɪ] *n* 寛大 [kandai]

generous ['dʒɛnərəs; 'dʒɛnrəs] *adj* 気前のよい [kimae no yoi]

genetic [dʒɪ'nɛtɪk] *adj* 遺伝子の [idenshi no]

genetically-modified [dʒɪ'nɛtɪklɪˌmɒdɪˌfaɪd] *adj* 遺伝子組み換えの [idenshi kumikae no]

genetics [dʒɪ'nɛtɪks] *n* 遺伝学 [idengaku]

genius ['dʒiːnɪəs; -njəs] *n* 天才 [tensai]

gentle ['dʒɛntəl] *adj* 優しい [yasashii]

gentleman ['dʒɛntəlmən] (gentlemen ['dʒɛntəlmɛn]) *n* 紳士 [shinshi]

gently ['dʒɛntlɪ] *adv* 優しく [yasashiku]

gents' [dʒɛnts] *n* 男性用トイレ [dansei you toire]; **Where is the gents?** 男性用トイレはどこですか? [dansei-you toire wa doko desu ka?]

genuine ['dʒɛnjʊɪn] *adj* 本物の [honmono no]

geography [dʒɪ'ɒgrəfɪ] *n* 地理学 [chirigaku]

geology [dʒɪ'ɒlədʒɪ] *n* 地質学 [chishitsugaku]

Georgia ['dʒɔːdʒə] *n* (country) グルジア [gurujia], (US state) ジョージア [joojia]

Georgian ['dʒɔːdʒjən] *adj* グルジアの [gurujia no] ▷ *n (inhabitant of Georgia)* グルジア人 [gurujiajin]

geranium [dʒɪ'reɪnɪəm] *n* ゼラニウム [zeraniumu]

gerbil ['dʒɜːbɪl] *n* アレチネズミ [arechinezumi]

geriatric [,dʒɛrɪ'ætrɪk] *adj* 老人病学の [roujinbyougaku no] ▷ *n* 老人病患者 [roujinbyou kanja]

germ [dʒɜːm] *n* 細菌 [saikin]

German ['dʒɜːmən] *adj* ドイツの [doitsu no] ▷ *n (language)* ドイツ語 [doitsugo], *(person)* ドイツ人 [doitsujin]; **German measles** *n* 風疹 [fuushin]

Germany ['dʒɜːmənɪ] *n* ドイツ [doitsu]

gesture ['dʒɛstʃə] *n* 身振り [miburi]

get [gɛt] *v* 得る [eru], *(to a place)* 着く [tsuku]; **How long will it take to get there?** そこに着くのに時間はどのくらいかかりますか? [soko ni tsuku no ni jikan wa dono kurai kakarimasu ka?]; **How long will it take to get to...?** ･･･に着くのに時間はどのくらいかかりますか? [...ni tsuku no ni jikan wa dono kurai kakarimasu ka?]

get away [gɛt ə'weɪ] *v* 逃げる [nigeru]

get back [gɛt bæk] *v* 戻る [modoru]

get in [gɛt ɪn] *v* 乗る [noru]

get into [gɛt 'ɪntə] *v* ･･･に到着する [...ni touchaku suru]

get off [gɛt ɒf] *v* 降りる [oriru]

get on [gɛt ɒn] *v* 乗る [noru]; **Can you help me get on, please?** 私が乗るのを手伝っていただけますか? [watashi ga noru nowo tetsudatte itadakemasuka?]

get out [gɛt aʊt] *v* 逃げる [nigeru]

get over [gɛt 'əʊvə] *v* 立ち直る [tachinaoru]

get through [gɛt θruː] *v* **I can't get through** つながりません [tsunagarimasen]

get together [gɛt tə'gɛðə] *v* 集まる [atsumaru]

get up [gɛt ʌp] *v* 起きる [okiru]

Ghana ['gɑːnə] *n* ガーナ [gaana]

Ghanaian [gɑː'neɪən] *adj* ガーナの [gaana no] ▷ *n* ガーナ人 [gaanajin]

ghost [gəʊst] *n* 幽霊 [yuurei]

giant ['dʒaɪənt] *adj* 巨大な [kyodai na] ▷ *n* 巨人 [kyojin]

gift [gɪft] *n* 贈り物 [okurimono]; **gift shop** *n* ギフトショップ [gifuto shoppu]; **gift voucher** *n* 商品券 [shouhinken]

gifted ['gɪftɪd] *adj* 生まれつき才能のある [umaretsuki sainou no aru]

gigantic [dʒaɪ'gæntɪk] *adj* 巨大な [kyodai na]

giggle ['gɪgəl] *v* くすくす笑う [kusukusu warau]

gin [dʒɪn] *n* ジン [jin]; **I'll have a gin and tonic, please** ジントニックをお願いします [jin-tonikku o o-negai shimasu]

ginger ['dʒɪndʒə] *adj* ショウガ色の [shouga iro no] ▷ *n* ショウガ [shouga]

giraffe [dʒɪ'rɑːf; -'ræf] *n* キリン [kirin]

girl [gɜːl] *n* 少女 [shoujo]

girlfriend ['gɜːl,frɛnd] *n* ガールフレンド [gaarufurendo]; **I have a girlfriend** 私にはガールフレンドがいます [watashi ni wa gaarufurendo ga imasu]

give [gɪv] *v* 与える [ataeru]

give back [gɪv bæk] *v* 返す [kaesu]

give in [gɪv ɪn] *v* 屈服する [kuppuku suru]

give out [gɪv aʊt] *v* 配布する [haifu suru]

give up [gɪv ʌp] *v* やめる [yameru] (よす)

glacier ['glæsɪə; 'gleɪs-] *n* 氷河 [hyouga]

glad [glæd] *adj* 嬉しい [ureshii]

glamorous ['glæmərəs] *adj* 魅力的な [miryokuteki na]

glance [glɑːns] *n* ちらっと見ること [chiratto miru koto] ▷ *v* ちらっと見る [chiratto miru]

gland [glænd] *n* 腺 [sen]

glare [glɛə] *v* にらみつける [niramitsukeru]

glaring ['glɛərɪŋ] *adj* 派手な [hade na]

glass [glɑːs] *n* ガラス [garasu], *(vessel)* ガラス [garasu]; **magnifying glass** *n* 拡大鏡 [kakudaikyou]; **stained glass** *n* ステンドグラス [sutendogurasu]

glasses ['glɑːsɪz] *npl* 眼鏡 [megane]

glazing [ˈgleɪzɪŋ] n **double glazing** n 複層ガラス [fukusou garasu]

glider [ˈglaɪdə] n グライダー [guraidaa]

gliding [ˈglaɪdɪŋ] n グライダー競技 [guraidaa kyougi]

global [ˈgləʊbəl] adj 地球の [chikyuu no]; **global warming** n 地球温暖化 [chikyuuondanka]

globalization [ˌgləʊbəlaɪˈzeɪʃən] n グローバル化 [guroobaruka]

globe [gləʊb] n 地球儀 [chikyuugi]

gloomy [ˈgluːmɪ] adj 憂鬱な [yuuutsu na]

glorious [ˈglɔːrɪəs] adj すばらしい [subarashii]

glory [ˈglɔːrɪ] n 栄誉 [eiyo]

glove [glʌv] n 手袋 [tebukuro]; **glove compartment** n グローブボックス [guroobubokkusu]; **oven glove** n オーブンミット [oobunmitto]; **rubber gloves** npl ゴム手袋 [gomu tebukuro]

glucose [ˈgluːkəʊz; -kəʊs] n グルコース [gurukoosu]

glue [gluː] n 接着剤 [setchakuzai] ▷ v 接着剤でつける [setchakuzai de tsukeru]

gluten [ˈgluːtᵊn] n グルテン [guruten]; **Could you prepare a meal without gluten?** グルテンを使わずに食事を用意していただけますか? [guruten o tsukawazu ni shokuji o youi shite itadakemasu ka?]; **Do you have gluten-free dishes?** グルテンを使っていない料理はありますか? [guruten o tsukatte inai ryouri wa arimasu ka?]

GM [dʒiː ɛm] abbr (= genetically modified) 遺伝子組み換えの [idenshi kumikae no]

go [gəʊ] v 行く [iku]; **Excuse me, which bus goes to...?** すみません、・・・へ行くバスはどれですか? [sumimasen, ... e iku basu wa dore desu ka?]; **Is it time to go?** もう行く時間ですか? [mou iku jikan desu ka?]

go after [gəʊ ˈɑːftə] v ・・・を追う [...-o ou]

go ahead [gəʊ əˈhɛd] v 先へ進む [saki-e susumu]

goal [gəʊl] n ゴール [gouru]

goalkeeper [ˈgəʊlˌkiːpə] n ゴールキーパー [gourukiipaa]

goat [gəʊt] n ヤギ [yagi]

go away [gəʊ əˈweɪ] v 立ち去る [tachisaru]

go back [gəʊ bæk] v 戻る [modoru]

go by [gəʊ baɪ] v 通過する [tsuuka suru]

god [gɒd] n 神 [kami]

godchild, godchildren [ˈgɒdˌtʃaɪld, ˈgɒdˌtʃɪldrən] n 教子 [kyouko] (男女)

goddaughter [ˈgɒdˌdɔːtə] n 教女 [kyoujo]

godfather [ˈgɒdˌfɑːðə] n (baptism) 教父 [kyoufu] (名づけ親), (criminal leader) ゴッドファーザー [goddofaazaa]

godmother [ˈgɒdˌmʌðə] n 教母 [kyoubo]

go down [gəʊ daʊn] v 下がる [sagaru]

godson [ˈgɒdˌsʌn] n 教子 [kyouko] (男子)

goggles [ˈgɒgᵊlz] npl ゴーグル [gougur I want to hire goggles** ゴーグルを借りたいのですが [googuru o karitai no desu ga]

go in [gəʊ ɪn] v 入る [hairu]

gold [gəʊld] n 金 [kin] (金属)

golden [ˈgəʊldən] adj 金製の [kinsei no

goldfish [ˈgəʊldˌfɪʃ] n 金魚 [kingyo]

gold-plated [ˈgəʊldˈpleɪtɪd] adj 金めっきの [kinmekki no]

golf [gɒlf] n ゴルフ [gorufu]; **golf club** n (game) ゴルフ用クラブ [gorufu you kurabu], (society) ゴルフクラブ [gorufukurabu]; **golf course** n ゴルフ場 [gorufujou]; **Do they hire out golf clubs?** ゴルフクラブを貸し出していますか? [gorufu-kurabu o kashidashite imasu ka?]; **Is there a public golf course near here?** この近くに公共のゴルフコースはありますか? [kono chikaku ni kookyou no gorufu-koosu wa arimasu ka?]; **Where can I play golf?** どこでゴルフができますか? [doko de gorufu ga dekimasu ka?]

gone [gɒn] adj いなくなって [inaku natt

good [gʊd] adj 良い [yoi]

oodbye [ˌɡʊdˈbaɪ] *excl* さようなら!
[sayounara]

ood-looking [ˈɡʊdˈlʊkɪŋ] *adj* 美貌の
[bibou no]

ood-natured [ˈɡʊdˈneɪtʃəd] *adj* 気だ
てのよい [kidate no yoi]

oods [ɡʊdz] *npl* 商品 [shouhin]

o off [ɡəʊ ɒf] *v* 止まる [tomaru]

oogle® [ˈɡuːɡəl] *v* グーグル®で調べる
[guuguru de shiraberu]

o on [ɡəʊ ɒn] *v* 続ける [tsuzukeru]

oose, geese [ɡuːs, ɡiːs] *n* ガチョウ
[gachou]; **goose pimples** *npl* 鳥肌
[torihada]

ooseberry [ˈɡʊzbərɪ; -brɪ] *n* グーズベ
リー [guuzuberii]

o out [ɡəʊ aʊt] *v* 外出する [gaishutsu
suru]

o past [ɡəʊ pɑːst] *v* ···を過ぎる [...-o
sugiru]

orgeous [ˈɡɔːdʒəs] *adj* 華麗な [karei
na]

orilla [ɡəˈrɪlə] *n* ゴリラ [gorira]

o round [ɡəʊ raʊnd] *v* 皆に行き渡る
[mina ni iki wataru]

ospel [ˈɡɒspəl] *n* 福音 [fukuin]

ossip [ˈɡɒsɪp] *n* うわさ話 [uwasabanashi]
▷ *v* うわさ話をする [uwasabanashi-o suru]

o through [ɡəʊ θruː] *v* 経験する
[keiken suru]

o up [ɡəʊ ʌp] *v* 上がる [agaru]

overnment [ˈɡʌvənmənt;
ˈɡʌvəmənt] *n* 政府 [seifu]

own [ɡaʊn] *n* **dressing gown** *n* ドレッ
シングガウン [doresshingugaun]

P [dʒiː piː] *abbr* 一般医 [ippan'i]

PS [dʒiː piː ɛs] *abbr* グローバル
ポジショニングシステム
[guroobarupojishoningushisutemu]

rab [ɡræb] *v* ひっつかむ [hittsukamu]

raceful [ˈɡreɪsfʊl] *adj* 優美な [yuubi na]

rade [ɡreɪd] *n* 等級 [toukyuu]

radual [ˈɡrædjʊəl] *adj* 徐々の
[jojo no]

radually [ˈɡrædjʊəlɪ] *adv* 徐々に
[jojo ni]

graduate [ˈɡrædjʊɪt] *n* 大学の卒業生
[daigaku no sotsugyousei]

graduation [ˌɡrædjʊˈeɪʃən] *n* 大学卒業
[daigaku sotsugyou]

graffiti, graffito [ɡræˈfiːtiː,
ɡræˈfiːtəʊ] *npl* 落書き [rakugaki]

grain [ɡreɪn] *n* 穀粒 [kokutsubu]

grammar [ˈɡræmə] *n* 文法 [bunpou]

grammatical [ɡrəˈmætɪkəl] *adj* 文法の
[bunpou no]

gramme [ɡræm] *n* グラム [guramu]

grand [ɡrænd] *adj* 壮大な [sodai na]

grandchild [ˈɡrænˌtʃaɪld] *n* 孫 [mago];
grandchildren *npl* 孫 [mago]

granddad [ˈɡrænˌdæd] *n* おじいちゃん
[ojiichan]

granddaughter [ˈɡrænˌdɔːtə] *n* 孫娘
[magomusume]

grandfather [ˈɡrænˌfɑːðə] *n* 祖父 [sofu]

grandma [ˈɡrænˌmɑː] *n* おばあちゃん
[obaachan]

grandmother [ˈɡrænˌmʌðə] *n* 祖母
[sobo]

grandpa [ˈɡrænˌpɑː] *n* おじいちゃん
[ojiichan]

grandparents [ˈɡrænˌpɛərəntz] *npl* 祖
父母 [sofubo]

grandson [ˈɡrænsʌn; ˈɡrænd-] *n* 孫息
子 [magomusuko]

granite [ˈɡrænɪt] *n* みかげ石
[mikageishi]

granny [ˈɡrænɪ] *n* おばあちゃん
[obaachan]

grant [ɡrɑːnt] *n* 助成金 [joseikin]

grape [ɡreɪp] *n* ブドウ [budou]

grapefruit [ˈɡreɪpˌfruːt] *n* グレープフル
ーツ [gureepufuruutsu]

graph [ɡrɑːf; ɡræf] *n* グラフ [gurafu]

graphics [ˈɡræfɪks] *npl* 画像 [gazou]

grasp [ɡrɑːsp] *v* しっかりつかむ [shikkari
tsukamu]

grass [ɡrɑːs] *n* (plant) 草 [kusa],
(informer) 密告者 [mikkokusha],
(marijuana) マリファナ [marifana]

grasshopper [ˈɡrɑːsˌhɒpə] *n*
イナゴ [inago]

grate [greɪt] v すりおろす [suriorosu]

grateful ['greɪtful] adj 感謝している [kansha shite iru]

grave [greɪv] n 墓 [haka]

gravel ['grævəl] n 砂利 [jari]

gravestone ['greɪvˌstəʊn] n 墓石 [hakaishi]

graveyard ['greɪvˌjɑːd] n 墓地 [bochi]

gravy ['greɪvɪ] n グレービーソース [gureebiisoosu]

grease [griːs] n 獣脂 [juushi]

greasy ['griːzɪ; -sɪ] adj 脂を含んだ [abura-o fukunda]

great [greɪt] adj 大きな [ooki na]

Great Britain ['greɪt 'brɪtən] n グレートブリテン [gureetoburiten]

great-grandfather ['greɪt'grænˌfɑːðə] n 曾祖父 [sousofu]

great-grandmother ['greɪt'grænˌmʌðə] n 曾祖母 [sousobo]

Greece [griːs] n ギリシャ [girisha]

greedy ['griːdɪ] adj 欲ばりの [yokubari no]

Greek [griːk] adj ギリシャの [girisha no] ▷ n (language) ギリシャ語 [girishago], (person) ギリシャ人 [girishajin]

green [griːn] adj (colour) 緑色の [midori iro no], (inexperienced) 未熟な [mijuku na] (経験不足) ▷ n 緑色 [ryokushoku]; **green salad** n グリーンサラダ [guriin sarada]

greengrocer's ['griːnˌgrəʊsəz] n 八百屋 [yaoya]

greenhouse ['griːnˌhaʊs] n 温室 [onshitsu]

Greenland ['griːnlənd] n グリーンランド [guriinrando]

greet [griːt] v …に挨拶する [...ni aisatsu suru]

greeting ['griːtɪŋ] n 挨拶 [aisatsu]; **greetings card** n グリーティングカード [guriitingukaado]

grey [greɪ] adj 灰色の [hai iro no]

grey-haired [ˌgreɪ'hɛəd] adj 白髪のある [shiraga no aru]

grid [grɪd] n グリッド [guriddo]

grief [griːf] n 深い悲しみ [fukai kanashimi]

grill [grɪl] n グリル [guriru] ▷ v グリルで焼く [guriru de yaku]

grilled [grɪld] adj 網焼きにする [amiyaki ni suru]

grim [grɪm] adj いやな [iya na]

grin [grɪn] n にこにこ笑い [nikoniko warai] ▷ v 歯を見せてにっこり笑う [ha-o misete nikkori warau]

grind [graɪnd] v 挽く [hiku]

grip [grɪp] v しっかりつかむ [shikkari tsukamu]

gripping [grɪpɪŋ] adj 心を強くとらえる [kokoro o tsuyoku toraeru]

grit [grɪt] n 粗い砂 [araisuna]

groan [grəʊn] v うなる [unaru]

grocer ['grəʊsə] n 食料雑貨商 [shokuryou zakkashou]

groceries ['grəʊsərɪz] npl 食料雑貨類 [shokuryou zakkarui]

grocer's ['grəʊsəz] n 食料雑貨店 [shokuryou zakkaten]

groom [gruːm; grʊm] n 馬の飼育係 [uma no shiikugakari], (bridegroom) 花婿 [hanamuko]

grope [grəʊp] v 手探りする [tesaguri suru]

gross [grəʊs] adj (fat) ひどい [hidoi], (income etc.) ひどい [hidoi]

grossly [grəʊslɪ] adv ひどく [hidoku]

ground [graʊnd] n 地面 [jimen] ▷ v 地面に置く [jimen ni oku]; **ground floor** n 一階 [ikkai]

group [gruːp] n グループ [guruupu]

grouse [graʊs] n (complaint) 不平 [fuhei], (game bird) ライチョウ [raichou]

grow [grəʊ] vi 成長する [seichou suru] ▷ vt 育てる [sodateru]

growl [graʊl] v 怒ってうなる [ikatte unaru]

grown-up [grəʊnʌp] n 成人 [seijin]

growth [grəʊθ] n 成長 [seichou]

grow up [grəʊ ʌp] v 大人になる [otona ni naru]

grub [grʌb] n 地虫 [jimushi]

grudge [grʌdʒ] n 恨み [urami]

gruesome ['gru:səm] adj ぞっとする [zotto suru]

grumpy ['grʌmpɪ] adj 気むずかしい [kimuzukashii]

guarantee [ˌgærən'ti:] n 保証 [hoshou] ▷ v 保証する [hoshou suru]; **It's still under guarantee** まだ保証期間内です [mada hoshou-kikan nai desu]

guard [gɑːd] n 見張り [mihari] ▷ v 見張る [miharu]; **security guard** n 警備員 [keibiin]

Guatemala [ˌgwɑːtə'mɑːlə] n グアテマラ [guatemara]

guess [gɛs] n 推測 [suisoku] ▷ v 推測する [suisoku suru]

guest [gɛst] n 客 [kyaku]

guesthouse ['gɛstˌhaʊs] n ゲストハウス [gesutohausu]

guide [gaɪd] n ガイド [gaido] ▷ v 案内する [annai suru]; **guide dog** n 盲導犬 [moudouken]; **guided tour** n ガイドツアー [gaidotsuaa]; **tour guide** n ツアーガイド [tsuaagaido]; **Do you have a guide book in...?** ･･･語のガイドブックはありますか？ [...go no gaidobukku wa arimasu ka?]; **Do you have a guide book in English?** 英語のガイドブックはありますか？ [eigo no gaidobukku wa arimasu ka?]; **Do you have a guide to local walks?** 地元のウォーキングのガイドはいますか？ [jimoto no wookingu no gaido wa imasu ka?]; **Is there a guide who speaks English?** 英語を話すガイドはいますか？ [eigo o hanasu gaido wa imasu ka?]

guidebook ['gaɪdˌbʊk] n ガイドブック [gaidobukku]

guilt [gɪlt] n 有罪 [yuuzai]

guilty ['gɪltɪ] adj 有罪の [yuuzai no]

Guinea ['gɪnɪ] n ギニア [ginia]; **guinea pig** n (for experiment) 実験台 [jikkendai], (rodent) モルモット [morumotto] (動物)

guitar [gɪ'tɑː] n ギター [gitaa]

gum [gʌm] n 粘性ゴム [nenseigomu];

chewing gum n チューインガム [chuuingamu]

gun [gʌn] n 銃 [juu]; **machine gun** n マシンガン [mashingan]

gust [gʌst] n 突風 [toppuu]

gut [gʌt] n 腸 [chou]

guy [gaɪ] n 男 [otoko]

Guyana [gaɪ'ænə] n ガイアナ [gaiana]

gym [dʒɪm] n ジム [jimu]; **Where is the gym?** ジムはどこですか？ [jimu wa doko desu ka?]

gymnast ['dʒɪmnæst] n 体操家 [taisouka]

gymnastics [dʒɪm'næstɪks] npl 体操 [taisou]

gynaecologist [ˌgaɪnɪ'kɒlədʒɪst] n 婦人科医 [fujinkai]

gypsy ['dʒɪpsɪ] n ジプシー [jipushii]

h

habit [ˈhæbɪt] *n* 癖 [kuse]

hack [hæk] *v* たたき切る [tatakikiru]

hacker [ˈhækə] *n* ハッカー [hakkaa]

haddock [ˈhædək] *n* ハドック [hadokku]

haemorrhoids [ˈhɛməˌrɔɪdz] *npl* 痔 [ji]

haggle [ˈhæg°l] *v* うるさく値切る [urusaku negiru]

hail [heɪl] *n* 雹 [hyou] ▷ *v* 呼び止める [yobitomeru]

hair [hɛə] *n* 髪 [kami]; **hair gel** *n* ヘアジェル [heajieru]; **hair spray** *n* ヘアスプレー [heasupuree]; **Can you dye my hair, please?** 髪を染めていただけますか？ [kami o somete itadakemasu ka?]; **Can you straighten my hair?** 髪をまっすぐにしてもらえますか？ [kami o massugu ni shite moraemasu ka?]; **I have greasy hair** 私の髪は脂性です [watashi no kami wa aburashou desu]; **What do you recommend for my hair?** 私の髪には何がいいと思いますか？ [watashi no kami ni wa nani ga ii to omoimasu ka?]

hairband [ˈhɛəˌbænd] *n* ヘアバンド [heabando]

hairbrush [ˈhɛəˌbrʌʃ] *n* ヘアブラシ [heaburashi]

haircut [ˈhɛəˌkʌt] *n* ヘアカット [heakatto]

hairdo [ˈhɛəˌduː] *n* ヘアスタイル [heasutairu]

hairdresser [ˈhɛəˌdrɛsə] *n* 美容師 [biyoushi]

hairdresser's [ˈhɛəˌdrɛsəz] *n* 美容院 [biyouin]

hairdryer [ˈhɛəˌdraɪə] *n* ヘアドライヤー [headoraiyaa]

hairgrip [ˈhɛəˌgrɪp] *n* ヘアピン [heapin]

hairstyle [ˈhɛəˌstaɪl] *n* ヘアスタイル [heasutairu]

hairy [ˈhɛərɪ] *adj* 毛深い [kebukai]

Haiti [ˈheɪtɪ; hɑːˈiːtɪ] *n* ハイチ [haichi]

half [hɑːf] *adj* 半分の [hanbun no] ▷ *adv* 半分だけ [hanbun dake] ▷ *n* 半分 [hanbun]; **half board** *n* 二食付き [nishokutsuki]

half-hour [ˈhɑːfˌaʊə] *n* 三十分 [sanjuppun]

half-price [ˈhɑːfˌpraɪs] *adj* 半額の [hangaku no] ▷ *adv* 半額で [hangaku de]

half-term [ˈhɑːfˌtɜːm] *n* 学期中の中間休暇 [gakkichuu no chuukan kyuuka]

half-time [ˈhɑːfˌtaɪm] *n* ハーフタイム [haafutaimu]

halfway [ˌhɑːfˈweɪ] *adv* 中程で [nakahodo de]

hall [hɔːl] *n* 入口の廊下 [iriguchi no rouka]; **town hall** *n* タウンホール [taunhooru]

hallway [ˈhɔːlˌweɪ] *n* 玄関 [genkan]

halt [hɔːlt] *n* 停止 [teishi]

ham [hæm] *n* ハム [hamu]

hamburger [ˈhæmˌbɜːgə] *n* ハンバーガー [hanbaagaa]

hammer [ˈhæmə] *n* ハンマー [hanmaa]

hammock [ˈhæmək] *n* ハンモック [hanmokku]

hamster [ˈhæmstə] *n* ハムスター [hamusutaa]

hand [hænd] *n* 手 [te] ▷ *v* 手渡す [tewatasu]; **hand luggage** *n* 手荷物 [tenimotsu]; **Where can I wash my hands?** どこで手を洗えばいいのですか？ [doko de te o araeba ii no desu ka?]

handbag ['hænd,bæg] n ハンドバッグ [handobaggu]

handball ['hænd,bɔːl] n ハンドボール [handobooru]

handbook ['hænd,bʊk] n ハンドブック [handobukku]

handbrake ['hænd,breɪk] n ハンドブレーキ [handobureeki]

handcuffs ['hænd,kʌfs] npl 手錠 [tejou]

handicap ['hændɪ,kæp] n **My handicap is...** 私のハンディーキャップは・・・です [watashi no handiikyappu wa ... desu]; **What's your handicap?** あなたのハンディーキャップはどのくらいですか? [anata no handiikyappu wa dono kurai desu ka?]

handkerchief ['hæŋkətʃɪf; -tʃiːf] n ハンカチ [hankachi]

handle ['hændəl] n ハンドル [handoru] (取っ手) ▷ v 取り扱う [toriatsukau]

handlebars ['hændəl,bɑːz] npl ハンドル [handoru] (自転車・バイク)

handmade [,hænd'meɪd] adj 手製の [tesei no]

hands-free ['hændz,friː] adj ハンズフリーの [hanzufurii no]; **hands-free kit** n ハンズフリーキット [hanzu furii kitto]

handsome ['hændsəm] adj ハンサムな [hansamu na]

handwriting ['hænd,raɪtɪŋ] n 手書き [tegaki]

handy ['hændɪ] adj 便利な [benri na]

hang [hæŋ] vi 掛かる [kaka ru] ▷ vt 掛ける [kakeru]

hanger ['hæŋə] n ハンガー [hangaa]

hang-gliding ['hæŋ'glaɪdɪŋ] n ハンググライディング [hanguguraideingu]; **I'd like to go hang-gliding** 私はハンググライディングをしたいのですが [watashi wa hanguguraidingu o shitai no desu ga]

hang on [hæŋ ɒn] v そのまま待つ [sono mama matsu]

hangover ['hæŋ,əʊvə] n 二日酔い [futsukayoi]

hang up [hæŋ ʌp] v 電話を切る [denwa o kiru]

hankie ['hæŋkɪ] n ハンカチ [hankachi]

happen ['hæpən] v 起こる [okoru]

happily ['hæpɪlɪ] adv 幸福に [koufuku ni]

happiness ['hæpɪnɪs] n 幸福 [koufuku]

happy ['hæpɪ] adj 幸福な [koufuku na]

harassment ['hærəsmənt] n いやがらせ [iyagarase]

harbour ['hɑːbə] n 港 [minato]

hard [hɑːd] adj (difficult) 困難な [konnan na], (firm, rigid) 堅い [katai] ▷ adv 懸命に [kenmei ni]; **hard disk** n ハードディスク [haadodisuku]; **hard shoulder** n 路肩 [rokata]

hardboard ['hɑːd,bɔːd] n ハードボード [haadoboodo]

hardly ['hɑːdlɪ] adv ほとんど・・・ない [hotondo ... nai]

hard up [hɑːd ʌp] adj 酔っぱらった [yopparatta]

hardware ['hɑːd,wɛə] n ハードウェア [haadouea]

hare [hɛə] n 野ウサギ [nousagi]

harm [hɑːm] v 害する [gai suru]

harmful ['hɑːmfʊl] adj 有害な [yuugai na]

harmless ['hɑːmlɪs] adj 無害な [mugai na]

harp [hɑːp] n ハープ [haapu]

harsh [hɑːʃ] adj 厳しい [kibishii]

harvest ['hɑːvɪst] n 収穫 [shuukaku] ▷ v 収穫する [shuukaku suru]

hastily [heɪstɪlɪ] adv 急いで [isoide]

hat [hæt] n 帽子 [boushi]

hatchback ['hætʃ,bæk] n ハッチバック [hatchibakku]

hate [heɪt] v 憎む [nikumu]

hatred ['heɪtrɪd] n 憎しみ [nikushimi]

haunted ['hɔːntɪd] adj 幽霊が出没する [yuurei ga shutsubotsu suru]

have [hæv] v 持っている [motte iru]

have to [hæv tʊ] v ・・・しなければならない [...shinakereba naranai]

hawthorn ['hɔː,θɔːn] n サンザシ [sanzashi]

hay [heɪ] n 干し草 [hoshikusa]; **hay fever** n 花粉症 [kafunshou]

haystack ['heɪ,stæk] n 干し草の山 [hoshikusa no yama]

hazelnut ['heɪzˌl,nʌt] n ヘーゼルナッツ [heezerunattsu]

he [hi:] pron 彼は [kare wa]

head [hɛd] n (body part) 頭 [atama], (principal) 長 [chou] (統率) ▷ v ···の先頭に立つ [...no sentou ni tatsu]; **deputy head** n 課長補佐 [kachouhosa]; **head office** n 本社 [honsha]

headache ['hɛdˌeɪk] n 頭痛 [zutsuu]; **I'd like something for a headache** 頭痛に効くものが欲しいのですが [zutsuu ni kiku mono ga hoshii no desu ga]

headlamp ['hɛdˌlæmp] n ヘッドランプ [heddoranpu]

headlight ['hɛdˌlaɪt] n ヘッドライト [heddoraito]

headline ['hɛdˌlaɪn] n 見出し [midashi]

headphones ['hɛdˌfəʊnz] npl ヘッドホン [heddohon]; **Does it have headphones?** ヘッドホンはついていますか? [heddohon wa tsuite imasu ka?]

headquarters [ˌhɛd'kwɔːtəz] npl 本社 [honsha]

headroom ['hɛdˌrʊm; -ˌruːm] n 頭上スペース [zujou supeesu]

headscarf, headscarves ['hɛdˌskɑːf, 'hɛdˌskɑːvz] n ヘッドスカーフ [heddosukaafu]

headteacher ['hɛdˌtiːtʃə] n 校長 [kouchou]

heal [hi:l] v 治る [naoru]

health [hɛlθ] n 健康 [kenkou]

healthy ['hɛlθɪ] adj 健康な [kenkou na]

heap [hi:p] n 積み重なったもの [tsumikasanatta mono]

hear [hɪə] v 聞く [kiku]

hearing ['hɪərɪŋ] n 聴力 [chouryoku]; **hearing aid** n 補聴器 [hochouki]

heart [hɑːt] n 心臓 [shinzou]; **heart attack** n 心臓発作 [shinzouhossa]; **I have a heart condition** 私は心臓病があります [watashi wa shinzou-byou ga arimasu]

heartbroken ['hɑːtˌbrəʊkən] adj 失恋した [shitsuren shita]

heartburn ['hɑːtˌbɜːn] n 胸焼け [muneyake]

heat [hi:t] n 熱 [netsu] ▷ v 熱する [nessuru]

heater ['hi:tə] n 暖房器具 [danbou kigu]

heather ['hɛðə] n ヘザー [hezaa]

heating ['hi:tɪŋ] n 暖房 [danbou]; **central heating** n セントラルヒーティング [sentoraruhiitingu]; **Does the room have heating?** その部屋に暖房はありますか? [sono heya ni danbou wa arimasu ka?]; **How does the heating work?** 暖房はどうやって使うのですか? [danbou wa dou-yatte tsukau no desu ka?]; **I can't turn the heating off** 暖房を切ることができません [danbou o kiru koto ga dekimasen]; **I can't turn the heating on** 暖房を入れることができません [danbou o ireru koto ga dekimasen]; **The heating doesn't work** 暖房がつきません [danbou ga tsukimasen]

heat up [hi:t ʌp] v 加熱する [kanetsu suru]

heaven ['hɛvən] n 天国 [tengoku]

heavily ['hɛvɪlɪ] adv 重く [omoku]

heavy ['hɛvɪ] adj 重い [omoi]

hedge [hɛdʒ] n 垣根 [kakine]

hedgehog ['hɛdʒ,hɒg] n ハリネズミ [harinezumi]

heel [hi:l] n かかと [kakato]; **high heels** npl ハイヒール [haihiiru]

height [haɪt] n 高さ [takasa]

heir [ɛə] n 相続人 [souzokunin]

heiress ['ɛərɪs] n 女相続人 [onna souzokunin]

helicopter ['hɛlɪˌkɒptə] n ヘリコプター [herikoputaa]

hell [hɛl] n 地獄 [jigoku]

hello [hɛ'ləʊ] excl こんにちは! [konnichi wa]

helmet ['hɛlmɪt] n ヘルメット [herumetto]; **Can I have a helmet?** ヘルメットをください [herumetto o kudasai]

help [hɛlp] n 援助 [enjo] ▷ v 助ける [tasukeru]

helpful ['hɛlpfʊl] adj 役に立つ [yaku ni tatsu]

helpline ['hɛlp,laɪn] n ヘルプライン [herupurain]

hen [hɛn] n めんどり [mendori]; **hen night** n ヘンパーティー [henpaatii]

hepatitis [,hɛpə'taɪtɪs] n 肝炎 [kanen]

her [hɜː] pron 彼女の [kanojo no], 彼女を [kanojo wo]

herbs [hɜːbz] npl ハーブ [haabu]

herd [hɜːd] n 群れ [mure]

here [hɪə] adv ここに [koko ni]

hereditary [hɪ'rɛdɪtərɪ; -trɪ] adj 遺伝的な [identeki na]

heritage ['hɛrɪtɪdʒ] n 先祖伝来のもの [senzo denrai no mono]

hernia ['hɜːnɪə] n ヘルニア [herunia]

hero ['hɪərəʊ] n ヒーロー [hiiroo]

heroin ['hɛrəʊɪn] n ヘロイン [heroin]

heroine ['hɛrəʊɪn] n ヒロイン [hiroin]

heron ['hɛrən] n サギ [sagi] (鳥)

herring ['hɛrɪŋ] n ニシン [nishin]

hers [hɜːz] pron 彼女のもの [kanojo no mono]

herself [hə'sɛlf] pron 彼女自身 [kanojojishin]

hesitate ['hɛzɪ,teɪt] v ためらう [tamerau]

heterosexual [,hɛtərəʊ'sɛksjʊəl] adj 異性愛の [iseiai no]

HGV [eɪtʃ dʒiː viː] abbr 大型輸送車 [ougata yusousha]

hi [haɪ] excl やあ! [yaa]

hiccups ['hɪkʌps] npl しゃっくり [shakkuri]

hidden ['hɪdən] adj 隠された [kakusareta]

hide [haɪd] vi 隠れる [kakureru] ▷ vt 隠す [kakusu]

hide-and-seek [,haɪdænd'siːk] n 隠れん坊 [kakurenbou]

hideous ['hɪdɪəs] adj ぞっとする [zotto suru]

hifi ['haɪ'faɪ] n ハイファイ装置 [haifai souchi]

high [haɪ] adj 高い [takai] (高低) ▷ adv 高く [takaku]; **high heels** npl ハイヒール [haihiiru]; **high jump** n 走り高跳び [hashiri takatobi]; **high season** n 最盛期 [saiseiki]

highchair ['haɪ,tʃɛə] n 小児用の食事椅子 [shouni you no shokuji isu]

high-heeled ['haɪ,hiːld] adj ハイヒールの [haihiiru no]

highlight ['haɪ,laɪt] n ハイライト [hairaito] (やま場) ▷ v 強調する [kyouchou suru]

highlighter ['haɪ,laɪtə] n ハイライト [hairaito] (化粧品)

high-rise ['haɪ,raɪz] n 高層建築 [kousou kenchiku]

hijack ['haɪ,dʒæk] v ハイジャックする [haijakku suru]

hijacker ['haɪ,dʒækə] n ハイジャックの犯人 [haijakku no hannin]

hike [haɪk] n ハイキング [haikingu]

hiking [haɪkɪŋ] n ハイキング [haikingu]

hilarious [hɪ'lɛərɪəs] adj 陽気な [youki na]

hill [hɪl] n 丘 [oka]

hill-walking ['hɪl,wɔːkɪŋ] n ヒルウォーキング [hiruuookingu]

him [hɪm] pron 彼を [kare wo]; **We must get him to hospital** 私たちは彼を病院に連れて行かなければなりません [watashi-tachi wa kare o byouin ni tsurete ikanakereba narimasen]

himself [hɪm'sɛlf; ɪm'sɛlf] pron 彼自身 [karejishin]

Hindu ['hɪnduː; hɪn'duː] adj ヒンズー教の [hinzuu kyou no] ▷ n ヒンズー教徒 [hinzuu kyouto]

Hinduism ['hɪndʊ,ɪzəm] n ヒンズー教 [hinzuukyou]

hinge [hɪndʒ] n ちょうつがい [choutsugai]

hint [hɪnt] n ヒント [hinto] ▷ v ほのめかす [honomekasu]

hip [hɪp] n 腰 [koshi]

hippie ['hɪpɪ] n ヒッピー [hippii]

hippo ['hɪpəʊ] n カバ [kaba] (植物)

hippopotamus, hippopotami

[ˌhɪpəˈpɒtəməs, ˌhɪpəˈpɒtəmaɪ] *n* カバ [kaba] (植物)

hire [ˈhaɪə] *n* 賃借り [chingari] ▷ *v* 賃借りする [chingari suru]; **car hire** *n* レンタカー [rentakaa]; **hire car** *n* レンタカー [rentakaa]

his [hɪz; ɪz] *adj* 彼の [kare no] ▷ *pron* 彼のもの [kare no mono]

historian [hɪˈstɔːrɪən] *n* 歴史家 [rekishika]

historical [hɪˈstɒrɪkəl] *adj* 歴史上の [rekishijou no]

history [ˈhɪstərɪ; ˈhɪstrɪ] *n* 歴史 [rekishi]

hit [hɪt] *n* 衝突 [shoutotsu] ▷ *v* 打つ [utsu]

hitch [hɪtʃ] *n* 障害 [shougai]

hitchhike [ˈhɪtʃhaɪk] *v* ヒッチハイクする [hitchihaiku suru]

hitchhiker [ˈhɪtʃhaɪkə] *n* ヒッチハイクをする人 [hitchihaiku o suru hito]

hitchhiking [ˈhɪtʃhaɪkɪŋ] *n* ヒッチハイク [hitchihaiku]

HIV-negative [eɪtʃ aɪ viː ˈnɛgətɪv] *adj* HIV陰性の [eichiaibui insei no]

HIV-positive [eɪtʃ aɪ viː ˈpɒzɪtɪv] *adj* HIV陽性の [eichiaibui yousei no]

hobby [ˈhɒbɪ] *n* 趣味 [shumi]

hockey [ˈhɒkɪ] *n* ホッケー [hokkee]; **ice hockey** *n* アイスホッケー [aisuhokkee]

hold [həʊld] *v* 手に持つ [te ni motsu]

holdall [ˈhəʊldˌɔːl] *n* 大型の旅行かばん [ougata no ryokou kaban]

hold on [həʊld ɒn] *v* しっかりつかまる [shikkari tsukamaru]

hold up [həʊld ʌp] *v* 持ちこたえる [mochikotaeru]

hold-up [həʊldʌp] *n* 強盗 [goutou] (量・程度)

hole [həʊl] *n* 穴 [ana]; **I have a hole in my shoe** 靴に穴があきました [kutsu ni ana ga akimashita]

holiday [ˈhɒlɪˌdeɪ; -dɪ] *n* 休暇 [kyuuka]; **activity holiday** *n* アクティブホリデー [akutibu horidee]; **bank holiday** *n* 祝祭日 [shukusaijitsu]; **holiday home** *n* 別荘 [bessou]; **holiday job** *n* 休日の仕事 [kyuujitsu no shigoto]; **package holiday** *n* パック旅行 [pakku ryokou]; **public holiday** *n* 祝祭日 [shukusaijitsu]; **Enjoy your holiday!** 楽しい休暇を！ [tanoshii kyuuka o!]; **I'm here on holiday** 私は休暇で来ています [watashi wa kyuuka de kite imasu]

Holland [ˈhɒlənd] *n* オランダ [oranda]

hollow [ˈhɒləʊ] *adj* 空洞の [kuudou no]

holly [ˈhɒlɪ] *n* セイヨウヒイラギ [seiyouhiiragi]

holy [ˈhəʊlɪ] *adj* 神聖な [shinsei na]

home [həʊm] *adv* 我が家へ [wagaya-e] ▷ *n* 自宅 [jitaku]; **home address** *n* 自宅住所 [jitaku juusho]; **home match** *n* ホームの試合 [hoomu no shiai]; **home page** *n* ホームページ [hoomupeeji]; **mobile home** *n* モビールハウス [mobiiruhausu]; **nursing home** *n* 老人ホーム [roujin hoomu]; **stately home** *n* 大邸宅 [daiteitaku]

homeland [ˈhəʊmˌlænd] *n* 祖国 [sokoku]

homeless [ˈhəʊmlɪs] *adj* 住む家のない [sumu ie no nai]

home-made [ˈhəʊmˈmeɪd] *adj* 自家製の [jikasei no]

homeopathic [ˌhəʊmɪˈɒpæθɪk] *adj* ホメオパシーの [homeopashii no]

homeopathy [ˌhəʊmɪˈɒpəθɪ] *n* ホメオパシー [homeopashii]

homesick [ˈhəʊmˌsɪk] *adj* ホームシックの [hoomushikku no]

homework [ˈhəʊmˌwɜːk] *n* 宿題 [shukudai]

Honduras [hɒnˈdjʊərəs] *n* ホンジュラス [honjurasu]

honest [ˈɒnɪst] *adj* 正直な [shoujiki na]

honestly [ˈɒnɪstlɪ] *adv* 正直に [shoujiki ni]

honesty [ˈɒnɪstɪ] *n* 正直 [shoujiki]

honey [ˈhʌnɪ] *n* 蜂蜜 [hachimitsu]

honeymoon [ˈhʌnɪˌmuːn] *n* ハネムーン [hanemuun]; **We are on our honeymoon** 私たちはハネムーン中です [watashi-tachi wa hanemuun-chuu desu]

honeysuckle ['hʌnɪˌsʌkᵊl] n スイカズラ [suikazura]

honour ['ɒnə] n 道義心 [dougishin]

hood [hʊd] n フード [fuudo]

hook [hʊk] n フック [fukku]

hooray [huːˈreɪ] excl 万歳! [banzai]

Hoover® ['huːvə] n フーバー® [fuubaa]; **hoover** v 掃除機で掃除する [soujiki de souji suru]

hope [həʊp] n 希望 [kibou] ▷ v 望む [nozomu]

hopeful ['həʊpfʊl] adj 希望が持てる [kibou ga moteru]

hopefully ['həʊpfʊlɪ] adv 希望を持って [kibou-o motte]

hopeless ['həʊplɪs] adj 希望を失って [kibou-o ushinatte]

horizon [həˈraɪzᵊn] n 地平線 [chiheisen]

horizontal [ˌhɒrɪˈzɒntᵊl] adj 水平な [suihei na]

hormone ['hɔːməʊn] n ホルモン [horumon]

horn [hɔːn] n 角 [kado] (動物); **French horn** n フレンチホルン [furenchihorun]

horoscope ['hɒrəˌskəʊp] n 星占い [hoshiuranai]

horrendous [hɒˈrɛndəs] adj 恐ろしい [osoroshii]

horrible ['hɒrəbᵊl] adj 実にひどい [jitsu ni hidoi]

horrifying ['hɒrɪˌfaɪɪŋ] adj ぞっとさせる [zotto saseru]

horror ['hɒrə] n 恐怖 [kyoufu]; **horror film** n ホラー映画 [horaa eiga]

horse [hɔːs] n 馬 [uma]; **horse racing** n 競馬 [keiba]; **horse riding** n 乗馬 [jouba]; **rocking horse** n 揺り木馬 [yurimokuba]; **Can we go horse riding?** 乗馬に行けますか? [jouba ni ikemasu ka?]; **I'd like to see a horse race** 私は競馬を観戦したいのですが [watashi wa keiba o kansen shitai no desu ga]; **Let's go horse riding** 乗馬に行きましょう [jouba ni ikimashou]

horseradish ['hɔːsˌrædɪʃ] n セイヨウワサビ [seiyouwasabi]

horseshoe ['hɔːsˌʃuː] n 蹄鉄 [teitetsu]

hose [həʊz] n ホース [hoosu]

hosepipe ['həʊzˌpaɪp] n ホース [hoosu]

hospital ['hɒspɪtᵊl] n 病院 [byouin]; **maternity hospital** n 産科病院 [sanka byouin]; **psychiatric hospital** n 精神病院 [seishinbyouin]; **How do I get to the hospital?** その病院へはどう行けばいいのですか? [sono byouin e wa dou ikeba ii no desu ka?]; **I work in a hospital** 私は病院で働いています [watashi wa byouin de hataraite imasu]; **We must get him to hospital** 私たちは彼を病院に連れて行かなければなりません [watashi-tachi wa kare o byouin ni tsurete ikanakereba narimasen]; **Where is the hospital?** 病院はどこですか? [byouin wa doko desu ka?]; **Will he have to go to hospital?** 彼は病院に行かなければなりませんか? [kare wa byouin ni ikanakereba narimasen ka?]

hospitality [ˌhɒspɪˈtælɪtɪ] n 歓待 [kantai]

host [həʊst] n (entertains) ホスト [hosuto], (multitude) 多数 [tasuu]

hostage ['hɒstɪdʒ] n 人質 [hitojichi]

hostel ['hɒstᵊl] n ホステル [hosuteru]; **Is there a youth hostel nearby?** 近くにユースホステルはありますか? [chikaku ni yuusu-hosuteru wa arimasu ka?]

hostess ['həʊstɪs] n air hostess n スチュワーデス [suchuwaadesu]

hostile ['hɒstaɪl] adj 敵意のある [teki-i no aru]

hot [hɒt] adj 熱い [atsui]; **hot dog** n ホットドック [hottodokku]

hotel [həʊˈtɛl] n ホテル [hoteru]; **Can you book me into a hotel?** 私のためにホテルの部屋を予約してもらえますか? [watashi no tame ni hoteru no heya o yoyaku shite moraemasu ka?]; **Can you recommend a hotel?** いいホテルを教えてもらえますか? [ii hoteru o oshiete moraemasu ka?]; **He runs the hotel** 彼がホテルの経営者です [kare ga hoteru no keieisha desu]; **I'm staying at a hotel** 私

はホテルに滞在しています [watashi wa hoteru ni taizai shite imasu]; **Is your hotel accessible to wheelchairs?** おたくのホテルは車椅子で利用できますか？ [otaku no hoteru wa kuruma-isu de riyou dekimasu ka?]; **We're looking for a hotel** 私たちはホテルを探しています [watashi-tachi wa hoteru o sagashite imasu]; **What's the best way to get to this hotel?** このホテルへ行く一番よい方法は何ですか？ [kono hoteru e iku ichiban yoi houhou wa nan desu ka?]

hour [aʊə] n 一時間 [ichijikan]; **office hours** npl 営業時間 [eigyoujikan]; **opening hours** npl 営業時間 [eigyoujikan]; **peak hours** npl ピーク時 [piikuji]; **rush hour** n ラッシュアワー [rasshuawaa]; **visiting hours** npl 面会時間 [menkaijikan]

hourly [ˈaʊəlɪ] adj 一時間ごとの [ichijikan goto no] ▷ adv 一時間ごとに [ichijikan goto ni]

house [haʊs] n 家 [ie]; **council house** n 公営住宅 [koueijuutaku]; **detached house** n 土地付き一戸建て家屋 [tochi tsuki ikkodate kaoku]; **semi-detached house** n 二戸建て住宅 [nikodate juutaku]; **Do we have to clean the house before we leave?** 出る前に家を掃除しなければなりませんか？ [deru mae ni ie o souji shinakereba narimasen ka?]

household [ˈhaʊsˌhəʊld] n 家族 [kazoku]

housewife, housewives [ˈhaʊsˌwaɪf, ˈhaʊsˌwaɪvz] n 主婦 [shufu]

housework [ˈhaʊsˌwɜːk] n 家事 [kaji]

hovercraft [ˈhɒvəˌkrɑːft] n ホバークラフト [hobaakurafuto]

how [haʊ] adv どのように [dono you ni]

however [haʊˈɛvə] adv いかに・・・であろうとも [ikani ... de aroutomo]

howl [haʊl] v 遠吠えする [tooboe suru]

HQ [eɪtʃ kjuː] abbr 本社 [honsha]

hubcap [ˈhʌbˌkæp] n ハブキャップ [habukyappu]

hug [hʌg] n 抱きしめること [dakishimeru

koto] ▷ v 抱きしめる [dakishimeru]

huge [hjuːdʒ] adj 巨大な [kyodai na]

hull [hʌl] n 船体 [sentai]

hum [hʌm] v ブンブンいう [bunbun iu]

human [ˈhjuːmən] adj 人間の [ningen no]; **human being** n 人間 [ningen]; **human rights** npl 人権 [jinken]

humanitarian [hjuːˌmænɪˈtɛərɪən] adj 人道主義の [jindou shugi no]

humble [ˈhʌmbəl] adj 謙虚な [kenkyo na]

humid [ˈhjuːmɪd] adj 湿気の多い [shikke no oui]

humidity [hjuːˈmɪdɪtɪ] n 湿気 [shikke]

humorous [ˈhjuːmərəs] adj ユーモアのある [yuumoa no aru]

humour [ˈhjuːmə] n ユーモア [yuumoa]; **sense of humour** n ユーモアのセンス [yuumoa no sensu]

hundred [ˈhʌndrəd] number 百 [hyaku]; **I'd like five hundred...** 五百・・・欲しいのですが [gohyaku ... hoshii no desu ga]

Hungarian [hʌŋˈgɛərɪən] adj ハンガリーの [hangarii no] ▷ n ハンガリー人 [hangariijin]

Hungary [ˈhʌŋgərɪ] n ハンガリー [hangarii]

hunger [ˈhʌŋgə] n 空腹 [kuufuku]

hungry [ˈhʌŋgrɪ] adj 腹の減った [hara no hetta]

hunt [hʌnt] n 狩り [kari] ▷ v 狩りをする [kari-o suru]

hunter [ˈhʌntə] n ハンター [hantaa]

hunting [ˈhʌntɪŋ] n 狩り [kari]

hurdle [ˈhɜːdəl] n ハードル [haadoru]

hurricane [ˈhʌrɪkən; -keɪn] n ハリケーン [harikeen]

hurry [ˈhʌrɪ] n 大急ぎ [ooisogi] ▷ v 急ぐ [isogu]

hurry up [ˈhʌrɪ ʌp] v 急ぐ [isogu]

hurt [hɜːt] adj 傷ついた [kizutsuita] ▷ v 傷つける [kizutsukeru]

husband [ˈhʌzbənd] n 夫 [otto]; **This is my husband** 私の夫です [watashi no otto desu]

hut [hʌt] n 小屋 [koya]; **Where is the**

nearest mountain hut? 一番近い山小屋はどこですか? [ichiban chikai yama-goya wa doko desu ka?]

hyacinth [ˈhaɪəsɪnθ] *n* ヒヤシンス [hiyashinsu]

hydrogen [ˈhaɪdrɪdʒən] *n* 水素 [suiso]

hygiene [ˈhaɪdʒiːn] *n* 衛生 [eisei]

hymn [hɪm] *n* 賛美歌 [sanbika]

hypermarket [ˈhaɪpəˌmɑːkɪt] *n* 郊外の大型スーパー [kougai no ougata suupaa]

hyphen [ˈhaɪfᵊn] *n* ハイフン [haifun]

I [aɪ] *pron* 私 [watashi]; **I don't like...** 私は・・・が好きではありません [watashi wa ... ga suki de wa arimasen]; **I have an appointment with...** 私は・・・さまとお約束をしています [watashi wa ... sama to o-yakusoku o shite imasu]; **I like...** 私は・・・が好きです [watashi wa ... ga suki desu]; **I love...** 私は・・・が大好きです [watashi wa ... ga daisuki desu]

ice [aɪs] *n* 氷 [kouri]; **black ice** *n* 路面の薄い透明な氷 [romen no usui toumei na kouri]; **ice cube** *n* アイスキューブ [aisukyuubu]; **ice hockey** *n* アイスホッケー [aisuhokkee]; **ice lolly** *n* アイスキャンディー [aisu kyandii]; **ice rink** *n* スケートリンク [sukeetorinku]; **With ice, please** 氷を入れてください [koori o irete kudsai]

iceberg [ˈaɪsbɜːg] *n* 氷山 [hyouzan]

icebox [ˈaɪsˌbɒks] *n* アイスボックス [aisu bokkusu]

ice cream [ˈaɪs ˈkriːm] *n* アイスクリーム [aisukuriimu]; **I'd like an ice cream** 私はアイスクリームをいただきます [watashi wa aisukuriimu o itadakimasu]

Iceland [ˈaɪslənd] *n* アイスランド [aisurando]

Icelandic [aɪsˈlændɪk] *adj* アイスランドの [aisurando no] ▷ *n* アイスランド人 [aisurandojin]

ice-skating [ˈaɪsˌskeɪtɪŋ] *n* アイススケート [aisusukeeto]

icing [ˈaɪsɪŋ] *n* アイシング [aishingu]; **icing sugar** *n* 粉砂糖 [konazatou]

icon [ˈaɪkɒn] *n* 聖像 [seizou]

icy [ˈaɪsɪ] *adj* 凍結した [touketsu shita]

idea [aɪˈdɪə] *n* 考え [kangae]

ideal [aɪˈdɪəl] *adj* 理想的な [risouteki na]

ideally [aɪˈdɪəlɪ] *adv* 理想的に [risouteki ni]

identical [aɪˈdɛntɪkəl] *adj* 同一の [douitsu no]

identification [aɪˌdɛntɪfɪˈkeɪʃən] *n* 身分証明 [mibun shoumei]

identify [aɪˈdɛntɪˌfaɪ] *v* 識別する [shikibetsu suru]

identity [aɪˈdɛntɪtɪ] *n* 身元 [mimoto]; **identity card** *n* 身分証明書 [mibunshomeisho]; **identity theft** *n* 個人情報泥棒 [kojin jouhou dorobou]

ideology [ˌaɪdɪˈɒlədʒɪ] *n* イデオロギー [ideorogii]

idiot [ˈɪdɪət] *n* ばか [baka]

idiotic [ˌɪdɪˈɒtɪk] *adj* ばかな [baka na]

idle [ˈaɪdəl] *adj* 何もしない [nanimo shinai]

i.e. [aɪ iː] *abbr* すなわち [sunawachi]

if [ɪf] *conj* もしも・・・ならば [moshimo ... naraba]

ignition [ɪgˈnɪʃən] *n* 点火装置 [tenkasouchi]

ignorance [ˈɪgnərəns] *n* 無知 [muchi]

ignorant [ˈɪgnərənt] *adj* 無知の [muchi no]

ignore [ɪgˈnɔː] *v* 無視する [mushi suru]

ill [ɪl] *adj* 病気の [byouki no]

illegal [ɪˈliːgəl] *adj* 不法な [fuhou na]

illegible [ɪˈlɛdʒɪbəl] *adj* 判読しにくい [handokushinikui]

illiterate [ɪˈlɪtərɪt] *adj* 読み書きのできない [yomikaki no dekinai]

illness [ˈɪlnɪs] *n* 病気 [byouki]

ill-treat [ɪlˈtriːt] *v* 虐待する [gyakutai suru]

illusion [ɪˈluːʒən] *n* 錯覚 [sakkaku]

illustration [ˌɪləˈstreɪʃən] *n* 挿絵 [sashie]

image [ˈɪmɪdʒ] *n* イメージ [imeeji]

imaginary [ɪˈmædʒɪnərɪ; -dʒɪnrɪ] *adj* 想像の [souzou no]

imagination [ɪˌmædʒɪˈneɪʃən] *n* 想像 [souzou]

imagine [ɪˈmædʒɪn] *v* 想像する [souzou suru]

imitate [ˈɪmɪˌteɪt] *v* 模倣する [mohou suru]

imitation [ˌɪmɪˈteɪʃən] *n* 模造品 [mozouhin]

immature [ˌɪməˈtjʊə; -ˈtʃʊə] *adj* 未成熟の [miseijuku no]

immediate [ɪˈmiːdɪət] *adj* 早速の [sassoku no]

immediately [ɪˈmiːdɪətlɪ] *adv* 早速 [sassoku]

immigrant [ˈɪmɪgrənt] *n* 移住者 [ijuusha]

immigration [ˌɪmɪˈgreɪʃən] *n* 移住 [ijuu]

immoral [ɪˈmɒrəl] *adj* 不道徳な [fudoutoku na]

impact [ˈɪmpækt] *n* 影響 [eikyou]

impaired [ɪmˈpɛəd] *adj* **I'm visually impaired** 私は視覚障害があります [watashi wa shikaku-shougai ga arimasu]

impartial [ɪmˈpɑːʃəl] *adj* 偏らない [katayoranai]

impatience [ɪmˈpeɪʃəns] *n* 短気 [tanki]

impatient [ɪmˈpeɪʃənt] *adj* いらいらしている [iraira shiteiru]

impatiently [ɪmˈpeɪʃəntlɪ] *adv* いらいらして [iraira shite]

impersonal [ɪmˈpɜːsənəl] *adj* 個人にかかわらない [kojin ni kakawaranai]

import *n* [ˈɪmpɔːt] 輸入 [yunyuu] ▷ *v* [ɪmˈpɔːt] 輸入する [yunyuu suru]

importance [ɪmˈpɔːtəns] *n* 重要性 [juuyousei]

important [ɪmˈpɔːtənt] *adj* 重要な [juuyou na]

impossible [ɪmˈpɒsəbəl] *adj* 不可能な [fukanou na]

practical [ɪmˈpræktɪkəl] *adj* 実際的
でない [jissaiteki denai]

press [ɪmˈprɛs] *v* 強く印象づける
[tsuyoku inshou zukeru]

pressed [ɪmˈprɛst] *adj* 感動した
[kandou shita]

pression [ɪmˈprɛʃən] *n* 印象 [inshou]

pressive [ɪmˈprɛsɪv] *adj* 印象的な
[inshouteki na]

prove [ɪmˈpruːv] *v* 改善する [kaizen
suru]

provement [ɪmˈpruːvmənt] *n* 改善
[kaizen]

[ɪn] *prep* ・・・の中に [...no naka ni]

accurate [ɪnˈækjʊrɪt; inˈaccurate]
adj 不正確な [fuseikaku na]

adequate [ɪnˈædɪkwɪt] *adj* 不十分な
[fujuubun na]

advertently [ˌɪnədˈvɜːtəntlɪ] *adv* 不
主意で [fuchuui de]

box [ˈɪnbɒks] *n* 書類受け [shoruiuke]

centive [ɪnˈsɛntɪv] *n* 奨励 [shourei]

ch [ɪntʃ] *n* インチ [inchi]

cident [ˈɪnsɪdənt] *n* 出来事 [dekigoto]

clude [ɪnˈkluːd] *v* 含む [fukumu]

cluded [ɪnˈkluːdɪd] *adj* 含まれた
[fukumareta]

cluding [ɪnˈkluːdɪŋ] *prep* ・・・を含め
て [...-o fukumete]

clusive [ɪnˈkluːsɪv] *adj* 含めた
[fukumeta]

come [ˈɪnkʌm; ˈɪnkəm] *n* 所得
[shotoku]; **income tax** *n* 所得税
[shotokuzei]

competent [ɪnˈkɒmpɪtənt] *adj* 無能
な [munou na]

complete [ˌɪnkəmˈpliːt] *adj* 不完全
な [fukanzen na]

consistent [ˌɪnkənˈsɪstənt] *adj* 一貫
性のない [ikkansei no nai]

convenience [ˌɪnkənˈviːnjəns;
-ˈviːnɪəns] *n* 不便 [fuben]

convenient [ˌɪnkənˈviːnjənt;
-ˈviːnɪənt] *adj* 不便な [fuben na]

correct [ˌɪnkəˈrɛkt] *adj* 不正確な
[fuseikaku na]

increase *n* [ˈɪnkriːs] 増加 [zouka] ▷ *v*
[ɪnˈkriːs] 増す [masu]

increasingly [ɪnˈkriːsɪŋlɪ] *adv* ますます
[masumasu]

incredible [ɪnˈkrɛdəbəl] *adj* 信じられな
い [shinjirarenai]

indecisive [ˌɪndɪˈsaɪsɪv] *adj* 優柔不断な
[yuujuu fudan na]

indeed [ɪnˈdiːd] *adv* 全く [mattaku]

independence [ˌɪndɪˈpɛndəns] *n* 独立
[dokuritsu]

independent [ˌɪndɪˈpɛndənt] *adj* 独立
した [dokuritsu shita]

index [ˈɪndɛks] *n (list)* 索引 [sakuin],
(numerical scale) 指数 [shisuu]; **index
finger** *n* 人差し指 [hitosashi yubi]

India [ˈɪndɪə] *n* インド [indo]

Indian [ˈɪndɪən] *adj* インドの [indo no]
▷ *n* インド人 [indojin]; **Indian Ocean** *n* イ
ンド洋 [indoyou]

indicate [ˈɪndɪˌkeɪt] *v* 示す [shimesu]

indicator [ˈɪndɪˌkeɪtə] *n* 指標
[shihyou]

indigestion [ˌɪndɪˈdʒɛstʃən] *n* 消化不
良 [shoukafuryou]

indirect [ˌɪndɪˈrɛkt] *adj* 間接的な
[kansetsuteki na]

indispensable [ˌɪndɪˈspɛnsəbəl] *adj* 不
可欠な [fukaketsu na]

individual [ˌɪndɪˈvɪdjʊəl] *adj* 個々の
[koko no]

Indonesia [ˌɪndəʊˈniːzɪə] *n* インドネシ
ア [indoneshia]

Indonesian [ˌɪndəʊˈniːzɪən] *adj* インド
ネシアの [indoneshia no] ▷ *n (person)* イン
ドネシア人 [indoneshiajin]

indoor [ˈɪnˌdɔː] *adj* 屋内の [okunai no]

indoors [ˌɪnˈdɔːz] *adv* 屋内で [okunai de]

industrial [ɪnˈdʌstrɪəl] *adj* 産業の
[sangyou no]; **industrial estate** *n* 工業
団地 [kougyoudanchi]

industry [ˈɪndəstrɪ] *n* 産業 [sangyou]

inefficient [ˌɪnɪˈfɪʃənt] *adj* 効率の悪い
[kouritsu no warui]

inevitable [ɪnˈɛvɪtəbəl] *adj* 避けられな
い [sakerarenai]

inexpensive [ˌɪnɪk'spɛnsɪv] *adj* 安い [yasui]

inexperienced [ˌɪnɪk'spɪərɪənst] *adj* 経験のない [keiken no nai]

infantry ['ɪnfəntrɪ] *n* 歩兵 [hohei]

infection [ɪn'fɛkʃən] *n* 感染 [kansen]

infectious [ɪn'fɛkʃəs] *adj* 感染性の [kansensei no]

inferior [ɪn'fɪərɪə] *adj* 劣った [ototta] ▷ *n* 目下の者 [meshita no mono]

infertile [ɪn'fɜːtaɪl] *adj* 繁殖力のない [hanshokuryoku no nai]

infinitive [ɪn'fɪnɪtɪv] *n* 不定詞 [futeishi]

infirmary [ɪn'fɜːmərɪ] *n* 診療所 [shinryoujo]

inflamed [ɪn'fleɪmd] *adj* 炎症を起こした [enshou-o okoshita]

inflammation [ˌɪnflə'meɪʃən] *n* 炎症 [enshou]

inflatable [ɪn'fleɪtəbᵊl] *adj* 膨張性の [bouchou sei no]

inflation [ɪn'fleɪʃən] *n* インフレーション [infureeshon]

inflexible [ɪn'flɛksəbᵊl] *adj* 頑固な [ganko na]

influence ['ɪnflʊəns] *n* 影響 [eikyou] ▷ *v* 影響を与える [eikyou-o ataeru]

influenza [ˌɪnflʊ'ɛnzə] *n* インフルエンザ [infuruenza]

inform [ɪn'fɔːm] *v* 知らせる [shiraseru]

informal [ɪn'fɔːməl] *adj* 形式ばらない [keishikibaranai]

information [ˌɪnfə'meɪʃən] *n* 知識 [chishiki]; **information office** *n* 案内所 [annaijo]

informative [ɪn'fɔːmətɪv] *adj* 知識を与える [chishiki-o ataeru]

infrastructure ['ɪnfrəˌstrʌktʃə] *n* インフラストラクチャー [infurasutorakuchaa]

infuriating [ɪn'fjʊərɪeɪtɪŋ] *adj* 腹立たしい [haradata shii]

ingenious [ɪn'dʒiːnjəs; -nɪəs] *adj* 独創的な [dokusouteki na]

ingredient [ɪn'griːdɪənt] *n* 材料 [zairyou]

inhabitant [ɪn'hæbɪtənt] *n* 住人 [juunin]

inhaler [ɪn'heɪlə] *n* 吸入器 [kyuunyuuki]

inherit [ɪn'hɛrɪt] *v* 相続する [souzoku suru]

inheritance [ɪn'hɛrɪtəns] *n* 相続 [souzoku]

inhibition [ˌɪnɪ'bɪʃən; ˌɪnhɪ-] *n* 抑圧 [yokuatsu]

initial [ɪ'nɪʃəl] *adj* 最初の [saisho no] ▷ *v* 頭文字で署名する [atamamoji de shomei suru]

initially [ɪ'nɪʃəlɪ] *adv* 最初に [saisho ni]

initials [ɪ'nɪʃəlz] *npl* 頭文字 [kashiramoji]

initiative [ɪ'nɪʃɪətɪv; -'nɪʃətɪv] *n* イニシアチブ [inishiachibu]

inject [ɪn'dʒɛkt] *v* 注射する [chuusha suru]

injection [ɪn'dʒɛkʃən] *n* 注射 [chuusha]; **I want an injection for the pain** 私は痛み止めの注射が欲しいのです [watashi wa itami-dome no chuusha ga hoshii no desu]; **Please give me an injection** 注射を打ってください [chuusha o utte kudasai]

injure ['ɪndʒə] *v* 傷つける [kizutsukeru]

injured ['ɪndʒəd] *adj* 傷ついた [kizutsuita]

injury ['ɪndʒərɪ] *n* 怪我 [kega]; **injury time** *n* サッカー・ラグビーなどで怪我の手当など needed などに要した分の延長時間 [sakkaa / ragubii nado de kega no teate nado ni youshita bun no enchou jikan]

injustice [ɪn'dʒʌstɪs] *n* 不公平 [fukouhei]

ink [ɪŋk] *n* インク [inku]

in-laws [ɪnlɔːz] *npl* 姻戚 [inseki]

inmate ['ɪnˌmeɪt] *n* 被収容者 [hishuuyousha]

inn [ɪn] *n* 宿屋 [yadoya]

inner ['ɪnə] *adj* 内側の [uchigawa no]; **inner tube** *n* インナーチューブ [innaachuubu]

innocent ['ɪnəsənt] *adj* 潔白な [keppaku na]

innovation [ˌɪnə'veɪʃən] *n* 革新 [kakushin]

innovative ['ɪnəˌveɪtɪv] *adj* 革新的な [kakushinteki na]

quest [ɪnˈkwɛst] n 検死審問 [kenshi hinmon]

quire [ɪnˈkwaɪə] v 尋ねる [tazuneru]

quiry [ɪnˈkwaɪərɪ] n 問い合わせ [toiawase]; **inquiries office** n 案内所 [annaijo]

quisitive [ɪnˈkwɪzɪtɪv] adj 詮索好き な [sensaku zuki na]

sane [ɪnˈseɪn] adj 正気でない [shouki de nai]

scription [ɪnˈskrɪpʃən] n 銘 [mei]

sect [ˈɪnsɛkt] n 昆虫 [konchuu]; **insect repellent** n 虫よけ [mushiyoke]; **stick insect** n ナナフシ [nanafushi]

sensitive [ɪnˈsɛnsɪtɪv] adj 鈍感な [donkan na]

side adv [ˌɪnˈsaɪd] 内側に [uchigawa ni] ▷ n [ˈɪnˈsaɪd] 内側 [uchigawa] ▷ prep ⋯の内側に [...no uchigawa ni]; **It's inside** 内側です [uchigawa desu]

sincere [ˌɪnsɪnˈsɪə] adj 誠意のない [seii no nai]

sist [ɪnˈsɪst] v 強要する [kyouyou suru]

somnia [ɪnˈsɒmnɪə] n 不眠症 [fuminshou]

spect [ɪnˈspɛkt] v 検査する [kensa suru]

spector [ɪnˈspɛktə] n 検査官 [kensakan]; **ticket inspector** n 検札係 [kensatsugakari]

stability [ˌɪnstəˈbɪlɪtɪ] n 不安定 [fuantei]

stalment [ɪnˈstɔːlmənt] n 分割払い [bunkatsu harai]

stance [ˈɪnstəns] n 事例 [jirei]

stant [ˈɪnstənt] adj 即座の [sokuza no]

stantly [ˈɪnstəntlɪ] adv 即座に [sokuza ni]

stead [ɪnˈstɛd] adv その代わりに [sono kawari ni]; **instead of** prep ⋯の代わり に [...no kawari ni]

stinct [ˈɪnstɪŋkt] n 本能 [honnou]

stitute [ˈɪnstɪˌtjuːt] n 学会 [gakkai]

stitution [ˌɪnstɪˈtjuːʃən] n 機関 [kikan] (組織)

struct [ɪnˈstrʌkt] v 指示する [shiji suru]

instructions [ɪnˈstrʌkʃənz] npl 指示 [shiji]

instructor [ɪnˈstrʌktə] n 指導者 [shidousha]; **driving instructor** n 自動 車教習指導員 [jidousha kyoushuu shidouin]

instrument [ˈɪnstrəmənt] n 器具 [kigu]; **musical instrument** n 楽器 [gakki]

insufficient [ˌɪnsəˈfɪʃənt] adj 不十分な [fujuubun na]

insulation [ˌɪnsjʊˈleɪʃən] n 絶縁材 [zetsuenzai]

insulin [ˈɪnsjʊlɪn] n インシュリン [inshurin]

insult n [ˈɪnsʌlt] 侮辱 [bujoku] ▷ v [ɪnˈsʌlt] 侮辱する [bujoku suru]

insurance [ɪnˈʃʊərəns; -ˈʃɔː-] n 保険 [hoken]; **accident insurance** n 事故保 険 [jiko hoken]; **car insurance** n 自動車 保険 [jidousha hoken]; **insurance certificate** n 保険契約書 [hoken keiyakusho]; **insurance policy** n 保険証 書 [hokenshousho]; **life insurance** n 生 命保険 [seimeihoken]; **third-party insurance** n 第三者賠償責任保険 [daisansha baishousekinin hoken]; **travel insurance** n 旅行保険 [ryokou hoken]; **Can I see your insurance certificate please?** あなたの保険証書を見せていた だけますか? [anata no hoken-shousho o misete itadakemasu ka?]; **Do you have insurance?** あなたは保険に入っていま すか? [anata wa hoken ni haitte imasu ka?]; **Give me your insurance details, please** あなたの保険の詳細を教えてく ださい [anata no hoken no shousai o oshiete kudasai]; **Here are my insurance details** 私の保険の詳細です [watashi no hoken no shousai desu]; **How much extra is comprehensive insurance cover?** 総合自動車保険に加 入する追加料金はいくらですか? [sougou-jidousha-hoken ni kanyuu suru tsuika-ryoukin wa ikura desu ka?]; **I don't have dental insurance** 私は歯科保険

に入っていません [watashi wa shika-hoken ni haitte imasen]; **I don't have health insurance** 私は医療保険に入っていません [watashi wa iryou-hoken ni haitte imasen]; **I have insurance** 私は保険に入っています [watashi wa hoken ni haitte imasu]; **I'd like to arrange personal accident insurance** 個人傷害保険をかけたいのですが [kojin-shougai-hoken o kaketai no desu ga]; **Is fully comprehensive insurance included in the price?** 料金には総合自動車保険が含まれていますか? [ryoukin ni wa sougou-jidousha-hoken ga fukumarete imasu ka?]; **Will the insurance pay for it?** 保険でそれが補償されますか? [hoken de sore ga hoshou saremasu ka?]

insure [ɪnˈʃʊə; -ˈʃɔː] v 保険をかける [hoken-o kakeru]

insured [ɪnˈʃʊəd; -ˈʃɔːd] adj 保険に入った [hoken ni haitta]

intact [ɪnˈtækt] adj 損なわれていない [sokonawareteinai]

intellectual [ˌɪntɪˈlɛktʃʊəl] adj 知的な [chiteki na] ▷ n 知識人 [chishikijin]

intelligence [ɪnˈtɛlɪdʒəns] n 知能 [chinou]

intelligent [ɪnˈtɛlɪdʒənt] adj 利口な [rikou na]

intend [ɪnˈtɛnd] v **intend to** v …するつもりだ [...suru tsumori da]

intense [ɪnˈtɛns] adj 強烈な [kyouretsu na]

intensive [ɪnˈtɛnsɪv] adj 集中的な [shuuchuuteki na]; **intensive care unit** n 集中治療室 [shuuchuuchiryoushitsu, ICU aishiiyuu]

intention [ɪnˈtɛnʃən] n 意図 [ito]

intentional [ɪnˈtɛnʃənəl] adj 意図的な [itoteki na]

intercom [ˈɪntəˌkɒm] n インターコム [intaakomu]

interest [ˈɪntrɪst; -tərɪst] n (curiosity) 興味 [kyoumi], (income) 利息 [risoku] ▷ v 興味を起こさせる [kyoumi-o okosaseru]; **interest rate** n 利率 [riritsu]

interested [ˈɪntrɪstɪd; -tərɪs-] adj 興味がある [kyoumi ga aru]

interesting [ˈɪntrɪstɪŋ; -tərɪs-] adj 興味深い [kyoumibukai]

interior [ɪnˈtɪərɪə] n 内側 [uchigawa]; **interior designer** n インテリアデザイナー [interiadezainaa]

intermediate [ˌɪntəˈmiːdɪɪt] adj 中間の [chuukan no]

internal [ɪnˈtɜːnəl] adj 内部の [naibu no]

international [ˌɪntəˈnæʃənəl] adj 国際的な [kokusaiteki na]

internet [ˈɪntəˌnɛt] n インターネット [intaanetto]; **internet café** n インターネットカフェ [intaanetto kafe]; **internet user** n インターネット利用者 [intaanetto riyousha]; **Are there any internet cafés here?** ここにインターネットカフェはありますか? [koko ni intaanetto-kafe wa arimasu ka?]; **Does the room have wireless internet access?** その部屋で無線インターネット接続を利用できますか? [sono heya de musen-intaanetto-setsuzoku o riyou dekimasu ka?]; **Is there an internet connection in the room?** その部屋にインターネットの接続ポイントはありますか? [sono heya ni intaanetto no setsuzoku-pointo wa arimasu ka?]

interpret [ɪnˈtɜːprɪt] v 解釈する [kaishaku suru]

interpreter [ɪnˈtɜːprɪtə] n 通訳者 [tsuuyakusha]

interrogate [ɪnˈtɛrəˌɡeɪt] v 質問する [shitsumon suru]

interrupt [ˌɪntəˈrʌpt] v 中断する [chuudan suru]

interruption [ˌɪntəˈrʌpʃən] n 中断 [chuudan]

interval [ˈɪntəvəl] n 間隔 [kankaku]

interview [ˈɪntəˌvjuː] n 面接 [mensetsu] ▷ v 面接する [mensetsu suru]

interviewer [ˈɪntəˌvjuːə] n 面接者 [mensetsusha]

intimate [ˈɪntɪmɪt] adj 親しい [shitashii]

intimidate [ɪnˈtɪmɪˌdeɪt] v おじけづかせる [ojikedukaseru]

into ['ɪntʊ:; 'ɪntə] *prep* ･･･の中へ [...no naka-e]; **bump into** *v* ばったり出会う [battari deau]

intolerant [ɪn'tɒlərənt] *adj* 耐えられない [taerarenai]

intranet ['ɪntrə,nɛt] *n* イントラネット [intouranetto]

introduce [,ɪntrə'dju:s] *v* 紹介する [shoukai suru]

introduction [,ɪntrə'dʌkʃən] *n* 紹介 [shoukai]

intruder [ɪn'tru:də] *n* 侵入者 [shinnyuusha]

intuition [,ɪntjʊ'ɪʃən] *n* 直感 [chokkan]

invade [ɪn'veɪd] *v* 侵略する [shinryaku suru]

invalid ['ɪnvə,li:d] *n* 病人 [byounin]

invent [ɪn'vɛnt] *v* 発明する [hatsumei suru]

invention [ɪn'vɛnʃən] *n* 発明 [hatsumei]

inventor [ɪn'vɛntə] *n* 発明者 [hatsumeisha]

inventory ['ɪnvəntərɪ; -trɪ] *n* 目録 [mokuroku]

invest [ɪn'vɛst] *v* 投資する [toushi suru]

investigation [ɪn,vɛstɪ'geɪʃən] *n* 調査 [chousa]

investment [ɪn'vɛstmənt] *n* 投資 [toushi]

investor [ɪn'vɛstə] *n* 投資者 [toushisha]

invigilator [ɪn'vɪdʒɪ,leɪtə] *n* 試験監督者 [shiken kantokusha]

invisible [ɪn'vɪzəbəl] *adj* 目に見えない [me ni mienai]

invitation [,ɪnvɪ'teɪʃən] *n* 招待 [shoutai]

invite [ɪn'vaɪt] *v* 誘う [sasou]

invoice ['ɪnvɔɪs] *n* インボイス [inboisu] ▷ *v* インボイスを送る [inboisu-o okuru]

involve [ɪn'vɒlv] *v* 伴う [tomonau]

iPod® ['aɪ,pɒd] *n* iPod® [ipod]

IQ [aɪ kju:] *abbr* 知能指数 [chinoushisuu]

Iran [ɪ'rɑ:n] *n* イラン [iran]

Iranian [ɪ'reɪnɪən] *adj* イランの [iran no] ▷ *n (person)* イラン人 [iranjin]

Iraq [ɪ'rɑ:k] *n* イラク [iraku]

Iraqi [ɪ'rɑ:kɪ] *adj* イラクの [iraku no] ▷ *n* イラク人 [irakujin]

Ireland ['aɪələnd] *n* アイルランド [airurando]; **Northern Ireland** *n* 北アイルランド [kita airurando]

iris ['aɪrɪs] *n* アヤメ [ayame]

Irish ['aɪrɪʃ] *adj* アイルランドの [airurando no] ▷ *n* アイルランド人 [airurandojin]

Irishman, Irishmen ['aɪrɪʃmən, 'aɪrɪʃmɛn] *n* アイルランド人 [airurandojin]

Irishwoman, Irishwomen ['aɪrɪʃwʊmən, 'aɪrɪʃwɪmɪn] *n* アイルランド人 [airurandojin]

iron ['aɪən] *n* 鉄 [tetsu] ▷ *v* アイロンをかける [airon-o kakeru]

ironic [aɪ'rɒnɪk] *adj* 皮肉な [hiniku na]

ironing ['aɪənɪŋ] *n* アイロンをかけるべきもの [airon-o kakerubeki mono]; **ironing board** *n* アイロン台 [airondai]

ironmonger's ['aɪən,mʌŋgəz] *n* 金物屋 [kanamonoya]

irony ['aɪrənɪ] *n* 皮肉 [hiniku]

irregular [ɪ'rɛgjʊlə] *adj* ふぞろいの [fuzoroi no]

irrelevant [ɪ'rɛləvənt] *adj* 無関係な [mukankei na]

irresponsible [,ɪrɪ'spɒnsəbəl] *adj* いい加減な [iikagen na]

irritable ['ɪrɪtəbəl] *adj* 怒りっぽい [okorippoi]

irritating ['ɪrɪ,teɪtɪŋ] *adj* いらいらさせる [iraira saseru]

Islam ['ɪzlɑ:m] *n* イスラム教 [isuramukyou]

Islamic ['ɪzləmɪk] *adj* イスラム教の [isuramukyou no]

island ['aɪlənd] *n* 島 [shima]; **desert island** *n* 無人島 [mujintou]

isolated ['aɪsə,leɪtɪd] *adj* 孤立した [koritsu shita]

ISP [aɪ ɛs pi:] *abbr* インターネットサービスプロバイダ [intaanetto saabisu purobaida]

Israel ['ɪzreɪəl; -rɪəl] *n* イスラエル [isuraeru]

Israeli [ɪz'reɪlɪ] *adj* イスラエルの [isuraeru no] ▷ *n* イスラエル人 [isuraerujin]

issue ['ɪʃjuː] *n* 論点 [ronten] ▷ *v* 公布する [koufu suru]

it [ɪt] *pron* それは [sore wa]; **I can't read it** それは読めません [sore wa yomemasen]; **Is it safe for children?** それは子供にも安全ですか? [sore wa kodomo ni mo anzen desu ka?]; **What is it?** それは何ですか? [sore wa nan desu ka?]

IT [aɪ tiː] *abbr* 情報技術 [jouho gijutsu]

Italian [ɪ'tæljən] *adj* イタリアの [itaria no] ▷ *n* (*language*) イタリア語 [itariago], (*person*) イタリア人 [itariajin]

Italy ['ɪtəlɪ] *n* イタリア [itaria]

itch [ɪtʃ] *v* かゆい [kayui]

itchy [ɪtʃɪ] *adj* かゆい [kayui]

item ['aɪtəm] *n* 項目 [koumoku]

itinerary [aɪ'tɪnərərɪ; ɪ-] *n* 旅程 [ryotei]

its [ɪts] *adj* それの [sore no]

itself [ɪt'sɛlf] *pron* それ自身 [sore jishin]

ivory ['aɪvərɪ; -vrɪ] *n* 象牙 [zouge]

ivy ['aɪvɪ] *n* ツタ [tsuta]

◆

J

jab [dʒæb] *n* 突き [tsuki]

jack [dʒæk] *n* ジャッキ [jakki]

jacket ['dʒækɪt] *n* ジャケット [jaketto]; **dinner jacket** *n* ディナージャケット [dinaa jaketto]; **jacket potato** *n* ジャケットポテト [jaketto poteto]; **life jacket** *n* 救命胴衣 [kyuumeidoui]

jackpot ['dʒæk,pɒt] *n* 多額の賞金 [tagaku no shoukin]

jail [dʒeɪl] *n* 刑務所 [keimusho] ▷ *v* 投獄する [tougoku suru]

jam [dʒæm] *n* ジャム [jamu]; **jam jar** *n* ジャムの瓶 [jamu no bin]; **traffic jam** *n* 交通渋滞 [koutsuujuutai]

Jamaican [dʒə'meɪkən] *adj* ジャマイカの [jamaika no] ▷ *n* (*person*) ジャマイカ人 [jamaikajin]

jammed [dʒæmd] *adj* ぎっしり詰め込んだ [gisshiri tsumekonda]

janitor ['dʒænɪtə] *n* 用務員 [youmuin]

January ['dʒænjʊərɪ] *n* 一月 [ichigatsu]

Japan [dʒə'pæn] *n* 日本 [nihon]

Japanese [,dʒæpə'niːz] *adj* 日本の [nihon no] ▷ *n* (*language*) 日本語 [nihongo], (*person*) 日本人 [nihonjin]

jar [dʒɑː] n 瓶 [bin]; **jam jar** n ジャムの瓶 [jamu no bin]

jaundice ['dʒɔːndɪs] n 黄疸 [oudan]

javelin ['dʒævlɪn] n 投げ槍 [nageyari]

jaw [dʒɔː] n あご [ago]

jazz [dʒæz] n ジャズ [jazu]

jealous ['dʒɛləs] adj 嫉妬深い [shittobukai]

jeans [dʒiːnz] npl ジーンズ [jiinzu]

jelly ['dʒɛlɪ] n ゼリー [zerii]

jellyfish ['dʒɛlɪˌfɪʃ] n クラゲ [kurage]; **Are there jellyfish here?** ここにクラゲはいますか? [koko ni kurage wa imasu ka?]

jersey ['dʒɜːzɪ] n ジャージー [jaajii]

Jesus ['dʒiːzəs] n イエス [iesu]

jet [dʒɛt] n ジェット機 [jettoki]; **jet lag** n 時差ぼけ [jisaboke]; **jumbo jet** n ジャンボジェット [janbojetto]

jetty ['dʒɛtɪ] n 突堤 [tottei]

Jew [dʒuː] n ユダヤ人 [yudayajin]

jewel ['dʒuːəl] n 宝石 [houseki]

jeweller ['dʒuːələ] n 宝石商 [housekishou]

jeweller's ['dʒuːələz] n 宝石商 [housekishou]

jewellery ['dʒuːəlrɪ] n 宝石類 [housekirui]

Jewish ['dʒuːɪʃ] adj ユダヤ人の [yudayajin no]

jigsaw ['dʒɪgˌsɔː] n ジグソーパズル [jigusoo pazuru]

job [dʒɒb] n 職 [shoku]; **job centre** n 公共職業安定所 [koukyoushokugyou anteisho]

jobless ['dʒɒblɪs; 'jobless] adj 失業中の [shitsugyouchuu no]

jockey ['dʒɒkɪ] n 競馬騎手 [keiba kishu]

jog [dʒɒg] v ジョギングする [jogingu suru]

jogging ['dʒɒgɪŋ] n ジョギング [jogingu]

join [dʒɔɪn] v 加わる [kuwawaru]

joiner ['dʒɔɪnə] n 建具屋 [tateguya]

joint [dʒɔɪnt] adj 共同の [kyoudou no] ▷ n (junction) 継ぎ目 [tsugime], (meat) 骨付き肉 [honetsuki niku]; **joint account** n 共同預金口座 [kyoudou yokin kouza]

joke [dʒəʊk] n 冗談 [joudan] ▷ v 冗談を言う [joudan o iu]

jolly ['dʒɒlɪ] adj 陽気な [youki na]

Jordan ['dʒɔːdən] n ヨルダン [yorudan]

Jordanian [dʒɔːˈdeɪnɪən] adj ヨルダンの [yorudan no] ▷ n ヨルダン人 [yorudanjin]

jot down [dʒɒt daʊn] v ちょっと書き留める [chotto kakitodomeru]

jotter ['dʒɒtə] n メモ帳 [memochou]

journalism ['dʒɜːnəˌlɪzəm] n ジャーナリズム [jaanarizumu]

journalist ['dʒɜːnəlɪst] n ジャーナリスト [jaanarisuto]

journey ['dʒɜːnɪ] n 旅行 [ryokou]

joy [dʒɔɪ] n 喜び [yorokobi]

joystick ['dʒɔɪˌstɪk] n 操縦桿 [soujuukan]

judge [dʒʌdʒ] n 裁判官 [saibankan] ▷ v 審査する [shinsa suru]

judo ['dʒuːdəʊ] n 柔道 [juudou]

jug [dʒʌg] n ジャグ [jagu]

juggler ['dʒʌglə] n 手品師 [tejinashi]

juice [dʒuːs] n ジュース [juusu]; **orange juice** n オレンジジュース [orenjijuusu]

July [dʒuːˈlaɪ; dʒə-; dʒʊ-] n 七月 [shichigatsu]

jump [dʒʌmp] n ジャンプ [janpu] ▷ v 跳びはねる [tobihaneru]; **high jump** n 走り高跳び [hashiri takatobi]; **jump leads** npl ブースターコード [buusutaakoodo]; **long jump** n 幅跳び [habatobi]

jumper ['dʒʌmpə] n セーター [seetaa]

jumping [dʒʌmpɪŋ] n show-jumping n 障害飛越 [shougaihietsu]

junction ['dʒʌŋkʃən] n 交差点 [kousaten]; **Go right at the next junction** 次の交差点で右に進んでください [tsugi no kousaten de migi ni susunde kudasai]

June [dʒuːn] n 六月 [rokugatsu]; **at the beginning of June** 六月の初めに [roku-gatsu no hajime ni]; **at the end of June** 六月の終わりに [roku-gatsu no owari ni]; **for the whole of June** 六月いっぱい [roku-gatsu ippai]; **It's Monday the fifteenth of June** 六月十五日の月

曜日です [roku-gatsu juugo-nichi no getsuyoubi desu]

jungle [ˈdʒʌŋgəl] *n* ジャングル [janguru]

junior [ˈdʒuːnjə] *adj* 下級の [kakyuu no]

junk [dʒʌŋk] *n* がらくた [garakuta]: **junk mail** *n* ジャンクメール [janku meeru]

jury [ˈdʒʊərɪ] *n* 陪審 [baishin]

just [dʒəst] *adv* たった今 [tatta ima]

justice [ˈdʒʌstɪs] *n* 正義 [seigi]

justify [ˈdʒʌstɪˌfaɪ] *v* 正当化する [seitouka suru]

kangaroo [ˌkæŋgəˈruː] *n* カンガルー [kangaruu]

karaoke [ˌkɑːrəˈəʊkɪ] *n* カラオケ [karaoke]

karate [kəˈrɑːtɪ] *n* 空手 [karate]

Kazakhstan [ˌkɑːzɑːkˈstæn; -ˈstɑːn] *n* カザフスタン [kazafusutan]

kebab [kəˈbæb] *n* カバブ [kababu]

keen [kiːn] *adj* 熱心な [nesshin na]

keep [kiːp] *v* 持ち続ける [mochitsudukeru]

keep-fit [ˈkiːpˌfɪt] *n* フィットネス運動 [fittonesu undou]

keep out [kiːp aʊt] *v* 中に入れない [naka ni irenai]

keep up [kiːp ʌp] *v* 維持する [iji suru]; **keep up with** *v* 維持する [iji suru]

kennel [ˈkɛnəl] *n* 犬小屋 [inugoya]

Kenya [ˈkɛnjə; ˈkiːnjə] *n* ケニア [kenia]

Kenyan [ˈkɛnjən; ˈkiːnjən] *adj* ケニアの [kenia no] ▷ *n* ケニア人 [keniajin]

kerb [kɜːb] *n* 縁石 [fuchiishi]

kerosene [ˈkɛrəˌsiːn] *n* 灯油 [touyu]

ketchup [ˈkɛtʃəp] *n* ケチャップ [kechappu]

kettle [ˈkɛtəl] *n* ケトル [ketoru]

key [kiː] n *(for lock)* 鍵 [kagi], *(music/computer)* キー [kii]; **car keys** npl 車の鍵 [kuruma no kagi]; **Can I have a key?** 鍵をもらえますか? [kagi o moraemasu ka?]; **I left the keys in the car** 私は車に鍵を置き忘れました [watashi wa kuruma ni kagi o okiwasuremashita]; **I'm having trouble with the key** 鍵に問題があります [kagi ni mondai ga arimasu]; **I've forgotten the key** 私は鍵を置き忘れました [watashi wa kagi o okiwasuremashita]; **the key for room number two hundred and two** 202号室の鍵 [nihyaku-ni-gou-shitsu no kagi]; **The key doesn't work** 鍵が開きません [kagi ga akimasen]; **We need a second key** 鍵がもう一つ必要です [kagi ga mou hitotsu hitsuyou desu]; **What's this key for?** この鍵は何のためですか? [kono kagi wa nan no tame desu ka?]; **Where do we get the key...?** ・・・の鍵はどこでもらえばいいのですか? [...no kagi wa doko de moraeba ii no desu ka?]; **Where do we hand in the key when we're leaving?** 出るときに鍵はどこに渡せばいいのですか? [deru toki ni kagi wa doko ni wataseba ii no desu ka?]; **Which is the key for the back door?** 裏口の鍵はどれですか? [uraguchi no kagi wa dore desu ka?]; **Which is the key for this door?** このドアの鍵はどれですか? [kono doa no kagi wa dore desu ka?]

keyboard ['kiːˌbɔːd] n キーボード [kiiboodo]

keyring ['kiːˌrɪŋ] n キーリング [kiiringu]

kick [kɪk] n 蹴り [keri] ▷ v 蹴る [keru]

kick off [kɪk ɒf] v キックオフする [kikkuofu suru]

kick-off [kɪkɒf] n キックオフ [kikkuofu]

kid [kɪd] n 子供 [kodomo] ▷ v ヤギが子を産む [yagi ga ko o umu]

kidnap ['kɪdnæp] v 誘拐する [yuukai suru]

kidney ['kɪdnɪ] n 腎臓 [jinzou]

kill [kɪl] v 殺す [korosu]

killer ['kɪlə] n 殺人者 [satsujinsha]

kilo ['kiːləʊ] n キロ [kiro]

kilometre [kɪ'lɒmɪtə; 'kɪləˌmiːtə] n キロメートル [kiromeetoru]

kilt [kɪlt] n キルト [kiruto] *(タータン)*

kind [kaɪnd] adj 親切な [shinsetsu na] ▷ n 種類 [shurui]

kindly ['kaɪndlɪ] adv 親切に [shinsetsu ni]

kindness ['kaɪndnɪs] n 親切 [shinsetsu]

king [kɪŋ] n 王 [ou]

kingdom ['kɪŋdəm] n 王国 [oukoku]

kingfisher ['kɪŋˌfɪʃə] n カワセミ [kawasemi]

kiosk ['kiːɒsk] n キオスク [kiosuku]

kipper ['kɪpə] n キッパー [kippaa]

kiss [kɪs] n キス [kisu] *(口)* ▷ v キスする [kisu suru]

kit [kɪt] n 用具一式 [yougu isshiki]; **hands-free kit** n ハンズフリーキット [hanzu furii kitto]; **repair kit** n 修理キット [shuuri kitto]

kitchen ['kɪtʃɪn] n 台所 [daidokoro]; **fitted kitchen** n 造り付けのキッチン [tsukuritsuke no kitchin]

kite [kaɪt] n 凧 [tako]

kitten ['kɪtᵊn] n 子猫 [koneko]

kiwi ['kiːwiː] n キーウィ [kiiui]

knee [niː] n ひざ [hiza]

kneecap ['niːˌkæp] n ひざがしら [hizagashira]

kneel [niːl] v ひざを曲げる [hiza-o mageru]

kneel down [niːl daʊn] v ひざまずく [hizamazuku]

knickers ['nɪkəz] npl ショーツ [shootsu]

knife [naɪf] n ナイフ [naifu]

knit [nɪt] v 編む [amu]

knitting ['nɪtɪŋ] n 編物 [amimono]; **knitting needle** n 編み棒 [amibou]

knob [nɒb] n ノブ [nobu]

knock [nɒk] n たたくこと [tataku koto] ▷ v たたく [tataku], *(on the door etc.)* たたく [tataku]

knock down [nɒk daʊn] v 打ち倒す [uchitaosu]

knock out [nɒk aʊt] v 打ち負かす [uchimakasu]

knot [nɒt] *n* 結び目 [musubime]

know [nəʊ] *v* 知っている [shitte iru]

know-all ['nəʊɔːl] *n* 知ったかぶりをする
人 [shitta kaburi o suru hito]

know-how ['nəʊˌhaʊ] *n* ノウハウ
[nouhau]

knowledge ['nɒlɪdʒ] *n* 知識 [chishiki]

knowledgeable ['nɒlɪdʒəbᵊl] *adj* ···
に精通している [...ni seitsuu shiteiru]

known [nəʊn] *adj* 知られている
[shirarete iru]

Koran [kɔː'rɑːn] *n* コーラン [kooran]

Korea [kə'riːə] *n* 朝鮮 [chousen]; **North
Korea** *n* 北朝鮮 [kita chousen]; **South
Korea** *n* 韓国 [kankoku]

Korean [kə'riːən] *adj* 朝鮮の [chousen
no] ▷ *n* (*language*) 朝鮮語 [chousengo],
(*person*) 朝鮮人 [chousenjin]

kosher ['kəʊʃə] *adj* ユダヤ教の掟に従っ
て料理された清浄な [yudaya kyou no
okite ni shitagatte ryouri sareta seijou na]

Kosovo ['kɔsɔvɒ; 'kɒsəvəʊ] *n* コソボ
[kosobo]

Kuwait [kʊ'weɪt] *n* クウェート [kuueeto]

Kuwaiti [kʊ'weɪtɪ] *adj* クウェートの
[kuueeto no] ▷ *n* クウェート人 [kuueetojin]

Kyrgyzstan ['kɪəgɪzˌstɑːn; -ˌstæn] *n*
キルギスタン [kirugisutan]

lab [læb] *n* ラボ [rabo]

label ['leɪbᵊl] *n* ラベル [raberu]

laboratory [lə'bɒrətrɪ; 'læbrəˌtɔːrɪ] *n*
実験室 [jikkenshitsu]; **language
laboratory** *n* 語学ラボ [gogaku rabo]

labour ['leɪbə] *n* 労働 [roudou]

labourer ['leɪbərə] *n* 労働者 [roudousha]

lace [leɪs] *n* レース [reesu] (*布*)

lack [læk] *n* 欠乏 [ketsubou]

lacquer ['lækə] *n* ラッカー [rakkaa]

lad [læd] *n* 少年 [shounen]

ladder ['lædə] *n* はしご [hashigo]

ladies ['leɪdɪz] *n* ladies' *n* 女性用トイレ
[joseiyou toire]; **Where is the ladies?** 女
性用トイレはどこですか? [josei-you toire
wa doko desu ka?]

ladle ['leɪdᵊl] *n* お玉 [otama]

lady ['leɪdɪ] *n* 婦人 [fujin]

ladybird ['leɪdɪˌbɜːd] *n* テントウムシ
[tentoumushi]

lag [læg] *n* jet lag *n* 時差ぼけ [jisaboke];
I'm suffering from jet lag 私は時差ぼ
けに悩んでいます [watashi wa jisaboke ni
nayande imasu]

lager ['lɑːgə] *n* ラガー [ragaa]

lagoon [lə'guːn] *n* 潟湖 [sekiko]

laid-back ['leɪdbæk] *adj* くつろいだ [kutsuroida]

lake [leɪk] *n* 湖 [mizu-umi]

lamb [læm] *n* 子羊 [kohitsuji]

lame [leɪm] *adj* びっこの [bikko no]

lamp [læmp] *n* ランプ [ranpu]; **bedside lamp** *n* ベッドサイドランプ [beddosaido ranpu]; **The lamp is not working** ランプがつきません [ranpu ga tsukimasen]

lamppost ['læmp,pəʊst] *n* 街灯柱 [gaitouchuu]

lampshade ['læmp,ʃeɪd] *n* ランプシェード [ranpusheedo]

land [lænd] *n* 陸 [riku] ▷ *v* 着陸する [chakuriku suru]

landing ['lændɪŋ] *n* 踊り場 [odoriba]

landlady ['lænd,leɪdɪ] *n* 女家主 [onna yanushi]

landlord ['lænd,lɔːd] *n* 家主 [yanushi]

landmark ['lænd,mɑːk] *n* ランドマーク [randomaaku]

landowner ['lænd,əʊnə] *n* 地主 [jinushi]

landscape ['lænd,skeɪp] *n* 風景 [fuukei]

landslide ['lænd,slaɪd] *n* 地すべり [jisuberi]

lane [leɪn] *n* 小道 [komichi], *(driving)* 車線 [shasen]; **cycle lane** *n* サイクルレーン [saikurureen]; **You are in the wrong lane** あなたは間違った車線にいます [anata wa machigatta shasen ni imasu]

language ['læŋgwɪdʒ] *n* 言葉 [kotoba]; **language laboratory** *n* 語学ラボ [gogaku rabo]; **language school** *n* 語学学校 [gogaku gakkou]; **sign language** *n* 手話 [shuwa]

lanky ['læŋkɪ] *adj* ひょろ長い [hyoro nagai]

Laos [laʊz; laʊs] *n* ラオス [raosu]

lap [læp] *n* ひざ [hiza]

laptop ['læp,tɒp] *n* ラップトップ [rapputoppu]; **Can I use my own laptop here?** ここで自分のラップトップを使えますか？ [koko de jibun no rappu-toppu o tsukaemasu ka?]

larder ['lɑːdə] *n* 食料置場 [shokuryou okiba]

large [lɑːdʒ] *adj* 大きい [ookii]

largely ['lɑːdʒlɪ] *adv* 主として [shutoshite]

laryngitis [,lærɪn'dʒaɪtɪs] *n* 喉頭炎 [koutouen]

laser ['leɪzə] *n* レーザー [reezaa]

lass [læs] *n* 少女 [shoujo]

last [lɑːst] *adj* 最後の [saigo no] ▷ *adv* 最後に [saigo ni] ▷ *v* 続く [tsuzuku]; **When does the last chair-lift go?** 最後のチェアリフトはいつ出ますか？ [saigo no chea-rifuto wa itsu demasu ka?]

lastly ['lɑːstlɪ] *adv* 最後に [saigo ni]

late [leɪt] *adj (dead)* 故・・・ [yue...], *(delayed)* 遅れた [okureta] ▷ *adv* 遅れて [okurete]; **Is the train running late?** 電車は遅れていますか？ [densha wa okurete imasu ka?]; **Sorry we're late** 遅れてすみません [okurete sumimasen]; **The train is running ten minutes late** 電車は十分遅れています [densha wa jup-pun okurete imasu]

lately ['leɪtlɪ] *adv* 最近 [saikin]

later ['leɪtə] *adv* あとで [ato de]; **Can you try again later?** あとでもう一度かけてもらえますか？ [ato de mou ichido kakete moraemasu ka?]; **I'll call back later** あとでかけなおします [ato de kakenaoshimasu]; **Shall I come back later?** あとで出直しましょうか？ [ato de denaoshimashou ka?]

Latin ['lætɪn] *n* ラテン語 [ratengo]

Latin America ['lætɪn ə'mɛrɪkə] *n* ラテンアメリカ [raten amerika]

Latin American ['lætɪn ə'mɛrɪkən] *adj* ラテンアメリカの [raten amerika no]

latitude ['lætɪ,tjuːd] *n* 緯度 [ido]

Latvia ['lætvɪə] *n* ラトビア [ratobia]

Latvian ['lætvɪən] *adj* ラトビアの [ratobia no] ▷ *n (language)* ラトビア語 [ratobiago], *(person)* ラトビア人 [ratobiajin]

laugh [lɑːf] *n* 笑い [warai] ▷ *v* 笑う [warau]

laughter ['lɑːftə] *n* 笑い声 [waraigoe]

launch [lɔːntʃ] *v* 打ち上げる [uchiage ru], 進水させる [shinsui saseru]

Launderette® [,lɔːndə'rɛt; lɔːn'drɛt] *n* ローンドレット® [roondoretto]

laundry ['lɔːndrɪ] *n* 洗濯物 [sentakumono]

lava ['lɑːvə] *n* 溶岩 [yougan]

lavatory ['lævətərɪ; -trɪ] *n* トイレ [toire]

lavender ['lævəndə] *n* ラベンダー [rabendaa]

law [lɔː] *n* 法律 [houritsu]; **law school** *n* ロースクール [roosukuuru]

lawn [lɔːn] *n* 芝生 [shibafu]

lawnmower ['lɔːnˌməʊə] *n* 芝刈り機 [shibakariki]

lawyer ['lɔːjə; 'lɔɪə] *n* 弁護士 [bengoshi]

laxative ['læksətɪv] *n* 緩下剤 [kangezai]

lay [leɪ] *v* 置く [oku]

layby ['leɪˌbaɪ] *n* 待避場所 [taihi basho]

layer ['leɪə] *n* 層 [sou]; **ozone layer** *n* オゾン層 [ozonsou]

lay off [leɪ ɒf] *v* 一時解雇する [ichiji kaiko suru]

layout ['leɪˌaʊt] *n* 配置 [haichi]

lazy ['leɪzɪ] *adj* 怠惰な [taida na]

lead[1] [liːd] *n* (*in play/film*) 主役 [shuyaku], (*position*) トップ記事 [toppu kiji] ▷ *v* 導く [michibiku]; **jump leads** *npl* ブースターコード [buusutaakoodo]; **lead singer** *n* リードシンガー [riidoshingaa]

lead[2] [lɛd] *n* (*metal*) 鉛 [namari]

leader ['liːdə] *n* リーダー [riidaa]

lead-free [ˌlɛd'friː] *adj* 無鉛の [muen no]

leaf [liːf] *n* 葉 [ha]; **bay leaf** *n* ローリエ [roorie]

leaflet ['liːflɪt] *n* ちらし [chirashi] (印刷物)

league [liːg] *n* 連盟 [renmei]

leak [liːk] *n* 漏れ口 [moreguchi] ▷ *v* 漏れる [moreru]

lean [liːn] *v* もたれる [motareru] (寄りかかる); **lean forward** *v* 前かがみになる [maekagami ni naru]

lean on [liːn ɒn] *v* おどす [odosu]

lean out [liːn aʊt] *v* ・・・から身を乗り出す [...kara mi-o noridasu]

leap [liːp] *v* 跳ねる [haneru]; **leap year** *n* うるう年 [uruudoshi]

learn [lɜːn] *v* 学ぶ [manabu]

learner ['lɜːnə; 'learner] *n* 学習者 [gakushuusha]; **learner driver** *n* 仮免許運転者 [karimenkyo untensha]

lease [liːs] *n* 賃貸借契約 [chintaishaku keiyaku] ▷ *v* 賃貸借する [chintaishaku suru]

least [liːst] *adj* 最も少ない [mottomo sukunai]; **at least** *adv* 少なくとも [sukunakutomo]

leather ['lɛðə] *n* 革 [kawa]

leave [liːv] *n* 許可 [kyoka] ▷ *v* 出発する [shuppatsu suru]; **maternity leave** *n* 出産休暇 [shussan kyuuka]; **paternity leave** *n* 父親の育児休暇 [chichioya no ikuji kyuuka]; **sick leave** *n* 病気休暇 [byoukikyuuka]

leave out [liːv aʊt] *v* 省く [habuku]

leaves [liːvz] *npl* 葉 [ha]

Lebanese [ˌlɛbə'niːz] *adj* レバノンの [rebanon no] ▷ *n* レバノン人 [rebanonjin]

Lebanon ['lɛbənən] *n* レバノン [rebanon]

lecture ['lɛktʃə] *n* 講義 [kougi] ▷ *v* 講義をする [kougi-o suru]

lecturer ['lɛktʃərə; 'lecturer] *n* 講師 [koushi]

leek [liːk] *n* ネギ [negi]

left [lɛft] *adj* 左の [hidari no] ▷ *adv* 左に [hidari no] ▷ *n* 左 [hidari]; **Go left at the next junction** 次の交差点で左に進んでください [tsugi no kousaten de hidari ni susunde kudasai]; **Turn left** 左に曲がってください [hidari ni magatte kudasai]

left-hand [ˌlɛft'hænd] *adj* 左側の [hidarigawa no]; **left-hand drive** *n* 左側通行 [hidarigawa tsuukou]

left-handed [ˌlɛft'hændɪd] *adj* 左利きの [hidarikiki no]

left-luggage [ˌlɛft'lʌgɪdʒ] *n* 預けた手荷物 [azuketa tenimotsu]; **left-luggage locker** *n* コインロッカー [koinrokkaa]; **left-luggage office** *n* 手荷物一時預かり所 [tenimotsu ichiji azukarisho]

leftovers ['lɛftˌəʊvəz] *npl* 食べ残し [tabenokoshi]

left-wing [ˌlɛft'wɪŋ] *adj* 左派の [saha no]

leg [lɛg] n 脚 [ashi]; **I can't move my leg** 私は脚を動かせません [watashi wa ashi o ugokasemasen]; **I've got cramp in my leg** 私は脚がつっています [watashi wa ashi ga tsutte imasu]; **My leg itches** 私は脚がかゆみます [watashi wa ashi ga kayumimasu]; **She has hurt her leg** 彼女は脚を痛めました [kanojo wa ashi o itamemashita]

legal ['li:gəl] adj 合法的な [gouhouteki na]

legend ['lɛdʒənd] n 伝説 [densetsu]

leggings ['lɛgɪŋz] npl レギングス [regingusu]

legible ['lɛdʒəbəl] adj 読みやすい [yomiyasui]

legislation [ˌlɛdʒɪs'leɪʃən] n 法律制定 [houritsu seitei]

leisure ['lɛʒə; 'li:ʒər] n 余暇 [yoka]; **leisure centre** n レジャーセンター [rejaasentaa]

lemon ['lɛmən] n レモン [remon]; **with lemon** レモン入りで [remon-iri de]

lemonade [ˌlɛmə'neɪd] n レモネード [remoneedo]

lend [lɛnd] v 貸す [kasu]

length [lɛŋkθ; lɛŋθ] n 長さ [nagasa]

lens [lɛnz] n レンズ [renzu]; **contact lenses** npl コンタクトレンズ [kontakutorenzu]; **zoom lens** n ズームレンズ [zuumurenzu]; **cleansing solution for contact lenses** コンタクトレンズの洗浄液 [kontakuto-renzu no senjou-eki]; **I wear contact lenses** 私はコンタクトレンズをはめています [watashi wa kontakuto-renzu o hamete imasu]

Lent [lɛnt] n 四旬節 [shijunsetsu]

lentils ['lɛntɪlz] npl ヒラマメ [hiramame]

Leo ['li:əʊ] n 獅子座 [shishiza]

leopard ['lɛpəd] n ヒョウ [hyou] (動物)

leotard ['lɪəˌtɑːd] n レオタード [reotaado]

less [lɛs] adv 少なく [sukunaku] ▷ pron より少量 [yori shouryou]

lesson ['lɛsən] n 授業 [jugyou]; **driving lesson** n 自動車教習 [jidoushakyoushuu]

let [lɛt] v ・・・させる [...saseru]

let down [lɛt daʊn] v がっかりさせる [gakkari saseru]

let in [lɛt ɪn] v 入れる [ireru]

letter ['lɛtə] n (a, b, c) 文字 [moji], (message) 手紙 [tegami]; **I'd like to send this letter** この手紙を送りたいのですが [kono tegami o okuritai no desu ga]

letterbox ['lɛtəˌbɒks] n 郵便受 [yuubinjuke]

lettuce ['lɛtɪs] n レタス [retasu]

leukaemia [luːˈkiːmɪə] n 白血病 [hakketsubyou]

level ['lɛvəl] adj 水平の [suihei no] ▷ n 水平 [suihei]; **level crossing** n 踏切 [fumikiri]; **sea level** n 海水面 [kaisui men]

lever ['liːvə] n レバー [rebaa] (操作ハンドル)

liar ['laɪə] n 嘘つき [usotsuki]

liberal ['lɪbərəl; 'lɪbrəl] adj リベラルな [riberaru na]

liberation [ˌlɪbə'reɪʃən] n 解放 [kaihou]

Liberia [laɪ'bɪərɪə] n リベリア [riberia]

Liberian [laɪ'bɪərɪən] adj リベリアの [riberia no] ▷ n リベリア人 [riberiajin]

Libra ['liːbrə] n 天秤座 [tenbinza]

librarian [laɪ'brɛərɪən] n 図書館員 [toshokan-in]

library ['laɪbrərɪ] n 図書館 [toshokan]

Libya ['lɪbɪə] n リビア [ribia]

Libyan ['lɪbɪən] adj リビアの [ribia no] ▷ n リビア人 [ribiajin]

lice [laɪs] npl シラミ [shirami]

licence ['laɪsəns] n 免許 [menkyo]; **driving licence** n 運転免許証 [untenmenkyoshou]; **I don't have my driving licence on me** 私は運転免許証を携帯していません [watashi wa unten-menkyoshou o keitai shite imasen]; **My driving licence number is...** 私の運転免許証番号は・・・です [watashi wa unten-menkyoshou bangou wa ... desu]

lick [lɪk] v なめる [nameru] (舌)

lid [lɪd] n 蓋 [futa]

lie [laɪ] n 嘘 [uso] ▷ v 嘘をつく [uso-o tsuku]

Liechtenstein ['lɪktən‚staɪn; 'lɪçtənʃtaɪn] n リヒテンシュタイン [rihitenshutain]

lie down [laɪ daʊn] v 横になる [yoko ni naru]

lie in [laɪ ɪn] v 朝寝坊 [asanebou]

lie-in [laɪɪn] n have a lie-in v 朝寝坊 [asanebou]

lieutenant [lɛfˈtɛnənt; luːˈtɛnənt] n 中尉 [chuui]

life [laɪf] n 生命 [seimei]; **life insurance** n 生命保険 [seimeihoken]; **life jacket** n 救命胴衣 [kyuumeidoui]

lifebelt ['laɪf‚bɛlt] n 救命ベルト [kyuumei beruto]

lifeboat ['laɪf‚bəʊt] n 救命ボート [kyuumeibooto]

lifeguard ['laɪf‚gɑːd] n 水泳場の救助員 [suieijou no kyuujoin]

life-saving ['laɪf-‚saɪvɪŋ] adj 救命の [kyuumei no]

lifestyle ['laɪf‚staɪl] n ライフスタイル [raifusutairu]

lift [lɪft] n (free ride) 人を車に乗せてあげること [hito-o kuruma ni nosete ageru koto], (up/down) エレベーター [erebeetaa] ▷ v 持ち上げる [mochiageru]; **ski lift** n スキー場のリフト [sukii jou no rifuto]; **Do you have a lift for wheelchairs?** 車椅子用のエレベーターはありますか? [kuruma-isu-you no erebeetaa wa arimasu ka?]; **Is there a lift in the building?** 建物内にエレベーターはありますか? [tatemono-nai ni erebeetaa wa arimasu ka?]; **Where is the lift?** エレベーターはどこですか? [erebeetaa wa doko desu ka?]

light [laɪt] adj (not dark) 明るい [akarui], (not heavy) 軽い [karui] ▷ n 光 [hikari] ▷ v ともす [tomosu]; **brake light** n ブレーキランプ [bureeki ranpu]; **hazard warning lights** npl 故障警告灯 [koshou keikokutou]; **light bulb** n 電球 [denkyuu]; **pilot light** n 口火 [kuchibi]; **traffic lights** npl 交通信号 [koutsuu shingou]; **May I take it over to the light?** 明るい

ところに持っていってもいいですか? [akarui tokoro ni motte itte mo ii desu ka?]

lighter ['laɪtə] n ライター [raitaa]

lighthouse ['laɪt‚haʊs] n 灯台 [toudai]

lighting ['laɪtɪŋ] n 照明 [shoumei]

lightning ['laɪtnɪŋ] n 雷 [kaminari]

like [laɪk] prep ···のような [...no you na] ▷ v 好む [konomu]

likely ['laɪklɪ] adj ···しそうな [...shisou na]

lilac ['laɪlək] adj ライラック色の [rairakku iro no] ▷ n ライラック [rairakku]

Lilo® ['laɪləʊ] n ライロー® [rairoo]

lily ['lɪlɪ] n ユリ [yuri]; **lily of the valley** n ドイツスズラン [doitsusuzuran]

lime [laɪm] n (compound) 石灰 [sekkai], (fruit) ライム [raimu]

limestone ['laɪm‚stəʊn] n 石灰岩 [sekkaigan]

limit ['lɪmɪt] n 限界 [genkai]; **age limit** n 年齢制限 [nenreiseigen]; **speed limit** n 制限速度 [seigensokudo]

limousine ['lɪmə‚ziːn; ‚lɪmə'ziːn] n リムジン [rimujin]

limp [lɪmp] v びっこをひく [bikko o hiku]

line [laɪn] n 線 [sen]; **washing line** n 物干し綱 [monohoshi tsuna]; **I want to make an outside call, can I have a line?** 外線電話をかけたいので、つないでもらえますか? [gaisen-denwa o kaketai no de, tsunaide moraemasu ka?]; **It's a bad line** 回線が悪いです [kaisen ga warui desu]; **Which line should I take for...?** ···へ行くにはどの路線を使えばいいのですか? [...e iku ni wa dono rosen o tsukaeba ii no desu ka?]

linen ['lɪnɪn] n 麻 [asa]; **bed linen** n ベッドリネン [beddorinen]

liner ['laɪnə] n 定期船 [teikisen]

lingerie ['lænʒərɪ] n ランジェリー [ranjerii]; **Where is the lingerie department?** ランジェリー売り場はどこですか? [ranjerii-uriba wa doko desu ka?]

linguist ['lɪŋgwɪst] n 言語学者 [gengogakusha]

nguistic [lɪŋ'gwɪstɪk] *adj* 言語の [gengo no]

ning ['laɪnɪŋ] *n* 裏地 [uraji]

nk [lɪŋk] *v* つなぐ [tsunagu]

no ['laɪnəʊ] *n* リノリウム [rinoriumu]

on ['laɪən] *n* ライオン [raion]

oness ['laɪənɪs] *n* 雌ライオン [mesuraion]

p [lɪp] *n* 唇 [kuchibiru]; **lip salve** *n* おべっか [obekka]

p-read ['lɪp,ri:d] *v* 読唇術で解する [dokushinjutsu de kaisuru]

pstick ['lɪp,stɪk] *n* 口紅 [kuchibeni]

queur [lɪ'kjʊə; likœr] *n* リキュール [rikyuuru]; **What liqueurs do you have?** どんなリキュールがありますか? [donna rikyuuru ga arimasu ka?]

quid ['lɪkwɪd] *n* 液体 [ekitai]; **washing-up liquid** *n* 食器洗い用液体洗剤 [shokkiarai you ekitai senzai]

quidizer ['lɪkwɪ,daɪzə] *n* ミキサー [mikisaa]

st [lɪst] *n* 一覧表 [ichiranhyou] ▷ *v* 一覧表を作る [ichiranhyou-o tsukuru]; **mailing list** *n* メーリングリスト [meeringurisuto]; **price list** *n* 価格表 [kakakuhyou]; **waiting list** *n* 順番待ち名簿 [junbanmachi meibo]; **wine list** *n* ワインリスト [wainrisuto]

isten ['lɪsən] *v* 聞く [kiku]; **listen to** *v* ・・・を聞く [...-o kiku]

istener ['lɪsnə] *n* 聞き手 [kikite]

iterally ['lɪtərəlɪ] *adv* 文字どおりに [mojidouri ni]

iterature ['lɪtərɪtʃə; 'lɪtrɪ-] *n* 文学 [bungaku]

ithuania [,lɪθjʊ'eɪnɪə] *n* リトアニア [ritoania]

ithuanian [,lɪθjʊ'eɪnɪən] *adj* リトアニアの [ritoania no] ▷ *n* (language) リトアニア語 [ritoaniago], (person) リトアニア人 [ritoaniajin]

itre ['li:tə] *n* リットル [rittoru]

itter ['lɪtə] *n* ごみ [gomi], (offspring) 動物の一腹子 [doubutsu no ippukushi]; **litter bin** *n* くずかご [kuzukago]

little ['lɪtəl] *adj* 小さい [chiisa na]

live[1] [lɪv] *v* 生きる [ikiru]

live[2] [laɪv] *adj* 生きている [ikite iru]

lively ['laɪvlɪ] *adj* 元気のよい [genki no yoi]

live on [lɪv ɒn] *v* ・・・にたよって暮らす [...ni tayotte kurasu]

liver ['lɪvə] *n* 肝臓 [kanzou]

live together [lɪv] *v* 同棲する [dousei suru]

living ['lɪvɪŋ] *n* 生活 [seikatsu]; **cost of living** *n* 生活費 [seikatsuhi]; **living room** *n* 居間 [ima]; **standard of living** *n* 生活水準 [seikatsusuijun]

lizard ['lɪzəd] *n* トカゲ [tokage]

load [ləʊd] *n* 荷 [ni] ▷ *v* 荷を積む [ni-o tsumu]

loaf, loaves [ləʊf, ləʊvz] *n* パンのひと塊 [pan no hitokatamari]

loan [ləʊn] *n* 貸し付け [kashizuke] ▷ *v* 貸し付ける [kashitsukeru]

loathe [ləʊð] *v* ひどく嫌う [hidoku kirau]

lobby ['lɒbɪ] *n* **I'll meet you in the lobby** ロビーでお会いしましょう [robii de o-ai shimashou]

lobster ['lɒbstə] *n* ロブスター [robusutaa]

local ['ləʊkəl] *adj* 局部の [kyokubu no]; **local anaesthetic** *n* 局所麻酔薬 [kyokusho masuiyaku]

location [ləʊ'keɪʃən] *n* 場所 [basho]; **My location is...** 今いる場所は・・・です [ima iru basho wa ... desu]

lock [lɒk] *n* (door) 錠 [jou], (hair) 髪のふさ [kami no fusa] ▷ *v* 鍵をかける [kagi-o kakeru]

locker ['lɒkə] *n* ロッカー [rokkaa]; **left-luggage locker** *n* コインロッカー [koinrokkaa]; **Are there any luggage lockers?** コインロッカーはありますか? [koin-rokkaa wa arimasu ka?]; **Where are the clothes lockers?** 服のロッカーはどこですか? [fuku no rokkaa wa doko desu ka?]; **Which locker is mine?** どれが私のロッカーですか? [dore ga watashi no rokkaa desu ka?]

locket ['lɒkɪt] *n* ロケット [roketto]

lock out [lɒk aʊt] v 締め出す [shimedasu]

locksmith ['lɒkˌsmɪθ] n 錠前屋 [joumaeya]

lodger ['lɒdʒə] n 下宿人 [geshukunin]

loft [lɒft] n 屋根裏 [yaneura]

log [lɒg] n 丸太 [maruta]

logical ['lɒdʒɪkəl] adj 論理的な [ronriteki na]

log in [lɒg ɪn] v ログインする [roguin suru]

logo ['ləʊgəʊ; 'lɒg-] n ロゴ [rogo]

log off [lɒg ɒf] v ログオフする [roguofu suru]

log on [lɒg ɒn] v ログオンする [roguon suru]; **How much is it to log on for an hour?** 1時間ログオンするのにいくらですか? [ichi-jikan roguon suru no ni ikura desu ka?]

log out [lɒg aʊt] v ログアウトする [roguauto suru]

lollipop ['lɒlɪˌpɒp] n 棒付きキャンデー [boutsuki kyandee]

lolly ['lɒlɪ] n 棒付きキャンデー [boutsuki kyandee]

London ['lʌndən] n ロンドン [rondon]

loneliness ['ləʊnlɪnɪs] n 孤独 [kodoku]

lonely ['ləʊnlɪ] adj 孤独の [kodoku no]

lonesome ['ləʊnsəm] adj 孤独の [kodoku no]

long [lɒŋ] adj 長い [nagai] ▷ adv 長く [nagaku] ▷ v 切望する [setsubou suru]; **long jump** n 幅跳び [habatobi]

longer [lɒŋə] adv より長く [yori nagaku]

longitude ['lɒndʒɪˌtjuːd; 'lɒŋg-] n 経度 [keido]

loo [luː] n トイレ [toire]

look [lʊk] n 目つき [metsuki] ▷ v 見る [miru]; **look at** v ・・・をよく見る [...-o yoku miru]

look after [lʊk ɑːftə] v ・・・の世話をする [...no sewa-o suru]

look for [lʊk fɔː] v ・・・をさがす [...-o sagasu]

look round [lʊk raʊnd] v あたりを見回す [atari-o miwatasu]

look up [lʊk ʌp] v 調べる [shiraberu]

loose [luːs] adj 緩い [yurui]

lorry ['lɒrɪ] n トラック [torakku]; **lorry driver** n トラック運転手 [torakku untenshu]

lose [luːz] vi 負ける [makeru] ▷ vt なくす [nakusu]

loser ['luːzə] n 敗者 [haisha]

loss [lɒs] n 喪失 [soushitsu]

lost [lɒst] adj 失った [utta]; **lost-property office** n 遺失物取扱所 [ishitsubutsu toriatsukaijo]

lost-and-found ['lɒstænd'faʊnd] n 遺失物 [ishitsubutsu]

lot [lɒt] n **a lot** n 群れ [mure]

lotion ['ləʊʃən] n ローション [rooshon]; **after sun lotion** n アフターサンローション [afutaasan rooshon]; **cleansing lotion** n クレンジングローション [kurenjingurooshon]; **suntan lotion** n サンタンローション [santanrooshon]

lottery ['lɒtərɪ] n 宝くじ [takarakuji]

loud [laʊd] adj 大声の [ougoe no]

loudly [laʊdlɪ] adv 大声で [ougoe de]

loudspeaker [ˌlaʊd'spiːkə] n スピーカー [supiikaa]

lounge [laʊndʒ] n ラウンジ [raunji]; **departure lounge** n 出発ラウンジ [shuppatsu raunji]; **transit lounge** n 通過ラウンジ [tsuuka raunji]; **Could we have coffee in the lounge?** ラウンジでコーヒーをいただけますか? [raunji de koohii o itadakemasu ka?]; **Is there a television lounge?** テレビラウンジはありますか? [terebi-raunji wa arimasu ka?]

lousy ['laʊzɪ] adj 卑劣な [hiretsu na]

love [lʌv] n 愛 [ai] ▷ v 愛する [ai suru]; **I love you** 私はあなたを愛しています [watashi wa anata o aishite imasu]

lovely ['lʌvlɪ] adj 美しい [utsukushii]

lover ['lʌvə] n 愛人 [aijin]

low [ləʊ] adj 低い [hikui] ▷ adv 低く [hikuku]; **low season** n シーズンオフ [shiizun'ofu]

low-alcohol ['ləʊˌælkəˌhɒl] adj 低アルコールの [tei arukooru no]

lower ['ləʊə] *adj* より低い [yori hikui] ▷ *v* 下げる [sageru]

low-fat ['ləʊ,fæt] *adj* 低脂肪の [teishibou no]

loyalty ['lɔɪəltɪ] *n* 忠誠 [chuusei]

luck [lʌk] *n* 運 [un]

luckily ['lʌkɪlɪ] *adv* 運よく [un yoku]

lucky ['lʌkɪ] *adj* 運のよい [un no yoi]

lucrative ['luːkrətɪv] *adj* 儲かる [moukaru]

luggage ['lʌɡɪdʒ] *n* 手荷物 [tenimotsu]; **hand luggage** *n* 手荷物 [tenimotsu]; **luggage rack** *n* 手荷物置き棚 [tenimotsu okidana]; **luggage trolley** *n* 手荷物カート [tenimotsu kaato]; **Are there any luggage trolleys?** 手荷物カートはありますか? [tenimotsu-kaato wa arimasu ka?]; **Can I insure my luggage?** 手荷物に保険をかけられますか? [tenimotsu ni hoken o kakeraremasu ka?]; **My luggage has been damaged** 私の手荷物が破損しています [watashi no tenimotsu ga hason shite imasu]; **My luggage has been lost** 私の手荷物が紛失しました [watashi no tenimotsu ga funshitsu shimashita]; **My luggage hasn't arrived** 私の手荷物が着いていません [watashi no tenimotsu ga tsuite imasen]; **Where do I check in my luggage?** 手荷物のチェックインはどこでするのですか? [tenimotsu no chekku-in wa doko de suru no desu ka?]; **Where is the luggage for the flight from...?** ・・・からのフライトの手荷物はどこですか? [...kara no furaito no tenimotsu wa doko desu ka?]

lukewarm [,luːk'wɔːm] *adj* なまぬるい [namanurui]

lullaby ['lʌlə,baɪ] *n* 子守歌 [komoriuta]

lump [lʌmp] *n* 塊 [katamari]

lunatic ['luː'nætɪk] *n* 愚人 [gujin]

lunch [lʌntʃ] *n* 昼食 [chuushoku]; **lunch break** *n* 昼休み [hiruyasumi]; **packed lunch** *n* 弁当 [bentou]; **Can we meet for lunch?** 昼食をご一緒できますか? [chuushoku o go-issho dekimasu ka?]; **I'm free for lunch** 昼食には時間があいています [chuushoku ni wa jikan ga aite imasu]; **The lunch was excellent** 昼食はすばらしかったです [chuushoku wa subarashikatta desu]; **When will lunch be ready?** 昼食はいつ用意できますか? [chuushoku wa itsu youi dekimasu ka?]; **Where do we stop for lunch?** 昼食にはどこで停まりますか? [chuushoku ni wa doko de tomarimasu ka?]

lunchtime ['lʌntʃ,taɪm] *n* ランチタイム [ranchitaimu]

lung [lʌŋ] *n* 肺 [hai]

lush [lʌʃ] *adj* 青々とした [aoao to shita]

lust [lʌst] *n* 性欲 [seiyoku]

Luxembourg ['lʌksəm,bɜːɡ] *n* ルクセンブルク [rukusenburuku]

luxurious [lʌɡ'zjʊərɪəs] *adj* 贅沢な [zeitaku na]

luxury ['lʌkʃərɪ] *n* 贅沢 [zeitaku]

lyrics ['lɪrɪks] *npl* 抒情詩 [jojoushi]

m

mac [mæk] *abbr* レインコート
[reinkooto]

macaroni [,mækə'rəʊnɪ] *npl* マカロニ
[makaroni]

machine [mə'ʃiːn] *n* 機械 [kikai];
answering machine *n* 留守番電話
[rusubandenwa]; **machine gun** *n* マシン
ガン [mashingan]; **machine washable**
adj 洗濯機で洗える [sentakuki de araeru];
sewing machine *n* ミシン [mishin]; **slot
machine** *n* スロットマシン
[surottomashin]; **ticket machine** *n* 券売
機 [kenbaiki]; **vending machine** *n* 自動
販売機 [jidouhanbaiki]; **washing
machine** *n* 洗濯機 [sentakuki]

machinery [mə'ʃiːnərɪ] *n* 機械類
[kikairui]

mackerel ['mækrəl] *n* サバ [saba]

mad [mæd] *adj (angry)* 腹を立てた
[hara-o tateta], *(insane)* 気の狂った [kino
kurutta]

Madagascar [,mædə'gæskə] *n* マダガ
スカル [madagasukaru]

madam ['mædəm] *n* 奥様 [okusama]

madly ['mædlɪ] *adv* 気違いのように
[kichigai no youni]

madman ['mædmən] *n* 気違い男
[kichigai otoko]

madness ['mædnɪs] *n* 狂気 [kyouki]

magazine [,mægə'ziːn] *n*
(ammunition) 弾薬 [dan-yaku],
(periodical) 雑誌 [zasshi]; **Where can I
buy a magazine?** どこで雑誌を買えま
すか? [doko de zasshi o kaemasu ka?]

maggot ['mægət] *n* うじ [uji] (虫)

magic ['mædʒɪk] *adj* 魔法の [mahou no]
▷ *n* 魔法 [mahou]

magical ['mædʒɪkəl] *adj* 魔術的な
[majutsuteki na]

magician [mə'dʒɪʃən] *n* 魔術師
[majutsushi]

magistrate ['mædʒɪ,streɪt; -strɪt] *n*
治安判事 [chian hanji]

magnet ['mægnɪt] *n* 磁石 [jishaku]

magnetic [mæg'nɛtɪk] *adj* 磁石の
[jishaku no]

magnificent [mæg'nɪfɪsənt] *adj* 壮大
な [sodai na]

magpie ['mæg,paɪ] *n* カササギ [kasasagi]

mahogany [mə'hɒgənɪ] *n* マホガニー
[mahoganii]

maid [meɪd] *n* お手伝い [otetsudai] (使
用人)

maiden ['meɪdən] *n* **maiden name** *n*
女性の結婚前の旧姓 [josei no kekkonmae
no kyuusei]

mail [meɪl] *n* 郵便 [yuubin] ▷ *v* 郵送する
[yuusou suru]; **junk mail** *n* ジャンクメー
ル [janku meeru]; **Is there any mail for
me?** 私あての郵便物がありますか?
[watashi ate no yuubinbutsu ga arimasu
ka?]; **Please send my mail on to this
address** 私あての郵便物をこの住所に
回送してください [watashi ate no
yuubinbutsu o kono juusho ni kaisou shite
kudasai]

mailbox ['meɪl,bɒks] *n* 郵便受
[yuubinju]

mailing list ['meɪlɪŋ 'lɪst] *n* **mailing
list** *n* メーリングリスト [meeringurisuto]

main [meɪn] *adj* 主な [omo na]; **main
course** *n* メインコース [meinkoosu];

main road n 幹線道路 [kansendouro]

mainland ['meɪnlənd] n 本土 [hondo]

mainly ['meɪnlɪ] adv 主に [omo ni]

maintain [meɪn'teɪn] v 維持する [iji suru]

maintenance ['meɪntɪnəns] n 維持 [iji]

maize [meɪz] n トウモロコシ [toumorokoshi]

majesty ['mædʒɪstɪ] n 威厳 [igen]

major ['meɪdʒə] adj 大きい方の [oukii hou no]

majority [mə'dʒɒrɪtɪ] n 大部分 [daibubun]

make [meɪk] v 作る [tsukuru]

makeover ['meɪkˌəʊvə] n 改造 [kaizou]

maker ['meɪkə] n 造り主 [tsukurinushi]

make up [meɪk ʌp] v 埋め合わせる [umeawaseru]

make-up [meɪkʌp] n メーキャップ [meekyappu]

malaria [mə'lɛərɪə] n マラリア [mararia]

Malawi [mə'lɑːwɪ] n マラウィ [maraui]

Malaysia [mə'leɪzɪə] n マレーシア [mareeshia]

Malaysian [mə'leɪzɪən] adj マレーシアの [mareeshia no] ▷ n マレーシア人 [mareeshiajin]

male [meɪl] adj 男性の [dansei no] ▷ n 男性 [dansei]

malicious [mə'lɪʃəs] adj 悪意のある [akui no aru]

malignant [mə'lɪgnənt] adj 悪意のある [akui no aru]

malnutrition [ˌmælnjuː'trɪʃən] n 栄養不良 [eiyou furyou]

Malta ['mɔːltə] n マルタ [maruta]

Maltese [mɔːl'tiːz] adj マルタの [maruta no] ▷ n (language) マルタ語 [marutago], (person) マルタ人 [marutajin]

mammal ['mæməl] n 哺乳動物 [honyuu doubutsu]

mammoth ['mæməθ] adj 巨大な [kyodai na] ▷ n マンモス [manmosu]

man, men [mæn, mɛn] n 男 [otoko]; **best man** n 新郎の付添い役 [shinrou no tsukisoiyaku]

manage ['mænɪdʒ] v うまく・・・する [umaku ... suru]

manageable ['mænɪdʒəbəl] adj 御しやすい [o shiyasui]

management ['mænɪdʒmənt] n 経営陣 [keieijin]

manager ['mænɪdʒə] n 経営者 [keieisha]

manageress [ˌmænɪdʒə'rɛs; 'mænɪdʒəˌrɛs] n 女性経営者 [josei keieisha]

mandarin ['mændərɪn] n (fruit) マンダリンオレンジ [mandarin orenji], (official) 上級官吏 [joukyuu kanri]

mangetout ['mɑ̃ʒ'tuː] n サヤエンドウ [sayaendou]

mango ['mæŋgəʊ] n マンゴー [mangou]

mania ['meɪnɪə] n ・・・熱 [...netsu] (熱狂)

maniac ['meɪnɪˌæk] n 狂人 [kyoujin]

manicure ['mænɪˌkjʊə] n マニキュア [manikyua] ▷ v マニキュアを塗る [manikyua-o nuru]

manipulate [mə'nɪpjʊˌleɪt] v 巧みに扱う [takumi ni atsukau]

mankind [ˌmæn'kaɪnd] n 人類 [jinrui]

man-made ['mænˌmeɪd] adj 人造の [jinzou no]

manner ['mænə] n 方法 [houhou]

manners ['mænəz] npl 行儀 [gyougi]

manpower ['mænˌpaʊə] n 労働力 [roudouryoku]

mansion ['mænʃən] n 大邸宅 [daiteitaku]

mantelpiece ['mæntəlˌpiːs] n マントルピース [mantorupiisu]

manual ['mænjʊəl] n マニュアル [manyuaru]; **A manual, please** マニュアル車をお願いします [manyuaru-sha o o-negai shimasu]

manufacture [ˌmænjʊ'fæktʃə] v 製造する [seizou suru]

manufacturer [ˌmænjʊ'fæktʃərə] n 製造業者 [seizougyousha]

manure [mə'njʊə] n 堆肥 [taihi]

manuscript ['mænjʊˌskrɪpt] n 原稿 [genkou]

many ['mɛnɪ] adj 多くの [ouku no] ▷ pron 多数 [tasuu]

Maori ['maʊrɪ] adj マオリの [maori no] ▷ n (language) マオリ語 [maorigo], (person) マオリ族 [maori zoku]

map [mæp] n 地図 [chizu]; **road map** n ロードマップ [roodomappu]; **street map** n 街路地図 [gairo chizu]; **Can you draw me a map with directions?** 道順を示す地図を書いてもらえますか? [michijun o shimesu chizu o kaite moraemasu ka?]; **Can you show me where it is on the map?** 地図でそれがどこにあるか教えてもらえますか? [chizu de sore ga doko ni aru ka oshiete moraemasu ka?]; **Have you got a map of...?** ···の地図はありますか? [...no chizu wa arimasu ka?]; **Where can I buy a map of the area?** どこでその地域の地図を買えますか? [doko de sono chiiki no chizu o kaemasu ka?]

maple ['meɪpəl] n カエデ [kaede]

marathon ['mærəθən] n マラソン [marason]

marble ['mɑ:bəl] n 大理石 [dairiseki]

march [mɑ:tʃ] n 行進 [koushin] ▷ v 行進する [koushin suru]

March [mɑ:tʃ] n 三月 [sangatsu]

mare [mɛə] n 雌馬 [meuma]

margarine [,mɑ,dʒə'ri:n; ,mɑ:gə-] n マーガリン [maagarin]

margin ['mɑ:dʒɪn] n へり [heri]

marigold ['mærɪ,gəʊld] n マリーゴールド [mariigourudo]

marijuana [,mærɪ'hwɑ:nə] n マリファナ [marifana]

marina [mə'ri:nə] n マリーナ [mariina]

marinade n [,mærɪ'neɪd] マリネ [marine] ▷ v ['mærɪ,neɪd] マリネにする [marine ni suru]

marital ['mærɪtəl] adj **marital status** n 婚姻関係の有無 [kon'in kankei no umu]

maritime ['mærɪ,taɪm] adj 海事の [kaiji no]

marjoram ['mɑ:dʒərəm] n マヨラナ [mayorana]

mark [mɑ:k] n 汚れの跡 [yogore no ato] ▷ v (grade) 採点する [saiten suru], (make sign) 汚れの跡をつける [yogore no ato-o tsukeru]; **exclamation mark** n 感嘆符 [kantanfu]; **question mark** n 疑問符 [gimonfu]; **quotation marks** npl 引用符 [in-youfu]

market ['mɑ:kɪt] n 市場 [ichiba]; **market research** n 市場調査 [shijouchousa]; **stock market** n 株式市場 [kabushikishijou]

marketing ['mɑ:kɪtɪŋ] n マーケティング [maaketeingu]

marketplace ['mɑ:kɪt,pleɪs] n 市場 [ichiba]

marmalade ['mɑ:mə,leɪd] n マーマレード [maamareedo]

maroon [mə'ru:n] adj 栗色の [kuri iro no]

marriage ['mærɪdʒ] n 結婚 [kekkon]; **marriage certificate** n 結婚証明書 [kekkonshoumeisho]

married ['mærɪd] adj 結婚している [kekkon shite iru]

marrow ['mærəʊ] n 骨髄 [kotsuzui]

marry ['mærɪ] v 結婚する [kekkon suru]

marsh [mɑ:ʃ] n 沼 [numa]

martyr ['mɑ:tə] n 殉教者 [junkyousha]

marvellous ['mɑ:vələs] adj すばらしい [subarashii]

Marxism ['mɑ:ksɪzəm] n マルクス主義 [marukusushugi]

marzipan ['mɑ:zɪ,pæn] n マジパン [majipan]

mascara [mæ'skɑ:rə] n マスカラ [masukara]

masculine ['mæskjʊlɪn] adj 男らしい [otokorashii]

mask [mɑ:sk] n マスク [masuku]

masked [mɑ:skt] adj マスクをした [masuku-o shita]

mass [mæs] n (amount) 大量 [tairyou], (church) ミサ [misa]; **When is mass?** ミサはいつですか? [misa wa itsu desu ka?]

massacre ['mæsəkə] n 大虐殺 [daigyakusatsu]

massage ['mæsɑːʒ; -sɑːdʒ] n マッサージ [massaaji]

massive ['mæsɪv] adj どっしりした [dosshiri shita]

mast [mɑːst] n マスト [masuto]

master ['mɑːstə] n 長 [chou] (統率) ▷ v 支配する [shihai suru]

masterpiece ['mɑːstə,piːs] n 傑作 [kessaku]

mat [mæt] n マット [matto]; **mouse mat** n マウスパッド [mausupaddo]

match [mætʃ] n (partnership) 縁組み [engumi], (sport) 試合 [shiai] ▷ v マッチさせる [matchi saseru]; **away match** n アウェーの試合 [auee no shiai]; **home match** n ホームの試合 [hoomu no shiai]; **I'd like to see a football match** 私はサッカーの試合が観たいのですが [watashi wa sakkaa no shiai ga mitai no desu ga]

matching [mætʃɪŋ] adj 合った [atta]

mate [meɪt] n 仲間 [nakama]

material [mə'tɪərɪəl] n 材料 [zairyou]; **What is the material?** 材料は何ですか? [zairyou wa nan desu ka?]

maternal [mə'tɜːnəl] adj 母性の [bosei no]

mathematical [,mæθə'mætɪkəl; ,mæθ'mæt-] adj 数学の [suugaku no]

mathematics [,mæθə'mætɪks; ,mæθ'mæt-] npl 数学 [suugaku]

maths [mæθs] npl 数学 [suugaku]

matter ['mætə] n 物質 [busshitsu] ▷ v 重要である [juuyou de aru]

mattress ['mætrɪs] n マットレス [mattoresu]

mature [mə'tjʊə; -'tʃʊə] adj 成熟した [seijuku shita]; **mature student** n 成人学生 [seijin gakusei]

Mauritania [,mɒrɪ'teɪnɪə] n モーリタニア [mooritania]

Mauritius [mə'rɪʃəs] n モーリシャス [moorishasu]

mauve [məʊv] adj 藤紫色の [fuji murasaki iro no]

maximum ['mæksɪməm] adj 最大の [saidai no] ▷ n 最大限 [saidaigen]

may [meɪ] v **May I call you tomorrow?** 明日電話してもいいですか? [asu denwa shite mo ii desu ka?]; **May I open the window?** 窓を開けてもいいですか? [mado o akete mo ii desu ka?]

May [meɪ] n 五月 [gogatsu]

maybe ['meɪ,biː] adv もしかしたら [moshikashitara]

mayonnaise [,meɪə'neɪz] n マヨネーズ [mayoneezu]

mayor, mayoress [mɛə, 'mɛərɪs] n 市長 [shichou]

maze [meɪz] n 迷路 [meiro]

me [miː] pron 私を [watashi o]

meadow ['mɛdəʊ] n 牧草地 [bokusouchi]

meal [miːl] n 食事 [shokuji]; **Could you prepare a meal without eggs?** 卵を使わずに食事を用意していただけますか? [tamago o tsukawazu ni shokuji o youi shite itadakemasu ka?]; **Could you prepare a meal without gluten?** グルテンを使わずに食事を用意していただけますか? [guruten o tsukawazu ni shokuji o youi shite itadakemasu ka?]; **Enjoy your meal!** お食事をお楽しみください! [o-shokuji o o-tanoshimi kudasai!]; **The meal was delicious** 食事はおいしかったです [shokuji wa oishikatta desu]

mealtime ['miːl,taɪm] n 食事時間 [shokuji jikan]

mean [miːn] adj けちな [kechi na] ▷ v 意味する [imi suru]

meaning ['miːnɪŋ] n 意味 [imi]

means [miːnz] npl 手段 [shudan]

meantime ['miːn,taɪm] adv その間に [sono aida ni]

meanwhile ['miːn,waɪl] adv その間に [sono aida ni]

measles ['miːzəlz] npl はしか [hashika]; **German measles** n 風疹 [fuushin]; **I had measles recently** 私は最近はしかにかかりました [watashi wa saikin hashika ni kakarimashita]

measure ['mɛʒə] v 測定する [sokutei suru]; **tape measure** n 巻尺 [makijaku]

measurements ['mɛʒəmənts] npl サイズ [saizu]

meat [miːt] n 肉 [niku]; **red meat** n 赤身肉 [akaminiku]; **Do you eat meat?** あなたは肉を食べますか？[anata wa niku o tabemasu ka?]; **I don't eat meat** 私は肉を食べません [watashi wa niku o tabemasen]; **I don't eat red meat** 私は赤身肉を食べません [watashi wa akaminiku o tabemasen]; **I don't like meat** 私は肉が好きではありません [watashi wa niku ga suki de wa arimasen]; **The meat is cold** 肉が冷たいです [niku ga tsumetai desu]; **This meat is off** この肉はいたんでいます [kono niku wa itande imasu]

meatball ['miːtˌbɔːl] n ミートボール [miitobooru]

Mecca ['mɛkə] n メッカ [mekka]

mechanic [mɪ'kænɪk] n 機械工 [kikaikou]

mechanical [mɪ'kænɪkəl] adj 機械の [kikai no]

mechanism ['mɛkəˌnɪzəm] n 機構 [kikou] (機械)

medal ['mɛdəl] n メダル [medaru]

medallion [mɪ'dæljən] n 大メダル [dai medaru]

media ['miːdɪə] npl マスメディア [masumedia]

mediaeval [ˌmɛdɪ'iːvəl] adj 中世の [chuusei no]

medical ['mɛdɪkəl] adj 医学の [igaku no] ▷ n 健康診断 [kenkoushindan]; **medical certificate** n 診断書 [shindansho]

medication [ˌmɛdɪ'keɪʃən] n **I'm on this medication** 私はこの薬を飲んでいます [watashi wa kono kusuri o nonde imasu]

medicine ['mɛdɪsɪn; 'mɛdsɪn] n 薬 [kusuri]; **I'm already taking this medicine** 私はすでにこの薬を飲んでいます [watashi wa sudeni kono kusuri o nonde imasu]

meditation [ˌmɛdɪ'teɪʃən] n 瞑想 [meisou]

Mediterranean [ˌmɛdɪtə'reɪnɪən] adj 地中海の [chichuukai no] ▷ n 地中海 [chichuukai]

medium ['miːdɪəm] adj (between extremes) 中くらいの [naka kurai no]

medium-sized ['miːdɪəmˌsaɪzd] adj 中サイズの [naka saizu no]

meet [miːt] vi 会う [au] ▷ vt ～に会う [~ ni au]

meeting ['miːtɪŋ] n 会議 [kaigi]

meet up [miːt ʌp] v 待ち合わせる [machiawaseru]

mega ['mɛgə] adj とても大きい [totemo ookii]

melody ['mɛlədɪ] n メロディー [merodii]

melon ['mɛlən] n メロン [meron]

melt [mɛlt] vi 溶ける [tokeru] ▷ vt 溶かす [tokasu]

member ['mɛmbə] n メンバー [menbaa] (会員)

membership ['mɛmbəˌʃɪp] n メンバー [menbaa] (会員資格); **membership card** n メンバーカード [menbaakaado]

meme [miːm] n ミーム [miimu]

memento [mɪ'mɛntəʊ] n 思い出の品 [omoide no shina]

memo ['mɛməʊ; 'miːməʊ] n メモ [memo]

memorial [mɪ'mɔːrɪəl] n 記念碑 [kinenhi]

memorize ['mɛməˌraɪz] v 記憶する [kioku suru]

memory ['mɛmərɪ] n 記憶 [kioku]; **memory card** n メモリカード [memorikaado]

mend [mɛnd] v 直す [naosu]

meningitis [ˌmɛnɪn'dʒaɪtɪs] n 髄膜炎 [zuimakuen]

menopause ['mɛnəʊˌpɔːz] n 閉経期 [heikeiki]

menstruation [ˌmɛnstrʊ'eɪʃən] n 月経 [gekkei]

mental ['mɛntəl] *adj* 精神の [seishin no]

mentality [mɛn'tælɪtɪ] *n* 精神構造 [seishin kouzou]

mention ['mɛnʃən] *v* 話に出す [hanashi ni dasu]

menu ['mɛnju:] *n* メニュー [menyuu]; **set menu** *n* 定食 [teishoku]; **Do you have a children's menu?** 子供用のメニューはありますか? [kodomo-you no menyuu wa arimasu ka?]; **Do you have a set-price menu?** セットメニューはありますか? [setto-menyuu wa arimasu ka?]; **How much is the set menu?** セットメニューはいくらですか? [setto-menyuu wa ikura desu ka?]; **The dessert menu, please** デザートのメニューをください [dezaato no menyuu o kudasai]; **The menu, please** メニューをください [menyuu o kudasai]; **We'll take the set menu** セットメニューをください [setto-menyuu o kudasai]

mercury ['mɜːkjʊrɪ] *n* 水銀 [suigin]

mercy ['mɜːsɪ] *n* 慈悲 [jihi]

mere [mɪə] *adj* ほんの [hon no]

merge [mɜːdʒ] *v* 合併する [gappei suru]

merger ['mɜːdʒə] *n* 合併 [gappei]

meringue [mə'ræŋ] *n* メレンゲ [merenge]

mermaid ['mɜː,meɪd] *n* 人魚 [ningyo]

merry ['mɛrɪ] *adj* 陽気な [youki na]

merry-go-round ['mɛrɪgəʊ'raʊnd] *n* 回転木馬 [kaitenmokuba]

mess [mɛs] *n* 乱雑 [sanran]

mess about [mɛs ə'baʊt] *v* 無為に過ごす [mui ni sugosu]

message ['mɛsɪdʒ] *n* 伝言 [dengon]; **text message** *n* テキストメッセージ [tekisutomesseeji]; **Are there any messages for me?** 私あての伝言がありますか? [watashi ate no dengon ga arimasu ka?]; **Can I leave a message with his secretary?** 彼の秘書に伝言を残すことはできますか? [kare no hisho ni dengon o nokosu koto wa dekimasu ka?]; **Can I leave a message?** 伝言をお願いできますか? [dengon o o-negai dekimasu ka?]

messenger ['mɛsɪndʒə] *n* 使者 [shisha]

mess up [mɛs ʌp] *v* 散らかす [chirakasu]

messy ['mɛsɪ] *adj* 散らかった [chira katta]

metabolism [mɪ'tæbə,lɪzəm] *n* 代謝 [taisha]

metal ['mɛtəl] *n* 金属 [kinzoku]

meteorite ['miːtɪə,raɪt] *n* 隕石 [inseki]

meter ['miːtə] *n* メーター [meetaa]; **parking meter** *n* パーキングメーター [paakingumeetaa]; **Do you have a meter?** *(taxi)* メーターはありますか? [meetaa wa arimasu ka?]; **Do you have change for the parking meter?** パーキングメーター用の小銭をお持ちですか? [paakingu-meetaa-you no kozeni o o-mochi desu ka?]; **It's more than on the meter** それではメーター料金より高いです [sore de wa meetaa-ryoukin yori takai desu]; **Please use the meter** メーターを使ってください [meetaa o tsukatte kudasai]; **The meter is broken** メーターが壊れています [meetaa ga kowarete imasu]; **The parking meter is broken** パーキングメーターが壊れています [paakingu-meetaa ga kowarete imasu]; **Where is the electricity meter?** 電気のメーターはどこですか? [denki no meetaa wa doko desu ka?]; **Where is the gas meter?** ガスのメーターはどこですか? [gasu no meetaa wa doko desu ka?]

method ['mɛθəd] *n* 方法 [houhou]

Methodist ['mɛθədɪst] *adj* メソジスト派の [mesojisuto ha no]

metre ['miːtə] *n* メートル [meetoru]

metric ['mɛtrɪk] *adj* メートル法の [meetoruhou no]

Mexican ['mɛksɪkən] *adj* メキシコの [mekishiko no] ▷ *n* メキシコ人 [mekishikojin]

Mexico ['mɛksɪ,kəʊ] *n* メキシコ [mekishiko]

microchip ['maɪkrəʊ,tʃɪp] *n* マイクロチップ [maikurochippu]

microphone ['maɪkrə,fəʊn] n マイクロホン [maikurohon]; **Does it have a microphone?** マイクロホンはついていますか? [maikurohon wa tsuite imasu ka?]

microscope ['maɪkrə,skəʊp] n 顕微鏡 [kenbikyou]

mid [mɪd] adj 中間の [chuukan no]

midday ['mɪd'deɪ] n 真昼 [mahiru]

middle ['mɪd°l] n 中央 [chuuou]; **Middle Ages** npl 中世 [chuusei]; **Middle East** n 中東 [chuutou]

middle-aged ['mɪd°l,eɪdʒɪd] adj 中年の [chuunen no]

middle-class ['mɪd°l,klɑːs] adj 中流階級の [chuuryuu kaikyuu no]

midge [mɪdʒ] n 小虫 [shou mushi]

midnight ['mɪd,naɪt] n 真夜中 [mayonaka]

midwife, midwives ['mɪd,waɪf, 'mɪd,waɪvz] n 助産婦 [josanpu]

migraine ['miːgreɪn; 'maɪ-] n 片頭痛 [henzutsuu]

migrant ['maɪgrənt] adj 移動性の [idousei no] ▷ n 移住者 [ijuusha]

migration [maɪ'greɪʃən] n 移住 [ijuu]

mike [maɪk] n マイク [maiku]

mild [maɪld] adj マイルドな [mairudo na]

mile [maɪl] n マイル [mairu]

mileage ['maɪlɪdʒ] n 総マイル数 [sou mairu suu]

mileometer [maɪ'lɒmɪtə] n 走行マイル計 [soukou mairu kei]

military ['mɪlɪtəri; -tri] adj 軍の [gun no]

milk [mɪlk] n 牛乳 [gyuunyuu] ▷ v 乳を搾る [chichi-o shiboru]; **milk chocolate** n ミルクチョコレート [mirukuchokoreeto]; **semi-skimmed milk** n 半脱脂乳 [han dasshi nyuu]; **skimmed milk** n 脱脂乳 [dasshinyuu]; **UHT milk** n 超高温殺菌牛乳 [choukouon sakkin gyuunyuu]; **Do you drink milk?** あなたは牛乳を飲みますか? [anata wa gyuunyuu o nomimasu ka?]; **Have you got real milk?** 本物の牛乳はありますか? [honmono no gyuunyuu wa arimasu ka?]; **Is it made with**

unpasteurised milk? それは低温殺菌していない牛乳を使って作られていますか? [sore wa teion-sakkin shite inai gyuunyuu o tsukatte tsukurarete imasu ka?]

milkshake ['mɪlk,ʃeɪk] n ミルクシェイク [mirukusheiku]

mill [mɪl] n 製粉所 [seifunjou]

millennium [mɪ'lɛnɪəm] n 千年間 [sennenkan]

millimetre ['mɪlɪ,miːtə] n ミリメートル [mirimeetoru]

million ['mɪljən] n 100万 [hyakuman]

millionaire [,mɪljə'nɛə] n 大金持ち [ooganemochi]

mimic ['mɪmɪk] v 物まねをする [monomane-o suru]

mince [mɪns] v 挽肉 [hikiniku]

mind [maɪnd] n 心 [kokoro] ▷ v いやだと思う [iyadato omou]

mine [maɪn] n 鉱山 [kouzan] ▷ pron 私のもの [watashi no mono]

miner ['maɪnə] n 炭坑労働者 [tankou roudousha]

mineral ['mɪnərəl; 'mɪnrəl] adj 鉱物の [koubutsu no] ▷ n 鉱物 [koubutsu]; **mineral water** n ミネラルウォーター [mineraru uootaa]

miniature ['mɪnɪtʃə] adj ミニチュアの [minichua no] ▷ n ミニチュア [minichua]

minibar ['mɪnɪ,bɑː] n ミニバー [minibaa]

minibus ['mɪnɪ,bʌs] n マイクロバス [maikurobasu]

minicab ['mɪnɪ,kæb] n 小型タクシー [kogata takushii]

minimal ['mɪnɪməl] adj 最小限の [saishougen no]

minimize ['mɪnɪ,maɪz] v 最小限度にする [saishougendo ni suru]

minimum ['mɪnɪməm] adj 最小の [saishou no] ▷ n 最小限 [saishougen]

mining ['maɪnɪŋ] n 鉱業 [kougyou]

miniskirt ['mɪnɪ,skɜːt] n ミニスカート [minisukaato]

minister ['mɪnɪstə] n (clergy) 聖職者 [seishokusha], (government) 大臣 [daijin]; **prime minister** n 首相 [shushou]

ministry ['mɪnɪstrɪ] n (government) 省 [shou], (religion) 聖職 [seishoku]

mink [mɪŋk] n ミンク [minku]

minor ['maɪnə] adj 小さい方の [chiisai hou no] ▷ n 未成年者 [miseinensha]

minority [maɪˈnɒrɪtɪ; mɪ-] n 少数派 [shousuuha]

mint [mɪnt] n (herb/sweet) ミント [minto], (coins) 貨幣鋳造所 [kahei chuuzoujo]

minus ['maɪnəs] prep ・・・を引いた [...-o hiita]

minute adj [maɪˈnjuːt] 微小な [bishou na] ▷ n ['mɪnɪt] 分 [fun]; **Can you wait here for a few minutes?** ここで数分待ってもらえますか? [koko de suu-fun matte moraemasu ka?]; **We are ten minutes late** 私たちは十分遅れました [watashi-tachi wa jup-pun okuremashita]

miracle ['mɪrəkəl] n 奇跡 [kiseki]

mirror ['mɪrə] n 鏡 [kagami]; **rear-view mirror** n バックミラー [bakkumiraa]; **wing mirror** n サイドミラー [saidomiraa]

misbehave [ˌmɪsbɪˈheɪv] v 不正を働く [fusei-o hataraku]

miscarriage [mɪsˈkærɪdʒ] n 流産 [ryuuzan]

miscellaneous [ˌmɪsəˈleɪnɪəs] adj 雑多な [zatta na]

mischief ['mɪstʃɪf] n いたずら [itazura]

mischievous ['mɪstʃɪvəs] adj いたずら好きな [itazura zuki na]

miser ['maɪzə] n どけち [dokechi]

miserable ['mɪzərəbəl; 'mɪzrə-] adj 惨めな [mijime na]

misery ['mɪzərɪ] n 惨めさ [mijimesa]

misfortune [mɪsˈfɔːtʃən] n 不運 [fuun]

mishap ['mɪshæp] n 不幸な出来事 [fukou na dekigoto]

misjudge [ˌmɪsˈdʒʌdʒ] v 判断を誤る [handan-o ayamaru]

mislay [mɪsˈleɪ] v 置き忘れる [okiwasureru]

misleading [mɪsˈliːdɪŋ] adj 誤解を招きやすい [gokai-o manekiyasui]

misprint ['mɪsˌprɪnt] n 誤植 [goshoku]

miss [mɪs] v 見逃す [minogasu]

Miss [mɪs] n 独身女性の名字の前に付ける敬称 [dokushin josei no myouji no mae ni tsukeru keishou]

missile ['mɪsaɪl] n ミサイル [misairu]

missing ['mɪsɪŋ] adj あるべき所にない [aru beki tokoro ni nai]

missionary ['mɪʃənərɪ] n 宣教師 [senkyoushi]

mist [mɪst] n もや [moya]

mistake [mɪˈsteɪk] n 間違い [machigai] ▷ v 間違える [machigaeru]

mistaken [mɪˈsteɪkən] adj 間違えた [machigaeta]

mistakenly [mɪˈsteɪkənlɪ] adv 間違って [machigatte]

mistletoe ['mɪsəlˌtəʊ] n ヤドリギ [yadorigi]

mistress ['mɪstrɪs] n 女性の愛人 [josei no aijin]

misty ['mɪstɪ] adj もやの立ち込めた [moya no tachikometa]

misunderstand [ˌmɪsʌndəˈstænd] v 誤解する [gokai suru]

misunderstanding [ˌmɪsʌndəˈstændɪŋ] n 誤解 [gokai]; **There's been a misunderstanding** 誤解があります [gokai ga arimasu]

mitten ['mɪtən] n ミトン [miton]

mix [mɪks] n 混合物 [kongoubutsu] ▷ v 混ぜる [mazeru]

mixed [mɪkst] adj 混合した [kongou shita]; **mixed salad** n ミックスサラダ [mikkususarada]

mixer ['mɪksə] n ミキサー [mikisaa]

mixture ['mɪkstʃə] n 混合物 [kongoubutsu]

mix up [mɪks ʌp] v 混同する [kondou suru]

mix-up [mɪksʌp] n 混同 [kondou]

MMS [ɛm ɛm ɛs] abbr マルチメディアメッセージングサービス [maruchimedia messeejingu saabisu]

moan [məʊn] v うめく [umeku]

moat [məʊt] n 濠 [hori]

mobile ['məʊbaɪl] adj 移動可能な

[idoukanou na]; **mobile home** n モビールハウス [mobiiruhausu]; **mobile number** n 携帯電話番号 [keitai denwa bangou]; **mobile phone** n 携帯電話 [keitai denwa]

mock [mɒk] adj まがいの [magai no] ▷ v あざける [azakeru]

mod cons ['mɒd kɒnz] npl 最新設備 [saishin setsubi]

model ['mɒdᵊl] adj 模範的な [mohanteki na] ▷ n 模型 [mokei] ▷ v 模型を作る [mokei-o tsukuru]

modem ['məʊdɛm] n モデム [modemu]

moderate ['mɒdərɪt] adj 適度の [tekido no]

moderation [ˌmɒdə'reɪʃən] n 適度 [tekido]

modern ['mɒdən] adj 現代の [gendai no]; **modern languages** npl 現代語 [gendaigo]

modernize ['mɒdəˌnaɪz] v 現代化する [gendaika suru]

modest ['mɒdɪst] adj 謙虚な [kenkyo na]

modification [ˌmɒdɪfɪ'keɪʃən] n 変更 [henkou]

modify ['mɒdɪˌfaɪ] v 変更する [henkou suru]

module ['mɒdju:l] n モジュール [mojuuru]

moist [mɔɪst] adj 湿った [shimetta]

moisture ['mɔɪstʃə] n 湿気 [shikke]

moisturizer ['mɔɪstʃəˌraɪzə] n モイスチャライザー [moisucharaizaa]

Moldova [mɒl'dəʊvə] n モルドバ [morudoba]

Moldovan [mɒl'dəʊvən] adj モルドバの [morudoba no] ▷ n モルドバ人 [morudobajin]

mole [məʊl] n (infiltrator) スパイ [supai], (mammal) モグラ [mogura], (skin) ほくろ [hokuro]

molecule ['mɒlɪ,kju:l] n 分子 [bunshi]

moment ['məʊmənt] n 瞬間 [shunkan]

momentarily ['məʊməntərəlɪ; -trɪlɪ] adv ちょっとの間 [chotto no aida]

momentary ['məʊməntərɪ; -trɪ] adj 瞬間の [shunkan no]

momentous [məʊ'mɛntəs] adj きわめて重大な [kiwamete juudai na]

Monaco ['mɒnə,kəʊ; mə'nɑ:kəʊ; mɔnako] n モナコ [monako]

monarch ['mɒnək] n 君主 [kunshu]

monarchy ['mɒnəkɪ] n 君主制 [kunshusei]

monastery ['mɒnəstərɪ; -strɪ] n 修道院 [shuudouin]; **Is the monastery open to the public?** その修道院は一般公開されていますか? [sono shuudouin wa ippan-koukai sarete imasu ka?]

Monday ['mʌndɪ] n 月曜日 [getsuyoubi]; **It's Monday the fifteenth of June** 六月十五日の月曜日です [roku-gatsu juugo-nichi no getsuyoubi desu]; **on Monday** 月曜日に [getsuyoubi ni]

monetary ['mʌnɪtərɪ; -trɪ] adj 通貨の [tsuuka no]

money ['mʌnɪ] n 金銭 [kinsen]; **money belt** n マネーベルト [maneeberuto]; **pocket money** n ポケットマネー [pokettomanee]

Mongolia [mɒŋ'gəʊlɪə] n モンゴル [mongoru]

Mongolian [mɒŋ'gəʊlɪən] adj モンゴルの [mongoru no] ▷ n (language) モンゴル語 [mongorugo], (person) モンゴル人 [mongorujin]

mongrel ['mʌŋgrəl] n 雑種の犬 [zasshu no inu]

monitor ['mɒnɪtə] n モニター [monitaa]

monk [mʌŋk] n 修道士 [shuudoushi]

monkey ['mʌŋkɪ] n サル [saru]

monopoly [mə'nɒpəlɪ] n 独占 [dokusen]

monotonous [mə'nɒtənəs] adj 単調な [tanchou na]

monsoon [mɒn'su:n] n モンスーン [monsuun]

monster ['mɒnstə] n 怪物 [kaibutsu]

month [mʌnθ] n 月 [tsuki] (暦); **a month ago** 一か月前 [ikkagetsu mae]; **in a month's time** 一か月後に [ikkagetsu go ni]

monthly ['mʌnθlɪ] *adj* 毎月の [maitsuki no]

monument ['mɒnjʊmənt] *n* 記念碑 [kinenhi]

mood [muːd] *n* 気分 [kibun]

moody ['muːdɪ] *adj* むっつりした [muttsuri shita]

moon [muːn] *n* 月 [tsuki] (天体); **full moon** *n* 満月 [mangetsu]

moor [mʊə; mɔː] *n* 荒野 [areno] ▷ *v* 停泊させる [teihaku saseru]

mop [mɒp] *n* モップ [moppu]

moped ['məʊpɛd] *n* モペッド [mopeddo]

mop up [mɒp ʌp] *v* モップでぬぐい取る [moppu de nuguitoru]

moral ['mɒrəl] *adj* 道徳の [doutoku no] ▷ *n* 教訓 [kyoukun]

morale [mɒ'rɑːl] *n* 士気 [shiki]

morals ['mɒrəlz] *npl* 品行 [hinkou]

more [mɔː] *adj* さらに多い [sarani oui] ▷ *adv* さらに多く [sara ni ooku] ▷ *pron* それ以上のこと [sore ijou nokoto]

morgue [mɔːg] *n* 死体保管所 [shitaihokanjo]

morning ['mɔːnɪŋ] *n* 午前 [gozen]; **morning sickness** *n* つわりの時期の朝の吐き気 [tsuwari no jiki no asa no hakike]; **in the morning** 午前中に [gozen-chuu ni]; **Is the museum open in the morning?** その博物館は午前中開いていますか? [sono hakubutsukan wa gozen-chuu hiraite imasu ka?]

Moroccan [mə'rɒkən] *adj* モロッコの [morokko no] ▷ *n* モロッコ人 [morokkojin]

Morocco [mə'rɒkəʊ] *n* モロッコ [morokko]

morphine ['mɔːfiːn] *n* モルヒネ [moruhine]

Morse [mɔːs] *n* モールス信号 [moorusu shingou]

mortar ['mɔːtə] *n* (military) 臼砲 [kyuuhou], (plaster) モルタル [morutaru]

mortgage ['mɔːɡɪdʒ] *n* 抵当 [teitou] ▷ *v* 抵当に入れる [teitou ni ireru]

mosaic [mə'zeɪɪk] *n* モザイク [mozaiku]

Moslem ['mɒzləm] *adj* イスラム教の [isuramukyou no] ▷ *n* イスラム教徒 [isuramukyouto]

mosque [mɒsk] *n* モスク [mosuku]; **Where is there a mosque?** どこかにモスクはありますか? [doko-ka ni mosuku wa arimasu ka?]

mosquito [mə'skiːtəʊ] *n* 蚊 [ka]

moss [mɒs] *n* コケ [koke]

most [məʊst] *adj* 最も多い [mottomo ooi] ▷ *adv* (superlative) 最も多く [mottomo ouku] ▷ *n* (majority) 最多数 [saitasuu]

mostly ['məʊstlɪ] *adv* たいてい [taitei]

MOT [ɛm əʊ tiː] *abbr* 車検 [shaken]

motel [məʊ'tɛl] *n* モーテル [mooteru]

moth [mɒθ] *n* 蛾 [ga]

mother ['mʌðə] *n* 母 [haha]; **mother tongue** *n* 母国語 [bokokugo]; **surrogate mother** *n* 代理母 [dairibo]

mother-in-law ['mʌðə ɪn lɔː] (mothers-in-law) *n* 義母 [gibo]

motionless ['məʊʃənlɪs] *adj* 動かない [ugokanai]

motivated ['məʊtɪˌveɪtɪd] *adj* 動機づけられた [douki zukerareta]

motivation [ˌməʊtɪ'veɪʃən] *n* 動機づけ [douki zuke]

motive ['məʊtɪv] *n* 動機 [douki]

motor ['məʊtə] *n* モーター [mootaa]; **motor mechanic** *n* 自動車整備士 [jidousha seibishi]; **motor racing** *n* モーターレース [mootaareesu]

motorbike ['məʊtəˌbaɪk] *n* モーターバイク [mootaabaiku]

motorboat ['məʊtəˌbəʊt] *n* モーターボート [mootaabooto]

motorcycle ['məʊtəˌsaɪkəl] *n* オートバイ [ootobai]

motorcyclist ['məʊtəˌsaɪklɪst] *n* オートバイ乗り [ootobainori]

motorist ['məʊtərɪst] *n* ドライバー [doraibaa] (人)

motorway ['məʊtəˌweɪ] *n* 高速道路 [kousokudouro]; **How do I get to the motorway?** 高速道路へはどう行くのですか? [kousoku-douro e wa dou iku no] desu ka?]; **Is there a toll on this motorway?** この高速道路は有料ですか? [kono kousoku-douro wa yuuryou desu ka?]

mould [məʊld] n (fungus) カビ [kabi], (shape) 型 [kata]

mouldy ['məʊldɪ] adj かびた [kabita]

mount [maʊnt] v のぼる [noboru]

mountain ['maʊntɪn] n 山 [yama]; **mountain bike** n マウンテンバイク [mauntenbaiku]; **Where is the nearest mountain rescue service post?** 一番近い山岳救助隊はどこですか? [ichiban chikai sangaku-kyuujo-tai wa doko desu ka?]

mountaineer [ˌmaʊntɪˈnɪə] n 登山者 [tozansha]

mountaineering [ˌmaʊntɪˈnɪərɪŋ] n 登山 [tozan]

mountainous ['maʊntɪnəs] adj 山の多い [yama no oui]

mount up [maʊnt ʌp] v かさむ [kasamu]

mourning ['mɔːnɪŋ] n 悲嘆 [hitan]

mouse, mice [maʊs; maɪs] n ハツカネズミ [hatsukanezumi]; **mouse mat** n マウスパッド [mausupaddo]

mousse [muːs] n ムース [muusu]

moustache [məˈstɑːʃ] n 口ひげ [kuchi hige]

mouth [maʊθ] n 口 [kuchi]; **mouth organ** n ハーモニカ [haamonika]

mouthwash ['maʊθˌwɒʃ] n マウスウォッシュ [mausu uosshu]

move [muːv] n 移動 [idou] ▷ vi 動く [ugoku] ▷ vt 動かす [ugokasu]

move back [muːv bæk] v 後ろに下がる [ushiro ni sagaru]

move forward [muːv fɔːwəd] v 前へ進む [mae-e susumu]

move in [muːv ɪn] v ···に転居する [...ni tenkyo suru]

movement ['muːvmənt] n 動き [douki]

movie ['muːvɪ] n 映画 [eiga]

moving ['muːvɪŋ] adj 感動させる [kandou saseru]

mow [məʊ] v 刈る [karu]

mower ['maʊə] n 草刈り機 [kusakariki]

Mozambique [ˌməʊzəmˈbiːk] n モザンビーク [mozanbiiku]

mph [maɪlz pə aʊə] abbr 毎時···マイル [maiji ... mairu]

Mr ['mɪstə] n 男性の名字の前に付ける敬称 [dansei no myouji no mae ni tsukeru keishou]

Mrs ['mɪsɪz] n 既婚女性の名字の前に付ける敬称 [kikonjosei no myouji no mae ni tsukeru keishou]

Ms [mɪz; məs] n 未婚・既婚にかかわらず、女性に対する敬称 [mikon / kikon ni kakawarazu, josei ni taisuru keishou]

MS [mɪz; məs] abbr 多発性硬化症 [tahatsusei koukashou]

much [mʌtʃ] adj 多くの [ouku no] ▷ adv たくさん [takusan], 大いに [ooi ni]

mud [mʌd] n 泥 [doro]

muddle ['mʌdəl] n 混乱状態 [konranjoutai]

muddy ['mʌdɪ] adj 泥だらけの [doro darake no]

mudguard ['mʌdˌgɑːd] n 泥よけ [doroyoke]

muesli ['mjuːzlɪ] n ミューズリー [myuuzurii]

muffler ['mʌflə] n マフラー [mafuraa]

mug [mʌg] n マグ [magu] ▷ v 襲って強奪する [osotte goudatsu suru]

mugger ['mʌgə] n 強盗 [goutou] (人)

mugging [mʌgɪŋ] n 強奪 [goudatsu]

muggy ['mʌgɪ] adj **It's muggy** 蒸し暑いです [mushiatsui desu]

mule [mjuːl] n ラバ [raba]

multinational [ˌmʌltɪˈnæʃənəl] adj 多国籍の [takokuseki no] ▷ n 多国籍企業 [takokuseki kigyou]

multiple ['mʌltɪpəl] adj **multiple sclerosis** n 多発性硬化症 [tahatsusei koukashou]

multiplication [ˌmʌltɪplɪˈkeɪʃən] n 掛け算 [kakezan]

multiply ['mʌltɪˌplaɪ] v 増す [masu]

mum [mʌm] n ママ [mama]

mummy [ˈmʌmɪ] n (body) ミイラ [miira], (mother) ママ [mama]

mumps [mʌmps] n おたふく風邪 [otafukukaze]

murder [ˈmɜːdə] n 殺人 [satsujin] ▷ v 殺害する [satsugai suru]

murderer [ˈmɜːdərə] n 殺人者 [satsujinsha]

muscle [ˈmʌsəl] n 筋肉 [kinniku]

muscular [ˈmʌskjʊlə] adj 筋骨たくましい [kinkotsu takumashii]

museum [mjuːˈzɪəm] n 博物館 [hakubutsukan]; **Is the museum open every day?** その博物館は毎日開いていますか? [sono hakubutsukan wa mainichi hiraite imasu ka?]; **When is the museum open?** その博物館はいつ開きますか? [sono hakubutsukan wa itsu hirakimasu ka?]

mushroom [ˈmʌʃruːm; -rʊm] n マッシュルーム [masshuruumu]

music [ˈmjuːzɪk] n 音楽 [ongaku]; **folk music** n フォークミュージック [fooku myuujikku]; **music centre** n システムコンポ [shisutemukonpo]

musical [ˈmjuːzɪkəl] adj 音楽の [ongaku no] ▷ n ミュージカル [myuujikaru]; **musical instrument** n 楽器 [gakki]

musician [mjuːˈzɪʃən] n 音楽家 [ongakuka]

Muslim [ˈmʊzlɪm; ˈmʌz-] adj イスラム教の [isuramukyou no] ▷ n イスラム教徒 [isuramukyouto]

mussel [ˈmʌsəl] n ムール貝 [muurugai]

must [mʌst] v …しなければならない [...shinakereba naranai]

mustard [ˈmʌstəd] n マスタード [masutaado]

mutter [ˈmʌtə] v ブツブツ言う [butsubutsu iu]

mutton [ˈmʌtən] n マトン [maton]

mutual [ˈmjuːtʃʊəl] adj 相互の [sougo no]

my [maɪ] pron 私の [watashi no]; **Here are my insurance details** 私の保険の詳細です [watashi no hoken no shousai desu]

Myanmar [ˈmaɪænmɑː; ˈmjænmɑː] n ミャンマー [myanmaa]

myself [maɪˈsɛlf] pron 私自身 [watashijishin]

mysterious [mɪˈstɪərɪəs] adj 謎めいた [nazomeita]

mystery [ˈmɪstərɪ] n 謎 [nazo]

myth [mɪθ] n 神話 [shinwa]

mythology [mɪˈθɒlədʒɪ] n 神話体系 [shinwa taikei]

n

naff [næf] *adj* 趣味が悪い [shumi ga warui]

nag [næg] *v* がみがみ小言を言う [gamigami kogoto-o iu]

nail [neɪl] *n* 釘 [kugi]; **nail polish** *n* マニキュア液 [manikyua eki]; **nail scissors** *npl* 爪切りばさみ [tsume kiri basami]; **nail varnish** *n* マニキュア液 [manikyua eki]; **nail-polish remover** *n* 除光液 [jokoueki]

nailbrush [ˈneɪlˌbrʌʃ] *n* 爪ブラシ [tsumeburashi]

nailfile [ˈneɪlˌfaɪl] *n* 爪やすり [tsumeyasuri]

naive [nɑːˈiːv; naɪˈiːv] *adj* うぶな [ubuna]

naked [ˈneɪkɪd] *adj* 裸の [hadaka no]

name [neɪm] *n* 名前 [namae]; **brand name** *n* ブランド名 [burando mei]; **first name** *n* ファーストネーム [faasutoneemu]; **maiden name** *n* 女性の結婚前の旧姓 [josei no kekkonmae no kyuusei]; **I booked a room in the name of...** ・・・の名前で部屋を予約しました [... no namae de heya o yoyaku shimashita]; **My name is...** 私の名前は・・・です

[watashi no namae wa ... desu]; **What's your name?** あなたのお名前は? [anata no o-namae wa?]

nanny [ˈnænɪ] *n* 乳母 [uba]

nap [næp] *n* うたたね [utatane]

napkin [ˈnæpkɪn] *n* ナプキン [napukin]

nappy [ˈnæpɪ] *n* おむつ [omutsu]

narrow [ˈnærəʊ] *adj* 狭い [semai]

narrow-minded [ˈnærəʊˈmaɪndɪd] *adj* 了見の狭い [ryouken no semai]

nasty [ˈnɑːstɪ] *adj* 嫌な [iya na]

nation [ˈneɪʃən] *n* 国民 [kokumin]; **United Nations** *n* 国際連合 [kokusairengou]

national [ˈnæʃənˀl] *adj* 国民の [kokumin no]; **national anthem** *n* 国歌 [kokka]; **national park** *n* 国立公園 [kokuritsu kouen]

nationalism [ˈnæʃənəˌlɪzəm; ˈnæʃnə-] *n* 国家主義 [kokkashugi]

nationalist [ˈnæʃənəlɪst] *n* 国家主義者 [kokkashugisha]

nationality [ˌnæʃəˈnælɪtɪ] *n* 国籍 [kokuseki]

nationalize [ˈnæʃənəˌlaɪz; ˈnæʃnə-] *v* 国営にする [kokuei ni suru]

native [ˈneɪtɪv] *adj* 出生地の [shusseichi no]; **native speaker** *n* 母国語とする人 [bokokugo to suru hito]

NATO [ˈneɪtəʊ] *abbr* 北大西洋条約機構 [kitataiseiyou jouyaku kikou]

natural [ˈnætʃrəl; -tʃərəl] *adj* 当然の [touzen no]; **natural gas** *n* 天然ガス [tennengasu]; **natural resources** *npl* 天然資源 [tennenshigen]

naturalist [ˈnætʃrəlɪst; -tʃərəl-] *n* 自然誌研究者 [shizenshi kenkyuusha]

naturally [ˈnætʃrəlɪ; -tʃərə-] *adv* 当然 [touzen]

nature [ˈneɪtʃə] *n* 自然 [shizen]

naughty [ˈnɔːtɪ] *adj* 腕白な [wanpaku na]

nausea [ˈnɔːzɪə; -sɪə] *n* 吐き気 [hakike]

naval [ˈneɪvˀl] *adj* 海軍の [kaigun no]

navel [ˈneɪvˀl] *n* へそ [heso]

navy [ˈneɪvɪ] *n* 海軍 [kaigun]

navy-blue ['neɪvɪ'blu:] *adj* 濃紺の [noukon no]

NB [ɛn bi:] *abbr (notabene)* 注意せよ [chuui seyo]

near [nɪə] *adj* 近い [chikai] ▷ *adv* 近くに [chikaku ni] ▷ *prep* ･･･の近くに [...no chikaku ni]; **Are there any good beaches near here?** この近くにいいビーチはありますか? [kono chikaku ni ii biichi wa arimasu ka?]; **How do I get to the nearest tube station?** 一番近い地下鉄の駅へはどう行けばいいのですか? [ichiban chikai chikatetsu no eki e wa dou ikeba ii no desu ka?]; **Where is the nearest bus stop?** 一番近いバス停はどこですか? [ichiban chikai basu-tei wa doko desu ka?]

nearby *adj* ['nɪəˌbaɪ] 近くの [chikaku no] ▷ *adv* [ˌnɪə'baɪ] 近くに [chikaku ni]; **Is there a bank nearby?** 近くに銀行はありますか? [chikaku ni ginkou wa arimasu ka?]

nearly ['nɪəlɪ] *adv* ほとんど [hotondo]

near-sighted [ˌnɪə'saɪtɪd] *adj* 近視の [kinshi no]

neat [ni:t] *adj* きちんとした [kichin to shita]

neatly [ni:tlɪ] *adv* きちんと [kichin to]

necessarily ['nɛsɪsərɪlɪ; ˌnɛsɪ'sɛrɪlɪ] *adv* 必ず [kanarazu]

necessary ['nɛsɪsərɪ] *adj* 必要な [hitsuyou na]

necessity [nɪ'sɛsɪtɪ] *n* 必要性 [hitsuyousei]

neck [nɛk] *n* 首 [kubi] (体)

necklace ['nɛklɪs] *n* ネックレス [nekkuresu]

nectarine ['nɛktərɪn] *n* ネクタリン [nekutarin]

need [ni:d] *n* 必要 [hitsuyou] ▷ *v* 必要とする [hitsuyou to suru]; **Do you need anything?** 何か必要ですか? [nani ka hitsuyou desu ka?]; **I need assistance** 私は介助が必要です [watashi wa kaijo ga hitsuyou desu]; **I need contraception** 私は避妊が必要です [watashi wa hinin ga hitsuyou desu]

needle ['ni:dəl] *n* 縫い針 [nuihari]; **knitting needle** *n* 編み棒 [amibou]

negative ['nɛgətɪv] *adj* 否定の [hitei no] ▷ *n* 否定の答え [hitei no kotae]

neglect [nɪ'glɛkt] *n* 怠慢 [taiman] ▷ *v* おろそかにする [orosoka ni suru]

neglected [nɪ'glɛktɪd] *adj* おろそかにされた [orosoka ni sareta]

negligee ['nɛglɪˌʒeɪ] *n* 化粧着 [keshougi]

negotiate [nɪ'gəʊʃɪˌeɪt] *v* 交渉する [koushou suru]

negotiations [nɪˌgəʊʃɪ'eɪʃənz] *npl* 交渉 [koushou]

negotiator [nɪ'gəʊʃɪˌeɪtə] *n* 交渉者 [koushousha]

neighbour ['neɪbə] *n* 近所の人 [kinjo no hito]

neighbourhood ['neɪbəˌhʊd] *n* 近所 [kinjo]

neither ['naɪðə; 'ni:ðə] *adv* ･･･もまた･･･でない [...momata ... denai] ▷ *conj* また･･･でない [mata ... denai] ▷ *pron* どちらも･･･でない [dochiramo ... denai]

neon ['ni:ɒn] *n* ネオン [neon]

Nepal [nɪ'pɔ:l] *n* ネパール [nepaaru]

nephew ['nɛvju:; 'nɛf-] *n* 甥 [oi]

nerve [nɜ:v] *n (boldness)* ずぶとさ [zubutosa], *(to/from brain)* 神経 [shinkei]

nerve-racking ['nɜ:vˈrækɪŋ] *adj* 神経を悩ます [shinkei-o nayamasu]

nervous ['nɜ:vəs] *adj* 神経質な [shinkeishitsu na]; **nervous breakdown** *n* 神経衰弱 [shinkeisuijaku]

nest [nɛst] *n* 巣 [su]

net [nɛt] *n* 網 [ami]

Net [nɛt] *n* 正味 [shoumi]

netball ['nɛtˌbɔ:l] *n* ネットボール [nettobooru]

Netherlands ['nɛðələndz] *npl* オランダ [oranda]

nettle ['nɛtəl] *n* イラクサ [irakusa]

network ['nɛtˌwɜ:k] *n* ネットワーク [nettowaaku]; **I can't get a network** ネットワークにつながりません [nettowaaku ni tsunagarimasen]

neurotic [njʊˈrɒtɪk] *adj* 神経過敏な [shinkeikabin na]

neutral [ˈnjuːtrəl] *adj* 中立の [chuuritsu no] ▷ *n* 中立国 [chuuritsukoku]

never [ˈnɛvə] *adv* ・・・したことがない [... shita koto ga nai]

nevertheless [ˌnɛvəðəˈlɛs] *adv* それでも [soredemo]

new [njuː] *adj* 新しい [atarashii]; **New Year** *n* 新年 [shinnen]; **New Zealand** *n* ニュージーランド [nyuujiirando]; **New Zealander** *n* ニュージーランド人 [nyuujiirandojin]

newborn [ˈnjuːˌbɔːn] *adj* 生まれたばかりの [umareta bakari no]

newcomer [ˈnjuːˌkʌmə] *n* 最近来た人 [saikin kita hito]

news [njuːz] *npl* ニュース [nyuusu]; **When is the news?** ニュースはいつですか? [nyuusu wa itsu desu ka?]

newsagent [ˈnjuːzˌeɪdʒənt] *n* 新聞販売店 [shinbunhanbaiten]

newspaper [ˈnjuːzˌpeɪpə] *n* 新聞 [shinbun]; **Do you have newspapers?** 新聞はありますか? [shinbun wa arimasu ka?]; **I would like a newspaper** 新聞をください [shinbun o kudasai]; **Where can I buy a newspaper?** どこで新聞を買えますか? [doko de shinbun o kaemasu ka?]; **Where is the nearest shop which sells newspapers?** 新聞を売っている一番近い店はどこですか? [shinbun o utte iru ichiban chikai mise wa doko desu ka?]

newsreader [ˈnjuːzˌriːdə] *n* ニュースキャスター [nyuusukyasutaa]

newt [njuːt] *n* イモリ [imori]

next [nɛkst] *adj* 次の [tsugi no] ▷ *adv* 次に [tsugi ni]; **next to** *prep* ・・・の隣に [...no tonari ni]; **What is the next stop?** 次の駅はどこですか? [tsugi no eki wa doko desu ka?]; **When is the next bus to...?** ・・・へ行く次のバスは何時ですか? [...e iku tsugi no basu wa nan-ji desu ka?]

next-of-kin [ˈnɛkstɒvˈkɪn] *n* 近親者 [kinshinsha]

Nicaragua [ˌnɪkəˈrægjʊə; nikaˈraɣwa] *n* ニカラグア [nikaragua]

Nicaraguan [ˌnɪkəˈrægjʊən; -gwən] *adj* ニカラグアの [nikaragua no] ▷ *n* ニカラグア人 [nikaraguajin]

nice [naɪs] *adj* すてきな [sutekina]

nickname [ˈnɪkˌneɪm] *n* ニックネーム [nikkuneemu]

nicotine [ˈnɪkəˌtiːn] *n* ニコチン [nikochin]

niece [niːs] *n* 姪 [mei]

Niger [ˈnaɪdʒɪər] *n* ニジェール [nijieeru]

Nigeria [naɪˈdʒɪərɪə] *n* ナイジェリア [naijeria]

Nigerian [naɪˈdʒɪərɪən] *adj* ナイジェリアの [naijeria no] ▷ *n* ナイジェリア人 [naijeriajin]

night [naɪt] *n* 夜 [yoru]; **hen night** *n* ヘンパーティー [henpaatii]; **night school** *n* 夜間学校 [yakangakkou]; **stag night** *n* スタッグパーティー [sutaggupaateii]; **at night** 夜に [yoru ni]; **last night** 昨夜 [sakuya]; **tomorrow night** 明日の夜 [asu no yoru]

nightclub [ˈnaɪtˌklʌb] *n* ナイトクラブ [naitokurabu]

nightdress [ˈnaɪtˌdrɛs] *n* ねまき [nemaki]

nightie [ˈnaɪtɪ] *n* ネグリジェ [negurije]

nightlife [ˈnaɪtˌlaɪf] *n* 歓楽街での夜の楽しみ [kanrakugai deno yoru no tanoshimi]

nightmare [ˈnaɪtˌmɛə] *n* 悪夢 [akumu]

night shift [ˈnaɪt ʃɪft] *n* 夜勤 [yakin]

nil [nɪl] *n* 零 [rei]

nine [naɪn] *number* 九 [kyuu]

nineteen [ˌnaɪnˈtiːn] *number* 十九 [juukyuu]

nineteenth [ˌnaɪnˈtiːnθ] *adj* 十九番目の [juukyuu banme no]

ninety [ˈnaɪntɪ] *number* 九十 [kyuujuu]

ninth [naɪnθ] *adj* 九番目の [kyuu banme no] ▷ *n* 九番目 [kyuubanme]

nitrogen [ˈnaɪtrədʒən] *n* 窒素 [chisso]

no [nəʊ] *pron* ない [nai]; **no!** *excl* なんてこ

とを! [nantekoto wo]; **no one** *pron* 誰も・・・ない [daremo ... nai]

nobody ['nəʊbədɪ] *pron* 誰も・・・ない [daremo ... nai]

nod [nɒd] *v* うなずく [unazuku]

noise [nɔɪz] *n* 騒音 [souon]

noisy ['nɔɪzɪ] *adj* やかましい [yakamashii]

nominate ['nɒmɪˌneɪt] *v* 指名する [shimei suru]

nomination [ˌnɒmɪ'neɪʃən] *n* 指名 [shimei]

none [nʌn] *pron* 誰も・・・ない [daremo ... nai]

nonsense ['nɒnsəns] *n* ナンセンス [nansensu]

non-smoker [nɒn'sməʊkə] *n* 非喫煙者 [hikitsuensha]

non-smoking [nɒn'sməʊkɪŋ] *adj* 禁煙の [kin'en no]

non-stop ['nɒn'stɒp] *adv* 直行で [chokkou de]

noodles ['nu:dəlz] *npl* ヌードル [nuudoru]

noon [nu:n] *n* 正午 [shougo]

nor [nɔ:; nə] *conj* ・・・もまた・・・ない [...momata...nai]

normal ['nɔ:məl] *adj* 普通の [futsuu no]

normally ['nɔ:məlɪ] *adv* 普通に [futsuu ni]

north [nɔ:θ] *adj* 北の [kita no] ▷ *adv* 北に [kita ni] ▷ *n* 北 [kita]; **North Africa** *n* 北アフリカ [kita afurika]; **North African** *n* 北アフリカ人 [kita afurikajin], 北アフリカの [kita afurika no]; **North America** *n* 北アメリカ [kita amerika]; **North American** *n* 北アメリカ人 [kita amerikajin], 北アメリカの [kita amerika no]; **North Korea** *n* 北朝鮮 [kita chousen]; **North Pole** *n* 北極 [hokkyoku]; **North Sea** *n* 北海 [hokkai]

northbound ['nɔ:θˌbaʊnd] *adj* 北行きの [kitayuki no]

northeast [ˌnɔ:θ'i:st; ˌnɔ:r'i:st] *n* 北東 [hokutou]

northern ['nɔ:ðən] *adj* 北の [kita no]; **Northern Ireland** *n* 北アイルランド [kita airurando]

northwest [ˌnɔ:θ'wɛst; ˌnɔ:'wɛst] *n* 北西 [hokusei]

Norway ['nɔ:ˌweɪ] *n* ノルウェー [noruwee]

Norwegian [nɔ:'wi:dʒən] *adj* ノルウェーの [noruwee no] ▷ *n* (*language*) ノルウェー語 [noruweego], (*person*) ノルウェー人 [noruweejin]

nose [nəʊz] *n* 鼻 [hana]

nosebleed ['nəʊzˌbli:d] *n* 鼻血 [hanaji]

nostril ['nɒstrɪl] *n* 鼻の穴 [hana no ana]

nosy ['nəʊzɪ] *adj* 詮索好きな [sensaku zuki na]

not [nɒt] *adv* ・・・でない [...denai]

note [nəʊt] *n* (*banknote*) 紙幣 [shihei], (*message*) メモ [memo], (*music*) 音符 [onpu]; **sick note** *n* 病欠届け [byouketsu todoke]; **Do you have change for this note?** この紙幣でお釣りがありますか? [kono shihei de o-tsuri ga arimasu ka?]

notebook ['nəʊtˌbʊk] *n* ノート [nooto]

note down [nəʊt daʊn] *v* 書き留める [kakitomeru]

notepad ['nəʊtˌpæd] *n* メモパッド [memopaddo]

notepaper ['nəʊtˌpeɪpə] *n* メモ用紙 [memoyoushi]

nothing ['nʌθɪŋ] *pron* 何も・・・ない [nanimo ... nai]

notice ['nəʊtɪs] *n* (*note*) 注意 [chuui], (*termination*) 通告 [tsuukoku] (解雇) ▷ *v* 気づく [kizuku]; **notice board** *n* 掲示板 [keijiban]

noticeable ['nəʊtɪsəbəl] *adj* 目立つ [medatsu]

notification [nəʊtɪfɪ'keɪʃən] *n* 通知 [tsuuchi]

notify ['nəʊtɪˌfaɪ] *v* 通知する [tsuuchi suru]

nought [nɔ:t] *n* 零 [rei]

noun [naʊn] *n* 名詞 [meishi]

novel ['nɒvəl] *n* 小説 [shousetsu]

novelist ['nɒvəlɪst] *n* 小説家 [shousetsuka]

November [nəʊ'vɛmbə] *n* 十一月 [juuichigatsu]

now [naʊ] *adv* 今 [ima]; **Do I pay now or later?** 払うのは今ですか、それとも後ですか？ [harau no wa ima desu ka, sore tomo ato desu ka?]

nowadays ['naʊəˌdeɪz] *adv* このごろは [konogoro wa]

nowhere ['nəʊˌwɛə] *adv* どこにも・・・ない [dokonimo ... nai]

nuclear ['njuːklɪə] *adj* 原子力の [genshiryoku no]

nude [njuːd] *adj* 裸の [hadaka no] ▷ *n* 裸体 [ratai]

nudist ['njuːdɪst] *n* 裸体主義者 [rataishugisha]

nuisance ['njuːsəns] *n* 厄介なもの [yakkai na mono]

numb [nʌm] *adj* 感覚のない [kankaku no nai]

number ['nʌmbə] *n* 数 [kazu]; **account number** *n* 口座番号 [kouzabangou]; **mobile number** *n* 携帯電話番号 [keitai denwa bangou]; **number plate** *n* ナンバープレート [nanbaapureeto]; **phone number** *n* 電話番号 [denwabangou]; **reference number** *n* 参照番号 [sanshou bangou]; **room number** *n* 客室番号 [kyakushitsu bangou]; **wrong number** *n* 間違い電話 [machigai denwa]

numerous ['njuːmərəs] *adj* 多数の [tasuu no]

nun [nʌn] *n* 尼僧 [nisou]

nurse [nɜːs] *n* 看護師 [kangoshi]; **I'd like to speak to a nurse** 看護師さんと話をしたいのですが [kangoshi-san to hanashi o shitai no desu ga]

nursery ['nɜːsrɪ] *n* 子供部屋 [kodomobeya]; **nursery rhyme** *n* 伝承童謡 [denshou douyou]; **nursery school** *n* 保育園 [hoikuen]

nursing home ['nɜːsɪŋ həʊm] *n* 老人ホーム [roujin hoomu]

nut [nʌt] *n* (device) ナット [natto], (food) ナッツ [nattsu]; **nut allergy** *n* ナッツアレルギー [nattsuarerugii]; **Could you prepare a meal without nuts?** ナッツを使わずに食事を用意していただけますか？ [nattsu o tsukawazu ni shokuji o youi shite itadakemasu ka?]

nutmeg ['nʌtmɛg] *n* ナツメグ [natsumegu]

nutrient ['njuːtrɪənt] *n* 栄養分 [eiyoubun]

nutrition [njuː'trɪʃən] *n* 栄養物摂取 [eiyoubutsu sesshu]

nutritious [njuː'trɪʃəs] *adj* 滋養のある [jiyou no aru]

nutter ['nʌtə] *n* 気違い [kichigai]

nylon ['naɪlɒn] *n* ナイロン [nairon]

O

oak [əʊk] *n* オーク [ooku]

oar [ɔː] *n* オール [ooru]

oasis, oases [əʊˈeɪsɪs, əʊˈeɪsiːz] *n* オアシス [oashisu]

oath [əʊθ] *n* 誓い [chikai]

oatmeal [ˈəʊtˌmiːl] *n* オートミール [ootomiiru]

oats [əʊts] *npl* オート麦 [ooto mugi]

obedient [əˈbiːdɪənt] *adj* 従順な [juujun na]

obese [əʊˈbiːs] *adj* 肥満した [himan shita]

obey [əˈbeɪ] *v* 従う [shitagau]

obituary [əˈbɪtjʊərɪ] *n* 死亡記事 [shiboukiji]

object [ˈɒbdʒɪkt] *n* 物 [mono]

objection [əbˈdʒɛkʃən] *n* 反対 [hantai]

objective [əbˈdʒɛktɪv] *n* 目的 [mokuteki]

oblong [ˈɒbˌlɒŋ] *adj* 長方形の [chouhoukei no]

obnoxious [əbˈnɒkʃəs] *adj* 不快な [fukai na]

oboe [ˈəʊbəʊ] *n* オーボエ [ooboe]

obscene [əbˈsiːn] *adj* 猥褻な [waisetu]

observant [əbˈzɜːvənt] *adj* 観察力の鋭い [kansatsuryoku no surudoi]

observatory [əbˈzɜːvətərɪ; -trɪ] *n* 観測所 [kansokujo]

observe [əbˈzɜːv] *v* 観察する [kansatsu suru]

observer [əbˈzɜːvə; obˈserver] *n* 観察者 [kansatsusha]

obsessed [əbˈsɛst] *adj* 執着した [shuuchaku shita]

obsession [əbˈsɛʃən] *n* 執着 [shuuchaku]

obsolete [ˈɒbsəˌliːt; ˌɒbsəˈliːt] *adj* すたれた [sutareta]

obstacle [ˈɒbstəkəl] *n* 障害物 [shougaibutsu]

obstinate [ˈɒbstɪnɪt] *adj* 頑固な [ganko na]

obstruct [əbˈstrʌkt] *v* ふさぐ [fusagu] (じゃま)

obtain [əbˈteɪn] *v* 手に入れる [te ni ireru]

obvious [ˈɒbvɪəs] *adj* 明らかな [akiraka na]

obviously [ˈɒbvɪəslɪ] *adv* 明らかに [akiraka ni]

occasion [əˈkeɪʒən] *n* 場合 [baai]

occasional [əˈkeɪʒənəl] *adj* 時折の [tokiori no]

occasionally [əˈkeɪʒənəlɪ] *adv* 時折 [tokiori]

occupation [ˌɒkjʊˈpeɪʃən] *n* (invasion) 占領 [senryou], (work) 職業 [shokugyou]

occupy [ˈɒkjʊˌpaɪ] *v* 占める [shimeru]

occur [əˈkɜː] *v* 起こる [okoru]

occurrence [əˈkʌrəns] *n* 出来事 [dekigoto]

ocean [ˈəʊʃən] *n* 海洋 [kaiyou]; **Arctic Ocean** *n* 北極海 [hokkyokukai]; **Indian Ocean** *n* インド洋 [indoyou]

Oceania [ˌəʊʃɪˈɑːnɪə] *n* オセアニア [oseania]

o'clock [əˈklɒk] *adv* **after eight o'clock** 八時過ぎに [hachi-ji sugi ni]; **at three o'clock** 三時に [san-ji ni]; **I'd like to book a table for four people for tonight at eight o'clock** 今晩八時に四人用のテーブルを予約したいのですが [konban hachi-ji ni yonin-you no teeburu o yoyaku shitai no desu ga]; **It's one o'clock**

一時です [ichi-ji desu]; **It's six o'clock** 六時です [roku-ji desu]

October [ɒk'təʊbə] n 十月 [juugatsu]; **It's Sunday the third of October** 十月三日の日曜日です [juu-gatsu mik-ka no nichiyoubi desu]

octopus ['ɒktəpəs] n タコ [tako] (動物)

odd [ɒd] adj 変な [hen na]

odour ['əʊdə] n におい [nioi]

of [ɒv; əv] prep ···の [...no]; **How do I get to the centre of...?** ···の中心部へはどう行けばいいのですか？ [...no chuushinbu e wa dou ikeba ii no desu ka?]

off [ɒf] adv 離れて [hanarete] ▷ prep ···を離れて [...o hanarete]; **time off** n 欠勤時間 [kekkin jikan]

offence [ə'fɛns] n 違反 [ihan]

offend [ə'fɛnd] v 不快感を与える [fukaikan-o ataeru]

offensive [ə'fɛnsɪv] adj 嫌な [iya na]

offer ['ɒfə] n 提供 [teikyou] ▷ v 提供する [teikyou suru]; **special offer** n 特別売り出し [tokubetsu uridashi]

office ['ɒfɪs] n オフィス [ofisu]; **booking office** n 予約オフィス [yoyaku ofisu]; **box office** n 切符売場 [kippu uriba]; **head office** n 本社 [honsha]; **information office** n 案内所 [annaijo]; **left-luggage office** n 手荷物一時預かり所 [tenimotsu ichiji azukarisho]; **lost-property office** n 遺失物取扱所 [ishitsubutsu toriatsukaijo]; **office hours** npl 営業時間 [eigyoujikan]; **post office** n 郵便局 [yuubinkyoku]; **registry office** n レジスターオフィス [rejisutaaofisu]; **ticket office** n 切符売場 [kippu uriba]; **tourist office** n ツーリストオフィス [tsuurisutoofisu]; **How do I get to your office?** 貴社のオフィスへ伺うにはどう行けばいいでしょうか？ [kisha no ofisu e ukagau ni wa dou ikeba ii deshou ka?]; **I work in an office** 私はオフィスで働いています [watashi wa ofisu de hataraite imasu]

officer ['ɒfɪsə] n 士官 [shikan]; **customs officer** n 税関係官 [zeikan kakarikan];

police officer n 警察官 [keisatsukan]; **prison officer** n 看守 [kanshu]

official [ə'fɪʃəl] adj 職務上の [shokumujou no]

off-licence ['ɒf,laɪsəns] n 酒類販売免許 [sakerui hanbai menkyo]

offline [ɒf'laɪn] adj オフラインの [ofurain no] ▷ adv オフラインで [ofurain de]

off-peak ['ɒf,piːk] adv ピーク時でなく [piikuji denaku]

off-season ['ɒf,siːzən] adj シーズンオフの [shiizun'ofu no] ▷ adv シーズンオフに [shiizun'ofu ni]

offside ['ɒf'saɪd] adj オフサイドの [ofusaido no]

often ['ɒfən; 'ɒftən] adv しばしば [shibashiba]

oil [ɔɪl] n 油 [abura] ▷ v 油を差す [abura-o sasu] (注油); **olive oil** n オリーブ油 [oriibuyu]; **This stain is oil** このしみは油です [kono shimi wa abura desu]

oil refinery [ɔɪl rɪ'faɪnərɪ] n 石油精製所 [sekiyu seiseijo]

oil rig [ɔɪl rɪg] n 石油掘削装置 [sekiyu kussakusouchi]

oil slick [ɔɪl slɪk] n 油膜 [yumaku]

oil well [ɔɪl wɛl] n 油井 [yusei]

ointment ['ɔɪntmənt] n 軟膏 [nankou]

OK [,əʊ'keɪ] excl オーケー！ [ookee]

okay [,əʊ'keɪ] adj オーケー [ookee]; **okay!** excl オーケー！ [ookee]

old [əʊld] adj 年取った [toshitotta]; **old-age pensioner** n 老齢年金受給者 [rourei nenkin jukyuusha]

old-fashioned ['əʊld'fæʃənd] adj 時代遅れの [jidaiokure no]

olive ['ɒlɪv] n オリーブ [oriibu]; **olive oil** n オリーブ油 [oriibuyu]; **olive tree** n オリーブ [oriibu]

Oman [əʊ'mɑːn] n オマーン [omaan]

omelette ['ɒmlɪt] n オムレツ [omuretsu]

on [ɒn] adv 物の上に載って [mono no ueni notte] ▷ prep ···の上に [...no ue ni]; **on behalf of** n 代理 [dairi]; **on time** adj 遅れずに [okurezu ni]

once [wʌns] adv 一度 [ichido]

ne [wʌn] *number* 一 [ichi] ▷ *pron* 一つ [hitotsu]; **no one** *pron* 誰も・・・ない [daremo ... nai]

ne-off [wʌnɒf] *n* 一回限りのこと [ikkai kagiri no koto]

nion [ˈʌnjən] *n* タマネギ [tamanegi]; **spring onion** *n* ネギ [negi]

nline [ˈɒnˌlaɪn] *adj* オンラインの [onrain no] ▷ *adv* オンラインで [onrain de]; **to go online** オンライン化する [onrainka suru]

nlooker [ˈɒnˌlʊkə] *n* 傍観者 [boukansha]

nly [ˈəʊnlɪ] *adj* 唯一の [yuiitsu no] ▷ *adv* 単にに [tan ni]

pen [ˈəʊpən] *adj* 開いた [aita] ▷ *v* 開ける [akeru]; **opening hours** *npl* 営業時間 [eigyoujikan]

pera [ˈɒpərə] *n* オペラ [opera]; **soap opera** *n* ソープオペラ [soopuopera]; **What's on tonight at the opera?** そのオペラ劇場で今晩何が上演されますか? [sono opera-gekijou de konban nani ga jouen saremasu ka?]

perate [ˈɒpəˌreɪt] *v* (*to function*) 操作する [sousa suru], (*to perform surgery*) 手術する [shujutsu suru]

perating theatre [ˈɒpəˌreɪtɪŋ ˈθɪətə] *n* 手術室 [shujutsushitsu]

peration [ˌɒpəˈreɪʃən] *n* (*surgery*) 手術 [shujutsu], (*undertaking*) 作業 [sagyou]

perator [ˈɒpəˌreɪtə] *n* オペレーター [opereetaa]

pinion [əˈpɪnjən] *n* 意見 [iken]; **opinion poll** *n* 世論調査 [yoronchousa]; **public opinion** *n* 世論 [yoron]

pponent [əˈpəʊnənt] *n* 敵対者 [tekitaisha]

pportunity [ˌɒpəˈtjuːnɪtɪ] *n* 機会 [kikai]

ppose [əˈpəʊz] *v* 反対する [hantai suru]

pposed [əˈpəʊzd] *adj* 反対した [hantai shita]

pposing [əˈpəʊzɪŋ] *adj* 反対する [hantai suru]

pposite [ˈɒpəzɪt; -sɪt] *adj* 向かい側の [mukaigawa no] ▷ *adv* 向かい側に [mukaigawa ni] ▷ *prep* ・・・の向かい側に [...no mukaigawa ni]

opposition [ˌɒpəˈzɪʃən] *n* 反対 [hantai]

optician [ɒpˈtɪʃən] *n* 眼鏡士 [meganeshi]

optimism [ˈɒptɪˌmɪzəm] *n* 楽観主義 [rakkanshugi]

optimist [ˈɒptɪˌmɪst] *n* 楽観主義者 [rakkan shugisha]

optimistic [ɒptɪˈmɪstɪk] *adj* 楽観的な [rakkanteki na]

option [ˈɒpʃən] *n* 選択 [sentaku]

optional [ˈɒpʃənəl] *adj* 自由選択の [jiyuusentakuno]

opt out [ɒpt aʊt] *v* ・・・から脱退する [...kara dattai suru]

or [ɔː] *conj* または [mata wa]; **either ... or** *conj* ・・・かまたは・・・か [...ka matawa ... ka]

oral [ˈɔːrəl; ˈɒrəl] *adj* 口頭の [koutou no] ▷ *n* 口頭試験 [koutou shiken]

orange [ˈɒrɪndʒ] *adj* オレンジ色の [orenjiiro no] ▷ *n* オレンジ [orenji]; **orange juice** *n* オレンジジュース [orenjijuusu]

orchard [ˈɔːtʃəd] *n* 果樹園 [kajuen]

orchestra [ˈɔːkɪstrə] *n* オーケストラ [ookesutora]

orchid [ˈɔːkɪd] *n* ラン [ran]

ordeal [ɔːˈdiːl] *n* 苦しい体験 [kurushii taiken]

order [ˈɔːdə] *n* 命令 [meirei] ▷ *v* (*command*) 命令する [meirei suru], (*request*) 注文する [chuumon suru]; **order form** *n* 注文用紙 [chuumon youshi]; **postal order** *n* 郵便為替 [yuubin kawase]; **standing order** *n* 自動振替 [jidoufurikae]

ordinary [ˈɔːdənrɪ] *adj* 普通の [futsuu no]

oregano [ˌɒrɪˈgɑːnəʊ] *n* オレガノ [oregano]

organ [ˈɔːɡən] *n* (*body part*) 臓器 [zouki], (*music*) オルガン [orugan]; **mouth organ** *n* ハーモニカ [haamonika]

organic [ɔːˈɡænɪk] *adj* 有機体の [yuukitai no]

organism ['ɔ:gə,nɪzəm] *n* 有機体 [yuukitai]

organization [,ɔ:gənaɪ'zeɪʃən] *n* 組織 [soshiki] (団体)

organize ['ɔ:gə,naɪz] *v* 組織する [soshiki suru]

organizer ['ɔ:gə,naɪzə] *n* **personal organizer** *n* システム手帳 [shisutemu techou]

orgasm ['ɔ:gæzəm] *n* オーガズム [oogazumu]

Orient ['ɔ:rɪənt] *n* 東洋 [touyou]

oriental [,ɔ:rɪ'ɛntəl] *adj* 東洋の [touyou no]

origin ['ɒrɪdʒɪn] *n* 起源 [kigen]

original [ə'rɪdʒɪnəl] *adj* 最初の [saisho no]

originally [ə'rɪdʒɪnəlɪ] *adv* 初めは [hajime wa]

ornament ['ɔ:nəmənt] *n* 装飾品 [soushokuhin]

orphan ['ɔ:fən] *n* 孤児 [koji]

ostrich ['ɒstrɪtʃ] *n* ダチョウ [dachou]

other ['ʌðə] *adj* ほかの [hoka no]; **Do you have any others?** ほかの部屋はありますか? [hoka no heya wa arimasu ka?]

otherwise ['ʌðə,waɪz] *adv* 別なふうに [betsu na fuuni] ▷ *conj* さもないと [sa mo nai to]

otter ['ɒtə] *n* カワウソ [kawauso]

ounce [aʊns] *n* オンス [onsu]

our [aʊə] *adj* 私たちの [watashi-tachi no]

ours [aʊəz] *pron* 私たちのもの [watashi-tachi no mono]

ourselves [aʊə'sɛlvz] *pron* 私たち自身 [watashi-tachi jishin]

out [aʊt] *adj* 外の [hoka no] ▷ *adv* 外に [hoka ni]

outbreak ['aʊt,breɪk] *n* 勃発 [boppatsu]

outcome ['aʊt,kʌm] *n* 結果 [kekka]

outdoor ['aʊt'dɔ:] *adj* 屋外の [okugai no]

outdoors [,aʊt'dɔ:z] *adv* 屋外で [okugai de]

outfit ['aʊt,fɪt] *n* 衣装一式 [ishou isshiki]

outgoing ['aʊt,gəʊɪŋ] *adj* 出て行く [deteiku]

outing ['aʊtɪŋ] *n* 遠足 [ensoku]

outline ['aʊt,laɪn] *n* 概要 [gaiyou]

outlook ['aʊt,lʊk] *n* 見通し [mitoushi]

out-of-date ['aʊtɒv'deɪt] *adj* 時代遅れの [jidaiokure no]

out-of-doors ['aʊtɒv'dɔ:z] *adv* 屋外で [okugai de]

outrageous [aʊt'reɪdʒəs] *adj* とんでもない [tonde mo nai]

outset ['aʊt,sɛt] *n* 最初 [saisho]

outside *adj* ['aʊt,saɪd] 外側の [sotogawa no] ▷ *adv* [,aʊt'saɪd] 外側に [sotogawa ni] ▷ *n* ['aʊt'saɪd] 外側 [sotogawa] ▷ *prep* ···の外側に [...no sotogawa ni]

outsize ['aʊt,saɪz] *adj* 特大の [tokudai no]

outskirts ['aʊt,skɜ:ts] *npl* 郊外 [kougai]

outspoken [,aʊt'spəʊkən] *adj* 遠慮のない [enryo no nai]

outstanding [,aʊt'stændɪŋ] *adj* 傑出した [kesshutsu shita]

oval ['əʊvəl] *adj* 卵形の [tamagogata no]

ovary ['əʊvərɪ] *n* 卵巣 [ransou]

oven ['ʌvən] *n* オーブン [oobun]; **microwave oven** *n* 電子レンジ [denshi renji]; **oven glove** *n* オーブンミット [oobunmitto]

ovenproof ['ʌvən,pru:f] *adj* オーブン耐熱性の [oobun tainetsusei no]

over ['əʊvə] *adj* 終わって [owatte] ▷ *prep* ···の上に [...no ue ni]

overall [,əʊvər'ɔ:l] *adv* 全体的に [zentaiteki ni]

overalls [,əʊvə'ɔ:lz] *npl* オーバーオール [oobaaooru]

overcast ['əʊvə,kɑ:st] *adj* 曇った [kumotta]

overcharge [,əʊvə'tʃɑ:dʒ] *v* 過大請求する [kadai seikyuu suru]

overcoat ['əʊvə,kəʊt] *n* オーバー [oobaa]

overcome [,əʊvə'kʌm] *v* 克服する [kokufuku suru]

overdone [,əʊvə'dʌn] *adj* やりすぎの [yarisugi no]

verdose ['əʊvəˌdəʊs] n 過量服用 [karyou fukuyou]

verdraft ['əʊvəˌdrɑːft] n 当座借越し [touzakarikoshi]

verdrawn [ˌəʊvəˈdrɔːn] adj 当座借越しをした [touza karikoshi-o shita]

verdue [ˌəʊvəˈdjuː] adj 遅れた [okureta]

verestimate [ˌəʊvərˈɛstɪˌmeɪt] v 過大評価する [kadai hyouka suru]

verheads ['əʊvəˌhɛdz] npl 諸経費 [shokeihi]

verlook [ˌəʊvəˈlʊk] v 見落とす [miotosu]

vernight ['əʊvəˌnaɪt] adv **Can I park here overnight?** ここに一晩駐車できますか? [koko ni hitoban chuusha dekimasu ka?]; **Can we camp here overnight?** ここで一晩キャンプできますか? [koko de hitoban kyanpu dekimasu ka?]; **Do I have to stay overnight?** 私は一晩入院しなければなりませんか? [watashi wa hitoban nyuuin shinakereba narimasen ka?]

verrule [ˌəʊvəˈruːl] v くつがえす [kutsugaesu]

verseas [ˌəʊvəˈsiːz] adv 海外に [kaigai ni]

versight ['əʊvəˌsaɪt] n (mistake) 見落とし [miotoshi], (supervision) 監督 [kantoku]

versleep [ˌəʊvəˈsliːp] v 寝過ごす [nesugosu]

vertake [ˌəʊvəˈteɪk] v 追い越す [oikosu]

vertime ['əʊvəˌtaɪm] n 超過勤務 [chouka kinmu]

verweight [ˌəʊvəˈweɪt] adj 太りすぎの [futori sugi no]

we [əʊ] v 借りがある [kari ga aru]

wing to ['əʊɪŋ tuː] prep ···のおかげで [no okagede]

wl [aʊl] n フクロウ [fukurou]

wn [əʊn] adj 自分自身の [jubunjishin no] ▷ v 所有する [shoyuu suru]

wner ['əʊnə] n 所有者 [shoyuusha]

own up [əʊn ʌp] v すっかり白状する [sukkari hakujou suru]

oxygen ['ɒksɪdʒən] n 酸素 [sanso]

oyster ['ɔɪstə] n 牡蠣 [kaki]

ozone ['əʊzəʊn; əʊ'zəʊn] n オゾン [ozon]; **ozone layer** n オゾン層 [ozonsou]

P

PA [piː eɪ] *abbr* 個人秘書 [kojin hisho]
pace [peɪs] *n* 歩調 [hochou]
pacemaker ['peɪsˌmeɪkə] *n* ペースメーカー [peesumeekaa]
Pacific [pəˈsɪfɪk] *n* 太平洋 [taiheiyou]
pack [pæk] *n* 荷物 [nimotsu] ▷ *v* 荷造りをする [nizukuri o suru]; **I need to pack now** これから荷物を詰めなければなりません [kore kara nimotsu o tsumenakereba narimasen]
package ['pækɪdʒ] *n* 小包 [kozutsumi]; **package holiday** *n* パック旅行 [pakku ryokou]; **package tour** *n* パック旅行 [pakku ryokou]
packaging ['pækɪdʒɪŋ] *n* パッケージ [pakkeeji]
packed [pækt] *adj* 荷造りが済んで [nizukuri ga sunde]; **packed lunch** *n* 弁当 [bentou]
packet ['pækɪt] *n* 小さな包み [chiisana tsutsumi]
pad [pæd] *n* パッド [paddo]
paddle ['pædəl] *n* パドル [padoru] ▷ *v* パドルで漕ぐ [padoru de kogu]
padlock ['pædˌlɒk] *n* 南京錠 [nankinjou]

paedophile ['piːdəʊˌfaɪl] *n* 小児性愛者 [shouniseiaimono]
page [peɪdʒ] *n* ページ [peeji] ▷ *v* ポケットベルで呼び出す [poketto beru de yobidasu]; **home page** *n* ホームページ [hoomupeeji]; **Yellow Pages®** *npl* イエローページ® [ieroopeeji]
pager ['peɪdʒə] *n* ポケットベル [poketto beru]
paid [peɪd] *adj* 支払い済みの [shiharaizumi no]
pail [peɪl] *n* バケツ [baketsu]
pain [peɪn] *n* 痛み [itami]; **back pain** *n* 腰痛 [youtsuu]; **Can you give me something for the pain?** 痛み止めに何かもらえますか? [itami-dome ni nani ka moraemasu ka?]; **I have a pain in my chest** 私は胸に痛みがあります [watashi wa mune ni itami ga arimasu]; **I want an injection for the pain** 私は痛み止めの注射が欲しいのです [watashi wa itami-dome no chuusha ga hoshii no desu]; **It hurts here** 私はここが痛みます [watashi wa koko ga itamimasu]
painful ['peɪnfʊl] *adj* 痛い [itai]
painkiller ['peɪnˌkɪlə] *n* 痛み止め [itamidome]
paint [peɪnt] *n* ペンキ [penki] ▷ *v* 絵を描く [e-o egaku]
paintbrush ['peɪntˌbrʌʃ] *n* 絵筆 [efude]
painter ['peɪntə] *n* 画家 [gaka]
painting ['peɪntɪŋ] *n* 絵画 [kaiga]
pair [pɛə] *n* ひと組 [hitokumi]
Pakistan [ˌpɑːkɪˈstɑːn] *n* パキスタン [pakisutan]
Pakistani [ˌpɑːkɪˈstɑːnɪ] *adj* パキスタンの [pakisutan no] ▷ *n* パキスタン人 [pakisutanjin]
pal [pæl] *n* 友だち [tomodachi]
palace ['pælɪs] *n* 宮殿 [kyuuden]; **Is the palace open to the public?** その宮殿は一般公開されていますか? [sono kyuuden wa ippan-koukai sarete imasu ka?]; **When is the palace open?** その宮殿はいつ開きますか? [sono kyuuden wa itsu hirakimasu ka?]

ale [peɪl] *adj* 薄い [usui] (住居)

alestine [ˈpælɪˌstaɪn] *n* パレスチナ
[paresuchina]

alestinian [ˌpælɪˈstɪnɪən] *adj* パレス
チナの [paresuchina no] ▷ *n* パレスチナ人
[paresuchinajin]

alm [pɑːm] *n* (*part of hand*) 手のひら
[tenohira], (*tree*) ヤシ [yashi]

amphlet [ˈpæmflɪt] *n* パンフレット
[panfuretto]

an [pæn] *n* 平なべ [taira nabe]; **frying
pan** *n* フライパン [furaipan]

anama [ˌpænəˈmɑː; ˈpænəˌmɑː] *n* パ
ナマ [panama]

ancake [ˈpænˌkeɪk] *n* パンケーキ
[pankeeki]

anda [ˈpændə] *n* パンダ [panda]

anic [ˈpænɪk] *n* パニック [panikku] ▷ *v* う
ろたえる [urotaeru]

anther [ˈpænθə] *n* ヒョウ [hyou]
(動物)

anties [ˈpæntɪz] *npl* パンティー [pantii]

antomime [ˈpæntəˌmaɪm] *n* パントマ
イム [pantomaimu]

ants [pænts] *npl* パンツ [pantsu] (洋服)

aper [ˈpeɪpə] *n* 紙 [kami]; **paper round**
n 新聞配達 [shinbun haitatsu]; **scrap
paper** *n* くず紙 [kuzugami]; **toilet paper**
n トイレットペーパー [toirettopeepaa];
tracing paper *n* トレース紙 [toreesushi];
wrapping paper *n* 包装紙 [housoushi];
writing paper *n* 便箋 [binsen]

aperback [ˈpeɪpəˌbæk] *n* ペーパーバ
ック [peepaabakku]

aperclip [ˈpeɪpəˌklɪp] *n* ペーパークリッ
プ [peepaakurippu]

aperweight [ˈpeɪpəˌweɪt] *n* ペーパー
ウェイト [peepaaueito]

aperwork [ˈpeɪpəˌwɜːk] *n* 机上事務
[kijou jimu]

aprika [ˈpæprɪkə; pæˈpriː-] *n* パプリ
カ [paprika]

aracetamol [ˌpærəˈsiːtəˌmɒl;
-ˈsɛtə-] *n* **I'd like some paracetamol**
パラセタモールが欲しいのですが
[parasetamooru ga hoshii no desu ga]

parachute [ˈpærəˌʃuːt] *n* パラシュート
[parashuuto]

parade [pəˈreɪd] *n* パレード [pareedo]

paradise [ˈpærəˌdaɪs] *n* 楽園 [rakuen]

paraffin [ˈpærəfɪn] *n* パラフィン
[parafin]

paragraph [ˈpærəˌgrɑːf; -ˌgræf] *n* 段
落 [danraku]

Paraguay [ˈpærəˌgwaɪ] *n* パラグアイ
[paraguai]

Paraguayan [ˌpærəˈgwaɪən] *adj* パラ
グアイの [paraguai no] ▷ *n* パラグアイ人
[paraguaijin]

parallel [ˈpærəˌlɛl] *adj* 平行の [heikou no]

paralysed [ˈpærəˌlaɪzd] *adj* 麻痺した
[mahi shita]

paramedic [ˌpærəˈmedɪk] *n* 救急救命
士 [kyuukyuu kyuumeishi]

parcel [ˈpɑːsəl] *n* 小包 [kozutsumi]; **How
much is it to send this parcel?** この小
包を送るのにいくらかかりますか? [kono
kozutsumi o okuru no ni ikura kakarimasu
ka?]; **I'd like to send this parcel** この小
包を送りたいのですが [kono kozutsumi o
okuritai no desu ga]

pardon [ˈpɑːdən] *n* 許し [yurushi]

parent [ˈpɛərənt] *n* 親 [oya]; **parents**
npl 両親 [ryoushin]; **single parent** *n* 片
親で子育てをする人 [kataoya de
kosodate-o suru hito]

parish [ˈpærɪʃ] *n* 教会区 [kyoukaiku]

park [pɑːk] *n* 公園 [kouen] ▷ *v* 駐車する
[chuusha suru]; **car park** *n* 駐車場
[chuushajou]; **national park** *n* 国立公園
[kokuritsu kouen]; **theme park** *n* テーマ
パーク [teemapaaku]

parking [ˈpɑːkɪŋ] *n* 駐車 [chuusha];
parking meter *n* パーキングメーター
[paakingumeetaa]; **parking ticket** *n* 駐車
違反切符 [chuushaihan kippu]; **Do I need
to buy a car-parking ticket?** 駐車チケ
ットを買わなければなりません [chuusha-chiketto o kawanakereba
narimasen ka?]

parliament [ˈpɑːləmənt] *n* 議会 [gikai]

parole [pəˈrəʊl] *n* 仮釈放 [kari shakuhou]

parrot ['pærət] n オウム [oumu]

parsley ['pɑːslɪ] n パセリ [paseri]

parsnip ['pɑːsnɪp] n パースニップ [paasunippu]

part [pɑːt] n 部分 [bubun]; **spare part** n スペアパーツ [supeapaatsu]

partial ['pɑːʃəl] adj 部分的な [bubunteki na]

participate [pɑːˈtɪsɪˌpeɪt] v 参加する [sanka suru]

particular [pəˈtɪkjʊlə] adj 特別の [tokubetsu no]

particularly [pəˈtɪkjʊlərlɪ] adv 特に [toku ni]

parting ['pɑːtɪŋ] n 別れ [wakare]

partly ['pɑːtlɪ] adv 部分的に [bubunteki ni]

partner ['pɑːtnə] n 相手 [aite]

partridge ['pɑːtrɪdʒ] n ヨーロッパヤマウズラ [yooroppayamauzura]

part-time ['pɑːtˌtaɪm] adj パートタイムの [paatotaimu no] ▷ adv パートタイムで [paatotaimu de]

part with [pɑːt wɪð] v ・・・を手放す [...-o tebanasu]

party ['pɑːtɪ] n (group) 一行 [ikkou] (集まり), (social gathering) パーティー [paateiji]; **dinner party** n ディナーパーティー [dinaa paatii]; **search party** n 捜索隊 [sousakutai]

pass [pɑːs] n (in mountains) 峠 [touge], (meets standard) 合格 [goukaku], (permit) 許可証 [kyokashou] ▷ vi 過ぎる [sugiru] ▷ vt 通過する [tsuuka suru], (an exam) 合格する [goukaku suru]; **boarding pass** n 搭乗券 [toujouken]; **ski pass** n スキー場のパス [sukii jou no pasu]

passage ['pæsɪdʒ] n (musical) 楽節 [gakusetsu], (route) 通路 [tsuuro]

passenger ['pæsɪndʒə] n 乗客 [joukyaku]

passion ['pæʃən] n 熱情 [netsujou]; **passion fruit** n パッションフルーツ [passhonfuruutsu]

passive ['pæsɪv] adj 受身の [ukemi no]

pass out [pɑːs aʊt] v 意識を失う [ishiki-o ushinau]

Passover ['pɑːsˌəʊvə] n 過越しの祭 [sugikoshi no matsuri]

passport ['pɑːspɔːt] n パスポート [pasupooto]; **passport control** n パスポート審査窓口 [pasupooto shinsa madoguchi]; **Here is my passport** 私のパスポートです [watashi no pasupooto desu]; **I've forgotten my passport** 私はパスポートを置き忘れました [watashi wa pasupooto o okiwasuremashita]; **I've lost my passport** 私はパスポートをなくしました [watashi wa pasupooto o nakushimashita]; **My passport has been stolen** 私のパスポートが盗まれました [watashi no pasupooto ga nusumaremashita]; **Please give me my passport back** 私のパスポートを返してください [watashi no pasupooto o kaeshite kudasai]; **The children are on this passport** 子供たちはこのパスポートに載っています [kodomo-tachi wa kono pasupooto ni notte imasu]

password ['pɑːsˌwɜːd] n パスワード [pasuwaado]

past [pɑːst] adj 過ぎ去った [sugisatta] ▷ n 過去 [kako] ▷ prep ・・・を過ぎて [...o sugite]

pasta ['pæstə] n パスタ [pasuta]; **I'd like pasta as a starter** スターターにパスタをいただきます [sutaataa ni pasuta o itadakimasu]

paste [peɪst] n ペースト [peesuto]

pasteurized ['pæstəˌraɪzd] adj 低温殺菌した [teion sakkin shita]

pastime ['pɑːsˌtaɪm] n 娯楽 [goraku]

pastry ['peɪstrɪ] n 生地 [kiji] (料理); **puff pastry** n パフペースト [pafupeesuto]; **shortcrust pastry** n ショートクラスト [shootokurasuto]

patch [pætʃ] n つぎ [tsugi] (布切れ)

patched [pætʃt] adj つぎを当てた [tsugi-o ateta]

path [pɑːθ] n 小道 [komichi]; **cycle path** n サイクルパス [saikuru pasu]

pathetic [pə'θɛtɪk] *adj* 哀れな [aware na]

patience ['peɪʃəns] *n* 忍耐 [nintai]

patient ['peɪʃənt] *adj* 忍耐強い [nintaizuyoi] ▷ *n* 患者 [kanja]

patio ['pætɪˌəʊ] *n* パティオ [pateio]

patriotic ['pætrɪəˌtɪk] *adj* 愛国的な [aikokuteki na]

patrol [pə'trəʊl] *n* パトロール [patorooru]; **patrol car** *n* パトロールカー [patoroorukaa]

pattern ['pætᵊn] *n* 模様 [moyou]

pause [pɔːz] *n* 小休止 [shoukyuushi]

pavement ['peɪvmənt] *n* 歩道 [hodou]

pavilion [pə'vɪljən] *n* 別館 [bekkan]

paw [pɔː] *n* 動物の足 [doubutsu no ashi]

pawnbroker ['pɔːnˌbrəʊkə] *n* 質屋 [shichiya]

pay [peɪ] *n* 給料 [kyuuryou] ▷ *v* 支払う [shiharau]; **sick pay** *n* 病気休暇中の手当て [byouki kyuukachuu no teate]

payable ['peɪəbᵊl] *adj* 支払うべき [shiharaubeki]

pay back [peɪ bæk] *v* 払い戻す [haraimodosu]

payment ['peɪmənt] *n* 支払い [shiharai]

payphone ['peɪˌfəʊn] *n* 公衆電話 [koushuudenwa]

PC [piː siː] *n* PC [piishii]

PDF [piː diː ɛf] *n* PDF [piidiiefu]

peace [piːs] *n* 平穏 [heion]

peaceful ['piːsfʊl] *adj* 平和な [heiwa na]

peach [piːtʃ] *n* モモ [momo]

peacock ['piːˌkɒk] *n* クジャク [kujaku]

peak [piːk] *n* 尖端 [sentan]; **peak hours** *npl* ピーク時 [piikuji]

peanut ['piːˌnʌt] *n* ピーナッツ [piinattsu]; **peanut allergy** *n* ピーナッツアレルギー [piinattsu arerugii]; **peanut butter** *n* ピーナッツバター [piinattsubataa]; **Does that contain peanuts?** それにはピーナッツが入っていますか? [sore ni wa piinattsu ga haitte imasu ka?]; **I'm allergic to peanuts** 私はピーナッツのアレルギーがあります [watashi wa piinattsu no arerugii ga arimasu]

pear [pɛə] *n* 西洋ナシ [seiyounashi]

pearl [pɜːl] *n* 真珠 [shinju]

peas [piːs] *npl* エンドウ [endou]

peat [piːt] *n* 泥炭 [deitan]

pebble ['pɛbᵊl] *n* 小石 [koishi]

peculiar [pɪ'kjuːlɪə] *adj* 変な [hen na]

pedal ['pɛdᵊl] *n* ペダル [pedaru]

pedestrian [pɪ'dɛstrɪən] *n* 歩行者 [hokousha]; **pedestrian crossing** *n* 横断歩道 [oudanhodou]; **pedestrian precinct** *n* 歩行者天国 [hokoushatengoku]

pedestrianized [pɪ'dɛstrɪəˌnaɪzd] *adj* 歩行者専用になった [hokousha sen'you ni natta]

pedigree ['pɛdɪˌgriː] *adj* 血統の明らかな [kettou no akiraka na]

peel [piːl] *n* 皮 [kawa] (果物・野菜) ▷ *v* 皮をむく [kawa-o muku]

peg [pɛg] *n* ペグ [pegu]

Pekinese [ˌpiːkɪŋ'iːz] *n* ペキニーズ [pekiniizu]

pelican ['pɛlɪkən] *n* ペリカン [perikan]; **pelican crossing** *n* 押しボタン信号式横断歩道 [oshibotan shingoushiki oudanhodou]

pellet ['pɛlɪt] *n* 小球 [shoukyuu]

pelvis ['pɛlvɪs] *n* 骨盤 [kotsuban]

pen [pɛn] *n* ペン [pen]; **ballpoint pen** *n* ボールペン [boorupen]; **felt-tip pen** *n* フェルトペン [ferutopen]; **fountain pen** *n* 万年筆 [mannenhitsu]; **Do you have a pen I could borrow?** ペンをお借りできますか? [pen o o-kari dekimasu ka?]

penalize ['piːnəˌlaɪz] *v* 罰する [bassuru]

penalty ['pɛnᵊltɪ] *n* 刑罰 [keibatsu]

pencil ['pɛnsᵊl] *n* 鉛筆 [enpitsu]; **pencil case** *n* 筆箱 [fudebako]; **pencil sharpener** *n* 鉛筆削り [enpitsukezuri]

pendant ['pɛndənt] *n* ペンダント [pendanto]

penfriend ['pɛnˌfrɛnd] *n* ペンパル [penparu]

penguin ['pɛŋgwɪn] *n* ペンギン [pengin]

penicillin [ˌpɛnɪ'sɪlɪn] *n* ペニシリン [penishirin]

peninsula [pɪ'nɪnsjʊlə] n 半島 [hantou]

penknife ['pɛn,naɪf] n ペンナイフ [pennaifu]

penny ['pɛnɪ] n ペニー [penii]

pension ['pɛnʃən] n 年金 [nenkin]

pensioner ['pɛnʃənə] n 年金受給者 [nenkin jukyuusha]; **old-age pensioner** n 老齢年金受給者 [rourei nenkin jukyuusha]

pentathlon [pɛn'tæθlən] n 五種競技 [goshu kyougi]

penultimate [pɪ'nʌltɪmɪt] adj 終わりから2番目の [owari kara ni banme no]

people ['piːp°l] npl 人々 [hitobito]

pepper ['pɛpə] n コショウ [koshou]

peppermill ['pɛpə,mɪl] n コショウひき [koshou hiki]

peppermint ['pɛpə,mɪnt] n ペパーミント [pepaaminto]

per [pɜː; pə] prep ・・・につき [...nitsuki]; **per cent** adv 百につき [hyaku ni tsuki]

percentage [pə'sɛntɪdʒ] n パーセンテージ [paasenteeji]

percussion [pə'kʌʃən] n 衝突 [shoutotsu]

perfect ['pɜːfɪkt] adj 完璧な [kanpeki na]

perfection [pə'fɛkʃən] n 完璧 [kanpeki]

perfectly ['pɜːfɪktlɪ] adv 完璧に [kanpeki ni]

perform [pə'fɔːm] v 行う [okonau]

performance [pə'fɔːməns] n (artistic) 演奏 [ensou], (functioning) 遂行 [suikou]

perfume ['pɜːfjuːm] n 香水 [kousui]

perhaps [pə'hæps; præps] adv ことによると [koto ni yoru to]

period ['pɪərɪəd] n 期間 [kikan]; **trial period** n 試用期間 [shiyou kikan]

perjury ['pɜːdʒərɪ] n 偽証 [gishou]

perm [pɜːm] n パーマ [paama]

permanent ['pɜːmənənt] adj 永久の [eikyuu no]

permanently ['pɜːmənəntlɪ] adv 永久に [eikyuu ni]

permission [pə'mɪʃən] n 許可 [kyoka]

permit n ['pɜːmɪt] 許可証 [kyokashou] ▷ v [pə'mɪt] 許可証 [kyokashou]; **work permit** n 労働許可証 [roudou kyokashou]

persecute ['pɜːsɪ,kjuːt] v 迫害する [hakugai suru]

persevere [,pɜːsɪ'vɪə] v 辛抱する [shinbou suru]

Persian ['pɜːʃən] adj ペルシャの [perusha no]

persistent [pə'sɪstənt] adj 持続性の [jizokusei no]

person ['pɜːs°n] n 人 [hito]; **How much is it per person?** それは一人あたりいくらですか? [sore wa hitori atari ikura desu ka?]

personal ['pɜːsən°l] adj 個人的な [kojinteki na]; **personal assistant** n 個人秘書 [kojin hisho]; **personal organizer** n システム手帳 [shisutemu techou]; **personal stereo** n パーソナルステレオ [paasonarusutereo]

personality [,pɜːsə'nælɪtɪ] n 個性 [kosei]

personally ['pɜːsənəlɪ] adv 直接自分で [chokusetsu jibun de]

personnel [,pɜːsə'nɛl] n 人員 [jin-in]

perspective [pə'spɛktɪv] n 観点 [kanten]

perspiration [,pɜːspə'reɪʃən] n 汗 [ase]

persuade [pə'sweɪd] v 説得する [settoku suru]

persuasive [pə'sweɪsɪv] adj 説得力のある [settokuryoku no aru]

Peru [pə'ruː] n ペルー [peruu]

Peruvian [pə'ruːvɪən] adj ペルーの [peruu no] ▷ n ペルー人 [peruujin]

pessimist ['pɛsɪ,mɪst] n 悲観主義者 [hikanshugisha]

pessimistic ['pɛsɪ,mɪstɪk] adj 悲観的な [hikanteki na]

pest [pɛst] n 害虫 [gaichuu]

pester ['pɛstə] v 悩ませる [nayamaseru]

pesticide ['pɛstɪ,saɪd] n 農薬 [nouyaku]

pet [pɛt] n ペット [petto]

petition [pɪ'tɪʃən] n 嘆願書 [tangansho]

petrified ['pɛtrɪ,faɪd] adj **to be petrified** すくむ [sukumu]

petrol ['pɛtrəl] n ガソリン [gasorin];
petrol station n ガソリンスタンド
[gasorinsutando]; **petrol tank** n ガソリン
タンク [gasorintanku]; **unleaded petrol**
n 無鉛ガソリン [muen gasorin]; **I've run
out of petrol** ガソリンが切れてしまいま
した [gasorin ga kirete shimaimashita]; **Is
there a petrol station near here?** こ
の近くにガソリンスタンドはありますか?
[kono chikaku ni gasorin-sutando wa
arimasu ka?]; **The petrol has run out** ガ
ソリンが切れてしまいました [gasorin ga
kirete shimaimashita]

pewter ['pjuːtə] n 白目 [shirome]

pharmacist ['fɑːməsɪst] n 薬剤師
[yakuzaishi]

pharmacy ['fɑːməsɪ] n 薬局 [yakkyoku];
**Which pharmacy provides
emergency service?** どの薬局が夜間
休日サービスを実施していますか?
[dono yakkyoku ga yakan-kyuujitsu-saabisu
o jisshi shite imasu ka?]

PhD [piː eɪtʃ diː] n 博士号 [hakasegou]

pheasant ['fɛzˀnt] n キジ [kiji]

philosophy [fɪ'lɒsəfɪ] n 哲学 [tetsugaku]

phobia ['fəʊbɪə] n 恐怖症 [kyoufushou]

phone [fəʊn] n 電話 [denwa] ▷ v 電話を
かける [denwa-o kakeru]; **camera
phone** n カメラ付き携帯電話 [kamera
tsuki keitai denwa]; **entry phone** n イン
ターホン [intaahon]; **mobile phone** n 携
帯電話 [keitai denwa]; **phone back** v 電
話をかけなおす [denwa-o kakenaosu];
phone bill n 電話の請求書 [denwa no
seikyuusho]; **phone number** n 電話番号
[denwabangou]; **smart phone** n スマー
トフォン [sumaatofon]; **Can I have your
phone number?** 電話番号を教えてもら
えますか? [denwa-bangou o oshiete
moraemasu ka?]; **Can I phone from
here?** ここから電話をかけられますか?
[koko kara denwa o kakeraremasu ka?];
**Can I phone internationally from
here?** ここから国際電話をかけられます
か? [koko kara kokusai-denwa o
kakeraremasu ka?]; **Can I use your**

phone, please? 電話をお借りできます
か? [denwa o o-kari dekimasu ka?]; **Do
you sell international phone cards?**
国際電話用のテレホンカードを売ってい
ますか? [kokusai-denwa-you no
terehon-kaado o utte imasu ka?]; **I must
make a phone call** 私は電話をかけな
ければなりません [watashi wa denwa o
kakenakereba narimasen]; **I want to
make a phone call** 電話をかけたいの
ですが [denwa o kaketai no desu ga]; **I'd
like some coins for the phone,
please** 電話に使うコインをいくらかお願
いします [denwa ni tsukau koin o ikura ka
o-negai shimasu]; **I'd like to phone my
embassy** 私は大使館に電話したいので
すが [watashi wa taishikan ni denwa shitai
no desu ga]; **I'm having trouble with
the phone** 電話に問題があります
[denwa ni mondai ga arimasu]; **May I
phone home?** 家に電話していいです
か? [ie ni denwa shite ii desu ka?]; **May I
use your phone?** 電話をお借りできま
すか? [denwa o o-kari dekimasu ka?];
**Where can I charge my mobile
phone?** どこで携帯電話を充電できます
か? [doko de keitai-denwa o juuden
dekimasu ka?]

phonebook ['fəʊnˌbʊk] n 電話帳
[denwachou]

phonebox ['fəʊnˌbɒks] n 電話ボックス
[denwa bokkusu]

phone call ['fəʊnˌkɔːl] n 電話をかける
こと [denwa-o kakeru koto]; **Where can I
make a phone call?** どこで電話をかけ
られますか? [doko de denwa o
kakeraremasu ka?]

phonecard ['fəʊnˌkɑːd] n テレホンカー
ド [terehon kaado]; **A phonecard,
please** テレホンカードをください
[terehon-kaado o kudasai]; **Where can I
buy a phonecard?** どこでテレホンカー
ドを買えますか? [doko de terehon-kaado
o kaemasu ka?]

photo ['fəʊtəʊ] n 写真 [shashin]; **photo
album** n アルバム [arubamu]; **Can I**

download photos to here? ここに写真をダウンロードできますか? [koko ni shashin o daunroodo dekimasu ka?]; **Can you put these photos on CD, please?** この写真をCDに焼き付けていただけますか? [kono shashin o shii-dii ni yakitsukete itadakemasu ka?]; **How much do the photos cost?** 写真代はいくらですか? [shashin-dai wa ikura desu ka?]; **I'd like the photos glossy** 写真は光沢仕上げにしてください [shashin wa koutaku-shiage ni shite kudasai]; **I'd like the photos matt** 写真はマット仕上げにしてください [shashin wa matto-shiage ni shite kudasai]; **When will the photos be ready?** 写真はいつできますか? [shashin wa itsu dekimasu ka?]

photocopier ['fəʊtəʊ,kɒpɪə] n コピー機 [kopiiki]

photocopy ['fəʊtəʊ,kɒpɪ] n コピー [kopii] (複写) ▷ v コピーする [kopii suru]; **I'd like a photocopy of this, please** このコピーをお願いします [kono kopii o o-negai shimasu]; **Where can I get some photocopying done?** どこでコピーを取ってもらえますか? [doko de kopii o totte moraemasu ka?]

photograph ['fəʊtə,grɑːf; -,græf] n 写真 [shashin] ▷ v 撮影する [satsuei suru]

photographer [fə'tɒgrəfə] n 写真家 [shashinka]

photography [fə'tɒgrəfɪ] n 写真撮影 [shashinsatsuei]

phrase [freɪz] n 慣用句 [kan'youku]

phrasebook ['freɪz,bʊk] n 外国語慣用句集 [gaikokugo kan'youku shuu]

physical ['fɪzɪkəl] adj 身体の [shintai no] ▷ n 身体検査 [shintai kensa]

physicist ['fɪzɪsɪst] n 物理学者 [butsurigakusha]

physics ['fɪzɪks] npl 物理学 [butsurigaku]

physiotherapist [,fɪzɪəʊ'θerəpɪst] n 理学療法士 [rigaku ryouhoushi]

physiotherapy [,fɪzɪəʊ'θerəpɪ] n 理学療法 [rigaku ryouhou]

pianist ['pɪənɪst] n ピアニスト [pianisuto]

piano [pɪ'ænəʊ] n ピアノ [piano]

pick [pɪk] n 選択 [sentaku] ▷ v 選ぶ [erabu]

pick on [pɪk ɒn] v いじめる [ijimeru]

pick out [pɪk aʊt] v 選ぶ [erabu]

pickpocket ['pɪk,pɒkɪt] n スリ [suri]

pick up [pɪk ʌp] v 持ち上げる [mochiageru]

picnic ['pɪknɪk] n ピクニック [pikunikku]

picture ['pɪktʃə] n 絵 [e]; **picture frame** n 額縁 [gakubuchi]

picturesque [,pɪktʃə'rɛsk] adj 絵のように美しい [e no youni utsukushii]

pie [paɪ] n パイ [pai]; **apple pie** n アップルパイ [appurupai]; **pie chart** n 円グラフ [engurafu]

piece [piːs] n 一つ [hitotsu]

pier [pɪə] n 埠頭 [futou]

pierce [pɪəs] v 穴をあける [ana-o akeru]

pierced [pɪəst] adj 穴をあけた [ana-o aketa]

piercing ['pɪəsɪŋ] n ピアス [piasu]

pig [pɪg] n 豚 [buta]; **guinea pig** n (for experiment) 実験台 [jikkendai], (rodent) モルモット [morumotto] (動物)

pigeon ['pɪdʒɪn] n 鳩 [hato]

piggybank ['pɪgɪ,bæŋk] n 貯金箱 [chokinbako]

pigtail ['pɪg,teɪl] n おさげ [osage]

pile [paɪl] n 積み重ね [tsumikasane]

piles [paɪlz] npl 痔 [di]

pile-up [paɪlʌp] n 山積み [yamazumi]

pilgrim ['pɪlgrɪm] n 巡礼者 [junreisha]

pilgrimage ['pɪlgrɪmɪdʒ] n 巡礼の旅 [junrei no tabi]

pill [pɪl] n 丸薬 [ganyaku]; **sleeping pill** n 睡眠薬 [suimin-yaku]

pillar ['pɪlə] n 柱 [hashira]

pillow ['pɪləʊ] n 枕 [makura]; **Please bring me an extra pillow** 追加の枕を持ってきてください [tsuika no makura o motte kite kudasai]

pillowcase ['pɪləʊ,keɪs] n 枕カバー [makurakabaa]

pilot ['paɪlət] n パイロット [pairotto]; **pilot light** n 口火 [kuchibi]

pimple ['pɪmpəl] n 吹き出物 [fukidemono]

pin [pɪn] n ピン [pin]; **drawing pin** n 画鋲 [gabyou]; **rolling pin** n 麺棒 [menbou]; **safety pin** n 安全ピン [anzenpin]; **I need a safety pin** 私は安全ピンが必要です [watashi wa anzen-pin ga hitsuyou desu]

PIN [pɪn] abbr (= personal identification number) 暗証番号 [anshobango]

pinafore ['pɪnəfɔː] n エプロン [epuron]

pinch [pɪntʃ] v つねる [tsuneru]

pine [paɪn] n マツ [matsu]

pineapple ['paɪnˌæpəl] n パイナップル [painappuru]

pink [pɪŋk] adj ピンク色の [pinkuiro no]

pint [paɪnt] n パイント [painto]

pip [pɪp] n 種 [shu] (果実)

pipe [paɪp] n パイプ [paipu]; **exhaust pipe** n エキゾーストパイプ [ekizoosutopaipu]

pipeline ['paɪpˌlaɪn] n パイプライン [paipurain]

pirate ['paɪrɪt] n 海賊 [kaizoku]

Pisces ['paɪsiːz; 'pɪ-] n 魚座 [uoza]

pistol ['pɪstəl] n ピストル [pisutoru]

piston ['pɪstən] n ピストン [pisuton]

pitch [pɪtʃ] n (sound) 調子 [choushi], (sport) ピッチ [pitchi] (競技場) ▷ v 投げる [nageru]

pity ['pɪtɪ] n 哀れみ [awaremi] ▷ v 哀れむ [awaremu]

pixel ['pɪksəl] n 画素 [gaso]

pizza ['piːtsə] n ピザ [piza]

place [pleɪs] n 場所 [basho] ▷ v 置く [oku]; **place of birth** n 出生地 [shusseichi]; **Where is the best place to dive?** ダイビングに最適の場所はどこですか? [daibingu ni saiteki no basho wa doko desu ka?]

placement ['pleɪsmənt] n 配置 [haichi]

plain [pleɪn] adj 平坦な [heitan na] ▷ n 平原 [heigen]; **plain chocolate** n ブラックチョコレート [burakku chokoreeto]

plait [plæt] n おさげ [osage]

plan [plæn] n 計画 [keikaku] ▷ v 計画する [keikaku suru]; **street plan** n 街路計画 [gairo keikaku]

plane [pleɪn] n (aeroplane) 飛行機 [hikouki], (surface) 平面 [heimen], (tool) かんな [kanna] (道具); **My plane leaves at...** 私の飛行機は・・・に出発します [watashi no hikouki wa ... ni shuppatsu shimasu]

planet ['plænɪt] n 惑星 [wakusei]

planning ['plænɪŋ] n 計画 [keikaku]

plant [plɑːnt] n 植物 [shokubutsu], (site/equipment) 製造工場 [seizou koujou] ▷ v 植える [ueru]; **plant pot** n 植木鉢 [uekibachi]; **pot plant** n 鉢植え植物 [hachiue shokubutsu]; **We'd like to see local plants and trees** 土地の植物と樹木を見たいのですが [tochi no shokubutsu to jumoku o mitai no desu ga]

plaque [plæk; plɑːk] n 記念銘板 [kinen meiban]

plaster ['plɑːstə] n (for wall) 漆喰 [shikkui], (for wound) 絆創膏 [iedomo chimakemu]

plastic ['plæstɪk] adj プラスチックの [purasuchikku no] ▷ n プラスチック [purasuchikku]; **plastic bag** n ビニール袋 [biniiru bukuro]; **plastic surgery** n 形成外科 [keisei geka]

plate [pleɪt] n 平皿 [taira sara]; **number plate** n ナンバープレート [nanbaapureeto]

platform ['plætfɔːm] n 演壇 [endan]

platinum ['plætɪnəm] n プラチナ [purachina]

play [pleɪ] n 劇 [geki] ▷ v (in sport) 競技を行う [kyougi-o okonau], (music) 演奏する [ensou suru]; **play truant** v サボる [saboru]; **playing card** n トランプ [toranpu]; **playing field** n グラウンド [guraundo]; **Where can we go to see a play?** どこに行けば観劇ができますか? [doko ni ikeba kangeki ga dekimasu ka?]

player ['pleɪə] n (instrumentalist) 演奏者 [ensousha], (of sport) 選手 [senshu]; **CD player** n CDプレーヤー [shiidii pureiyaa]; **MP3 player** n MP3プレーヤー

[emu pi surii pyreeyaa]; **MP4 player** n MP4プレーヤー [emu pi foa pyreeyaa]

playful ['pleɪfʊl] adj 陽気な [youki na]

playground ['pleɪˌɡraʊnd] n 遊び場 [asobiba]

playgroup ['pleɪˌɡruːp] n プレイグループ [pureiguruupu]

PlayStation® ['pleɪˌsteɪʃən] n プレイステーション® [pureisuteeshon]

playtime ['pleɪˌtaɪm] n 遊び時間 [asobi jikan]

playwright ['pleɪˌraɪt] n 脚本家 [kyakuhonka]

pleasant ['plɛzənt] adj 楽しい [tanoshii]

please [pliːz] excl お願い! #? I'd like to check in, please = チェックインをお願いします

pleased [pliːzd] adj 嬉しい [ureshii]

pleasure ['plɛʒə] n 楽しみ [tanoshimi]

plenty ['plɛntɪ] n たっぷり [tappuri]

pliers ['plaɪəz] npl プライヤー [puraiyaa]

plot [plɒt] n (piece of land) 小区画 [shou kukaku], (secret plan) たくらむ [takura-mu] (secret plan) ▷ v (conspire) たくらむ [takura-mu]

plough [plaʊ] n 鋤 [suki] ▷ v 耕す [tagayasu]

plug [plʌɡ] n 栓 [sen]; **spark plug** n スパークプラグ [supaakupuragu]

plughole ['plʌɡˌhəʊl] n 排水口 [haisuikou]

plug in [plʌɡ ɪn] v プラグで接続する [puragu de setsuzoku suru]

plum [plʌm] n プラム [puramu]

plumber ['plʌmə] n 配管工 [haikankou]

plumbing ['plʌmɪŋ] n 配管 [haikan]

plump [plʌmp] adj 丸々太った [marumaru futotta]

plunge [plʌndʒ] v 突っ込む [tsukkomu]

plural ['plʊərəl] n 複数 [fukusuu]

plus [plʌs] prep ···を加えて [...-o kuwaete]

plywood ['plaɪˌwʊd] n ベニヤ板 [beniyaita]

p.m. [piː ɛm] abbr 午後の [gogo no]

pneumonia [njuːˈməʊnɪə] n 肺炎 [haien]

poached [pəʊtʃt] adj (caught illegally) 密漁した [mitsuryou shita], (simmered gently) ポーチした [poochi shita]

pocket ['pɒkɪt] n ポケット [poketto]; **pocket calculator** n 電卓 [dentaku]; **pocket money** n ポケットマネー [pokettomanee]

podcast ['pɒdˌkɑːst] n ポッドキャスト [poddokyasuto]

poem ['pəʊɪm] n 詩 [shi]

poet ['pəʊɪt] n 詩人 [shijin]

poetry ['pəʊɪtrɪ] n 詩歌 [shiika]

point [pɔɪnt] n 要点 [youten] ▷ v 指し示す [sashishimesu]

pointless ['pɔɪntlɪs] adj 無意味な [muimi na]

point out [pɔɪnt aʊt] v 指摘する [shiteki suru]

poison ['pɔɪzən] n 毒 [doku] ▷ v 毒を盛る [doku-o moru]

poisonous ['pɔɪzənəs] adj 有毒な [yuudoku na]

poke [pəʊk] v つつく [tsutsuku]

poker ['pəʊkə] n ポーカー [pookaa]

Poland ['pəʊlənd] n ポーランド [poorando]

polar ['pəʊlə] adj 極地の [kyokuchi no]; **polar bear** n 北極グマ [hokkyokuguma]

pole [pəʊl] n 棒 [bou]; **North Pole** n 北極 [hokkyoku]; **pole vault** n 棒高跳び [bou taka tobi]; **South Pole** n 南極 [nankyoku]; **tent pole** n テントポール [tentopooru]

Pole [pəʊl] n ポーランド人 [poorandojin]

police [pəˈliːs] n 警察 [keisatsu]; **police officer** n 警察官 [keisatsukan]; **police station** n 警察署 [keisatsusho]; **Call the police** 警察を呼んでください [keisatsu o yonde kudasai]; **I need a police report for my insurance** 私は保険請求に警察の証明書が必要です [watashi wa hoken-seikyuu ni keisatsu no shoumeisho ga hitsuyou desu]; **We will have to report it to the police** 私たちはそれを警察に届け出なければなりません [watashi-tachi wa sore o keisatsu ni todokedenakereba narimasen]; **Where is the police station?** 警察署はどこですか? [keisatsusho wa doko desu ka?]

policeman, policemen [pə'li:smən, pə'li:smɛn] n 警官 [keikan]

policewoman, policewomen [pə'li:swʊmən, pə'li:swɪmɪn] n 婦人警官 [fujinkeikan]

policy ['pɒlɪsɪ] n **insurance policy** n 保険証書 [hokenshousho]

polio ['pəʊlɪəʊ] n ポリオ [porio]

polish ['pɒlɪʃ] n つや出し剤 [tsuyadashi zai] ▷ v つやを出す [tsuya-o dasu]; **nail polish** n マニキュア液 [manikyua eki]; **shoe polish** n 靴墨 [kutsuzumi]

Polish ['pəʊlɪʃ] adj ポーランドの [poorando no] ▷ n (language) ポーランド語 [poorandogo]

polite [pə'laɪt] adj 丁寧な [teinei na]

politely [pə'laɪtlɪ] adv 丁寧に [teinei ni]

politeness [pə'laɪtnɪs] n 丁寧 [teinei]

political [pə'lɪtɪkəl] adj 政治の [seiji no]

politician [ˌpɒlɪ'tɪʃən] n 政治家 [seijika]

politics ['pɒlɪtɪks] npl 政治 [seiji]

poll [pəʊl] n 世論調査 [yoronchousa]; **opinion poll** n 世論調査 [yoronchousa]

pollen ['pɒlən] n 花粉 [kafun]

pollute [pə'lu:t] v 汚染する [osen suru]

polluted [pə'lu:tɪd] adj 汚染された [osen sareta]

pollution [pə'lu:ʃən] n 汚染 [osen]

Polynesia [ˌpɒlɪ'ni:ʒə; -ʒɪə] n ポリネシア [porineshia]

Polynesian [ˌpɒlɪ'ni:ʒən; -ʒɪən] adj ポリネシアの [porineshia no] ▷ n (language) ポリネシア語 [porineshiago], (person) ポリネシア人 [porineshiajin]

pomegranate ['pɒmɪˌgrænɪt; 'pɒmˌgrænɪt] n ザクロ [zakuro]

pond [pɒnd] n 池 [ike]

pony ['pəʊnɪ] n ポニー [ponii]; **pony trekking** n ポニートレッキング [poniitorekkingu]

ponytail ['pəʊnɪˌteɪl] n ポニーテール [poniiteeru]

poodle ['pu:dəl] n プードル [puudoru]

pool [pu:l] n (resources) 共同資金 [kyoudou shikin], (water) プール [puuru] (水泳); **paddling pool** n 子供用プール [kodomoyou puuru]; **swimming pool** n スイミングプール [suimingupuuru]; **Is it an outdoor pool?** それは屋外プールですか? [sore wa okugai-puuru desu ka?]; **Is the pool heated?** プールは温水ですか? [puuru wa onsui desu ka?]; **Is there a children's pool?** 子供用のプールはありますか? [kodomo-you no puuru wa arimasu ka?]; **Is there a paddling pool for the children?** 子供用の浅いプールはありますか? [kodomo-you no asai puuru wa arimasu ka?]

poor [pʊə; pɔ:] adj 貧しい [mazushii]

poorly ['pʊəlɪ; 'pɔ:-] adj 体調が悪い [taichou ga warui]

popcorn ['pɒpˌkɔ:n] n ポップコーン [poppukoon]

pope [pəʊp] n ローマ法王 [rooma houou]

poplar ['pɒplə] n ポプラ [popura]

poppy ['pɒpɪ] n ケシ [keshi]

popular ['pɒpjʊlə] adj 人気のある [ninki no aru]

popularity ['pɒpjʊlærɪtɪ] n 人気 [ninki] (評判)

population [ˌpɒpjʊ'leɪʃən] n 人口 [jinkou]

pop-up book [pɒpʌp-] n 開くと絵が飛び出す本 [hiraku to e ga tobidasu hon]

porch [pɔ:tʃ] n ポーチ [poochi]

pork [pɔ:k] n ポーク [pooku]; **pork chop** n ポークチョップ [pookuchoppu]

porn [pɔ:n] n ポルノ [poruno]

pornographic [pɔ:'nɒgræfɪk] adj ポルノの [poruno no]

pornography [pɔ:'nɒgrəfɪ] n ポルノ [poruno]

porridge ['pɒrɪdʒ] n ポリッジ [porijji]

port [pɔ:t] n (ships) 港 [minato], (wine) ポートワイン [pootowain]

portable ['pɔ:təbəl] adj 持ち運びできる [mochihakobi dekiru]

porter ['pɔ:tə] n ポーター [pootaa]

portfolio [pɔːˈfəʊlɪəʊ] n 紙ばさみ [kamibasami]

portion [ˈpɔːʃən] n 部分 [bubun]

portrait [ˈpɔːtrɪt; -treɪt] n 肖像画 [shouzouga]

Portugal [ˈpɔːtjʊgəl] n ポルトガル [porutogaru]

Portuguese [ˌpɔːtjʊˈgiːz] adj ポルトガルの [porutogaru no] ▷ n (language) ポルトガル語 [porutogarugo], (person) ポルトガル人 [porutogarujin]

position [pəˈzɪʃən] n 位置 [ichi]

positive [ˈpɒzɪtɪv] adj 確信している [kakushin shite iru]

possess [pəˈzɛs] v 所有する [shoyuu suru]

possession [pəˈzɛʃən] n 所有 [shoyuu]

possibility [ˌpɒsɪˈbɪlɪtɪ] n 可能性 [kanousei]

possible [ˈpɒsɪbəl] adj 可能な [kanou na]

possibly [ˈpɒsɪblɪ] adv ことによると [koto ni yoru to]

post [pəʊst] n (mail) 郵便 [yuubin], (position) 地位 [chii], (stake) 柱 [hashira] ▷ v 郵送する [yuusou suru], (on social media) を投稿する [o toukou suru]; **post office** n 郵便局 [yuubinkyoku]; **How long will it take by registered post?** 書留郵便でどのくらいの日数がかかりますか? [kakitome-yuubin de dono kurai no nissuu ga kakarimasu ka?]; **When does the post office open?** 郵便局はいつ開きますか? [yuubinkyoku wa itsu hirakimasu ka?]

postage [ˈpəʊstɪdʒ] n 郵便料金 [yuubin ryoukin]

postbox [ˈpəʊstˌbɒks] n 郵便受 [yuubinju]

postcard [ˈpəʊstˌkaːd] n 郵便はがき [yuubin hagaki]; **Can I have stamps for four postcards to...** ・・・あての郵便はがき四枚分の切手をもらえますか? [...ate no yuubin-hagaki yonmai-bun no kitte o moraemasu ka?]; **Do you have any postcards?** 郵便はがきはありますか? [yuubin-hagaki wa arimasu ka?]; **I'm looking for postcards** 私は郵便はがきを探しています [watashi wa yuubin-hagaki o sagashite imasu]; **Where can I buy some postcards?** どこで郵便はがきを買えますか? [doko de yuubin-hagaki o o kaemasu ka?]

postcode [ˈpəʊstˌkəʊd] n 郵便番号 [yuubin bangou]

poster [ˈpəʊstə] n ポスター [posutaa]

postgraduate [pəʊstˈgrædjuɪt] n 大学院生 [daigakuinsei]

postman, postmen [ˈpəʊstmən, ˈpəʊstmɛn] n 郵便配達人 [yuubin haitatsunin]

postmark [ˈpəʊstˌmaːk] n 消印 [keshiin]

postpone [pəʊstˈpəʊn; pəˈspəʊn] v 延期する [enki suru]

postwoman, postwomen [ˈpəʊstwʊmən, ˈpəʊstwɪmɪn] n 女性郵便配達人 [josei yuubin haitatsunin]

pot [pɒt] n 深鍋 [shin nabe]; **plant pot** n 植木鉢 [uekibachi]; **pot plant** n 鉢植え植物 [hachiue shokubutsu]

potato, potatoes [pəˈteɪtəʊ, pəˈteɪtəʊz] n ジャガイモ [jagaimo]; **baked potato** n ベークドポテト [beekudopoteto]; **jacket potato** n ジャケットポテト [jaketto poteto]; **mashed potatoes** npl マッシュポテト [masshu poteto]; **potato peeler** n 皮むき器 [kawamukiki]

potential [pəˈtɛnʃəl] adj 可能性のある [kanousei no aru] ▷ n 可能性 [kanousei]

pothole [ˈpɒtˌhəʊl] n ポットホール [pottohooru]

pottery [ˈpɒtərɪ] n 陶器 [touki]

potty [ˈpɒtɪ] n 幼児用の便器 [youji-you no benki]; **Do you have a potty?** 幼児用の便器はありますか? [youji-you no benki wa arimasu ka?]

pound [paʊnd] n ポンド [pondo]; **pound sterling** n 英貨ポンド [eika pondo]

pour [pɔː] v 流す [nagasu]

poverty [ˈpɒvətɪ] n 貧困 [hinkon]

powder [ˈpaʊdə] n 粉 [kona]; **baking powder** n ベーキングパウダー [beekingupaudaa]; **soap powder** n 粉石

鹸 [kona sekken]; **talcum powder** n タルカムパウダー [tarukamupaudaa]; **washing powder** n 粉末洗剤 [funmatsusenzai]; **Do you have washing powder?** 粉末洗剤はあります か? [funmatsu-senzai wa arimasu ka?]

power ['pauə] n 能力 [nouryoku]; **power cut** n 停電 [teiden]; **solar power** n 太陽 エネルギー [taiyou enerugii]

powerful ['pauəful] adj 強力な [kyouryoku na]

practical ['præktɪkəl] adj 実際的な [jissaiteki na]

practically ['præktɪkəlɪ; -klɪ] adv 実 際に [jissai ni]

practice ['præktɪs] n 練習 [renshuu]

practise ['præktɪs] v 練習する [renshuu suru]

praise [preɪz] v ほめる [homeru]

pram [præm] n 乳母車 [ubaguruma]

prank [præŋk] n 戯れ [tawamure]

prawn [prɔːn] n クルマエビ [kurumaebi]

pray [preɪ] v 祈る [inoru]

prayer [preə] n 祈り [inori]

precaution [prɪˈkɔːʃən] n 用心 [youjin]

preceding [prɪˈsiːdɪŋ] adj 前の [mae no]

precinct ['priːsɪŋkt] n 指定地区 [shitei chiku]; **pedestrian precinct** n 歩行者天 国 [hokoushatengoku]

precious ['prɛʃəs] adj 貴重な [kichou na]

precise [prɪˈsaɪs] adj 正確な [seikaku na]

precisely [prɪˈsaɪslɪ] adv 正確に [seikaku ni]

predecessor ['priːdɪˌsɛsə] n 前任者 [zenninsha]

predict [prɪˈdɪkt] v 予想する [yosou suru]

predictable [prɪˈdɪktəbəl] adj 予想でき る [yosou dekiru]

prefect ['priːfɛkt] n 監督生 [kantokusei]

prefer [prɪˈfɜː] v ···の方を好む [...no hou o konomu]

preferably ['prɛfərəblɪ; 'prɛfrəblɪ] adv 好んで [kononde]

preference ['prɛfərəns; 'prɛfrəns] n 好み [konomi]

pregnancy ['prɛgnənsɪ] n 妊娠 [ninshin]

pregnant ['prɛgnənt] adj 妊娠した [ninshin shita]

prehistoric [ˌpriːhɪˈstɒrɪk] adj 有史前 の [yuushi mae no]

prejudice ['prɛdʒʊdɪs] n 偏見 [henken]

prejudiced ['prɛdʒʊdɪst] adj 偏見をも った [henken-o motta]

premature [ˌprɛməˈtjʊə; 'prɛmətjʊə] adj 時期尚早の [jikishousou no]

premiere ['prɛmɪˌɛə; 'prɛmɪə] n 初演 [shoen]

premises ['prɛmɪsɪz] npl 土地建物 [tochi tatemono]

premonition [ˌprɛməˈnɪʃən] n 予感 [yokan]

preoccupied [priːˈɒkjʊˌpaɪd] adj ···に 余念がない [...ni yonen ga nai]

prepaid [priːˈpeɪd] adj プリペイドの [puripeido no]

preparation [ˌprɛpəˈreɪʃən] n 準備 [junbi]

prepare [prɪˈpɛə] v 準備する [junbi suru]

prepared [prɪˈpɛəd] adj 用意ができた [youi ga dekita]

Presbyterian [ˌprɛzbɪˈtɪərɪən] adj 長 老派の [chourouha no] ▷ n 長老派の人 [chourouha no hito]

prescribe [prɪˈskraɪb] v 処方する [shohou suru]

prescription [prɪˈskrɪpʃən] n 処方箋 [shohousen]; **Where can I get this prescription made up?** どこでこの処方 箋の薬を出してもらえますか? [doko de kono shohousen no kusuri o dashite moraemasu ka?]

presence ['prɛzəns] n 存在 [sonzai]

present adj ['prɛz] 居る [iru] ▷ n ['prɛz] (gift) プレゼント [purezento], (time being) 現在 [genzai] ▷ v [prɪˈzɛnt] 紹介する [shoukai suru]; **I'm looking for a present for my husband** 私は夫への プレゼントを探しています [watashi wa otto e no purezento o sagashite imasu]

presentation [ˌprɛzənˈteɪʃən] n 紹介 [shoukai]

presenter [prɪˈzɛntə] n プレゼンター [purezentaa]

presently ['prɛzəntlɪ] *adv* やがて [yagate]

preservative [prɪ'zɜːvətɪv] *n* 保存料 [hozonryou]

president ['prɛzɪdənt] *n* 大統領 [daitouryou]

press [prɛs] *n* プレス機 [puresuki] ▷ *v* 押す [osu]; **press conference** *n* 記者会見 [kishakaiken]

press-up [prɛsʌp] *n* 腕立て伏せ [udetatefuse]

pressure ['prɛʃə] *n* 圧力 [atsuryoku] ▷ *v* 圧力を加える [atsuryoku-o kuwaeru]; **blood pressure** *n* 血圧 [ketsuatsu]

prestige [prɛ'stiːʒ] *n* 名声 [meisei]

prestigious [prɛ'stɪdʒəs] *adj* 名声のある [meisei no aru]

presumably [prɪ'zjuːməblɪ] *adv* 思うに [omou ni]

presume [prɪ'zjuːm] *v* 推定する [suitei suru]

pretend [prɪ'tɛnd] *v* ふりをする [furi o suru]

pretext ['priːtɛkst] *n* 口実 [koujitsu]

prettily ['prɪtɪlɪ] *adv* きれいに [kirei ni]

pretty ['prɪtɪ] *adj* きれいな [kirei na] ▷ *adv* かなり [kanari]

prevent [prɪ'vɛnt] *v* 防ぐ [fusegu]

prevention [prɪ'vɛnʃən] *n* 予防 [yobou]

previous ['priːvɪəs] *adj* 以前の [izen no]

previously ['priːvɪəslɪ] *adv* 以前に [izen ni]

prey [preɪ] *n* 餌食 [ejiki]

price [praɪs] *n* 価格 [kakaku]; **price list** *n* 価格表 [kakakuhyou]; **retail price** *n* 小売価格 [kourikakaku]; **selling price** *n* 販売価格 [hanbai kakaku]

prick [prɪk] *v* チクリと刺す [chikuri to sasu]

pride [praɪd] *n* 誇り [hokori]

priest [priːst] *n* 司祭 [shisai]

primarily ['praɪmərəlɪ] *adv* 主として [shutoshite]

primary ['praɪmərɪ] *adj* 第一の [daiichi no]; **primary school** *n* 小学校 [shougakkou]

primitive ['prɪmɪtɪv] *adj* 初期の [shoki no]

primrose ['prɪmˌrəʊz] *n* サクラソウ [sakurasou]

prince [prɪns] *n* 王子 [ouji]

princess [prɪn'sɛs] *n* 王女 [oujo]

principal ['prɪnsɪpəl] *adj* 主な [omo na] ▷ *n* 校長 [kouchou]

principle ['prɪnsɪpəl] *n* 主義 [shugi]

print [prɪnt] *n* 印刷物 [insatsubutsu] ▷ *v* 印刷する [insatsu suru]

printer ['prɪntə] *n* (machine) 印刷機 [insatsuki], (person) 印刷業者 [insatsu gyousha]

printing ['prɪntɪŋ] *n* **How much is printing?** 印刷はいくらですか? [insatsu wa ikura desu ka?]

printout ['prɪntaʊt] *n* ハードコピー [haadokopii]

priority [praɪ'ɒrɪtɪ] *n* 優先 [yuusen]; **How long will it take by priority post?** 優先郵便でどのくらいの日数がかかりますか? [yuusen-yuubin de dono kurai no nissuu ga kakarimasu ka?]

prison ['prɪzən] *n* 刑務所 [keimusho]; **prison officer** *n* 看守 [kanshu]

prisoner ['prɪzənə] *n* 囚人 [shuujin]

privacy ['praɪvəsɪ; 'prɪvəsɪ] *n* プライバシー [puraibashii]

private ['praɪvɪt] *adj* 個人的な [kojinteki na]; **private property** *n* 個人の所有物 [kojin no shoyuubutsu]

privatize ['praɪvɪˌtaɪz] *v* 民営化する [min'eika suru]

privilege ['prɪvɪlɪdʒ] *n* 特権 [tokken]

prize [praɪz] *n* 賞 [shou]

prize-giving ['praɪzˌgɪvɪŋ] *n* 授賞式 [jushoushiki]

prizewinner ['praɪzˌwɪnə] *n* 受賞者 [jushousha]

probability [ˌprɒbə'bɪlɪtɪ] *n* 見込み [mikomi]

probable ['prɒbəbəl] *adj* ありそうな [arisou na]

probably ['prɒbəblɪ] *adv* 多分 [tabun]

problem ['prɒbləm] *n* 問題 [mondai];

There's a problem with the room 部屋に問題があります [heya ni mondai ga arimasu]; **Who do we contact if there are problems?** 問題があったときに誰に連絡すればいいのですか? [mondai ga atta toki ni dare ni renraku sureba ii no desu ka?]

proceedings [prəˈsiːdɪŋz] *npl* 進行 [shinkou]

proceeds [ˈprəʊsiːdz] *npl* 収益 [shoueki]

process [ˈprəʊsɛs] *n* 過程 [katei]

procession [prəˈsɛʃən] *n* 行進 [koushin]

produce [prəˈdjuːs] *v* 生産する [seisan suru]

producer [prəˈdjuːsə] *n* プロデューサー [purodyuusaa]

product [ˈprɒdʌkt] *n* 製品 [seihin]

production [prəˈdʌkʃən] *n* 生産 [seisan]

productivity [ˌprɒdʌkˈtɪvɪtɪ] *n* 生産性 [seisansei]

profession [prəˈfɛʃən] *n* 職業 [shokugyou]

professional [prəˈfɛʃənəl] *adj* 職業的な [shokugyouteki na] ▷ *n* 専門家 [senmonka]

professionally [prəˈfɛʃənəlɪ] *adv* 職業的に [shokugyouteki ni]

professor [prəˈfɛsə] *n* 教授 [kyouju]

profile [ˈskrəʊl] *n* プロフィール [purofiiru]; **profile picture** *n* プロフィール写真 [purofiiru shashin]

profit [ˈprɒfɪt] *n* 収益 [shoueki]

profitable [ˈprɒfɪtəbəl] *adj* 収益の多い [shuueki no oui]

program [ˈprəʊɡræm] *n* プログラム [puroguramu] ▷ *v* プログラムを作成する [puroguramu-o sakusei suru]

programme [ˈprəʊɡræm] *n* プログラム [puroguramu]

programmer [ˈprəʊɡræmə] *n* プログラマー [puroguramaa]

programming [ˈprəʊɡræmɪŋ] *n* プログラム作成 [puroguramu sakusei]

progress [ˈprəʊɡrɛs] *n* 進歩 [shinpo]

prohibit [prəˈhɪbɪt] *v* 禁止する [kinshi suru]

prohibited [prəˈhɪbɪtɪd] *adj* 禁止された [kinshi sareta]

project [ˈprɒdʒɛkt] *n* 企画 [kikaku]

projector [prəˈdʒɛktə] *n* プロジェクター [purojekutaa]; **overhead projector** *n* オーバーヘッドプロジェクター [oobaaheddopurojekutaa]

promenade [ˌprɒməˈnɑːd] *n* 海岸の遊歩道 [kaigan no yuuhodou]

promise [ˈprɒmɪs] *n* 約束 [yakusoku] ▷ *v* 約束する [yakusoku suru]

promising [ˈprɒmɪsɪŋ] *adj* 将来有望な [shourai yuubou na]

promote [prəˈməʊt] *v* 促進する [sokushin suru]

promotion [prəˈməʊʃən] *n* 促進 [sokushin]

prompt [prɒmpt] *adj* 即座の [sokuza no]

promptly [ˈprɒmptlɪ] *adv* 即座に [sokuza ni]

pronoun [ˈprəʊˌnaʊn] *n* 代名詞 [daimeishi]

pronounce [prəˈnaʊns] *v* 発音する [hatsuon suru]

pronunciation [prəˌnʌnsɪˈeɪʃən] *n* 発音 [hatsuon]

proof [pruːf] *n* (*evidence*) 証拠 [shouko], (*for checking*) 校正刷り [kouseizuri]

propaganda [ˌprɒpəˈɡændə] *n* プロパガンダ [puropaganda]

proper [ˈprɒpə] *adj* 適切な [tekisetsu na]

properly [ˈprɒpəlɪ] *adv* 適切に [tekisetsu ni]

property [ˈprɒpətɪ] *n* 所有物 [shoyuubutsu]; **private property** *n* 個人の所有物 [kojin no shoyuubutsu]

proportion [prəˈpɔːʃən] *n* 比率 [hiritsu]

proportional [prəˈpɔːʃənəl] *adj* 比例した [hirei shita]

proposal [prəˈpəʊzəl] *n* 提案 [teian]

propose [prəˈpəʊz] *v* 提案する [teian suru]

prosecute [ˈprɒsɪˌkjuːt] *v* 起訴する [kiso suru]

prospect [ˈprɒspɛkt] *n* 見通し [mitoushi]

prospectus [prəˈspɛktəs] *n* 案内書 [annaisho]

prosperity [prɒˈspɛrɪtɪ] *n* 繁栄 [han-ei]

prostitute [ˈprɒstɪˌtjuːt] *n* 売春婦 [baishunfu]

protect [prəˈtɛkt] *v* 保護する [hogo suru]

protection [prəˈtɛkʃən] *n* 保護 [hogo]

protein [ˈprəʊtiːn] *n* 蛋白質 [tanpakushitsu]

protest *n* [ˈprəʊtɛst] 抗議 [kougi] ▷ *v* [prəˈtɛst] 抗議する [kougi suru]

Protestant [ˈprɒtɪstənt] *adj* プロテスタントの [purotesutanto no] ▷ *n* プロテスタント [purotesutanto]

proud [praʊd] *adj* 誇りに思う [hokori ni omou]

prove [pruːv] *v* 立証する [risshou suru]

proverb [ˈprɒvɜːb] *n* ことわざ [kotowaza]

provide [prəˈvaɪd] *v* 供給する [kyoukyuu suru]; **provide for** *v* 準備する [junbi suru]

provided [prəˈvaɪdɪd] *conj* もし・・・とすれば [moshi ... tosureba]

providing [prəˈvaɪdɪŋ] *conj* もし・・・とすれば [moshi ... tosureba]

provisional [prəˈvɪʒənəl] *adj* 暫定的な [zanteiteki na]

proximity [prɒkˈsɪmɪtɪ] *n* 近接 [kinsetsu]

prune [pruːn] *n* プルーン [puruun]

pry [praɪ] *v* 詮索する [sensaku suru]

pseudonym [ˈsjuːdəˌnɪm] *n* ペンネーム [penneemu]

psychiatric [ˌsaɪkɪˈætrɪk] *adj* 精神科の [seishinka no]

psychiatrist [saɪˈkaɪətrɪst] *n* 精神科医 [seishinka-i]

psychological [ˌsaɪkəˈlɒdʒɪkəl] *adj* 心理的な [shinriteki na]

psychologist [saɪˈkɒlədʒɪst] *n* 心理学者 [shinrigakusha]

psychology [saɪˈkɒlədʒɪ] *n* 心理学 [shinrigaku]

psychotherapy [ˌsaɪkəʊˈθɛrəpɪ] *n* 心理療法 [shinri ryouhou]

PTO [piː tiː əʊ] *abbr* (= *please turn over*) 次ページへ続く [jipeji he tsuduku]

pub [pʌb] *n* パブ [pabu]

public [ˈpʌblɪk] *adj* 公衆の [koushuu no] ▷ *n* 公衆 [koushuu]; **public holiday** *n* 祝祭日 [shukusaijitsu]; **public opinion** *n* 世論 [yoron]; **public relations** *npl* 広報 [kouhou]; **public school** *n* パブリックスクール [paburikkusukuuru]; **public transport** *n* 公共交通機関 [koukyou koutsuu kikan]

publican [ˈpʌblɪkən] *n* パブの主人 [pabu no shujin]

publication [ˌpʌblɪˈkeɪʃən] *n* 出版 [shuppan]

publish [ˈpʌblɪʃ] *v* 出版する [shuppan suru]

publisher [ˈpʌblɪʃə] *n* 出版業者 [shuppan gyousha]

pudding [ˈpʊdɪŋ] *n* プディング [pudingu]

puddle [ˈpʌdəl] *n* 水たまり [mizutamari]

Puerto Rico [ˈpwɜːtəʊ ˈriːkəʊ; ˈpwɛə-] *n* プエルトリコ [puerutoriko]

pull [pʊl] *v* 引く [hiku]

pull down [pʊl daʊn] *v* 取り壊す [torikowasu]

pull out [pʊl aʊt] *vi* 車線から出る [shasen kara deru]

pullover [ˈpʊlˌəʊvə] *n* プルオーバー [puruoobaa]

pull up [pʊl ʌp] *v* 止める [tomeru]

pulse [pʌls] *n* 脈拍 [myakuhaku]

pulses [pʌlsɪz] *npl* 豆類 [mamerui]

pump [pʌmp] *n* ポンプ [ponpu] ▷ *v* ポンプで注入する [ponpu de chuunyuu suru]; **bicycle pump** *n* 自転車ポンプ [jitensha ponpu]; **Pump number three, please** 3番のポンプをお願いします [san-ban no ponpu o o-negai shimasu]

pumpkin [ˈpʌmpkɪn] *n* カボチャ [kabocha]

pump up [pʌmp ʌp] *v* ポンプで膨らませる [ponpu de fukuramaseru]

punch [pʌntʃ] *n* (*blow*) パンチ [panchi] (殴打), (*hot drink*) パンチ [panchi] (飲み物) ▷ *v* げんこつをくらわす [genkotsu-o kurawasu]

punctual ['pʌŋktjʊəl] *adj* 時間厳守の [jikangenshu no]

punctuation [,pʌŋktjʊ'eɪʃən] *n* 句読 [kutou]

puncture ['pʌŋktʃə] *n* 刺し穴 [sashiana]

punish ['pʌnɪʃ] *v* 罰する [bassuru]

punishment ['pʌnɪʃmənt] *n* 処罰 [shobatsu]; **capital punishment** *n* 死刑 [shikei]; **corporal punishment** *n* 体刑 [taikei]

punk [pʌŋk] *n* チンピラ [chinpira]

pupil ['pjuːpəl] *n* (eye) 瞳孔 [doukou], (learner) 生徒 [seito]

puppet ['pʌpɪt] *n* あやつり人形 [ayatsuri ningyou]

puppy ['pʌpɪ] *n* 子犬 [koinu]

purchase ['pɜːtʃɪs] *v* 購入する [kounyuu suru]

pure [pjʊə] *adj* 純粋な [junsui na]

purple ['pɜːpəl] *adj* 紫色の [murasakiiro no]

purpose ['pɜːpəs] *n* 目的 [mokuteki]

purr [pɜː] *v* ゴロゴロとのどを鳴らす [gorogoro to nodo-o narasu]

purse [pɜːs] *n* 財布 [saifu]

pursue [pə'sjuː] *v* 追跡する [tsuiseki suru]

pursuit [pə'sjuːt] *n* 追跡 [tsuiseki]

pus [pʌs] *n* 膿 [umi]

push [pʊʃ] *v* 押す [osu]

pushchair ['pʊʃtʃɛə] *n* ベビーカー [bebiikaa]

push-up [pʊʃʌp] *n* 腕立て伏せ [udetatefuse]

put [pʊt] *v* 置く [oku]

put aside [pʊt ə'saɪd] *v* 取っておく [totteoku]

put away [pʊt ə'weɪ] *v* 取っておく [totteoku]

put back [pʊt bæk] *v* もとへ返す [moto-e kaesu]

put forward [pʊt fɔːwəd] *v* 提唱する [teishou suru]

put in [pʊt ɪn] *v* 投入する [tounyuu suru]

put off [pʊt ɒf] *v* 延期する [enki suru]

put up [pʊt ʌp] *v* 建てる [tateru]

puzzle ['pʌzəl] *n* 難問 [nanmon]

puzzled ['pʌzəld] *adj* 困った [komatta]

puzzling ['pʌzlɪŋ] *adj* 困らせる [komaraseru]

pyjamas [pə'dʒɑːməz] *npl* パジャマ [pajama]

pylon ['paɪlən] *n* 鉄塔 [tettou]

pyramid ['pɪrəmɪd] *n* ピラミッド [piramiddo]

q

Qatar [kæ'tɑ:] *n* カタール [kataaru]

quail [kweɪl] *n* ウズラ [uzura]

quaint [kweɪnt] *adj* 古風で趣のある [kofuu de omomuki no aru]

Quaker ['kweɪkə] *n* クエーカー [kueekaa]

qualification [ˌkwɒlɪfɪˈkeɪʃən] *n* 資格 [shikaku]

qualified ['kwɒlɪˌfaɪd] *adj* 資格のある [shikaku no aru]

qualify ['kwɒlɪˌfaɪ] *v* 資格を取る [shikaku o toru]

quality ['kwɒlɪtɪ] *n* 質 [shitsu]

quantify ['kwɒntɪˌfaɪ] *v* 量を決める [ryou-o kimeru]

quantity ['kwɒntɪtɪ] *n* 量 [ryou]

quarantine ['kwɒrənˌtiːn] *n* 検疫期間 [ken'eki kikan]

quarrel ['kwɒrəl] *n* 口論 [kouron] ▷ *v* 口論する [kouron suru]

quarry ['kwɒrɪ] *n* 採石場 [saisekijou]

quarter ['kwɔːtə] *n* 4分の1 [yonbun no ichi]; **quarter final** *n* 準々決勝 [junjunkesshou]

quartet [kwɔːˈtɛt] *n* 四重奏 [shijuusou]

quay [kiː] *n* 埠頭 [futou]

queen [kwiːn] *n* 女王 [joou]

query ['kwɪərɪ] *n* 疑問 [gimon] ▷ *v* 尋ねる [tazuneru]

question ['kwɛstʃən] *n* 質問 [shitsumon] ▷ *v* 質問する [shitsumon suru]; **question mark** *n* 疑問符 [gimonfu]

questionnaire [ˌkwɛstʃəˈnɛə; ˌkɛs-] *n* アンケート用紙 [ankeeto youshi]

queue [kjuː] *n* 列 [retsu] ▷ *v* 列を作る [retsu o tsukuru]; **Is this the end of the queue?** ここが列の最後ですか? [koko ga retsu no saigo desu ka?]

quick [kwɪk] *adj* 素早い [subayai]

quickly [kwɪklɪ] *adv* 素早く [subayaku]

quiet ['kwaɪət] *adj* 静かな [shizuka na]; **I'd like a quiet room** 静かな部屋がいいのですが [shizuka na heya ga ii no desu ga]; **Is there a quiet beach near here?** この近くに静かなビーチはありますか? [kono chikaku ni shizuka na biichi wa arimasu ka?]

quietly ['kwaɪətlɪ] *adv* 静かに [shizuka ni]

quilt [kwɪlt] *n* キルト [kiruto] (ベッドの上掛け)

quit [kwɪt] *v* やめる [yameru] (よす)

quite [kwaɪt] *adv* かなり [kanari]; **It's quite far** かなり遠いです [kanari tooi desu]

quiz, quizzes [kwɪz, 'kwɪzɪz] *n* クイズ [kuizu]

quota ['kwəʊtə] *n* 割当て [wariate]

quotation [kwəʊˈteɪʃən] *n* 引用文 [in-youbun]; **quotation marks** *npl* 引用符 [in-youfu]

quote [kwəʊt] *n* 引用文 [in-youbun] ▷ *v* 引用する [inyou suru]

r

rabbi ['ræbaɪ] *n* ラビ [rabi]

rabbit ['ræbɪt] *n* ウサギ [usagi]

rabies ['reɪbiːz] *n* 狂犬病 [kyoukenbyou]

race [reɪs] *n (contest)* レース [reesu] (競争), *(origin)* 人種 [jinshu] ▷ *v* 競争する [kyousou suru]

racecourse ['reɪsˌkɔːs] *n* 競馬場 [keibajou]

racehorse ['reɪsˌhɔːs] *n* 競走馬 [kyousouba]

racer ['reɪsə] *n* レーサー [reesaa]

racetrack ['reɪsˌtræk] *n* レーストラック [reesutorakku]

racial ['reɪʃəl] *adj* 人種の [jinshu no]

racing ['reɪsɪŋ] *n* **horse racing** *n* 競馬 [keiba]; **motor racing** *n* モーターレース [mootaareesu]; **racing car** *n* レーシングカー [reeshingukaa]; **racing driver** *n* レーシングドライバー [reeshingudoraibaa]

racism ['reɪsɪzəm] *n* 人種差別 [jinshusabetsu]

racist ['reɪsɪst] *adj* 人種差別主義者の [jinshu sabetsu shugisha no] ▷ *n* 人種差別主義者 [jinshusabetsushugisha]

rack [ræk] *n* ・・・掛け [...kake] (帽子や洋服); **luggage rack** *n* 手荷物置き棚 [tenimotsu okidana]

racket ['rækɪt] *n (racquet)* 騒ぎ [sawagi]; **tennis racket** *n* テニスラケット [tenisuraketto]

racoon [rə'kuːn] *n* アライグマ [araiguma]

racquet ['rækɪt] *n* ラケット [raketto]

radar ['reɪdɑː] *n* レーダー [reedaa]

radiation [ˌreɪdɪ'eɪʃən] *n* 放射 [housha]

radiator ['reɪdɪˌeɪtə] *n* ラジエーター [rajieetaa]; **There is a leak in the radiator** ラジエーターに漏れがあります [rajieetaa ni more ga arimasu]

radio ['reɪdɪəʊ] *n* ラジオ [rajio]; **digital radio** *n* デジタルラジオ [dejitaru rajio]; **radio station** *n* ラジオ局 [rajio kyoku]; **Can I switch the radio off?** ラジオを消してもいいですか? [rajio o keshite mo ii desu ka?]; **Can I switch the radio on?** ラジオをつけてもいいですか? [rajio o tsukete mo ii desu ka?]

radioactive [ˌreɪdɪəʊ'æktɪv] *adj* 放射性のある [houshasei no aru]

radio-controlled ['reɪdɪəʊ'kən'trəʊld] *adj* 無線制御の [musen seigyo no]

radish ['rædɪʃ] *n* ラディッシュ [radisshu]

raffle ['ræfəl] *n* 富くじ [tomikuji]

raft [rɑːft] *n* いかだ [ikada]

rag [ræg] *n* ぼろきれ [borokire]

rage [reɪdʒ] *n* 激怒 [gekido]; **road rage** *n* ドライバーが路上で激怒すること [doraibaa ga rojou de gekido suru koto]

raid [reɪd] *n* 襲撃 [shuugeki] ▷ *v* 襲撃する [shuugeki suru]

rail [reɪl] *n* 手すり [tesuri], 鉄道 [tetsudou]

railcard ['reɪlˌkɑːd] *n* 鉄道割引証 [tetsudou waribikishou]

railings ['reɪlɪŋz] *npl* 手すり [tesuri]

railway ['reɪlˌweɪ] *n* 鉄道 [tetsudou]; **railway station** *n* 鉄道駅 [tetsudoueki]

rain [reɪn] *n* 雨 [ame]; 雨が降る [ame ga furu]; **acid rain** *n* 酸性雨 [sanseiu]; **Do you think it's going to rain?** 雨が降ると思いますか? [ame ga furu to omoimasu ka?]; **It's raining** 雨が降っています [ame ga futte imasu]

rainbow ['reɪnˌbəʊ] *n* 虹 [niji]

raincoat ['reɪn,kəʊt] n レインコート [reinkooto]

rainforest ['reɪn,fɒrɪst] n 熱帯雨林 [nettai urin]

rainy ['reɪnɪ] adj 雨の [ame no]

raise [reɪz] v 上げる [ageru]

raisin ['reɪzᵊn] n レーズン [reezun]

rake [reɪk] n 熊手 [kumade]

rally ['rælɪ] n 大集会 [daishuukai]

ram [ræm] n 去勢していない雄羊 [kyosei shite inai ohitsuji] ▷ v 打ち固める [uchikatameru]

Ramadan [,ræmə'dɑːn] n ラマダーン [ramadaan]

rambler ['ræmblə] n ハイカー [haikaa]

ramp [ræmp] n 傾斜面 [keishamen]

random ['rændəm] adj 手当たり次第の [teatari shidai no]

range [reɪndʒ] n (limits) 範囲 [han-i], (mountains) 山脈 [sanmyaku] ▷ v 変化する [henka suru]

rank [ræŋk] n (line) 列 [retsu], (status) 階級 [kaikyuu] ▷ v ランク付けする [ranku zuke suru]

ransom ['rænsəm] n 身代金 [minoshirokin]

rape [reɪp] n (plant) セイヨウアブラナ [seiyouaburana], (sexual attack) レイプ [reipu] ▷ v レイプする [reipu suru]; **I've been raped** 私はレイプされました [watashi wa reipu saremashita]

rapids ['ræpɪdz] npl 早瀬 [hayase]

rapist ['reɪpɪst] n 強姦者 [goukansha]

rare [rɛə] adj (uncommon) 珍しい [mezurashii], (undercooked) 生焼けの [namayake no]

rarely ['rɛəlɪ] adv めったに···しない [mettani ... shinai]

rash [ræʃ] n 発疹 [hasshin]; **I have a rash** 私は発疹がでました [watashi wa hasshin ga demashita]

raspberry ['rɑːzbərɪ; -brɪ] n ラズベリー [razuberii]

rat [ræt] n ドブネズミ [dobunezumi]

rate [reɪt] n 割合 [wariai] ▷ v 評価する [hyouka suru]; **interest rate** n 利率 [riritsu]; **rate of exchange** n 為替レート [kawase reeto]

rather ['rɑːðə] adv かなり [kanari]

ratio ['reɪʃɪ,əʊ] n 比率 [hiritsu]

rational ['ræʃənᵊl] adj 理にかなった [ri ni kanatta]

rattle ['rætᵊl] n ガラガラいう音 [garagara iu oto]

rattlesnake ['rætᵊl,sneɪk] n ガラガラヘビ [garagarahebi]

rave [reɪv] n べたぼめ [betabome] ▷ v わめく [wameku]

raven ['reɪvᵊn] n カラス [karasu]

ravenous ['rævənəs] adj 飢えた [ueta]

ravine [rə'viːn] n 峡谷 [kyoukoku]

raw [rɔː] adj 生の [nama no]

razor ['reɪzə] n かみそり [kamisori]; **razor blade** n 安全かみそりの刃 [anzen kamisori no ha]

reach [riːtʃ] v 着く [tsuku]

react [rɪ'ækt] v 反応する [hannou suru]

reaction [rɪ'ækʃən] n 反応 [hannou]

reactor [rɪ'æktə] n 原子炉 [genshiro]

read [riːd] v 読む [yomu]

reader ['riːdə] n 読者 [dokusha]

readily ['rɛdɪlɪ] adv すぐに [sugu ni]

reading ['riːdɪŋ] n 読書 [dokusho]

read out [riːd] v 読み上げる [yomiageru]

ready ['rɛdɪ] adj 用意のできた [youi no dekita]

ready-cooked ['rɛdɪ'kʊkt] adj 調理済みの [chouri zumi no]

real ['rɪəl] adj 実在の [jitsuzai no]

realistic [,rɪə'lɪstɪk] adj 現実的な [genjitsuteki na]

reality [rɪ'ælɪtɪ] n 現実 [genjitsu]; **reality TV** n リアリティーテレビ番組 [riaritii terebi bangumi]; **virtual reality** n バーチャルリアリティー [baacharuriariiteii]

realize ['rɪə,laɪz] v 十分に理解する [juubun ni rikai suru]

really ['rɪəlɪ] adv 本当に [hontou ni]

rear [rɪə] adj 後ろの [ushiro no] ▷ n 後ろ [ushiro]; **rear-view mirror** n バックミラー [bakkumiraa]

reason ['riːzᵊn] n 理由 [riyuu]

reasonable [ˈriːzənəbəl] *adj* 理にかなった [ri ni kanatta]

reasonably [ˈriːzənəblɪ] *adv* 理にかなって [ri ni kanatte]

reassure [ˌriːəˈʃʊə] *v* 安心させる [anshin saseru]

reassuring [ˌriːəˈʃʊərɪŋ] *adj* 安心させる [anshin saseru]

rebate [ˈriːbeɪt] *n* リベート [ribeeto]

rebellious [rɪˈbɛljəs] *adj* 謀反の [muhon no]

rebuild [riːˈbɪld] *v* 再建する [saiken suru]

receipt [rɪˈsiːt] *n* 受領証 [juryoushou]

receive [rɪˈsiːv] *v* 受け取る [uketoru]

receiver [rɪˈsiːvə] *n* (electronic) 受信機 [jushinki], (person) 受取人 [uketorinin]

recent [ˈriːsənt] *adj* 最近の [saikin no]

recently [ˈriːsəntlɪ] *adv* 最近 [saikin]; **I had flu recently** 私は最近インフルエンザにかかりました [watashi wa saikin infuruenza ni kakarimashita]

reception [rɪˈsɛpʃən] *n* 受付 [uketsuke]

receptionist [rɪˈsɛpʃənɪst] *n* 受付係 [uketsukegakari]

recession [rɪˈsɛʃən] *n* 景気後退 [keikikoutai]

recharge [riːˈtʃɑːdʒ] *v* 再充電する [saijuuden suru]

recipe [ˈrɛsɪpɪ] *n* 調理法 [chourihou]

recipient [rɪˈsɪpɪənt] *n* 受取人 [uketorinin]

reckon [ˈrɛkən] *v* 判断する [handan suru]

reclining [rɪˈklaɪnɪŋ] *adj* リクライニング式の [rikurainingu shiki no]

recognizable [ˈrɛkəɡˌnaɪzəbəl] *adj* 認識できる [ninshiki dekiru]

recognize [ˈrɛkəɡˌnaɪz] *v* 分かる [wakaru]

recommend [ˌrɛkəˈmɛnd] *v* 勧める [susumeru]

recommendation [ˌrɛkəmɛnˈdeɪʃən] *n* 勧め [susume]

reconsider [ˌriːkənˈsɪdə] *v* 考え直す [kangaenaosu]

record *n* [ˈrɛkɔːd] 記録 [kiroku] ▷ *v* [rɪˈkɔːd] 記録する [kiroku suru]

recorded delivery [rɪˈkɔːdɪd dɪˈlɪvərɪ] *n* **recorded delivery** *n* 簡易書留 [kan-i kakitome]

recorder [rɪˈkɔːdə] *n* (music) リコーダー [rikoodaa], (scribe) 記録係 [kirokugakari]

recording [rɪˈkɔːdɪŋ] *n* 録音 [rokuon]

recover [rɪˈkʌvə] *v* 回復する [kaifuku suru]

recovery [rɪˈkʌvərɪ] *n* 回復 [kaifuku]

recruitment [rɪˈkruːtmənt] *n* 新人補充 [shinjin hojuu]

rectangle [ˈrɛkˌtæŋɡəl] *n* 長方形 [chouhoukei]

rectangular [rɛkˈtæŋɡjʊlə] *adj* 長方形の [chouhoukei no]

rectify [ˈrɛktɪˌfaɪ] *v* 修正する [shuusei suru]

recurring [rɪˈkʌrɪŋ] *adj* 繰り返し発生する [kurikaeshi hassei suru]

recycle [riːˈsaɪkəl] *v* 再生利用する [saisei riyou suru]

recycling [riːˈsaɪklɪŋ] *n* リサイクル [risaikuru]

red [rɛd] *adj* 赤い [akai]; **red meat** *n* 赤身肉 [akaminiku]; **red wine** *n* 赤ワイン [akawain]; **Red Cross** *n* 赤十字社 [sekijuujisha]; **Red Sea** *n* 紅海 [koukai]

redcurrant [ˈrɛdˈkʌrənt] *n* 赤スグリ [aka suguri]

redecorate [riːˈdɛkəˌreɪt] *v* 改装する [kaisou suru]

red-haired [ˈrɛdˌhɛəd] *adj* 赤毛の [akage no]

redhead [ˈrɛdˌhɛd] *n* 赤毛 [akage]

redo [riːˈduː] *v* やり直す [yarinaosu]

reduce [rɪˈdjuːs] *v* 減らす [herasu]

reduction [rɪˈdʌkʃən] *n* 減少 [genshou]

redundancy [rɪˈdʌndənsɪ] *n* 余剰人員の解雇 [yojou jin'in no kaiko]

redundant [rɪˈdʌndənt] *adj* 余剰人員として解雇された [yojou jin'in to shite kaiko sareta]

reed [riːd] *n* アシ [ashi] (植物)

reel [riːl; rɪəl] *n* リール [riiru]

refer [rɪˈfɜː] *v* 口に出す [kuchi ni dasu]

referee [ˌrɛfəˈriː] *n* レフェリー [referii]

reference ['rɛfərəns; 'rɛfrəns] *n* 参考 [sankou]; **reference number** *n* 参照番号 [sanshou bangou]

refill [ri:'fɪl] *v* 補充する [hojuu suru]

refinery [rɪ'faɪnərɪ] *n* 精製所 [seiseijo]; **oil refinery** *n* 石油精製所 [sekiyu seiseijo]

reflect [rɪ'flɛkt] *v* 反射する [hansha suru]

reflection [rɪ'flɛkʃən] *n* 反射 [hansha]

reflex ['ri:flɛks] *n* 反射作用 [hansha sayou]

refreshing [rɪ'frɛʃɪŋ] *adj* さわやかな [sawayaka na]

refreshments [rɪ'frɛʃmənts] *npl* 軽食 [keishoku]

refrigerator [rɪ'frɪdʒə,reɪtə] *n* 冷蔵庫 [reizouko]

refuel [ri:'fju:əl] *v* 燃料を補給する [nenryou o hokyuu suru]

refuge ['rɛfju:dʒ] *n* 避難所 [hinanjo]

refugee [,rɛfjʊ'dʒi:] *n* 避難者 [hinansha]

refund *n* ['ri:,fʌnd] 払い戻し [haraimodoshi] ▷ *v* [rɪ'fʌnd] 払い戻す [haraimodosu]; **Can I have a refund?** 払い戻してもらえますか? [haraimodoshite moraemasu ka?]

refusal [rɪ'fju:zəl] *n* 拒否 [kyohi]

refuse¹ [rɪ'fju:z] *v* 拒否する [kyohi suru]

refuse² ['rɛfju:s] *n* ごみ [gomi]

regain [rɪ'geɪn] *v* 回復する [kaifuku suru]

regard [rɪ'gɑ:d] *n* 敬意 [keii] ▷ *v* みなす [minasu]

regarding [rɪ'gɑ:dɪŋ] *prep* ･･･に関して [...ni kanshite]

regiment ['rɛdʒɪmənt] *n* 連隊 [rentai]

region ['ri:dʒən] *n* 地域 [chiiki]

regional ['ri:dʒənəl] *adj* 地域の [chiiki no]

register ['rɛdʒɪstə] *n* 登録簿 [tourokubo] ▷ *v* 登録する [touroku suru]; **cash register** *n* レジ [reji]; **Where do I register?** どこで登録するのですか? [doko de touroku suru no desu ka?]

registered ['rɛdʒɪstəd] *adj* 登録した [touroku shita]

registration [,rɛdʒɪ'streɪʃən] *n* 登録 [touroku]

regret [rɪ'grɛt] *n* 後悔 [koukai] ▷ *v* 後悔する [koukai suru]

regular ['rɛgjʊlə] *adj* 定期的な [teikiteki na]

regularly ['rɛgjʊləlɪ] *adv* 定期的に [teikiteki ni]

regulation [,rɛgjʊ'leɪʃən] *n* 規制 [kisei], 規則 [kisoku]

rehearsal [rɪ'h3:səl] *n* リハーサル [rihaasaru]

rehearse [rɪ'h3:s] *v* リハーサルをする [rihaasaru-o suru]

reimburse [,ri:ɪm'b3:s] *v* 弁済する [bensai suru]

reindeer ['reɪn,dɪə] *n* トナカイ [tonakai]

reins [reɪnz] *npl* 手綱 [tazuna]

reject [rɪ'dʒɛkt] *v* 拒否する [kyohi suru]

relapse ['ri:,læps] *n* 逆戻り [gyakumodori]

related [rɪ'leɪtɪd] *adj* 親類の [shinrui no]

relation [rɪ'leɪʃən] *n* 関係 [kankei]; **public relations** *npl* 広報 [kouhou]

relationship [rɪ'leɪʃənʃɪp] *n* 関係 [kankei]

relative ['rɛlətɪv] *n* 親戚 [shinseki]

relatively ['rɛlətɪvlɪ] *adv* 比較的 [hikakuteki]

relax [rɪ'læks] *v* くつろぐ [kutsurogu]

relaxation [,ri:læk'seɪʃən] *n* くつろぎ [kutsurogi]

relaxed [rɪ'lækst] *adj* くつろいだ [kutsuroida]

relaxing [rɪ'læksɪŋ] *adj* くつろがせる [kutsurogaseru]

relay ['ri:leɪ] *n* 交替班 [koutai han]

release [rɪ'li:s] *n* 解放 [kaihou] ▷ *v* 解放する [kaihou suru]

relegate ['rɛlɪ,geɪt] *v* 左遷する [sasen suru]

relevant ['rɛlɪvənt] *adj* 関連する [kanren suru]

reliable [rɪ'laɪəbəl] *adj* 信頼できる [shinrai dekiru]

relief [rɪ'li:f] *n* 安心 [anshin]

relieve [rɪ'li:v] *v* 安心させる [anshin saseru]

relieved [rɪˈliːvd] *adj* 安心した [anshin shita]

religion [rɪˈlɪdʒən] *n* 宗教 [shuukyou]

religious [rɪˈlɪdʒəs] *adj* 宗教の [shuukyou no]

reluctant [rɪˈlʌktənt] *adj* いやいやながらの [iyaiya nagara no]

reluctantly [rɪˈlʌktəntlɪ] *adv* いやいや [iyaiya]

rely [rɪˈlaɪ] *v* **rely on** *v* あてにする [ate ni suru]

remain [rɪˈmeɪn] *v* ・・・のままである [... no mama de aru]

remaining [rɪˈmeɪnɪŋ] *adj* 残りの [nokori no]

remains [rɪˈmeɪnz] *npl* 遺物 [ibutsu]

remake [ˈriːˌmeɪk] *n* リメイク [rimeiku]

remark [rɪˈmɑːk] *n* 意見 [iken]

remarkable [rɪˈmɑːkəbᵊl] *adj* 著しい [ichijirushii]

remarkably [rɪˈmɑːkəblɪ] *adv* 著しく [ichijirushiku]

remarry [riːˈmærɪ] *v* 再婚する [saikon suru]

remedy [ˈrɛmɪdɪ] *n* 治療 [chiryou]

remember [rɪˈmɛmbə] *v* 思い出す [omoidasu]

remind [rɪˈmaɪnd] *v* 思い出させる [omoidasaseru]

reminder [rɪˈmaɪndə] *n* 思い出させるもの [omoidasaseru mono]

remorse [rɪˈmɔːs] *n* 良心の呵責 [ryoushin no kashaku]

remote [rɪˈməʊt] *adj* 遠く離れた [touku hanareta]; **remote control** *n* リモコン [rimokon]

remotely [rɪˈməʊtlɪ] *adv* 遠く離れて [touku hanarete]

removable [rɪˈmuːvəbᵊl] *adj* 取り外せる [torihazuseru]

removal [rɪˈmuːvᵊl] *n* 移動 [idou]; **removal van** *n* 引越しトラック [hikkoshi torakku]

remove [rɪˈmuːv] *v* 移す [utsusu]

remover [rɪˈmuːvə] *n* **nail-polish remover** *n* 除光液 [jokoueki]

rendezvous [ˈrɒndɪˌvuː] *n* 会う約束 [au yakusoku]

renew [rɪˈnjuː] *v* 再開する [saikai suru]

renewable [rɪˈnjuːəbᵊl] *adj* 再び始められる [futatabi hajimerareru]

renovate [ˈrɛnəˌveɪt] *v* 修繕する [shuuzen suru]

renowned [rɪˈnaʊnd] *adj* 有名な [yuumei na]

rent [rɛnt] *n* 賃貸料 [chintairyou] ▷ *v* 賃貸する [chintai suru]

rental [ˈrɛntᵊl] *n* レンタル [rentaru]; **car rental** *n* レンタカー [rentakaa]; **rental car** *n* レンタカー [rentakaa]

reorganize [riːˈɔːgəˌnaɪz] *v* 再編成する [saihensei suru]

rep [rɛp] *n* レパートリー劇団 [repaatorii gekidan]

repair [rɪˈpɛə] *n* 修理 [shuuri] ▷ *v* 修理する [shuurisuru]; **repair kit** *n* 修理キット [shuuri kitto]; **Can you repair it?** 修理してもらえますか? [shuuri shite moraemasu ka?], それを修理できますか? [sore o shuuri dekimasu ka?]; **Can you repair my watch?** 私の時計を修理できますか? [watashi no tokei o shuuri dekimasu ka?]; **Can you repair this?** これを修理できますか? [kore o shuuri dekimasu ka?]; **Do you have a repair kit?** 修理キットはありますか? [shuuri-kitto wa arimasu ka?]; **How long will it take to repair?** 修理にどのくらいの時間がかかりますか? [shuuri ni dono kurai no jikan ga kakarimasu ka?]; **How much will the repairs cost?** 修理代はいくらかかりますか? [shuuri-dai wa ikura kakarimasu ka?]; **Where can I get this repaired?** どこでこれを修理してもらえますか? [doko de kore o shuuri shite moraemasu ka?]; **Where is the nearest bike repair shop?** 一番近い自転車修理店はどこですか? [ichiban chikai jitensha shuuri-ten wa doko desu ka?]

repay [rɪˈpeɪ] *v* 返済する [hensai suru]

repayment [rɪˈpeɪmənt] *n* 返済 [hensai]

repeat [rɪ'piːt] n 繰り返し [kurikaeshi] ▷ v 繰り返す [kurikaesu]

repeatedly [rɪ'piːtɪdlɪ] adv 繰り返して [kurikaeshite]

repellent [rɪ'pɛlənt] adj 嫌な [iya na]; **insect repellent** n 虫よけ [mushiyoke]

repercussions [ˌriːpə'kʌʃənz] npl 反動 [handou]

repetitive [rɪ'pɛtɪtɪv] adj 反復性の [hanpuku sei no]

replace [rɪ'pleɪs] v 取って代わる [tottekawaru]

replacement [rɪ'pleɪsmənt] n 置き換え [okikae]

replay n ['riː,pleɪ] 再生 [saisei] ▷ v [riː'pleɪ] 再生する [saisei suru]

replica ['rɛplɪkə] n レプリカ [repurika]

reply [rɪ'plaɪ] n 返事 [henji] ▷ v 返事をする [henji-o suru]

report [rɪ'pɔːt] n 報告 [houkoku] ▷ v 報告する [houkoku suru]; **report card** n 通知表 [tsuuchihyou]

reporter [rɪ'pɔːtə] n 取材記者 [shuzai kisha]

represent [ˌrɛprɪ'zɛnt] v 代表する [daihyou suru]

representative [ˌrɛprɪ'zɛntətɪv] adj 代表する [daihyou suru]

reproduction [ˌriːprə'dʌkʃən] n 繁殖 [hanshoku]

reptile ['rɛptaɪl] n 爬虫類 [hachuurui]

republic [rɪ'pʌblɪk] n 共和政体 [kyouwa seitai]

repulsive [rɪ'pʌlsɪv] adj むかつくような [mukatsuku you na] (腹が立つ)

reputable ['rɛpjʊtəb³l] adj 信頼できる [shinrai dekiru]

reputation [ˌrɛpjʊ'teɪʃən] n 評判 [hyouban]

request [rɪ'kwɛst] n 頼み [tanomi] ▷ v 頼む [tanomu]

require [rɪ'kwaɪə] v 必要とする [hitsuyou to suru]

requirement [rɪ'kwaɪəmənt] n 要求 [youkyuu]

rescue ['rɛskjuː] n 救助 [kyuujo] ▷ v 救う [sukuu]; **Where is the nearest mountain rescue service post?** 一番近い山岳救助隊はどこですか? [ichiban chikai sangaku-kyuujo-tai wa doko desu ka?]

research [rɪ'sɜːtʃ; 'riːsɜːtʃ] n 調査 [chousa]; **market research** n 市場調査 [shijouchousa]

resemblance [rɪ'zɛmbləns] n 類似 [ruiji]

resemble [rɪ'zɛmb³l] v 似ている [niteiru]

resent [rɪ'zɛnt] v 憤慨する [fungai suru]

resentful [rɪ'zɛntfʊl] adj 憤慨した [fungai shita]

reservation [ˌrɛzə'veɪʃən] n 懸念 [kenen]

reserve [rɪ'zɜːv] n (land) 保護区 [hogoku], (retention) 蓄え [takuwae] ▷ v 取っておく [totteoku]

reserved [rɪ'zɜːvd] adj 控えめの [hikaeme no]

reservoir ['rɛzə,vwɑː] n 貯水池 [chosuichi]

resident ['rɛzɪdənt] n 居住者 [kyojuusha]

residential [ˌrɛzɪ'dɛnʃəl] adj 住宅地の [juutakuchi no]

resign [rɪ'zaɪn] v 辞職する [jishoku suru]

resin ['rɛzɪn] n 樹脂 [jushi]

resist [rɪ'zɪst] v 抵抗する [teikou suru]

resistance [rɪ'zɪstəns] n 抵抗 [teikou]

resit [riː'sɪt] v 再受験する [saijuken suru]

resolution [ˌrɛzə'luːʃən] n 決意 [ketsui]

resort [rɪ'zɔːt] n 行楽地 [kourakuchi]; **resort to** v 頼る [tayoru]

resource [rɪ'zɔːs; -'sɔːs] n 資源 [shigen]; **natural resources** npl 天然資源 [tennenshigen]

respect [rɪ'spɛkt] n 尊重 [sonchou] ▷ v 尊重する [sonchou suru]

respectable [rɪ'spɛktəb³l] adj 尊敬すべき [sonkeisubeki]

respectively [rɪ'spɛktɪvlɪ] adv それぞれ [sorezore]

respond [rɪ'spɒnd] v 返答する [hentou suru]

response [rɪ'spɒns] n 返答 [hentou]

responsibility [rɪ,spɒnsə'bɪlɪtɪ] n 責任 [sekinin]

responsible [rɪ'spɒnsəbəl] adj 責任がある [sekinin ga aru]

rest [rɛst] n 休み [yasumi] ▷ v 休む [yasumu]; **the rest** n 休み [yasumi]

restaurant ['rɛstə,rɒn; 'rɛstrɒn; -rɒnt] n レストラン [resutoran]; **Are there any vegetarian restaurants here?** ここにベジタリアン用のレストランはありますか? [koko ni bejitarian-you no resutoran wa arimasu ka?]

restful ['rɛstfʊl] adj 落ち着いた [ochitsuita]

restless ['rɛstlɪs] adj 落ち着かない [ochitsukanai]

restore [rɪ'stɔː] v 修復する [shuufuku suru]

restrict [rɪ'strɪkt] v 制限する [seigen suru]

restructure [riː'strʌktʃə] v 再編成する [saihensei suru]

result [rɪ'zʌlt] n 結果 [kekka]; **result in** v 結果として生じる [kekka toshite shoujiru]

resume [rɪ'zjuːm] v 再開する [saikai suru]

retail ['riːteɪl] n 小売り [kouri] ▷ v 小売りする [kouri suru]; **retail price** n 小売価格 [kourikakaku]

retailer ['riːteɪlə] n 小売業者 [kourigyousha]

retire [rɪ'taɪə] v 退職する [taishoku suru]

retired [rɪ'taɪəd] adj 退職した [taishoku shita]

retirement [rɪ'taɪəmənt] n 退職 [taishoku]

retrace [rɪ'treɪs] v たどりなおす [tadorinaosu]

return [rɪ'tɜːn] n 帰ること [kaeru koto], (yield) 収益 [shoueki] ▷ vi 戻る [modoru] ▷ vt 戻す [modosu]; **day return** n 日帰り往復割引切符 [higaeri oufuku waribiki kippu]; **return ticket** n 往復切符 [oufuku kippu]; **tax return** n 所得申告 [shotoku shinkoku]

reunion [riː'juːnjən] n 再会 [saikai]

reuse [riː'juːz] v 再使用する [saishiyou suru]

reveal [rɪ'viːl] v 明らかにする [akiraka ni suru]

revenge [rɪ'vɛndʒ] n 復讐 [fukushuu]

revenue ['rɛvɪ,njuː] n 収入 [shuunyuu]

reverse [rɪ'vɜːs] n 逆 [gyaku] ▷ v 逆にする [gyaku ni suru]

review [rɪ'vjuː] n 批評 [hihyou]

revise [rɪ'vaɪz] v 修正する [shuusei suru]

revision [rɪ'vɪʒən] n 修正 [shuusei]

revive [rɪ'vaɪv] v 復活する [fukkatsu suru]

revolting [rɪ'vəʊltɪŋ] adj 実に嫌な [jitsu ni iya na]

revolution [,rɛvə'luːʃən] n 革命 [kakumei]

revolutionary [,rɛvə'luːʃənərɪ] adj 革命的な [kakumeiteki na]

revolver [rɪ'vɒlvə] n リボルバー [riborubaa]

reward [rɪ'wɔːd] n 報酬 [houshuu]

rewarding [rɪ'wɔːdɪŋ] adj 報いのある [mukui no aru]

rewind [riː'waɪnd] v 巻き戻す [makimodosu]

rheumatism ['ruːmə,tɪzəm] n リウマチ [riumachi]

rhubarb ['ruːbɑːb] n ルバーブ [rubaabu]

rhyme [raɪm] n **nursery rhyme** n 伝承童謡 [denshou douyou]

rhythm ['rɪðəm] n リズム [rizumu]

rib [rɪb] n 肋骨 [rokkotsu]

ribbon ['rɪbən] n リボン [ribon]

rice [raɪs] n 米 [kome]; **brown rice** n 玄米 [genmai]

rich [rɪtʃ] adj 金持ちの [kanemochi no]

ride [raɪd] n 乗ること [noru koto] ▷ v 乗る [noru]

rider ['raɪdə] n 乗り手 [norite]

ridiculous [rɪ'dɪkjʊləs] adj ばかげた [bakageta]

riding ['raɪdɪŋ] n 乗馬 [jouba]; **horse riding** n 乗馬 [jouba]; **Can we go horse riding?** 乗馬に行けますか? [jouba ni ikemasu ka?]

rifle ['raɪfᵊl] n ライフル銃 [raifuru juu]

rig [rɪg] n 掘削装置 [kussaku souchi]; **oil rig** n 石油掘削装置 [sekiyu kussakusouchi]

right [raɪt] adj (correct) 正しい [tadashii], (not left) 右の [migi no] ▷ n 権利 [kenri]; **civil rights** npl 公民権 [kouminken]; **human rights** npl 人権 [jinken]; **right angle** n 直角 [chokkaku]; **right of way** n 優先権 [yuusenken]

right-hand ['raɪt,hænd] adj 右側の [migigawa no]; **right-hand drive** n 右ハンドル [migi handoru]

right-handed ['raɪt,hændɪd] adj 右利きの [migikiki no]

rightly ['raɪtlɪ] adv 正しく [tadashiku]

right-wing ['raɪt,wɪŋ] adj 右派の [uha no]

rim [rɪm] n 縁 [en]

ring [rɪŋ] n 鳴らすこと [narasu koto] ▷ v 鳴らす [narasu]; **engagement ring** n 婚約指輪 [konyaku yubiwa]; **ring binder** n リングバインダー [ringubaindaa]; **ring road** n 環状道路 [kanjoudouro]; **wedding ring** n 結婚指輪 [kekkon yubiwa]

ring back [rɪŋ bæk] v 電話をかけなおす [denwa-o kakenaosu]

ringtone ['rɪŋ,təʊn] n 着信メロディ [chakushin merodi]

ring up [rɪŋ ʌp] v 電話をかける [denwa-o kakeru]

rink [rɪŋk] n スケートリンク [sukeetorinku]; **ice rink** n スケートリンク [sukeetorinku]; **skating rink** n スケートリンク [sukeetorinku]

rinse [rɪns] n すすぎ [susugi] ▷ v すすぐ [susugu]

riot ['raɪət] n 暴動 [boudou] ▷ v 暴動を起こす [boudou-o okosu]

rip [rɪp] v 引き裂く [hikisaku]

ripe [raɪp] adj 熟した [juku shita]

rip off [rɪp ɒf] v 法外な値をふっかける [hougai na ne-o fukkakeru]

rip-off [rɪpɒf] n 暴利 [bouri]

rip up [rɪp ʌp] v 破棄する [haki suru]

rise [raɪz] n 上昇 [joushou] ▷ v 立ち上がる [tachiagaru]

risk [rɪsk] n 危険 [kiken] ▷ vt 危険にさらす [kiken ni sarasu]

risky ['rɪskɪ] adj 危険な [kiken na]

ritual ['rɪtjʊəl] adj 儀式の [gishiki no] ▷ n 儀式 [gishiki]

rival ['raɪvᵊl] adj 競争する [kyousou suru] ▷ n 競争相手 [kyousouaite]

rivalry ['raɪvəlrɪ] n 競争 [kyousou]

river ['rɪvə] n 川 [kawa]; **Can one swim in the river?** その川で泳げますか? [sono kawa de oyogemasu ka?]

road [rəʊd] n 道路 [douro]; **main road** n 幹線道路 [kansendouro]; **ring road** n 環状道路 [kanjoudouro]; **road map** n ロードマップ [roodomappu]; **road rage** n ドライバーが路上で激怒すること [doraibaa ga rojou de gekido suru koto]; **road sign** n 道路標識 [dourohyoushiki]; **road tax** n 自動車の道路利用税 [jidousha no douro riyou zei]; **slip road** n 高速道路の進入退出路 [kousoku douro no shinnyuu taishutsuro]; **Are the roads icy?** 道路は凍結していますか? [douro wa touketsu shite imasu ka?]; **Do you have a road map of this area?** この地域の道路マップはありますか? [kono chiiki no douro-mappu wa arimasu ka?]; **I need a road map of...** 私は・・・の道路マップが必要です [watashi wa ... no douro-mappu ga hitsuyou desu]

roadblock ['rəʊd,blɒk] n 道路封鎖 [douro fuusa]

roadworks ['rəʊd,wɜ:ks] npl 道路工事 [dourokouji]

roast [rəʊst] adj 焼いた [yaita]

rob [rɒb] v 奪う [ubau]

robber [rɒbə] n 強盗 [goutou] (人)

robbery ['rɒbərɪ] n 強盗 [goutou] (行為)

robin ['rɒbɪn] n コマドリ [komadori]

robot ['rəʊbɒt] n ロボット [robotto]

rock [rɒk] n 岩 [iwa] ▷ v 揺れる [yureru]; **rock climbing** n ロッククライミング [rokkukuraimingu]

rocket ['rɒkɪt] n ロケット [roketto]

rod [rɒd] *n* 棒 [bou]

rodent ['rəʊdᵊnt] *n* 齧歯動物 [gesshi doubutsu]

role [rəʊl] *n* 役割 [yakuwari]

roll [rəʊl] *n* 転がり [korogari] ▷ *v* 転がる [korogaru]; **bread roll** *n* ロールパン [roorupan]; **roll call** *n* 点呼 [tenko]

roller ['rəʊlə] *n* ローラー [rooraa]

rollercoaster ['rəʊlə,kəʊstə] *n* ローラーコースター [rooraakoosutaa]

rollerskates ['rəʊlə,skeɪts] *npl* ローラースケート靴 [rooraa sukeeto kutsu]

rollerskating ['rəʊlə,skeɪtɪŋ] *n* ローラースケート [rooraasukeeto]

Roman ['rəʊmən] *adj* ローマの [rooma no]; **Roman Catholic** *n* ローマカトリック教会の [rooma katorikku kyoukai no], ローマカトリック教徒 [rooma katorikku kyouto]

romance ['rəʊmæns] *n* 恋愛 [ren-ai]

Romanesque [,rəʊmə'nɛsk] *adj* ロマネスク様式の [romanesuku youshiki no]

Romania [rəʊ'meɪnɪə] *n* ルーマニア [ruumania]

Romanian [rəʊ'meɪnɪən] *adj* ルーマニアの [ruumania no] ▷ *n (language)* ルーマニア語 [ruumaniago], *(person)* ルーマニア人 [ruumaniajin]

romantic [rəʊ'mæntɪk] *adj* ロマンチックな [romanchikku na]

roof [ru:f] *n* 屋根 [yane]

roof rack ['ru:f,ræk] *n* ルーフラック [ruufurakku]

room [ru:m; rʊm] *n* 部屋 [heya]; **changing room** *n* 更衣室 [kouishitsu]; **dining room** *n* ダイニングルーム [dainingu ruumu]; **double room** *n* ダブルルーム [dabururuumu]; **fitting room** *n* 試着室 [shichakushitsu]; **living room** *n* 居間 [ima]; **room number** *n* 客室番号 [kyakushitsu bangou]; **room service** *n* ルームサービス [ruumusaabisu]; **single room** *n* シングルルーム [shingururuumu]; **sitting room** *n* 居間 [ima]; **spare room** *n* 予備の寝室 [yobi no shinshitsu]; **twin room** *n* ツインルーム [tsuinruumu];

twin-bedded room *n* ツインベッドルーム [tsuinbeddoruumu]; **utility room** *n* ユーティリティールーム [yuutiritii ruumu]; **waiting room** *n* 待合室 [machiaishitsu]; **Can I see the room?** その部屋を見せてもらえますか? [sono heya o misete moraemasu ka?]; **Can I switch rooms?** 部屋を替えることができますか? [heya o kaeru koto ga dekimasu ka?]; **Can you clean the room, please?** 部屋を掃除してもらえますか? [heya o souji shite moraemasu ka?]; **Do you have a room for tonight?** 今晩部屋はありますか? [konban heya wa arimasu ka?]; **Does the room have air conditioning?** その部屋にエアコンはありますか? [sono heya ni eakon wa arimasu ka?]; **How much is the room?** その部屋はいくらですか? [sono heya wa ikura desu ka?]; **I booked a room in the name of...** ・・・の名前で部屋を予約しました [...no namae de heya o yoyaku shimashita]; **I need a room with wheelchair access** 私は車椅子で入れる部屋が必要です [watashi wa kuruma-isu de haireru heya ga hitsuyou desu]; **I'd like a no smoking room** 禁煙の部屋がいいのですが [kin'en no heya ga ii no desu ga]; **I'd like a room with a view of the sea** 海が見える部屋がいいのですが [umi ga mieru heya ga ii no desu ga]; **I'd like to rent a room** 部屋を借りたいのですが [heya o karitai no desu ga]; **Please charge it to my room** それを私の部屋の勘定につけておいてください [sore o watashi no heya no kanjou ni tsukete oite kudasai]; **The room is dirty** 部屋が汚れています [heya ga yogorete imasu]; **The room is too cold** 部屋が寒すぎます [heya ga samu-sugimasu]; **There's a problem with the room** 部屋に問題があります [heya ni mondai ga arimasu]

roommate ['ru:m,meɪt; 'rʊm-] *n* ルームメート [ruumumeeto]

root [ru:t] *n* 根 [kon]; **Can you dye my roots, please?** 根元を染めていただけ

ますか? [nemoto o somete itadakemasu ka?]

rope [rəʊp] n ロープ [roopu]

rope in [rəʊp ɪn] v 人を誘い込む [hito-o sasoi komu]

rose [rəʊz] n バラ [bara] (植物)

rosé ['rəʊzeɪ] n ロゼワイン [rozewain]; **Can you recommend a good rosé wine?** よいロゼワインを教えてもらえますか? [yoi roze-wain o oshiete moraemasu ka?]

rosemary ['rəʊzmərɪ] n ローズマリー [roozumarii]

rot [rɒt] v 腐る [kusaru]

rotten ['rɒtᵉn] adj 腐った [kusatta]

rough [rʌf] adj 粗い [arai]

roughly ['rʌflɪ] adv およそ [oyoso]

roulette [ruːˈlɛt] n ルーレット [ruuretto]

round [raʊnd] adj 丸い [marui] ▷ n (circle) 円 [en] (丸), (series) 連続 [renzoku] ▷ prep ···を囲んで [...o kakonde]; **paper round** n 新聞配達 [shinbun haitatsu]; **round trip** n 往復 [oufuku]

roundabout ['raʊndəˌbaʊt] n 環状交差路 [kanjou kousaro]

round up [raʊnd ʌp] v かき集める [kakiatsumeru]

route [ruːt] n ルート [ruuto]

routine [ruːˈtiːn] n 決まりきった仕事 [kimarikitta shigoto]

row[1] [rəʊ] n (line) 列 [retsu] ▷ v (in boat) 漕ぐ [kogu]

row[2] [raʊ] n (argument) 喧嘩 [kenka] ▷ v (to argue) 喧嘩する [kenka suru]

rowing [rəʊɪŋ] n ボートを漕ぐこと [booto-o kogu koto]; **rowing boat** n 漕ぎ舟 [kogibune]

royal ['rɔɪəl] adj 王室の [oushitsu no]

rub [rʌb] v こする [kosuru]

rubber ['rʌbə] n ゴム [gomu]; **rubber band** n 輪ゴム [wagomu]; **rubber gloves** npl ゴム手袋 [gomu tebukuro]

rubbish ['rʌbɪʃ] adj だめな [damena] ▷ n ごみ [gomi]; **rubbish dump** n ごみ捨て場 [gomi suteba]; **Where do we leave**

the rubbish? ごみはどこに出すのですか? [gomi wa doko ni dasu no desu ka?]

rucksack ['rʌkˌsæk] n リュックサック [ryukkusakku]

rude [ruːd] adj 失礼な [shitsurei na]

rug [rʌg] n ラグ [ragu]

rugby ['rʌgbɪ] n ラグビー [ragubii]

ruin ['ruːɪn] n 荒廃 [kouhai] ▷ v 荒廃させる [kouhai saseru]

rule [ruːl] n 規則 [kisoku]

rule out [ruːl aʊt] v 可能性を排除する [kanousei-o haijo suru]

ruler ['ruːlə] n (commander) 支配者 [shihaisha], (measure) 定規 [jougi]

rum [rʌm] n ラム [ramu] (酒)

rumour ['ruːmə] n うわさ [uwasa]

run [rʌn] n 走ること [hashiru koto] ▷ vi 走る [hashiru] ▷ vt を走る [-o hashiru]

run away [rʌn əˈweɪ] v 逃げ出す [nigedasu]

runner ['rʌnə] n ランナー [rannaa]; **runner bean** n ベニバナインゲン [benibanaingen]

runner-up ['rʌnəʌp] n 次点者 [jitensha]

running ['rʌnɪŋ] n ランニング [ranningu], 経営 [keiei]

run out [rʌn aʊt] v **The towels have run out** タオルが補充されていません [taoru ga hojuu sarete imasen]

run out of [rʌn aʊt ɒv] v ···を使い果たす [...-o tsukaihatasu]

run over [rʌn ˈəʊvə] v 轢く [hiku]

runway ['rʌnˌweɪ] n 滑走路 [kassouro]

rural ['rʊərəl] adj 田舎の [inaka no]

rush [rʌʃ] n 突進 [tosshin] ▷ v 急ぐ [isogu]; **rush hour** n ラッシュアワー [rasshuawaa]

rusk [rʌsk] n ラスク [rasuku]

Russia ['rʌʃə] n ロシア [roshia]

Russian ['rʌʃən] adj ロシアの [roshia no] ▷ n (language) ロシア語 [roshiago], (person) ロシア人 [roshiajin]

rust [rʌst] n さび [sabi] (腐食)

rusty ['rʌstɪ] adj さびた [sabita]

ruthless ['ruːθlɪs] adj 無慈悲な [mujihi na]

rye [raɪ] n ライ麦 [raimugi]

S

Sabbath ['sæbəθ] *n* 安息日 [ansokubi]

sabotage ['sæbətɑːʒ] *n* 故意の破壊 [koi no hakai] ▷ *v* 故意に破壊する [koi ni hakai suru]

sachet ['sæʃeɪ] *n* 小さな袋 [chiisana fukuro]

sack [sæk] *n (container)* 大袋 [oobukuro], *(dismissal)* 解雇 [kaiko] ▷ *v* 首にする [kubi ni suru]

sacred ['seɪkrɪd] *adj* 神聖な [shinsei na]

sacrifice ['sækrɪˌfaɪs] *n* 犠牲 [gisei]

sad [sæd] *adj* 悲しい [kanashii]

saddle ['sædᵊl] *n* サドル [sadoru]

saddlebag ['sædᵊlˌbæg] *n* サドルバッグ [sadorubaggu]

sadly [sædlɪ] *adv* 悲しんで [kanashinde]

safari [sə'fɑːrɪ] *n* サファリ [safari]

safe [seɪf] *adj* 安全な [anzen na] ▷ *n* 金庫 [kinko]; **I have some things in the safe** 金庫に入れたものがあります [kinko ni ireta mono ga arimasu]; **I would like to put my jewellery in the safe** 私はジュエリーを金庫に入れたいのですが [watashi wa juerii o kinko ni iretai no desu ga]; **Put that in the safe, please** それを金庫に入れてください [sore o kinko ni irete kudasai]

safety ['seɪftɪ] *n* 安全 [anzen]; **safety belt** *n* 安全ベルト [anzenberuto]; **safety pin** *n* 安全ピン [anzenpin]

saffron ['sæfrən] *n* サフラン [safuran]

Sagittarius [ˌsædʒɪ'tɛərɪəs] *n* 射手座 [iteza]

Sahara [sə'hɑːrə] *n* サハラ砂漠 [sahara sabaku]

sail [seɪl] *n* 帆 [ho] ▷ *v* 航海する [koukai suru]

sailing ['seɪlɪŋ] *n* 航海 [koukai]; **sailing boat** *n* ヨット [yotto]

sailor ['seɪlə] *n* 船員 [sen'in]

saint [seɪnt; sənt] *n* 聖人 [seijin]

salad ['sæləd] *n* サラダ [sarada]; **mixed salad** *n* ミックスサラダ [mikkususarada]; **salad dressing** *n* サラダドレッシング [saradadoresshingu]

salami [sə'lɑːmɪ] *n* サラミ [sarami]

salary ['sælərɪ] *n* 給料 [kyuuryou]

sale [seɪl] *n* 販売 [hanbai]; **sales assistant** *n* 販売スタッフ [hanbai sutaffu]; **sales rep** *n* 販売員 [hanbaiin]

salesman, salesmen ['seɪlzmən, 'seɪlzmɛn] *n* セールスマン [seerusuman]

salesperson ['seɪlzpɜːsᵊn] *n* 店員 [ten-in]

saleswoman, saleswomen ['seɪlzwʊmən, 'seɪlzwɪmɪn] *n* 女性店員 [josei ten'in]

saliva [sə'laɪvə] *n* 唾液 [daeki]

salmon ['sæmən] *n* サケ [sake] (魚)

salon ['sælɒn] *n* **beauty salon** *n* 美容院 [biyouin]

saloon [sə'luːn] *n* セダン [sedan]; **saloon car** *n* セダン [sedan]

salt [sɔːlt] *n* 塩 [shio]; **Pass the salt, please** 塩を取っていただけますか？ [shio o totte itadakemasu ka?]

saltwater ['sɔːltˌwɔːtə] *adj* 塩水の [shiomizu no]

salty ['sɔːltɪ] *adj* 塩気のある [shioke no aru]

salute [sə'luːt] *v* 挨拶する [aisatsu suru]

salve [sælv] *n* **lip salve** *n* おべっか [obekka]

same [seɪm] *adj* 同じ [onaji]; **I'll have the same** 私にも同じものをください [watashi ni mo onaji mono o kudasai]

sample ['sɑːmpᵊl] *n* 見本 [mihon]

sand [sænd] *n* 砂 [suna]; **sand dune** *n* 砂丘 [sakyuu]

sandal ['sændᵊl] *n* サンダル [sandaru]

sandcastle [sændkɑːsᵊl] *n* 砂のお城 [suna no oshiro]

sandpaper ['sænd,peɪpə] *n* サンドペーパー [sandopeepaa]

sandpit ['sænd,pɪt] *n* 砂場 [sunaba]

sandstone ['sænd,stəʊn] *n* 砂岩 [sagan]

sandwich ['sænwɪdʒ; -wɪtʃ] *n* サンドイッチ [sandoitchi]; **What kind of sandwiches do you have?** どんなサンドイッチがありますか? [donna sandoitchi ga arimasu ka?]

San Marino [ˌsæn məˈriːnəʊ] *n* サンマリノ [sanmarino]

sapphire ['sæfaɪə] *n* サファイア [safaia]

sarcastic [sɑːˈkæstɪk] *adj* 皮肉な [hiniku na]

sardine [sɑːˈdiːn] *n* サーディン [saadein]

satchel ['sætʃəl] *n* 肩掛けかばん [katakake kaban]

satellite ['sætᵊ,laɪt] *n* 人工衛星 [jinkou eisei]; **satellite dish** *n* 衛星放送用パラボラアンテナ [eisei housou you parabora antena]

satisfaction [ˌsætɪsˈfækʃən] *n* 満足 [manzoku]

satisfactory [ˌsætɪsˈfæktərɪ; -trɪ] *adj* 満足のいく [manzoku no iku]

satisfied ['sætɪs,faɪd] *adj* 満足した [manzoku shita]

sat nav ['sæt næv] *n* 衛星ナビゲーション [eisei nabigeeshon]

Saturday ['sætədɪ] *n* 土曜日 [doyoubi]; **every Saturday** 毎週土曜日に [maishuu doyoubi ni]; **last Saturday** 先週の土曜日に [senshuu no doyoubi ni]; **next Saturday** 来週の土曜日に [raishuu no doyoubi ni]; **on Saturday** 土曜日に [doyoubi ni]; **on Saturdays** 毎土曜日に [mai-doyoubi ni]; **this Saturday** 今週の土曜日に [konshuu no doyoubi ni]

sauce [sɔːs] *n* ソース [soosu]; **soy sauce** *n* 醤油 [shouyu]; **tomato sauce** *n* トマトソース [tomatosoosu]

saucepan ['sɔːspən] *n* ソースパン [soospan]

saucer ['sɔːsə] *n* 受け皿 [ukezara]

Saudi ['sɔːdɪ; 'saʊ-] *adj* サウジアラビアの [saujiarabia no] ▷ *n* サウジアラビア人 [saujiarabiajin]

Saudi Arabia ['sɔːdɪ; 'saʊ-] *n* サウジアラビア [saujiarabia]

Saudi Arabian ['sɔːdɪ əˈreɪbɪən] *adj* サウジアラビアの [saujiarabia no] ▷ *n* サウジアラビア人 [saujiarabiajin]

sauna ['sɔːnə] *n* サウナ [sauna]

sausage ['sɒsɪdʒ] *n* ソーセージ [sooseeji]

save [seɪv] *v* 救う [sukuu]

save up [seɪv ʌp] *v* 蓄える [takuwaeru]

savings ['seɪvɪŋz] *npl* 貯金 [chokin]

savoury ['seɪvərɪ] *adj* 塩味の [shioaji no]

saw [sɔː] *n* のこぎり [nokogiri]

sawdust ['sɔː,dʌst] *n* おがくず [ogakuzu]

saxophone ['sæksə,fəʊn] *n* サクソフォーン [sakusofoon]

say [seɪ] *v* 言う [iu]

saying ['seɪɪŋ] *n* ことわざ [kotowaza]

scaffolding ['skæfəldɪŋ] *n* 足場 [ashiba]

scale [skeɪl] *n (measure)* 尺度 [shakudo], *(tiny piece)* うろこ [uroko]

scales [skeɪlz] *npl* 天秤 [tenbin]

scallop ['skɒləp; 'skæl-] *n* ホタテガイ [hotategai]

scam [skæm] *n* 詐欺 [sagi]

scampi ['skæmpɪ] *npl* クルマエビ [kurumaebi]

scan [skæn] *n* 綿密な調査 [menmitsu na chousa] ▷ *v* 細かく調べる [komakaku shiraberu]

scandal ['skændᵊl] *n* スキャンダル [sukyandaru]

Scandinavia [ˌskændɪˈneɪvɪə] *n* スカンジナビア [sukanjinabia]

Scandinavian [ˌskændɪˈneɪvɪən] *adj* スカンジナビアの [sukanjinabia no]

scanner ['skænə] n スキャナー
[sukyanaa]

scar [skɑː] n 傷痕 [kizuato]

scarce [skɛəs] adj 不足して [fusoku shite]

scarcely ['skɛəslɪ] adv ほとんど···ない
[hotondo ... nai]

scare [skɛə] n 恐怖 [kyoufu] ▷ v 怖がらせ
る [kowagaraseru]

scarecrow ['skɛəˌkrəʊ] n かかし
[kakashi]

scared [skɛəd] adj 怖がった [kowagatta]

scarf, scarves [skɑːf, skɑːvz] n スカー
フ [sukaafu]

scarlet ['skɑːlɪt] adj 深紅色の
[shinkoushoku no]

scary ['skɛərɪ] adj 怖い [kowai]

scene [siːn] n 場面 [bamen]

scenery ['siːnərɪ] n 風景 [fuukei]

scent [sɛnt] n におい [nioi]

sceptical ['skɛptɪkəl] adj 疑い深い
[utagaibukai]

schedule ['ʃɛdjuːl; 'skɛdʒʊəl] n 予定
[yotei]; **We are on schedule** 私たちは予
定どおりです [watashi-tachi wa yotei
doori desu]; **We are slightly behind
schedule** 私たちは予定より少し遅れて
います [watashi-tachi wa yotei yori
sukoshi okurete imasu]

scheme [skiːm] n 計画 [keikaku]

schizophrenic [ˌskɪtsəʊ'frɛnɪk] adj 統
合失調症の [tougou shitchoushou no]

scholarship ['skɒləʃɪp] n 学問
[gakumon]

school [skuːl] n 学校 [gakkou]; **art
school** n 美術学校 [bijutsugakkou];
boarding school n 寄宿学校 [kishuku
gakkou]; **elementary school** n 小学校
[shougakkou]; **infant school** n 幼稚園
[youchien]; **language school** n 語学学
校 [gogaku gakkou]; **law school** n ロース
クール [roosukuuru]; **night school** n 夜
間学校 [yakangakkou]; **nursery school** n
保育園 [hoikuen]; **primary school** n 小
学校 [shougakkou]; **public school** n パブ
リックスクール [paburikkusukuuru];
school uniform n 学校の制服 [gakkou

no seifuku]; **secondary school** n 中学校
[chuugakkou]

schoolbag ['skuːlˌbæg] n 通学かばん
[tsuugaku kaban]

schoolbook ['skuːlˌbʊk] n 教科書
[kyoukasho]

schoolboy ['skuːlˌbɔɪ] n 男子生徒
[danshiseito]

schoolchildren ['skuːlˌtʃɪldrən] n 学童
[gakudou]

schoolgirl ['skuːlˌgɜːl] n 女子生徒
[joshiseito]

schoolteacher ['skuːlˌtiːtʃə] n 学校教
師 [gakkou kyoushi]

science ['saɪəns] n 科学 [kagaku];
science fiction n サイエンスフィクショ
ン [saiensu fikushon]

scientific [ˌsaɪən'tɪfɪk] adj 科学の
[kagaku no]

scientist ['saɪəntɪst] n 科学者
[kagakusha]

sci-fi ['saɪˌfaɪ] n サイエンスフィクション
[saiensu fikushon]

scissors ['sɪzəz] npl はさみ [hasami]; **nail
scissors** npl 爪切りばさみ [tsume kiri
basami]

sclerosis [sklɪə'rəʊsɪs] n **multiple
sclerosis** n 多発性硬化症 [tahatsusei
koukashou]

scoff [skɒf] v あざける [azakeru]

scold [skəʊld] v しかる [shikaru]

scooter ['skuːtə] n 片足スケート
[kataashi sukeeto]

score [skɔː] n (game/match) 得点
[tokuten], (of music) 楽譜 [gakufu nijuu]
▷ v 点を取る [ten-o toru]

Scorpio ['skɔːpɪˌəʊ] n 蠍座 [sasoriza]

scorpion ['skɔːpɪən] n サソリ [sasori]

Scot [skɒt] n スコットランド人
[sukottorandojin]

Scotland ['skɒtlənd] n スコットランド
[sukottorando]

Scots [skɒts] adj スコットランドの
[sukottorando no]

Scotsman, Scotsmen ['skɒtsmən,
'skɒtsmɛn] n スコットランド人男性

[sukottorandojin dansei]

Scotswoman, Scotswomen
['skɒts,wʊmən, 'skɒts,wɪmɪn] n スコットランド人女性 [sukottorandojin josei]

Scottish ['skɒtɪʃ] adj スコットランドの
[sukottorando no]

scout [skaʊt] n 偵察兵 [teisatsuhei]

scrap [skræp] n (dispute) けんか [kenka]
(争い), (small piece) 小片 [shouhen] ▷ v
廃棄する [haiki suru]; **scrap paper** n くず紙 [kuzugami]

scrapbook ['skræp,bʊk] n スクラップブック [sukurappubukku]

scratch [skrætʃ] n かき傷 [kakikizu] ▷ v
引っ掻く [hikkaku]

scream [skri:m] n 金切り声 [kanakirigoe]
▷ v 金切り声を上げる [kanagiri koe-o ageru]

screen [skri:n] n スクリーン [sukuriin];
plasma screen n プラズマスクリーン [purazumasukuriin]; **screen (off)** v 仕切りをする [shikiri-o suru]

screensaver ['skri:n,seɪvər] n スクリーンセーバー [sukuriinseebaa]

screw [skru:] n ねじ [neji]; **The screw has come loose** ねじがゆるくなっています [neji ga yuruku natte imasu]

screwdriver ['skru:,draɪvə] n ドライバー [doraibaa] (道具)

scribble ['skrɪbəl] v 走り書きする [hashirigaki suru]

scroll [skrəʊl] v スクロールする [sukurooru suru]

scrub [skrʌb] v ごしごし洗う [goshigoshi arau]

sculptor ['skʌlptə] n 彫刻家 [choukokuka]

sculpture ['skʌlptʃə] n 彫刻 [choukoku]

sea [si:] n 海 [umi]; **North Sea** n 北海 [hokkai]; **Red Sea** n 紅海 [koukai]; **sea level** n 海水面 [kaisui men]; **sea water** n 海水 [kaisui]; **Is the sea rough today?** 今日は海が荒れていますか? [kyou wa umi ga arete imasu ka?]

seafood ['si:,fu:d] n シーフード [shiifuudo]; **Do you like seafood?** シーフ

ードはお好きですか? [shii-fuudo wa o-suki desu ka?]

seagull ['si:,gʌl] n カモメ [kamome]

seal [si:l] n (animal) アザラシ [azarashi],
(mark) 封印 [fuuin] ▷ v 封をする [fuu-o suru]

seam [si:m] n 縫い目 [nuime]

seaman, seamen ['si:mən, 'si:mɛn] n
船乗り [funanori]

search [sɜ:tʃ] n 捜索 [sousaku] ▷ v 捜索する [sousaku suru]; **search engine** n 検索エンジン [kensaku enjin]; **search party** n 捜索隊 [sousakutai]

seashore ['si:,ʃɔ:] n 海岸 [kaigan]

seasick ['si:,sɪk] adj 船に酔った [fune ni yotta]

seaside ['si:,saɪd] n 海岸 [kaigan]

season ['si:zən] n 季節 [kisetsu]; **high season** n 最盛期 [saiseiki]; **low season** n シーズンオフ [shiizun'ofu]; **season ticket** n 定期券 [teikiken]

seasonal ['si:zənəl] adj 季節の [kisetsu no]

seasoning ['si:zənɪŋ] n 調味料 [choumiryou]

seat [si:t] n (constituency) 議席 [giseki],
(furniture) 座席 [zaseki]; **aisle seat** n 通路側の席 [tsuurogawa no seki]; **window seat** n 窓下の腰掛け [mado shita no koshikake]; **Can we have seats together?** 一緒の座席を取れますか? [issho no zaseki o toremasu ka?]; **I have a seat reservation** 私は座席予約をしてあります [watashi wa zaseki-yoyaku o shite arimasu]; **We'd like to reserve two seats for tonight** 今夜の座席を2つ予約したいのですが [kon'ya no zaseki o futatsu yoyaku shitai no desu ga]

seatbelt ['si:t,bɛlt] n シートベルト [shiitoberuto]

seaweed ['si:,wi:d] n 海藻 [kaisou]

second ['sɛkənd] adj 二番目の [ni banme no] ▷ n 二番目 [nibanme]; **second class** n 二等 [nitou]

second-class ['sɛkənd,klɑ:s] adj 二等の [nitou no]

secondhand ['sɛkənd,hænd] adj 中古
の [chuuko no]

secondly ['sɛkəndlɪ] adv 第二に [dai ni
ni]

second-rate ['sɛkənd,reɪt] adj 二流の
[niryuu no]

secret ['siːkrɪt] adj 秘密の [himitsu no]
▷ n 秘密 [himitsu]; **secret service** n 諜
報機関 [chouhou kikan]

secretary ['sɛkrətrɪ] n 秘書 [hisho]

secretly ['siːkrɪtlɪ] adv 秘密に [himitsu
ni]

sect [sɛkt] n 分派 [bunpa]

section ['sɛkʃən] n 部分 [bubun]

sector ['sɛktə] n 部門 [bumon]

secure [sɪ'kjʊə] adj 安全な [anzen na]

security [sɪ'kjʊərɪtɪ] n 防護 [bougo];
security guard n 警備員 [keibiin];
social security n 社会保障
[shakaihoshou]

sedative ['sɛdətɪv] n 鎮静剤 [chinseizai]

see [siː] v 見る [miru]

seed [siːd] n 種 [shu] (植物)

seek [siːk] v 捜す [sagasu]

seem [siːm] v ように思われる [youni
omowareru]

seesaw ['siː,sɔː] n シーソー [shiisoo]

see-through ['siː,θruː] adj 透けて見え
る [sukete mieru]

seize [siːz] v ぐいとつかむ [guito
tsukamu]

seizure ['siːʒə] n 発作 [hossa]

seldom ['sɛldəm] adv めったに···しな
い [mettani ... shinai]

select [sɪ'lɛkt] v 選ぶ [erabu]

selection [sɪ'lɛkʃən] n 選択 [sentaku]

self-assured ['sɛlfə'ʃʊəd] adj 自信のあ
る [jishin no aru]

self-catering ['sɛlf,keɪtərɪŋ] n 自炊
[jisui]

self-centred ['sɛlf,sɛntəd] adj 自己本
位の [jiko hon'i no]

self-conscious ['sɛlf,kɒnʃəs] adj 自意
識の強い [jiishiki no tsuyoi]

self-contained ['sɛlf,kən'teɪnd] adj 内
蔵型の [naizougata no]

self-control ['sɛlf,kən'trəʊl] n 自制
[jisei]

self-defence ['sɛlf,dɪ'fɛns] n 自衛 [jiei]

self-discipline ['sɛlf,dɪsɪplɪn] n 自己訓
練 [jiko kunren]

self-employed ['sɛlɪm'plɔɪd] adj 自営
業の [jieigyou no]

selfie ['sɛlfɪ] n 自撮り [jidori]

selfish ['sɛlfɪʃ] adj 利己的な [rikoteki na]

self-service ['sɛlf,sɜːvɪs] adj セルフサ
ービスの [serufusaabisu no]

sell [sɛl] v 売る [uru]; **sell-by date** n 販売
期限 [hanbai kigen]; **selling price** n 販売
価格 [hanbai kakaku]

sell off [sɛl ɒf] v 売り払う [uriharau]

Sellotape® ['sɛlə,teɪp] n セロテープ®
[seroteepu]

sell out [sɛl aʊt] v 売り尽くす [uritsukusu]

semester [sɪ'mɛstə] n 二学期制度の一
学期 [nigakki seido no ichigakki]

semi ['sɛmɪ] n 二戸建て住宅 [nikodate
juutaku]

semicircle ['sɛmɪ,sɜːkəl] n 半円 [han'en]

semicolon [,sɛmɪ'kəʊlən] n セミコロン
[semikoron]

semifinal [,sɛmɪ'faɪnəl] n 準決勝
[junkesshou]

send [sɛnd] v 送る [okuru]; **How much
is it to send this parcel?** この小包を送
るのにいくらかかりますか? [kono
kozutsumi o okuru no ni ikura kakarimasu
ka?]

send back [sɛnd bæk] v 送り返す
[okurikaesu]

sender ['sɛndə] n 送り主 [okurinushi]

send off [sɛnd ɒf] v 追い払う [oiharau]

send out [sɛnd aʊt] v 発送する [hassou
suru]

Senegal [,sɛnɪ'gɔːl] n セネガル
[senegaru]

Senegalese [,sɛnɪgə'liːz] adj セネガル
の [senegaru no] ▷ n セネガル人
[senegarujin]

senior ['siːnjə] adj 先輩の [senpai no];
senior citizen n 高齢者 [koureisha]

sensational [sɛn'seɪʃənəl] adj 世間をあ

っといわせるような [seken-o atto iwaseru you na]

sense [sɛns] *n* 感覚 [kankaku]; **sense of humour** *n* ユーモアのセンス [yuumoa no sensu]

senseless ['sɛnslɪs] *adj* 無意味な [muimi na]

sensible ['sɛnsɪbºl] *adj* 分別のある [bunbetsu no aru]

sensitive ['sɛnsɪtɪv] *adj* 傷つきやすい [kizutsukiyasui]

sensuous ['sɛnsjʊəs] *adj* 感覚に訴える [kankaku ni uttaeru]

sentence ['sɛntəns] *n* (*punishment*) 刑罰 [keibatsu], (*words*) 文 [bun] (言葉) ▷ *v* 判決を下す [hanketsu-o kudasu]

sentimental [ˌsɛntɪ'mɛntºl] *adj* 感傷的な [kanshouteki na]

separate *adj* ['sɛpərɪt] 単独の [tandoku no] ▷ *v* ['sɛpəˌreɪt] 分ける [wakeru]

separately ['sɛpərətlɪ] *adv* 別々に [betsubetsu ni]

separation [ˌsɛpə'reɪʃən] *n* 分離 [bunri]

September [sɛp'tɛmbə] *n* 九月 [kugatsu]

sequel ['si:kwəl] *n* 続篇 [zokuhen]

sequence ['si:kwəns] *n* 順序 [junjo]

Serbia ['sɜ:bɪə] *n* セルビア [serubia]

Serbian ['sɜ:bɪən] *adj* セルビアの [serubia no] ▷ *n* (*language*) セルビア語 [serubiago], (*person*) セルビア人 [serubiajin]

sergeant ['sɑ:dʒənt] *n* 軍曹 [gunsou]

serial ['sɪərɪəl] *n* 連続もの [renzokumono]

series ['sɪəri:z, -rɪz] *n* ひと続き [hitotsuduki]

serious ['sɪərɪəs] *adj* 深刻な [shinkoku na]

seriously ['sɪərɪəslɪ] *adv* 深刻に [shinkoku ni]

sermon ['sɜ:mən] *n* 説教 [sekkyou]

servant ['sɜ:vºnt] *n* 使用人 [shiyounin]; **civil servant** *n* 公務員 [koumuin]

serve [sɜ:v] *n* サーブ [saabu] ▷ *v* 仕える [tsukaeru]

server ['sɜ:və] *n* (*computer*) サーバー

[saabaa], (*person*) 給仕する人 [kyuuji suru hito]

service ['sɜ:vɪs] *n* サービス [saabisu] ▷ *v* サービスを提供する [saabisu-o teikyou suru]; **room service** *n* ルームサービス [ruumusaabisu]; **secret service** *n* 諜報機関 [chouhou kikan]; **service area** *n* サービスエリア [saabisu eria]; **service charge** *n* サービス料 [saabisuryou]; **service station** *n* ガソリンスタンド [gasorinsutando]; **social services** *npl* 政府の社会福祉事業 [seifu no shakai fukushi jigyou]; **Call the breakdown service, please** 故障時緊急修理サービスを呼んでください [koshou-ji kinkyuu-shuuri-saabisu o yonde kudasai]; **I want to complain about the service** 私はサービスについて苦情があります [watashi wa saabisu ni tsuite kujou ga arimasu]; **Is service included?** サービス料は入っていますか？ [saabisu-ryou wa haitte imasu ka?]; **Is there a charge for the service?** サービスに料金がかかりますか？ [saabisu ni ryoukin ga kakarimasu ka?]; **Is there a child-minding service?** 託児サービスはありますか？ [takuji saabisu wa arimasu ka?]; **Is there room service?** ルームサービスはありますか？ [ruumu-saabisu wa arimasu ka?]; **The service was terrible** サービスがひどかったです [saabisu ga hidokatta desu]

serviceman, servicemen ['sɜ:vɪsˌmæn, 'sɜ:vɪsˌmɛn] *n* 軍人 [gunjin]

servicewoman, servicewomen ['sɜ:vɪsˌwʊmən, 'sɜ:vɪsˌwɪmɪn] *n* 女性軍人 [josei gunjin]

serviette [ˌsɜ:vɪ'ɛt] *n* ナプキン [napukin]

session ['sɛʃən] *n* 会期 [kaiki]

set [sɛt] *n* ひとそろい [hitosoroi] ▷ *v* 定める [sadameru]

setback ['sɛtbæk] *n* 妨げ [samatage]

set menu [sɛt 'mɛnju:] *n* set menu 定食 [teishoku]

set off [sɛt ɒf] *v* 出発する [shuppatsu suru]

set out [sɛt aʊt] *v* 並べる [naraberu]

settee [sɛˈtiː] n 背付きの長椅子 [setsuki no nagaisu]

settle [ˈsɛtʰl] v 解決する [kaiketsu suru]

settle down [ˈsɛtʰl daʊn] v 落ち着く [ochitsuku] (住居)

seven [ˈsɛvˀn] number 七 [shichi]

seventeen [ˈsɛvˀnˈtiːn] number 十七 [juunana]

seventeenth [ˈsɛvˀnˈtiːnθ] adj 十七番目の [juushichi banme no]

seventh [ˈsɛvˀnθ] adj 七番目の [shichi banme no] ▷ n 七番目 [shichi banme]

seventy [ˈsɛvˀntɪ] number 七十 [shichijuu]

several [ˈsɛvrəl] adj いくつかの [ikutsuka no] ▷ pron 数個 [suuko]

sew [səʊ] v 縫う [nuu]

sewer [ˈsuːə] n 下水 [gesui]

sewing [ˈsəʊɪŋ] n 裁縫 [saihou]; **sewing machine** n ミシン [mishin]

sew up [səʊ ʌp] v 縫い合わせる [nuiawaseru]

sex [sɛks] n 性別 [seibetsu]

sexism [ˈsɛksɪzəm] n 性差別主義 [seisabetsu shugi]

sexist [ˈsɛksɪst] adj 性差別主義の [seisabetsu shugi no]

sexual [ˈsɛksjʊəl] adj 性的な [seiteki na]; **sexual intercourse** n 性交 [seikou]

sexuality [ˌsɛksjʊˈælɪtɪ] n 男女の別 [danjo no betsu]

sexy [ˈsɛksɪ] adj セクシーな [sekushii na]

shabby [ˈʃæbɪ] adj みすぼらしい [misuborashii]

shade [ʃeɪd] n 陰 [in]

shadow [ˈʃædəʊ] n 影 [kage]; **eye shadow** n アイシャドウ [aishadou]

shake [ʃeɪk] vi 揺れる [yureru] ▷ vt 振る [furu]

shaken [ˈʃeɪkən] adj 揺さぶられた [yusaburareta]

shaky [ˈʃeɪkɪ] adj よろよろする [yoroyoro suru]

shallow [ˈʃæləʊ] adj 浅い [asai]

shambles [ˈʃæmbˀlz] npl 乱雑な状態 [ranzatsu na joutai]

shame [ʃeɪm] n 恥ずかしい思い [hazukashii omoi]

shampoo [ʃæmˈpuː] n シャンプー [shanpuu]; **Do you sell shampoo?** シャンプーを売っていますか? [shanpuu o utte imasu ka?]

shape [ʃeɪp] n 形 [katachi]

share [ʃɛə] n 分け前 [wakemae] ▷ v 分ける [wakeru]

shareholder [ˈʃɛəˌhəʊldə] n 株主 [kabunushi]

share out [ʃɛə aʊt] v 分け合う [wakeau]

shark [ʃɑːk] n サメ [same]

sharp [ʃɑːp] adj 鋭い [surudoi]

shave [ʃeɪv] v 剃る [soru]; **shaving cream** n シェービングクリーム [sheebingukuriimu]; **shaving foam** n シェービングフォーム [shieebingufoomu]

shaver [ˈʃeɪvə] n シェーバー [shieebaa]

shawl [ʃɔːl] n ショール [shooru]

she [ʃiː] pron 彼女は [kanojo wa]

shed [ʃɛd] n 小屋 [koya]

sheep [ʃiːp] n 羊 [hitsuji]

sheepdog [ˈʃiːpˌdɒɡ] n 牧羊犬 [bokuyouken]

sheepskin [ˈʃiːpˌskɪn] n 羊の毛皮 [hitsuji no kegawa]

sheer [ʃɪə] adj 全くの [mattaku no]

sheet [ʃiːt] n シーツ [shiitsu]; **balance sheet** n 貸借対照表 [taishakutaishouhyou]; **fitted sheet** n マットレスにぴったり合うシーツ [mattoresu ni pittari au shiitsu]; **My sheets are dirty** 私のシーツは汚れています [watashi no shiitsu wa yogorete imasu]; **The sheets are dirty** シーツが汚れています [shiitsu ga yogorete imasu]; **We need more sheets** シーツがもっと必要です [shiitsu ga motto hitsuyou desu]

shelf, **shelves** [ʃɛlf, ʃɛlvz] n 棚 [tana]

shell [ʃɛl] n 殻 [kara]; **shell suit** n シェルスーツ [shierusuutsu]

shellfish [ˈʃɛlˌfɪʃ] n 貝 [kai]; **I'm allergic to shellfish** 私は貝類のアレルギーがあります [watashi wa kairui no arerugii ga arimasu]

shelter [ˈʃɛltə] n 避難所 [hinanjo]

shepherd [ˈʃɛpəd] n 羊飼い [hitsujikai]

sherry [ˈʃɛrɪ] n シェリー [shierii]

shield [ʃiːld] n 盾 [tate]

shift [ʃɪft] n 変化 [henka] ▷ v 移す [utsusu]

shifty [ˈʃɪftɪ] adj あてにならない [ate ni naranai]

Shiite [ˈʃiːaɪt] adj シーア派の信徒の [shiia ha no shinto no]

shin [ʃɪn] n むこうずね [mukouzune]

shine [ʃaɪn] v 光る [hikaru]

Shinto [ˈʃɪntəʊ] n 神道 [shintou]

shiny [ˈʃaɪnɪ] adj 光った [hikatta]

ship [ʃɪp] n 船 [fune]

shipbuilding [ˈʃɪpˌbɪldɪŋ] n 造船 [zousen]

shipment [ˈʃɪpmənt] n 積み荷 [tsumini]

shipwreck [ˈʃɪpˌrɛk] n 難破 [nanpa]

shipwrecked [ˈʃɪpˌrɛkt] adj 難破した [nanpa shita]

shipyard [ˈʃɪpˌjɑːd] n 造船所 [zousenjo]

shirt [ʃɜːt] n ワイシャツ [waishatsu]; **polo shirt** n ポロシャツ [poroshatsu]

shiver [ˈʃɪvə] v 震える [furueru]

shock [ʃɒk] n 衝撃 [shougeki] ▷ v 衝撃を与える [shougeki-o ataeru]; **electric shock** n 感電 [kanden]

shocking [ˈʃɒkɪŋ] adj ショッキングな [shokkingu na]

shoe [ʃuː] n 靴 [kutsu]; **shoe polish** n 靴墨 [kutsuzumi]; **shoe shop** n 靴屋 [kutsuya]; **Can you re-heel these shoes?** この靴のヒールを付け直すことができますか? [kono kutsu no hiiru o tsukenaosu koto ga dekimasu ka?]; **Can you repair these shoes?** この靴を修理できますか? [kono kutsu o shuuri dekimasu ka?]; **I have a hole in my shoe** 靴に穴があきました [kutsu ni ana ga akimashita]; **Which floor are shoes on?** 靴は何階にありますか? [kutsu wa nan-kai ni arimasu ka?]

shoelace [ˈʃuːˌleɪs] n 靴ひも [kutsuhimo]

shoot [ʃuːt] v 撃つ [utsu]

shooting [ˈʃuːtɪŋ] n 射撃 [shageki]

shop [ʃɒp] n 店 [mise]; **antique shop** n 骨董屋 [kottou ya]; **gift shop** n ギフトショップ [gifuto shoppu]; **shop assistant** n 店員 [ten-in]; **shop window** n ショーウィンドウ [shoouindou]; **What time do the shops close?** お店は何時に閉まりますか? [o-mise wa nan-ji ni shimarimasu ka?]

shopkeeper [ˈʃɒpˌkiːpə] n 店主 [tenshu]

shoplifting [ˈʃɒpˌlɪftɪŋ] n 万引き [manbiki]

shopping [ˈʃɒpɪŋ] n 買物 [kaimono]; **shopping bag** n 買物袋 [kaimonobukuro]; **shopping centre** n ショッピングセンター [shoppingu sentaa]; **shopping trolley** n ショッピングカート [shoppingukaato]

shore [ʃɔː] n 岸 [kishi]

short [ʃɔːt] adj 短い [mijikai]; **short story** n 短篇小説 [tanpen shousetsu]

shortage [ˈʃɔːtɪdʒ] n 不足 [fusoku]

shortcoming [ˈʃɔːtˌkʌmɪŋ] n 欠点 [ketten]

shortcut [ˈʃɔːtˌkʌt] n 近道 [chikamichi]

shortfall [ˈʃɔːtˌfɔːl] n 不足すること [fusoku suru koto]

shorthand [ˈʃɔːtˌhænd] n 速記 [sokki]

shortlist [ˈʃɔːtˌlɪst] n 選抜候補者リスト [senbatsu kouhosha risuto]

shortly [ˈʃɔːtlɪ] adv まもなく [mamonaku]

shorts [ʃɔːts] npl 半ズボン [hanzubon]

short-sighted [ˈʃɔːtˈsaɪtɪd] adj 近視の [kinshi no]

short-sleeved [ˈʃɔːtˌsliːvd] adj 半袖の [hansode no]

shot [ʃɒt] n 発砲 [happou]

shotgun [ˈʃɒtˌgʌn] n 散弾銃 [sandanjuu]

shoulder [ˈʃəʊldə] n 肩 [kata]; **hard shoulder** n 路肩 [rokata]; **shoulder blade** n 肩甲骨 [kenkoukotsu]; **I've hurt my shoulder** 私は肩を痛めました [watashi wa kata o itamemashita]

shout [ʃaʊt] n 叫び [sakebi] ▷ v 叫ぶ [sakebu]

shovel [ˈʃʌvəl] n シャベル [shaberu]

show [ʃəʊ] n ショー [shoo] ▷ v 見せる [miseru]; **show business** n ショービジネ

ス [shoobijinesu]; **Where can we go to see a show?** どこに行けばショーを見られますか? [doko ni ikeba shoo o miraremasu ka?]

shower ['ʃaʊə] n シャワー [shawaa]; **shower cap** n シャワーキャップ [shawaakyappu]; **shower gel** n シャワージェル [shawaajieru]; **Are there showers?** シャワーはありますか? [shawaa wa arimasu ka?]; **The shower doesn't work** シャワーが出ません [shawaa ga demasen]; **The shower is dirty** シャワーが汚れています [shawaa ga yogorete imasu]; **The showers are cold** シャワーが冷たいです [shawaa ga tsumetai desu]; **Where are the showers?** シャワーはどこですか? [shawaa wa doko desu ka?]

showerproof ['ʃaʊə,pruːf] adj ぬれても大丈夫な [nurete mo daijoubu na]

showing ['ʃəʊɪŋ] n 展示 [tenji]

show off [ʃəʊ ɒf] v 見せびらかす [misebirakasu]

show-off [ʃəʊɒf] n 見せびらかし [misebirakashi]

show up [ʃəʊ ʌp] v 現れる [arawareru]

shriek [ʃriːk] v 金切り声を出す [kanakirigoe o dasu]

shrimp [ʃrɪmp] n 小エビ [koebi]

shrine [ʃraɪn] n 神社 [jinja]

shrink [ʃrɪŋk] v 縮む [chijimu]

shrub [ʃrʌb] n 低木 [teiboku]

shrug [ʃrʌg] v 肩をすくめる [kata o sukumeru]

shrunk [ʃrʌŋk] adj 縮んだ [chijinda]

shudder ['ʃʌdə] v 身震いする [miburui suru]

shuffle ['ʃʌfəl] v 足をひきずって歩く [ashi-o hikizutte aruku]

shut [ʃʌt] v 閉める [shimeru]

shut down [ʃʌt daʊn] v 閉鎖する [heisa suru]

shutters ['ʃʌtəz] n シャッター [shattaa]

shuttle ['ʃʌtəl] n 定期往復便 [teiki oufuku bin]

shuttlecock ['ʃʌtəl,kɒk] n バドミントン

のシャトル [badminton no shatoru]

shut up [ʃʌt ʌp] v 黙る [damaru]

shy [ʃaɪ] adj 内気な [uchiki na]

Siberia [saɪ'bɪərɪə] n シベリア [shiberia]

siblings ['sɪblɪŋz] npl 兄弟姉妹 [kyoudaishimai]

sick [sɪk] adj 吐き気がする [hakike ga suru]; **sick leave** n 病気休暇 [byoukikyuuka]; **sick note** n 病欠届け [byouketsu todoke]; **sick pay** n 病気休暇中の手当て [byouki kyuukachuu no teate]

sickening ['sɪkənɪŋ] adj 吐き気をもよおさせる [hakike-o moyousaseru]

sickness ['sɪknɪs] n 病気 [byouki]; **morning sickness** n つわりの時期の朝の吐き気 [tsuwari no jiki no asa no hakike]; **travel sickness** n 乗物酔い [norimonoyoi]

side [saɪd] n 側 [gawa]; **side effect** n 副作用 [fukusayou]; **side street** n 横丁 [yokochou]

sideboard ['saɪd,bɔːd] n 食器棚 [shokkidana]

sidelight ['saɪd,laɪt] n 側灯 [sokutou]

sideways ['saɪd,weɪz] adv 横向きに [yokomuki ni]

sieve [sɪv] n ふるい [furui] (ざる)

sigh [saɪ] n ため息 [tameiki] ▷ v ため息をつく [tameiki o tsuku]

sight [saɪt] n 視力 [shiryoku]

sightseeing ['saɪt,siːɪŋ] n 観光 [kankou]; **Are there any sightseeing tours of the town?** その街の観光ツアーはありますか? [sono machi no kankou-tsuaa wa arimasu ka?]

sign [saɪn] n 兆候 [choukou] ▷ v 署名する [shomei suru]; **road sign** n 道路標識 [dourohyoushiki]; **sign language** n 手話 [shuwa]; **Where do I sign?** どこに署名するのですか? [doko ni shomei suru no desu ka?]

signal ['sɪgnəl] n 合図 [aizu] ▷ v 合図する [aizu suru]; **busy signal** n 話し中を示す信号 [hanashichuu-o shimesu shingou]

signature ['sɪgnɪtʃə] n 署名 [shomei]

significance [sɪg'nɪfɪkəns] *n* 重要性 [juuyousei]

significant [sɪg'nɪfɪkənt] *adj* 重要な [juuyou na]

sign on [saɪn ɒn] *v* 失業登録をする [shitsugyou touroku-o suru]

signpost ['saɪnˌpəʊst] *n* 道路標識 [dourohyoushiki]

Sikh [siːk] *adj* シーク教の [shiiku kyou no] ▷ *n* シーク教徒 [shiiku kyouto]

silence ['saɪləns] *n* 静けさ [shizukesa]

silencer ['saɪlənsə] *n* 消音装置 [shouon souchi]

silent ['saɪlənt] *adj* 寡黙な [kamoku na]

silk [sɪlk] *n* 絹 [kinu]

silly ['sɪlɪ] *adj* 愚かな [oroka na]

silver ['sɪlvə] *n* 銀 [gin]

similar ['sɪmɪlə] *adj* 類似した [ruiji shita]

similarity ['sɪmɪ'lærɪtɪ] *n* 類似 [ruiji]

simmer ['sɪmə] *v* 弱火でとろとろ煮る [yowabi de torotoro niru]

simple ['sɪmpəl] *adj* 簡単な [kantan na]

simplify ['sɪmplɪˌfaɪ] *v* 簡単にする [kantan ni suru]

simply ['sɪmplɪ] *adv* 簡単に [kantan ni]

simultaneous [ˌsɪməl'teɪnɪəs; ˌsaɪməl'teɪnɪəs] *adj* 同時の [douji no]

simultaneously [ˌsɪməl'teɪnɪəslɪ] *adv* 同時に [douji ni]

sin [sɪn] *n* 罪 [tsumi] (宗教・道徳)

since [sɪns] *adv* その時以来 [sono toki irai] ▷ *conj* •••して以来 [...shite irai] ▷ *prep* •••以来 [...irai]

sincere [sɪn'sɪə] *adj* 心からの [kokoro kara no]

sincerely [sɪn'sɪəlɪ] *adv* 心から [kokoro kara]

sing [sɪŋ] *v* 歌う [utau]

singer ['sɪŋə] *n* 歌手 [kashu]; **lead singer** *n* リードシンガー [riidoshingaa]

singing ['sɪŋɪŋ] *n* 歌うこと [utau koto]

single ['sɪŋɡəl] *adj* たった一つの [tatta hitotsu no] ▷ *n* シングル [shinguru]; **single bed** *n* シングルベッド [shingurubeddo]; **single parent** *n* 片親で子育てをする人 [kataoya de kosodate-o suru hito]; **single room** *n* シングルルーム [shingururuumu]; **single ticket** *n* 片道切符 [katamichi kippu]; **I want to reserve a single room** シングルルームを予約したいのですが [shinguru-ruumu o yoyaku shitai no desu ga]

singles ['sɪŋɡəlz] *npl* シングルス [shingurusu]

singular ['sɪŋɡjʊlə] *n* 単数 [tansuu]

sinister ['sɪnɪstə] *adj* 不吉な [fukitsu na]

sink [sɪŋk] *n* シンク [shinku] ▷ *v* 沈む [shizumu]

sinus ['saɪnəs] *n* 洞 [hora]

sir [sɜː] *n* あなた [anata]

siren ['saɪərən] *n* サイレン [sairen]

sister ['sɪstə] *n* 姉妹 [shimai]

sister-in-law ['sɪstə ɪn lɔː] *n* 義理の姉妹 [giri no shimai]

sit [sɪt] *v* 座る [suwaru]

sitcom ['sɪtˌkɒm] *n* シチュエーションコメディー [shichueeshonkomedii]

sit down [sɪt daʊn] *v* 着席する [chakuseki suru]

site [saɪt] *n* 敷地 [shikichi]; **building site** *n* 建設現場 [kensetsu genba]; **caravan site** *n* トレーラーハウスキャンプ場 [toreeraa hausu kyanpu jou]

situated ['sɪtjʊˌeɪtɪd] *adj* 位置している [ichi shite iru]

situation [ˌsɪtjʊ'eɪʃən] *n* 状況 [joukyou]

six [sɪks] *number* 六 [roku]; **It's six o'clock** 六時です [roku-ji desu]

sixteen ['sɪks'tiːn] *number* 十六 [juuroku]

sixteenth ['sɪks'tiːnθ] *adj* 十六番目の [juuroku banme no]

sixth [sɪksθ] *adj* 六番目の [roku banme no]

sixty ['sɪkstɪ] *number* 六十 [rokujuu]

size [saɪz] *n* サイズ [saizu]; **Do you have this in a bigger size?** これの大きなサイズはありますか? [kore no ooki-na saizu wa arimasu ka?]; **Do you have this in a smaller size?** これの小さなサイズはあり

ますか? [kore no chiisa-na saizu wa arimasu ka?]; **I'm a size 16** 私のサイズは十六号です [watashi no saizu wa jyuuroku-gou desu]

skate [skeɪt] v スケートをする [sukeeto o suru]

skateboard ['skeɪt,bɔ:d] n スケートボード [sukeetoboodo]; **I'd like to go skateboarding** 私はスケートボードをしたいのですが [watashi wa sukeetoboodo o shitai no desu ga]

skateboarding ['skeɪt,bɔ:dɪŋ] n スケートボーディング [sukeetoboodeingu]

skates [skeɪts] npl スケート靴 [sukeeto kutsu]; **Where can we hire skates?** どこでスケート靴を借りられますか? [doko de sukeeto-gutsu o kariraremasu ka?]

skating ['skeɪtɪŋ] n スケート [sukeeto]; **skating rink** n スケートリンク [sukeetorinku]

skeleton ['skɛlɪtən] n 骨格 [kokkaku]

sketch [skɛtʃ] n スケッチ [suketchi] ▷ v スケッチを描く [suketchi-o egaku]

skewer ['skjʊə] n 焼き串 [yakigushi]

ski [ski:] n スキー [sukii] ▷ v スキーをする [sukii o suru]; **ski lift** n スキー場のリフト [sukii jou no rifuto]; **ski pass** n スキー場のパス [sukii jou no pasu]; **Can we hire skis here?** ここでスキー板を借りられますか? [koko de sukii-ita o kariraremasu ka?]; **How much is a ski pass?** スキーパスはいくらですか? [sukii-pasu wa ikura desu ka?]; **I want to hire cross-country skis** クロスカントリースキーの板を借りたいのですが [kurosukantorii-sukii no ita o karitai no desu ga]; **I want to hire downhill skis** ダウンヒルスキーの板を借りたいのですが [daunhiru-sukii no ita o karitai no desu ga]; **I want to hire skis** スキー板を借りたいのですが [sukii-ita o karitai no desu ga]; **I'd like a ski pass for a day** 1日スキーパスが欲しいのですが [ichinichi sukii-pasu ga hoshii no desu ga]; **Is there a ski school?** スキースクールはありますか? [sukii-sukuuru wa arimasu ka?]; **Where can I buy a ski pass?** どこでスキーパスを買えますか? [doko de sukii-pasu o kaemasu ka?]

skid [skɪd] v 横すべりする [yokosuberi suru]

skier ['ski:ə] n スキーヤー [sukiiyaa]

skiing ['ski:ɪŋ] n スキー [sukii]; **Do you organise skiing lessons?** スキーのレッスンを企画していますか? [sukii no ressun o kikaku shite imasu ka?]; **I'd like to go skiing** スキーに行きたいのですが [sukii ni ikitai no desu ga]; **Is it possible to go cross-country skiing?** クロスカントリースキーに行くことは可能ですか? [kurosukantorii-sukii ni iku koto wa kanou desu ka?]; **Where can I hire skiing equipment?** どこでスキー用具を借りられますか? [doko de sukii-yougu o kariraremasu ka?]

skilful ['skɪlfʊl] adj 熟練した [jukuren shita]

skill [skɪl] n 熟練 [jukuren]

skilled [skɪld] adj 熟練した [jukuren shita]

skimpy ['skɪmpɪ] adj 不十分な [fujuubun na]

skin [skɪn] n 皮膚 [hifu]

skinhead ['skɪn,hɛd] n スキンヘッド [sukinheddo]

skinny ['skɪnɪ] adj やせこけた [yasekoketa]

skin-tight ['skɪn'taɪt] adj ぴったり体に合う [pittari karada ni au]

skip [skɪp] v 飛び跳ねる [tobihaneru]

skirt [skɜ:t] n スカート [sukaato]

skive [skaɪv] v 仕事をサボる [shigoto-o saboru]

skull [skʌl] n 頭蓋骨 [zugaikotsu]

sky [skaɪ] n 空 [sora] (天)

skyscraper ['skaɪ,skreɪpə] n 摩天楼 [matenrou]

slack [slæk] adj 緩い [yurui]

slag off [slæg ɒf] v けなす [kenasu]

slam [slæm] v バタンと閉める [batan to shimeru]

slang [slæŋ] n 俗語 [zokugo]

slap [slæp] v ピシャリと打つ [pishari to utsu]

slash [slæʃ] n **forward slash** n フォワードスラッシュ [fowaadosurasshu]

slate [sleɪt] n スレート [sureeto]

slave [sleɪv] n 奴隷 [dorei]; **slave away** v 奴隷のように働く [dorei no youni hataraku]

sledge [slɛdʒ] n そり [sori]; **Where can we go sledging?** どこに行けばそりに乗れますか? [doko ni ikeba sori ni noremasu ka?]

sledging ['slɛdʒɪŋ] n スレッジング [surejjingu]

sleep [sli:p] n 眠り [nemuri] ▷ v 眠る [nemuru]; **sleeping bag** n 寝袋 [nebukuro]; **sleeping car** n 寝台車 [shindaisha]; **sleeping pill** n 睡眠薬 [suimin-yaku]

sleep around [sli:p ə'raʊnd] v 誰とでも寝る [dare todemo neru]

sleeper ['sli:pə] n **Can I reserve a sleeper?** 寝台車を予約できますか? [shindai-sha o yoyaku dekimasu ka?]; **I want to book a sleeper to...** ···行きの寝台車を予約したいのですが [...iki no shindai-sha o yoyaku shitai no desu ga]

sleep in [sli:p ɪn] n 寝過ごす [nesugosu]

sleep together [sli:p tə'gɛðə] v いっしょに寝る [issho ni neru]

sleepwalk ['sli:p,wɔːk] v 夢遊病で歩く [muyuubyou de aruku]

sleepy ['sli:pɪ] adj 眠い [nemui]

sleet [sli:t] n みぞれ [mizore] ▷ v みぞれが降る [mizore ga furu]

sleeve [sli:v] n 袖 [sode]

sleeveless ['sli:vlɪs] adj 袖なしの [sode nashi no]

slender ['slɛndə] adj ほっそりした [hossori shita]

slice [slaɪs] n 薄切り [usugiri] ▷ v 薄く切る [usuku kiru]

slick [slɪk] n **oil slick** n 油膜 [yumaku]

slide [slaɪd] n 滑ること [suberu koto] ▷ v 滑る [suberu]

slight [slaɪt] adj わずかな [wazuka na]

slightly ['slaɪtlɪ] adv わずかに [wazuka ni]

slim [slɪm] adj ほっそりした [hossori shita]

sling [slɪŋ] n 吊り包帯 [tsuri houtai]

slip [slɪp] n (mistake) 間違い [machigai], (paper) 伝票 [denpyou], (underwear) スリップ [surippu] (下着) ▷ v 滑る [suberu]; **slip road** n 高速道路の進入退出路 [kousoku douro no shinnyuu taishutsuro]; **slipped disc** n 椎間板ヘルニア [tsuikanban herunia]

slipper ['slɪpə] n スリッパ [surippa]

slippery ['slɪpərɪ; -prɪ] adj 滑りやすい [suberiyasui]

slip up [slɪp ʌp] v 間違う [machigau]

slip-up [slɪpʌp] n 間違い [machigai]

slope [sləʊp] n 坂 [saka]; **nursery slope** n 初心者用ゲレンデ [shoshinshayou gerende]

sloppy ['slɒpɪ] adj ずさんな [zusanna]

slot [slɒt] n スロット [surotto]; **slot machine** n スロットマシン [surottomashin]

Slovak ['sləʊvæk] adj スロバキアの [surobakia no] ▷ n (language) スロバキア語 [surobakiago], (person) スロバキア人 [surobakiajin]

Slovakia [sləʊ'vækɪə] n スロバキア [surobakia]

Slovenia [sləʊ'vi:nɪə] n スロベニア [surobenia]

Slovenian [sləʊ'vi:nɪən] adj スロベニアの [surobenia no] ▷ n (language) スロベニア語 [surobeniago], (person) スロベニア人 [surobeniajin]

slow [sləʊ] adj 遅い [osoi]; **The connection seems very slow** 接続がとても遅いようです [setsuzoku ga totemo osoi you desu]

slow down [sləʊ daʊn] v もっとのんびりする [motto nonbiri suru]

slowly ['sləʊlɪ] adv 遅く [osoku]

slug [slʌg] n ナメクジ [namekuji]

slum [slʌm] n スラム街 [suramugai]

slush [slʌʃ] n ぬかるみ [nukarumi]

sly [slaɪ] adj ずるい [zurui]

smack [smæk] v ピシャリと打つ [pishari to utsu]

small [smɔːl] adj 小さい [chiisa na]; **small ads** npl 分類広告 [bunruikoukoku]

smart [smɑːt] adj スマートな [sumaato na]; **smart phone** n スマートフォン [sumaatofon] or スマホ [sumaho]

smash [smæʃ] v 打ち砕く [uchikudaku]

smashing ['smæʃɪŋ] adj すばらしい [subarashii]

smell [smɛl] n におい [nioi] ▷ vi においがする [nioi ga suru] ▷ vt においを嗅ぐ [nioi-o kagu]; **I can smell gas** ガスのにおいがします [gasu no nioi ga shimasu]; **My room smells of smoke** 私の部屋はタバコのにおいがします [watashi no heya wa tabako no nioi ga shimasu]; **There's a funny smell** 変なにおいがします [hen na nioi ga shimasu]

smelly ['smɛlɪ] adj いやなにおいのする [iya na nioino suru]

smile [smaɪl] n ほほ笑み [hohoemi] ▷ v ほほ笑む [hohoemu]

smiley ['smaɪlɪ] n スマイリー [sumairii]

smoke [sməʊk] n 煙 [kemuri] ▷ v 煙を出す [kemuri o dasu]; **smoke alarm** n 煙警報器 [kemuri keihouki]; **Where can I smoke?** どこで喫煙できますか？ [doko de kitsuen dekimasu ka?]

smoked ['sməʊkt] adj いぶした [ibushita]

smoker ['sməʊkə] n 喫煙者 [kitsuensha]

smoking ['sməʊkɪŋ] n 喫煙 [kitsuen]; **I'd like a seat in the smoking area** 喫煙エリアの席が欲しいのですが [kitsuen-eria no seki ga hoshii no desu ga]; **I'd like a smoking room** 喫煙できる部屋がいいのですが [kitsuen dekiru heya ga ii no desu ga]

smoky ['sməʊkɪ] adj **It's too smoky here** ここは煙たすぎます [koko wa kemuta-sugimasu]

smooth [smuːð] adj 滑らかな [nameraka na]

smoothie ['smuːðɪ] n スムージー [sumuujii]

SMS [ɛs ɛm ɛs] n ショートメッセージサービス [shootomesseejisaabisu]

smudge [smʌdʒ] n 汚れ [yogore]

smug [smʌɡ] adj 一人よがりの [hitori yogari no]

smuggle ['smʌɡəl] v 密輸する [mitsuyu suru]

smuggler ['smʌɡlə] n 密輸業者 [mitsuyu gyousha]

smuggling ['smʌɡlɪŋ] n 密輸 [mitsuyu]

snack [snæk] n 軽食 [keishoku]; **snack bar** n 軽食堂 [keishokudou]

snail [sneɪl] n カタツムリ [katatsumuri]

snake [sneɪk] n ヘビ [hebi]

snap [snæp] v ポキッと折る [pokitto oru]

snapshot ['snæpʃɒt] n スナップ写真 [sunappu shashin]

snarl [snɑːl] v 歯をむきだしてうなる [ha-o mukidashite unaru]

snatch [snætʃ] v ひったくる [hittakuru]

sneakers ['sniːkəz] npl スニーカー [suniikaa]

sneeze [sniːz] v くしゃみをする [kushami o suru]

sniff [snɪf] v 鼻で吸う [hana de suu]

snigger ['snɪɡə] v にやにや笑う [niyaniya warau]

snob [snɒb] n 紳士気取りの俗物 [shinshi kidori no zokubutsu]

snooker ['snuːkə] n スヌーカー [sunuukaa]

snooze [snuːz] n 居眠り [inemuri] ▷ v 居眠りをする [inemuri-o suru]

snore [snɔː] v いびきをかく [ibiki o kaku]

snorkel ['snɔːkəl] n シュノーケル [shunookeru]

snow [snəʊ] n 雪 [yuki] ▷ v 雪が降る [yuki ga furu]; **Do you think it will snow?** 雪が降ると思いますか？ [yuki ga furu to omoimasu ka?]; **It's snowing** 雪が降っています [yuki ga futte imasu]; **The snow is very heavy** 大雪です [ooyuki desu]; **What are the snow conditions?** 雪の状態はどうですか？ [yuki no joutai wa dou desu ka?]; **What is the snow like?** 雪はどんなものですか? [yuki wa donna mono desu ka?]

snowball ['snəʊ,bɔːl] n 雪つぶて [yukitsubute]

snowboard ['snəʊ,bɔːd] n **I want to hire a snowboard** スノーボードを借りたいのですが [sunooboodo o karitai no desu ga]

snowflake ['snəʊ,fleɪk] n ひとひらの雪 [hitohira no yuki]

snowman ['snəʊ,mæn] n 雪だるま [yukidaruma]

snowplough ['snəʊ,plaʊ] n 除雪車 [josetsusha]

snowstorm ['snəʊ,stɔːm] n 吹雪 [fubuki]

so [səʊ] adv そんなに [sonna ni]; **so (that)** conj ···するために [...suru tame ni]; **Why are you charging me so much?** なぜそんなにたくさん請求するのですか? [naze sonna ni takusan seikyuu suru no desu ka?]

soak [səʊk] v 浸す [hitasu]

soaked [səʊkt] adj ずぶぬれの [zubunure no]

soap [səʊp] n 石鹸 [sekken]; **soap dish** n 石鹸入れ [sekken ire]; **soap opera** n ソープオペラ [soopuopera]; **soap powder** n 粉石鹸 [kona sekken]; **There is no soap** 石鹸がありません [sekken ga arimasen]

sob [sɒb] v 泣きじゃくる [nakijakuru]

sober ['səʊbə] adj しらふの [shirafu no]

sociable ['səʊʃəbəl] adj 社交的な [shakouteki na]

social ['səʊʃəl] adj 社会の [shakai no]; **social media** n ソーシャルメディア [soosharu media]; **social security** n 社会保障 [shakaihoshou]; **social services** npl 政府の社会福祉事業 [seifu no shakai fukushi jigyou]; **social worker** n ソーシャルワーカー [soosharuwaakaa]

socialism ['səʊʃə,lɪzəm] n 社会主義 [shakaishugi]

socialist ['səʊʃəlɪst] adj 社会主義の [shakaishugi no] ▷ n 社会主義者 [shakaishugisha]

society [sə'saɪətɪ] n 社会 [shakai]

sociology [,səʊsɪ'ɒlədʒɪ] n 社会学 [shakaigaku]

sock [sɒk] n ソックス [sokkusu]

socket ['sɒkɪt] n コンセント [konsento]; **Where is the socket for my electric razor?** 電気カミソリのコンセントはどこですか? [denki-kamisori no konsento wa doko desu ka?]

sofa ['səʊfə] n ソファー [sofaa]; **sofa bed** n ソファーベッド [sofaabeddo]

soft [sɒft] adj 柔らかい [yawarakai]; **soft drink** n ソフトドリンク [sofutodorinku]

softener ['sɒfʰnə] n **Do you have softener?** 柔軟剤はありますか? [juunan-zai wa arimasu ka?]

software ['sɒft,wɛə] n ソフトウェア [sofutouea]

soggy ['sɒgɪ] adj ずぶぬれの [zubunure no]

soil [sɔɪl] n 土 [tsuchi]

solar ['səʊlə] adj 太陽の [taiyou no]; **solar power** n 太陽エネルギー [taiyou enerugii]; **solar system** n 太陽系 [taiyoukei]

soldier ['səʊldʒə] n 兵士 [heishi]

sold out ['səʊld aʊt] adj 売切れの [urikire no]

solicitor [sə'lɪsɪtə] n 事務弁護士 [jimubengoshi]

solid ['sɒlɪd] adj 固体の [kotai no]

solo ['səʊləʊ] n ソロ [soro]

soloist ['səʊləʊɪst] n ソリスト [sorisuto]

soluble ['sɒljʊbəl] adj 溶ける [tokeru]

solution [sə'luːʃən] n 解決 [kaiketsu]

solve [sɒlv] v 解決する [kaiketsu suru]

solvent ['sɒlvənt] n 溶剤 [youzai]

Somali [səʊ'mɑːlɪ] adj ソマリアの [somaria no] ▷ n (language) ソマリア語 [somariago], (person) ソマリア人 [somariajin]

Somalia [səʊ'mɑːlɪə] n ソマリア [somaria]

some [sʌm; səm] adj いくらかの

[ikuraka no] ▷ *pron* いくらか [ikuraka];
Could you lend me some money? お
金をいくらか貸していただけますか?
[o-kane o ikura ka kashite itadakemasu ka?]

somebody ['sʌmbədɪ] *pron* 誰か
[dareka]

somehow ['sʌm,haʊ] *adv* 何とか
[nantoka]

someone ['sʌm,wʌn; -wən] *pron* 誰か
[dareka]

someplace ['sʌm,pleɪs] *adv* どこかに
[dokoka ni]

something ['sʌmθɪŋ] *pron* 何か
[nanika]; **I'd like to order something
local** 何か郷土料理を注文したいのです
が [nani ka kyoudo-ryouri o chuumon shitai
no desu ga]; **Would you like
something to eat?** 何か召し上がりま
すか? [nani ka meshiagarimasu ka?];
**Would you like to do something
tomorrow?** 明日何かなさりたいです
か? [asu nani ka nasaritai desu ka?]

sometime ['sʌm,taɪm] *adv* いつか [itsu
ka]

sometimes ['sʌm,taɪmz] *adv* 時々
[tokidoki]

somewhere ['sʌm,wɛə] *adv* どこかに
[dokoka ni]

son [sʌn] *n* 息子 [musuko]; **My son is
lost** 息子の姿が見当たりません [musuko
no sugata ga miatarimasen]; **My son is
missing** 私の息子が行方不明です
[watashi no musuko ga yukue-fumei desu]

song [sɒŋ] *n* 歌 [uta]

son-in-law [sʌn ɪn lɔː] (sons-in-law)
n 娘の夫 [musume no otto]

soon [suːn] *adv* まもなく [mamonaku]

sooner ['suːnə] *adv* より早く [yori hayaku]

soot [sʊt] *n* すす [susu]

sophisticated [sə'fɪstɪ,keɪtɪd] *adj* 洗練
された [senren sareta]

soppy ['sɒpɪ] *adj* いやにセンチメンタル
な [iya ni senchimentaru na]

soprano [sə'prɑːnəʊ] *n* ソプラノ
[sopurano]

sorbet ['sɔːbeɪ; -bɪt] *n* ソルベ [sorube]

sorcerer ['sɔːsərə] *n* 魔法使い
[mahoutsukai]

sore [sɔː] *adj* 痛い [itai] ▷ *n* さわると痛い
ところ [sawaru to itai tokoro]; **cold sore** *n*
口辺ヘルペス [kouhenherupesu]

sorry ['sɒrɪ] *interj* sorry, I'm sorry ごめ
んなさい [gomen nasai]; **I'm sorry to
trouble you** ご迷惑をかけてすみません
[go-meiwaku o kakete sumimasen];
**I'm very sorry, I didn't know the
regulations** 大変申し訳ありませ
ん、規則を知りませんでした [taihen
moushiwake arimasen, kisoku o shirimasen
deshita]; **Sorry we're late** 遅れてすみま
せん [okurete sumimasen]; **Sorry,
I didn't catch that** ごめんなさい、
聞き取れませんでした [gomen nasai,
kikitoremasen deshita]; **Sorry, I'm not
interested** ごめんなさい、関心があ
りません [gomen nasai, kanshin ga
arimasen]

sort [sɔːt] *n* 種類 [shurui]

sort out [sɔːt aʊt] *v* 解決する [kaiketsu
suru]

SOS [ɛs əʊ ɛs] *n* 救難信号 [kyuunan
shingou]

so-so [səʊsəʊ] *adv* まあまあ [maamaa]

soul [səʊl] *n* 魂 [tamashii]

sound [saʊnd] *adj* 健全な [kenzen na]
▷ *n* 音 [oto]

soundtrack ['saʊnd,træk] *n* サウンド
トラック [saundotorakku]

soup [suːp] *n* スープ [suupu]; **What is
the soup of the day?** 今日のおすすめ
スープは何ですか? [kyou no osusume
suupu wa nan desu ka?]

sour ['saʊə] *adj* 酸っぱい [suppai]

south [saʊθ] *adj* 南の [minami no] ▷ *adv*
南に [minami ni] ▷ *n* 南 [minami]; **South
Africa** *n* 南アフリカ [minami afurika];
South African *n* 南アフリカの [minami
afurikajin], 南アフリカの [minami afurika
no]; **South America** *n* 南アメリカ
[minami amerika]; **South American** *n* 南
アメリカ人 [minami amerikajin], 南アメリ
カの [minami amerika no]; **South Korea**

n 韓国 [kankoku]; **South Pole** *n* 南極 [nankyoku]

southbound ['saʊθ,baʊnd] *adj* 南行き の [minami yuki no]

southeast [ˌsaʊθ'i:st; ˌsaʊ'i:st] *n* 南東 [nantou]

southern ['sʌðən] *adj* 南の [minami no]

southwest [ˌsaʊθ'wɛst; ˌsaʊ'wɛst] *n* 南西 [nansei]

souvenir [ˌsu:və'nɪə; 'su:və,nɪə] *n* 記 念品 [kinenhin]

soya ['sɔɪə] *n* 大豆 [daizu]

spa [spɑ:] *n* 鉱泉 [kousen]

space [speɪs] *n* 空間 [kuukan]

spacecraft ['speɪs,krɑ:ft] *n* 宇宙船 [uchuusen]

spade [speɪd] *n* 鋤 [suki]

spaghetti [spə'gɛtɪ] *n* スパゲッティ [supagetti]

Spain [speɪn] *n* スペイン [supein]

spam [spæm] *n* スパムメール [supamumeeru]

Spaniard ['spænjəd] *n* スペイン人 [supeinjin]

spaniel ['spænjəl] *n* スパニエル [supanieru]

Spanish ['spænɪʃ] *adj* スペインの [supein no] ▷ *n* スペイン人 [supeinjin]; *(language)* スペイン語 [supeingo]

spank [spæŋk] *v* ひっぱたく [hippataku]

spanner ['spænə] *n* スパナ [supana]

spare [speə] *adj* 余分の [yobun no] ▷ *v* 容 赦する [yousha suru]; **spare part** *n* スペ アパーツ [supeapaatsu]; **spare room** *n* 予備の寝室 [yobi no shinshitsu]; **spare time** *n* 余暇 [yoka]; **spare tyre** *n* スペア タイヤ [supeataiya]; **spare wheel** *n* スペ アホイール [supeahoiiru]

spark [spɑ:k] *n* 火花 [hibana]; **spark plug** *n* スパークプラグ [supaakupuragu]

sparrow ['spærəʊ] *n* スズメ [suzume]

spasm ['spæzəm] *n* 痙攣 [keirei]

speak [spi:k] *v* 話す [hanasu]

speaker ['spi:kə] *n* 話す人 [hanasu hito]; **native speaker** *n* 母国語とする人 [bokokugo to suru hito]

speak up [spi:k ʌp] *v* 遠慮なく話す [enryo naku hanasu]

special ['spɛʃəl] *adj* 特別の [tokubetsu no]; **special offer** *n* 特別売り出し [tokubetsu uridashi]

specialist ['spɛʃəlɪst] *n* 専門家 [senmonka]

speciality [ˌspɛʃɪ'ælɪtɪ] *n* 専門 [senmon]

specialize ['spɛʃə,laɪz] *v* 専門にする [senmon ni suru]

specially ['spɛʃəlɪ] *adv* 特別に [tokubetsu ni]

species ['spi:ʃi:z; 'spi:ʃɪ,i:z] *n* 種 [shu] (生物)

specific [spɪ'sɪfɪk] *adj* 特定の [tokutei no]

specifically [spɪ'sɪfɪklɪ] *adv* 特に [toku ni]

specify ['spɛsɪ,faɪ] *v* 明記する [meiki suru]

specs [spɛks] *npl* 眼鏡 [megane]

spectacles ['spɛktək⁹lz] *npl* 眼鏡 [megane]

spectacular [spɛk'tækjʊlə] *adj* 壮観な [soukan na]

spectator [spɛk'teɪtə] *n* 観客 [kankyaku]

speculate ['spɛkjʊ,leɪt] *v* 推測する [suisoku suru]

speech [spi:tʃ] *n* 言葉 [kotoba]

speechless ['spi:tʃlɪs] *adj* 口のきけない [kuchi no kikenai]

speed [spi:d] *n* 速さ [hayasa]; **speed limit** *n* 制限速度 [seigensokudo]

speedboat ['spi:d,bəʊt] *n* 快速モータ ーボート [kaisoku mootaabooto]

speeding ['spi:dɪŋ] *n* 高速進行 [kousoku shinkou]

speedometer [spɪ'dɒmɪtə] *n* 速度計 [sokudokei]

speed up [spi:d ʌp] *v* 速度を上げる [sokudo-o ageru]

spell [spɛl] *n* *(magic)* 呪文 [jumon], *(time)* 一時期 [ichijiki] ▷ *v* つづる [tsuduru]

spellchecker ['spɛl,tʃɛkə] *n* スペルチェ ッカー [superuchekkaa]

spelling ['spɛlɪŋ] n つづり [tsuzuri]

spend [spɛnd] v 費やす [tsuiyasu]

sperm [spɜːm] n 精子 [seishi]

spice [spaɪs] n 香辛料 [koushinryou]

spicy ['spaɪsɪ] adj 香辛料を入れた [koushinryou-o ireta]

spider ['spaɪdə] n クモ [kumo] (動物)

spill [spɪl] v こぼす [kobosu] (漏らす)

spinach ['spɪnɪdʒ; -ɪtʃ] n ほうれん草 [hourensou]

spine [spaɪn] n 脊椎 [sekitsui]

spinster ['spɪnstə] n 独身女性 [dokushinjosei]

spire [spaɪə] n 尖塔 [sentou]

spirit ['spɪrɪt] n 精神 [seishin]

spirits ['spɪrɪts] npl スピリッツ [supirittsu]

spiritual ['spɪrɪtjʊəl] adj 精神的な [seishinteki na]

spit [spɪt] n つば [tsuba] (唾液) ▷ v つばを吐く [tsuba o haku]

spite [spaɪt] n 意地悪 [ijiwaru] ▷ v 意地悪をする [ijiwaru-o suru]

spiteful ['spaɪtfʊl] adj 意地の悪い [iji no warui]

splash [splæʃ] v はねかける [hanekakeru]

splendid ['splɛndɪd] adj すばらしい [subarashii]

splint [splɪnt] n 添え木 [soegi]

splinter ['splɪntə] n 破片 [hahen]

split [splɪt] v 割る [waru]

split up [splɪt ʌp] v 分裂する [bunretsu suru]

spoil [spɔɪl] v 台無しにする [dainashi ni suru]

spoilsport ['spɔɪlˌspɔːt] n 人の興をそぐ人 [hito no kyou-o sogu hito]

spoilt [spɔɪlt] adj 台無しにされた [dainashi ni sareta]

spoke [spəʊk] n スポーク [supooku]

spokesman, spokesmen ['spəʊksmən, 'spəʊksmɛn] n スポークスマン [supookusuman]

spokesperson ['spəʊksˌpɜːsən] n スポークスパーソン [supookusupaason]

spokeswoman, spokeswomen ['spəʊksˌwʊmən, 'spəʊksˌwɪmɪn] n スポークスウーマン [supookusuuuman]

sponge [spʌndʒ] n (cake) スポンジケーキ [suponji keeki] (cake), (for washing) スポンジ [suponji]; **sponge bag** n 洗面用具入れ [senmen yougu ire]

sponsor ['spɒnsə] n 後援者 [kouensha] ▷ v 後援者となる [kouensha to naru]

sponsorship ['spɒnsəʃɪp] n 後援 [kouen]

spontaneous [spɒn'teɪnɪəs] adj 自発的な [jihatsuteki na]

spooky ['spuːkɪ; 'spooky] adj 気味の悪い [kimi no warui]

spoon [spuːn] n スプーン [supuun]; **Could I have a clean spoon, please?** 新しいスプーンをいただけますか? [atarashii supuun o itadakemasu ka?]

spoonful ['spuːnˌfʊl] n ひとさじ [hitosaji]

sport [spɔːt] n スポーツ [supootsu]; **winter sports** npl ウィンタースポーツ [uintaasupootsu]; **What sports facilities are there?** どんなスポーツ施設がありますか? [donna supootsu-shisetsu ga arimasu ka?]; **Which sporting events can we go to?** 私たちはどのスポーツイベントに行けますか? [watashi-tachi wa dono supootsu-ibento ni ikemasu ka?]

sportsman, sportsmen ['spɔːtsmən, 'spɔːtsmɛn] n スポーツマン [supootsuman]

sportswear ['spɔːtsˌwɛə] n スポーツウェア [supootsuuea]

sportswoman, sportswomen ['spɔːtsˌwʊmən, 'spɔːtsˌwɪmɪn] n スポーツウーマン [supootsuuuman]

sporty ['spɔːtɪ] adj スポーツ好きの [supootsuzuki no]

spot [spɒt] n (blemish) しみ [shimi], (place) 地点 [chiten] ▷ v 見つける [mitsukeru]

spotless ['spɒtlɪs] adj しみのない [shimi no nai]

spotlight ['spɒtˌlaɪt] n スポットライト [supottoraito]

spouse [spaʊs] n 配偶者 [haiguusha]

sprain [spreɪn] *n* 捻挫 [nenza] ▷ *v* くじく [kujiku]

spray [spreɪ] *n* 噴霧 [funmu] ▷ *v* 噴霧する [funmu suru]; **hair spray** *n* ヘアスプレー [heasupuree]

spread [sprɛd] *n* 広がること [hirogaru koto] ▷ *v* 広げる [hirogeru]

spread out [sprɛd aʊt] *v* 広げる [hirogeru]

spreadsheet ['sprɛd,ʃiːt] *n* スプレッドシート [supureddoshiito]

spring [sprɪŋ] *n (coil)* ばね [bane], *(season)* 春 [haru]; **spring onion** *n* ネギ [negi]

spring-cleaning ['sprɪŋ,kliːnɪŋ] *n* 春季の大掃除 [shunki no ousouji]

springtime ['sprɪŋ,taɪm] *n* 春季 [shunki]

sprinkler ['sprɪŋklə] *n* スプリンクラー [supurinkuraa]

sprint [sprɪnt] *n* 短距離競走 [tankyorikyousou] ▷ *v* 全力で走る [zenryoku de hashiru]

sprinter ['sprɪntə] *n* 短距離走者 [tankyori sousha]

sprouts [spraʊts] *npl* 新芽 [shinme]; **Brussels sprouts** *npl* 芽キャベツ [mekyabetsu]

spy [spaɪ] *n* スパイ [supai] ▷ *v* 見張る [miharu]

spying ['spaɪɪŋ] *n* スパイ行為 [supai koui]

squabble ['skwɒbəl] *v* つまらないことで口論する [tsumaranai koto de kouron suru]

squander ['skwɒndə] *v* 浪費する [rouhi suru]

square [skwɛə] *adj* 正方形の [seihoukei no] ▷ *n* 正方形 [seihoukei]

squash [skwɒʃ] *n* スカッシュ [sukasshu] ▷ *v* 押しつぶす [oshitsubusu]

squeak [skwiːk] *v* きしる [kishiru]

squeeze [skwiːz] *v* 強く押す [tsuyoku osu]

squeeze in [skwiːz ɪn] *v* 割り込む [warikomu]

squid [skwɪd] *n* イカ [ika]

squint [skwɪnt] *v* 斜視である [shashi de aru]

squirrel ['skwɪrəl; 'skwɜːrəl; 'skwʌrəl] *n* リス [risu]

Sri Lanka [ˌsriː 'læŋkə] *n* スリランカ [suriranka]

stab [stæb] *v* 突き刺す [tsukisasu]

stability [stə'bɪlɪtɪ] *n* 安定 [antei]

stable ['steɪbəl] *adj* 安定した [antei shita] ▷ *n* 馬小屋 [umagoya]

stack [stæk] *n* 積み重ね [tsumikasane]

stadium, stadia ['steɪdɪəm, 'steɪdɪə] *n* スタジアム [sutajiamu]; **How do we get to the stadium?** そのスタジアムにはどうやって行くのですか? [sono sutajiamu ni wa dou-yatte iku no desu ka?]

staff [stɑːf] *n (stick or rod)* 棒 [bou], *(workers)* 職員 [shokuin]

staffroom ['stɑːf,ruːm] *n* 職員室 [shokuinshitsu]

stage [steɪdʒ] *n* 段階 [dankai]

stagger ['stægə] *v* よろめく [yoromeku]

stain [steɪn] *n* しみ [shimi] ▷ *v* しみがつく [shimi ga tsuku]; **stain remover** *n* しみ抜き剤 [shiminuki zai]; **Can you remove this stain?** このしみを落とすことができますか? [kono shimi o otosu koto ga dekimasu ka?]; **This stain is coffee** このしみはコーヒーです [kono shimi wa koohii desu]; **This stain is wine** このしみはワインです [kono shimi wa wain desu]

staircase ['stɛə,keɪs] *n* 階段 [kaidan]

stairs [stɛəz] *npl* 階段 [kaidan]

stale [steɪl] *adj* 古くなった [furuku natta]

stalemate ['steɪl,meɪt] *n* ステイルメイト [suteirumeito]

stall [stɔːl] *n* 屋台 [yatai]

stamina ['stæmɪnə] *n* スタミナ [sutamina]

stammer ['stæmə] *v* どもる [domoru]

stamp [stæmp] *n* 切手 [kitte] ▷ *v* 踏みつける [fumitsukeru]; **Can I have stamps for four postcards to...** ···あての郵便はがき四枚分の切手をもらえますか? [... ate no yuubin-hagaki yonmai-bun no kitte o moraemasu ka?]; **Do you sell stamps?** 切手を売っていますか? [kitte o utte imasu ka?]; **Where can I buy stamps?** どこで切手を買えますか? [doko de kitte o kaemasu ka?]; **Where is the nearest shop which sells stamps?** 切手を売っている一番近い店はどこですか? [kitte o utte iru ichiban chikai mise wa doko desu ka?]

stand [stænd] v 立つ [tatsu]

standard ['stændəd] adj 標準の [hyoujun no] ▷ n 標準 [hyoujun]; **standard of living** n 生活水準 [seikatsusuijun]

stand for [stænd fɔː] v 表す [arawasu]

stand out [stænd aʊt] v 突出する [tosshutsu suru]

standpoint ['stænd,pɔɪnt] n 見地 [kenchi]

stands ['stændz] npl スタンド [sutando]

stand up [stænd ʌp] v 起立する [kiritsu suru]

staple ['steɪpᵊl] n (commodity) 主要産物 [shuyou sanbutsu], (wire) ステープル [suteepuru] ▷ v ステープルで留める [suteepuru de todomeru]

stapler ['steɪplə] n ステープラー [suteepuraa]

star [stɑː] n (person) スター [sutaa], (sky) 星 [hoshi] ▷ v 主演する [shuen suru]; **film star** n 映画スター [eigasutaa]

starch [stɑːtʃ] n 澱粉 [denpun]

stare [stɛə] v じっと見つめる [jitto mitsumeru]

stark [stɑːk] adj がらんとした [garan to shita]

start [stɑːt] n 開始 [kaishi] ▷ vi 始まる [hajimaru] ▷ vt 始める [hajimeru]

starter ['stɑːtə] n スターター [sutaataa]; **I'd like pasta as a starter** スターターにパスタをいただきます [sutaataa ni pasuta o itadakimasu]

startle ['stɑːtᵊl] v びっくりさせる [bikkuri saseru]

start off [stɑːt ɒf] v 旅立つ [tabidatsu]

starve [stɑːv] v 餓死する [gashi suru]

state [steɪt] n 状態 [joutai] ▷ v 述べる [noberu]

statement ['steɪtmənt] n 声明 [seimei]; **bank statement** n 銀行の明細書 [ginkou no meisaisho]

station ['steɪʃən] n 駅 [eki]; **bus station** n バスターミナル [basutaaminaru]; **metro station** n 地下鉄駅 [chikatetsu eki]; **petrol station** n ガソリンスタンド [gasorinsutando]; **police station** n 警察署 [keisatsusho]; **radio station** n ラジオ局 [rajio kyoku]; **railway station** n 鉄道駅 [tetsudoueki]; **service station** n ガソリンスタンド [gasorinsutando]; **tube station** n 地下鉄駅 [chikatetsu eki]; **Where is the nearest tube station?** 一番近い地下鉄の駅はどこですか? [ichiban chikai chikatetsu no eki wa doko desu ka?]

stationer's ['steɪʃənəz] n 文房具店 [bunbouguten]

stationery ['steɪʃənərɪ] n 文房具 [bunbougu]

statistics [stə'tɪstɪks] npl 統計 [toukei]

statue ['stætjuː] n 像 [zou]

status ['steɪtəs] n **marital status** n 婚姻関係の有無 [kon'in kankei no umu]

status quo ['steɪtəs kwəʊ] n 現状 [genjou]

stay [steɪ] n 滞在 [taizai] ▷ v とどまる [todomaru]; **I'm staying at a hotel** 私はホテルに滞在しています [watashi wa hoteru ni taizai shite imasu]

stay in [steɪ ɪn] v 家にいる [ie ni iru]

stay up [steɪ ʌp] v 起きている [okite iru]

steady ['stɛdɪ] adj しっかりした [shikkari shita]

steak [steɪk] n ステーキ [suteeki]; **rump steak** n ランプステーキ [ranpusuteeki]

steal [stiːl] v 盗む [nusumu]

steam [stiːm] n 蒸気 [jouki]

steel [stiːl] n 鋼鉄 [koutetsu]; **stainless steel** n ステンレススチール [sutenresusuchiiru]

steep [stiːp] adj 急な [kyuu na] (傾斜)

steeple ['stiːpᵊl] n 尖塔 [sentou]

steering ['stɪərɪŋ] n ステアリング

[suteoiringu]; **steering wheel** n ハンドル [handoru]

step [stɛp] n 歩み [ayumi]

stepbrother ['stɛpˌbrʌðə] n 継兄弟 [mama kyoudai]

stepdaughter ['stɛpˌdɔːtə] n 継娘 [mama musume]

stepfather ['stɛpˌfɑːðə] n 継父 [mama chichi]

stepladder ['stɛpˌlædə] n 脚立 [kyatatsu]

stepmother ['stɛpˌmʌðə] n 継母 [mama haha]

stepsister ['stɛpˌsɪstə] n 継姉妹 [mama shimai]

stepson ['stɛpˌsʌn] n 継子 [mamako]

stereo ['stɛrɪəʊ; 'stɪər-] n ステレオ [sutereo]; **personal stereo** n パーソナルステレオ [paasonarusutereo]; **Is there a stereo in the car?** 車にカーステレオはついていますか? [kuruma ni kaa-sutereo wa tsuite imasu ka?]

stereotype ['stɛrɪəˌtaɪp; 'stɪər-] n ステレオタイプ [sutereotaipu]

sterile ['stɛraɪl] adj 滅菌した [mekkin shita]

sterilize ['stɛrɪˌlaɪz] v 滅菌する [mekkin suru]

sterling ['stɜːlɪŋ] n 英貨 [eika]

steroid ['stɪərɔɪd; 'stɛr-] n ステロイド [suteroido]

stew [stjuː] n シチュー [shichuu]

steward ['stjʊəd] n スチュワード [suchuwaado]

stick [stɪk] n 棒切れ [bou kire]; **stick insect** n ナナフシ [nanafushi]; **walking stick** n ステッキ [sutekki]

sticker ['stɪkə] n ステッカー [sutekkaa]

stick out [stɪk aʊt] v 突き出す [tsukidasu]

sticky ['stɪkɪ] adj べとべとした [betobeto shita]

stiff [stɪf] adj 堅い [katai]

stifling ['staɪflɪŋ] adj むっとする [muttosuru] (息詰まる)

still [stɪl] adj 静かな [shizuka na] ▷ adv まだ [mada]; **I'm still studying** 私はまだ

学校に行っています [watashi wa mada gakkou ni itte imasu]; **The car is still under warranty** 車はまだ保証期間内です [kuruma wa mada hoshou-kikan nai desu]

sting [stɪŋ] n 刺し傷 [sashi kizu] ▷ v 刺す [sasu]

stingy ['stɪndʒɪ] adj けちな [kechi na]

stink [stɪŋk] n 悪臭 [akushuu] ▷ v 悪臭を放つ [akushuu-o hanatsu]

stir [stɜː] v かき混ぜる [kakimazeru]

stitch [stɪtʃ] n ひと針 [hitohari] ▷ v 縫う [nuu]

stock [stɒk] n 在庫品 [zaikohin] ▷ v 在庫を置く [zaiko-o oku]; **stock cube** n 固形スープの素 [kokei suupu no moto]; **stock exchange** n 証券取引所 [shouken torihikijo]; **stock market** n 株式市場 [kabushikishijou]

stockbroker ['stɒkˌbrəʊkə] n 株式仲買人 [kabushikinakagainin]

stockholder ['stɒkˌhəʊldə] n 株主 [kabunushi]

stocking ['stɒkɪŋ] n ストッキング [sutokkingu]

stock up [stɒk ʌp] v **stock up on** v 仕入れる [shiireru]

stomach ['stʌmək] n 胃 [i]

stomachache ['stʌməkˌeɪk] n 胃痛 [itsuu]

stone [stəʊn] n 石 [ishi]

stool [stuːl] n スツール [sutsuuru]

stop [stɒp] n 中止 [chuushi] ▷ vi 止まる [tomaru] ▷ vt 止める [tomeru]; **bus stop** n バス停 [basutei]; **full stop** n 終止符 [shuushifu]

stopover ['stɒpˌəʊvə] n 立ち寄ること [tachiyoru koto]

stopwatch ['stɒpˌwɒtʃ] n ストップウォッチ [sutoppuuotchi]

storage ['stɔːrɪdʒ] n 保管 [hokan]

store [stɔː] n 店 [mise] ▷ v 蓄える [takuwaeru]; **department store** n デパート [depaato]

storm [stɔːm] n 嵐 [arashi]; **Do you think there will be a storm?** 嵐になる

と思いますか? [arashi ni naru to omoimasu ka?]

tormy ['stɔːmɪ] *adj* 嵐の [arashi no]

tory ['stɔːrɪ] *n* 物語 [monogatari]; **short story** *n* 短篇小説 [tanpen shousetsu]

tove [stəʊv] *n* 料理用レンジ [ryouri you renji]

traight [streɪt] *adj* まっすぐな [massugu na]; **straight on** *adv* まっすぐに [massugu ni]

traighteners ['streɪtᵊnəz] *npl* ストレイトナー [sutoreitonaa]

traightforward [ˌstreɪtˈfɔːwəd] *adj* 率直な [sotchoku na]

train [streɪn] *n* 極度の緊張 [kyokudo no kinchou] ▷ *v* 緊張させる [kinchou saseru]

tranded ['strændɪd] *adj* 立ち往生した [tachioujou shita]

trange [streɪndʒ] *adj* 奇妙な [kimyou na]

tranger ['streɪndʒə] *n* 知らない人 [shiranai hito]

trangle ['stræŋgᵊl] *v* 絞め殺す [shimekorosu]

trap [stræp] *n* 革ひも [kawa himo]; **watch strap** *n* 腕時計のバンド [udedokei no bando]

trategic [strəˈtiːdʒɪk] *adj* 戦略的な [senryakuteki na]

trategy ['strætɪdʒɪ] *n* 戦略 [senryaku]

traw [strɔː] *n* 麦わら [mugiwara]

trawberry ['strɔːbərɪ; -brɪ] *n* イチゴ [ichigo]

tray [streɪ] *n* 迷い出た家畜 [mayoideta kachiku]

tream [striːm] *n* 小川 [ogawa]

treet [striːt] *n* 通り [touri]; **street map** *n* 街路地図 [gairo chizu]; **street plan** *n* 街路計画 [gairo keikaku]

treetlamp ['striːtˌlæmp] *n* 街灯 [gaitou]

treetwise ['striːtˌwaɪz] *adj* 世慣れた [yonareta]

rength [strɛŋθ] *n* 強さ [tsuyosa]

rengthen ['strɛŋθən] *v* 強くする [tsuyoku suru]

stress [strɛs] *n* ストレス [sutoresu] ▷ *v* 強調する [kyouchou suru]

stressed ['strɛst] *adj* ストレスがたまった [sutoresu ga tamatta]

stressful ['strɛsfʊl] *adj* ストレスの多い [sutoresu no oui]

stretch [strɛtʃ] *v* 伸びる [nobiru]

stretcher ['strɛtʃə] *n* 担架 [tanka]

stretchy ['strɛtʃɪ] *adj* 伸びる [nobiru]

strict [strɪkt] *adj* 厳しい [kibishii]

strictly [strɪktlɪ] *adv* 厳しく [kibishiku]

strike [straɪk] *n* ストライキ [sutoraiki] ▷ *vi* 襲う [osou], *(suspend work)* ストライキをする [sutoraiki o suru] ▷ *vt* 打つ [utsu]; **because of a strike** ストライキがあったからです [sutoraiki ga atta kara desu]

striker ['straɪkə] *n* ストライキ参加者 [sutoraiki sankasha]

striking ['straɪkɪŋ] *adj* 目立つ [medatsu]

string [strɪŋ] *n* ひも [himo]

strip [strɪp] *n* ストリップ [sutorippu] ▷ *v* はぐ [hagu]

stripe [straɪp] *n* 縞 [shima]

striped [straɪpt] *adj* 縞のある [shima no aru]

stripper ['strɪpə] *n* ストリッパー [sutorippaa]

stripy ['straɪpɪ] *adj* 縞の入った [shima no haitta]

stroke [strəʊk] *n* *(apoplexy)* 中風 [chuubuu], *(hit)* なでること [naderu koto] ▷ *v* なでる [naderu]

stroll [strəʊl] *n* ぶらぶら歩き [burabura aruki]

strong [strɒŋ] *adj* 強い [tsuyoi]; **I need something stronger** 私はもっと強い薬が必要です [watashi wa motto tsuyoi kusuri ga hitsuyou desu]

strongly [strɒŋlɪ] *adv* 強く [tsuyoku]

structure ['strʌktʃə] *n* 構造 [kouzou]

struggle ['strʌgᵊl] *v* 苦闘する [kutou suru]

stub [stʌb] *n* 使い残り [tsukainokori]

stubborn ['stʌbᵊn] *adj* 頑固な [ganko na]

stub out [stʌb aʊt] *v* 火をもみ消す [hi-o momikesu]

stuck [stʌk] *adj* 行きづまった [ikizumatta]

stuck-up [stʌkʌp] *adj* 高慢ちきな [koumanchiki na]

stud [stʌd] *n* 鋲 [byou]

student ['stjuːdənt] *n* 学生 [gakusei]; **student discount** *n* 学生割引 [gakusei waribiki]; **Are there any reductions for students?** 学生割引はありますか? [gakusei-waribiki wa arimasu ka?]; **I'm a student** 私は学生です [watashi wa gakusei desu]

studio ['stjuːdɪˌəʊ] *n* スタジオ [sutajio]; **studio flat** *n* スタジオフラット [sutajiofuratto]

study ['stʌdɪ] *v* 勉強する [benkyou suru]

stuff [stʌf] *n* もの [mono] (材料)

stuffy ['stʌfɪ] *adj* 風通しの悪い [kazetoushi no warui]

stumble ['stʌmbəl] *v* つまずく [tsumazuku]

stunned [stʌnd] *adj* どぎもを抜かれた [dogimo o nukareta]

stunning ['stʌnɪŋ] *adj* すばらしい [subarashii]

stunt [stʌnt] *n* 離れわざ [hanarewaza]

stuntman, stuntmen ['stʌntmən, 'stʌntmɛn] *n* スタントマン [sutantoman]

stupid ['stjuːpɪd] *adj* 愚かな [oroka na]

stutter ['stʌtə] *v* どもる [domoru]

style [staɪl] *n* スタイル [sutairu]

styling ['staɪlɪŋ] *n* **Do you sell styling products?** スタイリング用品を売っていますか? [sutairingu youhin o utte imasu ka?]

stylist ['staɪlɪst] *n* スタイリスト [sutairisuto]

subject ['sʌbdʒɪkt] *n* 主題 [shudai]

submarine ['sʌbməˌriːn; ˌsʌbməˈriːn] *n* 潜水艦 [sensuikan]

subscription [səbˈskrɪpʃən] *n* 定期購読 [teiki koudoku]

subsidiary [səbˈsɪdɪərɪ] *n* 子会社 [kogaisha]

subsidize ['sʌbsɪˌdaɪz] *v* 助成金を支給する [joseikin-o shikyuu suru]

subsidy ['sʌbsɪdɪ] *n* 助成金 [joseikin]

substance ['sʌbstəns] *n* 物質 [busshitsu]

substitute ['sʌbstɪˌtjuːt] *n* 代用 [daiyou] ▷ *v* 代用する [daiyou suru]

subtitled ['sʌbˌtaɪtəld] *adj* 字幕を入れた [jimaku-o ireta]

subtitles ['sʌbˌtaɪtəlz] *npl* 字幕 [jimaku]

subtle ['sʌtəl] *adj* 微妙な [bimyou na]

subtract [səbˈtrækt] *v* 引く [hiku]

suburb ['sʌbɜːb] *n* 郊外 [kougai]

suburban [səˈbɜːbən] *adj* 郊外の [kougai no]

subway ['sʌbˌweɪ] *n* 地下道 [chikadou]

succeed [səkˈsiːd] *v* 成功する [seikou suru]

success [səkˈsɛs] *n* 成功 [seikou]

successful [səkˈsɛsfʊl] *adj* 成功した [seikou shita]

successfully [səkˈsɛsfʊlɪ] *adv* うまく [umaku]

successive [səkˈsɛsɪv] *adj* 連続する [renzoku suru]

successor [səkˈsɛsə] *n* 後継者 [koukeisha]

such [sʌtʃ] *adj* そのような [sono youna] ▷ *adv* そんなに [sonna ni]

suck [sʌk] *v* 吸う [suu]

Sudan [suːˈdɑːn; -ˈdæn] *n* スーダン [suudan]

Sudanese [ˌsuːdəˈniːz] *adj* スーダンの [suudan no] ▷ *n* スーダン人 [suudanjin]

sudden ['sʌdən] *adj* 突然の [totsuzen no]

suddenly ['sʌdənlɪ] *adv* 突然に [totsuzen ni]

sue [sjuː; suː] *v* 訴える [uttaeru]

suede [sweɪd] *n* スエード [sueedo]

suffer ['sʌfə] *v* 被る [koumuru]

sufficient [səˈfɪʃənt] *adj* 十分な [juubun na]

suffocate ['sʌfəˌkeɪt] *v* 窒息する [chissoku suru]

sugar ['ʃʊgə] *n* 砂糖 [satou]; **icing sugar** *n* 粉砂糖 [konazatou]; **no sugar** 砂糖なしで [satou nashi de]

sugar-free ['ʃʊgəfriː] *adj* 砂糖を含まない [satou-o fukumanai]

uggest [səˈdʒɛst; səgˈdʒɛst] v 提案する [teian suru]

uggestion [səˈdʒɛstʃən] n 提案 [teian]

uicide [ˈsuːɪˌsaɪd; ˈsjuː-] n 自殺 [jisatsu]; **suicide bomber** n 自爆者 [jibakusha]

uit [suːt; sjuːt] n スーツ [suutsu] ▷ v 似合う [niau]; **bathing suit** n 水着 [mizugi]; **shell suit** n シェルスーツ [shierusuutsu]

uitable [ˈsuːtəbəl; ˈsjuːt-] adj 適切な [tekisetsu na]

uitcase [ˈsuːtˌkeɪs; ˈsjuːt-] n スーツケース [suutsukeesu]

uite [swiːt] n スイート [suiito]

ulk [sʌlk] v すねる [suneru]

ulky [ˈsʌlkɪ] adj すねた [suneta]

ultana [sʌlˈtɑːnə] n スルタナ [surutana]

um [sʌm] n 合計 [goukei]

ummarize [ˈsʌməˌraɪz] v 要約する [youyaku suru]

ummary [ˈsʌmərɪ] n 要約 [youyaku]

ummer [ˈsʌmə] n 夏 [natsu]; **summer holidays** npl 夏の休暇 [natsu no kyuuka]; **after summer** 夏の後に [natsu no ato ni]; **during the summer** 夏の間 [natsu no aida]; **in summer** 夏に [natsu ni]

ummertime [ˈsʌməˌtaɪm] n 夏季 [kaki]

ummit [ˈsʌmɪt] n 頂上 [choujou]

um up [sʌm ʌp] v 要約する [youyaku suru]

un [sʌn] n 太陽 [taiyou]

unbathe [ˈsʌnˌbeɪð] v 日光浴をする [nikkouyoku o suru]

unbed [ˈsʌnˌbɛd] n 日光浴用ベッド [nikkouyoku you beddo]

unblock [ˈsʌnˌblɒk] n 日焼け止め [hiyakedome]

unburn [ˈsʌnˌbɜːn] n 日焼け [hiyake]

unburnt [ˈsʌnˌbɜːnt] adj 日焼けした [hiyake shita]

uncream [ˈsʌnˌkriːm] n サンクリーム [sankuriimu]

unday [ˈsʌndɪ] n 日曜日 [nichiyoubi];
on Sunday 日曜日に [nichiyoubi ni]; **Is the museum open on Sundays?** その博物館は日曜日は開いていますか? [sono hakubutsukan wa nichiyoubi wa hiraite imasu ka?]

sunflower [ˈsʌnˌflaʊə] n ヒマワリ [himawari]

sunglasses [ˈsʌnˌglɑːsɪz] npl サングラス [sangurasu]

sunlight [ˈsʌnlaɪt] n 日光 [nikkou]

sunny [ˈsʌnɪ] adj 日当たりのよい [hiatari no yoi]

sunrise [ˈsʌnˌraɪz] n 日の出 [hi no de]

sunroof [ˈsʌnˌruːf] n サンルーフ [sanruufu]

sunscreen [ˈsʌnˌskriːn] n サンスクリーン [sansukuriin]

sunset [ˈsʌnˌsɛt] n 日没 [nichibotsu]

sunshine [ˈsʌnˌʃaɪn] n 日光 [nikkou]

sunstroke [ˈsʌnˌstrəʊk] n 日射病 [nisshabyou]

suntan [ˈsʌnˌtæn] n 小麦色の日焼け [komugi iro no hiyake]; **suntan lotion** n サンタンローション [santanrooshon]; **suntan oil** n サンタンオイル [santan oiru]

super [ˈsuːpə] adj すばらしい [subarashii]

superb [sʊˈpɜːb; sjuː-] adj すばらしい [subarashii]

superficial [ˌsuːpəˈfɪʃəl] adj 表面的な [hyoumenteki na]

superior [suːˈpɪərɪə] adj 優れた [sugureta] ▷ n 上役 [uwayaku]

supermarket [ˈsuːpəˌmɑːkɪt] n スーパーマーケット [suupaamaaketto]; **I need to find a supermarket** 私はスーパーマーケットをさがしています [watashi wa suupaamaaketto o sagashite imasu]

supernatural [ˌsuːpəˈnætʃrəl; -ˈnætʃərəl] adj 超自然の [choushizen no]

superstitious [ˌsuːpəˈstɪʃəs] adj 迷信的な [meishinteki na]

supervise [ˈsuːpəˌvaɪz] v 監督する [kantoku suru]

supervisor [ˈsuːpəˌvaɪzə] n 監督者 [kantokusha]

supper ['sʌpə] *n* 夕食 [yuushoku]

supplement ['sʌplɪmənt] *n* 補足 [hosoku]

supplier [sə'plaɪə] *n* 供給者 [kyoukyuusha]

supplies [sə'plaɪz] *npl* 食糧 [shokuryou]

supply [sə'plaɪ] *n* 供給 [kyoukyuu] ▷ *v* 供給する [kyoukyuu suru]; **supply teacher** *n* 臨時教員 [rinji kyouin]

support [sə'pɔːt] *n* 支え [sasae] ▷ *v* 支える [sasaeru] (支持)

supporter [sə'pɔːtə] *n* 支持者 [shijisha]

suppose [sə'pəʊz] *v* 想定する [soutei suru]

supposedly [sə'pəʊzɪdlɪ] *adv* おそらく [osoraku]

supposing [sə'pəʊzɪŋ] *conj* もし・・・と仮定するならば [moshi ... to katei surunaraba]

surcharge ['sɜːˌtʃɑːdʒ] *n* 追加料金 [tsuikaryoukin]

sure [ʃʊə; ʃɔː] *adj* 確信している [kakushin shite iru]

surely ['ʃʊəlɪ; 'ʃɔː-] *adv* 確かに [tashika ni]

surf [sɜːf] *n* 打ち寄せる波 [uchiyoseru nami] ▷ *v* サーフィンをする [saafin-o suru]

surface ['sɜːfɪs] *n* 表面 [hyoumen]

surfboard ['sɜːfˌbɔːd] *n* サーフボード [saafuboodo]

surfer ['sɜːfə] *n* サーファー [saafaa]

surfing ['sɜːfɪŋ] *n* サーフィン [saafin]

surge [sɜːdʒ] *n* 高まり [takamari]

surgeon ['sɜːdʒən] *n* 外科医 [gekai]

surgery ['sɜːdʒərɪ] *n (doctor's)* 診療所 [shinryoujo], *(operation)* 手術 [shujutsu]; **cosmetic surgery** *n* 美容外科 [biyou geka]; **plastic surgery** *n* 形成外科 [keisei geka]

surname ['sɜːˌneɪm] *n* 姓 [sei]

surplus ['sɜːpləs] *adj* 余分な [yobun na] ▷ *n* 余り [amari]

surprise [sə'praɪz] *n* 驚き [odoroki]

surprised [sə'praɪzd] *adj* 驚いた [odoroita]

surprising [sə'praɪzɪŋ] *adj* 意外な [igai na]

surprisingly [sə'praɪzɪŋlɪ] *adv* 驚くほど [odoroku hodo]

surrender [sə'rɛndə] *v* 降伏する [koufuku suru]

surround [sə'raʊnd] *v* 囲む [kakomu]

surroundings [sə'raʊndɪŋz] *npl* 環境 [kankyou]

survey ['sɜːveɪ] *n* 調査 [chousa]

surveyor [sɜː'veɪə] *n* 鑑定士 [kanteishi]

survival [sə'vaɪvəl] *n* 生存 [seizon]

survive [sə'vaɪv] *v* 生き残る [ikinokoru]

survivor [sə'vaɪvə] *n* 生存者 [seizonsha]

suspect *n* ['sʌspɛkt] 容疑者 [yougisha] ▷ *v* [sə'spɛkt] 疑いをかける [utagai-o kakeru]

suspend [sə'spɛnd] *v* つるす [tsurusu]

suspenders [sə'spɛndəz] *npl* 靴下留め [kutsushitadome]

suspense [sə'spɛns] *n* 不安 [fuan]

suspension [sə'spɛnʃən] *n* 一時停止 [ichiji teishi]; **suspension bridge** *n* 吊橋 [tsuribashi]

suspicious [sə'spɪʃəs] *adj* 疑わしい [utagawashii]

swallow ['swɒləʊ] *n* 飲むこと [nomu koto] ▷ *vi* 飲み込む [nomikomu] ▷ *vt* を飲み込む [-o nomikomu]

swamp [swɒmp] *n* 沼地 [numachi]

swan [swɒn] *n* 白鳥 [hakuchou]

swap [swɒp] *v* 交換する [koukan suru]

swat [swɒt] *v* ピシャリと打つ [pishari to utsu]

sway [sweɪ] *v* ゆさぶる [yusuburu]

Swaziland ['swɑːzɪˌlænd] *n* スワジランド [suwajirando]

swear [swɛə] *v* ののしる [nonoshiru]

swearword ['swɛəˌwɜːd] *n* ののしり [nonoshiri]

sweat [swɛt] *n* 汗 [ase] ▷ *v* 汗をかく [ase o kaku]

sweater ['swɛtə] *n* セーター [seetaa]; **polo-necked sweater** *n* とっくり襟のセーター [tokkuri eri no seetaa]

sweatshirt ['swɛtˌʃɜːt] *n* スエットシャツ [suettoshatsu]

sweaty ['swɛtɪ] adj 汗だらけの [ase darake no]

Swede [swi:d] n スウェーデンカブ [suueedenkabu]

Swede [swi:d] n スウェーデン人 [suueedenjin]

Sweden ['swi:dᵊn] n スウェーデン [suueeden]

Swedish ['swi:dɪʃ] adj スウェーデンの [suueeden no] ▷ n スウェーデン人 [suueedenjin]

sweep [swi:p] v 掃く [haku]

sweet [swi:t] adj (pleasing) 快い [kokoroyoi], (taste) 甘い [amai] ▷ n 甘いもの [amai mono]

sweetcorn ['swi:t,kɔ:n] n トウモロコシ [toumorokoshi]

sweetener ['swi:t²nə] n 甘味料 [kanmiryou]; **Do you have any sweetener?** 甘味料はありますか？ [kanmiryou wa arimasu ka?]

sweets [swi:tz] npl キャンデー [kyandee]

sweltering ['swɛltərɪŋ] adj うだるように暑い [udaru youni atsui]

swerve [swɜ:v] v 急にそれる [kyuu ni soreru]

swim [swɪm] v 泳ぐ [oyogu]

swimmer ['swɪmə] n 泳ぐ人 [oyogu hito]

swimming ['swɪmɪŋ] n 水泳 [suiei]; **swimming costume** n 水着 [mizugi]; **swimming pool** n スイミングプール [suimingupuuru]; **swimming trunks** npl スイミングトランクス [suimingutorankusu]

swimsuit ['swɪm,su:t; -,sju:t] n 水着 [mizugi]

swing [swɪŋ] n 揺れ [yure] ▷ v 揺れる [yureru]

Swiss [swɪs] adj スイスの [suisu no] ▷ n スイス人 [suisujin]

switch [swɪtʃ] n スイッチ [suitchi] ▷ v 変える [kaeru]

switchboard ['swɪtʃ,bɔ:d] n 電話交換台 [denwa koukandai]

switch off [swɪtʃ ɒf] v 切る [kiru]

switch on [swɪtʃ ɒn] v つける [tsukeru] (スイッチ); **How do you switch it on?** どうやってつけるのですか？ [dou-yatte tsukeru no desu ka?]

Switzerland ['swɪtsələnd] n スイス [suisu]

swollen ['swəʊlən] adj 腫れた [hareta]

sword [sɔ:d] n 剣 [tsurugi]

swordfish ['sɔ:d,fɪʃ] n メカジキ [mekajiki]

swot [swɒt] v ガリ勉する [gariben suru]

syllable ['sɪləbᵊl] n 音節 [onsetsu]

syllabus ['sɪləbəs] n 摘要 [tekiyou]

symbol ['sɪmbᵊl] n 象徴 [shouchou]

symmetrical [sɪ'mɛtrɪkᵊl] adj 左右対称の [sayuu taishou no]

sympathetic [,sɪmpə'θɛtɪk] adj 同情的な [doujouteki na]

sympathize ['sɪmpə,θaɪz] v 同情する [doujou suru]

sympathy ['sɪmpəθɪ] n 同情 [doujou]

symphony ['sɪmfənɪ] n 交響曲 [koukyoukyoku]

symptom ['sɪmptəm] n 症状 [shoujou]

synagogue ['sɪnə,gɒg] n シナゴーグ [shinagoogu]; **Where is there a synagogue?** どこかにシナゴーグはありますか？ [doko-ka ni shinagoogu wa arimasu ka?]

syndrome ['sɪndrəʊm] n **Down's syndrome** n ダウン症候群 [daun shoukougun]

Syria ['sɪrɪə] n シリア [shiria]

Syrian ['sɪrɪən] adj シリアの [shiria no] ▷ n シリア人 [shiriajin]

syringe ['sɪrɪndʒ; sɪ'rɪndʒ] n 注射器 [chuushaki]

syrup ['sɪrəp] n シロップ [shiroppu]

system ['sɪstəm] n 組織的な方法 [soshikiteki na houhou]; **immune system** n 免疫系 [men'ekikei]; **solar system** n 太陽系 [taiyoukei]; **systems analyst** n システムアナリスト [shisutemu anarisuto]

systematic [,sɪstɪ'mætɪk] adj 体系的な [taikeiteki na]

た

table ['teɪbᵊl] *n* (*chart*) 表 [omote], (*furniture*) テーブル [teeburu]; **bedside table** *n* ベッドサイドテーブル [beddosaido teeburu]; **coffee table** *n* コーヒーテーブル [koohii teeburu]; **dressing table** *n* 鏡台 [kyoudai]; **table tennis** *n* 卓球 [takkyuu]; **table wine** *n* テーブルワイン [teeburuwain]; **A table for four people, please** 四人用のテーブルをお願いします [yonin-you no teeburu o o-negai shimasu]; **I'd like to book a table for three people for tonight** 今晩三人用のテーブルを予約したいのですが [konban sannin-you no teeburu o yoyaku shitai no desu ga]; **I'd like to book a table for two people for tomorrow night** 明日の晩二人用のテーブルを予約したいのですが [asu no ban futari-you no teeburu o yoyaku shitai no desu ga]; **The table is booked for nine o'clock this evening** 今晩九時にテーブルを予約しました [konban ku-ji ni teeburu o yoyaku shimashita]

tablecloth ['teɪbᵊl,klɒθ] *n* テーブルクロス [teeburukurosu]

tablespoon ['teɪbᵊl,spu:n] *n* テーブルスプーン [teeburusupuun]

tablet ['tæblɪt] *n* 錠剤 [jouzai], (*computer*) タブレット [taburetto]

taboo [tə'bu:] *adj* タブーとなっている [tabuu to natte iru] ▷ *n* タブー [tabuu]

tackle ['tækᵊl; 'teɪkᵊl] *n* タックル [takkuru] ▷ *v* 取り組む [torikumu]; **fishing tackle** *n* 釣具 [tsurigu]

tact [tækt] *n* 機転 [kiten]

tactful ['tæktfʊl] *adj* 機転のきく [kiten no kiku]

tactics ['tæktɪks] *npl* 戦術 [senjutsu]

tactless ['teɪktlɪs] *adj* 機転のきかない [kiten no kikanai]

tadpole ['tæd,pəʊl] *n* オタマジャクシ [otamajakushi]

tag [tæg] *n* 付け札 [tsuke satsu]

Tahiti [tə'hi:tɪ] *n* タヒチ [tahichi]

tail [teɪl] *n* 尾 [o]

tailor ['teɪlə] *n* テーラー [teeraa]

Taiwan ['taɪ'wɑ:n] *n* 台湾 [taiwan]

Taiwanese [,taɪwɑ:'ni:z] *adj* 台湾の [taiwan no] ▷ *n* 台湾人 [taiwanjin]

Tajikistan [tɑ:,dʒɪkɪ'stɑ:n; -stæn] *n* タジキスタン [tajikisutan]

take [teɪk] *v* 手に取る [te ni toru], (*time*) 時間がかかる [jikan gakakaru]

take after [teɪk 'ɑ:ftə] *v* ···に似る [...ni niru]

take apart [teɪk ə'pɑ:t] *v* 分解する [bunkai suru]

take away [teɪk ə'weɪ] *v* 運び去る [hakobi saru]

takeaway ['teɪkə,weɪ] *n* テークアウト [teekuauto]

take back [teɪk bæk] *v* 取り消す [torikesu]

taken ['teɪkən] *adj* **Is this seat taken?** この席には誰か座っていますか? [kono seki ni wa dare ka suwatte imasu ka?]

take off [teɪk ɒf] *v* 脱ぐ [nugu]

takeoff ['teɪk,ɒf] *n* 離陸 [ririku]

take over [teɪk 'əʊvə] *v* 引き継ぐ [hikitsugu]

takeover ['teɪk,əʊvə] *n* 企業買収 [kigyou baishuu]

takings ['teɪkɪŋz] npl 収入 [shuunyuu]

tale [teɪl] n 話 [hanashi]

talent ['tælənt] n 才能 [sainou]

talented ['tæləntɪd] adj 才能のある [sainou no aru]

talk [tɔːk] n 話 [hanashi] ▷ v 話す [hanasu]; **talk to** v ･･･に話しかける [...ni hanashikakeru]

talkative ['tɔːkətɪv] adj 話好きな [hanashi zuki na]

tall [tɔːl] adj 高い [takai] (高低)

tame [teɪm] adj 飼いならされた [kainarasareta]

tampon ['tæmpɒn] n タンポン [tanpon]

tan [tæn] n 日焼け [hiyake]

tandem ['tændəm] n タンデム自転車 [tandemu jitensha]

tangerine [ˌtændʒəˈriːn] n タンジェリン [tanjierin]

tank [tæŋk] n (vehicle) 戦車 [sensha], (container) タンク [tanku]; **petrol tank** n ガソリンタンク [gasorintanku]; **septic tank** n 浄化槽 [joukasou]; **The petrol tank is leaking** ガソリンタンクが漏れています [gasorin-tanku ga morete imasu]

tanker ['tæŋkə] n タンカー [tankaa]

tanned [tænd] adj 日焼け色の [hiyake iro no]

tantrum ['tæntrəm] n かんしゃく [kanshaku]

Tanzania [ˌtænzəˈnɪə] n タンザニア [tanzania]

Tanzanian [ˌtænzəˈnɪən] adj タンザニアの [tanzania no] ▷ n (person) タンザニア人 [tanzaniajin]

tap [tæp] n 軽くたたくこと [karuku tataku koto]

tap-dancing ['tæpˌdɑːnsɪŋ] n タップダンス [tappudansu]

tape [teɪp] n テープ [teepu] ▷ v テープに記録する [teepu ni kiroku suru]; **tape measure** n 巻尺 [makijaku]; **tape recorder** n テープレコーダー [teepurekoodaa]; **Can I have a tape for this video camera, please?** このビデオカメラ用のテープをいただけますか? [kono bideo-kamera-you no teepu o itadakemasu ka?]

target ['tɑːgɪt] n 標的 [hyouteki]

tariff ['tærɪf] n 関税率 [kanzeiritsu]

tarmac ['tɑːmæk] n タールマカダム [taarumakadamu]

tarpaulin [tɑːˈpɔːlɪn] n タール塗り防水布 [taaru nuri bousuifu]

tarragon ['tærəgən] n タラゴン [taragon]

tart [tɑːt] n タルト [taruto]

tartan ['tɑːtᵊn] adj タータンの [taatan no]

task [tɑːsk] n 任務 [ninmu]

Tasmania [tæzˈmeɪnɪə] n タスマニア [tasumania]

taste [teɪst] n 味 [aji] ▷ v 味をみる [aji-o miru]; **It doesn't taste very nice** 味があまりよくありません [aji ga amari yoku arimasen]

tasteful ['teɪstfʊl] adj 趣味のよい [shumi no yoi]

tasteless ['teɪstlɪs] adj 味のない [aji no nai]

tasty ['teɪstɪ] adj 味のよい [aji no yoi]

tattoo [tæˈtuː] n 入れ墨 [irezumi]

Taurus ['tɔːrəs] n 牡牛座 [oushiza]

tax [tæks] n 税金 [zeikin]; **income tax** n 所得税 [shotokuzei]; **road tax** n 自動車の道路利用税 [jidousha no douro riyou zei]; **tax payer** n 納税者 [nouzeisha]; **tax return** n 所得申告 [shotoku shinkoku]

taxi ['tæksɪ] n タクシー [takushii]; **taxi driver** n タクシー運転手 [takushii untenshu]; **taxi rank** n タクシー乗り場 [takushii noriba]; **How much is the taxi fare into town?** 街までのタクシー料金はいくらですか? [machi made no takushii-ryoukin wa ikura desu ka?]; **I need a taxi** 私はタクシーが必要です [watashi wa takushii ga hitsuyou desu]; **Please order me a taxi for 8 o'clock** 八時にタクシーを呼んでください [hachi-ji ni takushii o yonde kudasai]; **Where is the taxi stand?** タクシー乗り場はどこです

か? [takushii-noriba wa doko desu ka?]

TB [ti: bi:] n 結核 [kekkaku]

tea [ti:] n お茶 [o-cha]; **herbal tea** n ハーブティー [haabuteii]; **tea bag** n ティーバッグ [tiibaggu]; **tea towel** n 布巾 [fukin]

teach [ti:tʃ] v 教える [oshieru]

teacher ['ti:tʃə] n 教師 [kyoushi]; **supply teacher** n 臨時教員 [rinji kyouin]; **I'm a teacher** 私は教師です [watashi wa kyoushi desu]

teaching ['ti:tʃɪŋ] n 教えること [oshieru koto]

teacup ['ti:ˌkʌp] n ティーカップ [tiikappu]

team [ti:m] n チーム [chiimu]

teapot ['ti:ˌpɒt] n ティーポット [tiipotto]

tear[1] [tɪə] n (from eye) 涙 [namida]

tear[2] [tɛə] n (split) 破れ目 [yabureme] ▷ v 破る [yaburu]; **tear up** v ずたずたに引き裂く [zutazuta ni hikisaku]

tear gas ['tɪəˌgæs] n 催涙ガス [sairuigasu]

tease [ti:z] v からかう [karakau]

teaspoon ['ti:ˌspu:n] n ティースプーン [tiisupuun]

teatime ['ti:ˌtaɪm] n ティータイム [tiitaimu]

technical ['tɛknɪkəl] adj 専門的な [senmonteki na]

technician [tɛk'nɪʃən] n 専門技術者 [senmon gijutsusha]

technique [tɛk'ni:k] n 専門技術 [senmon gijutsu]

techno music ['tɛknəʊ] n テクノポップ [tekunopoppu]

technological [tɛk'nɒlədʒɪkəl] adj 技術的な [gijutsuteki na]

technology [tɛk'nɒlədʒɪ] n 技術 [gijutsu]

tee [ti:] n ティー [tii] (ゴルフ)

teenager ['ti:ˌneɪdʒə] n ティーンエージャー [tiineejaa]

teens [ti:nz] npl 十代 [juudai]

tee-shirt ['ti:ˌʃɜːt] n Tシャツ [tiishatsu]

teethe [ti:ð] v 歯が生える [ha ga haeru]

teetotal [ti:'təʊtəl] adj 絶対禁酒の [zettai kinshu no]

telecommunications [ˌtɛlɪkəˌmju:nɪ'keɪʃənz] npl 電気通信 [denkitsuushin]

telegram ['tɛlɪˌgræm] n 電報 [denpou]; **Can I send a telegram from here?** ここから電報を送れますか? [koko kara denpou o okuremasu ka?]

telephone ['tɛlɪˌfəʊn] n 電話 [denwa]; **telephone directory** n 電話帳 [denwachou]; **How much is it to telephone...?** ・・・に電話するのはいくらですか? [...ni denwa suru no wa ikura desu ka?]; **I need to make an urgent telephone call** 私は緊急の電話をかけなければなりません [watashi wa kinkyuu no denwa o kakenakereba narimasen]; **What's the telephone number?** 電話番号は何番ですか? [denwa-bangou wa nan-ban desu ka?]

telesales ['tɛlɪˌseɪlz] npl 電話セールス [denwa seerusu]

telescope ['tɛlɪˌskəʊp] n 望遠鏡 [bouenkyou]

television ['tɛlɪˌvɪʒən] n テレビ [terebi]; **cable television** n ケーブルテレビ [keeburu terebi]; **colour television** n カラーテレビ [karaaterebi]; **digital television** n デジタルテレビ [dejitaru terebi]; **Where is the television?** テレビはどこですか? [terebi wa doko desu ka?]

tell [tɛl] v 告げる [tsugeru]

teller ['tɛlə] n 話し手 [hanashite]

tell off [tɛl ɒf] v しかる [shikaru]

telly ['tɛlɪ] n テレビ [terebi]

temp [tɛmp] n 臨時職員 [rinjishokuin]

temper ['tɛmpə] n かんしゃく [kanshaku]

temperature ['tɛmprɪtʃə] n 温度 [ondo]

temple ['tɛmpəl] n 寺院 [jiin]; **Is the temple open to the public?** その寺院は一般公開されていますか? [sono jiin wa ippan-koukai sarete imasu ka?]; **When is the temple open?** その寺院はいつ開きますか? [sono jiin wa itsu hirakimasu ka?]

temporary ['tɛmpərəri; 'tɛmprəri] *adj* 一時の [ichiji no]

tempt [tɛmpt] *v* 誘惑する [yuuwaku suru]

temptation [tɛmp'teiʃən] *n* 誘惑 [yuuwaku]

tempting ['tɛmptiŋ] *adj* 誘惑する [yuuwaku suru]

ten [tɛn] *number* 十 [juu]; **It's ten o'clock** 十時です [juu-ji desu]

tenant ['tɛnənt] *n* 賃借人 [chinshakunin]

tend [tɛnd] *v* 傾向がある [keikou ga aru]

tendency ['tɛndənsı] *n* 傾向 [keikou]

tender ['tɛndə] *adj* 柔らかい [yawarakai]

tendon ['tɛndən] *n* 腱 [kou]

tennis ['tɛnis] *n* テニス [tenisu]; **table tennis** *n* 卓球 [takkyuu]; **tennis player** *n* テニス選手 [tenisusenshu]; **tennis racket** *n* テニスラケット [tenisuraketto]; **How much is it to hire a tennis court?** テニスコートを借りるのはいくらですか? [tenisu-kooto o kariru no wa ikura desu ka?]; **Where can I play tennis?** どこでテニスができますか? [doko de tenisu ga dekimasu ka?]

tenor ['tɛnə] *n* テノール [tenooru]

tense [tɛns] *adj* 緊張した [kinchou shita] ▷ *n* 時制 [jisei]

tension ['tɛnʃən] *n* 緊張 [kinchou]

tent [tɛnt] *n* テント [tento]; **tent peg** *n* テントペグ [tentopegu]; **tent pole** *n* テントポール [tentopooru]; **Can we pitch our tent here?** ここにテントを張ってもいいですか? [koko ni tento o hatte mo ii desu ka?]; **How much is it per night for a tent?** テント一つにつき一晩でいくらですか? [tento hitotsu ni tsuki hitoban de ikura desu ka?]; **How much is it per week for a tent?** テント一つにつき1週間でいくらですか? [tento hitotsu ni tsuki isshuukan de ikura desu ka?]; **We'd like a site for a tent** テント用のサイトが欲しいのですが [tento-you no saito ga hoshii no desu ga]

tenth [tɛnθ] *adj* 十番目の [juu banme no] ▷ *n* 十番目 [juu banme]

term [tɜːm] *n* (*description*) 用語 [yougo], (*division of year*) 学期 [gakki]

terminal ['tɜːmɪnəl] *adj* 末期の [makki no] (*終わりの時期*) ▷ *n* ターミナル [taaminaru]

terminally ['tɜːmɪnəlɪ] *adv* 末期的に [makkiteki ni]

terrace ['tɛrəs] *n* テラスハウス [terasuhausu]

terraced ['tɛrəst] *adj* 段地作りの [danchizukuri no]

terrible ['tɛrəbəl] *adj* ひどい [hidoi]

terribly ['tɛrəblı] *adv* ひどく [hidoku]

terrier ['tɛrɪə] *n* テリア [teria]

terrific [təˈrɪfɪk] *adj* ものすごい [monosugoi]

terrified ['tɛrɪˌfaɪd] *adj* 怖がった [kowagatta]

terrify ['tɛrɪˌfaɪ] *v* 怖がらせる [kowagaraseru]

territory ['tɛrɪtərɪ; -trɪ] *n* 地域 [chiiki]

terrorism ['tɛrəˌrɪzəm] *n* テロリズム [terorizumu]

terrorist ['tɛrərɪst] *n* テロリスト [terorisuto]; **terrorist attack** *n* テロリストによる攻撃 [terorisuto niyoru kougeki]

test [tɛst] *n* 試験 [shiken] ▷ *v* 試験する [shiken suru]; **driving test** *n* 運転免許試験 [untenmenkyoshiken]; **smear test** *n* 塗沫検査 [tomatsu kensa]; **test tube** *n* 試験管 [shikenkan]

testicle ['tɛstɪkəl] *n* 精巣 [seisou]

tetanus ['tɛtənəs] *n* 破傷風 [hashoufuu]; **I need a tetanus shot** 私は破傷風予防の注射が必要です [watashi wa hashoufuu yobou no chuusha ga hitsuyou desu]

text [tɛkst] *n* 本文 [honbun] ▷ *v* テキストメッセージを送る [tekisuto messeeji-o okuru]; **text message** *n* テキストメッセージ [tekisutomesseeji]

textbook ['tɛkstˌbʊk] *n* 教科書 [kyoukasho]

textile ['tɛkstaɪl] *n* 織物 [orimono]

Thai [taɪ] *adj* タイの [tai no] ▷ *n*

(language) タイ語 [taigo], (person) タイ人 [taijin]

Thailand [ˈtaɪˌlænd] n タイ [tai] (国)

than [ðæn; ðən] conj …よりも [...yorimo]

thank [θæŋk] v 感謝する [kansha suru]

thanks [θæŋks] excl ありがとう! [arigatou]

that [ðæt; ðət] adj あの [ano] ▷ conj …ということ [...to iu koto] ▷ pron あの [ano], あれ [are]; **How much does that cost?** あれはいくらですか? [are wa ikura desu ka?]

thatched [θætʃt] adj 萱葺き屋根の [kayabuki yane no]

thaw [θɔ:] v **It's thawing** 雪解けしています [yukidoke shite imasu]

the [ðə] art その [sono]

theatre [ˈθɪətə] n 劇場 [gekijou]; **operating theatre** n 手術室 [shujutsushitsu]; **What's on at the theatre?** その劇場で何が上演されていますか? [sono gekijou de nani ga jouen sarete imasu ka?]

theft [θɛft] n 盗み [nusumi]; **identity theft** n 個人情報泥棒 [kojin jouhou dorobou]

their [ðɛə] pron 彼らの [karera no]

theirs [ðɛəz] pron 彼らのもの [karera no mono]

them [ðɛm; ðəm] pron 彼らを [karera wo]

theme [θi:m] n テーマ [teema]; **theme park** n テーマパーク [teemapaaku]

themselves [ðəmˈsɛlvz] pron 彼ら自身 [karera jishin]

then [ðɛn] adv その時 [sono toki] ▷ conj それなら [sorenara]

theology [θɪˈɒlədʒɪ] n 神学 [shingaku]

theory [ˈθɪərɪ] n 理論 [riron]

therapy [ˈθɛrəpɪ] n 療法 [ryouhou]

there [ðɛə] adv そこに [soko ni]

therefore [ˈðɛəˌfɔ:] adv 従って [shitagatte]

thermometer [θəˈmɒmɪtə] n 温度計 [ondokei]

Thermos® [ˈθɜ:məs] n サーモス® [saamosu]

thermostat [ˈθɜ:məˌstæt] n サーモスタット [saamosutatto]

these [ði:z] adj これらの [korera no] ▷ pron これら [korera]

they [ðeɪ] pron 彼らは [karera wa]

thick [θɪk] adj 厚い [atsui]

thickness [ˈθɪknɪs] n 厚さ [atsusa]

thief [θi:f] n 泥棒 [dorobou]

thigh [θaɪ] n 腿 [momo]

thin [θɪn] adj 薄い [usui] (厚み)

thing [θɪŋ] n 物 [mono]

think [θɪŋk] v 考える [kangaeru]

third [θɜ:d] adj 三番目の [san banme no] ▷ n 三番目 [san banme]; **third-party insurance** n 第三者賠償責任保険 [daisansha baishousekinin hoken]; **Third World** n 第三世界 [dai san sekai]

thirdly [ˈθɜ:dlɪ] adv 第三に [dai san ni]

thirst [θɜ:st] n のどの渇き [nodo no kawaki]

thirsty [ˈθɜ:stɪ] adj のどが渇いた [nodo ga kawaita]

thirteen [ˈθɜ:ˈti:n] number 十三 [juusan]

thirteenth [ˈθɜ:ˈti:nθ] adj 十三番目の [juusan banme no]

thirty [ˈθɜ:tɪ] number 三十 [sanjuu]

this [ðɪs] adj この [kono] ▷ pron これ [kore]; **I'll have this** 私はこれをいただきます [watashi wa kore o itadakimasu]; **This is your room** これがあなたの部屋です [kore ga anata no heya desu]; **What is in this?** これには何が入っていますか? [kore ni wa nani ga haitte imasu ka?]

thistle [ˈθɪsᵊl] n アザミ [azami]

thorn [θɔ:n] n とげ [toge]

thorough [ˈθʌrə] adj 徹底的な [tetteiteki na]

thoroughly [ˈθʌrəlɪ] adv 徹底的に [tetteiteki ni]

those [ðəʊz] adj それらの [sorera no] ▷ pron それら [sorera]

though [ðəʊ] adv でも [demo] ▷ conj …にもかかわらず [...nimokakawarazu]

thought [θɔ:t] n 思考 [shikou]

thoughtful ['θɔːtfʊl] *adj* 思慮深い [shiryobukai]

thoughtless ['θɔːtlɪs] *adj* 無思慮な [mushiryo na]

thousand ['θaʊzənd] *number* 千 [sen]

thousandth ['θaʊzənθ] *adj* 千番目の [sen banme no] ▷ *n* 千番目 [sen banme]

thread [θrɛd] *n* 糸 [ito]

threat [θrɛt] *n* 脅し [odoshi]

threaten ['θrɛtᵊn] *v* 脅す [odosu]

threatening ['θrɛtᵊnɪŋ] *adj* 脅すような [odosu you na]

three [θriː] *number* 三 [san]; **It's three o'clock** 三時です [san-ji desu]

three-dimensional [ˌθriːdɪˈmɛnʃənᵊl] *adj* 立体的な [rittaiteki na]

thrifty ['θrɪftɪ] *adj* 倹約な [kenyaku na]

thrill [θrɪl] *n* ぞくぞくする感じ [zokuzoku suru kanji]

thrilled [θrɪld] *adj* ぞくぞくした [zokuzoku shita]

thriller ['θrɪlə] *n* スリラー [suriraa]

thrilling ['θrɪlɪŋ] *adj* ぞくぞくさせる [zokuzoku saseru]

throat [θrəʊt] *n* のど [nodo]

throb [θrɒb] *v* 動悸を打つ [douki-o utsu]

throne [θrəʊn] *n* 王座 [ouza]

through [θruː] *prep* ・・・を通って [...o tootte]

throughout [θruːˈaʊt] *prep* ・・・の隅から隅まで [...no sumi kara sumi made]

throw [θrəʊ] *v* 投げる [nageru]

throw away [θrəʊ əˈweɪ] *v* 捨てる [suteru]

throw out [θrəʊ aʊt] *v* 拒否する [kyohi suru]

throw up [θrəʊ ʌp] *v* 吐く [haku]

thrush [θrʌʃ] *n* ツグミ [tsugumi]

thug [θʌɡ] *n* 凶悪犯 [kyouakuhan]

thumb [θʌm] *n* 親指 [oyayubi]

thumb tack ['θʌmˌtæk] *n* 画鋲 [gabyou]

thump [θʌmp] *v* ゴツンと打つ [gotsun to utsu]

thunder ['θʌndə] *n* 雷鳴 [raimei]

thunderstorm ['θʌndəˌstɔːm] *n* 雷雨 [raiu]

thundery ['θʌndərɪ] *adj* 雷鳴を伴った [raimei-o tomonatta]

Thursday ['θɜːzdɪ] *n* 木曜日 [mokuyoubi]; **on Thursday** 木曜日に [mokuyoubi ni]

thyme [taɪm] *n* タイム [taimu]

Tibet [tɪˈbɛt] *n* チベット [chibetto]

Tibetan [tɪˈbɛtᵊn] *adj* チベットの [chibetto no] ▷ *n* (*language*) チベット語 [chibettogo], (*person*) チベット人 [chibettojin]

tick [tɪk] *n* 照合の印 [shougou no in] ▷ *v* 照合の印をつける [shougou no in-o tsukeru]

ticket ['tɪkɪt] *n* チケット [chiketto]; **bus ticket** *n* バスの切符 [basu no kippu]; **one-way ticket** *n* 片道切符 [katamichi kippu]; **parking ticket** *n* 駐車違反切符 [chuushaihan no kippu]; **return ticket** *n* 往復切符 [oufuku kippu]; **season ticket** *n* 定期券 [teikiken]; **single ticket** *n* 片道切符 [katamichi kippu]; **stand-by ticket** *n* キャンセル待ちの切符 [kyanserumachi no kippu]; **ticket barrier** *n* 改札口 [kaisatsuguchi]; **ticket collector** *n* 改札係 [kaisatsugakari]; **ticket inspector** *n* 検札係 [kensatsugakari]; **ticket machine** *n* 券売機 [kenbaiki]; **ticket office** *n* 切符売場 [kippu uriba]; **a child's ticket** 子供のチケット [kodomo no chiketto]; **Can I buy the tickets here?** ここでそのチケットを買えますか? [koko de sono chiketto o kaemasu ka?]; **Can you book the tickets for us?** 私たちのためにそのチケットを予約してもらえますか? [watashi-tachi no tame ni sono chiketto o yoyaku shite moraemasu ka?]; **Do I need to buy a car-parking ticket?** 駐車チケットを買わなければなりませんか? [chuusha-chiketto o kawanakereba narimasen ka?]; **I've lost my ticket** 私はチケットをなくしました [watashi wa chiketto o nakushimashita]; **Two tickets for tonight, please** 今晩のチケットを2枚お願いします [konban no chiketto o nimai o-negai shimasu]; **Where can I buy**

tickets for the concert? どこでそのコンサートのチケットを買えますか? [doko de sono konsaato no chiketto o kaemasu ka?]

tickle ['tɪkᵊl] v くすぐる [kusuguru]

ticklish ['tɪklɪʃ] adj くすぐったがる [kusuguttagaru]

tick off [tɪk ɒf] v チェックする [chekku suru]

tide [taɪd] n 潮 [shio]; When is high tide? 満ち潮はいつですか? [michi-shio wa itsu desu ka?]

tidy ['taɪdɪ] adj きちんとした [kichin to shita] ▷ v 片付ける [katazukeru]

tidy up ['taɪdɪ ʌp] v 整頓する [seiton suru]

tie [taɪ] n ネクタイ [nekutai] ▷ v 縛る [shibaru]; bow tie n 蝶ネクタイ [chounekutai]

tie up [taɪ ʌp] v 固く縛る [kataku shibaru]

tiger ['taɪgə] n トラ [tora]

tight [taɪt] adj ぴんと張った [pin to hatta]

tighten ['taɪtᵊn] v 締める [shimeru]

tights [taɪts] npl タイツ [taitsu]

tile [taɪl] n タイル [tairu]

tiled [taɪld] adj タイルを張った [tairu-o hatta]

till [tɪl] conj ・・・する時まで [...suru toki made] ▷ prep ・・・まで [made] ▷ n レジ [reji]

timber ['tɪmbə] n 材木 [zaimoku]

time [taɪm] n 時間 [jikan]; closing time n 閉店時刻 [heiten jikoku]; dinner time n ディナーの時刻 [dinaa no jikoku]; on time adj 遅れずに [okurezu ni]; spare time n 余暇 [yoka]; time off n 欠勤時間 [kekkin jikan]; time zone n 標準時間帯 [hyoujun jikantai]; Is it time to go? もう行く時間ですか? [mou iku jikan desu ka?]; What's the minimum amount of time? 最低利用時間はどれだけですか? [saitei-riyou-jikan wa dore dake desu ka?]

time bomb ['taɪmˌbɒm] n 時限爆弾 [jigenbakudan]

timer ['taɪmə] n タイマー [taimaa]

timeshare ['taɪmˌʃɛə] n 休暇施設の共同所有権 [kyuuka shisetsu no kyoudou shoyuuken]

timetable ['taɪmˌteɪbᵊl] n 時刻表 [jikokuhyou]; Can I have a timetable, please? 時刻表をいただけますか? [jikokuhyou o itadakemasu ka?]

tin [tɪn] n 錫 [suzu]; tin-opener n 缶切り [kankiri]

tinfoil ['tɪnˌfɔɪl] n アルミ箔 [arumihaku]

tinned [tɪnd] adj 缶詰にした [kanzume ni shita]

tinsel ['tɪnsəl] n 装飾用のぴかぴか光る金属片や糸 [soushoku you no pikapika hikaru kinzokuhen ya ito]

tinted ['tɪntɪd] adj 薄く色を着けた [usuku iro-o tsuketa]

tiny ['taɪnɪ] adj 小さな [chiisa na]

tip [tɪp] n (end of object) 先端 [sentan], (reward) チップ [chippu] (心づけ), (suggestion) 助言 [jogen] ▷ v (incline) 傾ける [katamukeru], (reward) チップをやる [chippu-o yaru] (心づけ); How much should I give as a tip? チップはいくら渡せばよいですか? [chippu wa ikura wataseba yoi desu ka?]; Is it usual to give a tip? チップを渡すのは一般的なことですか? [chippu o watasu no wa ippan-teki na koto desu ka?]

tipsy ['tɪpsɪ] adj ほろ酔いの [horo yoi no]

tiptoe ['tɪpˌtəʊ] n つまさき [tsumasaki]

tired ['taɪəd] adj 疲れた [tsukareta]

tiring ['taɪərɪŋ] adj 疲れる [tsukareru]

tissue ['tɪsjuː; 'tɪʃuː] n (anatomy, paper) 組織 [soshiki]

title ['taɪtᵊl] n 題名 [daimei]

to [tuː; tʊ; tə] prep ・・・に [...ni]

toad [təʊd] n ヒキガエル [hikigaeru]

toadstool ['təʊdˌstuːl] n 毒キノコ [doku kinoko]

toast [təʊst] n (bread) トースト [toosuto], (tribute) 乾杯 [kanpai]

toaster ['təʊstə] n トースター [toosutaa]

tobacco [təˈbækəʊ] n タバコ [tabako]

tobacconist's [təˈbækənɪsts] n タバコ屋 [tabakoya]

tobogganing [təˈbɒgənɪŋ] n トボガン [tobogan]

today [təˈdeɪ] adv 今日 [kyou]; What

day is it today? 今日は何曜日ですか？ [kyou wa nan-youbi desu ka?]; **What is today's date?** 今日は何日ですか？ [kyou wa nan-nichi desu ka?]

toddler ['tɒdlə] n よちよち歩きの幼児 [yochiyochi aruki no youji]

toe [təʊ] n 足の指 [ashi no yubi]

toffee ['tɒfɪ] n トフィー [tofii]

together [tə'gɛðə] adv 一緒に [issho ni]; **All together, please** 全部一緒にお勘定をお願いします [zenbu issho ni o-kanjou o o-negai shimasu]

Togo ['təʊgəʊ] n トーゴ [toogo]

toilet ['tɔɪlɪt] n トイレ [toire]; **toilet bag** n 洗面用具バッグ [senmen yougu baggu]; **toilet paper** n トイレットペーパー [toirettopeepaa]; **toilet roll** n トイレットペーパーロール [toirettopeepaarooru]; **Are there any accessible toilets?** 身体障害者用のトイレはありますか？ [shintai-shougaisha-you no toire wa arimasu ka?]; **Can I use the toilet?** トイレをお借りできますか？ [toire o o-kari dekimasu ka?]; **Is there a toilet on board?** 車内にトイレはありますか？ [shanai ni toire wa arimasu ka?]; **The toilet won't flush** トイレが流れません [toire ga nagaremasen]; **There is no toilet paper** トイレットペーパーがありません [toiretto-peepaa ga arimasen]; **Where are the toilets?** トイレはどこですか？ [toire wa doko desu ka?]

toiletries ['tɔɪltriːs] npl 洗面化粧品 [senmen keshou youhin]

token ['təʊkən] n しるし [shirushi] (現れ)

tolerant ['tɒlərənt] adj 寛容な [kan'you na]

toll [təʊl] n 鐘の音 [kane no oto]

tomato, tomatoes [tə'mɑːtəʊ, tə'mɑːtəʊz] n トマト [tomato]; **tomato sauce** n トマトソース [tomatosoosu]

tomb [tuːm] n 墓 [haka]

tomboy ['tɒmˌbɔɪ] n おてんば娘 [otemba musume]

tomorrow [tə'mɒrəʊ] adv 明日 [asu]; **Is it open tomorrow?** それは明日開きますか？ [sore wa asu hirakimasu ka?]; **tomorrow morning** 明日の朝 [asu no asa]

ton [tʌn] n トン [ton]

tone [təʊn] n **dialling tone** n 発信音 [hasshin-on]; **engaged tone** n 話し中の信号音 [hanashichuu no shingouon]

Tonga ['tɒŋgə] n トンガ [tonga]

tongue [tʌŋ] n 舌 [shita]; **mother tongue** n 母国語 [bokokugo]

tonic ['tɒnɪk] n 強壮剤 [kyousouzai]

tonight [tə'naɪt] adv 今夜 [konya]

tonsillitis [ˌtɒnsɪ'laɪtɪs] n 扁桃腺炎 [hentousen'en]

tonsils ['tɒnsəlz] npl 扁桃 [hentou]

too [tuː] adv また [mata] (おなじく), とても [totemo]

tool [tuːl] n 道具 [dougu]

tooth, teeth ['tuːθ, tiːθ] n 歯 [ha]; **wisdom tooth** n 親知らず [oyashirazu]; **I've broken a tooth** 私は歯を折りました [watashi wa ha o orimashita]; **This tooth hurts** この歯が痛みます [kono ha ga itamimasu]

toothache ['tuːθˌeɪk] n 歯痛 [shitsuu]

toothbrush ['tuːθˌbrʌʃ] n 歯ブラシ [haburashi]

toothpaste ['tuːθˌpeɪst] n 練り歯ミガキ [neri hamigaki]

toothpick ['tuːθˌpɪk] n つま楊枝 [tsuma youji]

top [tɒp] adj 一番上の [ichiban ue no] ▷ n 上 [ue]

topic ['tɒpɪk] n 話題 [wadai]

topical ['tɒpɪkəl] adj 時事的な [jijiteki na]

top-secret ['tɒp'siːkrɪt] adj 最高機密の [saikou kimitsu no]

top up [tɒp ʌp] v **Can you top up the windscreen washers?** フロントガラスのウォッシャー液を補充してもらえますか？ [furonto-garasu no wosshaa-eki o hojuu shite moraemasu ka?]; **Where can I buy a top-up card?** どこでトップアップカードを買えますか？ [doko de toppu-appu-kaado o kaemasu ka?]

torch [tɔːtʃ] n 懐中電灯 [kaichuudentou]

tornado [tɔː'neɪdəʊ] n 竜巻 [tatsumaki]

tortoise ['tɔːtəs] n カメ [kame] (動物)

torture ['tɔːtʃə] n 拷問 [goumon] ▷ v 拷問にかける [goumon ni kakeru]

toss [tɒs] v 軽く投げる [karuku nageru]

total ['təʊtˀl] adj 完全な [kanzen na] ▷ n 合計 [goukei]

totally ['təʊtˀlɪ] adv 完全に [kanzen ni]

touch [tʌtʃ] v 触れる [fureru]

touchdown ['tʌtʃˌdaʊn] n 着地 [chakuchi]

touched [tʌtʃt] adj 感動した [kandou shita]

touching ['tʌtʃɪŋ] adj 感動的な [kandouteki na]

touchline ['tʌtʃˌlaɪn] n タッチライン [tatchirain]

touch pad ['tʌtʃˌpæd] n タッチパッド [tatchipaddo]

touchy ['tʌtʃɪ] adj 怒りっぽい [okorippoi]

tough [tʌf] adj 丈夫な [joubu na]

toupee ['tuːpeɪ] n かつら [katsura]

tour [tʊə] n 旅行 [ryokou] ▷ v 旅行する [ryokou suru]; **guided tour** n ガイドツアー [gaidotsuaa]; **package tour** n パック旅行 [pakku ryokou]; **tour guide** n ツアーガイド [tsuaagaido]; **tour operator** n 旅行業者 [ryokougyousha]

tourism ['tʊərɪzəm] n 旅行業 [ryokou gyou]

tourist ['tʊərɪst] n 旅行者 [ryokousha]; **tourist office** n ツーリストオフィス [tsuurisutoofisu]

tournament ['tʊənəmənt; 'tɔː-; 'tɜː-] n トーナメント [toonamento]

towards [tə'wɔːdz; tɔːdz] prep ・・・の方へ [...no hou e]

tow away [təʊ ə'weɪ] v レッカー移動する [rekkaa idou suru]

towel ['taʊəl] n タオル [taoru]; **bath towel** n バスタオル [basutaoru]; **dish towel** n 布巾 [fukin]; **sanitary towel** n 生理用ナプキン [seiriyou napukin]; **tea towel** n 布巾 [fukin]; **Could you lend me a towel?** タオルを貸していただけますか? [taoru o kashite itadakemasu ka?]; **Please bring me more towels** タオル をもっと持ってきてください [taoru o motto motte kite kudasai]

tower ['taʊə] n 塔 [tou]

town [taʊn] n 町 [machi]; **town centre** n 町の中心部 [machi no chuushinbu]; **town hall** n タウンホール [taunhooru]; **town planning** n 都市計画 [toshikeikaku]

toxic ['tɒksɪk] adj 有毒な [yuudoku na]

toy [tɔɪ] n おもちゃ [omocha]

trace [treɪs] n 跡 [ato]

tracing paper ['treɪsɪŋ 'peɪpə] n **tracing paper** n トレース紙 [toreesushi]

track [træk] n 小道 [komichi]

track down [træk daʊn] v 跡をたどって見つけ出す [ato-o tadotte mitsukedasu]

tracksuit ['trækˌsuːt; -ˌsjuːt] n トラックスーツ [torakkusuutsu]

tractor ['træktə] n トラクター [torakutaa]

trade [treɪd] n 商売 [shoubai]; **trade union** n 労働組合 [roudoukumiai]; **trade unionist** n 労働組合主義者 [roudoukumiai shugisha]

trademark ['treɪdˌmɑːk] n 商標 [shouhyou]

tradition [trə'dɪʃən] n 伝統 [dentou]

traditional [trə'dɪʃənˀl] adj 伝統的な [dentouteki na]

traffic ['træfɪk] n 交通 [koutsuu]; **traffic jam** n 交通渋滞 [koutsuujuutai]; **traffic lights** npl 交通信号 [koutsuu shingou]; **traffic warden** n 交通監視員 [koutsuu kanshiin]; **Is the traffic heavy on the motorway?** 高速道路は交通量が多いですか? [kousoku-douro wa koutsuu-ryou ga ooi desu ka?]

tragedy ['trædʒɪdɪ] n 悲惨な出来事 [hisan na dekigoto]

tragic ['trædʒɪk] adj 悲惨な [hisan na]

trailer ['treɪlə] n トレーラー [toreeraa]

train [treɪn] n 列車 [ressha] ▷ v 訓練する [kunren suru]

trained ['treɪnd] adj 訓練された [kunren sareta]

trainee [treɪ'niː] n 訓練を受けている人 [kunren-o ukete iru hito]

trainer ['treɪnə] n コーチ [koochi]

trainers ['treɪnəz] npl トレーニングシューズ [toreeningushuuzu]

training ['treɪnɪŋ] n トレーニング [toreeningu]; **training course** n トレーニングコース [toreeningukoosu]

tram [træm] n 路面電車 [romendensha]

tramp [træmp] n (beggar) 浮浪者 [furousha], (long walk) 徒歩旅行 [tohoryokou]

trampoline ['træmpəlɪn; -,li:n] n トランポリン [toranporin]

tranquillizer ['træŋkwɪ,laɪzə] n 精神安定剤 [seishin anteizai]

transaction [træn'zækʃən] n 取引 [torihiki]

transcript ['trænskrɪpt] n 写し [utsushi]

transfer n ['trænsfɜ:] 移転 [iten] ▷ v [træns'fɜ:] 移転する [iten suru]

transform [træns'fɔ:m] v 変容させる [hen'you saseru]

transfusion [træns'fju:ʒən] n 輸血 [yuketsu]; **blood transfusion** n 輸血 [yuketsu]

transistor [træn'zɪstə] n トランジスター [toranjisutaa]

transit ['trænsɪt; 'trænz-] n 輸送 [yusou]; **transit lounge** n 通過ラウンジ [tsuuka raunji]

transition [træn'zɪʃən] n 移行 [ikou]

translate [træns'leɪt; trænz-] v 訳す [yakusu]

translation [træns'leɪʃən; trænz-] n 翻訳 [honyaku]

translator [træns'leɪtə; trænz-] n 翻訳者 [hon'yakusha]

transparent [træns'pærənt; -'pɛər-] adj 透明な [toumei na]

transplant ['træns,plɑ:nt] n 移植 [ishoku]

transport n ['træns,pɔ:t] 輸送 [yusou] ▷ v [træns'pɔ:t] 輸送する [yusou suru]; **public transport** n 公共交通機関 [koukyou koutsuu kikan]

transvestite [trænz'vɛstaɪt] n 服装倒錯 [fukusou tousaku]

trap [træp] n わな [wana]

trash [træʃ] n くだらないこと [kudaranai koto]

traumatic ['trɔːməˌtɪk] adj 外傷性の [gaishou sei no]

travel ['trævəl] n 旅行 [ryokou] ▷ v 移動する [idou suru]; **travel agency** n 旅行代理店 [ryokoudairiten]; **travel agent's** n 旅行代理店 [ryokoudairiten]; **travel sickness** n 乗物酔い [norimonoyoi]; **I don't have travel insurance** 私は旅行保険に入っていません [watashi wa ryokou-hoken ni haitte imasen]; **I'm travelling alone** 私は一人で旅行しています [watashi wa hitori de ryokou shite imasu]

traveller ['trævələ; 'trævlə] n 旅行者 [ryokousha]; **traveller's cheque** n 旅行者用小切手 [ryokousha you kogitte]

travelling ['trævəlɪŋ] n 旅行 [ryokou]

tray [treɪ] n 盆 [bon] (台所用品)

treacle ['tri:kəl] n 糖蜜 [toumitsu]

tread [trɛd] **tread on** v 踏む [fumu]

treasure ['trɛʒə] n 財宝 [zaihou]

treasurer ['trɛʒərə] n 会計係 [kaikeigakari]

treat [tri:t] n 歓待 [kantai] ▷ v 扱う [atsukau]

treatment ['tri:tmənt] n 治療 [chiryou]

treaty ['tri:tɪ] n 条約 [jouyaku]

treble ['trɛbəl] v 三倍にする [sanbai ni suru]

tree [tri:] n 木 [ki]

trek [trɛk] n 苦難に満ちた旅 [kunan ni michita tabi] ▷ v 苦難に耐えつつ旅をする [kunan ni taetsutsu tabi-o suru]

trekking ['trɛkɪŋ] n **I'd like to go pony trekking** 私はポニートレッキングに行きたいのですが [watashi wa ponii-torekkingu ni ikitai no desu ga]

tremble ['trɛmbəl] v 震える [furueru]

tremendous [trɪ'mɛndəs] adj 巨大な [kyodai na]

trench [trɛntʃ] n 深くて細長い溝 [fukakute hosonagai mizo]

trend [trɛnd] n 傾向 [keikou]

trendy ['trɛndɪ] adj 今はやりの [ima hayari no]

trial ['traɪəl] n 裁判 [saiban], 試み [kokoromi]; **trial period** n 試用期間 [shiyou kikan]

triangle ['traɪˌæŋgəl] n 三角形 [sankakkei]

tribe [traɪb] n 部族 [buzoku]

tribunal [traɪˈbjuːnəl; trɪ-] n 裁定委員会 [saitei iinkai]

trick [trɪk] n 策略 [sakuryaku] ▷ v だます [damasu]

tricky ['trɪkɪ] adj 油断のならない [yudan no naranai]

tricycle ['traɪsɪkəl] n 三輪車 [sanrinsha]

trifle ['traɪfəl] n つまらないもの [tsumaranai mono]

trim [trɪm] v 整える [totonoeru]

Trinidad and Tobago ['trɪnɪˌdæd ænd təˈbeɪgəʊ] n トリニダード・トバゴ [torinidaado tobago]

trip [trɪp] n 旅行 [ryokou]; **business trip** n 出張 [shutchou]; **round trip** n 往復 [oufuku]; **trip (up)** v つまずく [tsumazuku]; **Have a good trip!** よいご旅行を! [yoi go-ryokou o!]; **This is my first trip to...** ・・・への旅行はこれが初めてです [...e no ryokou wa kore ga hajimete desu]

triple ['trɪpəl] adj 三重の [mie no]

triplets ['trɪplɪts] npl 三つ子 [mitsugo]

triumph ['traɪəmf] n 勝利 [shouri] ▷ v 勝利を収める [shouri-o osameru]

trivial ['trɪvɪəl] adj 些細な [sasai na]

trolley ['trɒlɪ] n ワゴン [wagon]; **luggage trolley** n 手荷物カート [tenimotsu kaato]; **shopping trolley** n ショッピングカート [shoppingukaato]

trombone [trɒmˈbəʊn] n トロンボーン [toronboon]

troops ['truːps] npl 軍隊 [guntai]

trophy ['trəʊfɪ] n トロフィー [torofii]

tropical ['trɒpɪkəl] adj 熱帯の [nettai no]

trot [trɒt] v 速足で駆ける [hayaashi de kakeru]

trouble ['trʌbəl] n 困難 [konnan]

troublemaker ['trʌbəlˌmeɪkə] n もめごとを起こす人 [momegoto-o okosu hito]

trough [trɒf] n かいば桶 [kaibaoke]

trousers ['traʊzəz] npl ズボン [zubon]; **Can I try on these trousers?** このズボンを試着していいですか? [kono zubon o shichaku shite ii desu ka?]

trout [traʊt] n マス [masu] (魚)

trowel ['traʊəl] n 移植ごて [ishokugote]

truant ['truːənt] n play truant v サボる [saboru]

truce [truːs] n 休戦 [kyuusen]

truck [trʌk] n 無蓋貨車 [mugai kasha]; **breakdown truck** n レッカー車 [rekkaasha]; **truck driver** n トラック運転手 [torakku untenshu]

true [truː] adj 本当の [hontou no]

truly ['truːlɪ] adv 偽りなく [itsuwari naku]

trumpet ['trʌmpɪt] n トランペット [toranpetto]

trunk [trʌŋk] n 幹 [miki]; **swimming trunks** npl スイミングトランクス [suimingutorankusu]

trunks [trʌŋks] npl トランクス [torankusu]

trust [trʌst] n 信頼 [shinrai] ▷ v 信頼する [shinrai suru]

trusting ['trʌstɪŋ] adj 信じている [shinjite iru]

truth [truːθ] n 事実 [jijitsu]

truthful ['truːθfʊl] adj 正直な [shoujiki na]

try [traɪ] n 努力 [doryoku] ▷ v 努める [tsutomeru]

try on [traɪ ɒn] v 試着する [shichaku suru]

try out [traɪ aʊt] v 試してみる [tameshite miru]

T-shirt ['tiːˌʃɜːt] n Tシャツ [tiishatsu]

tsunami [tsʊˈnæmɪ] n 津波 [tsunami]

tube [tjuːb] n 管 [kan]; **inner tube** n インナーチューブ [innaachuubu]; **test tube** n 試験管 [shikenkan]; **tube station** n 地下鉄駅 [chikatetsu eki]

tuberculosis [tjʊˌbɜːkjʊˈləʊsɪs] n 結核 [kekkaku]

Tuesday ['tjuːzdɪ] n 火曜日 [kayoubi]; **Shrove Tuesday** n 告解火曜日 [kokkai kayoubi]; **on Tuesday** 火曜日に [kayoubi ni]

tug-of-war ['tʌɡɒv'wɔː] n 綱引き [tsunahiki]

tuition [tjuːˈɪʃən] n 授業 [jugyou]; **tuition fees** npl 授業料 [jugyouryou]

tulip ['tjuːlɪp] n チューリップ [chuurippu]

tummy ['tʌmɪ] n おなか [onaka]

tumour ['tjuːmə] n 腫瘍 [shuyou]

tuna ['tjuːnə] n マグロ [maguro]

tune [tjuːn] n 曲 [kyoku]

Tunisia [tjuːˈnɪzɪə; -ˈnɪsɪə] n チュニジア [chunijia]

Tunisian [tjuːˈnɪzɪən; -ˈnɪsɪən] adj チュニジアの [chunijia no] ▷ n チュニジア人 [chunijiajin]

tunnel ['tʌnəl] n トンネル [tonneru]

turbulence ['tɜːbjʊləns] n 激動 [gekidou]

Turk [tɜːk] n トルコ人 [torukojin]

turkey ['tɜːkɪ] n 七面鳥 [shichimenchou]

Turkey ['tɜːkɪ] n トルコ [toruko]

Turkish ['tɜːkɪʃ] adj トルコの [toruko no] ▷ n トルコ語 [torukogo]

turn [tɜːn] n 逸れること [soreru koto] ▷ v 向きを変える [muki o kaeru]

turn around [tɜːn əˈraʊnd] v 方向転換する [houkoutenkan suru]

turn back [tɜːn bæk] v 引き返す [hikikaesu]

turn down [tɜːn daʊn] v 小さくする [chiisaku suru]

turning ['tɜːnɪŋ] n 分かれ道 [wakaremichi]

turnip ['tɜːnɪp] n カブ [kabu] (食べ物)

turn off [tɜːn ɒf] v わき道へ入る [wakimichi-e hairu]

turn on [tɜːn ɒn] v つける [tsukeru] (スイッチ)

turn out [tɜːn aʊt] v 消す [kesu] (切る)

turnover ['tɜːnˌəʊvə] n 総売上高 [souuriagedaka]

turn round [tɜːn raʊnd] v 方向転換する [houkoutenkan suru]

turnstile ['tɜːnˌstaɪl] n 回転式改札口 [kaitenshiki kaisatsuguchi]

turn up [tɜːn ʌp] v 姿を現す [sugata-o arawasu]

turquoise ['tɜːkwɔɪz; -kwɑːz] adj 青緑色の [aomidori iro no]

turtle ['tɜːtəl] n カメ [kame] (動物)

tutor ['tjuːtə] n 個別指導教官 [kobetsu shidou kyoukan]

tutorial [tjuːˈtɔːrɪəl] n 個別指導 [kobetsu shidou]

tuxedo [tʌkˈsiːdəʊ] n タキシード [takishiido]

TV [tiː viː] n テレビ [terebi]; **plasma TV** n プラズマテレビ [purazumaterebi]; **reality TV** n リアリティーテレビ番組 [riaritii terebi bangumi]; **Does the room have a TV?** その部屋にテレビはありますか? [sono heya ni terebi wa arimasu ka?]

tweet [twiːt] v をツイートする [o tsuiito suru]

tweezers ['twiːzəz] npl ピンセット [pinsetto]

twelfth [twɛlfθ] adj 十二番目の [juuni banme no]

twelve [twɛlv] number 十二 [juuni]

twentieth ['twɛntɪɪθ] adj 二十番目の [nijuu banme no]

twenty ['twɛntɪ] number 二十 [nijuu]

twice [twaɪs] adv 二度 [nido]

twin [twɪn] n 双子 [futago]; **twin beds** npl ツインベッド [tsuinbeddo]; **twin room** n ツインルーム [tsuinruumu]; **twin-bedded room** n ツインベッドルーム [tsuinbeddoruumu]

twinned ['twɪnd] adj 対になった [tsui ni natta]

twist [twɪst] v ねじる [nejiru]

twit [twɪt] n ばか [baka]

two [tuː] num 二 [ni]; **I'd like two hundred...** 二百・・・欲しいのですが [nihyaku ... hoshii no desu ga]

type [taɪp] n 種類 [shurui] ▷ v タイプする [taipu suru]

typewriter ['taɪpˌraɪtə] n タイプライター [taipuraitaa]

typhoid [ˈtaɪfɔɪd] *n* 腸チフス
[chouchifusu]

typical [ˈtɪpɪkəl] *adj* 典型的な [tenkeiteki na]

typist [ˈtaɪpɪst] *n* タイピスト [taipisuto]

tyre [ˈtaɪə] *n* タイヤ [taiya]; **spare tyre** *n* スペアタイヤ [supeataiya]; **Can you check the tyres, please?** タイヤを点検してもらえますか? [taiya o tenken shite moraemasu ka?]; **I have a flat tyre** タイヤがパンクしました [taiya ga panku shimashita]; **The tyre has burst** タイヤが破裂しました [taiya ga haretsu shimashita]; **What should the tyre pressure be?** 適正なタイヤ圧はどのくらいですか? [tekisei na taiya-atsu wa dono kurai desu ka?]

UFO [ˈjuːfəʊ] *abbr* 未確認飛行物体 [mikakunin hikoubuttai]

Uganda [juːˈɡændə] *n* ウガンダ [uganda]

Ugandan [juːˈɡændən] *adj* ウガンダの [uganda no] ▷ *n* ウガンダ人 [ugandajin]

ugh [ʊx; ʊh; ʌh] *excl* ウッ [utsu]

ugly [ˈʌɡlɪ] *adj* 醜い [minikui]

UK [juː keɪ] *n* (= United Kingdom) 英国 [eikoku]

Ukraine [juːˈkreɪn] *n* ウクライナ [ukuraina]

Ukrainian [juːˈkreɪnɪən] *adj* ウクライナの [ukuraina no] ▷ *n* (language) ウクライナ語 [ukurainago], (person) ウクライナ人 [ukurainajin]

ulcer [ˈʌlsə] *n* 潰瘍 [kaiyou]

Ulster [ˈʌlstə] *n* アルスター [arusutaa]

ultimate [ˈʌltɪmɪt] *adj* 最終的な [saishuuteki na]

ultimately [ˈʌltɪmɪtlɪ] *adv* 最終的に [saishuuteki ni]

ultimatum [ˌʌltɪˈmeɪtəm] *n* 最後通牒 [saigo tsuuchou]

ultrasound [ˈʌltrəˌsaʊnd] *n* 超音波 [chouonpa]

umbrella [ʌm'brɛlə] n 傘 [kasa]

umpire ['ʌmpaɪə] n アンパイア [anpaia]

UN [juː ɛn] abbr 国際連合 [kokusairengou]

unable [ʌn'eɪbᵊl] adj **unable to** adj ・・・できない [...dekinai]

unacceptable [ʌnək'sɛptəbᵊl] adj 容認できない [younin dekinai]

unanimous [juː'nænɪməs] adj 満場一致の [manjouitchi no]

unattended [ʌnə'tɛndɪd] adj 番人のいない [bannin no inai]

unavoidable [ʌnə'vɔɪdəbᵊl] adj 避けられない [sakerarenai]

unbearable [ʌn'bɛərəbᵊl] adj 耐えられない [taerarenai]

unbeatable [ʌn'biːtəbᵊl] adj 太刀打ちできない [tachiuchi dekinai]

unbelievable [ʌnbɪ'liːvəbᵊl] adj 信じられない [shinjirarenai]

unbreakable [ʌn'breɪkəbᵊl] adj 壊すことのできない [kowasu koto no dekinai]

uncanny [ʌn'kænɪ] adj 薄気味悪い [usukimiwarui]

uncertain [ʌn'sɜːtᵊn] adj 不確実な [fukakujitsu na]

uncertainty [ʌn'sɜːtᵊntɪ] n 不確実 [fukakujitsu]

unchanged [ʌn'tʃeɪndʒd] adj 変わっていない [kawatteinai]

uncivilized [ʌn'sɪvɪˌlaɪzd] adj 未開の [mikai no]

uncle ['ʌŋkᵊl] n おじ [oji] (伯父・叔父)

unclear [ʌn'klɪə] adj 不明瞭な [fumeiryou na]

uncomfortable [ʌn'kʌmftəbᵊl] adj 心地よくない [kokochi yokunai]

unconditional [ʌnkən'dɪʃənᵊl] adj 無条件の [mujouken no]

unconscious [ʌn'kɒnʃəs] adj 意識を失った [ishiki o ushinatta]

uncontrollable [ʌnkən'trəʊləbᵊl] adj 制御できない [seigyodekinai]

unconventional [ʌnkən'vɛnʃənᵊl] adj 慣例に従わない [kanrei ni shitagawanai]

undecided [ʌndɪ'saɪdɪd] adj 決心がつ

いていない [kesshin ga tsuite inai]

undeniable [ʌndɪ'naɪəbᵊl] adj 否定できない [hitei dekinai]

under ['ʌndə] prep ・・・の下に [...no shita ni]

underage [ʌndər'eɪdʒ] adj 未成年の [miseinen no]

underestimate [ʌndərɛstɪ'meɪt] v 過小評価する [kashouhyouka suru]

undergo [ʌndə'gəʊ] v 経験する [keiken suru]

undergraduate [ʌndə'grædjuɪt] n 学部学生 [gakubu gakusei]

underground ['ʌndə'graʊnd] adj 地下に [chika ni]; **underground movement** n 地下運動 [chika undou]

underline [ʌndə'laɪn] v 下線を引く [kasen-o hiku]

underneath [ʌndə'niːθ] adv 下に [shita ni] ▷ prep ・・・の下に [...no shita ni]

underpaid [ʌndə'peɪd] adj 十分な額が払われていない [juubun na gaku ga harawarete inai]

underpants ['ʌndəˌpænts] npl パンツ [pantsu] (下着)

underpass ['ʌndəˌpɑːs] n アンダーパス [andaapasu]

underskirt ['ʌndəˌskɜːt] n アンダースカート [andaasukaato]

understand [ʌndə'stænd] v 理解する [rikai suru]

understandable [ʌndə'stændəbᵊl] adj 理解できる [rikai dekiru]

understanding [ʌndə'stændɪŋ] adj 話がわかる [hanashi ga wakaru]

undertaker ['ʌndəˌteɪkə] n 葬儀屋 [sougiya]

underwater ['ʌndə'wɔːtə] adv 水中に [suichuu ni]

underwear ['ʌndəˌwɛə] n 下着 [shitagi]

undisputed [ʌndɪ'spjuːtɪd] adj 異議のない [igi no nai]

undo [ʌn'duː] v ほどく [hodoku]

undoubtedly [ʌn'daʊtɪdlɪ] adv 疑いなく [utagainaku]

undress [ʌn'drɛs] v 服を脱ぐ [fuku o nugu]

unemployed [ˌʌnɪmˈplɔɪd] *adj* 失業している [shitsugyou shite iru]

unemployment [ˌʌnɪmˈplɔɪmənt] *n* 失業 [shitsugyou]

unexpected [ˌʌnɪkˈspɛktɪd] *adj* 予期しない [yoki shinai]

unexpectedly [ˌʌnɪkˈspɛktɪdlɪ] *adv* 思いがけなく [omoigakenaku]

unfair [ʌnˈfɛə] *adj* 不公平な [fukouhei na]

unfaithful [ʌnˈfeɪθfʊl] *adj* 不貞な [futei na]

unfamiliar [ˌʌnfəˈmɪljə] *adj* 不慣れの [funare no]

unfashionable [ʌnˈfæʃənəbəl] *adj* はやらない [hayaranai]

unfavourable [ʌnˈfeɪvərəbəl; -ˈfeɪvrə-] *adj* 好ましくない [konomashikunai]

unfit [ʌnˈfɪt] *adj* 不向きな [fumuki na]

unfollow [ʌnˈfɒləʊ] *v* のフォローを解除する [no foroo o kaijo suru]

unforgettable [ˌʌnfəˈgɛtəbəl] *adj* 忘れられない [wasurerarenai]

unfortunately [ʌnˈfɔːtʃənɪtlɪ] *adv* 運悪く [unwaruku]

unfriend [ʌnˈfrɛnd] *v* を友達から削除する [o tomodachi kara sakujo suru]

unfriendly [ʌnˈfrɛndlɪ] *adj* 不親切な [fushinsetsu na]

ungrateful [ʌnˈgreɪtfʊl] *adj* 感謝を表さない [kansha-o arawasanai]

unhappy [ʌnˈhæpɪ] *adj* 不幸な [fukou na]

unhealthy [ʌnˈhɛlθɪ] *adj* 不健康な [fukenkou na]

unhelpful [ʌnˈhɛlpfʊl] *adj* 役に立たない [yaku ni tatanai]

uni [ˈjuːnɪ] *n* 大学 [daigaku]

unidentified [ˌʌnaɪˈdɛntɪˌfaɪd] *adj* 身元不詳の [mimoto fushou no]

uniform [ˈjuːnɪˌfɔːm] *n* 制服 [seifuku]; **school uniform** *n* 学校の制服 [gakkou no seifuku]

unimportant [ˌʌnɪmˈpɔːtənt] *adj* 重要でない [juuyou de nai]

uninhabited [ˌʌnɪnˈhæbɪtɪd] *adj* 人の住んでいない [hito no sunde inai]

unintentional [ˌʌnɪnˈtɛnʃənəl] *adj* 故意でない [koi de nai]

union [ˈjuːnjən] *n* 結合 [ketsugou]; **European Union** *n* 欧州連合 [oushuu rengou]; **trade union** *n* 労働組合 [roudoukumiai]

unique [juːˈniːk] *adj* 独特の [dokutoku no]

unit [ˈjuːnɪt] *n* 単一体 [tan'itsutai]

unite [juːˈnaɪt] *v* 結合する [ketsugou suru]

United Kingdom [juːˈnaɪtɪd ˈkɪŋdəm] *n* 英国 [eikoku]

United States [juːˈnaɪtɪd steɪts] *n* 米国 [beikoku]

universe [ˈjuːnɪˌvɜːs] *n* 宇宙 [uchuu]

university [ˌjuːnɪˈvɜːsɪtɪ] *n* 大学 [daigaku]

unknown [ʌnˈnəʊn] *adj* 未知の [michi no]

unleaded [ʌnˈlɛdɪd] *n* 無鉛ガソリン [muen gasorin]; **unleaded petrol** *n* 無鉛ガソリン [muen gasorin]

unless [ʌnˈlɛs] *conj* もし・・・でなければ [moshi ... denakereba]

unlike [ʌnˈlaɪk] *prep* ・・・と違って [... tochigatte]

unlikely [ʌnˈlaɪklɪ] *adj* ありそうもない [arisou mo nai]

unlisted [ʌnˈlɪstɪd] *adj* 目録に載っていない [mokuroku ni notte inai]

unload [ʌnˈləʊd] *v* 荷を降ろす [ni-o orosu]

unlock [ʌnˈlɒk] *v* 錠をあける [jou-o akeru]

unlucky [ʌnˈlʌkɪ] *adj* 運の悪い [un no warui]

unmarried [ʌnˈmærɪd] *adj* 未婚の [mikon no]

unnecessary [ʌnˈnɛsɪsərɪ; -ɪsrɪ] *adj* 不必要な [fuhitsuyou na]

unofficial [ˌʌnəˈfɪʃəl] *adj* 非公認の [hikounin no]

unpack [ʌnˈpæk] *v* 荷を解く [ni-o toku]

unpaid [ʌnˈpeɪd] *adj* 無給の [mukyuu no]

unpleasant [ʌnˈplɛzᵊnt] *adj* 不愉快な [fuyukai na]

unplug [ʌnˈplʌg] *v* プラグを抜いて電源を断つ [puragu-o nuite dengen-o tatsu]

unpopular [ʌnˈpɒpjʊlə] *adj* 人気のない [hitoke no nai]

unprecedented [ʌnˈprɛsɪˌdɛntɪd] *adj* 先例のない [senrei no nai]

unpredictable [ˌʌnprɪˈdɪktəbᵊl] *adj* 予測できない [yosoku dekinai]

unreal [ʌnˈrɪəl] *adj* 現実のものではない [genjitsu no mono dewa nai]

unrealistic [ˌʌnrɪəˈlɪstɪk] *adj* 非現実的な [higenjitsuteki na]

unreasonable [ʌnˈriːznəbᵊl] *adj* 不当な [futou na]

unreliable [ˌʌnrɪˈlaɪəbᵊl] *adj* あてにならない [ate ni naranai]

unroll [ʌnˈrəʊl] *v* 広げる [hirogeru]

unsatisfactory [ˌʌnsætɪsˈfæktəri; -trɪ] *adj* 不満足な [fumanzoku na]

unscrew [ʌnˈskruː] *v* ねじを緩める [neji-o yurumeru]

unshaven [ʌnˈʃeɪvᵊn] *adj* ひげを剃っていない [hige-o sotte inai]

unskilled [ʌnˈskɪld] *adj* 熟練していない [jukuren shite inai]

unstable [ʌnˈsteɪbᵊl] *adj* 不安定な [fuantei na]

unsteady [ʌnˈstɛdɪ] *adj* 不安定な [fuantei na]

unsuccessful [ˌʌnsəkˈsɛsfʊl] *adj* 不成功に終わった [fuseikou ni owatta]

unsuitable [ʌnˈsuːtəbᵊl; ʌnˈsjuːt-] *adj* 不適切な [futekisetsu na]

unsure [ʌnˈʃʊə] *adj* 確信のない [kakushin no nai]

untidy [ʌnˈtaɪdɪ] *adj* だらしのない [darashi no nai]

untie [ʌnˈtaɪ] *v* ほどく [hodoku]

until [ʌnˈtɪl] *conj* •••の時まで [...no toki made] ▷ *prep* •••まで [made]

unusual [ʌnˈjuːʒʊəl] *adj* 普通でない [futsuu de nai]

unwell [ʌnˈwɛl] *adj* 気分のすぐれない [kibun no sugurenai]

unwind [ʌnˈwaɪnd] *v* ほどく [hodoku]

unwise [ʌnˈwaɪz] *adj* 分別のない [funbetsu no nai]

unwrap [ʌnˈræp] *v* 包装を解く [housou-o toku]

unzip [ʌnˈzɪp] *v* ファスナーを開ける [fasunaa-o hirakeru]

up [ʌp] *adv* 上へ [ue-e]

upbringing [ˈʌpˌbrɪŋɪŋ] *n* しつけ [shitsuke]

upcycle [ˈʌpsaɪkl] *v* をアップサイクルする [o appusaikuru suru]

update *n* [ˈʌpˌdeɪt] 更新する [koushin suru] ▷ *v* [ʌpˈdeɪt] 更新する [koushin suru]

upgrade [ʌpˈgreɪd] *n* **I want to upgrade my ticket** 切符をアップグレードしたいのですが [kippu o appugureedo shitai no desu ga]

uphill [ˈʌpˈhɪl] *adv* 坂の上へ [saka no ue-e]

upload [ʌpˈləʊd] *v* をアップロードする [o appuroodo suru]

upper [ˈʌpə] *adj* 上の [ue no]

upright [ˈʌpˌraɪt] *adv* まっすぐ上に [massugu ueni]

upset *adj* [ʌpˈsɛt] 狼狽した [roubai shita] ▷ *v* [ʌpˈsɛt] *(knock over)* ひっくり返す [hikkurigaesu]

upside down [ˈʌpˌsaɪd daʊn] *adv* 逆さまに [sakasama ni]

upstairs [ˈʌpˈstɛəz] *adv* 上の階に [ueno kai ni]

uptight [ʌpˈtaɪt] *adj* 緊張しきった [kinchou shikitta]

up-to-date [ʌptʊdeɪt] *adj* 最新の [saishin no]

upwards [ˈʌpwədz] *adv* 上へ向かって [ue he mukatte]

uranium [jʊˈreɪnɪəm] *n* ウラニウム [uraniumu]

urgency [ˈɜːdʒənsɪ] *n* 緊急 [kinkyuu]

urgent [ˈɜːdʒənt] *adj* 緊急の [kinkyuu no]; **I need to make an urgent phone call** 私は緊急の電話をかけなければなりません [watashi wa kinkyuu no denwa o kakenakereba narimasen]

urine ['jʊərɪn] *n* 尿 [nyou]

URL [ju: ɑ: ɛl] *n* URL [yuuaarueru]

Uruguay ['jʊərə,gwaɪ] *n* ウルグアイ [uruguai]

Uruguayan [,jʊərə'gwaɪən] *adj* ウルグアイの [uruguai no] ▷ *n* ウルグアイ人 [uruguaijin]

us [ʌs] *pron* 私たちを [watashi-tachi-o]

US [ju: ɛs] *n* 米国 [beikoku]

USA [ju: ɛs eɪ] *n* 米国 [beikoku]

USB stick [ju: ɛs bi:-] *n* USBメモリー [yuuesubii memorii]

use *n* [ju:s] 使用 [shiyou] ▷ *v* [ju:z] 使用する [shiyou suru]

used [ju:zd] *adj* 中古の [chuuko no]

useful ['ju:sfʊl] *adj* 役に立つ [yaku ni tatsu]

useless ['ju:slɪs] *adj* 役に立たない [yaku ni tatanai]

user ['ju:zə] *n* 使用者 [shiyousha]; **internet user** *n* インターネット利用者 [intaanetto riyousha]

user-friendly ['ju:zə,frɛndlɪ] *adj* 使いやすい [tsukaiyasui]

use up [ju:z ʌp] *v* 使い果たす [tsukaihatasu]

usual ['ju:ʒʊəl] *adj* 普通の [futsuu no]

usually ['ju:ʒʊəlɪ] *adv* 普通は [futsuu wa]

U-turn ['ju:,tɜ:n] *n* Uターン [yuutaan]

Uzbekistan [,ʌzbɛkɪ'stɑ:n] *n* ウズベキスタン [uzubekisutan]

vacancy ['veɪkənsɪ] *n* 欠員 [ketsuin]

vacant ['veɪkənt] *adj* 空いている [aite iru]

vacate [və'keɪt] *v* 立ち退く [tachishirizoku]

vaccinate ['væksɪ,neɪt] *v* 予防接種をする [yobou sesshu-o suru]

vaccination [,væksɪ'neɪʃən] *n* 予防接種 [yobou sesshu]; **I need a vaccination** 私は予防接種が必要です [watashi wa yobou-sesshu ga hitsuyou desu]

vacuum ['vækjʊəm] *v* 電気掃除機で掃除する [denki soujiki de souji suru]; **vacuum cleaner** *n* 電気掃除機 [denki soujiki]

vague [veɪg] *adj* 曖昧な [aimai na]

vain [veɪn] *adj* うぬぼれの強い [unubore no tsuyoi]

valid ['vælɪd] *adj* 正当な [seitou na]

valley ['vælɪ] *n* 谷間 [taniai]

valuable ['væljʊəbəl] *adj* 高価な [kouka na]

valuables ['væljʊəbəlz] *npl* 貴重品 [kichouhin]; **I'd like to put my valuables in the safe** 私は貴重品を金庫に入れたいのですが [watashi wa

kichouhin o kinko ni iretai no desu ga];
Where can I leave my valuables?
貴重品はどこに置いておけますか？
[kichouhin wa doko ni oite okemasu ka?]

value ['vælju:] *n* 価値 [kachi]

vampire ['væmpaɪə] *n* 吸血鬼
[kyuuketsuki]

van [væn] *n* バン [ban] (自動車);
breakdown van *n* レッカー車
[rekkaasha]; **removal van** *n* 引越しトラッ
ク [hikkoshi torakku]

vandal ['vændəl] *n* 破壊者 [hakaisha]

vandalism ['vændə.lɪzəm] *n* 破壊行為
[hakai koui]

vandalize ['vændə.laɪz] *v* 故意に破壊す
る [koi ni hakai suru]

vanilla [və'nɪlə] *n* バニラ [banira]

vanish ['vænɪʃ] *v* 消える [kieru]

vape [veɪp] *v* 電子タバコを吸う [denshi
tabako o suu]

variable ['vɛərɪəbəl] *adj* 変わりやすい
[kawariyasui]

varied ['vɛərɪd] *adj* さまざまな
[samazama na]

variety [və'raɪɪtɪ] *n* 多様性 [tayousei]

various ['vɛərɪəs] *adj* さまざまな
[samazama na]

varnish ['vɑːnɪʃ] *n* ニス [nisu] ▷ *v* ニスを
塗る [nisu-o nuru]; **nail varnish** *n* マニキ
ュア液 [manikyua eki]

vary ['vɛərɪ] *v* 変わる [kawaru]

vase [vɑːz] *n* 花瓶 [kabin]

VAT [væt] *abbr* 付加価値税 [fukakachizei];
Is VAT included? 付加価値税は含まれ
ていますか？ [fukakachi-zei wa
fukumarete imasu ka?]

Vatican ['vætɪkən] *n* バチカン
[bachikan]

vault [vɔːlt] *n* **pole vault** *n* 棒高跳び
[bou taka tobi]

veal [viːl] *n* 子牛の肉 [koushi no niku]

vegan ['viːɡən] *n* ビーガン [biigan];
Do you have any vegan dishes?
ビーガン料理はありますか？
[biigan-ryouri wa arimasu ka?]

vegetable ['vɛdʒtəbəl] *n* 野菜 [yasai];

**Are the vegetables fresh or
frozen?** 野菜は生鮮品ですか、それと
も冷凍品ですか？ [yasai wa seisen-hin
desu ka, sore tomo reitou-hin desu ka?];
Are the vegetables included? 野菜も
付いてきますか？ [yasai mo tsuite kimasu
ka?]

vegetarian [,vɛdʒɪ'tɛərɪən] *adj* ベジタ
リアンの [bejitarian no] ▷ *n* ベジタリアン
[bejitarian]; **Do you have any
vegetarian dishes?** ベジタリアン料理
はありますか？ [bejitarian-ryouri wa
arimasu ka?]; **I'm vegetarian** 私はベジタ
リアンです [watashi wa bejitarian desu]

vegetation [,vɛdʒɪ'teɪʃən] *n* 草木
[soumoku]

vehicle ['viːɪkəl] *n* 乗り物 [norimono]

veil [veɪl] *n* ベール [beeru]

vein [veɪn] *n* 静脈 [joumyaku]

Velcro® ['vɛlkrəʊ] *n* ベルクロ®
[berukuro]

velvet ['vɛlvɪt] *n* ビロード [biroodo]

vendor ['vɛndɔː] *n* 売る人 [uru hito]

Venezuela [,vɛnɪ'zweɪlə] *n* ベネズエラ
[benezuera]

Venezuelan [,vɛnɪ'zweɪlən] *adj* ベネズ
エラの [benezuera no] ▷ *n* ベネズエラ人
[benezuerajin]

venison ['vɛnɪzən; -sən] *n* 鹿肉 [shika
niku]

venom ['vɛnəm] *n* 悪意 [akui]

ventilation [,vɛntɪ'leɪʃən] *n* 風通し
[kazetooshi]

venue ['vɛnjuː] *n* 会場 [kaijou]

verb [vɜːb] *n* 動詞 [doushi]

verdict ['vɜːdɪkt] *n* 評決 [hyouketsu]

versatile ['vɜːsə,taɪl] *adj* 多方面の
[tahoumen no]

version ['vɜːʃən; -ʒən] *n* 版 [han]

versus ['vɜːsəs] *prep* ⋯対 [...tai]

vertical ['vɜːtɪkəl] *adj* 垂直の [suichoku
no]

vertigo ['vɜːtɪ,ɡəʊ] *n* めまい [memai]

very ['vɛrɪ] *adv* 非常に [hijou ni]

vest [vɛst] *n* 肌着 [hadagi]

vet [vɛt] *n* 獣医 [juui]

veteran ['vɛtərən; 'vɛtrən] *adj* 老練な [rouren na] ▷ *n* 老練な人 [rouren na hito]

veto ['vi:təʊ] *n* 拒否権 [kyohiken]

via [vaɪə] *prep* ･･･経由で [...keiyu de]

vicar ['vɪkə] *n* 教区牧師 [kyouku bokushi]

vice [vaɪs] *n* 悪徳 [akutoku]

vice versa ['vaɪsɪ 'vɜːsə] *adv* 逆に [gyaku ni]

vicinity [vɪ'sɪnɪtɪ] *n* 近所 [kinjo]

vicious ['vɪʃəs] *adj* ひどい [hidoi]

victim ['vɪktɪm] *n* 犠牲 [gisei]

victory ['vɪktərɪ] *n* 勝利 [shouri]

video ['vɪdɪ,əʊ] *n* ビデオ [bideo]; **video camera** *n* ビデオカメラ [bideokamera]

videophone ['vɪdɪə,fəʊn] *n* テレビ電話 [terebi denwa]

Vietnam [,vjɛt'næm] *n* ベトナム [betonamu]

Vietnamese [,vjɛtnə'mi:z] *adj* ベトナムの [betonamu no] ▷ *n* (*language*) ベトナム語 [betonamugo], (*person*) ベトナム人 [betonamujin]

view [vju:] *n* 見解 [kenkai]

viewer ['vju:ə] *n* 見る人 [miru hito]

viewpoint ['vju:,pɔɪnt] *n* 観点 [kanten]

vile [vaɪl] *adj* 堕落した [daraku shita]

villa ['vɪlə] *n* 大邸宅 [daiteitaku]

village ['vɪlɪdʒ] *n* 村 [mura]

villain ['vɪlən] *n* 悪党 [akutou]

vinaigrette [,vɪneɪ'grɛt] *n* ビネグレットドレッシング [binegurettodoresshingu]

vine [vaɪn] *n* つる植物 [tsuru shokubutsu]

vinegar ['vɪnɪgə] *n* 酢 [su]

vineyard ['vɪnjəd] *n* ブドウ園 [budouen]

viola [vɪ'əʊlə] *n* ビオラ [biora]

violence ['vaɪələns] *n* 暴力 [bouryoku]

violent ['vaɪələnt] *adj* 暴力的な [bouryokuteki na]

violin [,vaɪə'lɪn] *n* バイオリン [baiorin]

violinist [,vaɪə'lɪnɪst] *n* バイオリン奏者 [baiorinsousha]

viral ['vaɪərəl] *adj* **to go viral** (*video*) 頻繁に共有される [hinpan ni kyouyuu sareru]

virgin ['vɜːdʒɪn] *n* 処女 [shojo]

Virgo ['vɜːgəʊ] *n* 乙女座 [otomeza]

virtual ['vɜːtʃʊəl] *adj* 実質上の [jisshitsujou no]; **virtual reality** *n* バーチャルリアリティー [baacharuriariteii]

virus ['vaɪrəs] *n* ウイルス [uirusu]

visa ['vi:zə] *n* ビザ [biza]; **Here is my visa** 私のビザです [watashi no biza desu]; **I have an entry visa** 入国ビザを持っています [nyuukoku-biza o motte imasu]

visibility [,vɪzɪ'bɪlɪtɪ] *n* 視界 [shikai]

visible ['vɪzɪbəl] *adj* 目に見える [me ni mieru]

visit ['vɪzɪt] *n* 訪問 [houmon] ▷ *v* 訪問する [houmon suru]; **visiting hours** *npl* 面会時間 [menkaijikan]

visitor ['vɪzɪtə] *n* 訪問者 [houmonsha]; **visitor centre** *n* ビジターセンター [bijitaasentaa]

visual ['vɪʒʊəl; -zjʊ-] *adj* 視覚の [shikaku no]

visualize ['vɪʒʊə,laɪz; -zjʊ-] *v* 思い描く [omoiegaku]

vital ['vaɪtəl] *adj* きわめて重大な [kiwamete juudai na]

vitamin ['vɪtəmɪn; 'vaɪ-] *n* ビタミン [bitamin]

vivid ['vɪvɪd] *adj* 鮮やかな [azayaka na]

vlog [veɪp] *n* ブイログ [buirogu]; **vlogger** ['vlɒgə] *n* ビデオブロガー [bideo burogaa]

vocabulary [və'kæbjʊlərɪ] *n* 語彙 [goi]

vocational [və'keɪʃənəl] *adj* 職業上の [shokugyou jou no]

vodka ['vɒdkə] *n* ウォッカ [uokka]

voice [vɔɪs] *n* 声 [koe]

voicemail ['vɔɪs,meɪl] *n* ボイスメール [boisumeeru]

void [vɔɪd] *adj* 無効の [mukou no] ▷ *n* 空虚な感じ [kuukyo na kanji]

volcano, volcanoes [vɒl'keɪnəʊ, vɒl'keɪnəʊz] *n* 噴火口 [funkakou]

volleyball ['vɒlɪ,bɔ:l] *n* バレーボール [bareebooru]

volt [vəʊlt] *n* ボルト [boruto] (*電圧*)

voltage ['vəʊltɪdʒ] *n* 電圧 [den-atsu]; **What's the voltage?** 電圧は何ボルトですか? [denatsu wa nan-boruto desu ka?]

volume ['vɒlju:m] *n* 容積 [youseki]

voluntarily [ˈvɒləntərɪlɪ] *adv* 自発的に [jihatsuteki ni]

voluntary [ˈvɒləntərɪ; -trɪ] *adj* 自発的な [jihatsuteki na]

volunteer [ˌvɒlənˈtɪə] *n* 志願者 [shigansha] ▷ *v* 自発的に申し出る [jihatsuteki ni moushideru]

vomit [ˈvɒmɪt] *v* 吐く [haku]

vote [vəʊt] *n* 投票 [touhyou] ▷ *v* 投票する [touhyou suru]

voucher [ˈvaʊtʃə] *n* 引換券 [hikikaeken]; **gift voucher** *n* 商品券 [shouhinken]

vowel [ˈvaʊəl] *n* 母音 [boin]

vulgar [ˈvʌlɡə] *adj* 低俗な [teizoku na]

vulnerable [ˈvʌlnərəbᵊl] *adj* 傷つきやすい [kizutsukiyasui]

vulture [ˈvʌltʃə] *n* ハゲワシ [hagewashi]

wafer [ˈweɪfə] *n* ウエハース [uehaasu]

waffle [ˈwɒfᵊl] *n* ワッフル [waffuru] ▷ *v* たわごとを並べる [tawagoto-o naraberu]

wage [weɪdʒ] *n* 賃金 [chingin]

waist [weɪst] *n* ウエスト [uesuto]

waistcoat [ˈweɪsˌkəʊt] *n* ウエストコート [uesutokooto]

wait [weɪt] *v* 待つ [matsu]; **wait for** *v* 待つ [matsu]; **waiting list** *n* 順番待ち名簿 [junbanmachi meibo]; **waiting room** *n* 待合室 [machiaishitsu]

waiter [ˈweɪtə] *n* ウェイター [weitaa]

waitress [ˈweɪtrɪs] *n* ウェイトレス [weitoresu]

wait up [weɪt ʌp] *v* 寝ないで待つ [nenaide matsu]

waive [weɪv] *v* 放棄する [houki suru]

wake up [weɪk ʌp] *v* 目が覚める [me ga sameru]

Wales [weɪlz] *n* ウェールズ [weeruzu]

walk [wɔːk] *n* 散歩 [sanpo] ▷ *v* 歩く [aruku]

walkie-talkie [ˌwɔːkɪˈtɔːkɪ] *n* トランシーバー [toranshiibaa]

walking [ˈwɔːkɪŋ] *n* 歩行 [hokou]; **walking stick** *n* ステッキ [sutekki]

walkway ['wɔːkˌweɪ] n 歩行者用通路 [hokoushayou tsuuro]

wall [wɔːl] n 壁 [kabe]

wallet ['wɒlɪt] n 財布 [saifu]; **I've lost my wallet** 私は財布をなくしました [watashi wa saifu o nakushimashita]; **My wallet has been stolen** 私の財布が盗まれました [watashi no saifu ga nusumaremashita]

wallpaper ['wɔːlˌpeɪpə] n 壁紙 [kabegami]

walnut ['wɔːlˌnʌt] n クルミ [kurumi]

walrus ['wɔːlrəs; 'wɒl-] n セイウチ [seiuchi]

waltz [wɔːls] n ワルツ [warutsu] ▷ v ワルツを踊る [warutsu o odoru]

wander ['wɒndə] v 歩き回る [arukimawaru]

want [wɒnt] v 欲しい [hoshii]; **I want something cheaper** もっと安いものが欲しいのです [motto yasui mono ga hoshii no desu]

war [wɔː] n 戦争 [sensou]; **civil war** n 内戦 [naisen]

ward [wɔːd] n (area) 区 [ku], (hospital room) 病棟 [byoutou]; **Which ward is ... in?** ・・・はどの病棟に入院していますか? [...wa dono byoutou ni nyuuin shite imasu ka?]

warden ['wɔːdən] n 管理者 [kanrisha]; **traffic warden** n 交通監視員 [koutsuu kanshiin]

wardrobe ['wɔːdrəʊb] n 洋服だんす [youfukudansu]

warehouse ['wɛəˌhaʊs] n 倉庫 [souko]

warm [wɔːm] adj 暖かい [atatakai]

warm up [wɔːm ʌp] v 暖まる [atatamaru]

warn [wɔːn] v 警告する [keikoku suru]

warning ['wɔːnɪŋ] n 警告 [keikoku]; **hazard warning lights** npl 故障警告灯 [koshou keikokutou]; **The oil warning light won't go off** オイル警告灯が消えません [oiru keikoku-tou ga kiemasen]

warranty ['wɒrəntɪ] n 保証 [hoshou]; **The car is still under warranty** 車はまだ保証期間内です [kuruma wa mada hoshou-kikan nai desu]

wart [wɔːt] n いぼ [ibo]

wash [wɒʃ] v 洗う [arau]; **car wash** n 洗車機 [senshaki]

washable ['wɒʃəbᵊl] adj **machine washable** adj 洗濯機で洗える [sentakuki de araeru]; **Is it washable?** それは洗えますか? [sore wa araemasu ka?]

washbasin ['wɒʃˌbeɪsᵊn] n 洗面台 [senmendai]; **The washbasin is dirty** 洗面台が汚れています [senmendai ga yogorete imasu]

washing ['wɒʃɪŋ] n 洗濯物 [sentakumono]; **washing line** n 物干し綱 [monohoshi tsuna]; **washing machine** n 洗濯機 [sentakuki]; **washing powder** n 粉末洗剤 [funmatsusenzai]

washing-up ['wɒʃɪŋʌp] n 食器洗い [shokkiarai]; **washing-up liquid** n 食器洗い用液体洗剤 [shokkiarai you ekitai senzai]

wash up [wɒʃ ʌp] v 洗って片付ける [aratte katazukeru]

wasp [wɒsp] n スズメバチ [suzumebachi]

waste [weɪst] n 浪費 [rouhi] ▷ v 浪費する [rouhi suru]

watch [wɒtʃ] n 腕時計 [udedokei] ▷ v じっと見る [jitto miru]; **digital watch** n デジタル時計 [dejitaru tokei]

watch out [wɒtʃ aʊt] v 気をつける [ki o tsukeru]

water ['wɔːtə] n 水 [mizu] ▷ v 水をやる [mizu-o yaru]; **drinking water** n 飲料水 [inryousui]; **mineral water** n ミネラルウォーター [mineraru uootaa]; **sea water** n 海水 [kaisui]; **sparkling water** n たんさんすい [tansansui]; **watering can** n じょうろ [jouro]; **a glass of water** コップ一杯の水 [koppu ippai no mizu]; **Can you check the water, please?** 冷却水を点検してもらえますか? [reikyakusui o tenken shite moraemasu ka?]; **Please bring more water** 水をもっと持ってきてください [mizu o motto motte kite kudasai]

watercolour [ˈwɔːtəˌkʌlə] *n* 水彩絵の具 [suisai enogu]

watercress [ˈwɔːtəˌkrɛs] *n* クレソン [kureson]

waterfall [ˈwɔːtəˌfɔːl] *n* 滝 [taki]

watermelon [ˈwɔːtəˌmɛlən] *n* スイカ [suika]

waterproof [ˈwɔːtəˌpruːf] *adj* 防水の [bousui no]

water-skiing [ˈwɔːtəˌskiːɪŋ] *n* 水上スキー [suijousukii]; **Is it possible to go water-skiing here?** ここで水上スキーはできますか？ [koko de suijou-sukii wa dekimasu ka?]

wave [weɪv] *n* 波 [nami] ▷ *v* 手を振る [te o furu]

wavelength [ˈweɪvˌlɛŋθ] *n* 波長 [hachou]

wavy [ˈweɪvɪ] *adj* 波状の [hajou no]

wax [wæks] *n* 蝋 [rou]

way [weɪ] *n* 方法 [houhou]; **right of way** *n* 優先権 [yuusenken]; **What's the best way to get to the railway station?** 鉄道駅へ行く一番よい方法は何ですか？ [tetsudou-eki e iku ichiban yoi houhou wa nan desu ka?]

way in [weɪ ɪn] *n* 入口 [iriguchi]

way out [weɪ aʊt] *n* 出口 [deguchi]

we [wiː] *pron* 私たちは [watashi-tachi wa]; **We live in...** 私たちは・・・に住んでいます [watashi-tachi wa ... ni sunde imasu]

weak [wiːk] *adj* 弱い [yowai]

weakness [ˈwiːknɪs] *n* 弱いこと [yowai koto]

wealth [wɛlθ] *n* 富裕 [fuyuu]

wealthy [ˈwɛlθɪ] *adj* 富裕な [fuyuu na]

weapon [ˈwɛpən] *n* 武器 [buki]

wear [wɛə] *v* 身に着けている [mi ni tsukete iru]

weasel [ˈwiːzəl] *n* イタチ [itachi]

weather [ˈwɛðə] *n* 天気 [tenki]; **weather forecast** *n* 天気予報 [tenkiyohou]; **Is the weather going to change?** 天気は変わりますか？ [tenki wa kawarimasu ka?]; **What awful weather!** なんてひどい天気でしょう！ [nante hidoi tenki deshou!]; **What will the weather be like tomorrow?** 明日はどんな天気でしょう？ [asu wa donna tenki deshou?]

web [wɛb] *n* (*spiderweb*) クモの巣 [kumo no su]; **web address** *n* ウェブアドレス [webuadoresu]; **web browser** *n* ウェブブラウザ [webuburauza]

webcam [ˈwɛbˌkæm] *n* ウェブカム [webu kamu]

webmaster [ˈwɛbˌmɑːstə] *n* ウェブマスター [webumasutaa]

website [ˈwɛbˌsaɪt] *n* ウェブサイト [webu saito]

webzine [ˈwɛbˌziːn] *n* ウェブジン [webujin]

wedding [ˈwɛdɪŋ] *n* 結婚式 [kekkonshiki]; **wedding anniversary** *n* 結婚記念日 [kekkon kinenbi]; **wedding dress** *n* ウェディングドレス [wedingudoresu]; **wedding ring** *n* 結婚指輪 [kekkon yubiwa]; **We are here for a wedding** 私たちは結婚式で来ています [watashi-tachi wa kekkon-shiki de kite imasu]

Wednesday [ˈwɛnzdɪ] *n* 水曜日 [suiyoubi]; **Ash Wednesday** *n* 灰の水曜日 [hai no suiyoubi]; **on Wednesday** 水曜日に [suiyoubi ni]

weed [wiːd] *n* 雑草 [zassou]

weedkiller [ˈwiːdˌkɪlə] *n* 除草剤 [josouzai]

week [wiːk] *n* 週 [shuu]; **a week ago** 一週間前 [isshuukan mae]; **How much is it for a week?** 1週間でいくらですか？ [isshuukan de ikura desu ka?]; **last week** 先週 [senshuu]; **next week** 来週 [raishuu]

weekday [ˈwiːkˌdeɪ] *n* 平日 [heijitsu]

weekend [ˌwiːkˈɛnd] *n* 週末 [shuumatsu]; **I want to hire a car for the weekend** 車を週末借りたいのですが [kuruma o shuumatsu karitai no desu ga]

weep [wiːp] *v* 泣く [naku]

weigh [weɪ] *v* 重さが・・・ある [omosa ga ... aru]

weight [weɪt] *n* 重さ [omosa]

weightlifter ['weɪt,lɪftə] *n* 重量挙げ選手 [juuryouage senshu]

weightlifting ['weɪt,lɪftɪŋ] *n* 重量挙げ [juuryouage]

weird [wɪəd] *adj* 変な [hen na]

welcome ['wɛlkəm] *n* 歓迎 [kangei] ▷ *v* 歓迎する [kangei suru]; **welcome!** *excl* ようこそ! [youkoso]

well [wɛl] *adj* 申し分ない [moushibun nai] ▷ *adv* 申し分なく [moushibun naku] ▷ *n* 井戸 [ido]; **oil well** *n* 油井 [yusei]; **well done!** *excl* おみごと! [omigoto]

well-behaved ['wɛl'bɪ'heɪvd] *adj* 行儀のよい [gyougi no yoi]

wellies ['wɛlɪz] *npl* ウェリントンブーツ [werintonbuutsu]

wellingtons ['wɛlɪŋtənz] *npl* ウェリントンブーツ [werintonbuutsu]

well-known ['wɛl'nəʊn] *adj* 有名な [yuumei na]

well-off ['wɛl'ɒf] *adj* 裕福な [yuufuku na]

well-paid ['wɛl'peɪd] *adj* 給料のよい [kyuuryou no yoi]

Welsh [wɛlʃ] *adj* ウェールズの [ueeruzu no] ▷ *n (language)* ウェールズ語 [ueeruzugo]

west [wɛst] *adj* 西の [nishi no] ▷ *adv* 西に [nishi ni] ▷ *n* 西 [nishi]; **West Indian** *n* 西インド諸島の [nishiindoshotou no], 西インド諸島の人 [nishiindoshotou no hito]; **West Indies** *npl* 西インド諸島 [nishiindoshotou]

westbound ['wɛst,baʊnd] *adj* 西行きの [nishi yuki no]

western ['wɛstən] *adj* 西の [nishi no] ▷ *n* ウェスタン [uesutan]

wet [wɛt] *adj* 濡れた [nureta]

wetsuit ['wɛt,su:t] *n* ウェットスーツ [uettosuutsu]

whale [weɪl] *n* クジラ [kujira]

what [wɒt; wət] *adj* 何の [nan no] ▷ *pron* 何 [nan]; **What do you do?** お仕事は何をなさっていますか? [o-shigoto wa nani o nasatte imasu ka?]; **What is it?** それは何ですか? [sore wa nan desu ka?];

What is the word for...? ・・・は何といいますか? [...wa nan to iimasu ka?];

What time is it, please? 今何時か教えていただけますか? [ima nan-ji ka oshiete itadakemasu ka?]

wheat [wi:t] *n* 小麦 [komugi]; **wheat intolerance** *n* 小麦アレルギー [komugi arerugii]

wheel [wi:l] *n* 車輪 [sharin]; **spare wheel** *n* スペアホイール [supeahoiiru]; **steering wheel** *n* ステアリングホイール [sutearinguhoiiru]

wheelbarrow ['wi:l,bærəʊ] *n* 手押し車 [teoshiguruma]

wheelchair ['wi:l,tʃɛə] *n* 車椅子 [kurumaisu]; **Can you visit ... in a wheelchair?** 車椅子で・・・を訪れることができますか? [kuruma-isu de ... o otozureru koto ga dekimasu ka?]; **Do you have a lift for wheelchairs?** 車椅子用のエレベーターはありますか? [kuruma-isu-you no erebeetaa wa arimasu ka?]; **Do you have wheelchairs?** おたくには車椅子がありますか? [otaku ni wa kuruma-isu ga arimasu ka?]; **I need a room with wheelchair access** 私は車椅子で入れる部屋が必要です [watashi wa kuruma-isu de haireru heya ga hitsuyou desu]; **I use a wheelchair** 私は車椅子を使っています [watashi wa kuruma-isu o tsukatte imasu]; **Is there wheelchair-friendly transport available to...?** ・・・へ行くのに車椅子で利用しやすい交通手段はありますか? [...e iku no ni kuruma-isu de riyou shiyasui koutsuu-shudan wa arimasu ka?]; **Is your hotel accessible to wheelchairs?** おたくのホテルは車椅子で利用できますか? [otaku no hoteru wa kuruma-isu de riyou dekimasu ka?]; **Where is the nearest repair shop for wheelchairs?** 一番近くの車椅子修理店はどこですか? [ichiban chikaku no kuruma-isu shuuri-ten wa doko desu ka?]; **Where is the wheelchair-accessible entrance?** 車椅子で利用できる入口はどこですか?

[kuruma-isu de riyou dekiru iriguchi wa doko desu ka?]

when [wɛn] *adv* いつ [itsu] ▷ *conj* ・・・する時は [...suru toki ni]; **When does it begin?** いつ始まりますか? [itsu hajimarimasu ka?]; **When does it finish?** いつ終わりますか? [itsu owarimasu ka?]; **When is it due?** いつ到着する予定ですか? [itsu touchaku suru yotei desu ka?]

where [wɛə] *adv* どこに [doko ni] ▷ *conj* ・・・する所に [...suru tokoro ni]; **Where can you go...?** どこに行けば・・・ができますか? [doko ni ikeba ... ga dekimasu ka?]; **Where do I sign?** どこに署名するのですか? [doko ni shomei suru no desu ka?]

whether [ˈwɛðə] *conj* ・・・かどうか [... kadouka]

which [wɪtʃ] *pron* どの [dono], どれ [dore]; **Which is the key for this door?** このドアの鍵はどれですか? [kono doa no kagi wa dore desu ka?]

while [waɪls] *conj* ・・・する間 [...suru aida] ▷ *n* 間 [aida]

whip [wɪp] *n* 鞭 [muchi]; **whipped cream** *n* ホイップクリーム [hoippukuriimu]

whisper [ˈwɪspə] *v* ささやく [sasayaku]

whistle [ˈwɪsᵊl] *n* 口笛 [kuchibue] ▷ *v* 口笛を吹く [kuchibue o fuku]

white [waɪt] *adj* 白い [shiroi]; **egg white** *n* 卵の白身 [tamago no shiromi]

whiteboard [ˈwaɪtˌbɔːd] *n* ホワイトボード [howaitoboodo]

whitewash [ˈwaɪtˌwɒʃ] *v* 漆喰を塗る [shikkui-o nuru]

whiting [ˈwaɪtɪŋ] *n* ホワイティング [howaitingu] (魚)

who [huː] *pron* 誰 [dare]

whole [həʊl] *adj* 全体の [zentai no] ▷ *n* 全体 [zentai]

wholefoods [ˈhəʊlˌfuːdz] *npl* 自然食品 [shizen shokuhin]

wholemeal [ˈhəʊlˌmiːl] *adj* 全粒小麦の [zenryuu komugi no]

wholesale [ˈhəʊlˌseɪl] *adj* 卸売りの [oroshiuri no] ▷ *n* 卸売り [oroshiuri]

whom [huːm] *pron* 誰を [dare-o]

whose [huːz] *adj* 誰の [dare no] ▷ *pron* 誰のもの [dare no mono]; **Whose round is it?** 誰の番ですか? [dare no ban desu ka?]

why [waɪ] *adv* なぜ [naze]

wicked [ˈwɪkɪd] *adj* 邪悪な [jaaku na]

wide [waɪd] *adj* 広い [hiroi] ▷ *adv* 広く [hiroku]

widespread [ˈwaɪdˌsprɛd] *adj* 広まった [hiromatta]

widow [ˈwɪdəʊ] *n* 未亡人 [miboujin]

widower [ˈwɪdəʊə] *n* 男やもめ [otokoyamome]

width [wɪdθ] *n* 幅 [haba]

wife, wives [waɪf, waɪvz] *n* 妻 [tsuma]; **This is my wife** 私の妻です [watashi no tsuma desu]

WiFi [waɪ faɪ] *n* ワイファイ [waifai]

wig [wɪg] *n* かつら [katsura]

wild [waɪld] *adj* 野生の [yasei no]

wildlife [ˈwaɪldˌlaɪf] *n* 野生生物 [yaseiseibutsu]; **We'd like to see wildlife** 野生生物を見たいのですが [yasei-seibutsu o mitai no desu ga]

will [wɪl] *n* (document) 遺言 [yuigon], (motivation) 意志 [ishi]

willing [ˈwɪlɪŋ] *adj* いとわない [itowanai]

willingly [ˈwɪlɪŋlɪ] *adv* 進んで [susunde]

willow [ˈwɪləʊ] *n* ヤナギ [yanagi]

willpower [ˈwɪlˌpaʊə] *n* 意志の力 [ishi no chikara]

wilt [wɪlt] *v* しおれる [shioreru]

win [wɪn] *v* 勝つ [katsu]

wind[1] [wɪnd] *n* 風 [kaze] ▷ *vt* (with a blow etc.) 巻く [maku]

wind[2] [waɪnd] *v* (coil around) 巻く [maku]

windmill [ˈwɪndˌmɪl; ˈwɪnˌmɪl] *n* 風車小屋 [fuushagoya]

whisk [wɪsk] *n* 泡立て器 [awatateki]

whiskers [ˈwɪskəz] *npl* ひげ [hige]

whisky [ˈwɪskɪ] *n* ウイスキー [uisukii]; **malt whisky** *n* モルトウイスキー [moruto uisukii]; **a whisky and soda** ウイスキーのソーダ割り [uisukii no sooda wari]; **I'll have a whisky** ウイスキーをください [uisukii o kudasai]

window ['wɪndəʊ] *n* 窓 [mado]; **shop window** *n* ショーウィンドウ [shoouindou]; **window pane** *n* 窓ガラス [madogarasu]; **window seat** *n* 窓下の腰掛け [mado shita no koshikake]; **I can't open the window** 窓を開けられません [mado o akeraremasen]; **I'd like a window seat** 窓側の席をお願いします [mado-gawa no seki o o-negai shimasu]; **May I close the window?** 窓を閉めてもいいですか？ [mado o shimete mo ii desu ka?]; **May I open the window?** 窓を開けてもいいですか？ [mado o akete mo ii desu ka?]

windowsill ['wɪndəʊˌsɪl] *n* 窓の下枠 [mado no shitawaku]

windscreen ['wɪndˌskriːn] *n* フロントガラス [furontogarasu]; **windscreen wiper** *n* フロントガラスのワイパー [furonto garasu no waipaa]; **Can you top up the windscreen washers?** フロントガラスのウォッシャー液を補充してもらえますか？ [furonto-garasu no wosshaa-eki o hojuu shite moraemasu ka?]; **Could you clean the windscreen?** フロントガラスを拭いてもらえますか？ [furonto-garasu o fuite moraemasu ka?]; **The windscreen is broken** フロントガラスが割れています [furonto-garasu ga warete imasu]

windsurfing ['wɪndˌsɜːfɪŋ] *n* ウインドサーフィン [uindosaafin]

windy ['wɪndɪ] *adj* 風の強い [kaze no tsuyoi]

wine [waɪn] *n* ワイン [wain]; **house wine** *n* ハウスワイン [hausuwain]; **red wine** *n* 赤ワイン [akawain]; **table wine** *n* テーブルワイン [teeburuwain]; **wine list** *n* ワインリスト [wainrisuto]; **a bottle of white wine** 白ワインのボトルを1本 [shiro-wain no botoru o ippon]; **Can you recommend a good wine?** よいワインを教えてもらえますか？ [yoi wain o oshiete moraemasu ka?]; **Is the wine chilled?** ワインは冷えていますか？ [wain wa hiete imasu ka?]; **The wine list, please** ワインリストをください [wain-risuto o kudasai]; **This stain is wine** このしみはワインです [kono shimi wa wain desu]; **This wine is not chilled** このワインは冷えていません [kono wain wa hiete imasen]

wineglass ['waɪnˌɡlɑːs] *n* ワイングラス [waingurasu]

wing [wɪŋ] *n* 翼 [tsubasa]; **wing mirror** *n* サイドミラー [saidomiraa]

wink [wɪŋk] *v* ウインクする [uinku suru]

winner ['wɪnə] *n* 勝者 [shousha]

winning ['wɪnɪŋ] *adj* 勝利を得た [shouri-o eta]

winter ['wɪntə] *n* 冬 [fuyu]; **winter sports** *npl* ウィンタースポーツ [wintaasupootsu]

wipe [waɪp] *v* 拭く [fuku]; **baby wipe** *n* 赤ちゃん用ウェットティシュー [akachanyouuettotishuu]

wipe up [waɪp ʌp] *v* 皿拭きをする [sarafuki-o suru]

wire [waɪə] *n* 針金 [harigane]; **barbed wire** *n* 有刺鉄線 [yuushitessen]

wisdom ['wɪzdəm] *n* 賢明 [kenmei]; **wisdom tooth** *n* 親知らず [oyashirazu]

wise [waɪz] *adj* 賢い [kashikoi]

wish [wɪʃ] *n* 願い [negai] ▷ *v* 願う [negau]

wit [wɪt] *n* 機知 [kichi]

witch [wɪtʃ] *n* 魔女 [majo]

with [wɪð; wɪθ] *prep* ···と一緒に [...to issho ni]

withdraw [wɪð'drɔː] *v* 抜き取る [nukitoru]

withdrawal [wɪð'drɔːəl] *n* 引っ込めること [hikkomeru koto]

within [wɪ'ðɪn] *prep (space)* ···以内で [...inai de], *(term)* ···以内で [...inai de]

without [wɪ'ðaʊt] *prep* ···なしで [...nashide]; **I'd like it without..., please** ···なしでお願いします [...nashi de o-negai shimasu]

witness ['wɪtnɪs] *n* 目撃者 [mokugekisha]; **Jehovah's Witness** *n* エホバの証人 [ehoba no shounin]; **Can you be a witness for me?** 私の目撃者になってもらえますか？ [watashi no mokugeki sha ni natte moraemasu ka?]

witty ['wɪtɪ] *adj* 機知に富んだ [kichi ni tonda]

wolf, wolves [wʊlf, wʊlvz] *n* オオカミ [ookami]

woman, women ['wʊmən, 'wɪmɪn] *n* 女性 [josei]

wonder ['wʌndə] *v* 怪しむ [ayashimu]

wonderful ['wʌndəfʊl] *adj* すばらしい [subarashii]

wood [wʊd] *n (forest)* 森 [mori], *(material)* 材木 [zaimoku]

wooden ['wʊdᵊn] *adj* 木製の [mokusei no]

woodwind ['wʊd,wɪnd] *n* 木管楽器 [mokkangakki]

woodwork ['wʊd,wɜːk] *n* 木工部 [mokkoubu]

wool [wʊl] *n* 羊毛 [youmou]; **cotton wool** *n* 脱脂綿 [dasshimen]

woollen ['wʊlən] *adj* 毛織りの [keori no]

woollens ['wʊlənz] *npl* 毛織物衣類 [keorimono irui]

word [wɜːd] *n* 単語 [tango]

work [wɜːk] *n* 労働 [roudou] ▷ *v* 働く [hataraku]; **work experience** *n* 労働体験 [roudou taiken]; **work of art** *n* 美術品 [bijutsuhin]; **work permit** *n* 労働許可証 [roudou kyokashou]; **work station** *n* ワークステーション [waakusuteeshon]

worker ['wɜːkə] *n* 働く人 [hatarakuhito]; **social worker** *n* ソーシャルワーカー [soosharuwaakaa]

workforce ['wɜːk,fɔːs] *n* 作業要員 [sagyou youin]

working-class ['wɜːkɪŋklɑːs] *adj* 労働者階級の [roudoushakaikyuu no]

workman, workmen ['wɜːkmən, 'wɜːkmɛn] *n* 肉体労働者 [nikutairoudousha]

work out [wɜːk aʊt] *v* 考え出す [kangaedasu]

workplace ['wɜːk,pleɪs] *n* 職場 [shokuba]

workshop ['wɜːk,ʃɒp] *n* 仕事場 [shigotoba]

workspace ['wɜːk,speɪs] *n* 作業スペース [sagyou supeesu]

workstation ['wɜːk,steɪʃən] *n* ワークステーション [waakusuteeshon]

world [wɜːld] *n* 世界 [sekai]; **Third World** *n* 第三世界 [dai san sekai]; **World Cup** *n* ワールドカップ [waarudokappu]

worm [wɜːm] *n* 虫 [mushi]

worn [wɔːn] *adj* 着古した [kifurushita]

worried ['wʌrɪd] *adj* 心配している [shinpai shite iru]

worry ['wʌrɪ] *v* 心配する [shinpai suru]

worrying ['wʌrɪɪŋ] *adj* 気がもめる [ki ga momeru]

worse [wɜːs] *adj* 一層悪い [issou warui] ▷ *adv* 一層悪く [issou waruku]

worsen ['wɜːsᵊn] *v* 悪化する [akka suru]

worship ['wɜːʃɪp] *v* 礼拝する [reihai suru]

worst [wɜːst] *adj* 最悪の [saiaku no]

worth [wɜːθ] *n* 資産 [shisan]

worthless ['wɜːθlɪs] *adj* 価値のない [kachi no nai]

would [wʊd; wəd] *v* I would like to wash the car 車を洗いたいのですが [kuruma o araitai no desu ga]; We would like to go cycling 私たちはサイクリングに行きたいのですが [watashi-tachi wa saikuringu ni ikitai no desu ga]

wound [wuːnd] *n* 傷 [kizu] ▷ *v* 傷つける [kizutsukeru]

wrap [ræp] *v* 包む [tsutsumu]; **wrapping paper** *n* 包装紙 [housoushi]

wrap up [ræp ʌp] *v* 包む [tsutsumu]

wreck [rɛk] *n* 大破 [taiha] ▷ *v* 大破する [taiha suru]

wreckage ['rɛkɪdʒ] *n* 残骸 [zangai]

wren [rɛn] *n* ミソサザイ [misosazai]

wrench [rɛntʃ] *n* ねじり [nejiri] ▷ *v* ねじる [nejiru]

wrestler ['rɛslə] *n* レスラー [resuraa]

wrestling ['rɛslɪŋ] *n* レスリング [resuringu]

wrinkle ['rɪŋkᵊl] *n* しわ [shiwa]

wrinkled ['rɪŋkᵊld] *adj* しわの寄った [shiwa no yotta]

wrist [rɪst] *n* 手首 [tekubi]

write [raɪt] *v* 書く [kaku]

write down [raɪt daʊn] *v* 書き留める [kakitomeru]

writer ['raɪtə] *n* 作家 [sakka]

writing ['raɪtɪŋ] *n* 書いたもの [kaita mono]; **writing paper** *n* 便箋 [binsen]

wrong [rɒŋ] *adj* 間違った [machigatta] ▷ *adv* 間違って [machigatte]; **wrong number** *n* 間違い電話 [machigai denwa]; **I think you've given me the wrong change** お釣りが間違っていると思います [o-tsuri ga machigatte iru to omoimasu]; **The bill is wrong** 請求書が間違っています [seikyuusho ga machigatte imasu]

Xmas ['ɛksməs; 'krɪsməs] *n* クリスマス [kurisumasu]

X-ray [ɛksreɪ] *n* X線 [ekkususen] ▷ *v* X線写真を撮る [x-sen shashin-o toru]

xylophone ['zaɪlə,fəʊn] *n* シロホン [shirohon]

yacht [jɒt] *n* ヨット [yotto]

yard [jɑːd] *n (enclosure)* 庭 [niwa], *(measurement)* ヤード [yaado]

yawn [jɔːn] *v* あくびをする [akubi-o suru]

year [jɪə] *n* 年 [nen, toshi]; **academic year** *n* 学年 [gakunen]; **financial year** *n* 会計年度 [kaikeinendo]; **leap year** *n* うるう年 [uruudoshi]; **New Year** *n* 新年 [shinnen]; **last year** 去年 [kyonen]; **next year** 来年 [rainen]; **this year** 今年 [kotoshi]

yearly [ˈjɪəlɪ] *adj* 年に一度の [nen ni ichido no] ▷ *adv* 年に一度 [nen ni ichido]

yeast [jiːst] *n* 酵母菌 [koubokin]

yell [jɛl] *v* 叫ぶ [sakebu]

yellow [ˈjɛləʊ] *adj* 黄色の [ki iro no]; **Yellow Pages®** *npl* イエローページ® [ieroopeeji]

Yemen [ˈjɛmən] *n* イエメン [iemen]

yes [jɛs] *excl* はい [hai]

yesterday [ˈjɛstədɪ; -ˌdeɪ] *adv* 昨日 [kinou, sakujitsu]

yet [jɛt] *adv (interrogative)* もう [mou], *(with negative)* まだ [mada] ▷ *conj (nevertheless)* それにもかかわらず [sorenimokakawarazu]

yew [juː] *n* イチイ [ichii]

yield [jiːld] *v* 生む [umu] *(利益)*

yoga [ˈjəʊɡə] *n* ヨガ [yoga]

yoghurt [ˈjəʊɡət; ˈjɒɡ-] *n* ヨーグルト [yooguruto]

yolk [jəʊk] *n* 卵の黄身 [tamago no kimi]

you [juː; jʊ] *pron (plural)* あなた方 [anatagata], *(singular)* あなた [anata]

young [jʌŋ] *adj* 若い [wakai]

younger [jʌŋə] *adj* 年下の方の [toshishita no hou no]

youngest [jʌŋɪst] *adj* 一番若い [ichiban wakai]

your [jɔː; jʊə; jə] *adj (plural)* あなた方の [anatagata no], *(singular)* あなたの [anata no]

yours [jɔːz; jʊəz] *pron (plural)* あなた方の [anatagata no], *(singular)* あなたの [anata no]

yourself [jɔːˈsɛlf; jʊə-] *pron* あなた自身 [anata jishin], *(intensifier)* ご自分で [go jibun de]

yourselves [jɔːˈsɛlvz] *pron (intensifier)* ご自分で [go jibun de], *(polite)* あなた自身 [anata jishin], *(reflexive)* あなた方自身 [anatagata jishin]

youth [juːθ] *n* 青春時代 [seishun jidai]; **youth club** *n* ユースクラブ [yuusukurabu]; **youth hostel** *n* ユースホステル [yuusuhosuteru]

Z

zoology [zəʊˈɒlədʒɪ; zu...]
[doubutsugaku]
zoom [zuːm] *n* **zoom lens** *n* ズームレン
ズ [zuumurenzu]
zucchini [tsuːˈkiːnɪ; zuː-] *n* ズッキーニ
[zukkiini]

Zambia [ˈzæmbɪə] *n* ザンビア [zanbia]
Zambian [ˈzæmbɪən] *adj* ザンビアの
[zanbia no] ▷ *n* ザンビア人 [zanbiajin]
zebra [ˈziːbrə; ˈzɛbrə] *n* シマウマ
[shimauma]; **zebra crossing** *n* 太い白線
の縞模様で示した横断歩道 [futoi
hakusen no shimamoyou de shimeshita
oudanhodou]
zero, zeroes [ˈzɪərəʊ, ˈzɪərəʊz] *n* 零 [rei]
zest [zɛst] *n* (*excitement*) 沸き立つ喜び
[wakitatsu yorokobi]; **lemon zest** *n* レモ
ンゼスト [remonzesuto]
Zimbabwe [zɪmˈbɑːbwɪ; -weɪ] *n* ジン
バブウェ [jinbabuwe]
Zimbabwean [zɪmˈbɑːbwɪən;
-weɪən] *adj* ジンバブウェの [jinbabuwe
no] ▷ *n* (*person*) ジンバブウェ人
[jinbabuwejin]
zinc [zɪŋk] *n* 亜鉛 [aen]
zip [zɪp] *n* ファスナー [fasunaa]; **zip (up)** *v*
ファスナーを締める [fasunaa-o shimeru]
zit [zɪt] *n* にきび [nikibi]
zodiac [ˈzəʊdɪˌæk] *n* 十二宮 [juunikyuu]
zone [zəʊn] *n* 地帯 [chitai]; **time zone** *n*
標準時間帯 [hyoujun jikantai]
zoo [zuː] *n* 動物園 [doubutsuen]